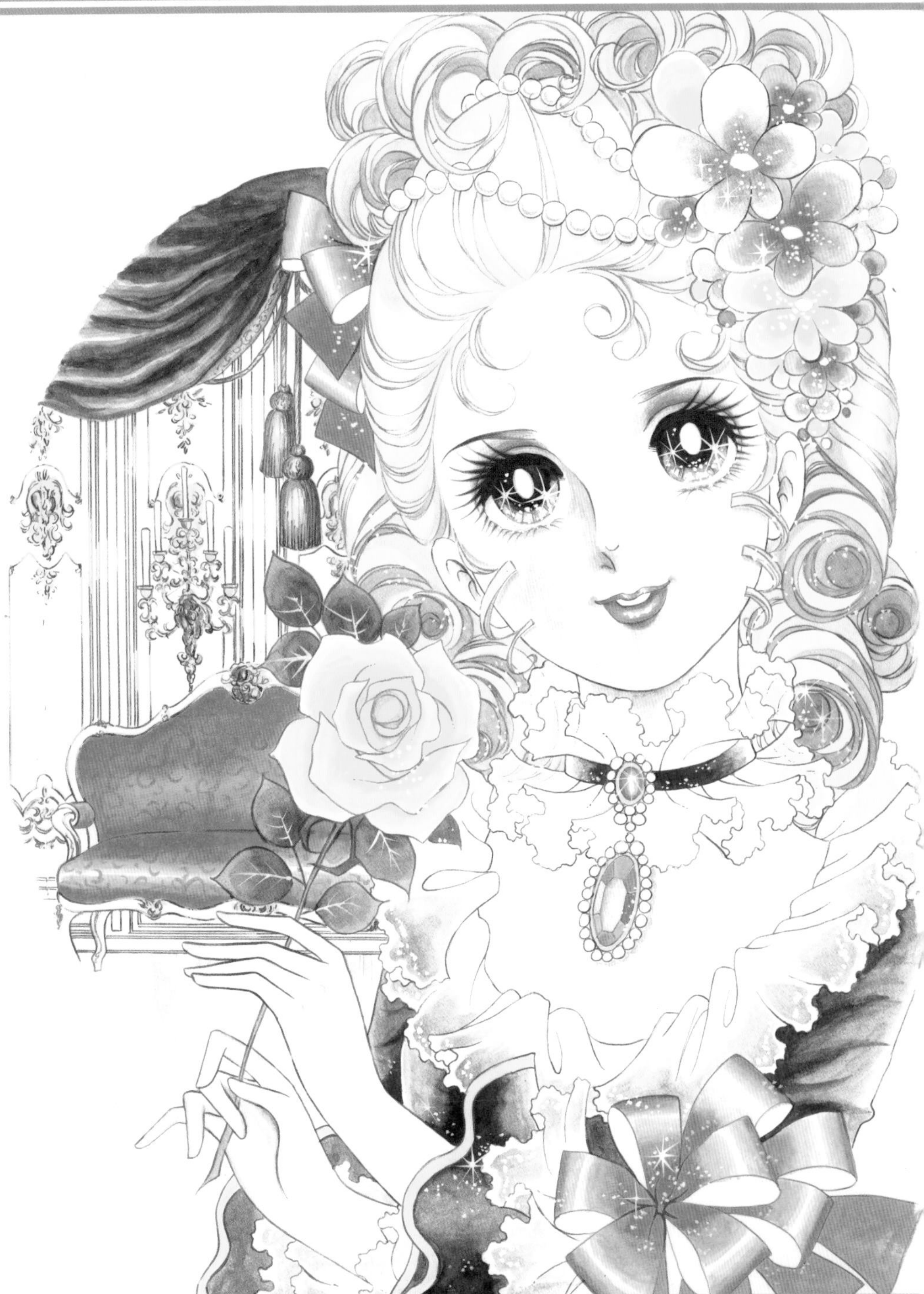

the ROSE of VERSAILLES

ベルサイユのばら

Riyoko Ikeda

the ROSE of VERSAILLES ベルサイユのばら
Volume 1

Special Colorized Art (Made by Shueisha for the Perfect Edition)
P.5-9, 142, 187-191, 254-257, 429-433, 472
Additional Art Gallery
P.28, 52, 120, 164, 186, 208, 232, 296, 318, 340, 362, 406, 450

English Edition Staff:

Translation: Mari Morimoto
Lettering and Touch Up: Jeannie Lee
Editor: Erica Friedman
Cover Design: Andy Tsang

Chief of Operations: Erik Ko
Director of Publishing: Matt Moylan
Associate Editor: M. Chandler
Project Manager: Janice Leung

VP of Business Development: Cory Casoni
Director of Marketing: Megan Maiden
Japanese Liaisons: Steven Cummings
Anna Kawashima

Special Thanks to: Ms. Yayoi Arima and the staff at Shueisha Inc.
Chigusa Ogino and Alisa Sunago at Tuttle-Mori Agency.

This English edition was re-edited and revised based on
the Perfect Edition published by SHUEISHA Inc. Tokyo

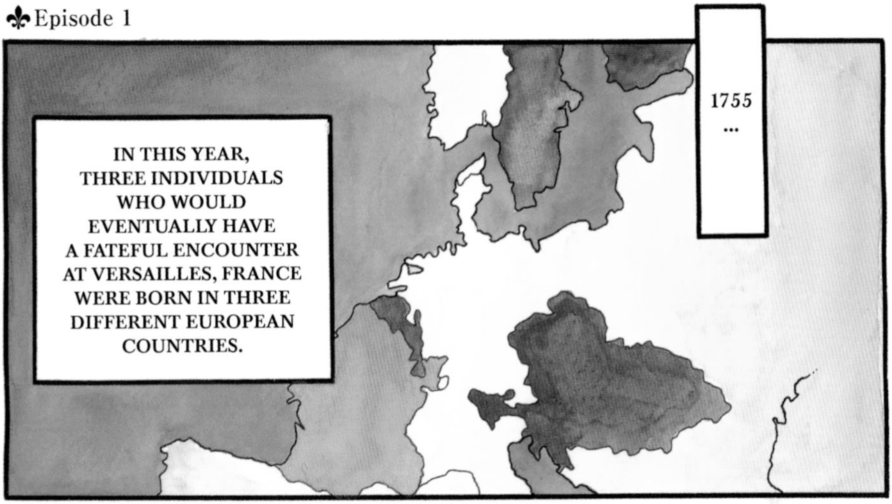
1755 ...
IN THIS YEAR, THREE INDIVIDUALS WHO WOULD EVENTUALLY HAVE A FATEFUL ENCOUNTER AT VERSAILLES, FRANCE WERE BORN IN THREE DIFFERENT EUROPEAN COUNTRIES.

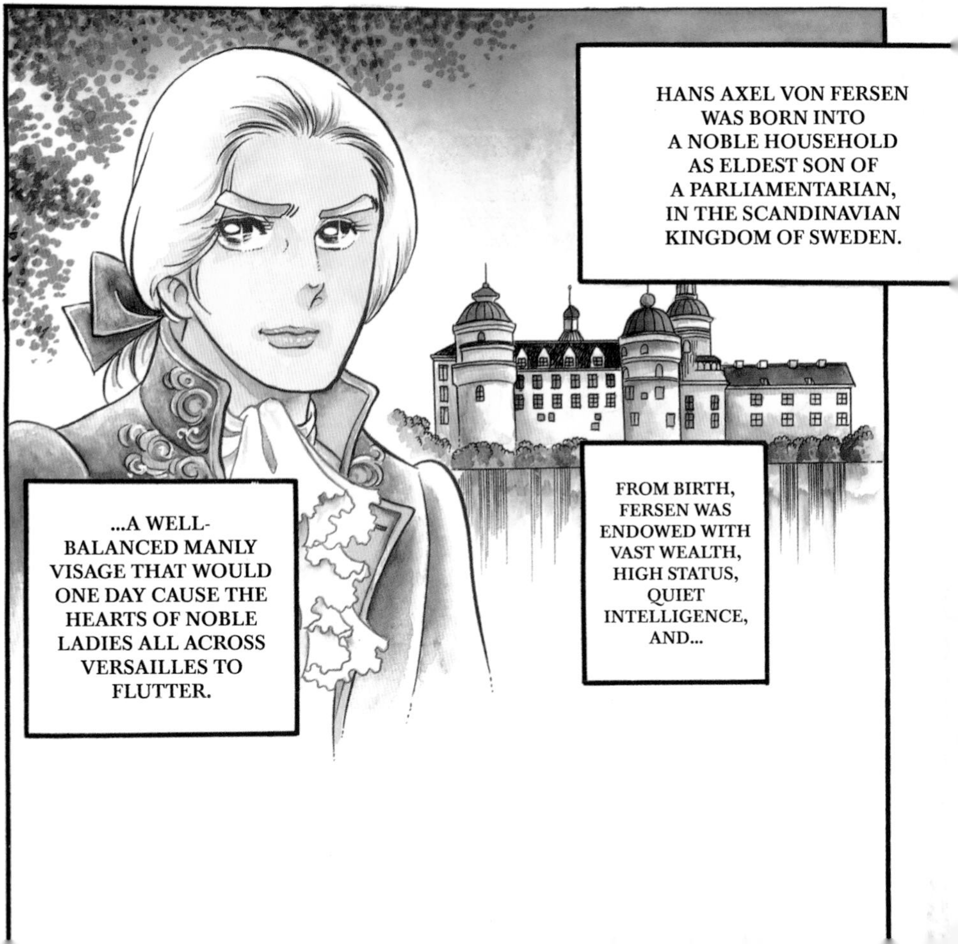
HANS AXEL VON FERSEN WAS BORN INTO A NOBLE HOUSEHOLD AS ELDEST SON OF A PARLIAMENTARIAN, IN THE SCANDINAVIAN KINGDOM OF SWEDEN.
FROM BIRTH, FERSEN WAS ENDOWED WITH VAST WEALTH, HIGH STATUS, QUIET INTELLIGENCE, AND...
...A WELL-BALANCED MANLY VISAGE THAT WOULD ONE DAY CAUSE THE HEARTS OF NOBLE LADIES ALL ACROSS VERSAILLES TO FLUTTER.

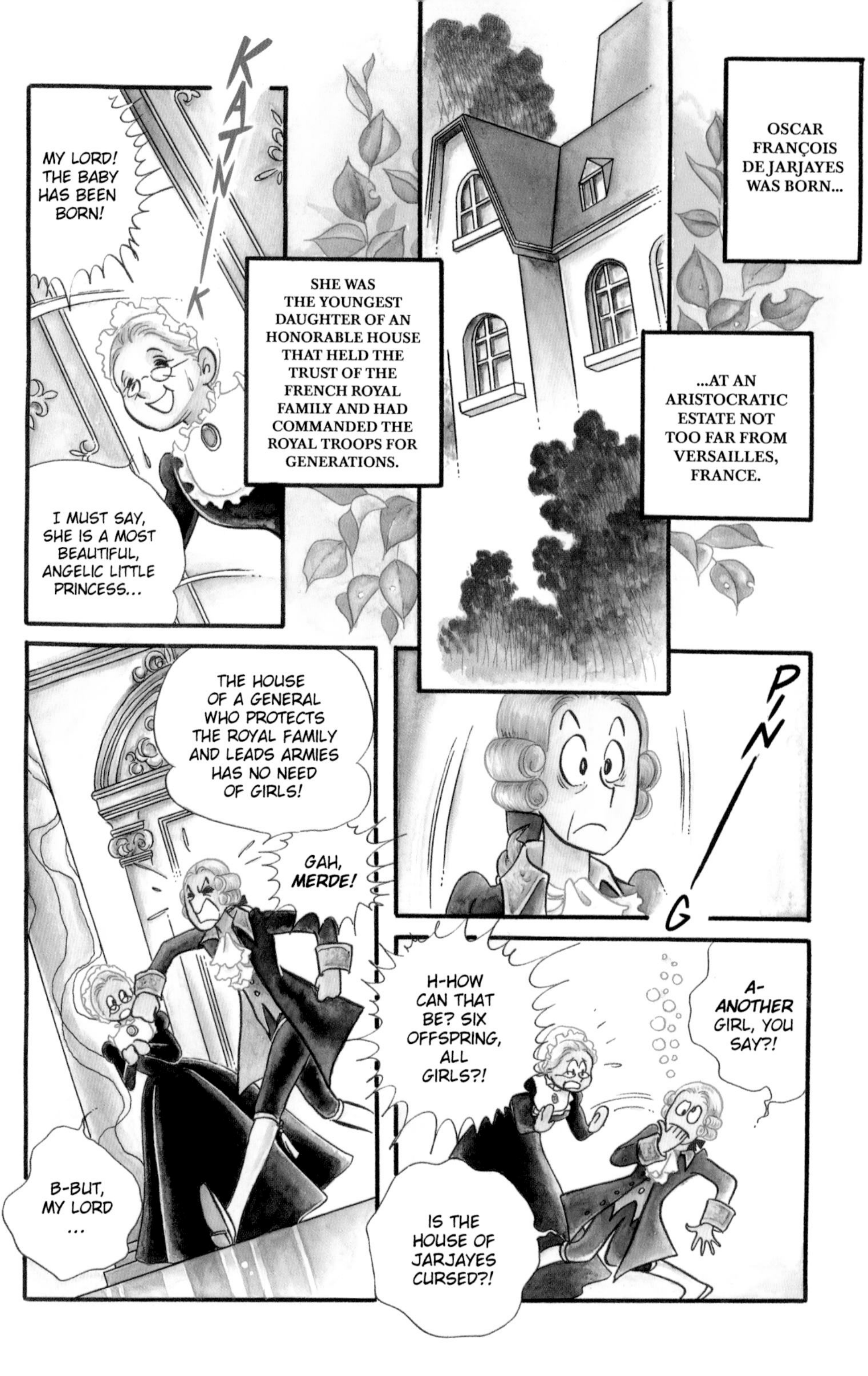
OSCAR FRANÇOIS DE JARJAYES WAS BORN...
...AT AN ARISTOCRATIC ESTATE NOT TOO FAR FROM VERSAILLES, FRANCE.
SHE WAS THE YOUNGEST DAUGHTER OF AN HONORABLE HOUSE THAT HELD THE TRUST OF THE FRENCH ROYAL FAMILY AND HAD COMMANDED THE ROYAL TROOPS FOR GENERATIONS.
KATNIK
MY LORD! THE BABY HAS BEEN BORN!
I MUST SAY, SHE IS A MOST BEAUTIFUL, ANGELIC LITTLE PRINCESS...
PING
A-ANOTHER GIRL, YOU SAY?!
H-HOW CAN THAT BE? SIX OFFSPRING, ALL GIRLS?!
IS THE HOUSE OF JARJAYES CURSED?!
THE HOUSE OF A GENERAL WHO PROTECTS THE ROYAL FAMILY AND LEADS ARMIES HAS NO NEED OF GIRLS!
GAH, *MERDE!*
B-BUT, MY LORD ...

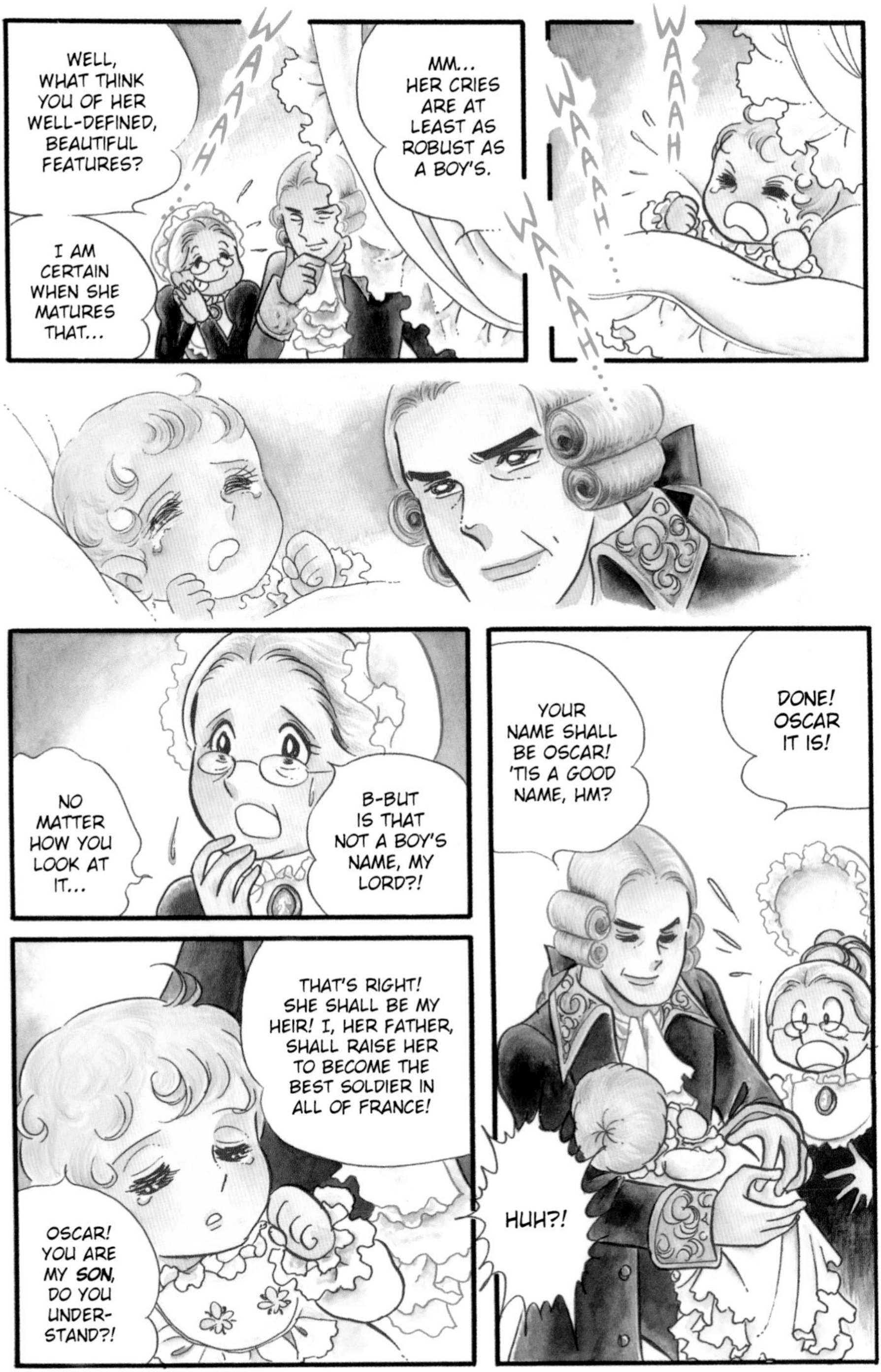
WAAAH
WAAAAH...
WAAAAAH...
WAAAAH...
MM... HER CRIES ARE AT LEAST AS ROBUST AS A BOY'S.
WELL, WHAT THINK YOU OF HER WELL-DEFINED, BEAUTIFUL FEATURES?
I AM CERTAIN WHEN SHE MATURES THAT...
DONE! OSCAR IT IS!
YOUR NAME SHALL BE OSCAR! 'TIS A GOOD NAME, HM?
HUH?!
B-BUT IS THAT NOT A BOY'S NAME, MY LORD?!
NO MATTER HOW YOU LOOK AT IT...
THAT'S RIGHT! SHE SHALL BE MY HEIR! I, HER FATHER, SHALL RAISE HER TO BECOME THE BEST SOLDIER IN ALL OF FRANCE!
OSCAR! YOU ARE MY SON, DO YOU UNDERSTAND?!

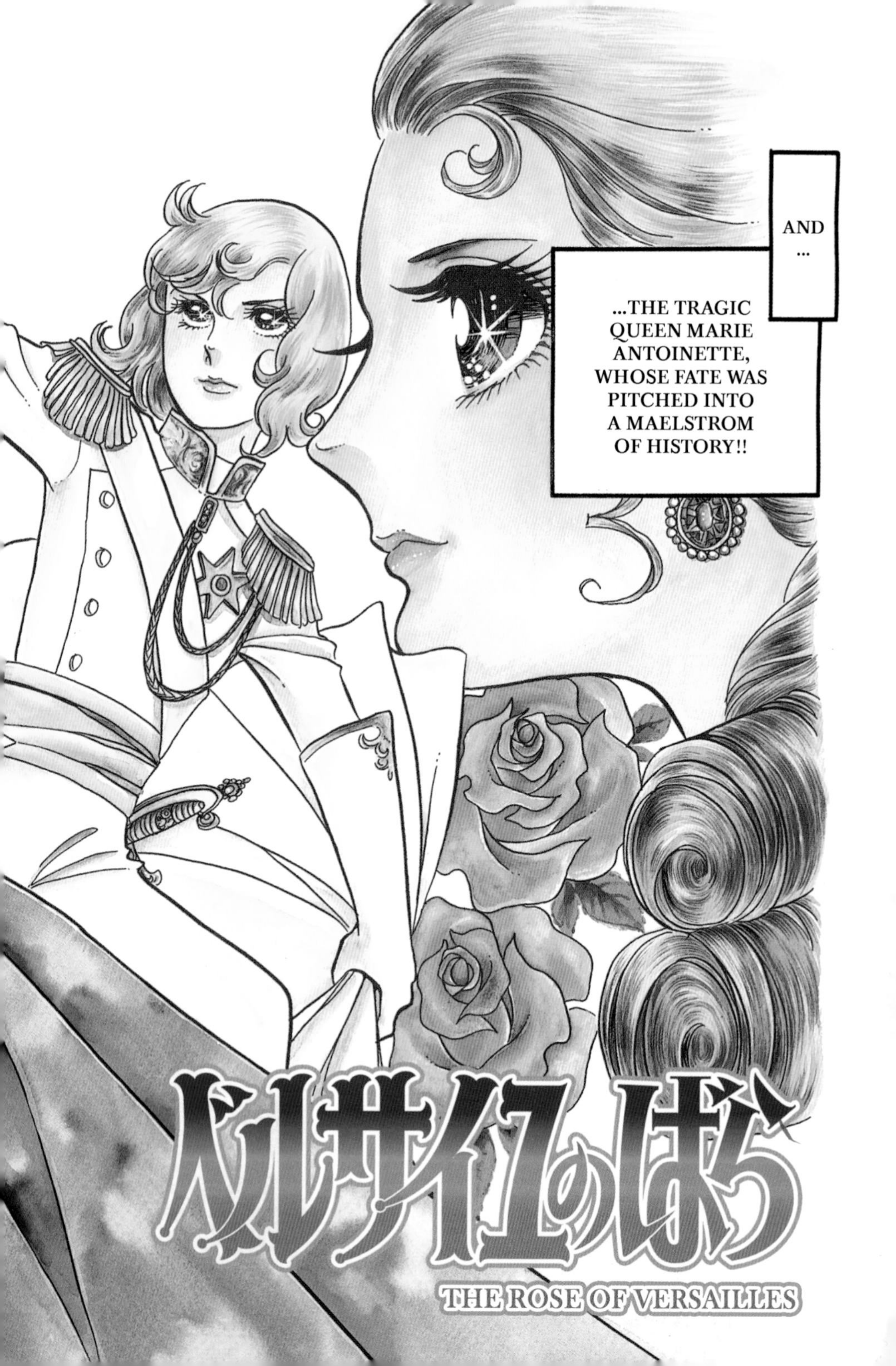
AND ...
...THE TRAGIC QUEEN MARIE ANTOINETTE, WHOSE FATE WAS PITCHED INTO A MAELSTROM OF HISTORY!!
ベルサイユのばら
THE ROSE OF VERSAILLES

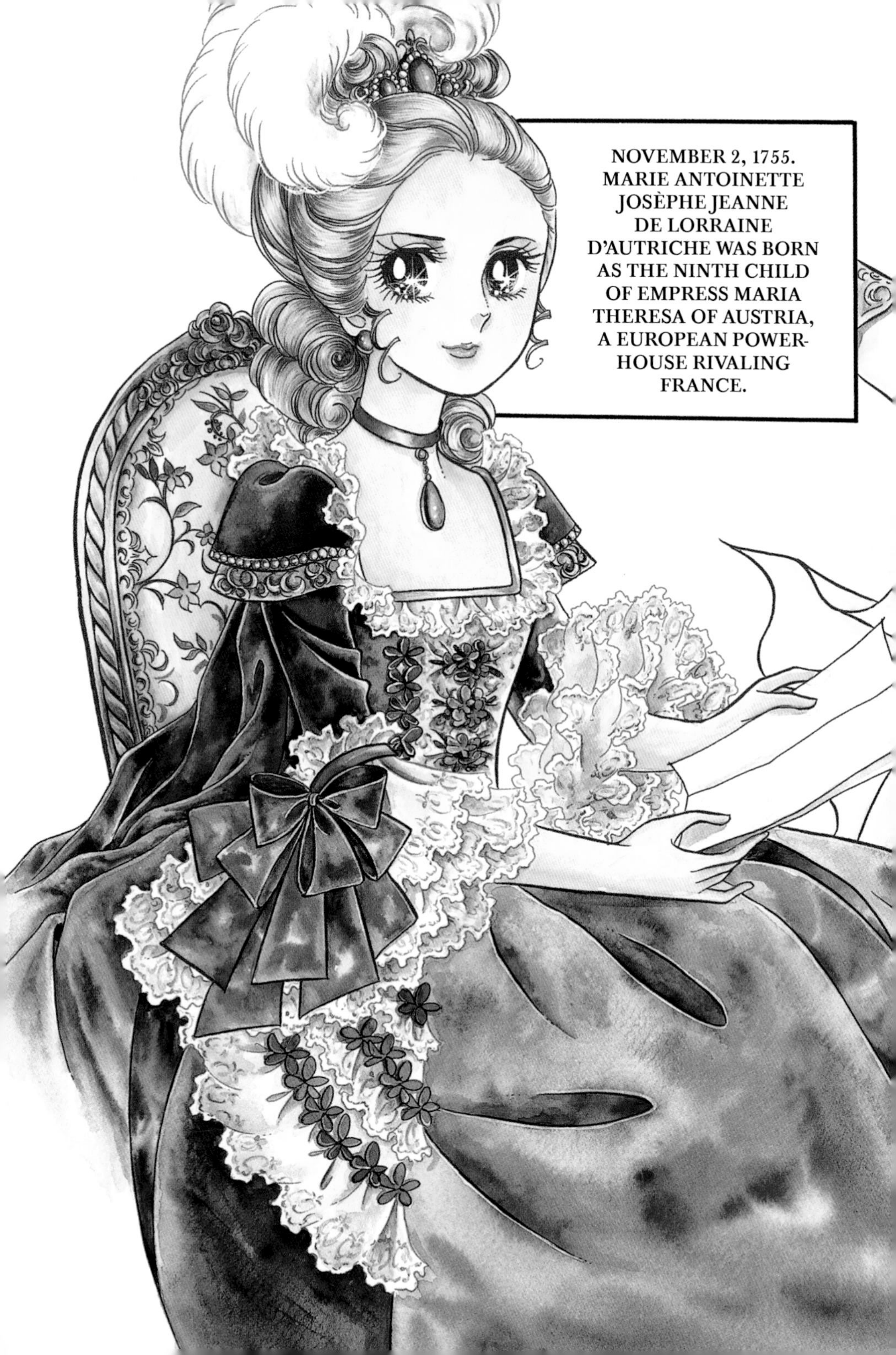
NOVEMBER 2, 1755. MARIE ANTOINETTE JOSÈPHE JEANNE DE LORRAINE D'AUTRICHE WAS BORN AS THE NINTH CHILD OF EMPRESS MARIA THERESA OF AUSTRIA, A EUROPEAN POWER-HOUSE RIVALING FRANCE.

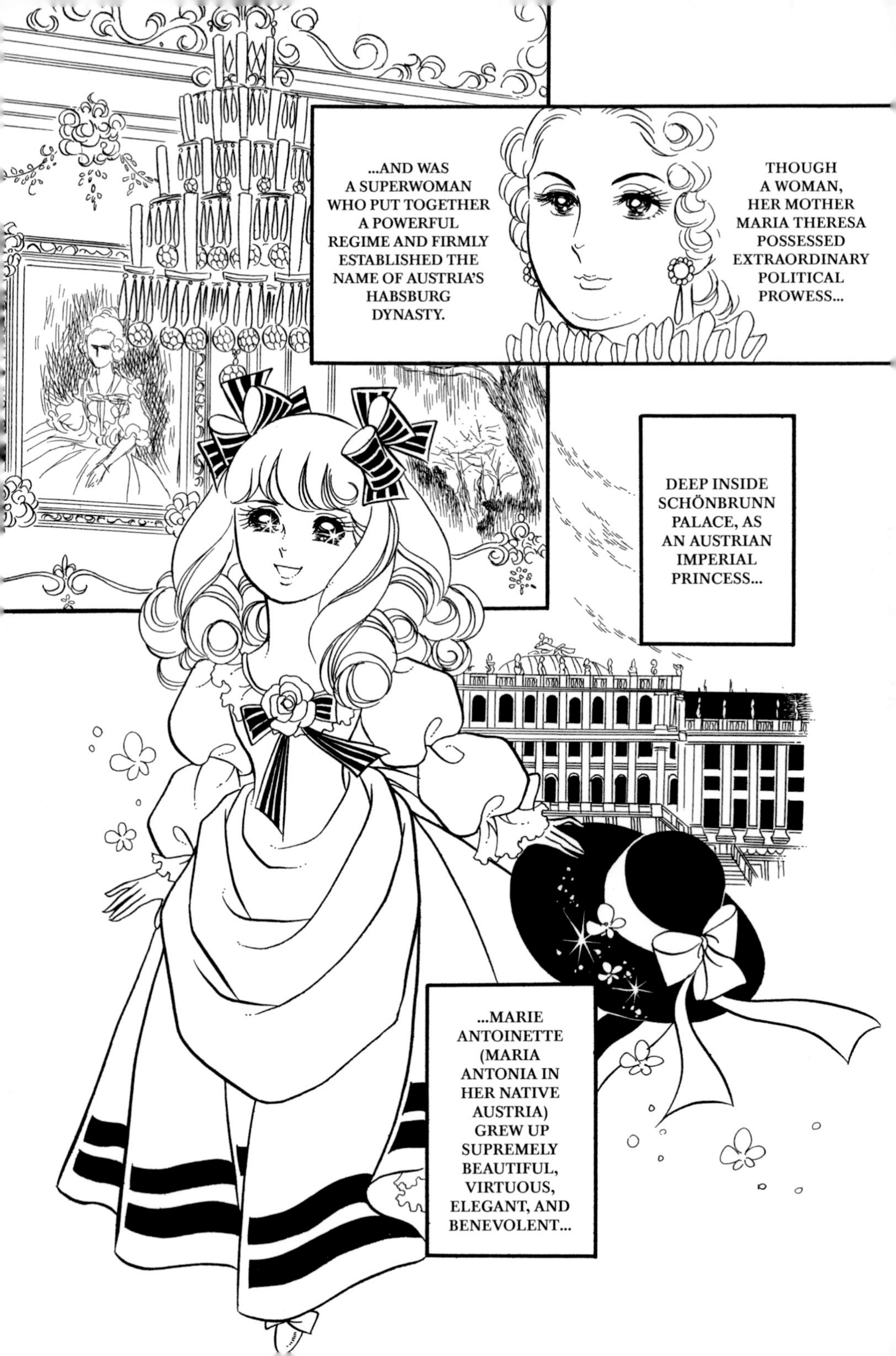
THOUGH A WOMAN, HER MOTHER MARIA THERESA POSSESSED EXTRAORDINARY POLITICAL PROWESS...
...AND WAS A SUPERWOMAN WHO PUT TOGETHER A POWERFUL REGIME AND FIRMLY ESTABLISHED THE NAME OF AUSTRIA'S HABSBURG DYNASTY.
DEEP INSIDE SCHÖNBRUNN PALACE, AS AN AUSTRIAN IMPERIAL PRINCESS...
...MARIE ANTOINETTE (MARIA ANTONIA IN HER NATIVE AUSTRIA) GREW UP SUPREMELY BEAUTIFUL, VIRTUOUS, ELEGANT, AND BENEVOLENT...

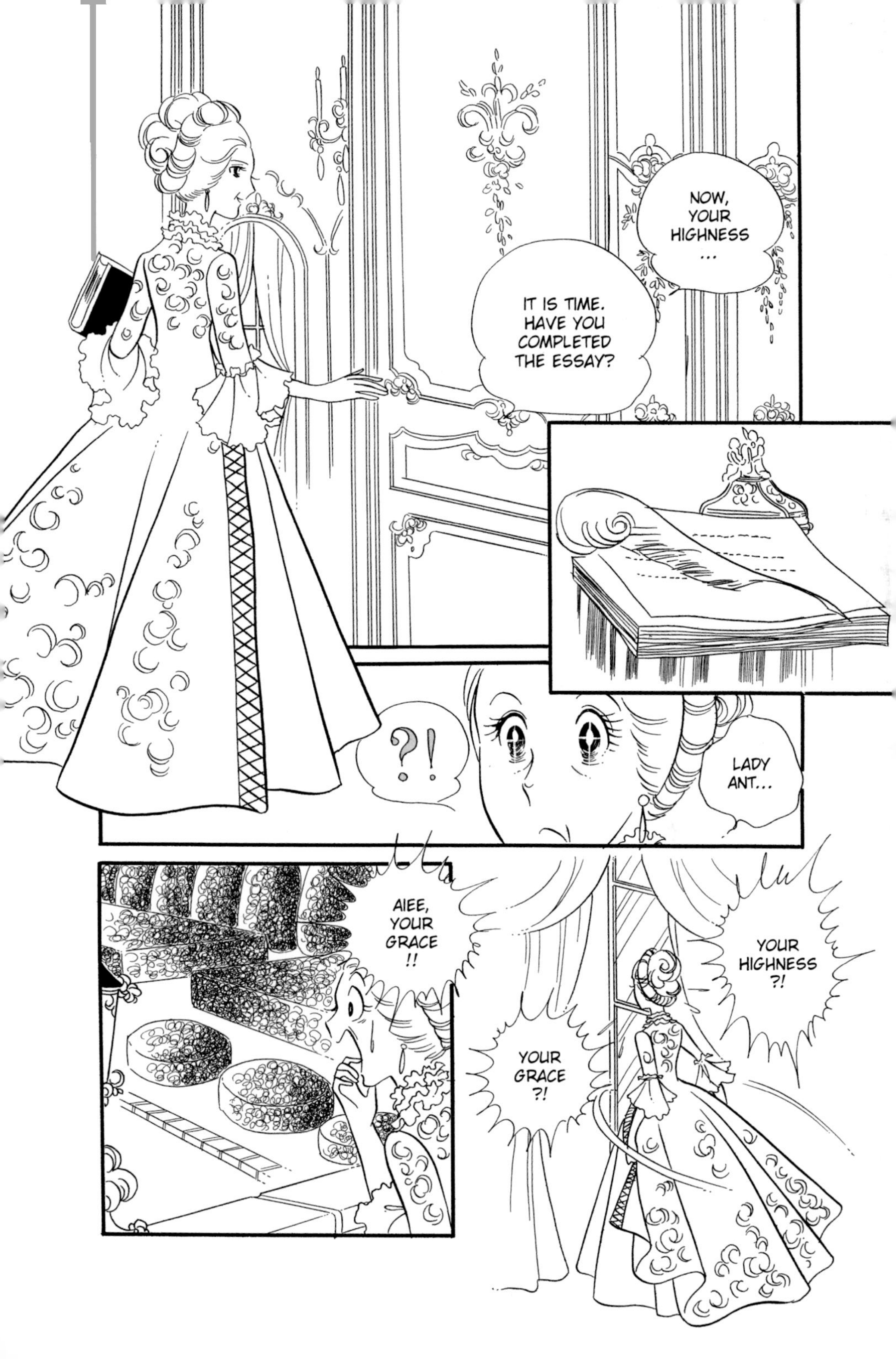
NOW, YOUR HIGHNESS ...
IT IS TIME. HAVE YOU COMPLETED THE ESSAY?
LADY ANT...
?!
YOUR HIGHNESS ?!
YOUR GRACE ?!
AIEE, YOUR GRACE !!

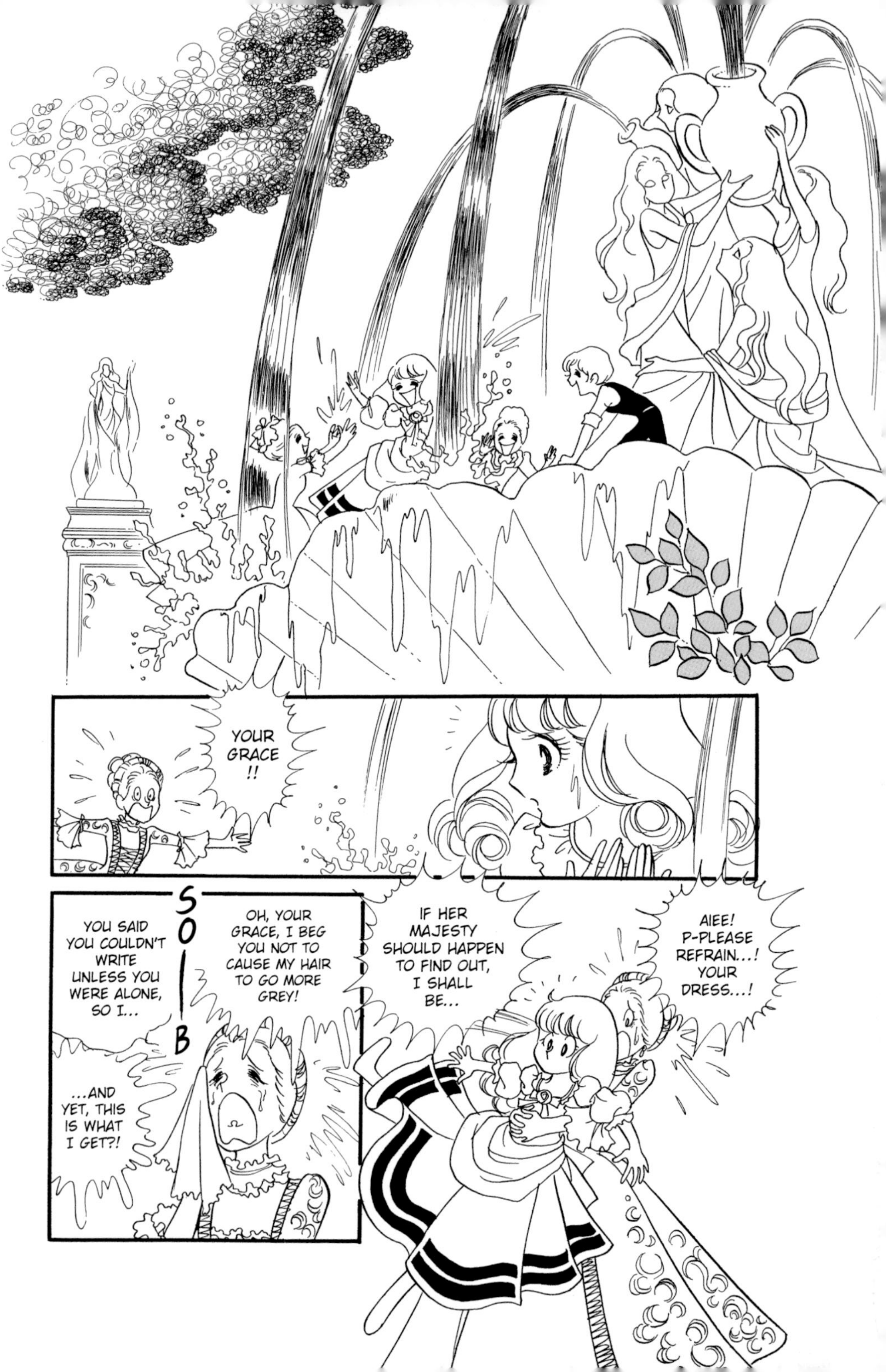
YOUR GRACE !!
AIEE! P-PLEASE REFRAIN...! YOUR DRESS...!
IF HER MAJESTY SHOULD HAPPEN TO FIND OUT, I SHALL BE...
OH, YOUR GRACE, I BEG YOU NOT TO CAUSE MY HAIR TO GO MORE GREY!
SOB
YOU SAID YOU COULDN'T WRITE UNLESS YOU WERE ALONE, SO I...
...AND YET, THIS IS WHAT I GET?!

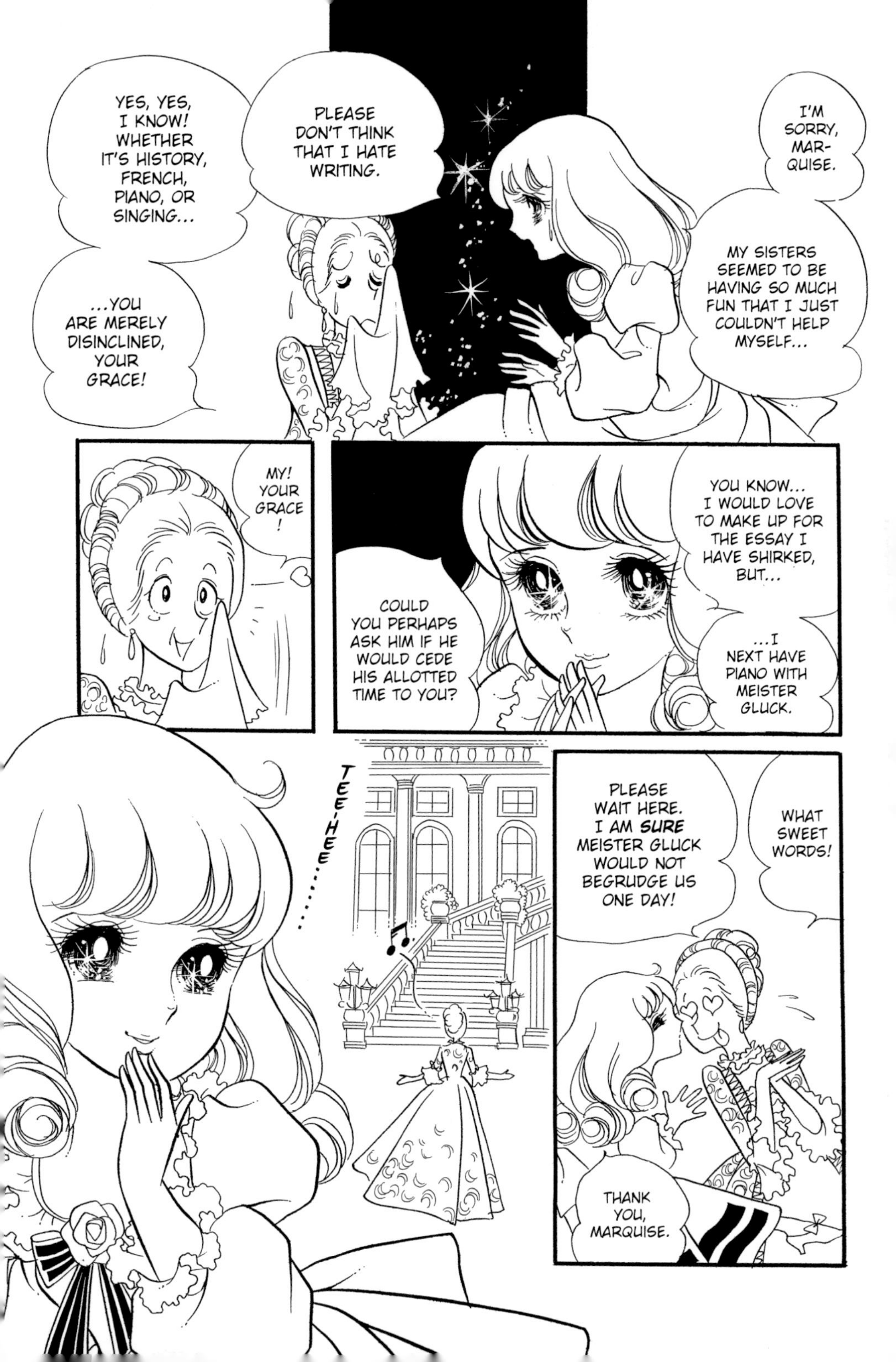
I'M SORRY, MARQUISE.
MY SISTERS SEEMED TO BE HAVING SO MUCH FUN THAT I JUST COULDN'T HELP MYSELF...
PLEASE DON'T THINK THAT I HATE WRITING.
YES, YES, I KNOW! WHETHER IT'S HISTORY, FRENCH, PIANO, OR SINGING...
...YOU ARE MERELY DISINCLINED, YOUR GRACE!
YOU KNOW... I WOULD LOVE TO MAKE UP FOR THE ESSAY I HAVE SHIRKED, BUT...
...I NEXT HAVE PIANO WITH MEISTER GLUCK.
COULD YOU PERHAPS ASK HIM IF HE WOULD CEDE HIS ALLOTTED TIME TO YOU?
MY! YOUR GRACE!
WHAT SWEET WORDS!
PLEASE WAIT HERE. I AM **SURE** MEISTER GLUCK WOULD NOT BEGRUDGE US ONE DAY!
THANK YOU, MARQUISE.
TEE-HEE......

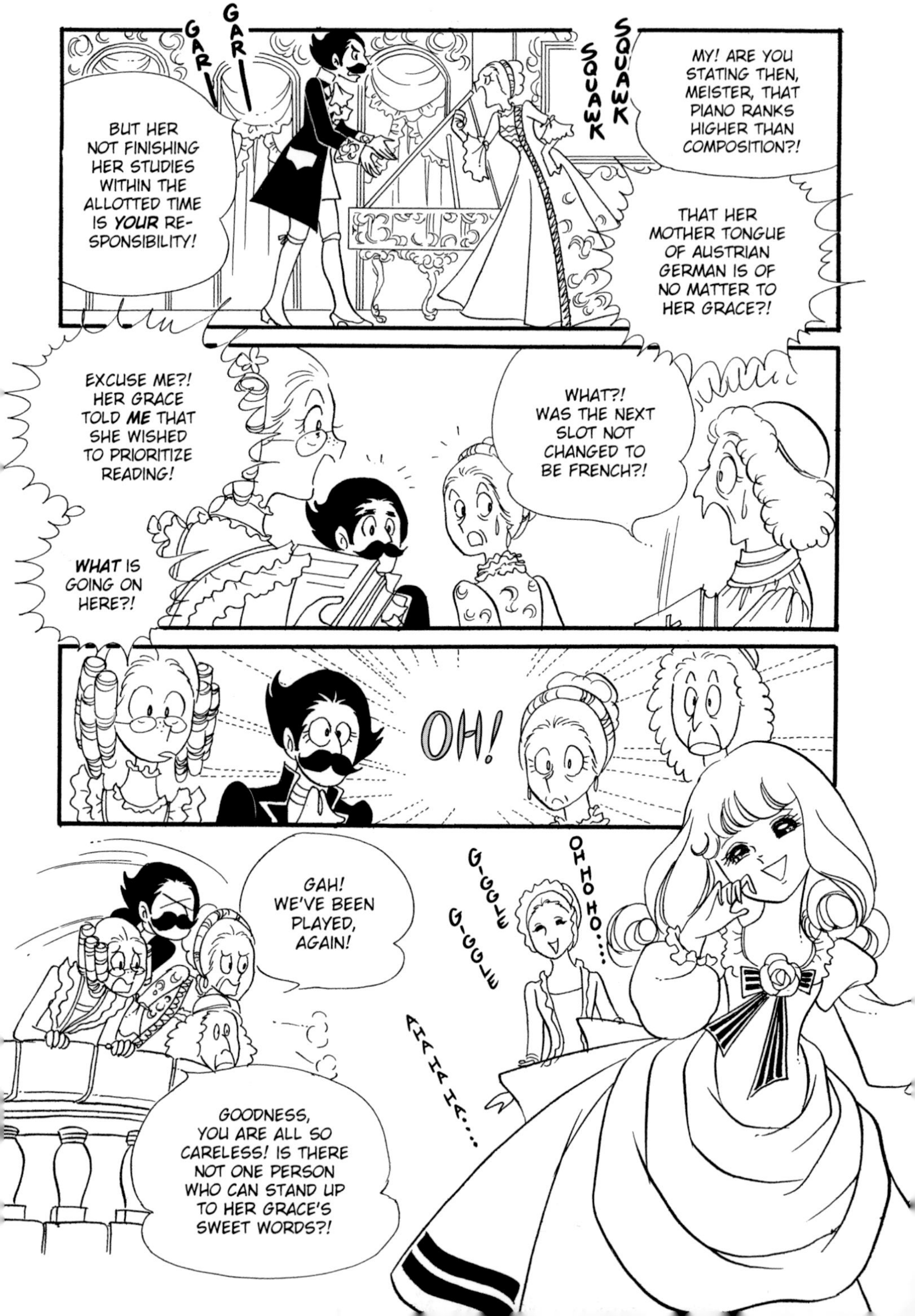
SQUAWK SQUAWK
MY! ARE YOU STATING THEN, MEISTER, THAT PIANO RANKS HIGHER THAN COMPOSITION?!
THAT HER MOTHER TONGUE OF AUSTRIAN GERMAN IS OF NO MATTER TO HER GRACE?!
GARI GARI
BUT HER NOT FINISHING HER STUDIES WITHIN THE ALLOTTED TIME IS *YOUR* RESPONSIBILITY!
WHAT?! WAS THE NEXT SLOT NOT CHANGED TO BE FRENCH?!
EXCUSE ME?! HER GRACE TOLD *ME* THAT SHE WISHED TO PRIORITIZE READING!
WHAT IS GOING ON HERE?!
OH!
OHHOHO....
GIGGLE GIGGLE
GAH! WE'VE BEEN PLAYED, AGAIN!
AHAHAHA....
GOODNESS, YOU ARE ALL SO CARELESS! IS THERE NOT ONE PERSON WHO CAN STAND UP TO HER GRACE'S SWEET WORDS?!

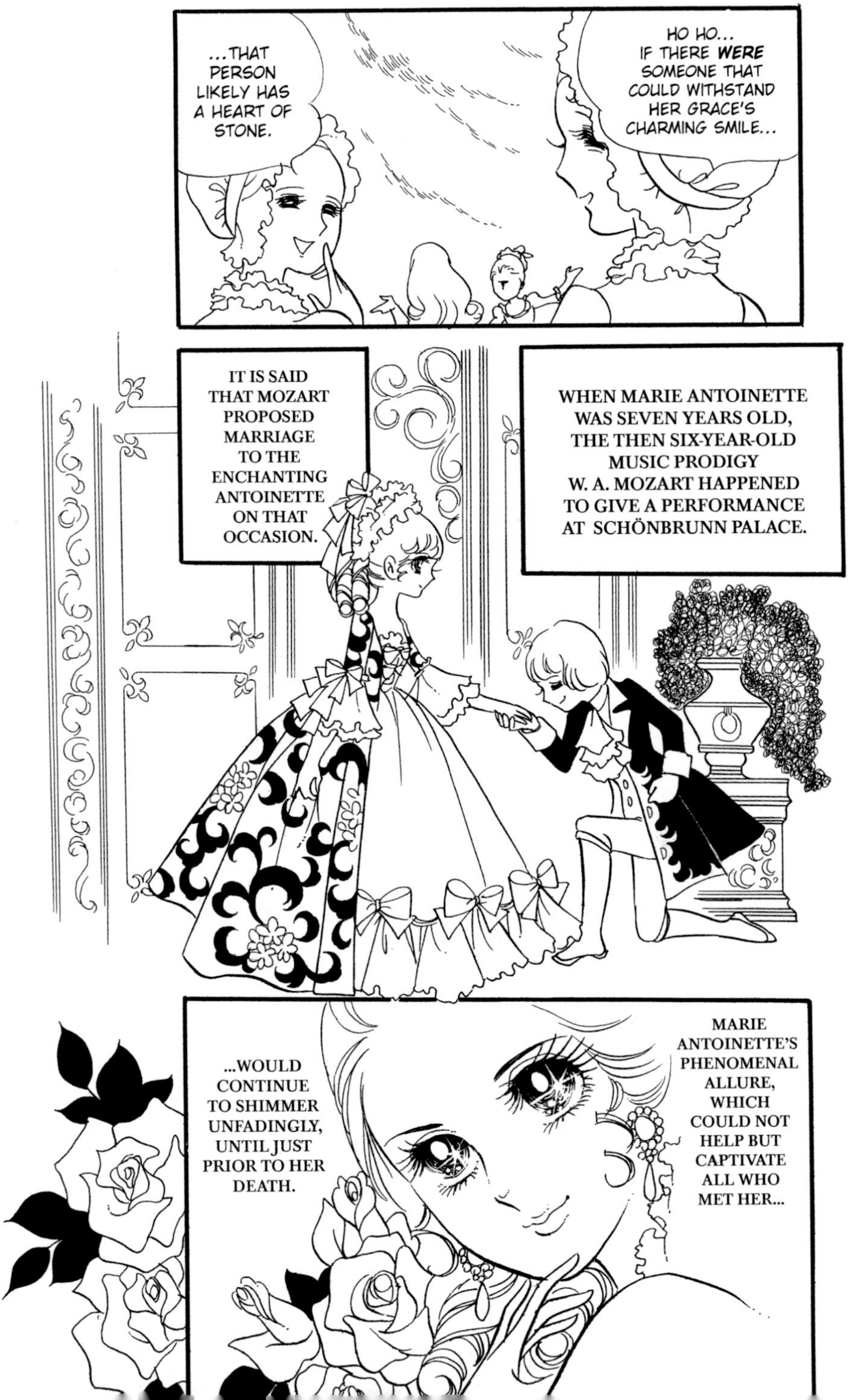
HO HO...
IF THERE **WERE** SOMEONE THAT COULD WITHSTAND HER GRACE'S CHARMING SMILE...
...THAT PERSON LIKELY HAS A HEART OF STONE.
WHEN MARIE ANTOINETTE WAS SEVEN YEARS OLD, THE THEN SIX-YEAR-OLD MUSIC PRODIGY W. A. MOZART HAPPENED TO GIVE A PERFORMANCE AT SCHÖNBRUNN PALACE.
IT IS SAID THAT MOZART PROPOSED MARRIAGE TO THE ENCHANTING ANTOINETTE ON THAT OCCASION.
MARIE ANTOINETTE'S PHENOMENAL ALLURE, WHICH COULD NOT HELP BUT CAPTIVATE ALL WHO MET HER...
...WOULD CONTINUE TO SHIMMER UNFADINGLY, UNTIL JUST PRIOR TO HER DEATH.

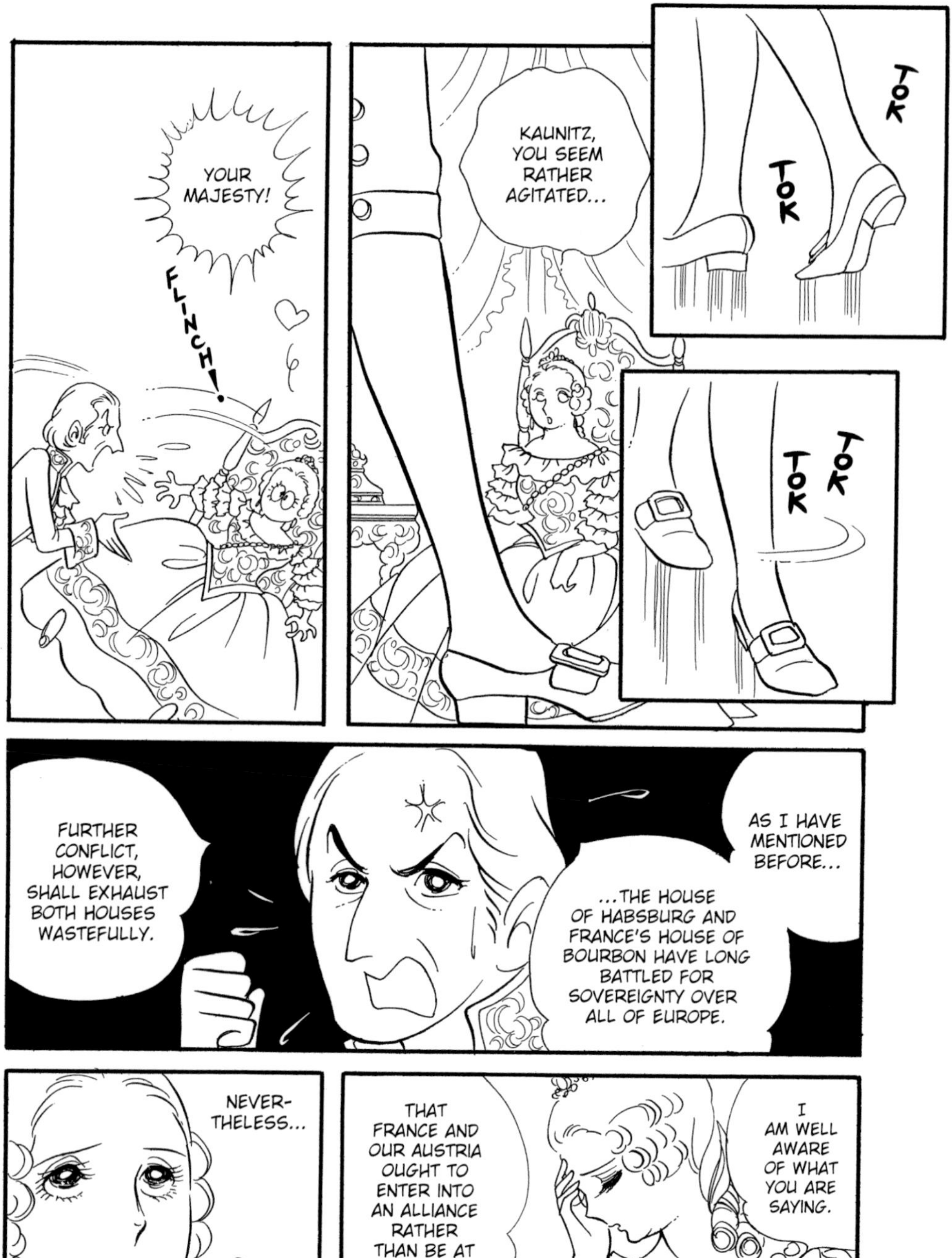
TOK
TOK
TOK
TOK
KAUNITZ, YOU SEEM RATHER AGITATED...
YOUR MAJESTY!
FLINCH!
AS I HAVE MENTIONED BEFORE...
...THE HOUSE OF HABSBURG AND FRANCE'S HOUSE OF BOURBON HAVE LONG BATTLED FOR SOVEREIGNTY OVER ALL OF EUROPE.
FURTHER CONFLICT, HOWEVER, SHALL EXHAUST BOTH HOUSES WASTEFULLY.
I AM WELL AWARE OF WHAT YOU ARE SAYING.
THAT FRANCE AND OUR AUSTRIA OUGHT TO ENTER INTO AN ALLIANCE RATHER THAN BE AT ODDS...
NEVER-THELESS...

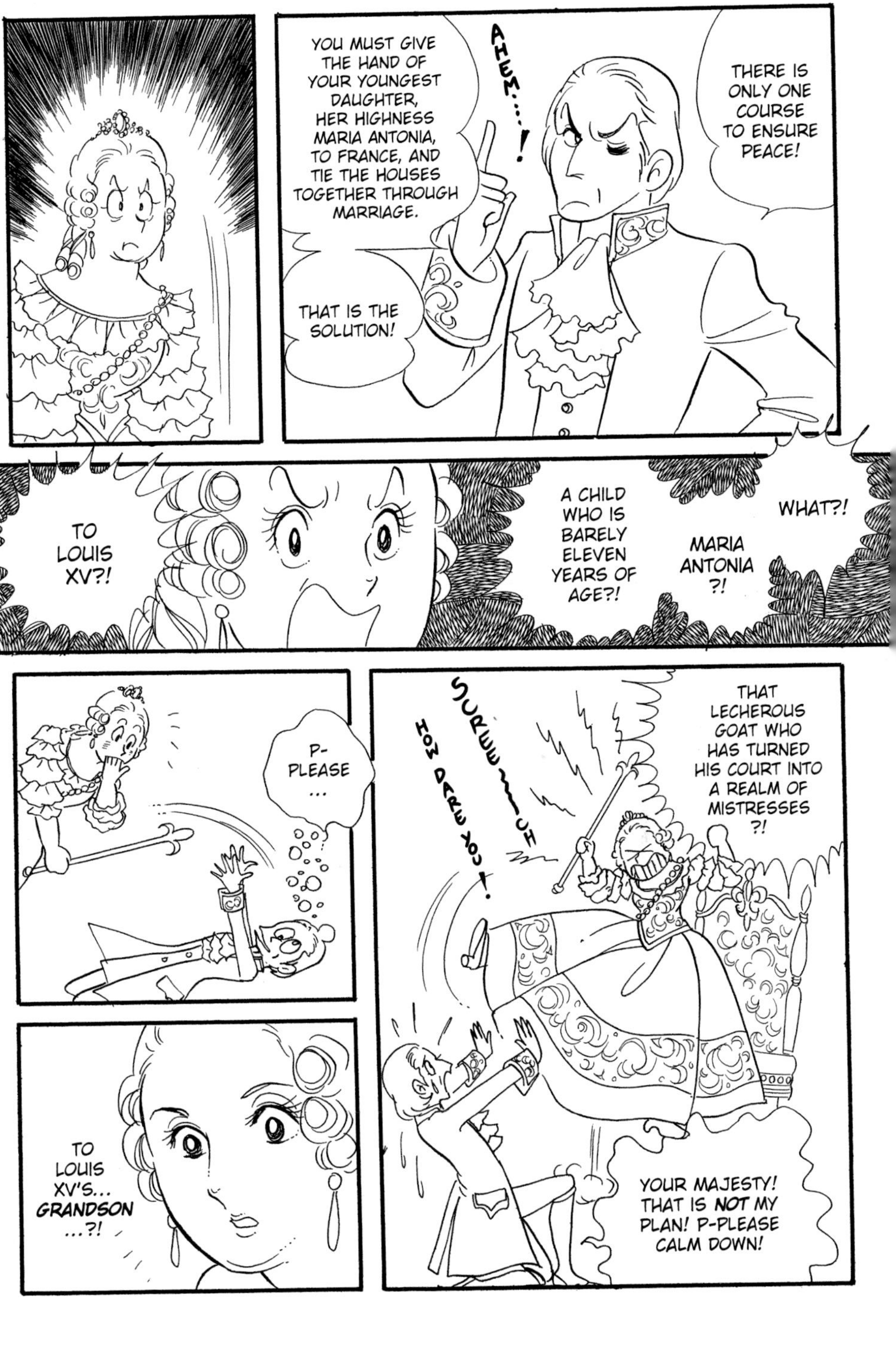
THERE IS ONLY ONE COURSE TO ENSURE PEACE!
AHEM...!
YOU MUST GIVE THE HAND OF YOUR YOUNGEST DAUGHTER, HER HIGHNESS MARIA ANTONIA, TO FRANCE, AND TIE THE HOUSES TOGETHER THROUGH MARRIAGE.
THAT IS THE SOLUTION!
WHAT?!
MARIA ANTONIA ?!
A CHILD WHO IS BARELY ELEVEN YEARS OF AGE?!
TO LOUIS XV?!
THAT LECHEROUS GOAT WHO HAS TURNED HIS COURT INTO A REALM OF MISTRESSES ?!
SWREE~ICH
HOW DARE YOU!
YOUR MAJESTY! THAT IS **NOT** MY PLAN! P-PLEASE CALM DOWN!
P-PLEASE ...
TO LOUIS XV'S... **GRANDSON** ...?!

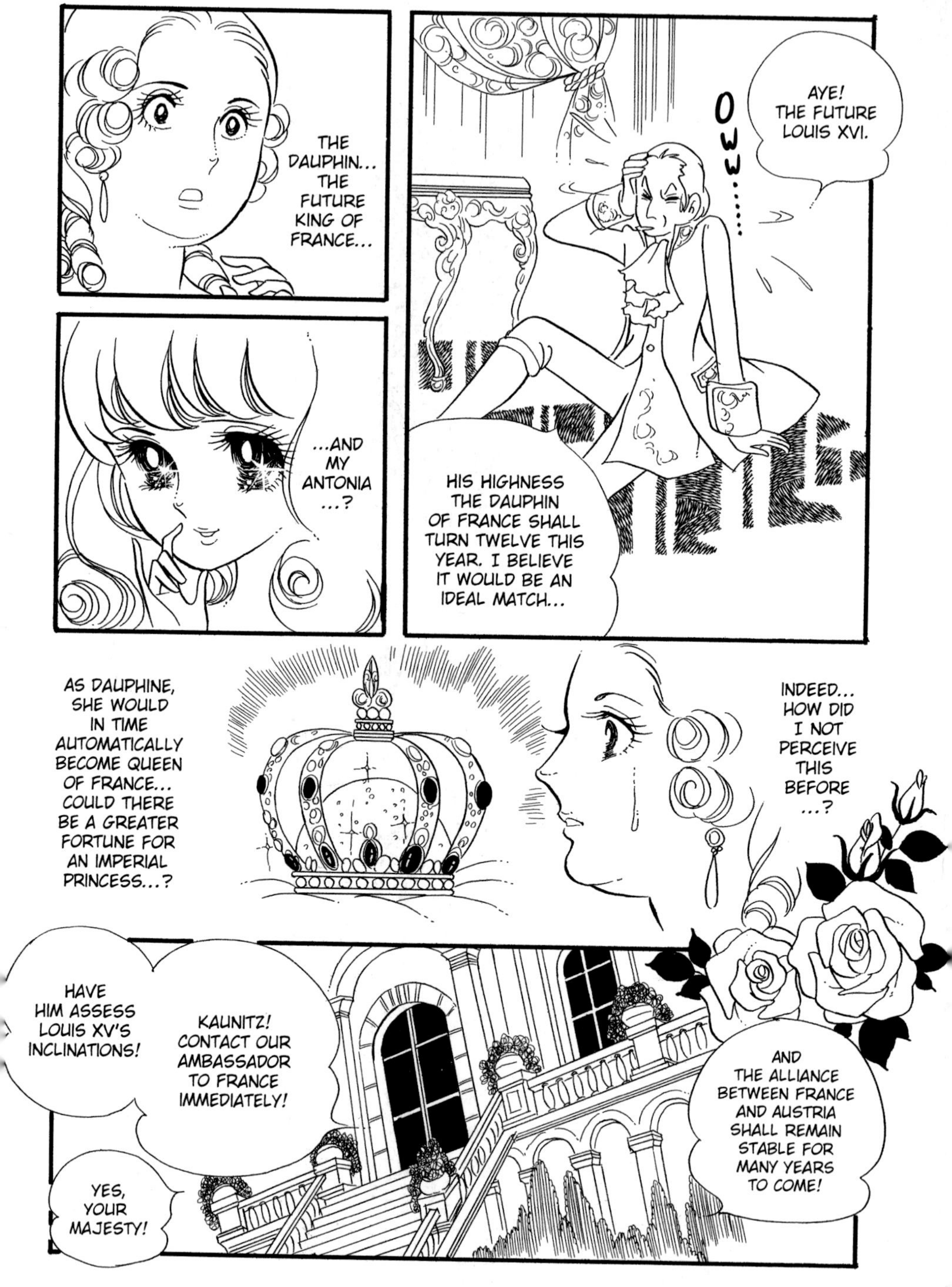
AYE! THE FUTURE LOUIS XVI.
OWW......
HIS HIGHNESS THE DAUPHIN OF FRANCE SHALL TURN TWELVE THIS YEAR. I BELIEVE IT WOULD BE AN IDEAL MATCH...
THE DAUPHIN... THE FUTURE KING OF FRANCE...
...AND MY ANTONIA ...?
INDEED... HOW DID I NOT PERCEIVE THIS BEFORE ...?
AS DAUPHINE, SHE WOULD IN TIME AUTOMATICALLY BECOME QUEEN OF FRANCE... COULD THERE BE A GREATER FORTUNE FOR AN IMPERIAL PRINCESS...?
AND THE ALLIANCE BETWEEN FRANCE AND AUSTRIA SHALL REMAIN STABLE FOR MANY YEARS TO COME!
KAUNITZ! CONTACT OUR AMBASSADOR TO FRANCE IMMEDIATELY!
HAVE HIM ASSESS LOUIS XV'S INCLINATIONS!
YES, YOUR MAJESTY!

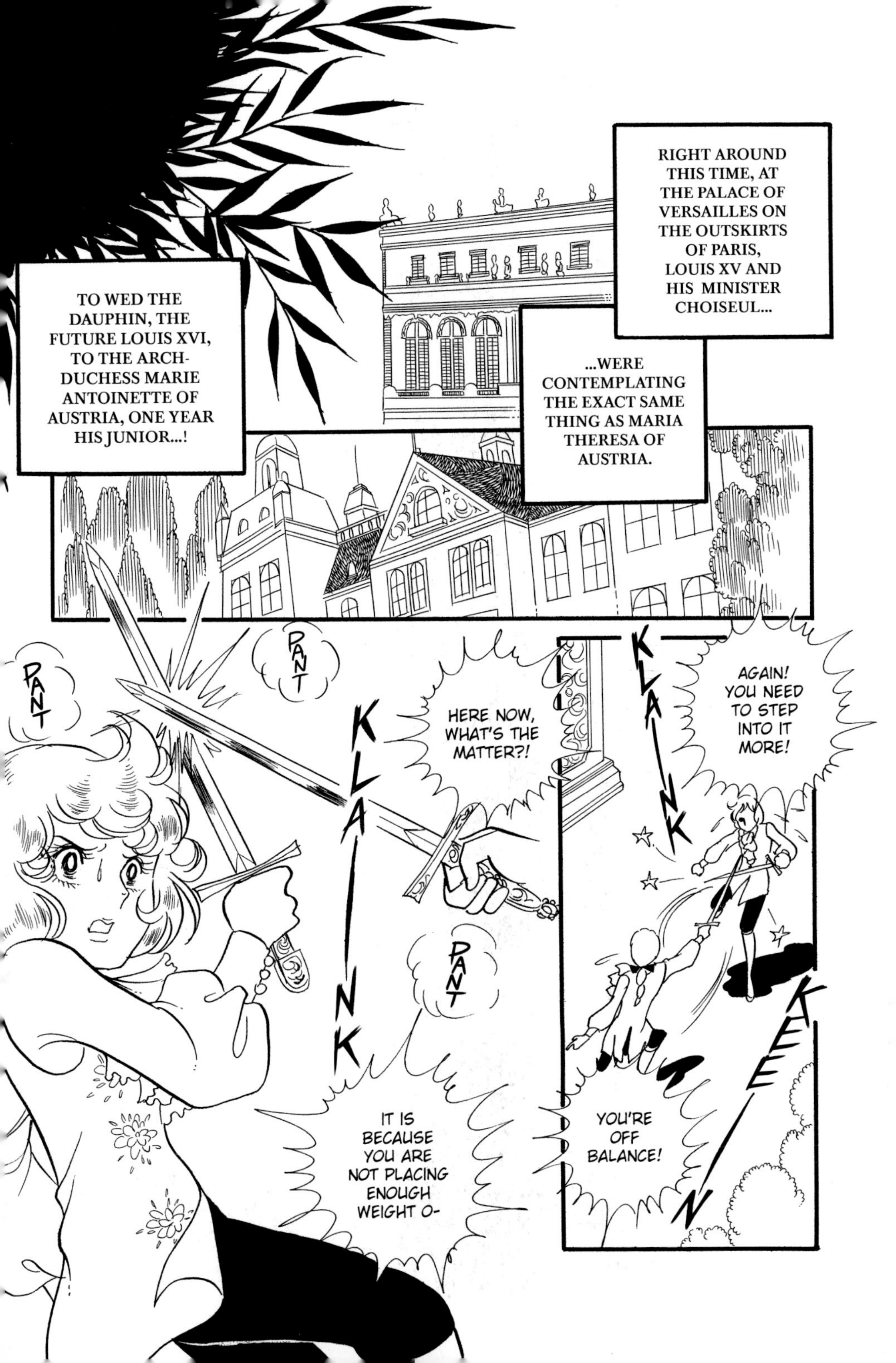
RIGHT AROUND THIS TIME, AT THE PALACE OF VERSAILLES ON THE OUTSKIRTS OF PARIS, LOUIS XV AND HIS MINISTER CHOISEUL...
...WERE CONTEMPLATING THE EXACT SAME THING AS MARIA THERESA OF AUSTRIA.
TO WED THE DAUPHIN, THE FUTURE LOUIS XVI, TO THE ARCH-DUCHESS MARIE ANTOINETTE OF AUSTRIA, ONE YEAR HIS JUNIOR...!
KLANK
AGAIN! YOU NEED TO STEP INTO IT MORE!
YOU'RE OFF BALANCE!
KEEEN
HERE NOW, WHAT'S THE MATTER?!
PANT
PANT
KLANK
PANT
IT IS BECAUSE YOU ARE NOT PLACING ENOUGH WEIGHT O-

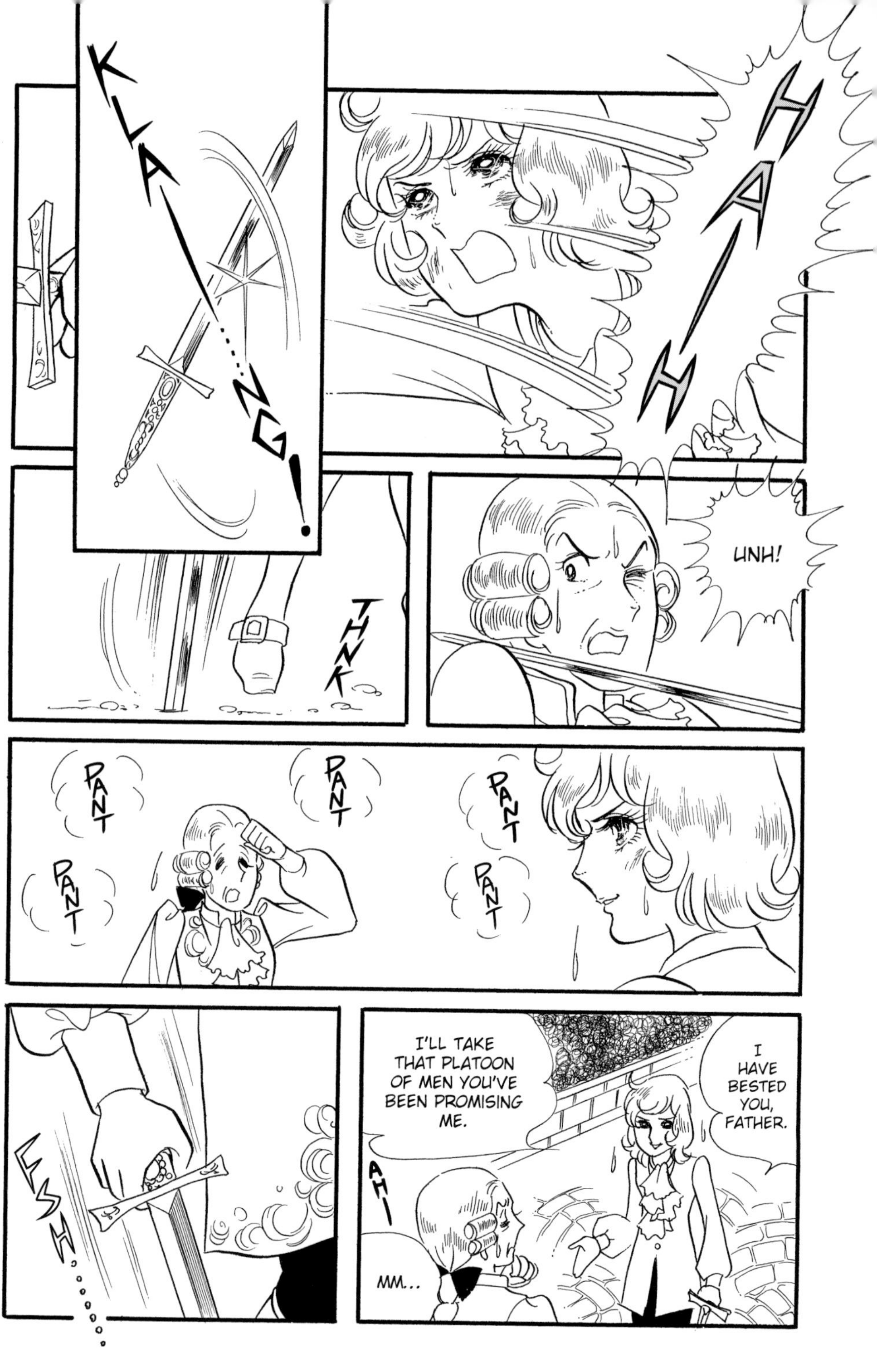
HAH
KLA...NG!
UNH!
THNK
PANT
PANT
PANT
PANT
I HAVE BESTED YOU, FATHER.
I'LL TAKE THAT PLATOON OF MEN YOU'VE BEEN PROMISING ME.
AH!
MM...
FSH......

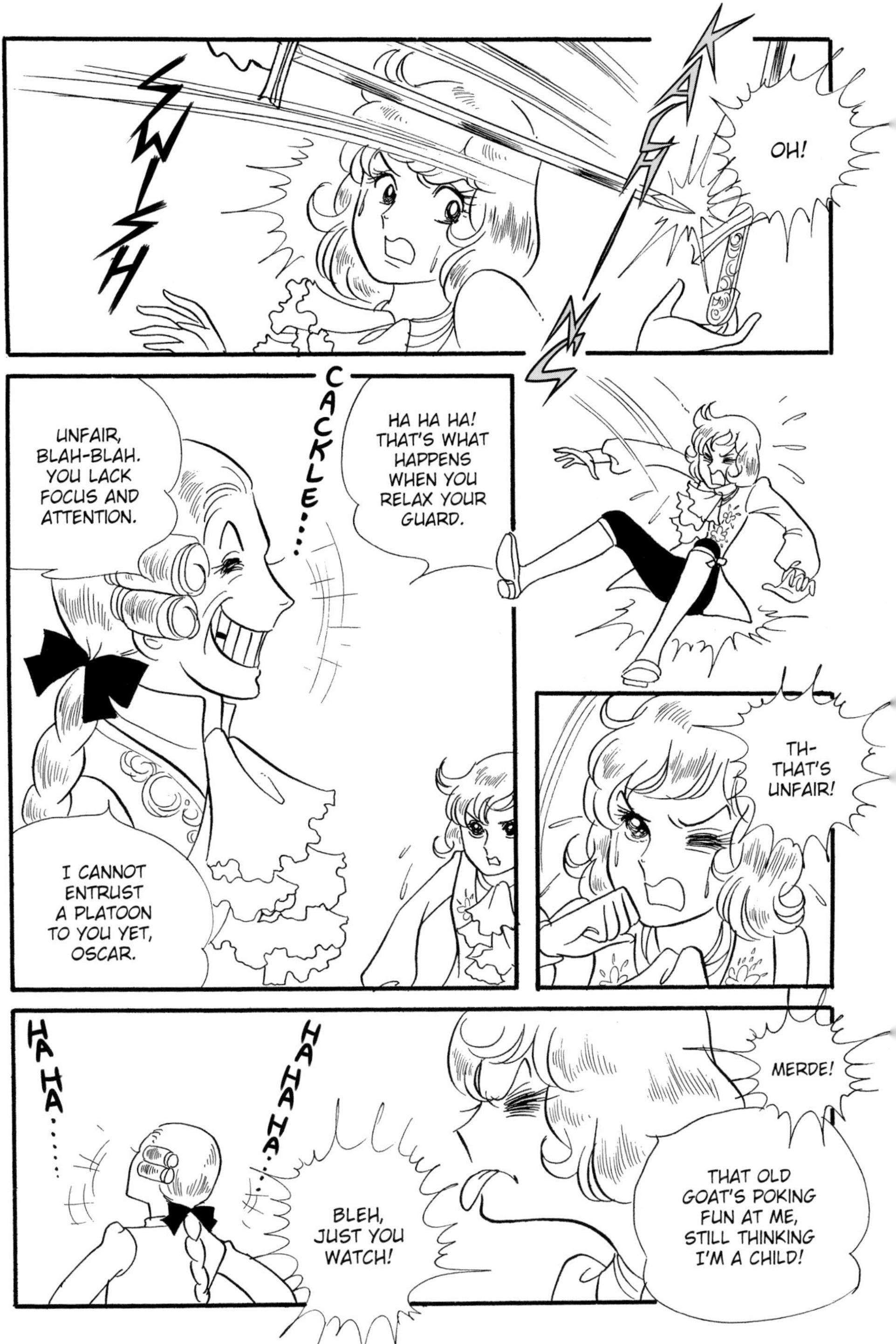
OH!
KASH
SWISH
TH- THAT'S UNFAIR!
HA HA HA! THAT'S WHAT HAPPENS WHEN YOU RELAX YOUR GUARD.
CACKLE...
UNFAIR, BLAH-BLAH. YOU LACK FOCUS AND ATTENTION.
I CANNOT ENTRUST A PLATOON TO YOU YET, OSCAR.
MERDE!
THAT OLD GOAT'S POKING FUN AT ME, STILL THINKING I'M A CHILD!
BLEH, JUST YOU WATCH!
HAHAHAHA...
HAHA......

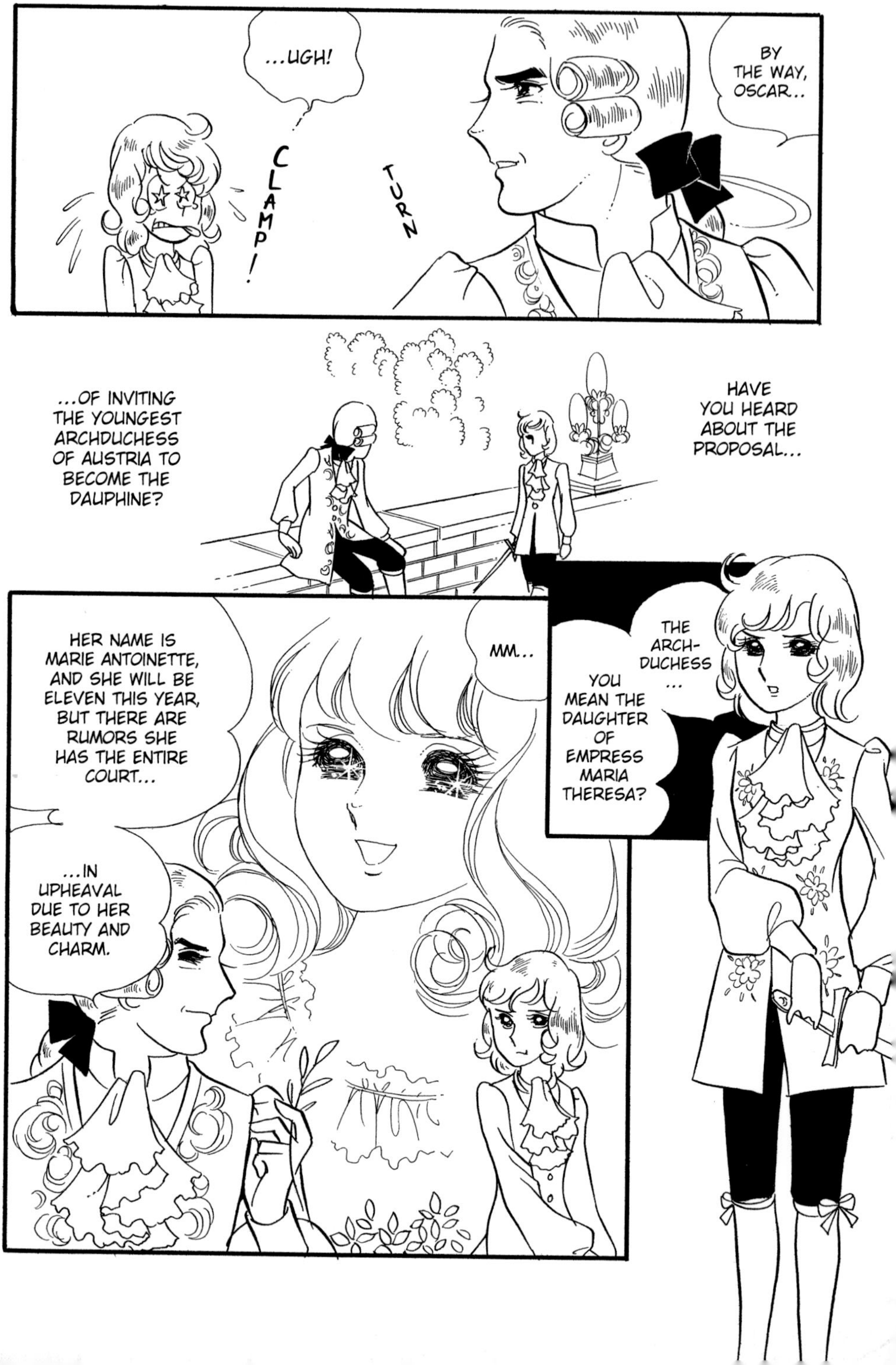

BY THE WAY, OSCAR...
...UGH!
TURN
CLAMP!
HAVE YOU HEARD ABOUT THE PROPOSAL...
...OF INVITING THE YOUNGEST ARCHDUCHESS OF AUSTRIA TO BECOME THE DAUPHINE?
THE ARCH-DUCHESS...
YOU MEAN THE DAUGHTER OF EMPRESS MARIA THERESA?
MM...
HER NAME IS MARIE ANTOINETTE, AND SHE WILL BE ELEVEN THIS YEAR, BUT THERE ARE RUMORS SHE HAS THE ENTIRE COURT...
...IN UPHEAVAL DUE TO HER BEAUTY AND CHARM.

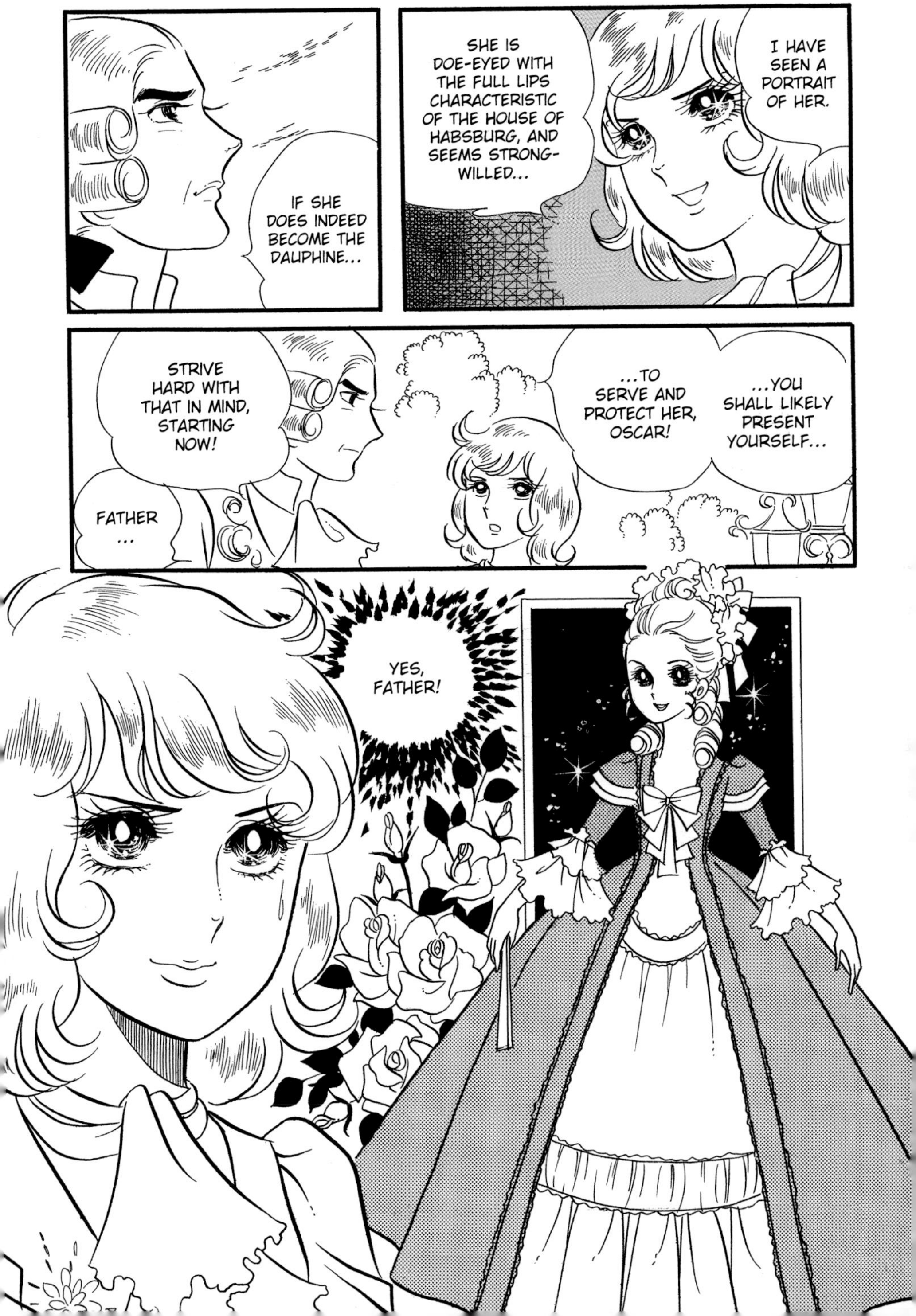
I HAVE SEEN A PORTRAIT OF HER.
SHE IS DOE-EYED WITH THE FULL LIPS CHARACTERISTIC OF THE HOUSE OF HABSBURG, AND SEEMS STRONG-WILLED...
IF SHE DOES INDEED BECOME THE DAUPHINE...
...YOU SHALL LIKELY PRESENT YOURSELF...
...TO SERVE AND PROTECT HER, OSCAR!
STRIVE HARD WITH THAT IN MIND, STARTING NOW!
FATHER ...
YES, FATHER!

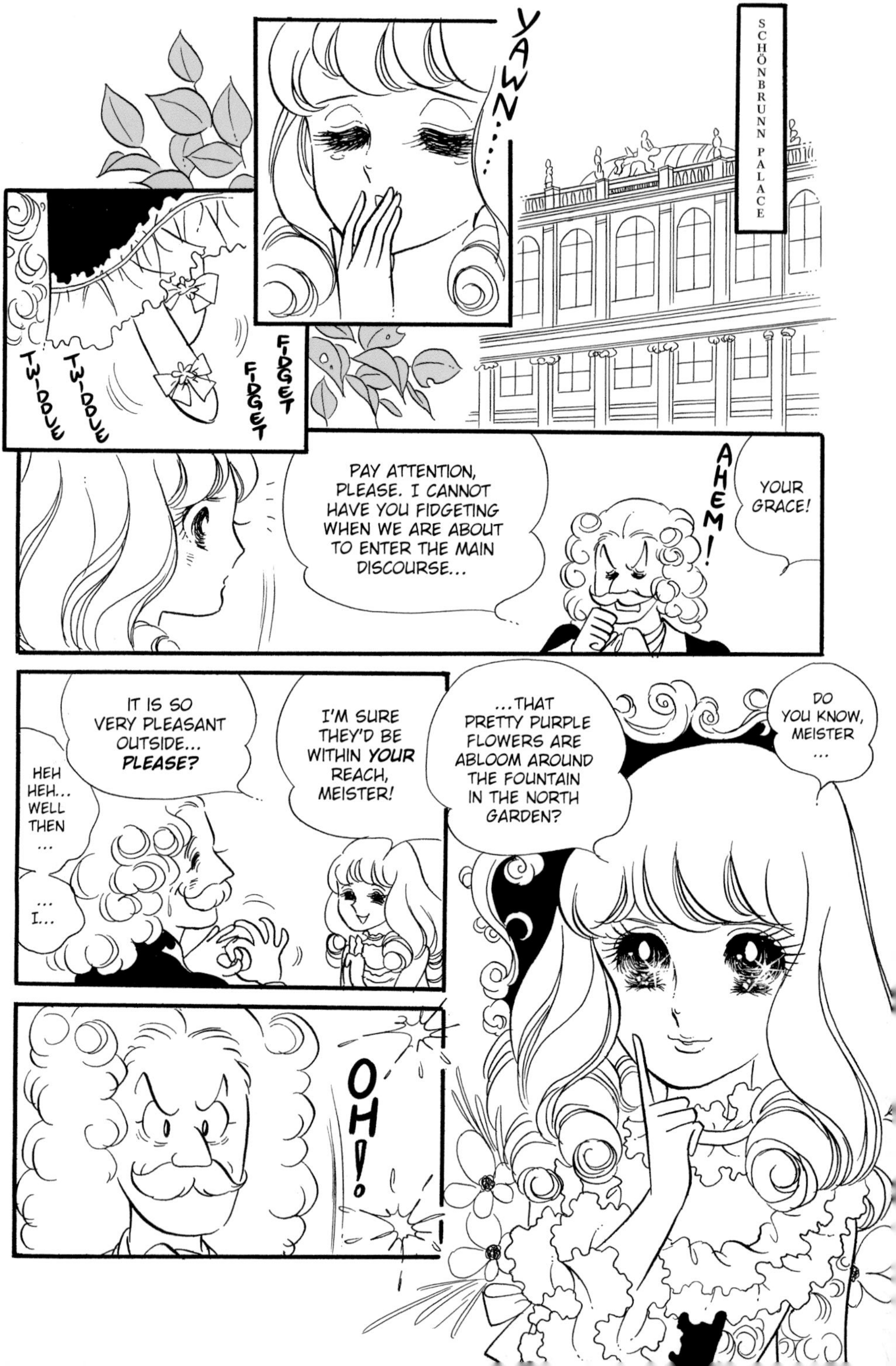
SCHÖNBRUNN PALACE
YAWN...
FIDGET FIDGET
TWIDDLE TWIDDLE
YOUR GRACE!
AHEM!
PAY ATTENTION, PLEASE. I CANNOT HAVE YOU FIDGETING WHEN WE ARE ABOUT TO ENTER THE MAIN DISCOURSE...
DO YOU KNOW, MEISTER ...
...THAT PRETTY PURPLE FLOWERS ARE ABLOOM AROUND THE FOUNTAIN IN THE NORTH GARDEN?
I'M SURE THEY'D BE WITHIN *YOUR* REACH, MEISTER!
IT IS SO VERY PLEASANT OUTSIDE... ***PLEASE?***
HEH HEH... WELL THEN ...
... I...
OH!!

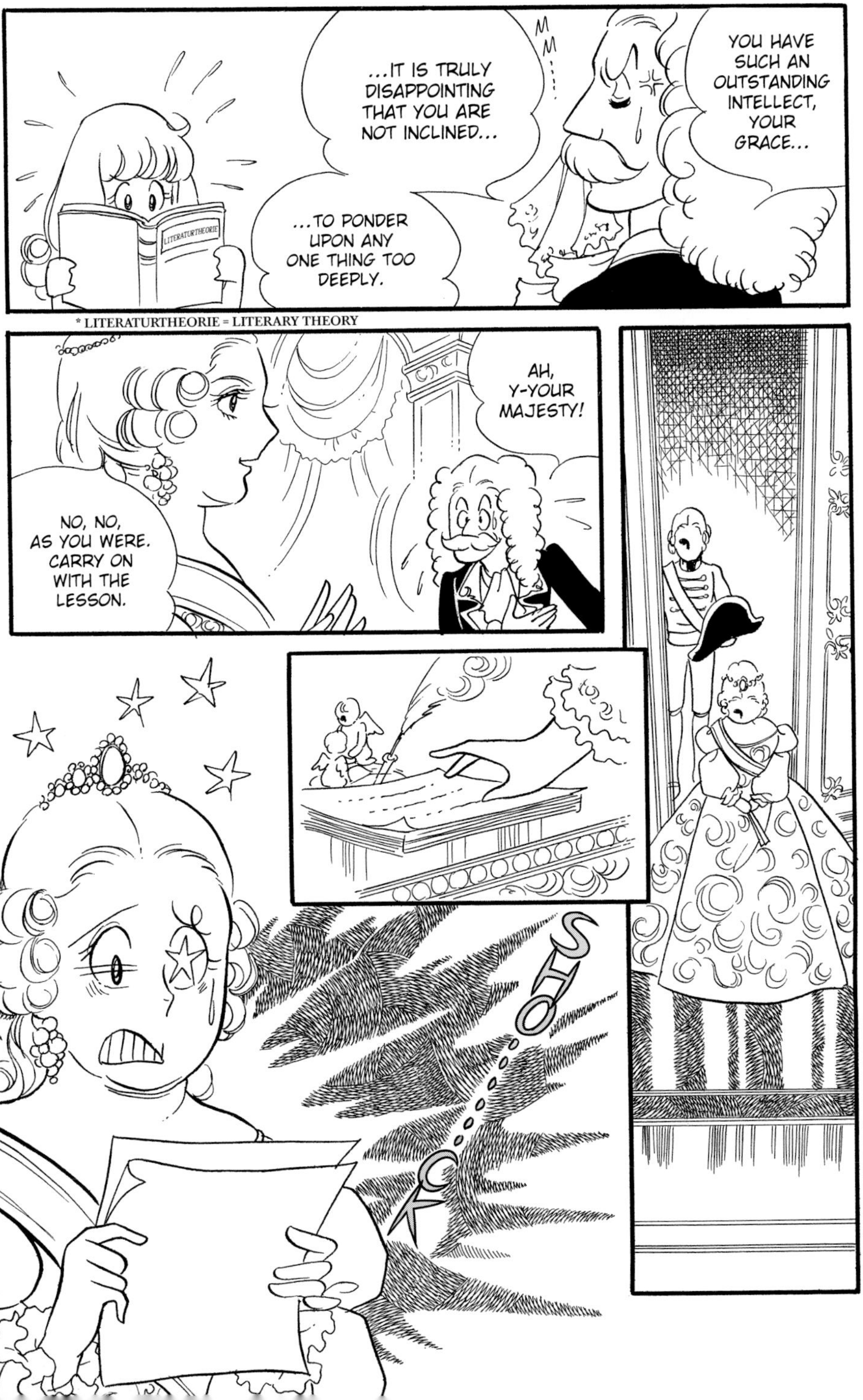
YOU HAVE SUCH AN OUTSTANDING INTELLECT, YOUR GRACE...
MM...
...IT IS TRULY DISAPPOINTING THAT YOU ARE NOT INCLINED...
...TO PONDER UPON ANY ONE THING TOO DEEPLY.
LITERATURTHEORIE
* LITERATURTHEORIE = LITERARY THEORY
AH, Y-YOUR MAJESTY!
NO, NO, AS YOU WERE. CARRY ON WITH THE LESSON.
SHOOOOOOCK

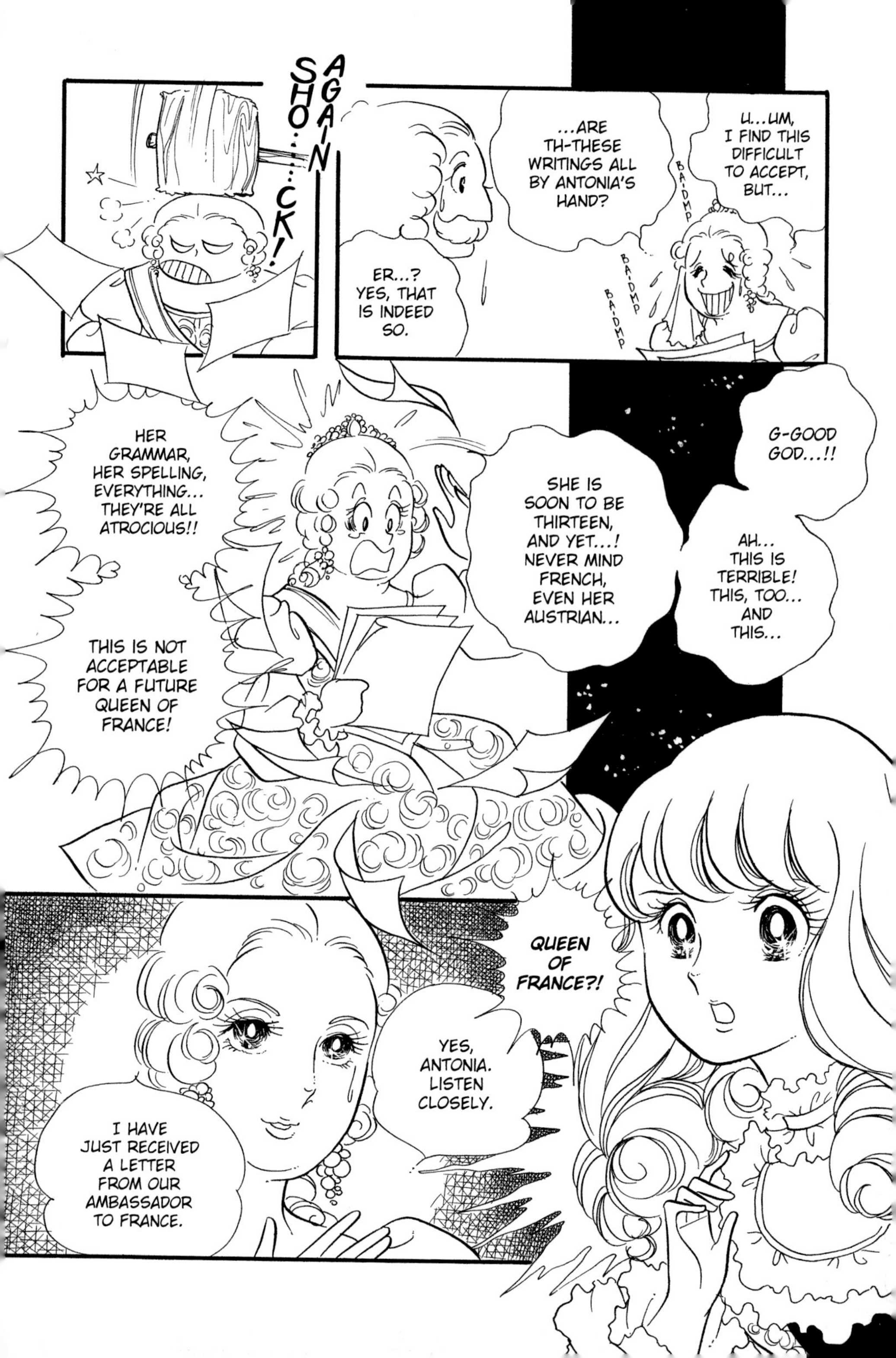
U...UM, I FIND THIS DIFFICULT TO ACCEPT, BUT...
BA-DMP
BA-DMP
BA-DMP
...ARE TH-THESE WRITINGS ALL BY ANTONIA'S HAND?
ER...? YES, THAT IS INDEED SO.
AGAIN
SHO...CK!
G-GOOD GOD...!!
AH... THIS IS TERRIBLE! THIS, TOO... AND THIS...
SHE IS SOON TO BE THIRTEEN, AND YET...! NEVER MIND FRENCH, EVEN HER AUSTRIAN...
HER GRAMMAR, HER SPELLING, EVERYTHING... THEY'RE ALL ATROCIOUS!!
THIS IS NOT ACCEPTABLE FOR A FUTURE QUEEN OF FRANCE!
QUEEN OF FRANCE?!
YES, ANTONIA. LISTEN CLOSELY.
I HAVE JUST RECEIVED A LETTER FROM OUR AMBASSADOR TO FRANCE.

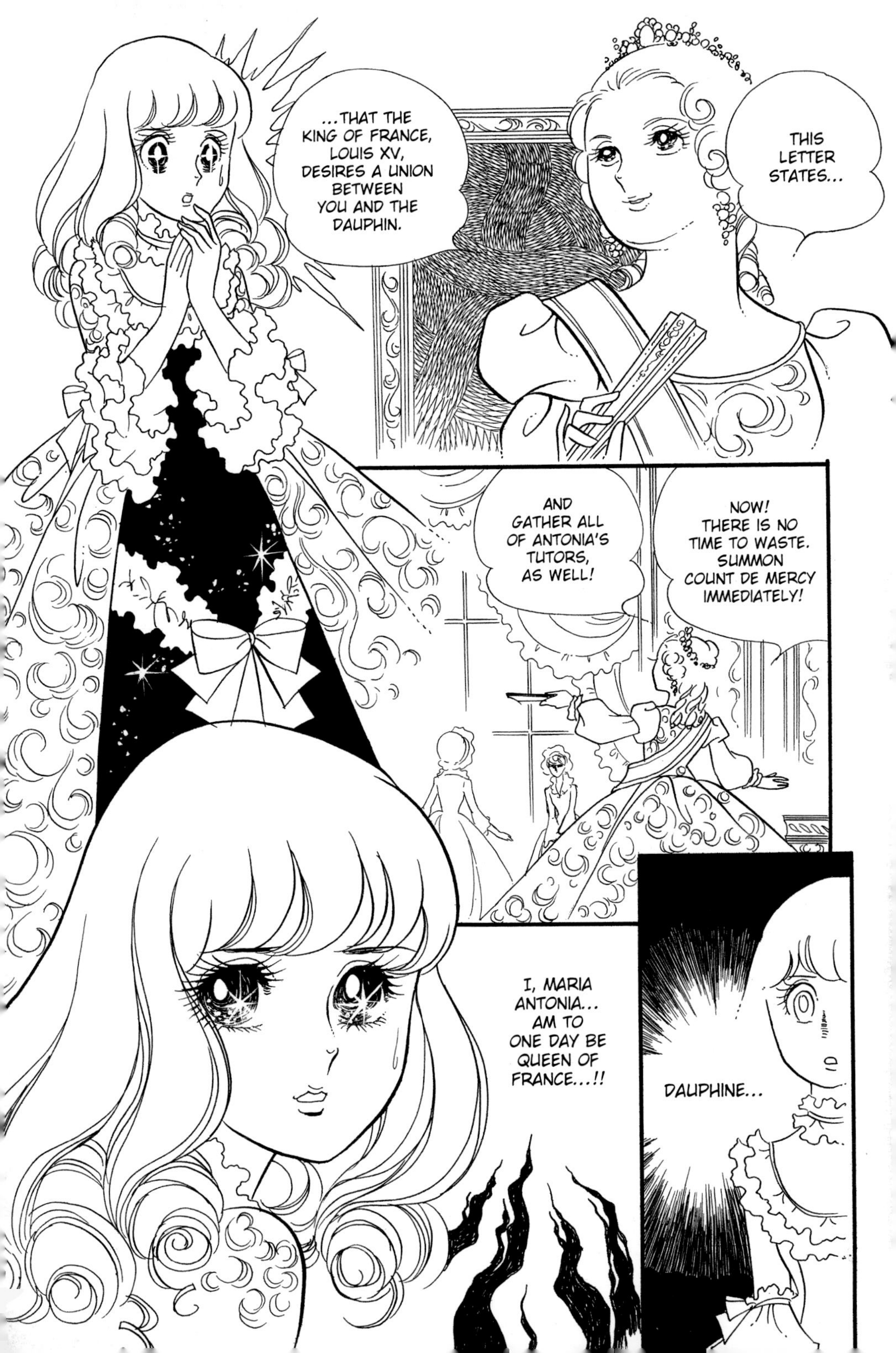

THIS LETTER STATES...
...THAT THE KING OF FRANCE, LOUIS XV, DESIRES A UNION BETWEEN YOU AND THE DAUPHIN.
NOW! THERE IS NO TIME TO WASTE. SUMMON COUNT DE MERCY IMMEDIATELY!
AND GATHER ALL OF ANTONIA'S TUTORS, AS WELL!
DAUPHINE...
I, MARIA ANTONIA... AM TO ONE DAY BE QUEEN OF FRANCE...!!

1972 WEEKLY MARGARET MAGAZINE
ISSUE 20 PREVIEW ART

◆はやくも**大評判**!!

♥11歳のオーストリア皇女、アントワネットに、フランス王太子との結婚の話が…!!

ベルサイユのばら

池田理代子

♦ALREADY A HUGE SENSATION!
♥AN ARRANGED MARRIAGE WITH THE CROWN PRINCE OF FRANCE IS
PROPOSED TO ANTOINETTE, THE 11 YEAR OLD PRINCESS OF AUSTRIA...!!

EPISODE 02

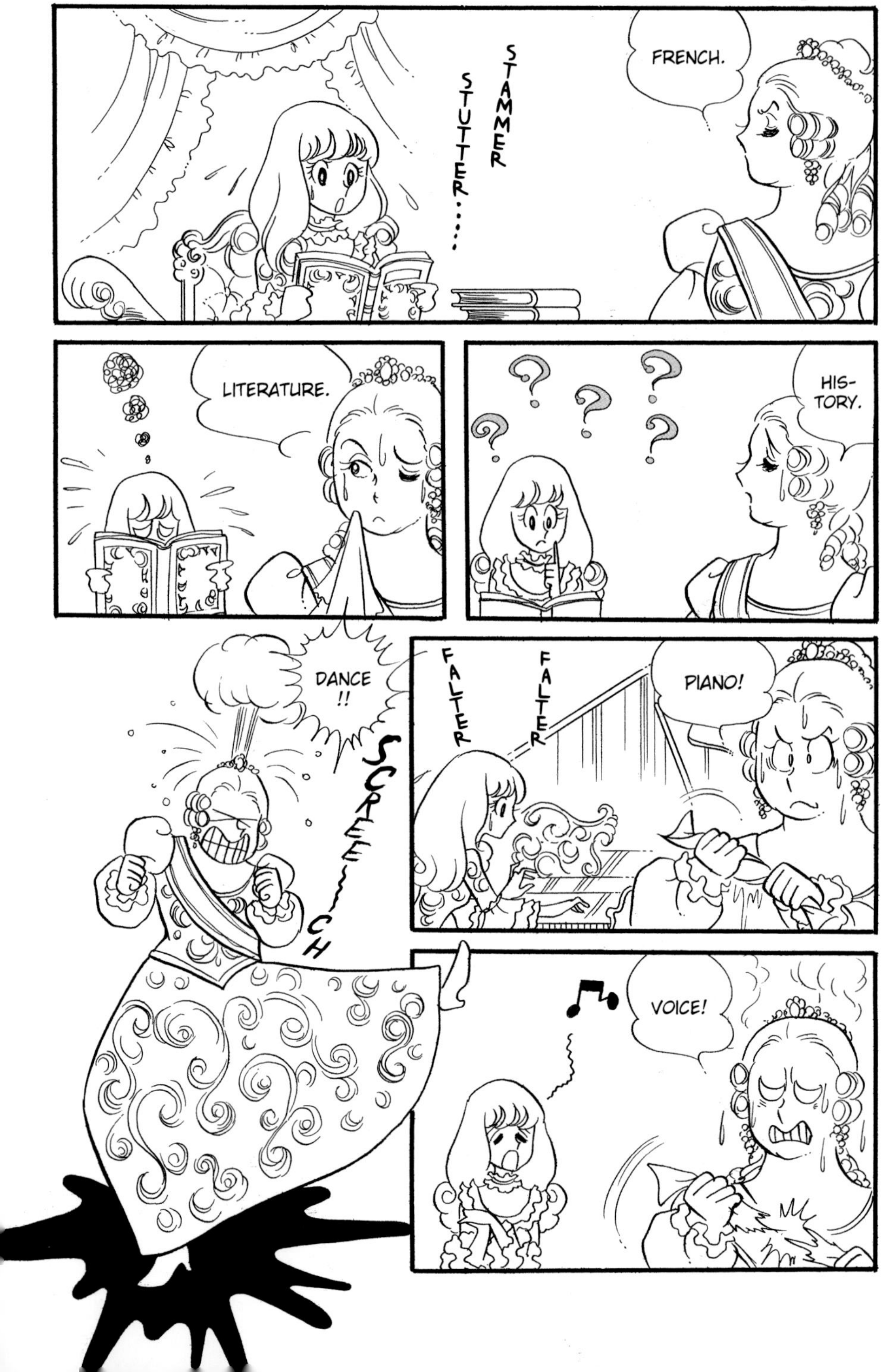
FRENCH.
STAMMER
STUTTER.....
HIS-
TORY.
LITERATURE.
PIANO!
FALTER
FALTER
VOICE!
DANCE !!
SCREEE~CH

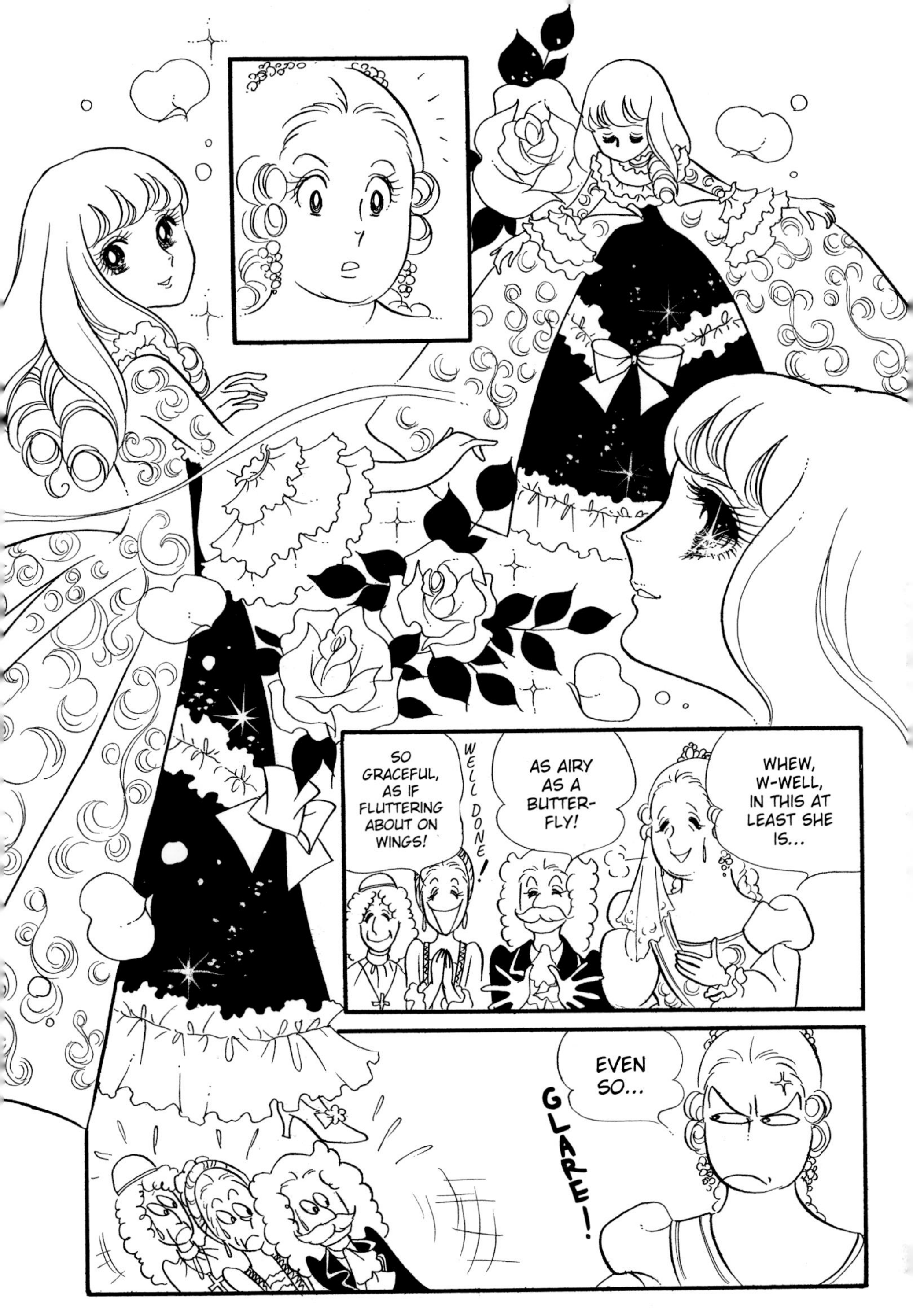
WHEW, W-WELL, IN THIS AT LEAST SHE IS...
AS AIRY AS A BUTTERFLY!
WELL DONE!
SO GRACEFUL, AS IF FLUTTERING ABOUT ON WINGS!
EVEN SO...
GLARE!

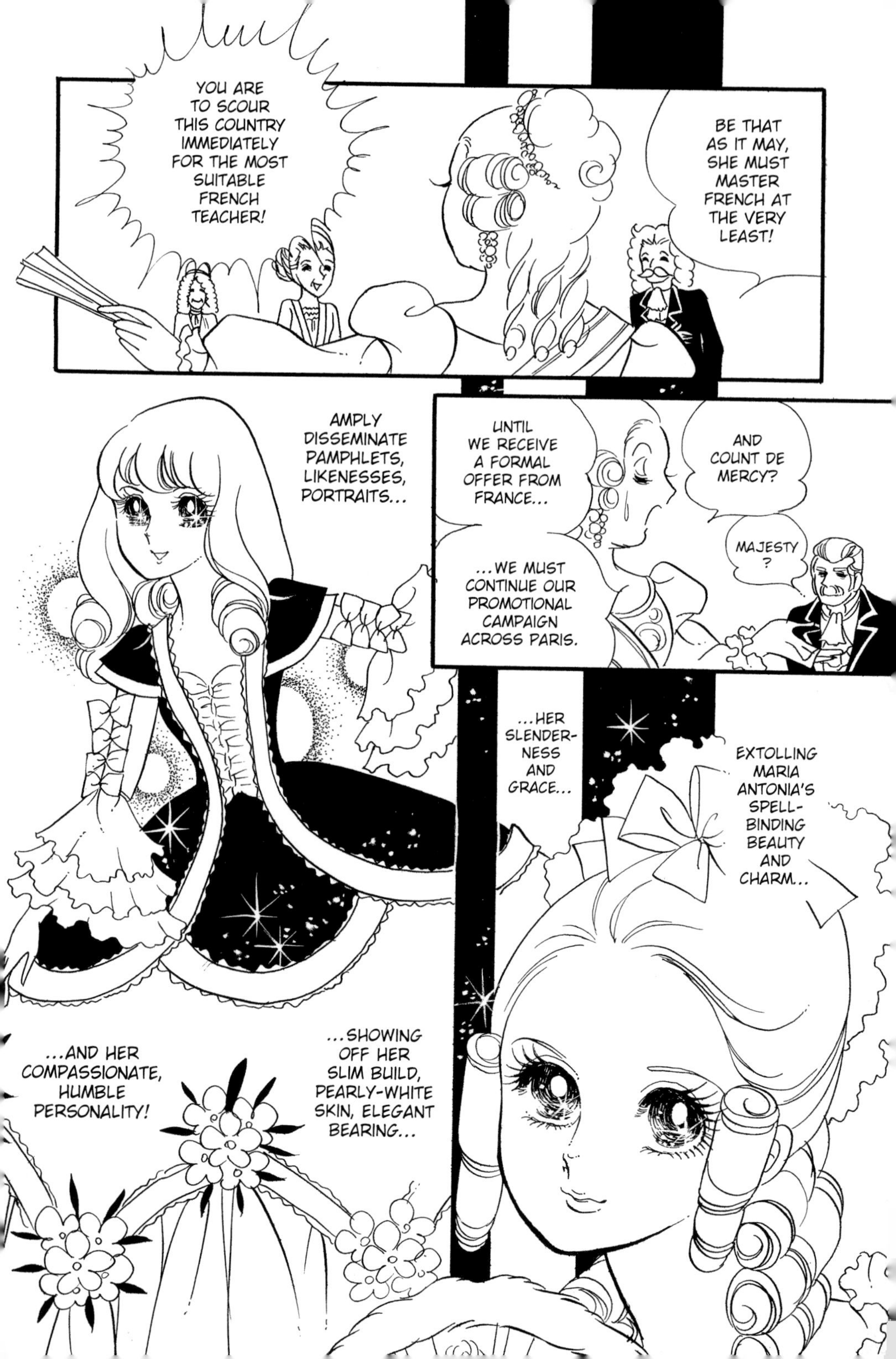
BE THAT AS IT MAY, SHE MUST MASTER FRENCH AT THE VERY LEAST!
YOU ARE TO SCOUR THIS COUNTRY IMMEDIATELY FOR THE MOST SUITABLE FRENCH TEACHER!
AND COUNT DE MERCY?
MAJESTY?
UNTIL WE RECEIVE A FORMAL OFFER FROM FRANCE...
...WE MUST CONTINUE OUR PROMOTIONAL CAMPAIGN ACROSS PARIS.
AMPLY DISSEMINATE PAMPHLETS, LIKENESSES, PORTRAITS...
EXTOLLING MARIA ANTONIA'S SPELL-BINDING BEAUTY AND CHARM...
...HER SLENDER-NESS AND GRACE...
...SHOWING OFF HER SLIM BUILD, PEARLY-WHITE SKIN, ELEGANT BEARING...
...AND HER COMPASSIONATE, HUMBLE PERSONALITY!

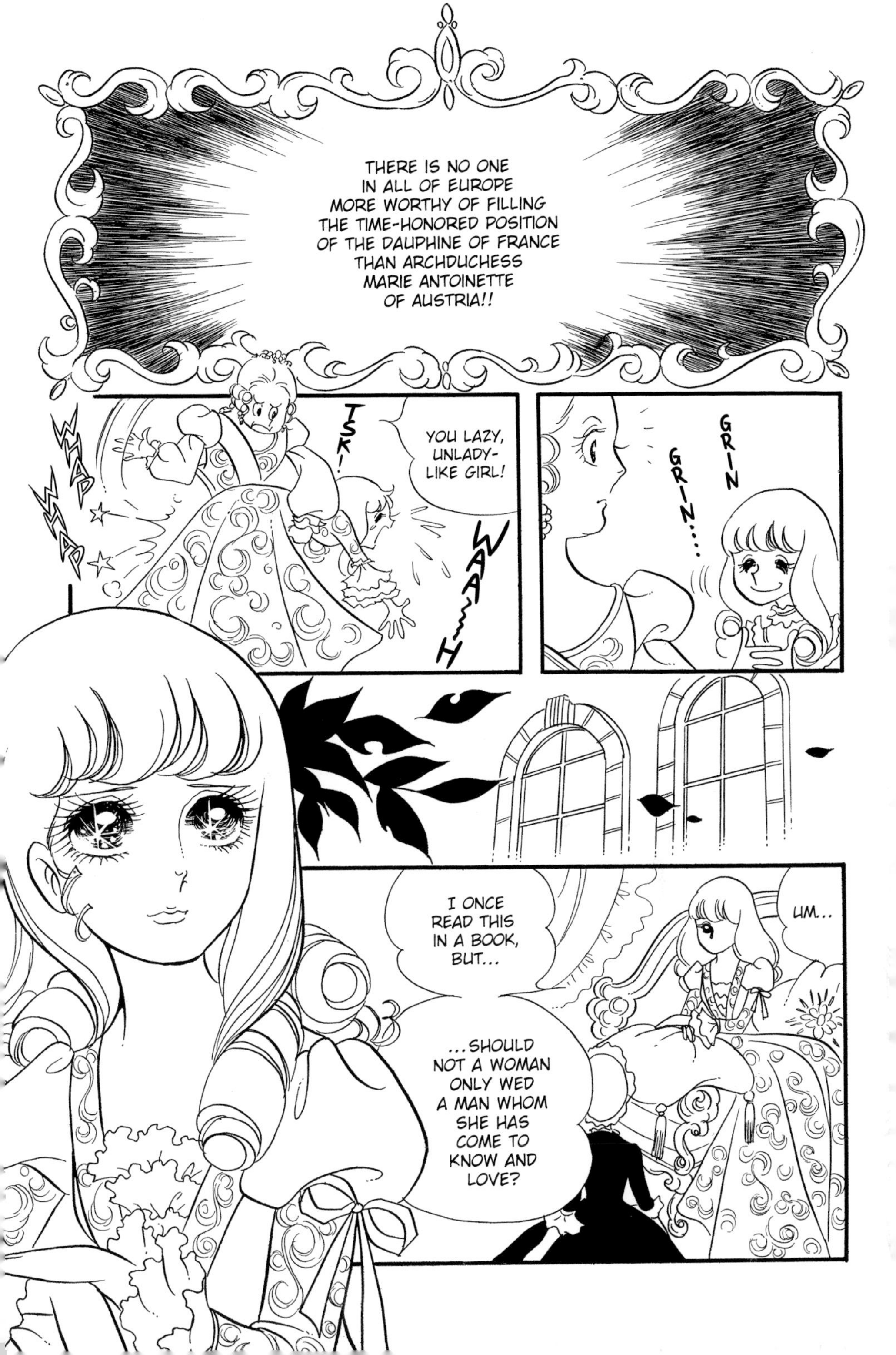
THERE IS NO ONE IN ALL OF EUROPE MORE WORTHY OF FILLING THE TIME-HONORED POSITION OF THE DAUPHINE OF FRANCE THAN ARCHDUCHESS MARIE ANTOINETTE OF AUSTRIA!!
GRIN GRIN....
YOU LAZY, UNLADY-LIKE GIRL!
TSK!
WAAAAH
WHAP WHAP
UM...
I ONCE READ THIS IN A BOOK, BUT...
...SHOULD NOT A WOMAN ONLY WED A MAN WHOM SHE HAS COME TO KNOW AND LOVE?

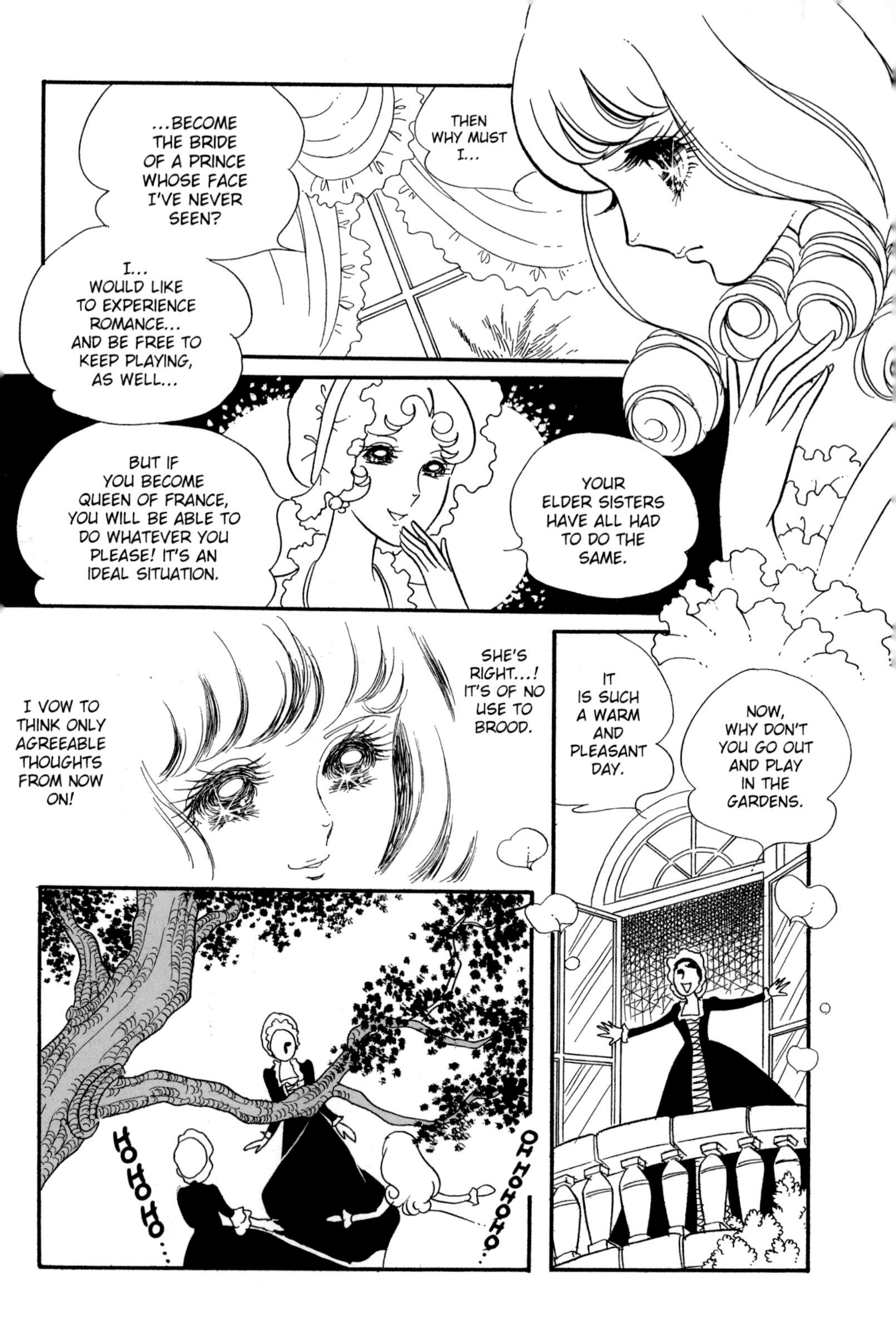
THEN WHY MUST I...
...BECOME THE BRIDE OF A PRINCE WHOSE FACE I'VE NEVER SEEN?
I... WOULD LIKE TO EXPERIENCE ROMANCE... AND BE FREE TO KEEP PLAYING, AS WELL...
YOUR ELDER SISTERS HAVE ALL HAD TO DO THE SAME.
BUT IF YOU BECOME QUEEN OF FRANCE, YOU WILL BE ABLE TO DO WHATEVER YOU PLEASE! IT'S AN IDEAL SITUATION.
IT IS SUCH A WARM AND PLEASANT DAY.
NOW, WHY DON'T YOU GO OUT AND PLAY IN THE GARDENS.
SHE'S RIGHT...! IT'S OF NO USE TO BROOD.
I VOW TO THINK ONLY AGREEABLE THOUGHTS FROM NOW ON!
OHOHOHOHO...
HOHOHO...

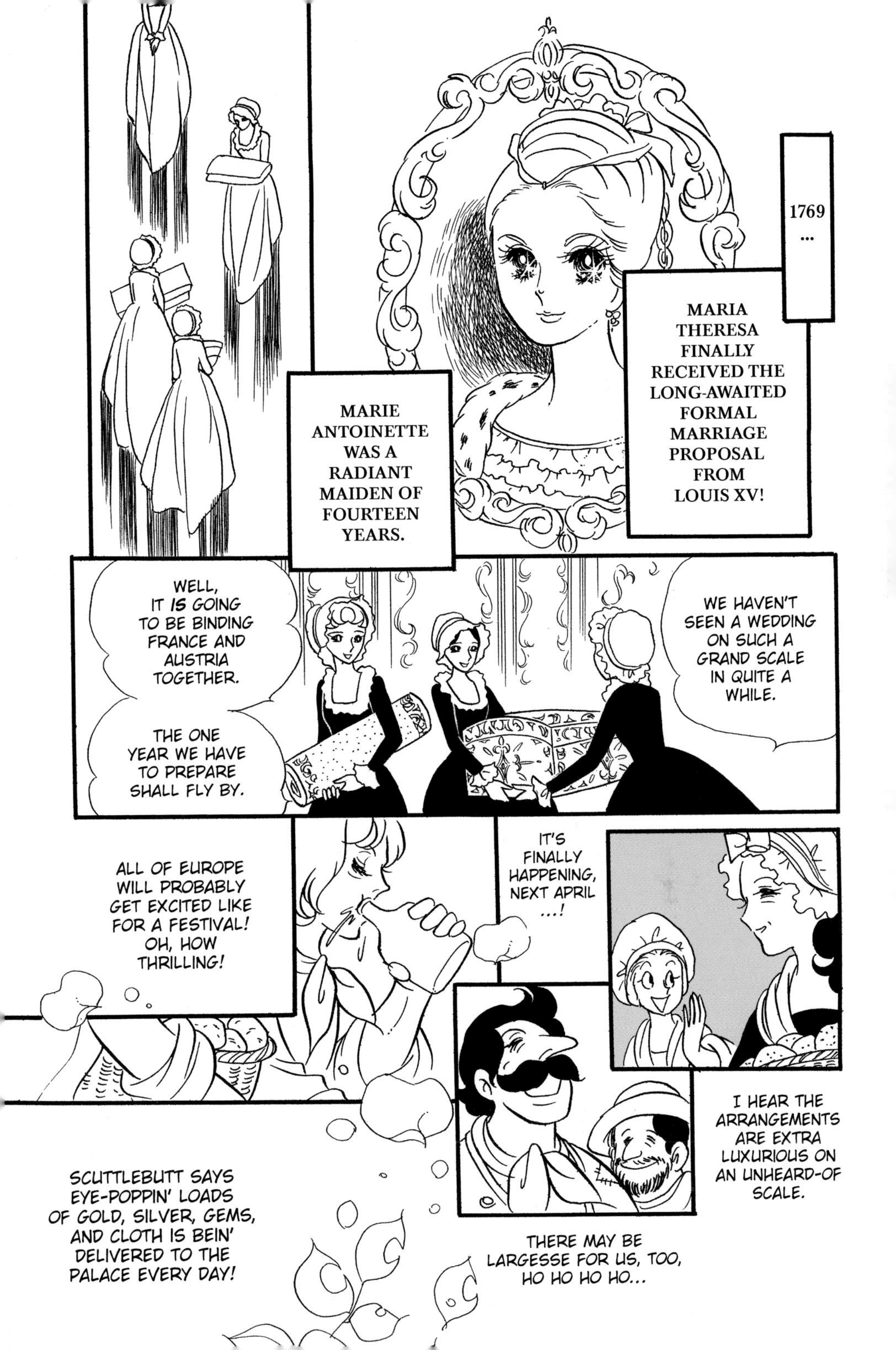
1769 ...
MARIA THERESA FINALLY RECEIVED THE LONG-AWAITED FORMAL MARRIAGE PROPOSAL FROM LOUIS XV!
MARIE ANTOINETTE WAS A RADIANT MAIDEN OF FOURTEEN YEARS.
WE HAVEN'T SEEN A WEDDING ON SUCH A GRAND SCALE IN QUITE A WHILE.
WELL, IT *IS* GOING TO BE BINDING FRANCE AND AUSTRIA TOGETHER.
THE ONE YEAR WE HAVE TO PREPARE SHALL FLY BY.
IT'S FINALLY HAPPENING, NEXT APRIL ...!
ALL OF EUROPE WILL PROBABLY GET EXCITED LIKE FOR A FESTIVAL! OH, HOW THRILLING!
I HEAR THE ARRANGEMENTS ARE EXTRA LUXURIOUS ON AN UNHEARD-OF SCALE.
THERE MAY BE LARGESSE FOR US, TOO, HO HO HO HO...
SCUTTLEBUTT SAYS EYE-POPPIN' LOADS OF GOLD, SILVER, GEMS, AND CLOTH IS BEIN' DELIVERED TO THE PALACE EVERY DAY!

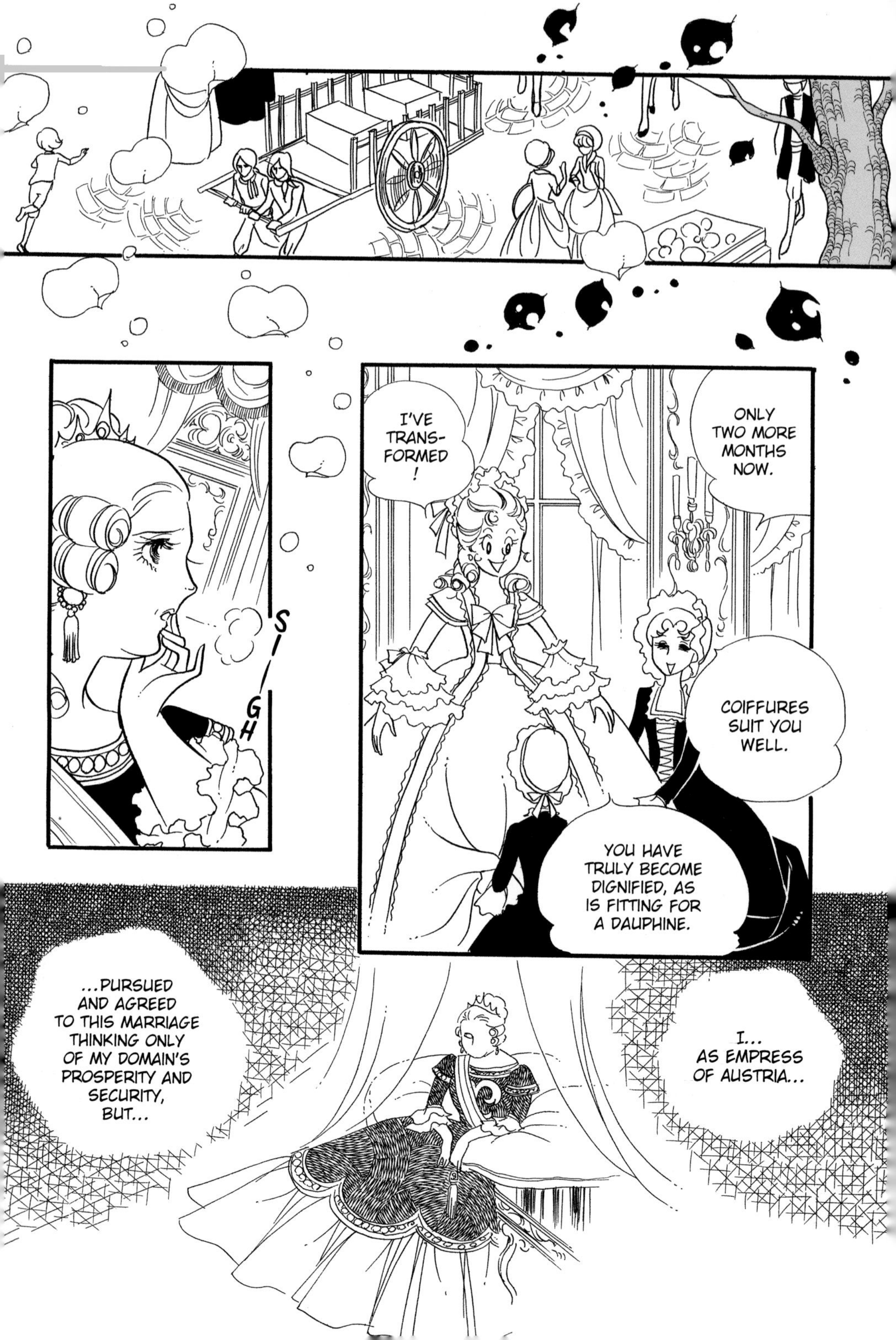
ONLY TWO MORE MONTHS NOW.
I'VE TRANS-FORMED!
COIFFURES SUIT YOU WELL.
YOU HAVE TRULY BECOME DIGNIFIED, AS IS FITTING FOR A DAUPHINE.
SIGH
I... AS EMPRESS OF AUSTRIA...
...PURSUED AND AGREED TO THIS MARRIAGE THINKING ONLY OF MY DOMAIN'S PROSPERITY AND SECURITY, BUT...

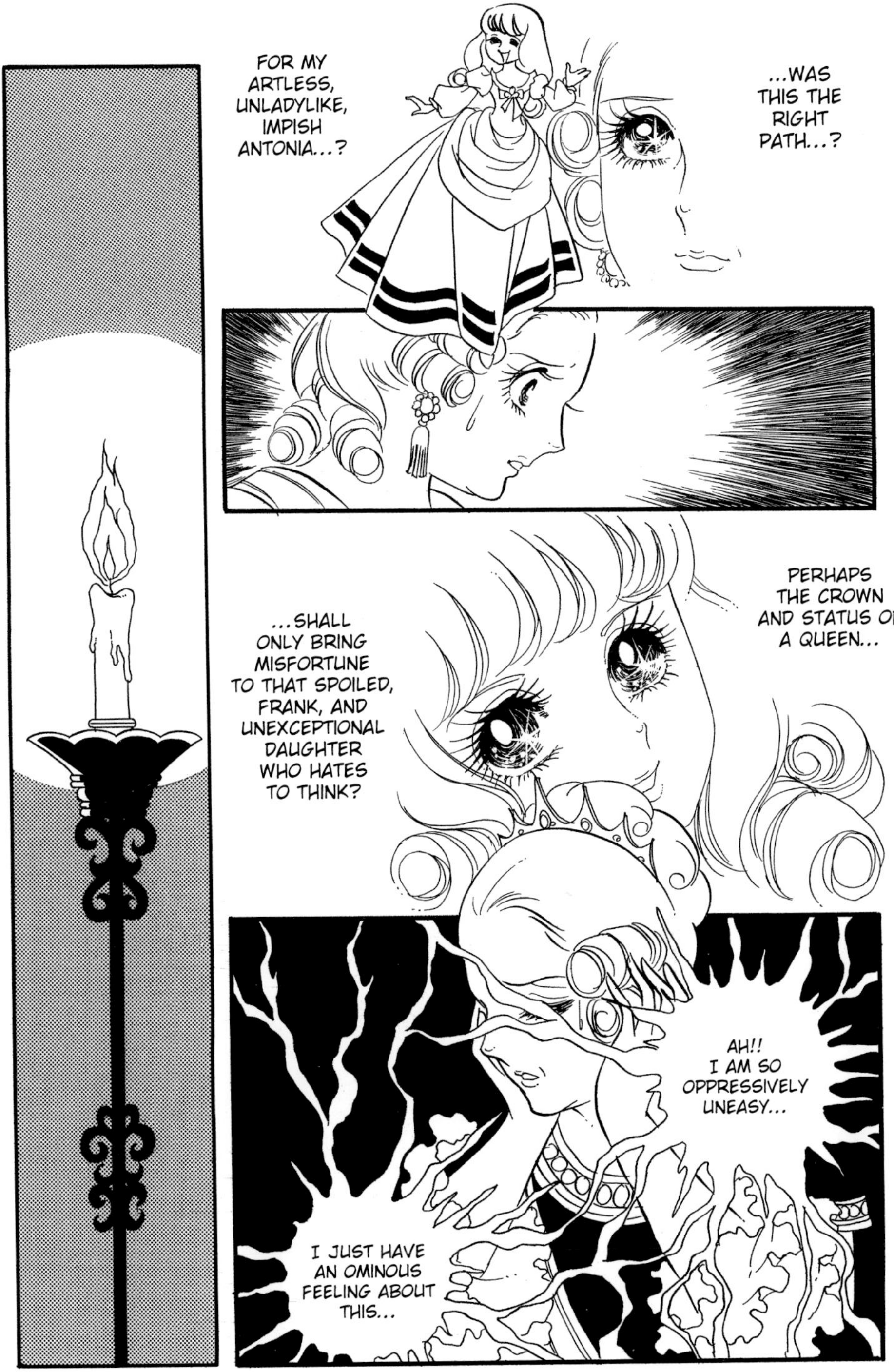
...WAS THIS THE RIGHT PATH...?
FOR MY ARTLESS, UNLADYLIKE, IMPISH ANTONIA...?
PERHAPS THE CROWN AND STATUS OF A QUEEN...
...SHALL ONLY BRING MISFORTUNE TO THAT SPOILED, FRANK, AND UNEXCEPTIONAL DAUGHTER WHO HATES TO THINK?
AH!! I AM SO OPPRESSIVELY UNEASY...
I JUST HAVE AN OMINOUS FEELING ABOUT THIS...

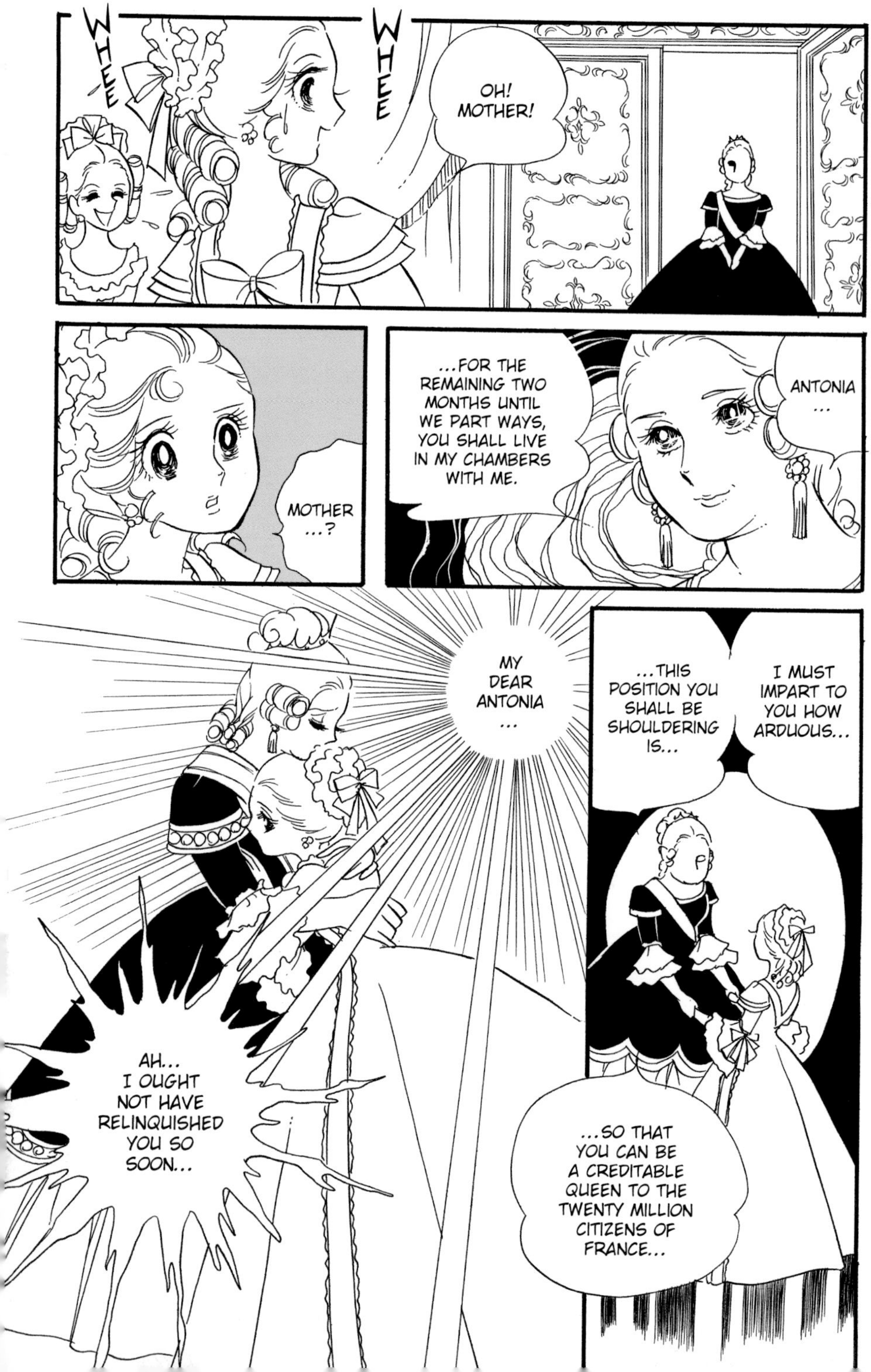
OH! MOTHER!
WHEE
WHEE
ANTONIA ...
...FOR THE REMAINING TWO MONTHS UNTIL WE PART WAYS, YOU SHALL LIVE IN MY CHAMBERS WITH ME.
MOTHER ...?
I MUST IMPART TO YOU HOW ARDUOUS...
...THIS POSITION YOU SHALL BE SHOULDERING IS...
...SO THAT YOU CAN BE A CREDITABLE QUEEN TO THE TWENTY MILLION CITIZENS OF FRANCE...
MY DEAR ANTONIA ...
AH... I OUGHT NOT HAVE RELINQUISHED YOU SO SOON...

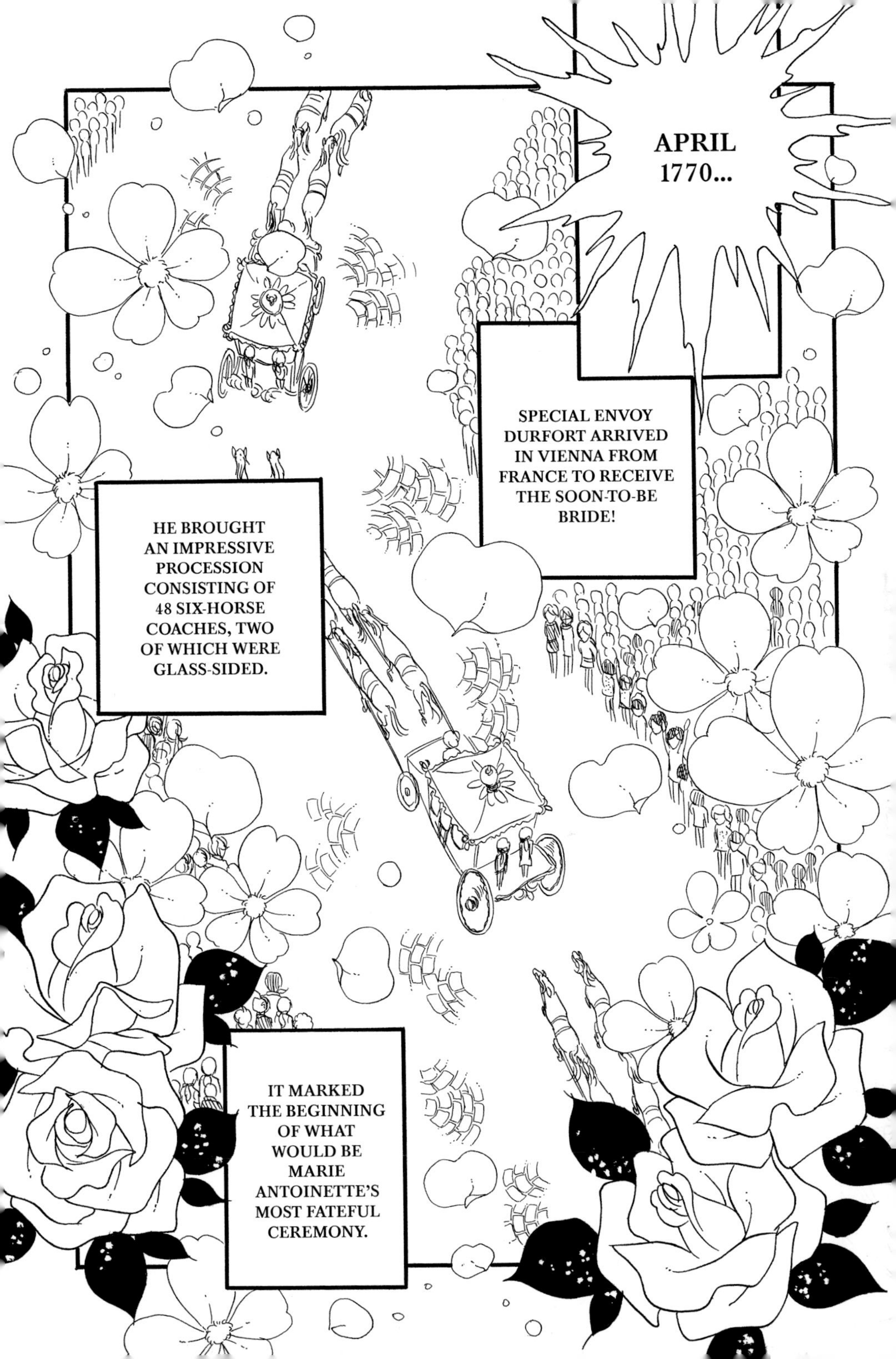
APRIL 1770...
SPECIAL ENVOY DURFORT ARRIVED IN VIENNA FROM FRANCE TO RECEIVE THE SOON-TO-BE BRIDE!
HE BROUGHT AN IMPRESSIVE PROCESSION CONSISTING OF 48 SIX-HORSE COACHES, TWO OF WHICH WERE GLASS-SIDED.
IT MARKED THE BEGINNING OF WHAT WOULD BE MARIE ANTOINETTE'S MOST FATEFUL CEREMONY.

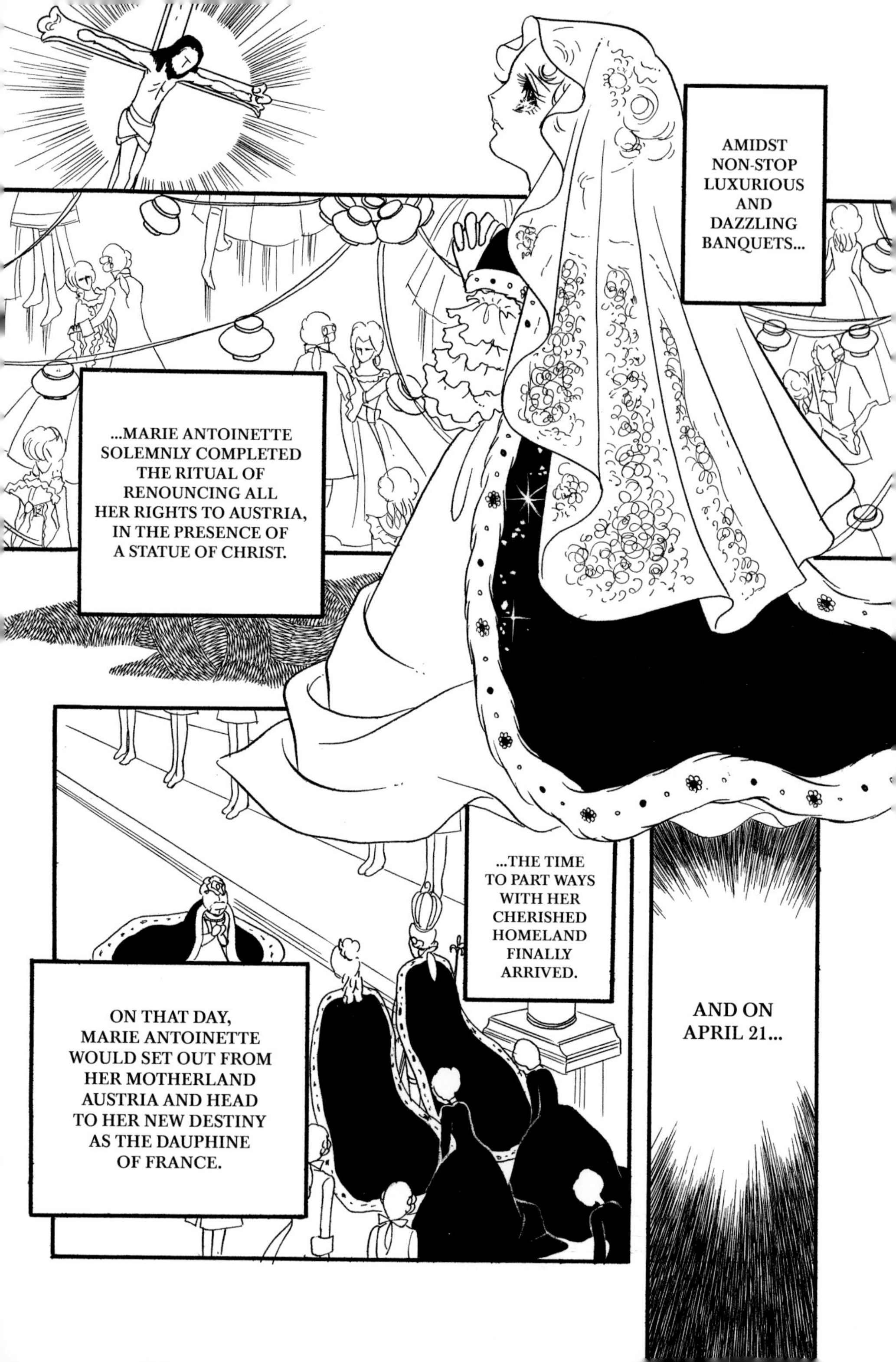
AMIDST NON-STOP LUXURIOUS AND DAZZLING BANQUETS...
...MARIE ANTOINETTE SOLEMNLY COMPLETED THE RITUAL OF RENOUNCING ALL HER RIGHTS TO AUSTRIA, IN THE PRESENCE OF A STATUE OF CHRIST.
AND ON APRIL 21...
...THE TIME TO PART WAYS WITH HER CHERISHED HOMELAND FINALLY ARRIVED.
ON THAT DAY, MARIE ANTOINETTE WOULD SET OUT FROM HER MOTHERLAND AUSTRIA AND HEAD TO HER NEW DESTINY AS THE DAUPHINE OF FRANCE.

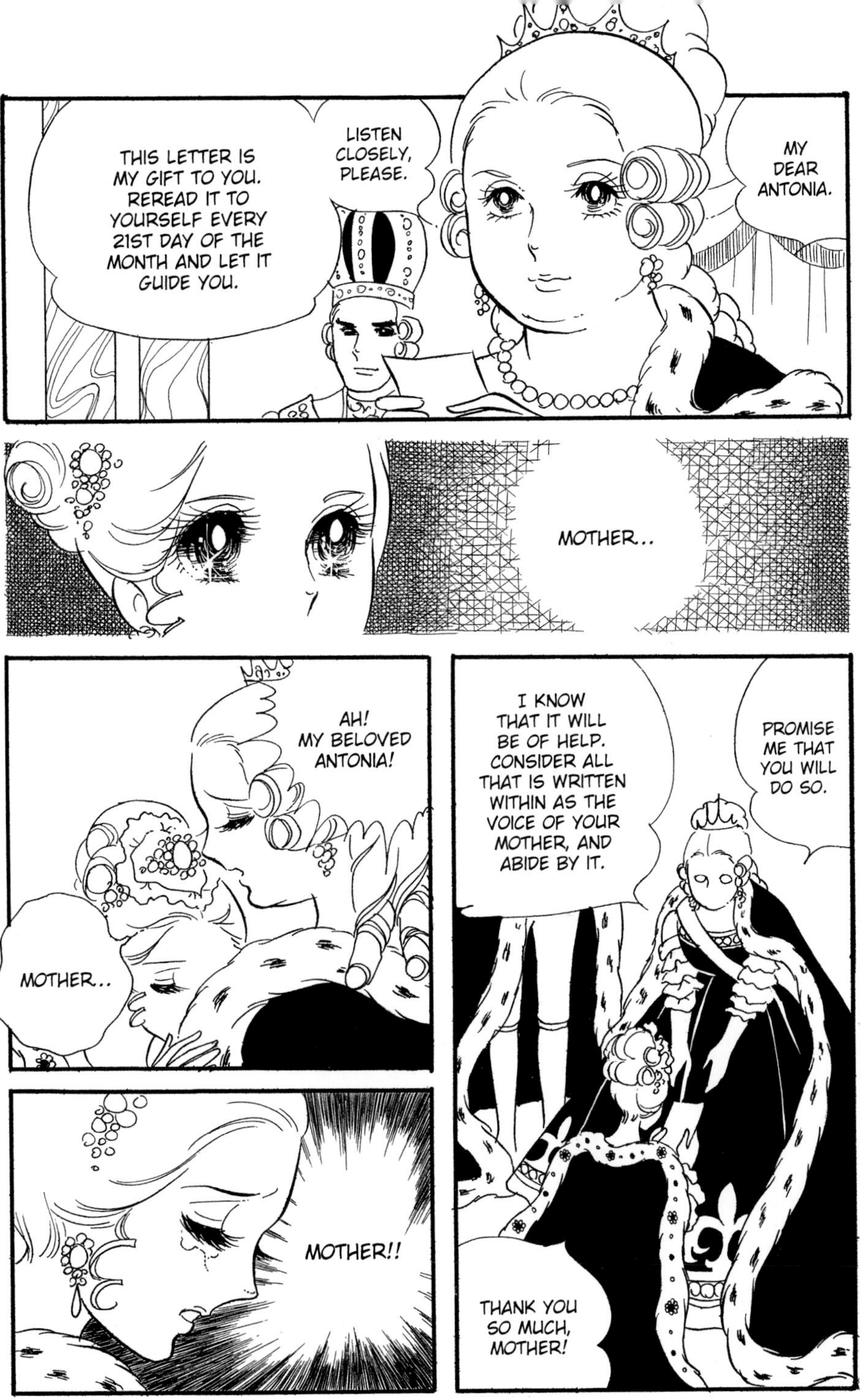
MY DEAR ANTONIA.
LISTEN CLOSELY, PLEASE.
THIS LETTER IS MY GIFT TO YOU. REREAD IT TO YOURSELF EVERY 21ST DAY OF THE MONTH AND LET IT GUIDE YOU.
MOTHER...
PROMISE ME THAT YOU WILL DO SO.
I KNOW THAT IT WILL BE OF HELP. CONSIDER ALL THAT IS WRITTEN WITHIN AS THE VOICE OF YOUR MOTHER, AND ABIDE BY IT.
THANK YOU SO MUCH, MOTHER!
AH! MY BELOVED ANTONIA!
MOTHER...
MOTHER!!

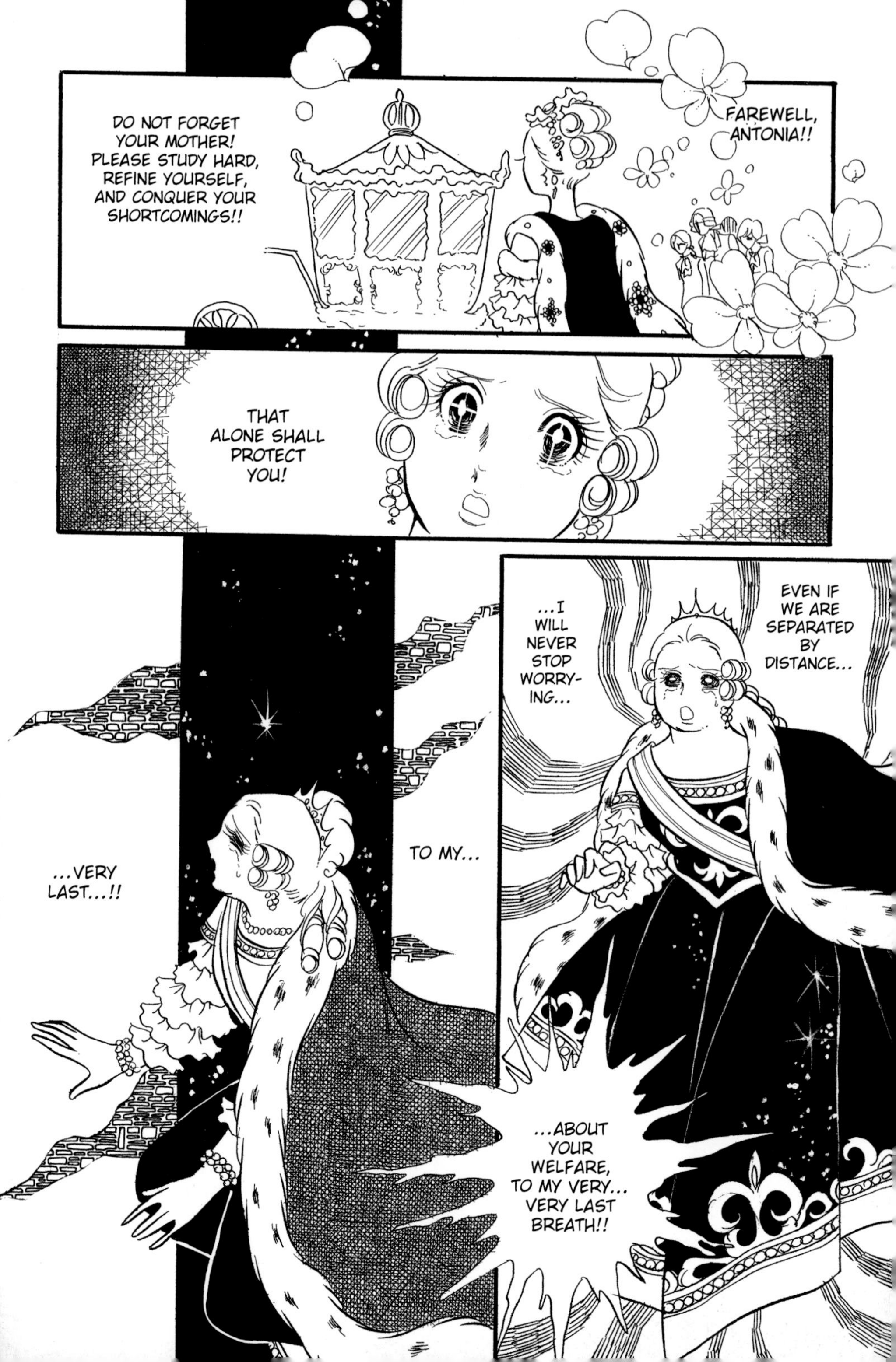
FAREWELL, ANTONIA!!
DO NOT FORGET YOUR MOTHER! PLEASE STUDY HARD, REFINE YOURSELF, AND CONQUER YOUR SHORTCOMINGS!!
THAT ALONE SHALL PROTECT YOU!
EVEN IF WE ARE SEPARATED BY DISTANCE...
...I WILL NEVER STOP WORRYING...
...ABOUT YOUR WELFARE, TO MY VERY... VERY LAST BREATH!!
TO MY...
...VERY LAST...!!

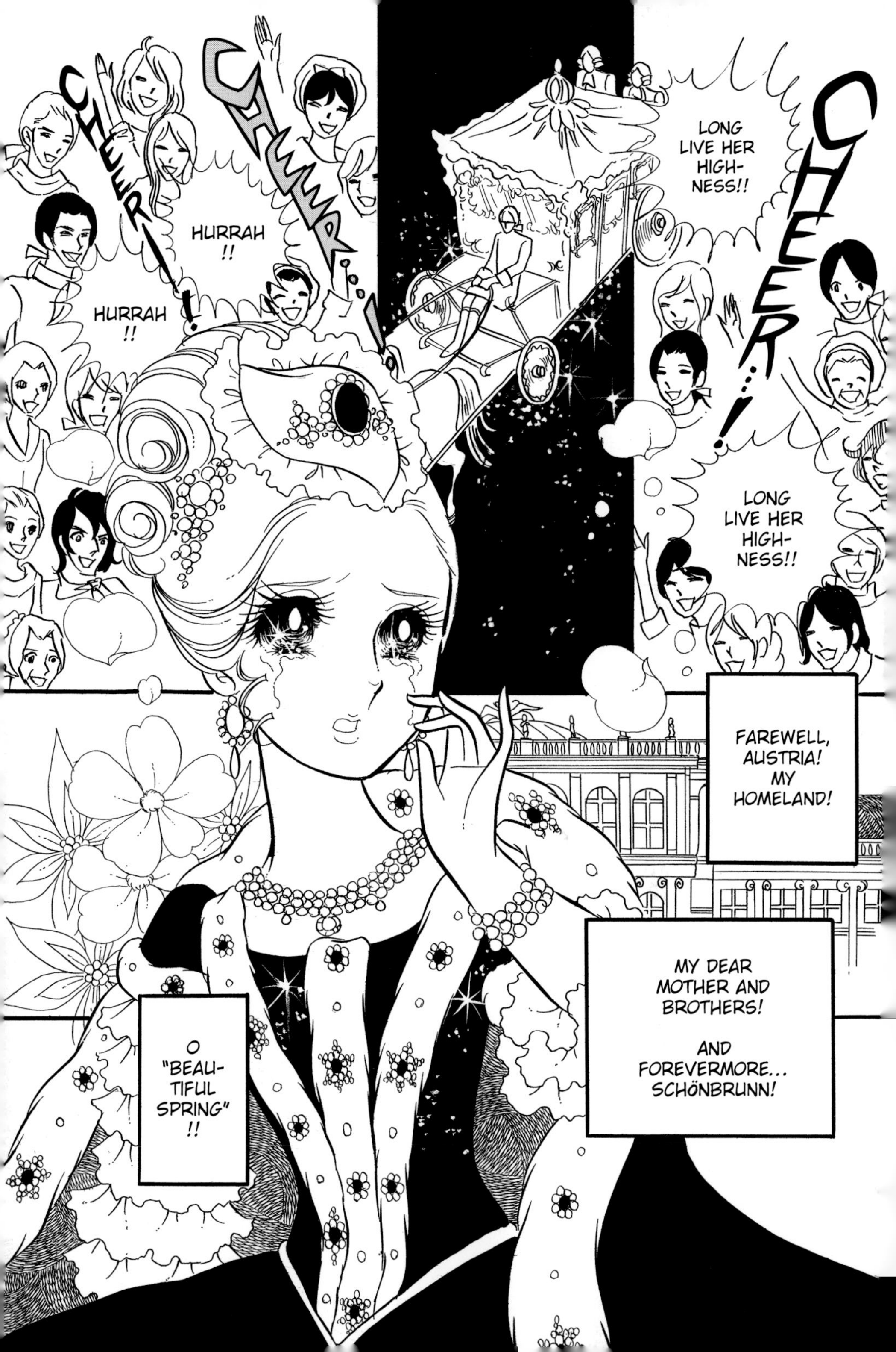

CHEER...!
LONG LIVE HER HIGH-NESS!!
LONG LIVE HER HIGH-NESS!!
CHWWAR...!
CHEER!!
HURRAH!!
HURRAH!!
FAREWELL, AUSTRIA! MY HOMELAND!
MY DEAR MOTHER AND BROTHERS!
AND FOREVERMORE... SCHÖNBRUNN!
O "BEAU-TIFUL SPRING"!!

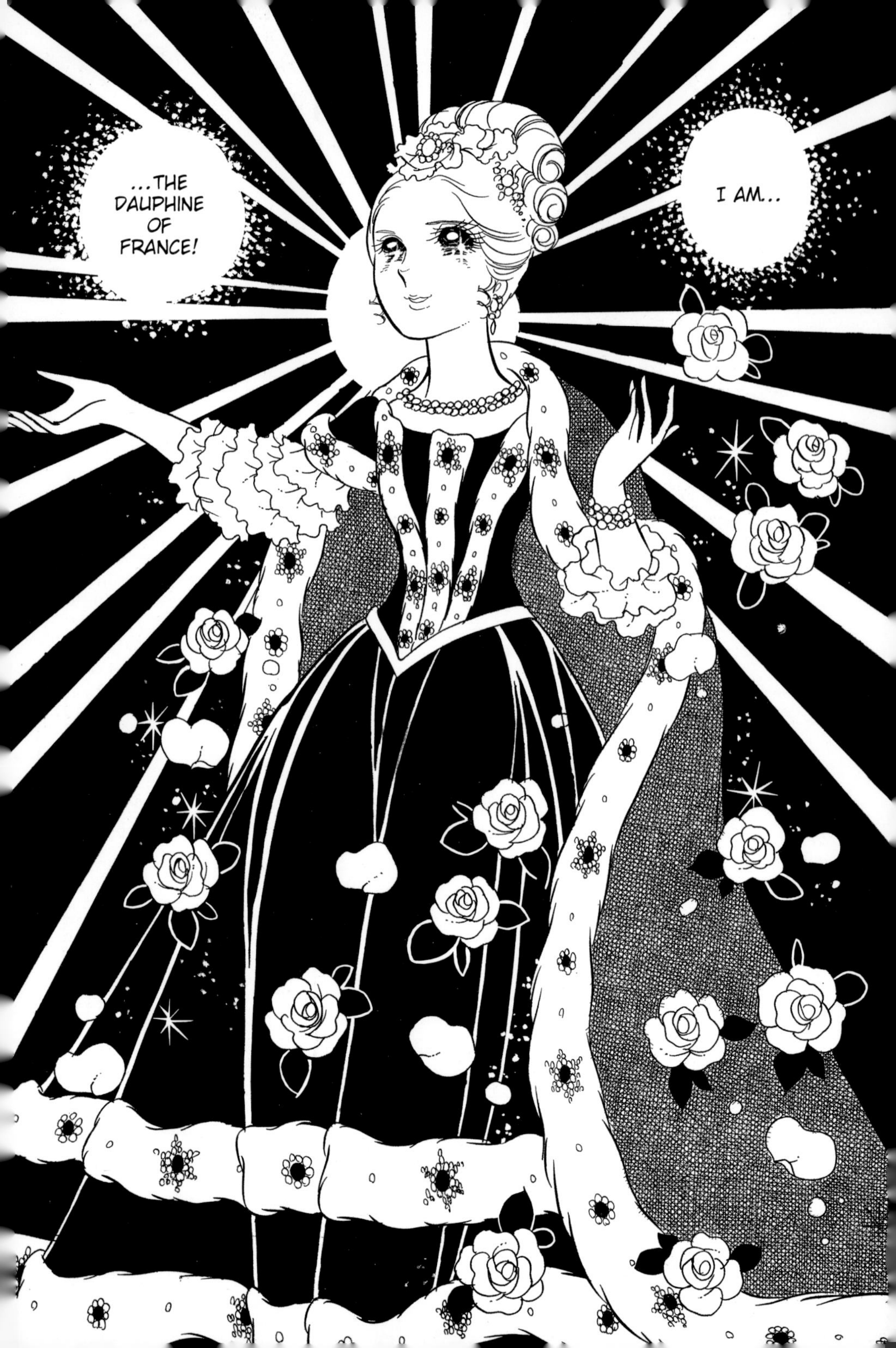
I AM...
...THE DAUPHINE OF FRANCE!

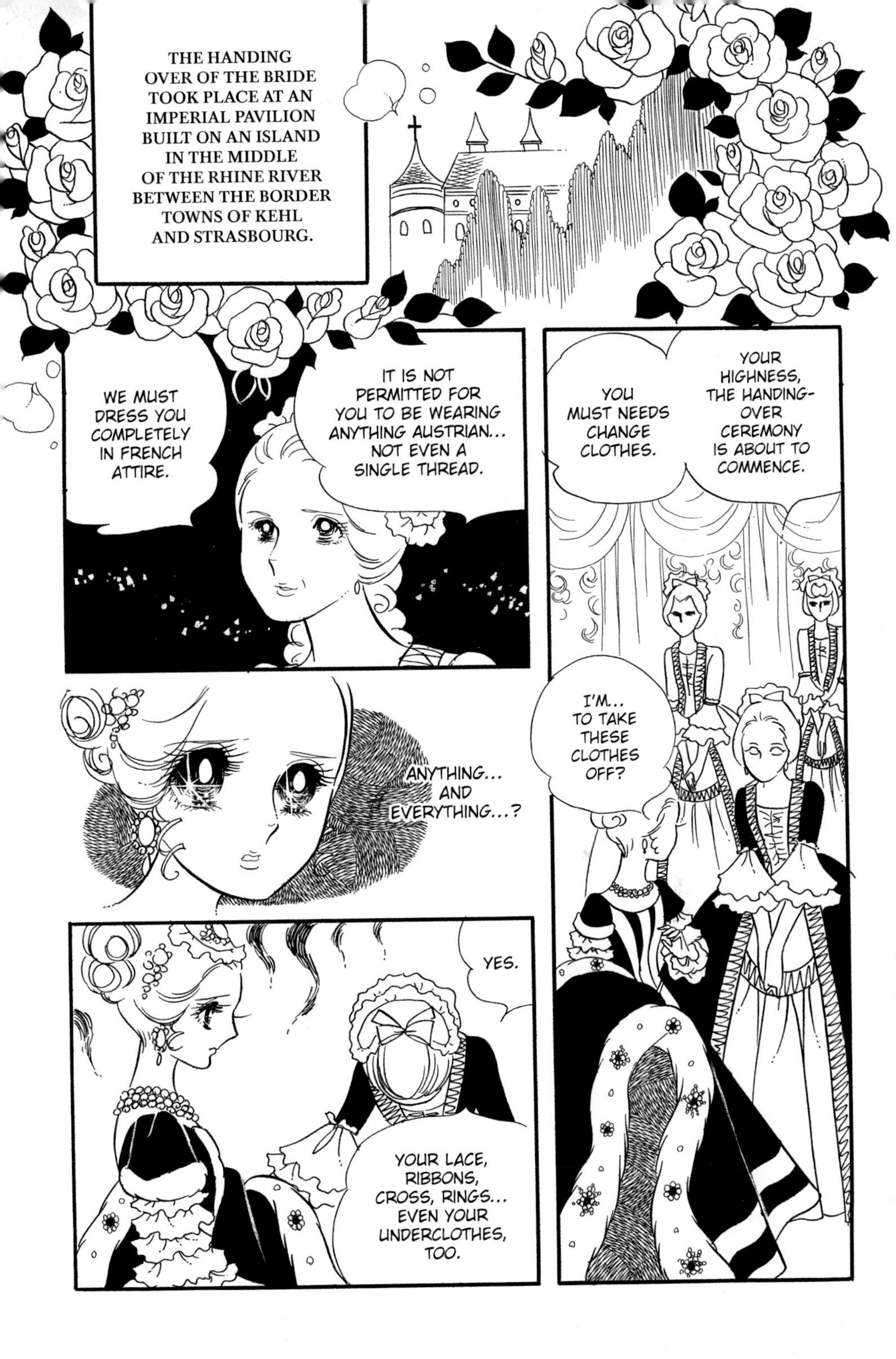
THE HANDING OVER OF THE BRIDE TOOK PLACE AT AN IMPERIAL PAVILION BUILT ON AN ISLAND IN THE MIDDLE OF THE RHINE RIVER BETWEEN THE BORDER TOWNS OF KEHL AND STRASBOURG.
YOUR HIGHNESS, THE HANDING-OVER CEREMONY IS ABOUT TO COMMENCE.
YOU MUST NEEDS CHANGE CLOTHES.
I'M... TO TAKE THESE CLOTHES OFF?
IT IS NOT PERMITTED FOR YOU TO BE WEARING ANYTHING AUSTRIAN... NOT EVEN A SINGLE THREAD.
WE MUST DRESS YOU COMPLETELY IN FRENCH ATTIRE.
ANYTHING... AND EVERYTHING...?
YES.
YOUR LACE, RIBBONS, CROSS, RINGS... EVEN YOUR UNDERCLOTHES, TOO.

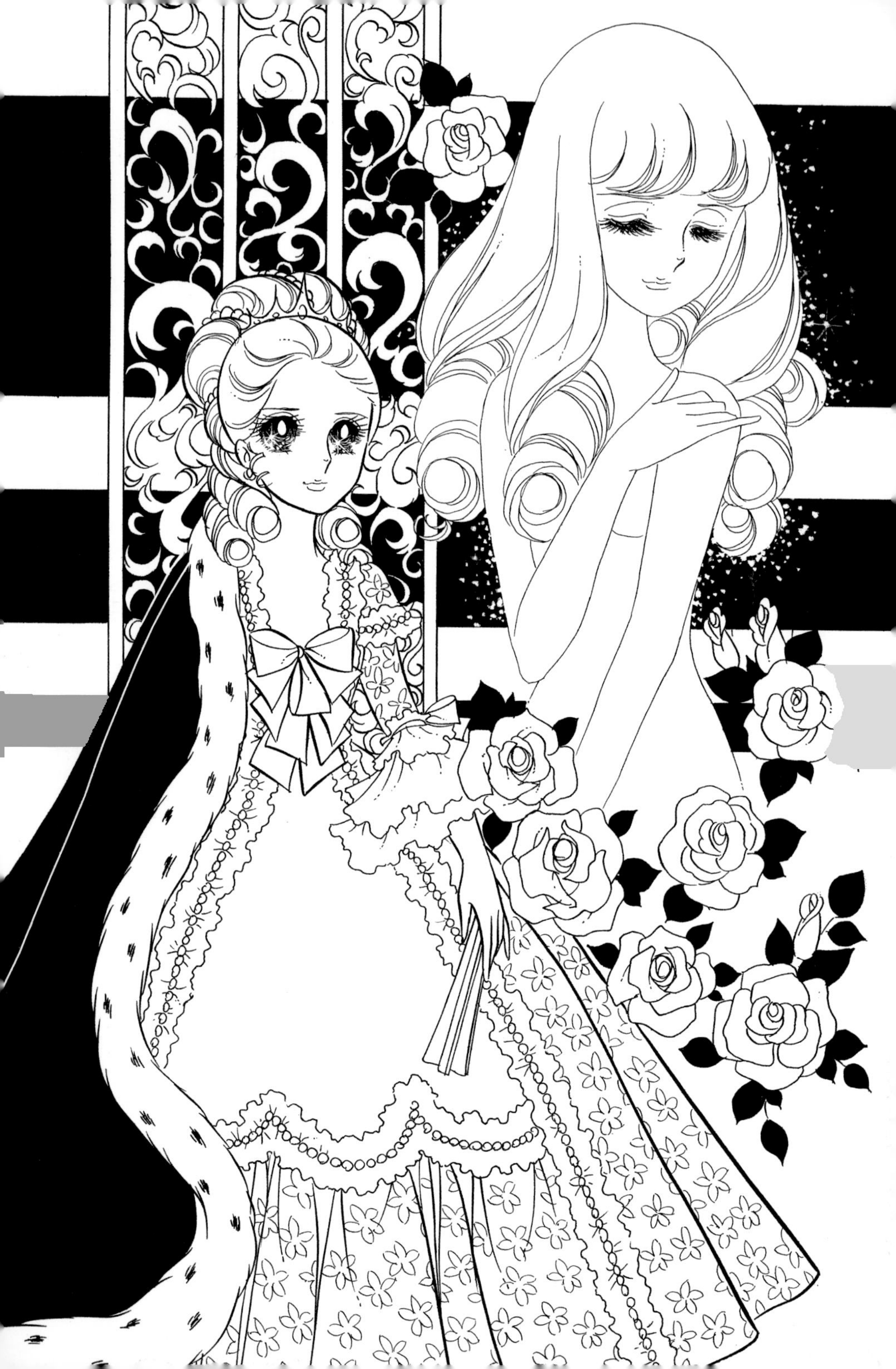

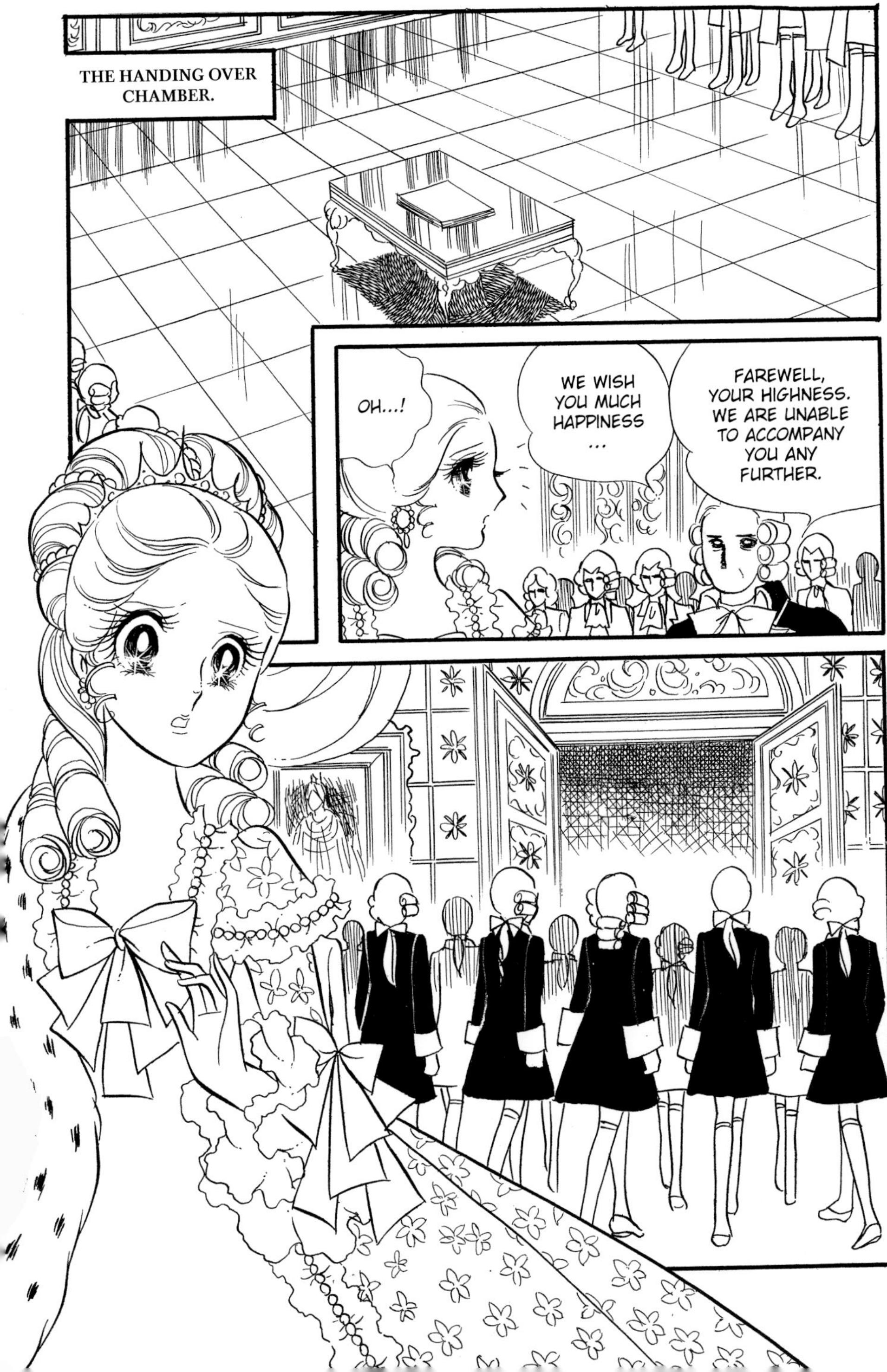
THE HANDING OVER CHAMBER.
FAREWELL, YOUR HIGHNESS. WE ARE UNABLE TO ACCOMPANY YOU ANY FURTHER.
WE WISH YOU MUCH HAPPINESS ...
OH...!

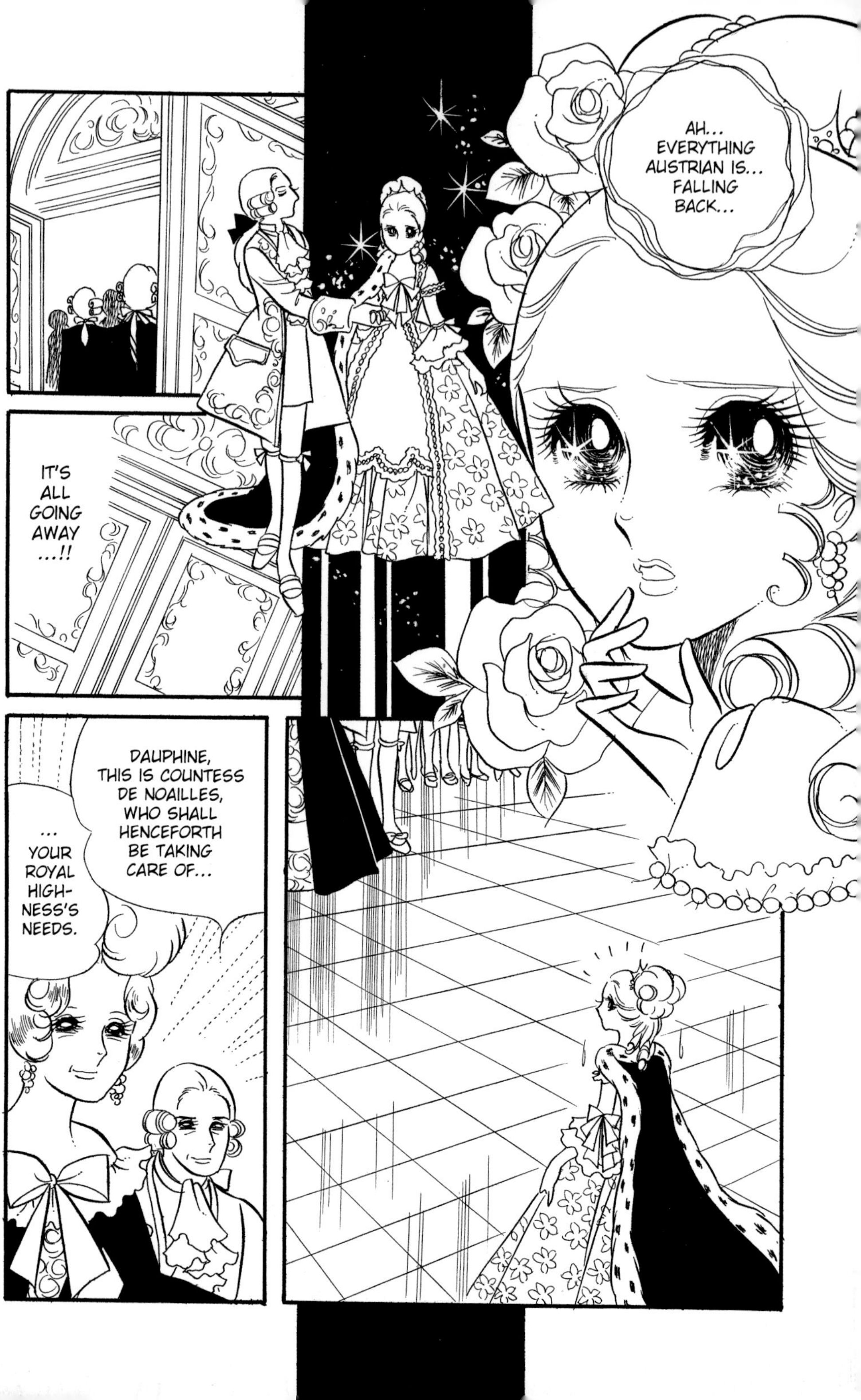
AH... EVERYTHING AUSTRIAN IS... FALLING BACK...
IT'S ALL GOING AWAY...!!
DAUPHINE, THIS IS COUNTESS DE NOAILLES, WHO SHALL HENCEFORTH BE TAKING CARE OF...
... YOUR ROYAL HIGH-NESS'S NEEDS.

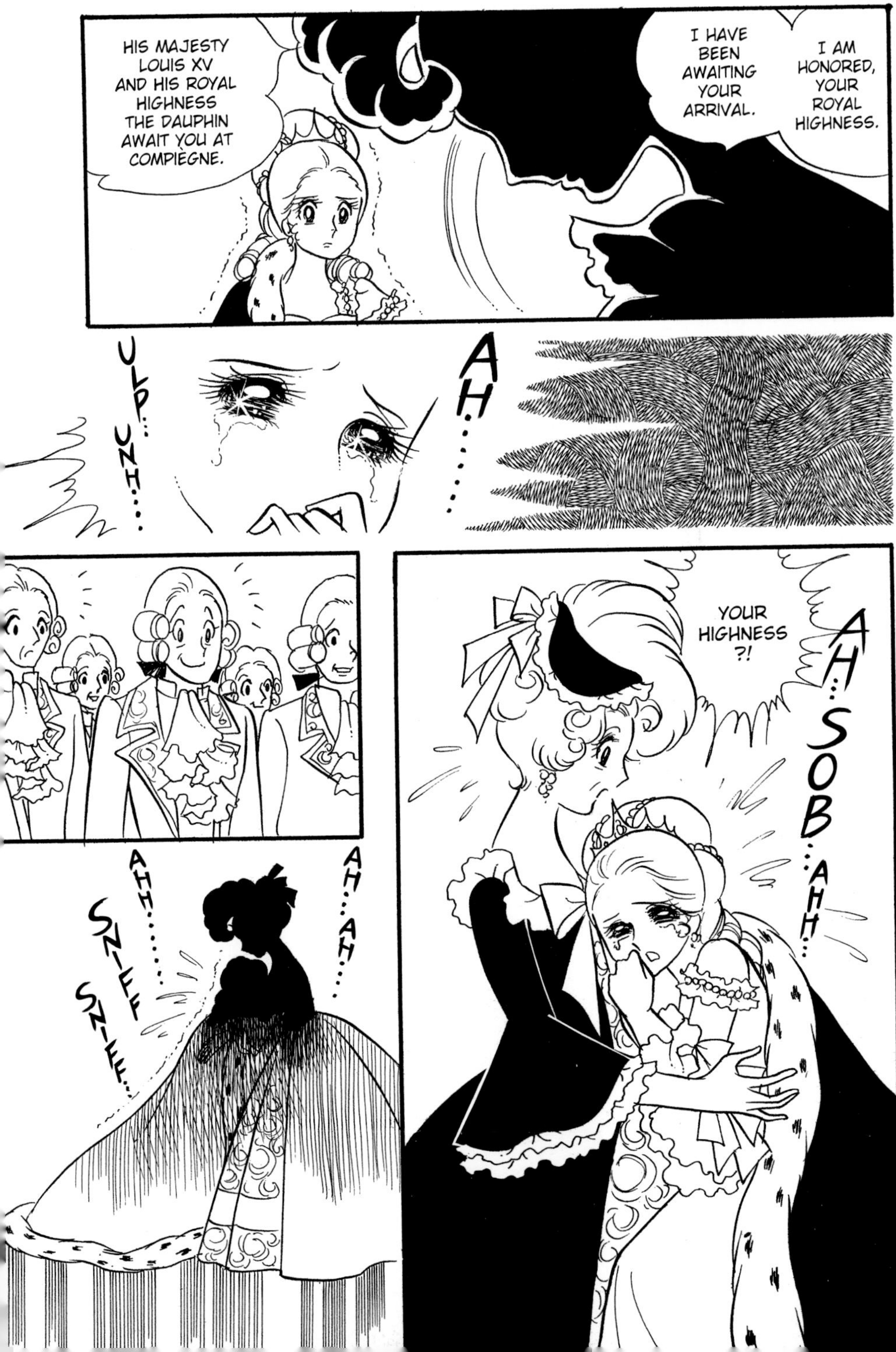
I AM HONORED, YOUR ROYAL HIGHNESS.
I HAVE BEEN AWAITING YOUR ARRIVAL.
HIS MAJESTY LOUIS XV AND HIS ROYAL HIGHNESS THE DAUPHIN AWAIT YOU AT COMPIÈGNE.
AH......
ULP... UNH....
YOUR HIGHNESS ?!
AH...SOB...AHH...
AH...AH...
AHH......
SNIFF SNIFF...

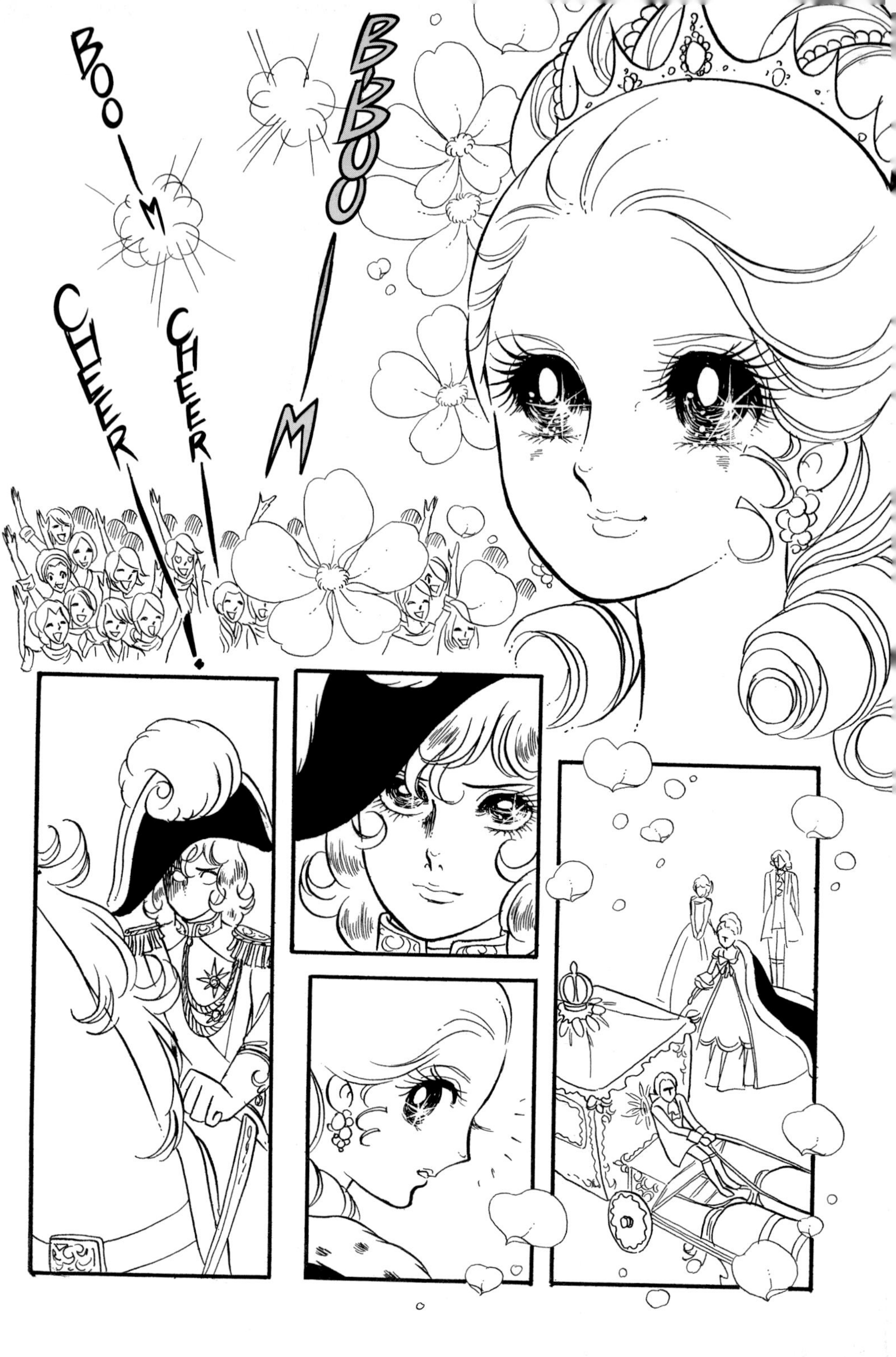
BBBOO—M
BOO—M
CHEER
CHEER!

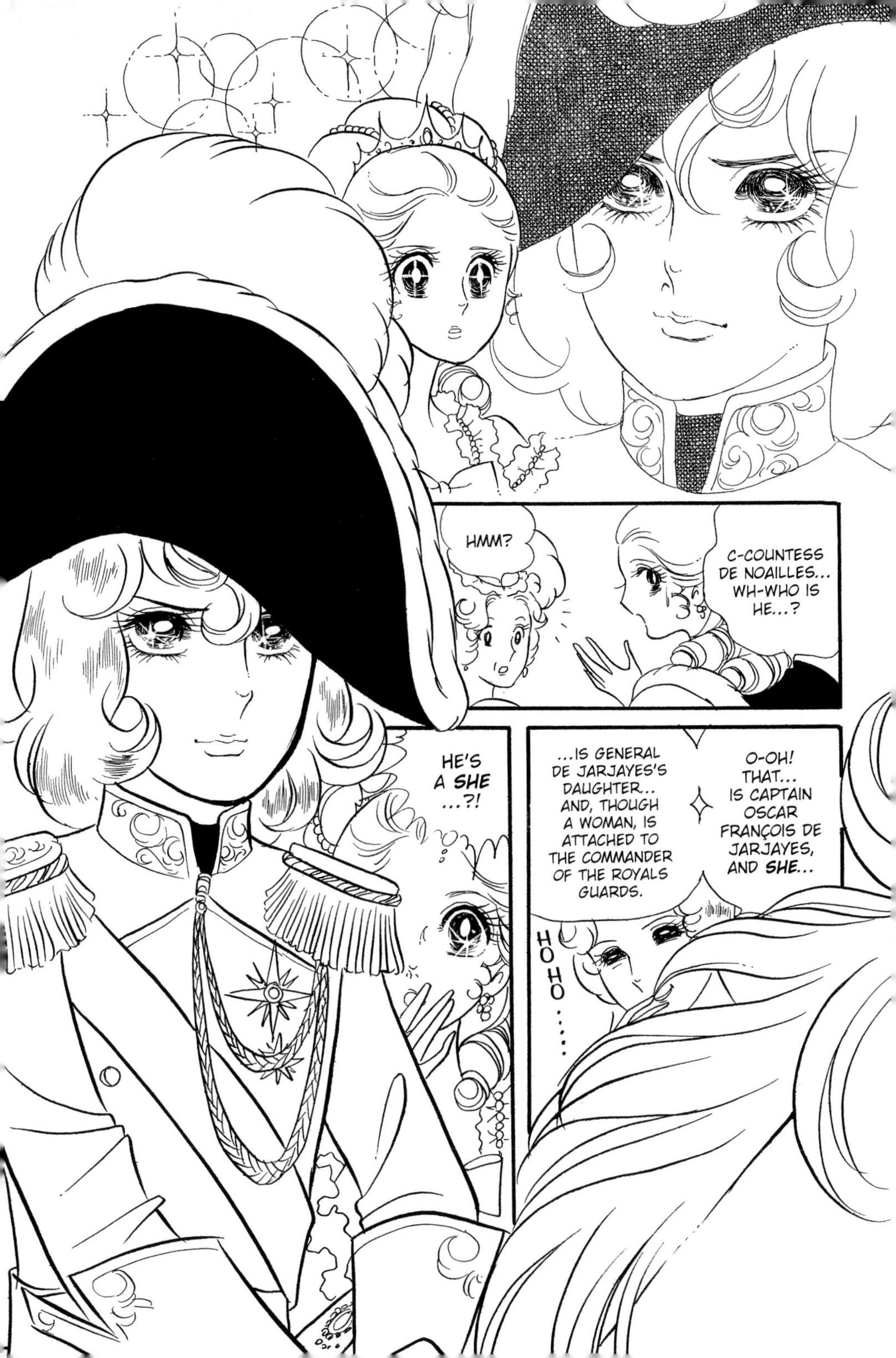
C-COUNTESS DE NOAILLES... WH-WHO IS HE...?
HMM?
O-OH! THAT... IS CAPTAIN OSCAR FRANÇOIS DE JARJAYES, AND SHE...
...IS GENERAL DE JARJAYES'S DAUGHTER... AND, THOUGH A WOMAN, IS ATTACHED TO THE COMMANDER OF THE ROYALS GUARDS.
HO HO......
HE'S A SHE ...?!

1972 WEEKLY MARGARET MAGAZINE
ISSUE 20 PREVIEW ART

◆ THE HOT TOPIC OF DISCUSSION AMONG READERS ACROSS THE NATION!!
♥ ANTOINETTE FINALLY BECOMES THE DAUPHINE...!!

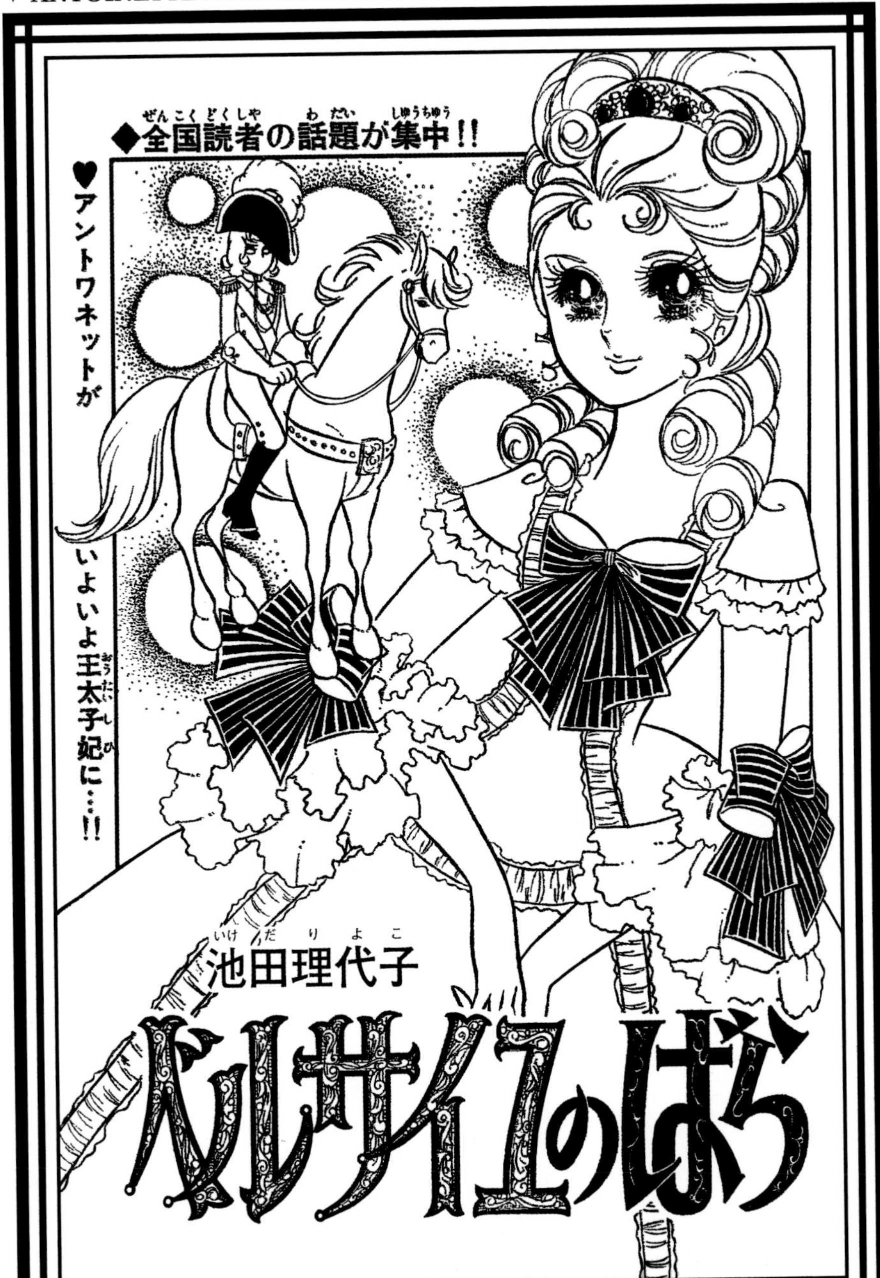
◆全国読者の話題が集中!!
♥アントワネットが いよいよ王太子妃に…!!
池田理代子
ベルサイユのばら
EPISODE 03

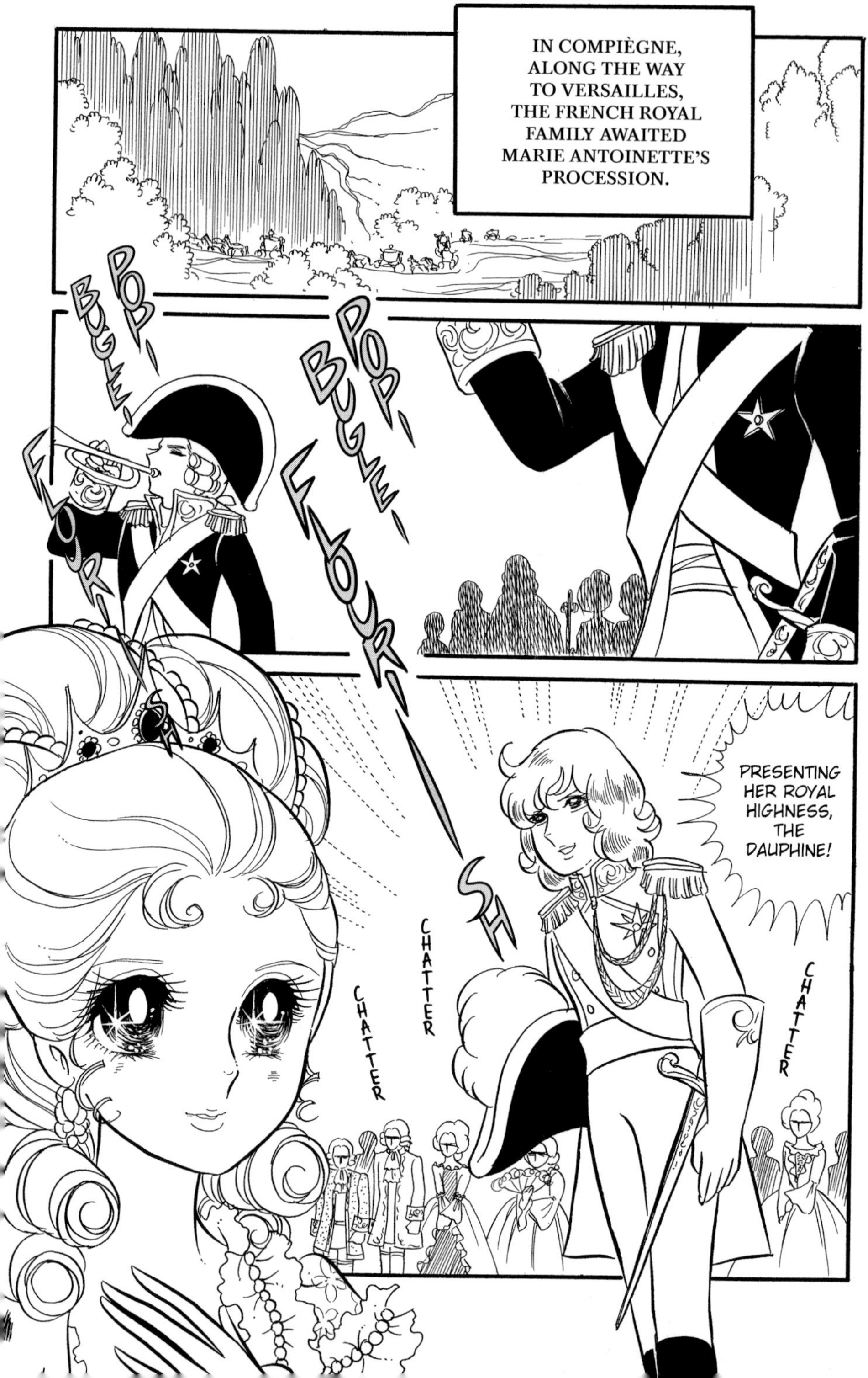
IN COMPIÈGNE, ALONG THE WAY TO VERSAILLES, THE FRENCH ROYAL FAMILY AWAITED MARIE ANTOINETTE'S PROCESSION.
POP! BUGLE! FLOURI—SH
POP! BUGLE! FLOUR!—SH
PRESENTING HER ROYAL HIGHNESS, THE DAUPHINE!
CHATTER
CHATTER
CHATTER

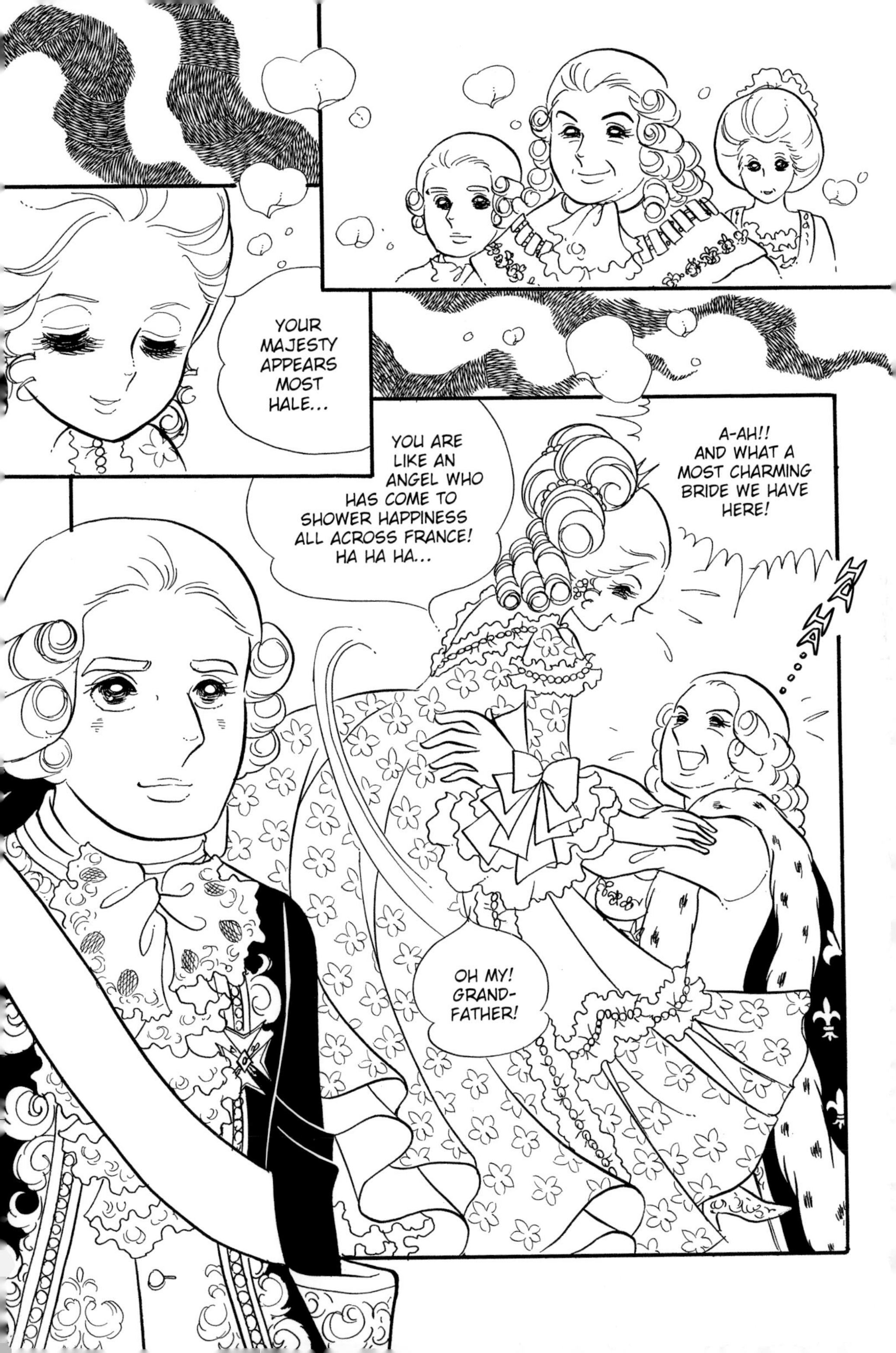
YOUR MAJESTY APPEARS MOST HALE...
A-AH!! AND WHAT A MOST CHARMING BRIDE WE HAVE HERE!
HA HA
YOU ARE LIKE AN ANGEL WHO HAS COME TO SHOWER HAPPINESS ALL ACROSS FRANCE! HA HA HA...
OH MY! GRAND-FATHER!

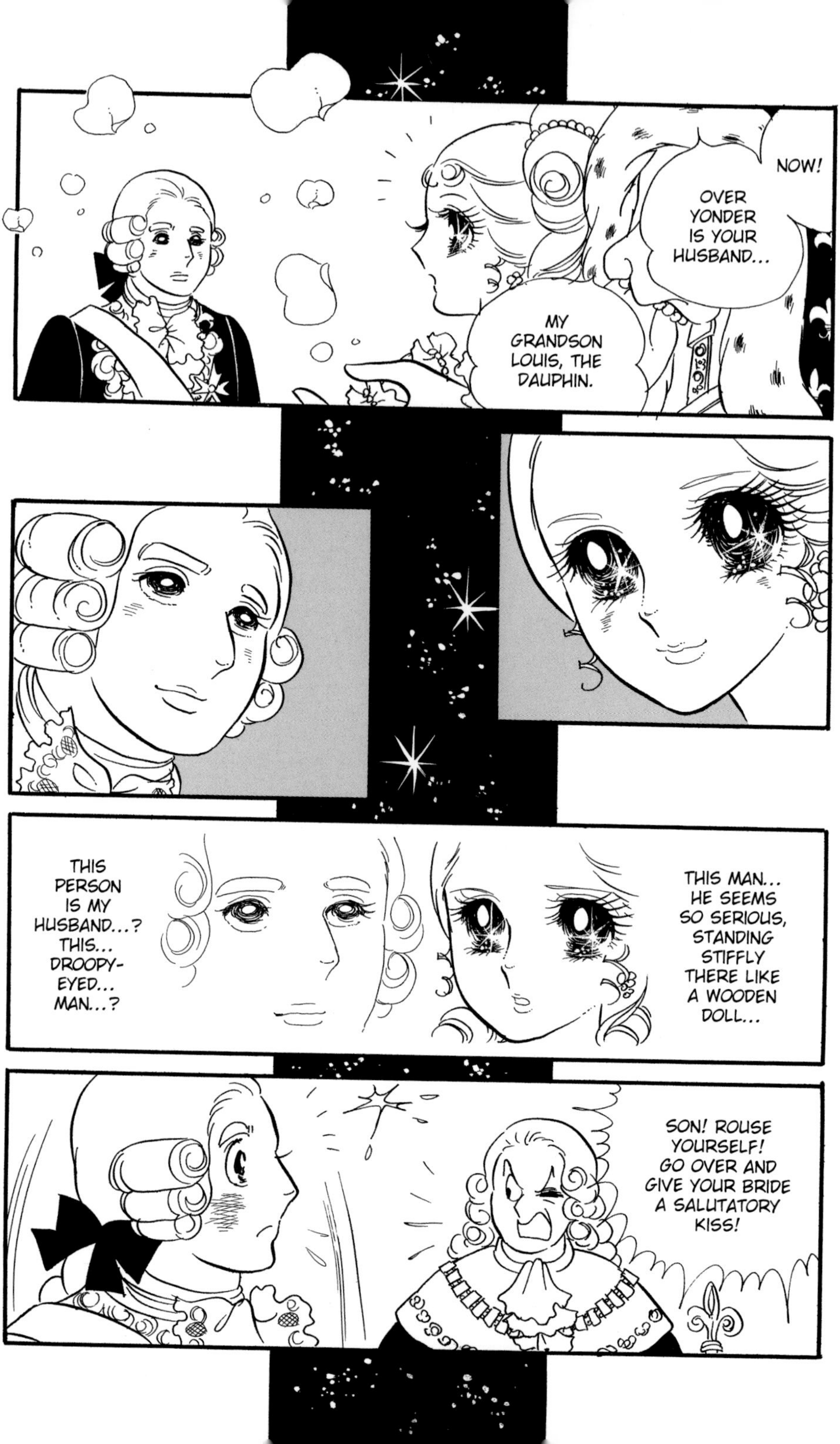
NOW!
OVER YONDER IS YOUR HUSBAND...
MY GRANDSON LOUIS, THE DAUPHIN.
THIS MAN... HE SEEMS SO SERIOUS, STANDING STIFFLY THERE LIKE A WOODEN DOLL...
THIS PERSON IS MY HUSBAND...? THIS... DROOPY-EYED... MAN...?
SON! ROUSE YOURSELF! GO OVER AND GIVE YOUR BRIDE A SALUTATORY KISS!

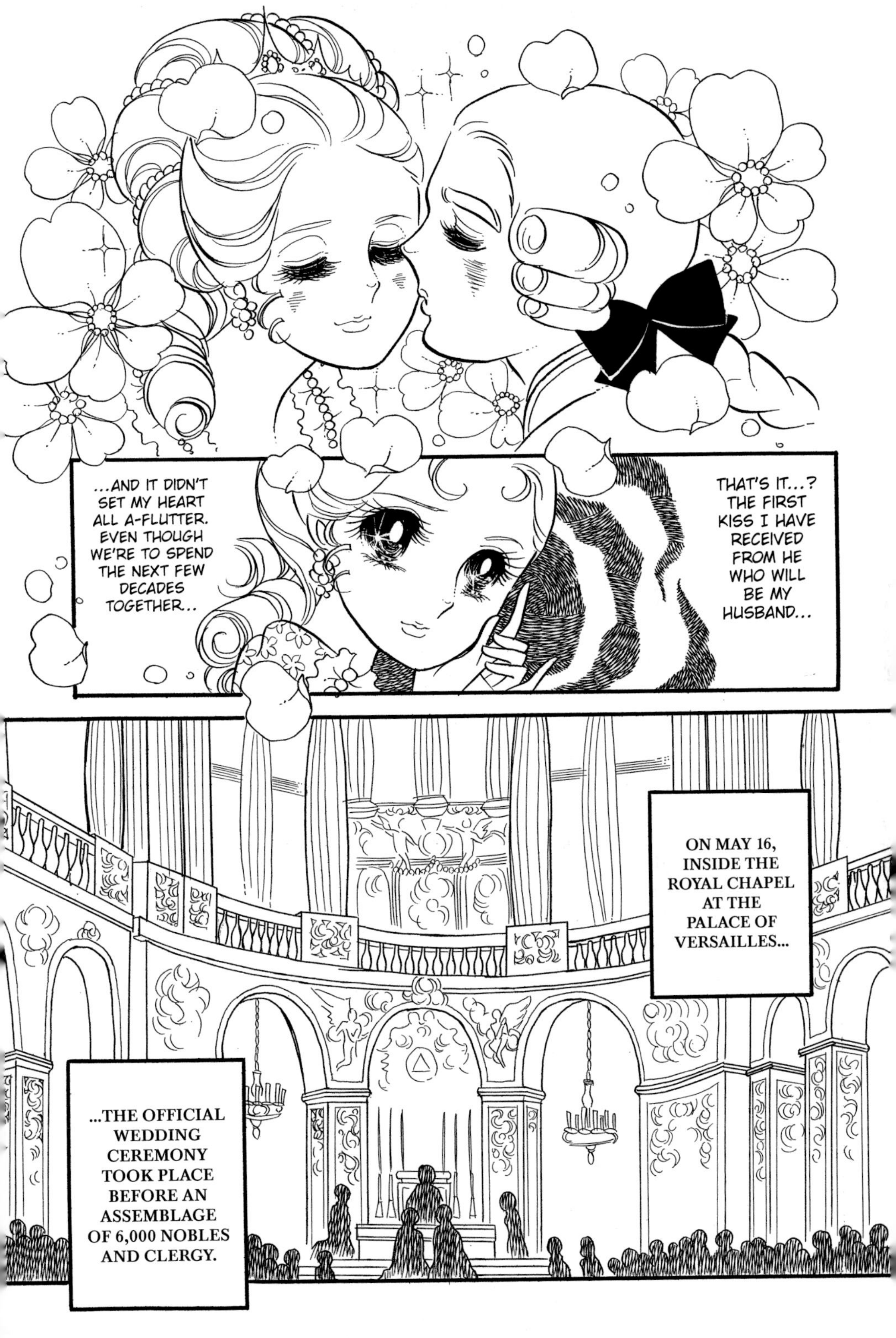
THAT'S IT...? THE FIRST KISS I HAVE RECEIVED FROM HE WHO WILL BE MY HUSBAND...
...AND IT DIDN'T SET MY HEART ALL A-FLUTTER. EVEN THOUGH WE'RE TO SPEND THE NEXT FEW DECADES TOGETHER...
ON MAY 16, INSIDE THE ROYAL CHAPEL AT THE PALACE OF VERSAILLES...
...THE OFFICIAL WEDDING CEREMONY TOOK PLACE BEFORE AN ASSEMBLAGE OF 6,000 NOBLES AND CLERGY.

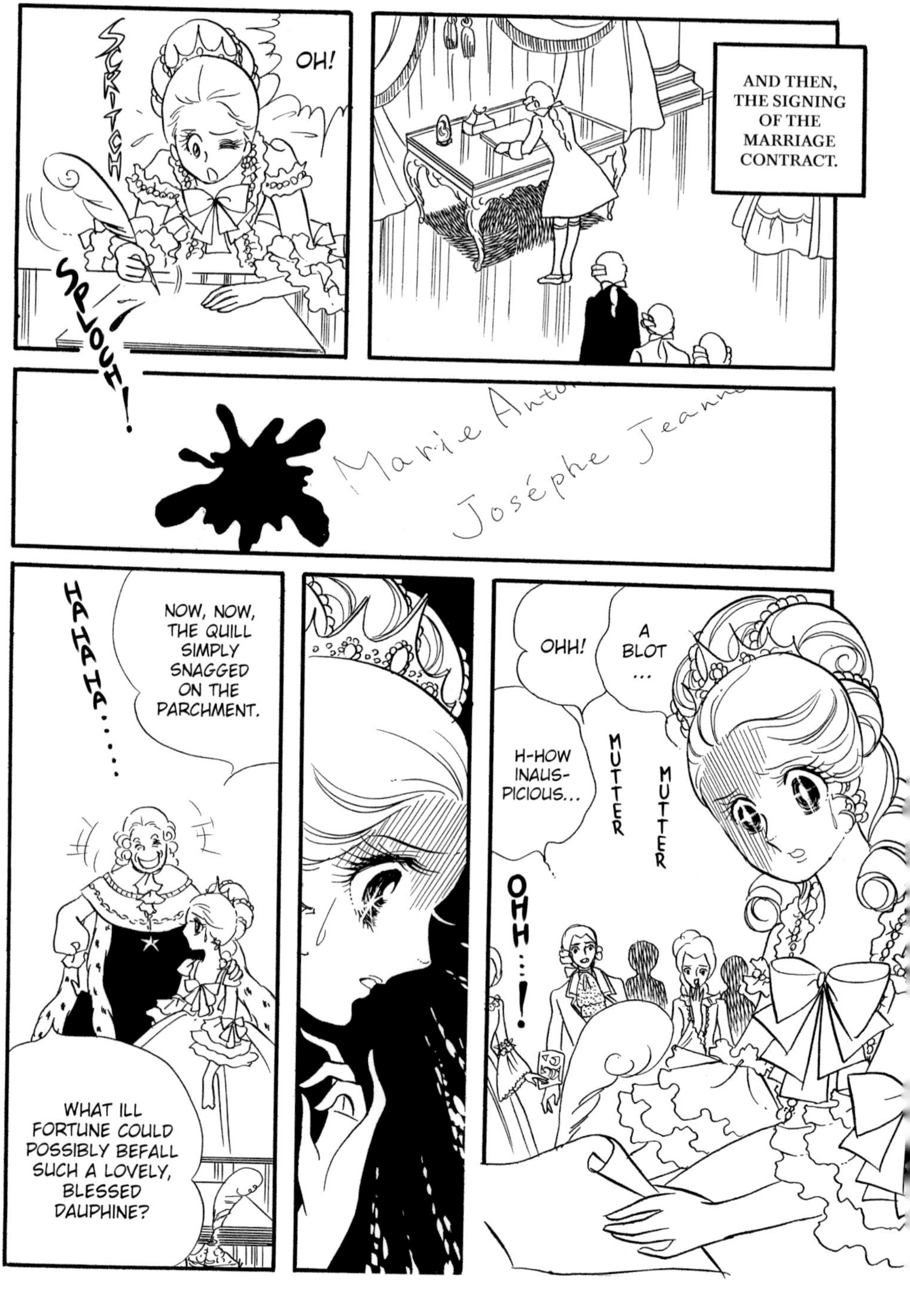
AND THEN, THE SIGNING OF THE MARRIAGE CONTRACT.
SCRITCH
OH!
SPLOUCH!
Marie Anto
Josèphe Jeann
OHH!
A BLOT...
H-HOW INAUSPICIOUS...
MUTTER
MUTTER
OHH...!
HAHAHA.....
NOW, NOW, THE QUILL SIMPLY SNAGGED ON THE PARCHMENT.
WHAT ILL FORTUNE COULD POSSIBLY BEFALL SUCH A LOVELY, BLESSED DAUPHINE?

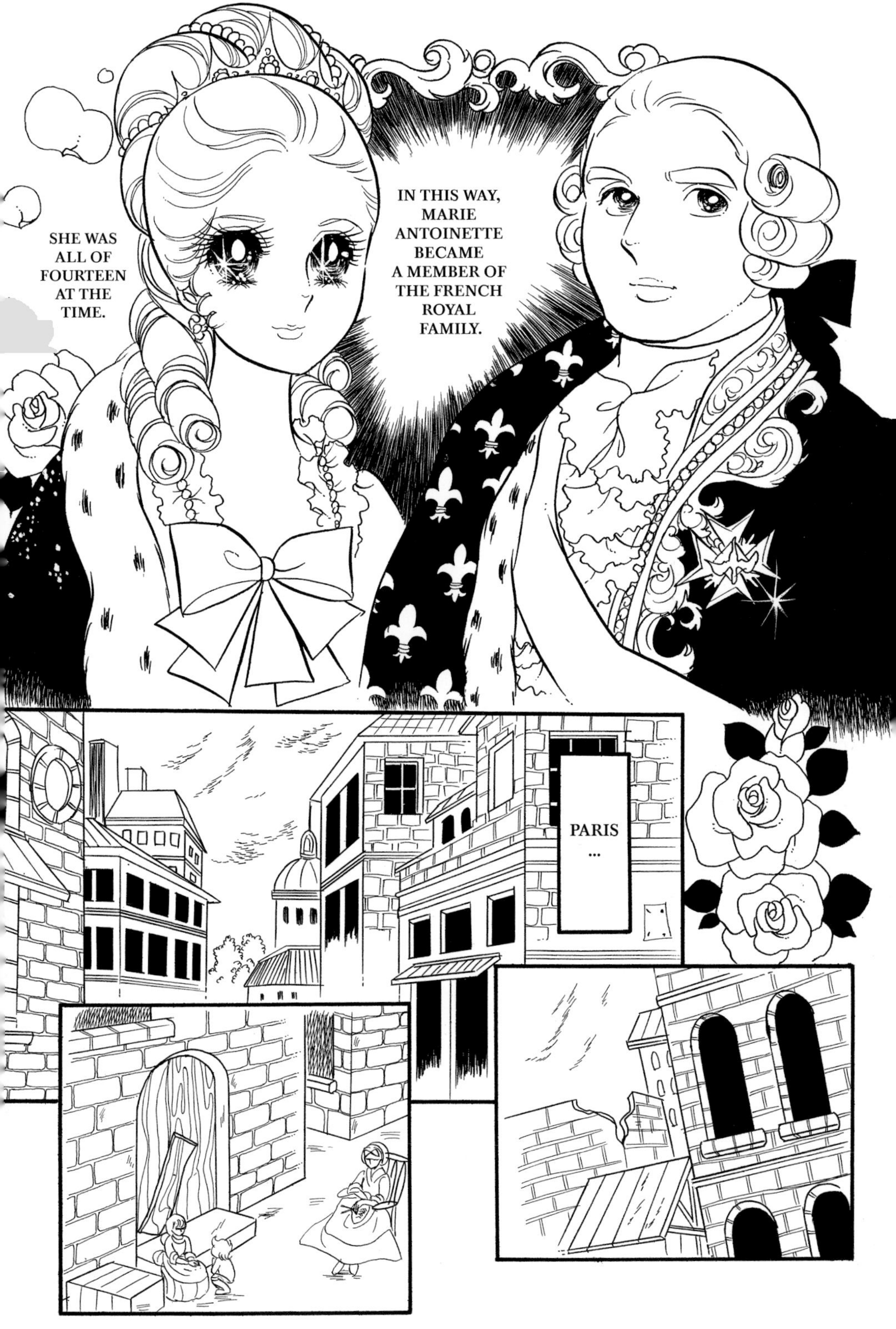
IN THIS WAY, MARIE ANTOINETTE BECAME A MEMBER OF THE FRENCH ROYAL FAMILY.
SHE WAS ALL OF FOURTEEN AT THE TIME.
PARIS ...

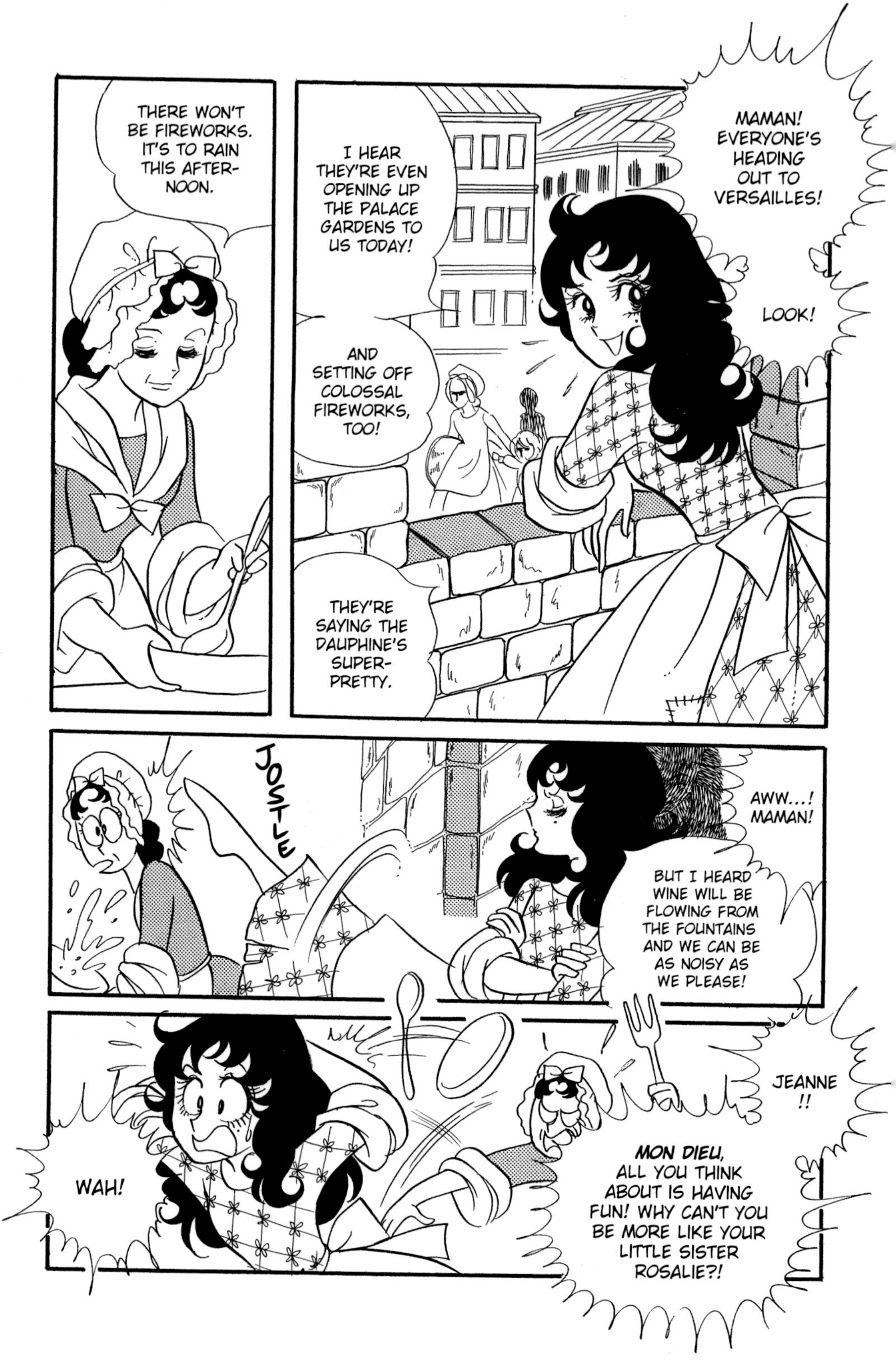
MAMAN! EVERYONE'S HEADING OUT TO VERSAILLES!
LOOK!
I HEAR THEY'RE EVEN OPENING UP THE PALACE GARDENS TO US TODAY!
AND SETTING OFF COLOSSAL FIREWORKS, TOO!
THEY'RE SAYING THE DAUPHINE'S SUPER-PRETTY.
THERE WON'T BE FIREWORKS. IT'S TO RAIN THIS AFTERNOON.
AWW...! MAMAN!
BUT I HEARD WINE WILL BE FLOWING FROM THE FOUNTAINS AND WE CAN BE AS NOISY AS WE PLEASE!
JOSTLE
JEANNE !!
MON DIEU, ALL YOU THINK ABOUT IS HAVING FUN! WHY CAN'T YOU BE MORE LIKE YOUR LITTLE SISTER ROSALIE?!
WAH!

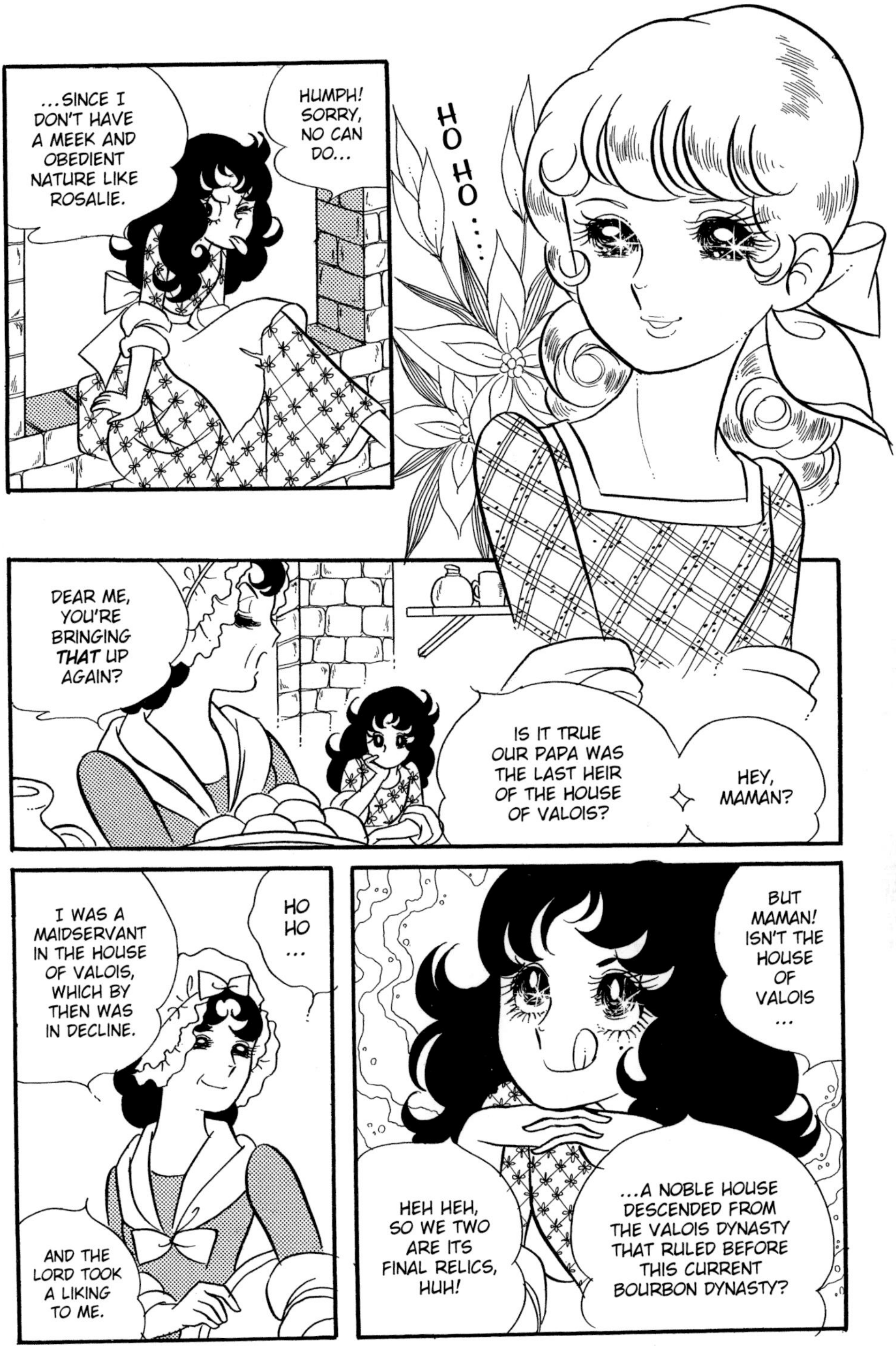
HO HO.....
HUMPH! SORRY, NO CAN DO...
...SINCE I DON'T HAVE A MEEK AND OBEDIENT NATURE LIKE ROSALIE.
HEY, MAMAN?
IS IT TRUE OUR PAPA WAS THE LAST HEIR OF THE HOUSE OF VALOIS?
DEAR ME, YOU'RE BRINGING *THAT* UP AGAIN?
BUT MAMAN! ISN'T THE HOUSE OF VALOIS ...
...A NOBLE HOUSE DESCENDED FROM THE VALOIS DYNASTY THAT RULED BEFORE THIS CURRENT BOURBON DYNASTY?
HEH HEH, SO WE TWO ARE ITS FINAL RELICS, HUH!
HO HO ...
I WAS A MAIDSERVANT IN THE HOUSE OF VALOIS, WHICH BY THEN WAS IN DECLINE.
AND THE LORD TOOK A LIKING TO ME.

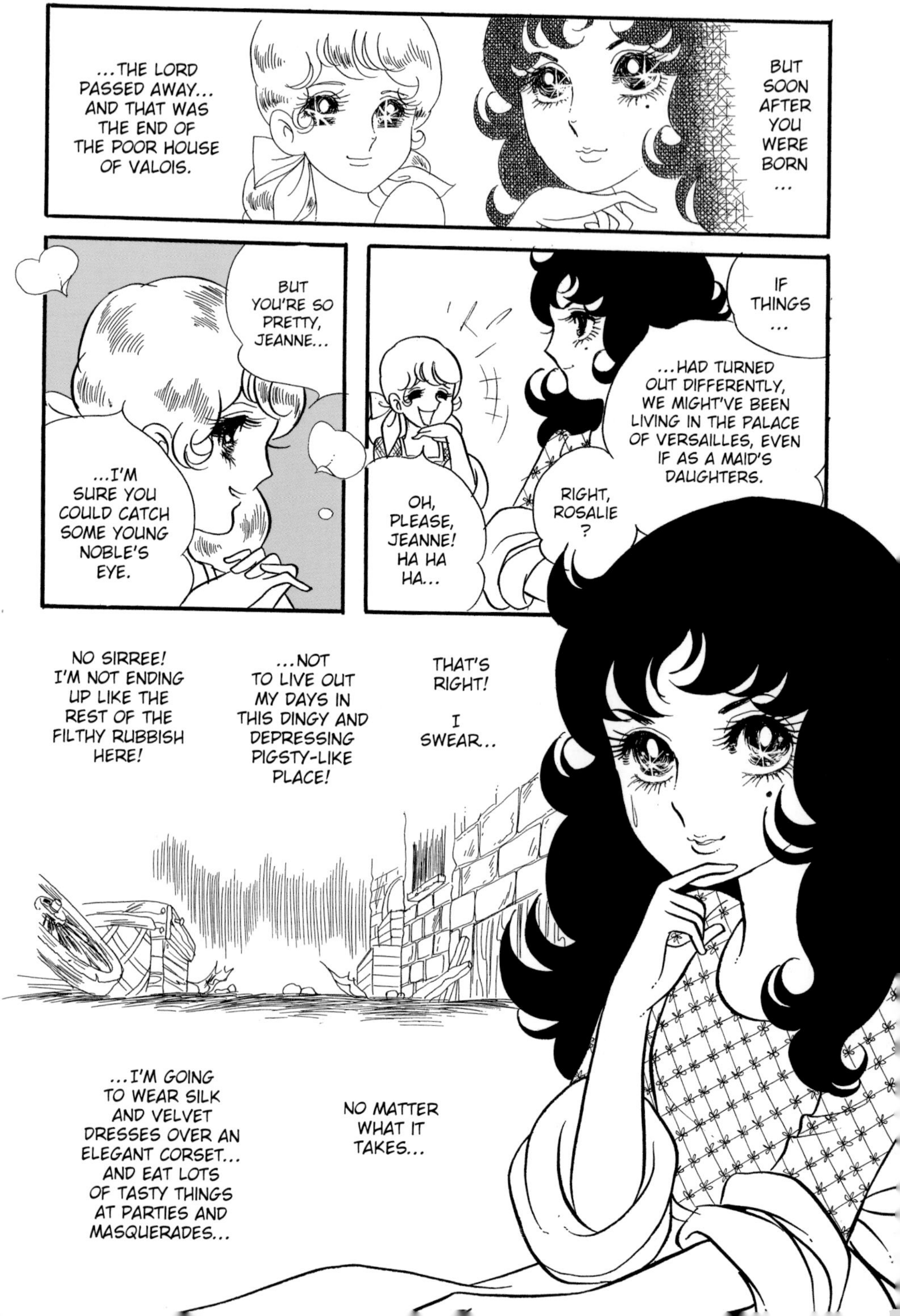
BUT SOON AFTER YOU WERE BORN...
...THE LORD PASSED AWAY... AND THAT WAS THE END OF THE POOR HOUSE OF VALOIS.
IF THINGS...
...HAD TURNED OUT DIFFERENTLY, WE MIGHT'VE BEEN LIVING IN THE PALACE OF VERSAILLES, EVEN IF AS A MAID'S DAUGHTERS.
RIGHT, ROSALIE?
OH, PLEASE, JEANNE! HA HA HA...
BUT YOU'RE SO PRETTY, JEANNE...
...I'M SURE YOU COULD CATCH SOME YOUNG NOBLE'S EYE.
THAT'S RIGHT!
I SWEAR...
...NOT TO LIVE OUT MY DAYS IN THIS DINGY AND DEPRESSING PIGSTY-LIKE PLACE!
NO SIRREE! I'M NOT ENDING UP LIKE THE REST OF THE FILTHY RUBBISH HERE!
NO MATTER WHAT IT TAKES...
...I'M GOING TO WEAR SILK AND VELVET DRESSES OVER AN ELEGANT CORSET... AND EAT LOTS OF TASTY THINGS AT PARTIES AND MASQUERADES...

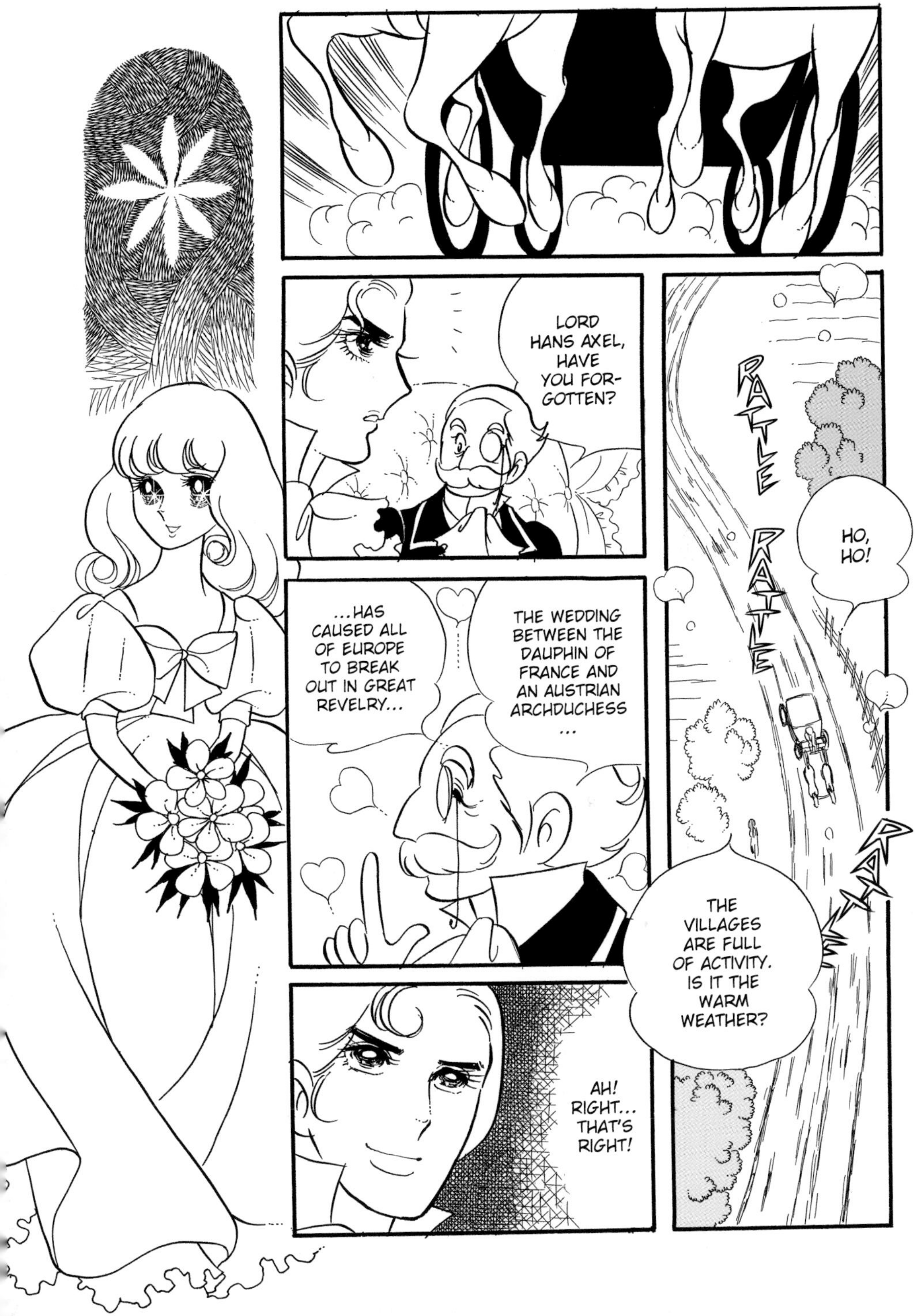
RATTLE
RATTLE
HO, HO!
RATTLE
THE VILLAGES ARE FULL OF ACTIVITY. IS IT THE WARM WEATHER?
LORD HANS AXEL, HAVE YOU FOR-GOTTEN?
THE WEDDING BETWEEN THE DAUPHIN OF FRANCE AND AN AUSTRIAN ARCHDUCHESS ...
...HAS CAUSED ALL OF EUROPE TO BREAK OUT IN GREAT REVELRY...
AH! RIGHT... THAT'S RIGHT!

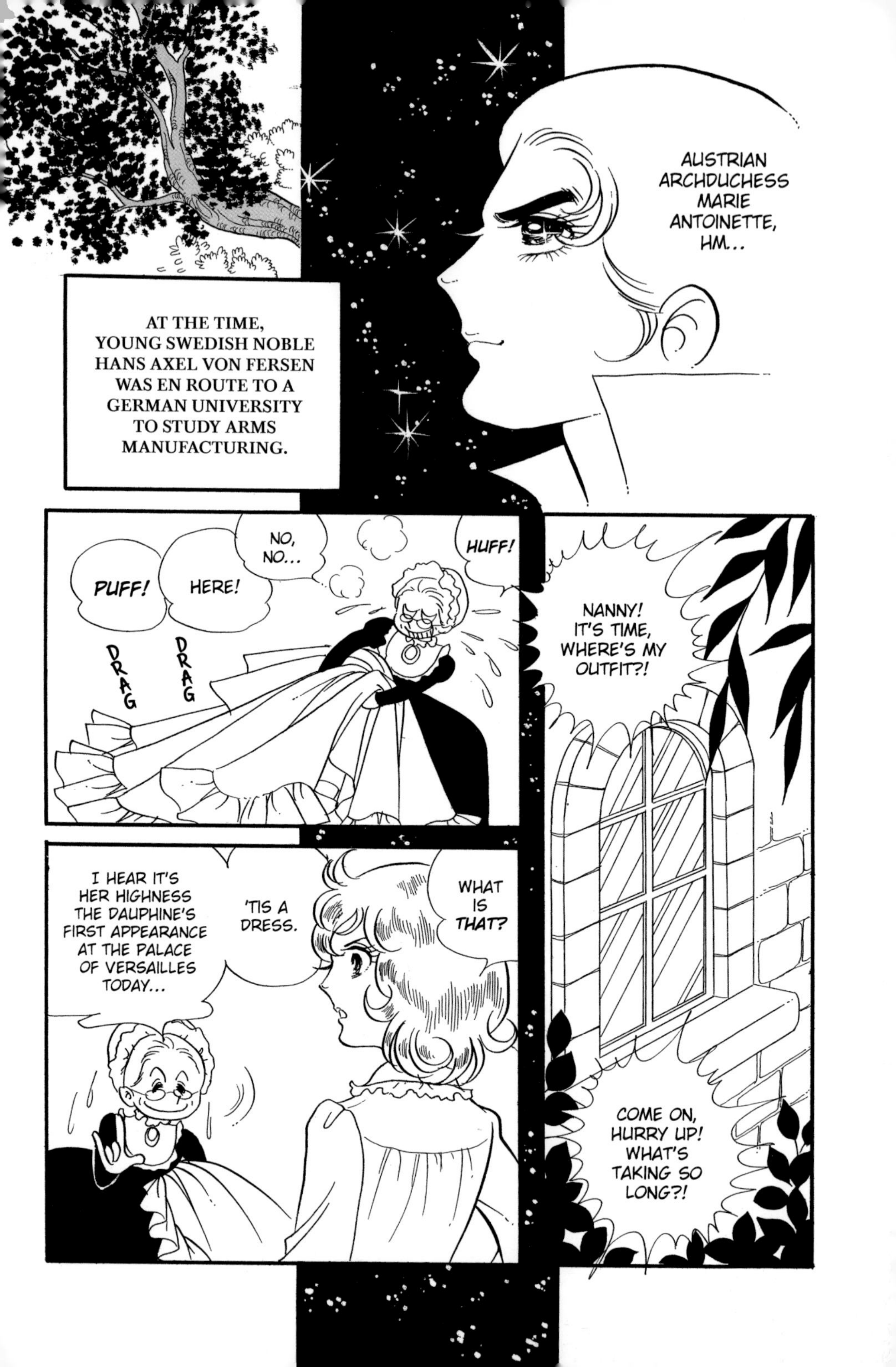
AUSTRIAN ARCHDUCHESS MARIE ANTOINETTE, HM...
AT THE TIME, YOUNG SWEDISH NOBLE HANS AXEL VON FERSEN WAS EN ROUTE TO A GERMAN UNIVERSITY TO STUDY ARMS MANUFACTURING.
NANNY! IT'S TIME, WHERE'S MY OUTFIT?!
COME ON, HURRY UP! WHAT'S TAKING SO LONG?!
HUFF!
NO, NO...
HERE!
PUFF!
DRAG
DRAG
WHAT IS THAT?
'TIS A DRESS.
I HEAR IT'S HER HIGHNESS THE DAUPHINE'S FIRST APPEARANCE AT THE PALACE OF VERSAILLES TODAY...

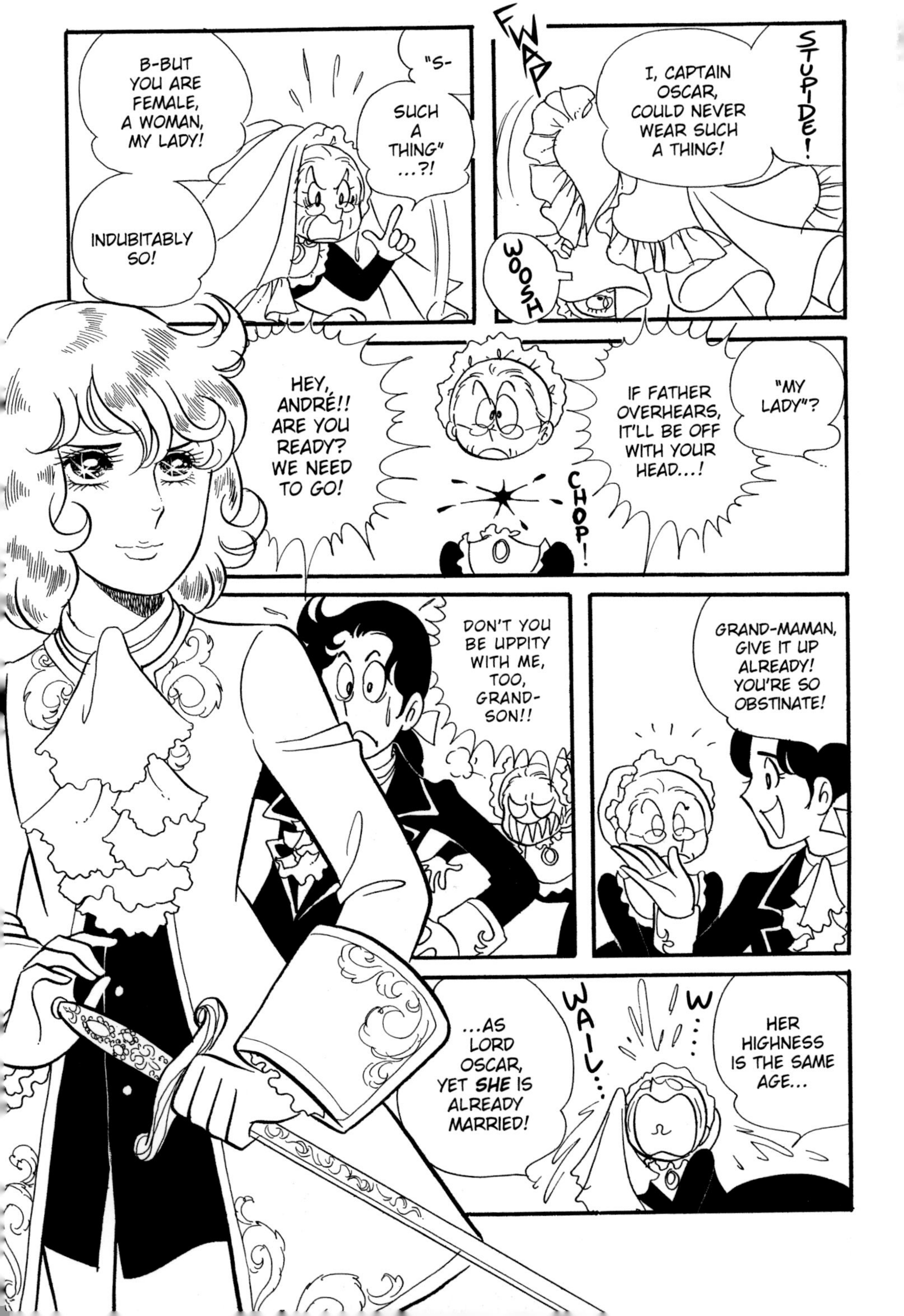
STUPIDE!
FWAP
I, CAPTAIN OSCAR, COULD NEVER WEAR SUCH A THING!
WOOSH
"S-
SUCH A THING" ...?!
B-BUT YOU ARE FEMALE, A WOMAN, MY LADY!
INDUBITABLY SO!
"MY LADY"?
IF FATHER OVERHEARS, IT'LL BE OFF WITH YOUR HEAD...!
CHOP!
HEY, ANDRÉ!! ARE YOU READY? WE NEED TO GO!
GRAND-MAMAN, GIVE IT UP ALREADY! YOU'RE SO OBSTINATE!
DON'T YOU BE UPPITY WITH ME, TOO, GRAND-SON!!
HER HIGHNESS IS THE SAME AGE...
W...
WAIL...
...AS LORD OSCAR, YET **SHE** IS ALREADY MARRIED!

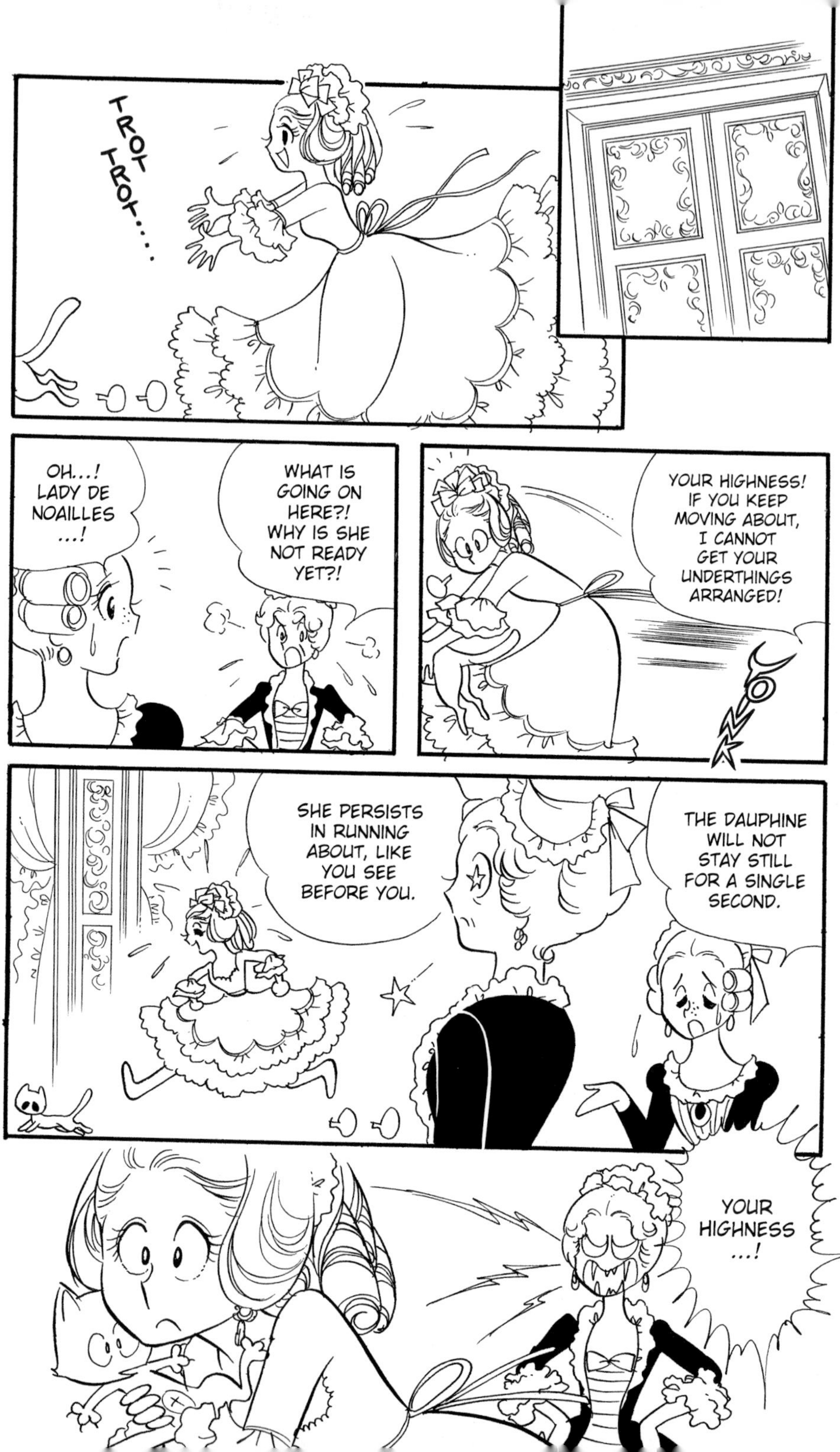
TROT TROT....
YOUR HIGHNESS! IF YOU KEEP MOVING ABOUT, I CANNOT GET YOUR UNDERTHINGS ARRANGED!
WHAT IS GOING ON HERE?! WHY IS SHE NOT READY YET?!
OH...! LADY DE NOAILLES ...!
THE DAUPHINE WILL NOT STAY STILL FOR A SINGLE SECOND.
SHE PERSISTS IN RUNNING ABOUT, LIKE YOU SEE BEFORE YOU.
YOUR HIGHNESS ...!

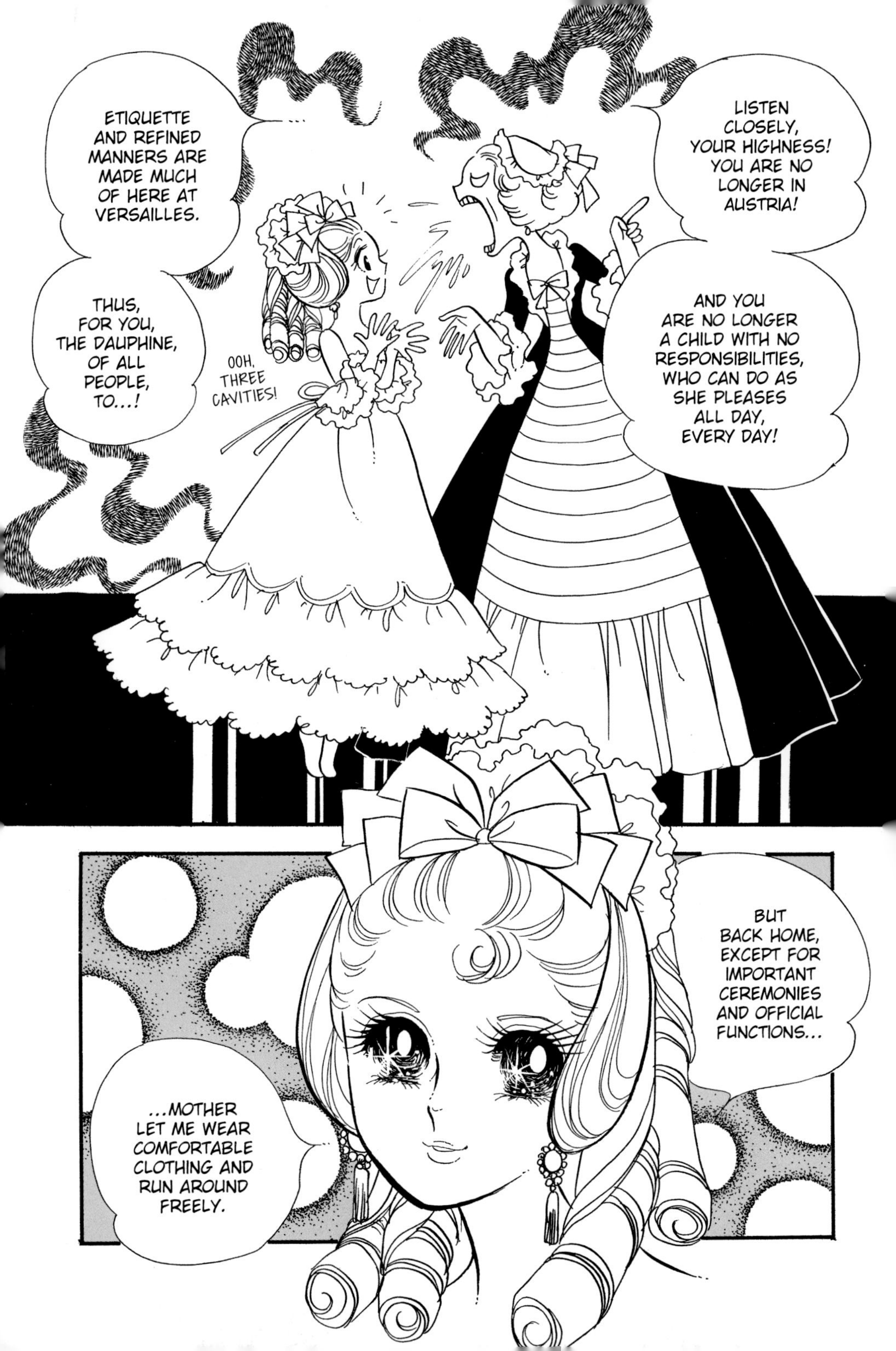
LISTEN CLOSELY, YOUR HIGHNESS! YOU ARE NO LONGER IN AUSTRIA!
AND YOU ARE NO LONGER A CHILD WITH NO RESPONSIBILITIES, WHO CAN DO AS SHE PLEASES ALL DAY, EVERY DAY!
ETIQUETTE AND REFINED MANNERS ARE MADE MUCH OF HERE AT VERSAILLES.
THUS, FOR YOU, THE DAUPHINE, OF ALL PEOPLE, TO...!
OOH, THREE CAVITIES!
BUT BACK HOME, EXCEPT FOR IMPORTANT CEREMONIES AND OFFICIAL FUNCTIONS...
...MOTHER LET ME WEAR COMFORTABLE CLOTHING AND RUN AROUND FREELY.

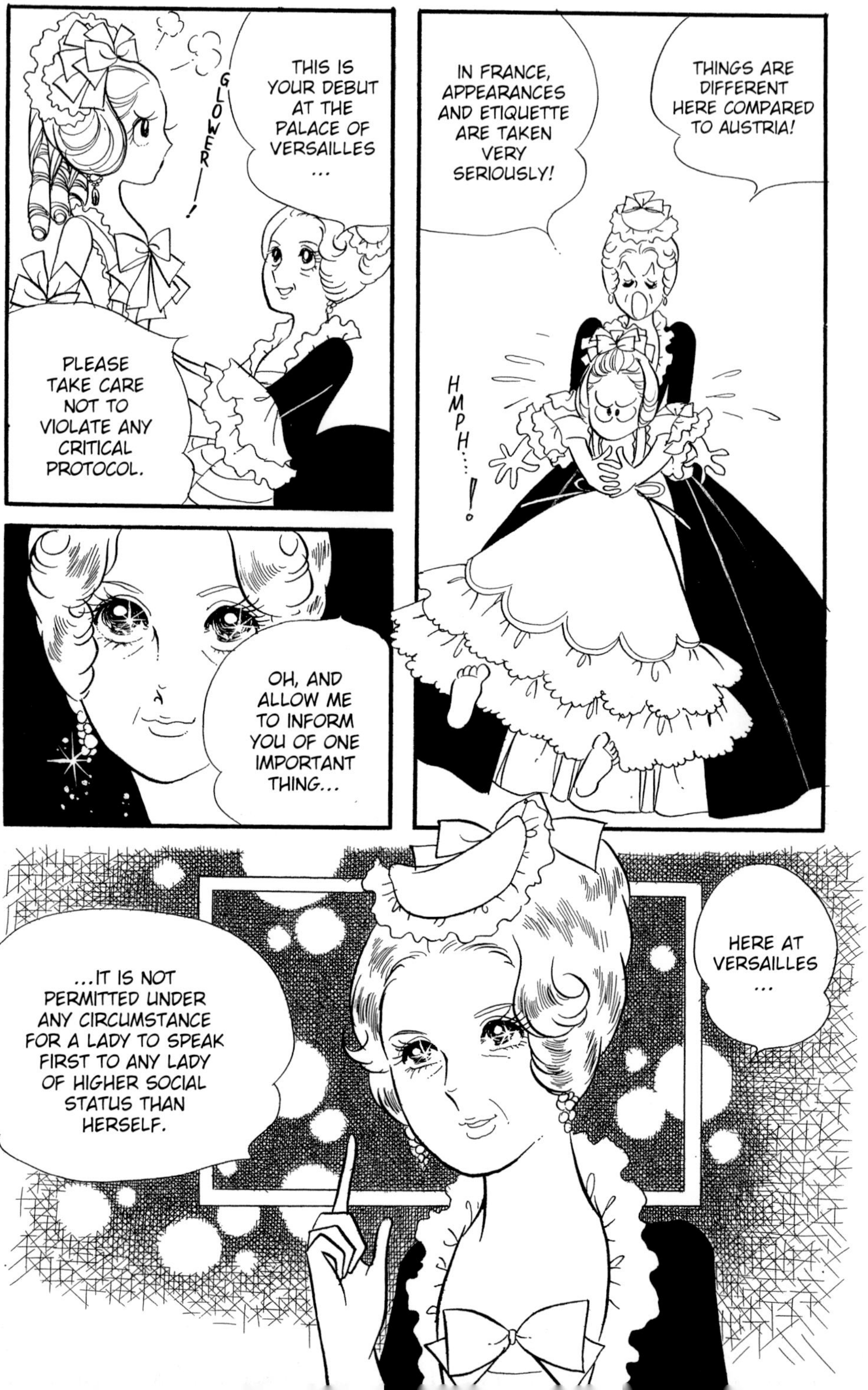
THINGS ARE DIFFERENT HERE COMPARED TO AUSTRIA!
IN FRANCE, APPEARANCES AND ETIQUETTE ARE TAKEN VERY SERIOUSLY!
HMPH...!
THIS IS YOUR DEBUT AT THE PALACE OF VERSAILLES ...
GLOWER!
PLEASE TAKE CARE NOT TO VIOLATE ANY CRITICAL PROTOCOL.
OH, AND ALLOW ME TO INFORM YOU OF ONE IMPORTANT THING...
HERE AT VERSAILLES ...
...IT IS NOT PERMITTED UNDER ANY CIRCUMSTANCE FOR A LADY TO SPEAK FIRST TO ANY LADY OF HIGHER SOCIAL STATUS THAN HERSELF.

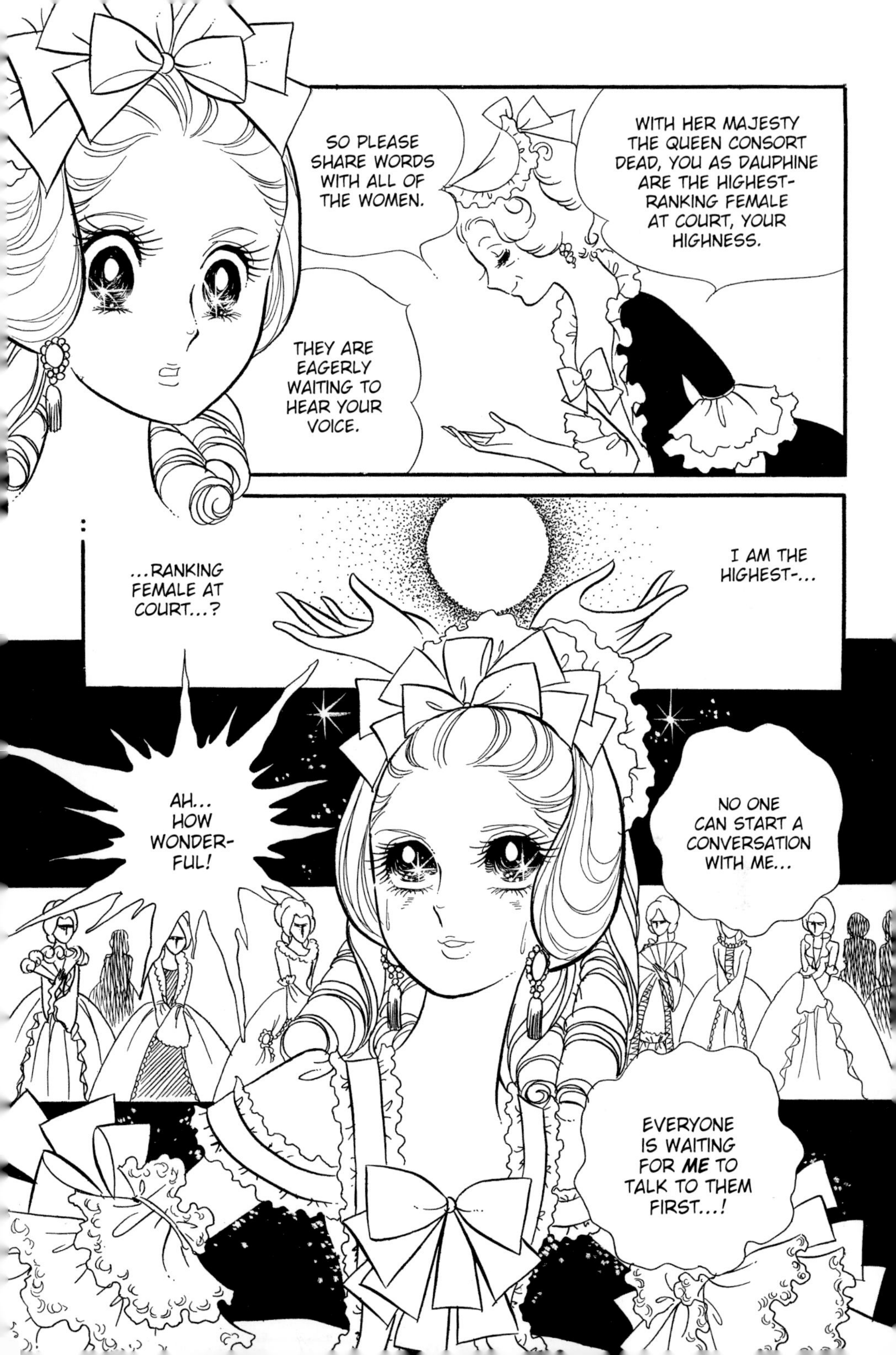
WITH HER MAJESTY THE QUEEN CONSORT DEAD, YOU AS DAUPHINE ARE THE HIGHEST-RANKING FEMALE AT COURT, YOUR HIGHNESS.
SO PLEASE SHARE WORDS WITH ALL OF THE WOMEN.
THEY ARE EAGERLY WAITING TO HEAR YOUR VOICE.
I AM THE HIGHEST-...
...RANKING FEMALE AT COURT...?
NO ONE CAN START A CONVERSATION WITH ME...
EVERYONE IS WAITING FOR *ME* TO TALK TO THEM FIRST...!
AH... HOW WONDER-FUL!

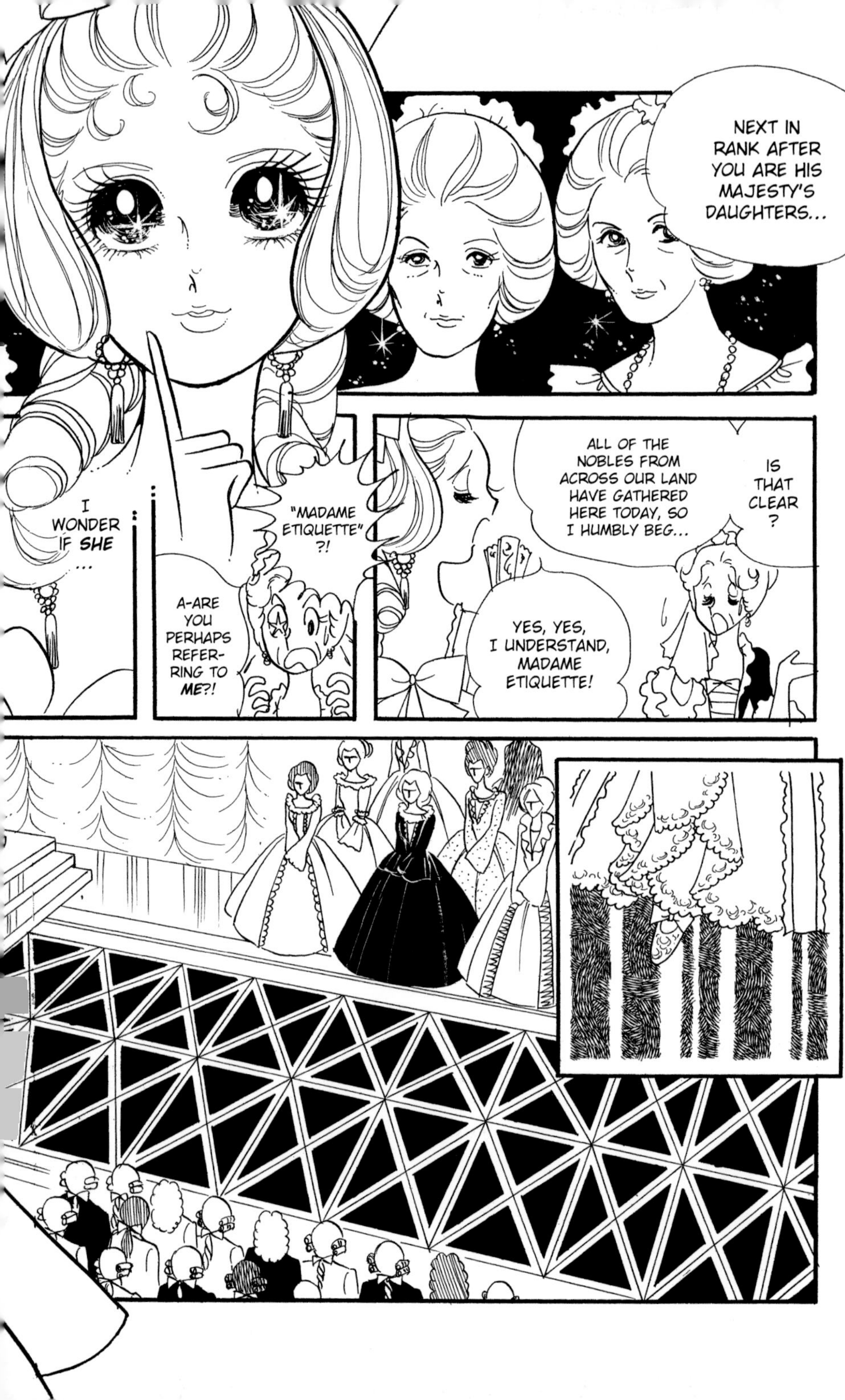
NEXT IN RANK AFTER YOU ARE HIS MAJESTY'S DAUGHTERS...
ALL OF THE NOBLES FROM ACROSS OUR LAND HAVE GATHERED HERE TODAY, SO I HUMBLY BEG...
IS THAT CLEAR?
YES, YES, I UNDERSTAND, MADAME ETIQUETTE!
"MADAME ETIQUETTE"?!
A-ARE YOU PERHAPS REFERRING TO ME?!
I WONDER IF SHE...

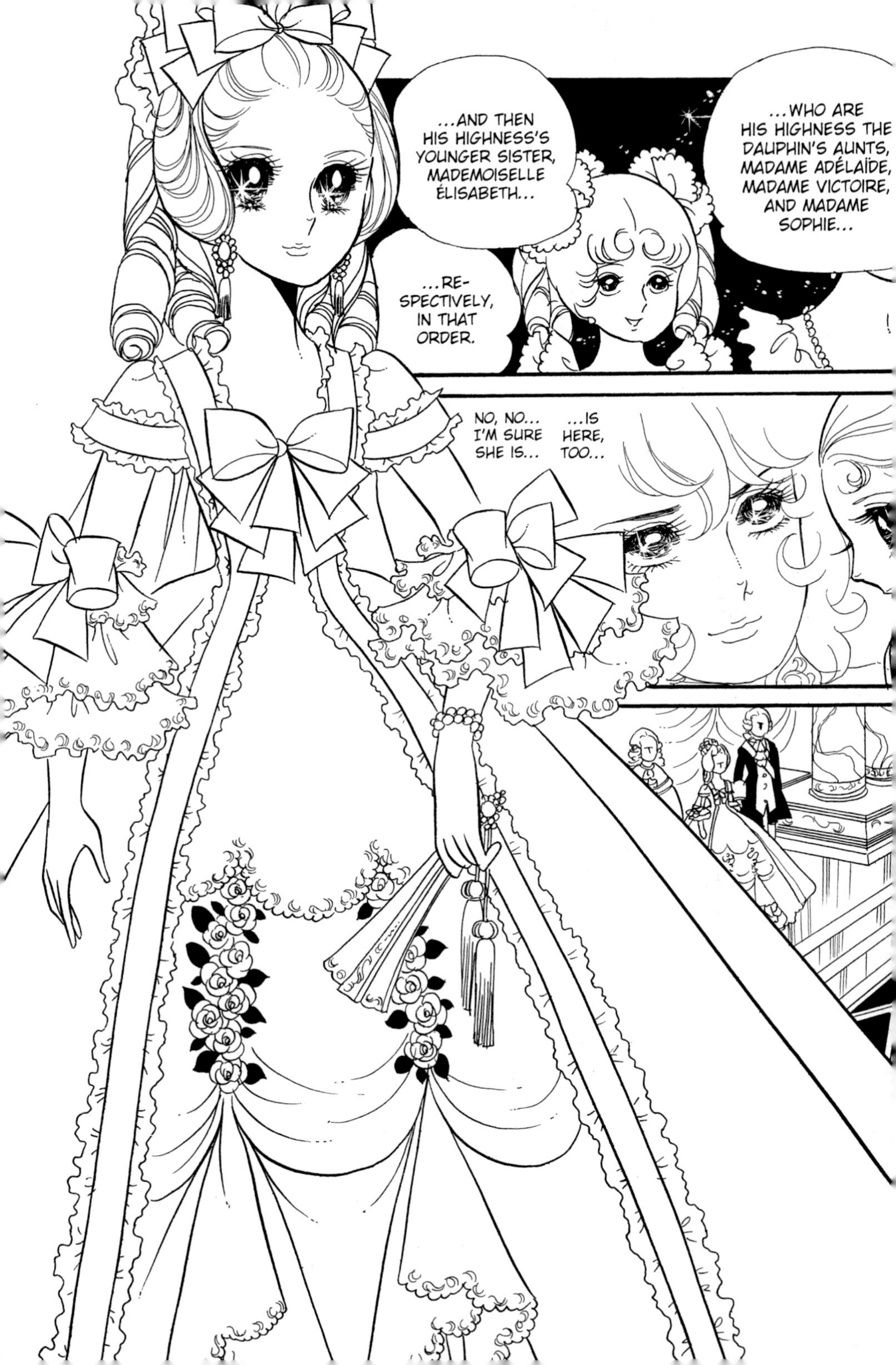
...WHO ARE HIS HIGHNESS THE DAUPHIN'S AUNTS, MADAME ADÉLAÏDE, MADAME VICTOIRE, AND MADAME SOPHIE...
...AND THEN HIS HIGHNESS'S YOUNGER SISTER, MADEMOISELLE ÉLISABETH...
...RE-SPECTIVELY, IN THAT ORDER.
...IS HERE, TOO...
NO, NO... I'M SURE SHE IS...

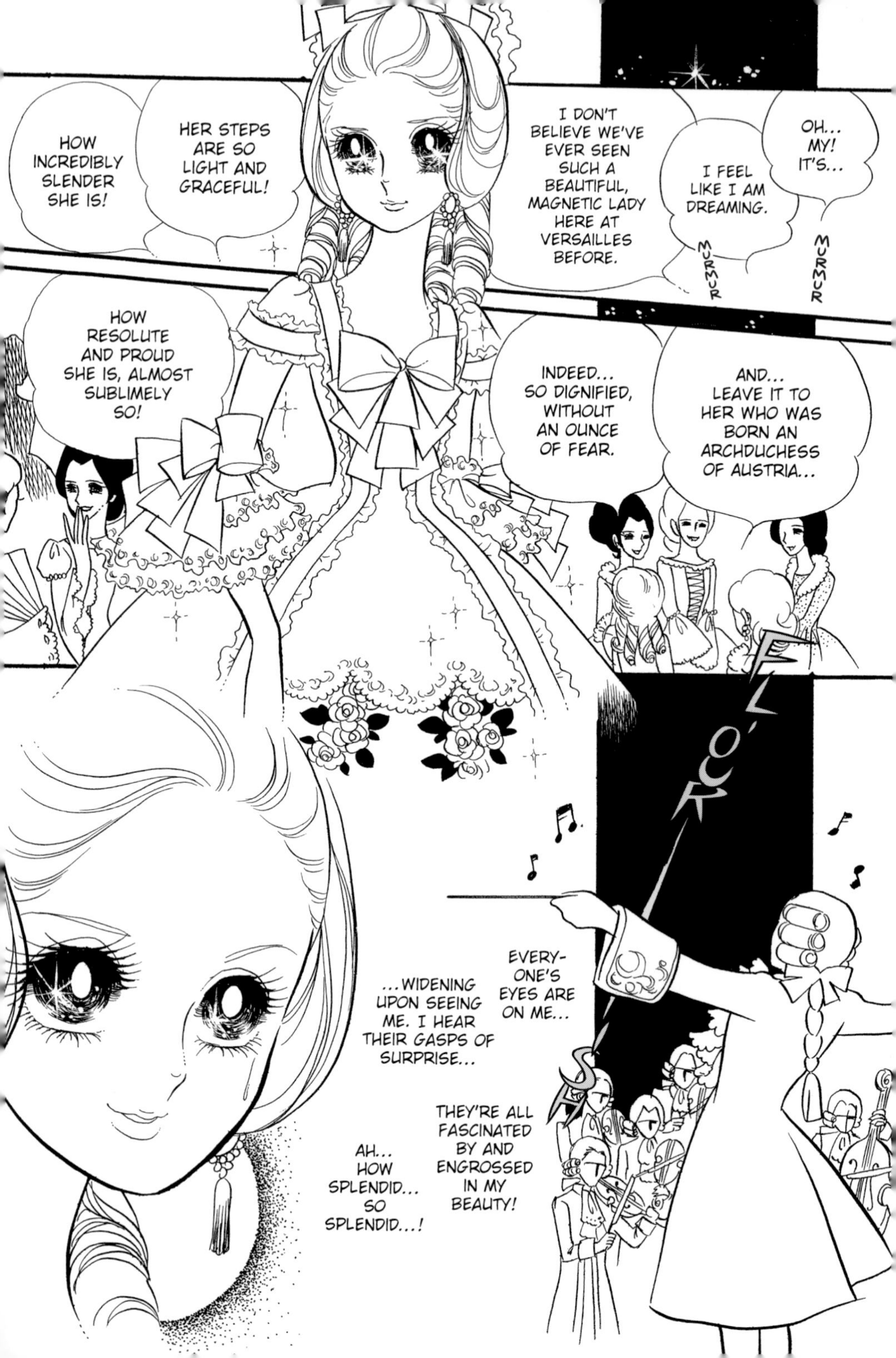
OH... MY! IT'S...
MURMUR
I FEEL LIKE I AM DREAMING.
MURMUR
I DON'T BELIEVE WE'VE EVER SEEN SUCH A BEAUTIFUL, MAGNETIC LADY HERE AT VERSAILLES BEFORE.
HER STEPS ARE SO LIGHT AND GRACEFUL!
HOW INCREDIBLY SLENDER SHE IS!
AND... LEAVE IT TO HER WHO WAS BORN AN ARCHDUCHESS OF AUSTRIA...
INDEED... SO DIGNIFIED, WITHOUT AN OUNCE OF FEAR.
HOW RESOLUTE AND PROUD SHE IS, ALMOST SUBLIMELY SO!
FLOURISH
EVERY-ONE'S EYES ARE ON ME...
...WIDENING UPON SEEING ME. I HEAR THEIR GASPS OF SURPRISE...
THEY'RE ALL FASCINATED BY AND ENGROSSED IN MY BEAUTY!
AH... HOW SPLENDID... SO SPLENDID...!

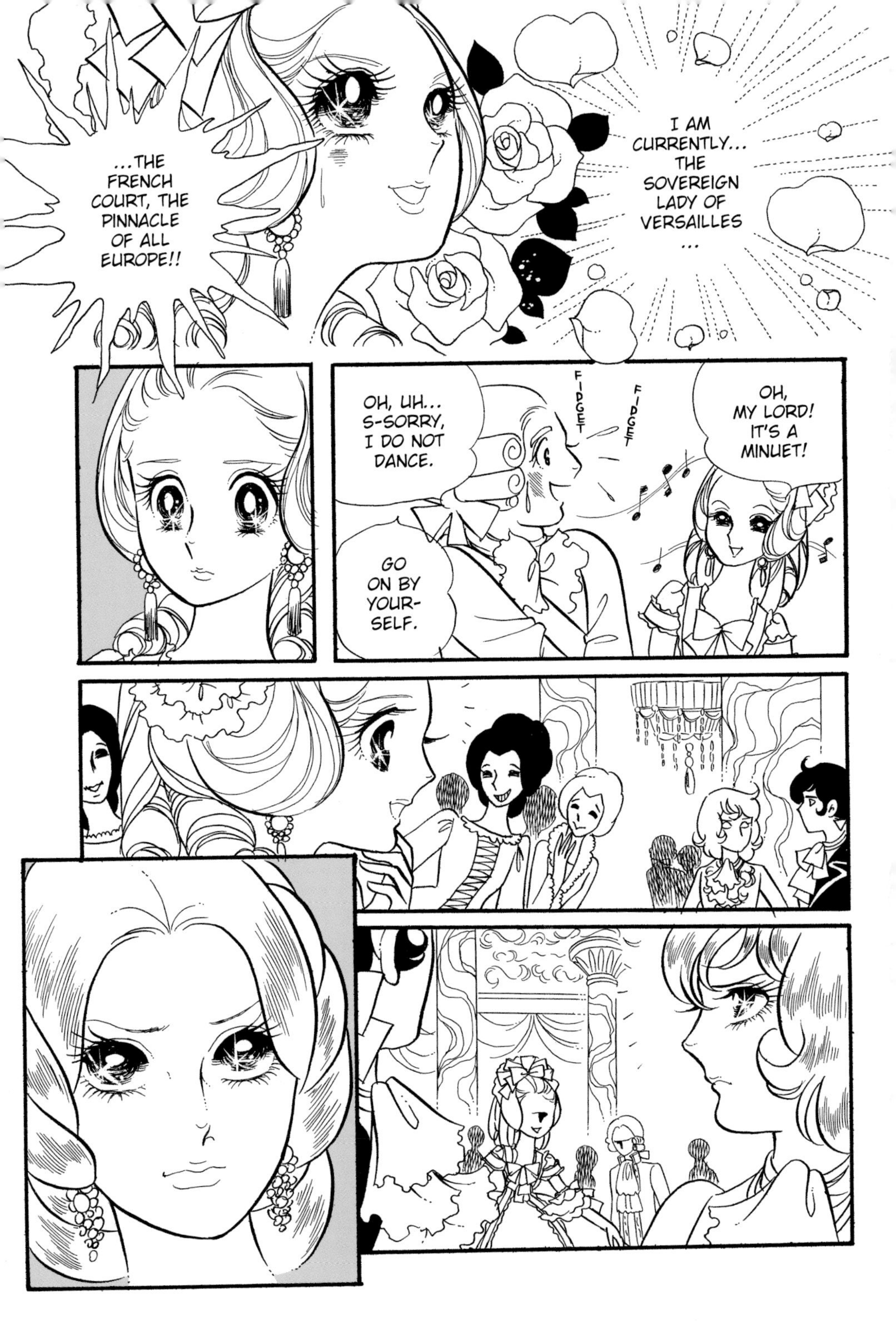
I AM CURRENTLY... THE SOVEREIGN LADY OF VERSAILLES ...
...THE FRENCH COURT, THE PINNACLE OF ALL EUROPE!!
OH, MY LORD! IT'S A MINUET!
FIDGET
FIDGET
OH, UH... S-SORRY, I DO NOT DANCE.
GO ON BY YOURSELF.

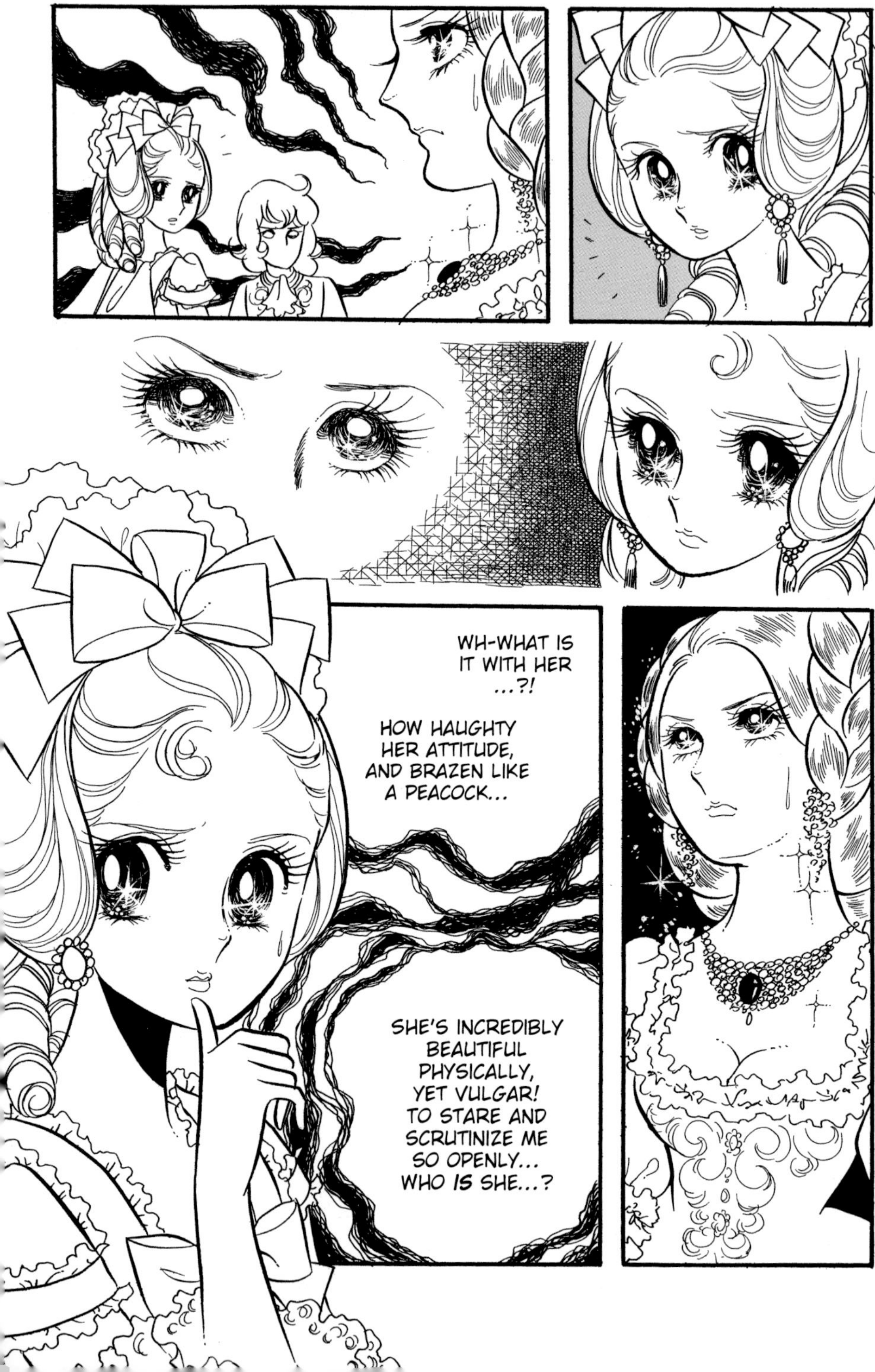
WH-WHAT IS IT WITH HER ...?!
HOW HAUGHTY HER ATTITUDE, AND BRAZEN LIKE A PEACOCK...
SHE'S INCREDIBLY BEAUTIFUL PHYSICALLY, YET VULGAR! TO STARE AND SCRUTINIZE ME SO OPENLY... WHO *IS* SHE...?

♥ **ANTOINETTE'S HEART IS DRAWN TO OSCAR. HOWEVER, THERE ARE STERN EYES GAZING AT HER...!?**

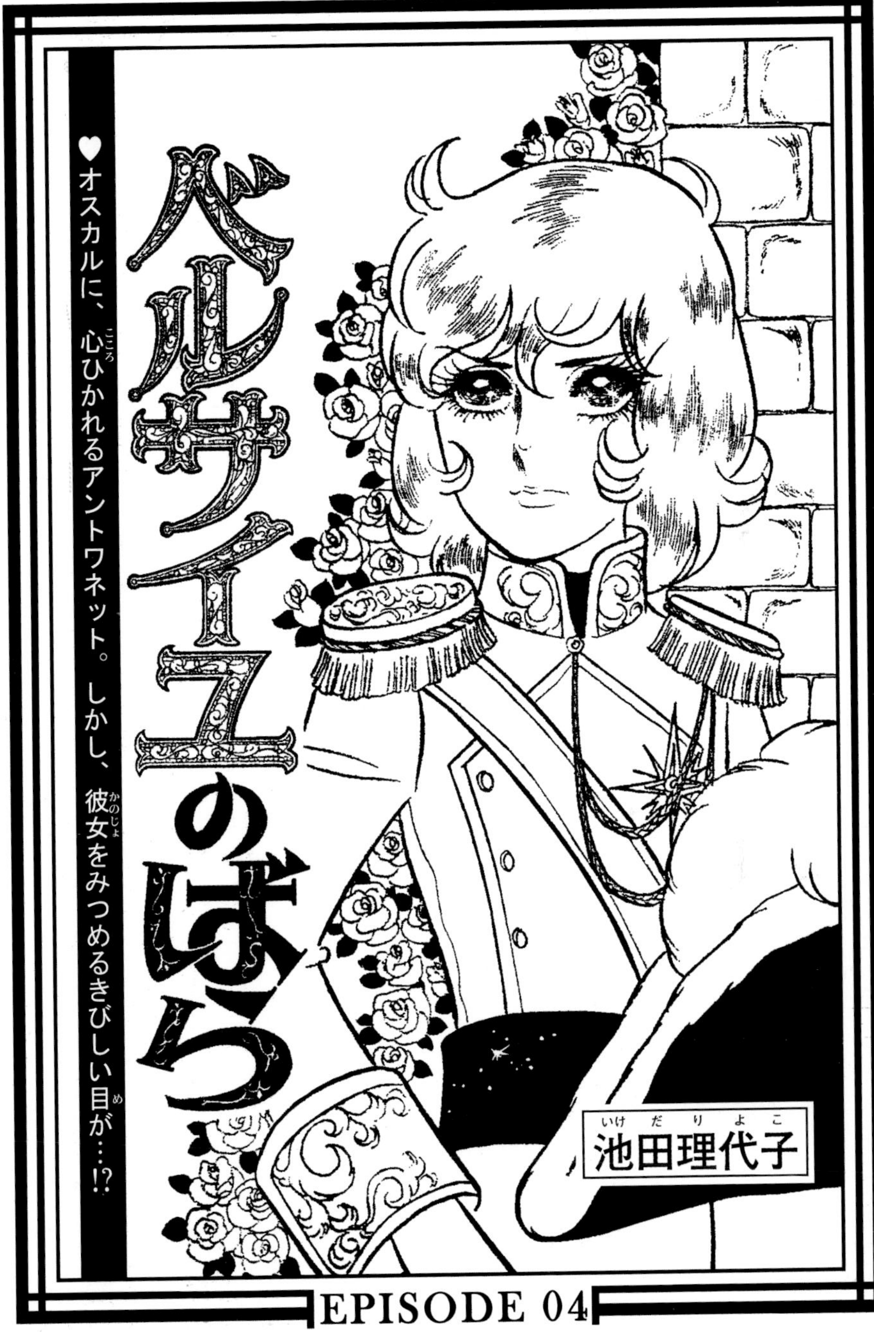
ベルサイユのばら
♥オスカルに、心ひかれるアントワネット。しかし、彼女をみつめるきびしい目が…!?
池田理代子

EPISODE 04

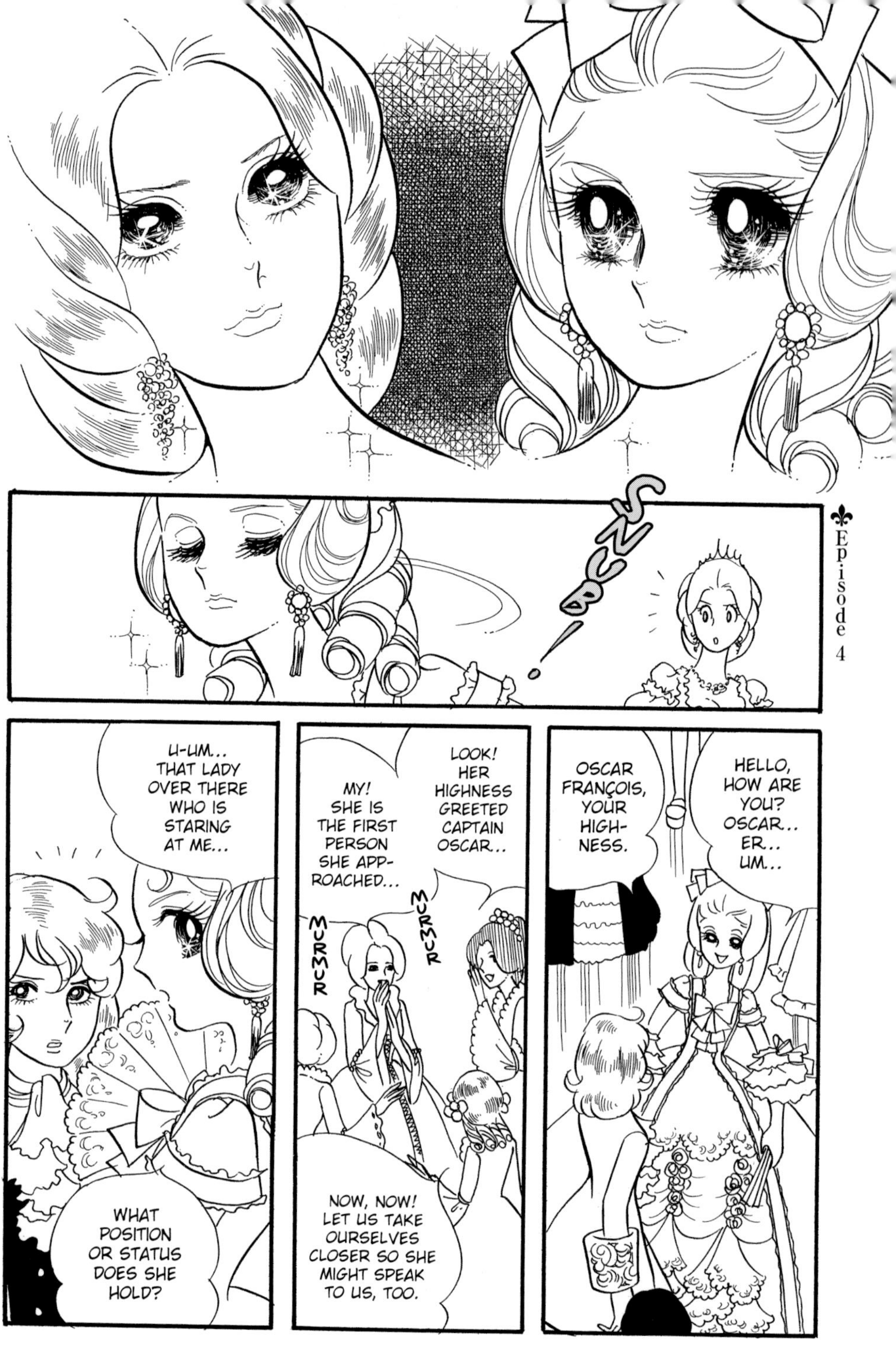
SNUB!
HELLO, HOW ARE YOU? OSCAR... ER... UM...
OSCAR FRANÇOIS, YOUR HIGHNESS.
LOOK! HER HIGHNESS GREETED CAPTAIN OSCAR...
MY! SHE IS THE FIRST PERSON SHE APPROACHED...
MURMUR
MURMUR
NOW, NOW! LET US TAKE OURSELVES CLOSER SO SHE MIGHT SPEAK TO US, TOO.
U-UM... THAT LADY OVER THERE WHO IS STARING AT ME...
WHAT POSITION OR STATUS DOES SHE HOLD?

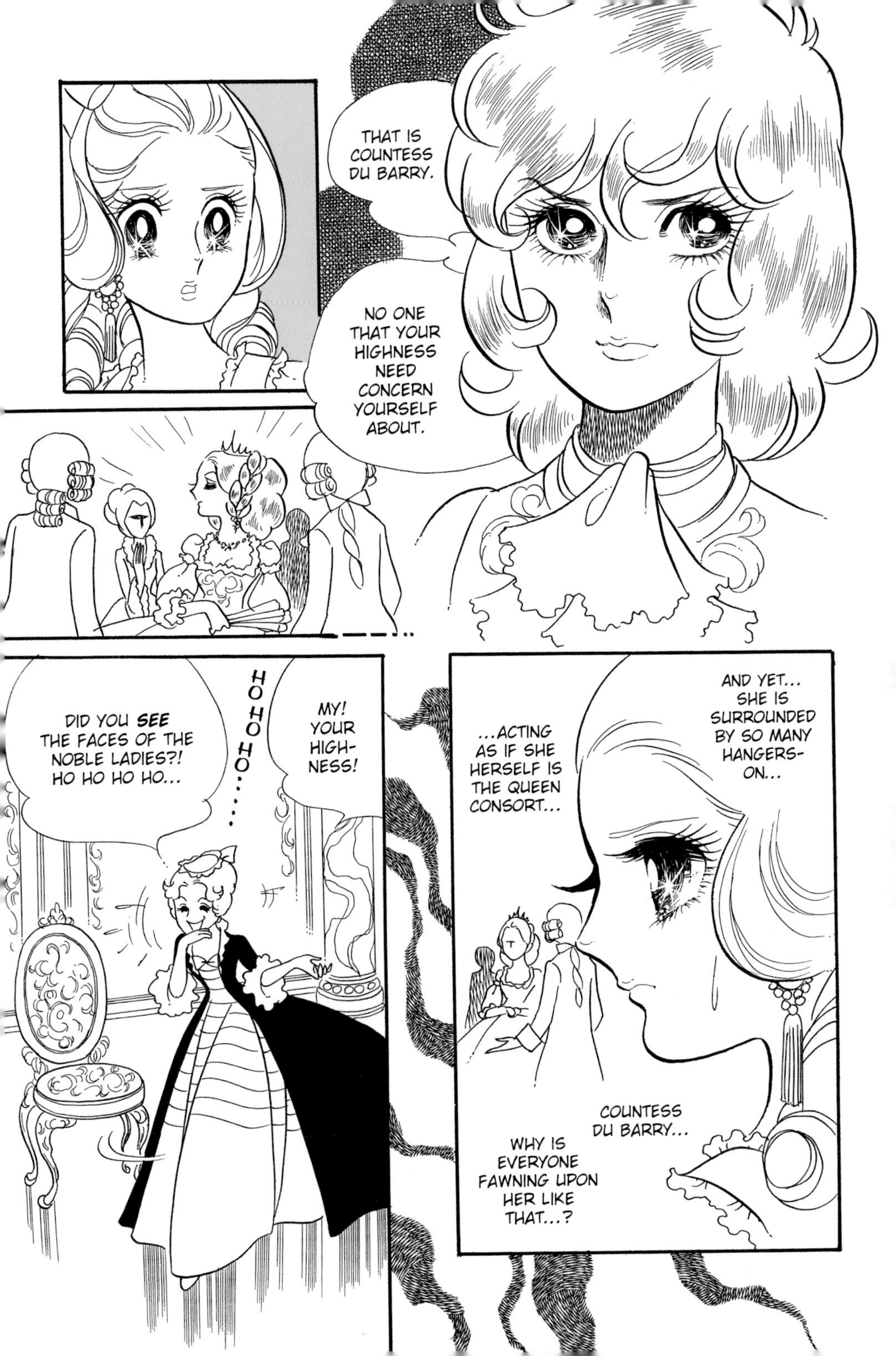
THAT IS COUNTESS DU BARRY.
NO ONE THAT YOUR HIGHNESS NEED CONCERN YOURSELF ABOUT.
AND YET... SHE IS SURROUNDED BY SO MANY HANGERS-ON...
...ACTING AS IF SHE HERSELF IS THE QUEEN CONSORT...
COUNTESS DU BARRY...
WHY IS EVERYONE FAWNING UPON HER LIKE THAT...?
MY! YOUR HIGH-NESS!
HO HO HO HO...
DID YOU **SEE** THE FACES OF THE NOBLE LADIES?! HO HO HO HO...

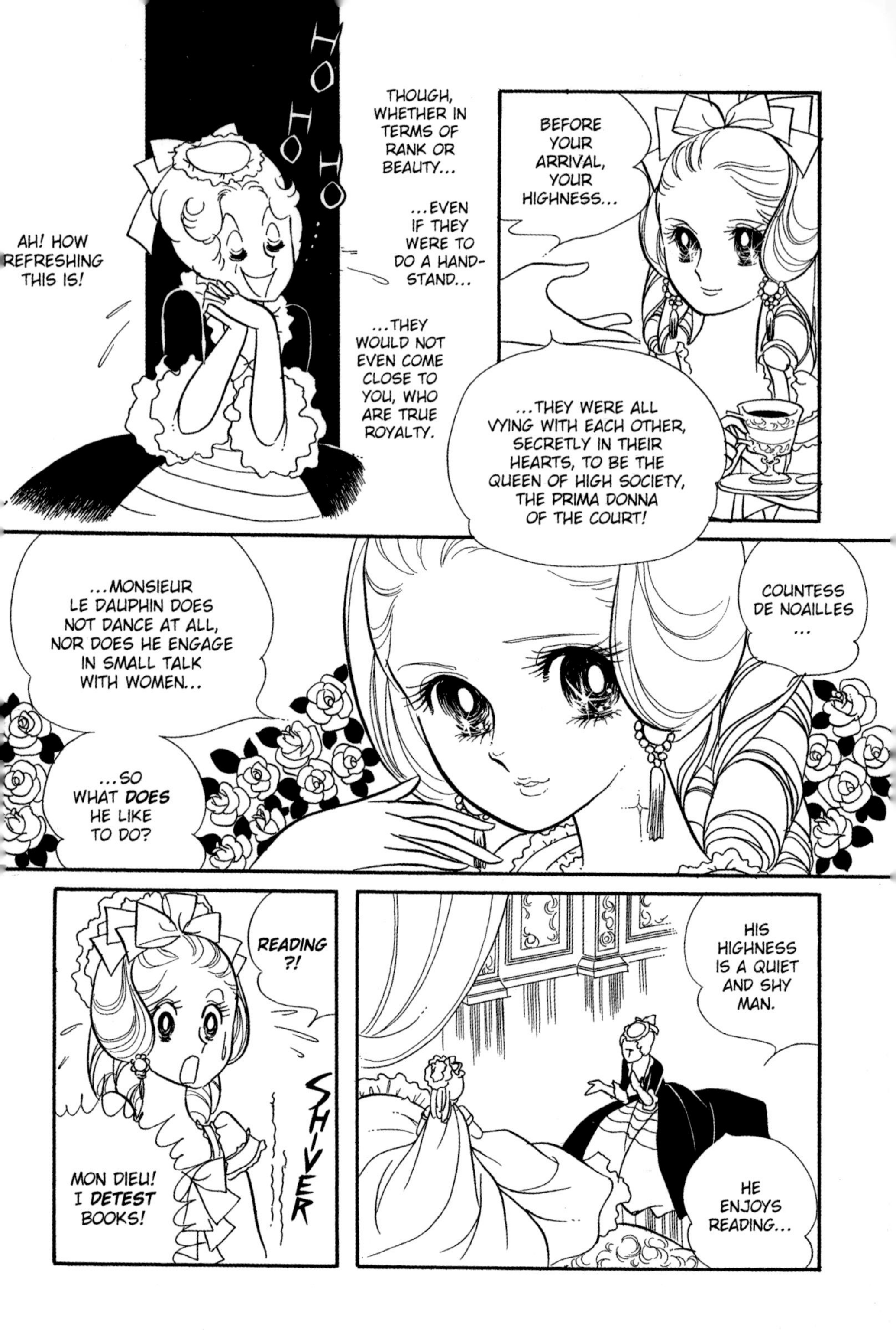
BEFORE YOUR ARRIVAL, YOUR HIGHNESS...
...THEY WERE ALL VYING WITH EACH OTHER, SECRETLY IN THEIR HEARTS, TO BE THE QUEEN OF HIGH SOCIETY, THE PRIMA DONNA OF THE COURT!
THOUGH, WHETHER IN TERMS OF RANK OR BEAUTY...
...EVEN IF THEY WERE TO DO A HAND-STAND...
...THEY WOULD NOT EVEN COME CLOSE TO YOU, WHO ARE TRUE ROYALTY.
HO HO HO
AH! HOW REFRESHING THIS IS!
COUNTESS DE NOAILLES...
...MONSIEUR LE DAUPHIN DOES NOT DANCE AT ALL, NOR DOES HE ENGAGE IN SMALL TALK WITH WOMEN...
...SO WHAT **DOES** HE LIKE TO DO?
HIS HIGHNESS IS A QUIET AND SHY MAN.
HE ENJOYS READING...
READING?!
SHIVER
MON DIEU! I **DETEST** BOOKS!

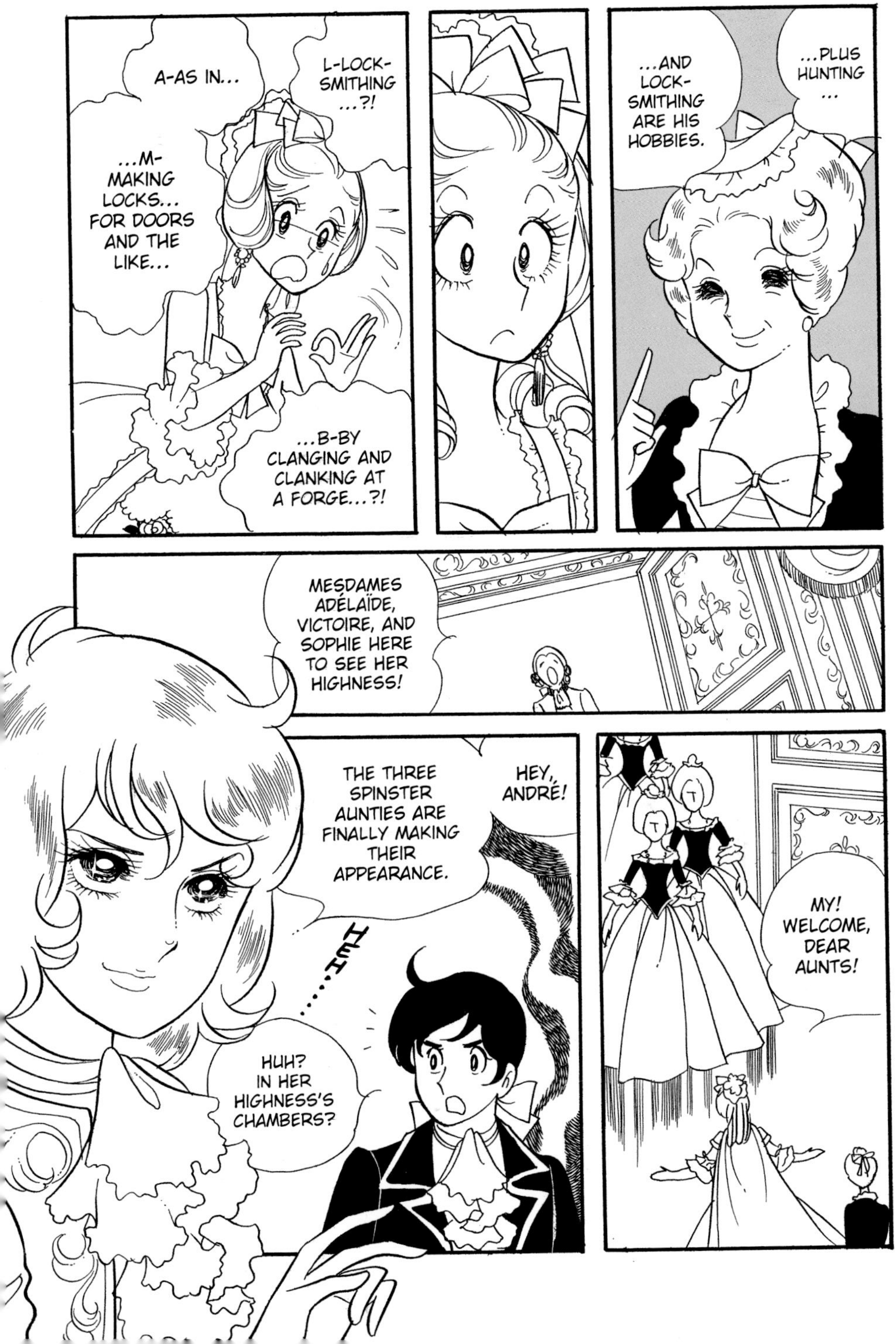
...PLUS HUNTING ...
...AND LOCK-SMITHING ARE HIS HOBBIES.
L-LOCK-SMITHING ...?!
A-AS IN...
...M-MAKING LOCKS... FOR DOORS AND THE LIKE...
...B-BY CLANGING AND CLANKING AT A FORGE...?!
MESDAMES ADÉLAÏDE, VICTOIRE, AND SOPHIE HERE TO SEE HER HIGHNESS!
MY! WELCOME, DEAR AUNTS!
HEY, ANDRÉ!
THE THREE SPINSTER AUNTIES ARE FINALLY MAKING THEIR APPEARANCE.
HEH...
HUH? IN HER HIGHNESS'S CHAMBERS?

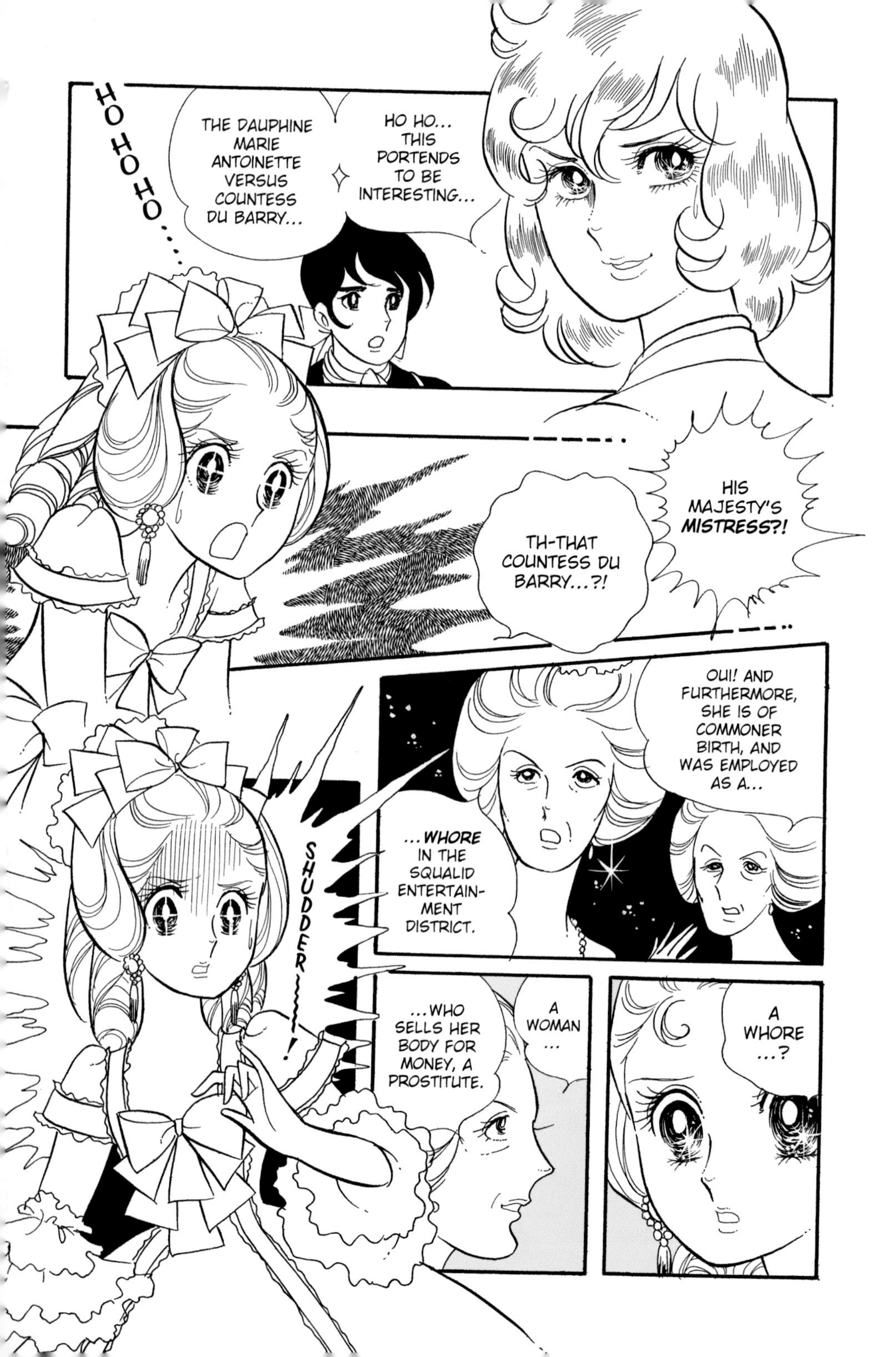

HO HO... THIS PORTENDS TO BE INTERESTING...
THE DAUPHINE MARIE ANTOINETTE VERSUS COUNTESS DU BARRY...
HO HO HO HO...
HIS MAJESTY'S **MISTRESS?!**
TH-THAT COUNTESS DU BARRY...?!
OUI! AND FURTHERMORE, SHE IS OF COMMONER BIRTH, AND WAS EMPLOYED AS A...
...**WHORE** IN THE SQUALID ENTERTAIN-MENT DISTRICT.
A WHORE ...?
A WOMAN ...
...WHO SELLS HER BODY FOR MONEY, A PROSTITUTE.
SHUDDER!

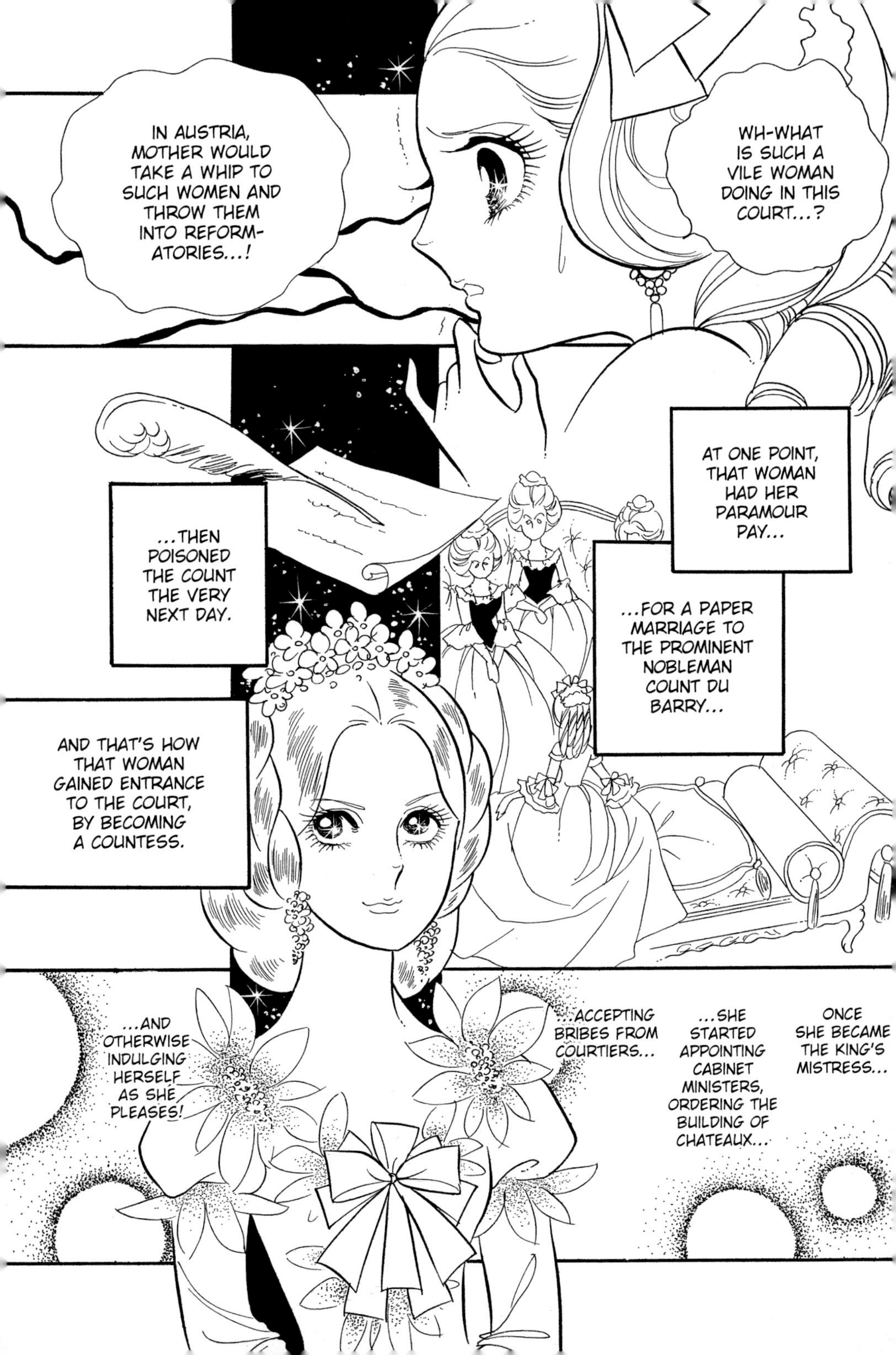
WH-WHAT IS SUCH A VILE WOMAN DOING IN THIS COURT...?
IN AUSTRIA, MOTHER WOULD TAKE A WHIP TO SUCH WOMEN AND THROW THEM INTO REFORM-ATORIES...!
AT ONE POINT, THAT WOMAN HAD HER PARAMOUR PAY...
...FOR A PAPER MARRIAGE TO THE PROMINENT NOBLEMAN COUNT DU BARRY...
...THEN POISONED THE COUNT THE VERY NEXT DAY.
AND THAT'S HOW THAT WOMAN GAINED ENTRANCE TO THE COURT, BY BECOMING A COUNTESS.
ONCE SHE BECAME THE KING'S MISTRESS...
...SHE STARTED APPOINTING CABINET MINISTERS, ORDERING THE BUILDING OF CHATEAUX...
...ACCEPTING BRIBES FROM COURTIERS...
...AND OTHERWISE INDULGING HERSELF AS SHE PLEASES!

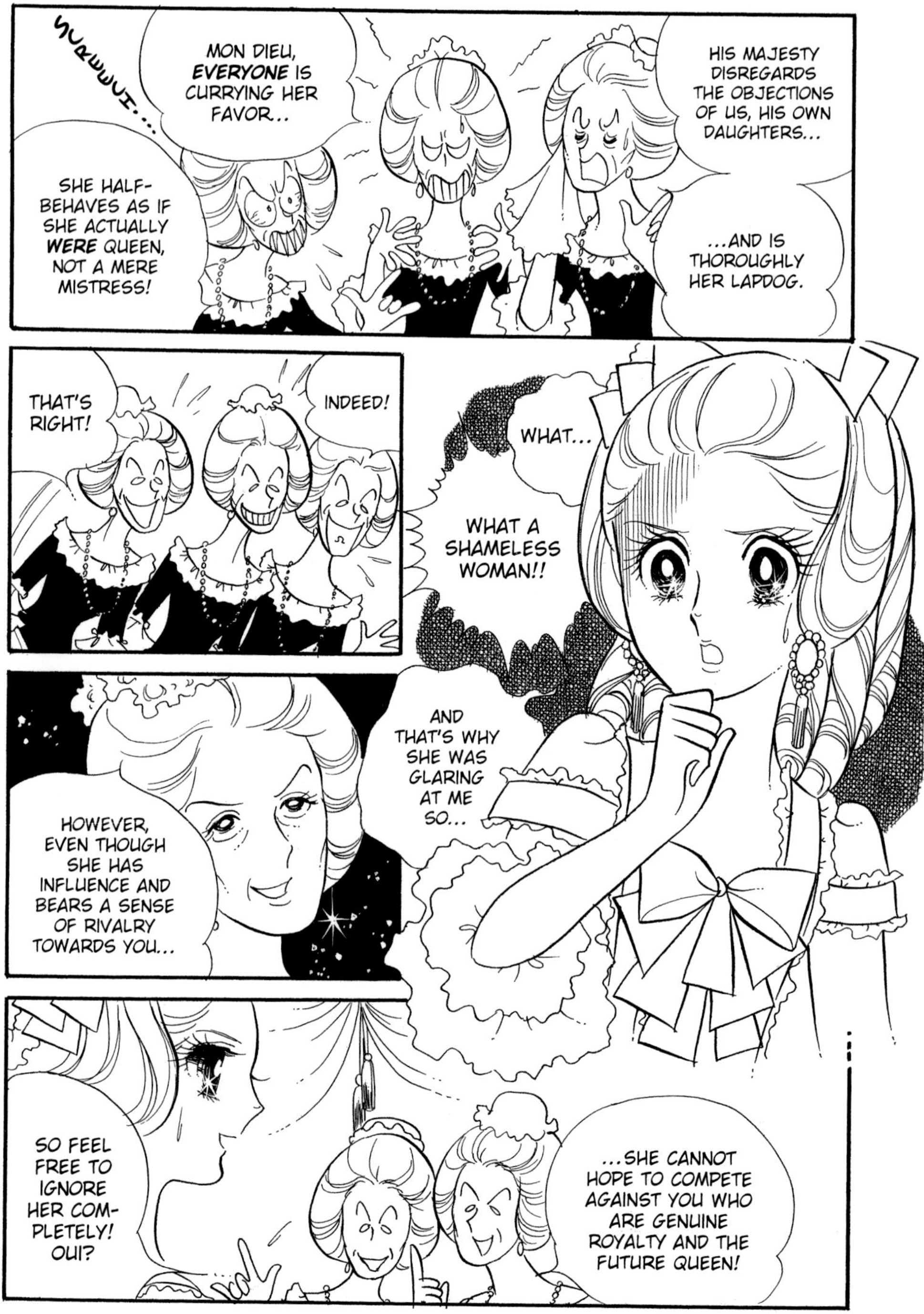

HIS MAJESTY DISREGARDS THE OBJECTIONS OF US, HIS OWN DAUGHTERS...
...AND IS THOROUGHLY HER LAPDOG.
MON DIEU, **EVERYONE** IS CURRYING HER FAVOR...
SHE HALF-BEHAVES AS IF SHE ACTUALLY ***WERE*** QUEEN, NOT A MERE MISTRESS!
SURWWUI...
WHAT...
WHAT A SHAMELESS WOMAN!!
AND THAT'S WHY SHE WAS GLARING AT ME SO...
INDEED!
THAT'S RIGHT!
HOWEVER, EVEN THOUGH SHE HAS INFLUENCE AND BEARS A SENSE OF RIVALRY TOWARDS YOU...
...SHE CANNOT HOPE TO COMPETE AGAINST YOU WHO ARE GENUINE ROYALTY AND THE FUTURE QUEEN!
SO FEEL FREE TO IGNORE HER COM-PLETELY! OUI?

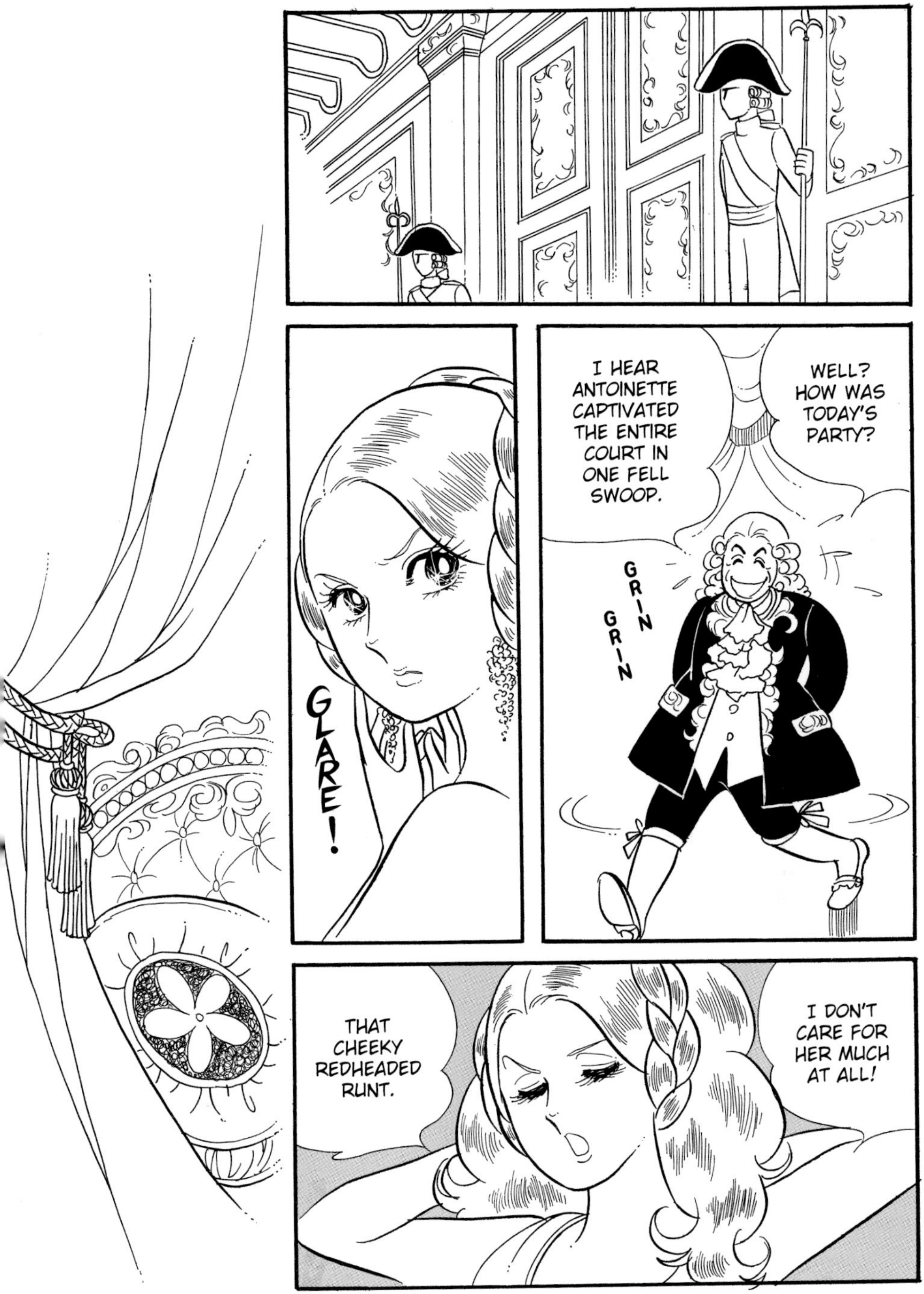
WELL? HOW WAS TODAY'S PARTY?
I HEAR ANTOINETTE CAPTIVATED THE ENTIRE COURT IN ONE FELL SWOOP.
GRIN GRIN
GLARE!
I DON'T CARE FOR HER MUCH AT ALL!
THAT CHEEKY REDHEADED RUNT.

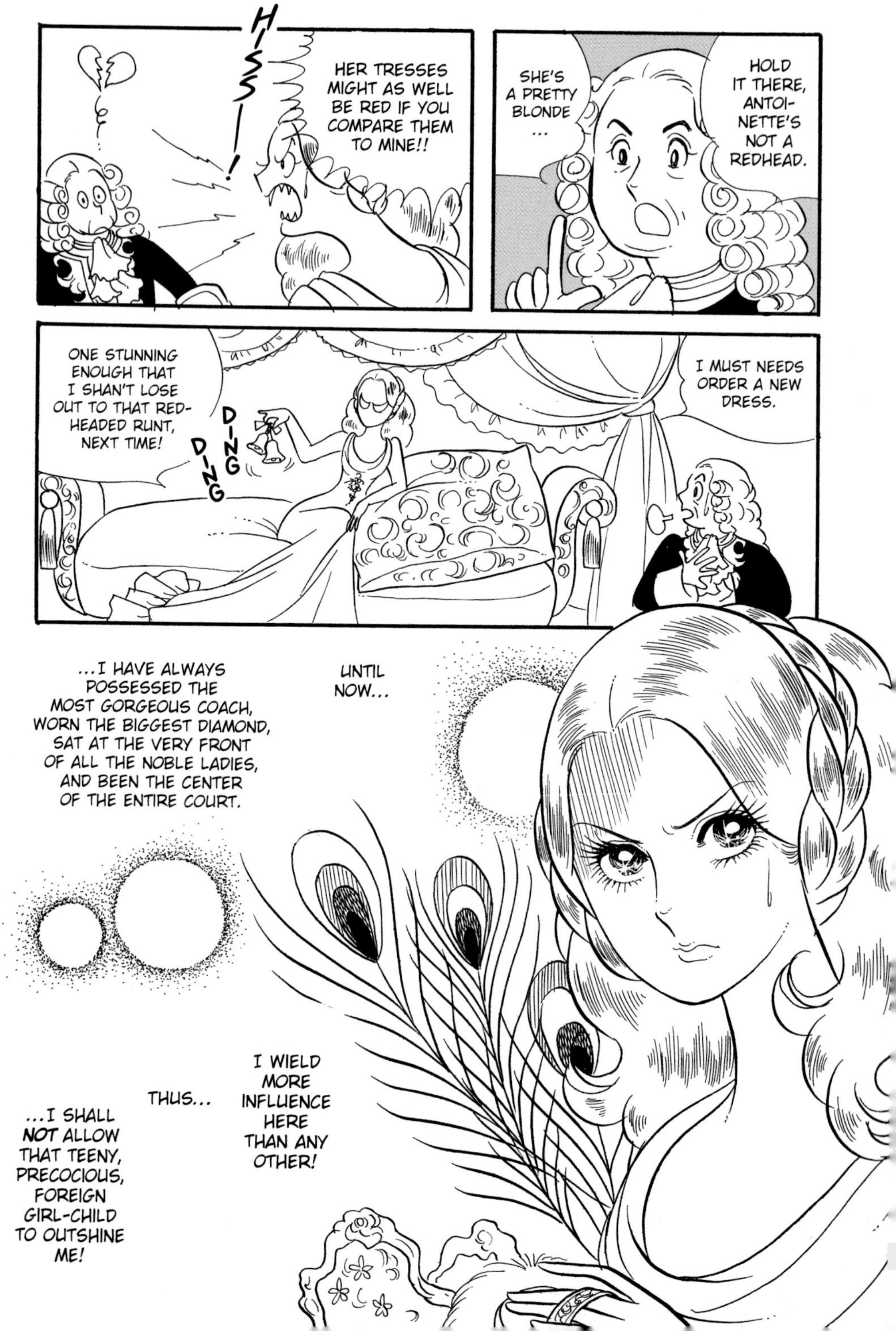
HOLD IT THERE, ANTOINETTE'S NOT A REDHEAD.
SHE'S A PRETTY BLONDE ...
HER TRESSES MIGHT AS WELL BE RED IF YOU COMPARE THEM TO MINE!!
HISS!
I MUST NEEDS ORDER A NEW DRESS.
ONE STUNNING ENOUGH THAT I SHAN'T LOSE OUT TO THAT RED-HEADED RUNT, NEXT TIME!
DING DING
UNTIL NOW...
...I HAVE ALWAYS POSSESSED THE MOST GORGEOUS COACH, WORN THE BIGGEST DIAMOND, SAT AT THE VERY FRONT OF ALL THE NOBLE LADIES, AND BEEN THE CENTER OF THE ENTIRE COURT.
I WIELD MORE INFLUENCE HERE THAN ANY OTHER!
THUS...
...I SHALL **NOT** ALLOW THAT TEENY, PRECOCIOUS, FOREIGN GIRL-CHILD TO OUTSHINE ME!

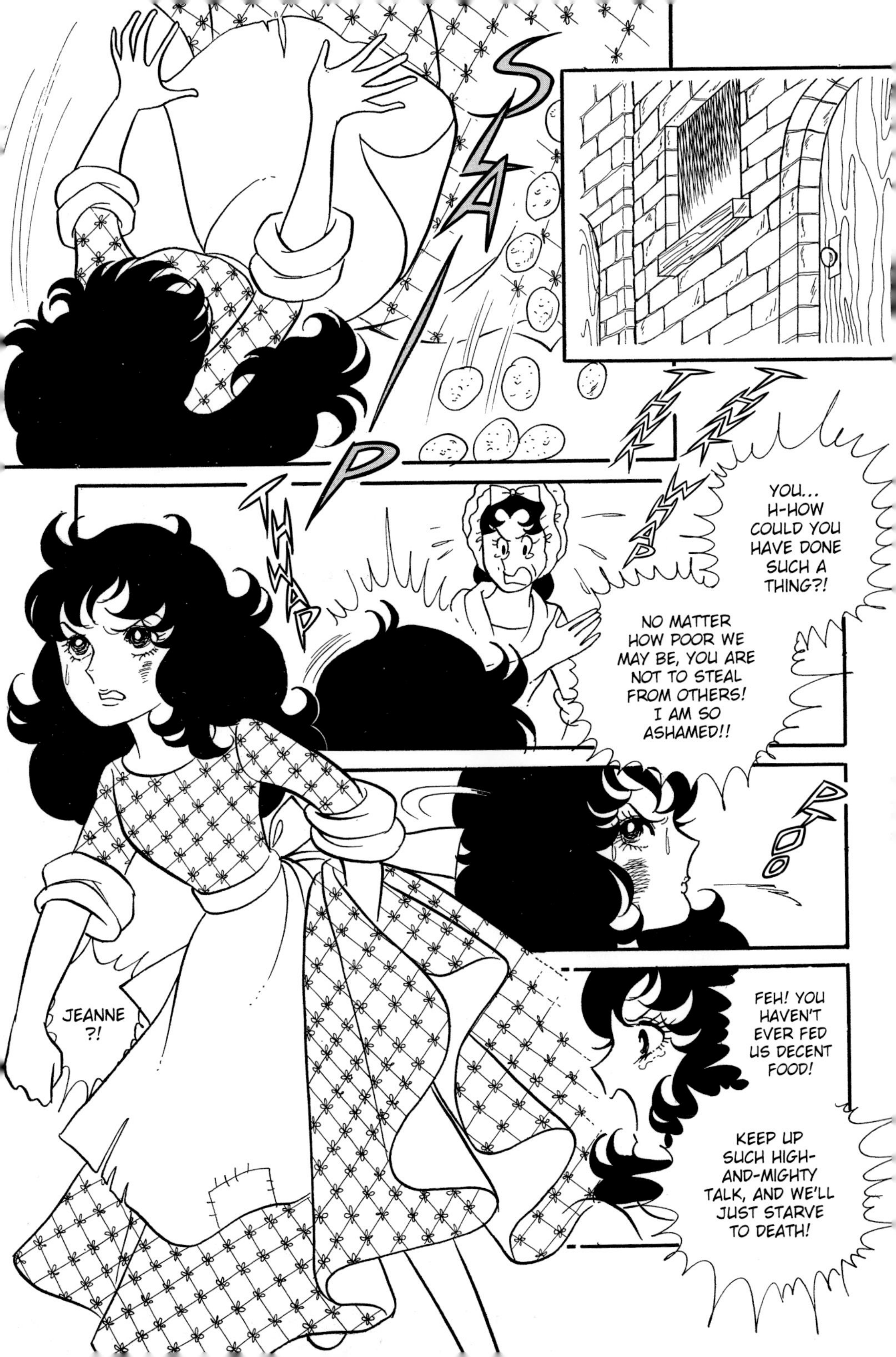
SLAP
THWAP
THWAP
THWAP
YOU... H-HOW COULD YOU HAVE DONE SUCH A THING?!
NO MATTER HOW POOR WE MAY BE, YOU ARE NOT TO STEAL FROM OTHERS! I AM SO ASHAMED!!
FEH! YOU HAVEN'T EVER FED US DECENT FOOD!
KEEP UP SUCH HIGH-AND-MIGHTY TALK, AND WE'LL JUST STARVE TO DEATH!
JEANNE ?!

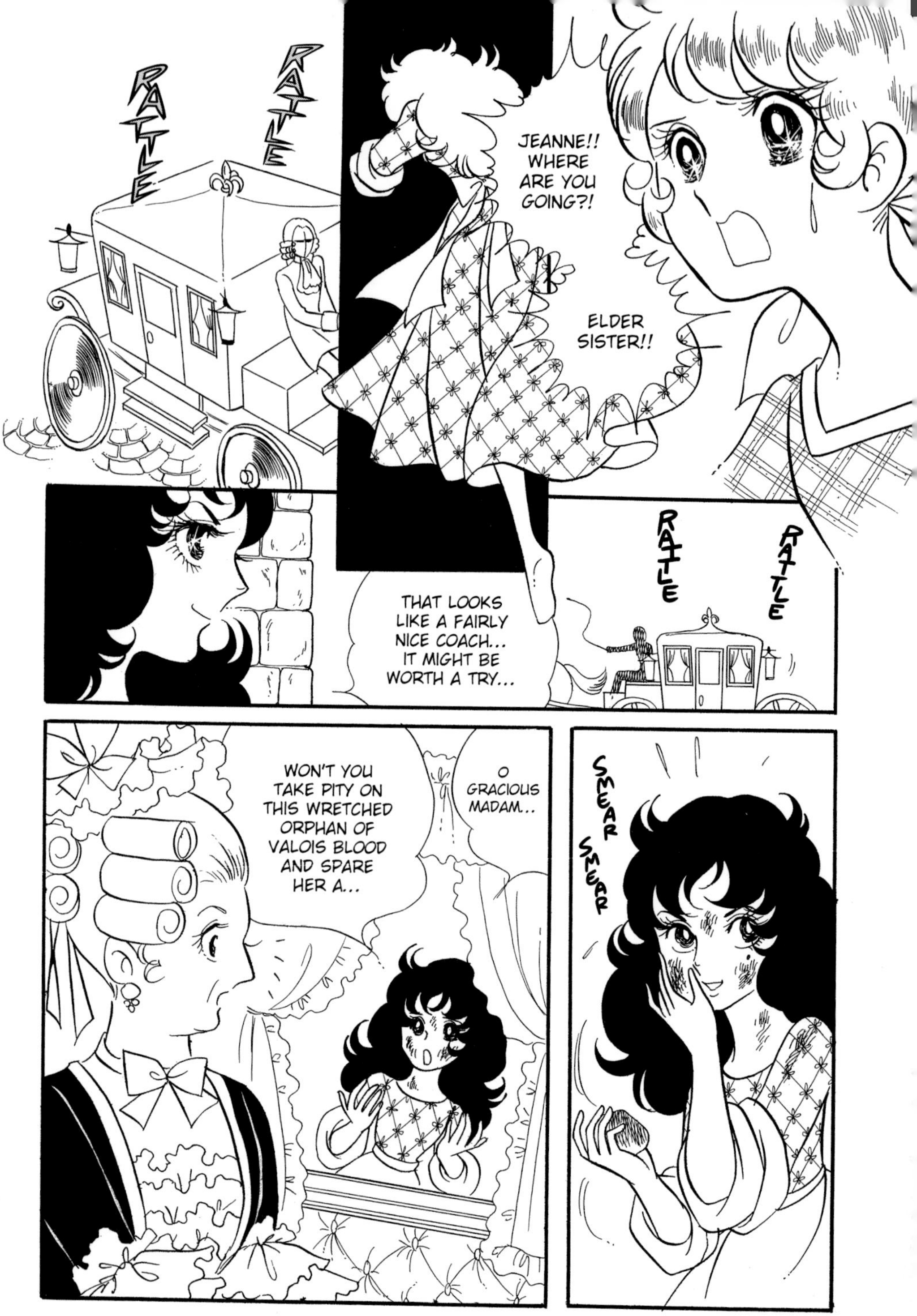
JEANNE!! WHERE ARE YOU GOING?!
ELDER SISTER!!
RATTLE
RATTLE
RATTLE
RATTLE
THAT LOOKS LIKE A FAIRLY NICE COACH... IT MIGHT BE WORTH A TRY...
SMEAR
SMEAR
O GRACIOUS MADAM...
WON'T YOU TAKE PITY ON THIS WRETCHED ORPHAN OF VALOIS BLOOD AND SPARE HER A...

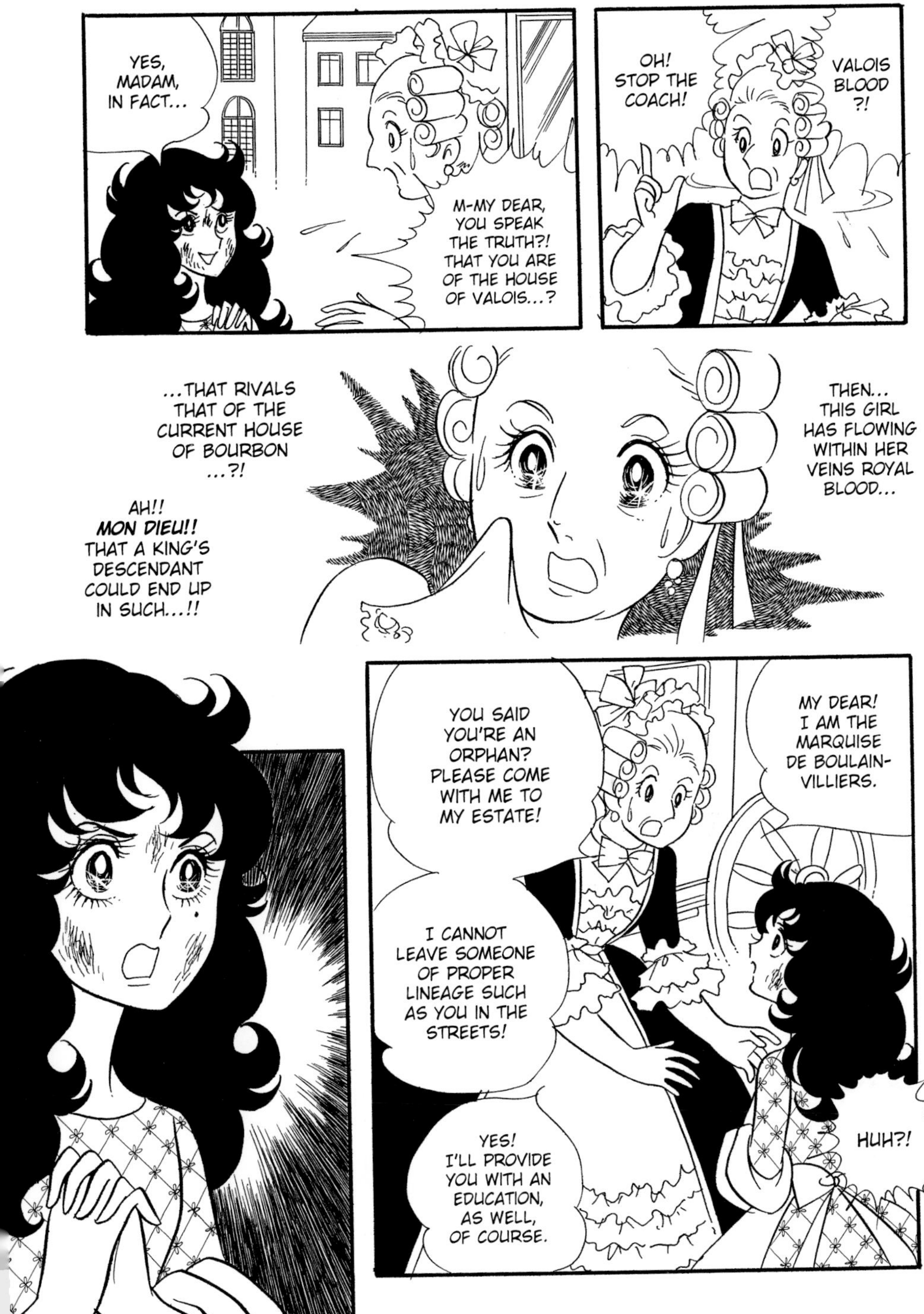
VALOIS BLOOD ?!
OH! STOP THE COACH!
YES, MADAM, IN FACT...
M-MY DEAR, YOU SPEAK THE TRUTH?! THAT YOU ARE OF THE HOUSE OF VALOIS...?
THEN... THIS GIRL HAS FLOWING WITHIN HER VEINS ROYAL BLOOD...
...THAT RIVALS THAT OF THE CURRENT HOUSE OF BOURBON ...?!
AH!! ***MON DIEU!!*** THAT A KING'S DESCENDANT COULD END UP IN SUCH...!!
MY DEAR! I AM THE MARQUISE DE BOULAIN-VILLIERS.
YOU SAID YOU'RE AN ORPHAN? PLEASE COME WITH ME TO MY ESTATE!
HUH?!
I CANNOT LEAVE SOMEONE OF PROPER LINEAGE SUCH AS YOU IN THE STREETS!
YES! I'LL PROVIDE YOU WITH AN EDUCATION, AS WELL, OF COURSE.

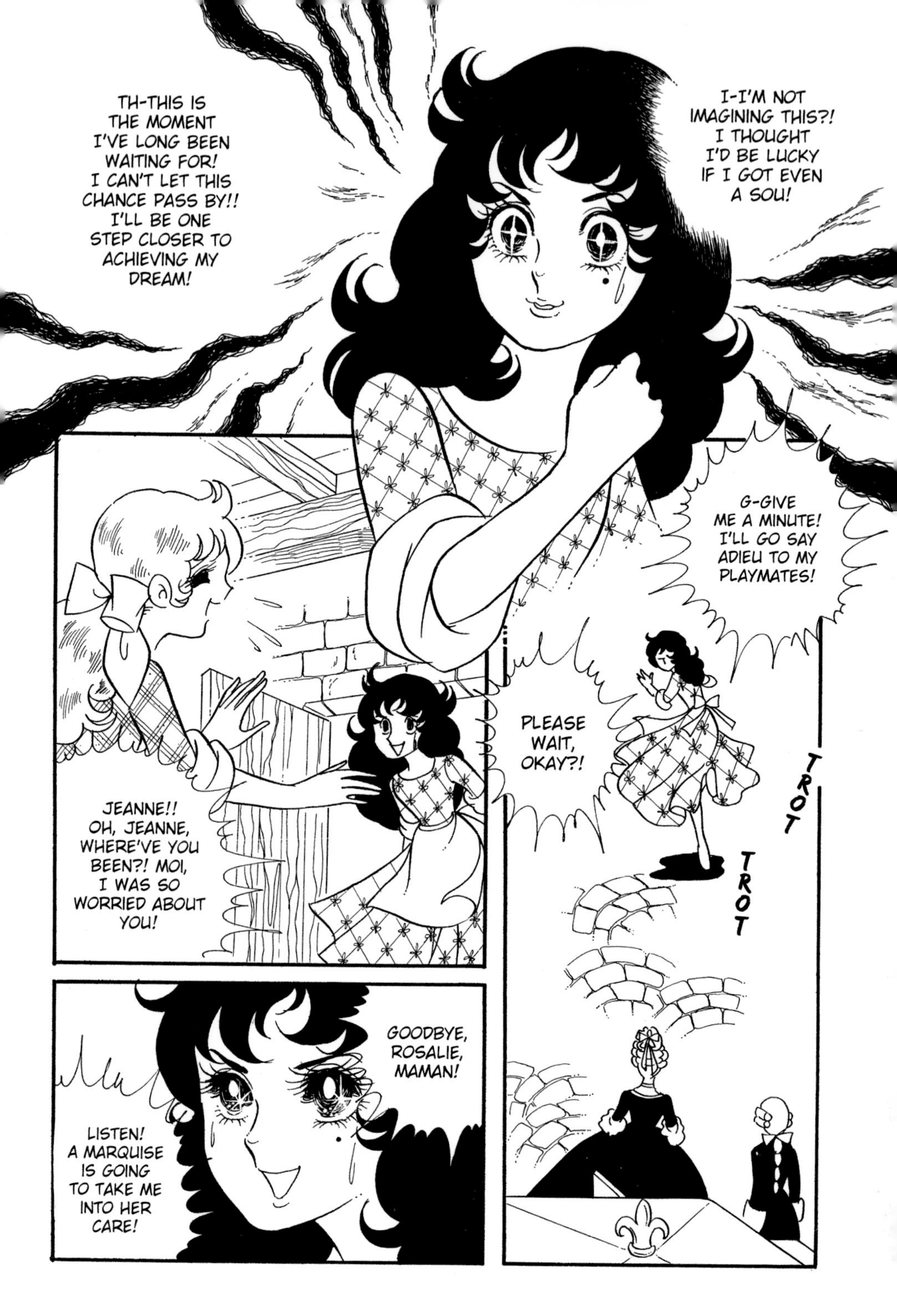
I-I'M NOT IMAGINING THIS?! I THOUGHT I'D BE LUCKY IF I GOT EVEN A SOU!
TH-THIS IS THE MOMENT I'VE LONG BEEN WAITING FOR! I CAN'T LET THIS CHANCE PASS BY!! I'LL BE ONE STEP CLOSER TO ACHIEVING MY DREAM!
G-GIVE ME A MINUTE! I'LL GO SAY ADIEU TO MY PLAYMATES!
PLEASE WAIT, OKAY?!
TROT
TROT
JEANNE!! OH, JEANNE, WHERE'VE YOU BEEN?! MOI, I WAS SO WORRIED ABOUT YOU!
GOODBYE, ROSALIE, MAMAN!
LISTEN! A MARQUISE IS GOING TO TAKE ME INTO HER CARE!

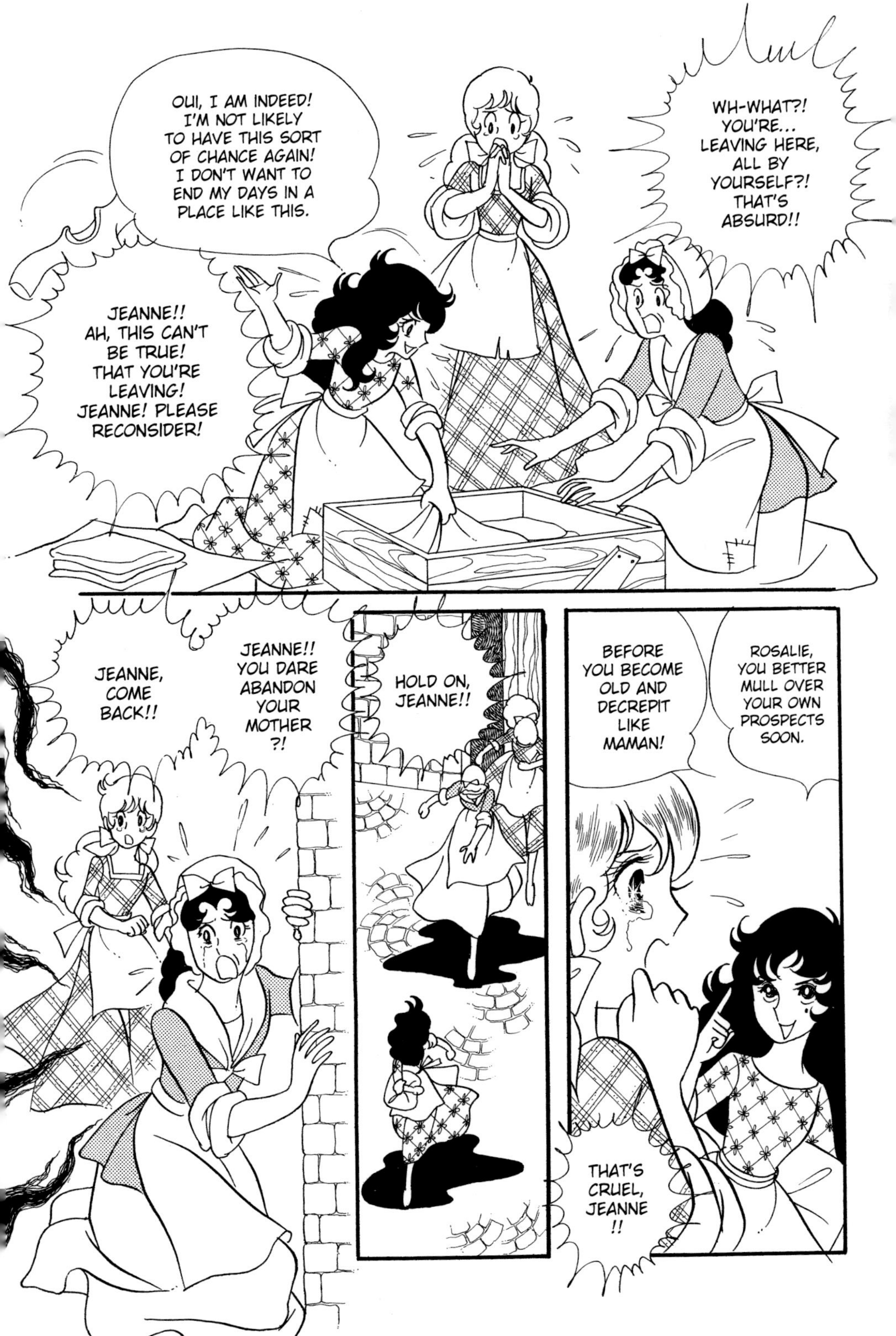
WH-WHAT?! YOU'RE... LEAVING HERE, ALL BY YOURSELF?! THAT'S ABSURD!!
OUI, I AM INDEED! I'M NOT LIKELY TO HAVE THIS SORT OF CHANCE AGAIN! I DON'T WANT TO END MY DAYS IN A PLACE LIKE THIS.
JEANNE!! AH, THIS CAN'T BE TRUE! THAT YOU'RE LEAVING! JEANNE! PLEASE RECONSIDER!
ROSALIE, YOU BETTER MULL OVER YOUR OWN PROSPECTS SOON.
BEFORE YOU BECOME OLD AND DECREPIT LIKE MAMAN!
THAT'S CRUEL, JEANNE !!
HOLD ON, JEANNE!!
JEANNE!! YOU DARE ABANDON YOUR MOTHER ?!
JEANNE, COME BACK!!

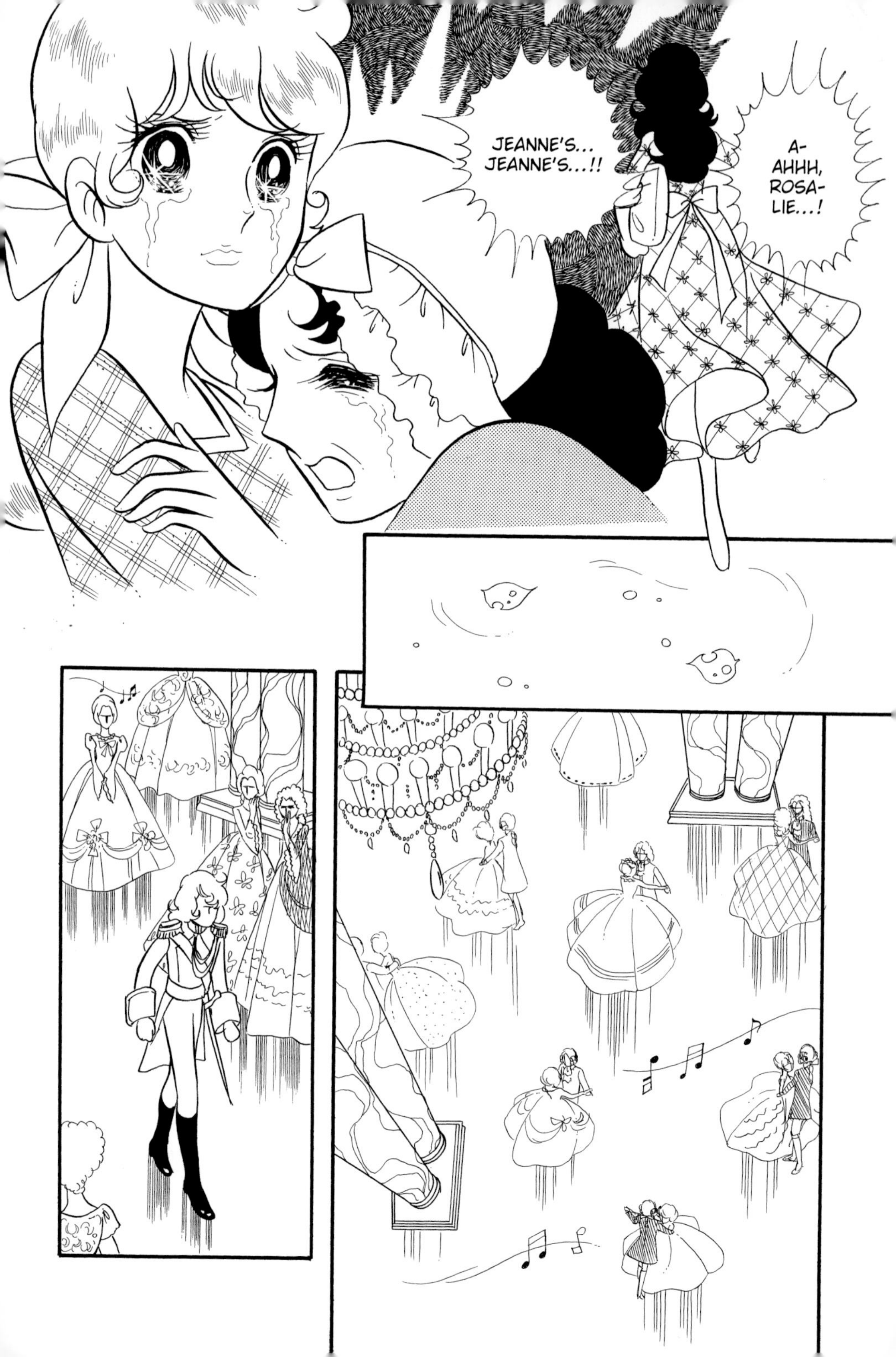
A-AHHH, ROSA-LIE...!
JEANNE'S... JEANNE'S...!!

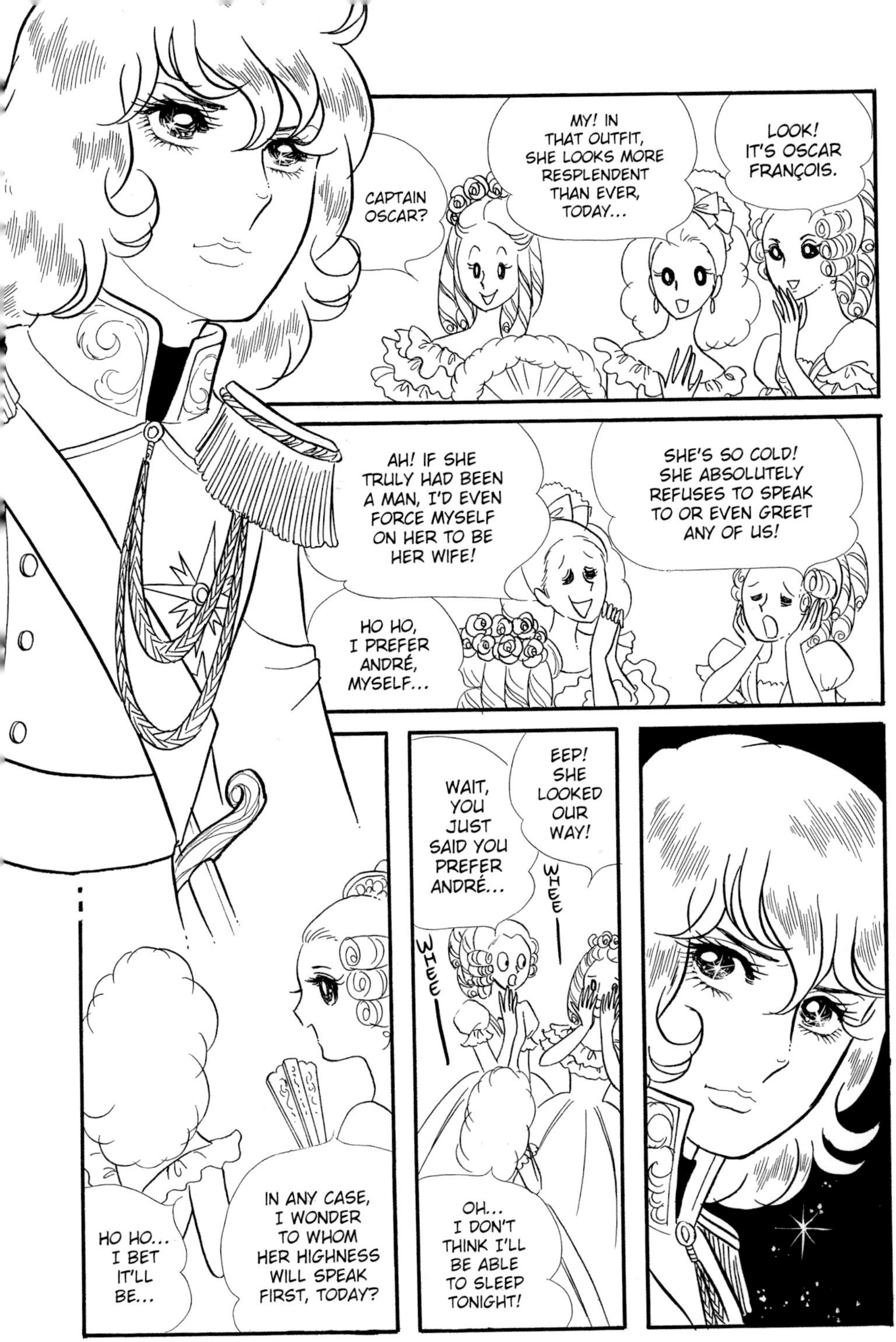
LOOK! IT'S OSCAR FRANÇOIS.
MY! IN THAT OUTFIT, SHE LOOKS MORE RESPLENDENT THAN EVER, TODAY...
CAPTAIN OSCAR?
SHE'S SO COLD! SHE ABSOLUTELY REFUSES TO SPEAK TO OR EVEN GREET ANY OF US!
AH! IF SHE TRULY HAD BEEN A MAN, I'D EVEN FORCE MYSELF ON HER TO BE HER WIFE!
HO HO, I PREFER ANDRÉ, MYSELF...
EEP! SHE LOOKED OUR WAY!
WAIT, YOU JUST SAID YOU PREFER ANDRÉ...
WHEE—
WHEE—
OH... I DON'T THINK I'LL BE ABLE TO SLEEP TONIGHT!
IN ANY CASE, I WONDER TO WHOM HER HIGHNESS WILL SPEAK FIRST, TODAY?
HO HO... I BET IT'LL BE...

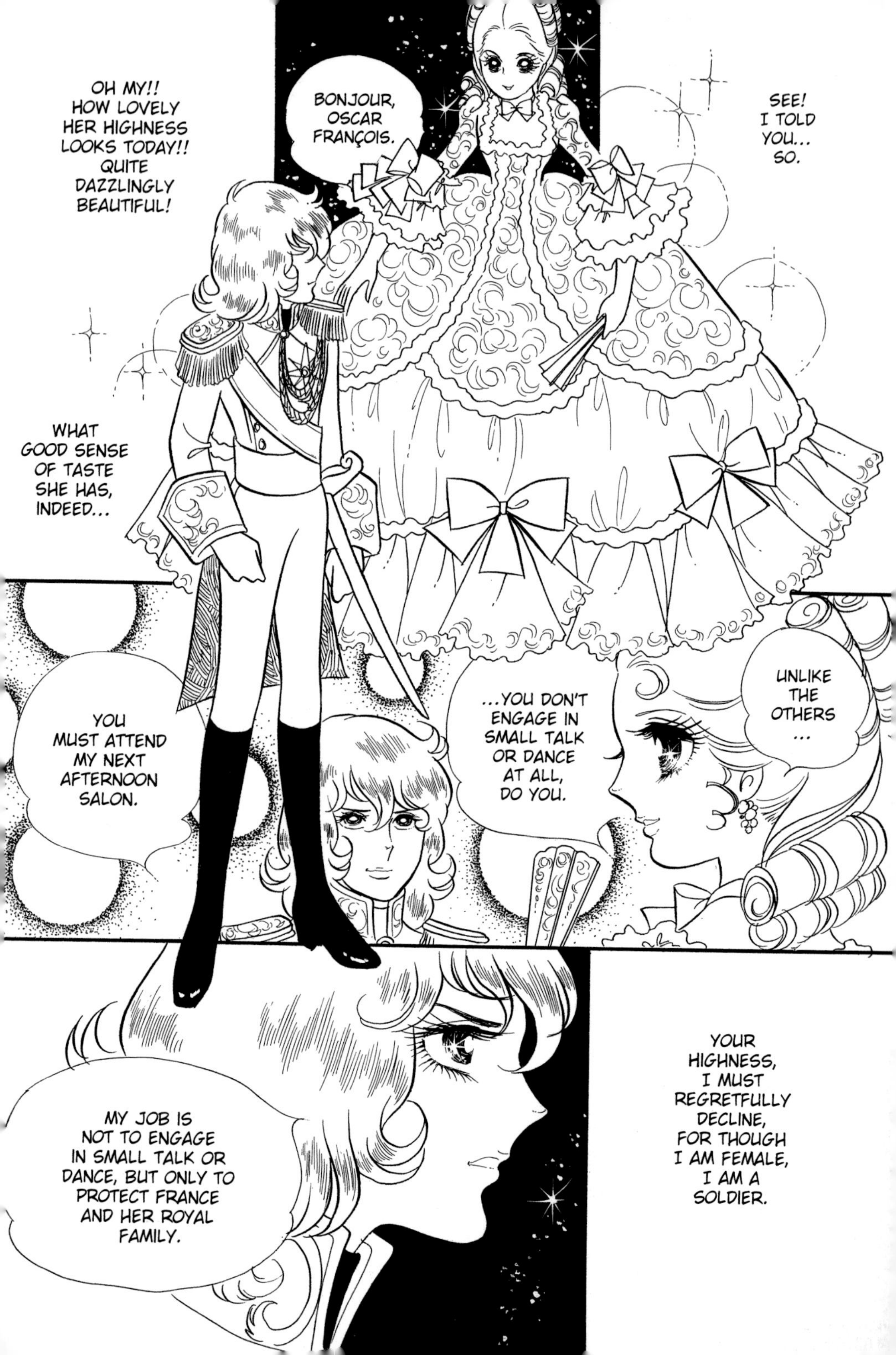
SEE! I TOLD YOU... SO.
BONJOUR, OSCAR FRANÇOIS.
OH MY!! HOW LOVELY HER HIGHNESS LOOKS TODAY!! QUITE DAZZLINGLY BEAUTIFUL!
WHAT GOOD SENSE OF TASTE SHE HAS, INDEED...
UNLIKE THE OTHERS ...
...YOU DON'T ENGAGE IN SMALL TALK OR DANCE AT ALL, DO YOU.
YOU MUST ATTEND MY NEXT AFTERNOON SALON.
YOUR HIGHNESS, I MUST REGRETFULLY DECLINE, FOR THOUGH I AM FEMALE, I AM A SOLDIER.
MY JOB IS NOT TO ENGAGE IN SMALL TALK OR DANCE, BUT ONLY TO PROTECT FRANCE AND HER ROYAL FAMILY.

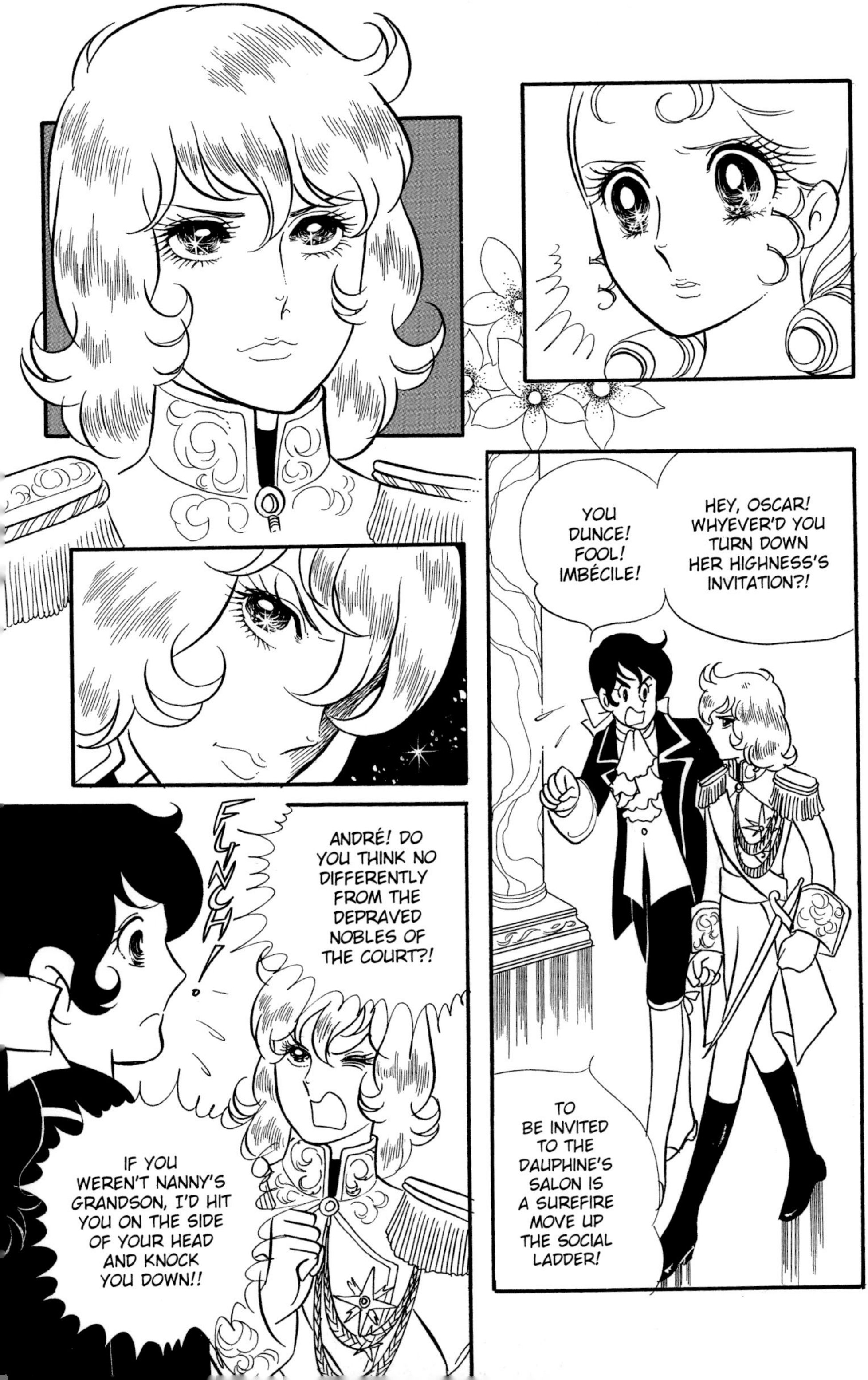
HEY, OSCAR! WHYEVER'D YOU TURN DOWN HER HIGHNESS'S INVITATION?!
YOU DUNCE! FOOL! IMBÉCILE!
TO BE INVITED TO THE DAUPHINE'S SALON IS A SUREFIRE MOVE UP THE SOCIAL LADDER!
ANDRÉ! DO YOU THINK NO DIFFERENTLY FROM THE DEPRAVED NOBLES OF THE COURT?!
FLINCH!
IF YOU WEREN'T NANNY'S GRANDSON, I'D HIT YOU ON THE SIDE OF YOUR HEAD AND KNOCK YOU DOWN!!

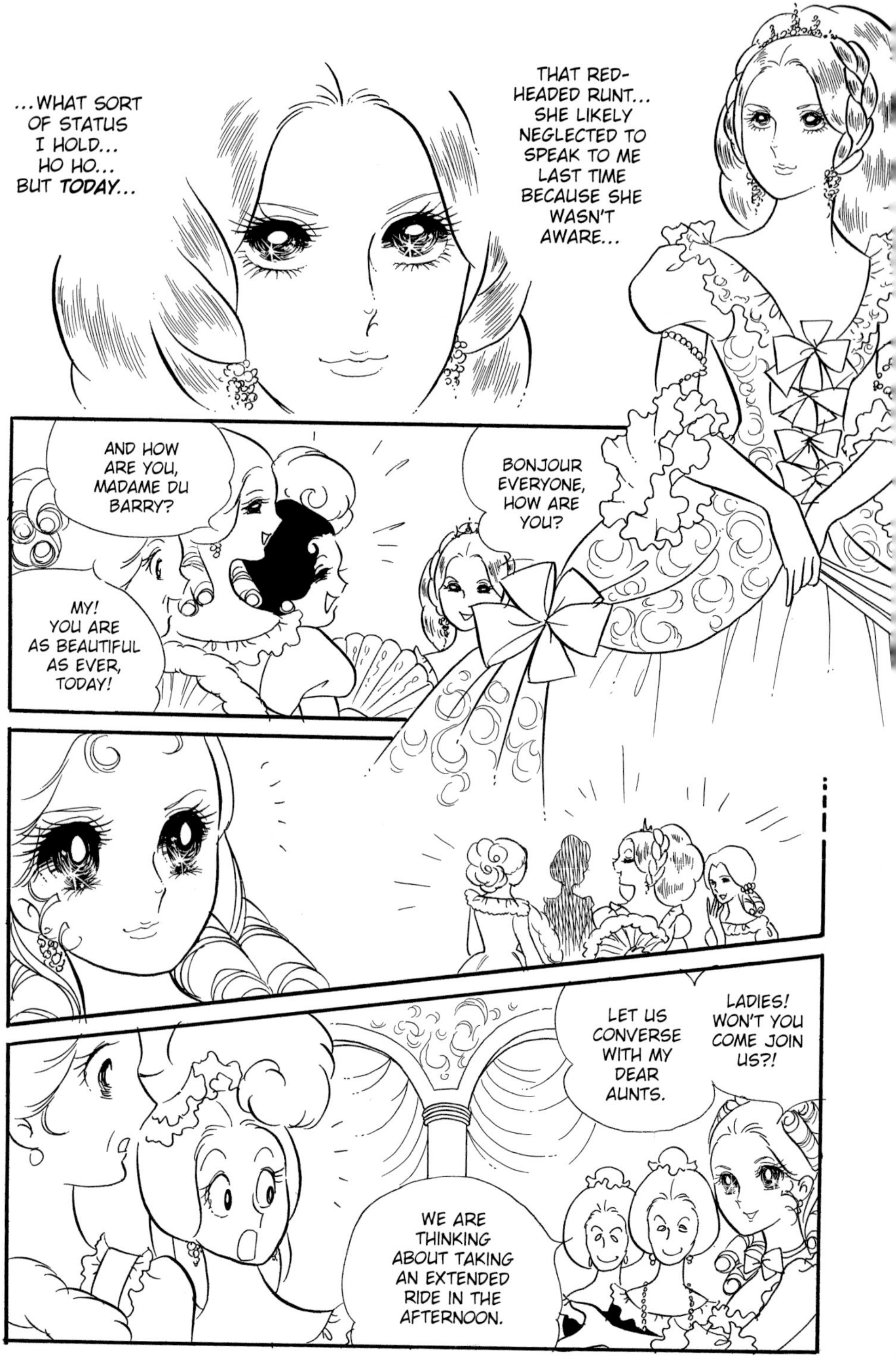
THAT RED-HEADED RUNT... SHE LIKELY NEGLECTED TO SPEAK TO ME LAST TIME BECAUSE SHE WASN'T AWARE...
...WHAT SORT OF STATUS I HOLD... HO HO... BUT *TODAY*...
BONJOUR EVERYONE, HOW ARE YOU?
AND HOW ARE YOU, MADAME DU BARRY?
MY! YOU ARE AS BEAUTIFUL AS EVER, TODAY!
LADIES! WON'T YOU COME JOIN US?!
LET US CONVERSE WITH MY DEAR AUNTS.
WE ARE THINKING ABOUT TAKING AN EXTENDED RIDE IN THE AFTERNOON.

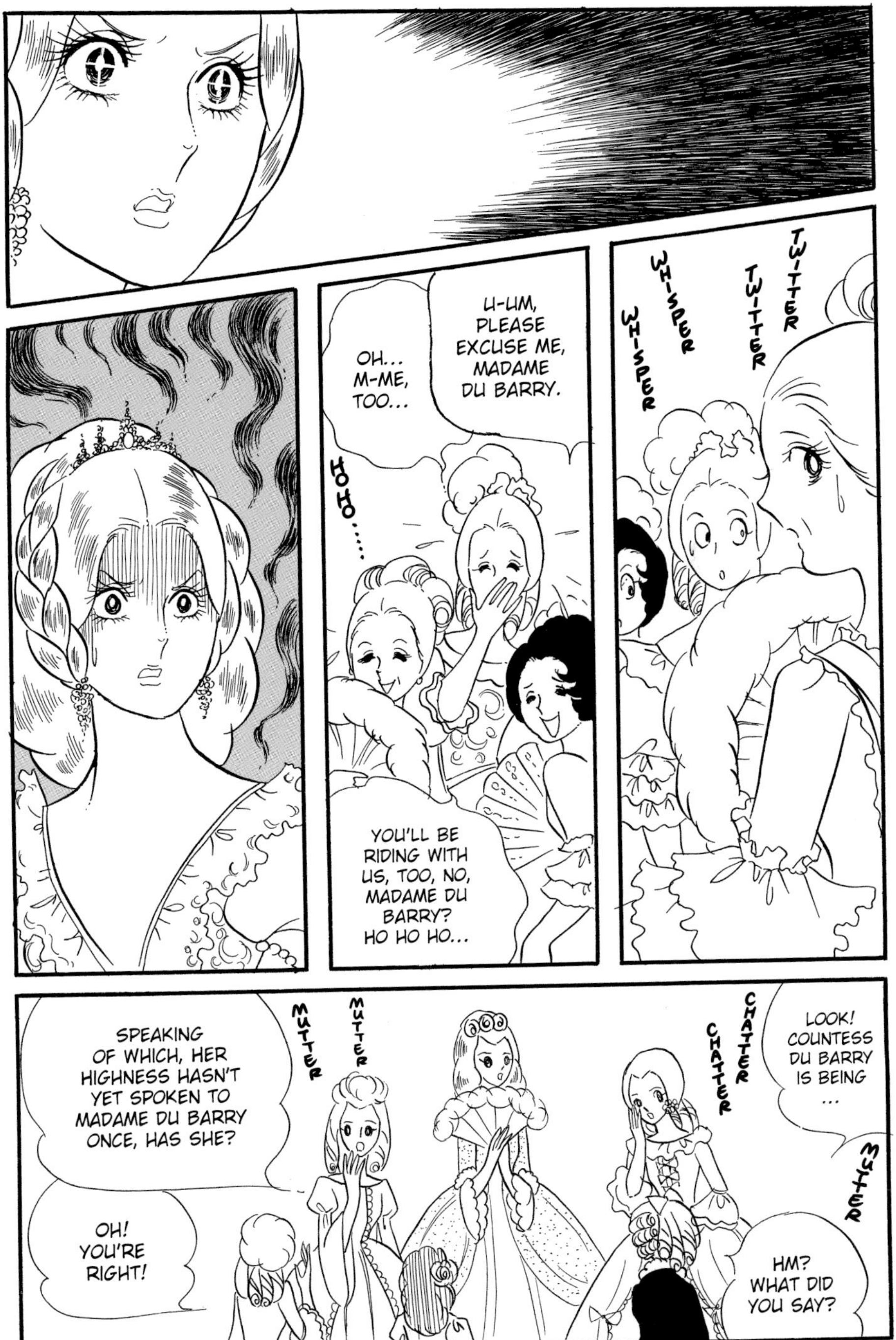
TWITTER
TWITTER
WHISPER
WHISPER
U-UM, PLEASE EXCUSE ME, MADAME DU BARRY.
OH... M-ME, TOO...
HO HO.....
YOU'LL BE RIDING WITH US, TOO, NO, MADAME DU BARRY? HO HO HO...
LOOK! COUNTESS DU BARRY IS BEING ...
CHATTER
CHATTER
MUTTER
HM? WHAT DID YOU SAY?
MUTTER
MUTTER
SPEAKING OF WHICH, HER HIGHNESS HASN'T YET SPOKEN TO MADAME DU BARRY ONCE, HAS SHE?
OH! YOU'RE RIGHT!

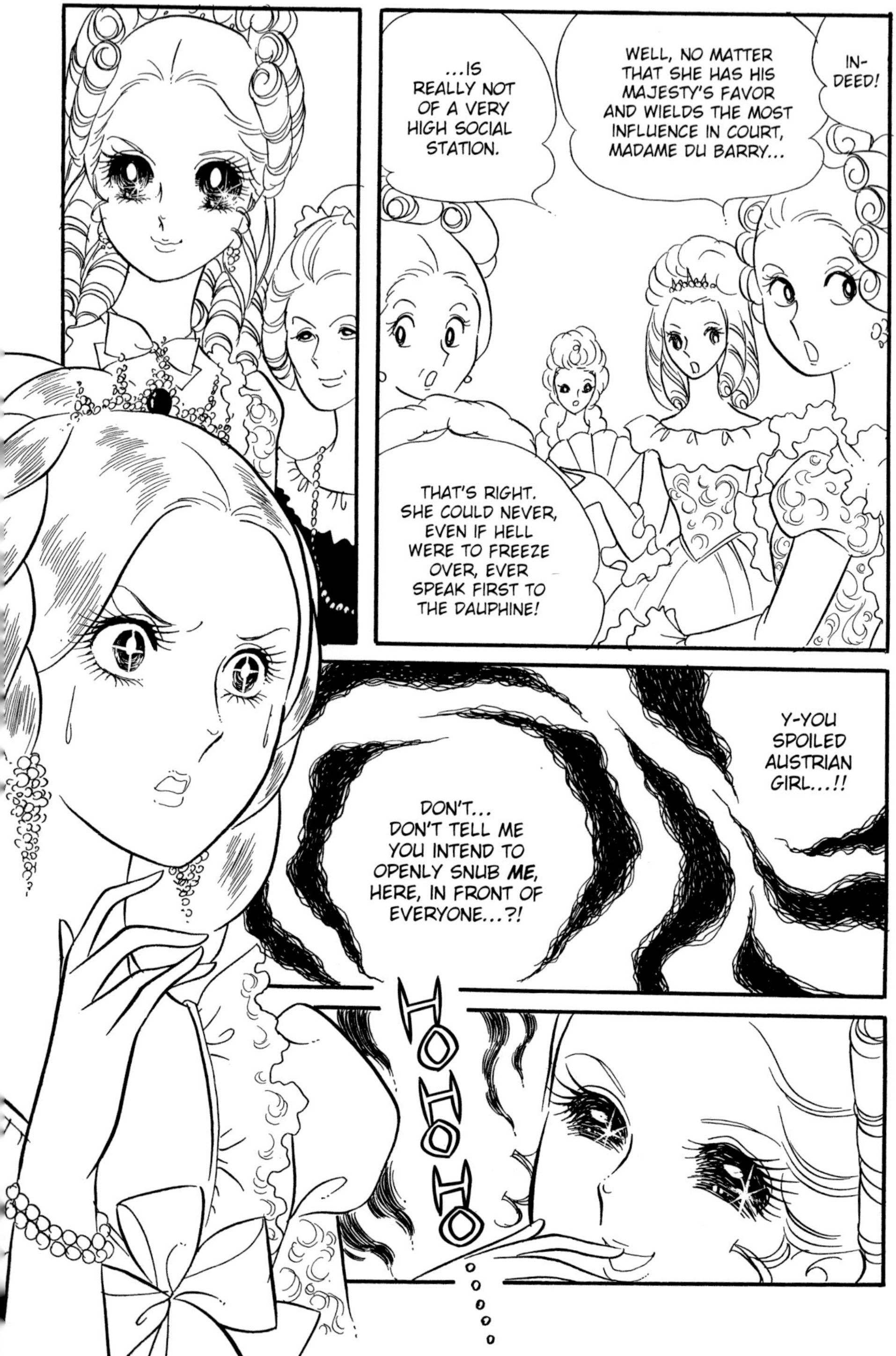
WELL, NO MATTER THAT SHE HAS HIS MAJESTY'S FAVOR AND WIELDS THE MOST INFLUENCE IN COURT, MADAME DU BARRY...
...IS REALLY NOT OF A VERY HIGH SOCIAL STATION.
IN-DEED!
THAT'S RIGHT. SHE COULD NEVER, EVEN IF HELL WERE TO FREEZE OVER, EVER SPEAK FIRST TO THE DAUPHINE!
Y-YOU SPOILED AUSTRIAN GIRL...!!
DON'T... DON'T TELL ME YOU INTEND TO OPENLY SNUB **ME**, HERE, IN FRONT OF EVERYONE...?!
HOHOHOHO

♥ HUGELY POPULAR, AND A HUGE SENSATION!!
FACED WITH MADAME DU BARRY, WHAT WILL ANTOINETTE DO!?

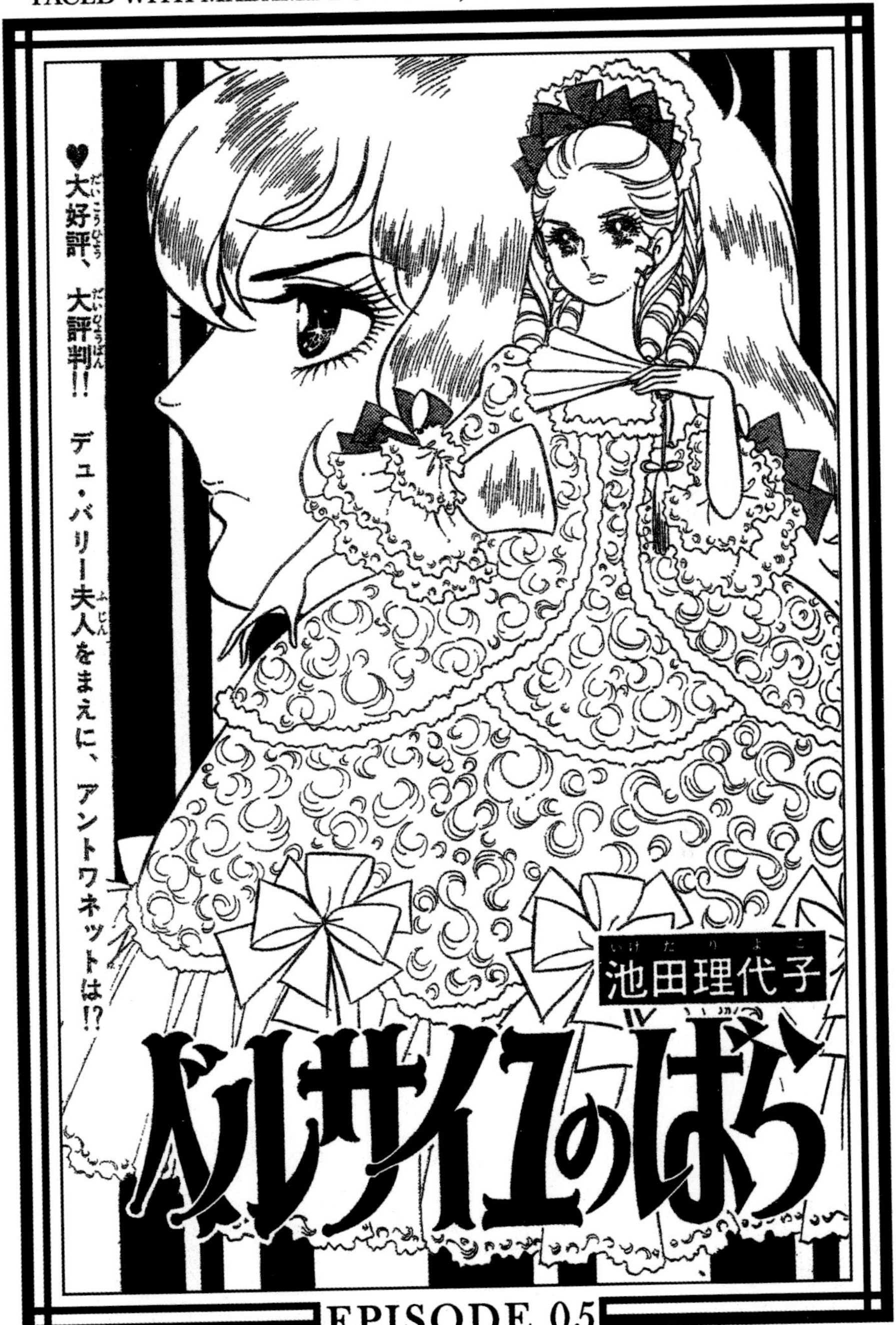
♥大好評、大評判!! デュ・バリー夫人をまえに、アントワネットは!?
池田理代子
ベルサイユのばら
EPISODE 05

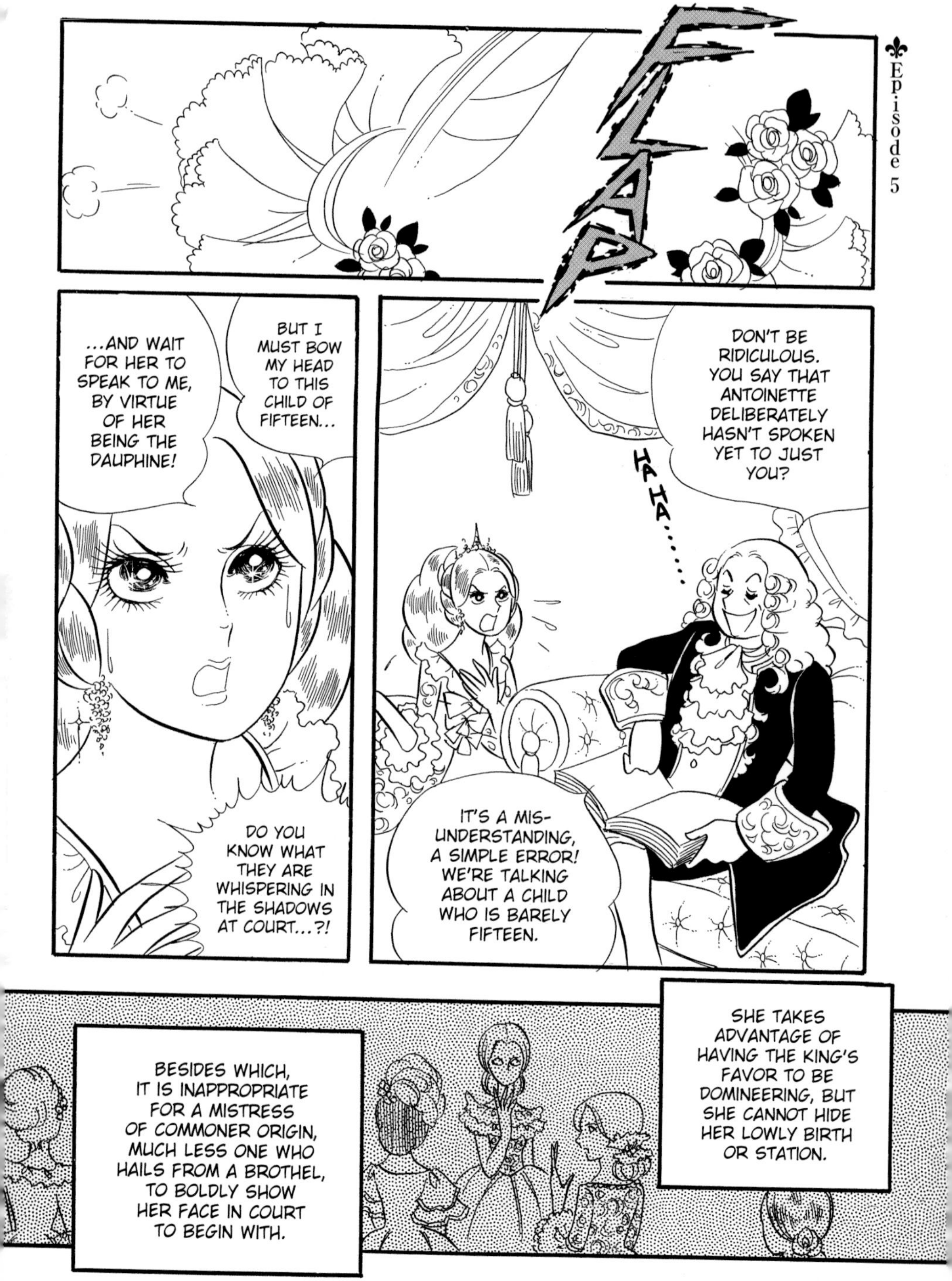
FLAP
DON'T BE RIDICULOUS. YOU SAY THAT ANTOINETTE DELIBERATELY HASN'T SPOKEN YET TO JUST YOU?
HA HA......
IT'S A MIS-UNDERSTANDING, A SIMPLE ERROR! WE'RE TALKING ABOUT A CHILD WHO IS BARELY FIFTEEN.
BUT I MUST BOW MY HEAD TO THIS CHILD OF FIFTEEN...
...AND WAIT FOR HER TO SPEAK TO ME, BY VIRTUE OF HER BEING THE DAUPHINE!
DO YOU KNOW WHAT THEY ARE WHISPERING IN THE SHADOWS AT COURT...?!
SHE TAKES ADVANTAGE OF HAVING THE KING'S FAVOR TO BE DOMINEERING, BUT SHE CANNOT HIDE HER LOWLY BIRTH OR STATION.
BESIDES WHICH, IT IS INAPPROPRIATE FOR A MISTRESS OF COMMONER ORIGIN, MUCH LESS ONE WHO HAILS FROM A BROTHEL, TO BOLDLY SHOW HER FACE IN COURT TO BEGIN WITH.

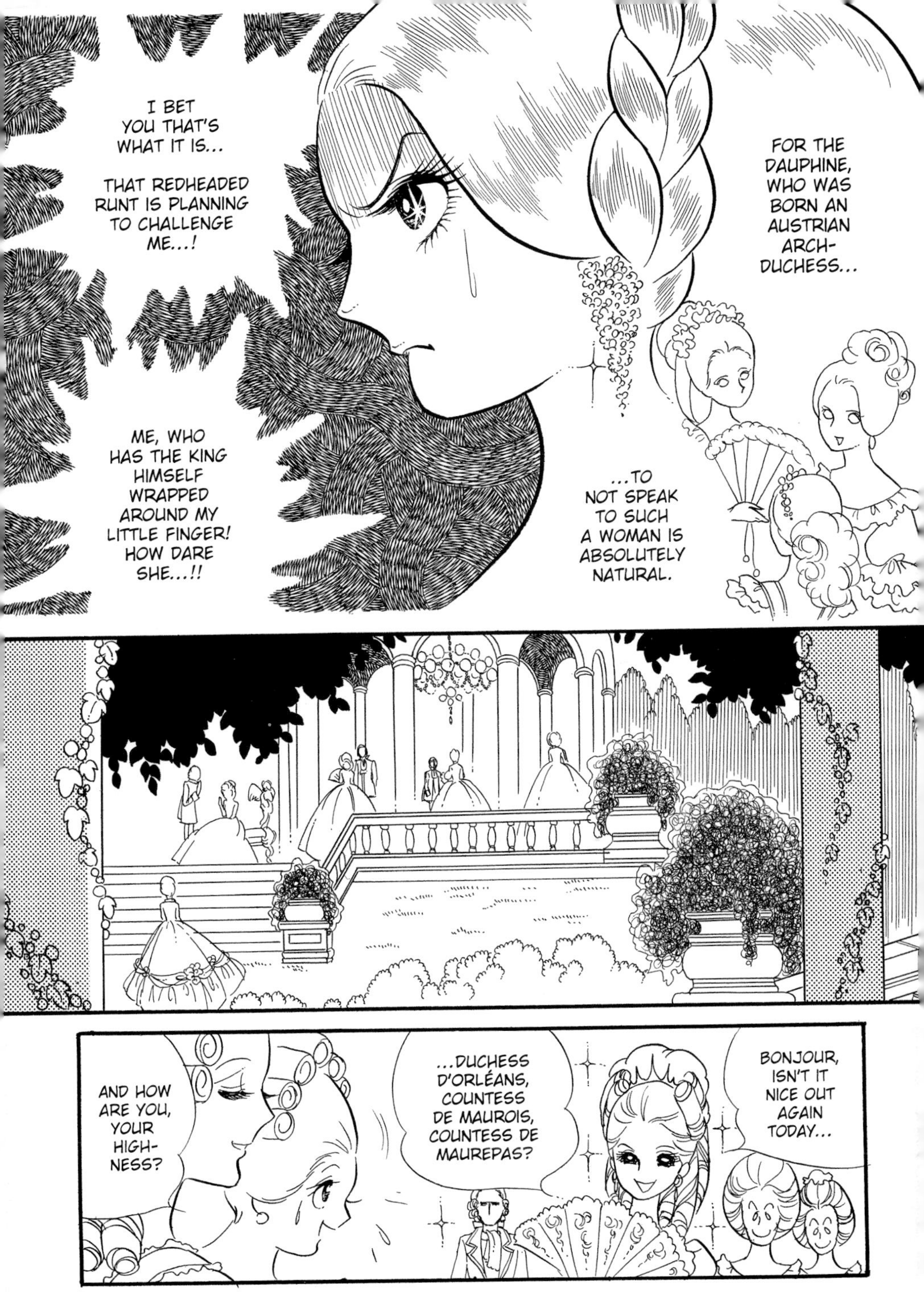
FOR THE DAUPHINE, WHO WAS BORN AN AUSTRIAN ARCH-DUCHESS...
...TO NOT SPEAK TO SUCH A WOMAN IS ABSOLUTELY NATURAL.
I BET YOU THAT'S WHAT IT IS...
THAT REDHEADED RUNT IS PLANNING TO CHALLENGE ME...!
ME, WHO HAS THE KING HIMSELF WRAPPED AROUND MY LITTLE FINGER! HOW DARE SHE...!!
BONJOUR, ISN'T IT NICE OUT AGAIN TODAY...
...DUCHESS D'ORLÉANS, COUNTESS DE MAUROIS, COUNTESS DE MAUREPAS?
AND HOW ARE YOU, YOUR HIGH-NESS?

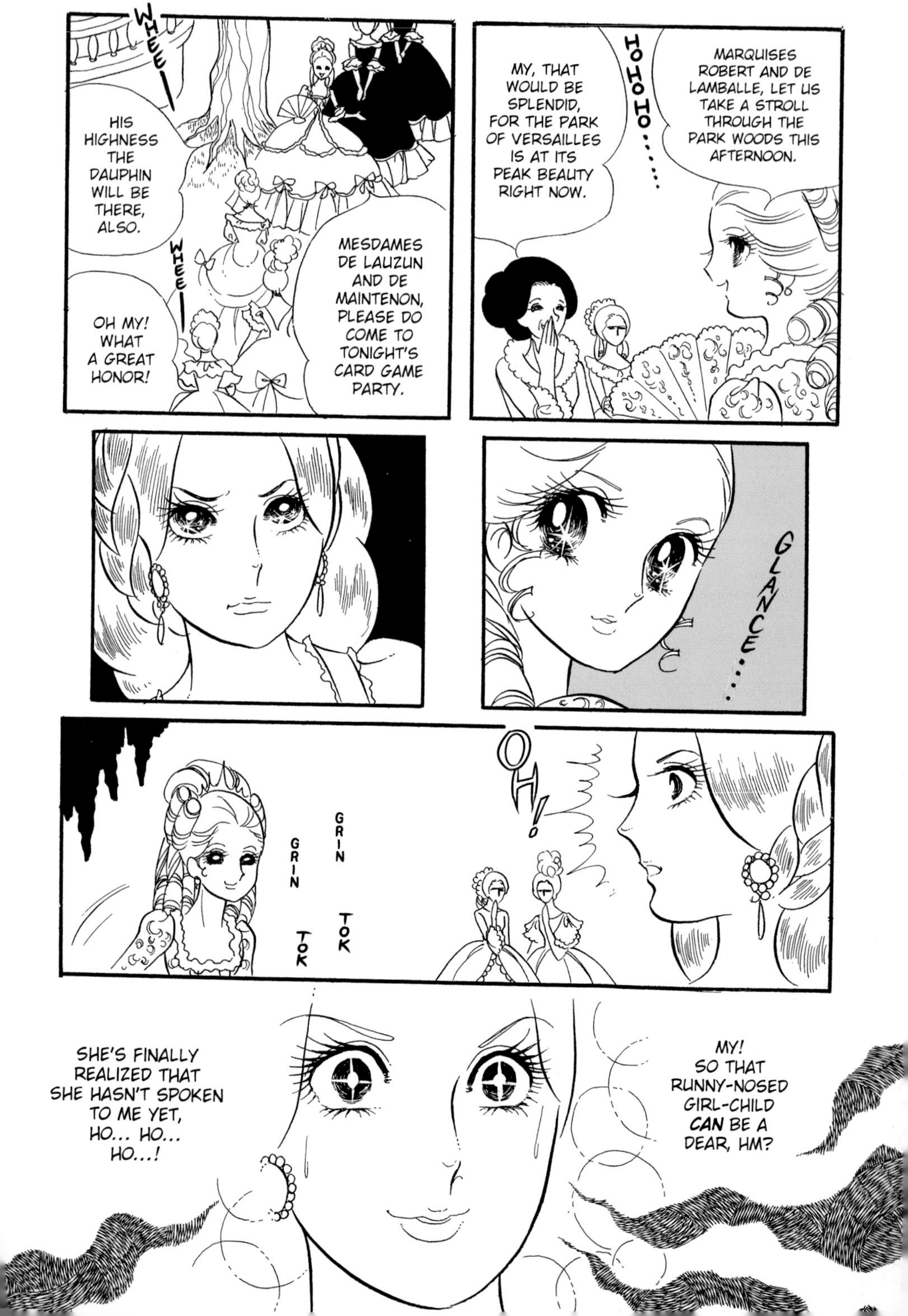
MARQUISES ROBERT AND DE LAMBALLE, LET US TAKE A STROLL THROUGH THE PARK WOODS THIS AFTERNOON.
HO HO HO......
MY, THAT WOULD BE SPLENDID, FOR THE PARK OF VERSAILLES IS AT ITS PEAK BEAUTY RIGHT NOW.
WHEE!
MESDAMES DE LAUZUN AND DE MAINTENON, PLEASE DO COME TO TONIGHT'S CARD GAME PARTY.
WHEE!
OH MY! WHAT A GREAT HONOR!
HIS HIGHNESS THE DAUPHIN WILL BE THERE, ALSO.
GLANCE...
OH!
GRIN GRIN
TOK TOK
MY! SO THAT RUNNY-NOSED GIRL-CHILD **CAN** BE A DEAR, HM?
SHE'S FINALLY REALIZED THAT SHE HASN'T SPOKEN TO ME YET, HO... HO... HO...!

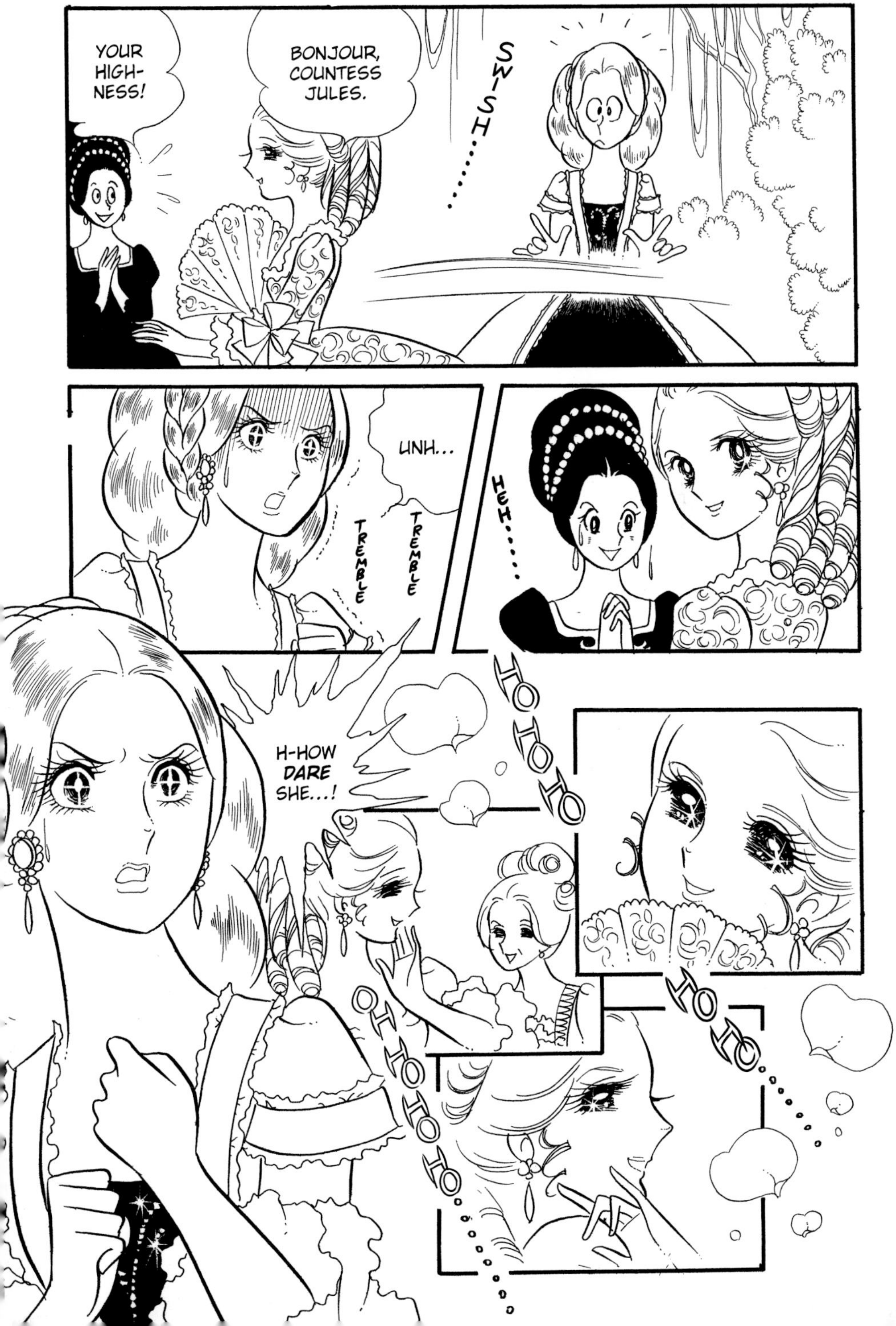
SWISH...
BONJOUR, COUNTESS JULES.
YOUR HIGH-NESS!
HEH...
UNH...
TREMBLE TREMBLE
HO HO HO HO
HO HO HO...
OH HO HO HO HO...
H-HOW DARE SHE...!

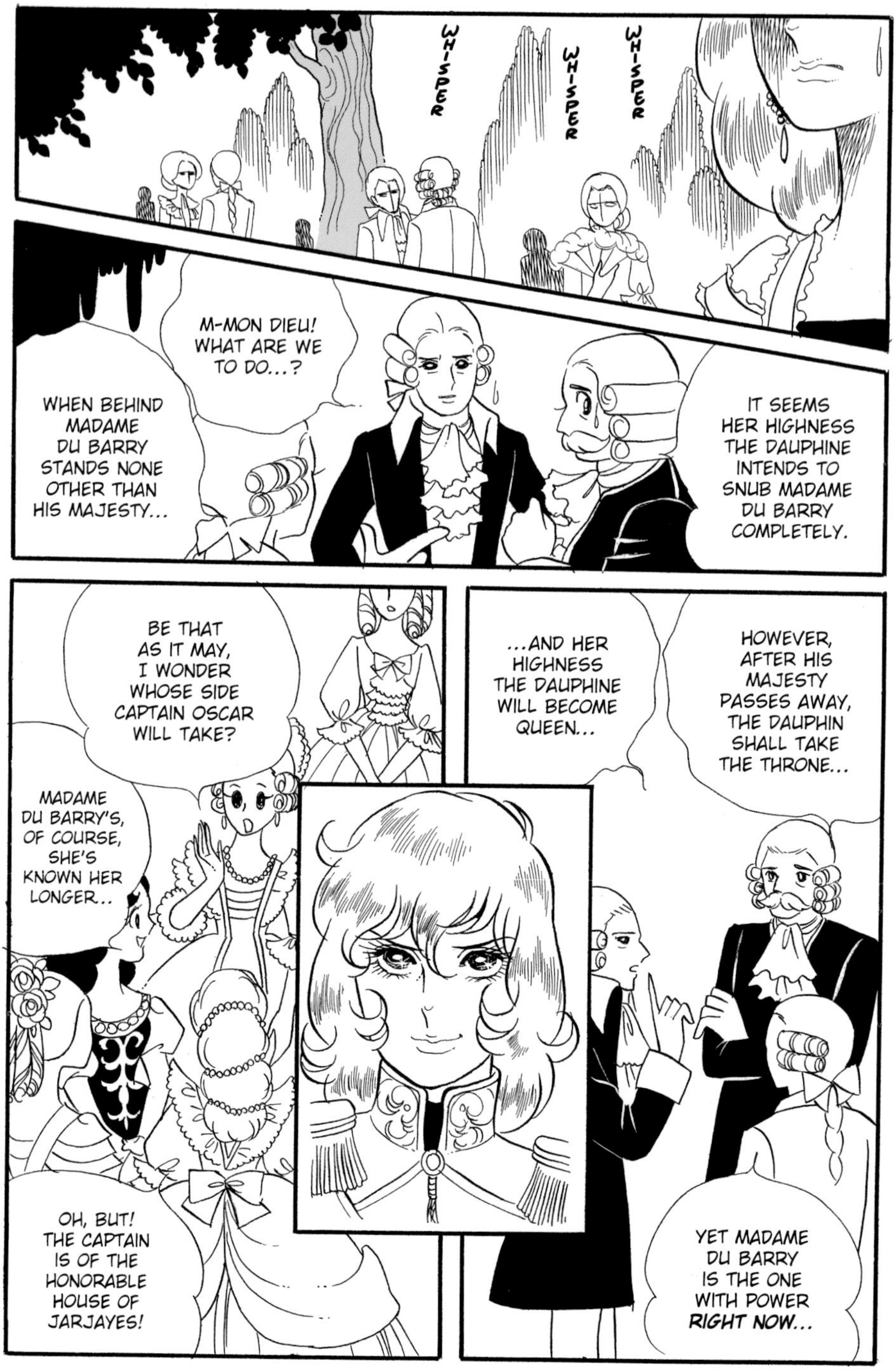
WHISPER
WHISPER
WHISPER
IT SEEMS HER HIGHNESS THE DAUPHINE INTENDS TO SNUB MADAME DU BARRY COMPLETELY.
M-MON DIEU! WHAT ARE WE TO DO...?
WHEN BEHIND MADAME DU BARRY STANDS NONE OTHER THAN HIS MAJESTY...
HOWEVER, AFTER HIS MAJESTY PASSES AWAY, THE DAUPHIN SHALL TAKE THE THRONE...
...AND HER HIGHNESS THE DAUPHINE WILL BECOME QUEEN...
YET MADAME DU BARRY IS THE ONE WITH POWER **RIGHT NOW...**
BE THAT AS IT MAY, I WONDER WHOSE SIDE CAPTAIN OSCAR WILL TAKE?
MADAME DU BARRY'S, OF COURSE, SHE'S KNOWN HER LONGER...
OH, BUT! THE CAPTAIN IS OF THE HONORABLE HOUSE OF JARJAYES!

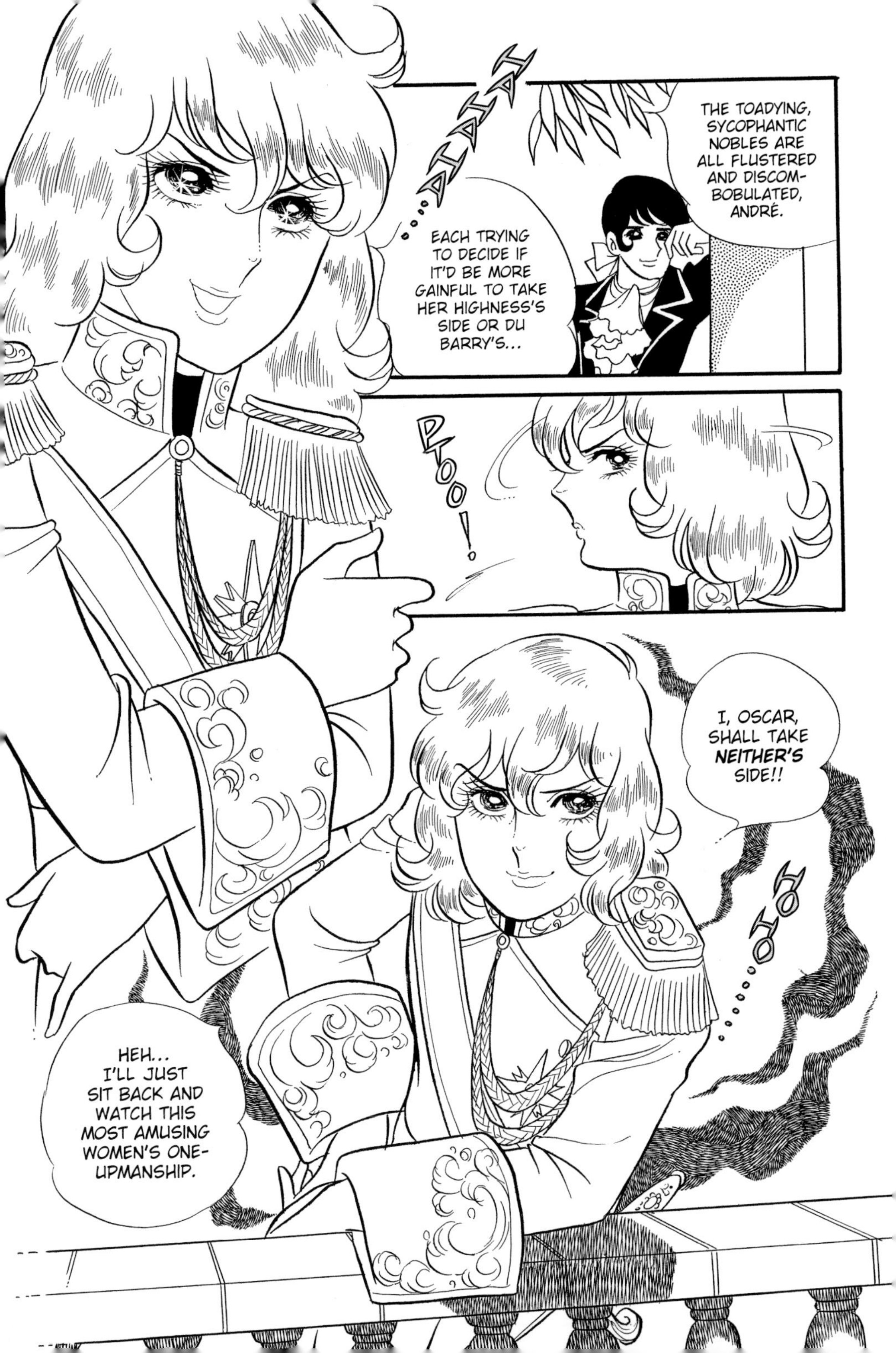
THE TOADYING, SYCOPHANTIC NOBLES ARE ALL FLUSTERED AND DISCOM-BOBULATED, ANDRÉ.
EACH TRYING TO DECIDE IF IT'D BE MORE GAINFUL TO TAKE HER HIGHNESS'S SIDE OR DU BARRY'S...
...AHAHAHA
PTOO!
I, OSCAR, SHALL TAKE **NEITHER'S** SIDE!!
...HOHO
HEH... I'LL JUST SIT BACK AND WATCH THIS MOST AMUSING WOMEN'S ONE-UPMANSHIP.

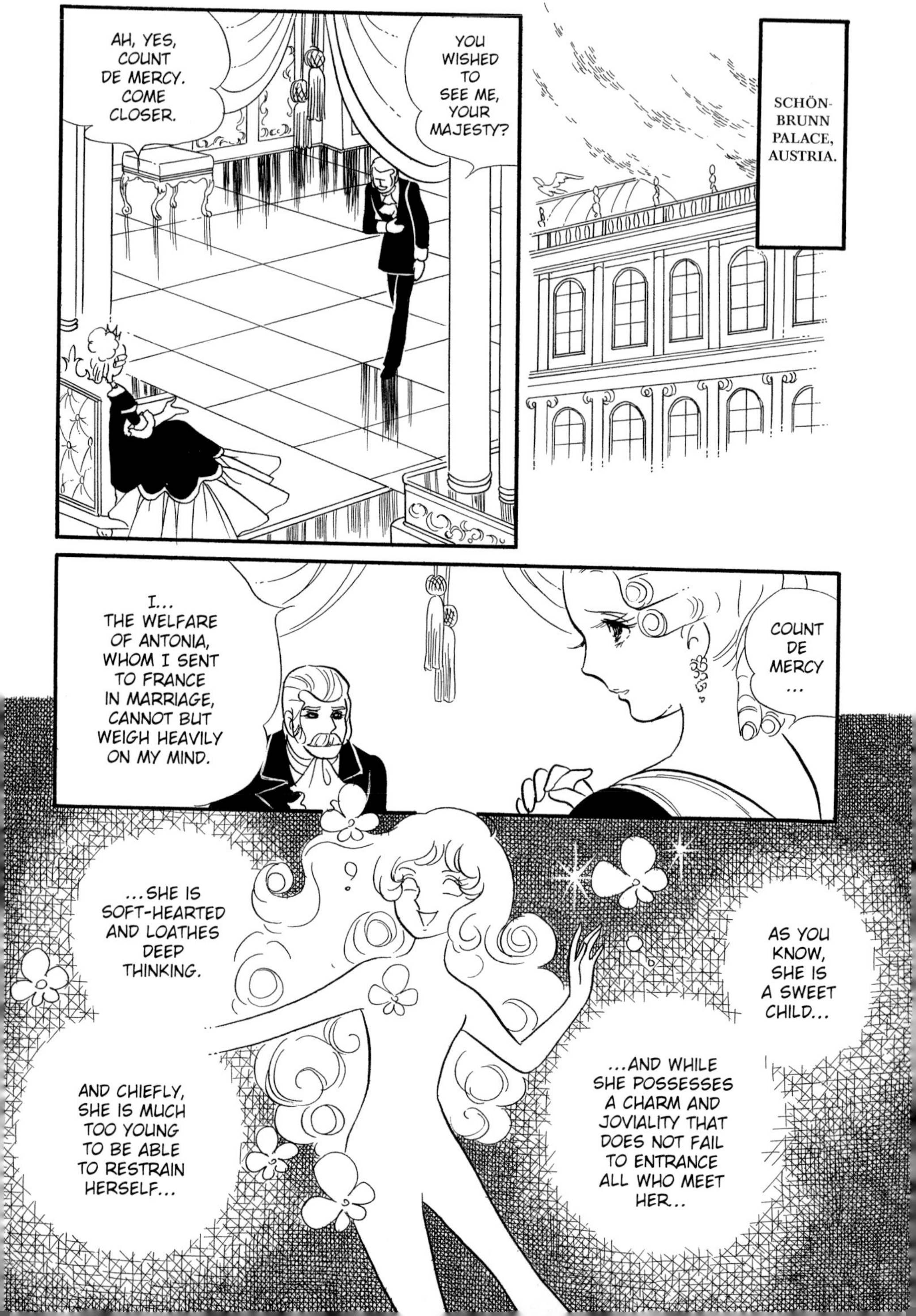
SCHÖN-BRUNN PALACE, AUSTRIA.
YOU WISHED TO SEE ME, YOUR MAJESTY?
AH, YES, COUNT DE MERCY. COME CLOSER.
COUNT DE MERCY ...
I... THE WELFARE OF ANTONIA, WHOM I SENT TO FRANCE IN MARRIAGE, CANNOT BUT WEIGH HEAVILY ON MY MIND.
AS YOU KNOW, SHE IS A SWEET CHILD...
...AND WHILE SHE POSSESSES A CHARM AND JOVIALITY THAT DOES NOT FAIL TO ENTRANCE ALL WHO MEET HER..
...SHE IS SOFT-HEARTED AND LOATHES DEEP THINKING.
AND CHIEFLY, SHE IS MUCH TOO YOUNG TO BE ABLE TO RESTRAIN HERSELF...

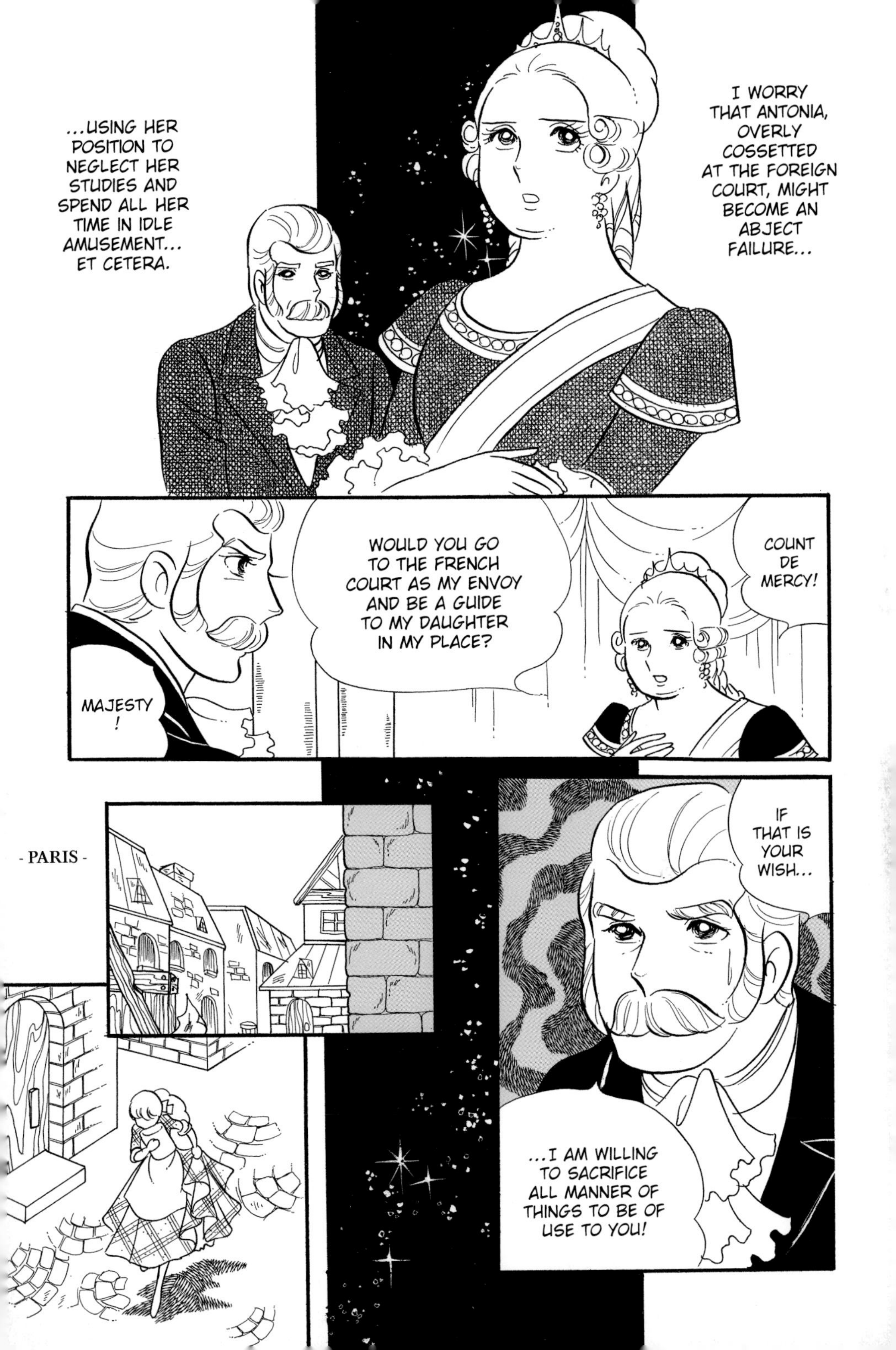
I WORRY THAT ANTONIA, OVERLY COSSETTED AT THE FOREIGN COURT, MIGHT BECOME AN ABJECT FAILURE...
...USING HER POSITION TO NEGLECT HER STUDIES AND SPEND ALL HER TIME IN IDLE AMUSEMENT... ET CETERA.
COUNT DE MERCY!
WOULD YOU GO TO THE FRENCH COURT AS MY ENVOY AND BE A GUIDE TO MY DAUGHTER IN MY PLACE?
MAJESTY!
IF THAT IS YOUR WISH...
...I AM WILLING TO SACRIFICE ALL MANNER OF THINGS TO BE OF USE TO YOU!
- PARIS -

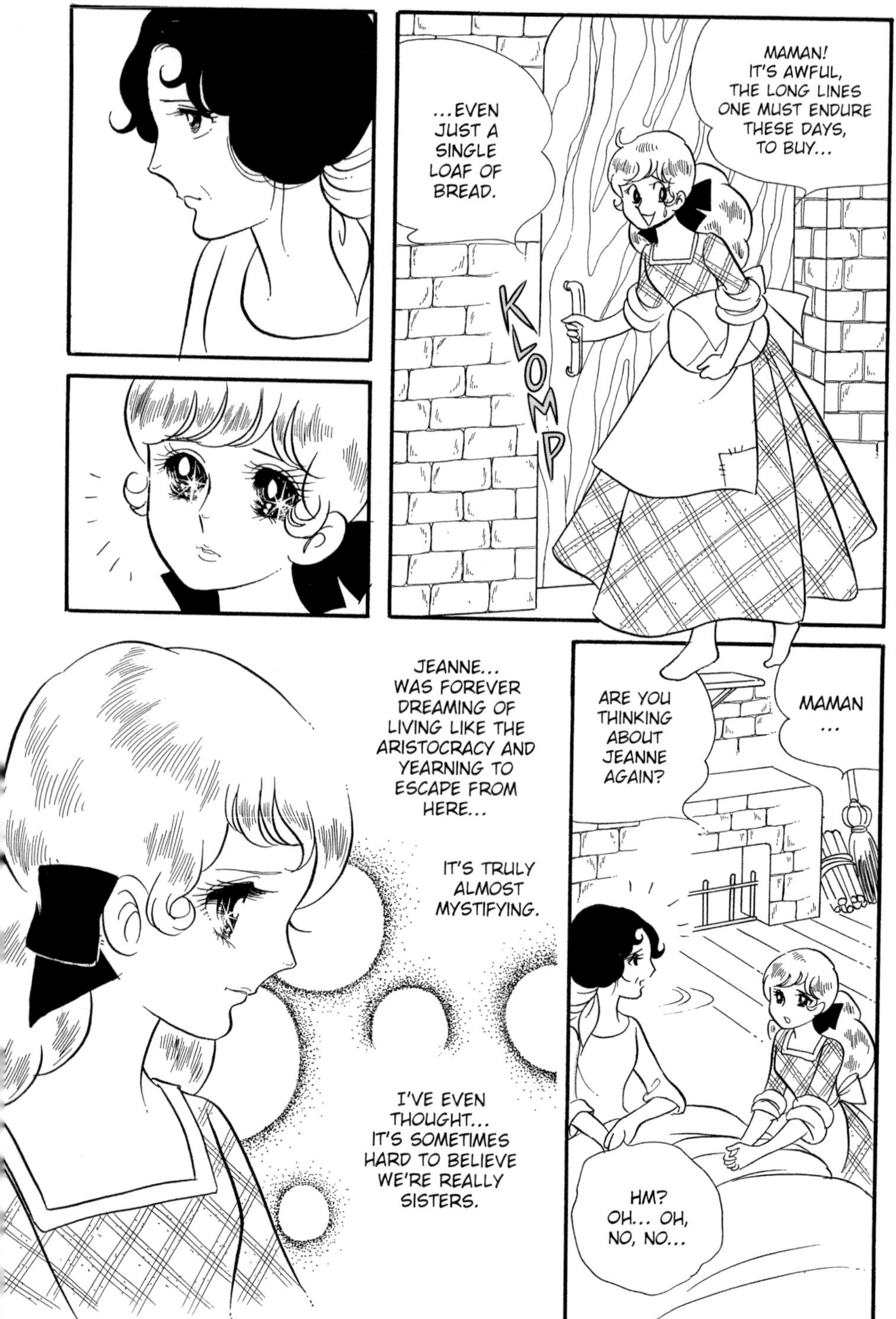
MAMAN! IT'S AWFUL, THE LONG LINES ONE MUST ENDURE THESE DAYS, TO BUY...
...EVEN JUST A SINGLE LOAF OF BREAD.
KLOMP
MAMAN ...
ARE YOU THINKING ABOUT JEANNE AGAIN?
HM? OH... OH, NO, NO...
JEANNE... WAS FOREVER DREAMING OF LIVING LIKE THE ARISTOCRACY AND YEARNING TO ESCAPE FROM HERE...
IT'S TRULY ALMOST MYSTIFYING.
I'VE EVEN THOUGHT... IT'S SOMETIMES HARD TO BELIEVE WE'RE REALLY SISTERS.

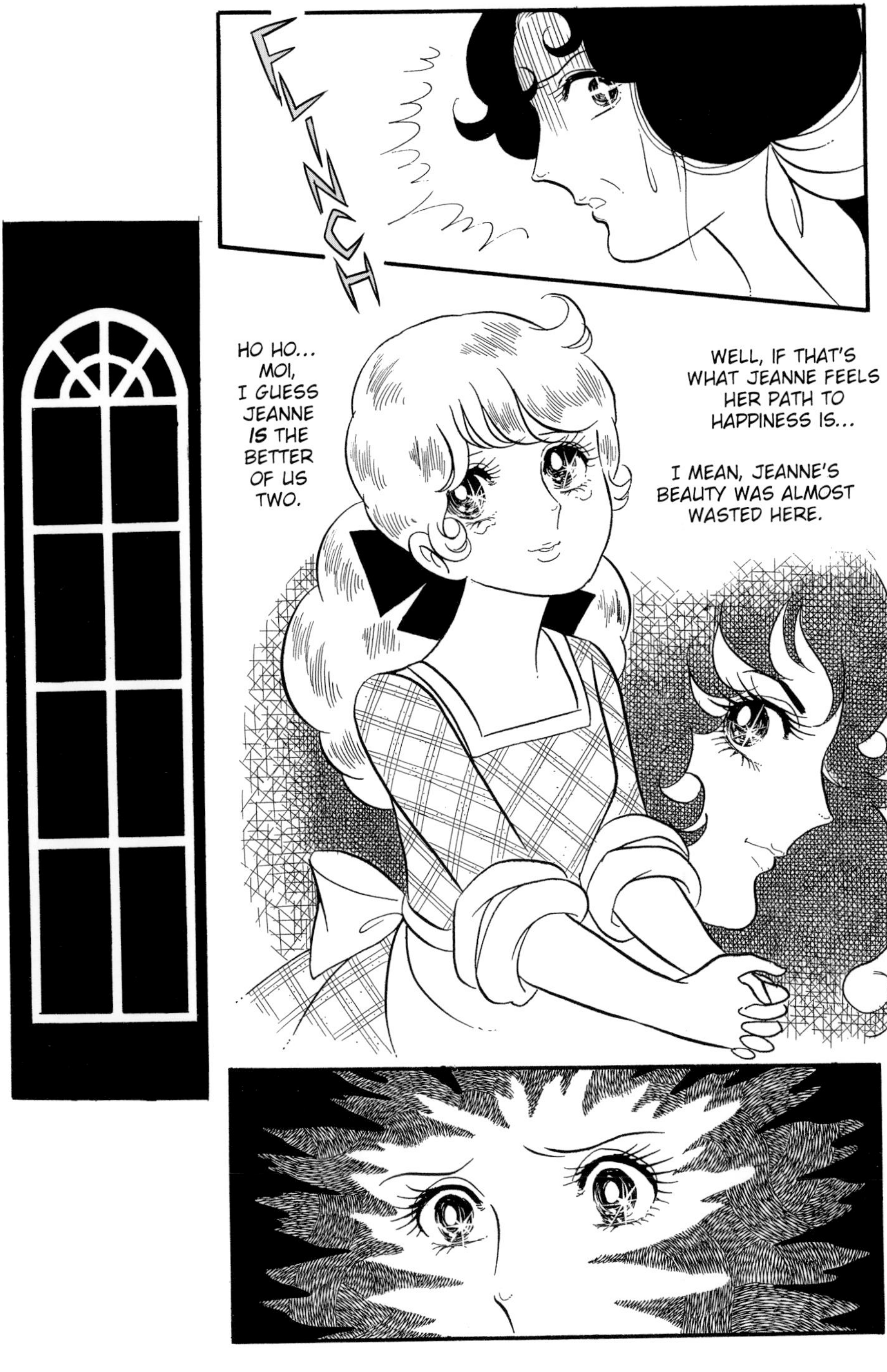
FLINCH
WELL, IF THAT'S WHAT JEANNE FEELS HER PATH TO HAPPINESS IS...
I MEAN, JEANNE'S BEAUTY WAS ALMOST WASTED HERE.
HO HO... MOI, I GUESS JEANNE **IS** THE BETTER OF US TWO.

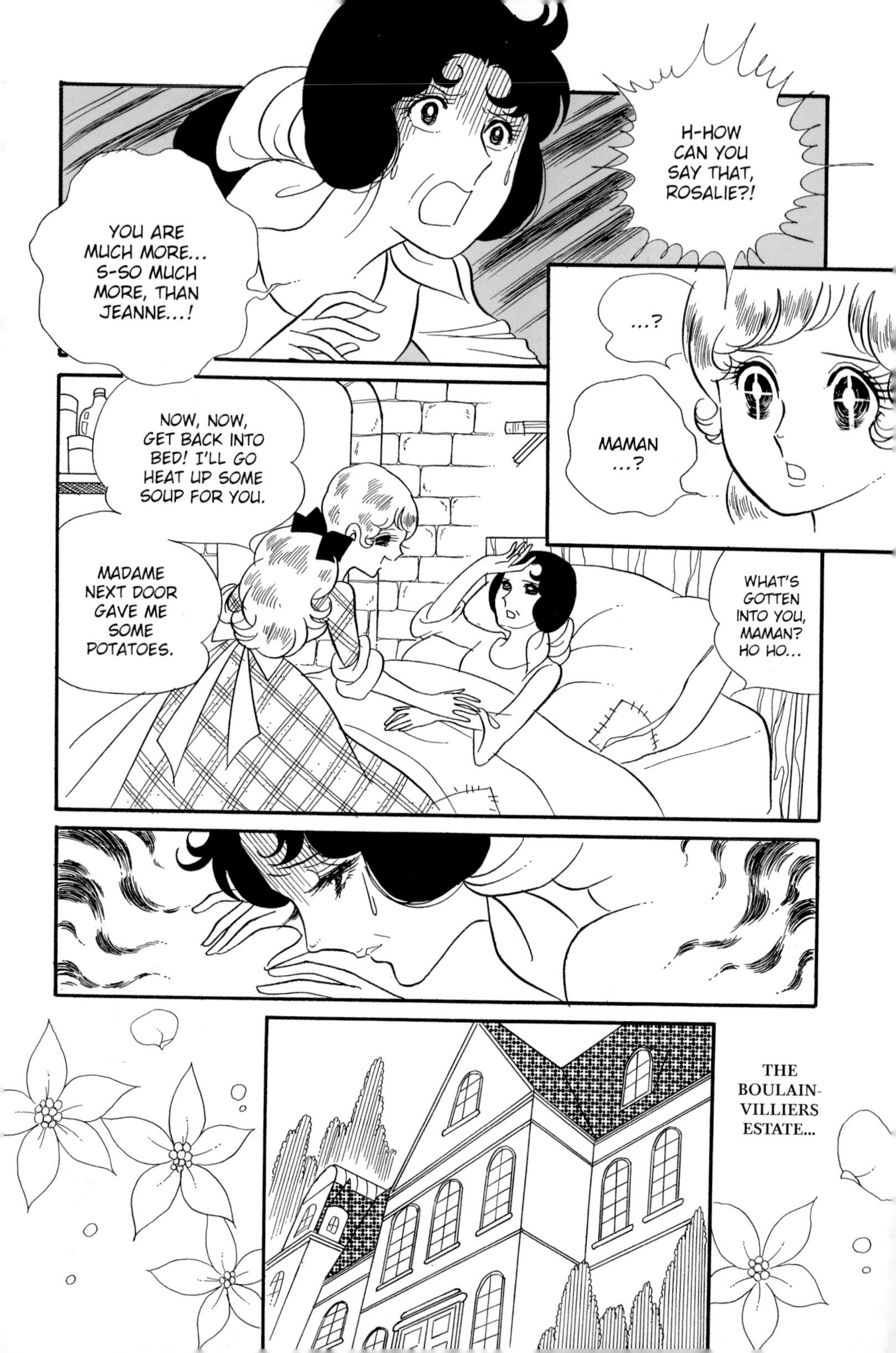
H-HOW CAN YOU SAY THAT, ROSALIE?!
YOU ARE MUCH MORE... S-SO MUCH MORE, THAN JEANNE...!
...?
MAMAN ...?
WHAT'S GOTTEN INTO YOU, MAMAN? HO HO...
NOW, NOW, GET BACK INTO BED! I'LL GO HEAT UP SOME SOUP FOR YOU.
MADAME NEXT DOOR GAVE ME SOME POTATOES.
THE BOULAIN-VILLIERS ESTATE...

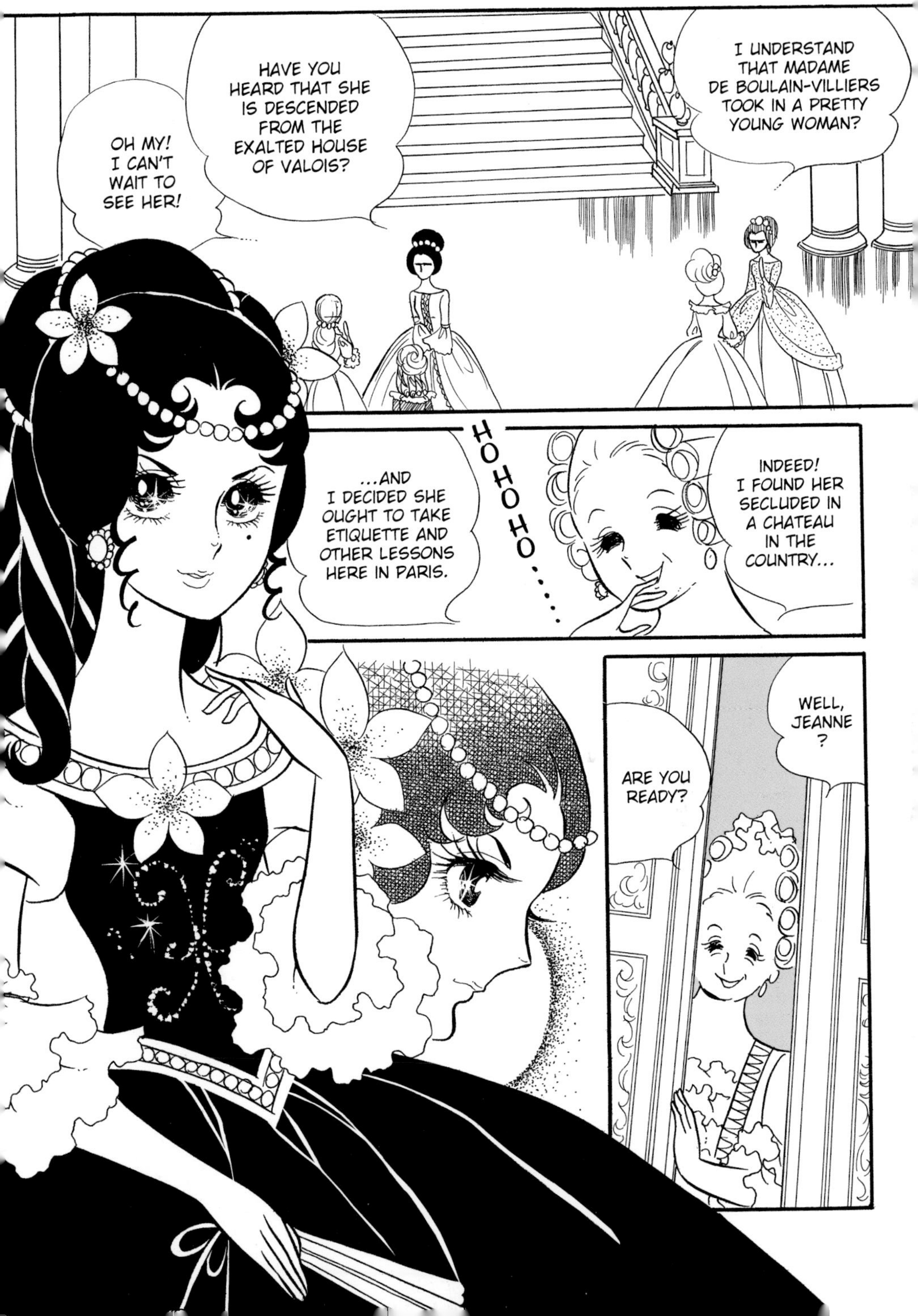
I UNDERSTAND THAT MADAME DE BOULAIN-VILLIERS TOOK IN A PRETTY YOUNG WOMAN?
HAVE YOU HEARD THAT SHE IS DESCENDED FROM THE EXALTED HOUSE OF VALOIS?
OH MY! I CAN'T WAIT TO SEE HER!
INDEED! I FOUND HER SECLUDED IN A CHATEAU IN THE COUNTRY...
HOHOHO......
...AND I DECIDED SHE OUGHT TO TAKE ETIQUETTE AND OTHER LESSONS HERE IN PARIS.
WELL, JEANNE?
ARE YOU READY?

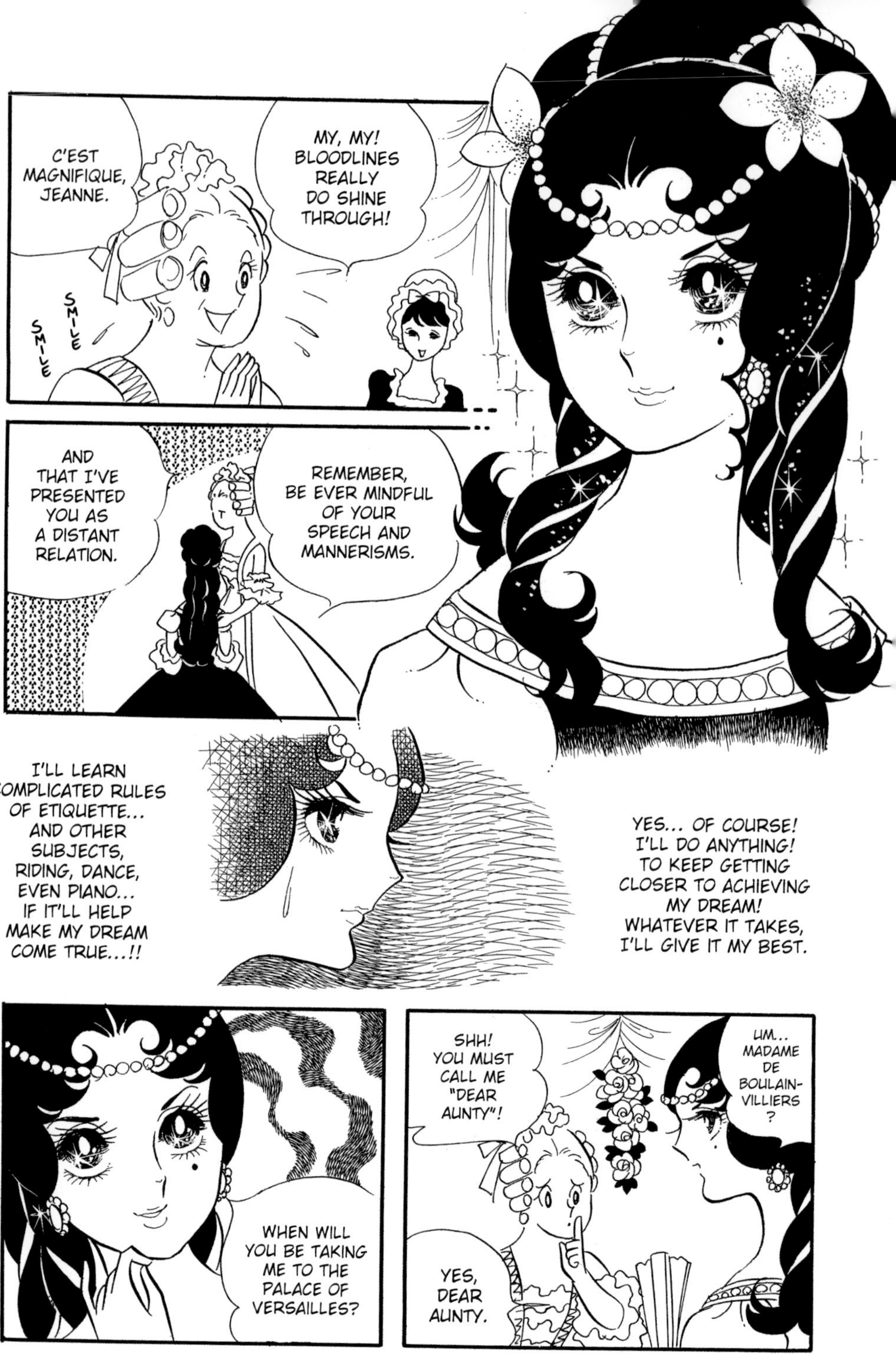
MY, MY! BLOODLINES REALLY DO SHINE THROUGH!
C'EST MAGNIFIQUE, JEANNE.
SMILE SMILE
REMEMBER, BE EVER MINDFUL OF YOUR SPEECH AND MANNERISMS.
AND THAT I'VE PRESENTED YOU AS A DISTANT RELATION.
YES... OF COURSE! I'LL DO ANYTHING! TO KEEP GETTING CLOSER TO ACHIEVING MY DREAM! WHATEVER IT TAKES, I'LL GIVE IT MY BEST.
I'LL LEARN COMPLICATED RULES OF ETIQUETTE... AND OTHER SUBJECTS, RIDING, DANCE, EVEN PIANO... IF IT'LL HELP MAKE MY DREAM COME TRUE...!!
UM... MADAME DE BOULAIN-VILLIERS?
SHH! YOU MUST CALL ME "DEAR AUNTY"!
YES, DEAR AUNTY.
WHEN WILL YOU BE TAKING ME TO THE PALACE OF VERSAILLES?

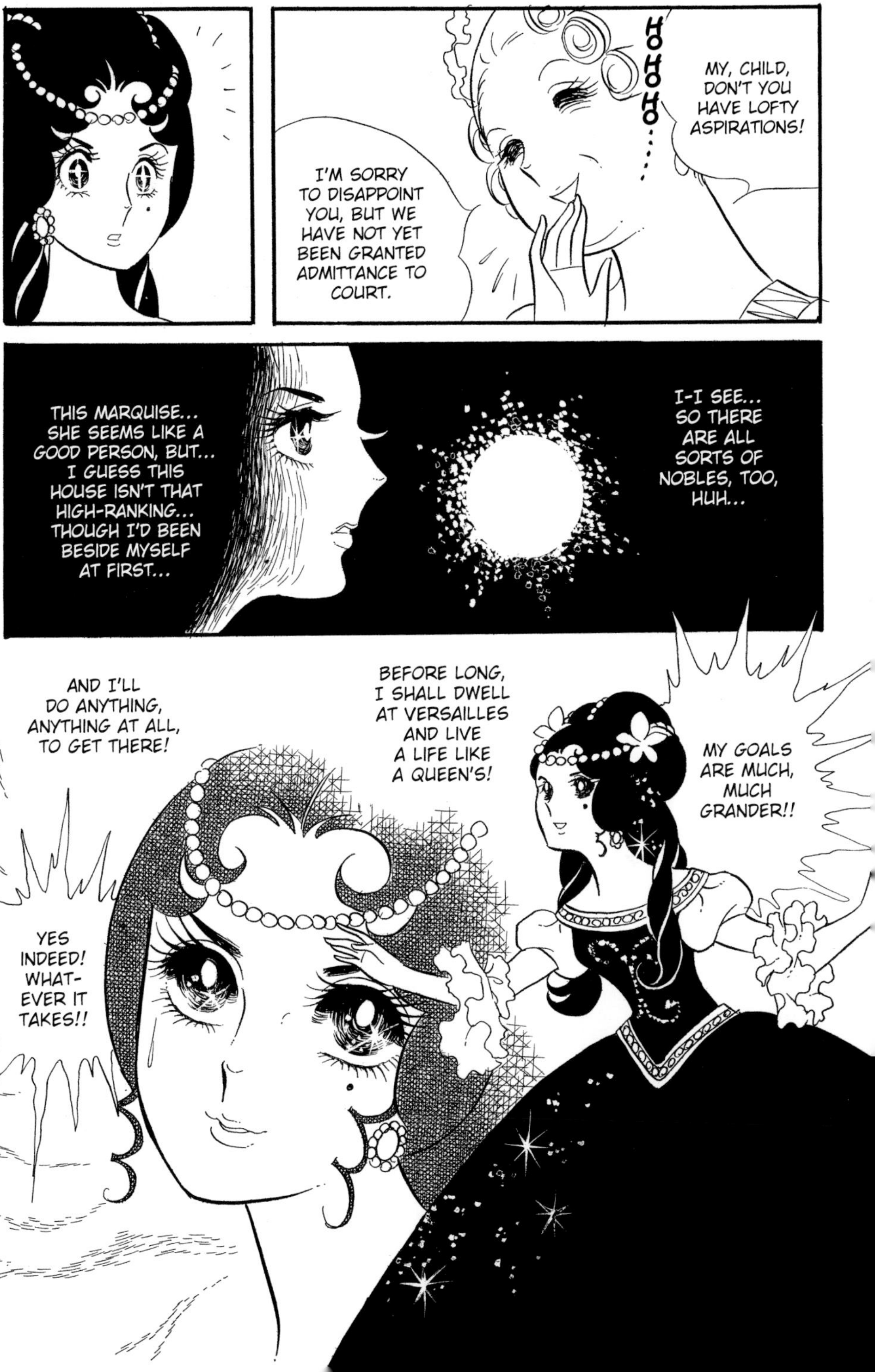
HO HO HO...
MY, CHILD, DON'T YOU HAVE LOFTY ASPIRATIONS!
I'M SORRY TO DISAPPOINT YOU, BUT WE HAVE NOT YET BEEN GRANTED ADMITTANCE TO COURT.
I-I SEE... SO THERE ARE ALL SORTS OF NOBLES, TOO, HUH...
THIS MARQUISE... SHE SEEMS LIKE A GOOD PERSON, BUT... I GUESS THIS HOUSE ISN'T THAT HIGH-RANKING... THOUGH I'D BEEN BESIDE MYSELF AT FIRST...
MY GOALS ARE MUCH, MUCH GRANDER!!
BEFORE LONG, I SHALL DWELL AT VERSAILLES AND LIVE A LIFE LIKE A QUEEN'S!
AND I'LL DO ANYTHING, ANYTHING AT ALL, TO GET THERE!
YES INDEED! WHAT-EVER IT TAKES!!

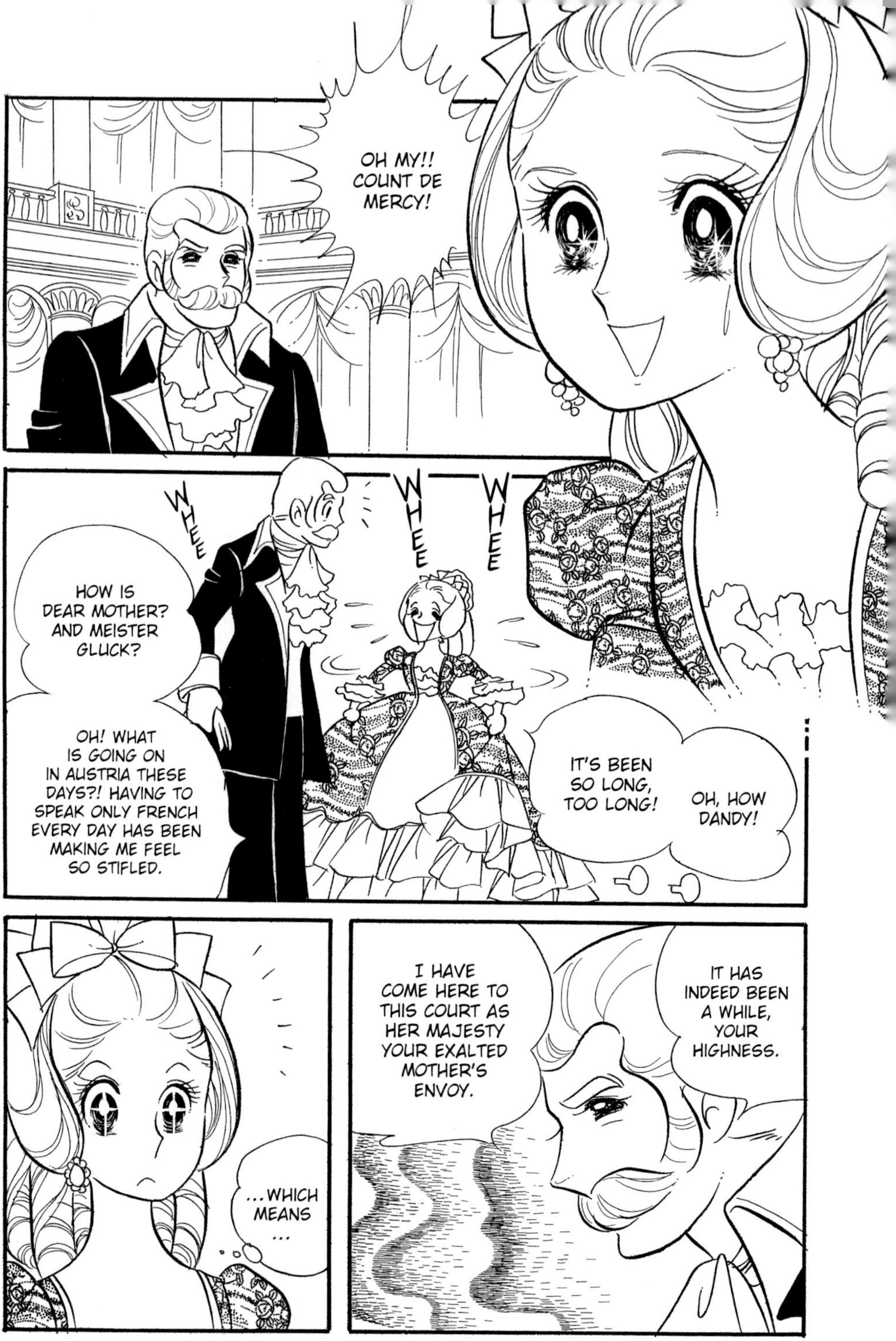
OH MY!! COUNT DE MERCY!
WHEE
WHEE
WHEE
OH, HOW DANDY!
IT'S BEEN SO LONG, TOO LONG!
HOW IS DEAR MOTHER? AND MEISTER GLUCK?
OH! WHAT IS GOING ON IN AUSTRIA THESE DAYS?! HAVING TO SPEAK ONLY FRENCH EVERY DAY HAS BEEN MAKING ME FEEL SO STIFLED.
IT HAS INDEED BEEN A WHILE, YOUR HIGHNESS.
I HAVE COME HERE TO THIS COURT AS HER MAJESTY YOUR EXALTED MOTHER'S ENVOY.
...WHICH MEANS ...

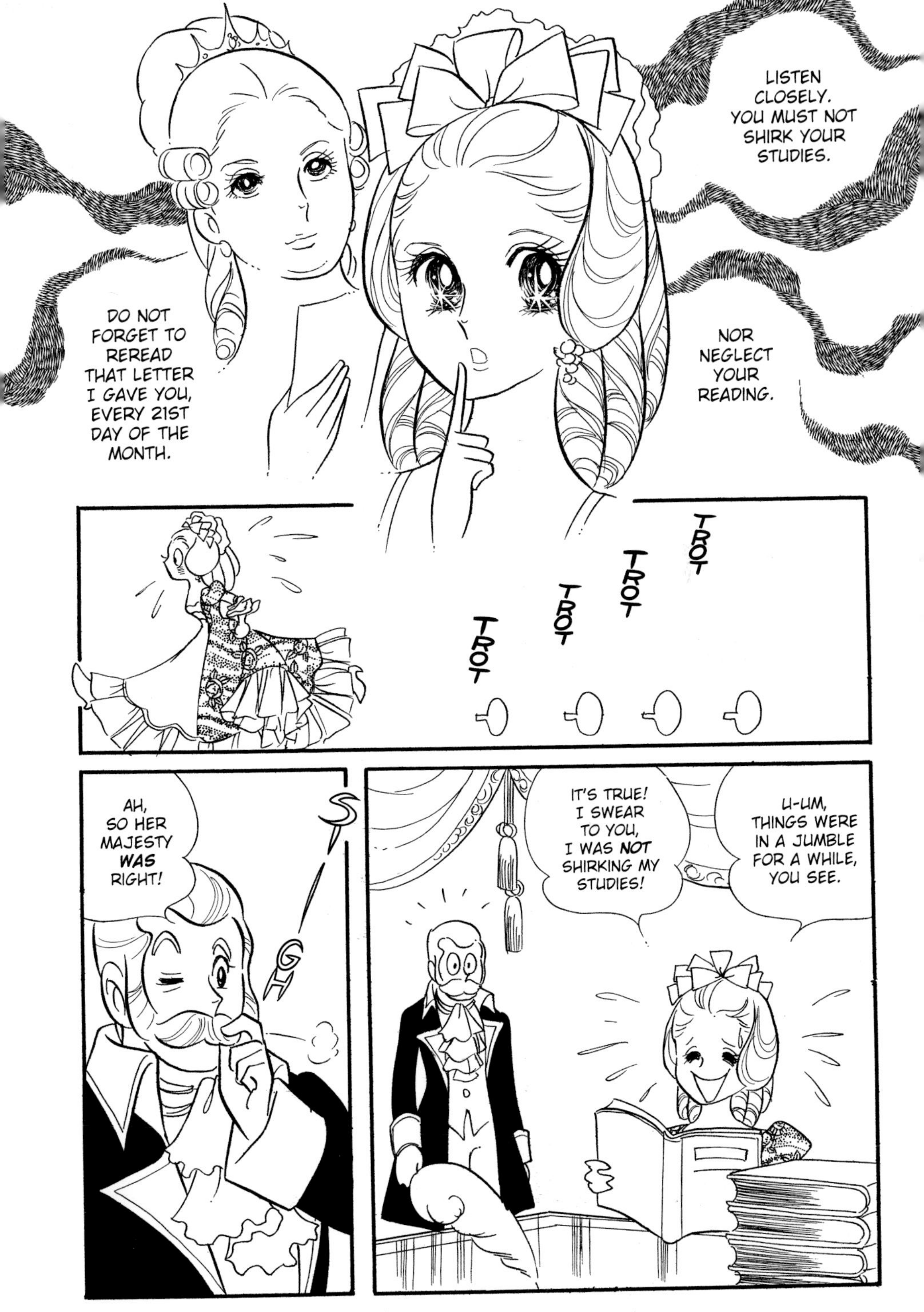
LISTEN CLOSELY. YOU MUST NOT SHIRK YOUR STUDIES.
NOR NEGLECT YOUR READING.
DO NOT FORGET TO REREAD THAT LETTER I GAVE YOU, EVERY 21ST DAY OF THE MONTH.
TROT
TROT
TROT
TROT
U-UM, THINGS WERE IN A JUMBLE FOR A WHILE, YOU SEE.
IT'S TRUE! I SWEAR TO YOU, I WAS **NOT** SHIRKING MY STUDIES!
AH, SO HER MAJESTY **WAS** RIGHT!
SIGH

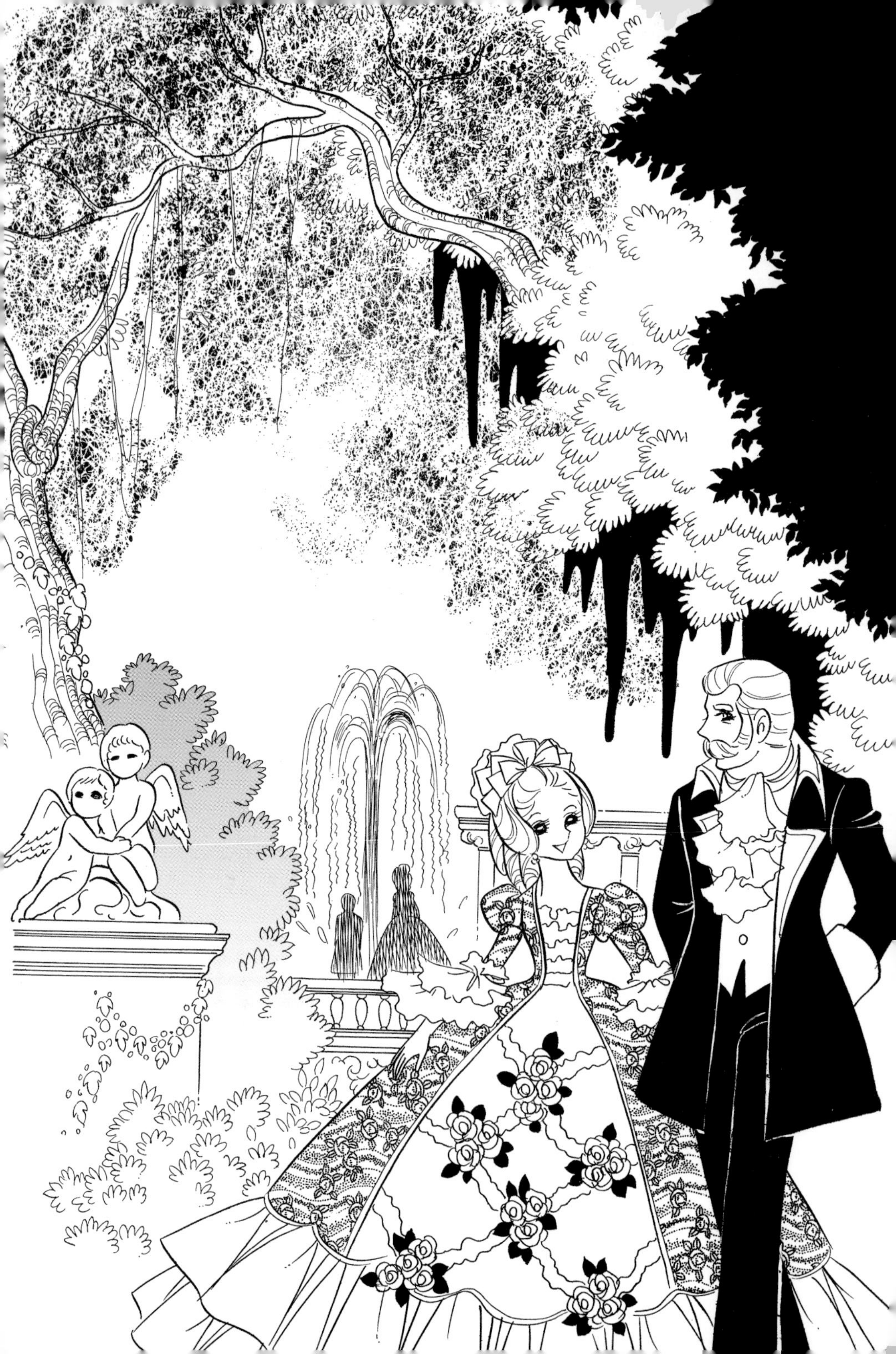

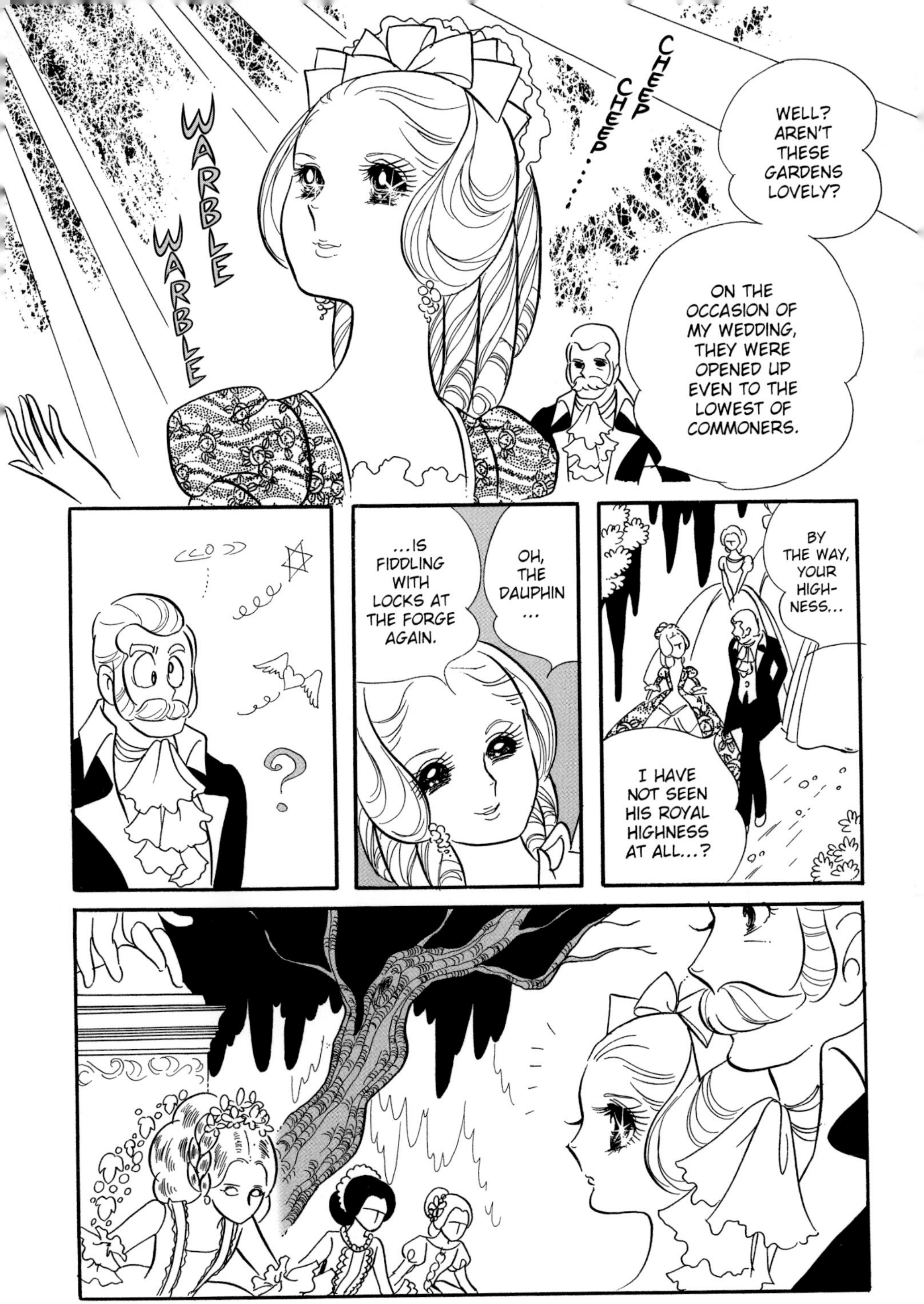
WELL? AREN'T THESE GARDENS LOVELY?
ON THE OCCASION OF MY WEDDING, THEY WERE OPENED UP EVEN TO THE LOWEST OF COMMONERS.
CHEEP CHEEP...
WARBLE WARBLE
BY THE WAY, YOUR HIGHNESS...
I HAVE NOT SEEN HIS ROYAL HIGHNESS AT ALL...?
OH, THE DAUPHIN...
...IS FIDDLING WITH LOCKS AT THE FORGE AGAIN.

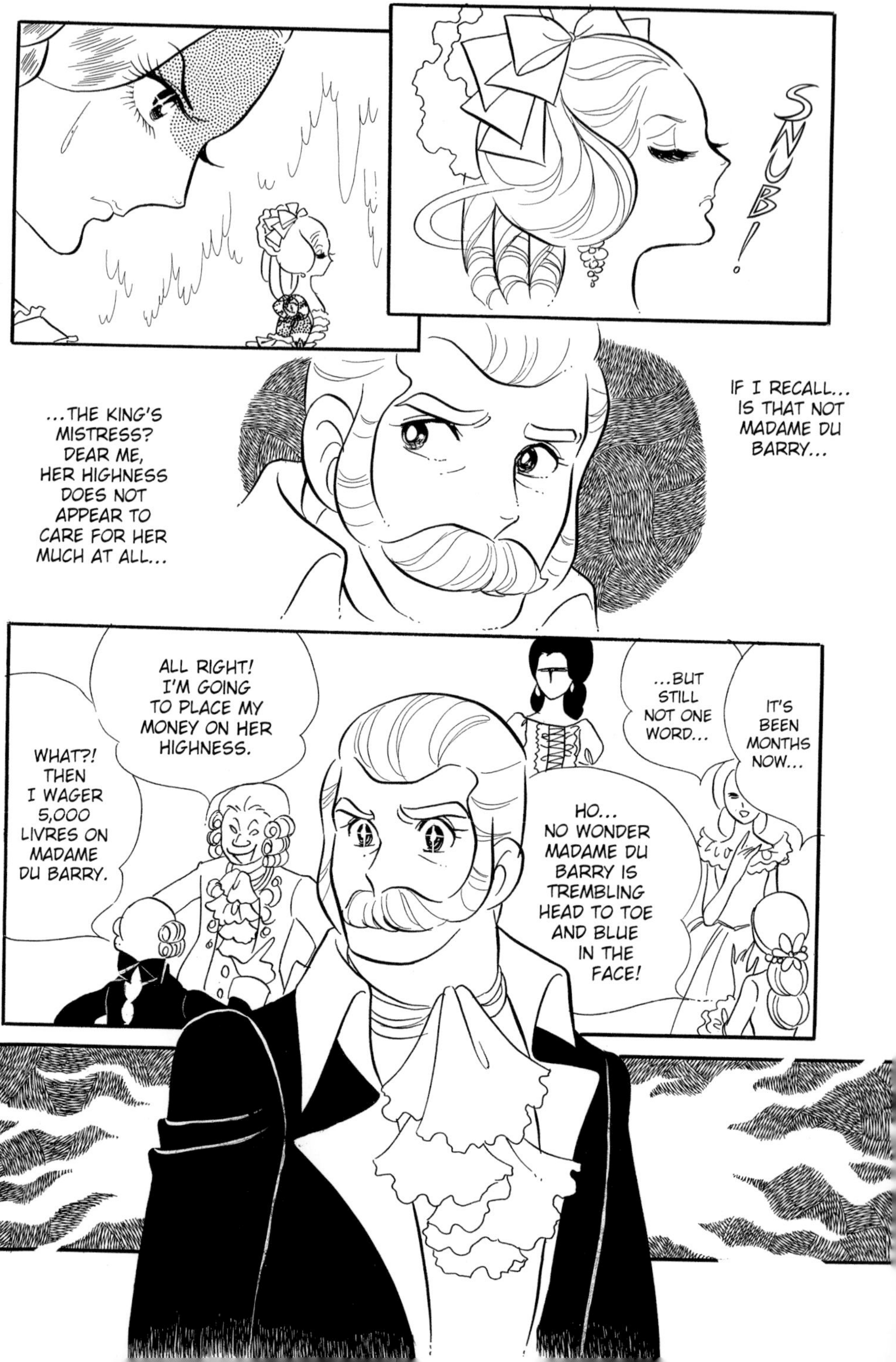
SNUB!
IF I RECALL... IS THAT NOT MADAME DU BARRY...
...THE KING'S MISTRESS? DEAR ME, HER HIGHNESS DOES NOT APPEAR TO CARE FOR HER MUCH AT ALL...
IT'S BEEN MONTHS NOW...
...BUT STILL NOT ONE WORD...
HO... NO WONDER MADAME DU BARRY IS TREMBLING HEAD TO TOE AND BLUE IN THE FACE!
ALL RIGHT! I'M GOING TO PLACE MY MONEY ON HER HIGHNESS.
WHAT?! THEN I WAGER 5,000 LIVRES ON MADAME DU BARRY.

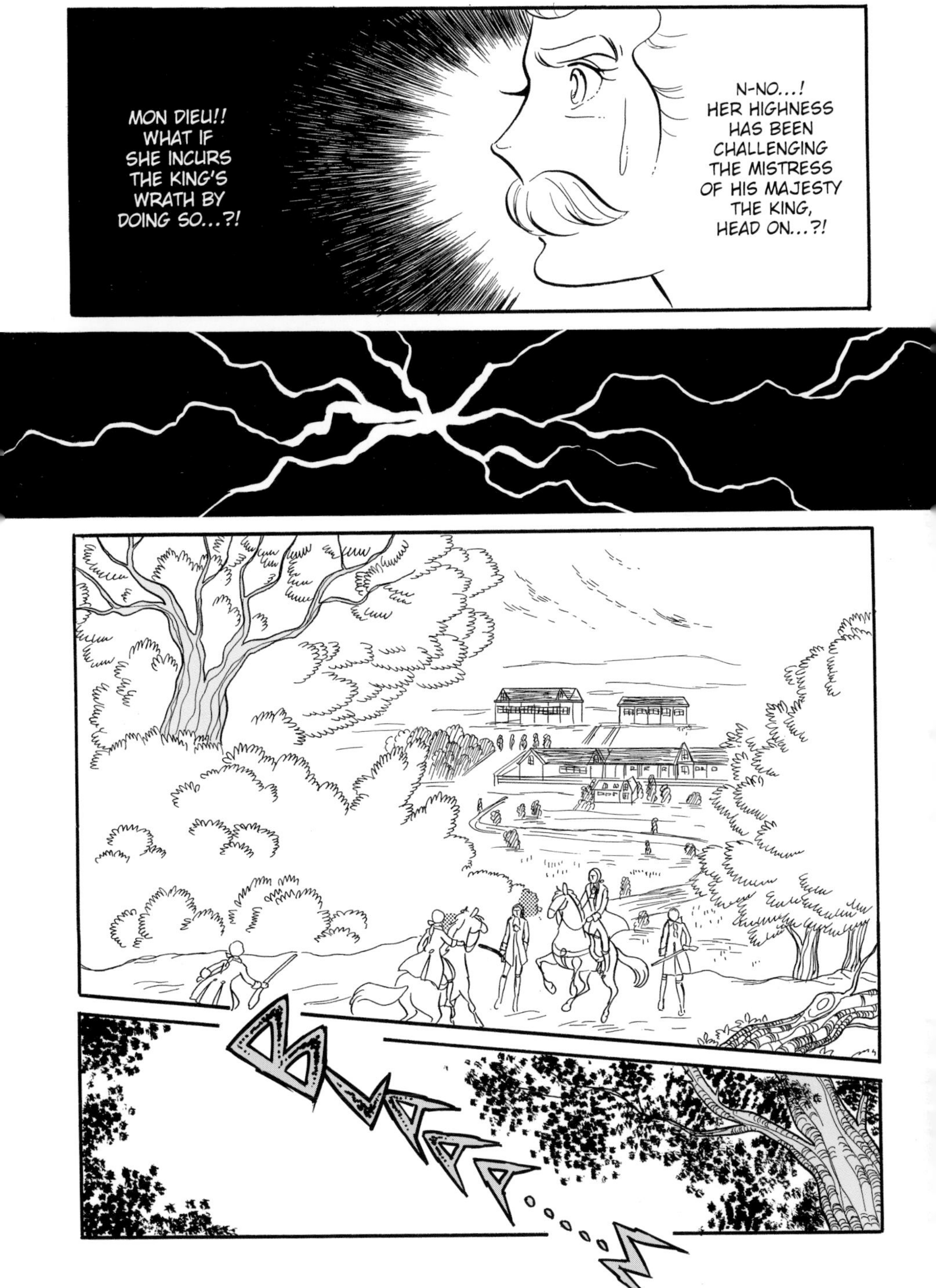
N-NO...! HER HIGHNESS HAS BEEN CHALLENGING THE MISTRESS OF HIS MAJESTY THE KING, HEAD ON...?!
MON DIEU!! WHAT IF SHE INCURS THE KING'S WRATH BY DOING SO...?!
BWAAA.....M

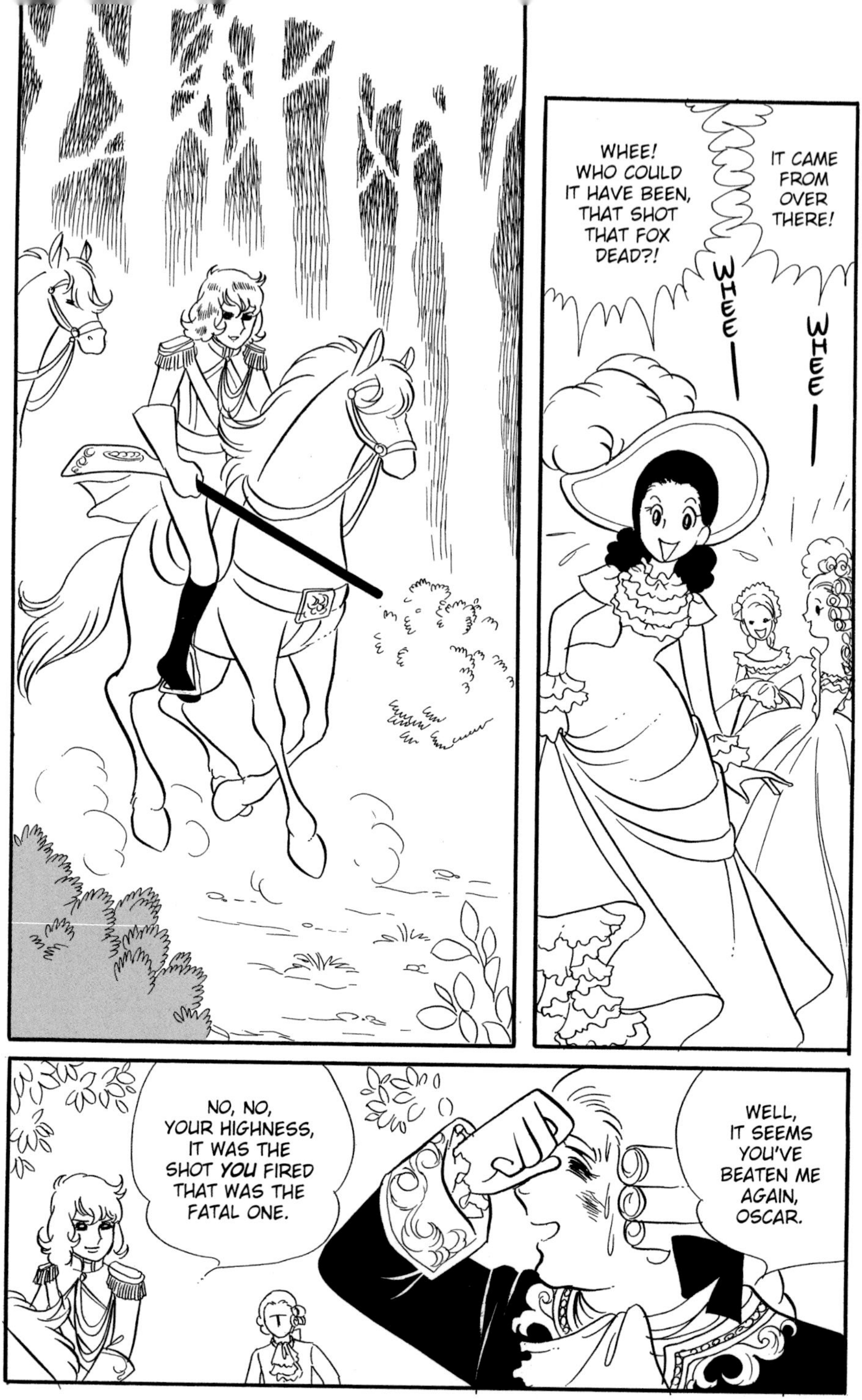
IT CAME FROM OVER THERE!
WHEE! WHO COULD IT HAVE BEEN, THAT SHOT THAT FOX DEAD?!
WHEE—
WHEE—
WELL, IT SEEMS YOU'VE BEATEN ME AGAIN, OSCAR.
NO, NO, YOUR HIGHNESS, IT WAS THE SHOT *YOU* FIRED THAT WAS THE FATAL ONE.

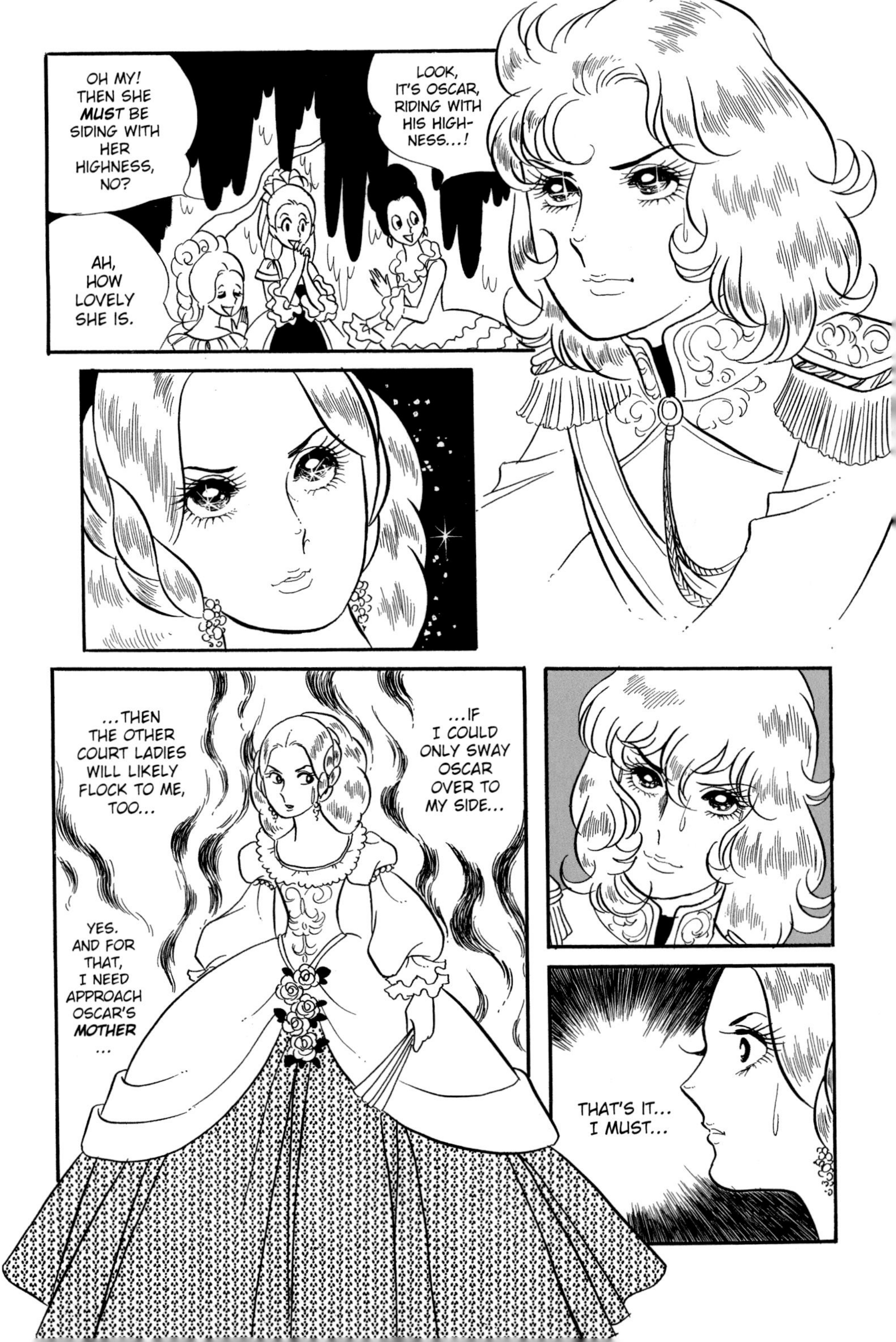
LOOK, IT'S OSCAR, RIDING WITH HIS HIGHNESS...!
OH MY! THEN SHE *MUST* BE SIDING WITH HER HIGHNESS, NO?
AH, HOW LOVELY SHE IS.
THAT'S IT... I MUST...
...IF I COULD ONLY SWAY OSCAR OVER TO MY SIDE...
...THEN THE OTHER COURT LADIES WILL LIKELY FLOCK TO ME, TOO...
YES. AND FOR THAT, I NEED APPROACH OSCAR'S *MOTHER* ...

1972 WEEKLY MARGARET MAGAZINE
ISSUE 21 SPINE ART EXCERPT

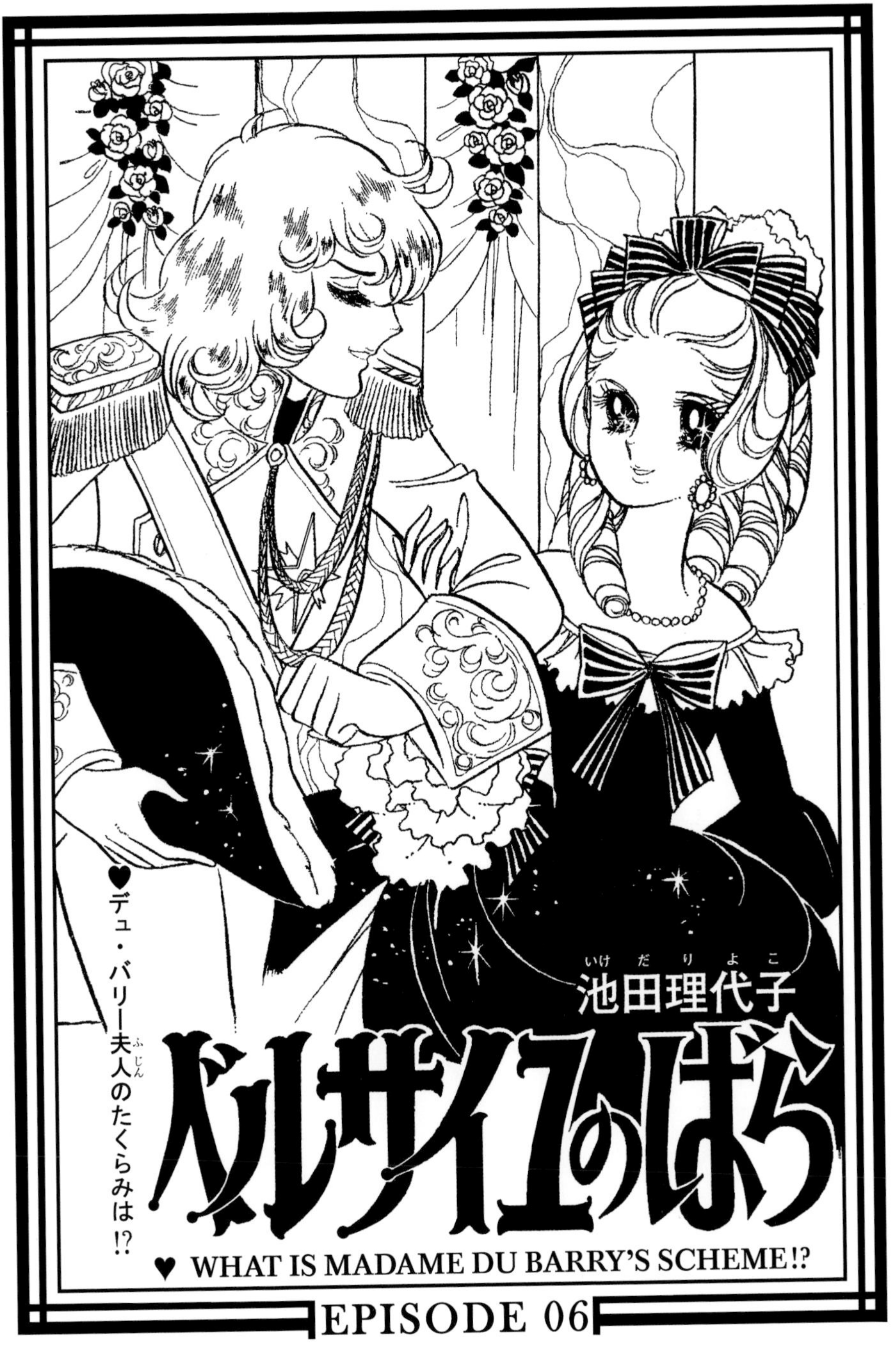

♥デュ・バリー夫人のたくらみは!?
池田理代子
ベルサイユのばら
♥ WHAT IS MADAME DU BARRY'S SCHEME!?
EPISODE 06

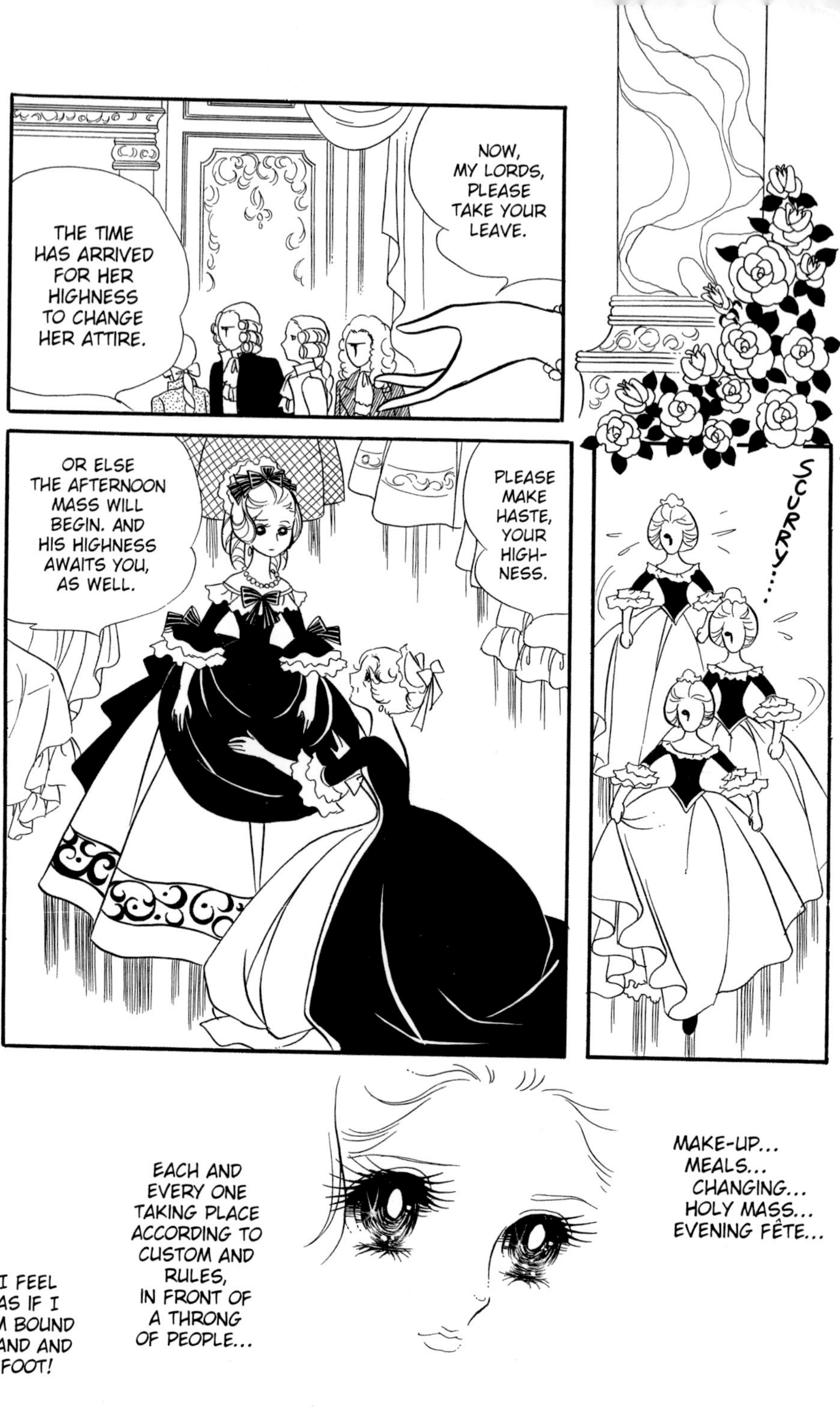
NOW, MY LORDS, PLEASE TAKE YOUR LEAVE.
THE TIME HAS ARRIVED FOR HER HIGHNESS TO CHANGE HER ATTIRE.
SCURRY...
PLEASE MAKE HASTE, YOUR HIGH-NESS.
OR ELSE THE AFTERNOON MASS WILL BEGIN. AND HIS HIGHNESS AWAITS YOU, AS WELL.
MAKE-UP... MEALS... CHANGING... HOLY MASS... EVENING FÊTE...
EACH AND EVERY ONE TAKING PLACE ACCORDING TO CUSTOM AND RULES, IN FRONT OF A THRONG OF PEOPLE...
I FEEL AS IF I AM BOUND HAND AND FOOT!

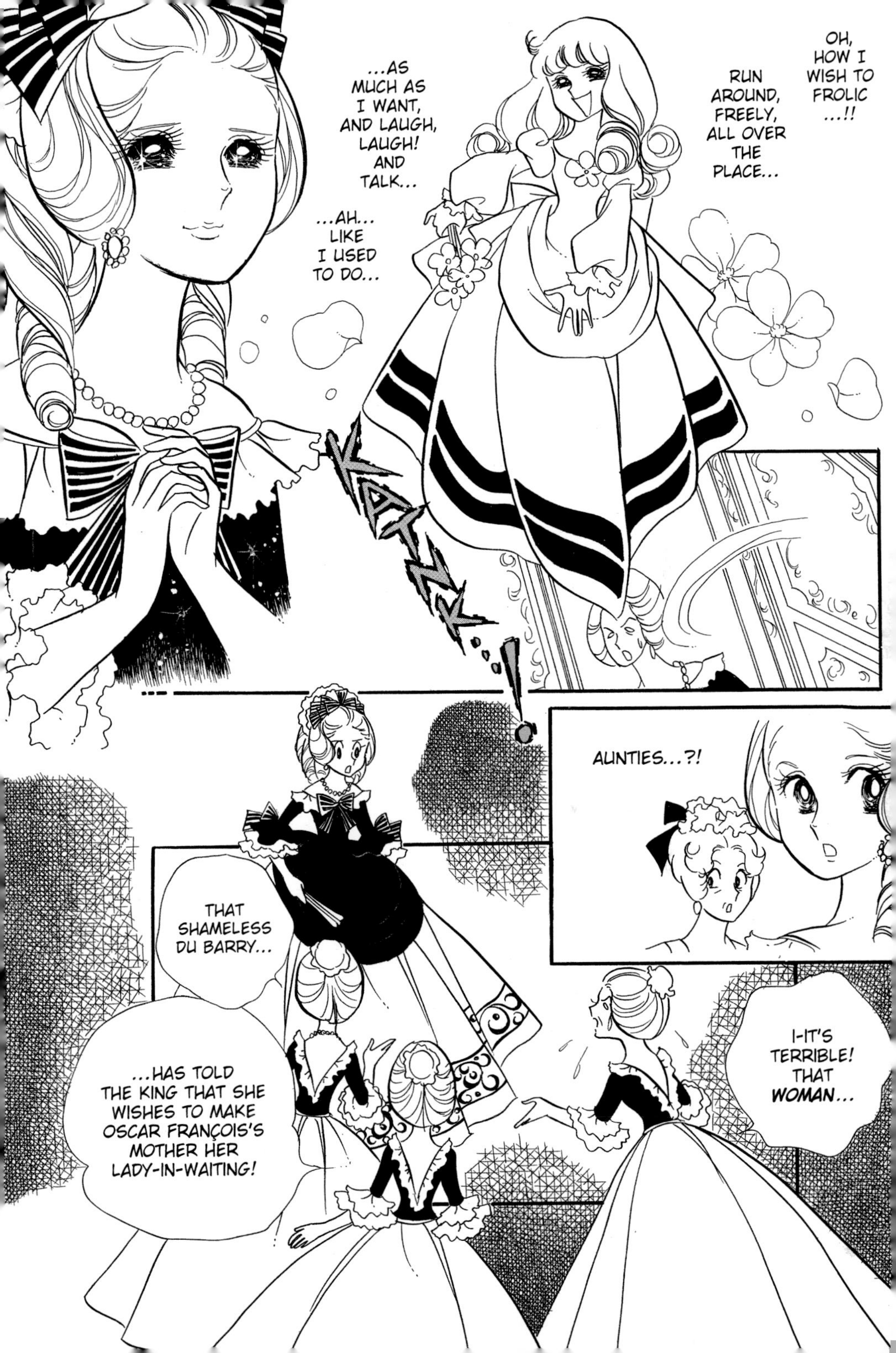
OH, HOW I WISH TO FROLIC...!!
RUN AROUND, FREELY, ALL OVER THE PLACE...
...AS MUCH AS I WANT, AND LAUGH, LAUGH! AND TALK...
...AH... LIKE I USED TO DO...
KATANK...!
AUNTIES...?!
I-IT'S TERRIBLE! THAT **WOMAN**...
THAT SHAMELESS DU BARRY...
...HAS TOLD THE KING THAT SHE WISHES TO MAKE OSCAR FRANÇOIS'S MOTHER HER LADY-IN-WAITING!

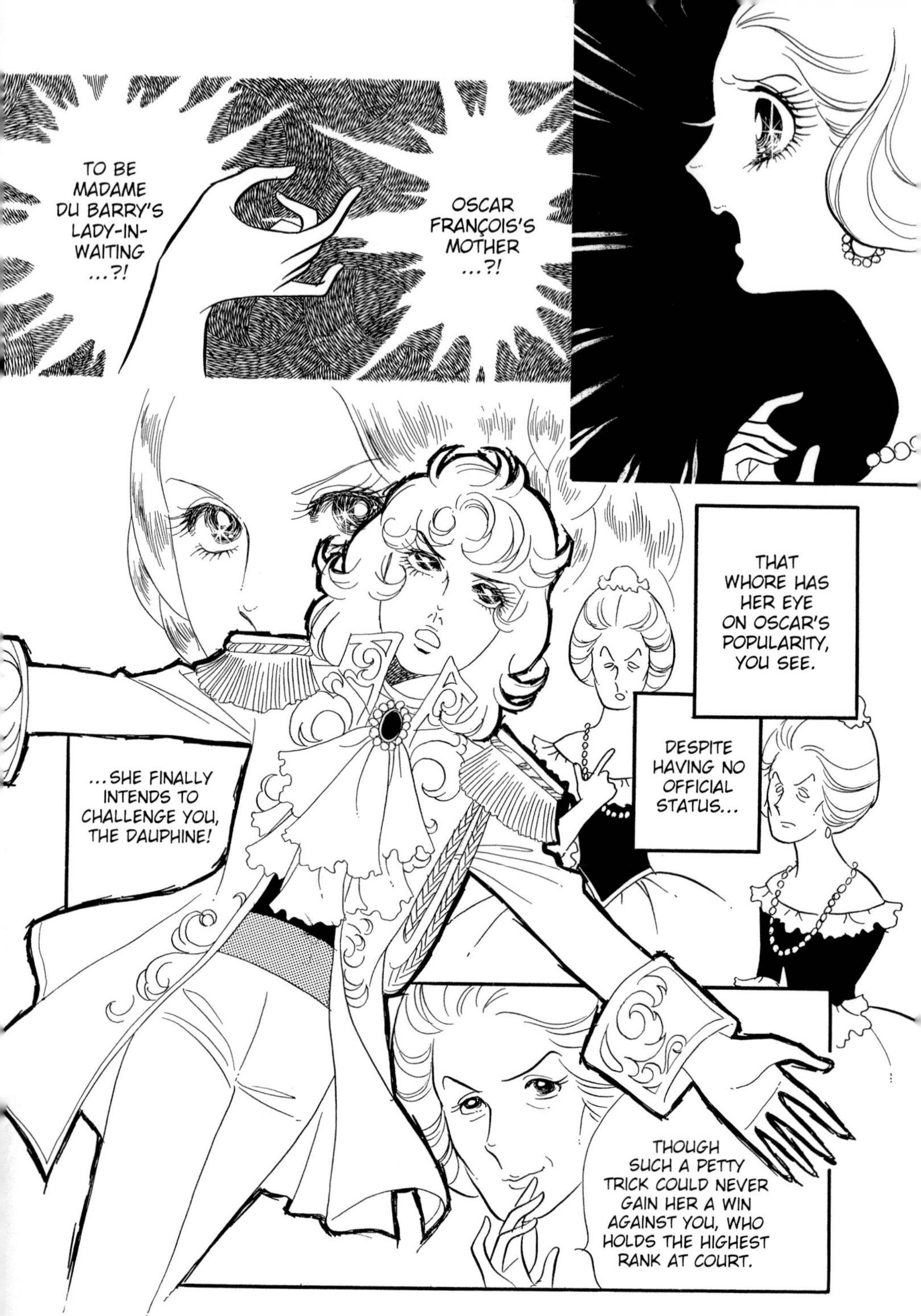
OSCAR FRANÇOIS'S MOTHER ...?!
TO BE MADAME DU BARRY'S LADY-IN-WAITING ...?!
THAT WHORE HAS HER EYE ON OSCAR'S POPULARITY, YOU SEE.
DESPITE HAVING NO OFFICIAL STATUS...
...SHE FINALLY INTENDS TO CHALLENGE YOU, THE DAUPHINE!
THOUGH SUCH A PETTY TRICK COULD NEVER GAIN HER A WIN AGAINST YOU, WHO HOLDS THE HIGHEST RANK AT COURT.

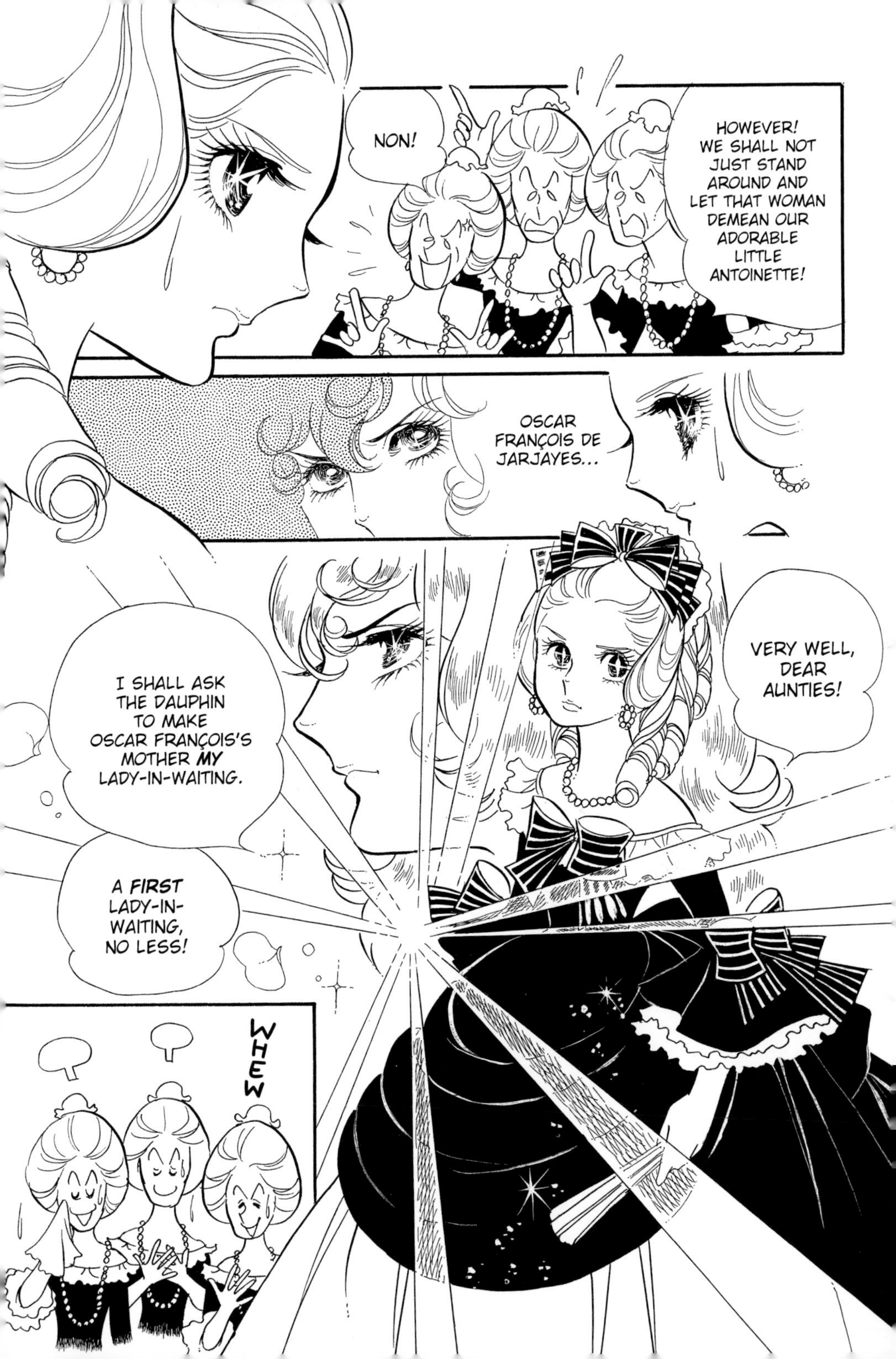
HOWEVER! WE SHALL NOT JUST STAND AROUND AND LET THAT WOMAN DEMEAN OUR ADORABLE LITTLE ANTOINETTE!
NON!
OSCAR FRANÇOIS DE JARJAYES...
VERY WELL, DEAR AUNTIES!
I SHALL ASK THE DAUPHIN TO MAKE OSCAR FRANÇOIS'S MOTHER **MY** LADY-IN-WAITING.
A **FIRST** LADY-IN-WAITING, NO LESS!
WHEW

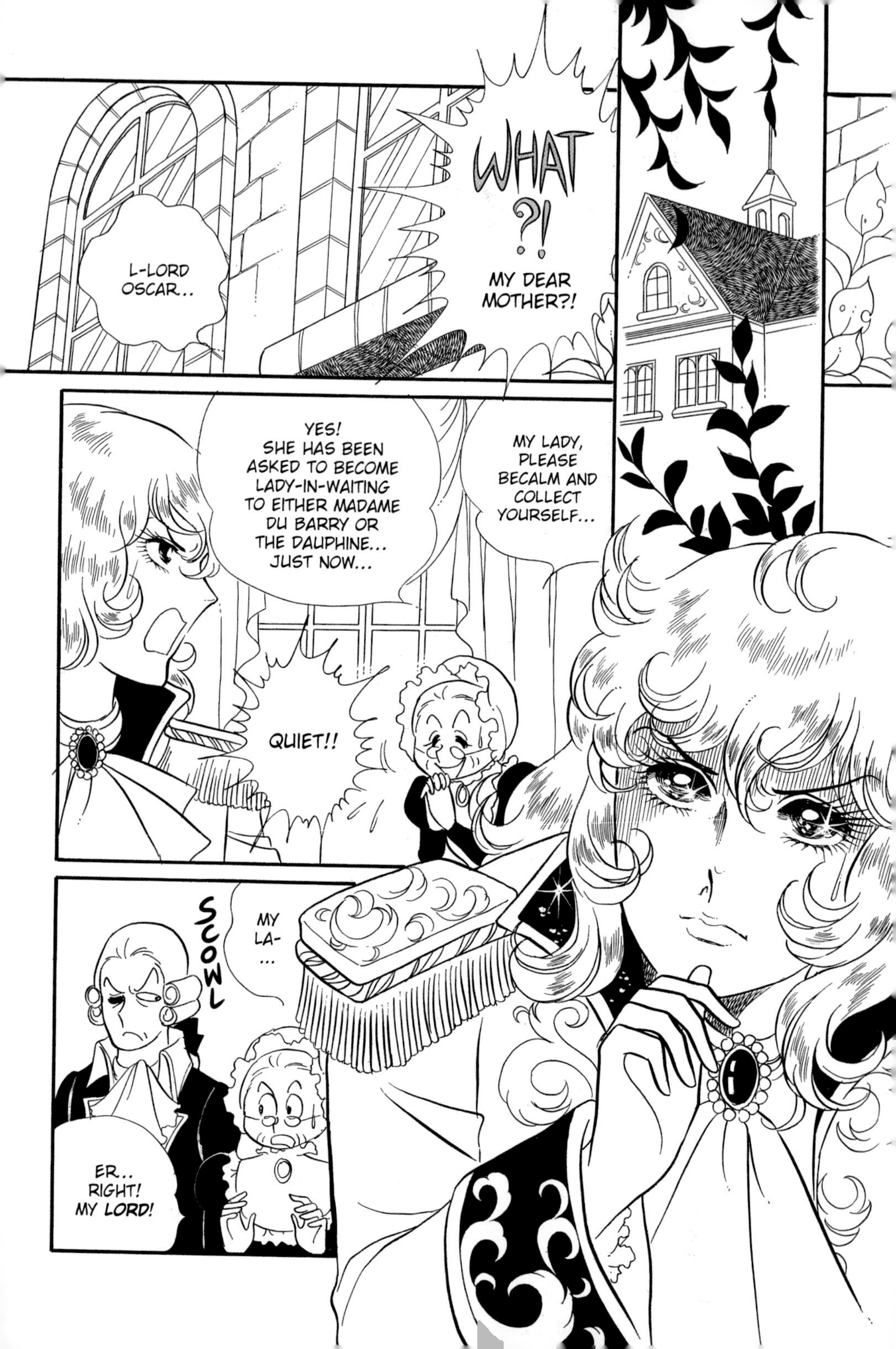
WHAT ?!
MY DEAR MOTHER?!
L-LORD OSCAR...
MY LADY, PLEASE BECALM AND COLLECT YOURSELF...
YES! SHE HAS BEEN ASKED TO BECOME LADY-IN-WAITING TO EITHER MADAME DU BARRY OR THE DAUPHINE... JUST NOW...
QUIET!!
MY LA- ...
SCOWL
ER... RIGHT! MY LORD!

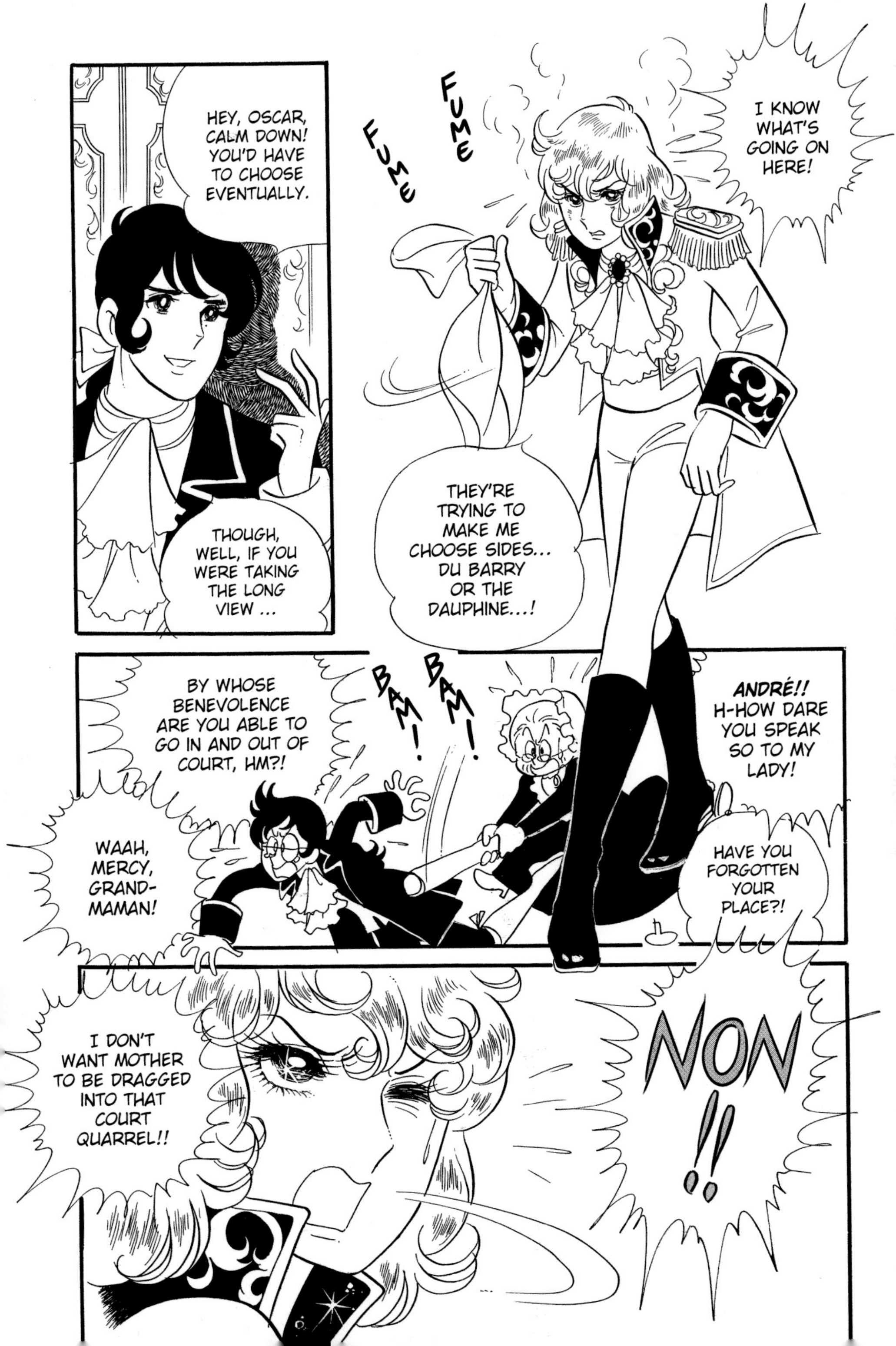
FUME FUME
I KNOW WHAT'S GOING ON HERE!
THEY'RE TRYING TO MAKE ME CHOOSE SIDES... DU BARRY OR THE DAUPHINE...!
HEY, OSCAR, CALM DOWN! YOU'D HAVE TO CHOOSE EVENTUALLY.
THOUGH, WELL, IF YOU WERE TAKING THE LONG VIEW ...
ANDRÉ!! H-HOW DARE YOU SPEAK SO TO MY LADY!
BAM! BAM!
BY WHOSE BENEVOLENCE ARE YOU ABLE TO GO IN AND OUT OF COURT, HM?!
HAVE YOU FORGOTTEN YOUR PLACE?!
WAAH, MERCY, GRAND-MAMAN!
NON!!
I DON'T WANT MOTHER TO BE DRAGGED INTO THAT COURT QUARREL!!

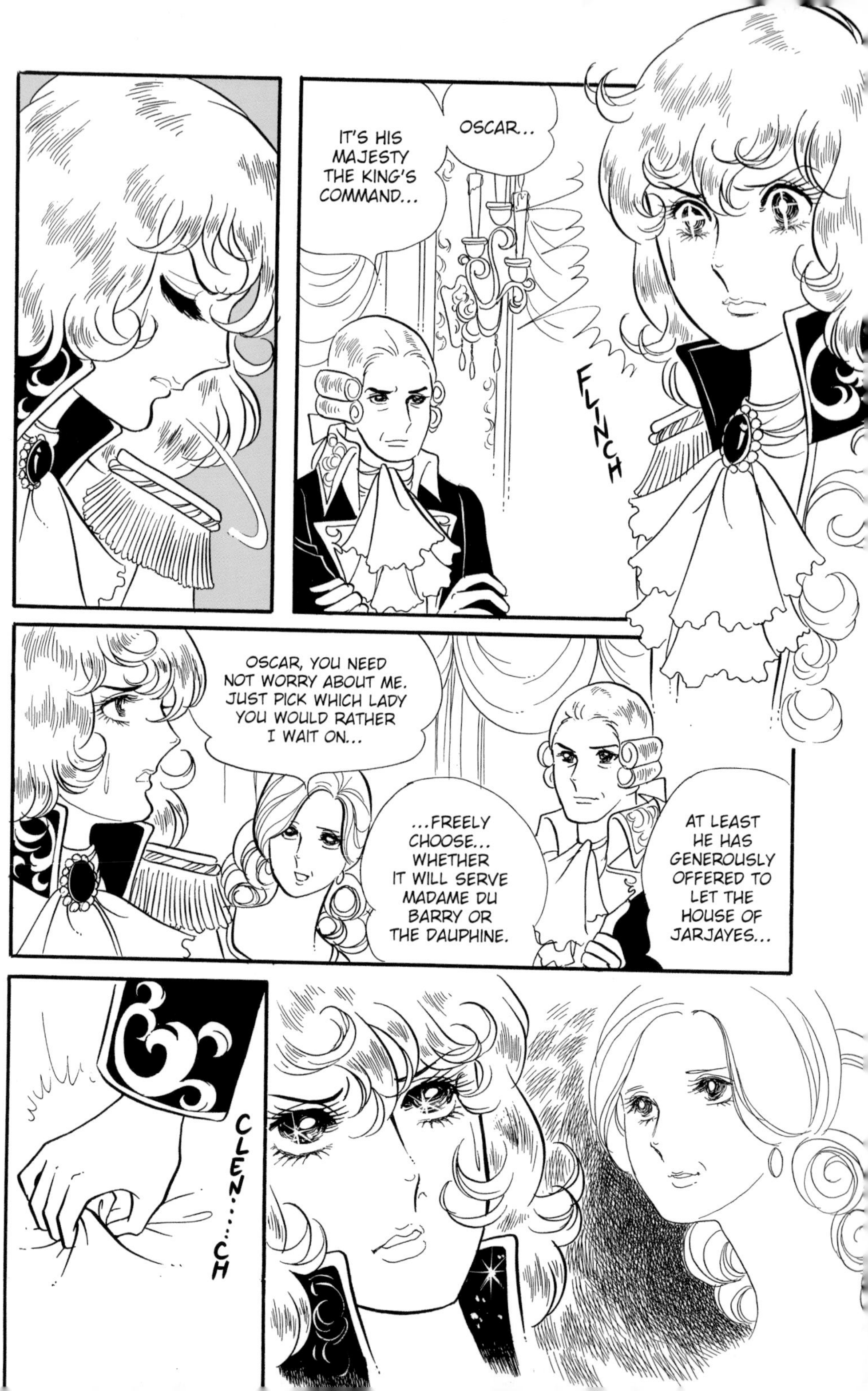
FLINCH
OSCAR...
IT'S HIS MAJESTY THE KING'S COMMAND...
AT LEAST HE HAS GENEROUSLY OFFERED TO LET THE HOUSE OF JARJAYES...
...FREELY CHOOSE... WHETHER IT WILL SERVE MADAME DU BARRY OR THE DAUPHINE.
OSCAR, YOU NEED NOT WORRY ABOUT ME. JUST PICK WHICH LADY YOU WOULD RATHER I WAIT ON...
CLEN....CH

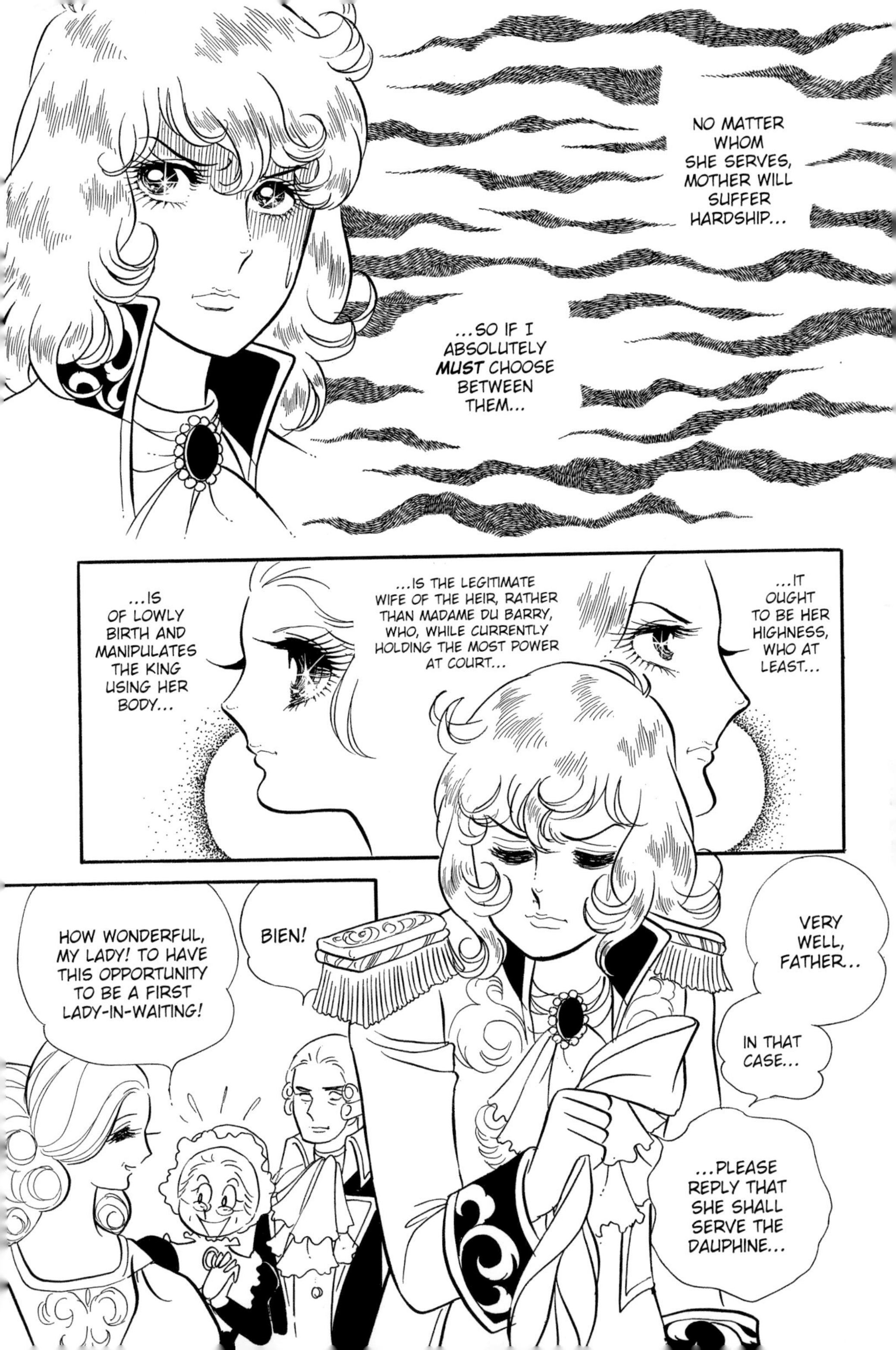
NO MATTER WHOM SHE SERVES, MOTHER WILL SUFFER HARDSHIP...
...SO IF I ABSOLUTELY **MUST** CHOOSE BETWEEN THEM...
...IT OUGHT TO BE HER HIGHNESS, WHO AT LEAST...
...IS THE LEGITIMATE WIFE OF THE HEIR, RATHER THAN MADAME DU BARRY, WHO, WHILE CURRENTLY HOLDING THE MOST POWER AT COURT...
...IS OF LOWLY BIRTH AND MANIPULATES THE KING USING HER BODY...
VERY WELL, FATHER...
IN THAT CASE...
...PLEASE REPLY THAT SHE SHALL SERVE THE DAUPHINE...
BIEN!
HOW WONDERFUL, MY LADY! TO HAVE THIS OPPORTUNITY TO BE A FIRST LADY-IN-WAITING!

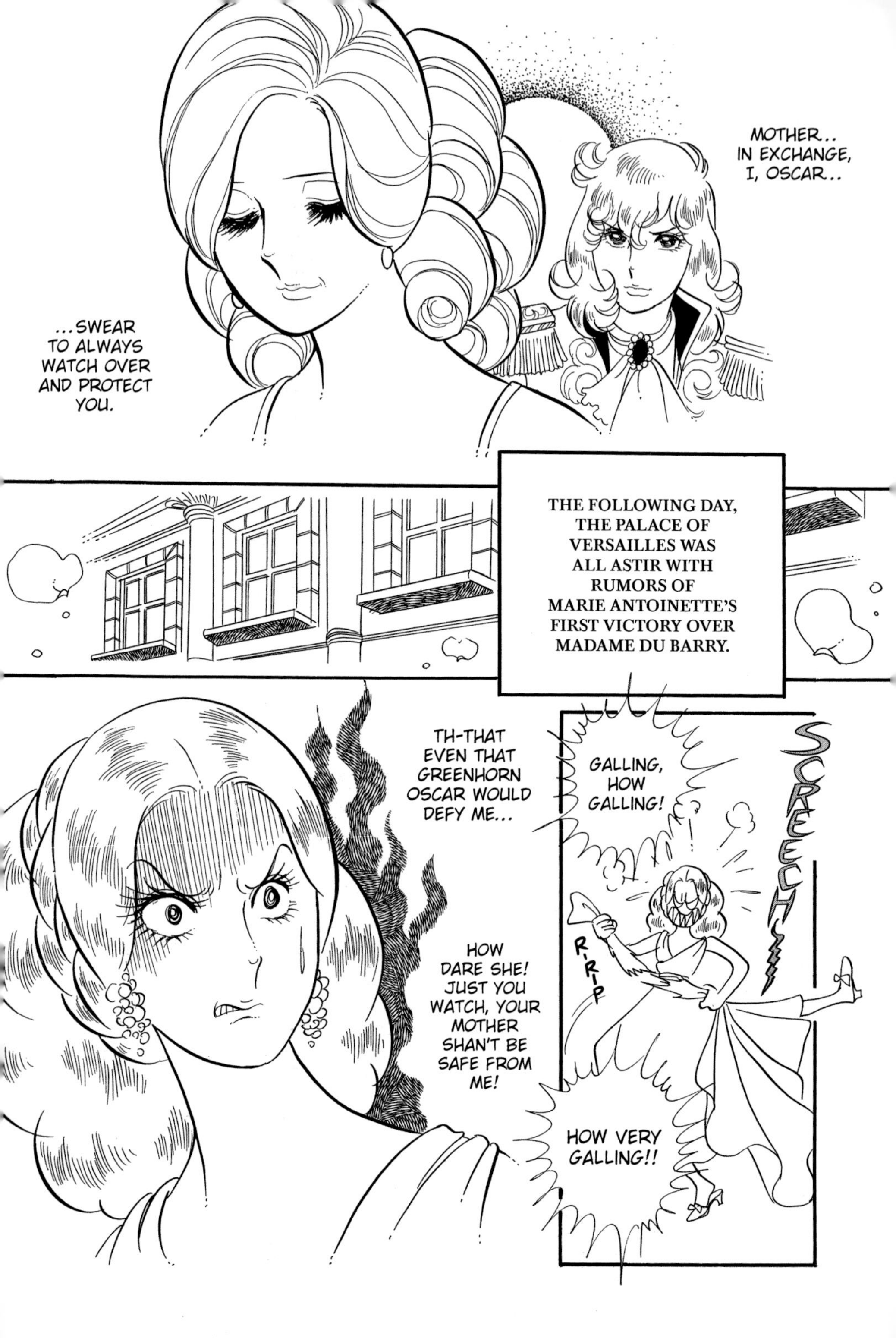
MOTHER.. IN EXCHANGE, I, OSCAR..
...SWEAR TO ALWAYS WATCH OVER AND PROTECT YOU.
THE FOLLOWING DAY, THE PALACE OF VERSAILLES WAS ALL ASTIR WITH RUMORS OF MARIE ANTOINETTE'S FIRST VICTORY OVER MADAME DU BARRY.
SCREECH
GALLING, HOW GALLING!
R-R-IP
HOW VERY GALLING!!
TH-THAT EVEN THAT GREENHORN OSCAR WOULD DEFY ME...
HOW DARE SHE! JUST YOU WATCH, YOUR MOTHER SHAN'T BE SAFE FROM ME!

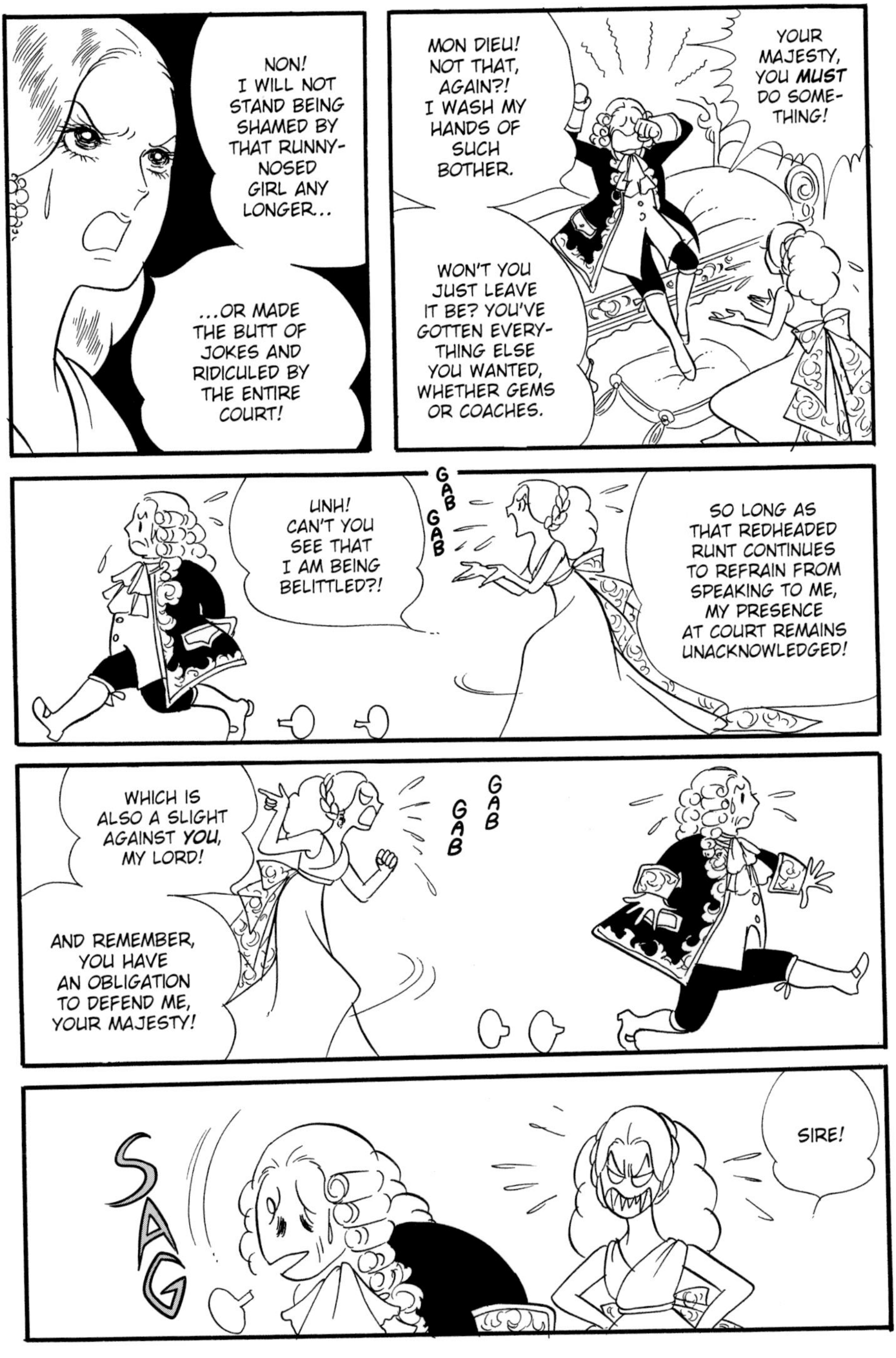
YOUR MAJESTY, YOU MUST DO SOMETHING!
MON DIEU! NOT THAT, AGAIN?! I WASH MY HANDS OF SUCH BOTHER.
WON'T YOU JUST LEAVE IT BE? YOU'VE GOTTEN EVERYTHING ELSE YOU WANTED, WHETHER GEMS OR COACHES.
NON! I WILL NOT STAND BEING SHAMED BY THAT RUNNY-NOSED GIRL ANY LONGER...
...OR MADE THE BUTT OF JOKES AND RIDICULED BY THE ENTIRE COURT!
SO LONG AS THAT REDHEADED RUNT CONTINUES TO REFRAIN FROM SPEAKING TO ME, MY PRESENCE AT COURT REMAINS UNACKNOWLEDGED!
GAB GAB
UNH! CAN'T YOU SEE THAT I AM BEING BELITTLED?!
GAB
GAB
WHICH IS ALSO A SLIGHT AGAINST YOU, MY LORD!
AND REMEMBER, YOU HAVE AN OBLIGATION TO DEFEND ME, YOUR MAJESTY!
SIRE!
SAG

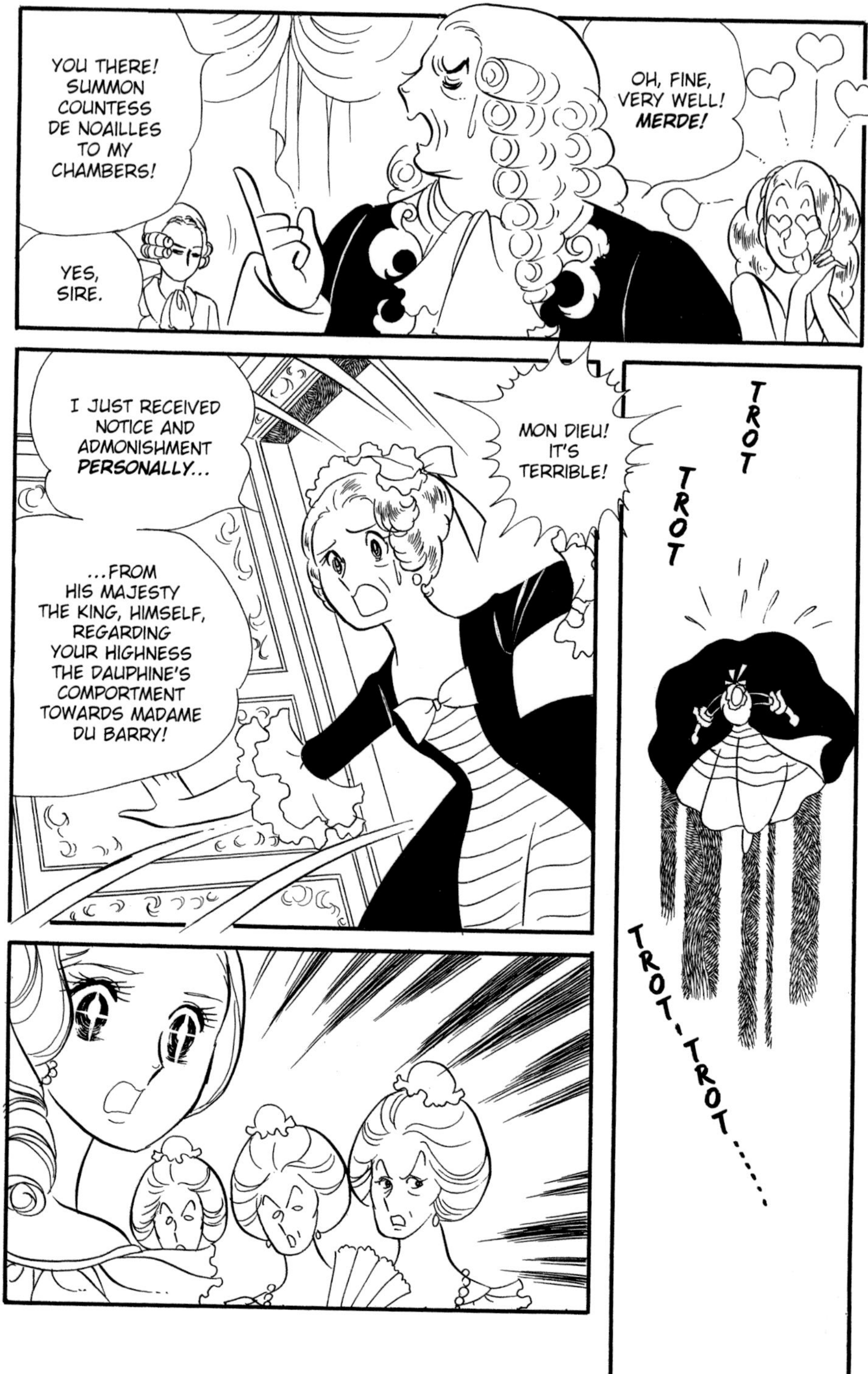
OH, FINE, VERY WELL! MERDE!
YOU THERE! SUMMON COUNTESS DE NOAILLES TO MY CHAMBERS!
YES, SIRE.
TROT
TROT
TROT-TROT-TROT......
MON DIEU! IT'S TERRIBLE!
I JUST RECEIVED NOTICE AND ADMONISHMENT PERSONALLY...
...FROM HIS MAJESTY THE KING, HIMSELF, REGARDING YOUR HIGHNESS THE DAUPHINE'S COMPORTMENT TOWARDS MADAME DU BARRY!

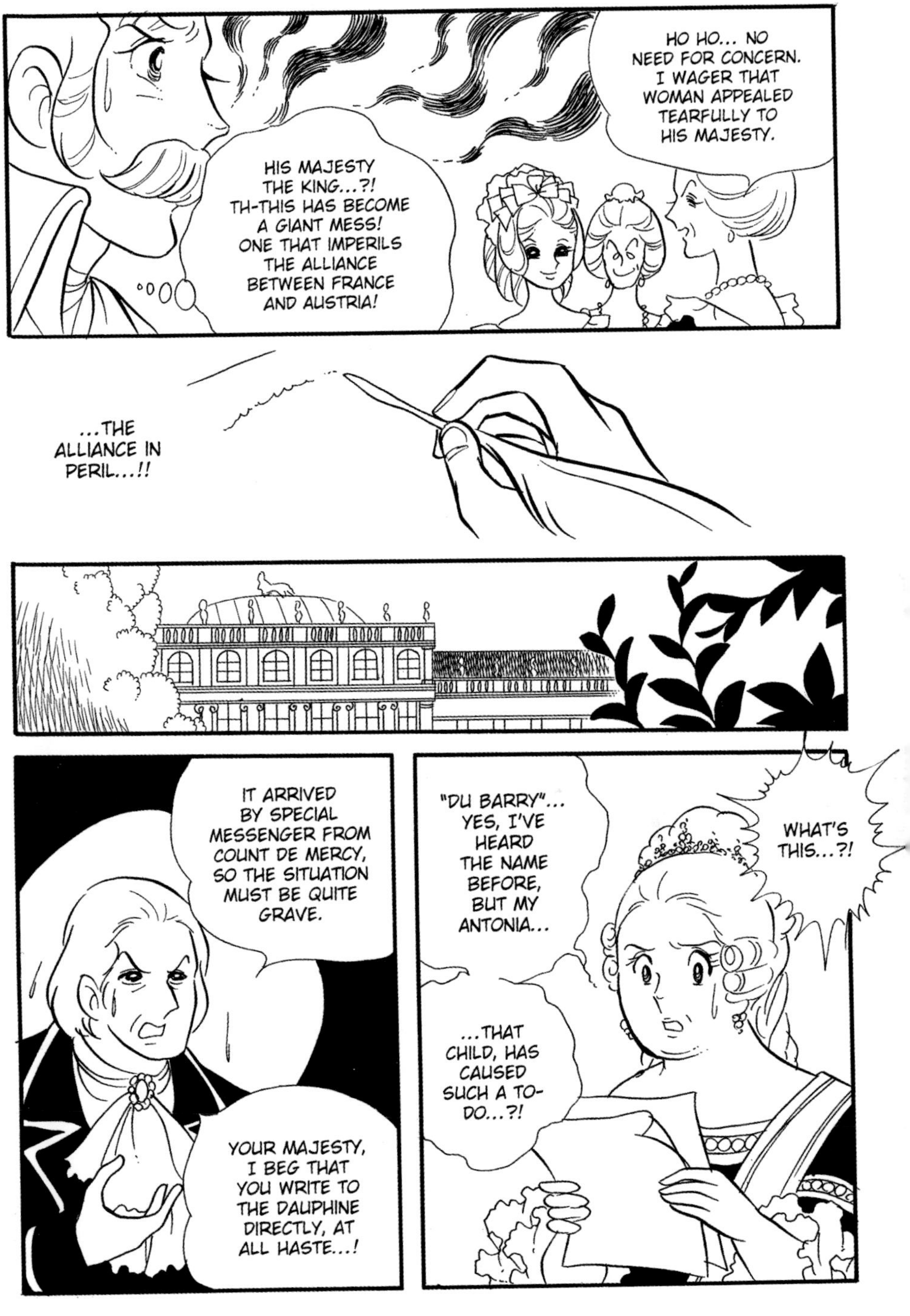
HO HO... NO NEED FOR CONCERN. I WAGER THAT WOMAN APPEALED TEARFULLY TO HIS MAJESTY.
HIS MAJESTY THE KING...?! TH-THIS HAS BECOME A GIANT MESS! ONE THAT IMPERILS THE ALLIANCE BETWEEN FRANCE AND AUSTRIA!
...THE ALLIANCE IN PERIL...!!
WHAT'S THIS...?!
"DU BARRY"... YES, I'VE HEARD THE NAME BEFORE, BUT MY ANTONIA...
...THAT CHILD, HAS CAUSED SUCH A TO-DO...?!
IT ARRIVED BY SPECIAL MESSENGER FROM COUNT DE MERCY, SO THE SITUATION MUST BE QUITE GRAVE.
YOUR MAJESTY, I BEG THAT YOU WRITE TO THE DAUPHINE DIRECTLY, AT ALL HASTE...!

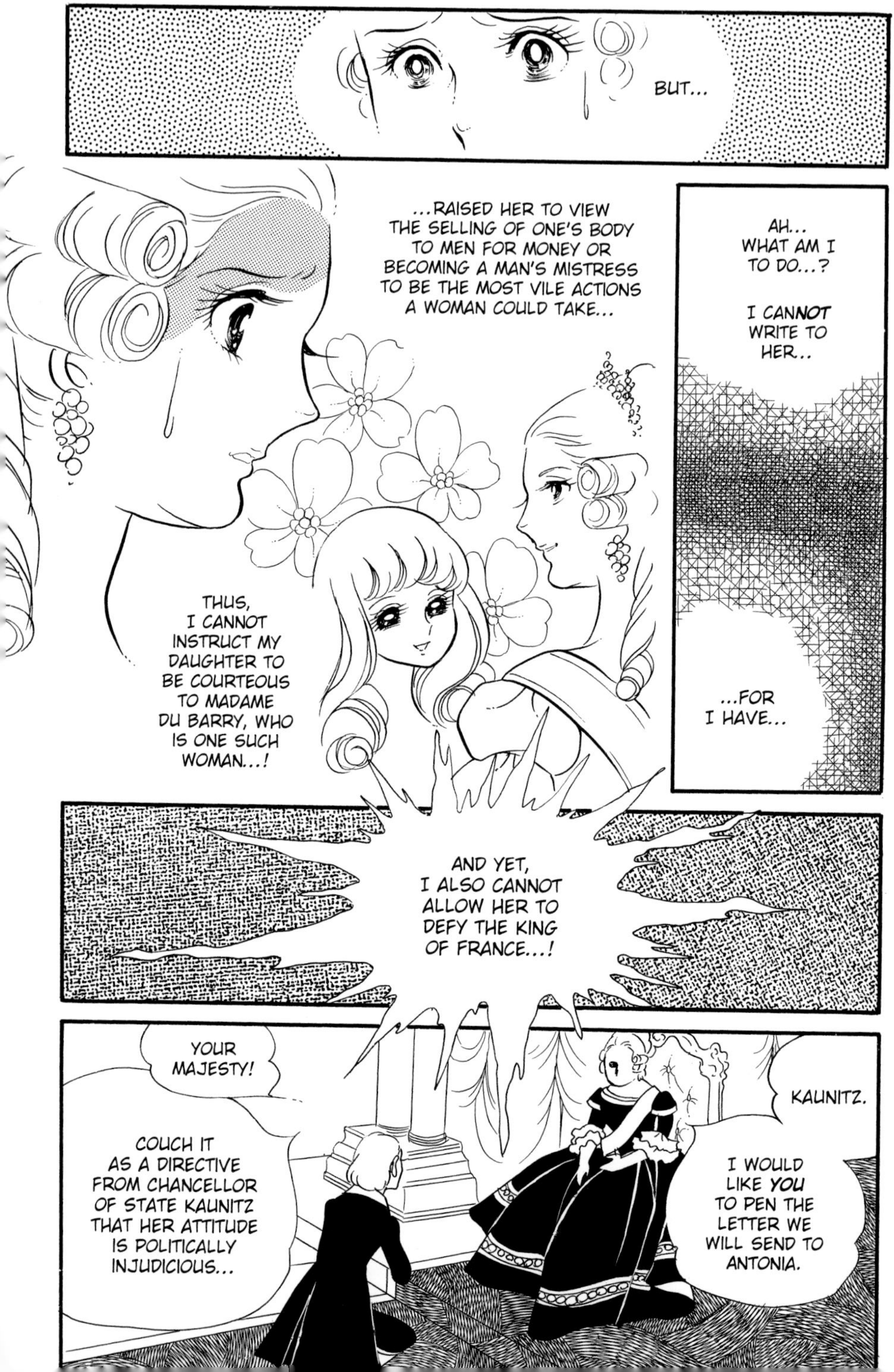
BUT...
AH... WHAT AM I TO DO...?
I CANNOT WRITE TO HER...
...FOR I HAVE...
...RAISED HER TO VIEW THE SELLING OF ONE'S BODY TO MEN FOR MONEY OR BECOMING A MAN'S MISTRESS TO BE THE MOST VILE ACTIONS A WOMAN COULD TAKE...
THUS, I CANNOT INSTRUCT MY DAUGHTER TO BE COURTEOUS TO MADAME DU BARRY, WHO IS ONE SUCH WOMAN...!
AND YET, I ALSO CANNOT ALLOW HER TO DEFY THE KING OF FRANCE...!
KAUNITZ.
I WOULD LIKE YOU TO PEN THE LETTER WE WILL SEND TO ANTONIA.
YOUR MAJESTY!
COUCH IT AS A DIRECTIVE FROM CHANCELLOR OF STATE KAUNITZ THAT HER ATTITUDE IS POLITICALLY INJUDICIOUS...

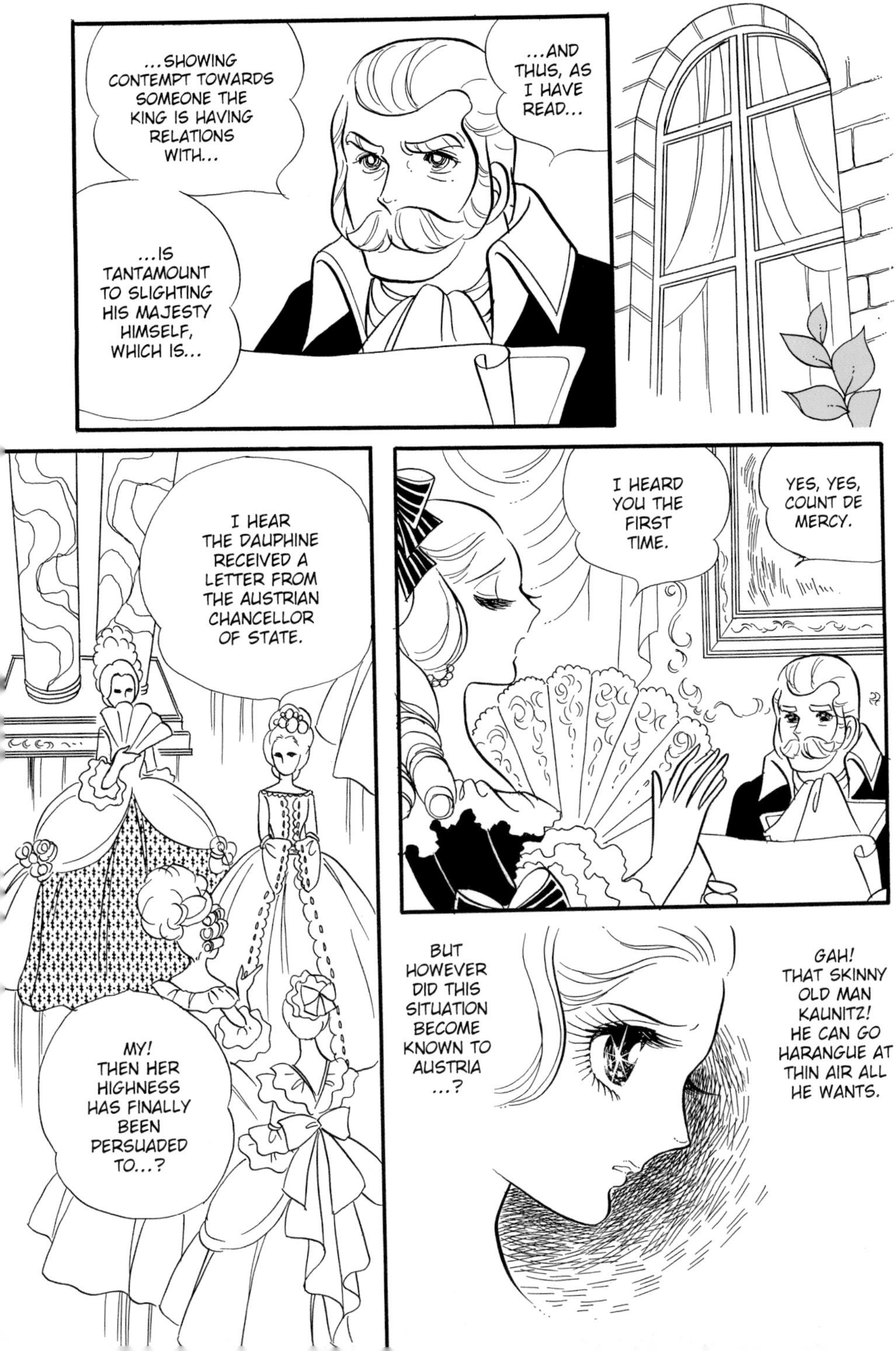
...AND THUS, AS I HAVE READ...
...SHOWING CONTEMPT TOWARDS SOMEONE THE KING IS HAVING RELATIONS WITH...
...IS TANTAMOUNT TO SLIGHTING HIS MAJESTY HIMSELF, WHICH IS...
YES, YES, COUNT DE MERCY.
I HEARD YOU THE FIRST TIME.
GAH! THAT SKINNY OLD MAN KAUNITZ! HE CAN GO HARANGUE AT THIN AIR ALL HE WANTS.
BUT HOWEVER DID THIS SITUATION BECOME KNOWN TO AUSTRIA ...?
I HEAR THE DAUPHINE RECEIVED A LETTER FROM THE AUSTRIAN CHANCELLOR OF STATE.
MY! THEN HER HIGHNESS HAS FINALLY BEEN PERSUADED TO...?

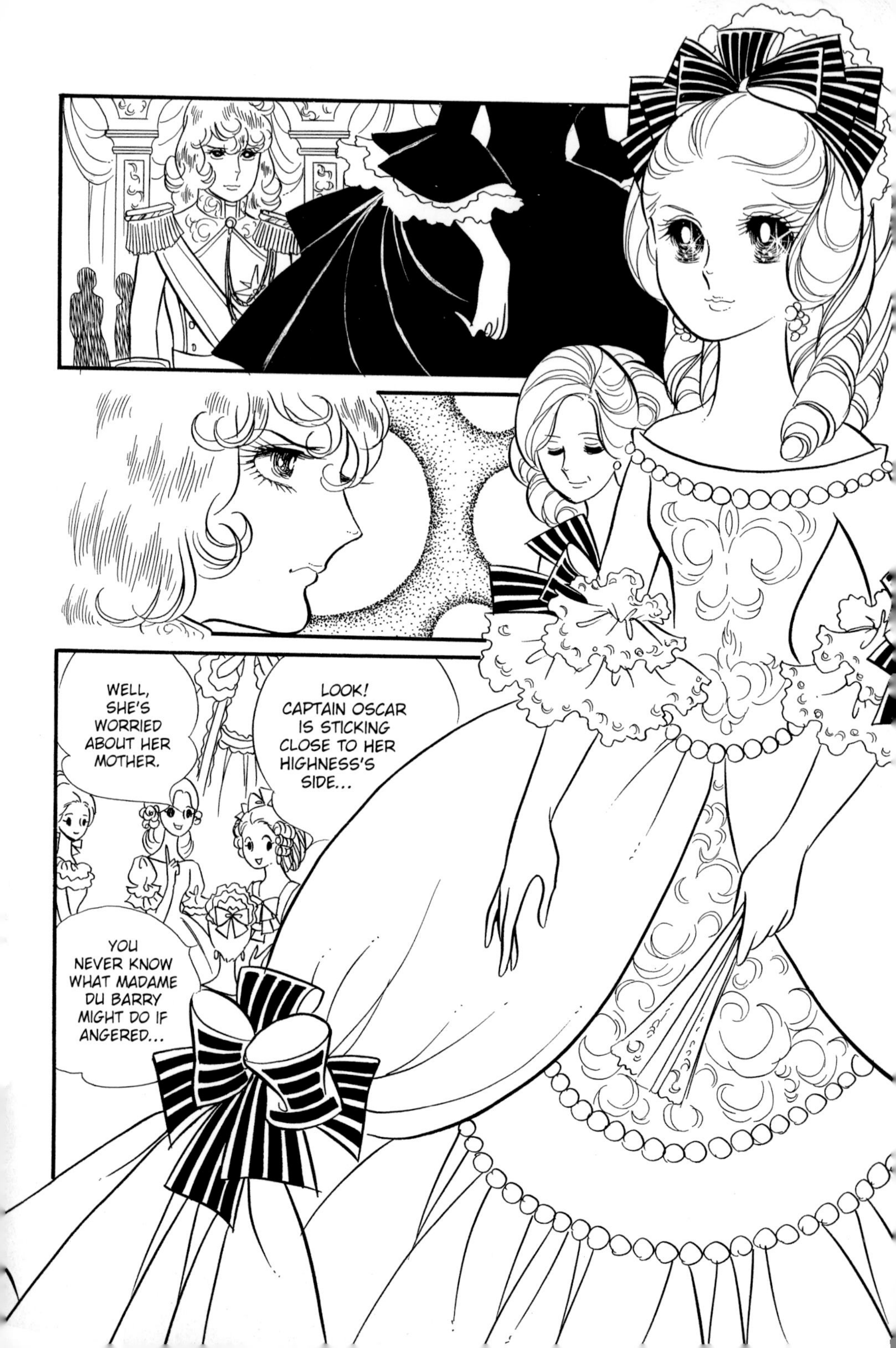
LOOK! CAPTAIN OSCAR IS STICKING CLOSE TO HER HIGHNESS'S SIDE...
WELL, SHE'S WORRIED ABOUT HER MOTHER.
YOU NEVER KNOW WHAT MADAME DU BARRY MIGHT DO IF ANGERED...

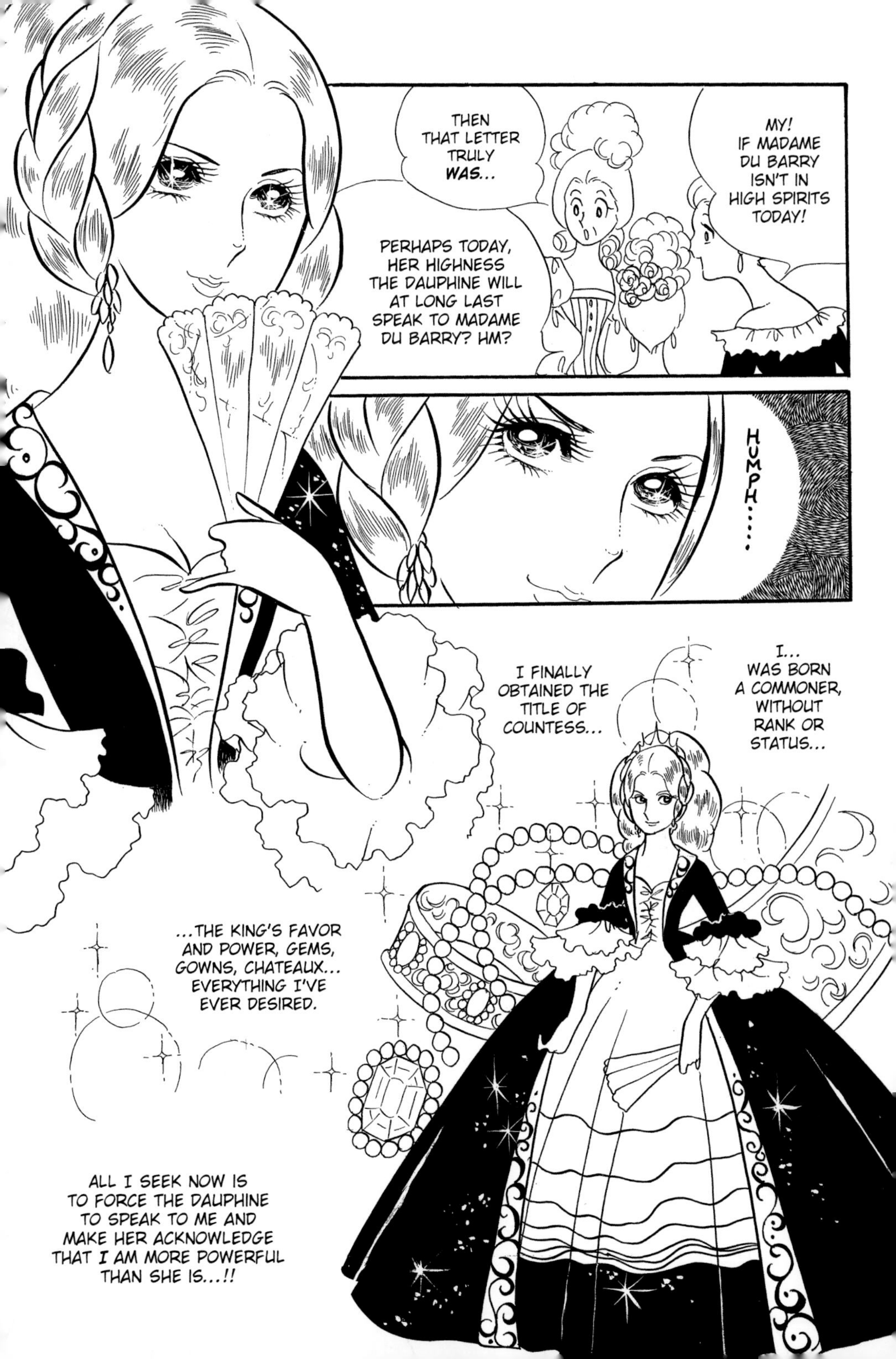
MY! IF MADAME DU BARRY ISN'T IN HIGH SPIRITS TODAY!
THEN THAT LETTER TRULY WAS...
PERHAPS TODAY, HER HIGHNESS THE DAUPHINE WILL AT LONG LAST SPEAK TO MADAME DU BARRY? HM?
HUMPH....
I... WAS BORN A COMMONER, WITHOUT RANK OR STATUS...
I FINALLY OBTAINED THE TITLE OF COUNTESS...
...THE KING'S FAVOR AND POWER, GEMS, GOWNS, CHATEAUX... EVERYTHING I'VE EVER DESIRED.
ALL I SEEK NOW IS TO FORCE THE DAUPHINE TO SPEAK TO ME AND MAKE HER ACKNOWLEDGE THAT I AM MORE POWERFUL THAN SHE IS...!!

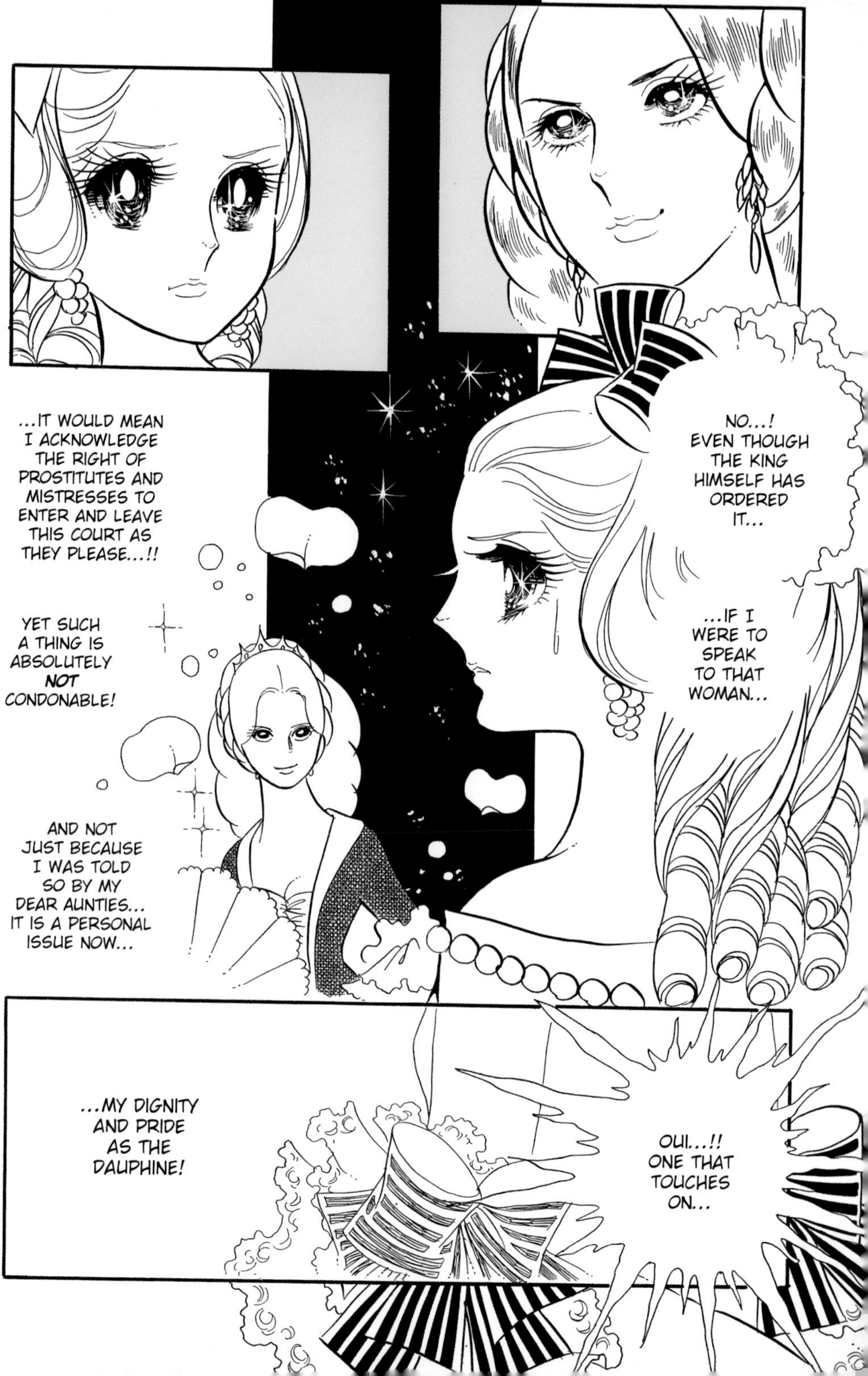
NO...! EVEN THOUGH THE KING HIMSELF HAS ORDERED IT...
...IF I WERE TO SPEAK TO THAT WOMAN...
...IT WOULD MEAN I ACKNOWLEDGE THE RIGHT OF PROSTITUTES AND MISTRESSES TO ENTER AND LEAVE THIS COURT AS THEY PLEASE...!!
YET SUCH A THING IS ABSOLUTELY **NOT** CONDONABLE!
AND NOT JUST BECAUSE I WAS TOLD SO BY MY DEAR AUNTIES... IT IS A PERSONAL ISSUE NOW...
OUI...!! ONE THAT TOUCHES ON...
...MY DIGNITY AND PRIDE AS THE DAUPHINE!

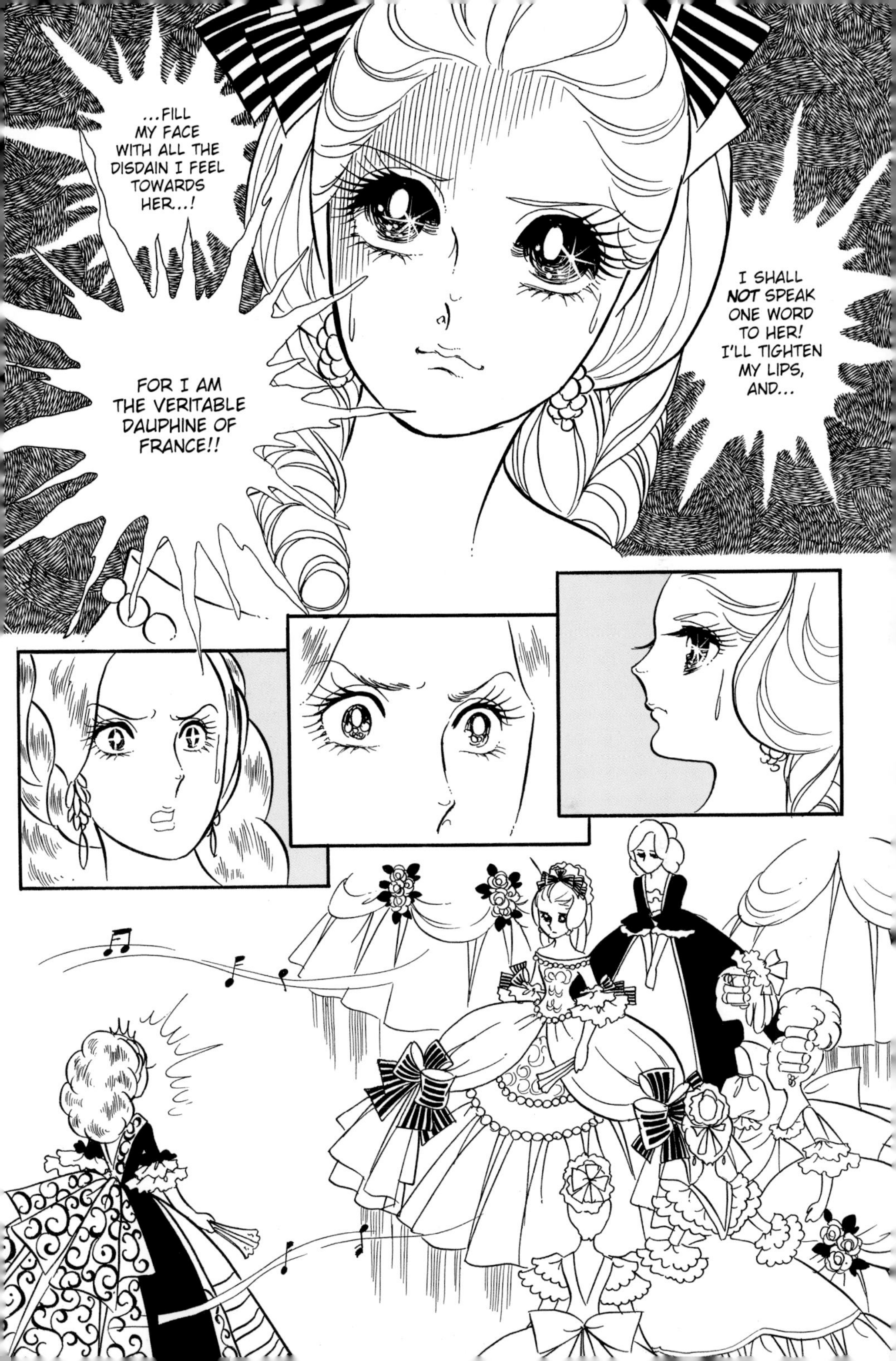
I SHALL **NOT** SPEAK ONE WORD TO HER! I'LL TIGHTEN MY LIPS, AND...
...FILL MY FACE WITH ALL THE DISDAIN I FEEL TOWARDS HER...!
FOR I AM THE VERITABLE DAUPHINE OF FRANCE!!

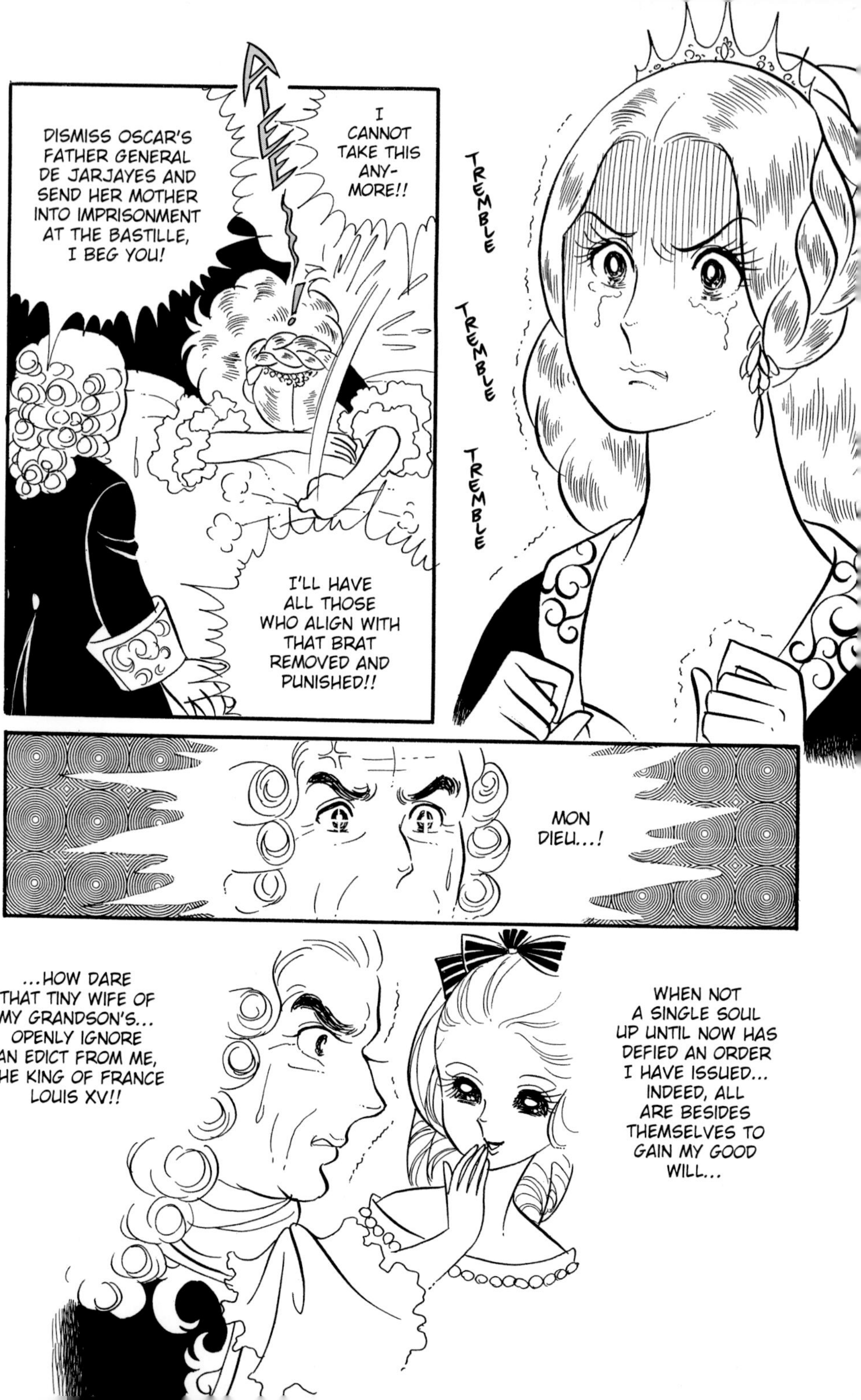
TREMBLE
TREMBLE
TREMBLE
I CANNOT TAKE THIS ANYMORE!!
AIEE!
DISMISS OSCAR'S FATHER GENERAL DE JARJAYES AND SEND HER MOTHER INTO IMPRISONMENT AT THE BASTILLE, I BEG YOU!
I'LL HAVE ALL THOSE WHO ALIGN WITH THAT BRAT REMOVED AND PUNISHED!!
MON DIEU...!
WHEN NOT A SINGLE SOUL UP UNTIL NOW HAS DEFIED AN ORDER I HAVE ISSUED... INDEED, ALL ARE BESIDES THEMSELVES TO GAIN MY GOOD WILL...
...HOW DARE THAT TINY WIFE OF MY GRANDSON'S... OPENLY IGNORE AN EDICT FROM ME, THE KING OF FRANCE LOUIS XV!!

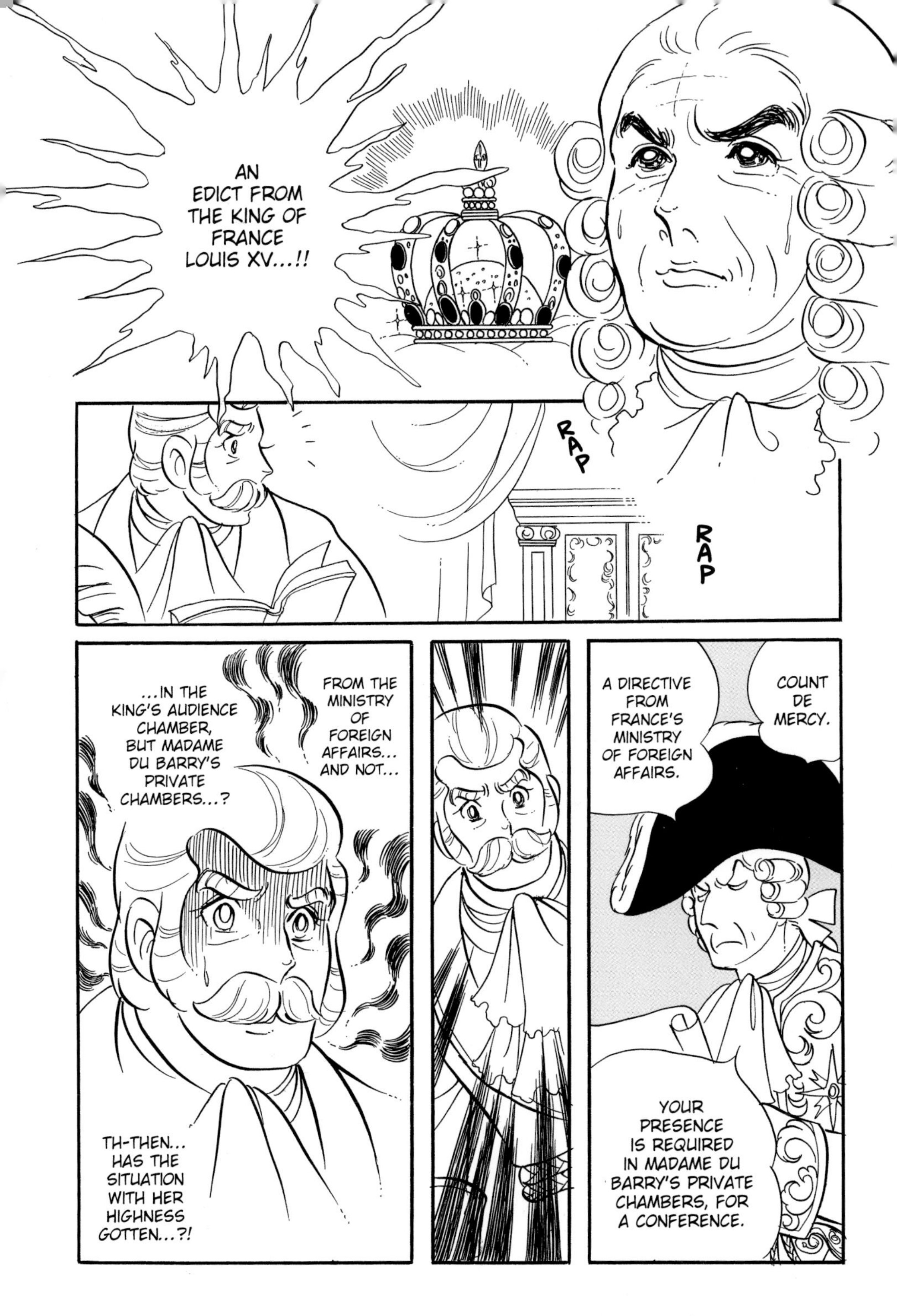
AN EDICT FROM THE KING OF FRANCE LOUIS XV...!!
RAP
RAP
COUNT DE MERCY.
A DIRECTIVE FROM FRANCE'S MINISTRY OF FOREIGN AFFAIRS.
YOUR PRESENCE IS REQUIRED IN MADAME DU BARRY'S PRIVATE CHAMBERS, FOR A CONFERENCE.
FROM THE MINISTRY OF FOREIGN AFFAIRS... AND NOT...
...IN THE KING'S AUDIENCE CHAMBER, BUT MADAME DU BARRY'S PRIVATE CHAMBERS...?
TH-THEN... HAS THE SITUATION WITH HER HIGHNESS GOTTEN...?!

THE ROSE OF VERSAILLES

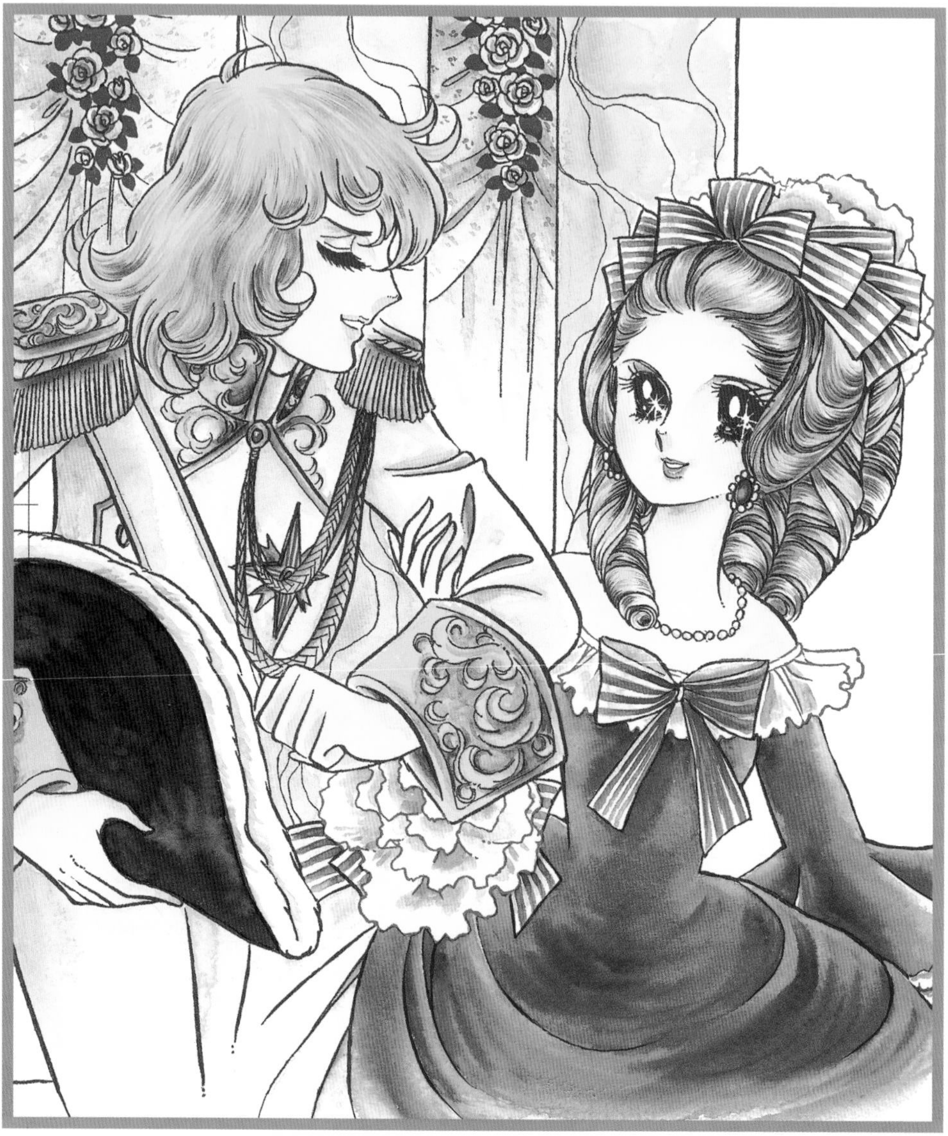

1972 - WEEKLY MARGARET MAGAZINE ISSUE 26 COVER PAGE (SPECIAL COLORIZED VERSION)

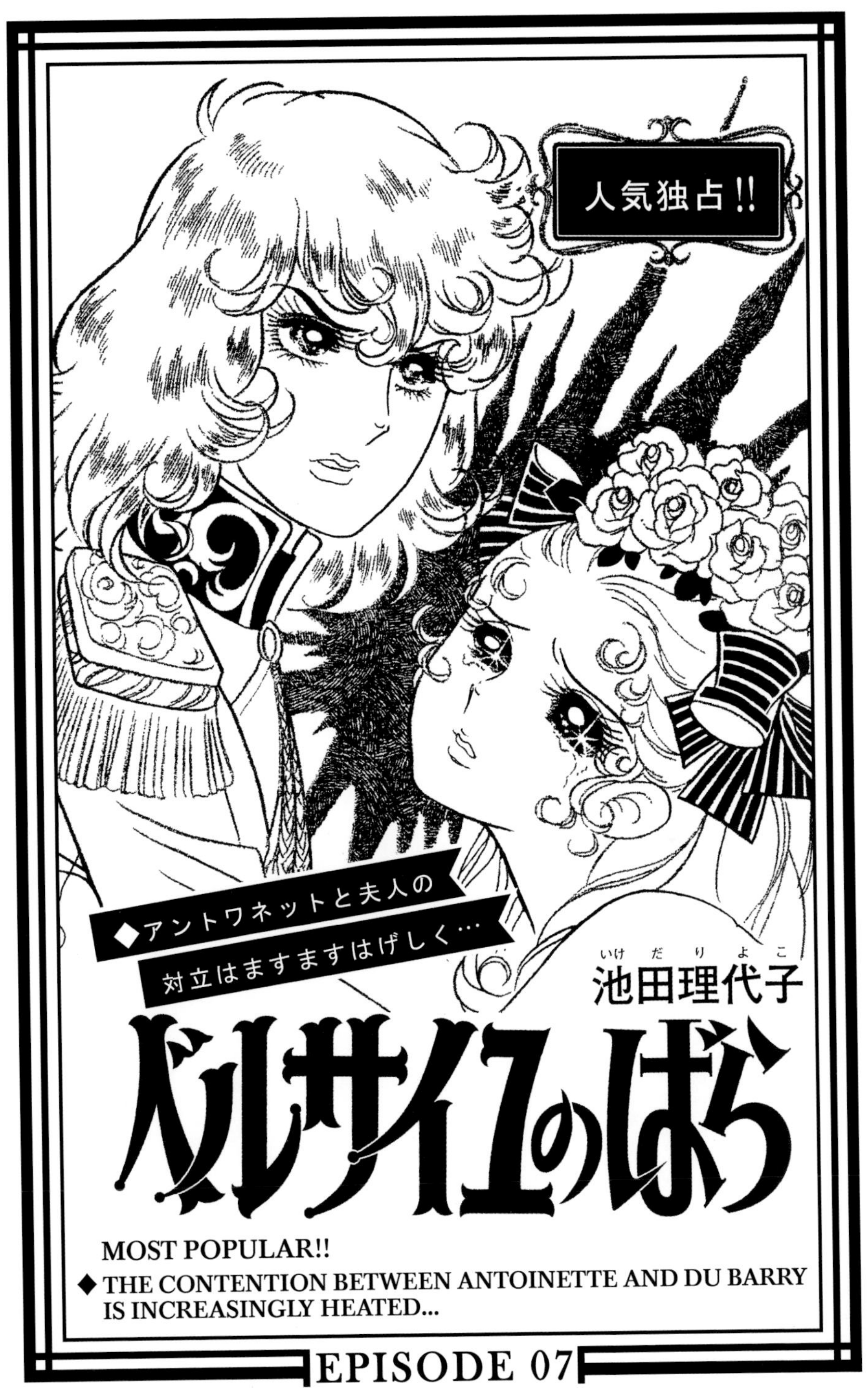
人気独占!!
◆アントワネットと夫人の
対立はますますはげしく…
いけだりよこ
池田理代子
ベルサイユのばら

MOST POPULAR!!

◆ THE CONTENTION BETWEEN ANTOINETTE AND DU BARRY IS INCREASINGLY HEATED...

EPISODE 07

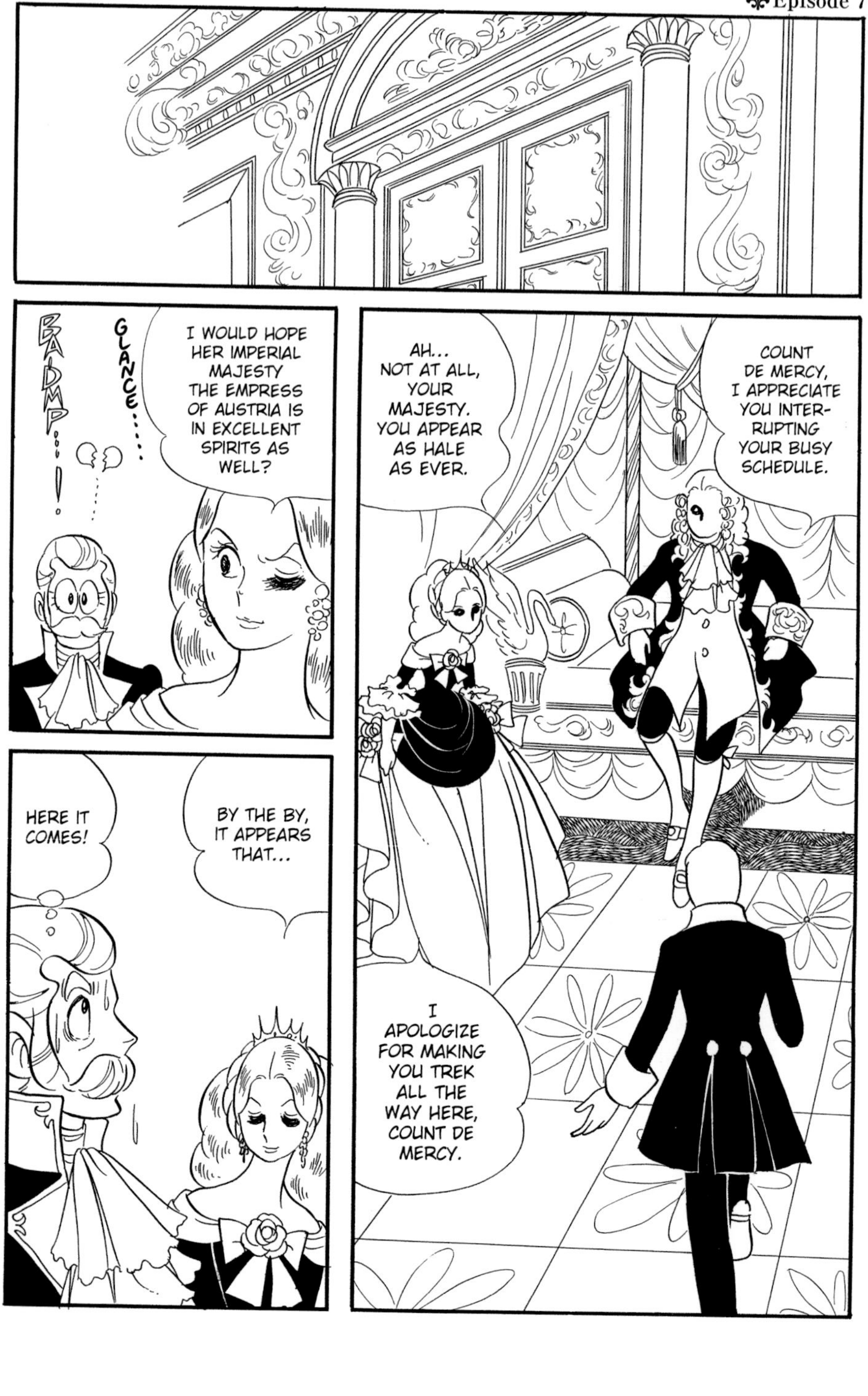
COUNT DE MERCY, I APPRECIATE YOU INTER-RUPTING YOUR BUSY SCHEDULE.
AH... NOT AT ALL, YOUR MAJESTY. YOU APPEAR AS HALE AS EVER.
I APOLOGIZE FOR MAKING YOU TREK ALL THE WAY HERE, COUNT DE MERCY.
I WOULD HOPE HER IMPERIAL MAJESTY THE EMPRESS OF AUSTRIA IS IN EXCELLENT SPIRITS AS WELL?
GLANCE.....
BADMP...!
BY THE BY, IT APPEARS THAT...
HERE IT COMES!

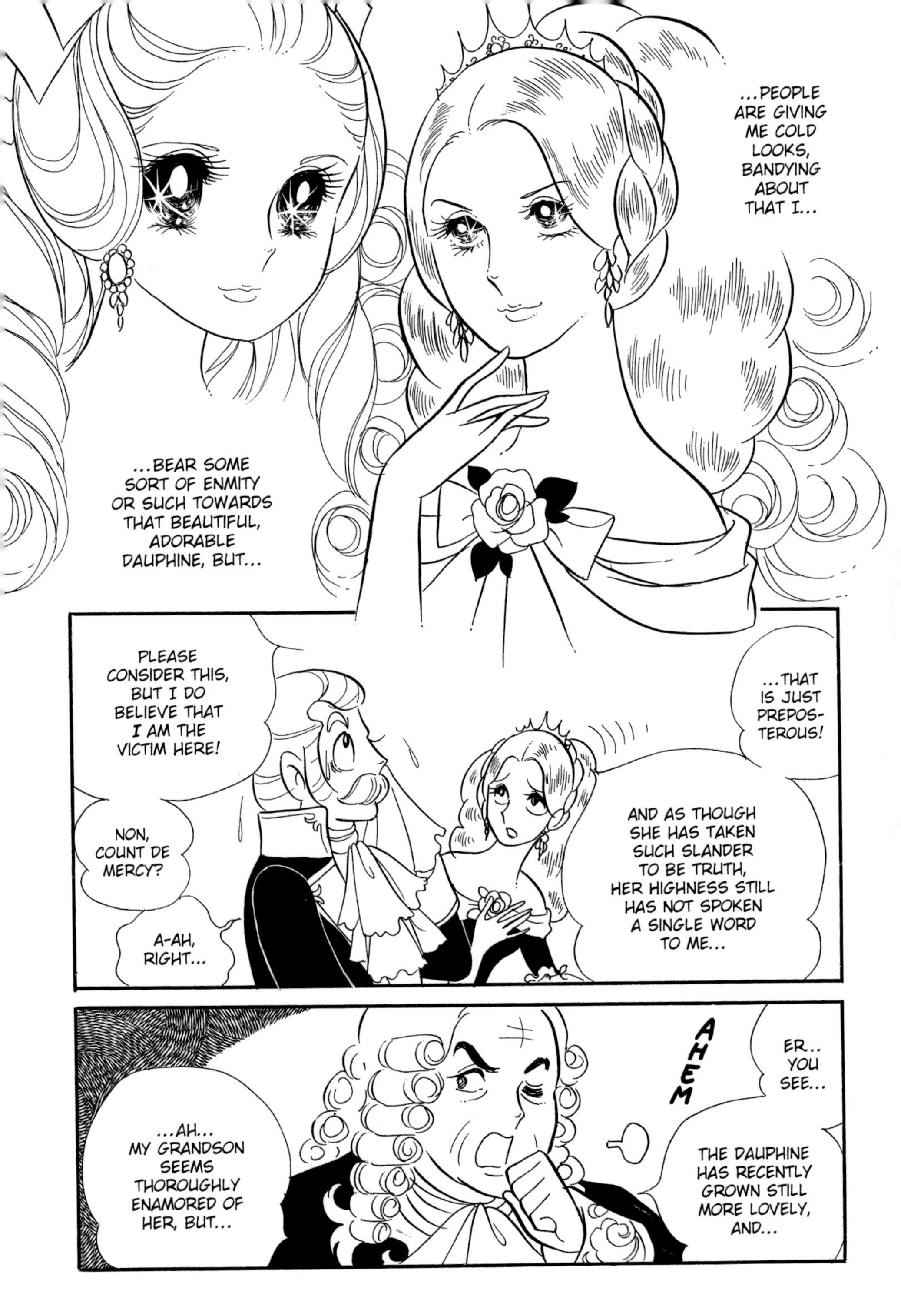
...PEOPLE ARE GIVING ME COLD LOOKS, BANDYING ABOUT THAT I...
...BEAR SOME SORT OF ENMITY OR SUCH TOWARDS THAT BEAUTIFUL, ADORABLE DAUPHINE, BUT...
...THAT IS JUST PREPOSTEROUS!
AND AS THOUGH SHE HAS TAKEN SUCH SLANDER TO BE TRUTH, HER HIGHNESS STILL HAS NOT SPOKEN A SINGLE WORD TO ME...
PLEASE CONSIDER THIS, BUT I DO BELIEVE THAT I AM THE VICTIM HERE!
NON, COUNT DE MERCY?
A-AH, RIGHT...
ER... YOU SEE...
AHEM
THE DAUPHINE HAS RECENTLY GROWN STILL MORE LOVELY, AND...
...AH... MY GRANDSON SEEMS THOROUGHLY ENAMORED OF HER, BUT...

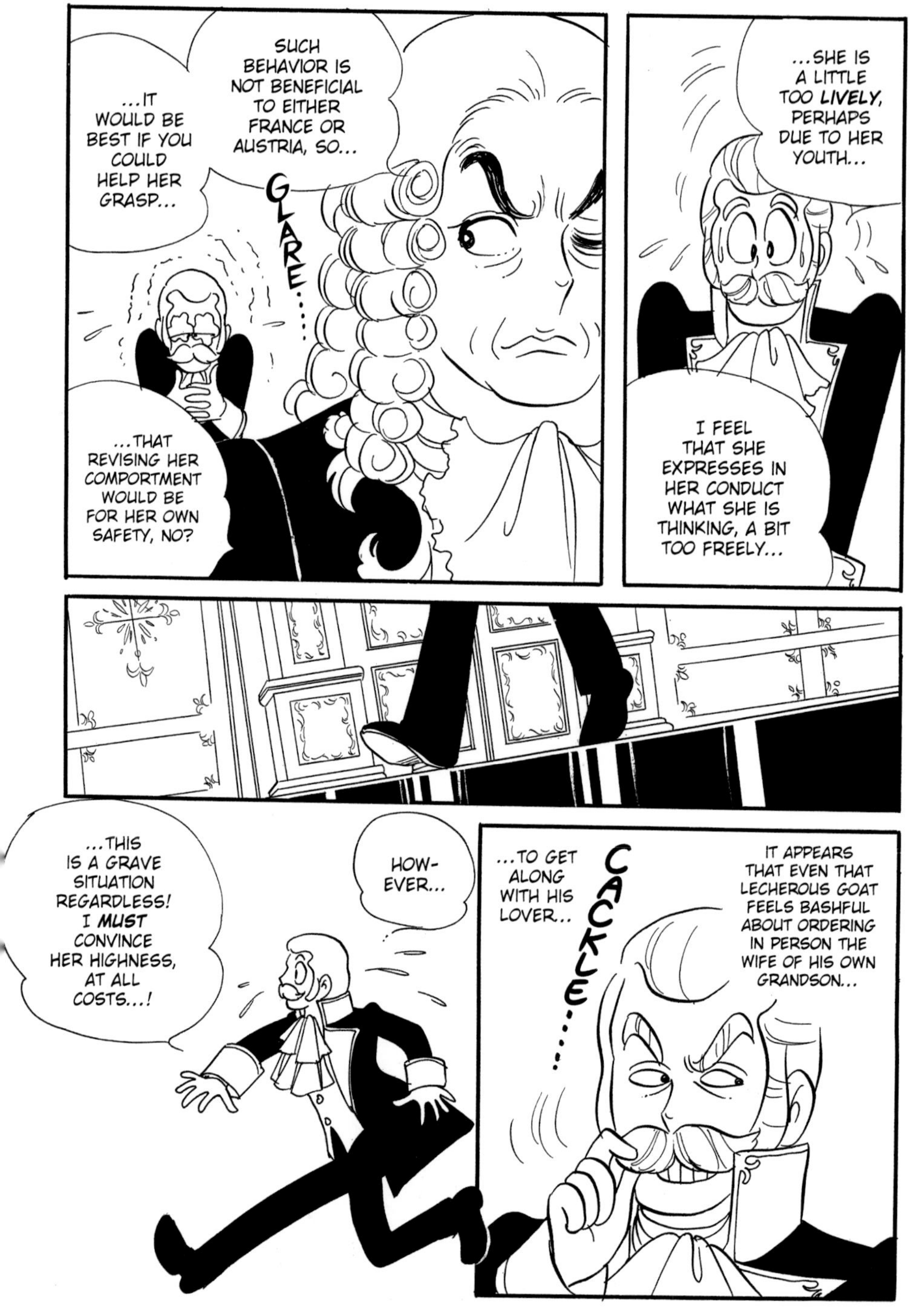
...SHE IS A LITTLE TOO LIVELY, PERHAPS DUE TO HER YOUTH...
I FEEL THAT SHE EXPRESSES IN HER CONDUCT WHAT SHE IS THINKING, A BIT TOO FREELY...
SUCH BEHAVIOR IS NOT BENEFICIAL TO EITHER FRANCE OR AUSTRIA, SO...
...IT WOULD BE BEST IF YOU COULD HELP HER GRASP...
GLARE...
...THAT REVISING HER COMPORTMENT WOULD BE FOR HER OWN SAFETY, NO?
IT APPEARS THAT EVEN THAT LECHEROUS GOAT FEELS BASHFUL ABOUT ORDERING IN PERSON THE WIFE OF HIS OWN GRANDSON...
CACKLE...
...TO GET ALONG WITH HIS LOVER...
HOW-EVER...
...THIS IS A GRAVE SITUATION REGARDLESS! I MUST CONVINCE HER HIGHNESS, AT ALL COSTS...!

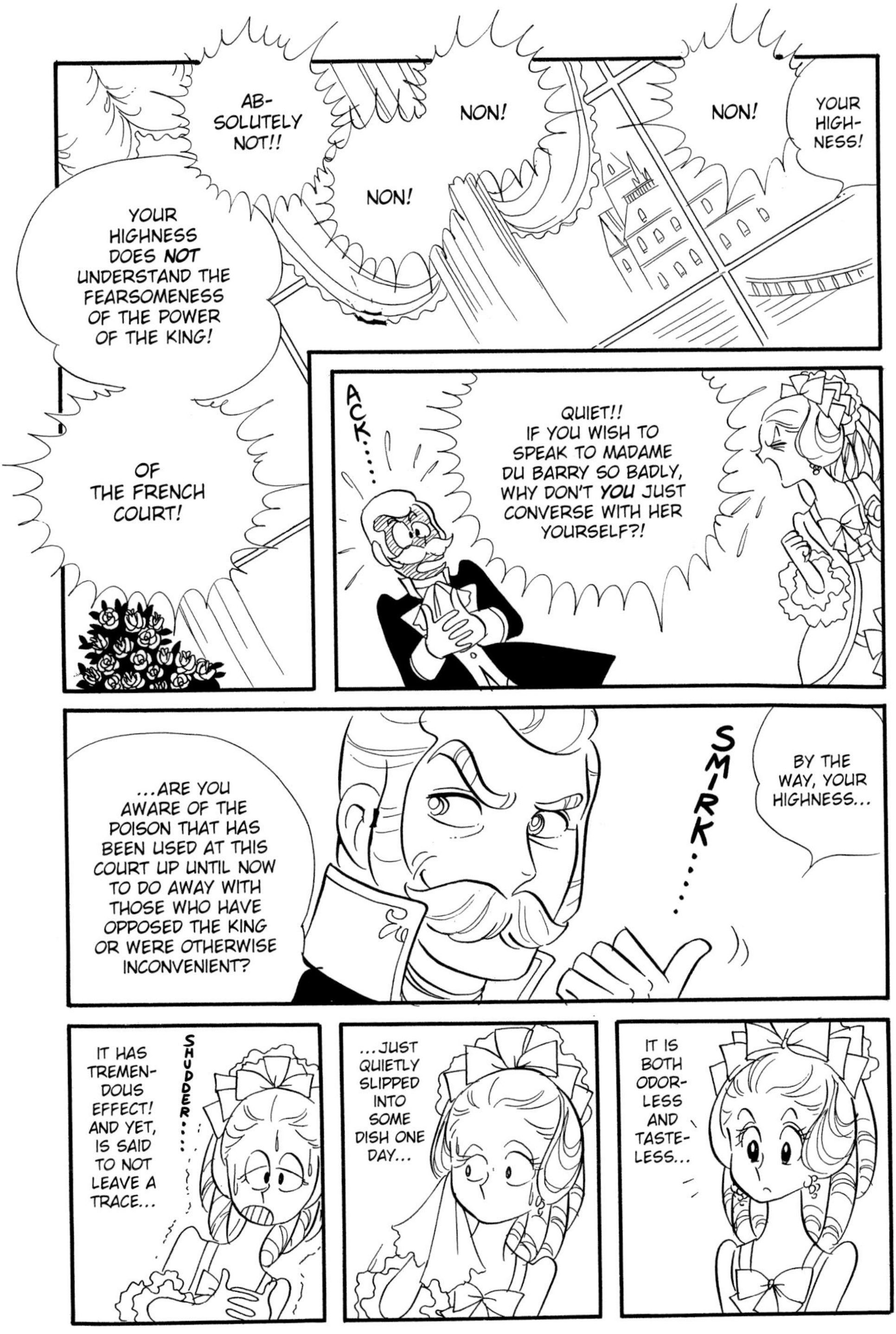
YOUR HIGH-NESS!
NON!
NON!
NON!
AB-SOLUTELY NOT!!
YOUR HIGHNESS DOES NOT UNDERSTAND THE FEARSOMENESS OF THE POWER OF THE KING!
OF THE FRENCH COURT!
QUIET!! IF YOU WISH TO SPEAK TO MADAME DU BARRY SO BADLY, WHY DON'T YOU JUST CONVERSE WITH HER YOURSELF?!
ACK....
BY THE WAY, YOUR HIGHNESS...
SMIRK...
...ARE YOU AWARE OF THE POISON THAT HAS BEEN USED AT THIS COURT UP UNTIL NOW TO DO AWAY WITH THOSE WHO HAVE OPPOSED THE KING OR WERE OTHERWISE INCONVENIENT?
IT IS BOTH ODOR-LESS AND TASTE-LESS...
...JUST QUIETLY SLIPPED INTO SOME DISH ONE DAY...
IT HAS TREMEN-DOUS EFFECT! AND YET, IS SAID TO NOT LEAVE A TRACE...
SHUDDER...

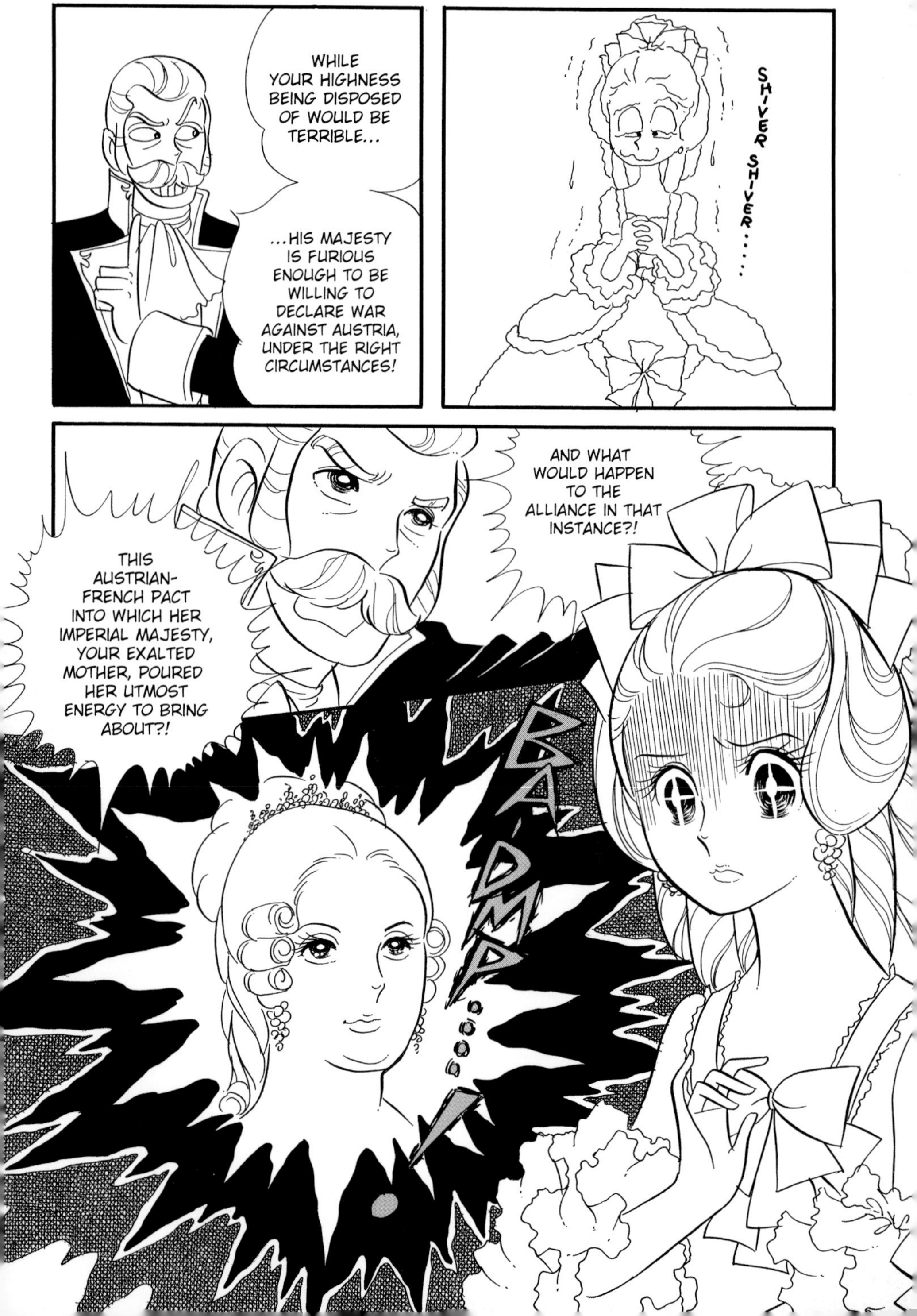
SHIVER SHIVER.....
WHILE YOUR HIGHNESS BEING DISPOSED OF WOULD BE TERRIBLE...
...HIS MAJESTY IS FURIOUS ENOUGH TO BE WILLING TO DECLARE WAR AGAINST AUSTRIA, UNDER THE RIGHT CIRCUMSTANCES!
AND WHAT WOULD HAPPEN TO THE ALLIANCE IN THAT INSTANCE?!
THIS AUSTRIAN-FRENCH PACT INTO WHICH HER IMPERIAL MAJESTY, YOUR EXALTED MOTHER, POURED HER UTMOST ENERGY TO BRING ABOUT?!
BA-DMP....

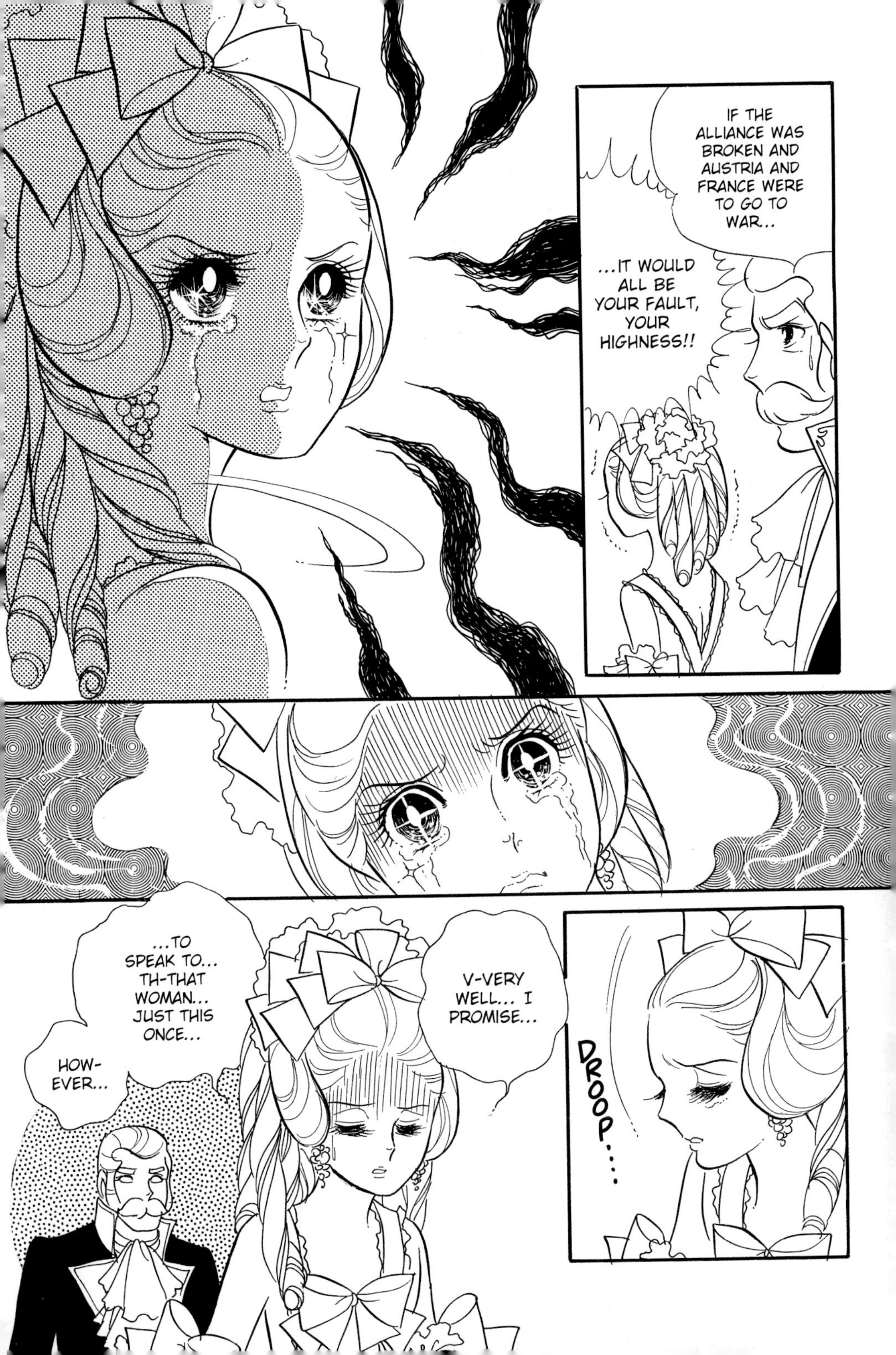
IF THE ALLIANCE WAS BROKEN AND AUSTRIA AND FRANCE WERE TO GO TO WAR...
...IT WOULD ALL BE YOUR FAULT, YOUR HIGHNESS!!
DROOP....
V-VERY WELL... I PROMISE...
...TO SPEAK TO... TH-THAT WOMAN... JUST THIS ONCE...
HOW-EVER...

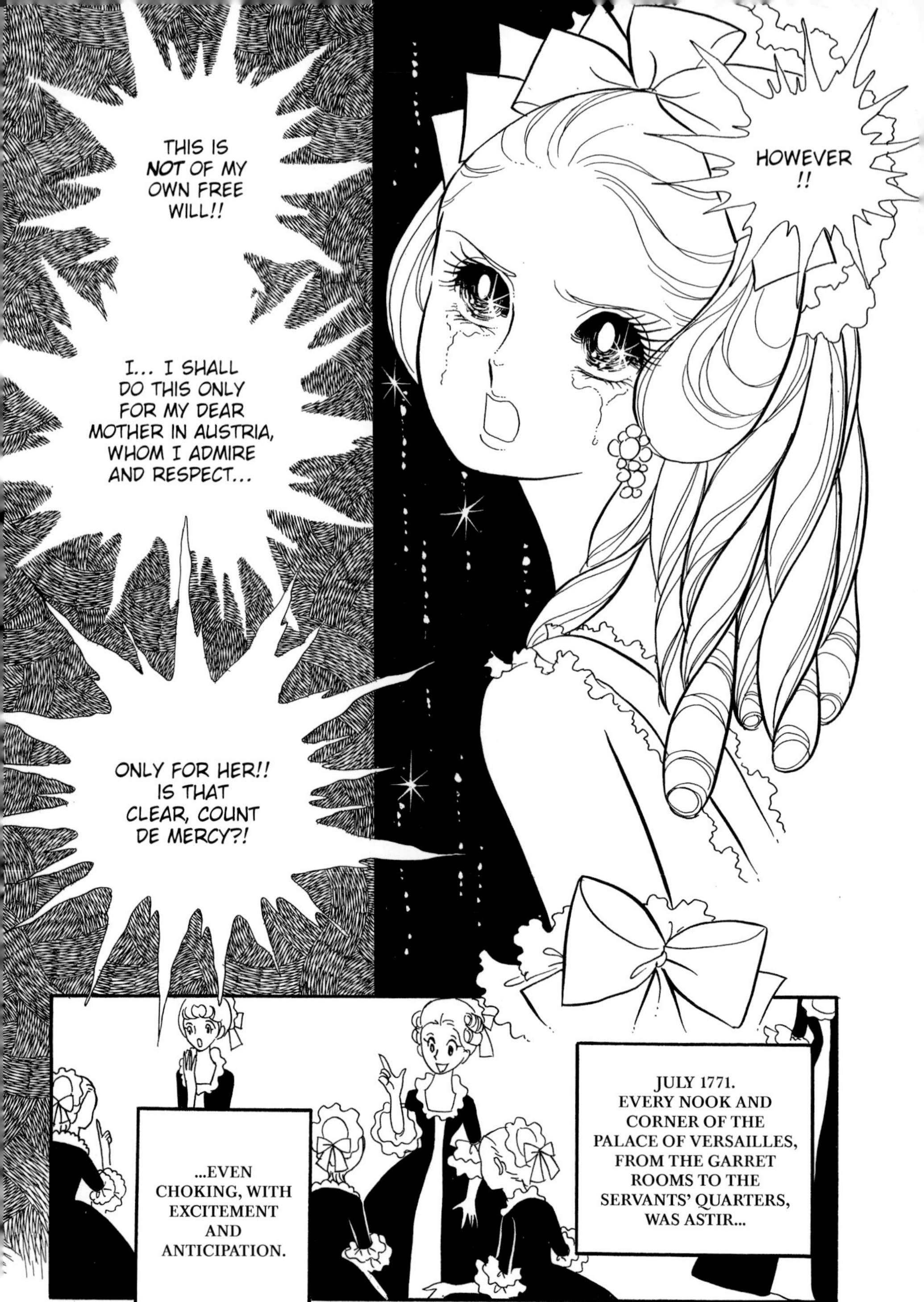
HOWEVER !!
THIS IS NOT OF MY OWN FREE WILL!!
I... I SHALL DO THIS ONLY FOR MY DEAR MOTHER IN AUSTRIA, WHOM I ADMIRE AND RESPECT...
ONLY FOR HER!! IS THAT CLEAR, COUNT DE MERCY?!
JULY 1771. EVERY NOOK AND CORNER OF THE PALACE OF VERSAILLES, FROM THE GARRET ROOMS TO THE SERVANTS' QUARTERS, WAS ASTIR...
...EVEN CHOKING, WITH EXCITEMENT AND ANTICIPATION.

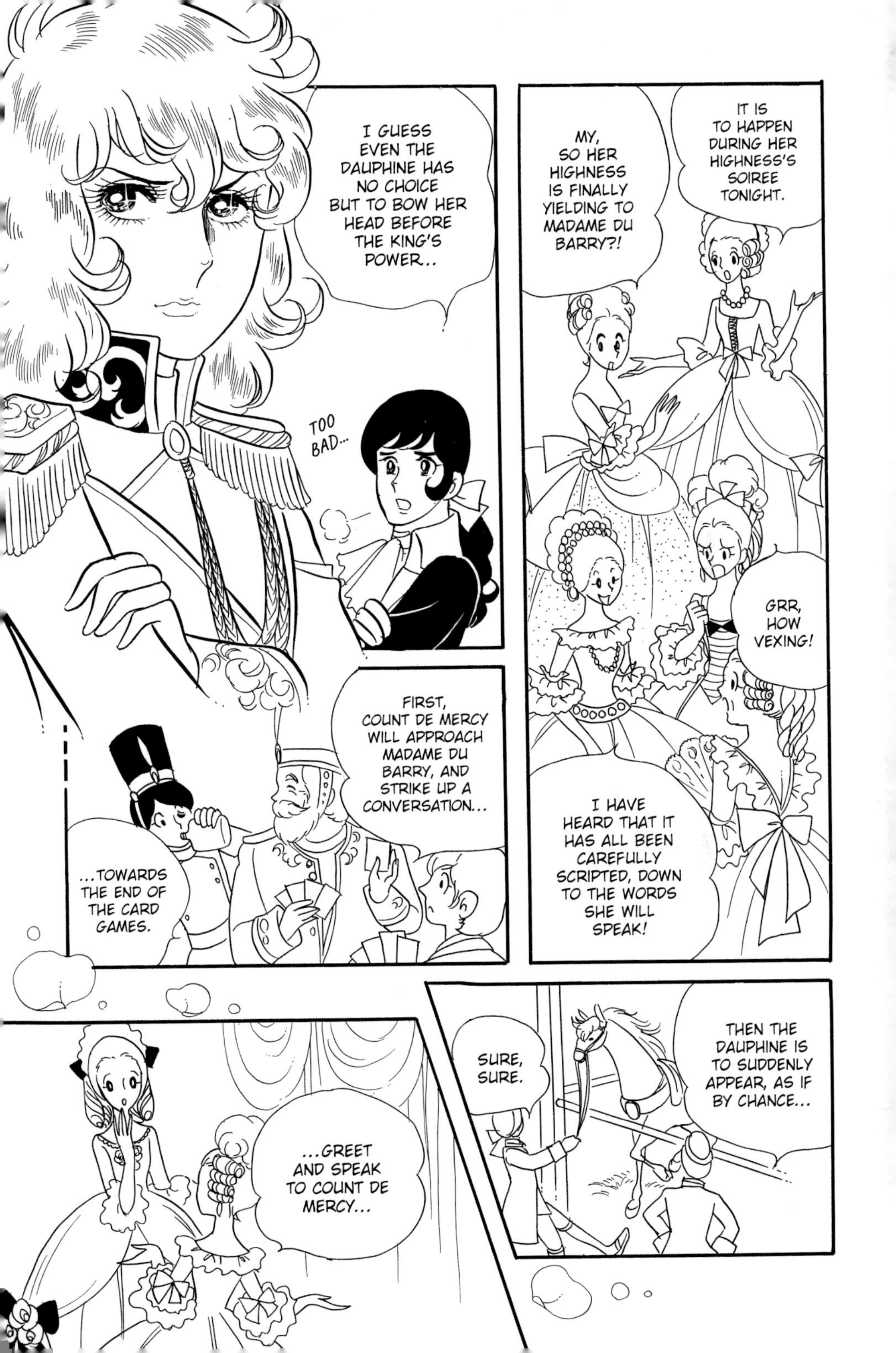
IT IS TO HAPPEN DURING HER HIGHNESS'S SOIREE TONIGHT.
MY, SO HER HIGHNESS IS FINALLY YIELDING TO MADAME DU BARRY?!
GRR, HOW VEXING!
I HAVE HEARD THAT IT HAS ALL BEEN CAREFULLY SCRIPTED, DOWN TO THE WORDS SHE WILL SPEAK!
I GUESS EVEN THE DAUPHINE HAS NO CHOICE BUT TO BOW HER HEAD BEFORE THE KING'S POWER...
TOO BAD...
FIRST, COUNT DE MERCY WILL APPROACH MADAME DU BARRY, AND STRIKE UP A CONVERSATION...
...TOWARDS THE END OF THE CARD GAMES.
THEN THE DAUPHINE IS TO SUDDENLY APPEAR, AS IF BY CHANCE...
SURE, SURE.
...GREET AND SPEAK TO COUNT DE MERCY...

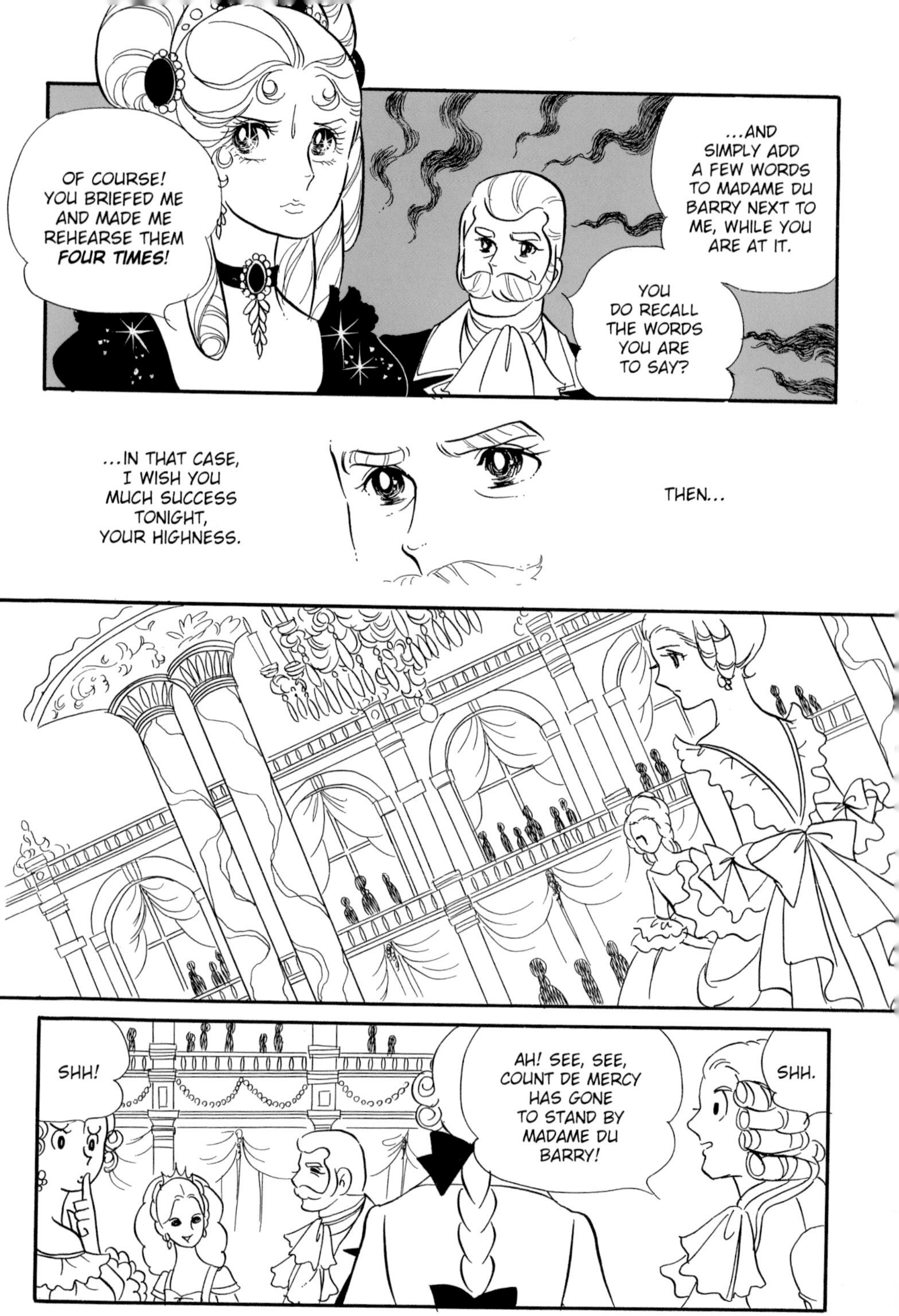
...AND SIMPLY ADD A FEW WORDS TO MADAME DU BARRY NEXT TO ME, WHILE YOU ARE AT IT.
YOU DO RECALL THE WORDS YOU ARE TO SAY?
OF COURSE! YOU BRIEFED ME AND MADE ME REHEARSE THEM **FOUR TIMES!**
...IN THAT CASE, I WISH YOU MUCH SUCCESS TONIGHT, YOUR HIGHNESS.
THEN...
SHH.
AH! SEE, SEE, COUNT DE MERCY HAS GONE TO STAND BY MADAME DU BARRY!
SHH!

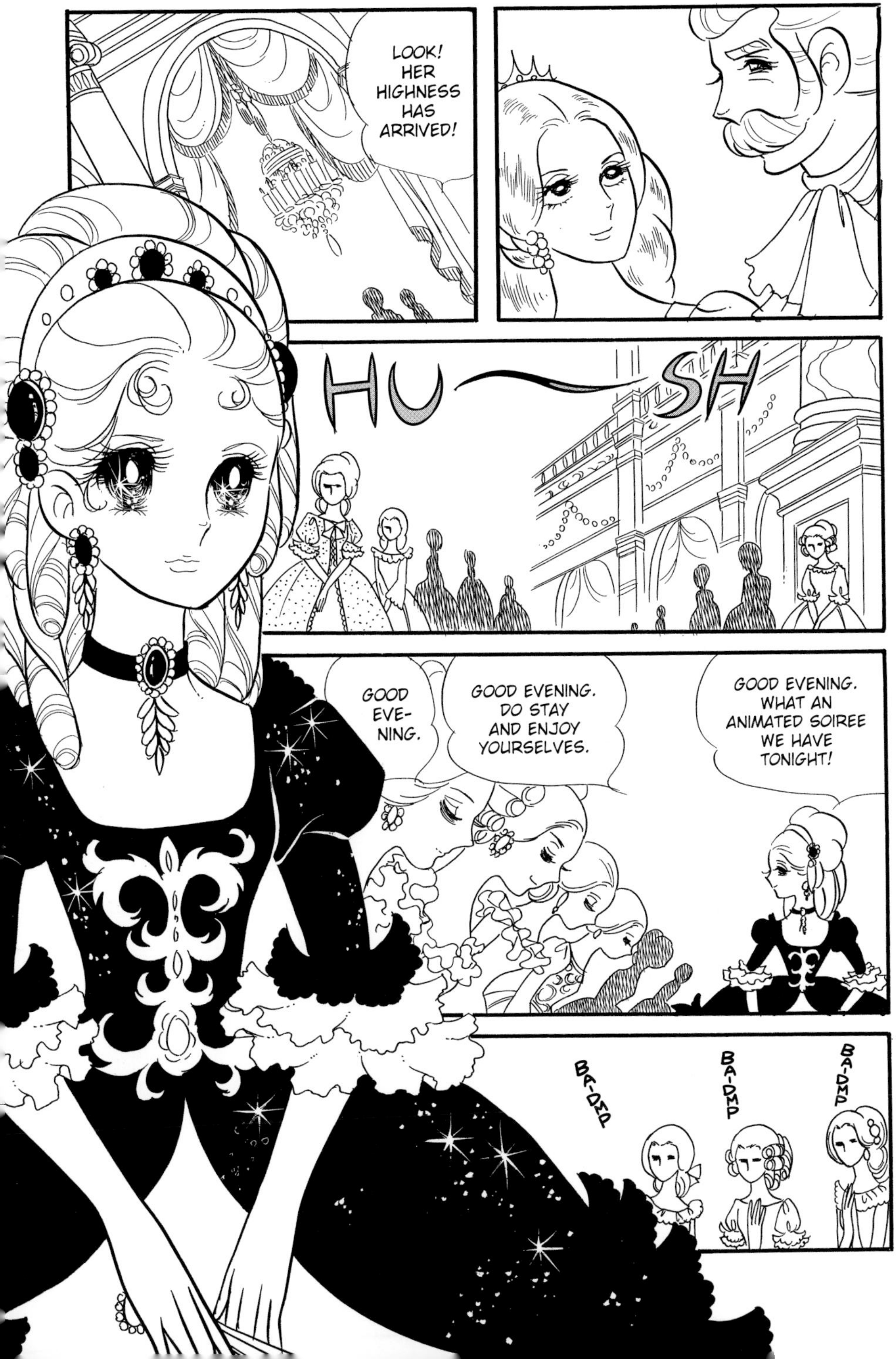
LOOK! HER HIGHNESS HAS ARRIVED!
HU—SH
GOOD EVENING. WHAT AN ANIMATED SOIREE WE HAVE TONIGHT!
GOOD EVENING. DO STAY AND ENJOY YOURSELVES.
GOOD EVE-NING.
BA-DMP
BA-DMP
BA-DMP

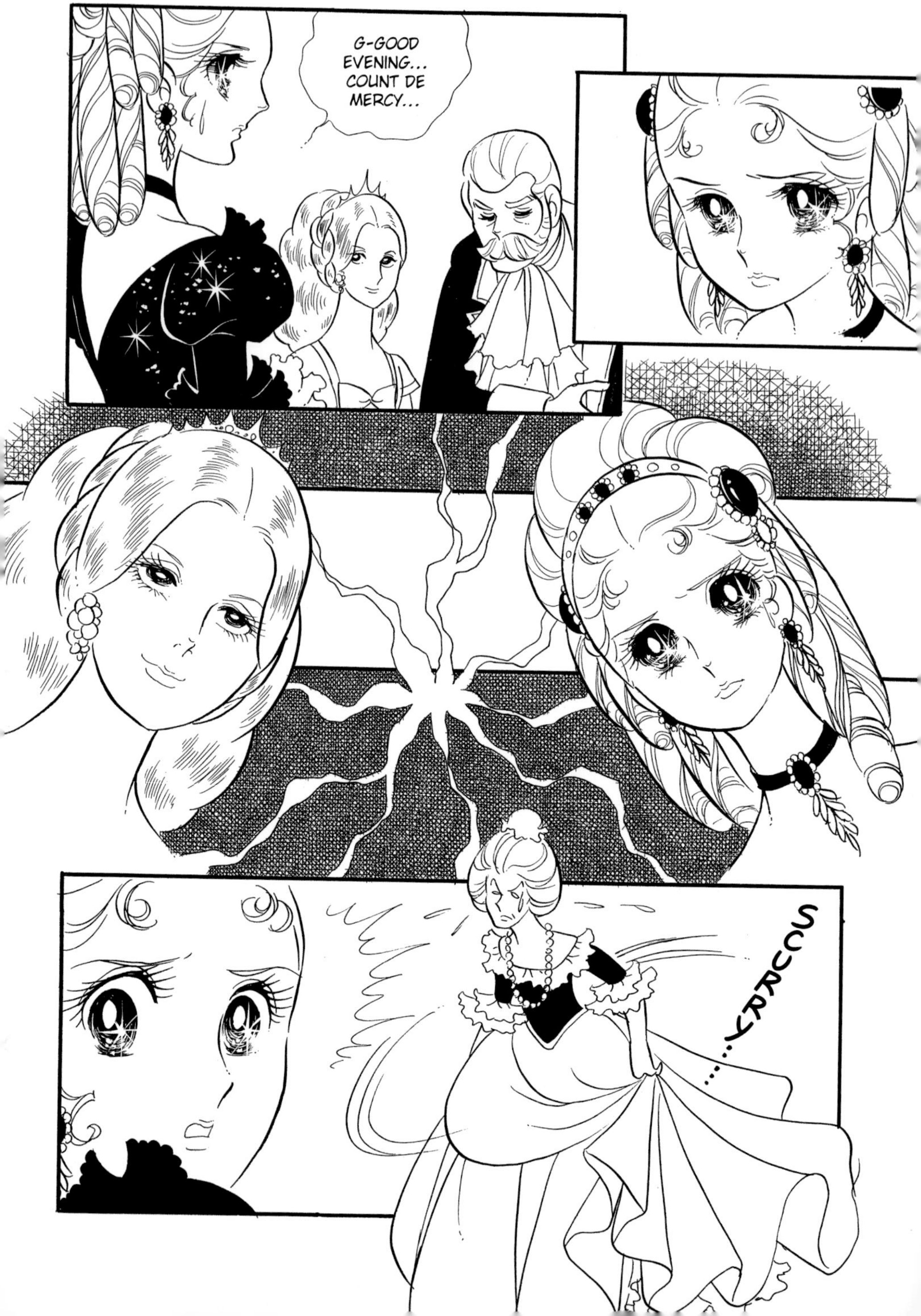
G-GOOD EVENING... COUNT DE MERCY...
SCURRY....

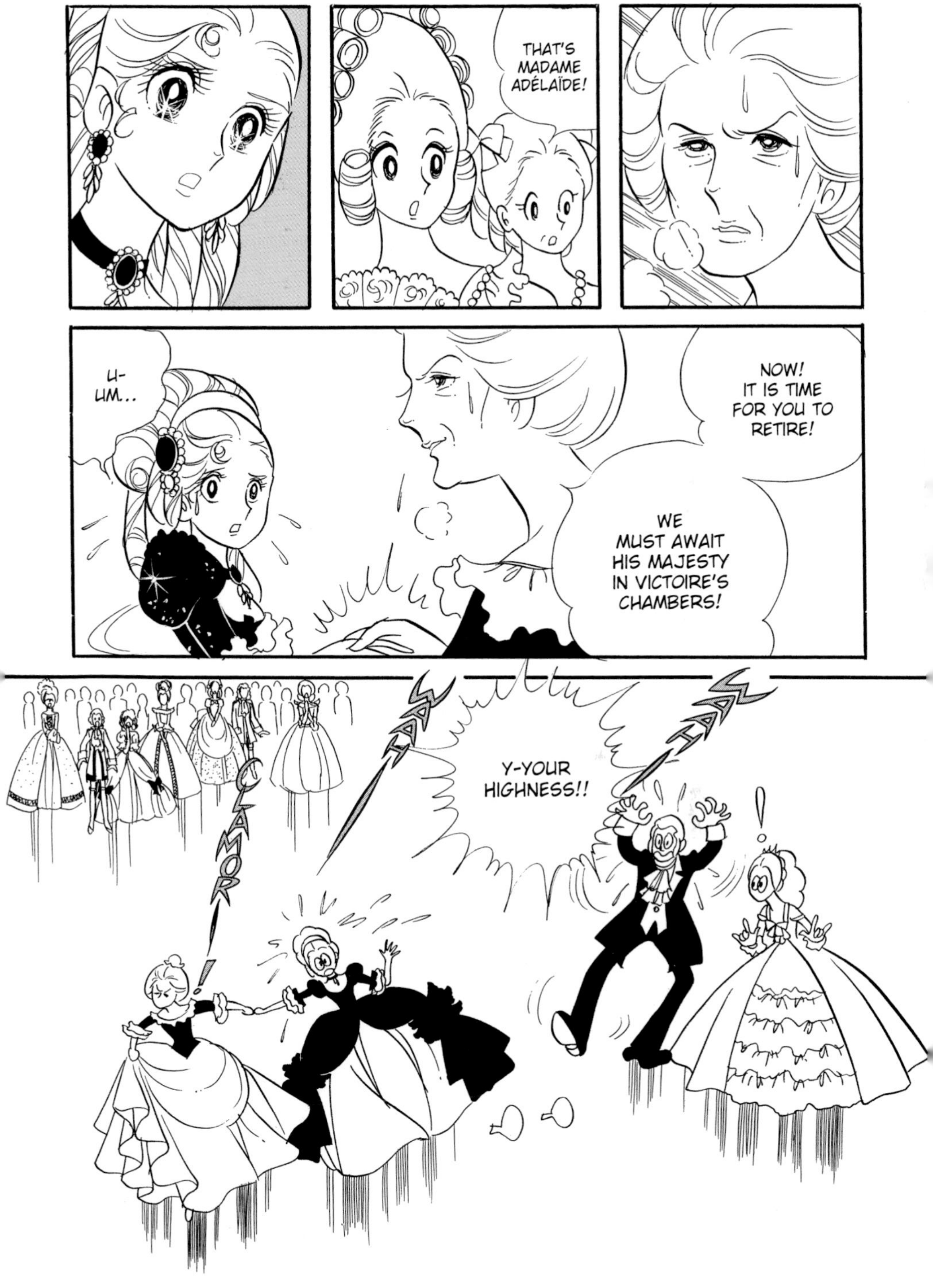
THAT'S MADAME ADÉLAÏDE!
NOW! IT IS TIME FOR YOU TO RETIRE!
WE MUST AWAIT HIS MAJESTY IN VICTOIRE'S CHAMBERS!
U-UM...
WHAA
WHAA
Y-YOUR HIGHNESS!!
CLAMOR!
!

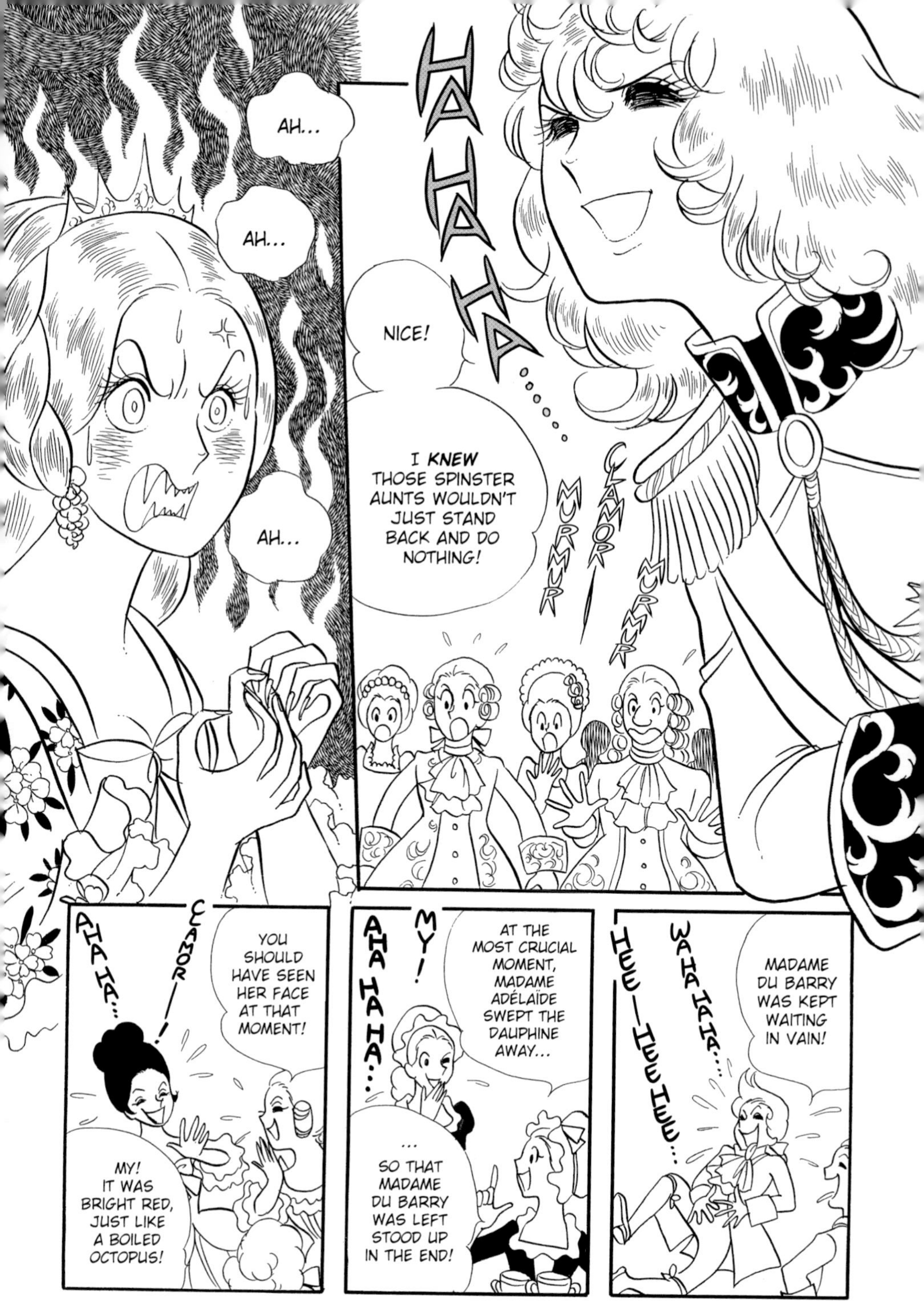
HAHAHAHA.....
NICE!
I **KNEW** THOSE SPINSTER AUNTS WOULDN'T JUST STAND BACK AND DO NOTHING!
CLAMOR
MURMUR
MURMUR
AH...
AH...
AH...
WAHAHAHA...
HEE HEE HEE...
MADAME DU BARRY WAS KEPT WAITING IN VAIN!
MY!
AT THE MOST CRUCIAL MOMENT, MADAME ADÉLAÏDE SWEPT THE DAUPHINE AWAY...
AHAHAHA...
... SO THAT MADAME DU BARRY WAS LEFT STOOD UP IN THE END!
CLAMOR!
YOU SHOULD HAVE SEEN HER FACE AT THAT MOMENT!
AHAHA...
MY! IT WAS BRIGHT RED, JUST LIKE A BOILED OCTOPUS!

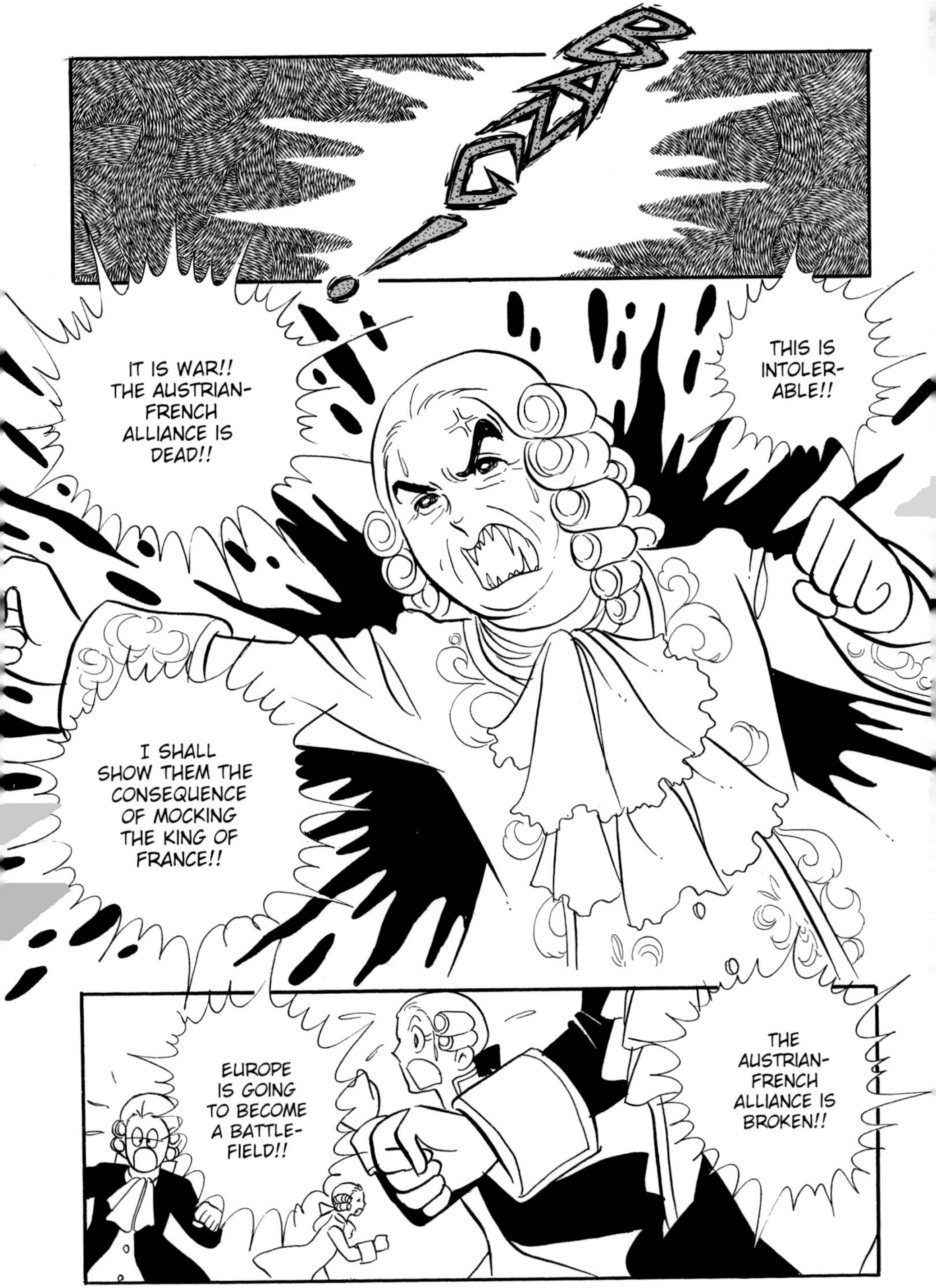
THIS IS INTOLER-ABLE!!
IT IS WAR!! THE AUSTRIAN-FRENCH ALLIANCE IS DEAD!!
I SHALL SHOW THEM THE CONSEQUENCE OF MOCKING THE KING OF FRANCE!!
THE AUSTRIAN-FRENCH ALLIANCE IS BROKEN!!
EUROPE IS GOING TO BECOME A BATTLE-FIELD!!

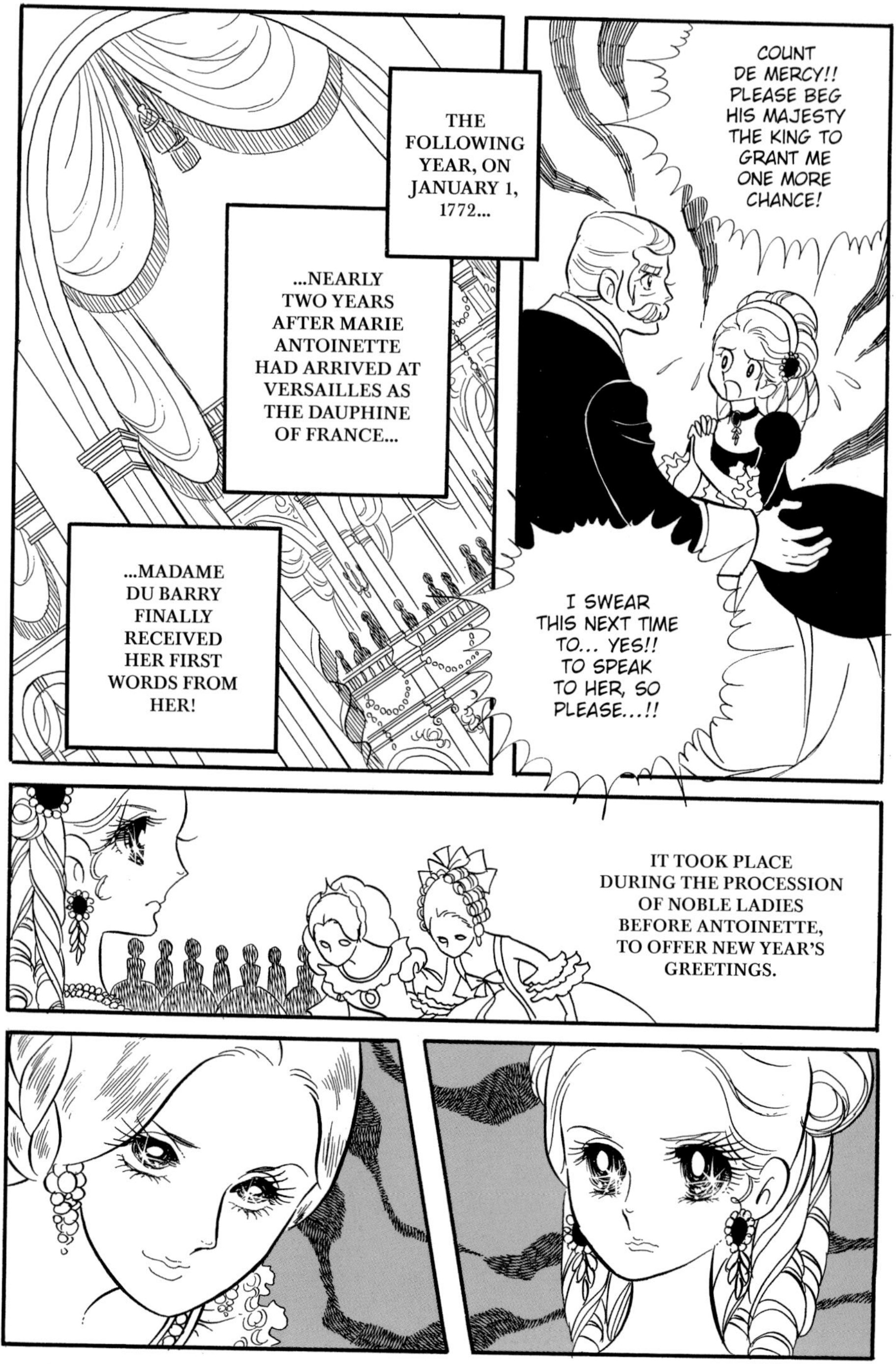
COUNT DE MERCY!! PLEASE BEG HIS MAJESTY THE KING TO GRANT ME ONE MORE CHANCE!
I SWEAR THIS NEXT TIME TO... YES!! TO SPEAK TO HER, SO PLEASE...!!
THE FOLLOWING YEAR, ON JANUARY 1, 1772...
...NEARLY TWO YEARS AFTER MARIE ANTOINETTE HAD ARRIVED AT VERSAILLES AS THE DAUPHINE OF FRANCE...
...MADAME DU BARRY FINALLY RECEIVED HER FIRST WORDS FROM HER!
IT TOOK PLACE DURING THE PROCESSION OF NOBLE LADIES BEFORE ANTOINETTE, TO OFFER NEW YEAR'S GREETINGS.

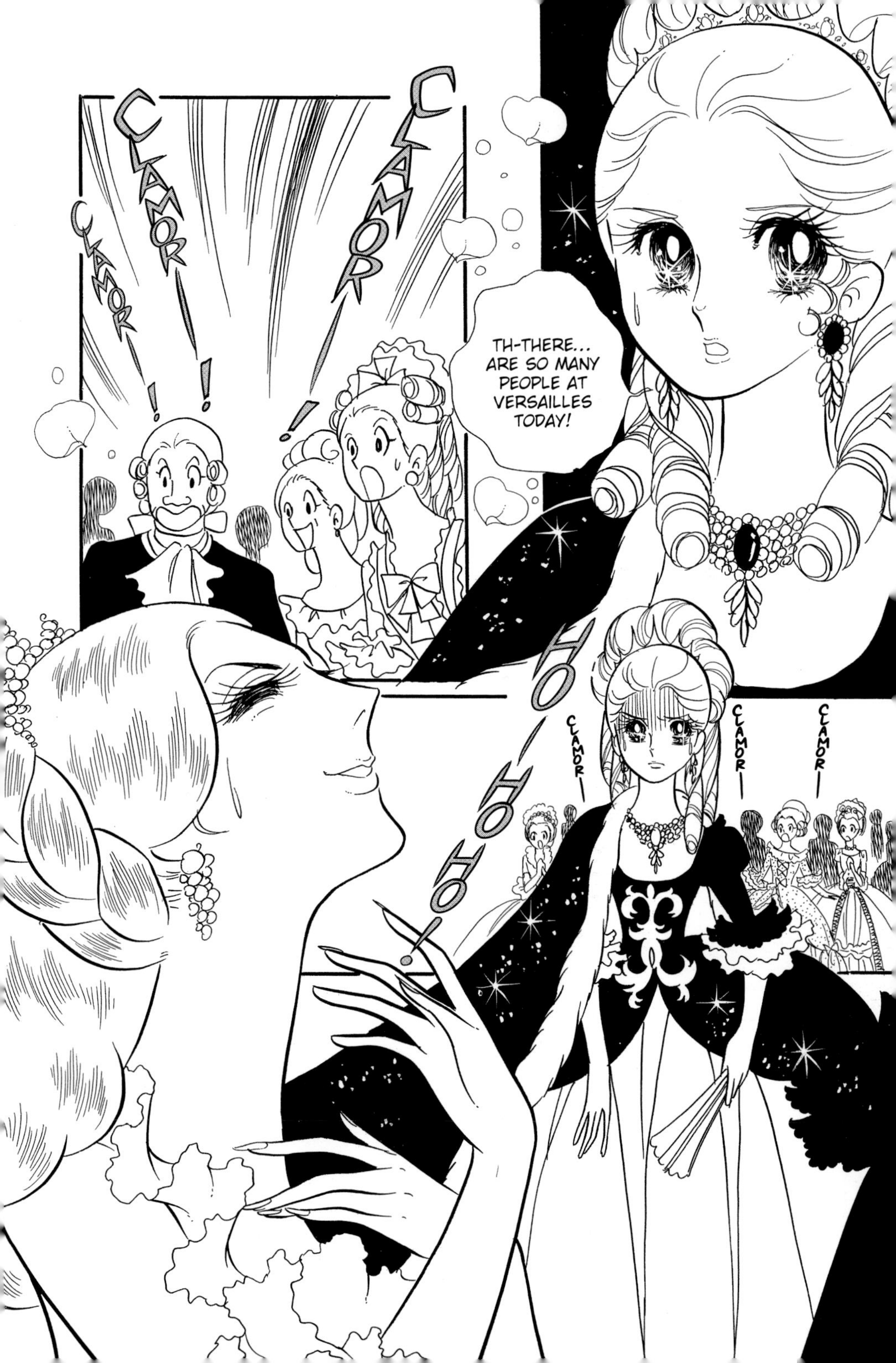
TH-THERE... ARE SO MANY PEOPLE AT VERSAILLES TODAY!
CLAMOR!
CLAMOR!
CLAMOR!
CLAMOR
CLAMOR
CLAMOR
HO-HO-HO-HO!

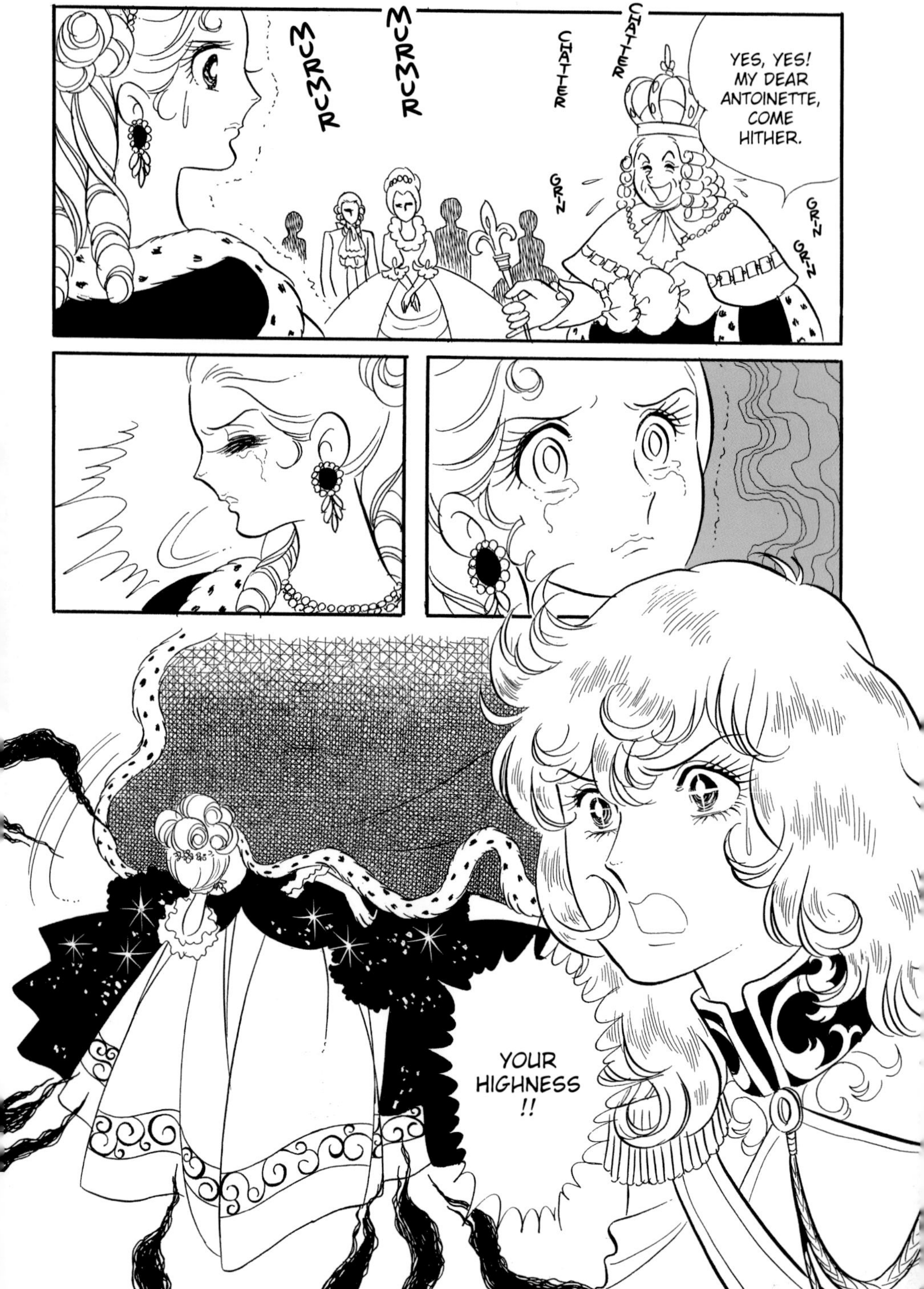
YES, YES! MY DEAR ANTOINETTE, COME HITHER.
GRIN GRIN
CHATTER
CHATTER
GRIN
MURMUR
MURMUR
YOUR HIGHNESS !!

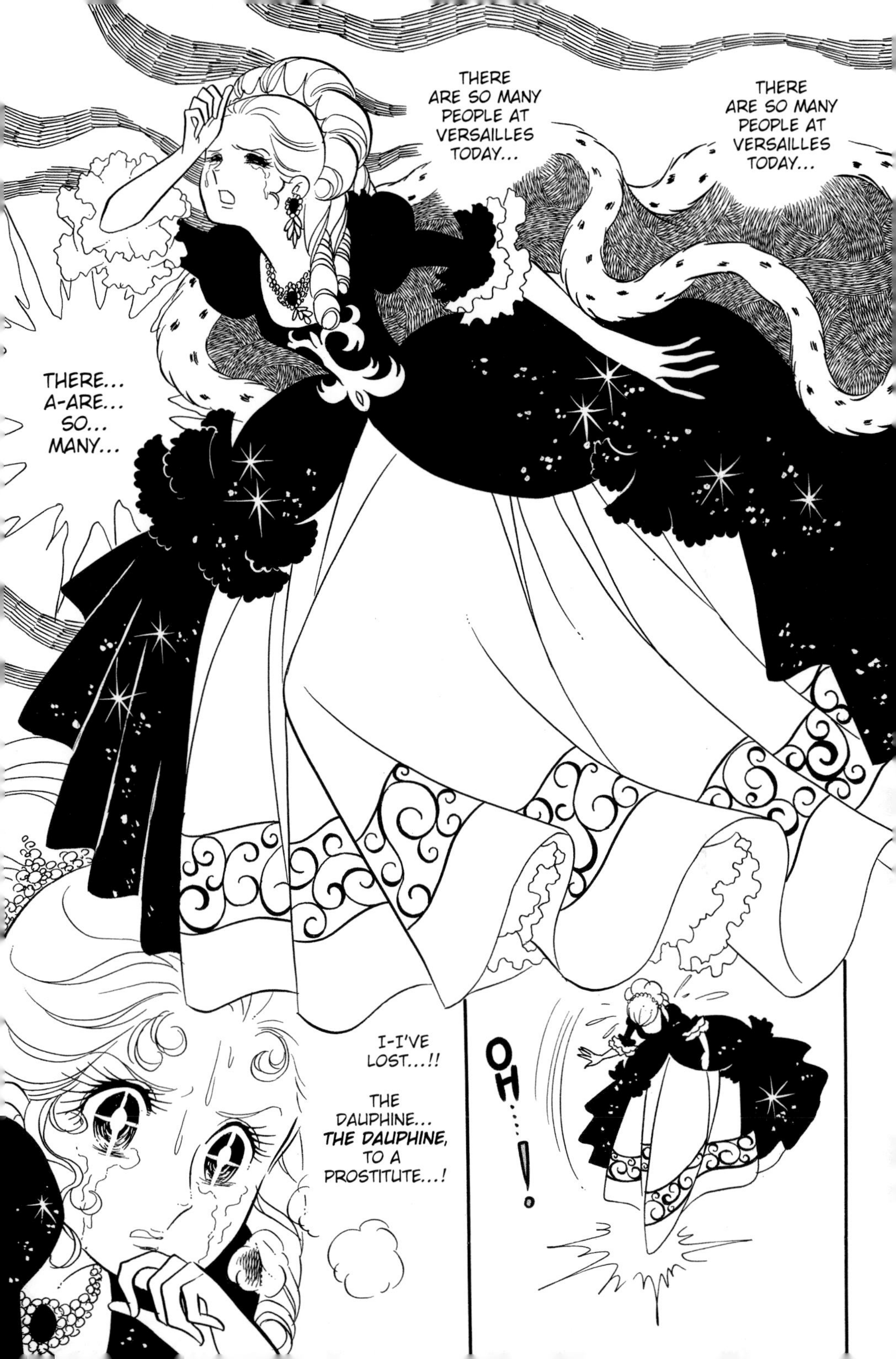
THERE ARE SO MANY PEOPLE AT VERSAILLES TODAY...
THERE ARE SO MANY PEOPLE AT VERSAILLES TODAY...
THERE... A-ARE... SO... MANY...
OH...!
I-I'VE LOST...!!
THE DAUPHINE... THE DAUPHINE, TO A PROSTITUTE...!

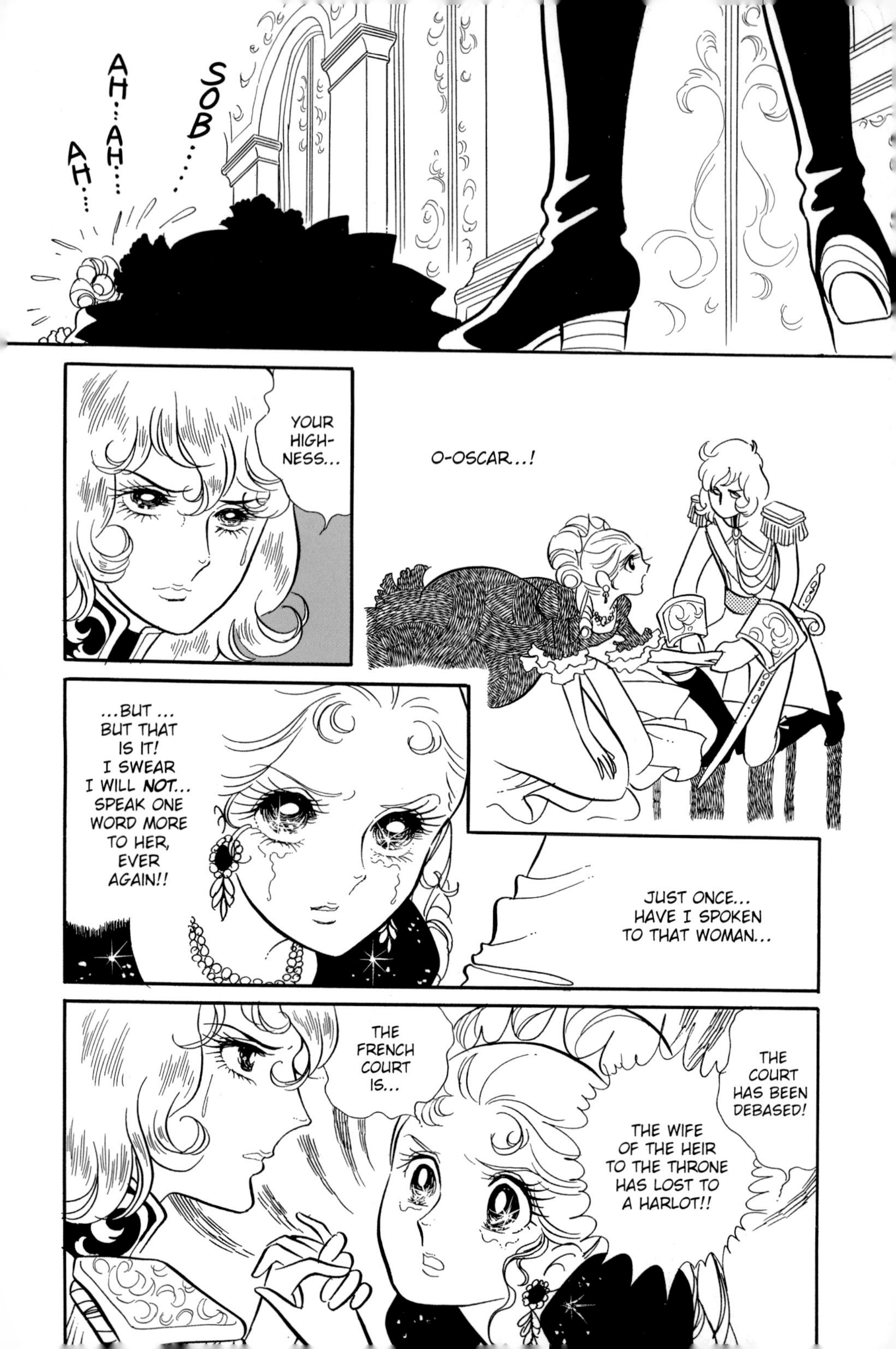
SOB...
AH...AH...
AH...
O-OSCAR...!
YOUR HIGHNESS...
JUST ONCE... HAVE I SPOKEN TO THAT WOMAN...
...BUT ... BUT THAT IS IT! I SWEAR I WILL **NOT**... SPEAK ONE WORD MORE TO HER, EVER AGAIN!!
THE COURT HAS BEEN DEBASED!
THE FRENCH COURT IS...
THE WIFE OF THE HEIR TO THE THRONE HAS LOST TO A HARLOT!!

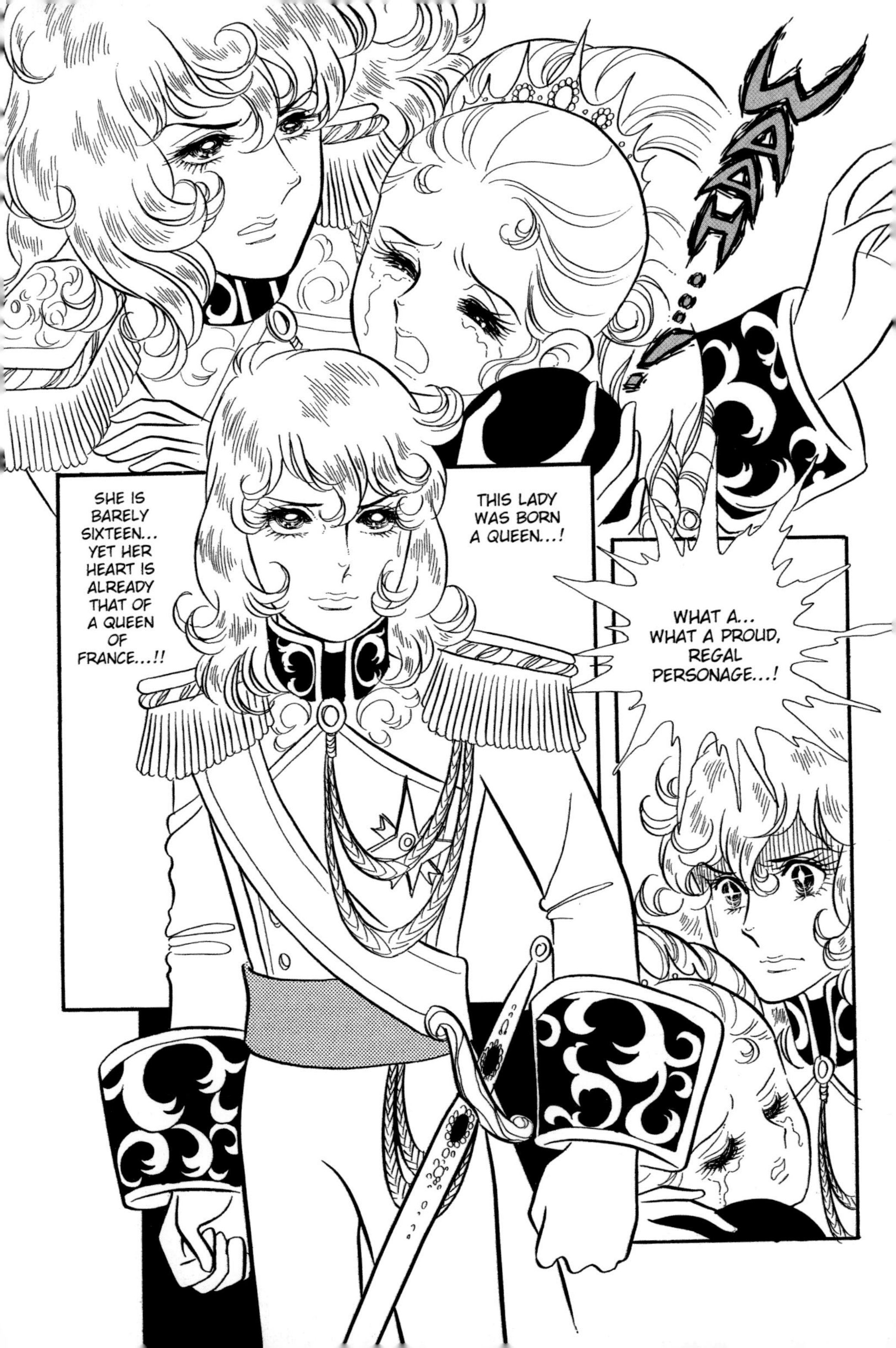
WAAH...!
WHAT A... WHAT A PROUD, REGAL PERSONAGE...!
THIS LADY WAS BORN A QUEEN...!
SHE IS BARELY SIXTEEN... YET HER HEART IS ALREADY THAT OF A QUEEN OF FRANCE...!!

1972 WEEKLY MARGARET MAGAZINE
ISSUE 22 PREVIEW ART

◆ A MAGNIFICENT GRAND ROMANCE SET IN
THE 18TH CENTURY FRENCH ROYAL COURT!!

◆18世紀、フランス宮廷を舞台に描く華麗なる大ロマン

池田理代子

バルサイユのばら

EPISODE 08

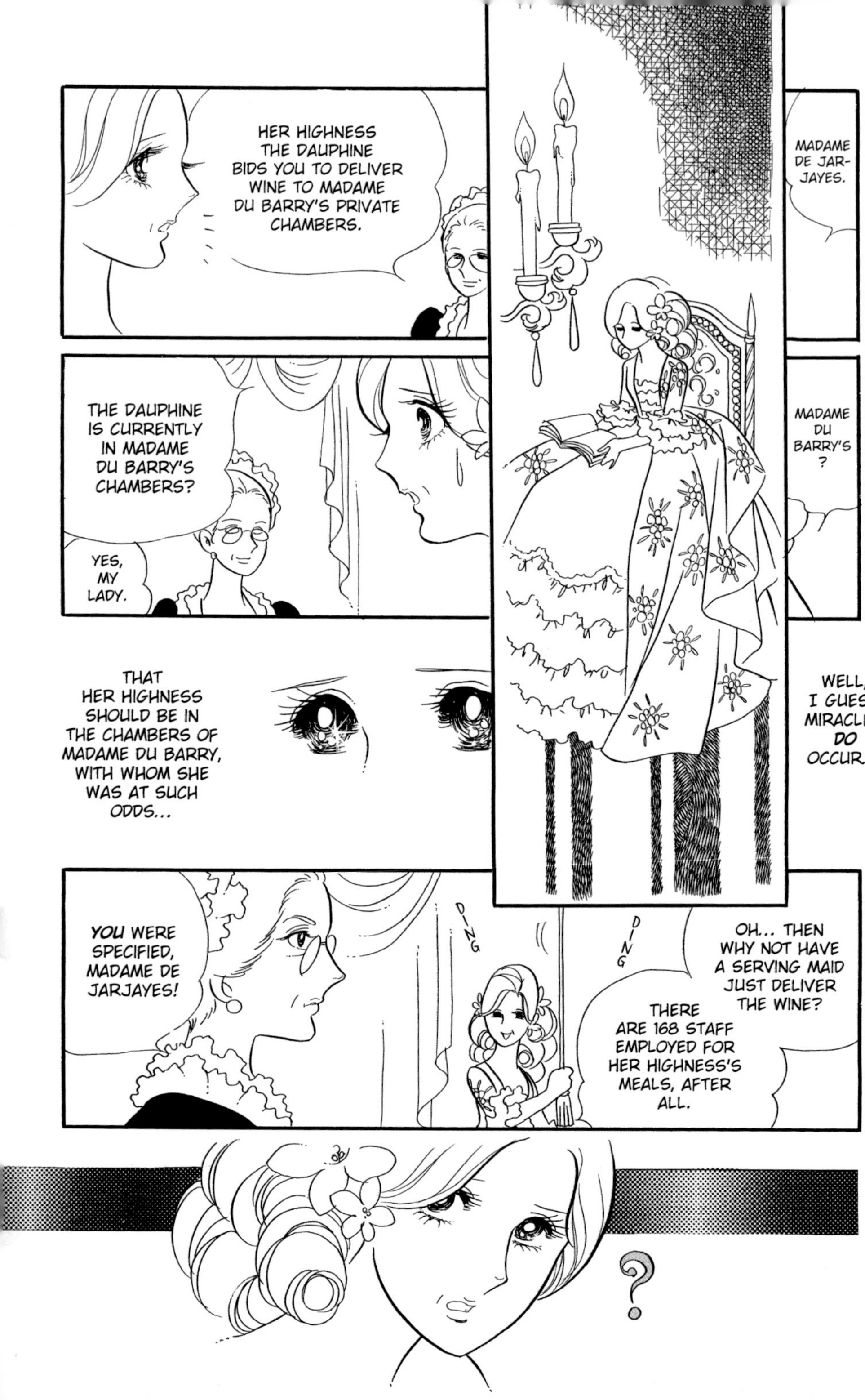
MADAME DE JARJAYES.
HER HIGHNESS THE DAUPHINE BIDS YOU TO DELIVER WINE TO MADAME DU BARRY'S PRIVATE CHAMBERS.
MADAME DU BARRY'S ?
THE DAUPHINE IS CURRENTLY IN MADAME DU BARRY'S CHAMBERS?
YES, MY LADY.
WELL, I GUESS MIRACLES DO OCCUR...
THAT HER HIGHNESS SHOULD BE IN THE CHAMBERS OF MADAME DU BARRY, WITH WHOM SHE WAS AT SUCH ODDS...
OH... THEN WHY NOT HAVE A SERVING MAID JUST DELIVER THE WINE?
THERE ARE 168 STAFF EMPLOYED FOR HER HIGHNESS'S MEALS, AFTER ALL.
DING
DING
YOU WERE SPECIFIED, MADAME DE JARJAYES!
?

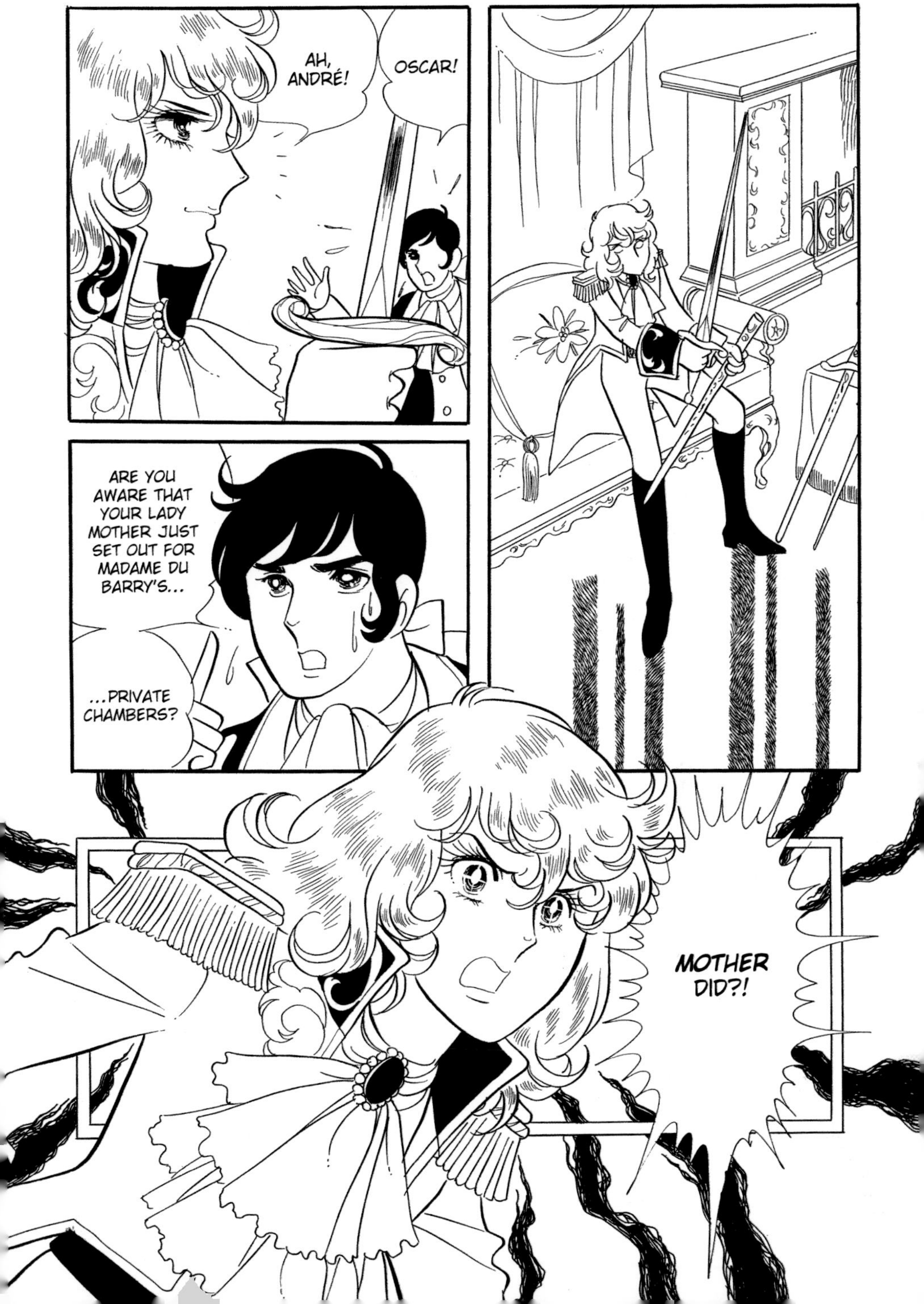
OSCAR!
AH, ANDRÉ!
ARE YOU AWARE THAT YOUR LADY MOTHER JUST SET OUT FOR MADAME DU BARRY'S...
...PRIVATE CHAMBERS?
MOTHER DID?!

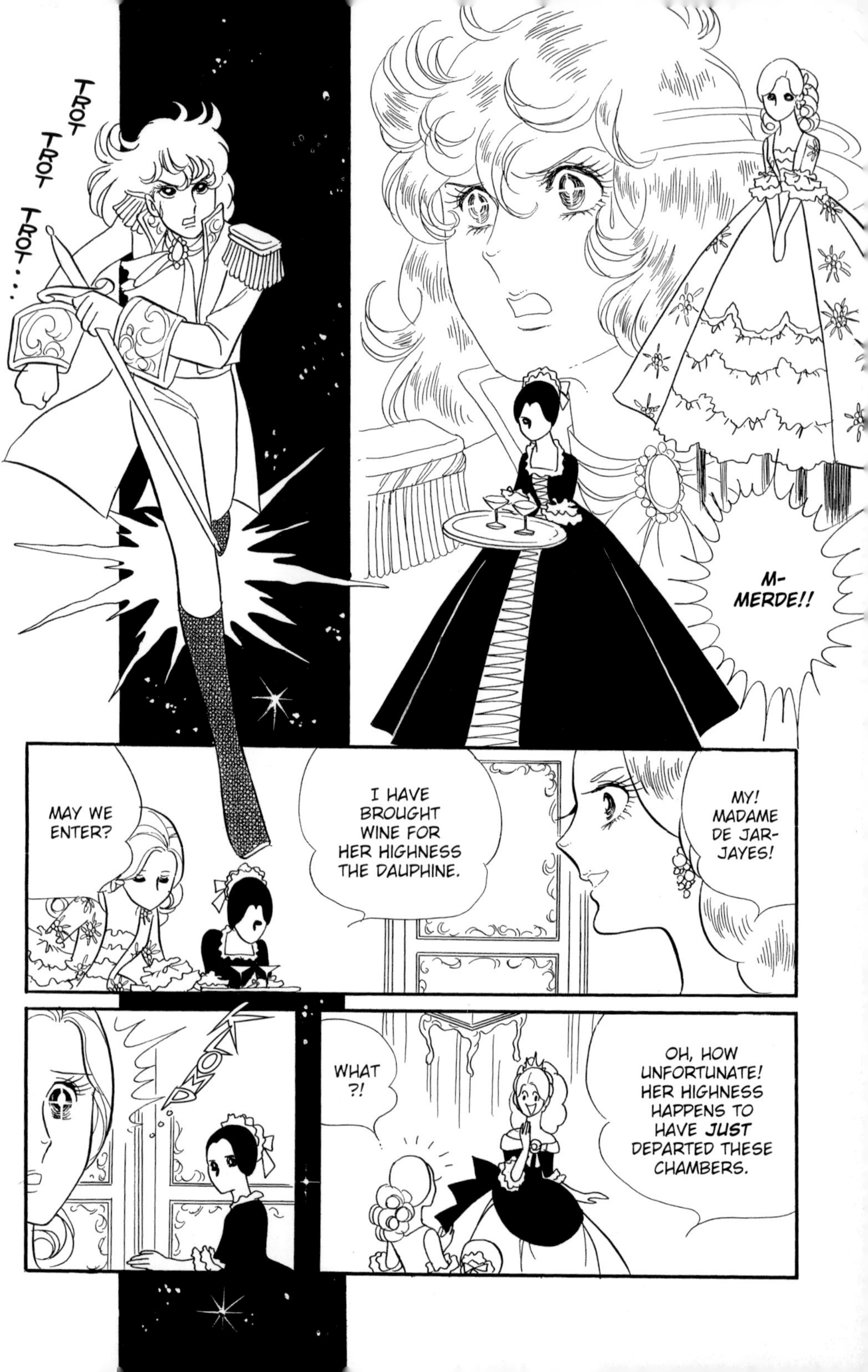
M-
MERDE!!
TROT
TROT
TROT...
MY! MADAME DE JAR-JAYES!
I HAVE BROUGHT WINE FOR HER HIGHNESS THE DAUPHINE.
MAY WE ENTER?
OH, HOW UNFORTUNATE! HER HIGHNESS HAPPENS TO HAVE **JUST** DEPARTED THESE CHAMBERS.
WHAT ?!

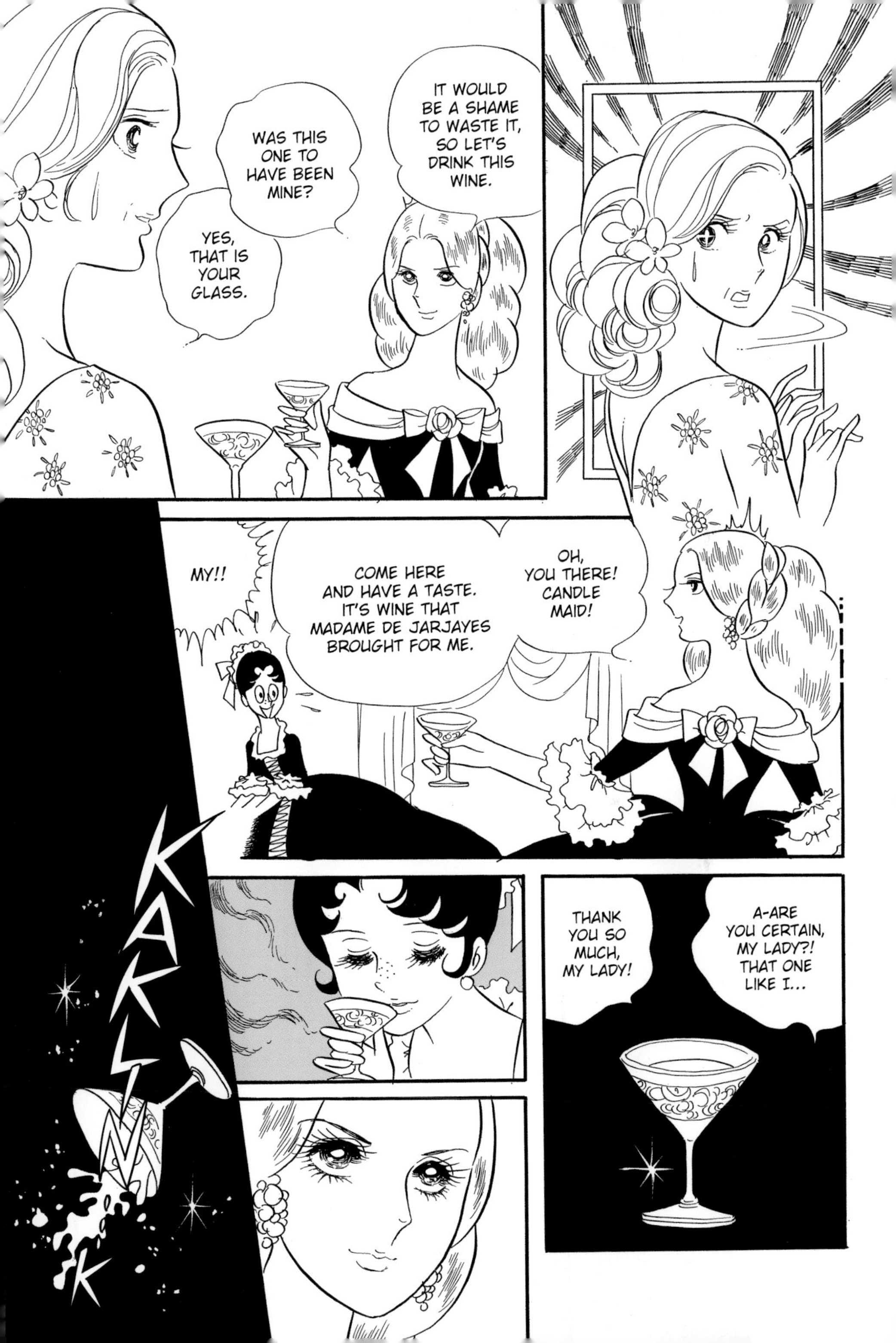
IT WOULD BE A SHAME TO WASTE IT, SO LET'S DRINK THIS WINE.
WAS THIS ONE TO HAVE BEEN MINE?
YES, THAT IS YOUR GLASS.
OH, YOU THERE! CANDLE MAID!
COME HERE AND HAVE A TASTE. IT'S WINE THAT MADAME DE JARJAYES BROUGHT FOR ME.
MY!!
A-ARE YOU CERTAIN, MY LADY?! THAT ONE LIKE I...
THANK YOU SO MUCH, MY LADY!
KAKLINK

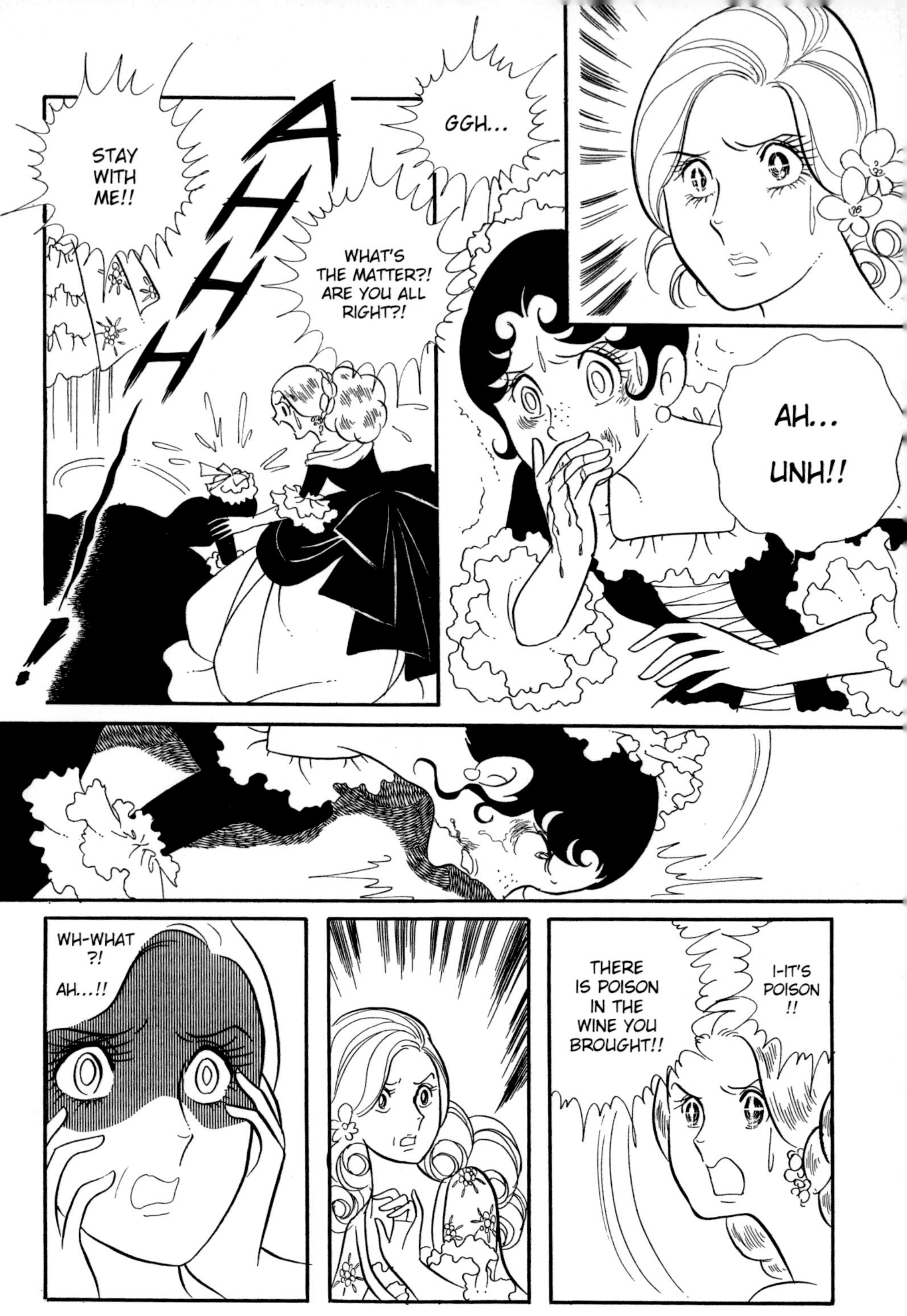
AH... UNH!!
GGH...
AHHHH!
STAY WITH ME!!
WHAT'S THE MATTER?! ARE YOU ALL RIGHT?!
I-IT'S POISON!!
THERE IS POISON IN THE WINE YOU BROUGHT!!
WH-WHAT?!
AH...!!

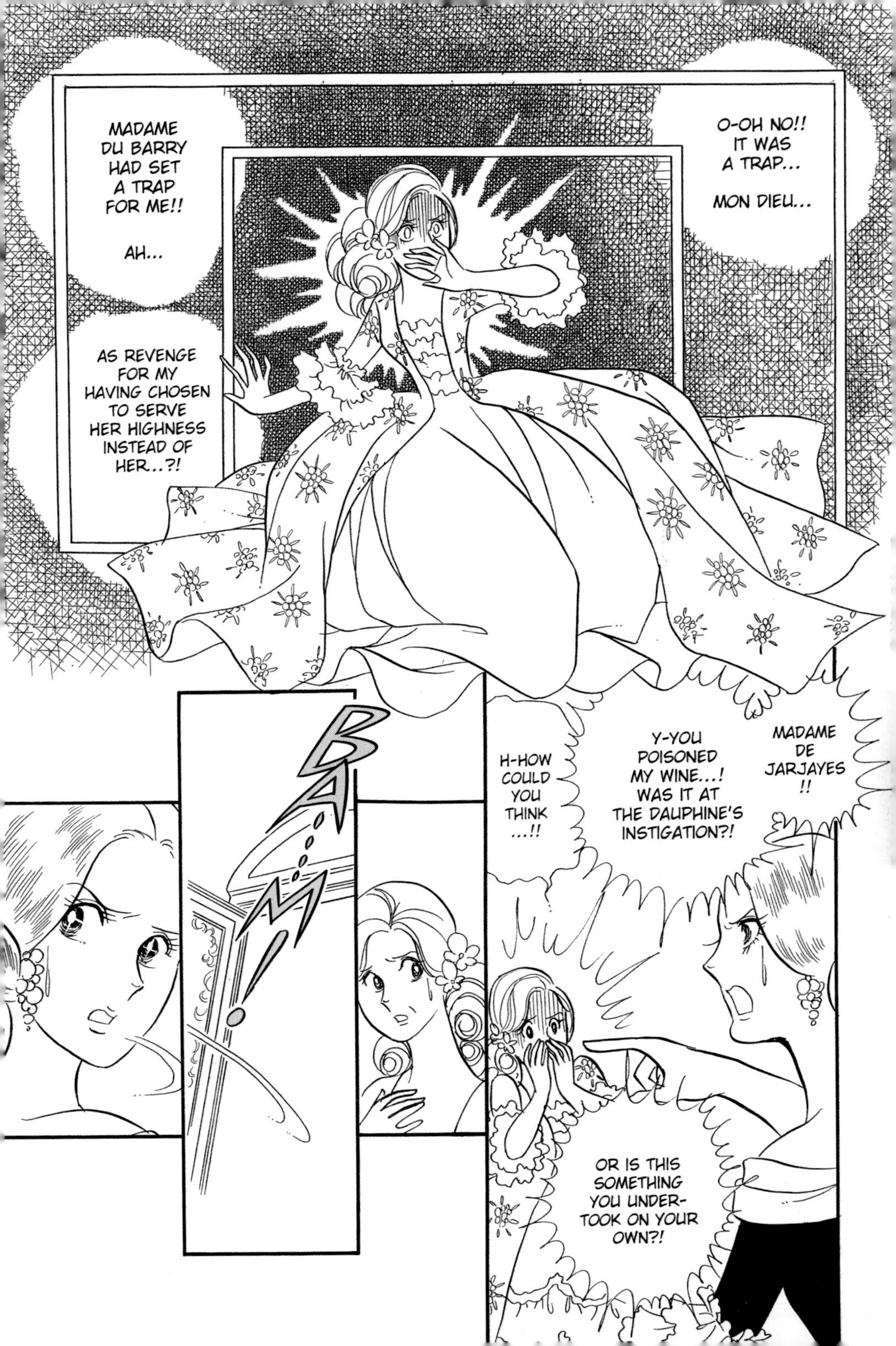
O-OH NO!! IT WAS A TRAP... MON DIEU...
MADAME DU BARRY HAD SET A TRAP FOR ME!! AH...
AS REVENGE FOR MY HAVING CHOSEN TO SERVE HER HIGHNESS INSTEAD OF HER...?!
MADAME DE JARJAYES!!
Y-YOU POISONED MY WINE...! WAS IT AT THE DAUPHINE'S INSTIGATION?!
H-HOW COULD YOU THINK...!!
OR IS THIS SOMETHING YOU UNDER-TOOK ON YOUR OWN?!
BAM...!

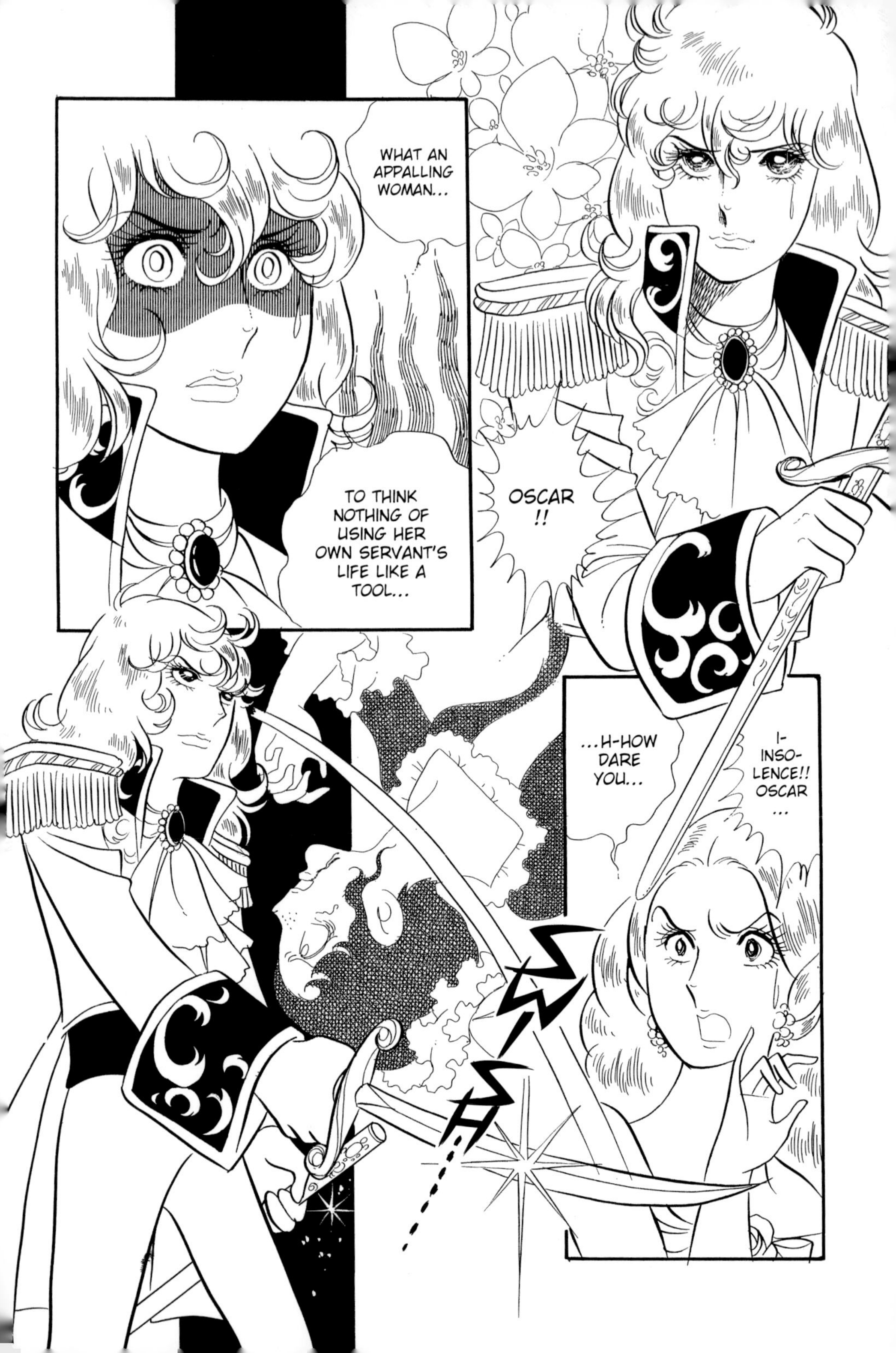
WHAT AN APPALLING WOMAN...
TO THINK NOTHING OF USING HER OWN SERVANT'S LIFE LIKE A TOOL...
OSCAR !!
I- INSO- LENCE!! OSCAR ...
...H-HOW DARE YOU...

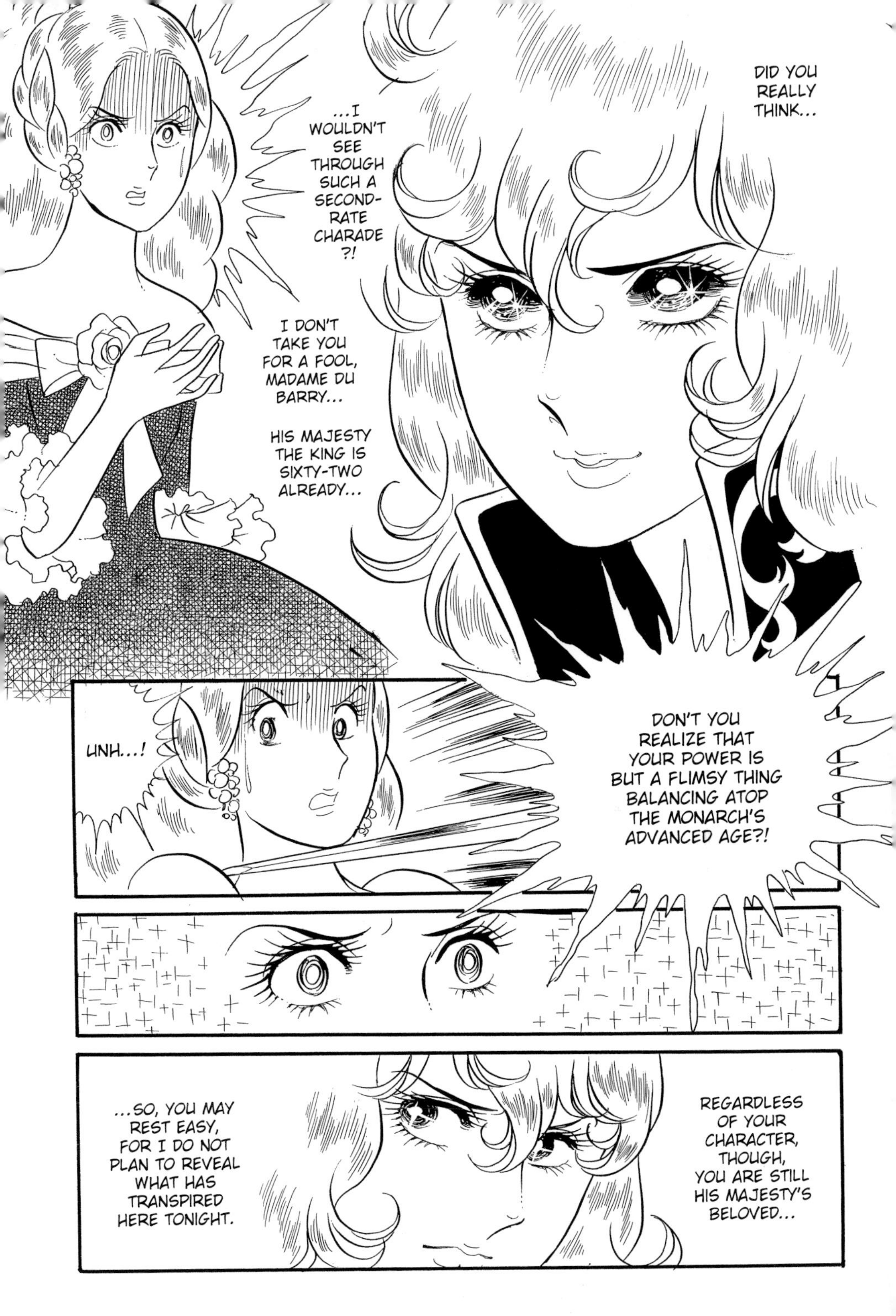
DID YOU REALLY THINK...
...I WOULDN'T SEE THROUGH SUCH A SECOND-RATE CHARADE?!
I DON'T TAKE YOU FOR A FOOL, MADAME DU BARRY...
HIS MAJESTY THE KING IS SIXTY-TWO ALREADY...
DON'T YOU REALIZE THAT YOUR POWER IS BUT A FLIMSY THING BALANCING ATOP THE MONARCH'S ADVANCED AGE?!
UNH...!
REGARDLESS OF YOUR CHARACTER, THOUGH, YOU ARE STILL HIS MAJESTY'S BELOVED...
...SO, YOU MAY REST EASY, FOR I DO NOT PLAN TO REVEAL WHAT HAS TRANSPIRED HERE TONIGHT.

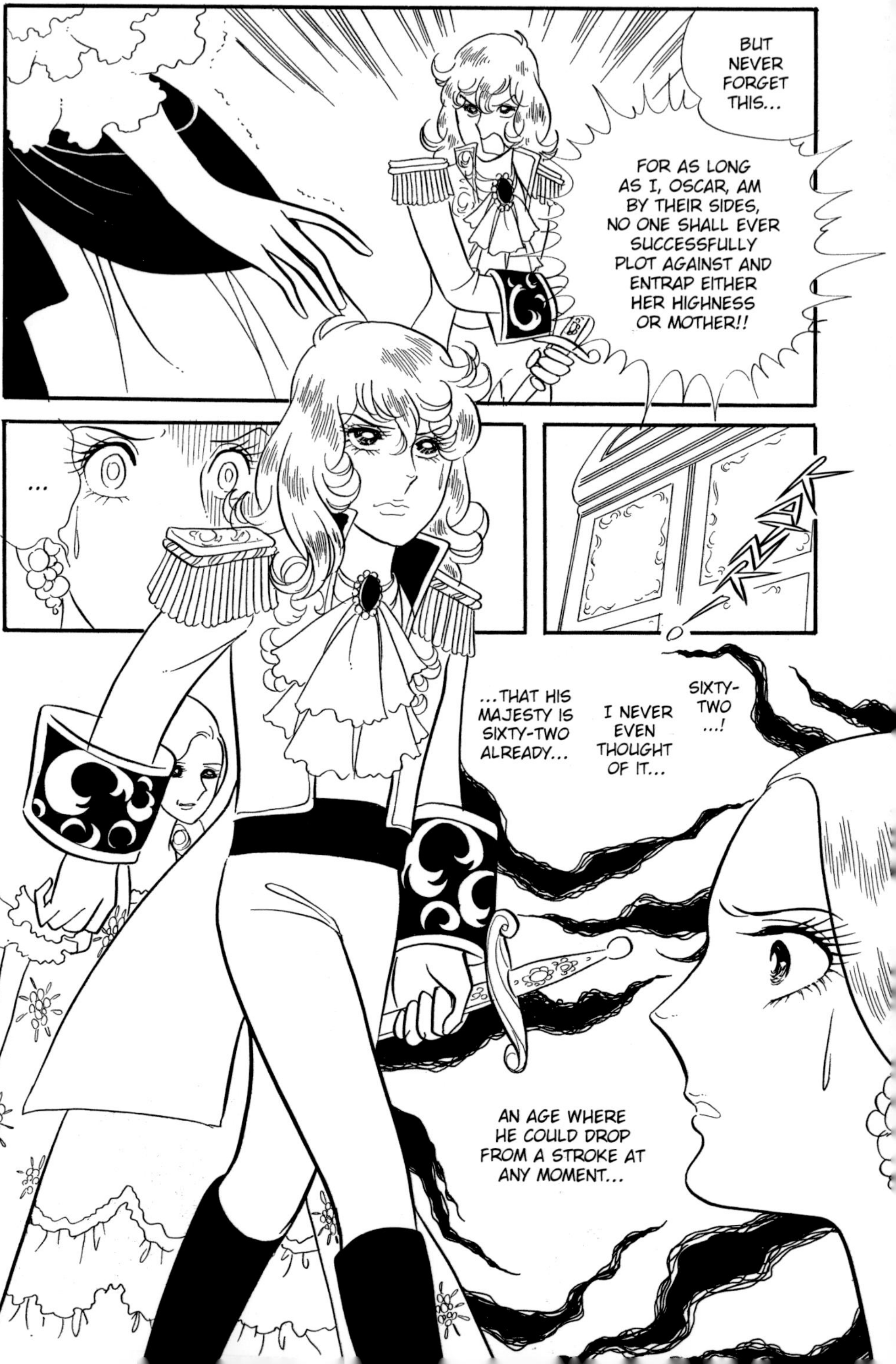

BUT NEVER FORGET THIS...
FOR AS LONG AS I, OSCAR, AM BY THEIR SIDES, NO ONE SHALL EVER SUCCESSFULLY PLOT AGAINST AND ENTRAP EITHER HER HIGHNESS OR MOTHER!!
KRAK
...
SIXTY-TWO...!
I NEVER EVEN THOUGHT OF IT...
...THAT HIS MAJESTY IS SIXTY-TWO ALREADY...
AN AGE WHERE HE COULD DROP FROM A STROKE AT ANY MOMENT...

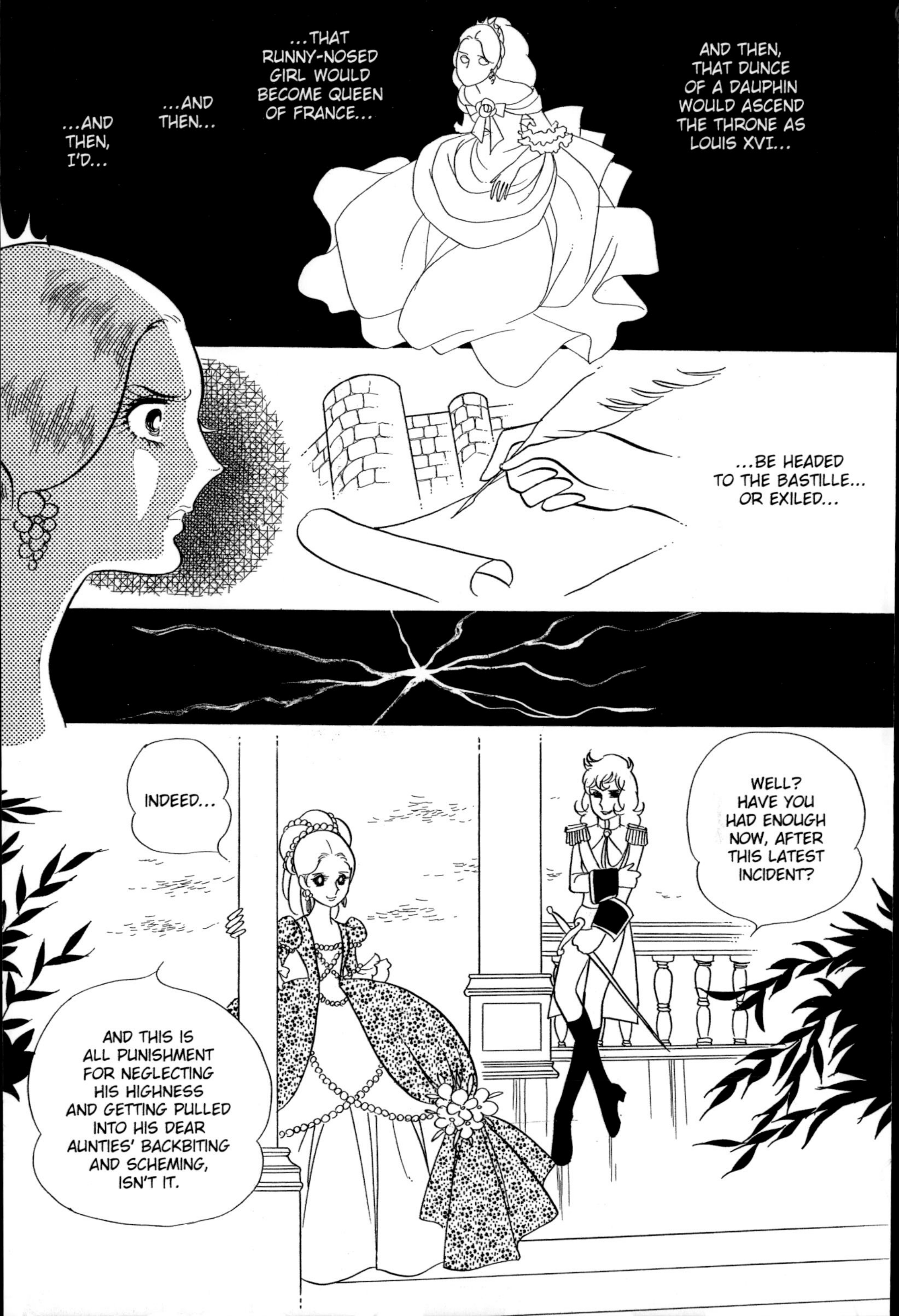
AND THEN, THAT DUNCE OF A DAUPHIN WOULD ASCEND THE THRONE AS LOUIS XVI...
...THAT RUNNY-NOSED GIRL WOULD BECOME QUEEN OF FRANCE...
...AND THEN...
...AND THEN, I'D...
...BE HEADED TO THE BASTILLE... OR EXILED...
WELL? HAVE YOU HAD ENOUGH NOW, AFTER THIS LATEST INCIDENT?
INDEED...
AND THIS IS ALL PUNISHMENT FOR NEGLECTING HIS HIGHNESS AND GETTING PULLED INTO HIS DEAR AUNTIES' BACKBITING AND SCHEMING, ISN'T IT.

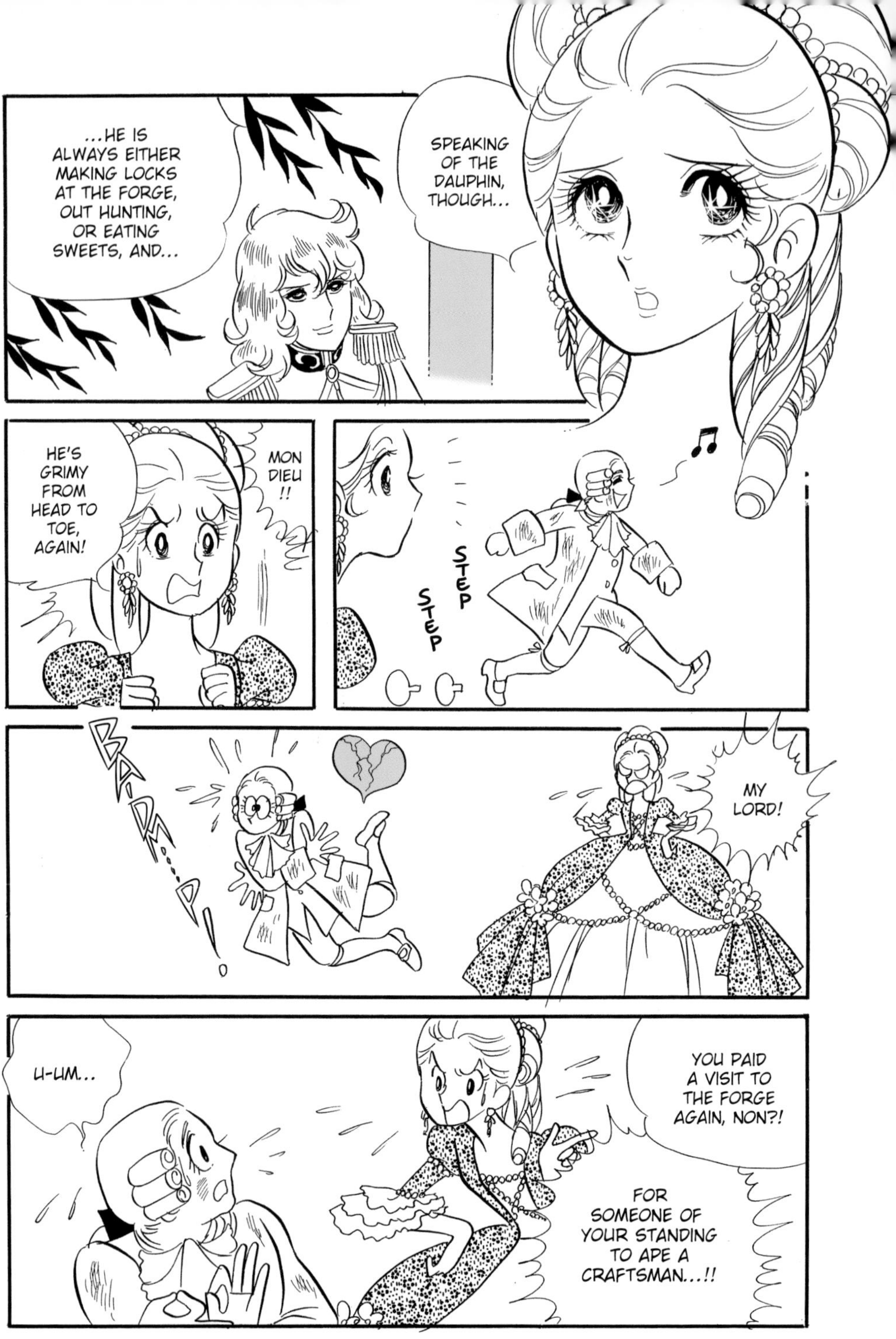
SPEAKING OF THE DAUPHIN, THOUGH...
...HE IS ALWAYS EITHER MAKING LOCKS AT THE FORGE, OUT HUNTING, OR EATING SWEETS, AND...
STEP STEP
MON DIEU!!
HE'S GRIMY FROM HEAD TO TOE, AGAIN!
MY LORD!
BA-DM...P!
YOU PAID A VISIT TO THE FORGE AGAIN, NON?!
FOR SOMEONE OF YOUR STANDING TO APE A CRAFTSMAN...!!
U-UM...

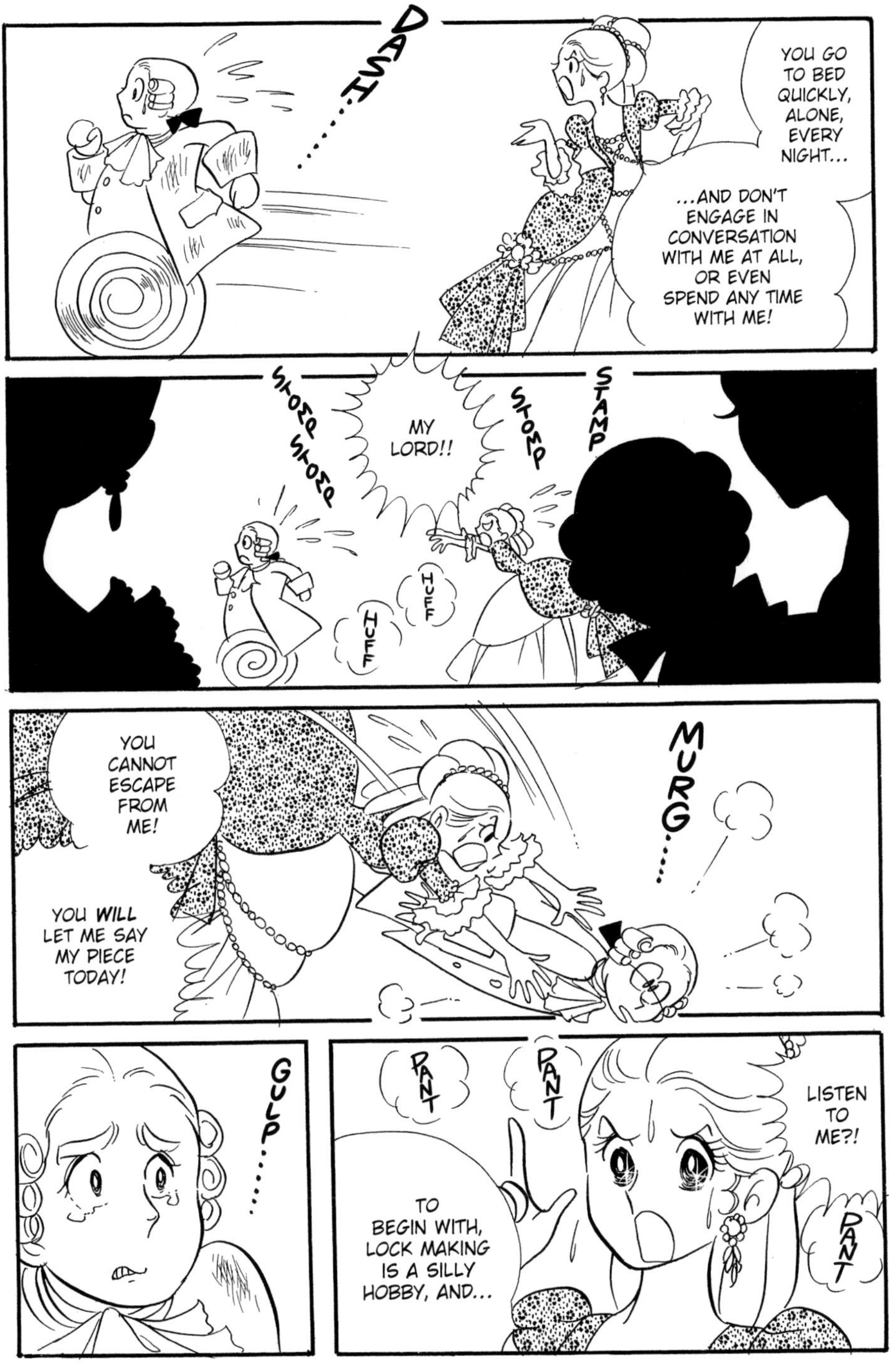
YOU GO TO BED QUICKLY, ALONE, EVERY NIGHT...
...AND DON'T ENGAGE IN CONVERSATION WITH ME AT ALL, OR EVEN SPEND ANY TIME WITH ME!
DASH...
STAMP
STOMP
MY LORD!!
HUFF
HUFF
MURG...
YOU CANNOT ESCAPE FROM ME!
YOU **WILL** LET ME SAY MY PIECE TODAY!
LISTEN TO ME?!
PANT
PANT
PANT
TO BEGIN WITH, LOCK MAKING IS A SILLY HOBBY, AND...
GULP...

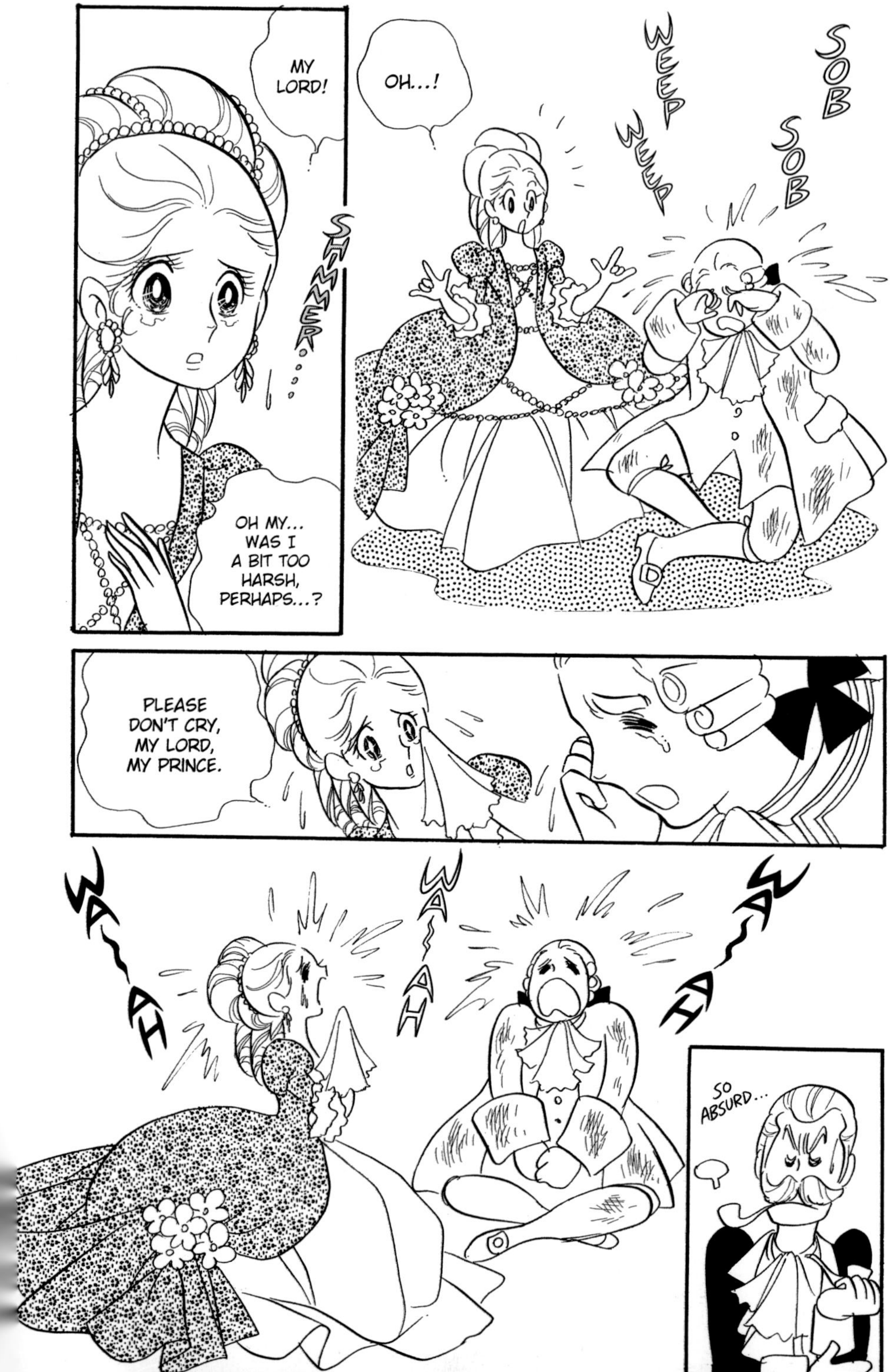
OH...!
WEEP WEEP
SOB SOB
MY LORD!
SHIMMER
OH MY... WAS I A BIT TOO HARSH, PERHAPS...?
PLEASE DON'T CRY, MY LORD, MY PRINCE.
WA-AH
WA-AH
WA-AH
SO ABSURD...

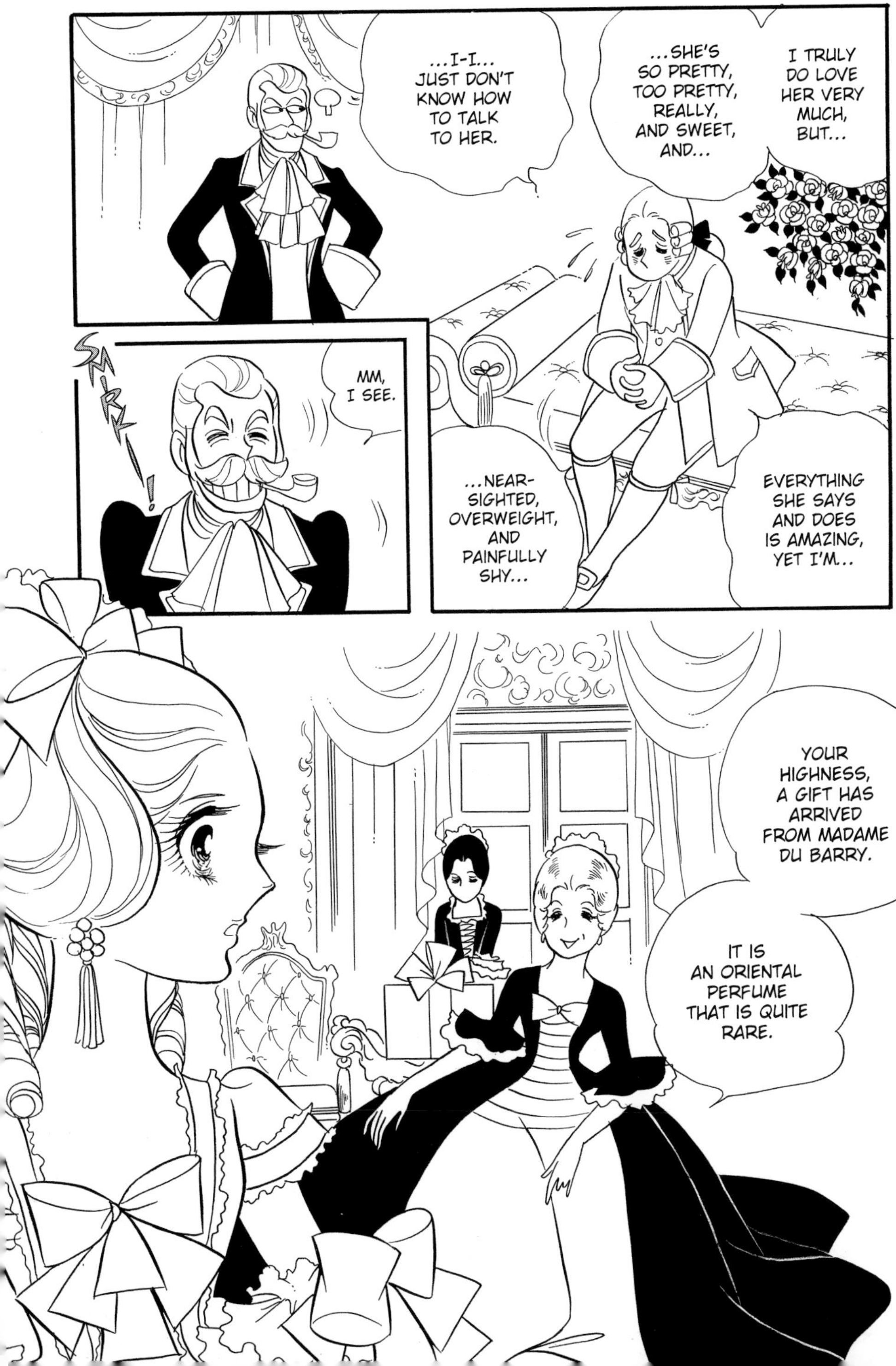
I TRULY DO LOVE HER VERY MUCH, BUT...
...SHE'S SO PRETTY, TOO PRETTY, REALLY, AND SWEET, AND...
EVERYTHING SHE SAYS AND DOES IS AMAZING, YET I'M...
...NEAR-SIGHTED, OVERWEIGHT, AND PAINFULLY SHY...
...I-I... JUST DON'T KNOW HOW TO TALK TO HER.
MM, I SEE.
SMIRK!
YOUR HIGHNESS, A GIFT HAS ARRIVED FROM MADAME DU BARRY.
IT IS AN ORIENTAL PERFUME THAT IS QUITE RARE.

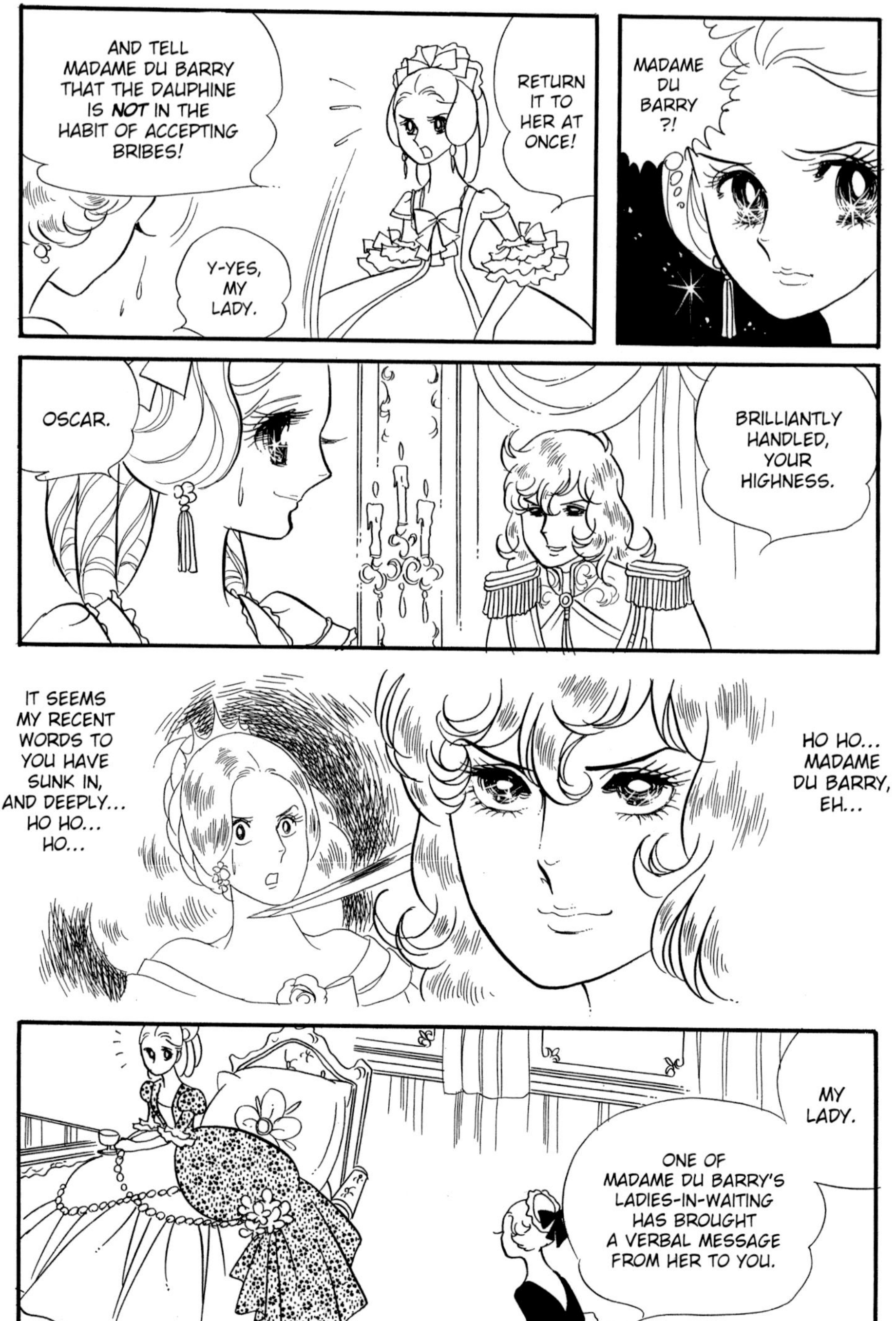
MADAME DU BARRY ?!
RETURN IT TO HER AT ONCE!
AND TELL MADAME DU BARRY THAT THE DAUPHINE IS **NOT** IN THE HABIT OF ACCEPTING BRIBES!
Y-YES, MY LADY.
BRILLIANTLY HANDLED, YOUR HIGHNESS.
OSCAR.
HO HO... MADAME DU BARRY, EH...
IT SEEMS MY RECENT WORDS TO YOU HAVE SUNK IN, AND DEEPLY... HO HO... HO...
MY LADY.
ONE OF MADAME DU BARRY'S LADIES-IN-WAITING HAS BROUGHT A VERBAL MESSAGE FROM HER TO YOU.

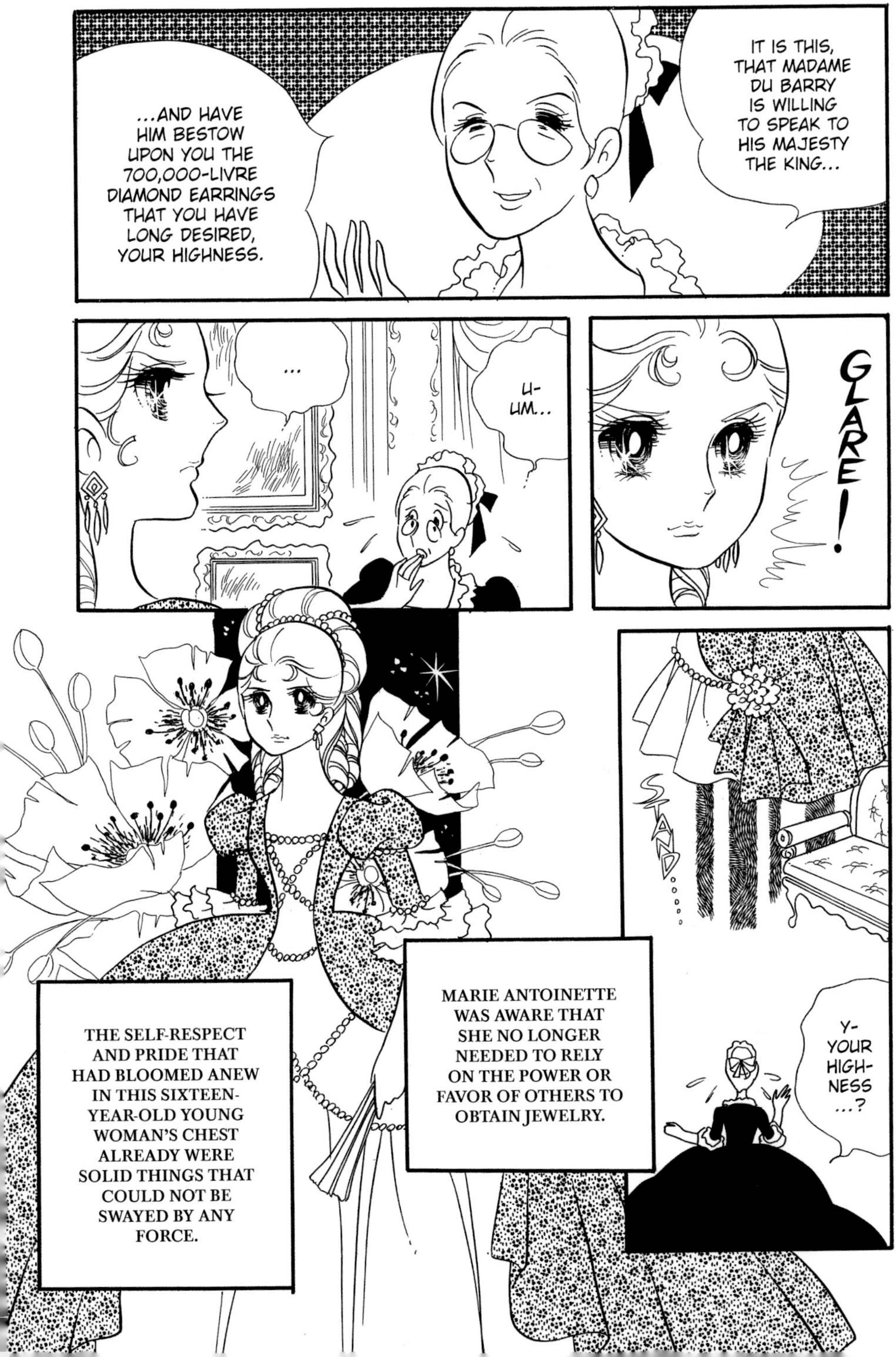
IT IS THIS, THAT MADAME DU BARRY IS WILLING TO SPEAK TO HIS MAJESTY THE KING...
...AND HAVE HIM BESTOW UPON YOU THE 700,000-LIVRE DIAMOND EARRINGS THAT YOU HAVE LONG DESIRED, YOUR HIGHNESS.
GLARE!
...
U-UM...
STAND...
Y-YOUR HIGH-NESS...?
MARIE ANTOINETTE WAS AWARE THAT SHE NO LONGER NEEDED TO RELY ON THE POWER OR FAVOR OF OTHERS TO OBTAIN JEWELRY.
THE SELF-RESPECT AND PRIDE THAT HAD BLOOMED ANEW IN THIS SIXTEEN-YEAR-OLD YOUNG WOMAN'S CHEST ALREADY WERE SOLID THINGS THAT COULD NOT BE SWAYED BY ANY FORCE.

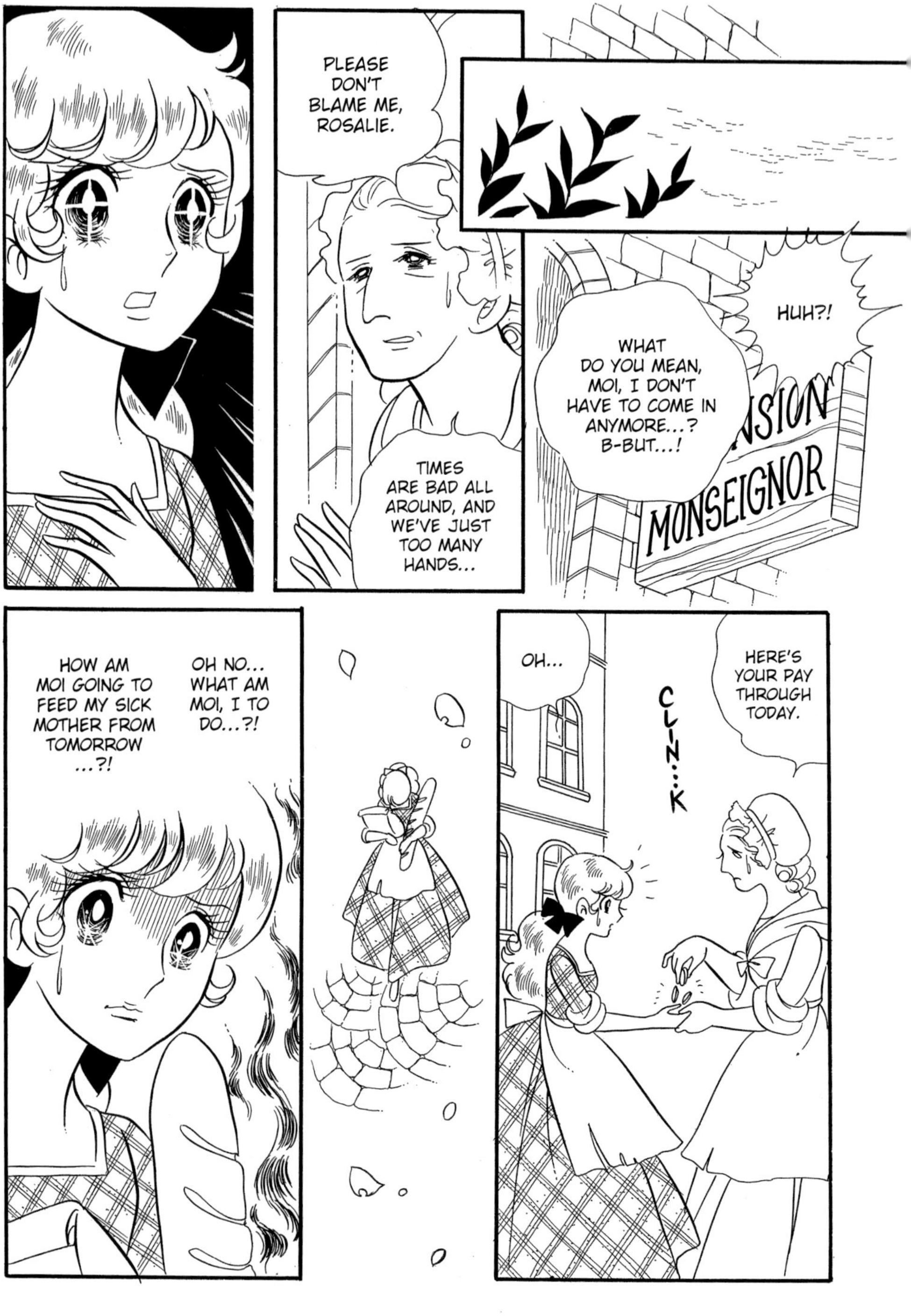
HUH?!
WHAT DO YOU MEAN, MOI, I DON'T HAVE TO COME IN ANYMORE...? B-BUT...!
NSION
MONSEIGNOR
PLEASE DON'T BLAME ME, ROSALIE.
TIMES ARE BAD ALL AROUND, AND WE'VE JUST TOO MANY HANDS...
HERE'S YOUR PAY THROUGH TODAY.
CLIN...K
OH...
OH NO... WHAT AM MOI, I TO DO...?!
HOW AM MOI GOING TO FEED MY SICK MOTHER FROM TOMORROW ...?!

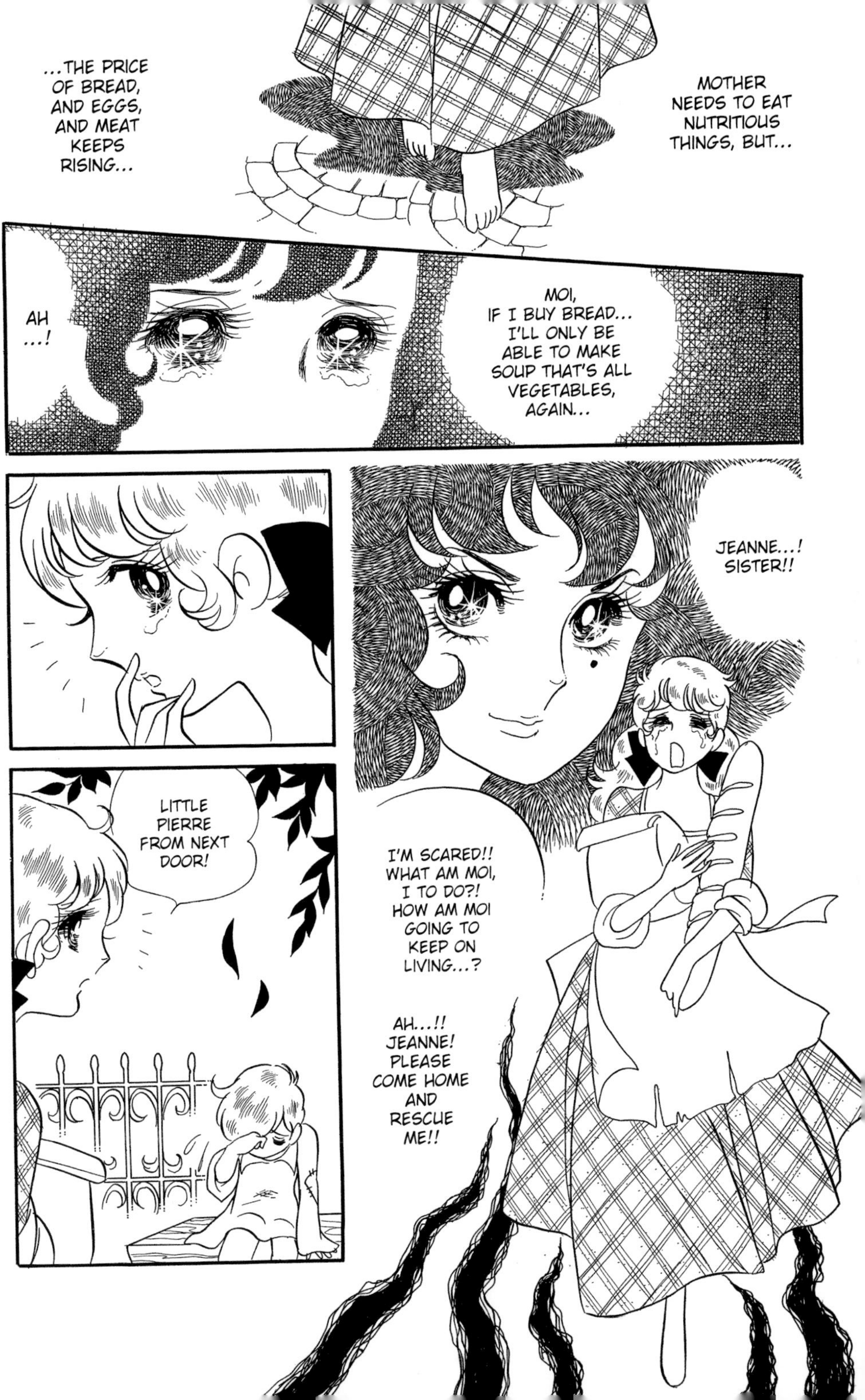
MOTHER NEEDS TO EAT NUTRITIOUS THINGS, BUT...
...THE PRICE OF BREAD, AND EGGS, AND MEAT KEEPS RISING...
MOI, IF I BUY BREAD... I'LL ONLY BE ABLE TO MAKE SOUP THAT'S ALL VEGETABLES, AGAIN...
AH ...!
JEANNE...! SISTER!!
I'M SCARED!! WHAT AM MOI, I TO DO?! HOW AM MOI GOING TO KEEP ON LIVING...?
AH...!! JEANNE! PLEASE COME HOME AND RESCUE ME!!
LITTLE PIERRE FROM NEXT DOOR!

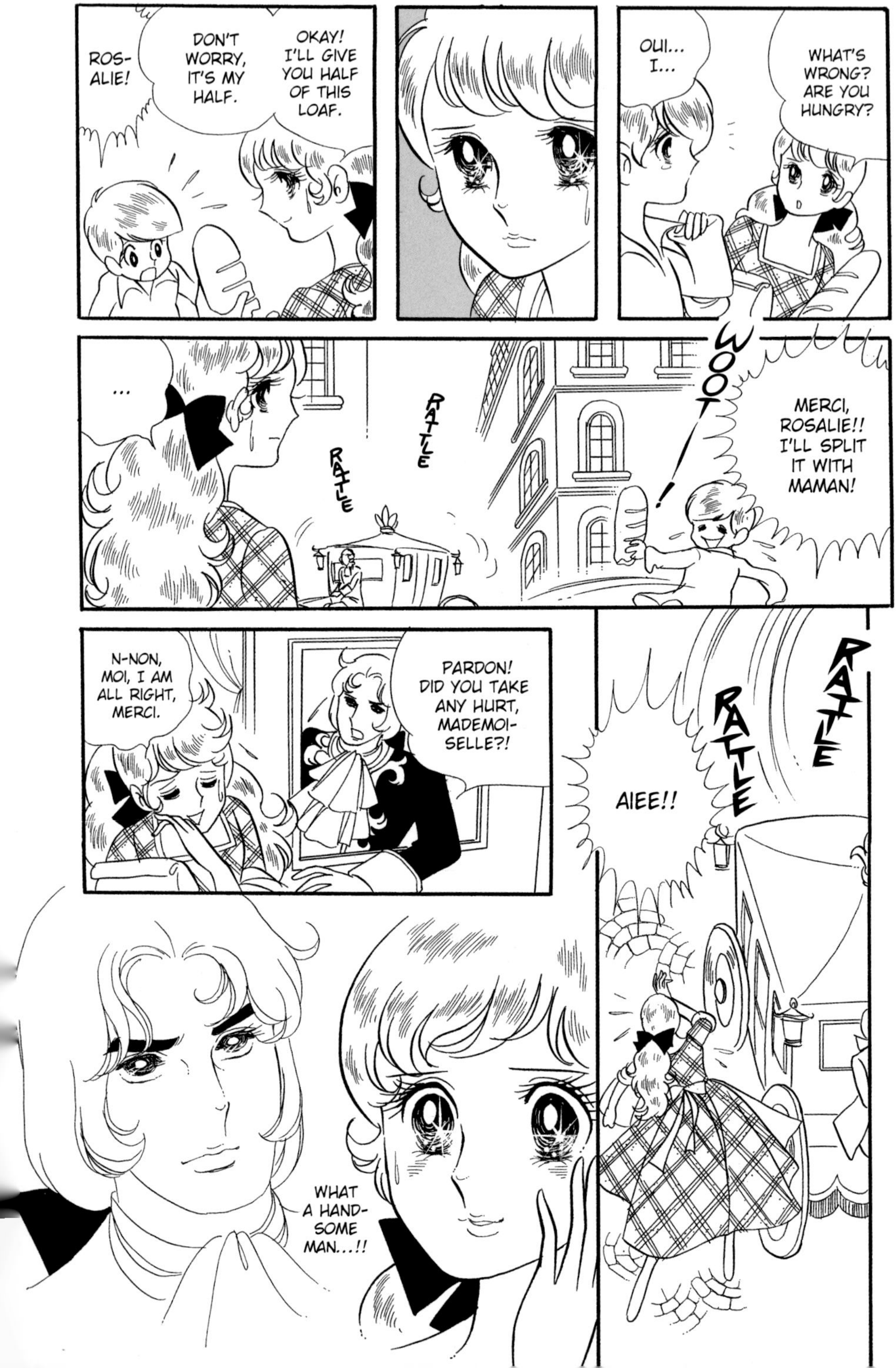
WHAT'S WRONG? ARE YOU HUNGRY?
OUI... I...
OKAY! I'LL GIVE YOU HALF OF THIS LOAF.
DON'T WORRY, IT'S MY HALF.
ROS-ALIE!
WOOT!!
MERCI, ROSALIE!! I'LL SPLIT IT WITH MAMAN!
RATTLE
RATTLE
...
RATTLE
RATTLE
AIEE!!
PARDON! DID YOU TAKE ANY HURT, MADEMOI-SELLE?!
N-NON, MOI, I AM ALL RIGHT, MERCI.
WHAT A HAND-SOME MAN...!!

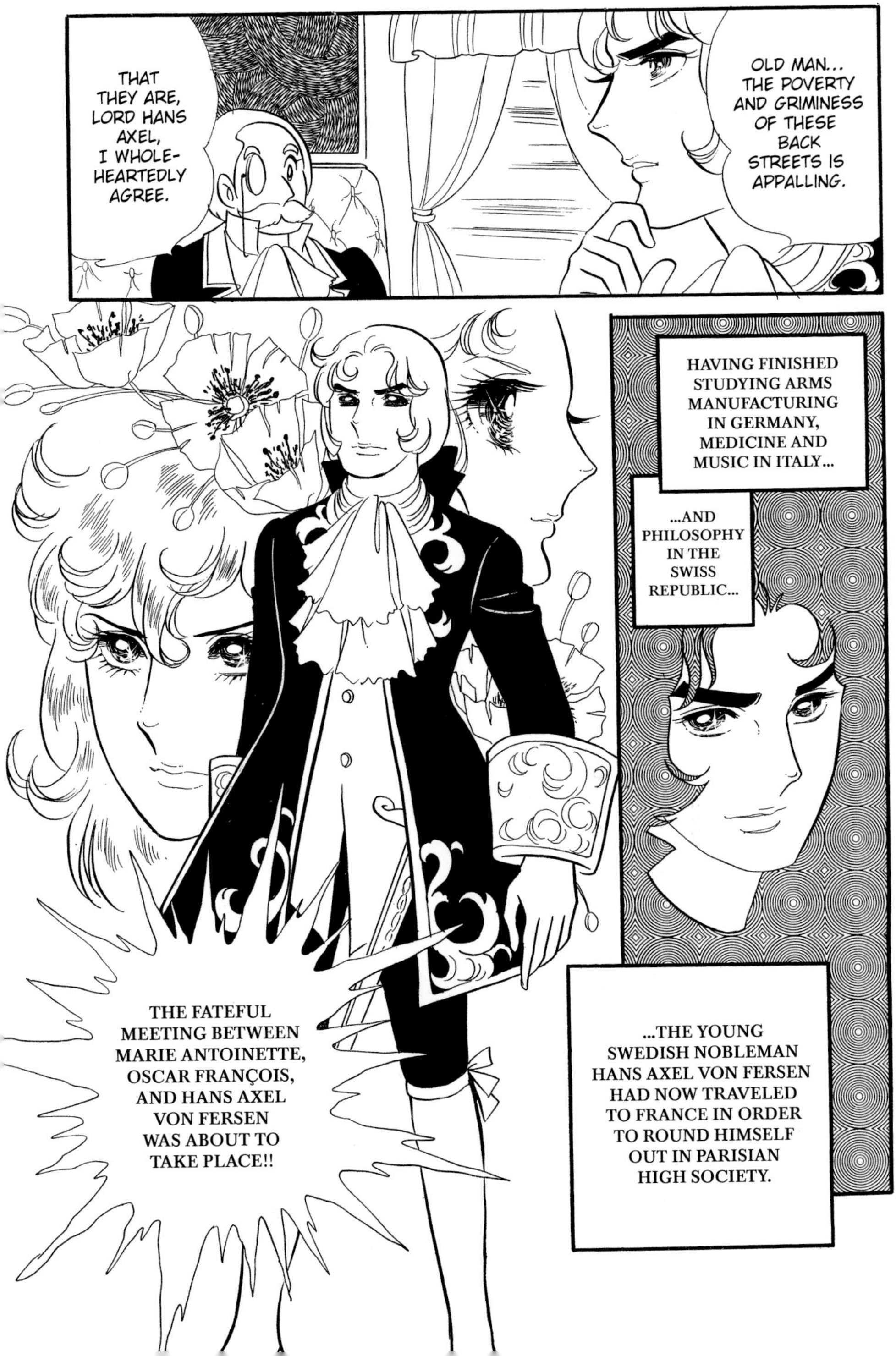
OLD MAN... THE POVERTY AND GRIMINESS OF THESE BACK STREETS IS APPALLING.
THAT THEY ARE, LORD HANS AXEL, I WHOLE-HEARTEDLY AGREE.
HAVING FINISHED STUDYING ARMS MANUFACTURING IN GERMANY, MEDICINE AND MUSIC IN ITALY...
...AND PHILOSOPHY IN THE SWISS REPUBLIC...
...THE YOUNG SWEDISH NOBLEMAN HANS AXEL VON FERSEN HAD NOW TRAVELED TO FRANCE IN ORDER TO ROUND HIMSELF OUT IN PARISIAN HIGH SOCIETY.
THE FATEFUL MEETING BETWEEN MARIE ANTOINETTE, OSCAR FRANÇOIS, AND HANS AXEL VON FERSEN WAS ABOUT TO TAKE PLACE!!

1972 WEEKLY MARGARET MAGAZINE
ISSUE 22 COVER INSERT ART

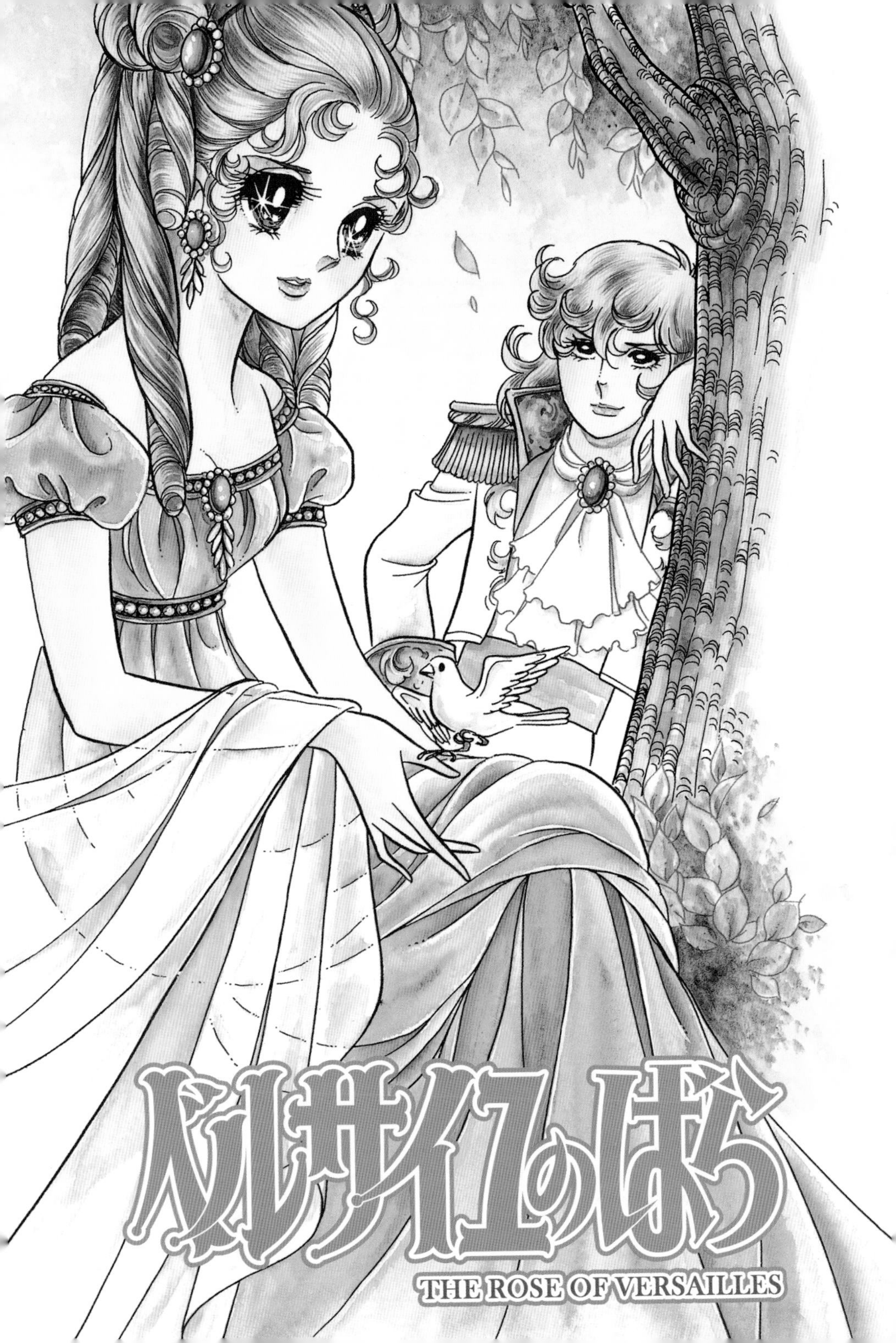
ベルサイユのばら
THE ROSE OF VERSAILLES

⚜Episode 9

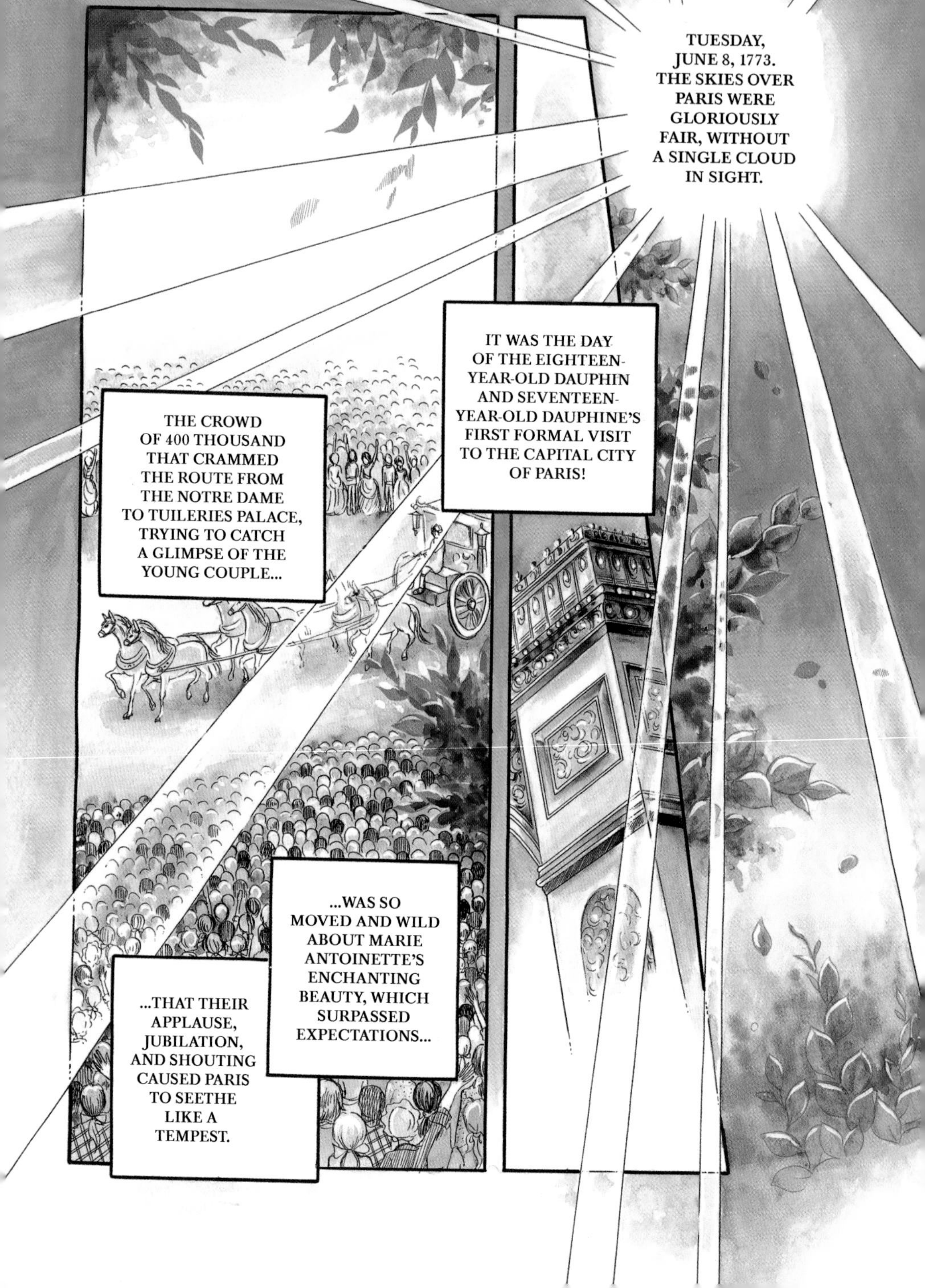
TUESDAY, JUNE 8, 1773. THE SKIES OVER PARIS WERE GLORIOUSLY FAIR, WITHOUT A SINGLE CLOUD IN SIGHT.
IT WAS THE DAY OF THE EIGHTEEN-YEAR-OLD DAUPHIN AND SEVENTEEN-YEAR-OLD DAUPHINE'S FIRST FORMAL VISIT TO THE CAPITAL CITY OF PARIS!
THE CROWD OF 400 THOUSAND THAT CRAMMED THE ROUTE FROM THE NOTRE DAME TO TUILERIES PALACE, TRYING TO CATCH A GLIMPSE OF THE YOUNG COUPLE...
...WAS SO MOVED AND WILD ABOUT MARIE ANTOINETTE'S ENCHANTING BEAUTY, WHICH SURPASSED EXPECTATIONS...
...THAT THEIR APPLAUSE, JUBILATION, AND SHOUTING CAUSED PARIS TO SEETHE LIKE A TEMPEST.

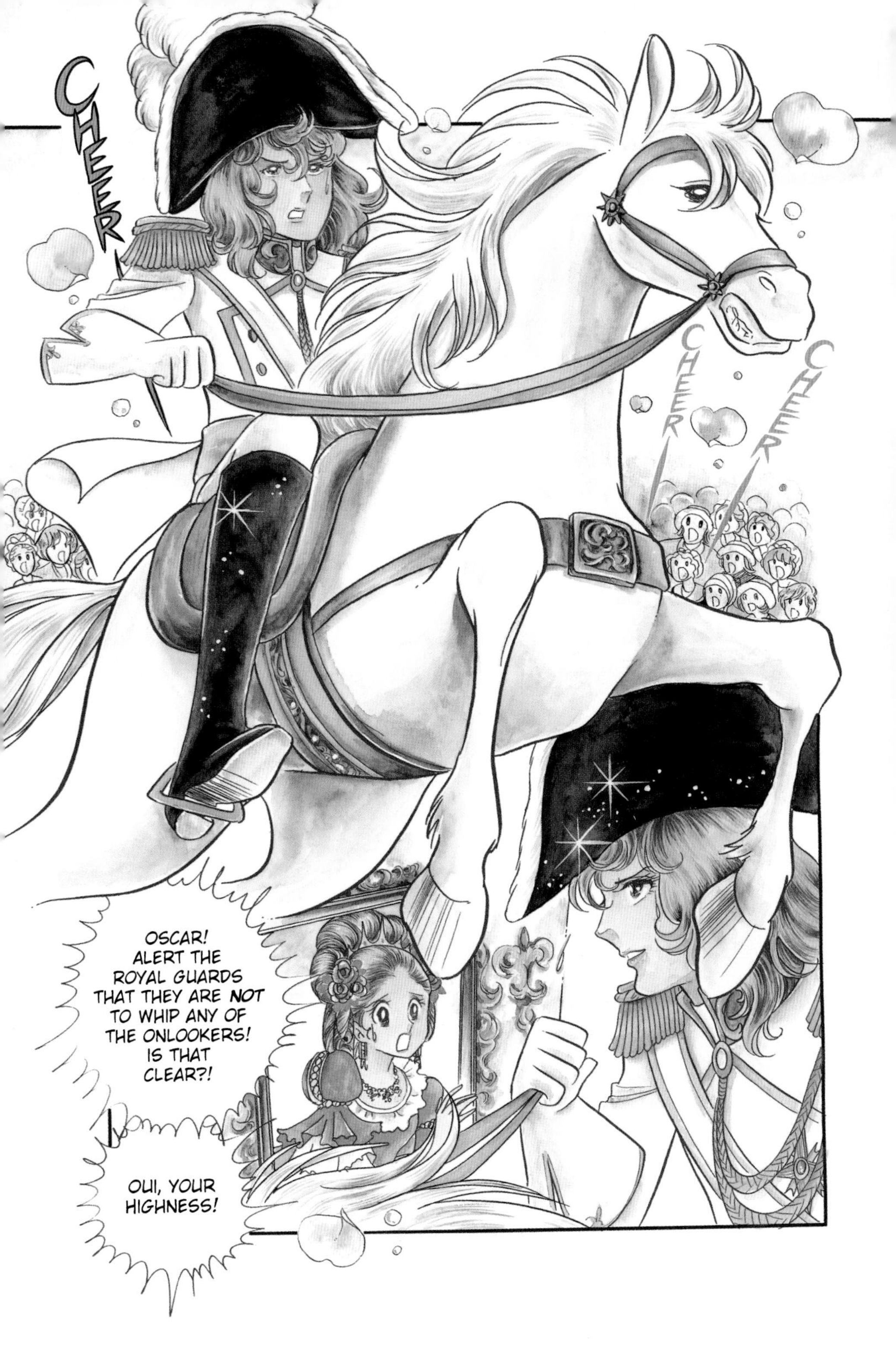
CHEER
CHEER
CHEER
OSCAR! ALERT THE ROYAL GUARDS THAT THEY ARE **NOT** TO WHIP ANY OF THE ONLOOKERS! IS THAT CLEAR?!
OUI, YOUR HIGHNESS!

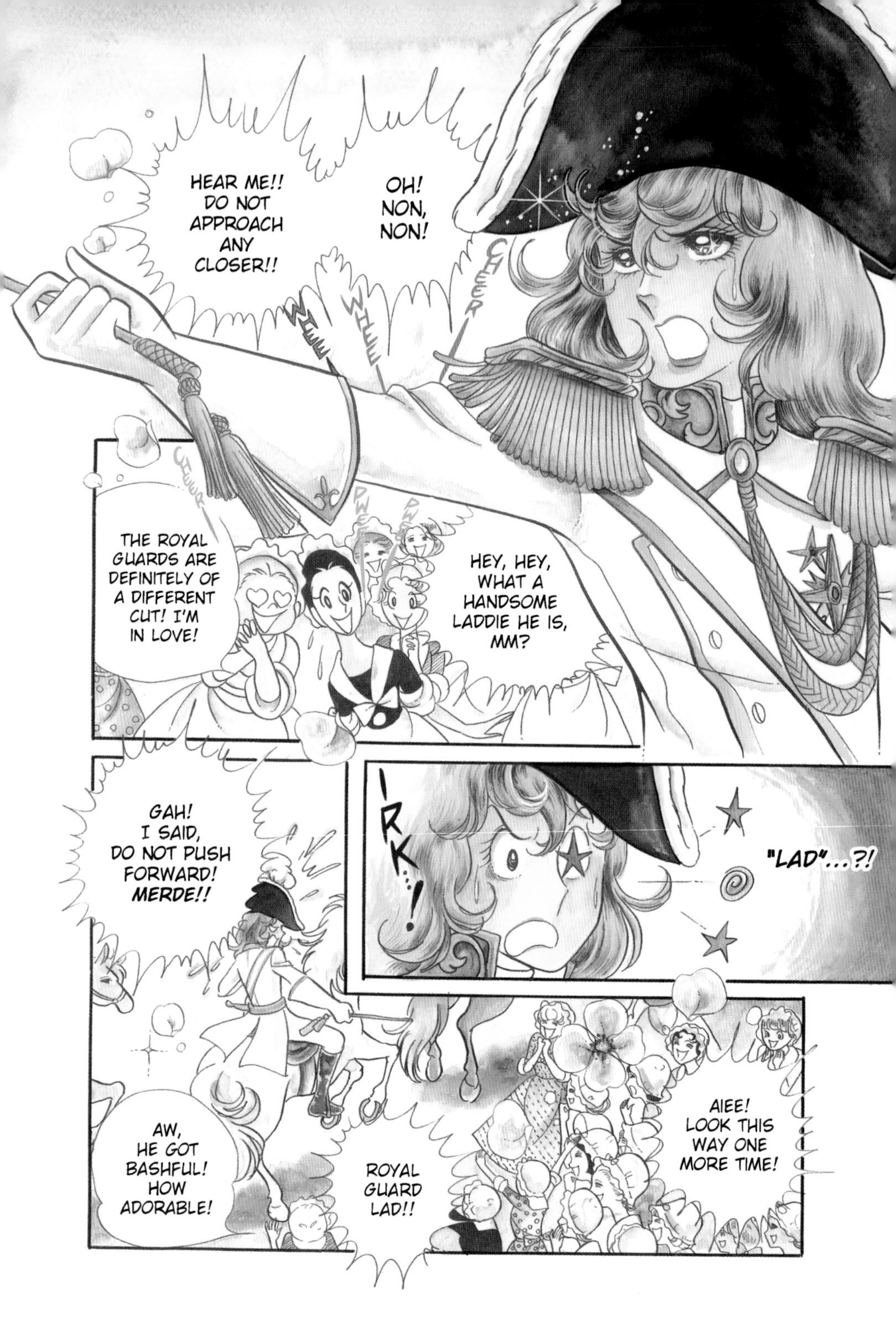
OH! NON, NON!
HEAR ME!! DO NOT APPROACH ANY CLOSER!!
CHEER
WHEE
WEE
HEY, HEY, WHAT A HANDSOME LADDIE HE IS, MM?
PWEE
PWEE
THE ROYAL GUARDS ARE DEFINITELY OF A DIFFERENT CUT! I'M IN LOVE!
CHEER
"LAD"...?!
IRK...!
GAH! I SAID, DO NOT PUSH FORWARD! **MERDE!!**
AIEE! LOOK THIS WAY ONE MORE TIME!
ROYAL GUARD LAD!!
AW, HE GOT BASHFUL! HOW ADORABLE!

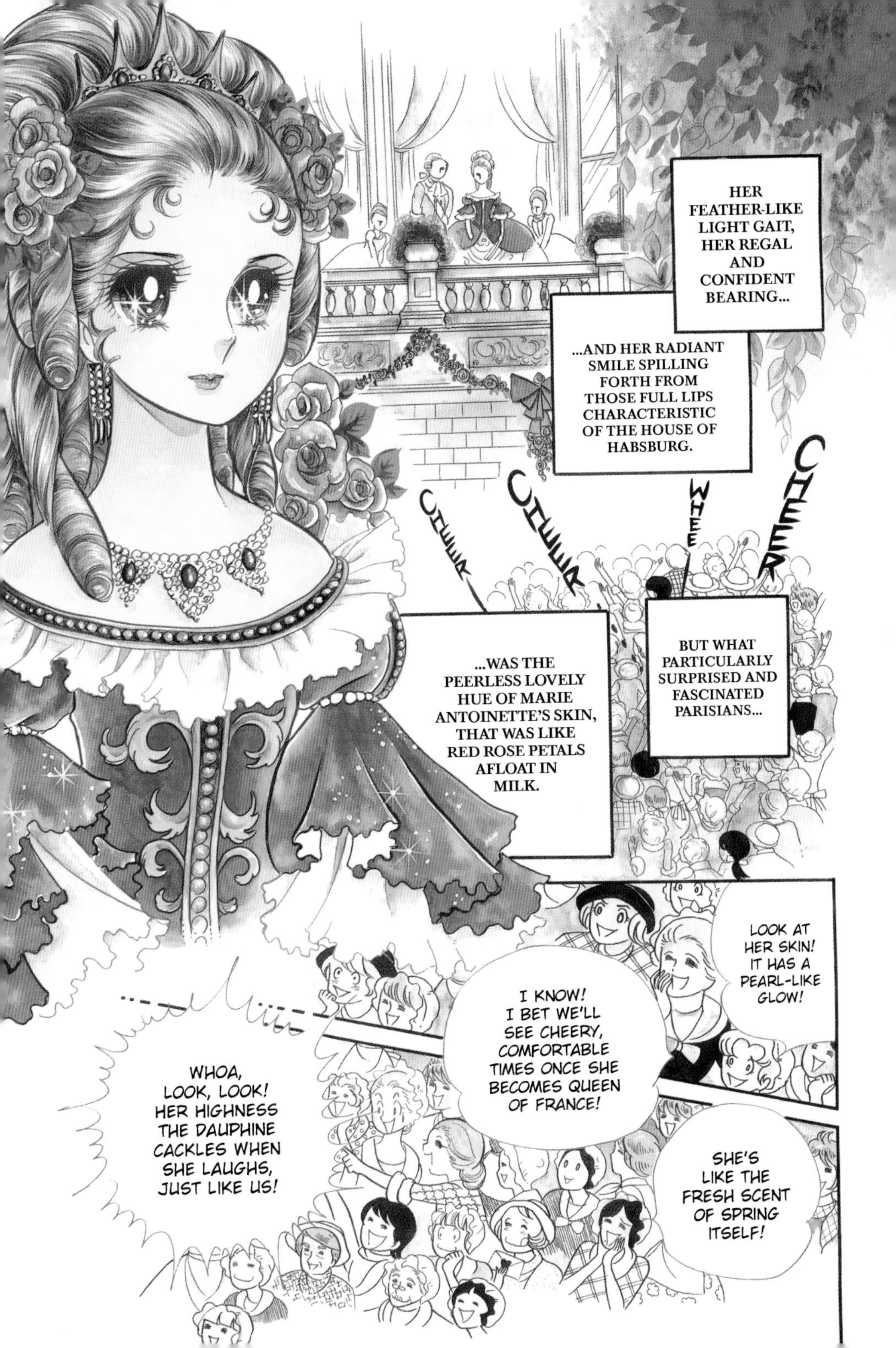
HER FEATHER-LIKE LIGHT GAIT, HER REGAL AND CONFIDENT BEARING...
...AND HER RADIANT SMILE SPILLING FORTH FROM THOSE FULL LIPS CHARACTERISTIC OF THE HOUSE OF HABSBURG.
CHEER
WHEE
CHEER
CHEER
BUT WHAT PARTICULARLY SURPRISED AND FASCINATED PARISIANS...
...WAS THE PEERLESS LOVELY HUE OF MARIE ANTOINETTE'S SKIN, THAT WAS LIKE RED ROSE PETALS AFLOAT IN MILK.
LOOK AT HER SKIN! IT HAS A PEARL-LIKE GLOW!
I KNOW! I BET WE'LL SEE CHEERY, COMFORTABLE TIMES ONCE SHE BECOMES QUEEN OF FRANCE!
SHE'S LIKE THE FRESH SCENT OF SPRING ITSELF!
WHOA, LOOK, LOOK! HER HIGHNESS THE DAUPHINE CACKLES WHEN SHE LAUGHS, JUST LIKE US!

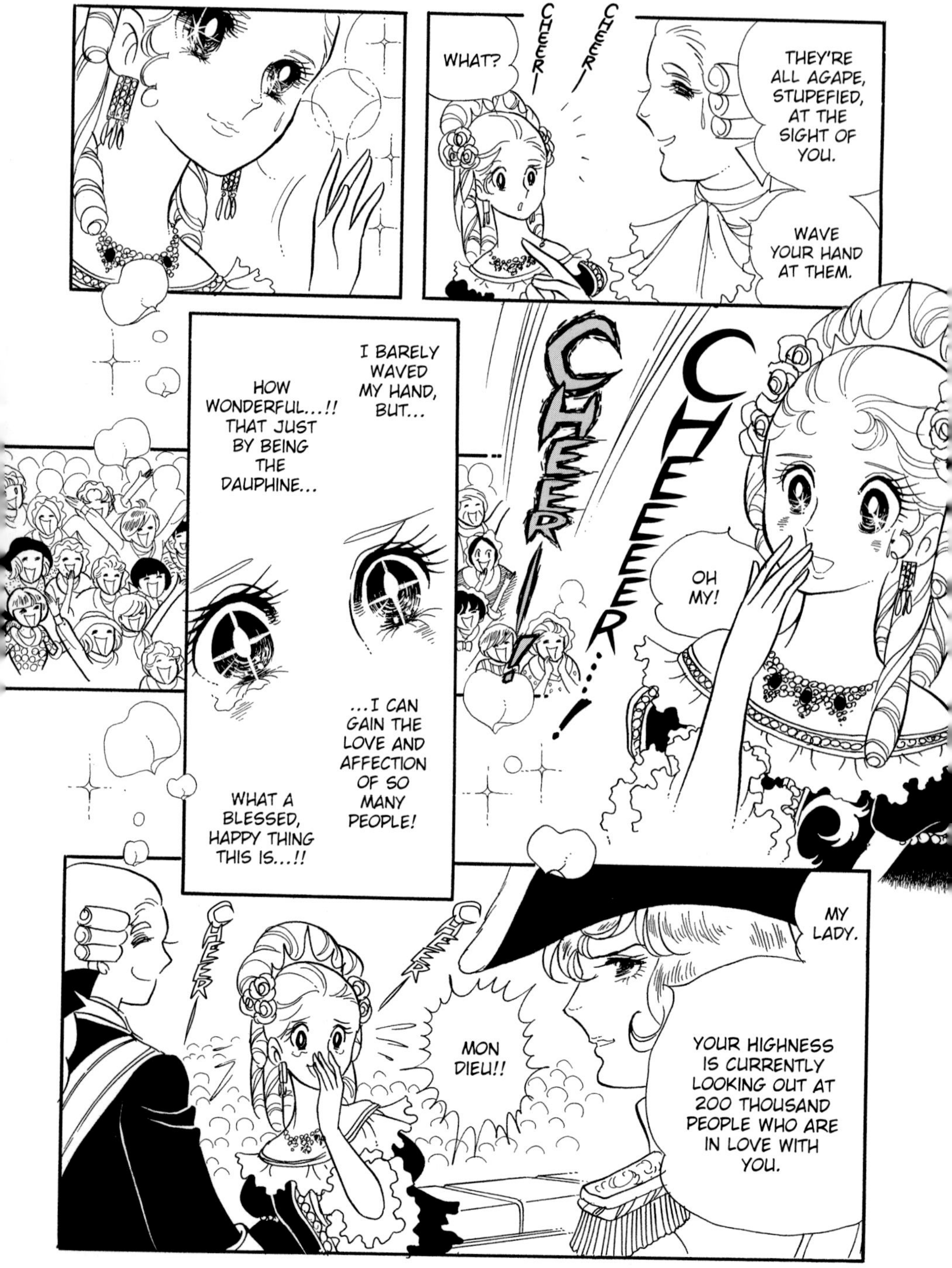

THEY'RE ALL AGAPE, STUPEFIED, AT THE SIGHT OF YOU.
WAVE YOUR HAND AT THEM.
CHEER—
CHEER—
WHAT?
CHEEEER...!
CHEER!!
OH MY!
I BARELY WAVED MY HAND, BUT...
HOW WONDERFUL...!! THAT JUST BY BEING THE DAUPHINE...
...I CAN GAIN THE LOVE AND AFFECTION OF SO MANY PEOPLE!
WHAT A BLESSED, HAPPY THING THIS IS...!!
MY LADY.
YOUR HIGHNESS IS CURRENTLY LOOKING OUT AT 200 THOUSAND PEOPLE WHO ARE IN LOVE WITH YOU.
CHEER
CHEER
MON DIEU!!

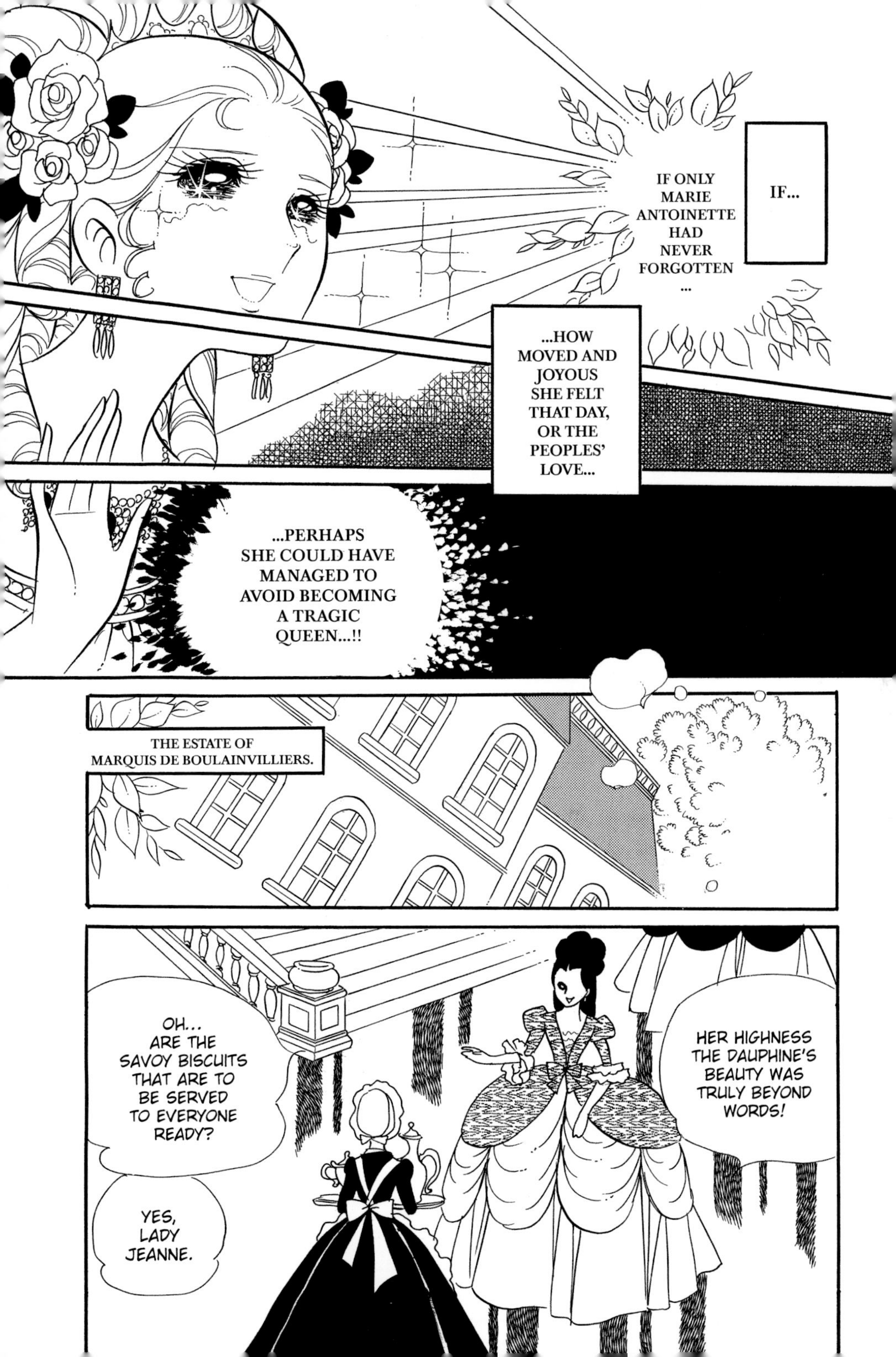
IF...
IF ONLY MARIE ANTOINETTE HAD NEVER FORGOTTEN ...
...HOW MOVED AND JOYOUS SHE FELT THAT DAY, OR THE PEOPLES' LOVE...
...PERHAPS SHE COULD HAVE MANAGED TO AVOID BECOMING A TRAGIC QUEEN...!!
THE ESTATE OF MARQUIS DE BOULAINVILLIERS.
HER HIGHNESS THE DAUPHINE'S BEAUTY WAS TRULY BEYOND WORDS!
OH... ARE THE SAVOY BISCUITS THAT ARE TO BE SERVED TO EVERYONE READY?
YES, LADY JEANNE.

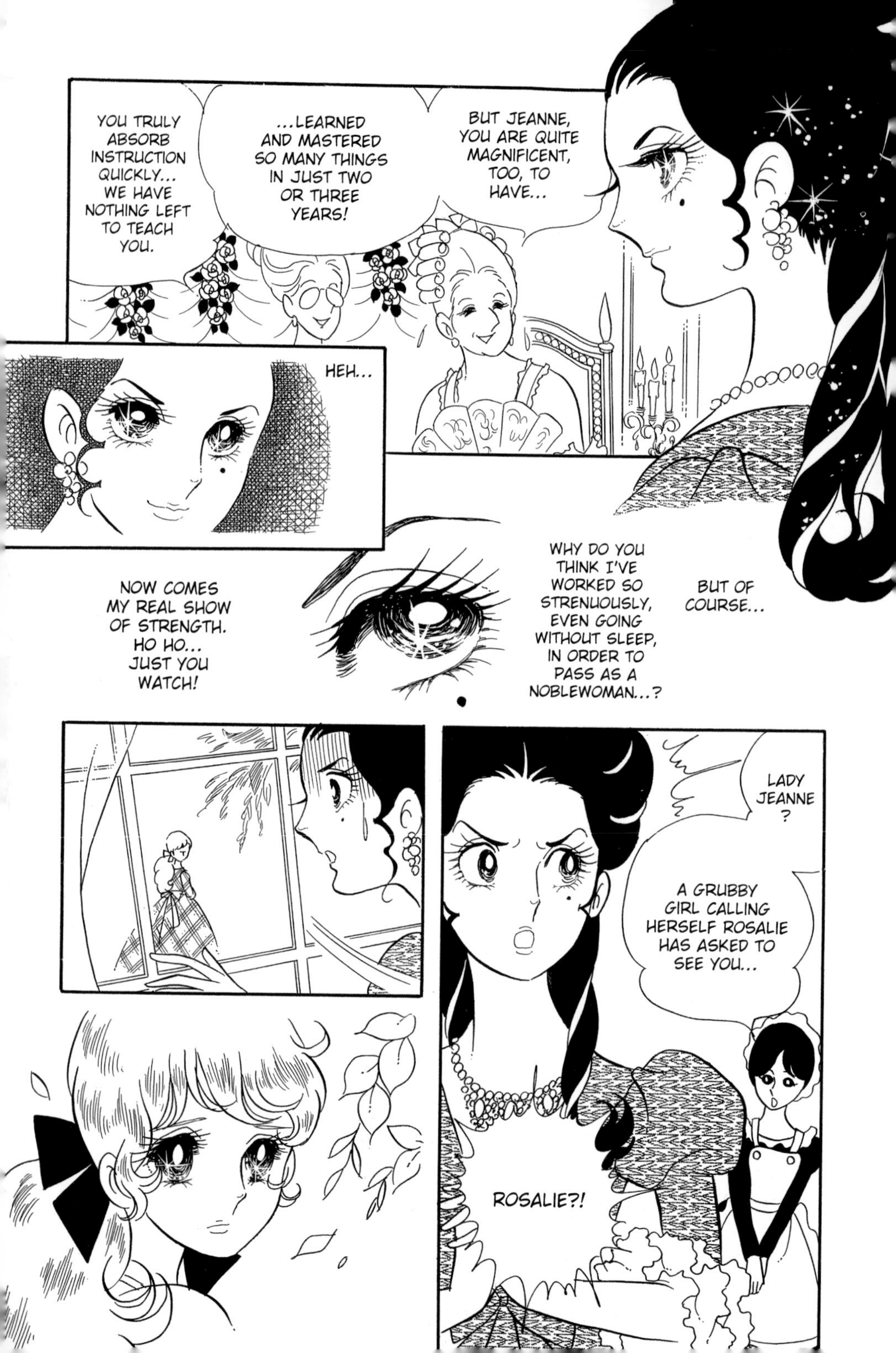

BUT JEANNE, YOU ARE QUITE MAGNIFICENT, TOO, TO HAVE...
...LEARNED AND MASTERED SO MANY THINGS IN JUST TWO OR THREE YEARS!
YOU TRULY ABSORB INSTRUCTION QUICKLY... WE HAVE NOTHING LEFT TO TEACH YOU.
HEH...
BUT OF COURSE...
WHY DO YOU THINK I'VE WORKED SO STRENUOUSLY, EVEN GOING WITHOUT SLEEP, IN ORDER TO PASS AS A NOBLEWOMAN...?
NOW COMES MY REAL SHOW OF STRENGTH. HO HO... JUST YOU WATCH!
LADY JEANNE ?
A GRUBBY GIRL CALLING HERSELF ROSALIE HAS ASKED TO SEE YOU...
ROSALIE?!

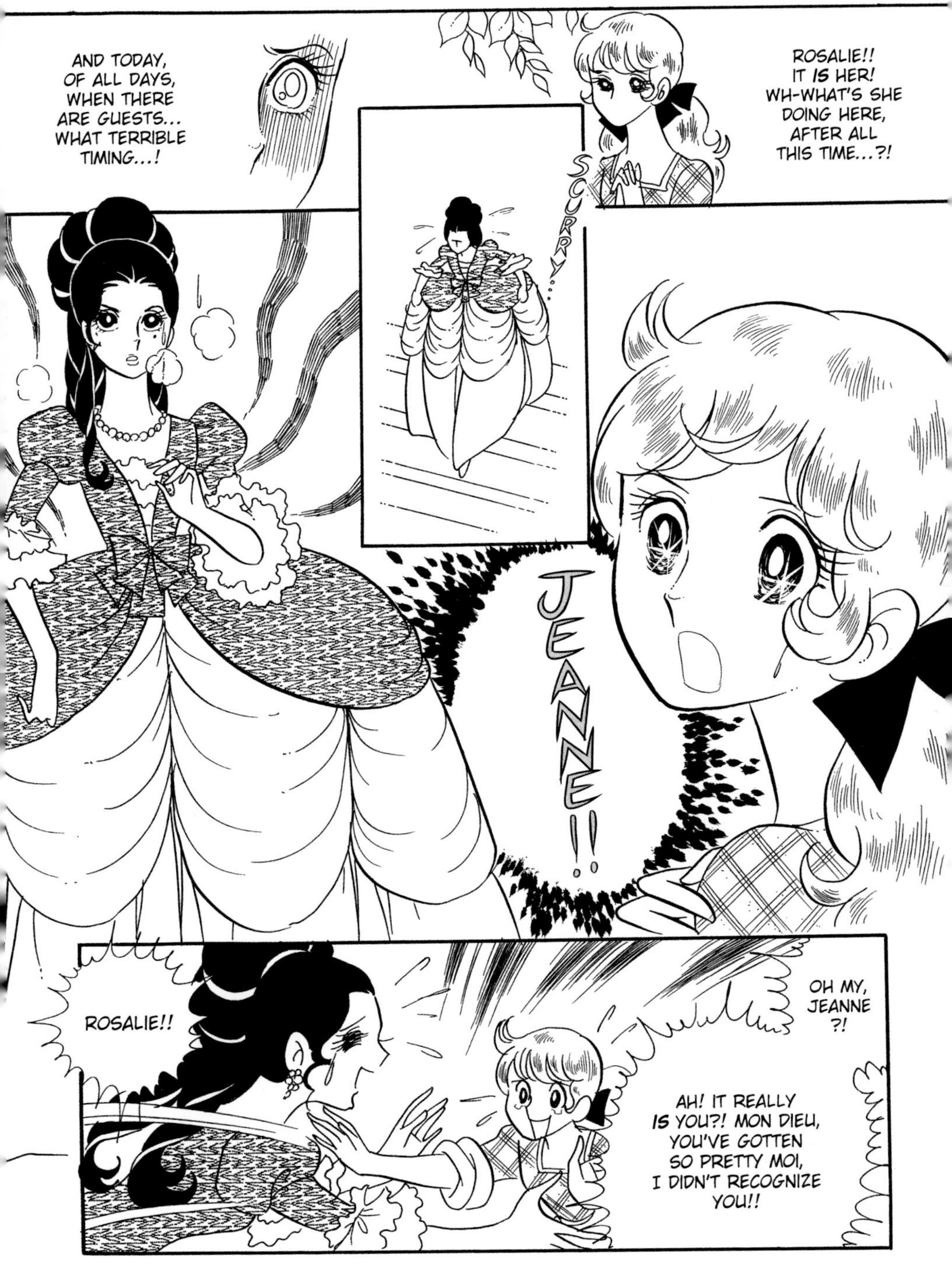
ROSALIE!! IT IS HER! WH-WHAT'S SHE DOING HERE, AFTER ALL THIS TIME...?!
AND TODAY, OF ALL DAYS, WHEN THERE ARE GUESTS... WHAT TERRIBLE TIMING...!
JEANNE!!
SCURRY...
OH MY, JEANNE?!
AH! IT REALLY IS YOU?! MON DIEU, YOU'VE GOTTEN SO PRETTY MOI, I DIDN'T RECOGNIZE YOU!!
ROSALIE!!

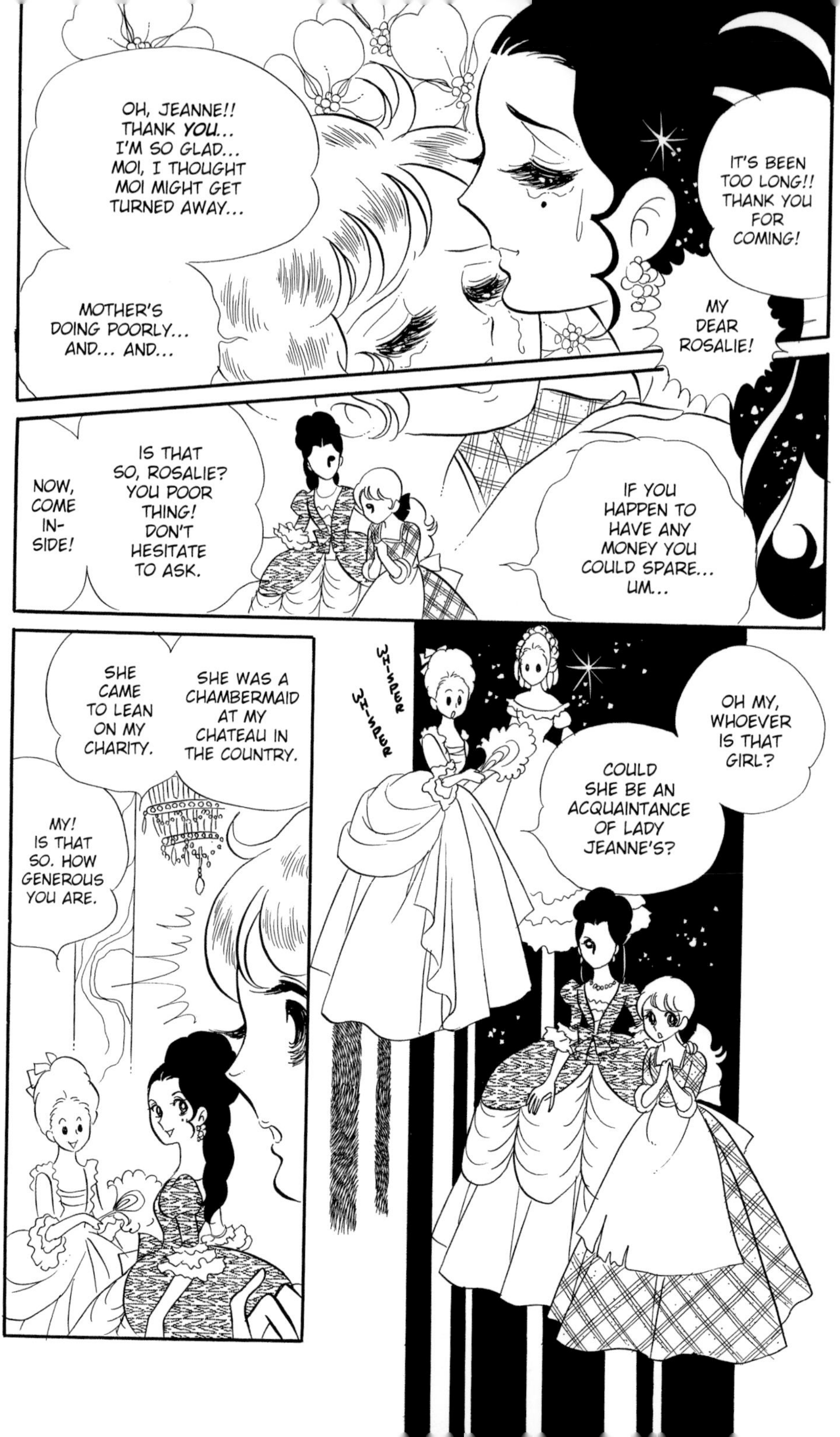
IT'S BEEN TOO LONG!! THANK YOU FOR COMING!
MY DEAR ROSALIE!
OH, JEANNE!! THANK *YOU*... I'M SO GLAD... MOI, I THOUGHT MOI MIGHT GET TURNED AWAY...
MOTHER'S DOING POORLY... AND... AND...
IF YOU HAPPEN TO HAVE ANY MONEY YOU COULD SPARE... UM...
IS THAT SO, ROSALIE? YOU POOR THING! DON'T HESITATE TO ASK.
NOW, COME IN-SIDE!
OH MY, WHOEVER IS THAT GIRL?
COULD SHE BE AN ACQUAINTANCE OF LADY JEANNE'S?
WHISPER
WHISPER
SHE WAS A CHAMBERMAID AT MY CHATEAU IN THE COUNTRY.
SHE CAME TO LEAN ON MY CHARITY.
MY! IS THAT SO. HOW GENEROUS YOU ARE.

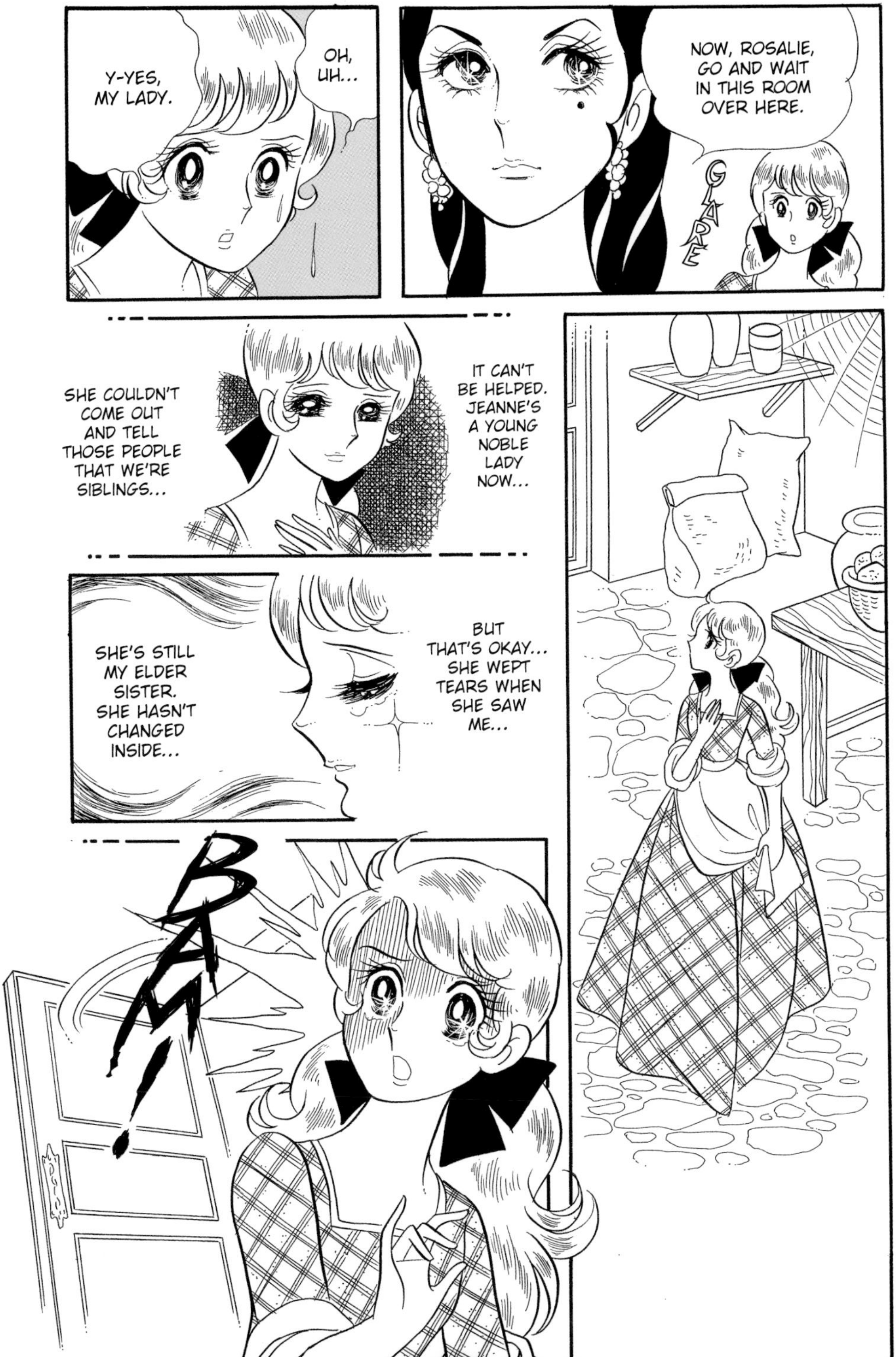
NOW, ROSALIE, GO AND WAIT IN THIS ROOM OVER HERE.
GLARE
OH, UH...
Y-YES, MY LADY.
IT CAN'T BE HELPED. JEANNE'S A YOUNG NOBLE LADY NOW...
SHE COULDN'T COME OUT AND TELL THOSE PEOPLE THAT WE'RE SIBLINGS...
BUT THAT'S OKAY... SHE WEPT TEARS WHEN SHE SAW ME...
SHE'S STILL MY ELDER SISTER. SHE HASN'T CHANGED INSIDE...
BAM!

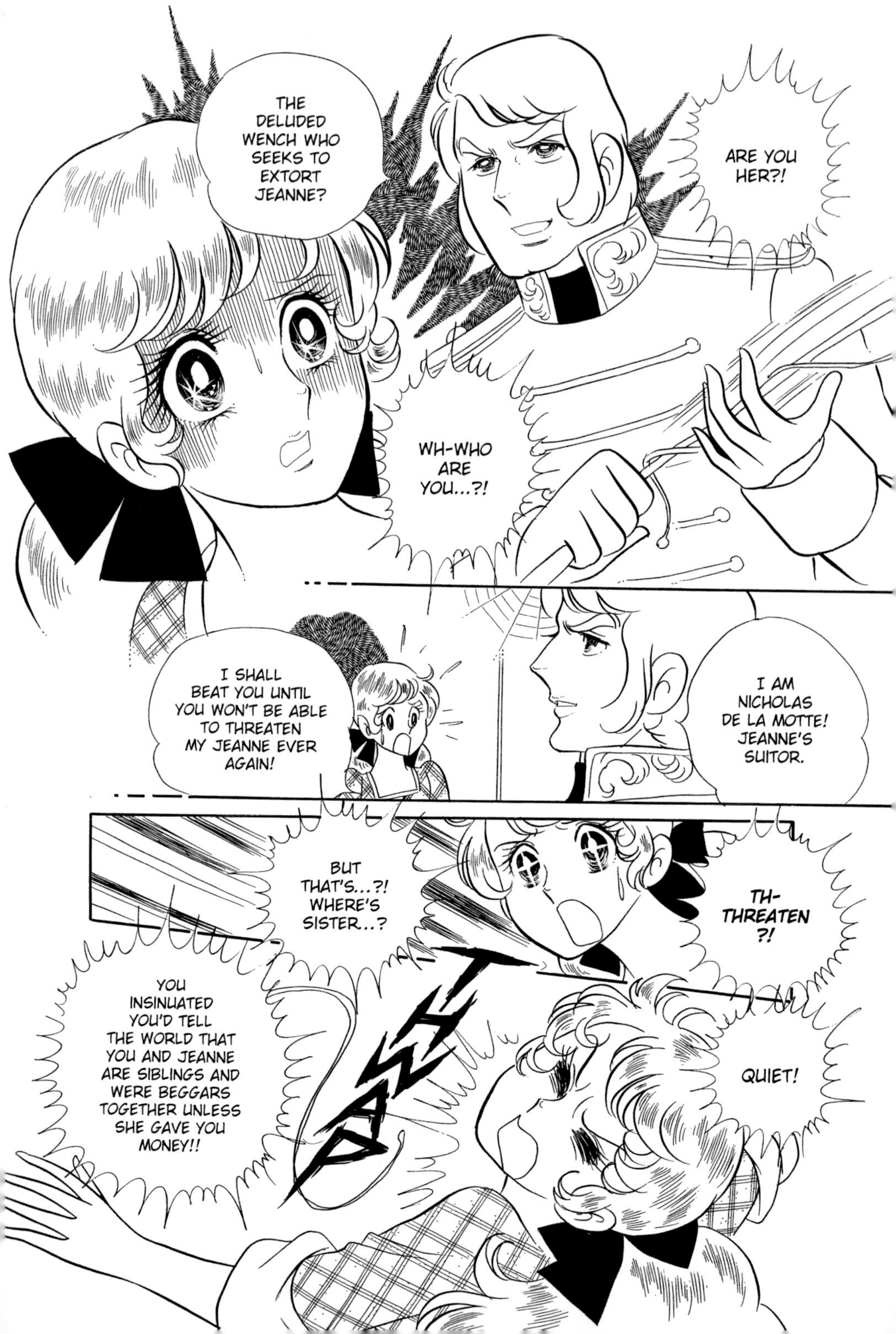

ARE YOU HER?!
THE DELUDED WENCH WHO SEEKS TO EXTORT JEANNE?
WH-WHO ARE YOU...?!
I AM NICHOLAS DE LA MOTTE! JEANNE'S SUITOR.
I SHALL BEAT YOU UNTIL YOU WON'T BE ABLE TO THREATEN MY JEANNE EVER AGAIN!
TH-THREATEN?!
BUT THAT'S...?! WHERE'S SISTER...?
QUIET!
YOU INSINUATED YOU'D TELL THE WORLD THAT YOU AND JEANNE ARE SIBLINGS AND WERE BEGGARS TOGETHER UNLESS SHE GAVE YOU MONEY!!
THWAP

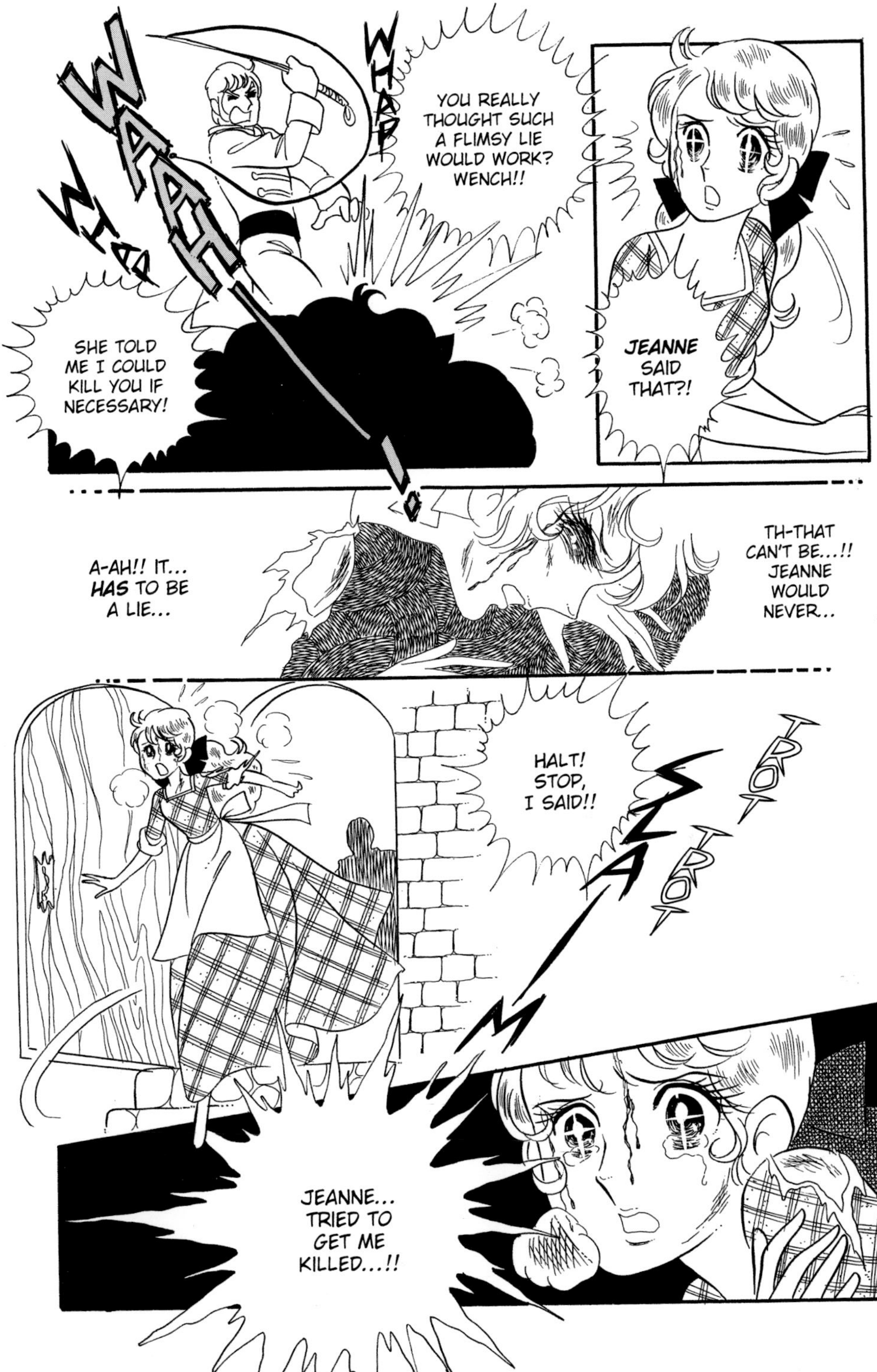
JEANNE SAID THAT?!
WHAP
YOU REALLY THOUGHT SUCH A FLIMSY LIE WOULD WORK? WENCH!!
SHE TOLD ME I COULD KILL YOU IF NECESSARY!
TH-THAT CAN'T BE...!! JEANNE WOULD NEVER...
A-AH!! IT... **HAS** TO BE A LIE...
TROT TROT
HALT! STOP, I SAID!!
SLAM
JEANNE... TRIED TO GET ME KILLED...!!

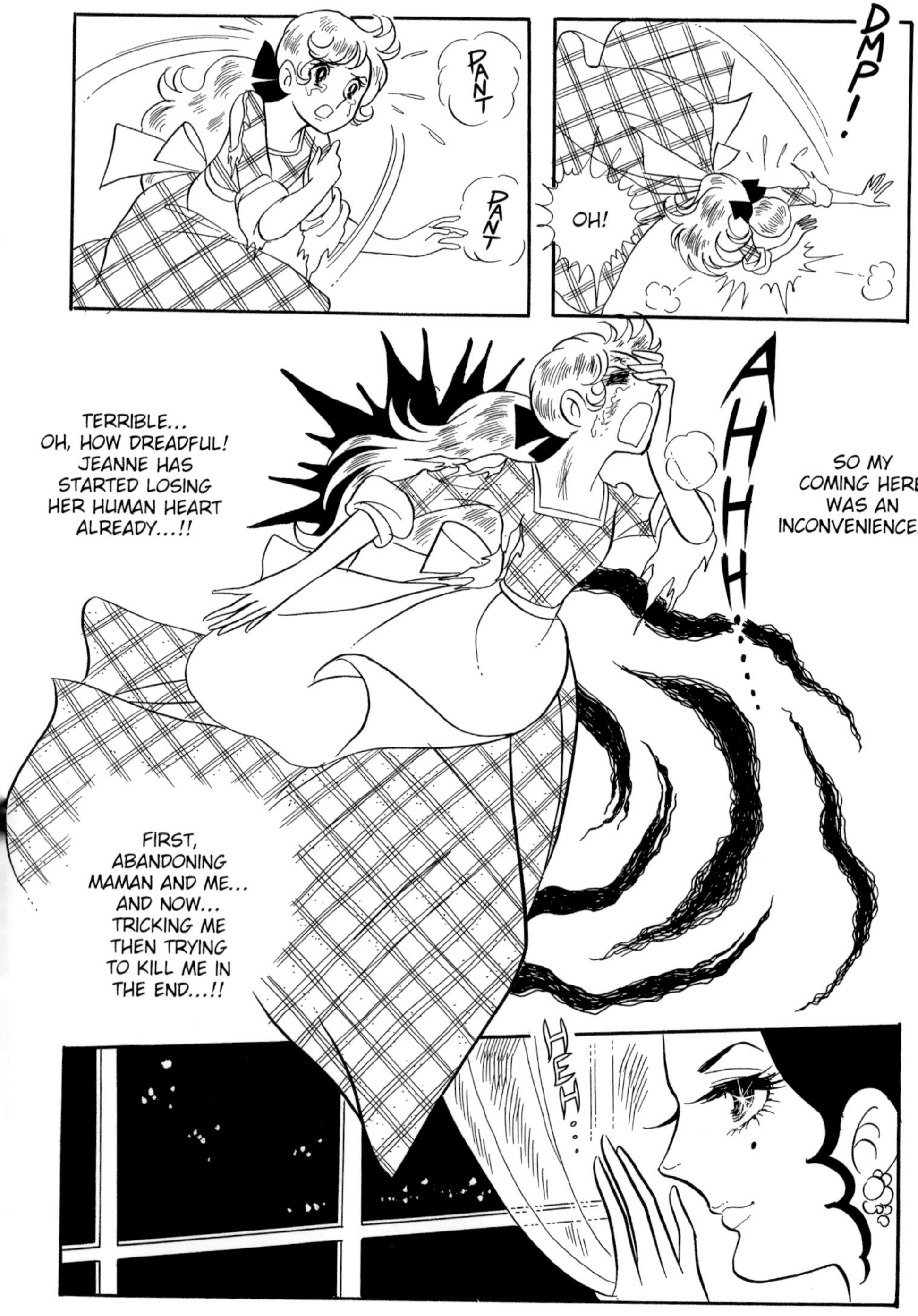
DMP!
OH!
PANT
PANT
AHHH...
SO MY COMING HERE WAS AN INCONVENIENCE...!
TERRIBLE... OH, HOW DREADFUL! JEANNE HAS STARTED LOSING HER HUMAN HEART ALREADY...!!
FIRST, ABANDONING MAMAN AND ME... AND NOW... TRICKING ME THEN TRYING TO KILL ME IN THE END...!!
HEH...

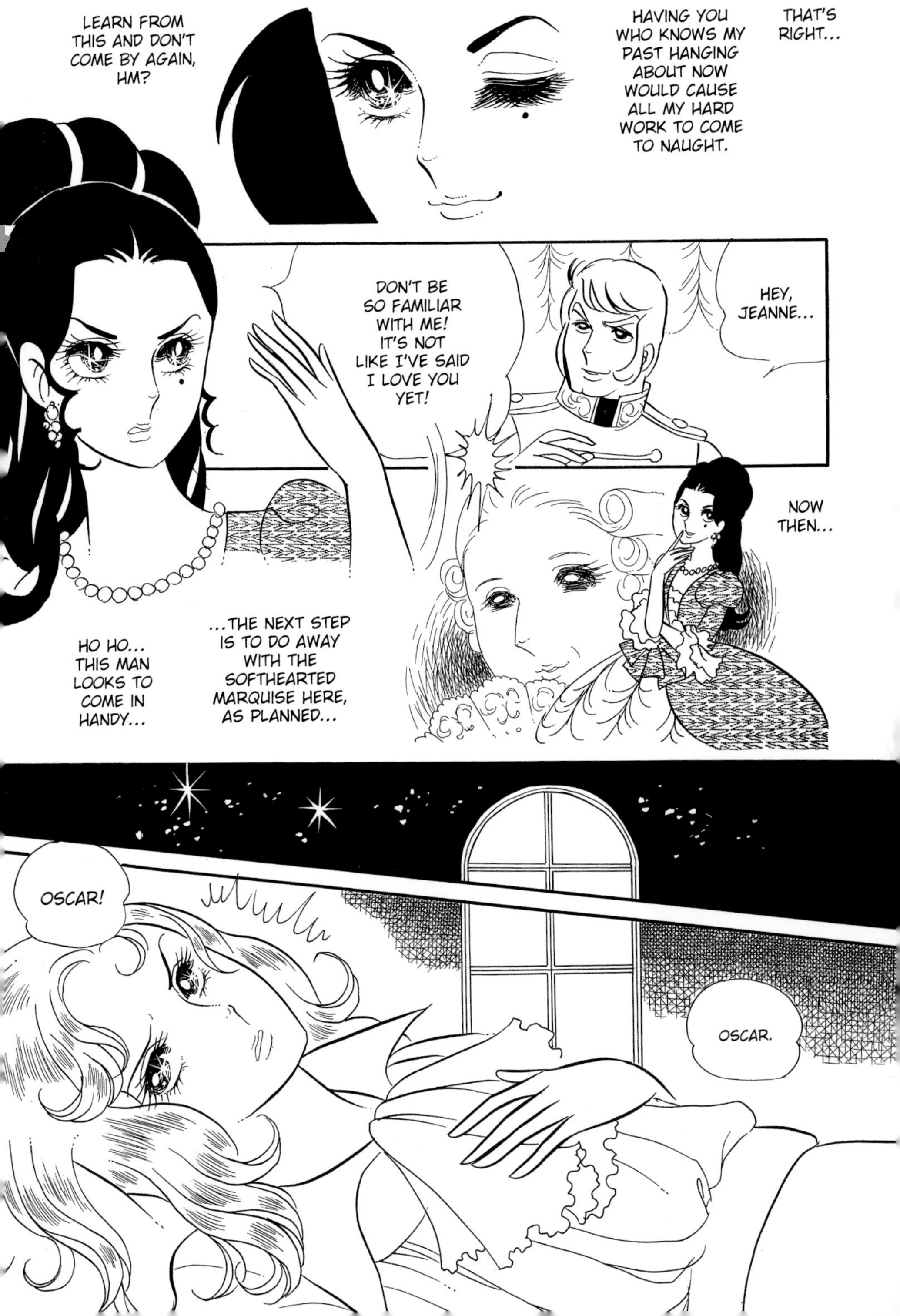
THAT'S RIGHT...
HAVING YOU WHO KNOWS MY PAST HANGING ABOUT NOW WOULD CAUSE ALL MY HARD WORK TO COME TO NAUGHT.
LEARN FROM THIS AND DON'T COME BY AGAIN, HM?
HEY, JEANNE...
DON'T BE SO FAMILIAR WITH ME! IT'S NOT LIKE I'VE SAID I LOVE YOU YET!
NOW THEN...
...THE NEXT STEP IS TO DO AWAY WITH THE SOFTHEARTED MARQUISE HERE, AS PLANNED...
HO HO... THIS MAN LOOKS TO COME IN HANDY...
OSCAR.
OSCAR!

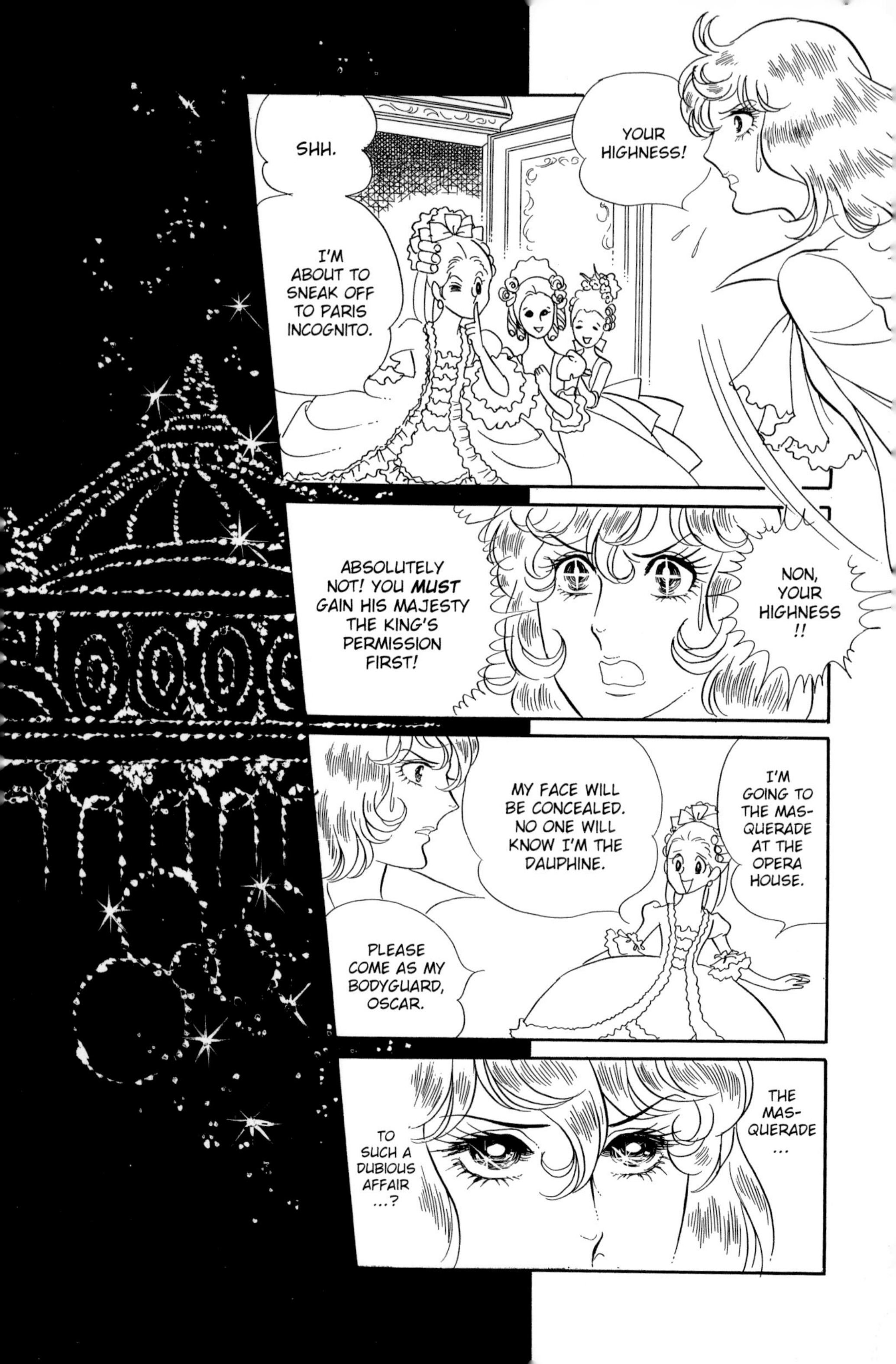
YOUR HIGHNESS!
SHH.
I'M ABOUT TO SNEAK OFF TO PARIS INCOGNITO.
NON, YOUR HIGHNESS !!
ABSOLUTELY NOT! YOU **MUST** GAIN HIS MAJESTY THE KING'S PERMISSION FIRST!
I'M GOING TO THE MASQUERADE AT THE OPERA HOUSE.
MY FACE WILL BE CONCEALED. NO ONE WILL KNOW I'M THE DAUPHINE.
PLEASE COME AS MY BODYGUARD, OSCAR.
THE MASQUERADE ...
TO SUCH A DUBIOUS AFFAIR ...?

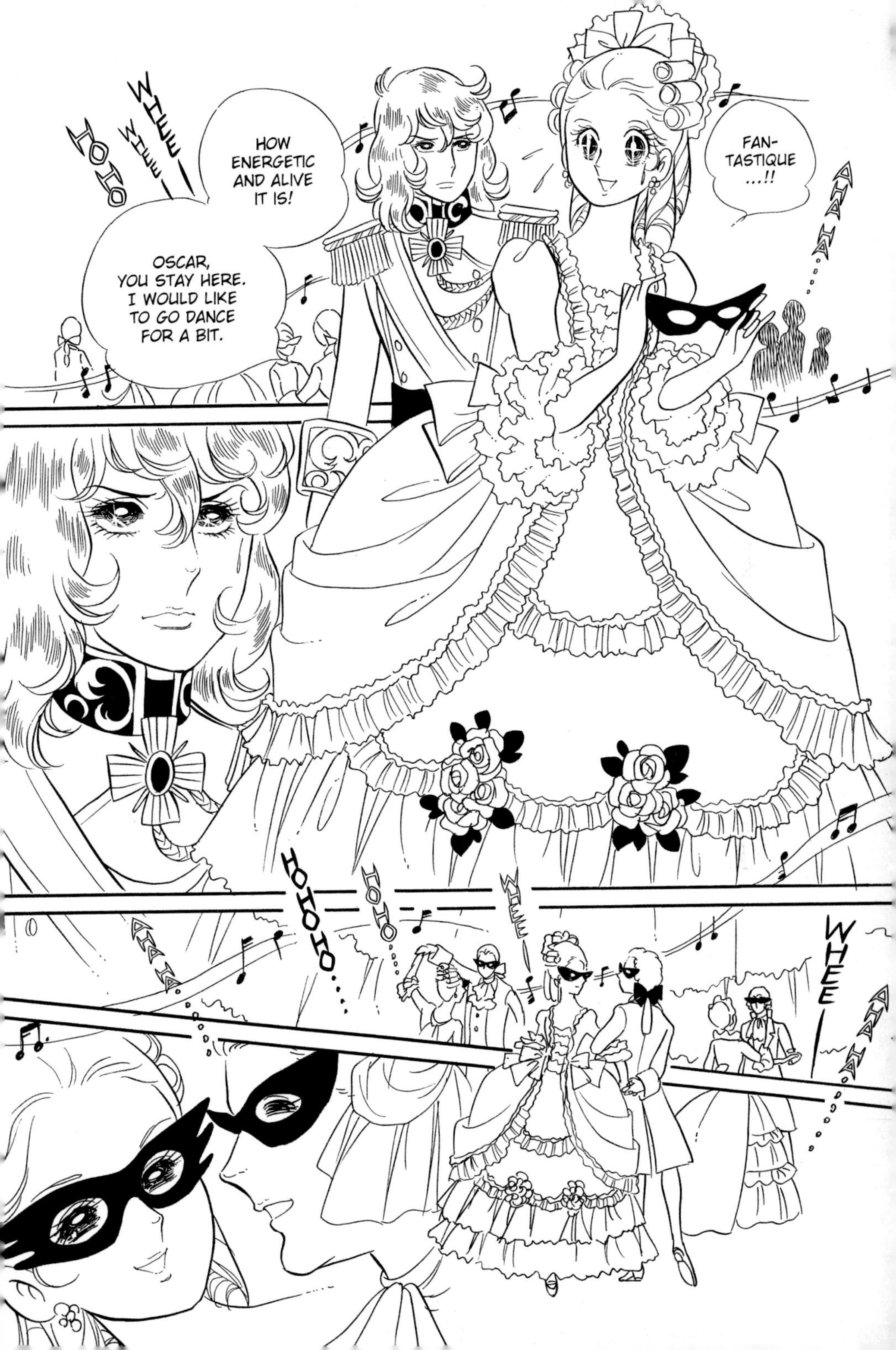
FAN-TASTIQUE ...!!
AHAHAHA...
HOW ENERGETIC AND ALIVE IT IS!
WHEE—
WHEE—
HOHO
OSCAR, YOU STAY HERE. I WOULD LIKE TO GO DANCE FOR A BIT.
AHAHAHA...
WHEE—
WHEE—
HOHO...
HOHOHO...
AHAHA...

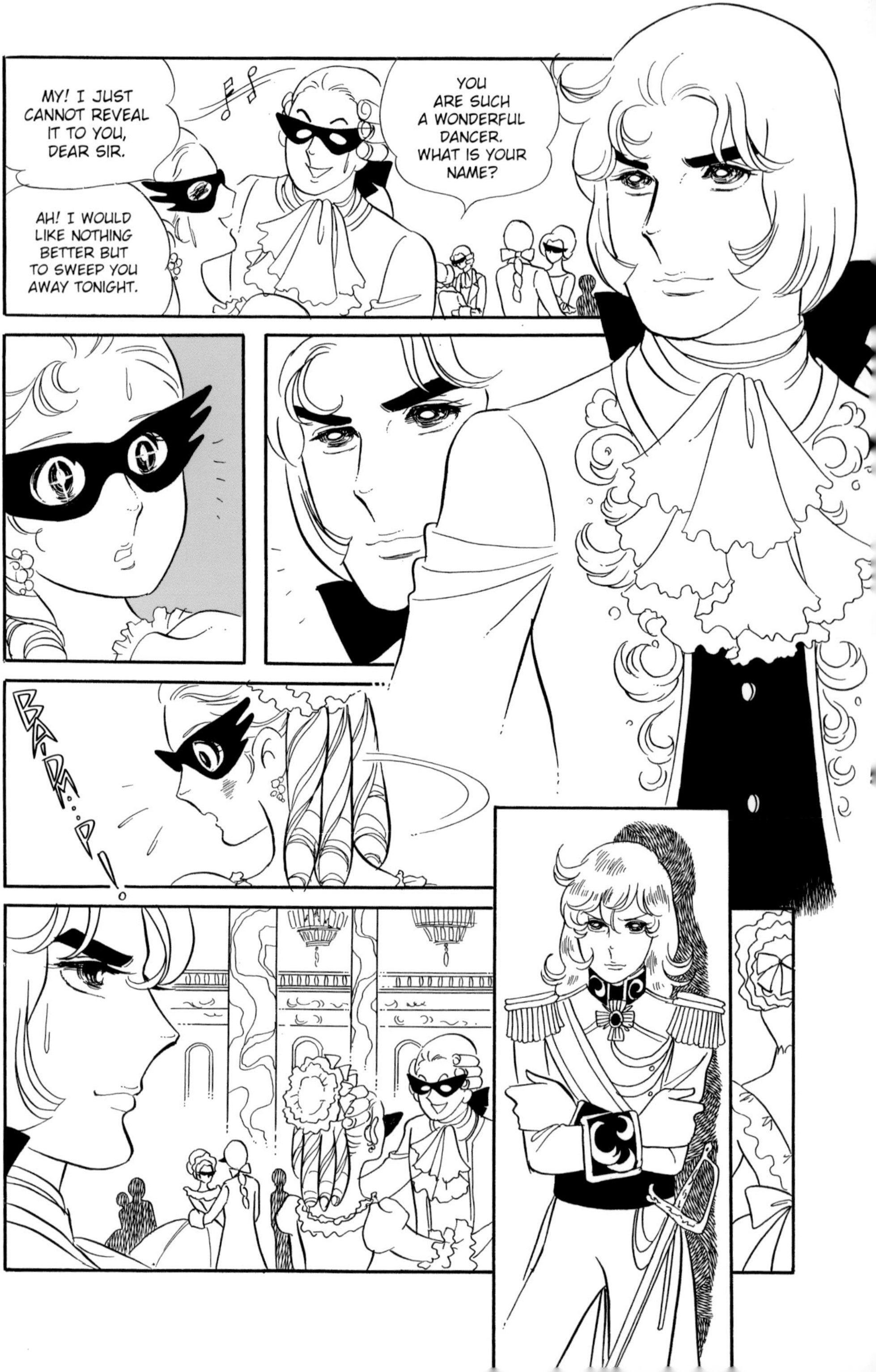
YOU ARE SUCH A WONDERFUL DANCER. WHAT IS YOUR NAME?
MY! I JUST CANNOT REVEAL IT TO YOU, DEAR SIR.
AH! I WOULD LIKE NOTHING BETTER BUT TO SWEEP YOU AWAY TONIGHT.
BA-DM...P!

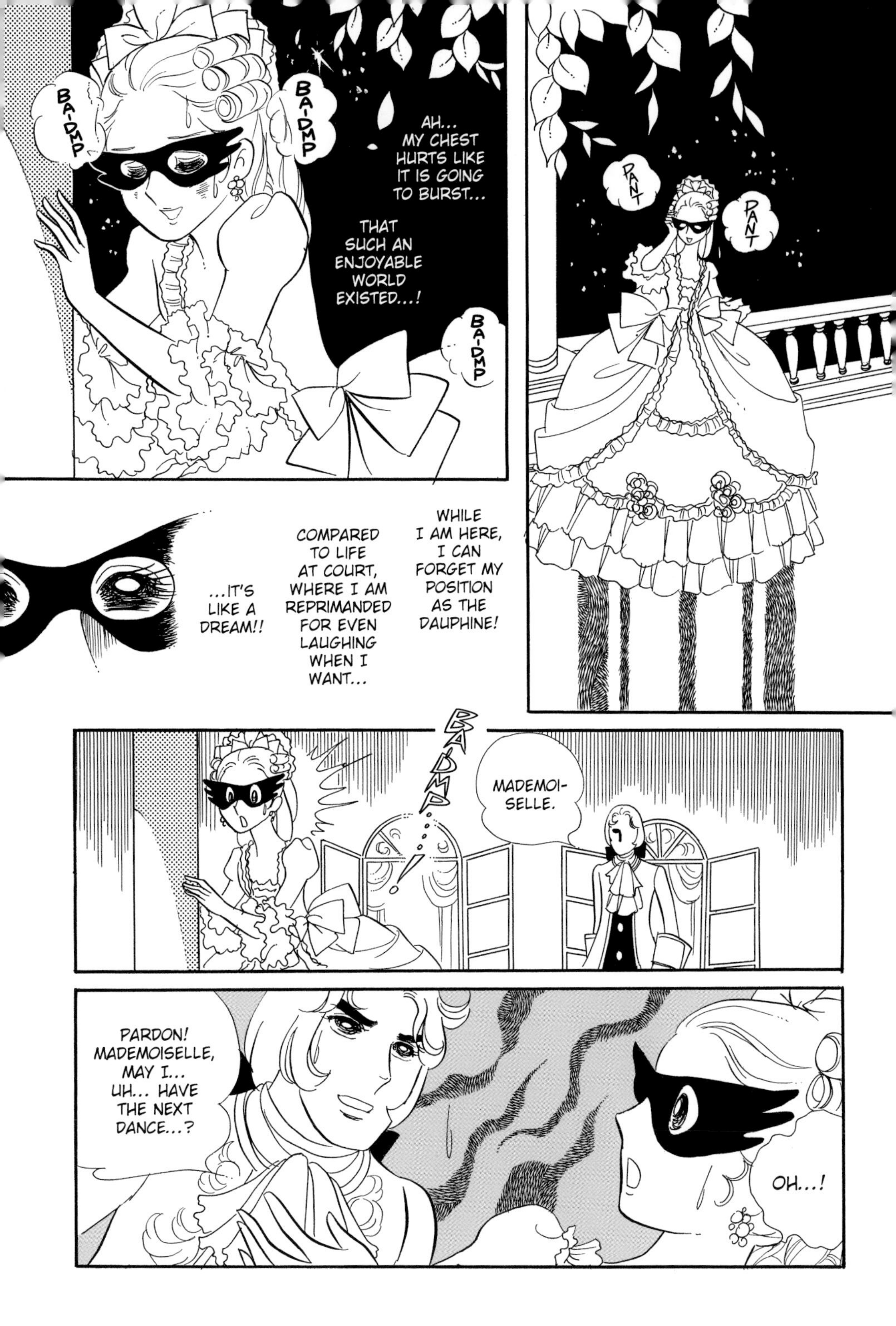
PANT
PANT
BA-DMP
BA-DMP
AH... MY CHEST HURTS LIKE IT IS GOING TO BURST...
THAT SUCH AN ENJOYABLE WORLD EXISTED...!
BA-DMP
WHILE I AM HERE, I CAN FORGET MY POSITION AS THE DAUPHINE!
COMPARED TO LIFE AT COURT, WHERE I AM REPRIMANDED FOR EVEN LAUGHING WHEN I WANT...
...IT'S LIKE A DREAM!!
MADEMOI-SELLE.
BA-DMP!
OH...!
PARDON! MADEMOISELLE, MAY I... UH... HAVE THE NEXT DANCE...?

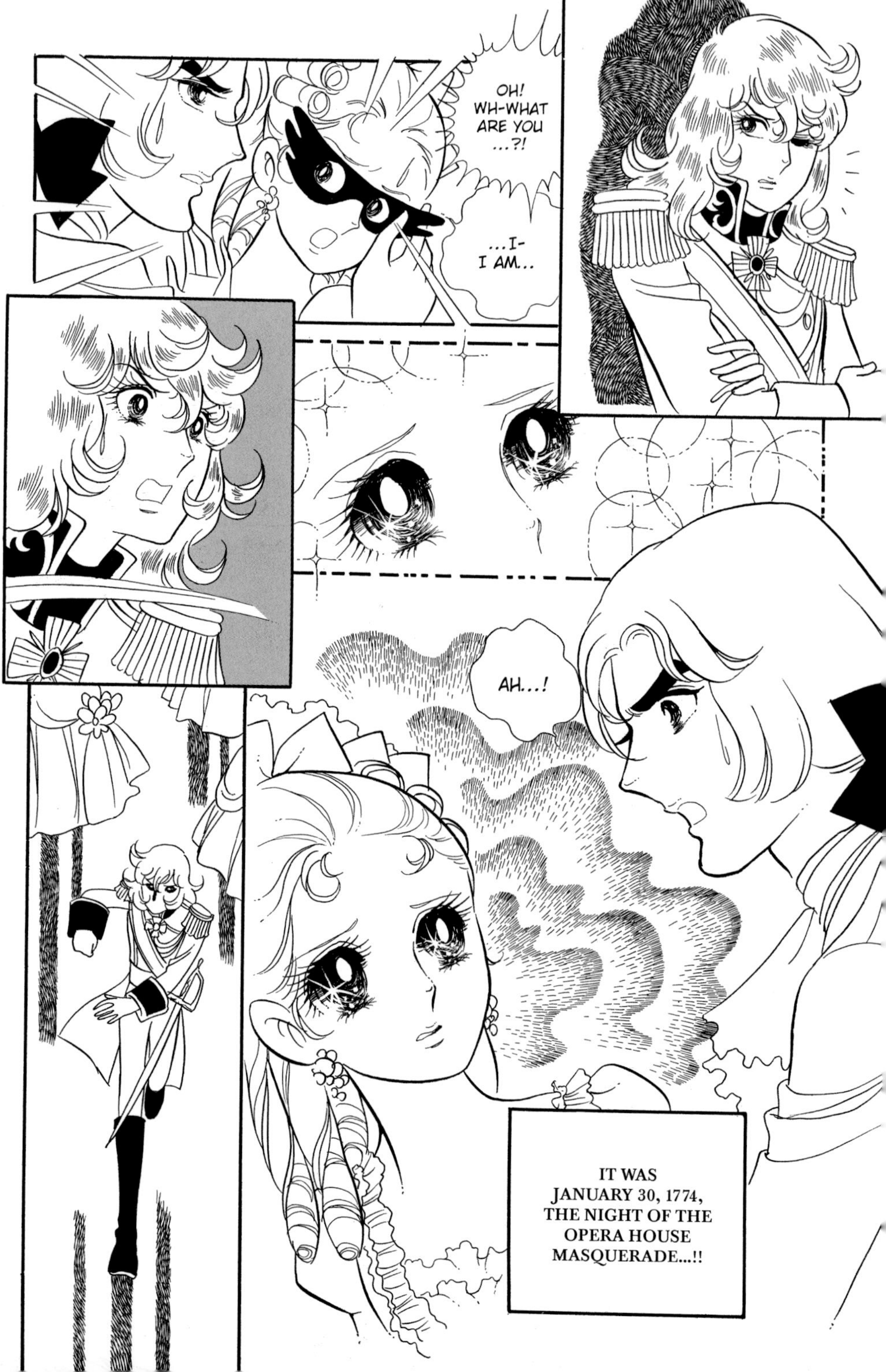
OH! WH-WHAT ARE YOU ...?!
...I- I AM...
AH...!
IT WAS JANUARY 30, 1774, THE NIGHT OF THE OPERA HOUSE MASQUERADE...!!

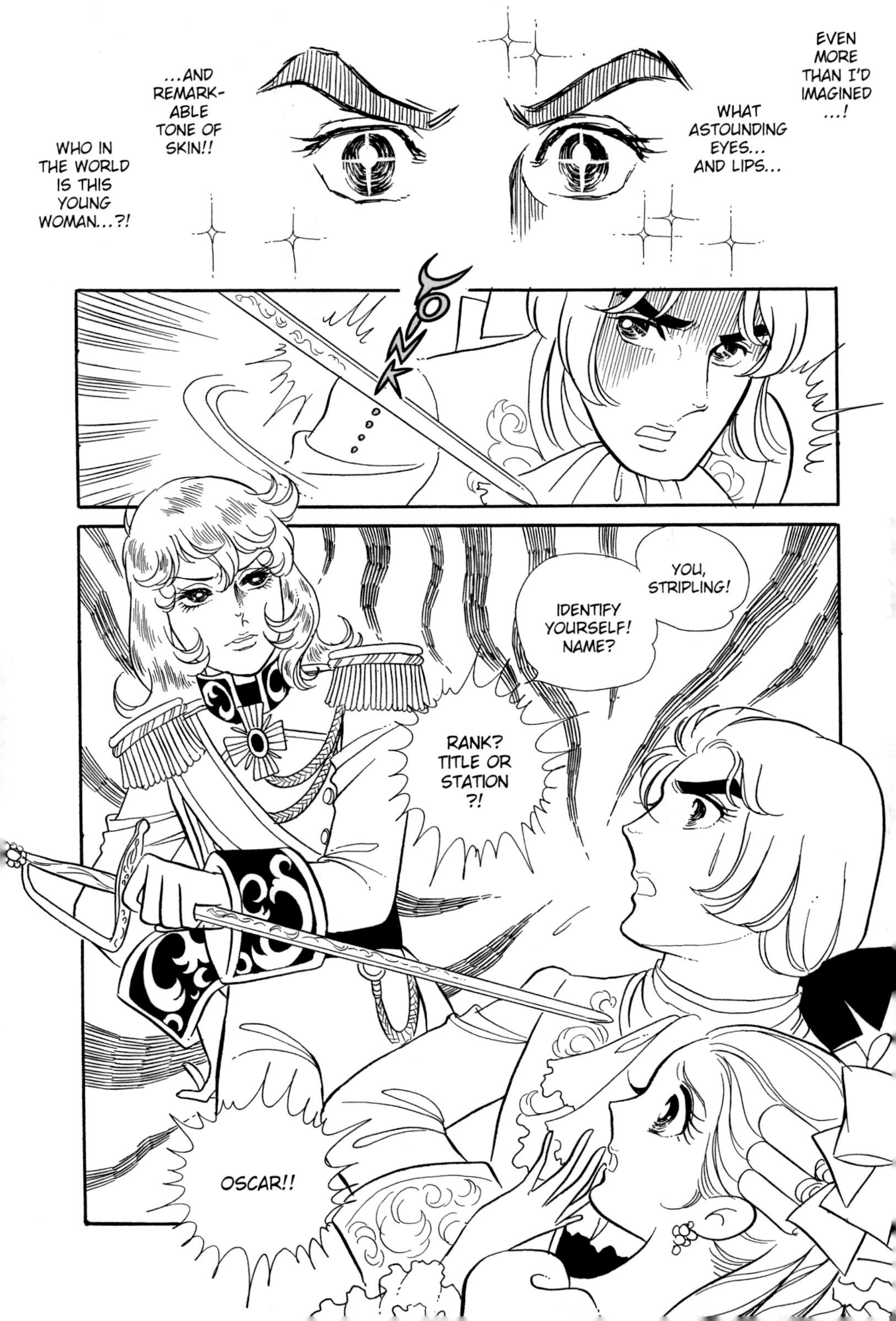
EVEN MORE THAN I'D IMAGINED ...!
WHAT ASTOUNDING EYES... AND LIPS...
...AND REMARK-ABLE TONE OF SKIN!!
WHO IN THE WORLD IS THIS YOUNG WOMAN...?!
CONK
YOU, STRIPLING!
IDENTIFY YOURSELF! NAME?
RANK? TITLE OR STATION ?!
OSCAR!!

1972 WEEKLY MARGARET MAGAZINE
ISSUE 30 BOOKMARK INSERT ART

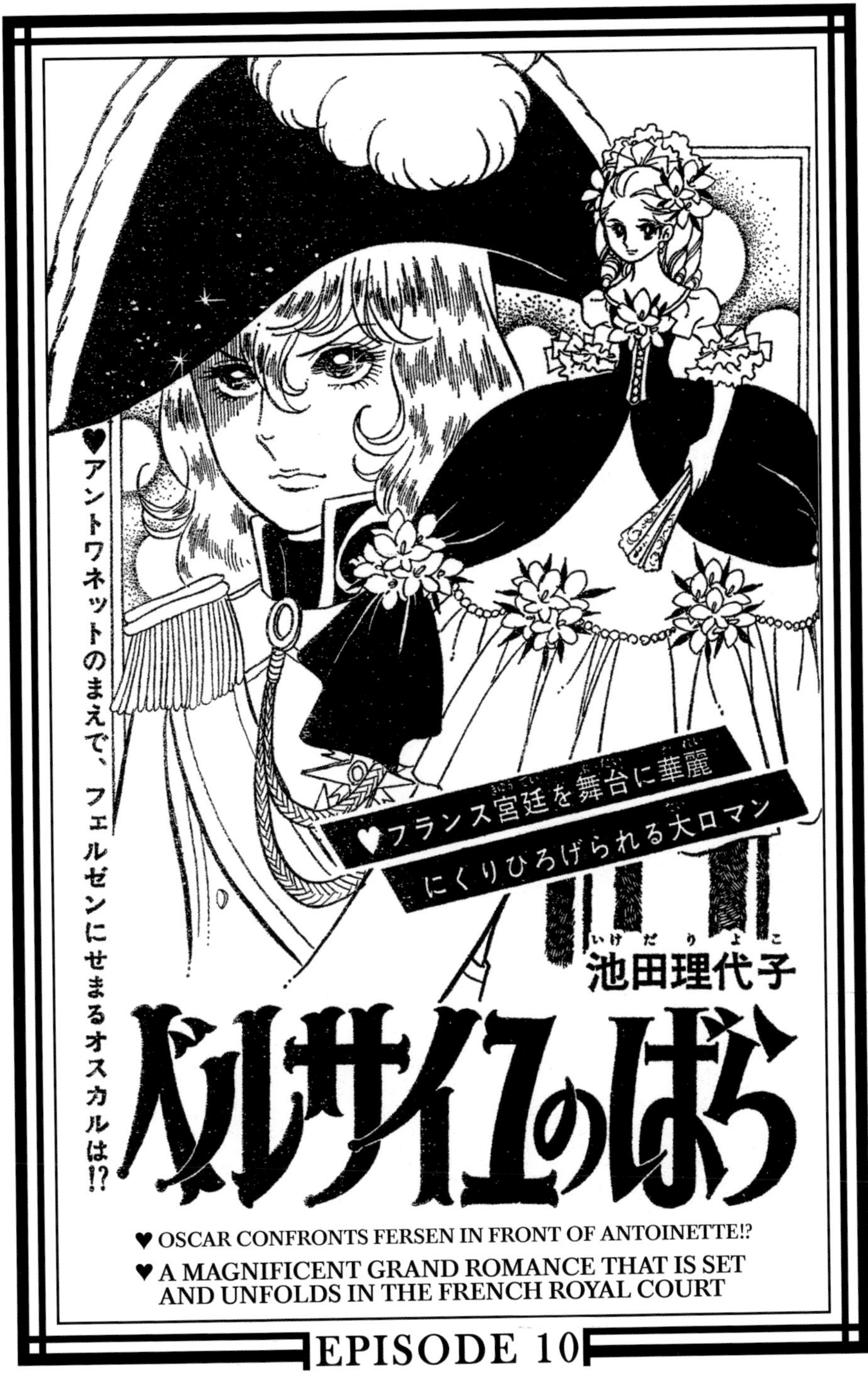
♥アントワネットのまえで、フェルゼンにせまるオスカルは!?
♥フランス宮廷を舞台に華麗にくりひろげられる大ロマン
池田理代子
ベルサイユのばら
♥ OSCAR CONFRONTS FERSEN IN FRONT OF ANTOINETTE!?
♥ A MAGNIFICENT GRAND ROMANCE THAT IS SET AND UNFOLDS IN THE FRENCH ROYAL COURT
EPISODE 10

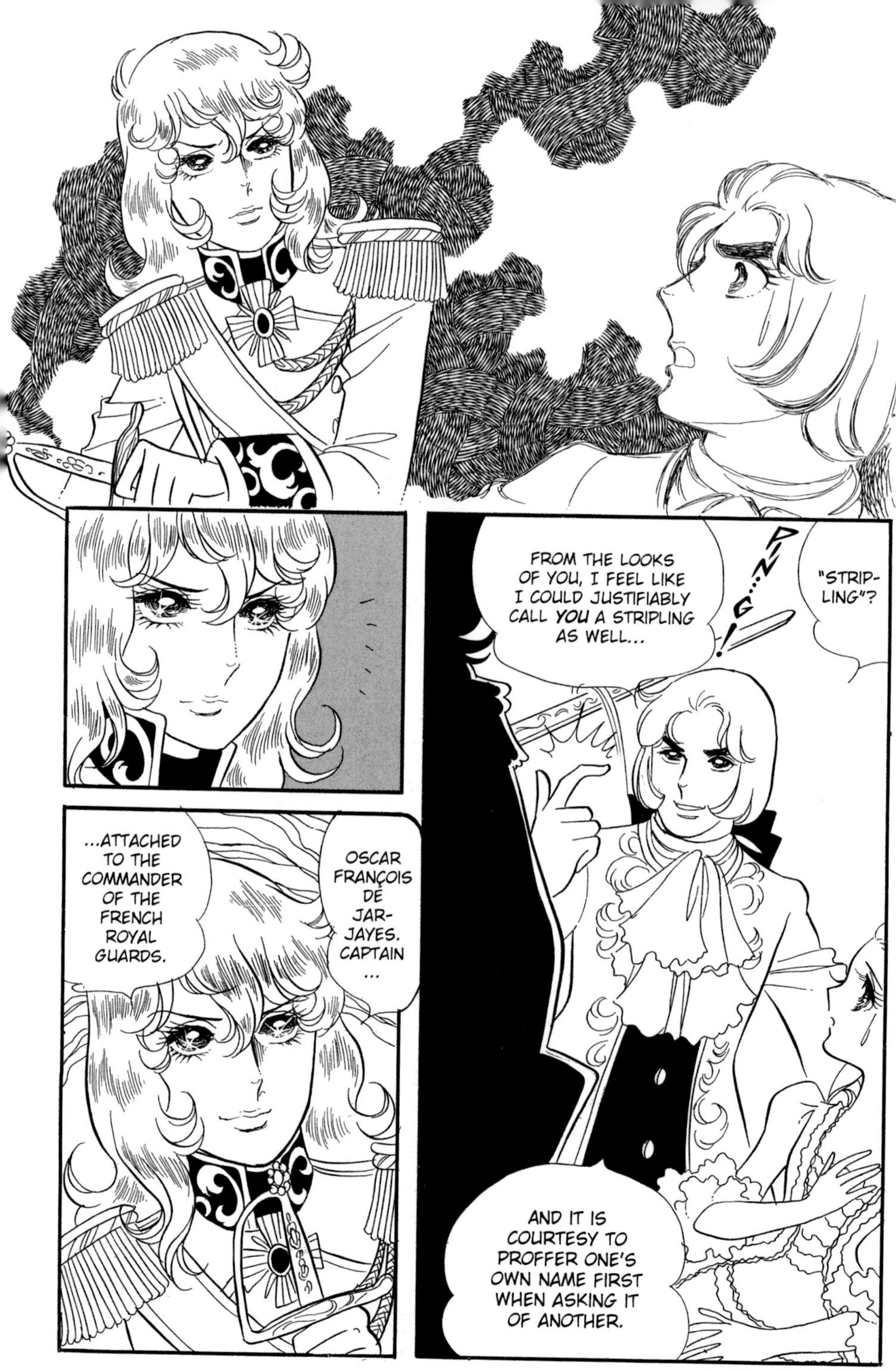
"STRIP-LING"?
D-I-N-G...!
FROM THE LOOKS OF YOU, I FEEL LIKE I COULD JUSTIFIABLY CALL *YOU* A STRIPLING AS WELL...
AND IT IS COURTESY TO PROFFER ONE'S OWN NAME FIRST WHEN ASKING IT OF ANOTHER.
OSCAR FRANÇOIS DE JAR-JAYES. CAPTAIN ...
...ATTACHED TO THE COMMANDER OF THE FRENCH ROYAL GUARDS.

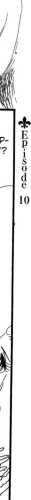

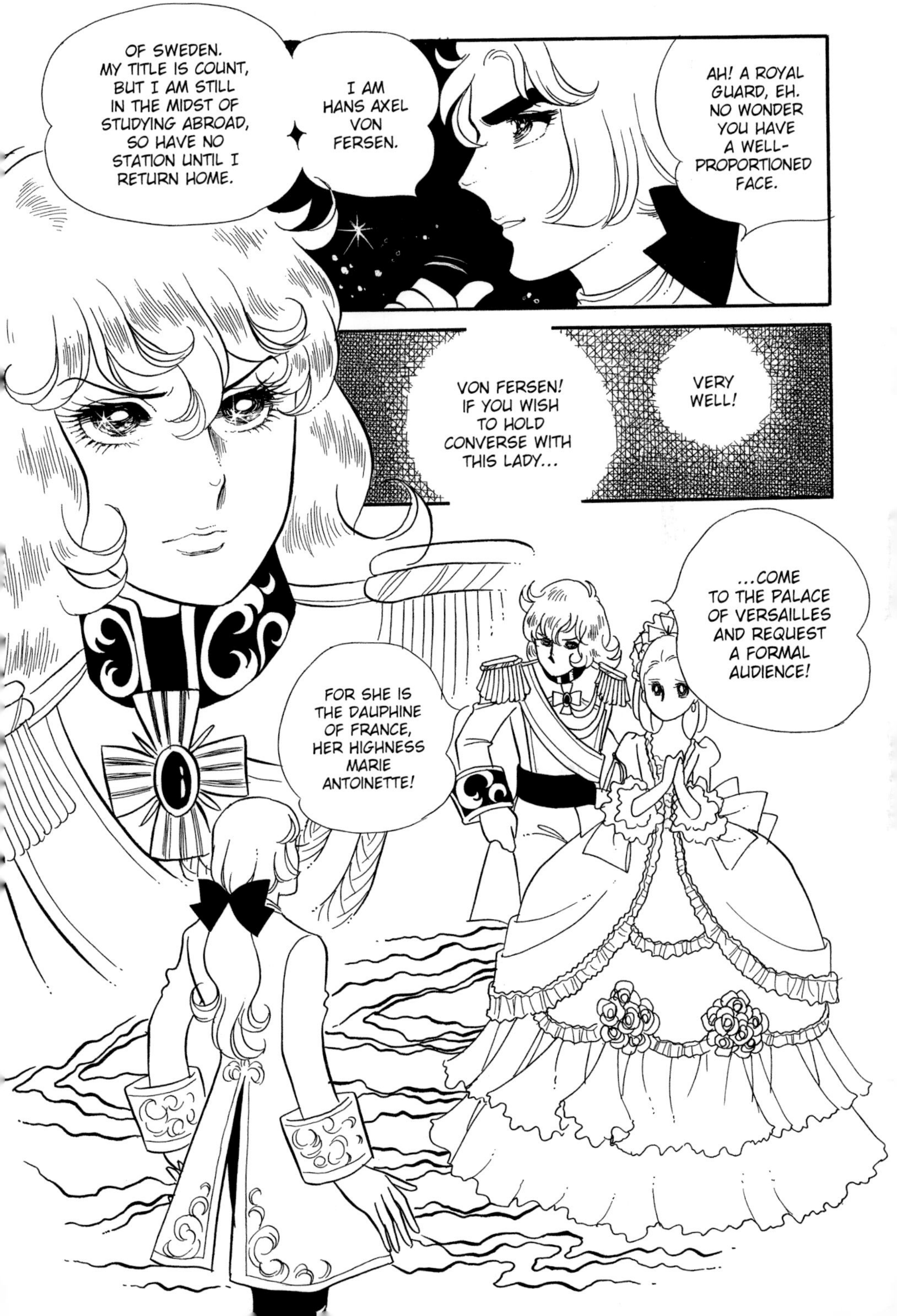
AH! A ROYAL GUARD, EH. NO WONDER YOU HAVE A WELL-PROPORTIONED FACE.
I AM HANS AXEL VON FERSEN.
OF SWEDEN. MY TITLE IS COUNT, BUT I AM STILL IN THE MIDST OF STUDYING ABROAD, SO HAVE NO STATION UNTIL I RETURN HOME.
VERY WELL!
VON FERSEN! IF YOU WISH TO HOLD CONVERSE WITH THIS LADY...
...COME TO THE PALACE OF VERSAILLES AND REQUEST A FORMAL AUDIENCE!
FOR SHE IS THE DAUPHINE OF FRANCE, HER HIGHNESS MARIE ANTOINETTE!

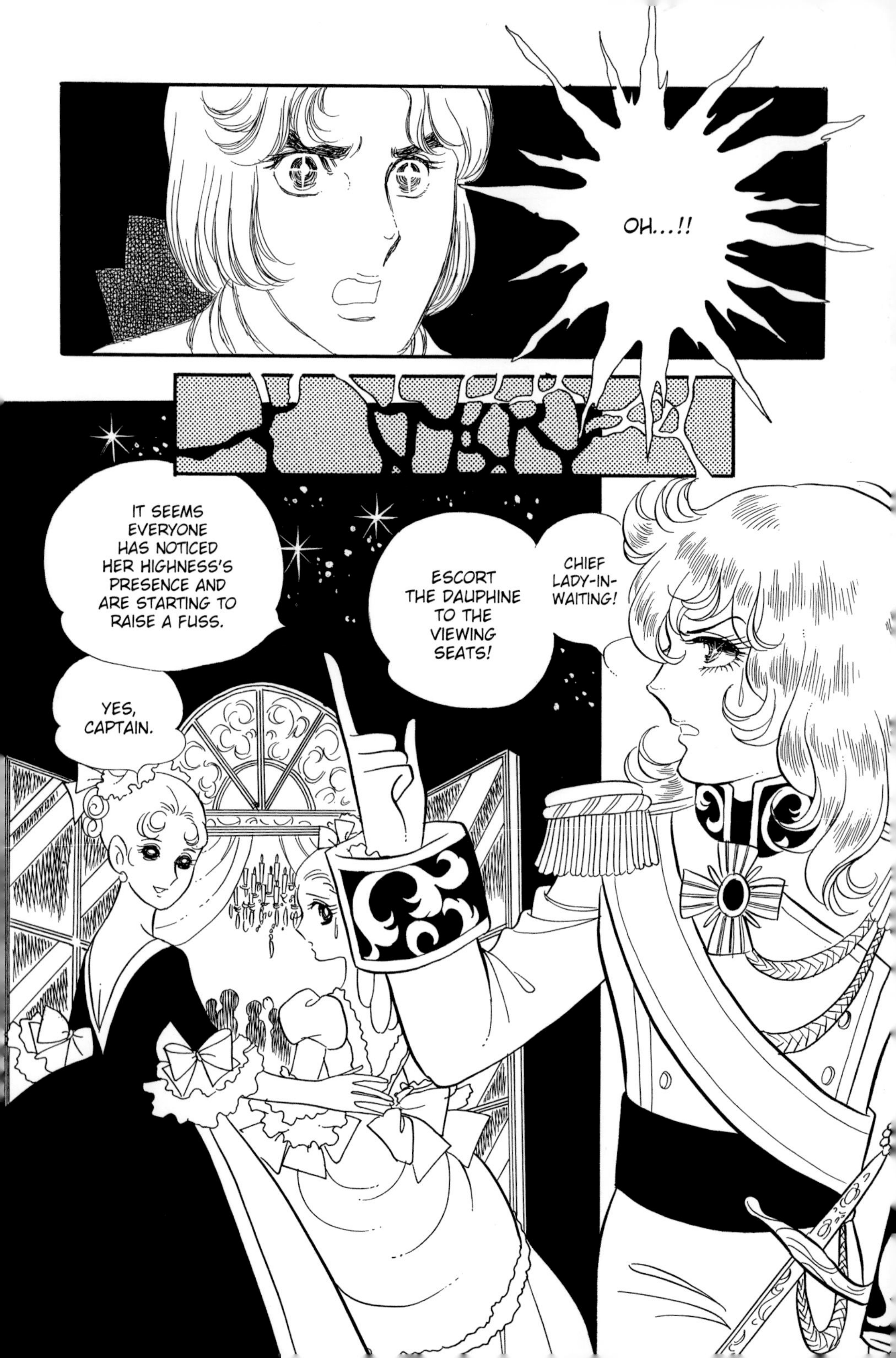
OH...!!
CHIEF LADY-IN-WAITING!
ESCORT THE DAUPHINE TO THE VIEWING SEATS!
IT SEEMS EVERYONE HAS NOTICED HER HIGHNESS'S PRESENCE AND ARE STARTING TO RAISE A FUSS.
YES, CAPTAIN.

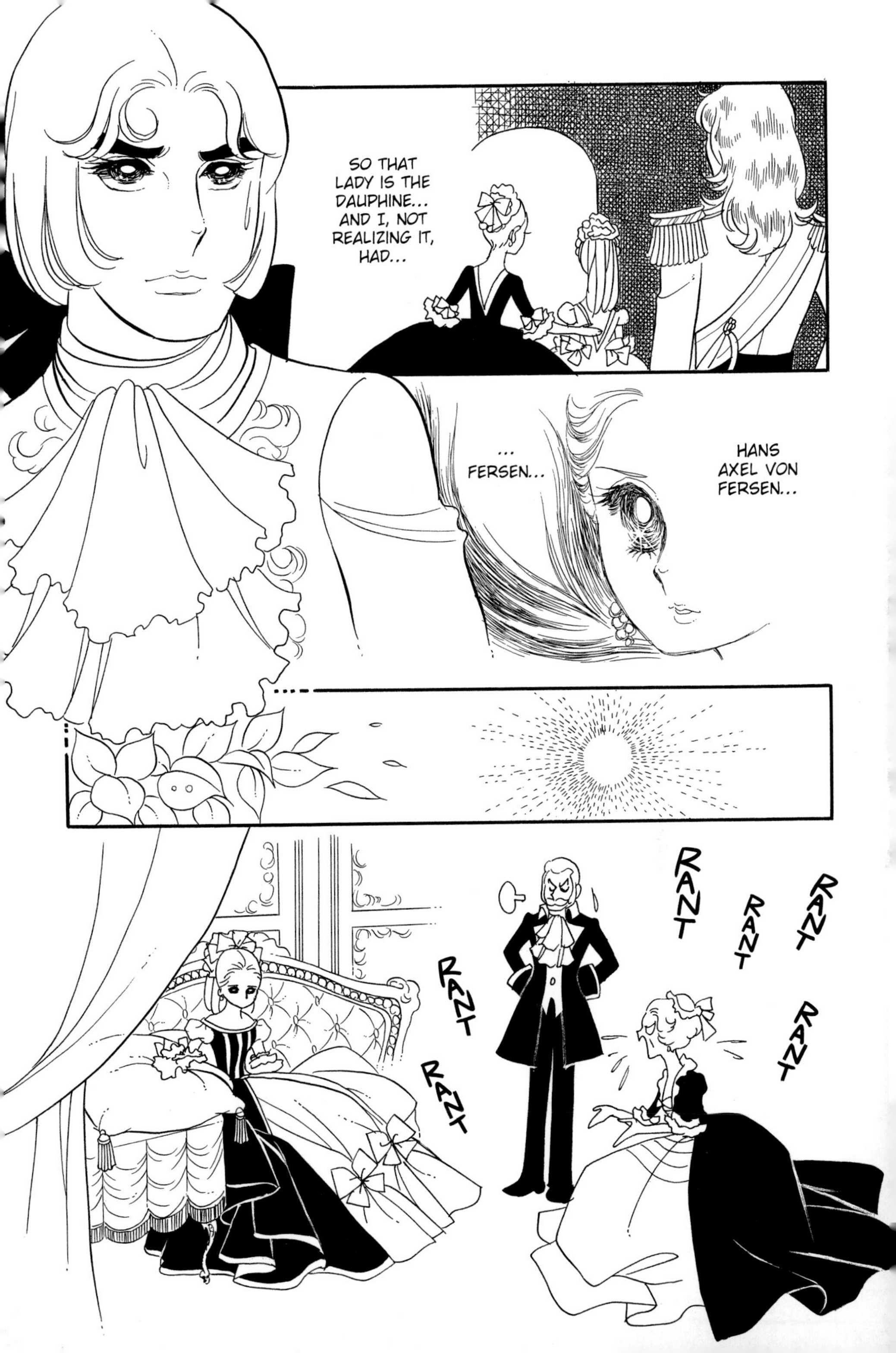
SO THAT LADY IS THE DAUPHINE... AND I, NOT REALIZING IT, HAD...
HANS AXEL VON FERSEN...
... FERSEN...
RANT
RANT
RANT
RANT
RANT
RANT

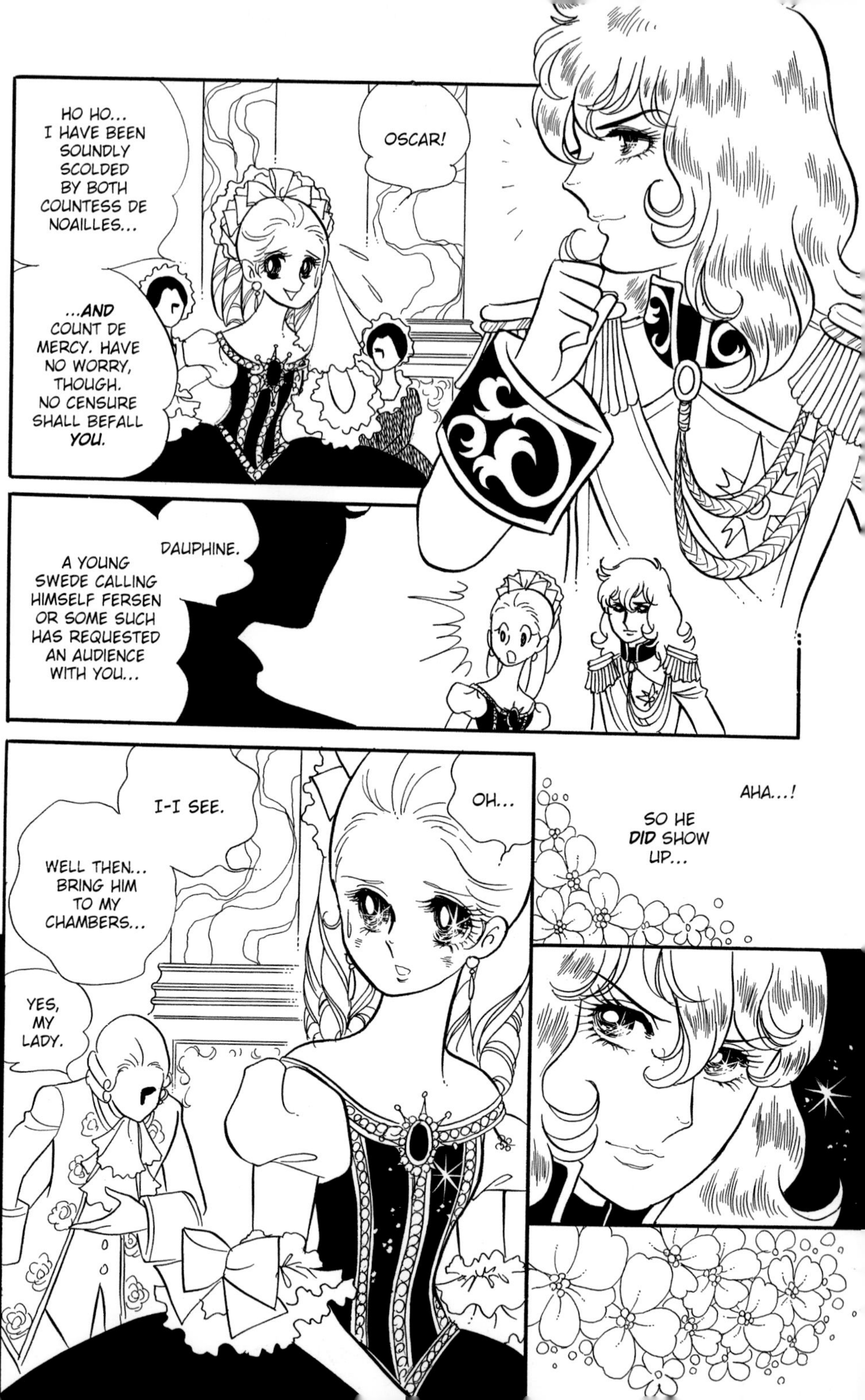
OSCAR!
HO HO... I HAVE BEEN SOUNDLY SCOLDED BY BOTH COUNTESS DE NOAILLES...
...**AND** COUNT DE MERCY. HAVE NO WORRY, THOUGH. NO CENSURE SHALL BEFALL **YOU**.
DAUPHINE.
A YOUNG SWEDE CALLING HIMSELF FERSEN OR SOME SUCH HAS REQUESTED AN AUDIENCE WITH YOU...
AHA...!
SO HE **DID** SHOW UP...
OH...
I-I SEE.
WELL THEN... BRING HIM TO MY CHAMBERS...
YES, MY LADY.

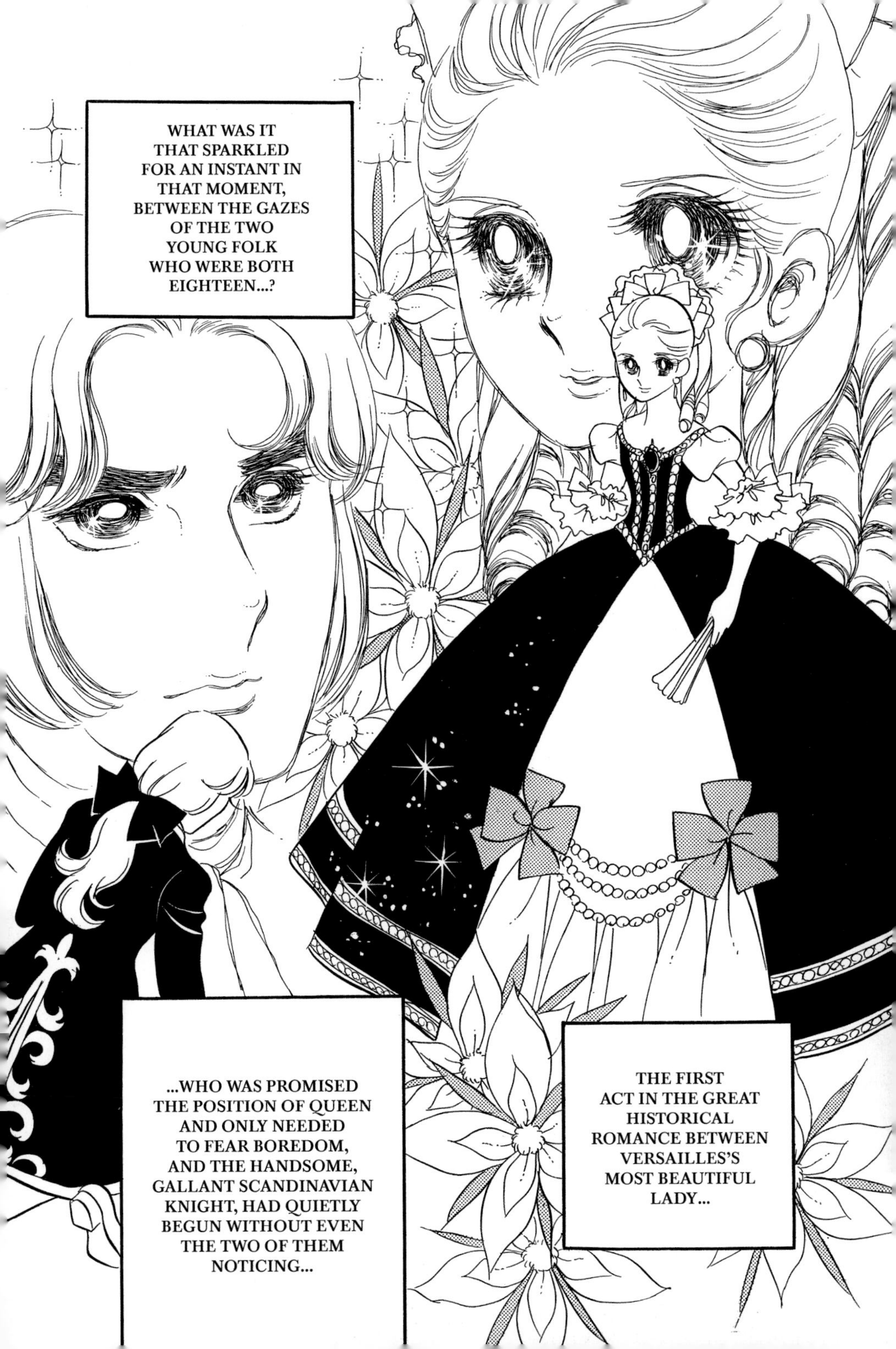
WHAT WAS IT THAT SPARKLED FOR AN INSTANT IN THAT MOMENT, BETWEEN THE GAZES OF THE TWO YOUNG FOLK WHO WERE BOTH EIGHTEEN...?
THE FIRST ACT IN THE GREAT HISTORICAL ROMANCE BETWEEN VERSAILLES'S MOST BEAUTIFUL LADY...
...WHO WAS PROMISED THE POSITION OF QUEEN AND ONLY NEEDED TO FEAR BOREDOM, AND THE HANDSOME, GALLANT SCANDINAVIAN KNIGHT, HAD QUIETLY BEGUN WITHOUT EVEN THE TWO OF THEM NOTICING...

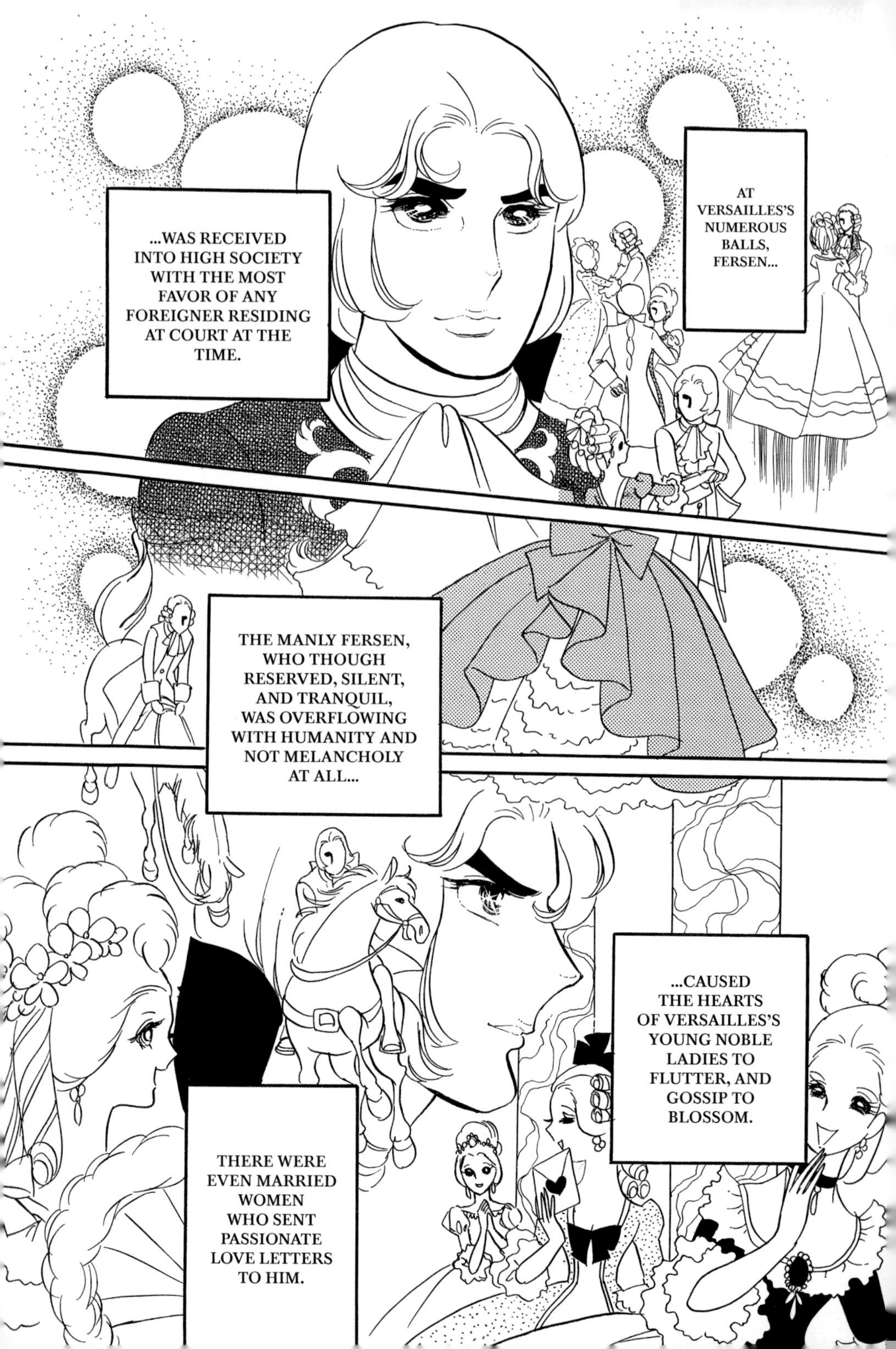
AT VERSAILLES'S NUMEROUS BALLS, FERSEN...
...WAS RECEIVED INTO HIGH SOCIETY WITH THE MOST FAVOR OF ANY FOREIGNER RESIDING AT COURT AT THE TIME.
THE MANLY FERSEN, WHO THOUGH RESERVED, SILENT, AND TRANQUIL, WAS OVERFLOWING WITH HUMANITY AND NOT MELANCHOLY AT ALL...
...CAUSED THE HEARTS OF VERSAILLES'S YOUNG NOBLE LADIES TO FLUTTER, AND GOSSIP TO BLOSSOM.
THERE WERE EVEN MARRIED WOMEN WHO SENT PASSIONATE LOVE LETTERS TO HIM.

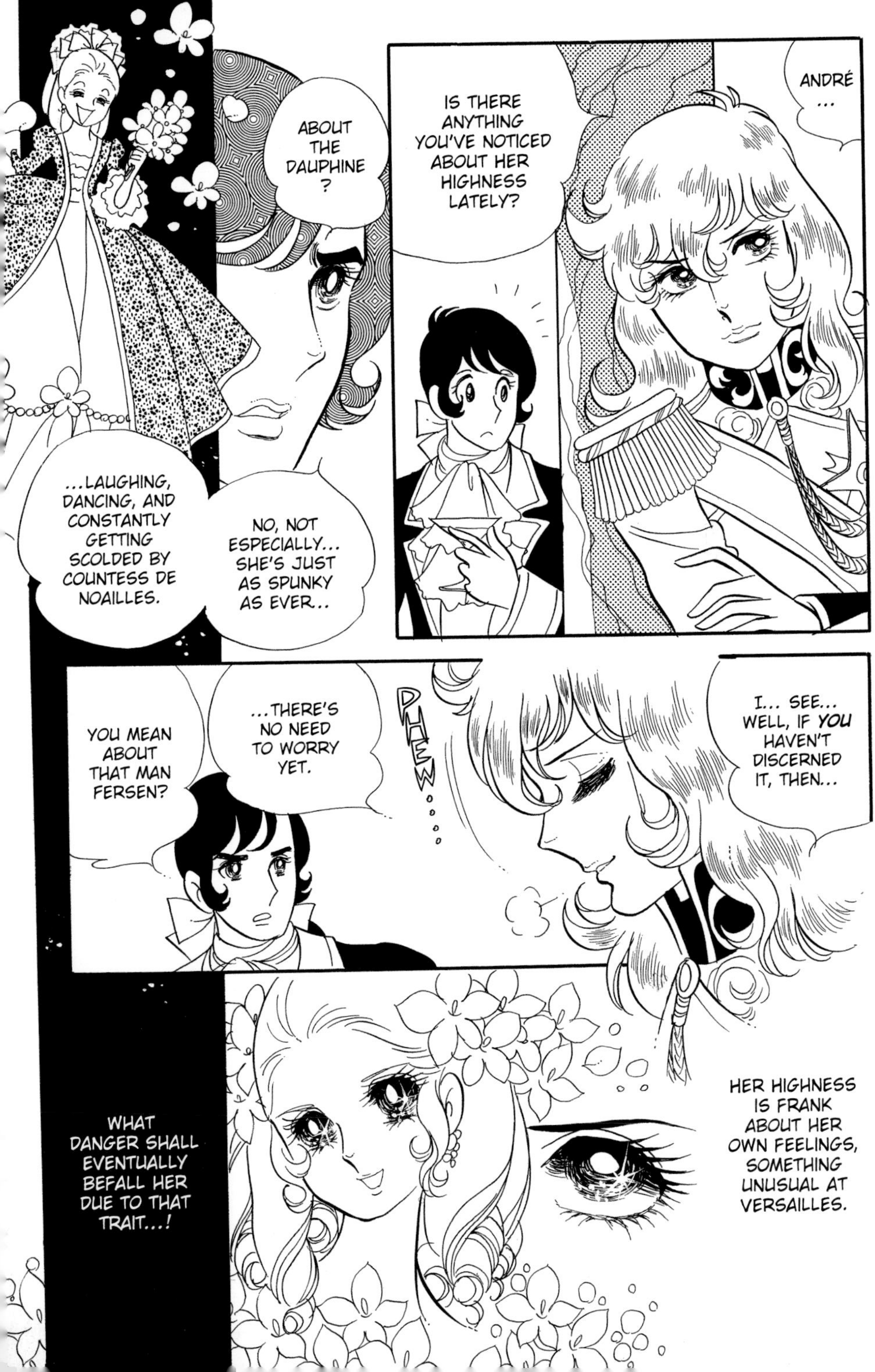
ANDRÉ ...
IS THERE ANYTHING YOU'VE NOTICED ABOUT HER HIGHNESS LATELY?
ABOUT THE DAUPHINE ?
NO, NOT ESPECIALLY... SHE'S JUST AS SPUNKY AS EVER...
...LAUGHING, DANCING, AND CONSTANTLY GETTING SCOLDED BY COUNTESS DE NOAILLES.
I... SEE... WELL, IF *YOU* HAVEN'T DISCERNED IT, THEN...
PHEW...
...THERE'S NO NEED TO WORRY YET.
YOU MEAN ABOUT THAT MAN FERSEN?
HER HIGHNESS IS FRANK ABOUT HER OWN FEELINGS, SOMETHING UNUSUAL AT VERSAILLES.
WHAT DANGER SHALL EVENTUALLY BEFALL HER DUE TO THAT TRAIT...!

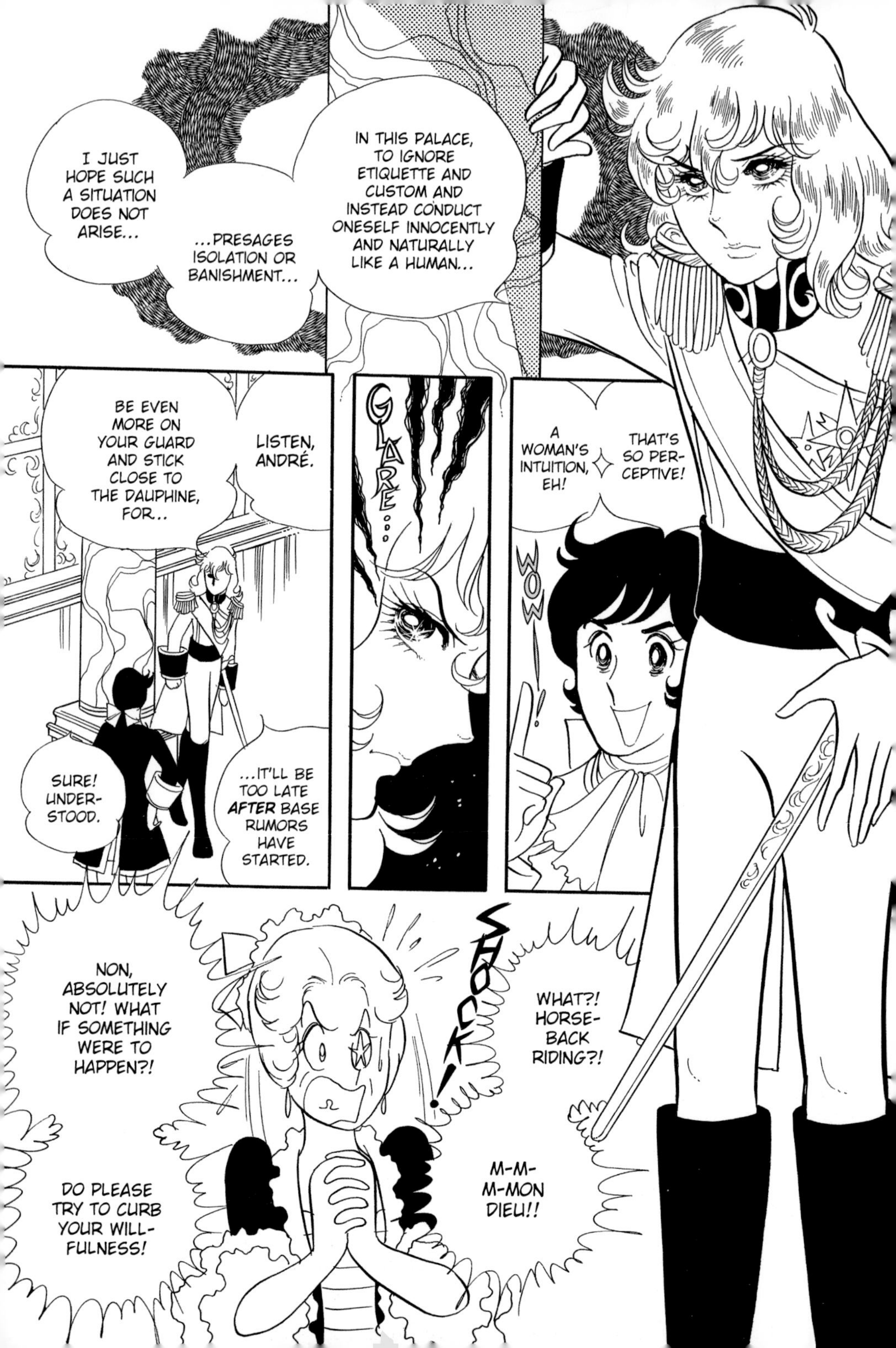
IN THIS PALACE, TO IGNORE ETIQUETTE AND CUSTOM AND INSTEAD CONDUCT ONESELF INNOCENTLY AND NATURALLY LIKE A HUMAN...
...PRESAGES ISOLATION OR BANISHMENT...
I JUST HOPE SUCH A SITUATION DOES NOT ARISE...
THAT'S SO PERCEPTIVE!
A WOMAN'S INTUITION, EH!
WOW!!
GLARE...
LISTEN, ANDRÉ.
BE EVEN MORE ON YOUR GUARD AND STICK CLOSE TO THE DAUPHINE, FOR...
...IT'LL BE TOO LATE **AFTER** BASE RUMORS HAVE STARTED.
SURE! UNDERSTOOD.
WHAT?! HORSEBACK RIDING?!
SHOCK!
NON, ABSOLUTELY NOT! WHAT IF SOMETHING WERE TO HAPPEN?!
M-M-M-MON DIEU!!
DO PLEASE TRY TO CURB YOUR WILLFULNESS!

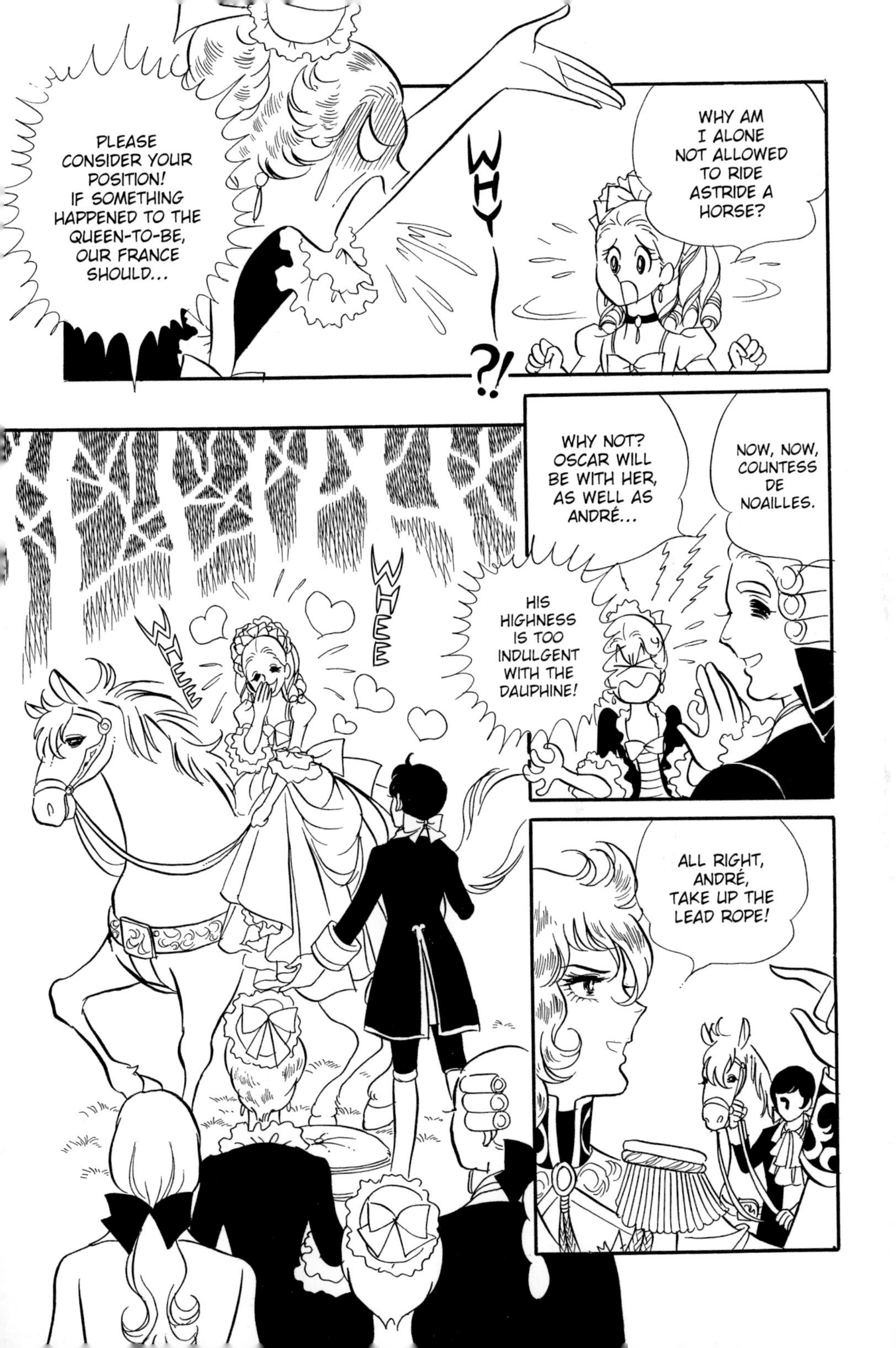
WHY AM I ALONE NOT ALLOWED TO RIDE ASTRIDE A HORSE?
WHY—?!
PLEASE CONSIDER YOUR POSITION! IF SOMETHING HAPPENED TO THE QUEEN-TO-BE, OUR FRANCE SHOULD...
NOW, NOW, COUNTESS DE NOAILLES.
WHY NOT? OSCAR WILL BE WITH HER, AS WELL AS ANDRÉ...
HIS HIGHNESS IS TOO INDULGENT WITH THE DAUPHINE!
ALL RIGHT, ANDRÉ, TAKE UP THE LEAD ROPE!
WHEE
WHEE

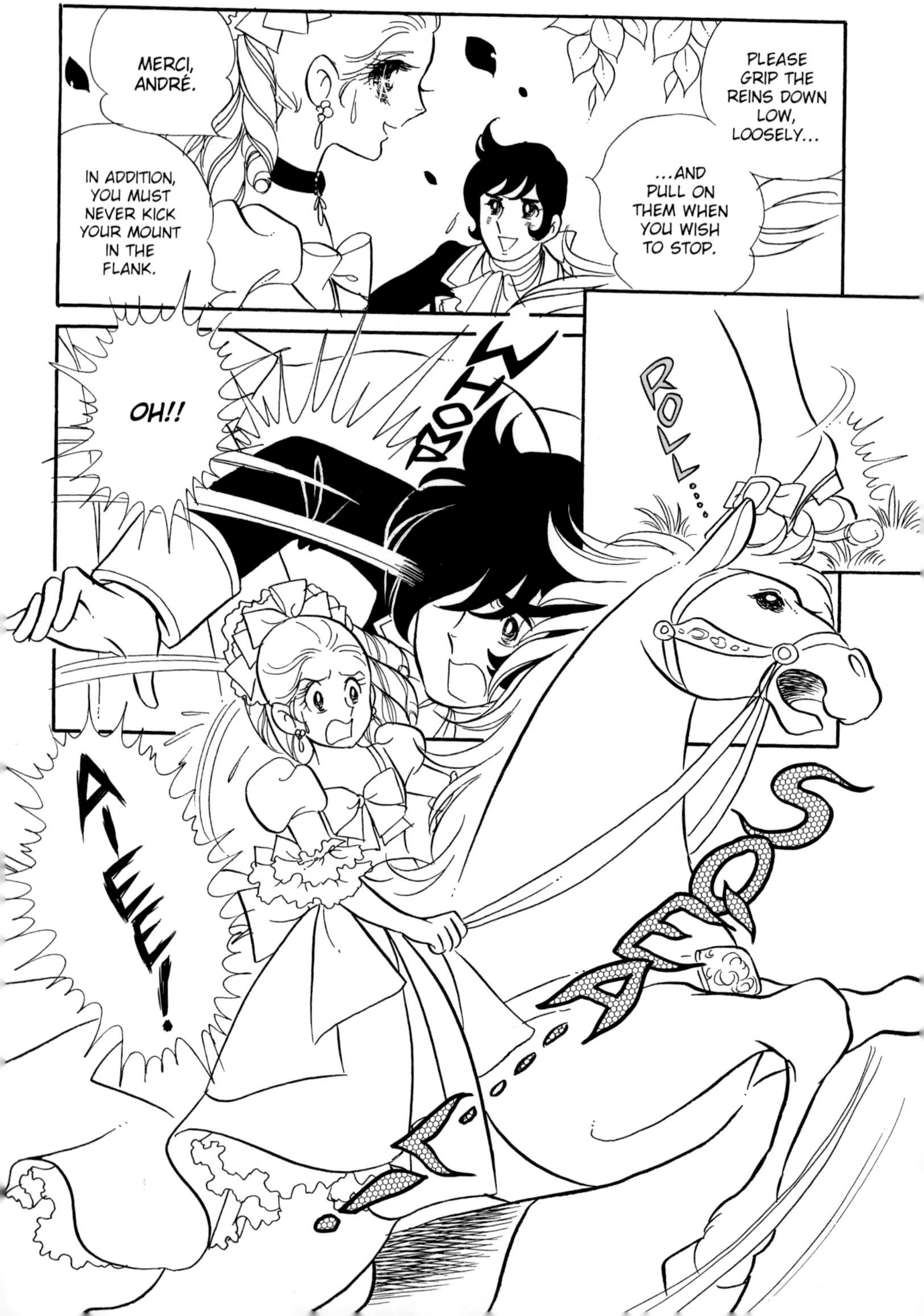
PLEASE GRIP THE REINS DOWN LOW, LOOSELY...
...AND PULL ON THEM WHEN YOU WISH TO STOP.
MERCI, ANDRÉ.
IN ADDITION, YOU MUST NEVER KICK YOUR MOUNT IN THE FLANK.
ROLL...
WHOOM
OH!!
A-EEE!

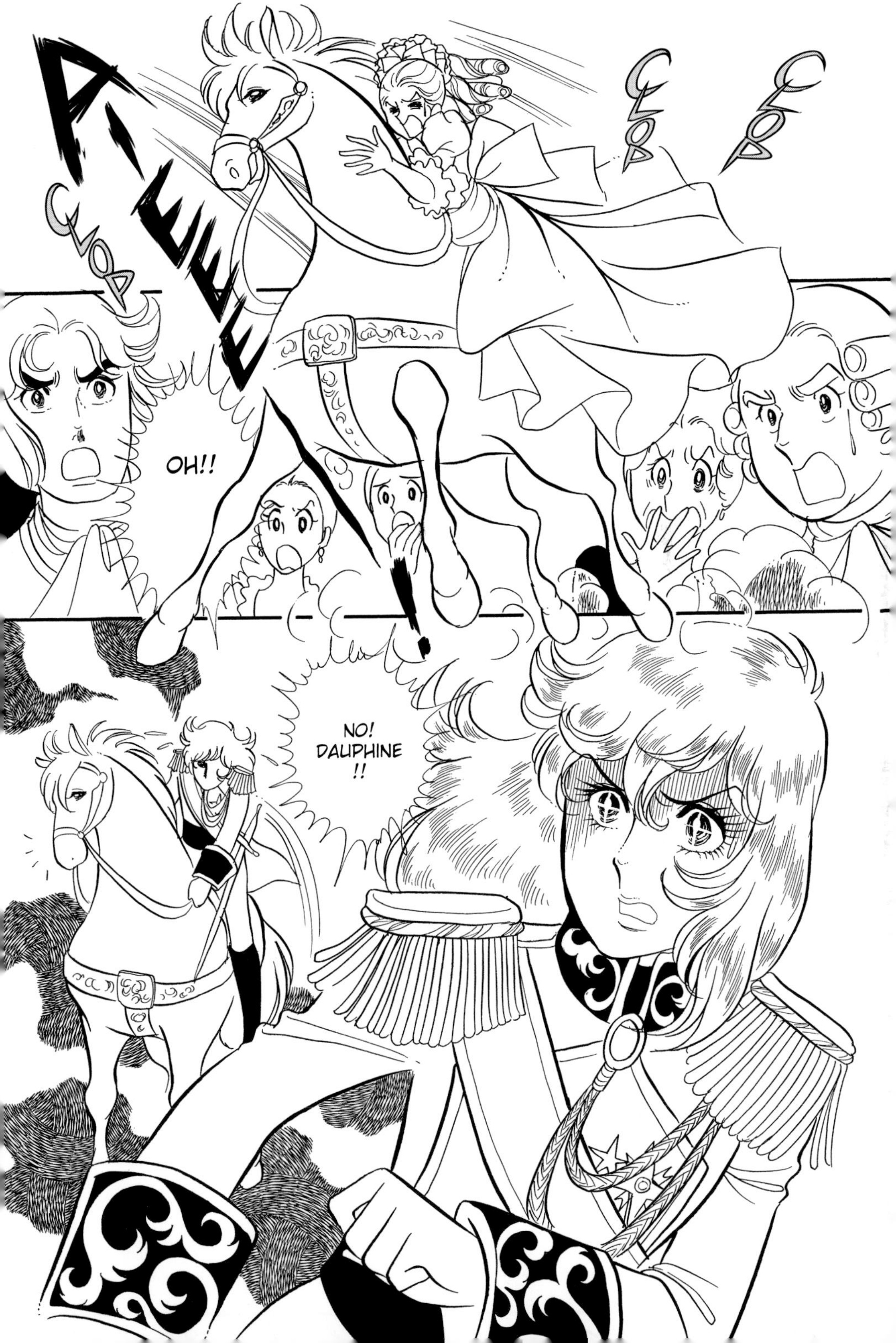

CLOP
CLOP
AIEEEE
CLOP
OH!!
NO! DAUPHINE !!

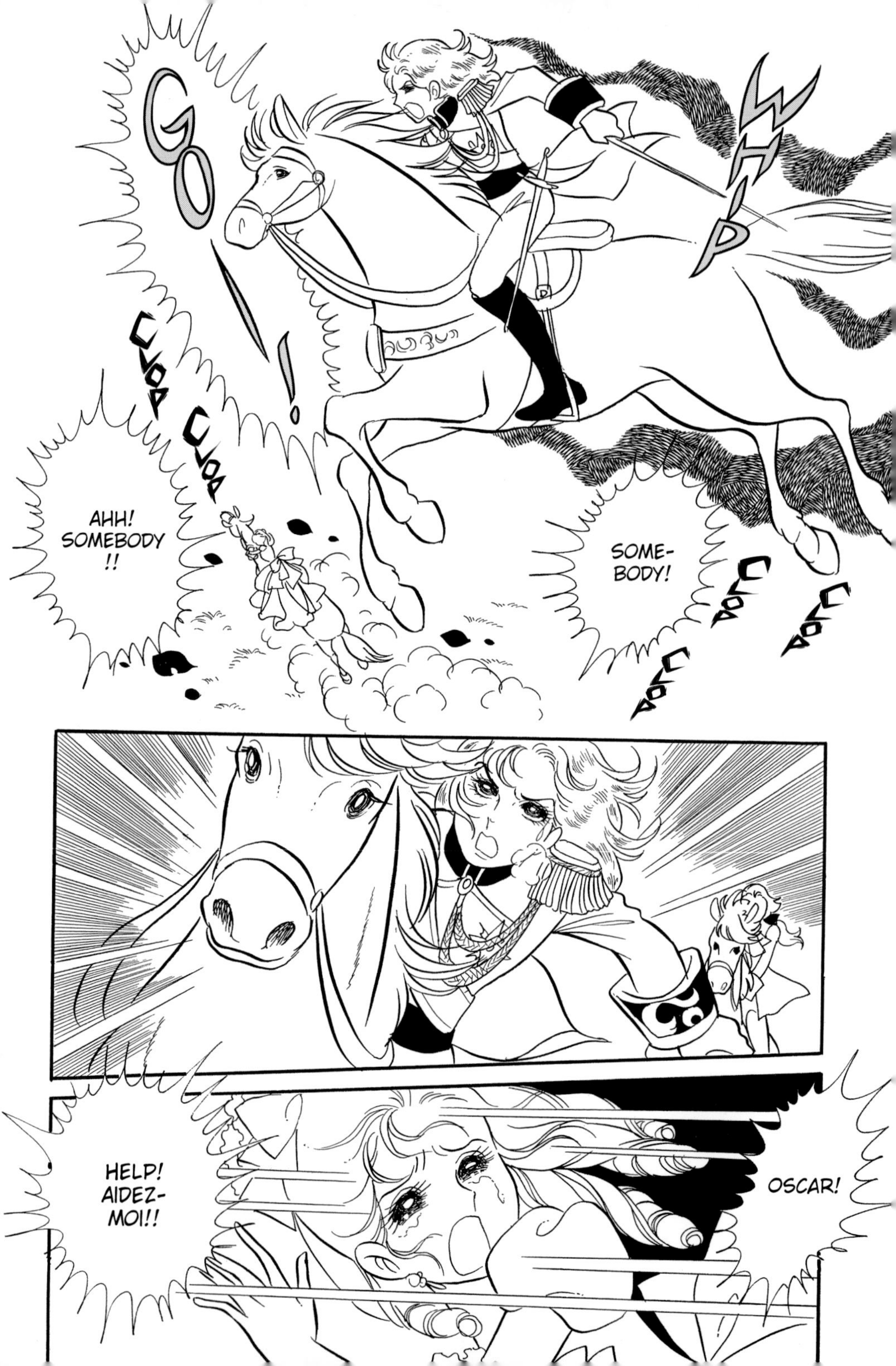

WHIP
GO!!
SOME-
BODY!
CLOP CLOP CLOP
CLOP CLOP
AHH!
SOMEBODY
!!
OSCAR!
HELP!
AIDEZ-
MOI!!

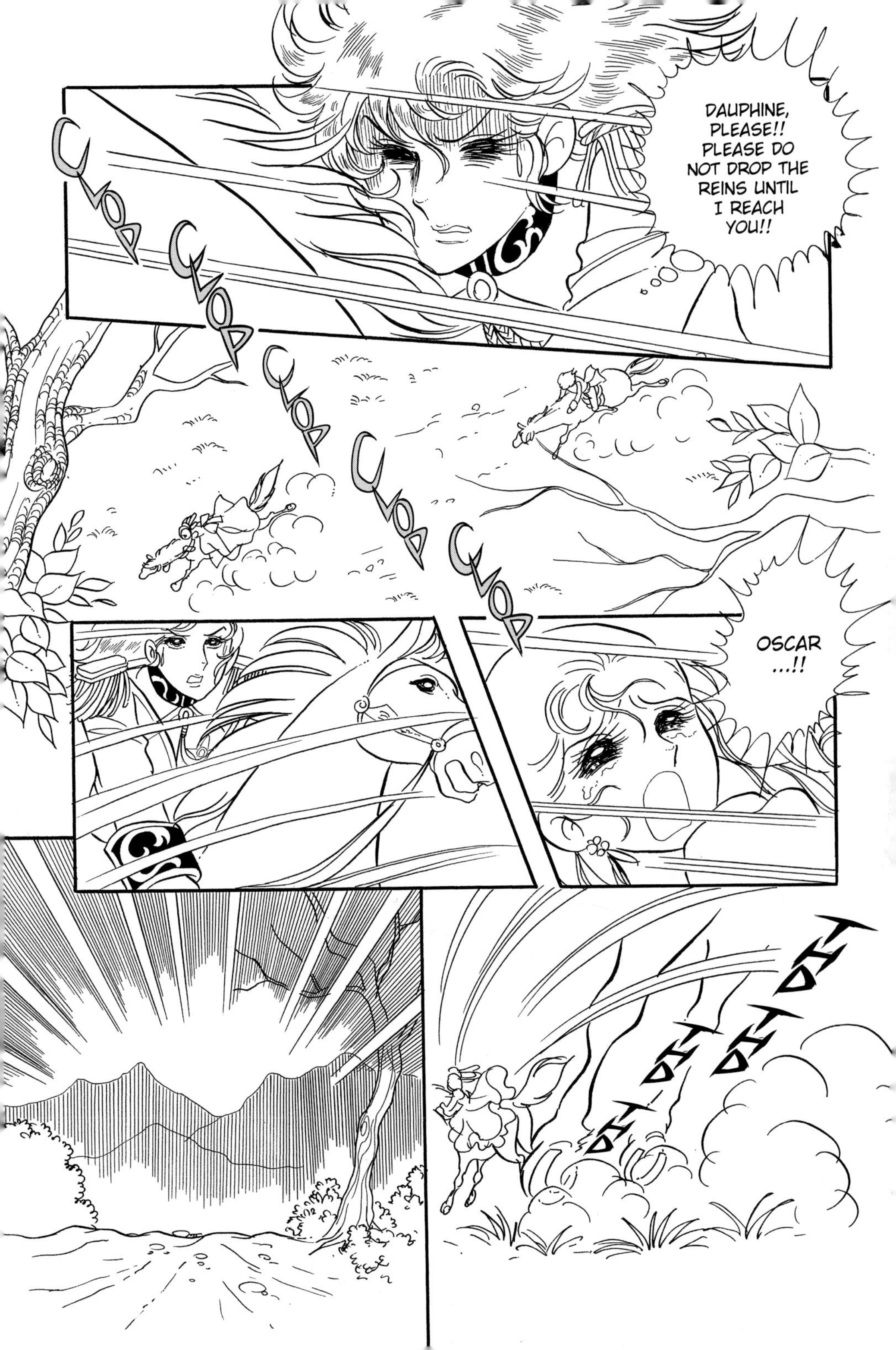
DAUPHINE, PLEASE!! PLEASE DO NOT DROP THE REINS UNTIL I REACH YOU!!
CLOP CLOP CLOP CLOP CLOP CLOP
OSCAR ...!!
THD THD
THD THD

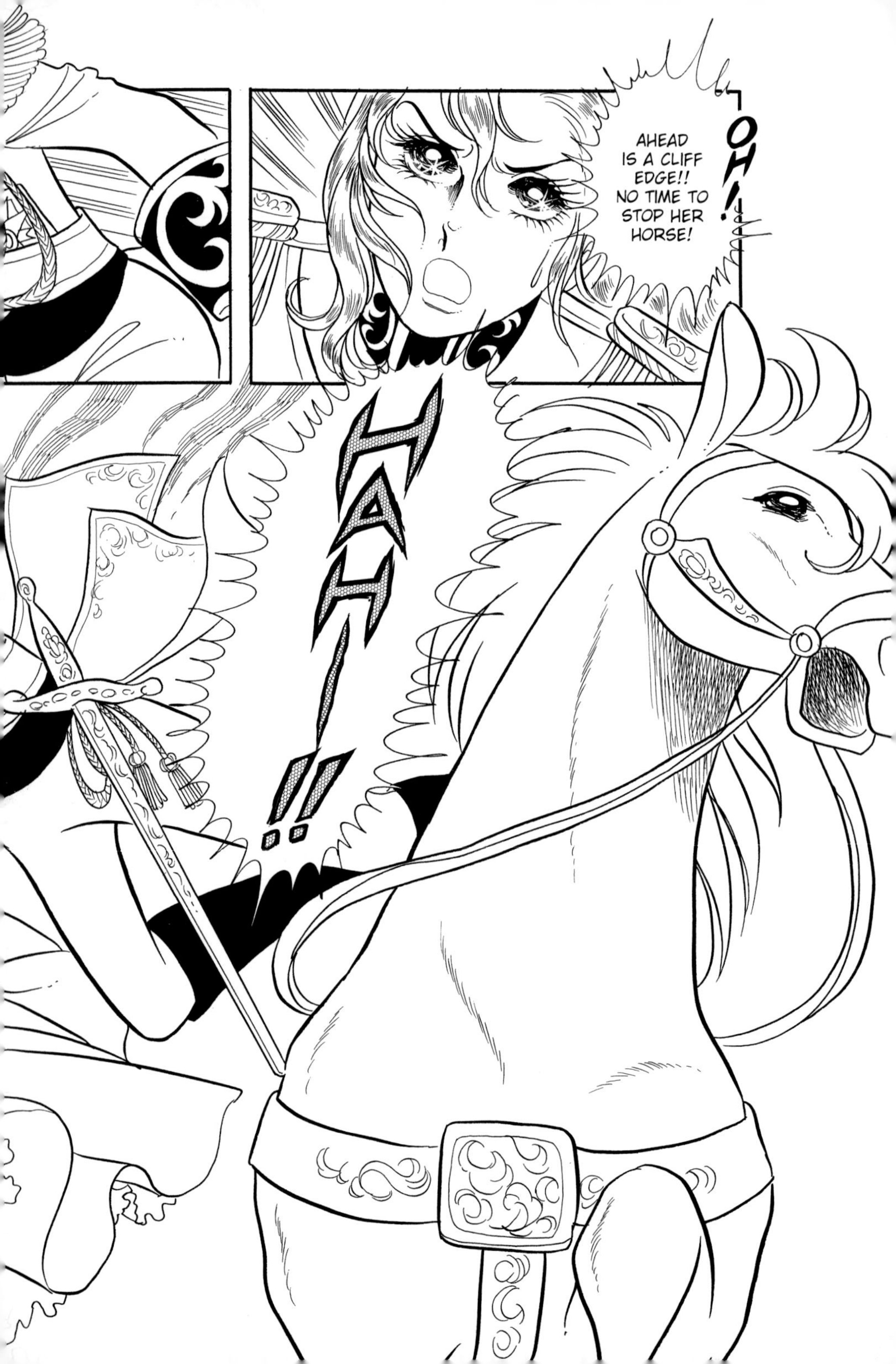
OH!
AHEAD IS A CLIFF EDGE!! NO TIME TO STOP HER HORSE!
HAAH!!!

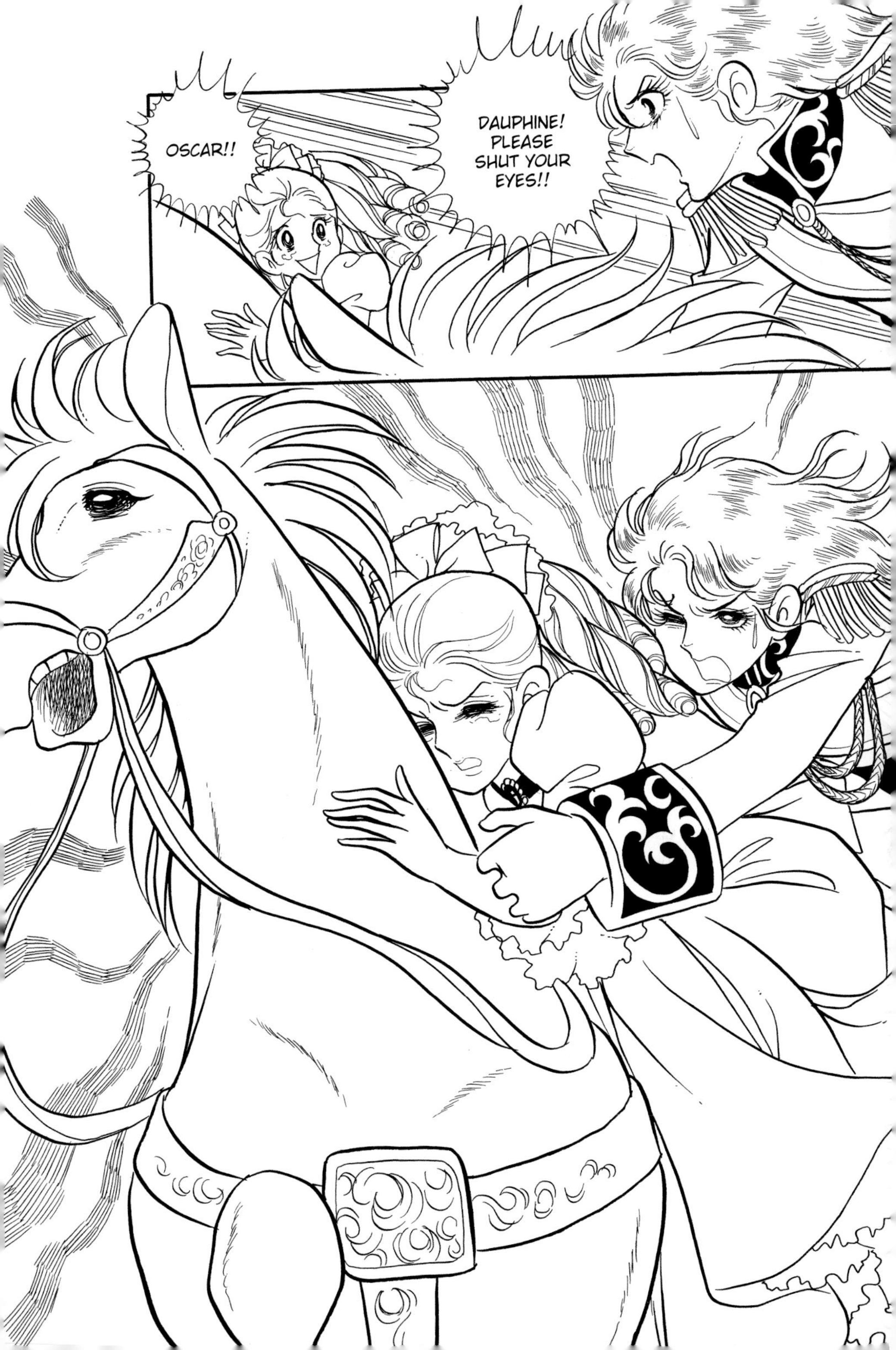
DAUPHINE! PLEASE SHUT YOUR EYES!!
OSCAR!!

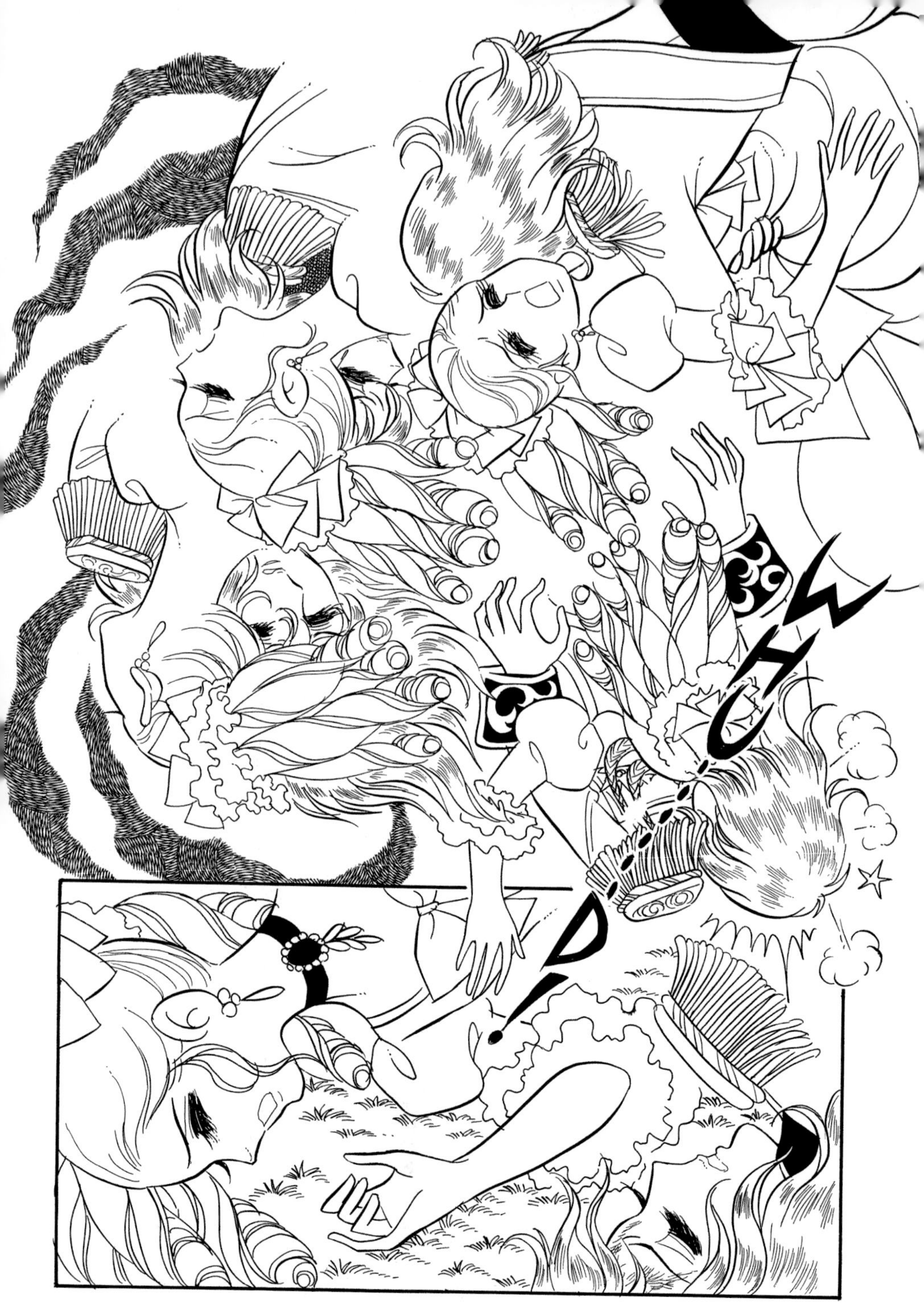
WHUD!

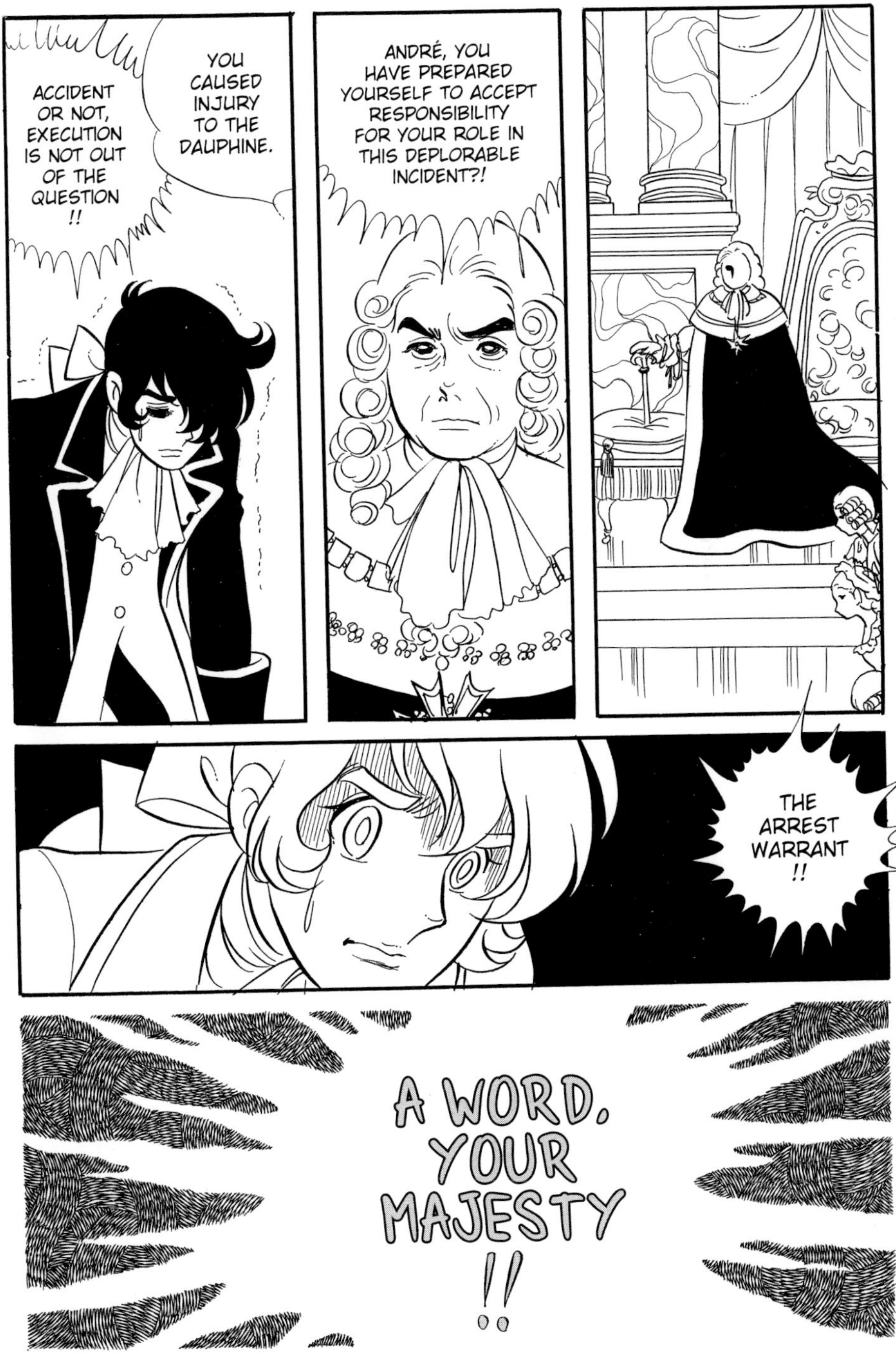
ANDRÉ, YOU HAVE PREPARED YOURSELF TO ACCEPT RESPONSIBILITY FOR YOUR ROLE IN THIS DEPLORABLE INCIDENT?!
YOU CAUSED INJURY TO THE DAUPHINE.
ACCIDENT OR NOT, EXECUTION IS NOT OUT OF THE QUESTION!!
THE ARREST WARRANT!!
A WORD, YOUR MAJESTY!!

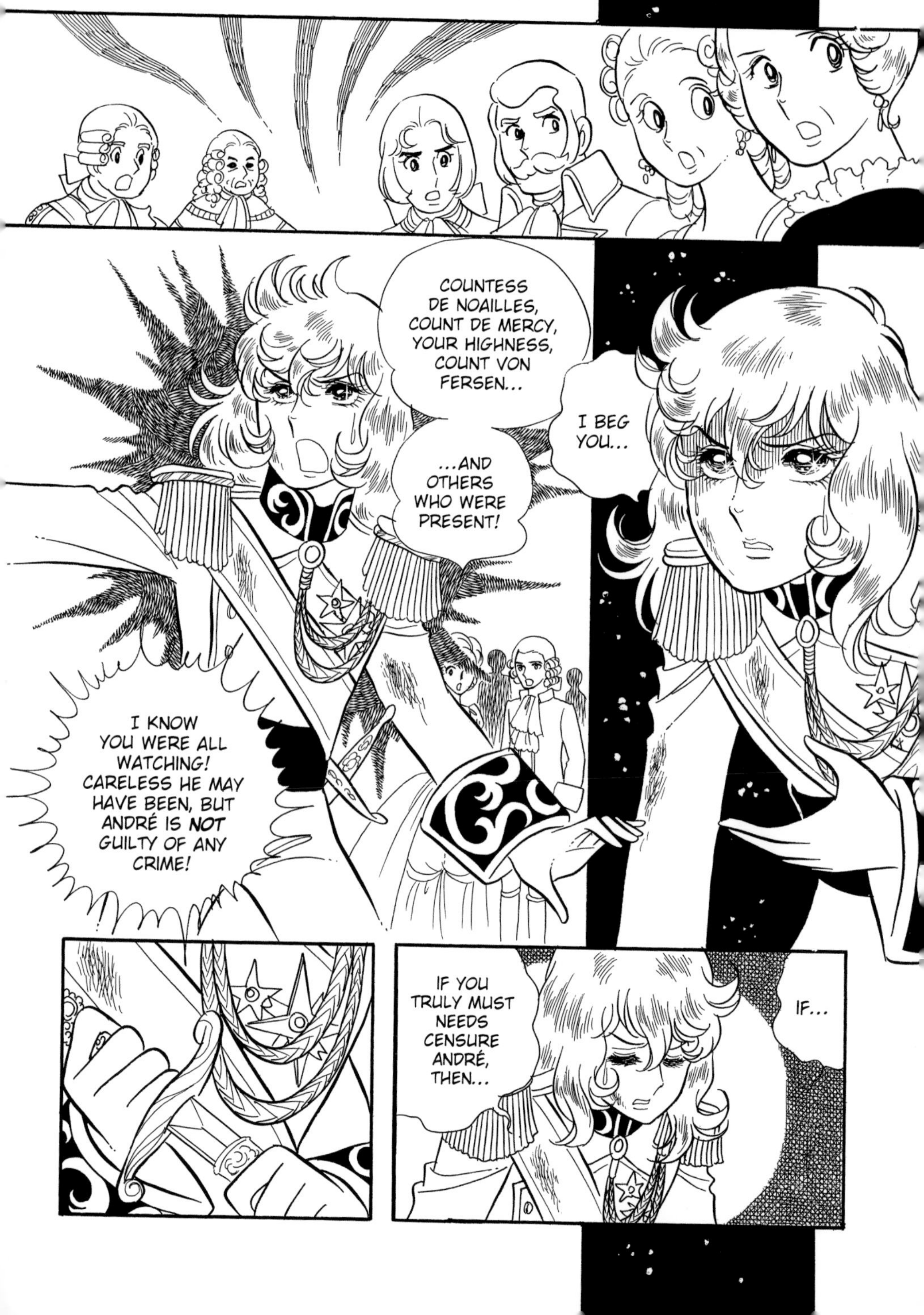
I BEG YOU...
COUNTESS DE NOAILLES, COUNT DE MERCY, YOUR HIGHNESS, COUNT VON FERSEN...
...AND OTHERS WHO WERE PRESENT!
I KNOW YOU WERE ALL WATCHING! CARELESS HE MAY HAVE BEEN, BUT ANDRÉ IS **NOT** GUILTY OF ANY CRIME!
IF...
IF YOU TRULY MUST NEEDS CENSURE ANDRÉ, THEN...

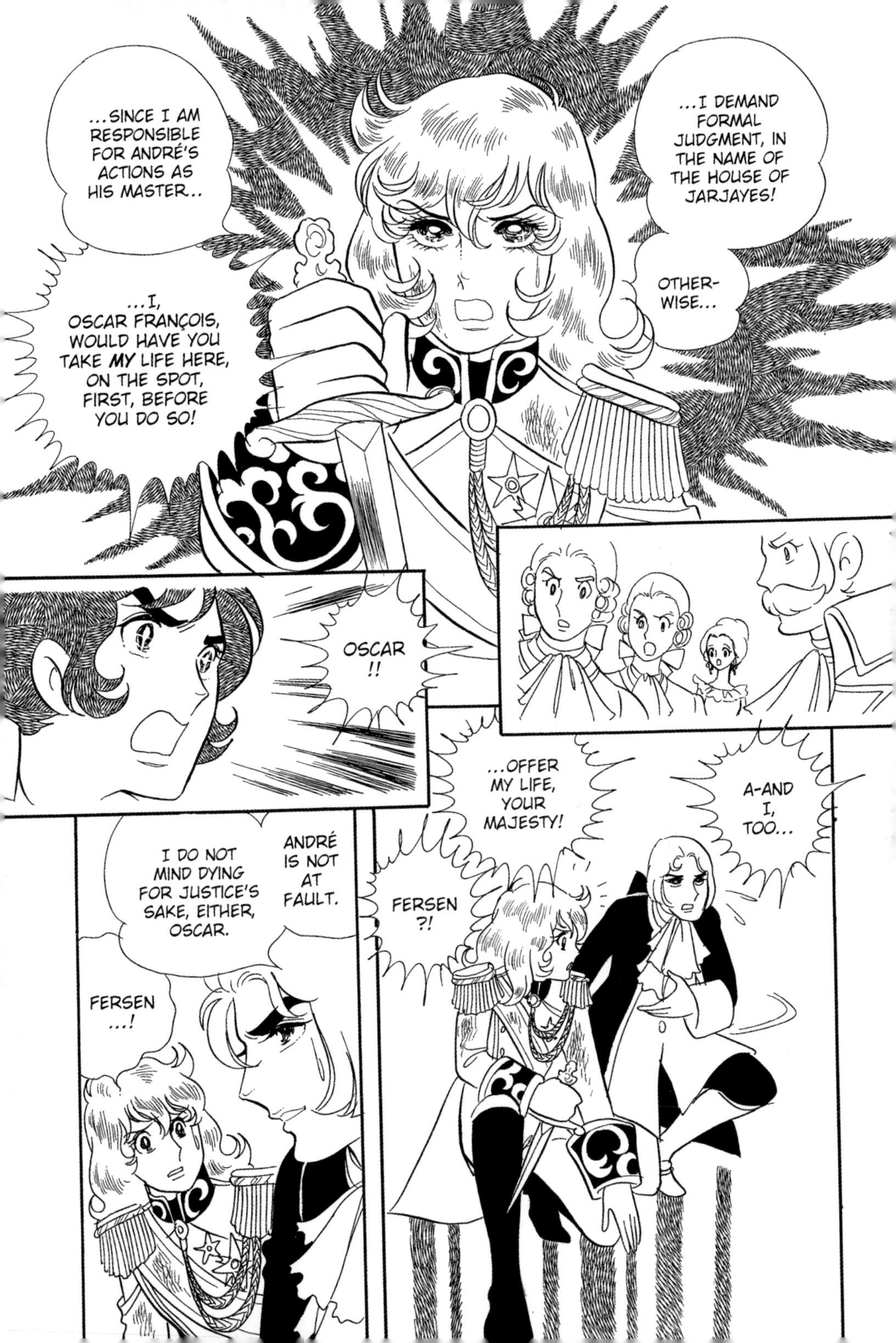

...SINCE I AM RESPONSIBLE FOR ANDRÉ'S ACTIONS AS HIS MASTER...
...I DEMAND FORMAL JUDGMENT, IN THE NAME OF THE HOUSE OF JARJAYES!
OTHER-WISE...
...I, OSCAR FRANÇOIS, WOULD HAVE YOU TAKE *MY* LIFE HERE, ON THE SPOT, FIRST, BEFORE YOU DO SO!
OSCAR !!
A-AND I, TOO...
...OFFER MY LIFE, YOUR MAJESTY!
FERSEN ?!
ANDRÉ IS NOT AT FAULT.
I DO NOT MIND DYING FOR JUSTICE'S SAKE, EITHER, OSCAR.
FERSEN ...!

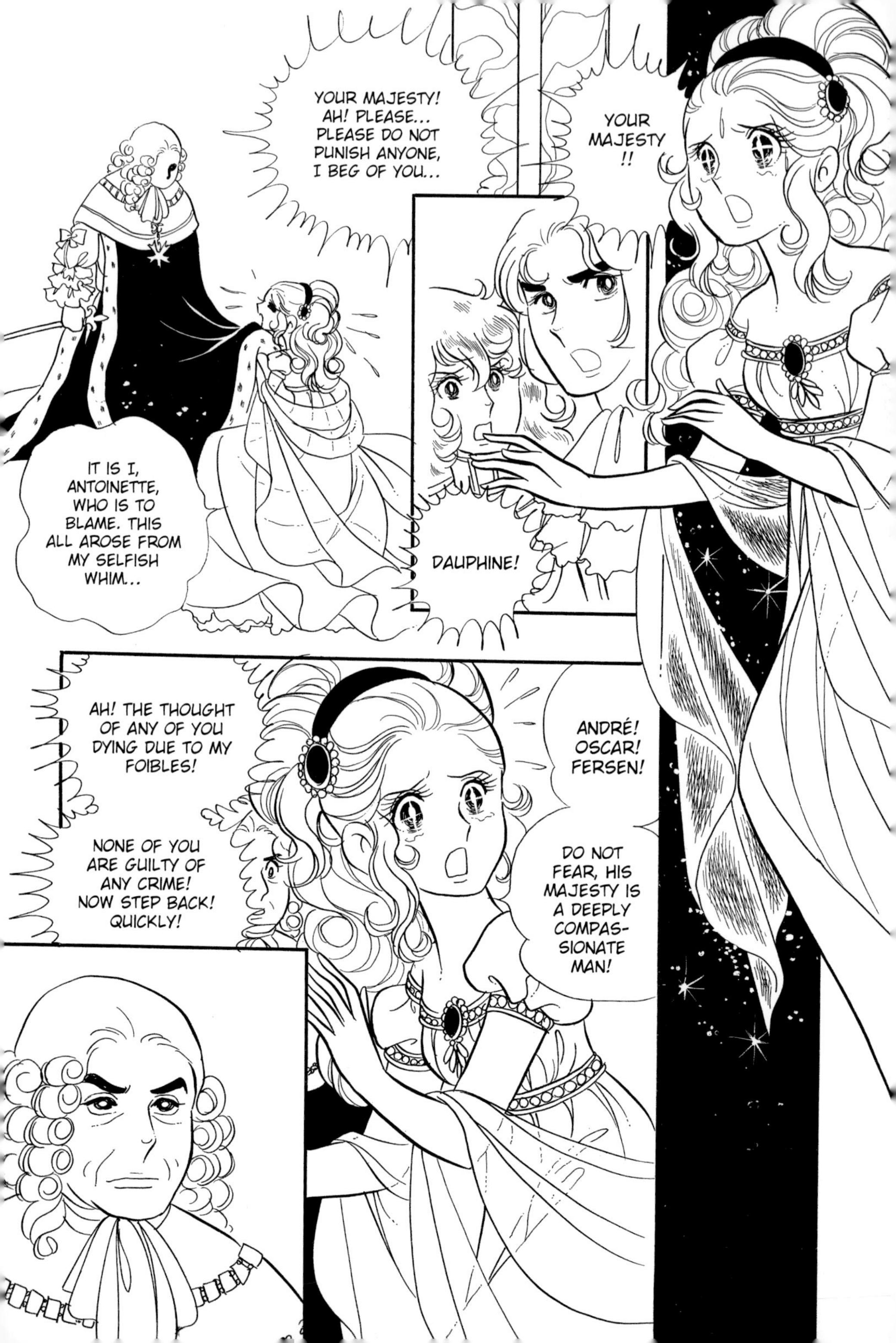
YOUR MAJESTY !!
DAUPHINE!
YOUR MAJESTY! AH! PLEASE... PLEASE DO NOT PUNISH ANYONE, I BEG OF YOU...
IT IS I, ANTOINETTE, WHO IS TO BLAME. THIS ALL AROSE FROM MY SELFISH WHIM...
ANDRÉ! OSCAR! FERSEN!
DO NOT FEAR, HIS MAJESTY IS A DEEPLY COMPAS-SIONATE MAN!
AH! THE THOUGHT OF ANY OF YOU DYING DUE TO MY FOIBLES!
NONE OF YOU ARE GUILTY OF ANY CRIME! NOW STEP BACK! QUICKLY!

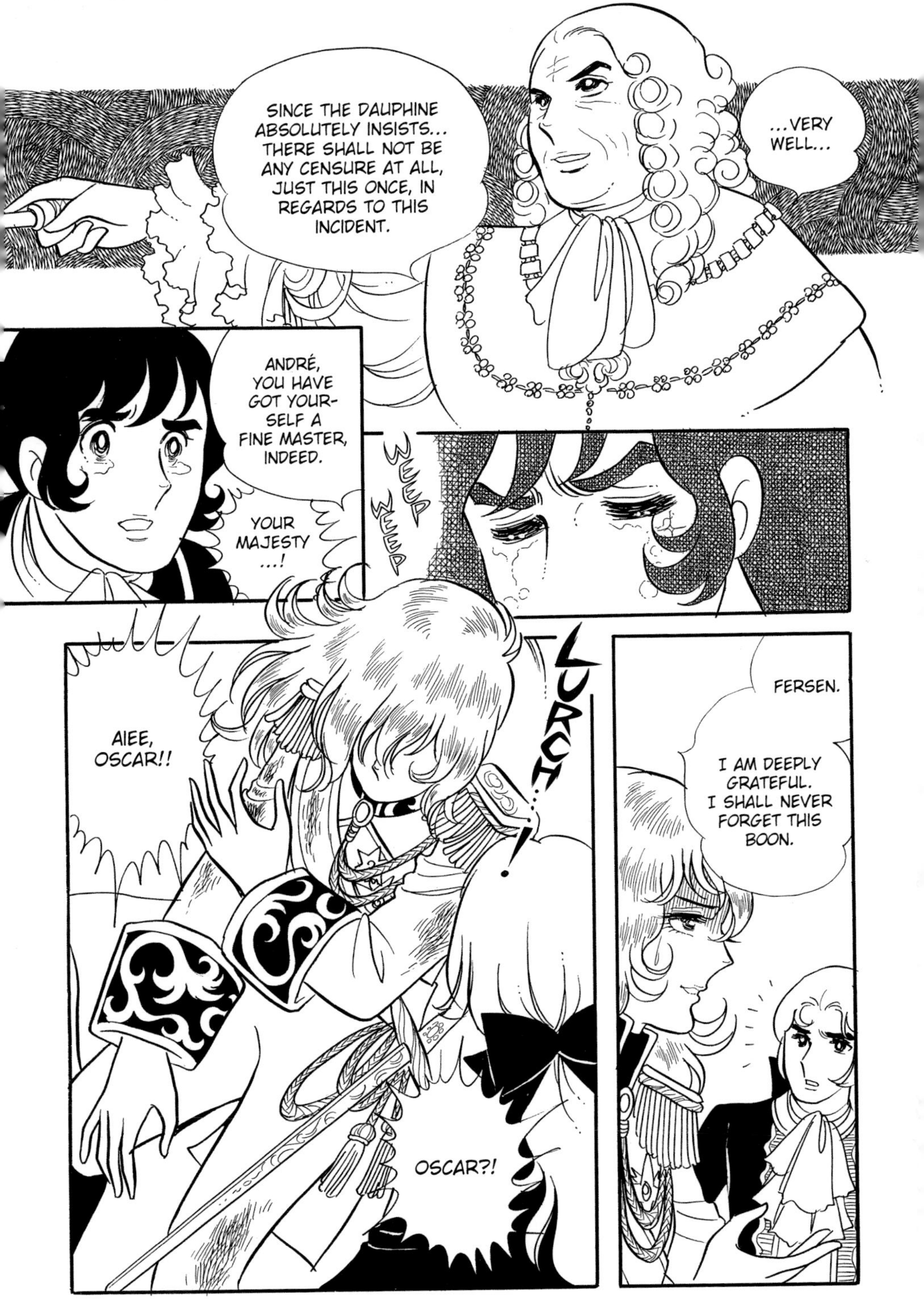
...VERY WELL...
SINCE THE DAUPHINE ABSOLUTELY INSISTS... THERE SHALL NOT BE ANY CENSURE AT ALL, JUST THIS ONCE, IN REGARDS TO THIS INCIDENT.
WEEP WEEP
ANDRÉ, YOU HAVE GOT YOURSELF A FINE MASTER, INDEED.
YOUR MAJESTY ...!
FERSEN.
I AM DEEPLY GRATEFUL. I SHALL NEVER FORGET THIS BOON.
LURCH...!
AIEE, OSCAR!!
OSCAR?!

THE ROSE OF VERSAILLES

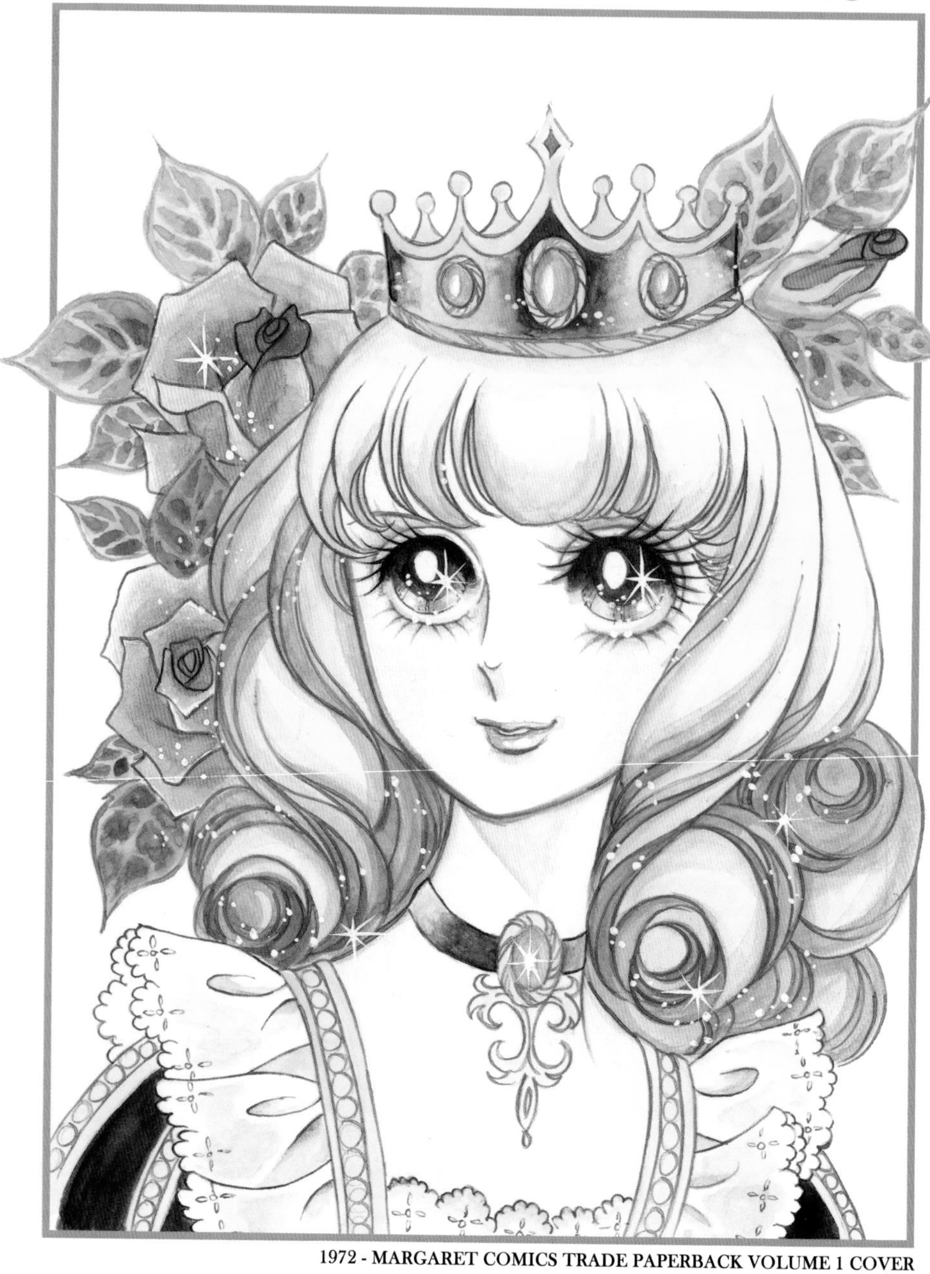

1972 - MARGARET COMICS TRADE PAPERBACK VOLUME 1 COVER

◆18世紀、フランス宮廷を舞台に描く華麗なる大ロマン!!

ベルサイユのばら

♥身をていしてアントワネットの危機をすくったオスカル。しかし、そのオスカルが!?

池田理代子

◆ A MAGNIFICENT GRAND ROMANCE SET IN THE 18TH CENTURY FRENCH ROYAL COURT!!
♥OSCAR RISKS HER OWN LIFE TO RESCUE ANTOINETTE FROM DANGER.
HOWEVER, WHAT OF OSCAR HERSELF!?

EPISODE 11

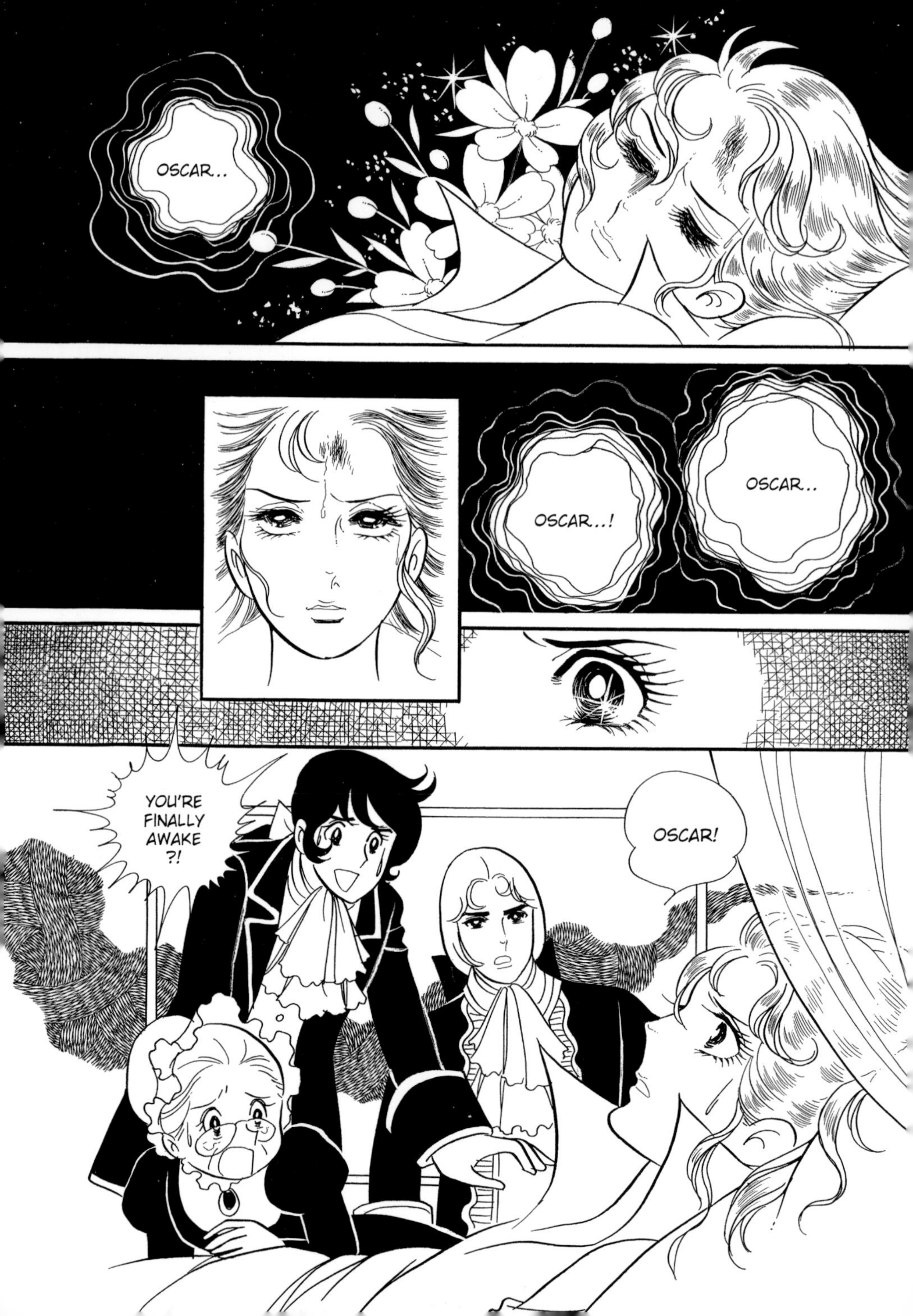
OSCAR...
OSCAR..
OSCAR...!
OSCAR!
YOU'RE FINALLY AWAKE ?!

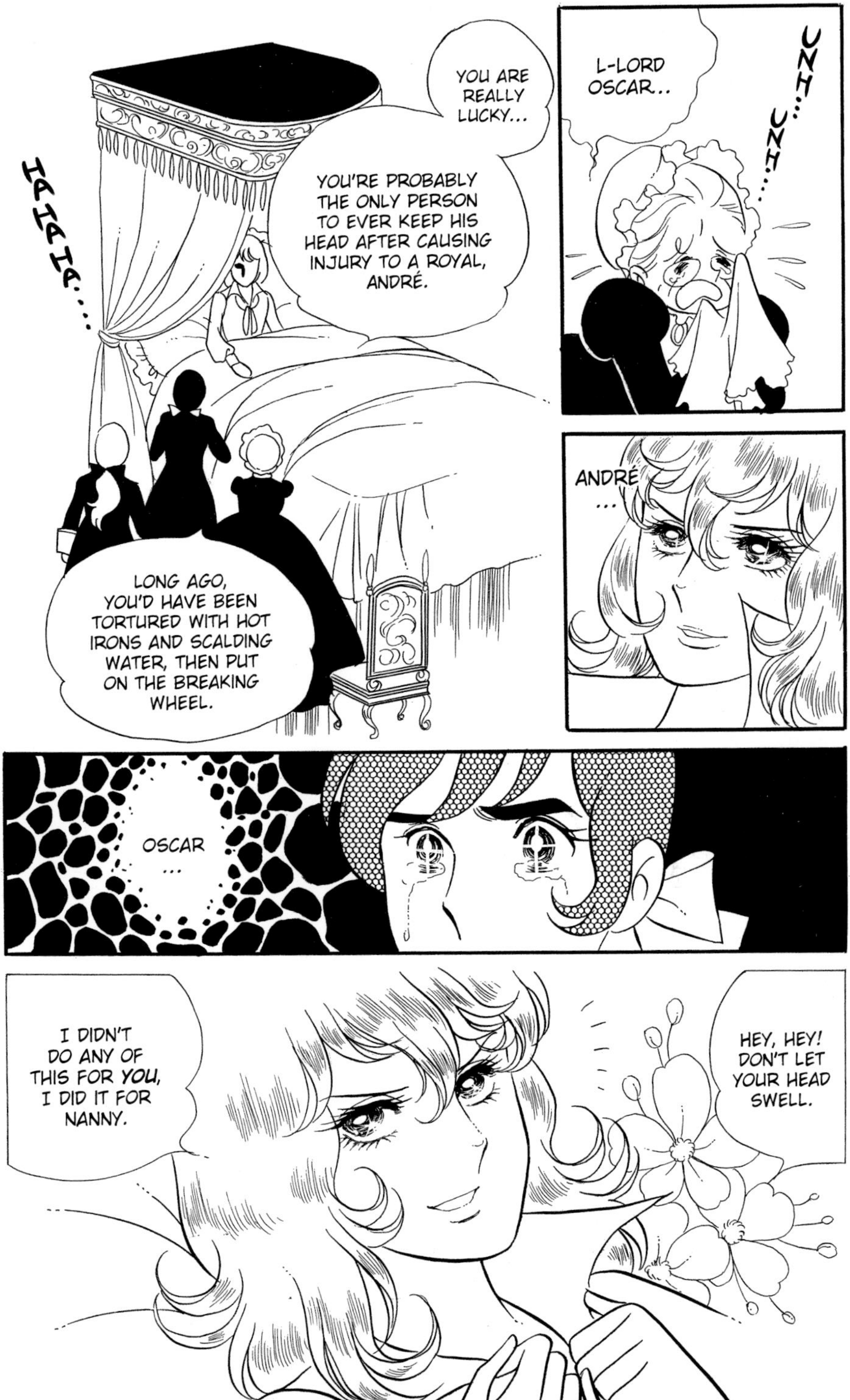

UNH... UNH...
L-LORD OSCAR...
ANDRÉ ...
YOU ARE REALLY LUCKY...
YOU'RE PROBABLY THE ONLY PERSON TO EVER KEEP HIS HEAD AFTER CAUSING INJURY TO A ROYAL, ANDRÉ.
HAHAHA...
LONG AGO, YOU'D HAVE BEEN TORTURED WITH HOT IRONS AND SCALDING WATER, THEN PUT ON THE BREAKING WHEEL.
OSCAR ...
HEY, HEY! DON'T LET YOUR HEAD SWELL.
I DIDN'T DO ANY OF THIS FOR *YOU*, I DID IT FOR NANNY.

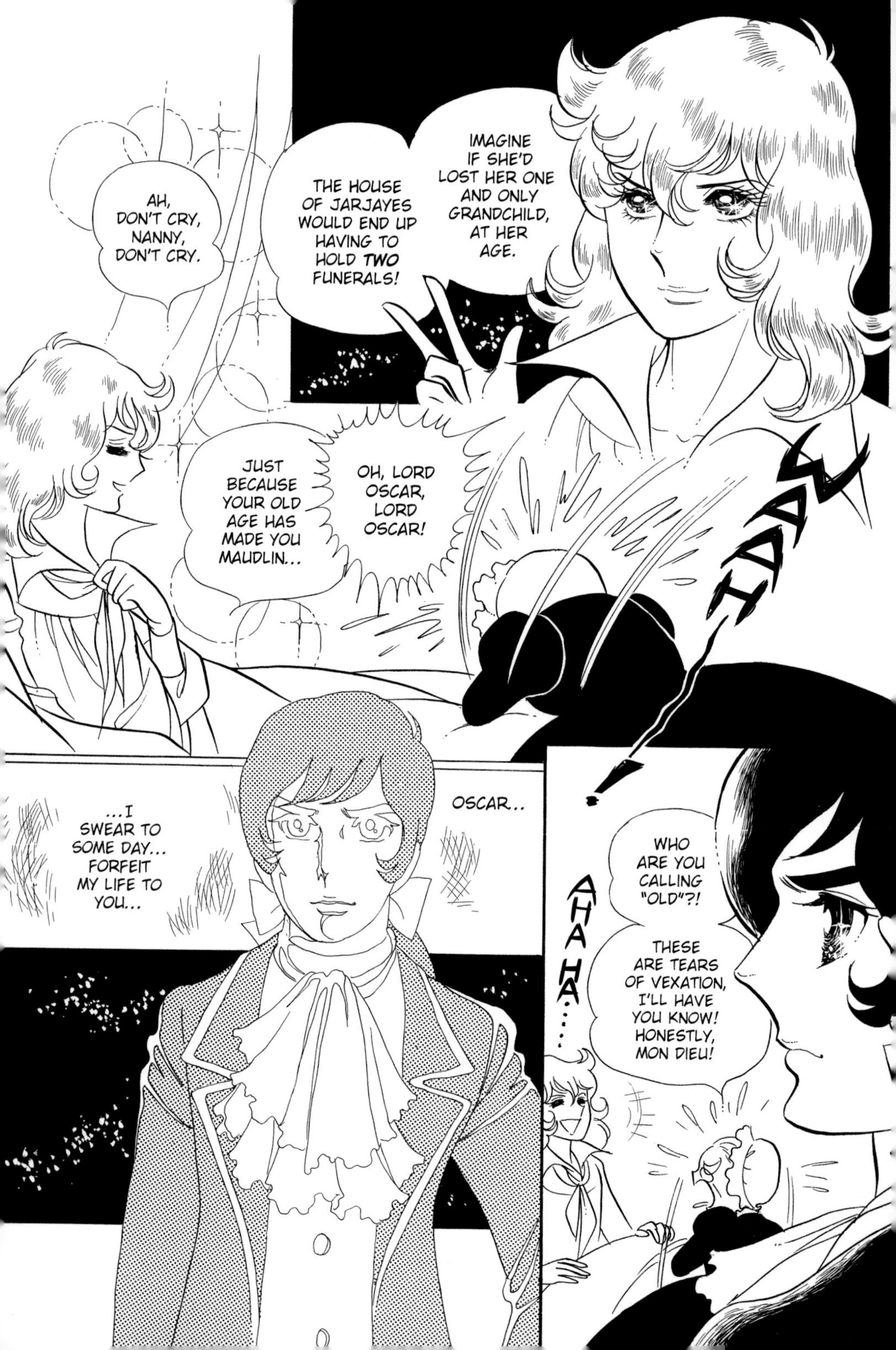

IMAGINE IF SHE'D LOST HER ONE AND ONLY GRANDCHILD, AT HER AGE.
THE HOUSE OF JARJAYES WOULD END UP HAVING TO HOLD **TWO** FUNERALS!
WAAAH!
OH, LORD OSCAR, LORD OSCAR!
AH, DON'T CRY, NANNY, DON'T CRY.
JUST BECAUSE YOUR OLD AGE HAS MADE YOU MAUDLIN...
WHO ARE YOU CALLING "OLD"?!
THESE ARE TEARS OF VEXATION, I'LL HAVE YOU KNOW! HONESTLY, MON DIEU!
AHAHA....
OSCAR..
...I SWEAR TO SOME DAY... FORFEIT MY LIFE TO YOU...

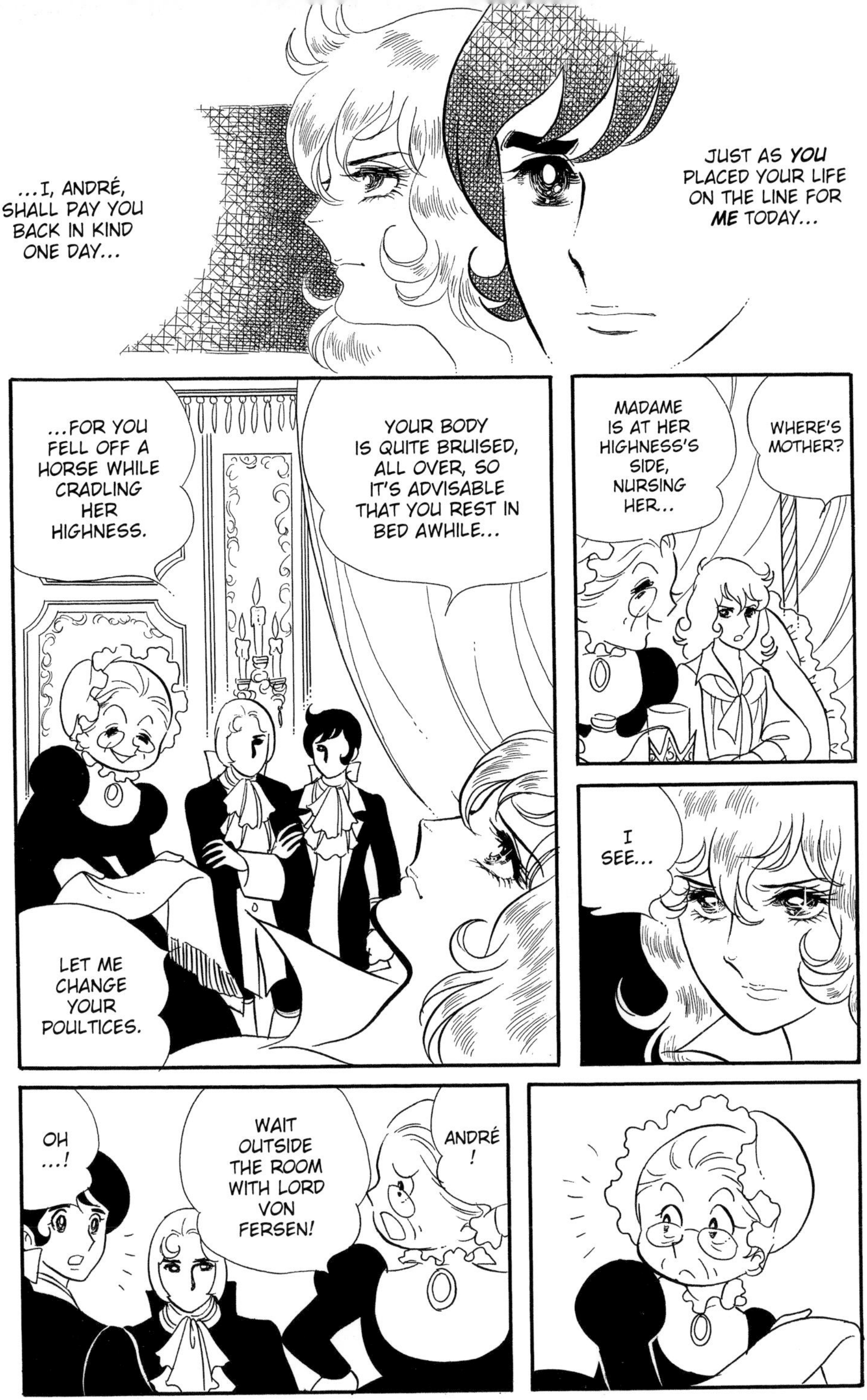
JUST AS *YOU* PLACED YOUR LIFE ON THE LINE FOR *ME* TODAY...
...I, ANDRÉ, SHALL PAY YOU BACK IN KIND ONE DAY...
WHERE'S MOTHER?
MADAME IS AT HER HIGHNESS'S SIDE, NURSING HER...
I SEE...
YOUR BODY IS QUITE BRUISED, ALL OVER, SO IT'S ADVISABLE THAT YOU REST IN BED AWHILE...
...FOR YOU FELL OFF A HORSE WHILE CRADLING HER HIGHNESS.
LET ME CHANGE YOUR POULTICES.
ANDRÉ!
WAIT OUTSIDE THE ROOM WITH LORD VON FERSEN!
OH...!

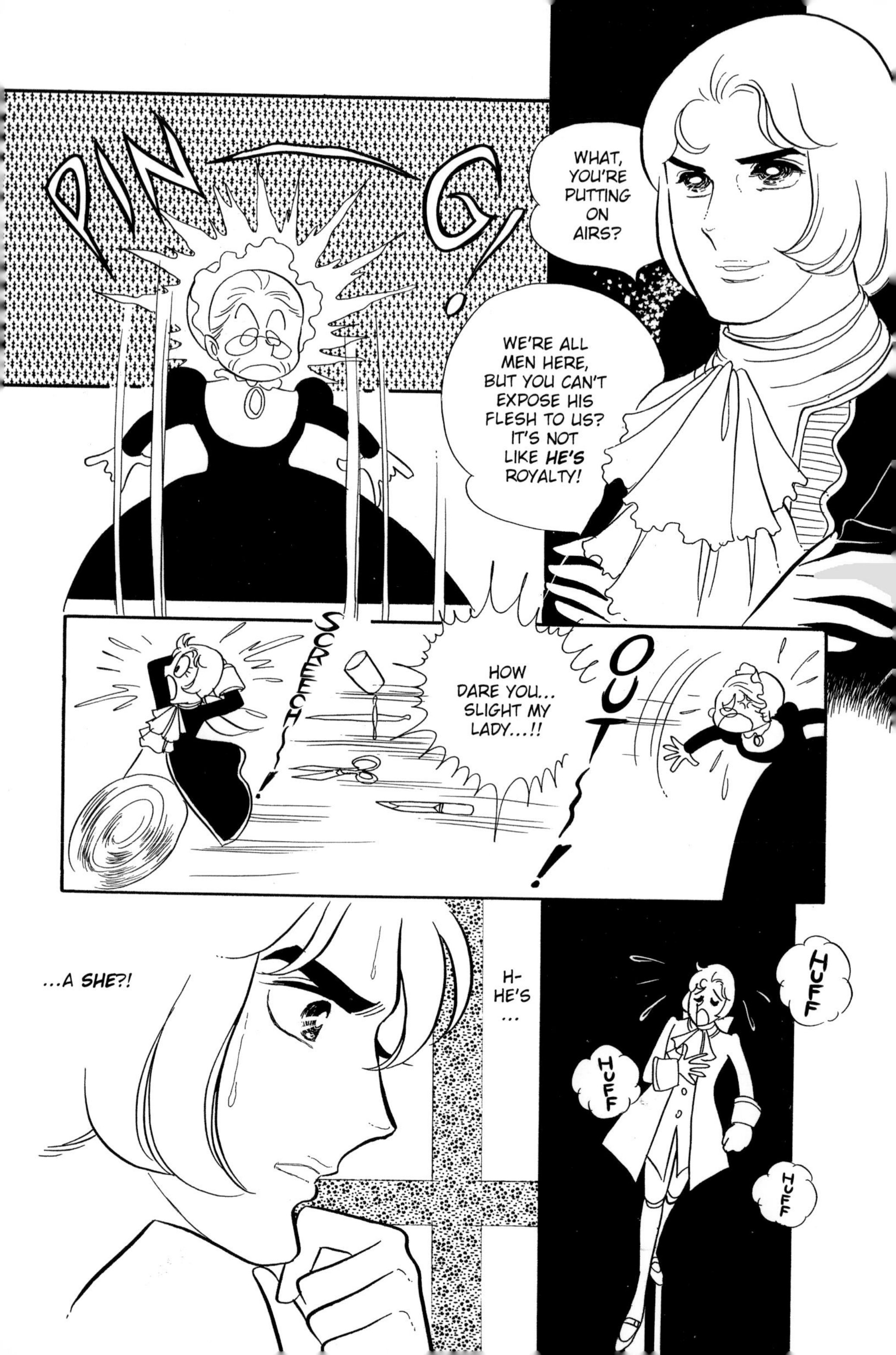
WHAT, YOU'RE PUTTING ON AIRS?
WE'RE ALL MEN HERE, BUT YOU CAN'T EXPOSE HIS FLESH TO US? IT'S NOT LIKE **HE'S** ROYALTY!
PING!
OUT!!
HOW DARE YOU... SLIGHT MY LADY...!!
SCREECH!
HUFF
HUFF
HUFF
H-HE'S...
...A **SHE**?!

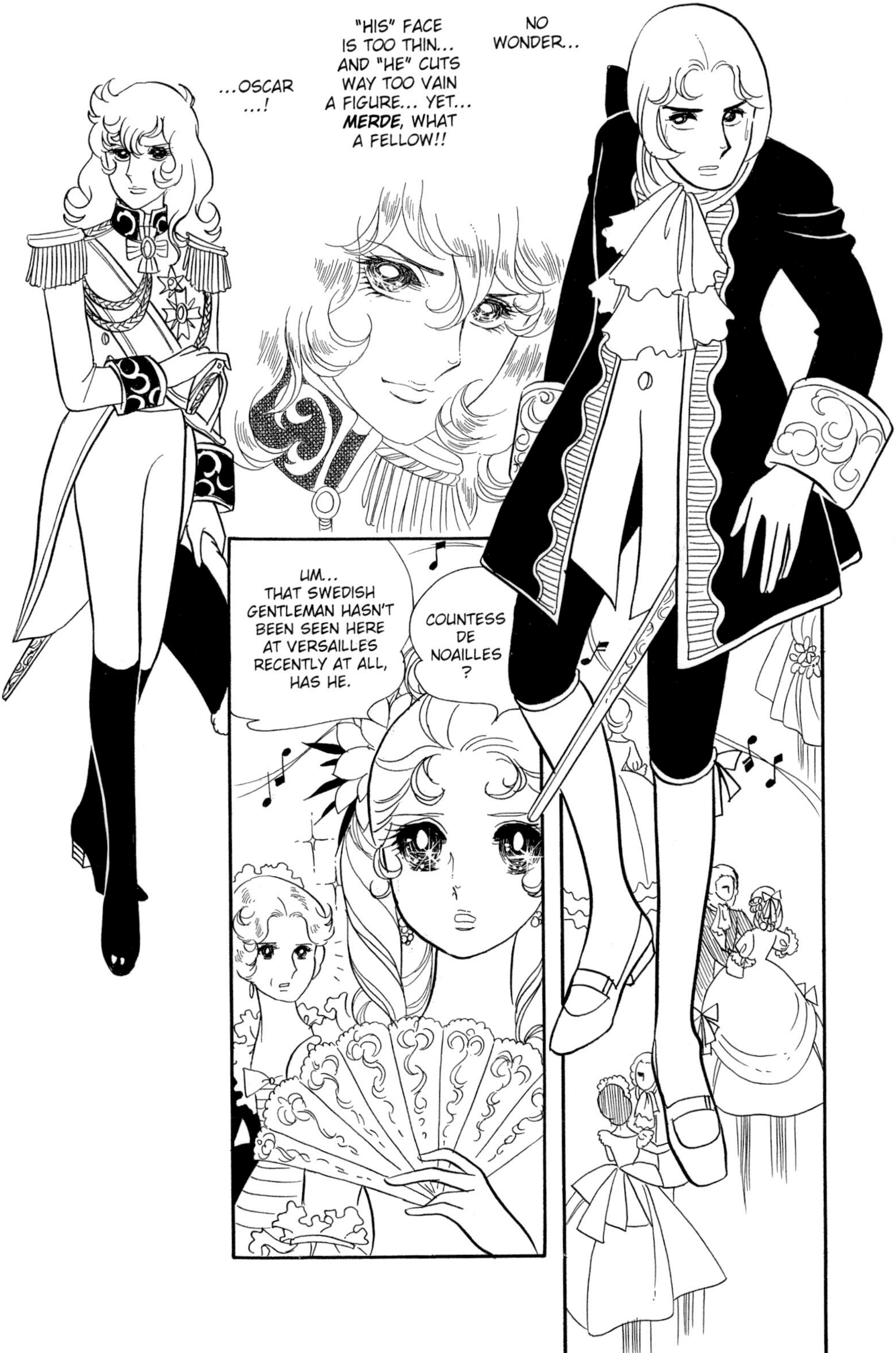
NO WONDER...
"HIS" FACE IS TOO THIN... AND "HE" CUTS WAY TOO VAIN A FIGURE... YET... **MERDE**, WHAT A FELLOW!!
...OSCAR ...!
COUNTESS DE NOAILLES ?
UM... THAT SWEDISH GENTLEMAN HASN'T BEEN SEEN HERE AT VERSAILLES RECENTLY AT ALL, HAS HE.

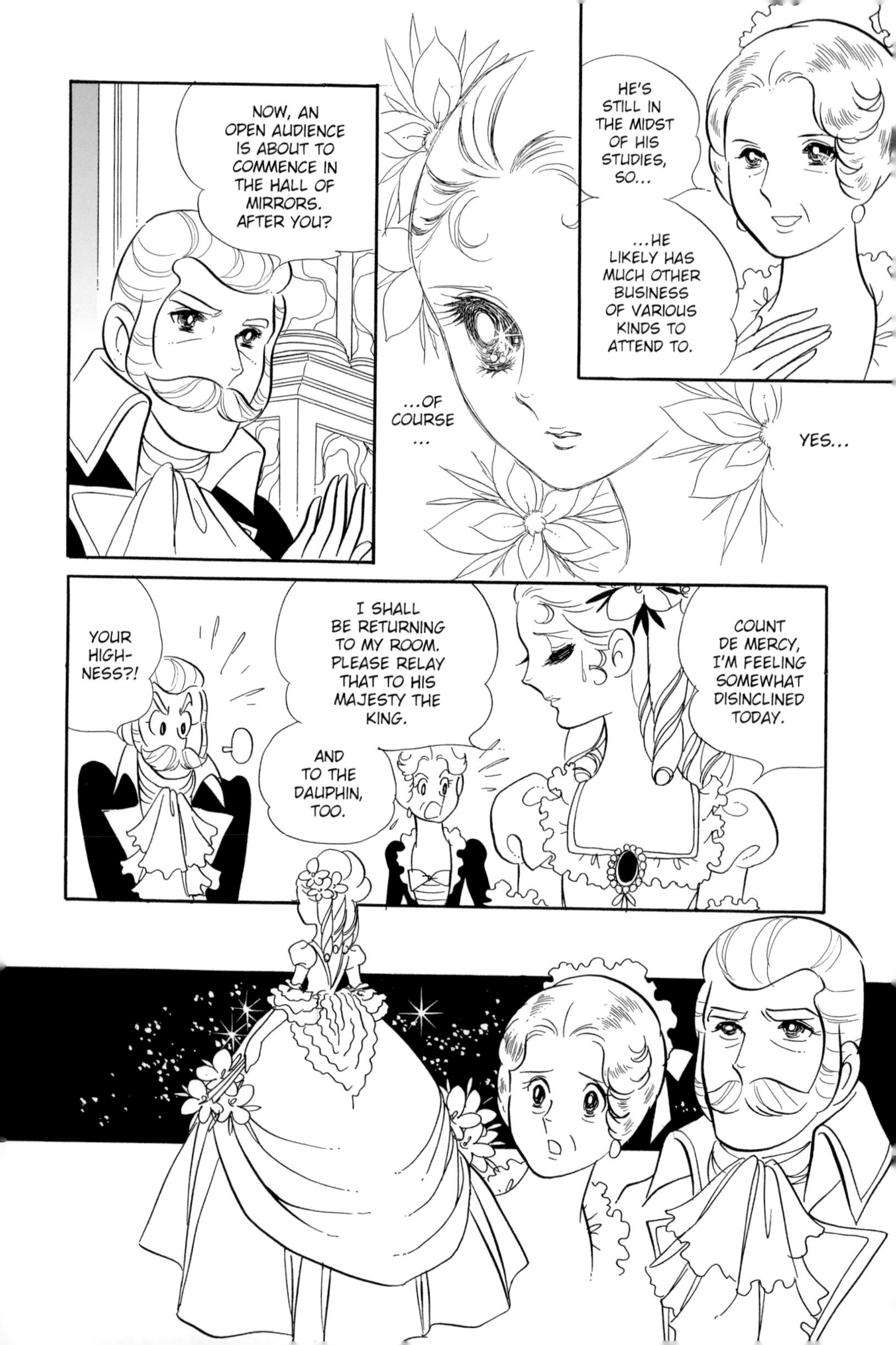
HE'S STILL IN THE MIDST OF HIS STUDIES, SO...
...HE LIKELY HAS MUCH OTHER BUSINESS OF VARIOUS KINDS TO ATTEND TO.
YES...
...OF COURSE ...
NOW, AN OPEN AUDIENCE IS ABOUT TO COMMENCE IN THE HALL OF MIRRORS. AFTER YOU?
COUNT DE MERCY, I'M FEELING SOMEWHAT DISINCLINED TODAY.
I SHALL BE RETURNING TO MY ROOM. PLEASE RELAY THAT TO HIS MAJESTY THE KING.
AND TO THE DAUPHIN, TOO.
YOUR HIGH-NESS?!

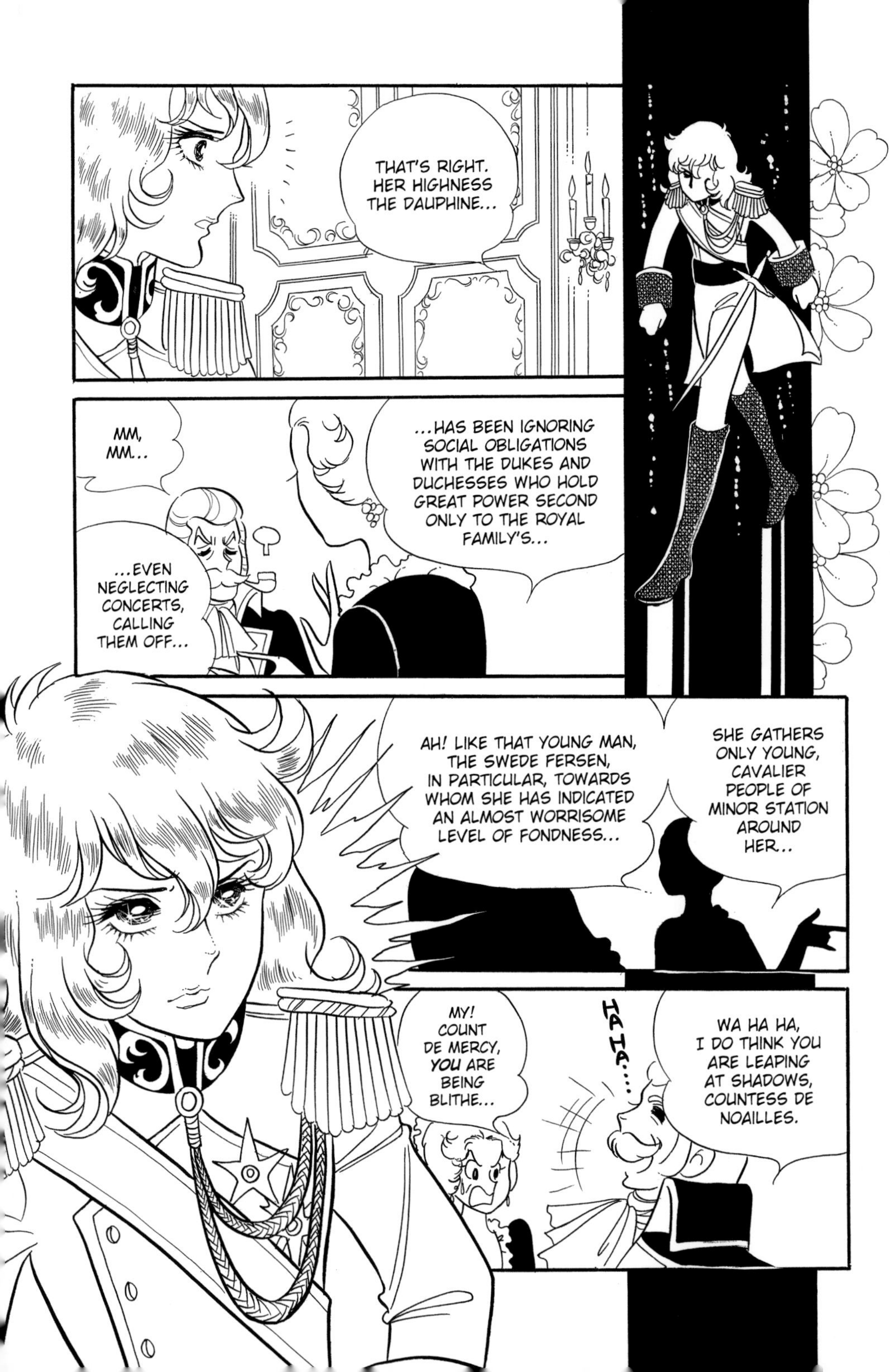
THAT'S RIGHT. HER HIGHNESS THE DAUPHINE...
...HAS BEEN IGNORING SOCIAL OBLIGATIONS WITH THE DUKES AND DUCHESSES WHO HOLD GREAT POWER SECOND ONLY TO THE ROYAL FAMILY'S...
MM, MM...
...EVEN NEGLECTING CONCERTS, CALLING THEM OFF...
SHE GATHERS ONLY YOUNG, CAVALIER PEOPLE OF MINOR STATION AROUND HER...
AH! LIKE THAT YOUNG MAN, THE SWEDE FERSEN, IN PARTICULAR, TOWARDS WHOM SHE HAS INDICATED AN ALMOST WORRISOME LEVEL OF FONDNESS...
WA HA HA, I DO THINK YOU ARE LEAPING AT SHADOWS, COUNTESS DE NOAILLES.
HA HA...
MY! COUNT DE MERCY, *YOU* ARE BEING BLITHE...

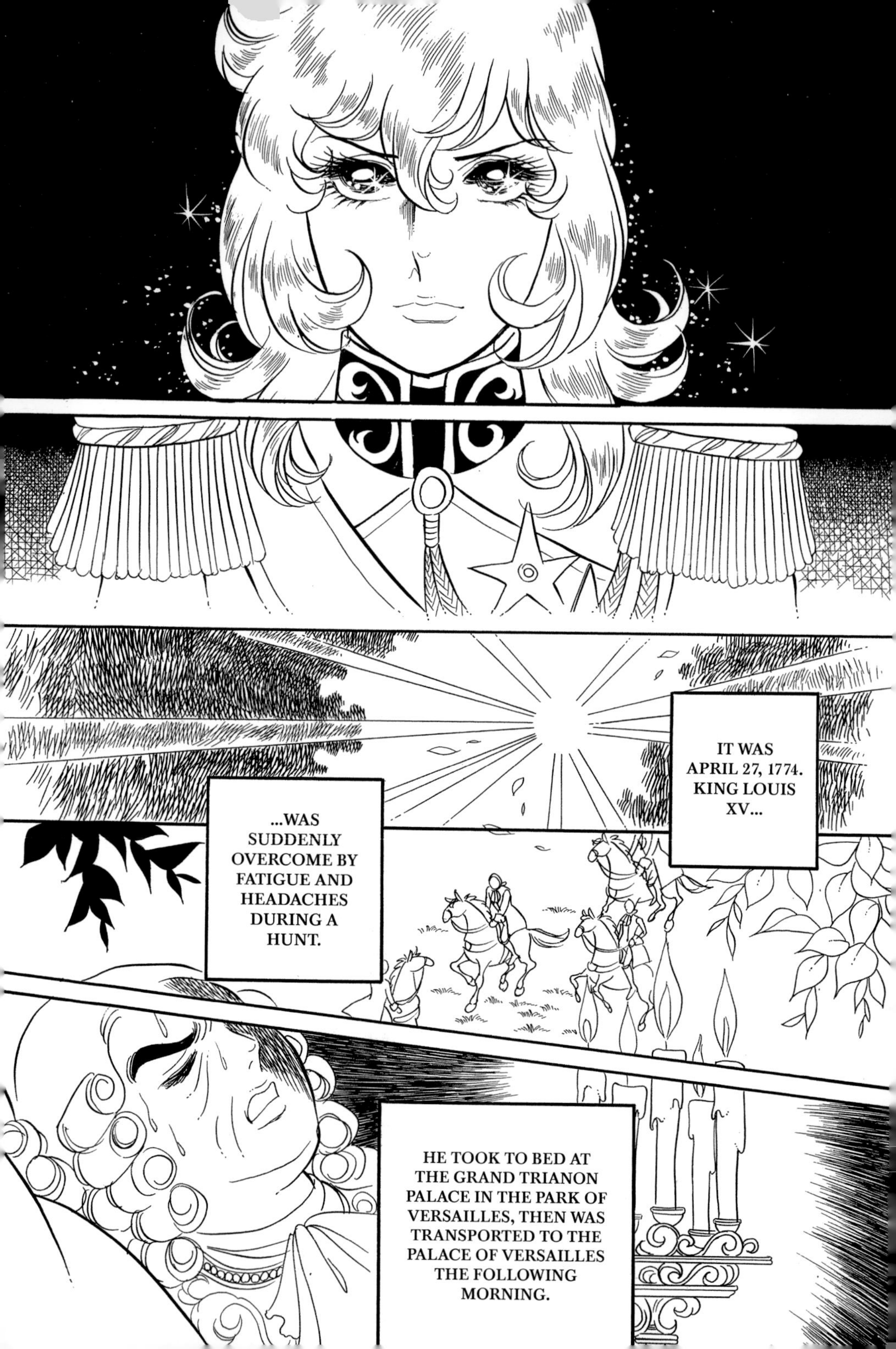
IT WAS APRIL 27, 1774. KING LOUIS XV...
...WAS SUDDENLY OVERCOME BY FATIGUE AND HEADACHES DURING A HUNT.
HE TOOK TO BED AT THE GRAND TRIANON PALACE IN THE PARK OF VERSAILLES, THEN WAS TRANSPORTED TO THE PALACE OF VERSAILLES THE FOLLOWING MORNING.

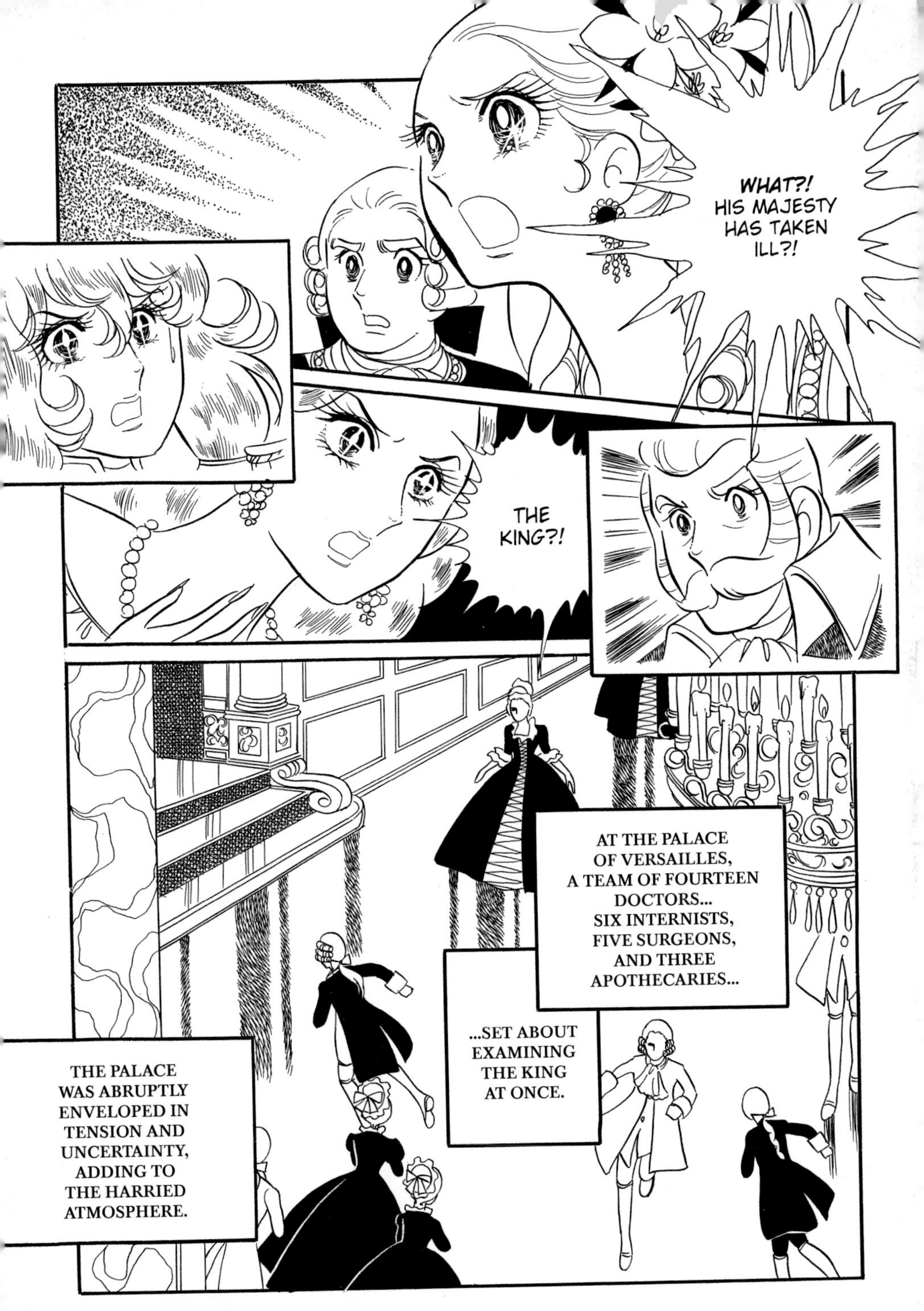
WHAT?! HIS MAJESTY HAS TAKEN ILL?!
THE KING?!
AT THE PALACE OF VERSAILLES, A TEAM OF FOURTEEN DOCTORS... SIX INTERNISTS, FIVE SURGEONS, AND THREE APOTHECARIES...
...SET ABOUT EXAMINING THE KING AT ONCE.
THE PALACE WAS ABRUPTLY ENVELOPED IN TENSION AND UNCERTAINTY, ADDING TO THE HARRIED ATMOSPHERE.

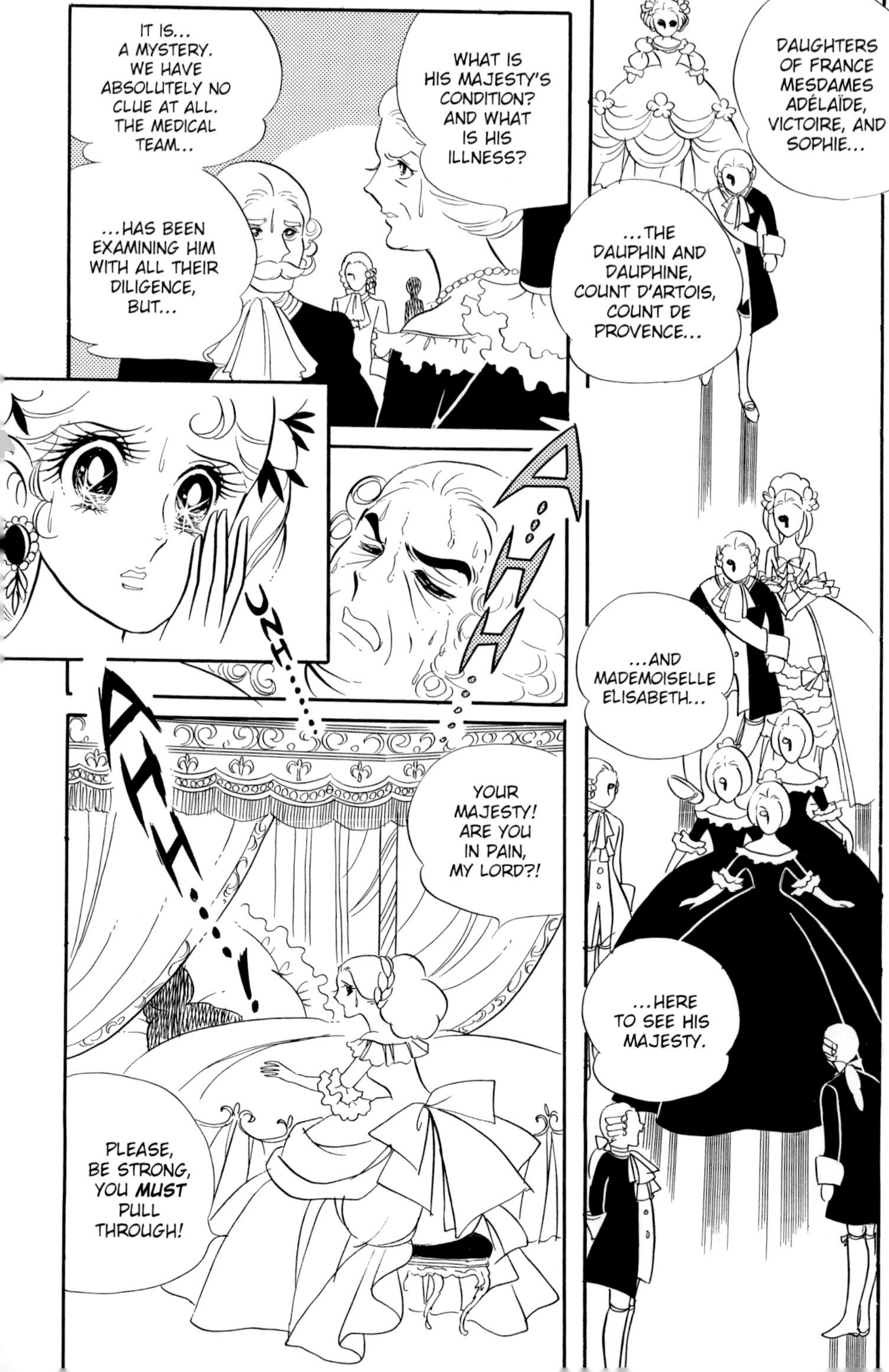
DAUGHTERS OF FRANCE MESDAMES ADÉLAÏDE, VICTOIRE, AND SOPHIE...
...THE DAUPHIN AND DAUPHINE, COUNT D'ARTOIS, COUNT DE PROVENCE...
...AND MADEMOISELLE ELISABETH...
...HERE TO SEE HIS MAJESTY.
WHAT IS HIS MAJESTY'S CONDITION? AND WHAT IS HIS ILLNESS?
IT IS... A MYSTERY. WE HAVE ABSOLUTELY NO CLUE AT ALL. THE MEDICAL TEAM...
...HAS BEEN EXAMINING HIM WITH ALL THEIR DILIGENCE, BUT...
AHHH....
AHH...!
YOUR MAJESTY! ARE YOU IN PAIN, MY LORD?!
PLEASE, BE STRONG, YOU **MUST** PULL THROUGH!

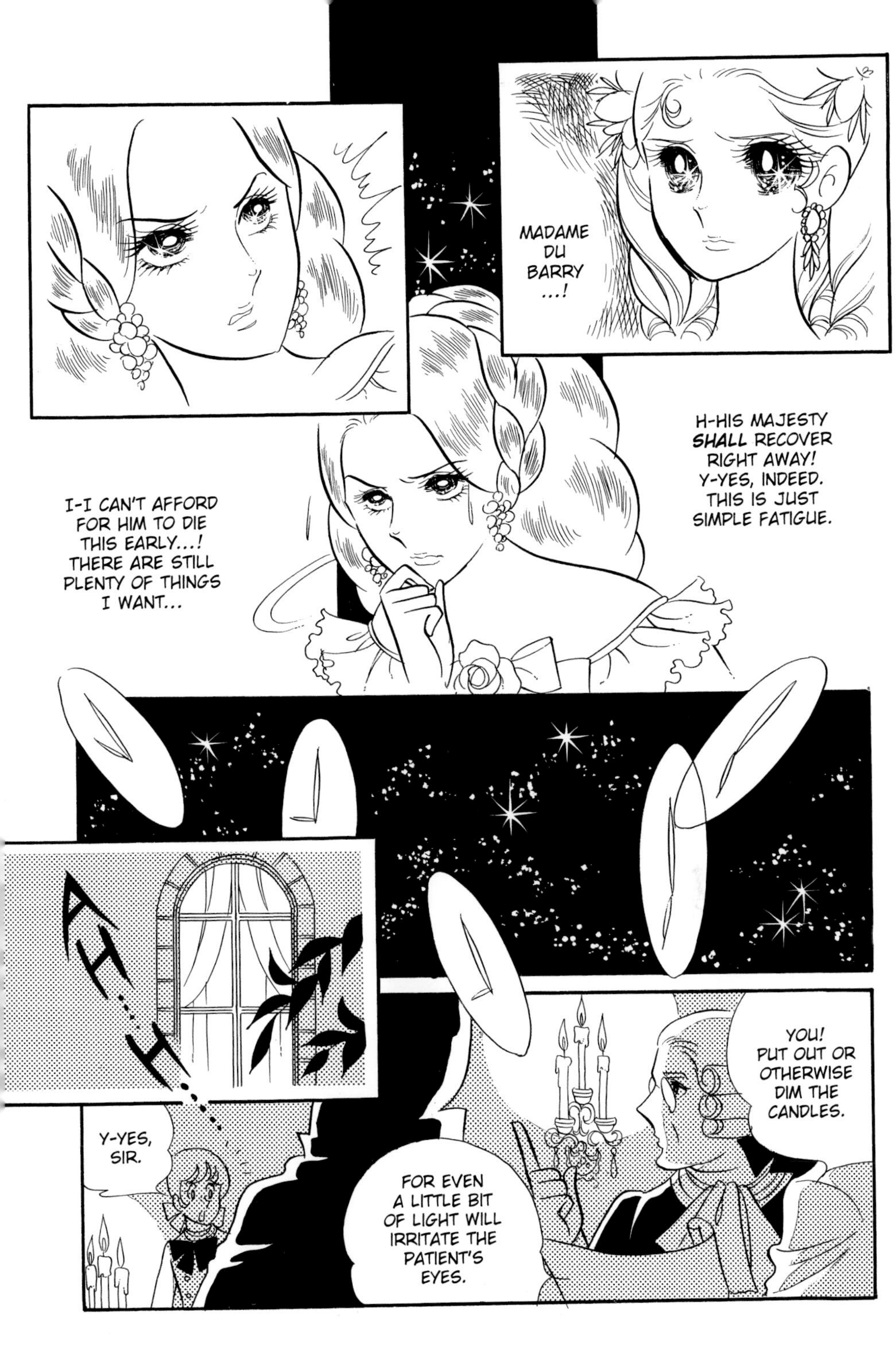
MADAME DU BARRY ...!
H-HIS MAJESTY **SHALL** RECOVER RIGHT AWAY! Y-YES, INDEED. THIS IS JUST SIMPLE FATIGUE.
I-I CAN'T AFFORD FOR HIM TO DIE THIS EARLY...! THERE ARE STILL PLENTY OF THINGS I WANT...
AH...H...
YOU! PUT OUT OR OTHERWISE DIM THE CANDLES.
FOR EVEN A LITTLE BIT OF LIGHT WILL IRRITATE THE PATIENT'S EYES.
Y-YES, SIR.

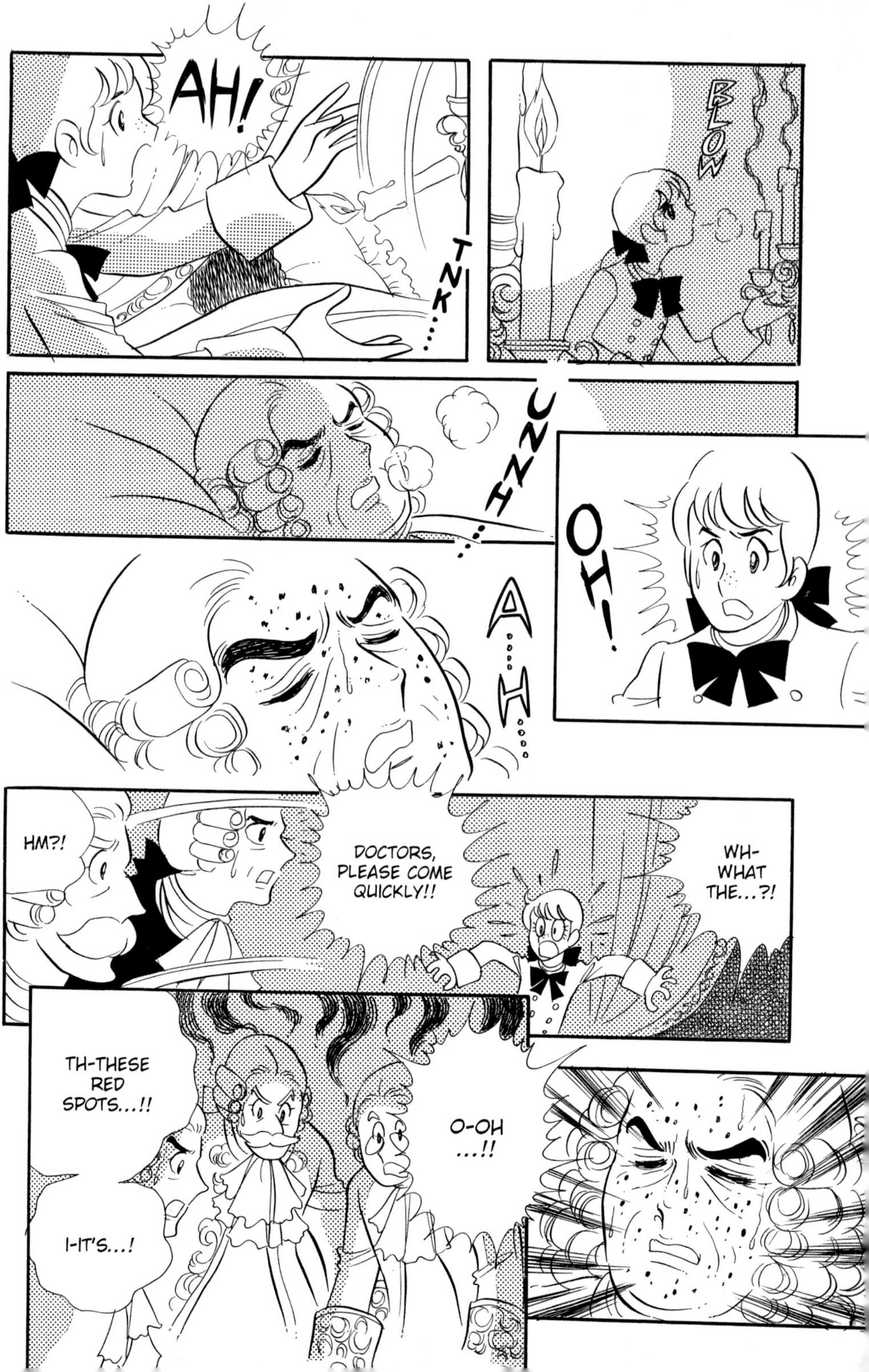
BLOW
AH!
TNK...
OH!
UNNNH...
AH...H...
WH- WHAT THE...?!
DOCTORS, PLEASE COME QUICKLY!!
HM?!
O-OH ...!!
TH-THESE RED SPOTS...!!
I-IT'S...!

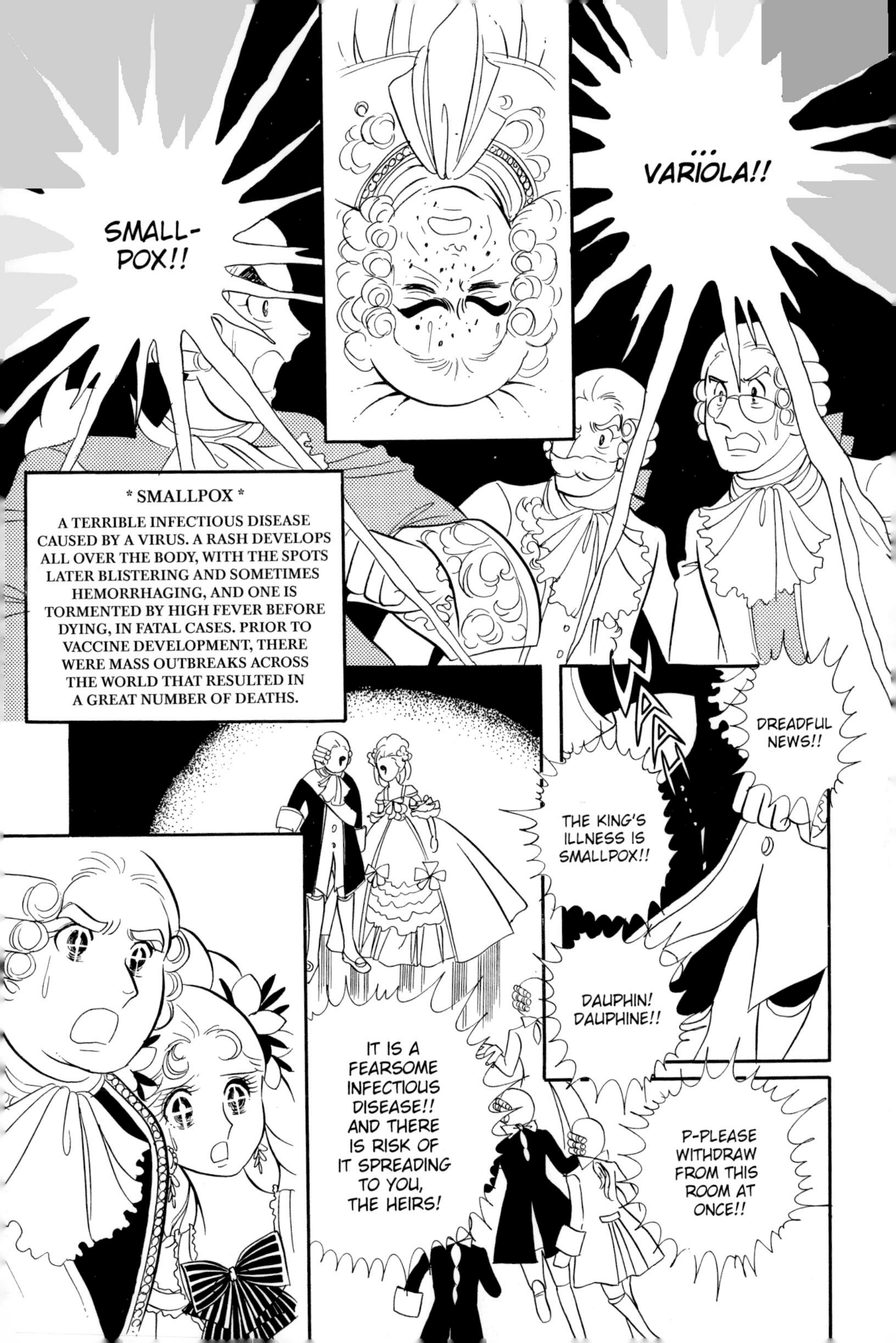
...VARIOLA!!
SMALL-POX!!
* SMALLPOX *
A TERRIBLE INFECTIOUS DISEASE CAUSED BY A VIRUS. A RASH DEVELOPS ALL OVER THE BODY, WITH THE SPOTS LATER BLISTERING AND SOMETIMES HEMORRHAGING, AND ONE IS TORMENTED BY HIGH FEVER BEFORE DYING, IN FATAL CASES. PRIOR TO VACCINE DEVELOPMENT, THERE WERE MASS OUTBREAKS ACROSS THE WORLD THAT RESULTED IN A GREAT NUMBER OF DEATHS.
DREADFUL NEWS!!
THE KING'S ILLNESS IS SMALLPOX!!
DAUPHIN! DAUPHINE!!
P-PLEASE WITHDRAW FROM THIS ROOM AT ONCE!!
IT IS A FEARSOME INFECTIOUS DISEASE!! AND THERE IS RISK OF IT SPREADING TO YOU, THE HEIRS!

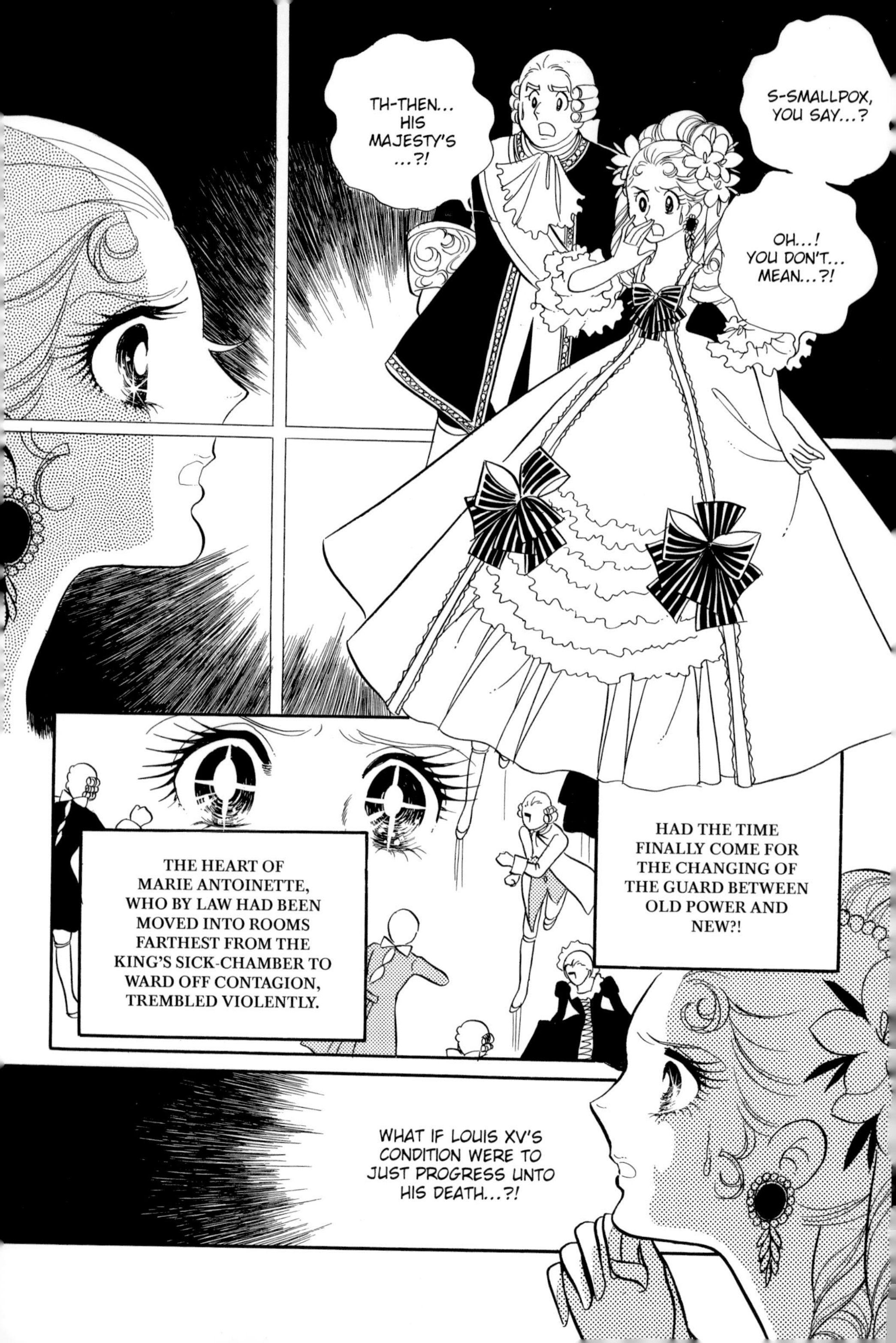
S-SMALLPOX, YOU SAY...?
OH...! YOU DON'T... MEAN...?!
TH-THEN... HIS MAJESTY'S ...?!
HAD THE TIME FINALLY COME FOR THE CHANGING OF THE GUARD BETWEEN OLD POWER AND NEW?!
THE HEART OF MARIE ANTOINETTE, WHO BY LAW HAD BEEN MOVED INTO ROOMS FARTHEST FROM THE KING'S SICK-CHAMBER TO WARD OFF CONTAGION, TREMBLED VIOLENTLY.
WHAT IF LOUIS XV'S CONDITION WERE TO JUST PROGRESS UNTO HIS DEATH...?!

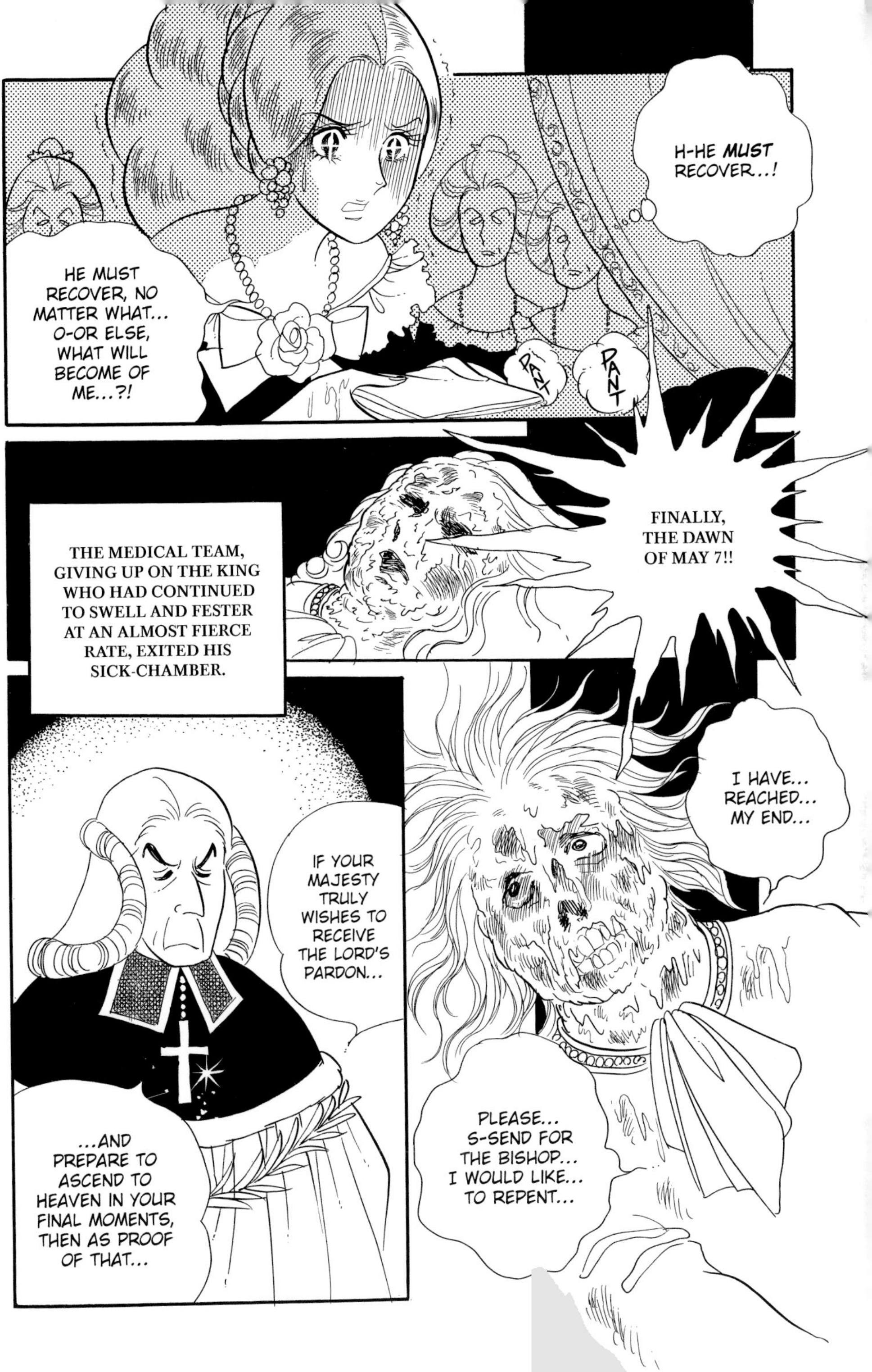
H-HE MUST RECOVER...!
HE MUST RECOVER, NO MATTER WHAT... O-OR ELSE, WHAT WILL BECOME OF ME...?!
PANT
PANT
FINALLY, THE DAWN OF MAY 7!!
THE MEDICAL TEAM, GIVING UP ON THE KING WHO HAD CONTINUED TO SWELL AND FESTER AT AN ALMOST FIERCE RATE, EXITED HIS SICK-CHAMBER.
I HAVE... REACHED... MY END...
PLEASE... S-SEND FOR THE BISHOP... I WOULD LIKE... TO REPENT...
IF YOUR MAJESTY TRULY WISHES TO RECEIVE THE LORD'S PARDON...
...AND PREPARE TO ASCEND TO HEAVEN IN YOUR FINAL MOMENTS, THEN AS PROOF OF THAT...

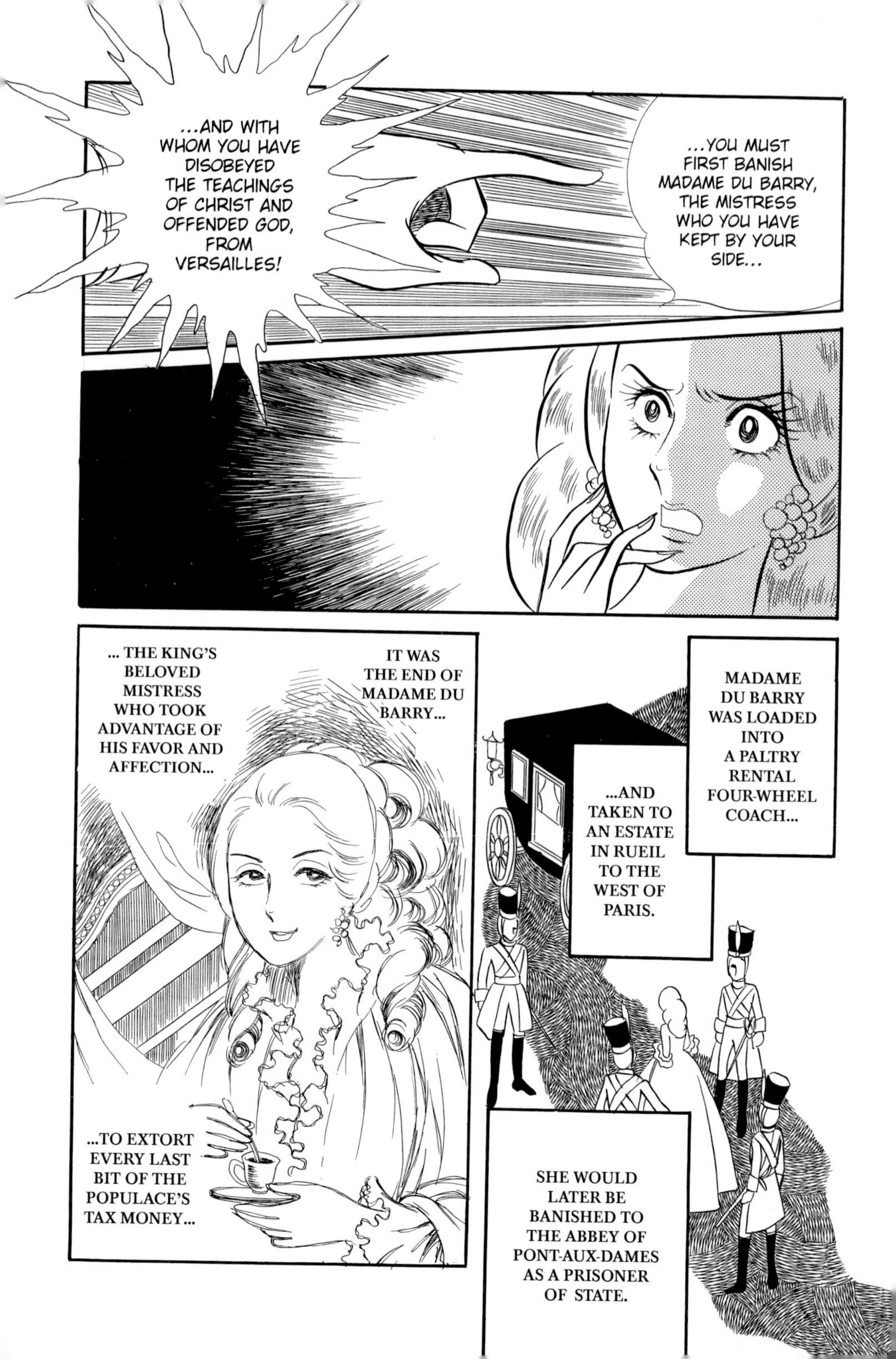
...YOU MUST FIRST BANISH MADAME DU BARRY, THE MISTRESS WHO YOU HAVE KEPT BY YOUR SIDE...
...AND WITH WHOM YOU HAVE DISOBEYED THE TEACHINGS OF CHRIST AND OFFENDED GOD, FROM VERSAILLES!
MADAME DU BARRY WAS LOADED INTO A PALTRY RENTAL FOUR-WHEEL COACH...
...AND TAKEN TO AN ESTATE IN RUEIL TO THE WEST OF PARIS.
SHE WOULD LATER BE BANISHED TO THE ABBEY OF PONT-AUX-DAMES AS A PRISONER OF STATE.
IT WAS THE END OF MADAME DU BARRY...
... THE KING'S BELOVED MISTRESS WHO TOOK ADVANTAGE OF HIS FAVOR AND AFFECTION...
...TO EXTORT EVERY LAST BIT OF THE POPULACE'S TAX MONEY...

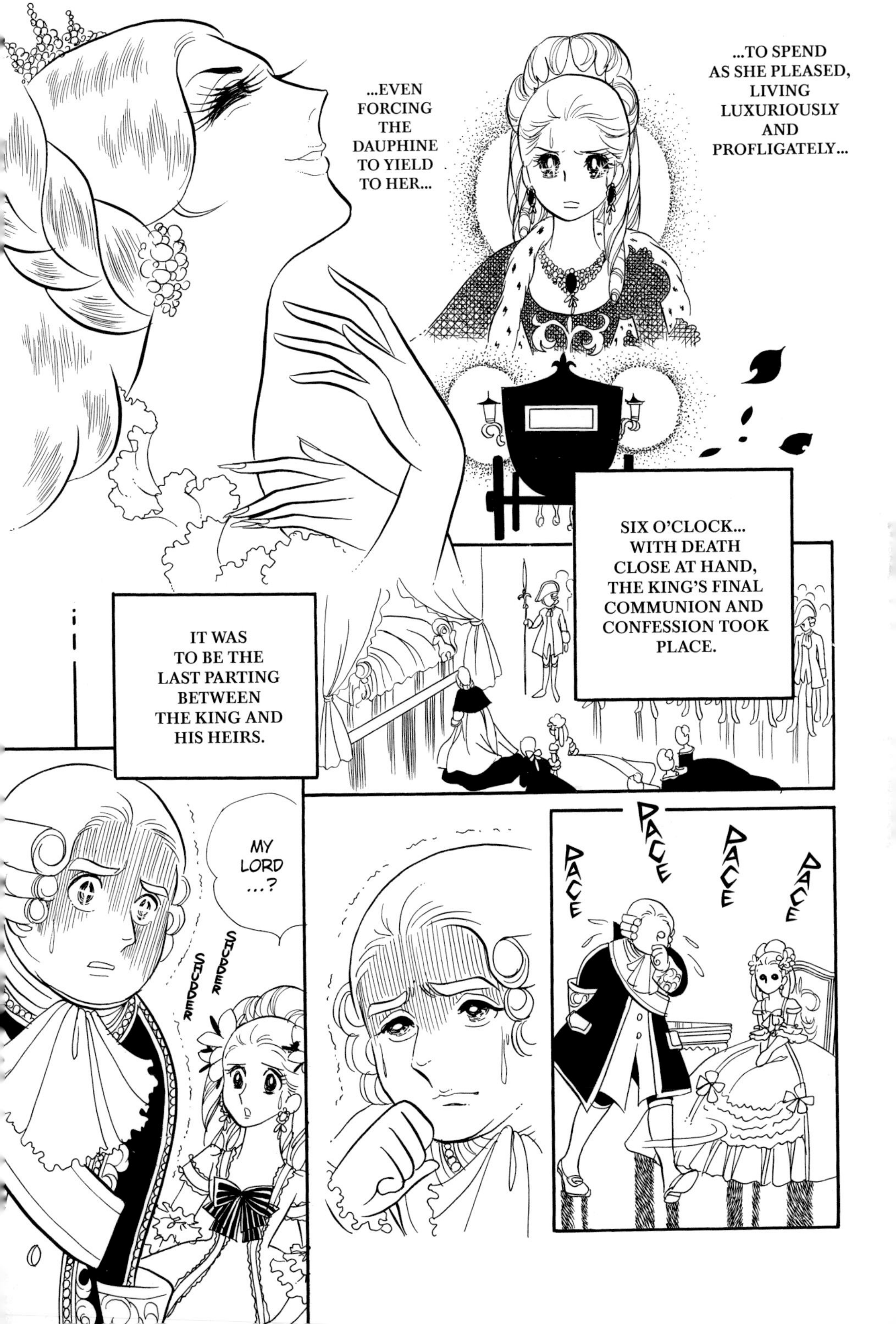

...TO SPEND AS SHE PLEASED, LIVING LUXURIOUSLY AND PROFLIGATELY...
...EVEN FORCING THE DAUPHINE TO YIELD TO HER...
SIX O'CLOCK... WITH DEATH CLOSE AT HAND, THE KING'S FINAL COMMUNION AND CONFESSION TOOK PLACE.
IT WAS TO BE THE LAST PARTING BETWEEN THE KING AND HIS HEIRS.
PACE
PACE
PACE
PACE
MY LORD ...?
SHUDDER
SHUDDER

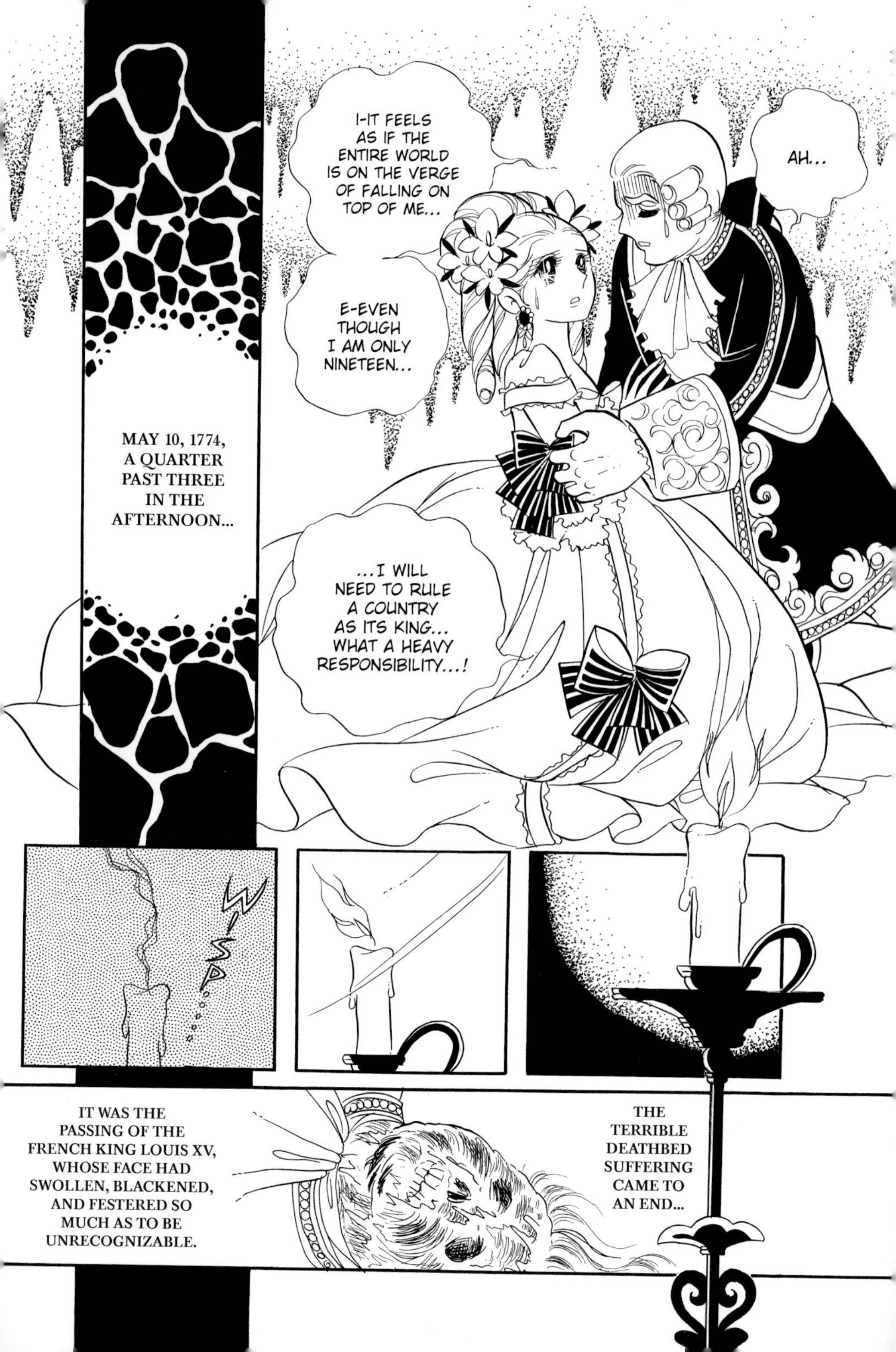
AH...
I-IT FEELS AS IF THE ENTIRE WORLD IS ON THE VERGE OF FALLING ON TOP OF ME...
E-EVEN THOUGH I AM ONLY NINETEEN...
...I WILL NEED TO RULE A COUNTRY AS ITS KING... WHAT A HEAVY RESPONSIBILITY...!
MAY 10, 1774, A QUARTER PAST THREE IN THE AFTERNOON...
WISP
THE TERRIBLE DEATHBED SUFFERING CAME TO AN END...
IT WAS THE PASSING OF THE FRENCH KING LOUIS XV, WHOSE FACE HAD SWOLLEN, BLACKENED, AND FESTERED SO MUCH AS TO BE UNRECOGNIZABLE.

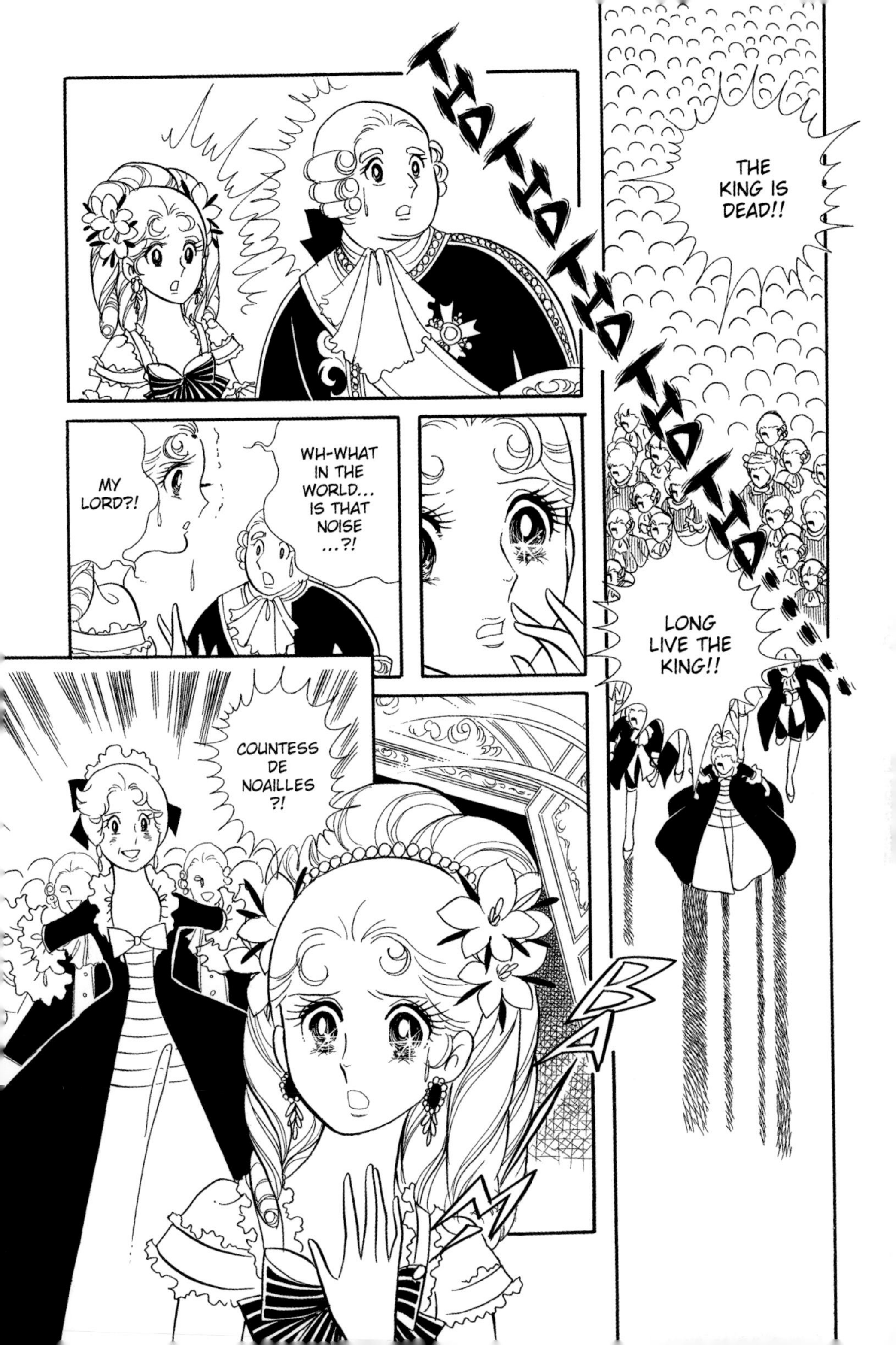
THE KING IS DEAD!!
THO THO THO THO THO THO THO
LONG LIVE THE KING!!
WH-WHAT IN THE WORLD... IS THAT NOISE ...?!
MY LORD?!
COUNTESS DE NOAILLES ?!

THE ROSE OF VERSAILLES

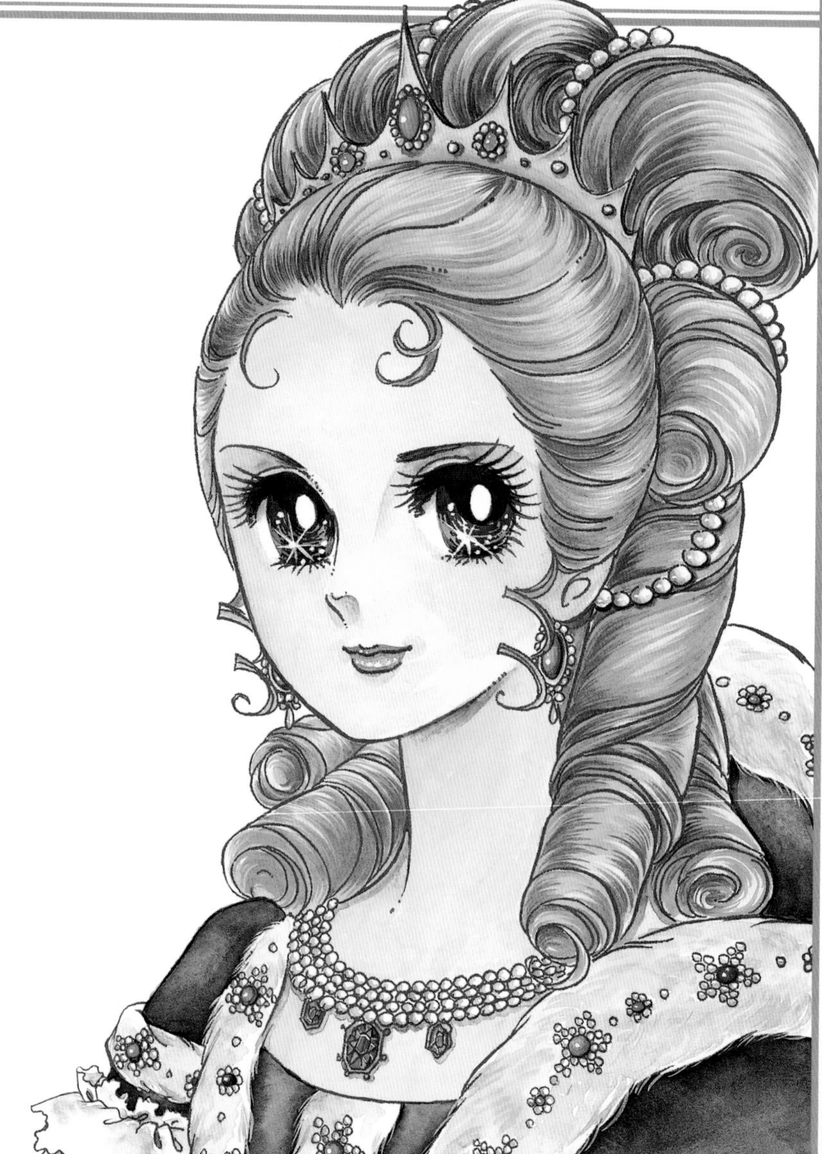

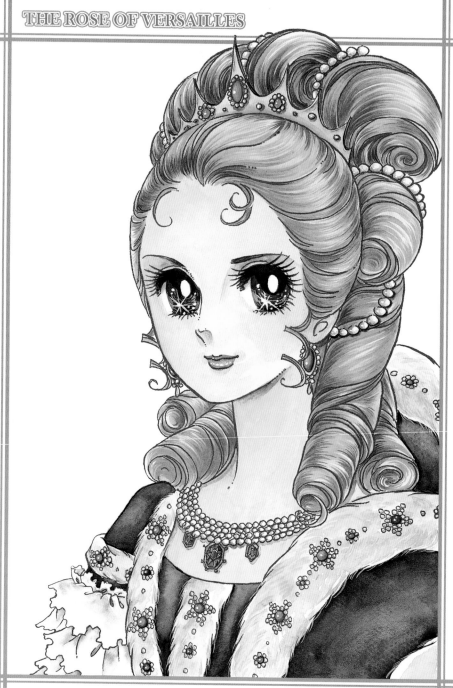

1972 WEEKLY MARGARET MAGAZINE ISSUE 22 COVER PAGE
(SPECIAL COLORIZED VERSION)

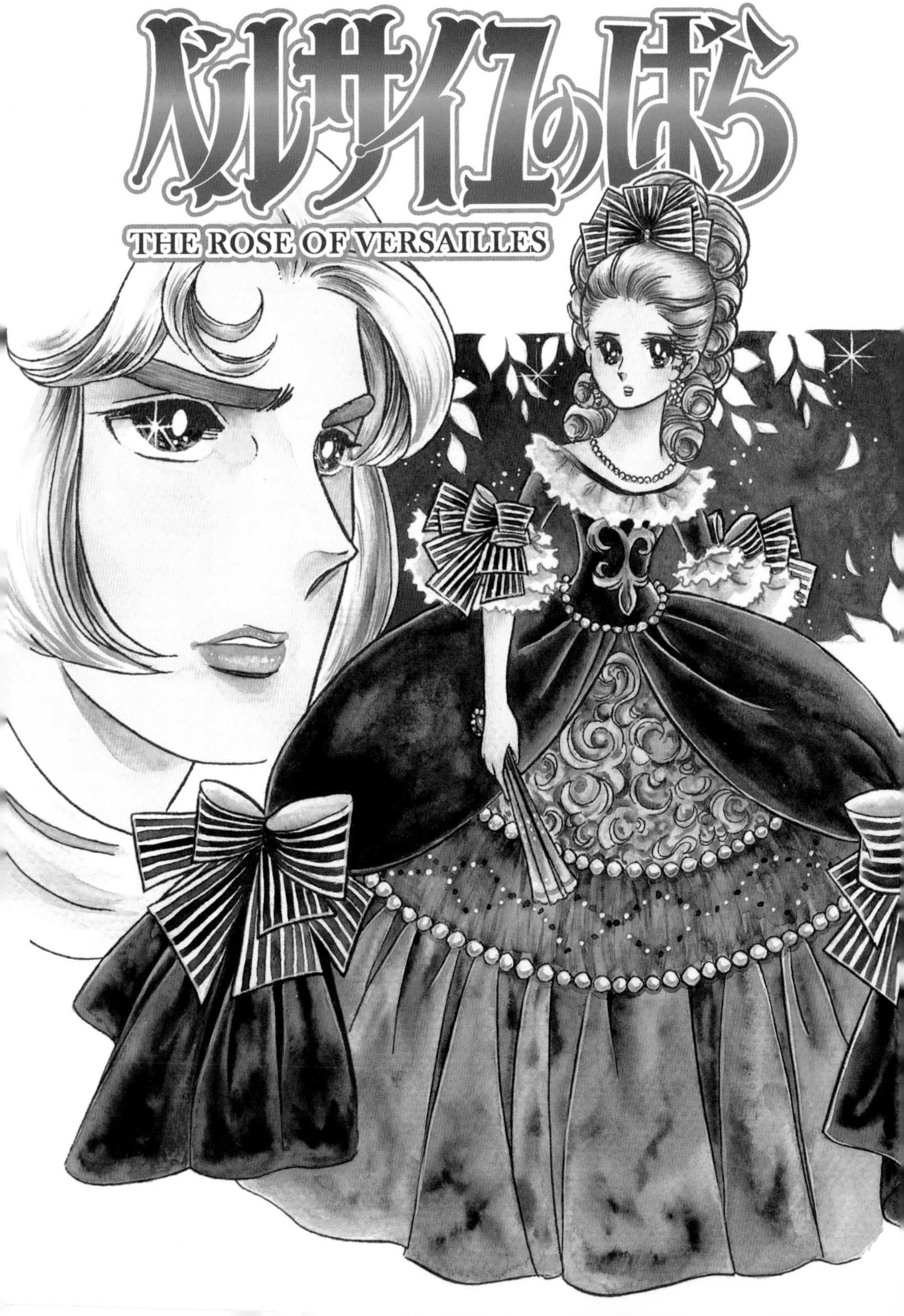
ベルサイユのばら
THE ROSE OF VERSAILLES

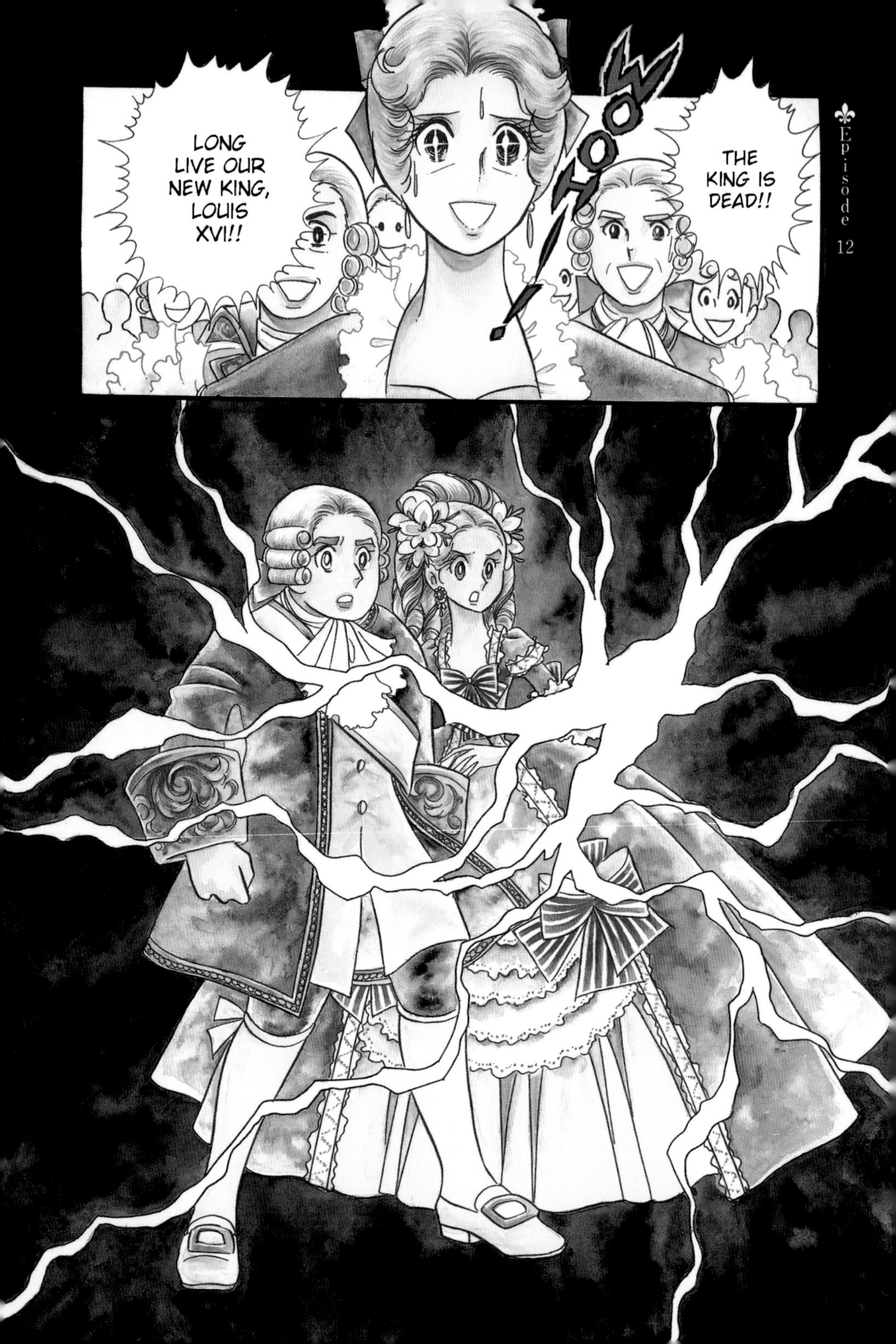
THE KING IS DEAD!!
WOOH!!!
LONG LIVE OUR NEW KING, LOUIS XVI!!

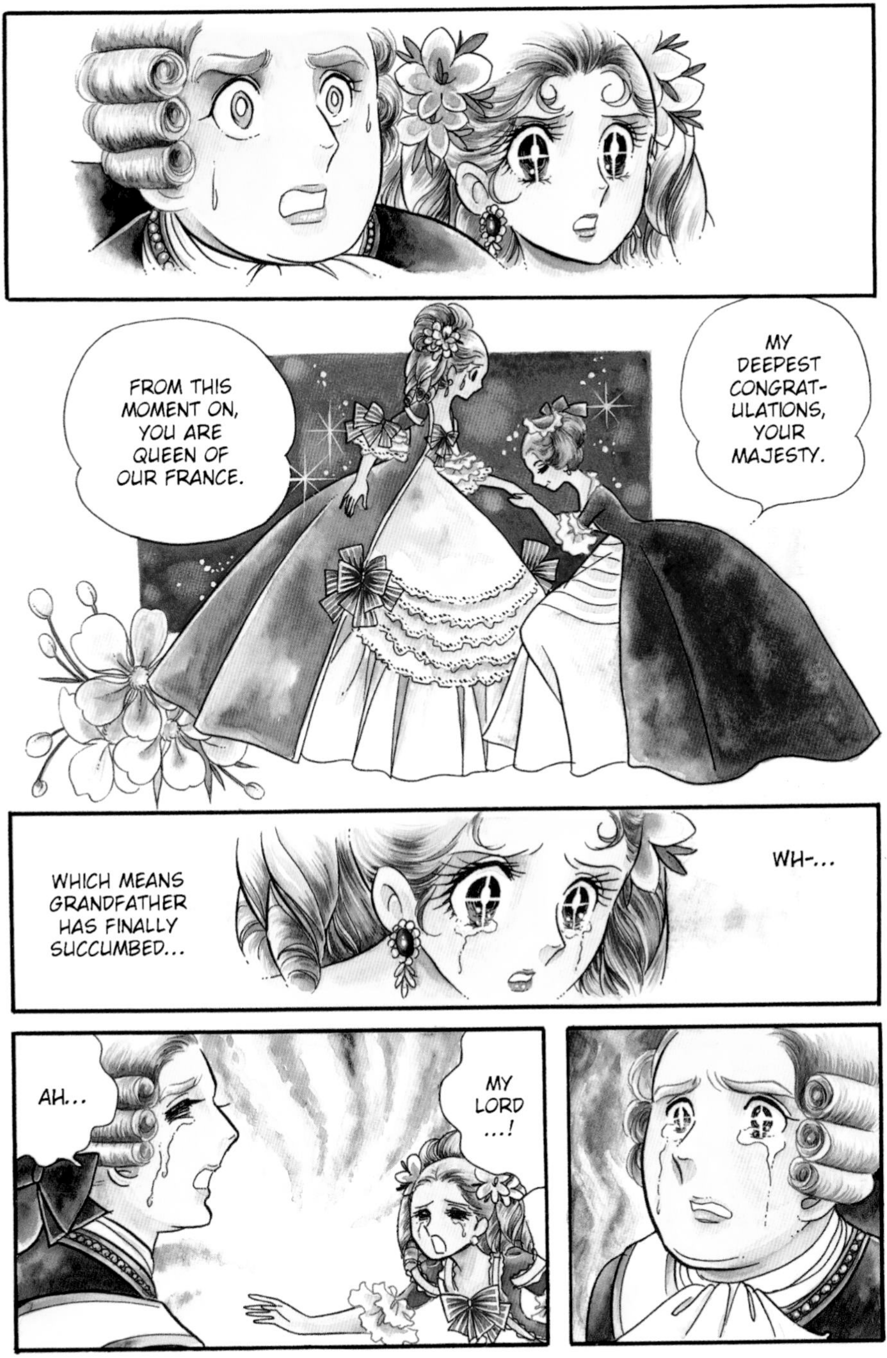
MY DEEPEST CONGRAT-ULATIONS, YOUR MAJESTY.
FROM THIS MOMENT ON, YOU ARE QUEEN OF OUR FRANCE.
WH-...
WHICH MEANS GRANDFATHER HAS FINALLY SUCCUMBED...
MY LORD ...!
AH...

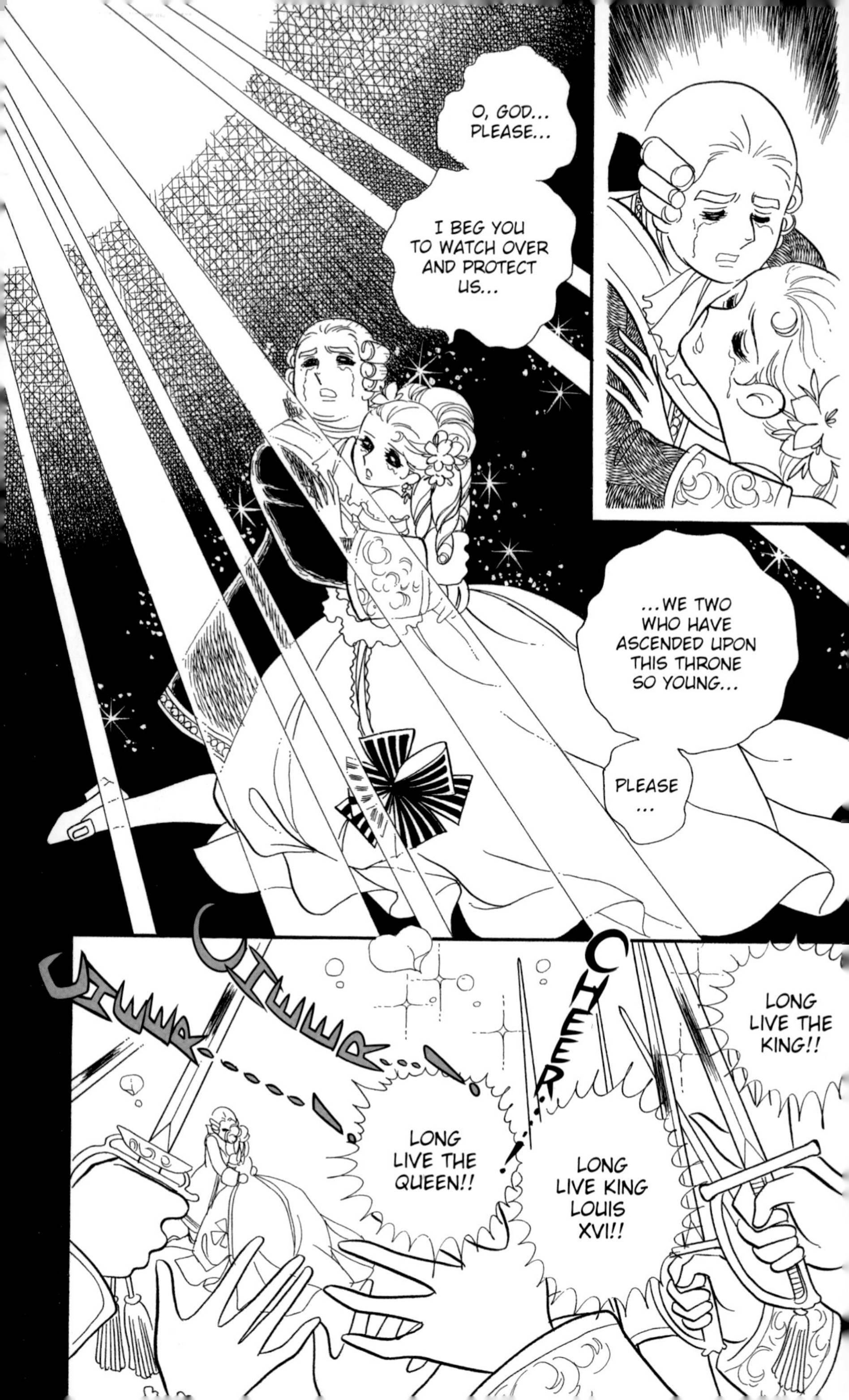
O, GOD... PLEASE...
I BEG YOU TO WATCH OVER AND PROTECT US...
...WE TWO WHO HAVE ASCENDED UPON THIS THRONE SO YOUNG...
PLEASE ...
LONG LIVE THE KING!!
CHEER
LONG LIVE KING LOUIS XVI!!
LONG LIVE THE QUEEN!!

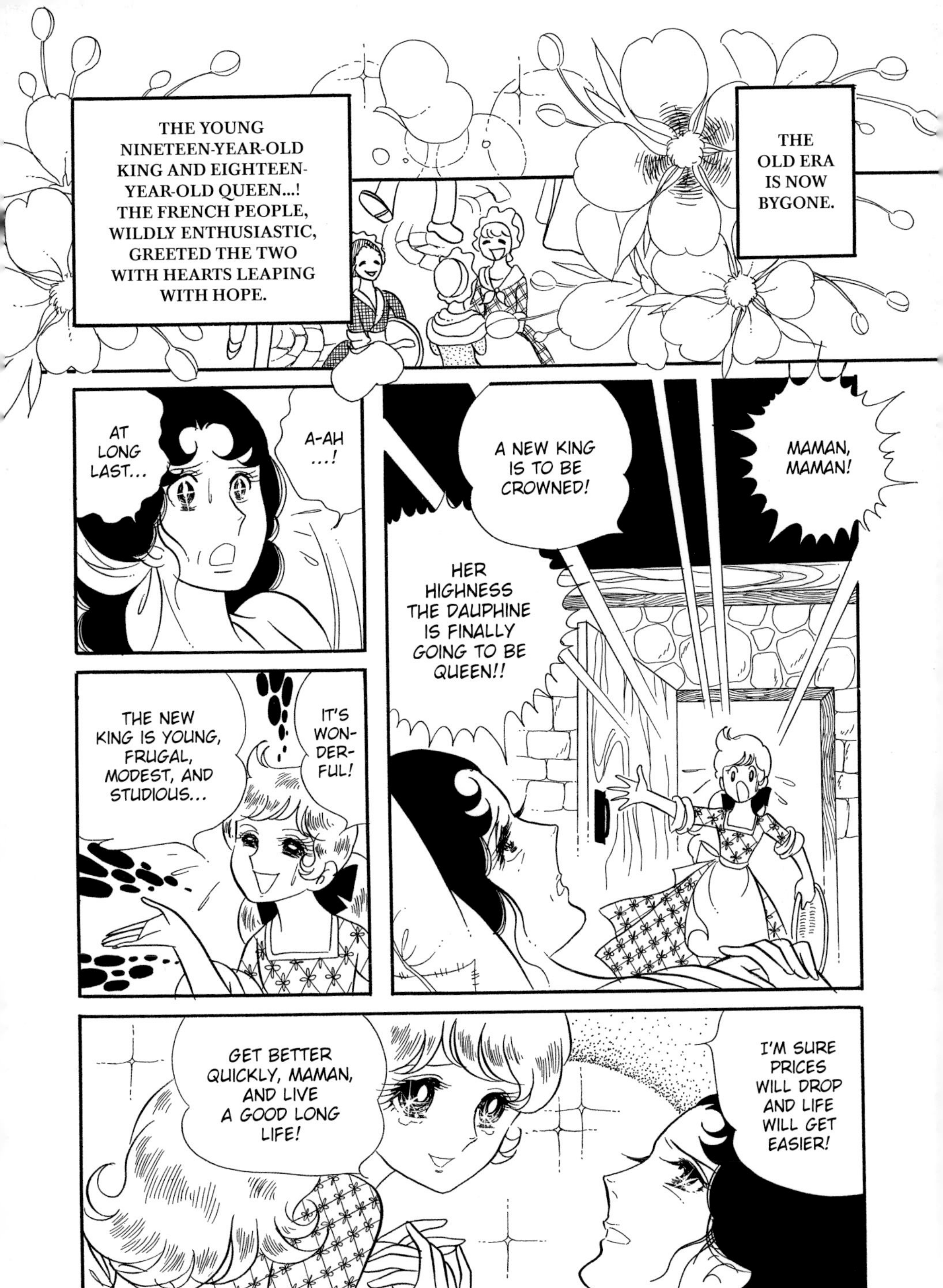
THE OLD ERA IS NOW BYGONE.
THE YOUNG NINETEEN-YEAR-OLD KING AND EIGHTEEN-YEAR-OLD QUEEN...! THE FRENCH PEOPLE, WILDLY ENTHUSIASTIC, GREETED THE TWO WITH HEARTS LEAPING WITH HOPE.
MAMAN, MAMAN!
A NEW KING IS TO BE CROWNED!
HER HIGHNESS THE DAUPHINE IS FINALLY GOING TO BE QUEEN!!
A-AH ...!
AT LONG LAST...
IT'S WONDERFUL!
THE NEW KING IS YOUNG, FRUGAL, MODEST, AND STUDIOUS...
I'M SURE PRICES WILL DROP AND LIFE WILL GET EASIER!
GET BETTER QUICKLY, MAMAN, AND LIVE A GOOD LONG LIFE!

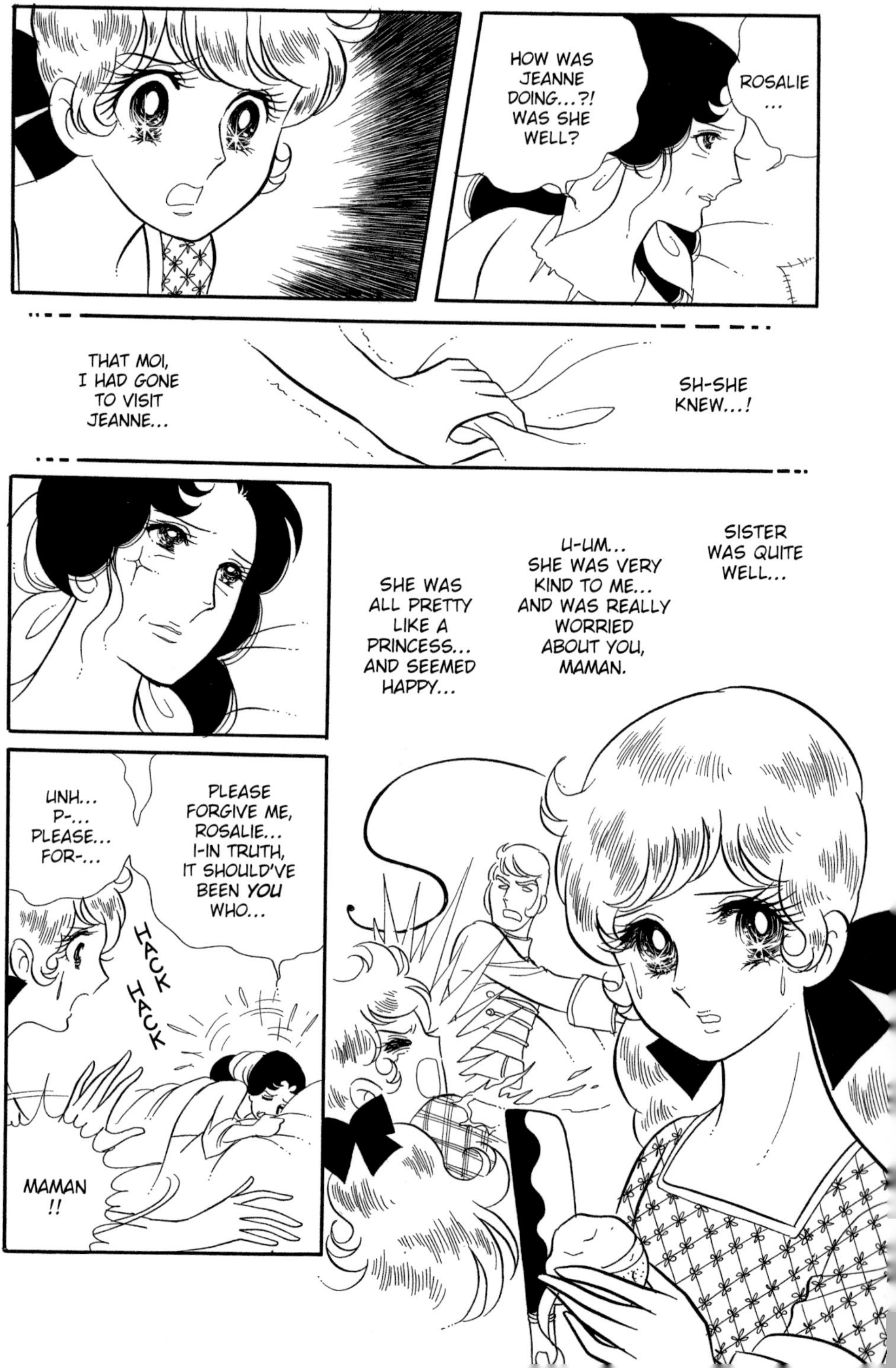
ROSALIE ...
HOW WAS JEANNE DOING...?! WAS SHE WELL?
SH-SHE KNEW...!
THAT MOI, I HAD GONE TO VISIT JEANNE...
SISTER WAS QUITE WELL...
U-UM.. SHE WAS VERY KIND TO ME... AND WAS REALLY WORRIED ABOUT YOU, MAMAN.
SHE WAS ALL PRETTY LIKE A PRINCESS... AND SEEMED HAPPY...
PLEASE FORGIVE ME, ROSALIE... I-IN TRUTH, IT SHOULD'VE BEEN *YOU* WHO...
UNH... P-... PLEASE... FOR-...
HACK HACK
MAMAN !!

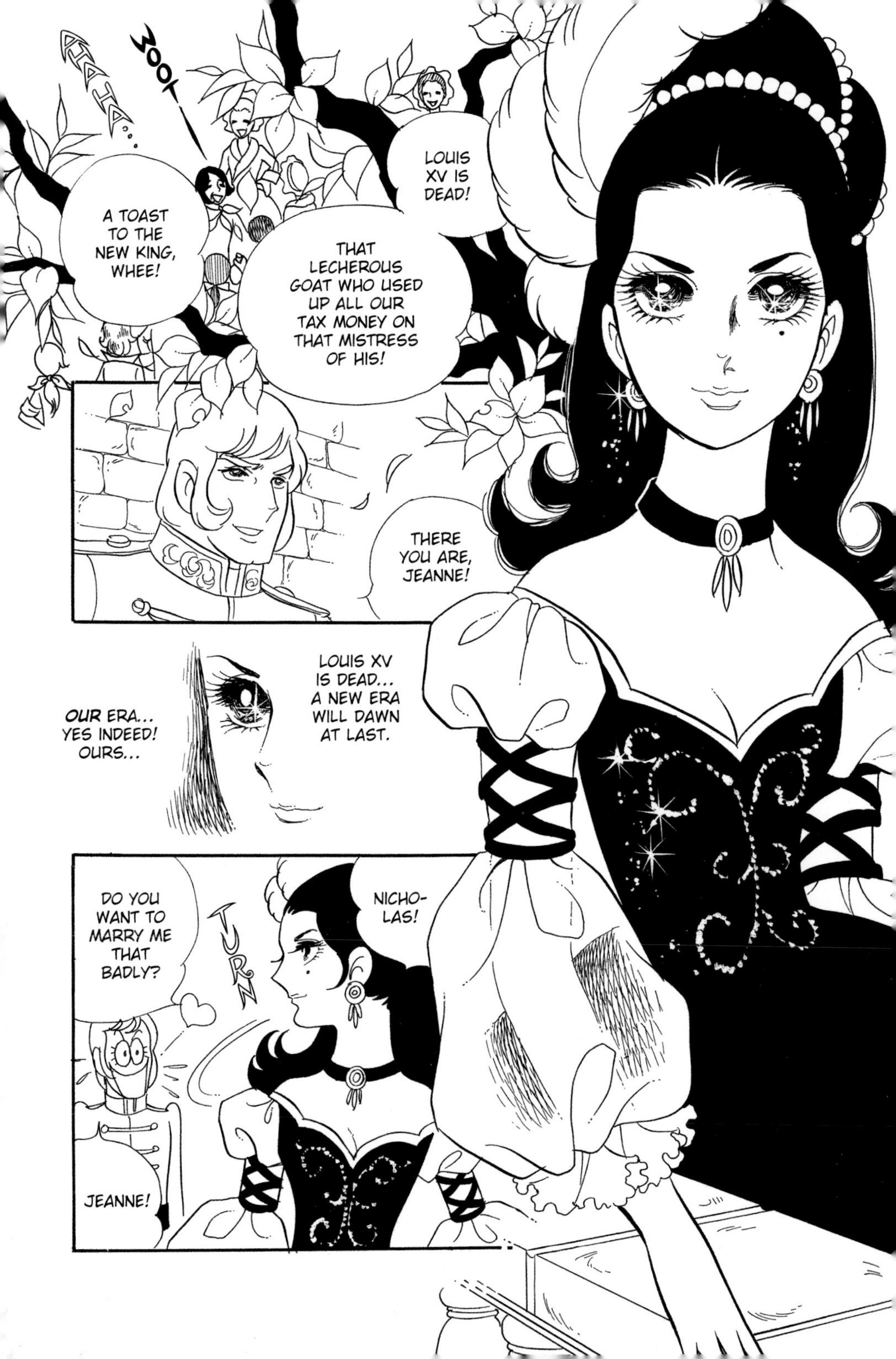
LOUIS XV IS DEAD!
THAT LECHEROUS GOAT WHO USED UP ALL OUR TAX MONEY ON THAT MISTRESS OF HIS!
WOOT
A TOAST TO THE NEW KING, WHEE!
AHAHAHA...
THERE YOU ARE, JEANNE!
LOUIS XV IS DEAD... A NEW ERA WILL DAWN AT LAST.
OUR ERA... YES INDEED! OURS...
NICHO-LAS!
TURN
DO YOU WANT TO MARRY ME THAT BADLY?
JEANNE!

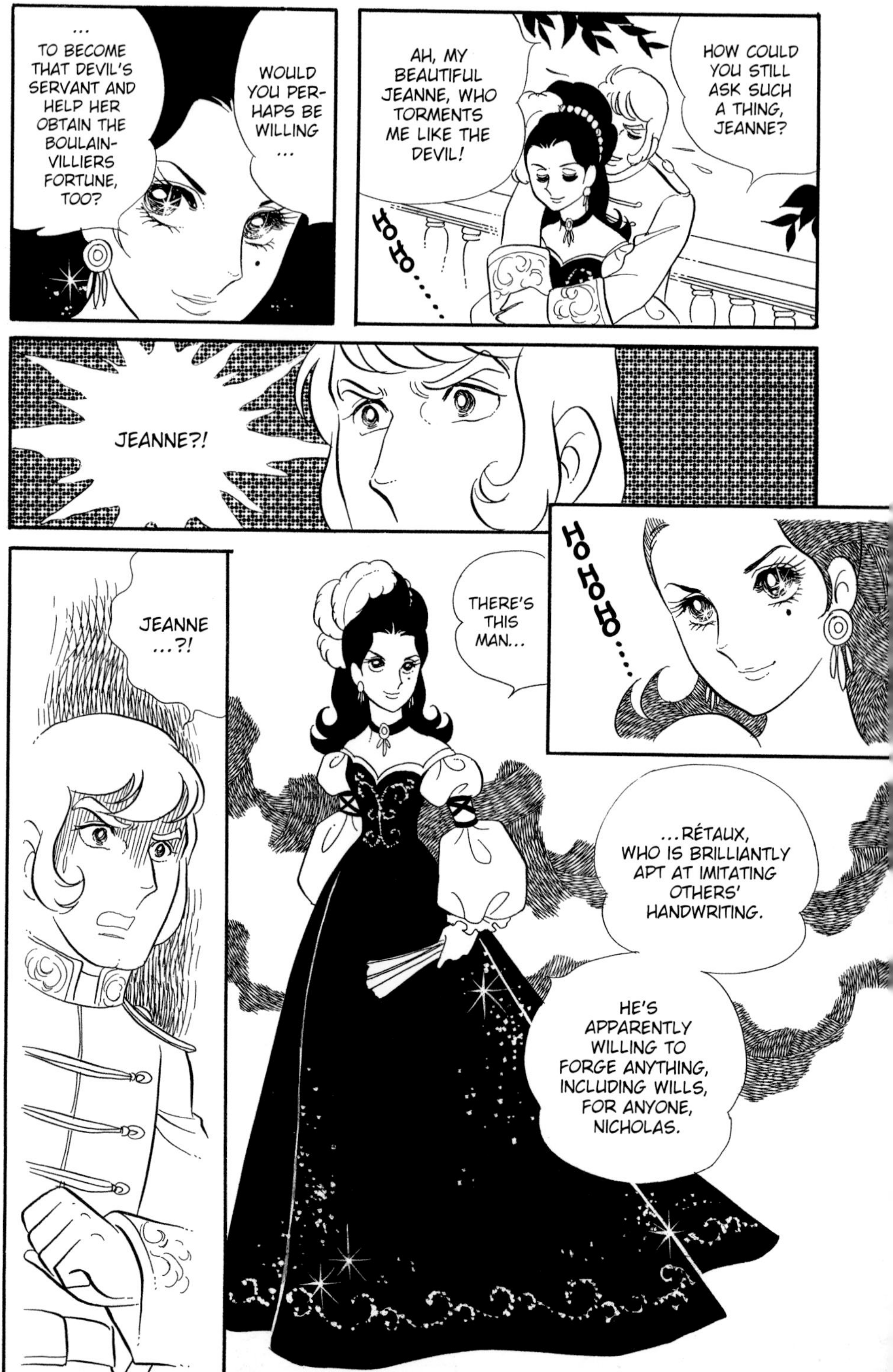
WOULD YOU PERHAPS BE WILLING ...
... TO BECOME THAT DEVIL'S SERVANT AND HELP HER OBTAIN THE BOULAIN-VILLIERS FORTUNE, TOO?
HOW COULD YOU STILL ASK SUCH A THING, JEANNE?
AH, MY BEAUTIFUL JEANNE, WHO TORMENTS ME LIKE THE DEVIL!
HO HO......
JEANNE?!
JEANNE ...?!
HO HO HO....
THERE'S THIS MAN...
...RÉTAUX, WHO IS BRILLIANTLY APT AT IMITATING OTHERS' HANDWRITING.
HE'S APPARENTLY WILLING TO FORGE ANYTHING, INCLUDING WILLS, FOR ANYONE, NICHOLAS.

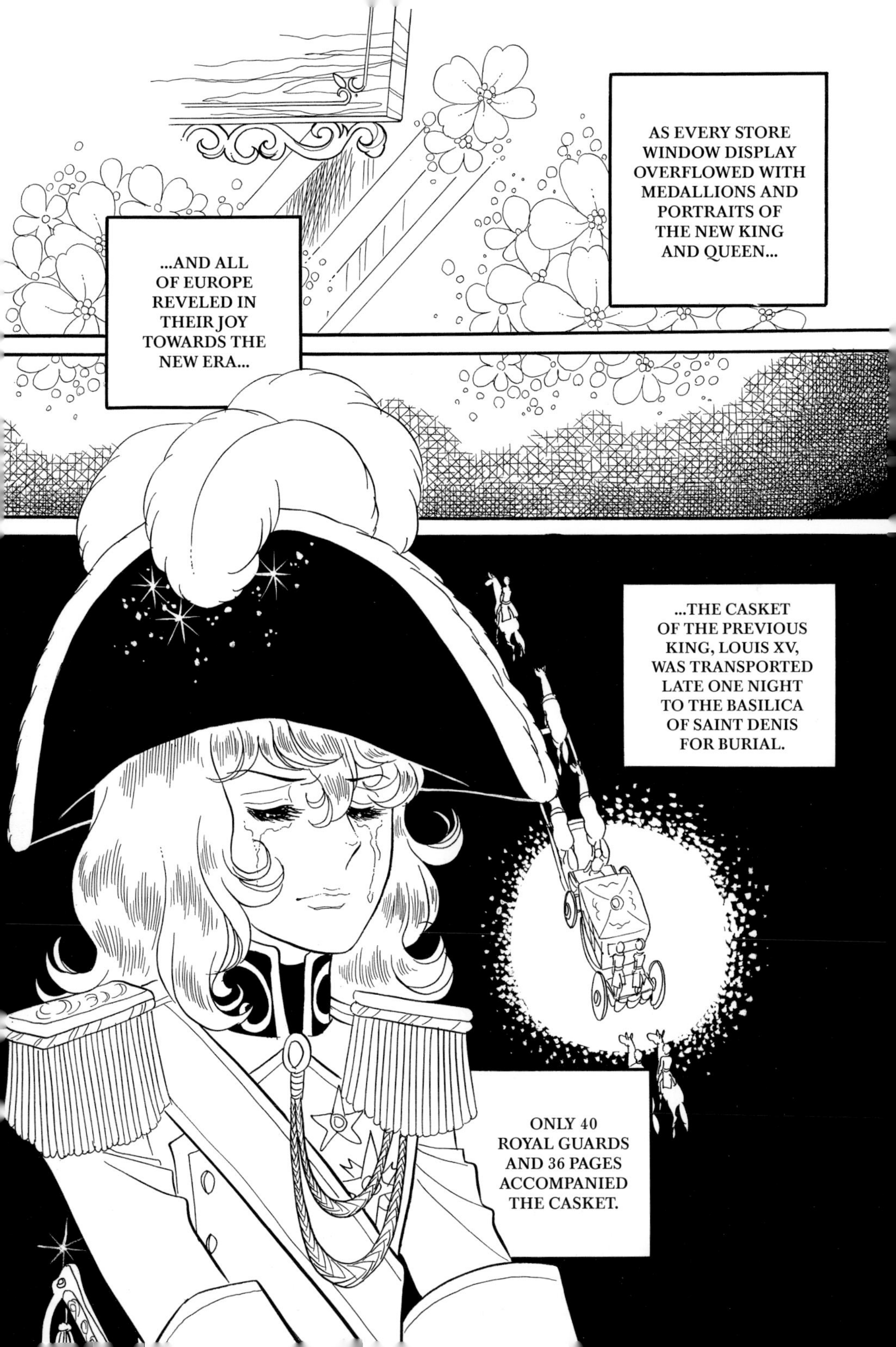
AS EVERY STORE WINDOW DISPLAY OVERFLOWED WITH MEDALLIONS AND PORTRAITS OF THE NEW KING AND QUEEN...
...AND ALL OF EUROPE REVELED IN THEIR JOY TOWARDS THE NEW ERA...
...THE CASKET OF THE PREVIOUS KING, LOUIS XV, WAS TRANSPORTED LATE ONE NIGHT TO THE BASILICA OF SAINT DENIS FOR BURIAL.
ONLY 40 ROYAL GUARDS AND 36 PAGES ACCOMPANIED THE CASKET.

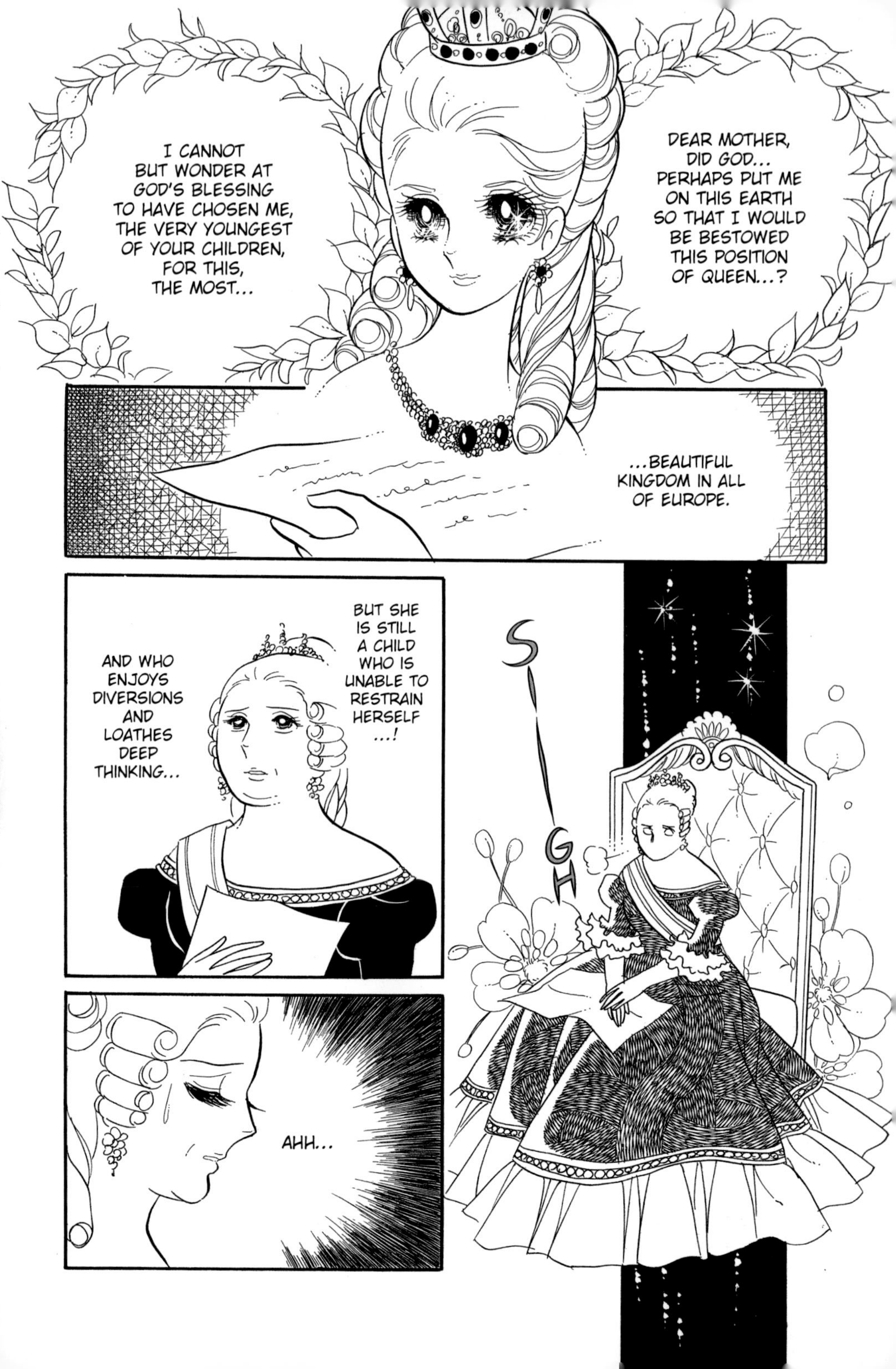
DEAR MOTHER, DID GOD... PERHAPS PUT ME ON THIS EARTH SO THAT I WOULD BE BESTOWED THIS POSITION OF QUEEN...?
I CANNOT BUT WONDER AT GOD'S BLESSING TO HAVE CHOSEN ME, THE VERY YOUNGEST OF YOUR CHILDREN, FOR THIS, THE MOST...
...BEAUTIFUL KINGDOM IN ALL OF EUROPE.
SIGH
BUT SHE IS STILL A CHILD WHO IS UNABLE TO RESTRAIN HERSELF ...!
AND WHO ENJOYS DIVERSIONS AND LOATHES DEEP THINKING...
AHH...

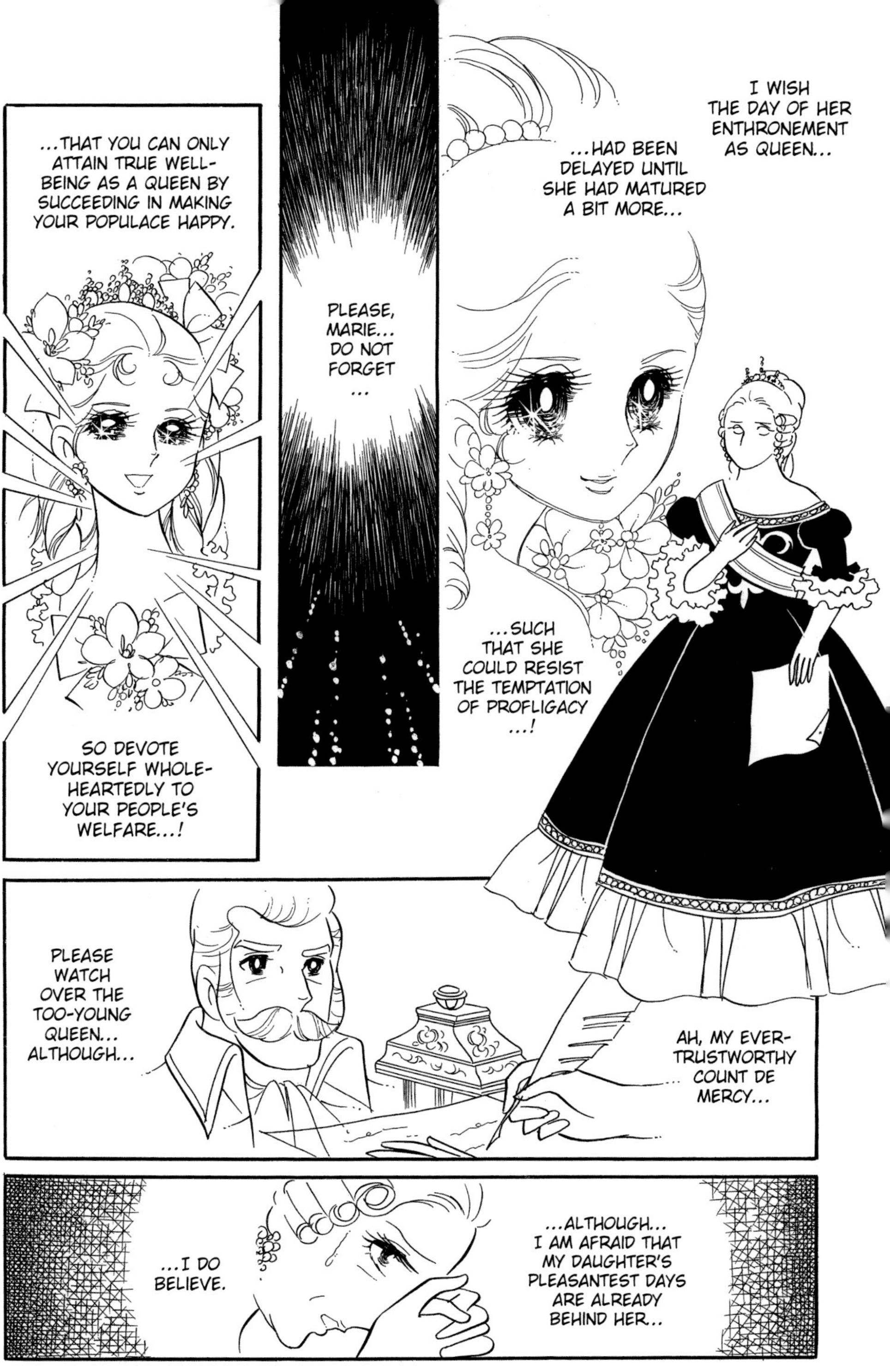
I WISH THE DAY OF HER ENTHRONEMENT AS QUEEN...
...HAD BEEN DELAYED UNTIL SHE HAD MATURED A BIT MORE...
...SUCH THAT SHE COULD RESIST THE TEMPTATION OF PROFLIGACY ...!
PLEASE, MARIE... DO NOT FORGET ...
...THAT YOU CAN ONLY ATTAIN TRUE WELL-BEING AS A QUEEN BY SUCCEEDING IN MAKING YOUR POPULACE HAPPY.
SO DEVOTE YOURSELF WHOLE-HEARTEDLY TO YOUR PEOPLE'S WELFARE...!
AH, MY EVER-TRUSTWORTHY COUNT DE MERCY...
PLEASE WATCH OVER THE TOO-YOUNG QUEEN... ALTHOUGH...
...ALTHOUGH... I AM AFRAID THAT MY DAUGHTER'S PLEASANTEST DAYS ARE ALREADY BEHIND HER...
...I DO BELIEVE.

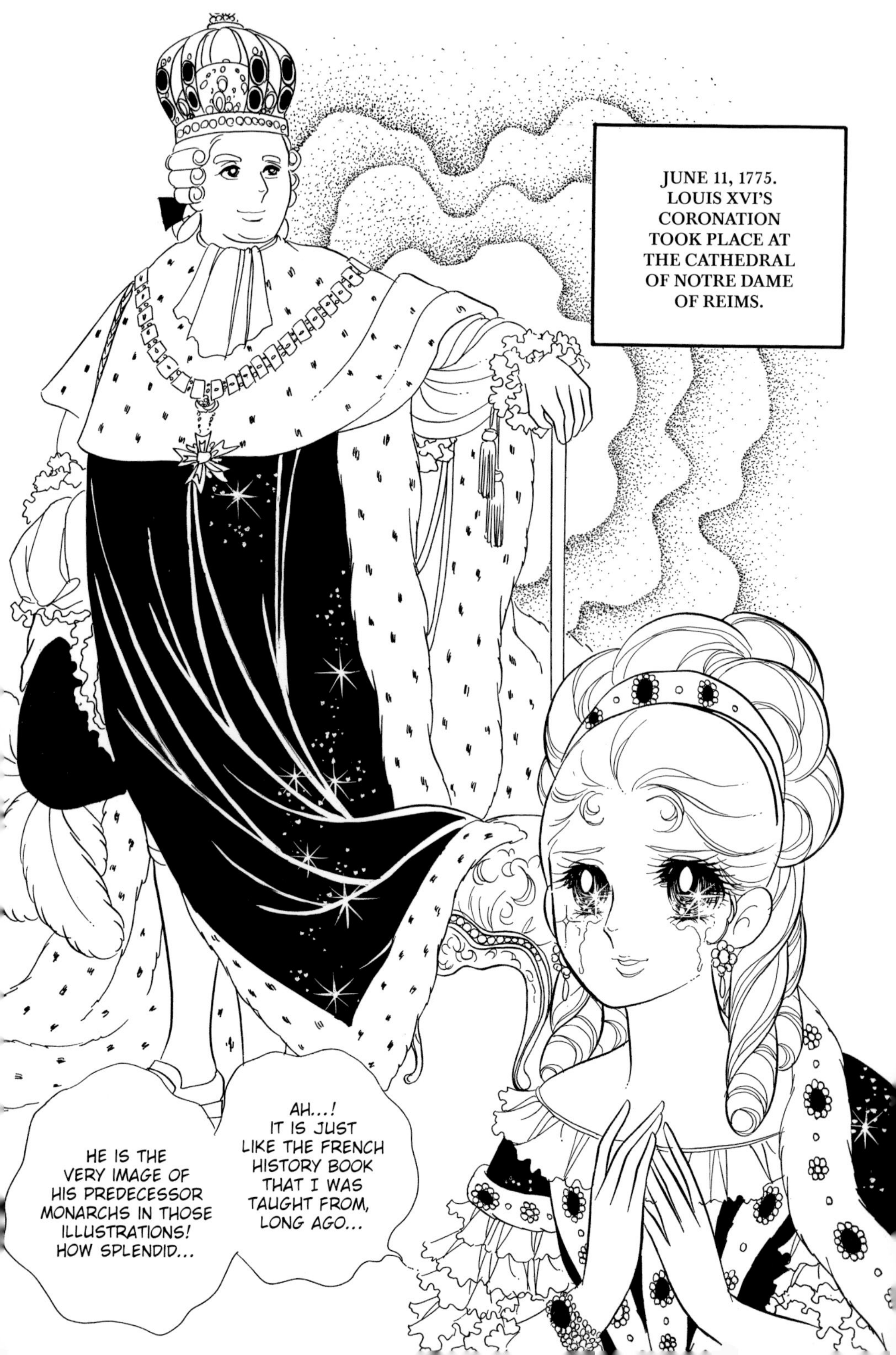
JUNE 11, 1775. LOUIS XVI'S CORONATION TOOK PLACE AT THE CATHEDRAL OF NOTRE DAME OF REIMS.
AH...! IT IS JUST LIKE THE FRENCH HISTORY BOOK THAT I WAS TAUGHT FROM, LONG AGO...
HE IS THE VERY IMAGE OF HIS PREDECESSOR MONARCHS IN THOSE ILLUSTRATIONS! HOW SPLENDID...

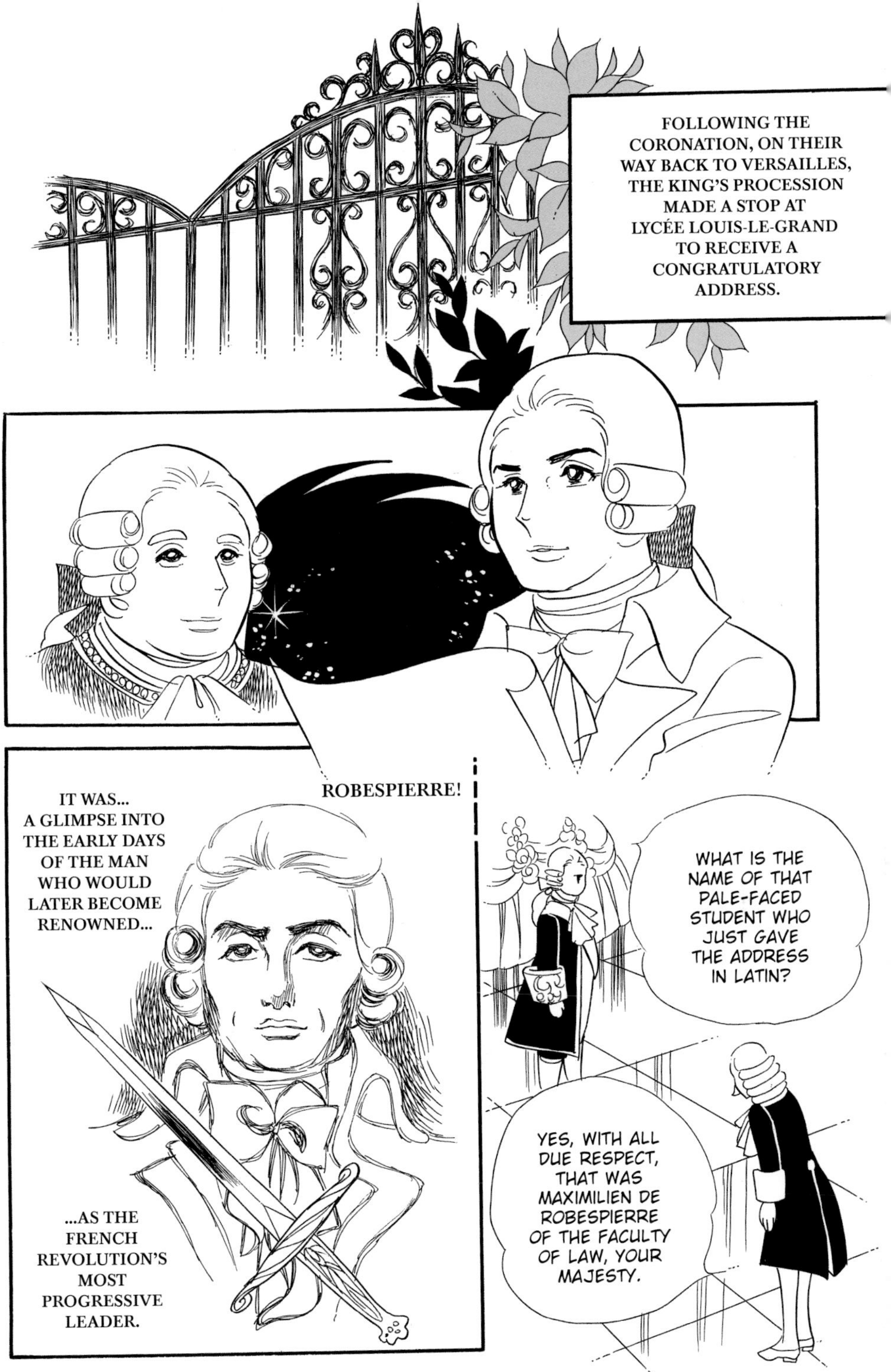
FOLLOWING THE CORONATION, ON THEIR WAY BACK TO VERSAILLES, THE KING'S PROCESSION MADE A STOP AT LYCÉE LOUIS-LE-GRAND TO RECEIVE A CONGRATULATORY ADDRESS.
WHAT IS THE NAME OF THAT PALE-FACED STUDENT WHO JUST GAVE THE ADDRESS IN LATIN?
YES, WITH ALL DUE RESPECT, THAT WAS MAXIMILIEN DE ROBESPIERRE OF THE FACULTY OF LAW, YOUR MAJESTY.
ROBESPIERRE!
IT WAS... A GLIMPSE INTO THE EARLY DAYS OF THE MAN WHO WOULD LATER BECOME RENOWNED...
...AS THE FRENCH REVOLUTION'S MOST PROGRESSIVE LEADER.

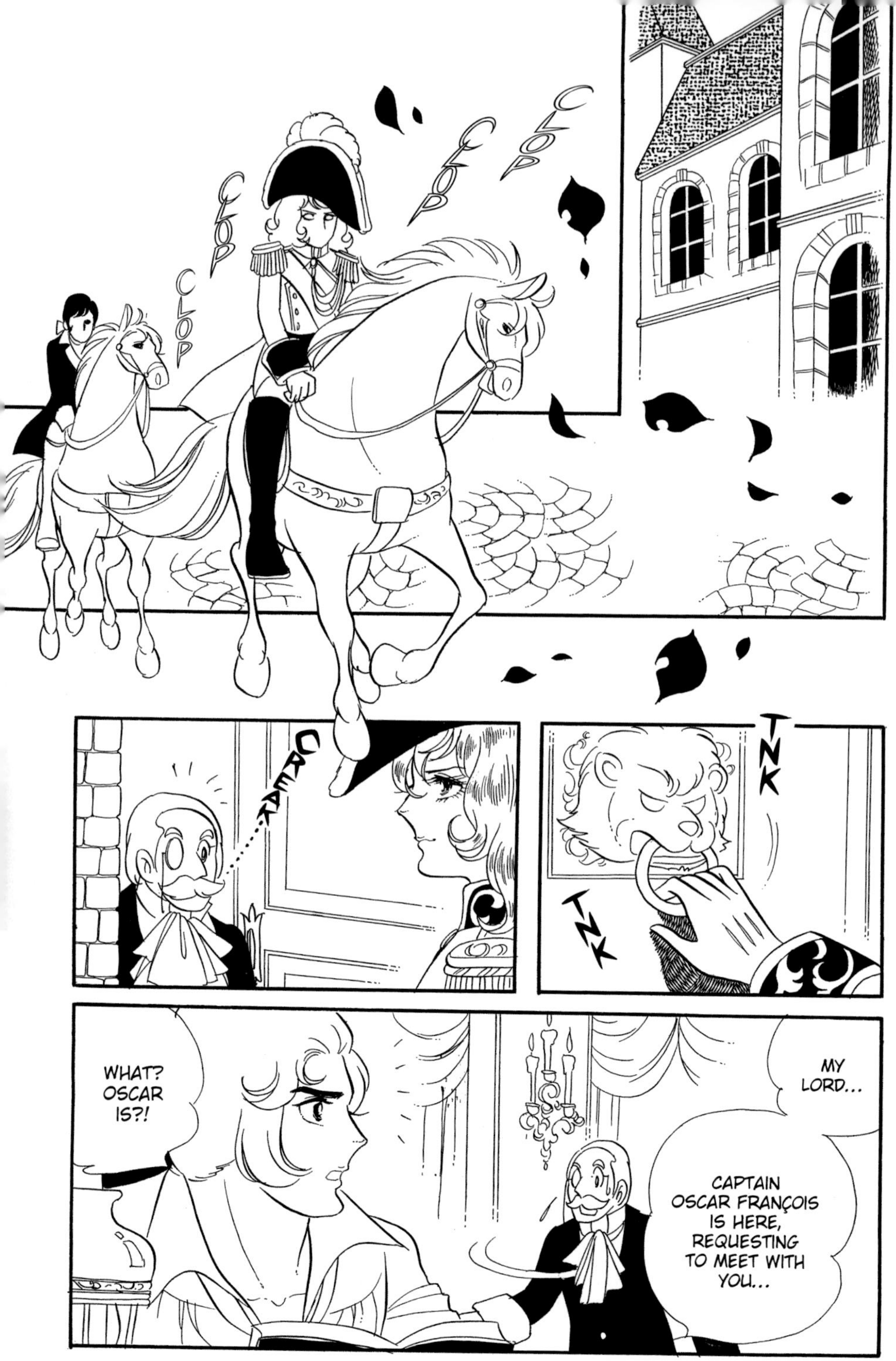
CLOP
CLOP
CLOP
CLOP
TNK
TNK
CREAK
MY LORD...
CAPTAIN OSCAR FRANÇOIS IS HERE, REQUESTING TO MEET WITH YOU...
WHAT? OSCAR IS?!

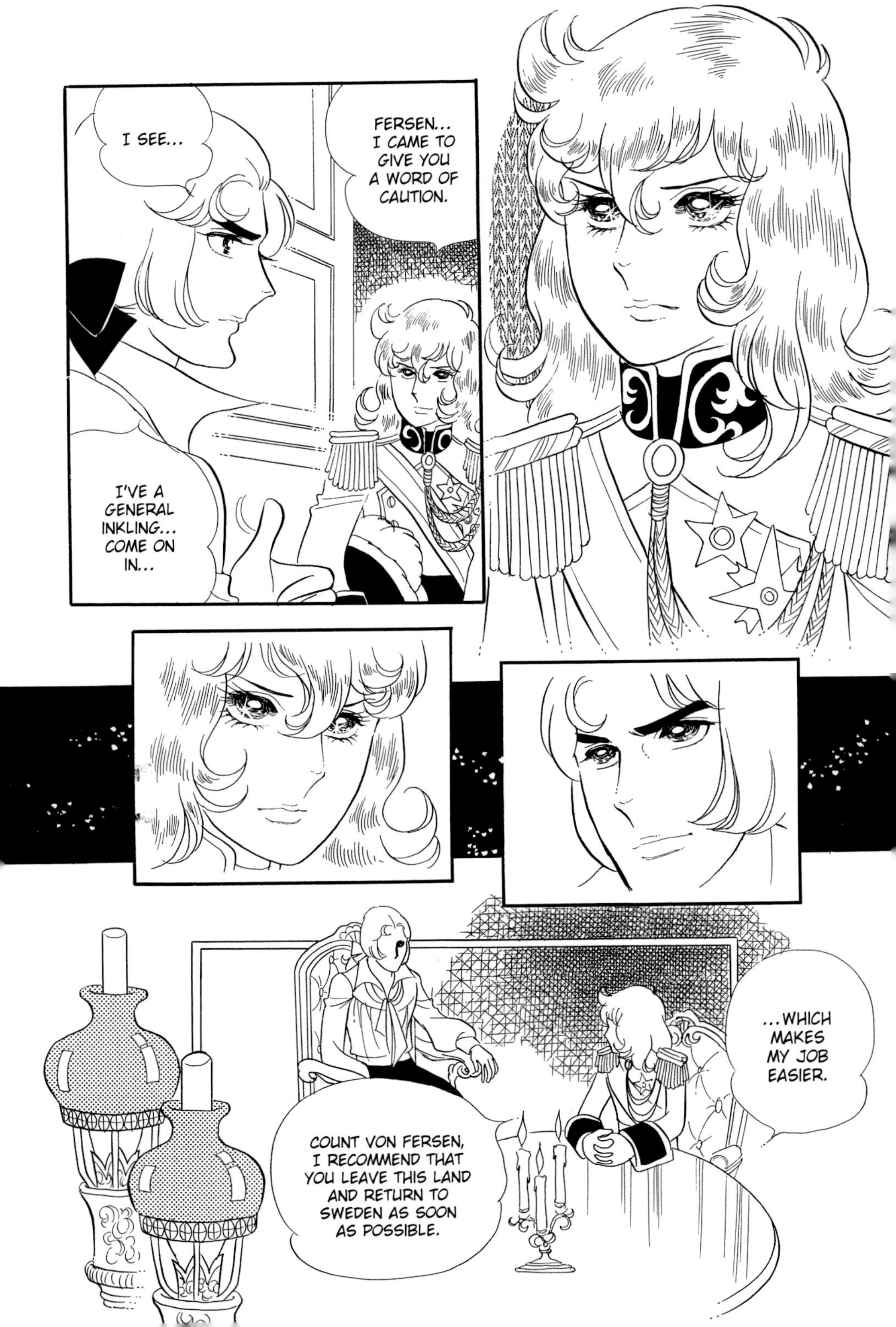
FERSEN... I CAME TO GIVE YOU A WORD OF CAUTION.
I SEE...
I'VE A GENERAL INKLING... COME ON IN...
COUNT VON FERSEN, I RECOMMEND THAT YOU LEAVE THIS LAND AND RETURN TO SWEDEN AS SOON AS POSSIBLE.
...WHICH MAKES MY JOB EASIER.

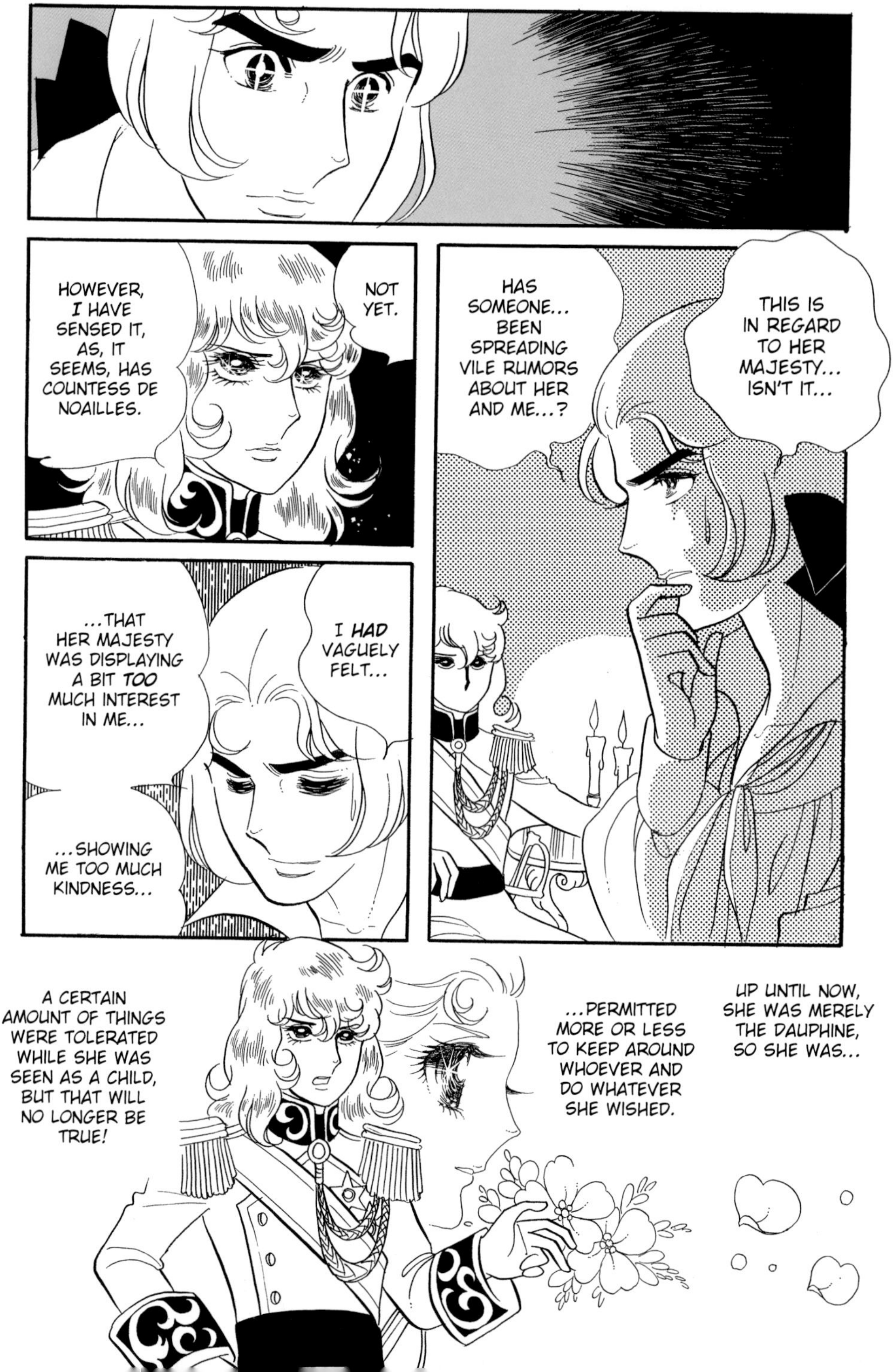
THIS IS IN REGARD TO HER MAJESTY... ISN'T IT...
HAS SOMEONE... BEEN SPREADING VILE RUMORS ABOUT HER AND ME...?
NOT YET.
HOWEVER, *I* HAVE SENSED IT, AS, IT SEEMS, HAS COUNTESS DE NOAILLES.
I *HAD* VAGUELY FELT...
...THAT HER MAJESTY WAS DISPLAYING A BIT *TOO* MUCH INTEREST IN ME...
...SHOWING ME TOO MUCH KINDNESS...
UP UNTIL NOW, SHE WAS MERELY THE DAUPHINE, SO SHE WAS...
...PERMITTED MORE OR LESS TO KEEP AROUND WHOEVER AND DO WHATEVER SHE WISHED.
A CERTAIN AMOUNT OF THINGS WERE TOLERATED WHILE SHE WAS SEEN AS A CHILD, BUT THAT WILL NO LONGER BE TRUE!

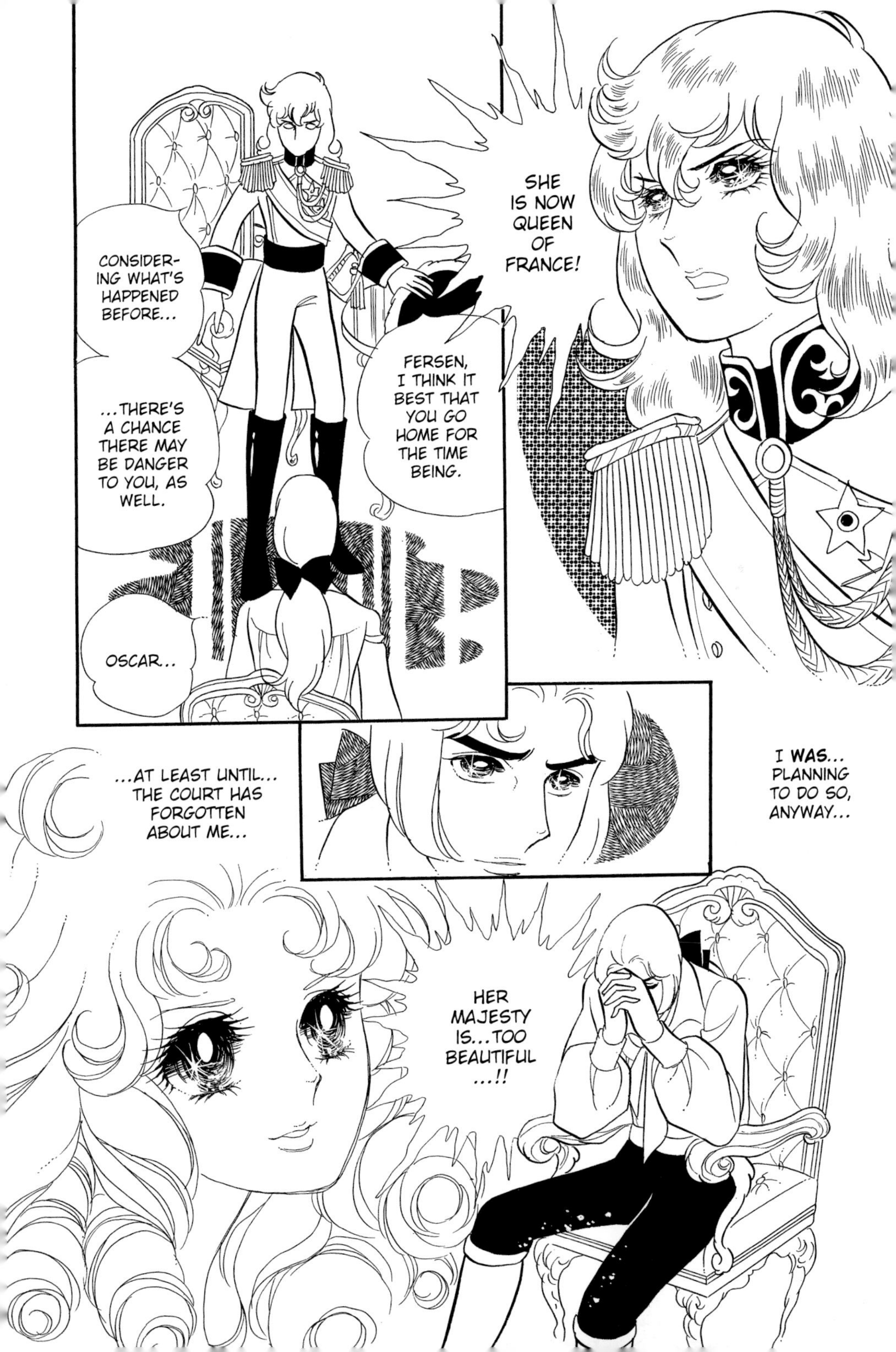

SHE IS NOW QUEEN OF FRANCE!
FERSEN, I THINK IT BEST THAT YOU GO HOME FOR THE TIME BEING.
CONSIDER-ING WHAT'S HAPPENED BEFORE...
...THERE'S A CHANCE THERE MAY BE DANGER TO YOU, AS WELL.
OSCAR...
I WAS... PLANNING TO DO SO, ANYWAY...
...AT LEAST UNTIL... THE COURT HAS FORGOTTEN ABOUT ME...
HER MAJESTY IS...TOO BEAUTIFUL ...!!

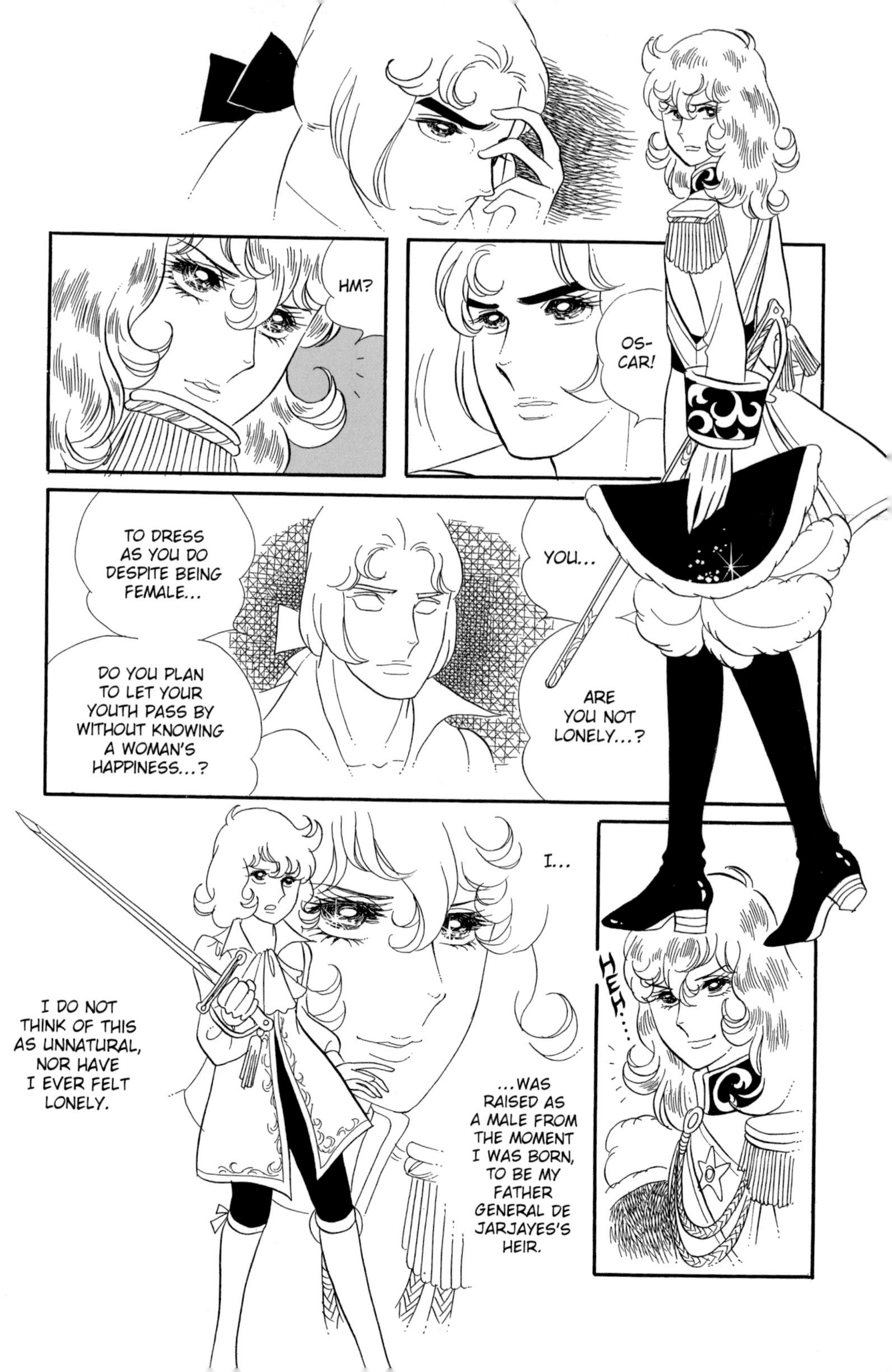
OS-CAR!
HM?
YOU...
TO DRESS AS YOU DO DESPITE BEING FEMALE...
DO YOU PLAN TO LET YOUR YOUTH PASS BY WITHOUT KNOWING A WOMAN'S HAPPINESS...?
ARE YOU NOT LONELY...?
HEH...
I...
...WAS RAISED AS A MALE FROM THE MOMENT I WAS BORN, TO BE MY FATHER GENERAL DE JARJAYES'S HEIR.
I DO NOT THINK OF THIS AS UNNATURAL, NOR HAVE I EVER FELT LONELY.

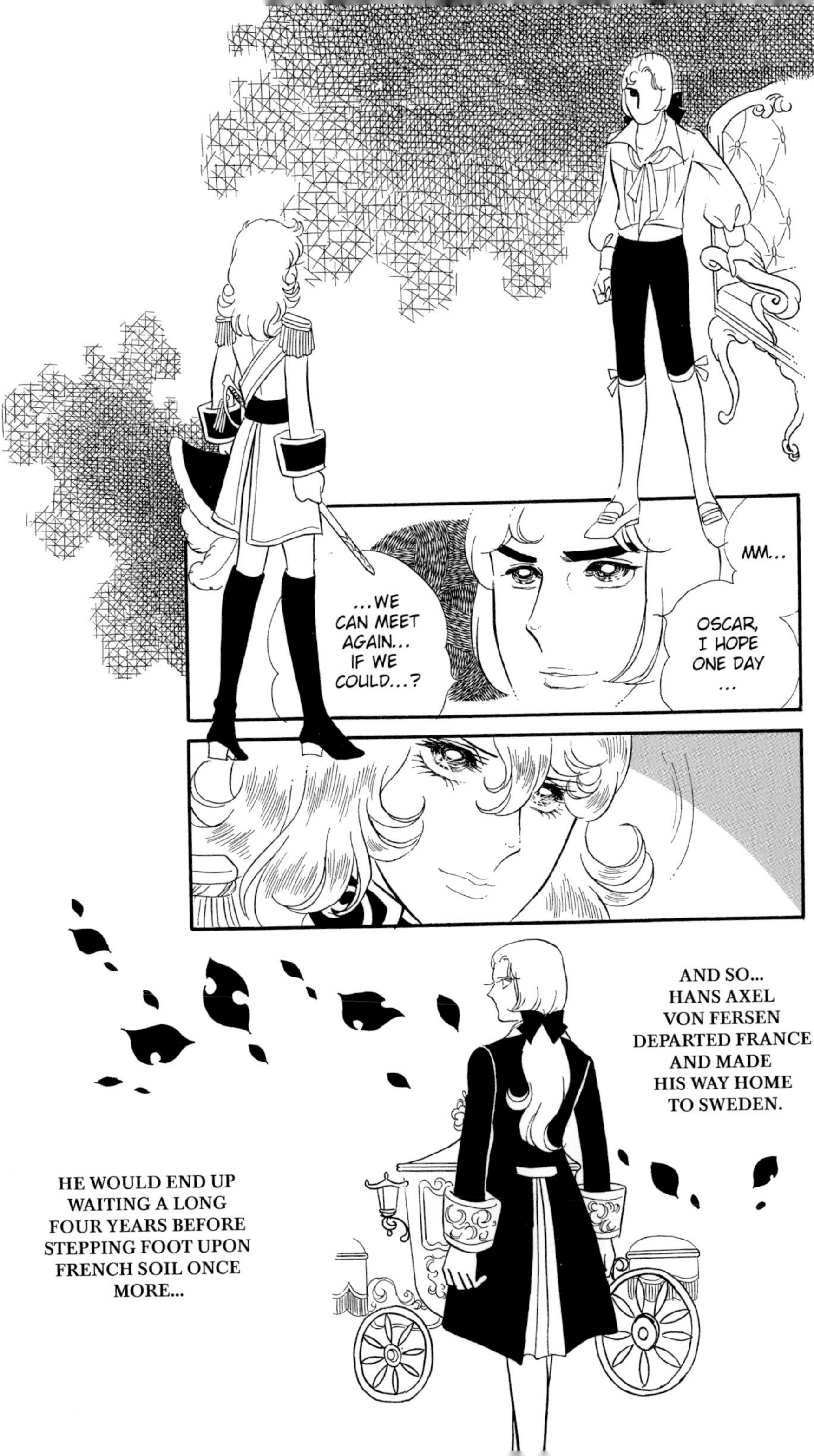
MM...
OSCAR, I HOPE ONE DAY ...
...WE CAN MEET AGAIN... IF WE COULD...?
AND SO... HANS AXEL VON FERSEN DEPARTED FRANCE AND MADE HIS WAY HOME TO SWEDEN.
HE WOULD END UP WAITING A LONG FOUR YEARS BEFORE STEPPING FOOT UPON FRENCH SOIL ONCE MORE...

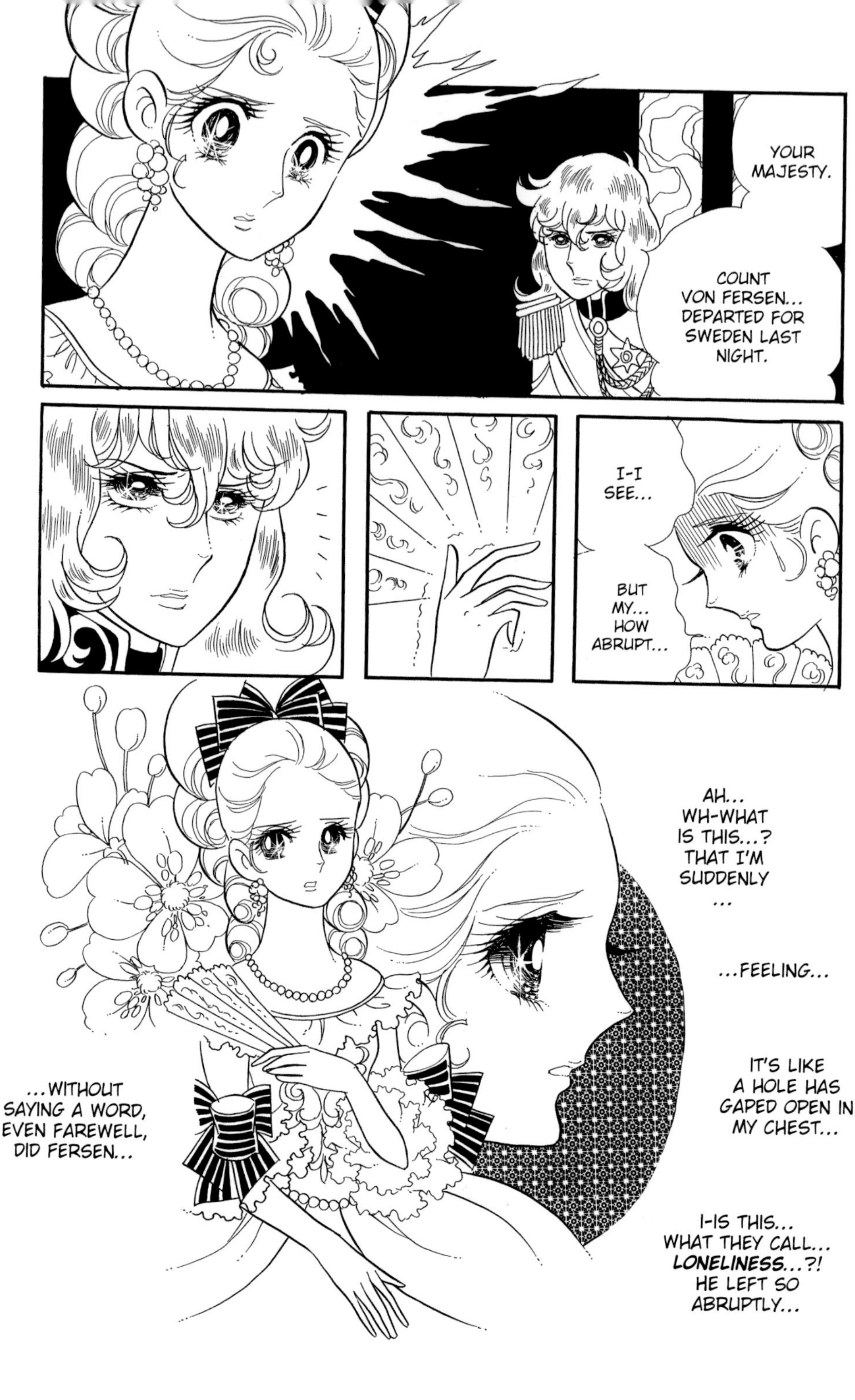
YOUR MAJESTY.
COUNT VON FERSEN... DEPARTED FOR SWEDEN LAST NIGHT.
I-I SEE...
BUT MY... HOW ABRUPT...
AH... WH-WHAT IS THIS...? THAT I'M SUDDENLY ...
...FEELING...
IT'S LIKE A HOLE HAS GAPED OPEN IN MY CHEST...
I-IS THIS... WHAT THEY CALL... **LONELINESS**...?! HE LEFT SO ABRUPTLY...
...WITHOUT SAYING A WORD, EVEN FAREWELL, DID FERSEN...

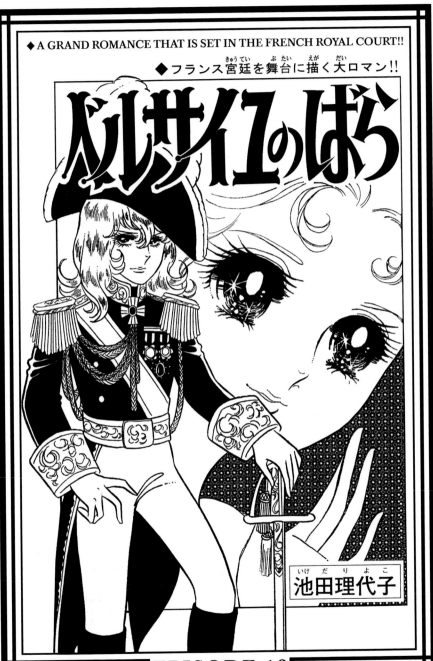

◆A GRAND ROMANCE THAT IS SET IN THE FRENCH ROYAL COURT!!

◆フランス宮廷を舞台に描く大ロマン!!

バルサイユのばら

池田理代子

EPISODE 13

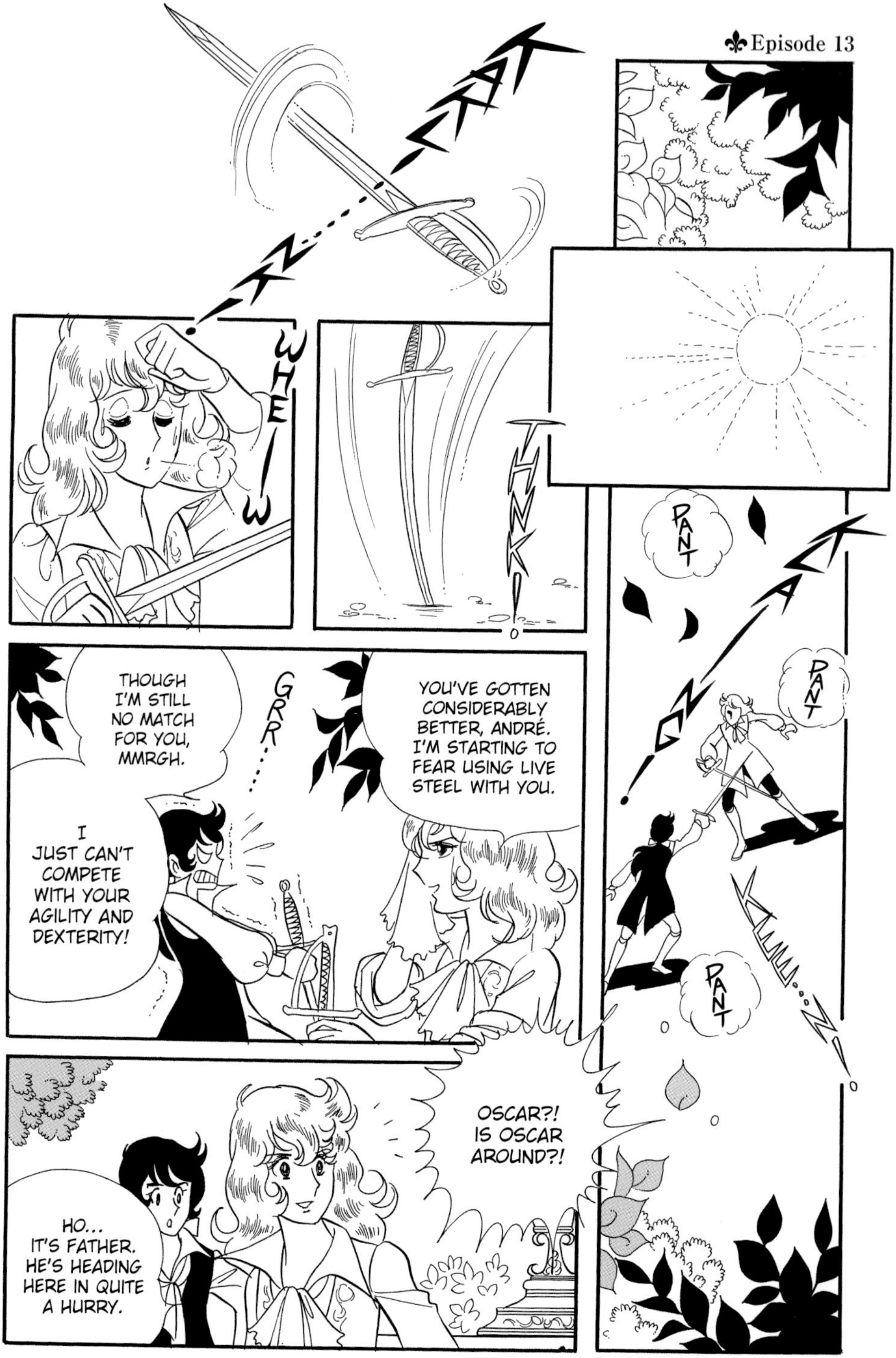
PANT
PANT
PANT
THNK!
WHEW
YOU'VE GOTTEN CONSIDERABLY BETTER, ANDRÉ. I'M STARTING TO FEAR USING LIVE STEEL WITH YOU.
GRR...
THOUGH I'M STILL NO MATCH FOR YOU, MMRGH.
I JUST CAN'T COMPETE WITH YOUR AGILITY AND DEXTERITY!
OSCAR?! IS OSCAR AROUND?!
HO... IT'S FATHER. HE'S HEADING HERE IN QUITE A HURRY.

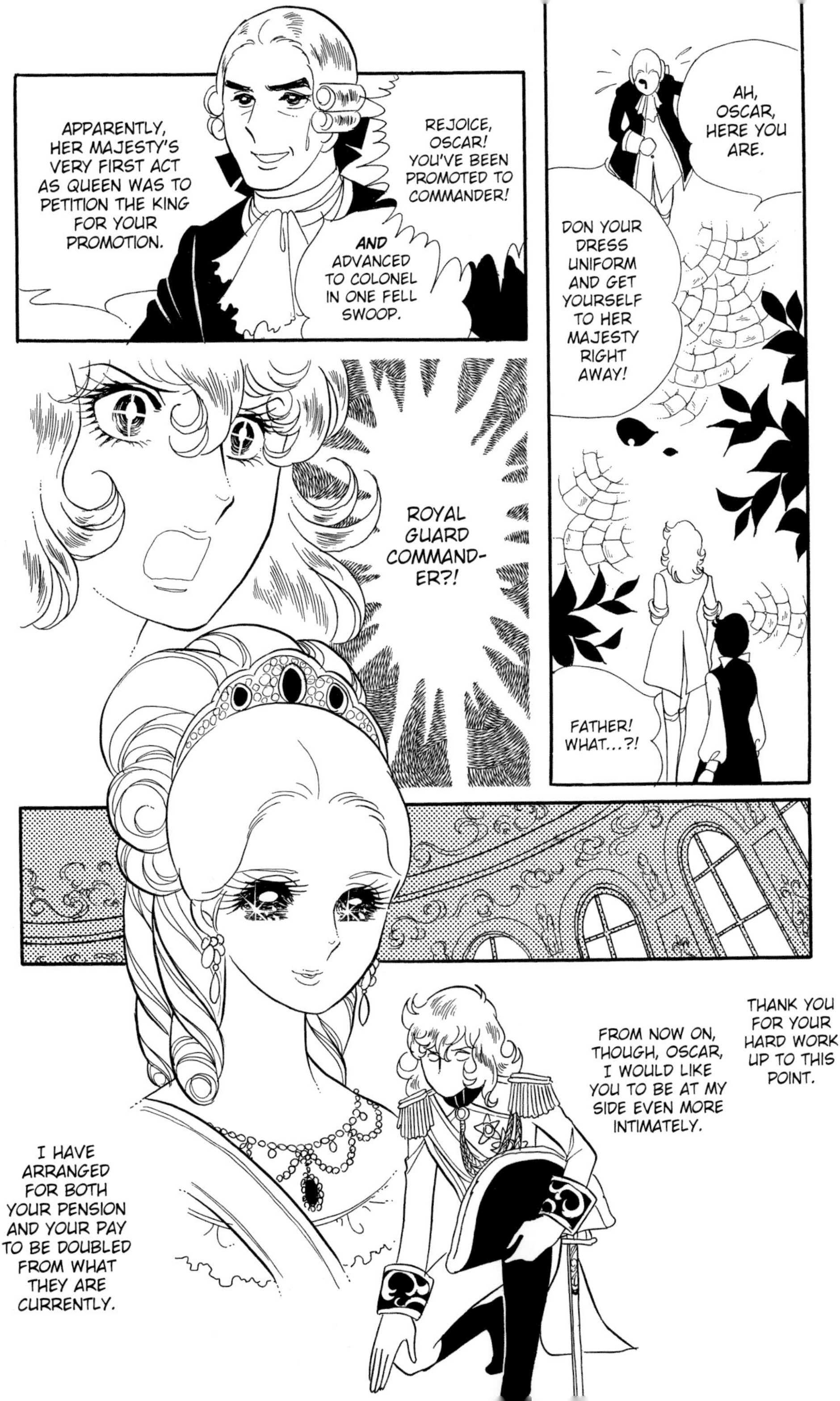
AH, OSCAR, HERE YOU ARE.
DON YOUR DRESS UNIFORM AND GET YOURSELF TO HER MAJESTY RIGHT AWAY!
FATHER! WHAT...?!
REJOICE, OSCAR! YOU'VE BEEN PROMOTED TO COMMANDER!
AND ADVANCED TO COLONEL IN ONE FELL SWOOP.
APPARENTLY, HER MAJESTY'S VERY FIRST ACT AS QUEEN WAS TO PETITION THE KING FOR YOUR PROMOTION.
ROYAL GUARD COMMANDER?!
THANK YOU FOR YOUR HARD WORK UP TO THIS POINT.
FROM NOW ON, THOUGH, OSCAR, I WOULD LIKE YOU TO BE AT MY SIDE EVEN MORE INTIMATELY.
I HAVE ARRANGED FOR BOTH YOUR PENSION AND YOUR PAY TO BE DOUBLED FROM WHAT THEY ARE CURRENTLY.

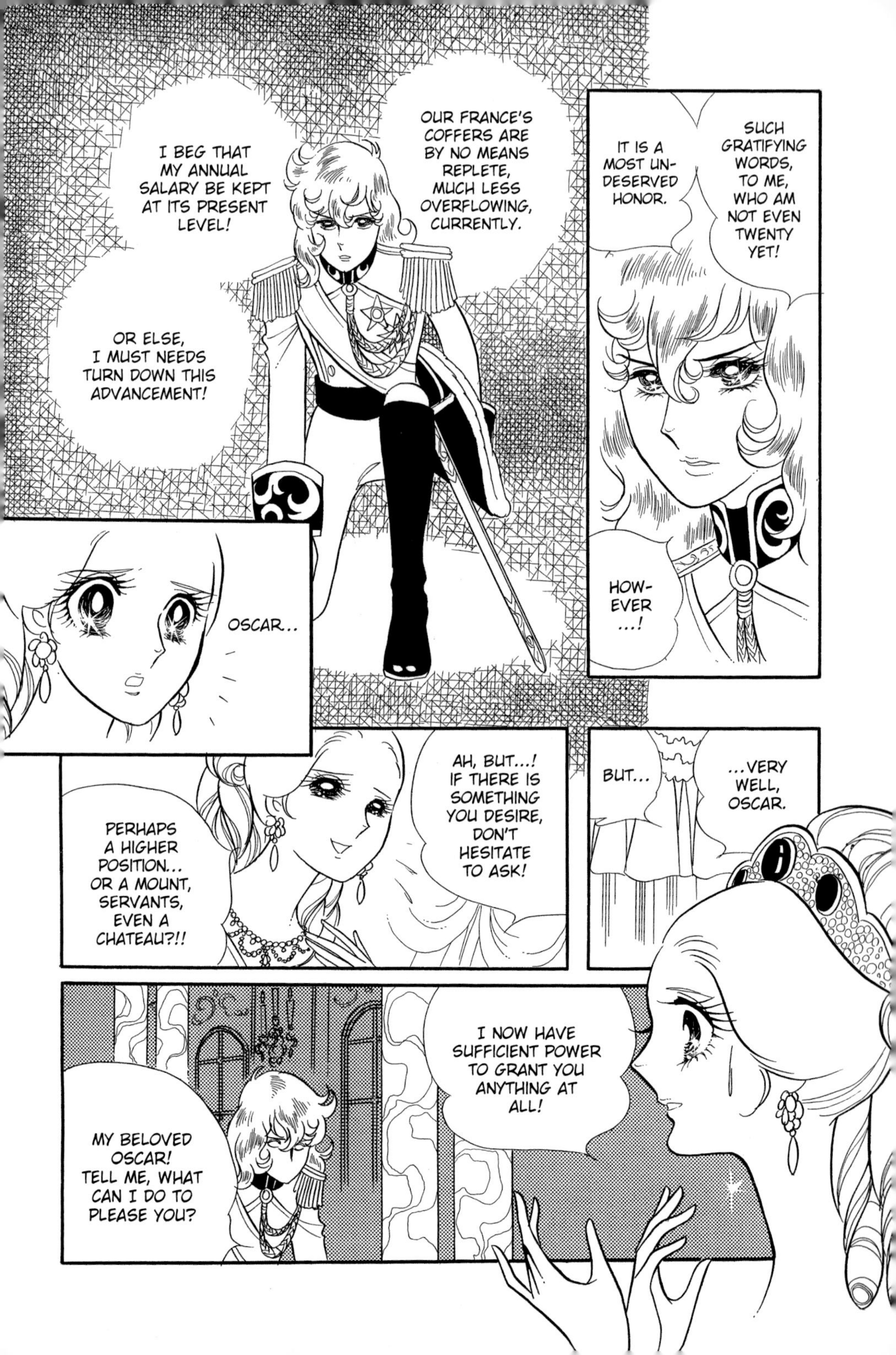
SUCH GRATIFYING WORDS, TO ME, WHO AM NOT EVEN TWENTY YET!
IT IS A MOST UN-DESERVED HONOR.
HOW-EVER ...!
OUR FRANCE'S COFFERS ARE BY NO MEANS REPLETE, MUCH LESS OVERFLOWING, CURRENTLY.
I BEG THAT MY ANNUAL SALARY BE KEPT AT ITS PRESENT LEVEL!
OR ELSE, I MUST NEEDS TURN DOWN THIS ADVANCEMENT!
OSCAR...
...VERY WELL, OSCAR.
BUT...
AH, BUT...! IF THERE IS SOMETHING YOU DESIRE, DON'T HESITATE TO ASK!
PERHAPS A HIGHER POSITION... OR A MOUNT, SERVANTS, EVEN A CHATEAU?!!
I NOW HAVE SUFFICIENT POWER TO GRANT YOU ANYTHING AT ALL!
MY BELOVED OSCAR! TELL ME, WHAT CAN I DO TO PLEASE YOU?

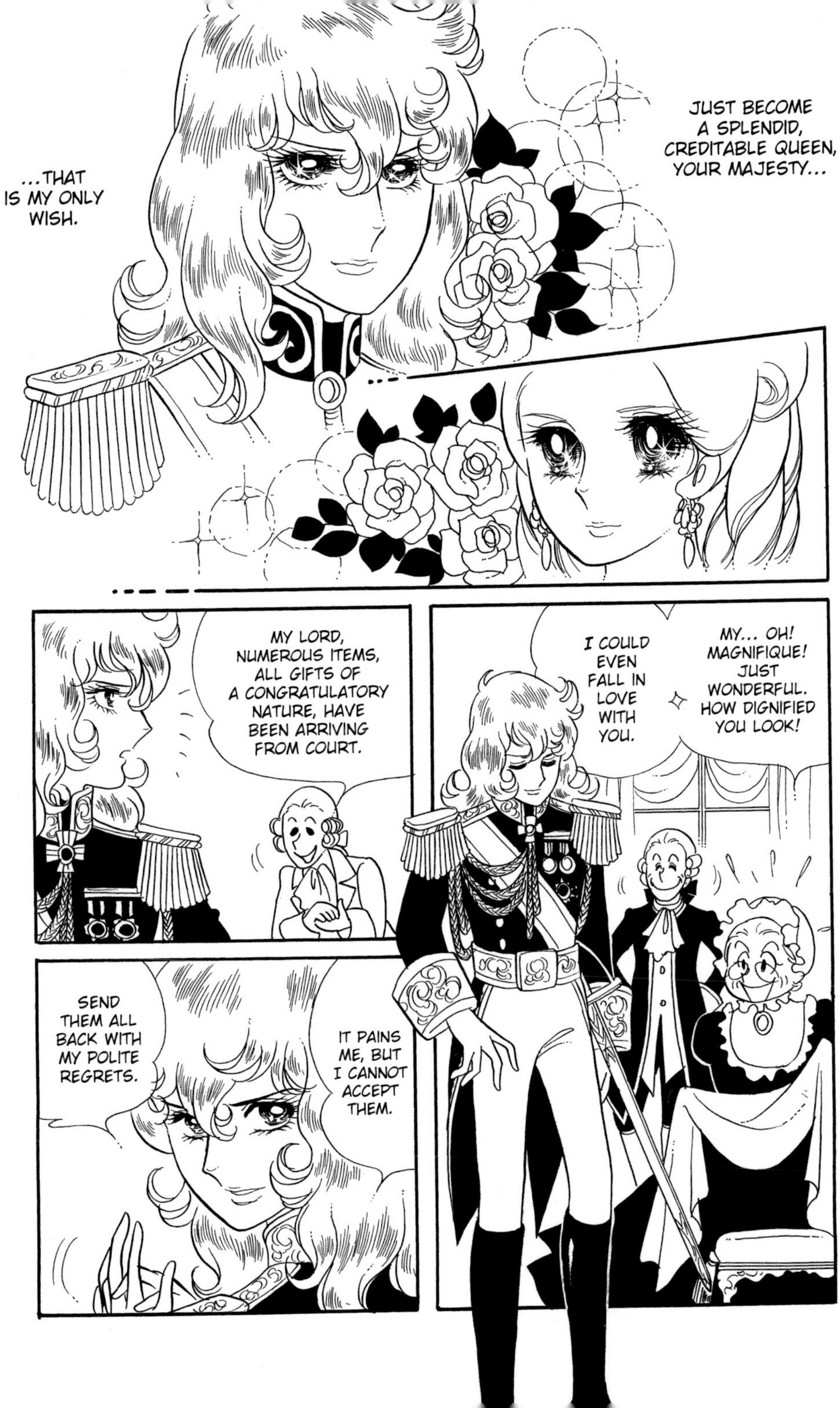
JUST BECOME A SPLENDID, CREDITABLE QUEEN, YOUR MAJESTY...
...THAT IS MY ONLY WISH.
MY... OH! MAGNIFIQUE! JUST WONDERFUL. HOW DIGNIFIED YOU LOOK!
I COULD EVEN FALL IN LOVE WITH YOU.
MY LORD, NUMEROUS ITEMS, ALL GIFTS OF A CONGRATULATORY NATURE, HAVE BEEN ARRIVING FROM COURT.
IT PAINS ME, BUT I CANNOT ACCEPT THEM.
SEND THEM ALL BACK WITH MY POLITE REGRETS.

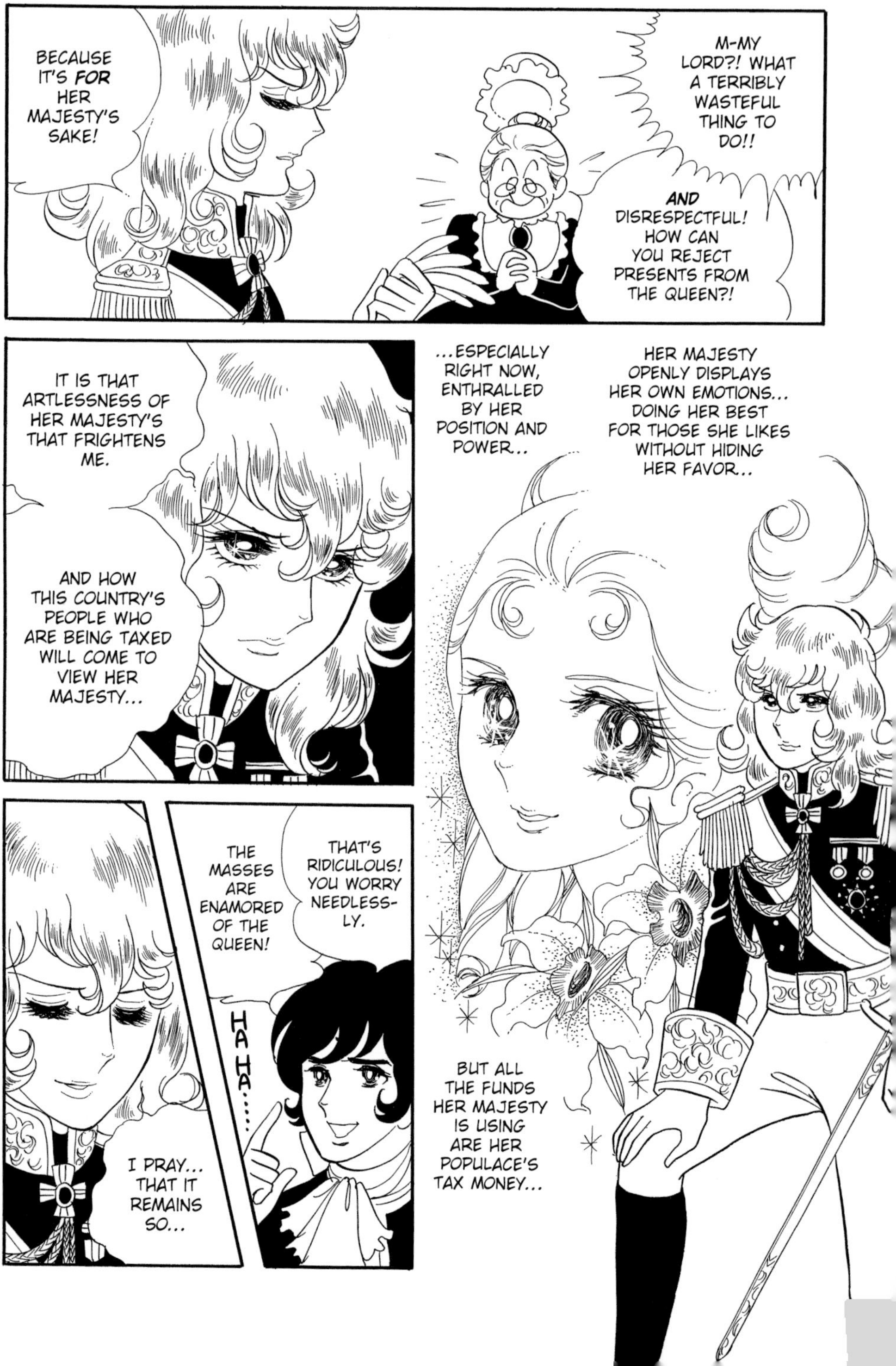
M-MY LORD?! WHAT A TERRIBLY WASTEFUL THING TO DO!!
AND DISRESPECTFUL! HOW CAN YOU REJECT PRESENTS FROM THE QUEEN?!
BECAUSE IT'S **FOR** HER MAJESTY'S SAKE!
HER MAJESTY OPENLY DISPLAYS HER OWN EMOTIONS... DOING HER BEST FOR THOSE SHE LIKES WITHOUT HIDING HER FAVOR...
...ESPECIALLY RIGHT NOW, ENTHRALLED BY HER POSITION AND POWER...
BUT ALL THE FUNDS HER MAJESTY IS USING ARE HER POPULACE'S TAX MONEY...
IT IS THAT ARTLESSNESS OF HER MAJESTY'S THAT FRIGHTENS ME.
AND HOW THIS COUNTRY'S PEOPLE WHO ARE BEING TAXED WILL COME TO VIEW HER MAJESTY...
THAT'S RIDICULOUS! YOU WORRY NEEDLESS-LY.
THE MASSES ARE ENAMORED OF THE QUEEN!
HA HA....
I PRAY... THAT IT REMAINS SO...

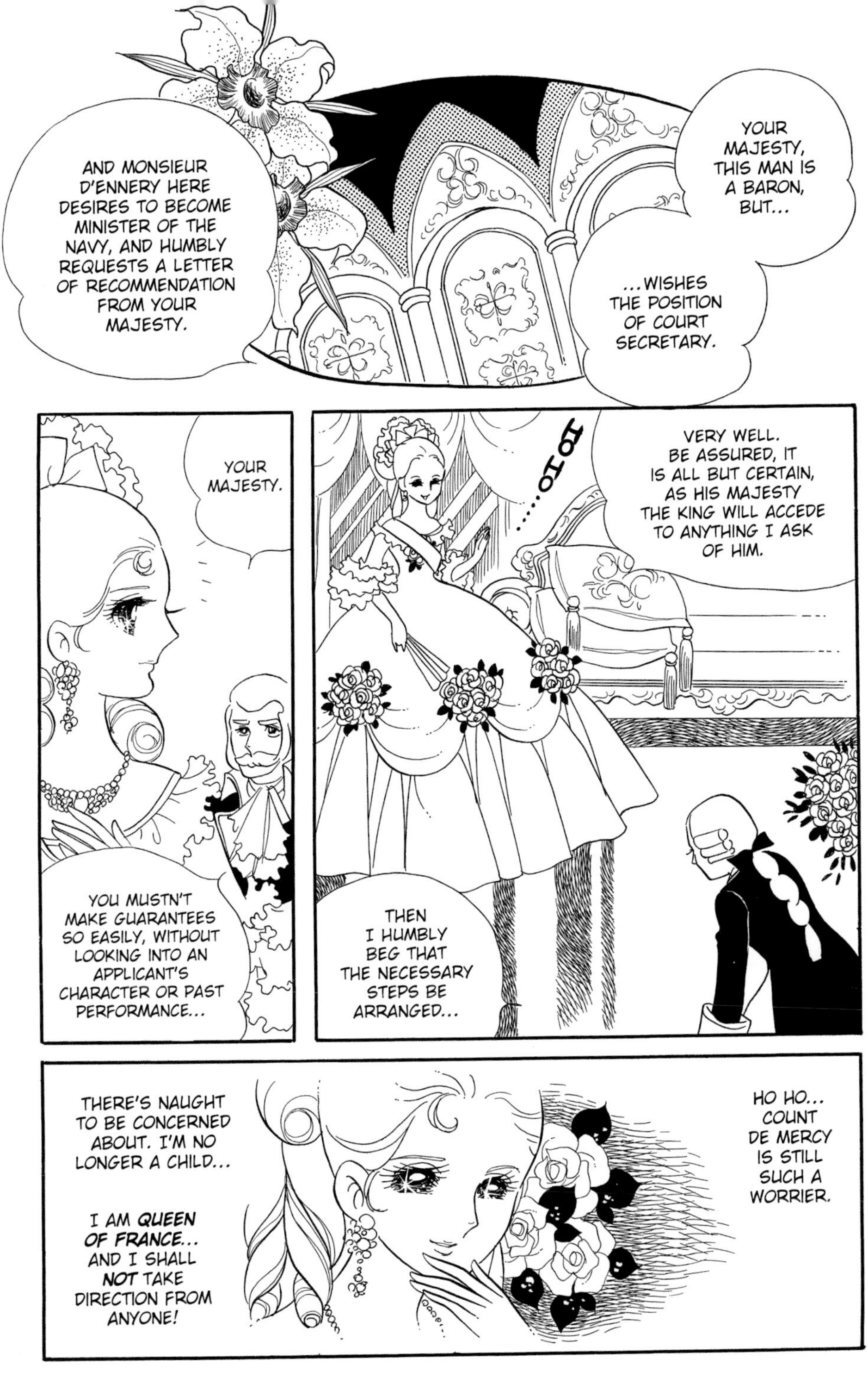
YOUR MAJESTY, THIS MAN IS A BARON, BUT...
...WISHES THE POSITION OF COURT SECRETARY.
AND MONSIEUR D'ENNERY HERE DESIRES TO BECOME MINISTER OF THE NAVY, AND HUMBLY REQUESTS A LETTER OF RECOMMENDATION FROM YOUR MAJESTY.
VERY WELL. BE ASSURED, IT IS ALL BUT CERTAIN, AS HIS MAJESTY THE KING WILL ACCEDE TO ANYTHING I ASK OF HIM.
HOHO.....
THEN I HUMBLY BEG THAT THE NECESSARY STEPS BE ARRANGED...
YOUR MAJESTY.
YOU MUSTN'T MAKE GUARANTEES SO EASILY, WITHOUT LOOKING INTO AN APPLICANT'S CHARACTER OR PAST PERFORMANCE...
HO HO... COUNT DE MERCY IS STILL SUCH A WORRIER.
THERE'S NAUGHT TO BE CONCERNED ABOUT. I'M NO LONGER A CHILD...
I AM *QUEEN OF FRANCE*... AND I SHALL *NOT* TAKE DIRECTION FROM ANYONE!

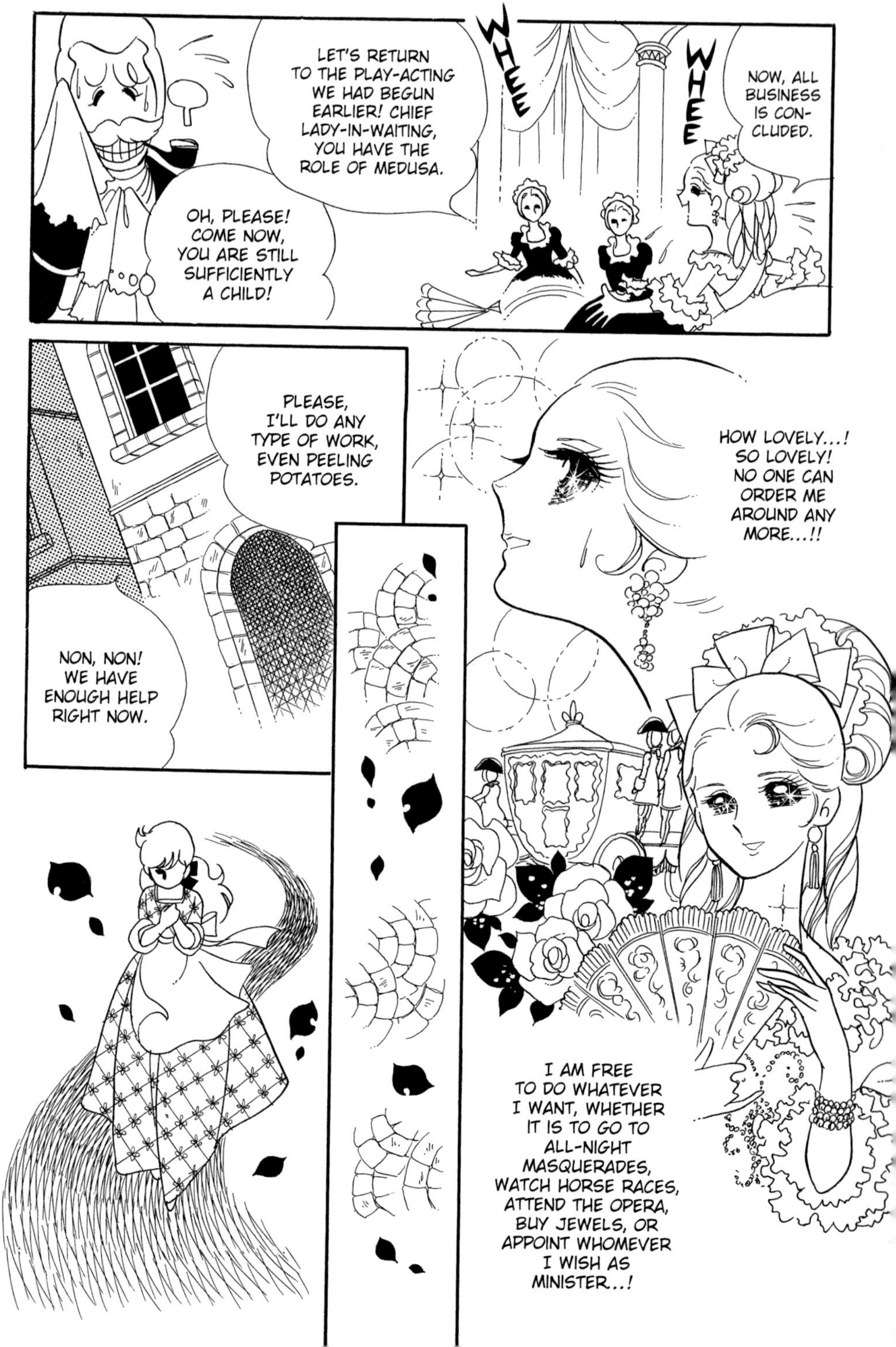
NOW, ALL BUSINESS IS CON- CLUDED.
WHEE
WHEE
LET'S RETURN TO THE PLAY-ACTING WE HAD BEGUN EARLIER! CHIEF LADY-IN-WAITING, YOU HAVE THE ROLE OF MEDUSA.
OH, PLEASE! COME NOW, YOU ARE STILL SUFFICIENTLY A CHILD!
HOW LOVELY...! SO LOVELY! NO ONE CAN ORDER ME AROUND ANY MORE...!!
I AM FREE TO DO WHATEVER I WANT, WHETHER IT IS TO GO TO ALL-NIGHT MASQUERADES, WATCH HORSE RACES, ATTEND THE OPERA, BUY JEWELS, OR APPOINT WHOMEVER I WISH AS MINISTER...!
PLEASE, I'LL DO ANY TYPE OF WORK, EVEN PEELING POTATOES.
NON, NON! WE HAVE ENOUGH HELP RIGHT NOW.

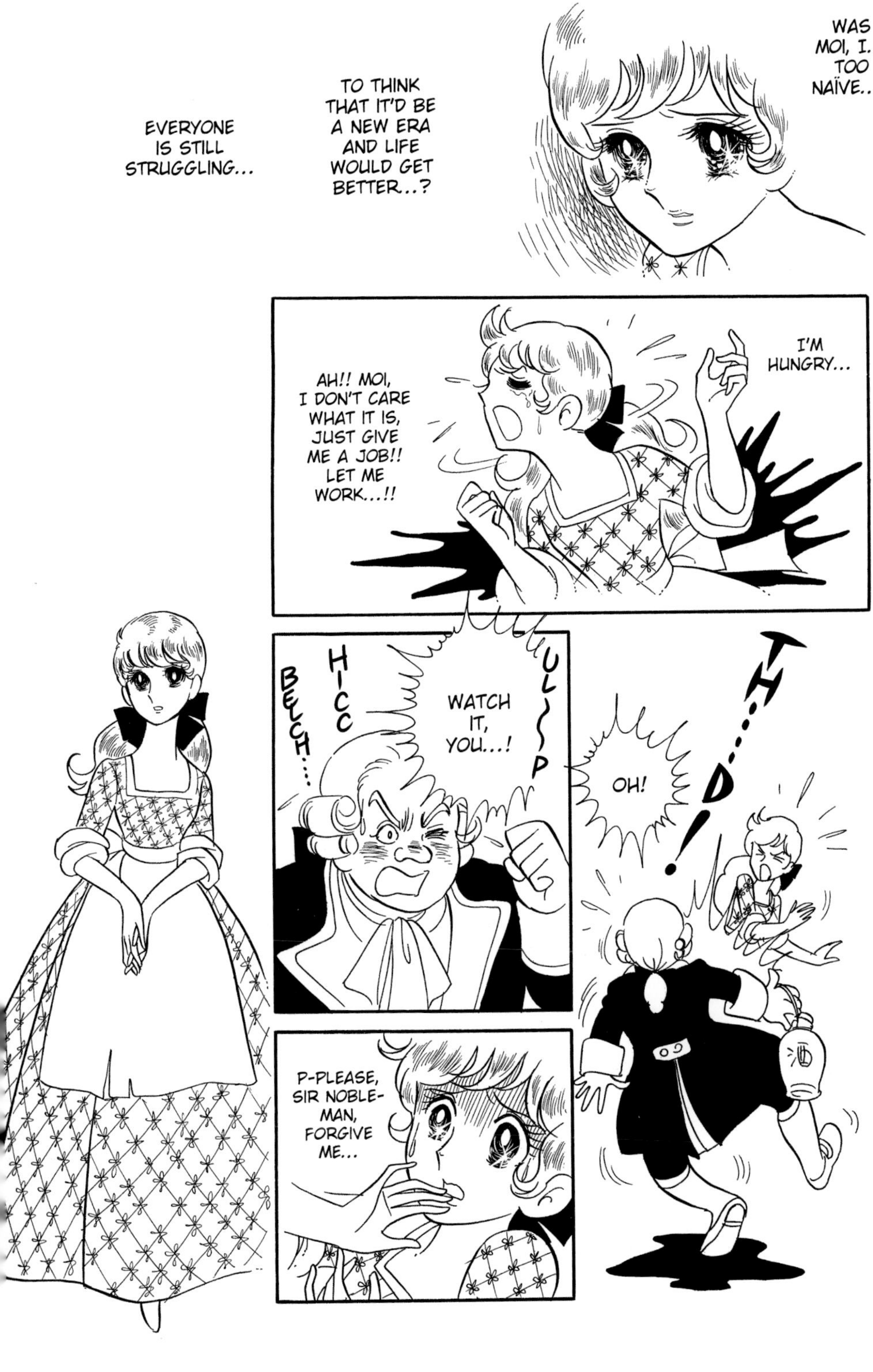
WAS MOI, I... TOO NAÏVE...?
TO THINK THAT IT'D BE A NEW ERA AND LIFE WOULD GET BETTER..?
EVERYONE IS STILL STRUGGLING...
I'M HUNGRY...
AH!! MOI, I DON'T CARE WHAT IT IS, JUST GIVE ME A JOB!! LET ME WORK...!!
TH...D!
OH!
UL~P
WATCH IT, YOU...!
HICC
BELCH...
P-PLEASE, SIR NOBLEMAN, FORGIVE ME...

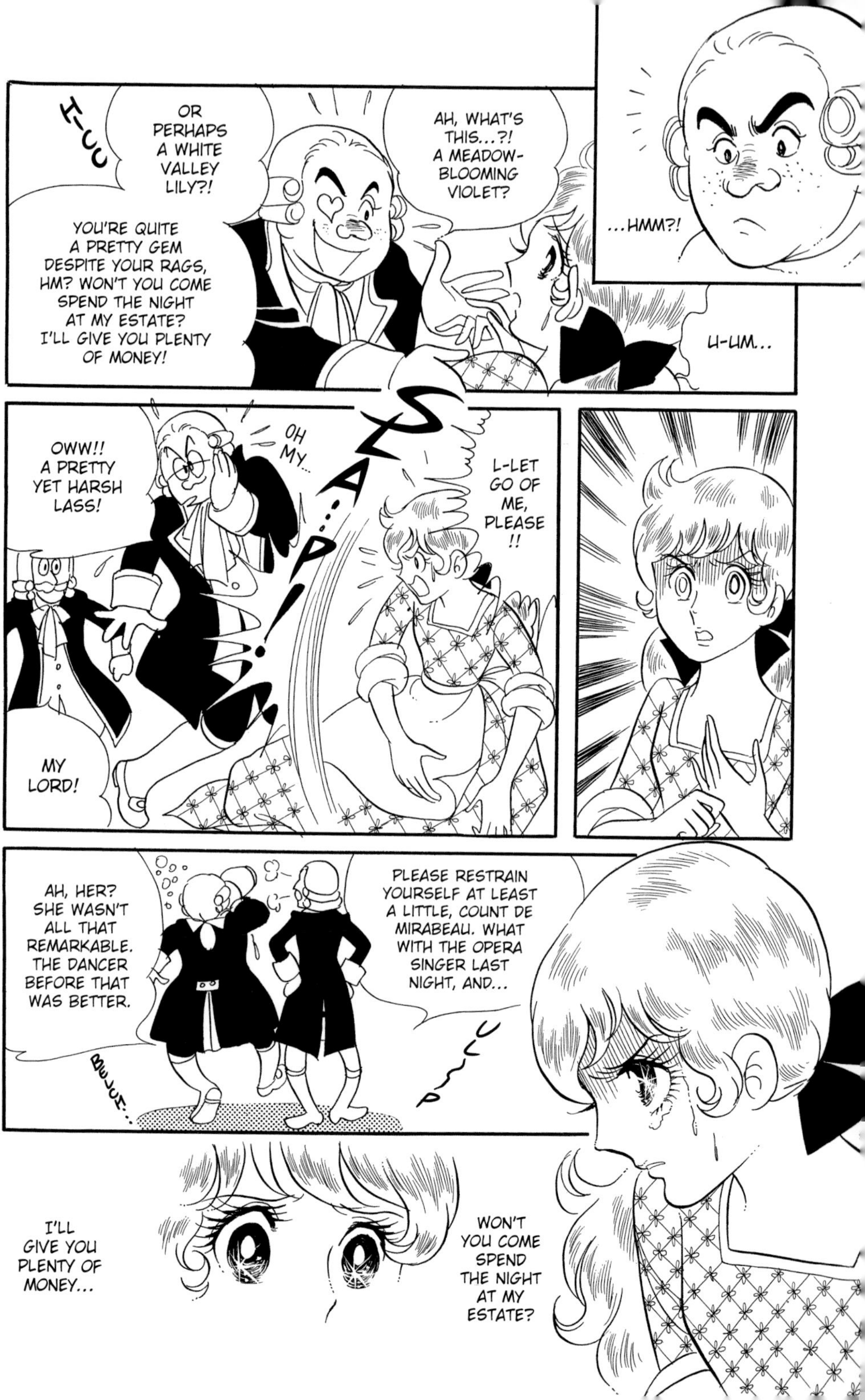
...HMM?!
U-UM...
AH, WHAT'S THIS...?! A MEADOW-BLOOMING VIOLET?
OR PERHAPS A WHITE VALLEY LILY?!
YOU'RE QUITE A PRETTY GEM DESPITE YOUR RAGS, HM? WON'T YOU COME SPEND THE NIGHT AT MY ESTATE? I'LL GIVE YOU PLENTY OF MONEY!
H-CC
L-LET GO OF ME, PLEASE!!
SLAP!!
OH MY...
OWW!! A PRETTY YET HARSH LASS!
MY LORD!
PLEASE RESTRAIN YOURSELF AT LEAST A LITTLE, COUNT DE MIRABEAU. WHAT WITH THE OPERA SINGER LAST NIGHT, AND...
AH, HER? SHE WASN'T ALL THAT REMARKABLE. THE DANCER BEFORE THAT WAS BETTER.
BELCH...
WON'T YOU COME SPEND THE NIGHT AT MY ESTATE?
I'LL GIVE YOU PLENTY OF MONEY...

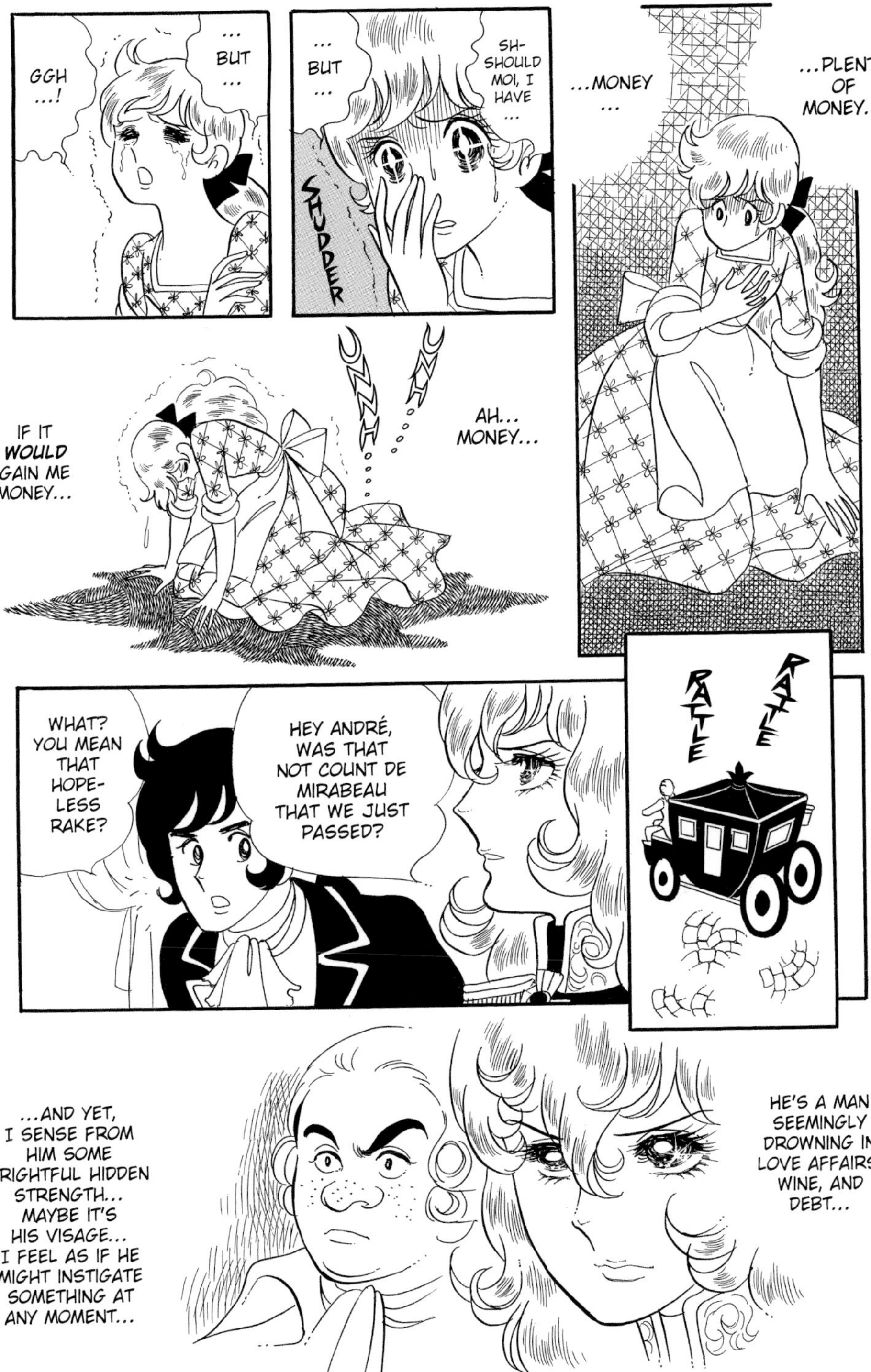
...PLENTY OF MONEY...
...MONEY...
SH-SHOULD MOI, I HAVE...
...BUT...
SHUDDER
...BUT...
GGH...!
AH... MONEY...
UNH
UNNH
IF IT *WOULD* GAIN ME MONEY...
RATTLE
RATTLE
HEY ANDRÉ, WAS THAT NOT COUNT DE MIRABEAU THAT WE JUST PASSED?
WHAT? YOU MEAN THAT HOPE-LESS RAKE?
HE'S A MAN SEEMINGLY DROWNING IN LOVE AFFAIRS, WINE, AND DEBT...
...AND YET, I SENSE FROM HIM SOME FRIGHTFUL HIDDEN STRENGTH... MAYBE IT'S HIS VISAGE... I FEEL AS IF HE MIGHT INSTIGATE SOMETHING AT ANY MOMENT...

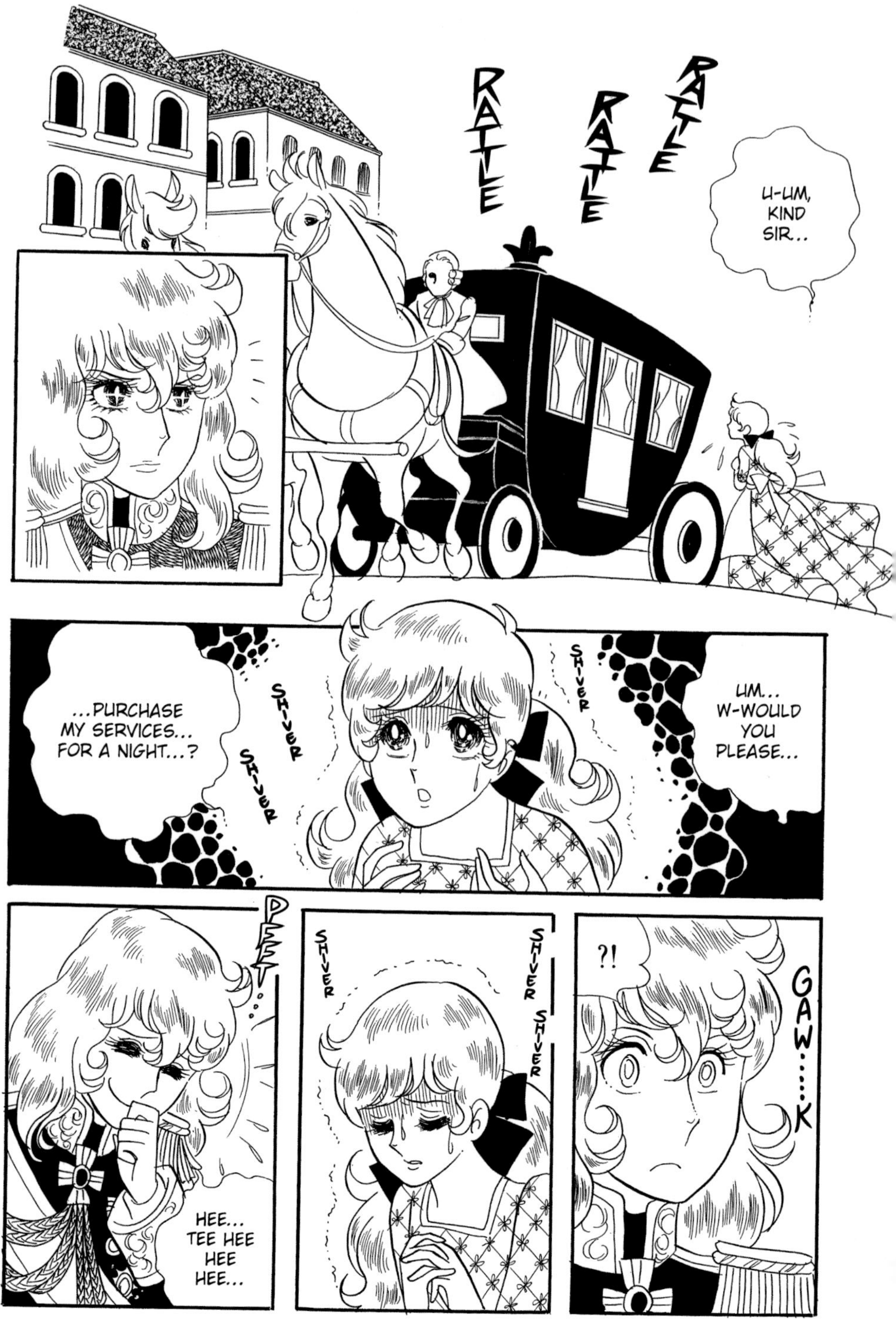
RATTLE
RATTLE
RATTLE
U-UM, KIND SIR...
UM... W-WOULD YOU PLEASE...
SHIVER
SHIVER
SHIVER
...PURCHASE MY SERVICES... FOR A NIGHT...?
GAW...K
?!
SHIVER
SHIVER
SHIVER
PFFT
HEE... TEE HEE HEE HEE...

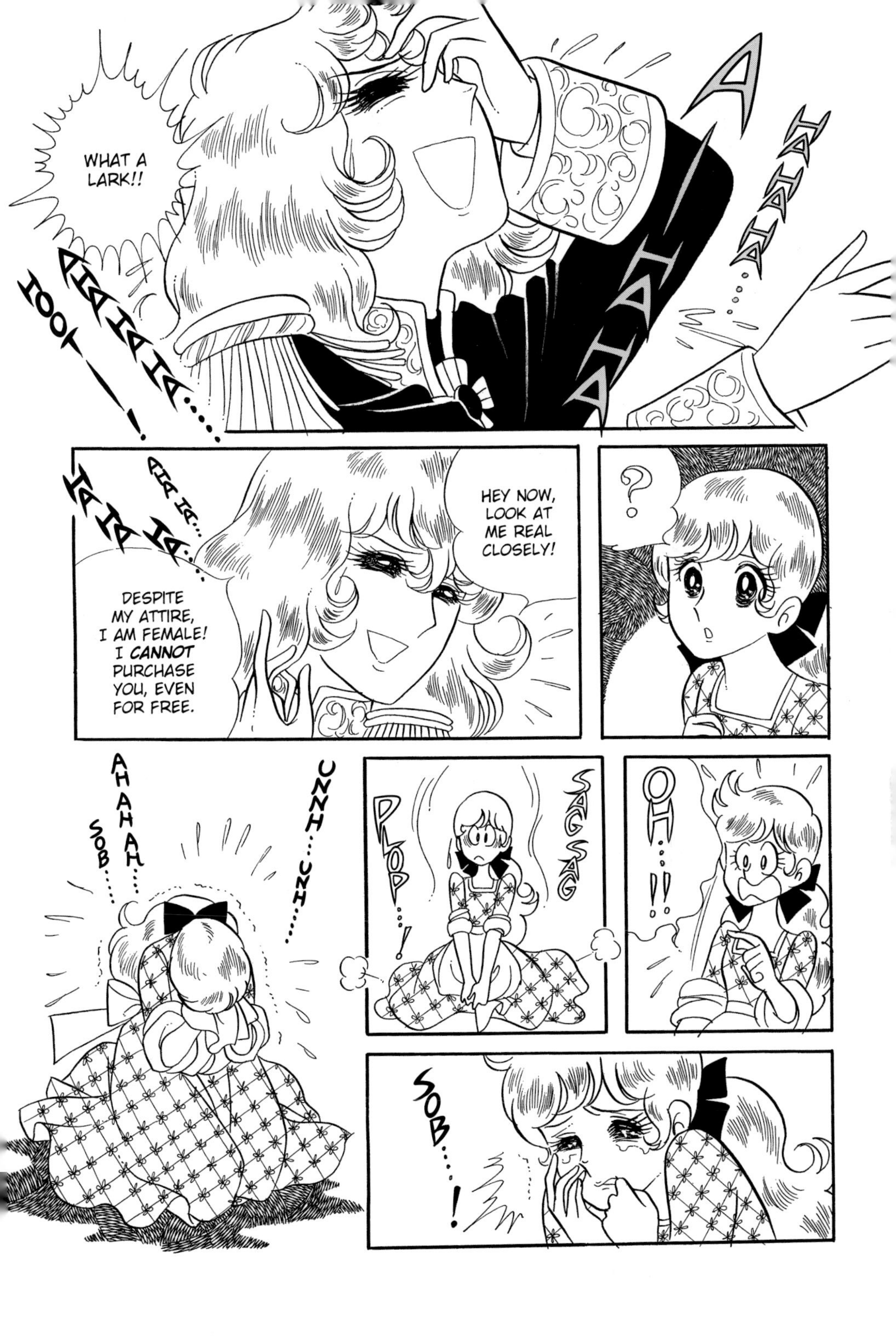

AHAHAHA...
AHAHA
WHAT A LARK!!
AHAHAHA......
HOOT—!!
?
HEY NOW, LOOK AT ME REAL CLOSELY!
DESPITE MY ATTIRE, I AM FEMALE! I CANNOT PURCHASE YOU, EVEN FOR FREE.
AHA HA...
HAHAHA...
OH...!!
SAG SAG
PLOP...!
SOB...!
UNNH... UNH......
AHAHAH...
SOB...

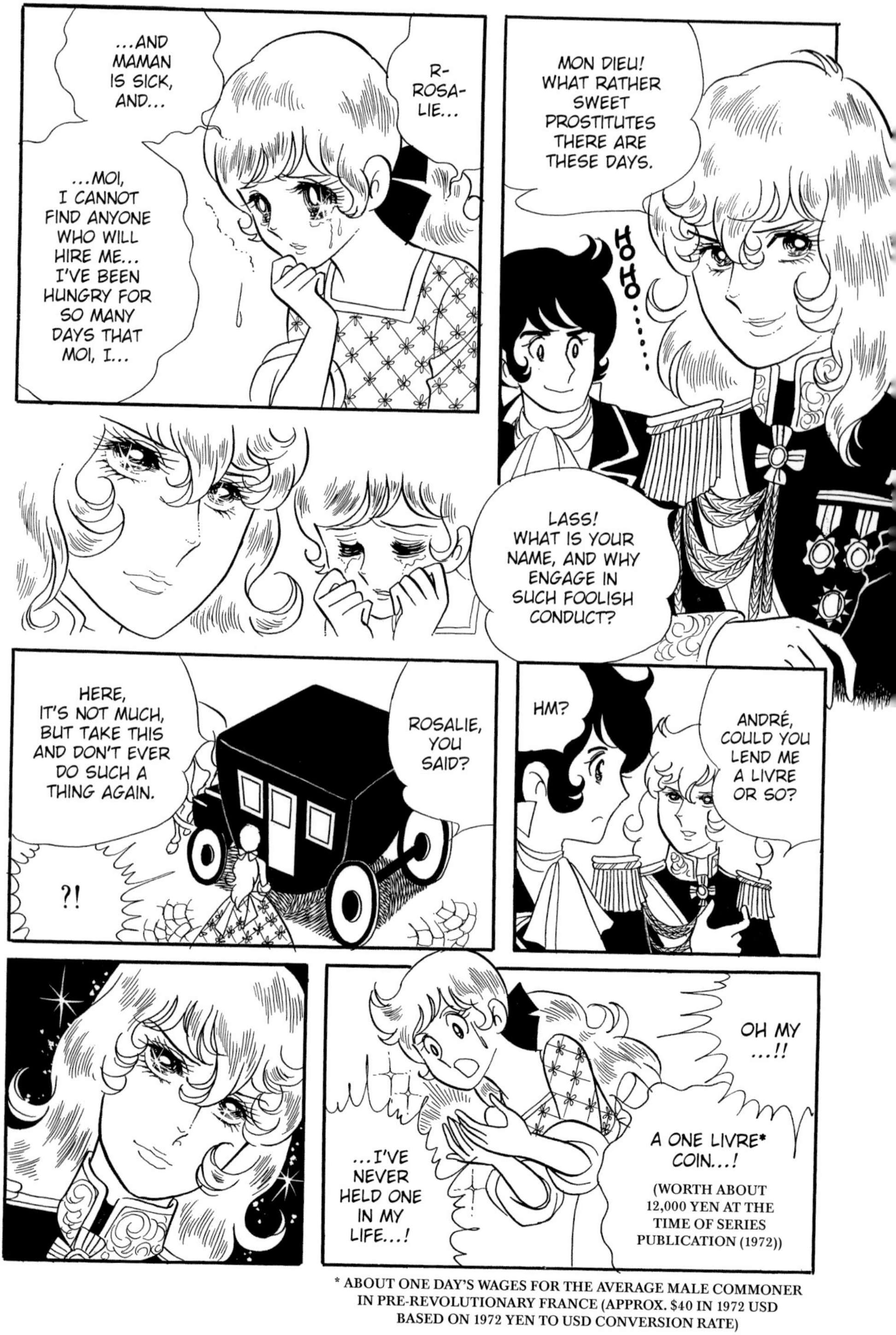
MON DIEU! WHAT RATHER SWEET PROSTITUTES THERE ARE THESE DAYS.
HO HO......
R-ROSALIE...
...AND MAMAN IS SICK, AND...
...MOI, I CANNOT FIND ANYONE WHO WILL HIRE ME... I'VE BEEN HUNGRY FOR SO MANY DAYS THAT MOI, I...
LASS! WHAT IS YOUR NAME, AND WHY ENGAGE IN SUCH FOOLISH CONDUCT?
ANDRÉ, COULD YOU LEND ME A LIVRE OR SO?
HM?
ROSALIE, YOU SAID?
HERE, IT'S NOT MUCH, BUT TAKE THIS AND DON'T EVER DO SUCH A THING AGAIN.
?!
OH MY ...!!
A ONE LIVRE* COIN...!
(WORTH ABOUT 12,000 YEN AT THE TIME OF SERIES PUBLICATION (1972))
...I'VE NEVER HELD ONE IN MY LIFE...!

* ABOUT ONE DAY'S WAGES FOR THE AVERAGE MALE COMMONER IN PRE-REVOLUTIONARY FRANCE (APPROX. $40 IN 1972 USD BASED ON 1972 YEN TO USD CONVERSION RATE)

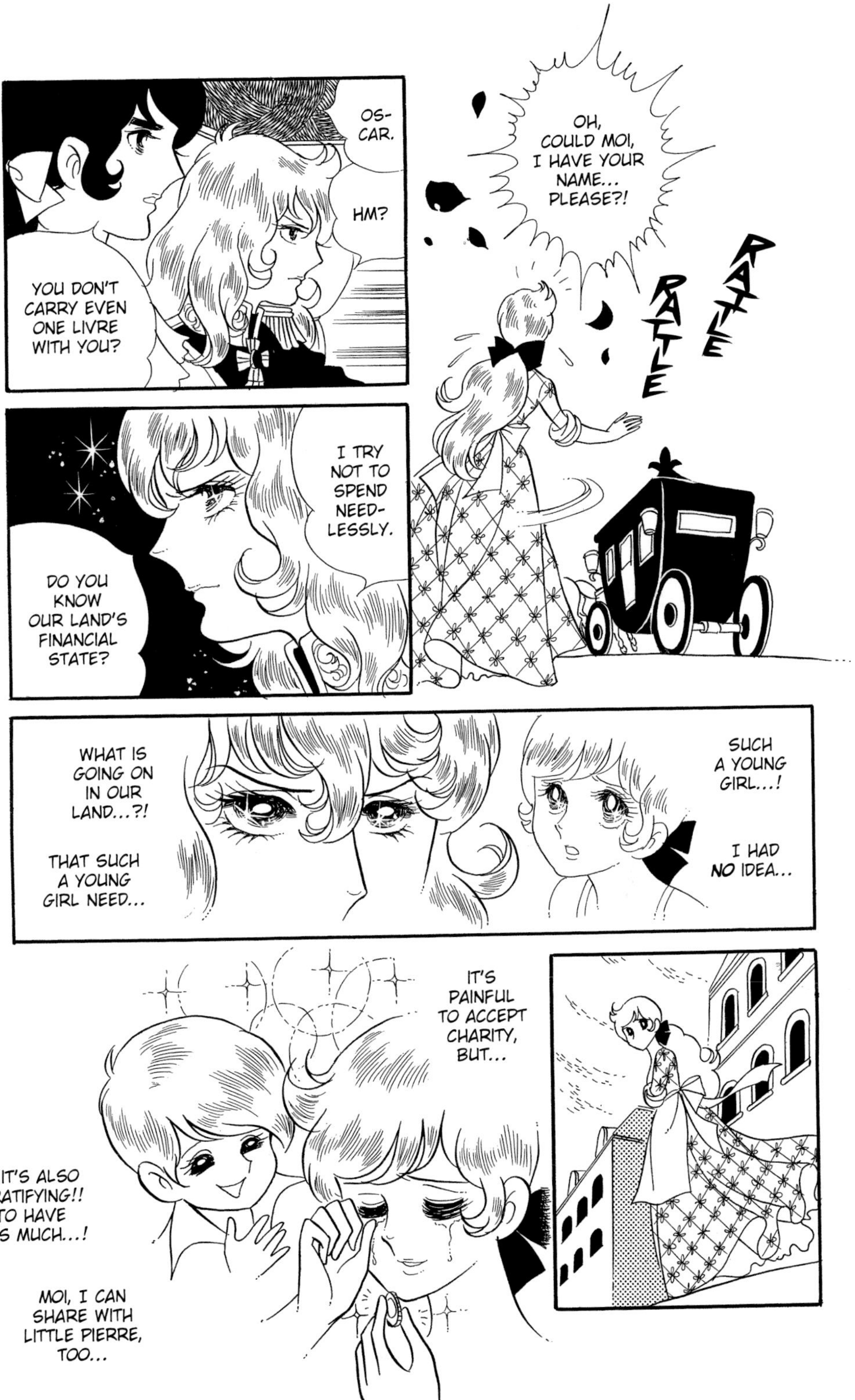
OH, COULD MOI, I HAVE YOUR NAME... PLEASE?!
RATTLE
RATTLE
OS-CAR.
HM?
YOU DON'T CARRY EVEN ONE LIVRE WITH YOU?
I TRY NOT TO SPEND NEED-LESSLY.
DO YOU KNOW OUR LAND'S FINANCIAL STATE?
SUCH A YOUNG GIRL...!
I HAD NO IDEA...
WHAT IS GOING ON IN OUR LAND...?!
THAT SUCH A YOUNG GIRL NEED...
IT'S PAINFUL TO ACCEPT CHARITY, BUT...
...IT'S ALSO GRATIFYING!! TO HAVE THIS MUCH...!
MOI, I CAN SHARE WITH LITTLE PIERRE, TOO...

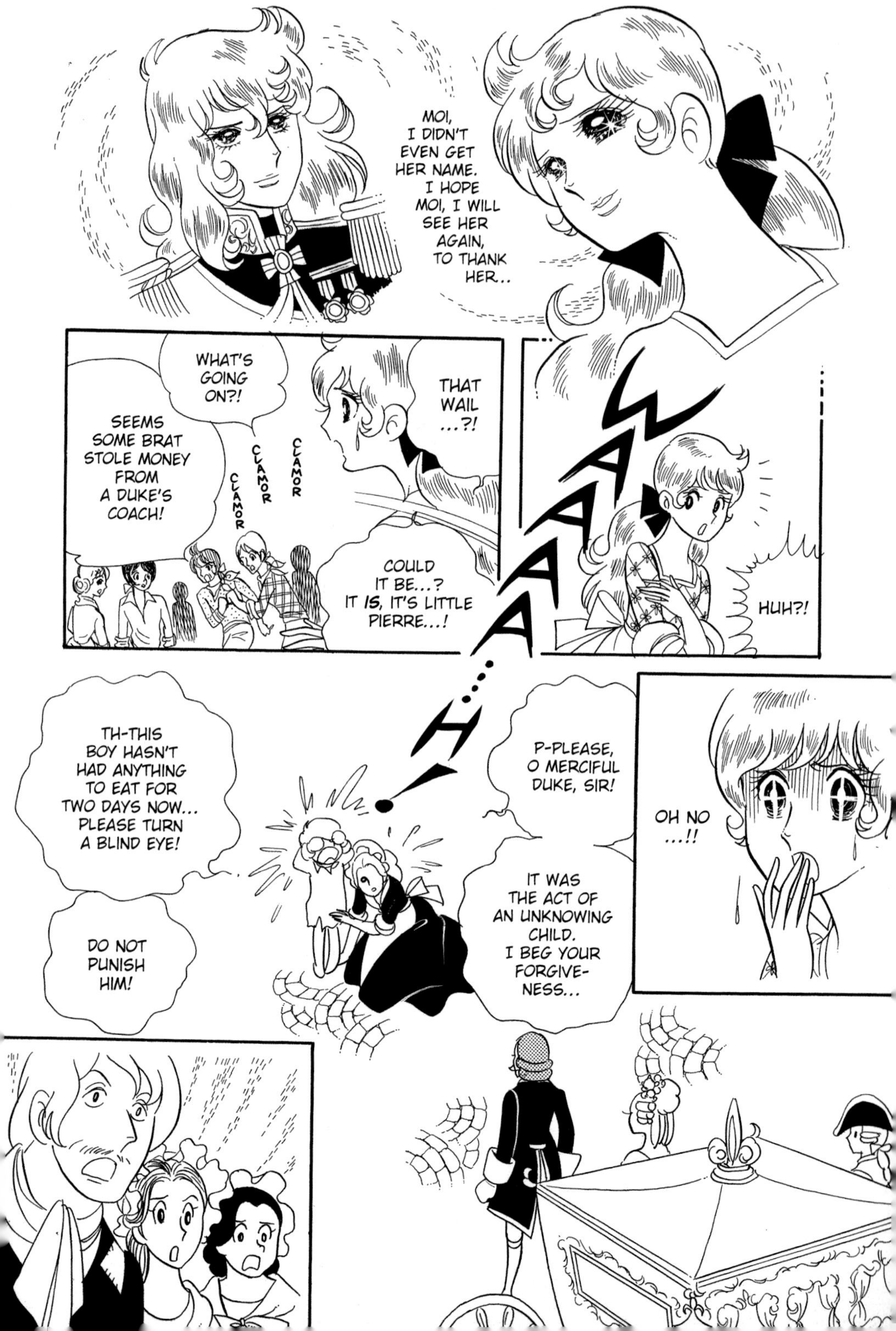
MOI, I DIDN'T EVEN GET HER NAME. I HOPE MOI, I WILL SEE HER AGAIN, TO THANK HER..
WAAAAH...!
HUH?!
THAT WAIL ...?!
WHAT'S GOING ON?!
SEEMS SOME BRAT STOLE MONEY FROM A DUKE'S COACH!
CLAMOR
CLAMOR
CLAMOR
COULD IT BE...? IT *IS*, IT'S LITTLE PIERRE...!
OH NO ...!!
P-PLEASE, O MERCIFUL DUKE, SIR!
IT WAS THE ACT OF AN UNKNOWING CHILD. I BEG YOUR FORGIVE-NESS...
TH-THIS BOY HASN'T HAD ANYTHING TO EAT FOR TWO DAYS NOW... PLEASE TURN A BLIND EYE!
DO NOT PUNISH HIM!

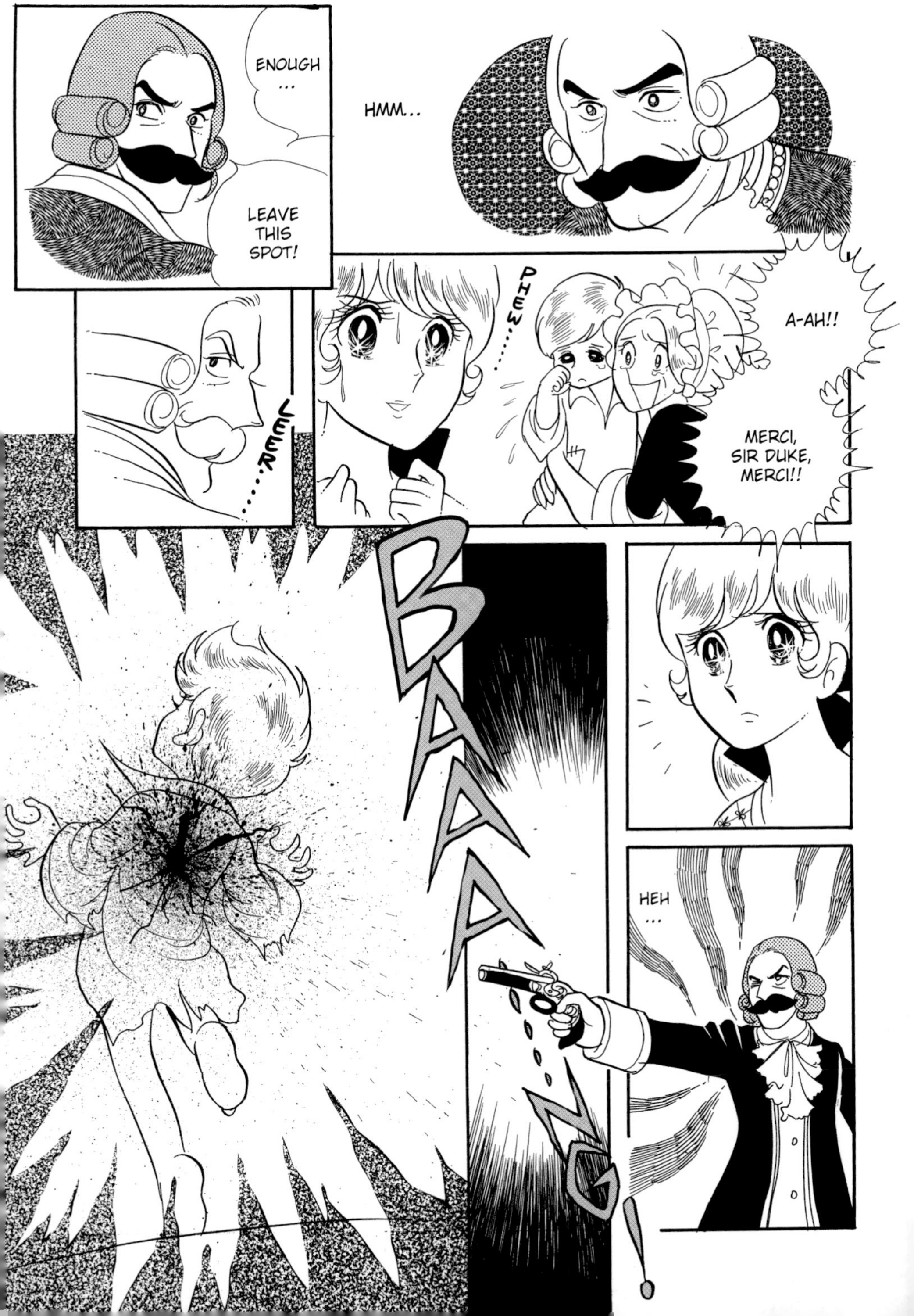
HMM...
ENOUGH ...
LEAVE THIS SPOT!
A-AH!!
MERCI, SIR DUKE, MERCI!!
PHEW...
LEER...
HEH ...
BAAAANG!

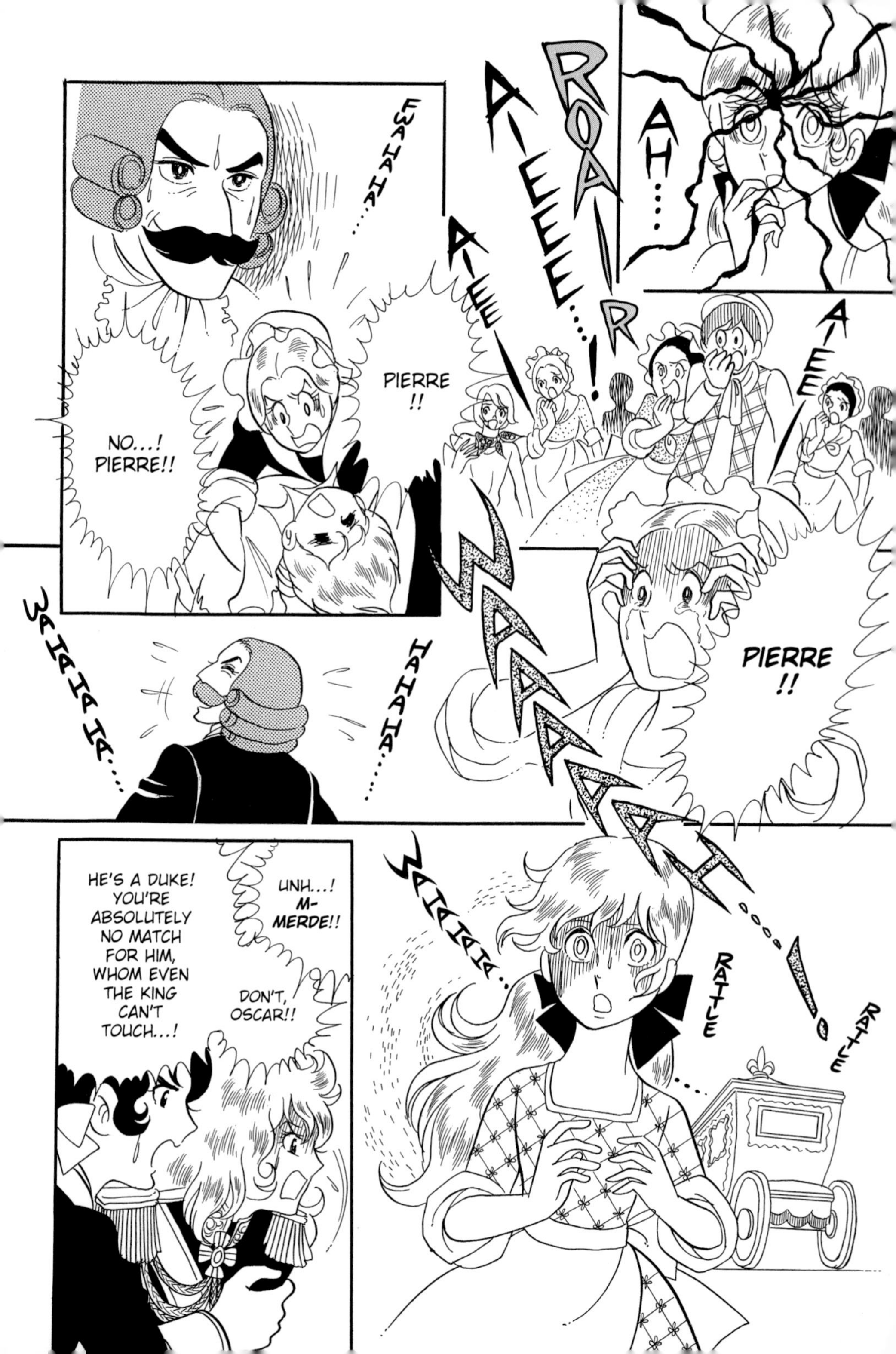
AH...
ROAR
AIEEE...!
AIEE...!
AIEE...
FWAHAHAHA...
PIERRE!!
NO...! PIERRE!!
PIERRE!!
WAAAAAH...!
HAHAHA...
WAHAHAHA...
WAHAHAHA...
RATTLE
RATTLE
UNH...! M-MERDE!!
HE'S A DUKE! YOU'RE ABSOLUTELY NO MATCH FOR HIM, WHOM EVEN THE KING CAN'T TOUCH...!
DON'T, OSCAR!!

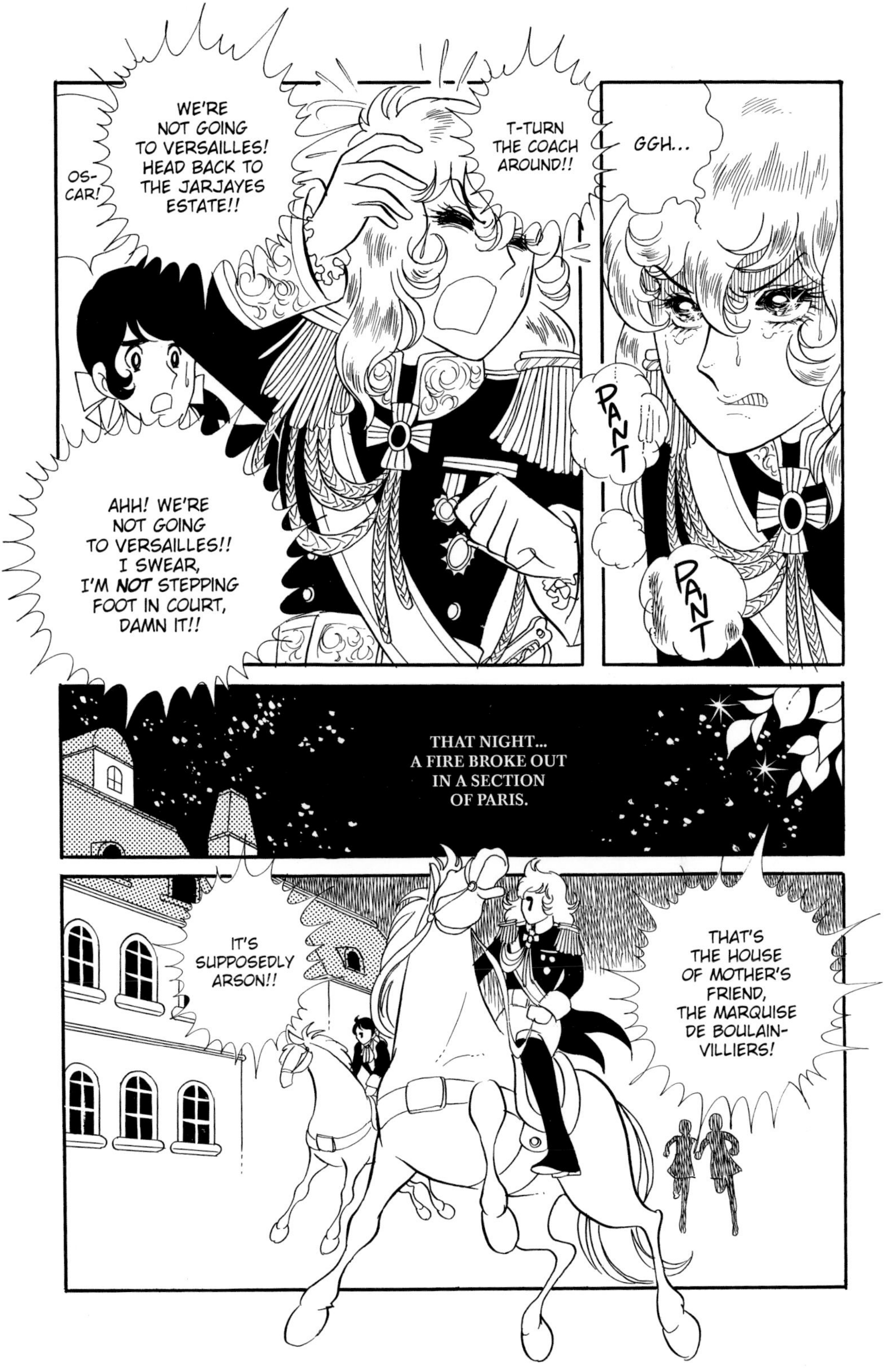
GGH...
PANT
PANT
T-TURN THE COACH AROUND!!
WE'RE NOT GOING TO VERSAILLES! HEAD BACK TO THE JARJAYES ESTATE!!
OS-CAR!
AHH! WE'RE NOT GOING TO VERSAILLES!! I SWEAR, I'M **NOT** STEPPING FOOT IN COURT, DAMN IT!!
THAT NIGHT... A FIRE BROKE OUT IN A SECTION OF PARIS.
THAT'S THE HOUSE OF MOTHER'S FRIEND, THE MARQUISE DE BOULAIN-VILLIERS!
IT'S SUPPOSEDLY ARSON!!

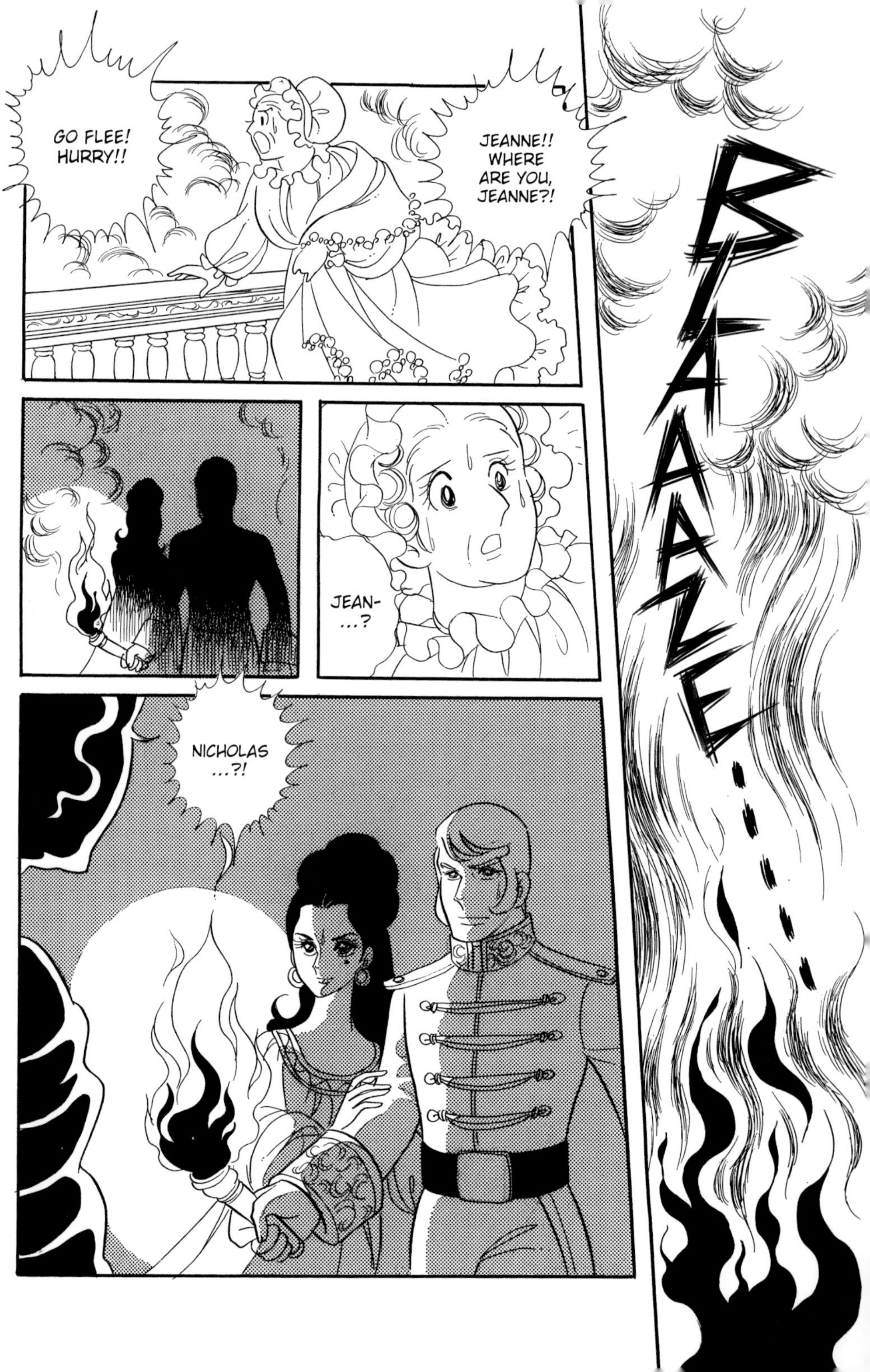
BLAAAZE...
JEANNE!! WHERE ARE YOU, JEANNE?!
GO FLEE! HURRY!!
JEAN-...?
NICHOLAS ...?!

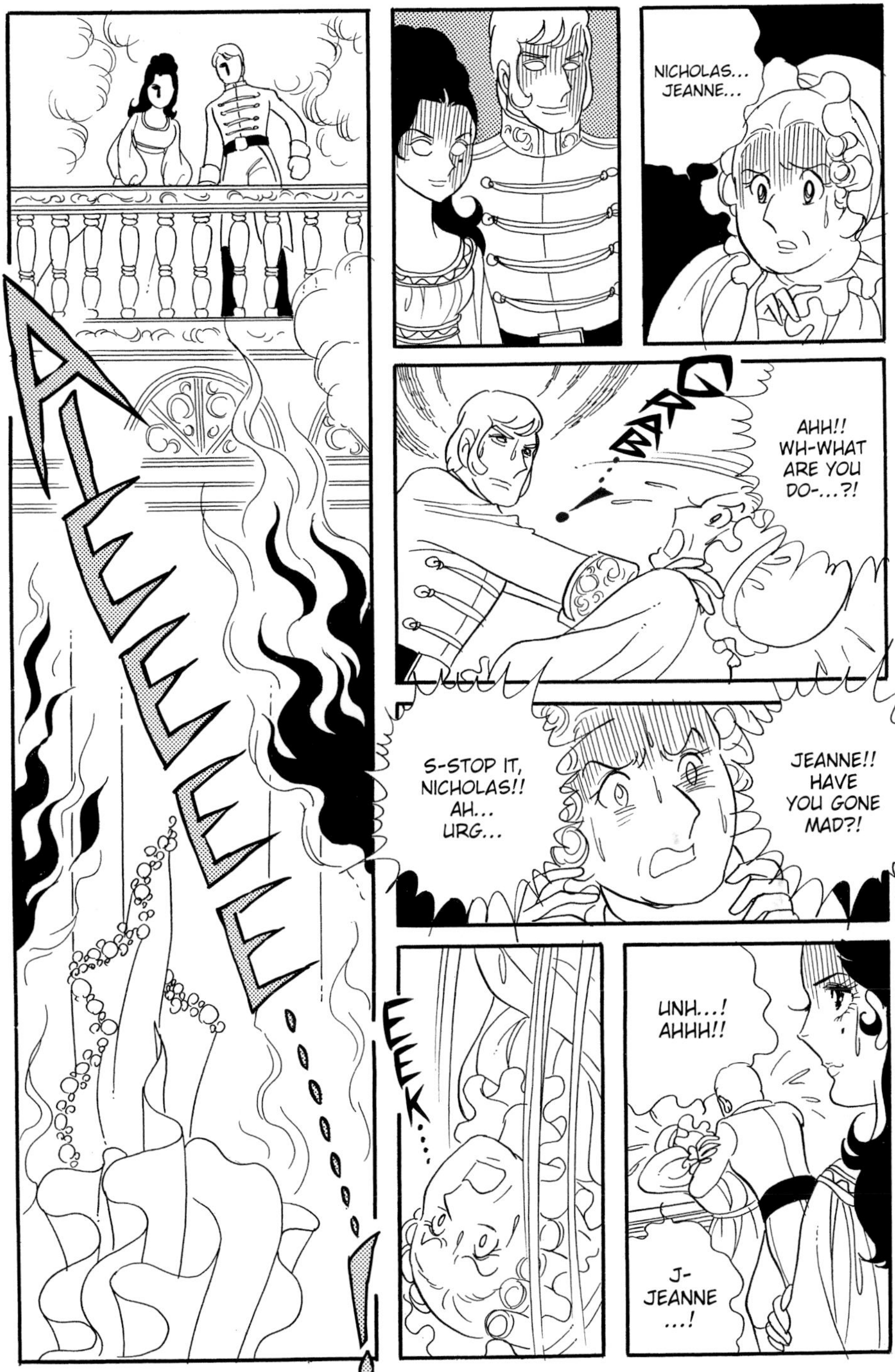
NICHOLAS... JEANNE...
GRAB...!
AHH!! WH-WHAT ARE YOU DO-...?!
JEANNE!! HAVE YOU GONE MAD?!
S-STOP IT, NICHOLAS!! AH... URG...
UNH...! AHHH!!
J-JEANNE...!
EEEK...
AIEEEEEE..........!!

1972 MARGARET COMICS
VOLUME 1 INSERT ART

♥宮廷への野心にもえるジャンヌのたくらみのために、ブーレンビリエ候夫人は!?

池田理代子

バルサイユのばら

♥THANKS TO THE INTRIGUE OF JEANNE, WHO BURNS WITH AMBITION
TO JOIN THE COURT, WHAT OF THE MARQUISE DE BOULAINVILLIERS!?

EPISODE 14

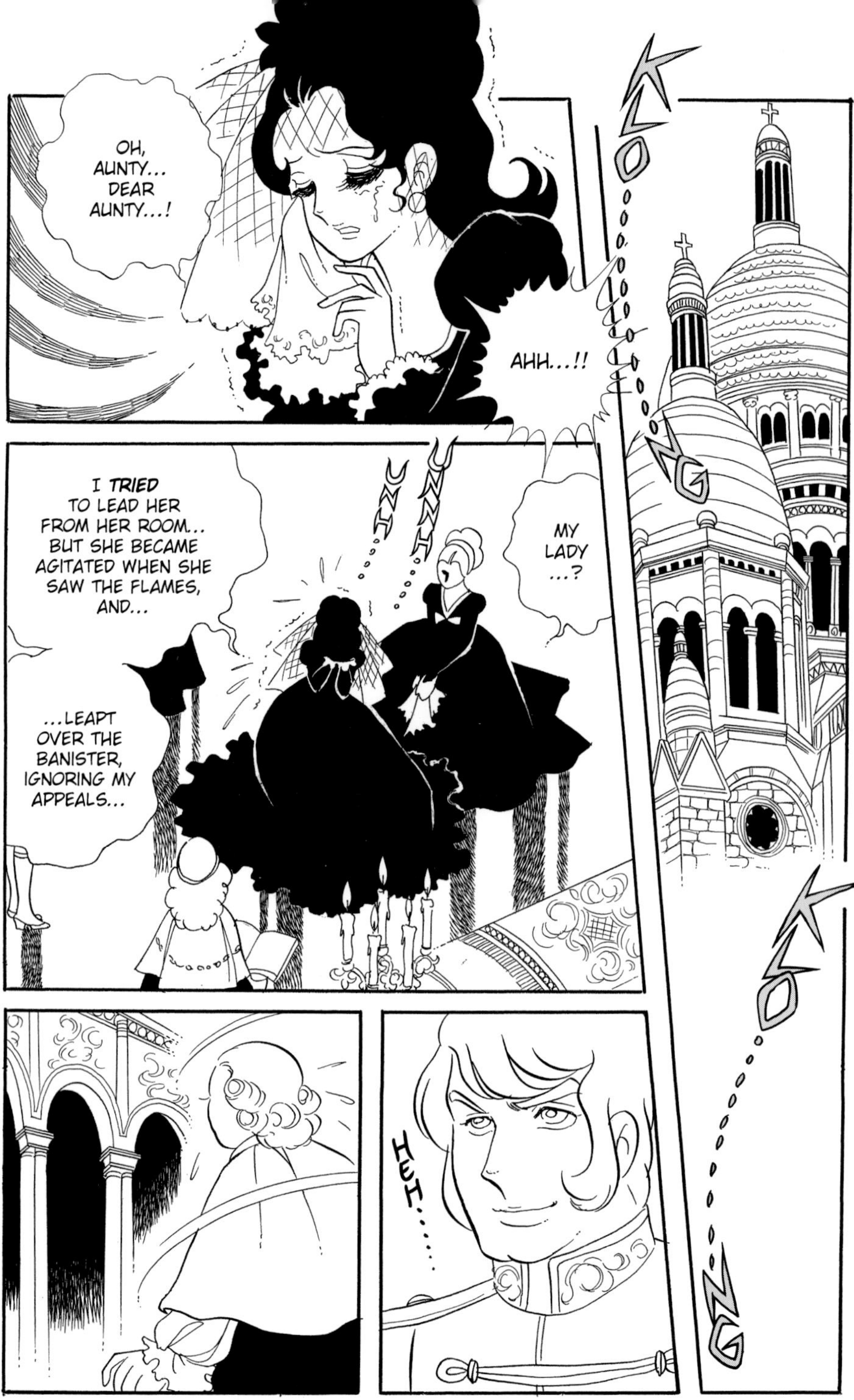
KLOOOOOOOONG
KLOOOOOOOOONG
OH, AUNTY... DEAR AUNTY...!
AHH...!!
MY LADY ...?
UNNH
UNNH
I TRIED TO LEAD HER FROM HER ROOM... BUT SHE BECAME AGITATED WHEN SHE SAW THE FLAMES, AND...
...LEAPT OVER THE BANISTER, IGNORING MY APPEALS...
HEH.....

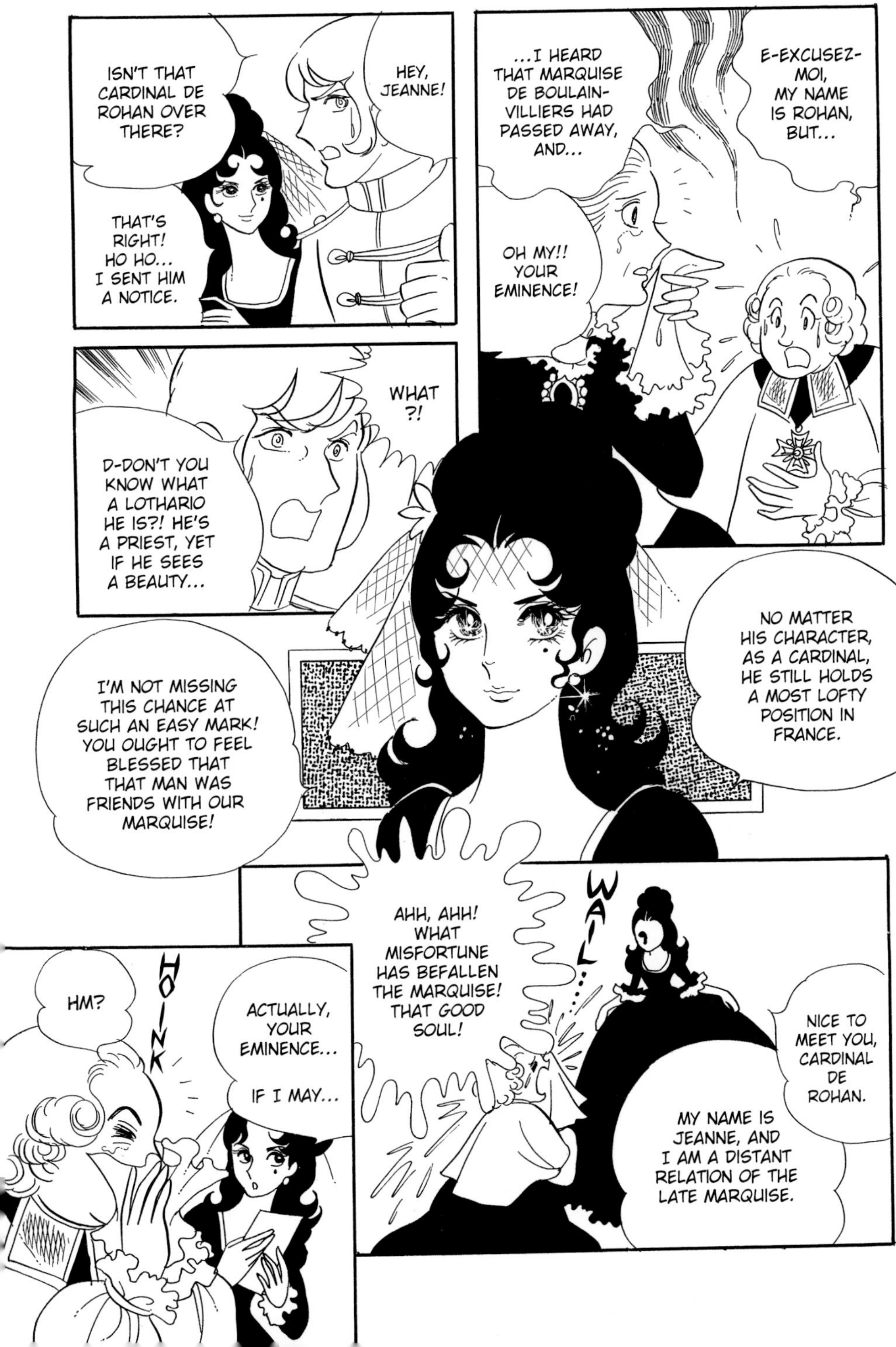
E-EXCUSEZ-MOI, MY NAME IS ROHAN, BUT...
...I HEARD THAT MARQUISE DE BOULAIN-VILLIERS HAD PASSED AWAY, AND...
OH MY!! YOUR EMINENCE!
HEY, JEANNE!
ISN'T THAT CARDINAL DE ROHAN OVER THERE?
THAT'S RIGHT! HO HO... I SENT HIM A NOTICE.
WHAT ?!
D-DON'T YOU KNOW WHAT A LOTHARIO HE IS?! HE'S A PRIEST, YET IF HE SEES A BEAUTY...
NO MATTER HIS CHARACTER, AS A CARDINAL, HE STILL HOLDS A MOST LOFTY POSITION IN FRANCE.
I'M NOT MISSING THIS CHANCE AT SUCH AN EASY MARK! YOU OUGHT TO FEEL BLESSED THAT THAT MAN WAS FRIENDS WITH OUR MARQUISE!
NICE TO MEET YOU, CARDINAL DE ROHAN.
MY NAME IS JEANNE, AND I AM A DISTANT RELATION OF THE LATE MARQUISE.
WAIL...
AHH, AHH! WHAT MISFORTUNE HAS BEFALLEN THE MARQUISE! THAT GOOD SOUL!
ACTUALLY, YOUR EMINENCE...
IF I MAY...
HOINK
HM?

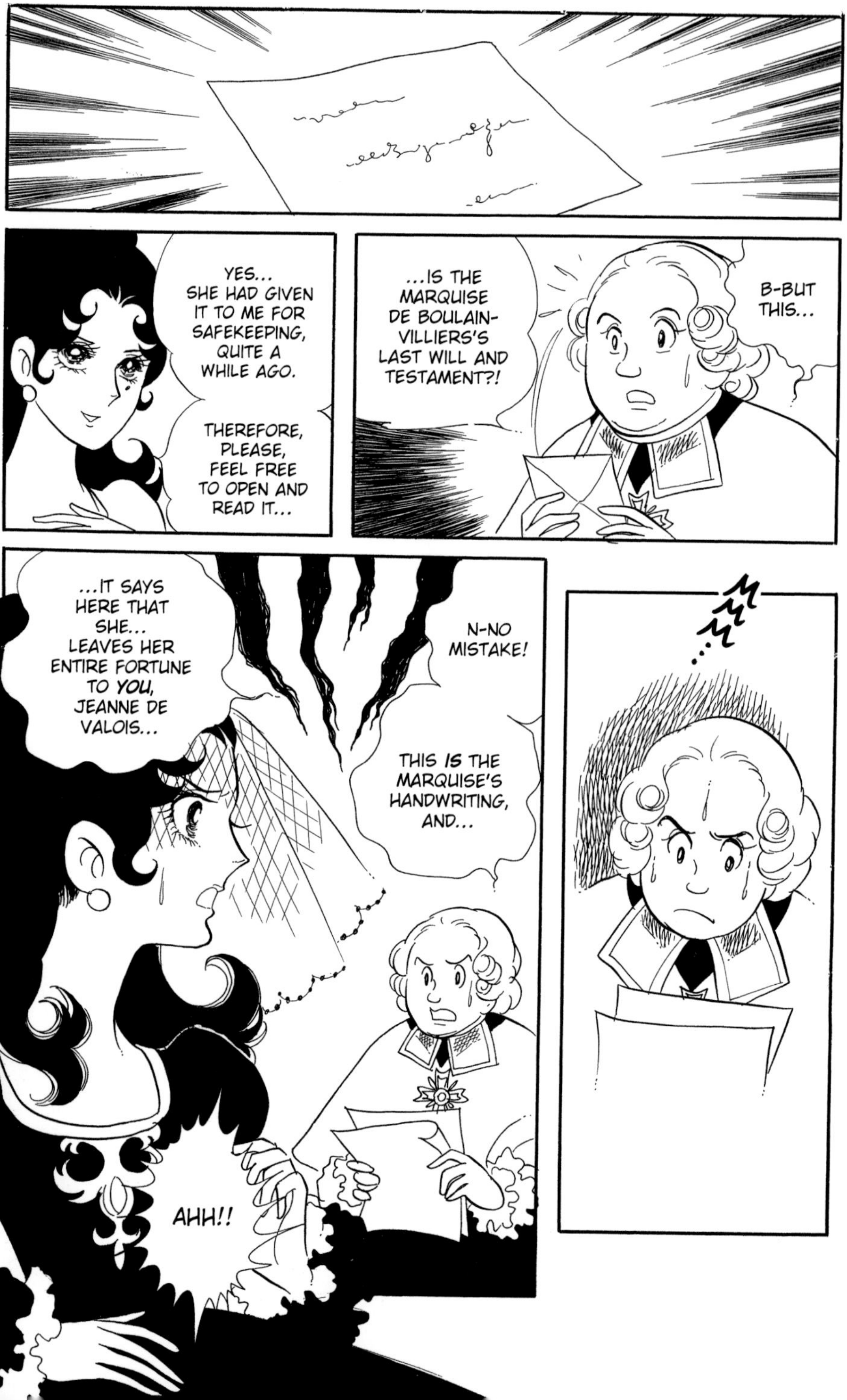
B-BUT THIS...
...IS THE MARQUISE DE BOULAIN-VILLIERS'S LAST WILL AND TESTAMENT?!
YES... SHE HAD GIVEN IT TO ME FOR SAFEKEEPING, QUITE A WHILE AGO.
THEREFORE, PLEASE, FEEL FREE TO OPEN AND READ IT...
MMM...
N-NO MISTAKE!
THIS *IS* THE MARQUISE'S HANDWRITING, AND...
...IT SAYS HERE THAT SHE... LEAVES HER ENTIRE FORTUNE TO *YOU*, JEANNE DE VALOIS...
AHH!!

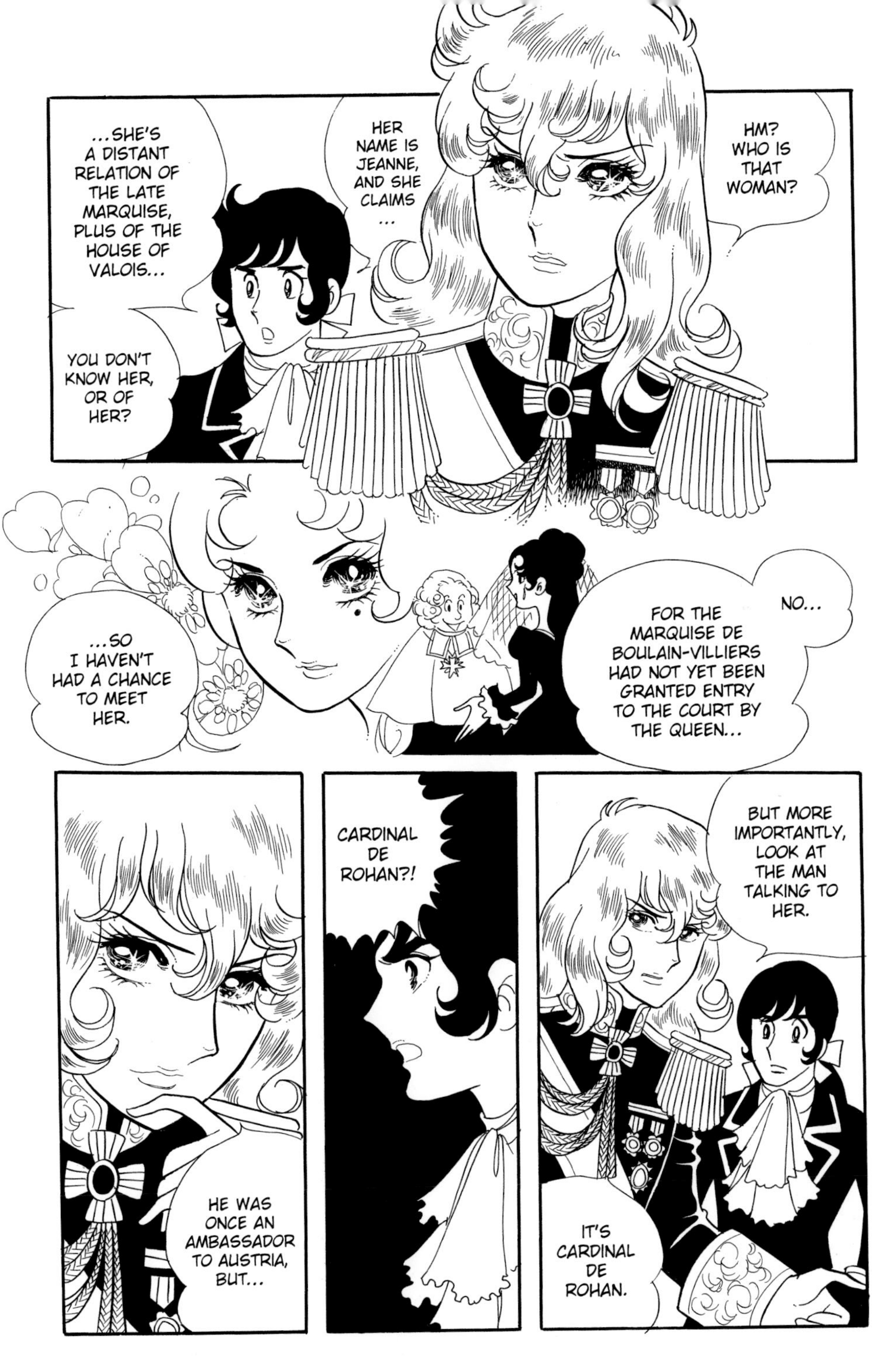
HM? WHO IS THAT WOMAN?
HER NAME IS JEANNE, AND SHE CLAIMS ...
...SHE'S A DISTANT RELATION OF THE LATE MARQUISE, PLUS OF THE HOUSE OF VALOIS...
YOU DON'T KNOW HER, OR OF HER?
NO... FOR THE MARQUISE DE BOULAIN-VILLIERS HAD NOT YET BEEN GRANTED ENTRY TO THE COURT BY THE QUEEN...
...SO I HAVEN'T HAD A CHANCE TO MEET HER.
BUT MORE IMPORTANTLY, LOOK AT THE MAN TALKING TO HER.
IT'S CARDINAL DE ROHAN.
CARDINAL DE ROHAN?!
HE WAS ONCE AN AMBASSADOR TO AUSTRIA, BUT...

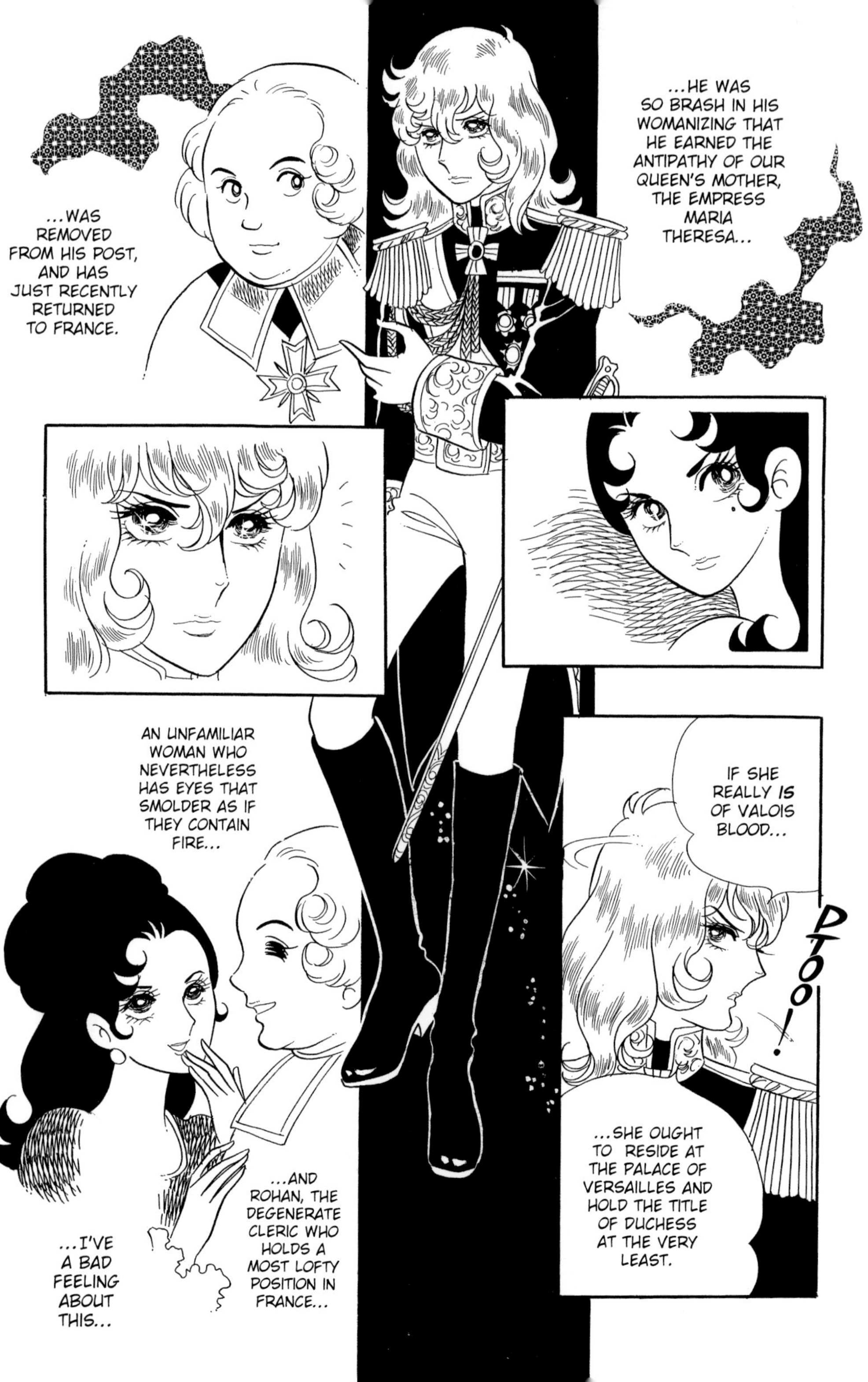
...HE WAS SO BRASH IN HIS WOMANIZING THAT HE EARNED THE ANTIPATHY OF OUR QUEEN'S MOTHER, THE EMPRESS MARIA THERESA...
...WAS REMOVED FROM HIS POST, AND HAS JUST RECENTLY RETURNED TO FRANCE.
IF SHE REALLY **IS** OF VALOIS BLOOD...
DTOO!
...SHE OUGHT TO RESIDE AT THE PALACE OF VERSAILLES AND HOLD THE TITLE OF DUCHESS AT THE VERY LEAST.
AN UNFAMILIAR WOMAN WHO NEVERTHELESS HAS EYES THAT SMOLDER AS IF THEY CONTAIN FIRE...
...AND ROHAN, THE DEGENERATE CLERIC WHO HOLDS A MOST LOFTY POSITION IN FRANCE...
...I'VE A BAD FEELING ABOUT THIS...

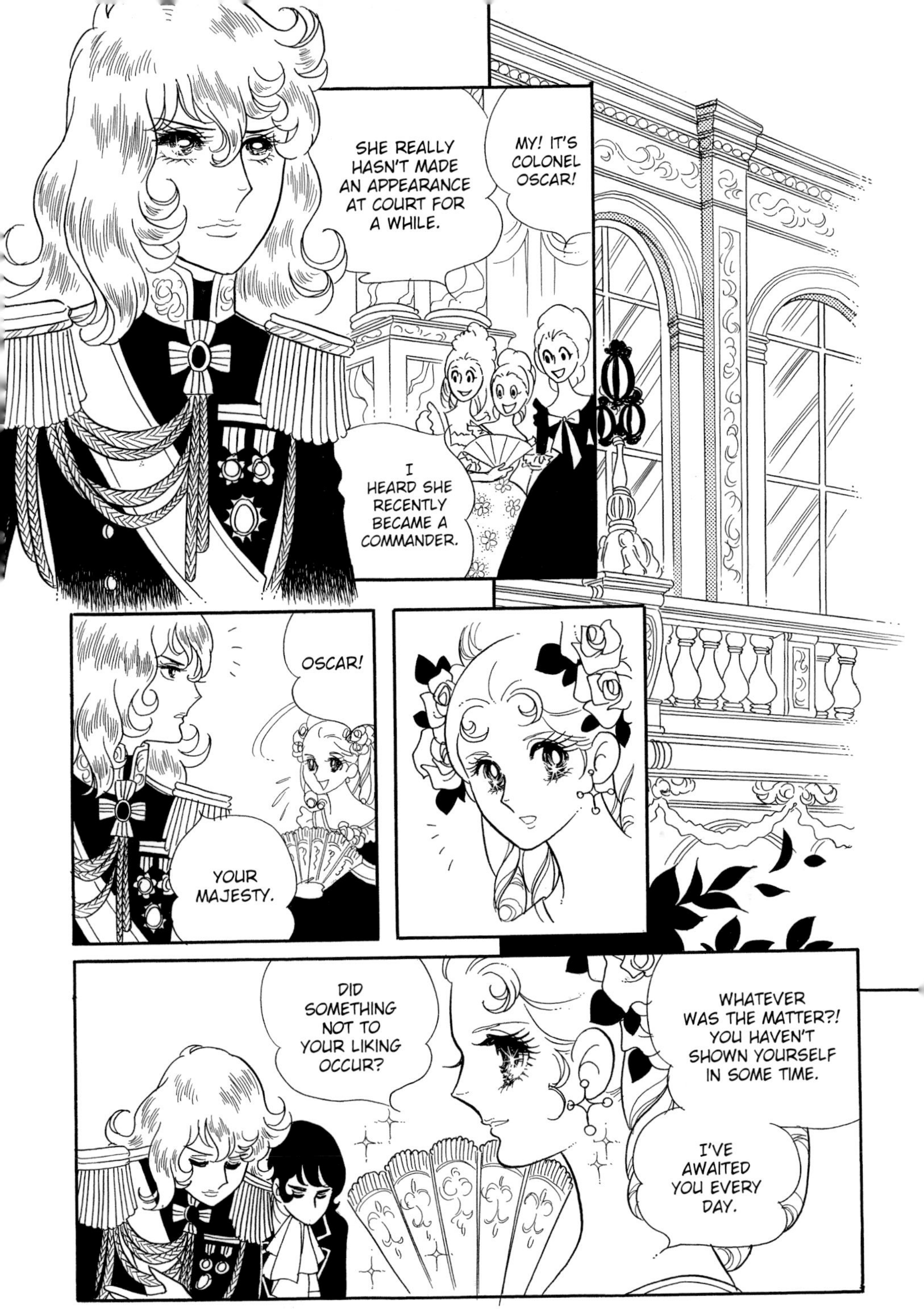
MY! IT'S COLONEL OSCAR!
SHE REALLY HASN'T MADE AN APPEARANCE AT COURT FOR A WHILE.
I HEARD SHE RECENTLY BECAME A COMMANDER.
OSCAR!
YOUR MAJESTY.
WHATEVER WAS THE MATTER?! YOU HAVEN'T SHOWN YOURSELF IN SOME TIME.
DID SOMETHING NOT TO YOUR LIKING OCCUR?
I'VE AWAITED YOU EVERY DAY.

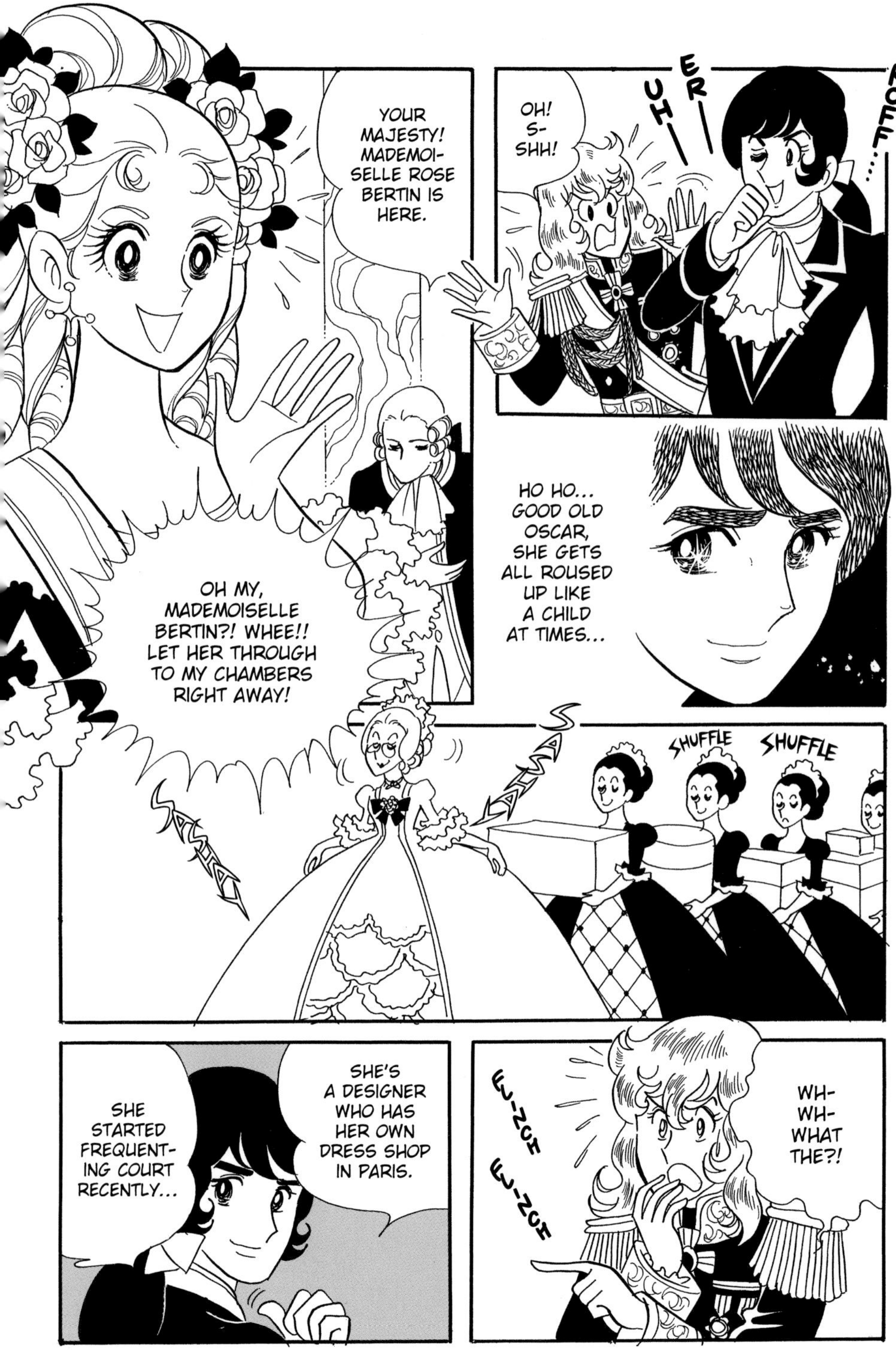
OH! S-SHH!
UH ER
KOFF...
HO HO... GOOD OLD OSCAR, SHE GETS ALL ROUSED UP LIKE A CHILD AT TIMES...
YOUR MAJESTY! MADEMOISELLE ROSE BERTIN IS HERE.
OH MY, MADEMOISELLE BERTIN?! WHEE!! LET HER THROUGH TO MY CHAMBERS RIGHT AWAY!
SHUFFLE
SHUFFLE
SASHAY
WH-WH-WHAT THE?!
EW-ZCH
EW-ZCH
SHE'S A DESIGNER WHO HAS HER OWN DRESS SHOP IN PARIS.
SHE STARTED FREQUENT-ING COURT RECENTLY...

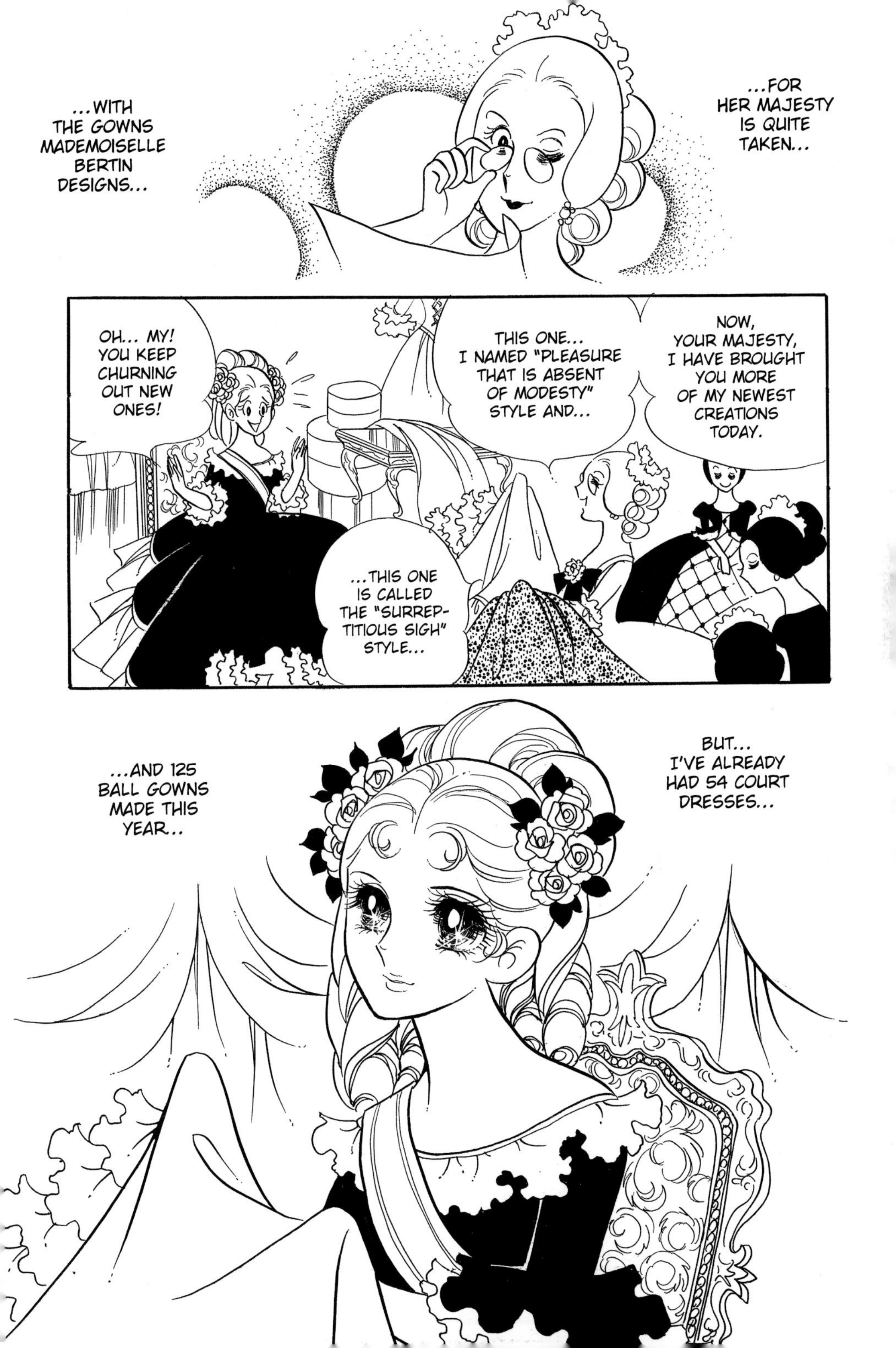
...FOR HER MAJESTY IS QUITE TAKEN...
...WITH THE GOWNS MADEMOISELLE BERTIN DESIGNS...
NOW, YOUR MAJESTY, I HAVE BROUGHT YOU MORE OF MY NEWEST CREATIONS TODAY.
THIS ONE... I NAMED "PLEASURE THAT IS ABSENT OF MODESTY" STYLE AND...
...THIS ONE IS CALLED THE "SURREP-TITIOUS SIGH" STYLE...
OH... MY! YOU KEEP CHURNING OUT NEW ONES!
BUT... I'VE ALREADY HAD 54 COURT DRESSES...
...AND 125 BALL GOWNS MADE THIS YEAR...

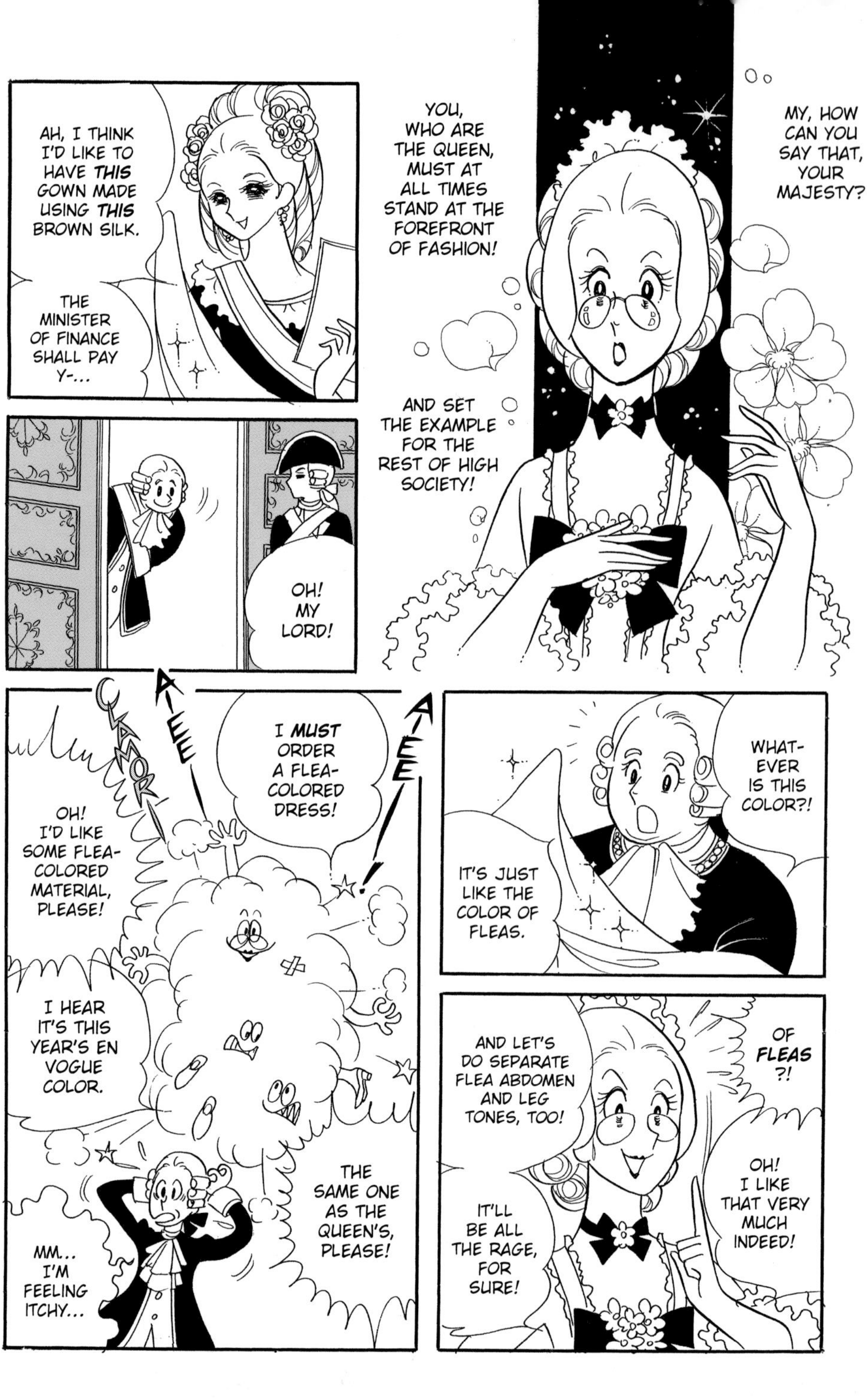
MY, HOW CAN YOU SAY THAT, YOUR MAJESTY?
YOU, WHO ARE THE QUEEN, MUST AT ALL TIMES STAND AT THE FOREFRONT OF FASHION!
AND SET THE EXAMPLE FOR THE REST OF HIGH SOCIETY!
AH, I THINK I'D LIKE TO HAVE **THIS** GOWN MADE USING **THIS** BROWN SILK.
THE MINISTER OF FINANCE SHALL PAY Y-...
OH! MY LORD!
WHAT-EVER IS THIS COLOR?!
IT'S JUST LIKE THE COLOR OF FLEAS.
OF **FLEAS**?!
AND LET'S DO SEPARATE FLEA ABDOMEN AND LEG TONES, TOO!
OH! I LIKE THAT VERY MUCH INDEED!
IT'LL BE ALL THE RAGE, FOR SURE!
AIEE!
I **MUST** ORDER A FLEA-COLORED DRESS!
AIEE!
CLAMOR
OH! I'D LIKE SOME FLEA-COLORED MATERIAL, PLEASE!
THE SAME ONE AS THE QUEEN'S, PLEASE!
I HEAR IT'S THIS YEAR'S EN VOGUE COLOR.
MM... I'M FEELING ITCHY...

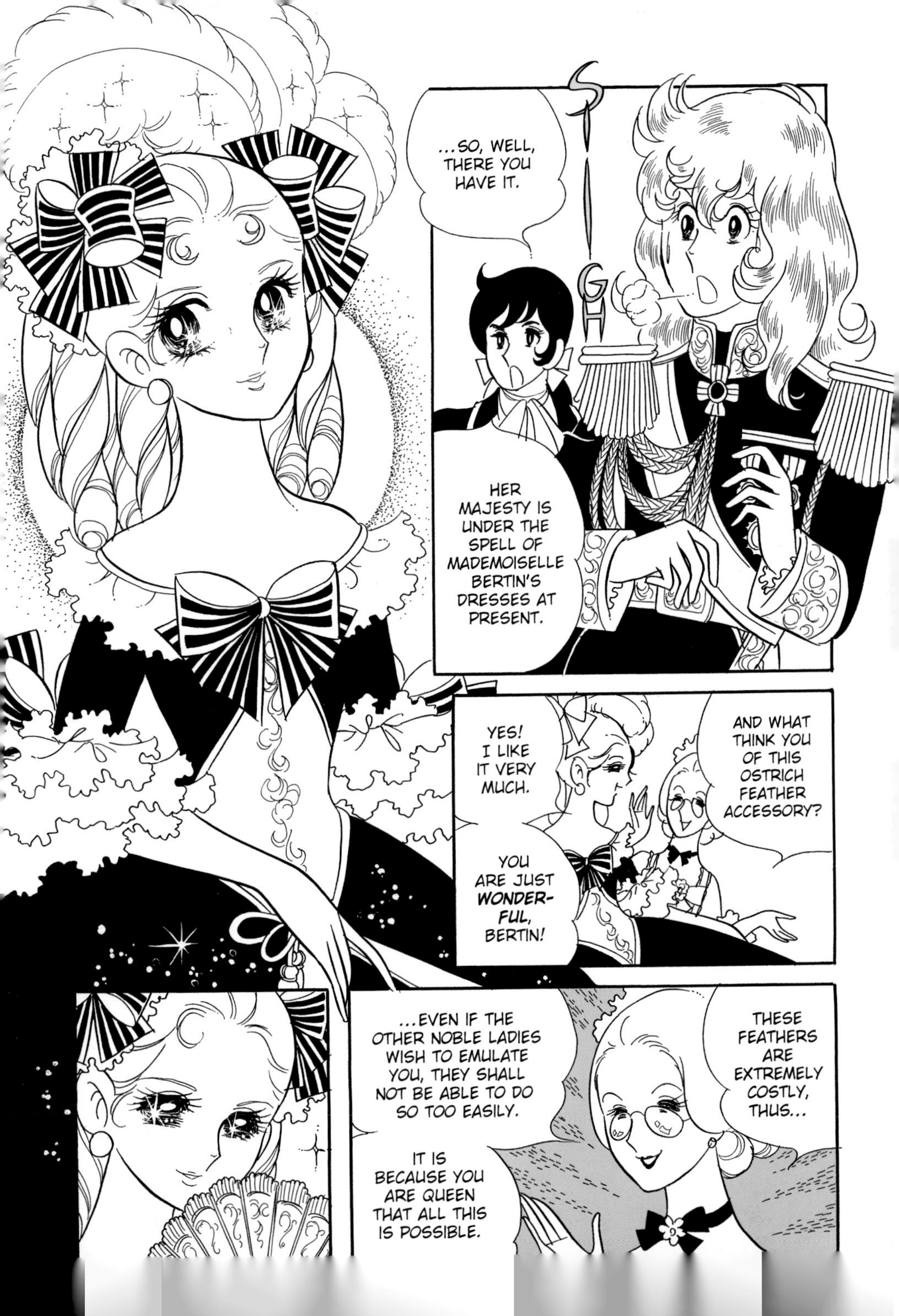
SIGH
...SO, WELL, THERE YOU HAVE IT.
HER MAJESTY IS UNDER THE SPELL OF MADEMOISELLE BERTIN'S DRESSES AT PRESENT.
AND WHAT THINK YOU OF THIS OSTRICH FEATHER ACCESSORY?
YES! I LIKE IT VERY MUCH.
YOU ARE JUST *WONDERFUL*, BERTIN!
THESE FEATHERS ARE EXTREMELY COSTLY, THUS...
...EVEN IF THE OTHER NOBLE LADIES WISH TO EMULATE YOU, THEY SHALL NOT BE ABLE TO DO SO TOO EASILY.
IT IS BECAUSE YOU ARE QUEEN THAT ALL THIS IS POSSIBLE.

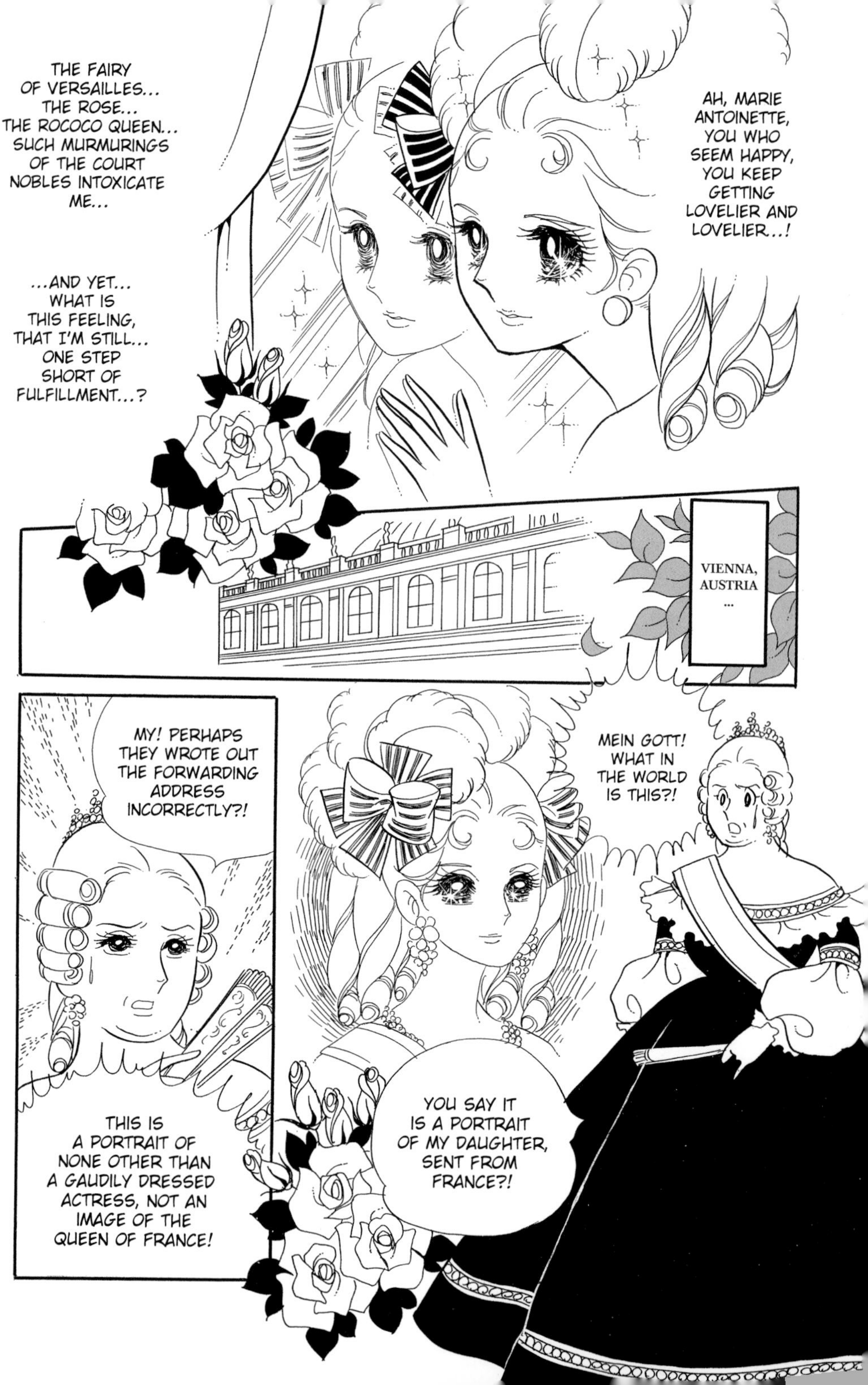
AH, MARIE ANTOINETTE, YOU WHO SEEM HAPPY, YOU KEEP GETTING LOVELIER AND LOVELIER...!
THE FAIRY OF VERSAILLES... THE ROSE... THE ROCOCO QUEEN... SUCH MURMURINGS OF THE COURT NOBLES INTOXICATE ME...
...AND YET... WHAT IS THIS FEELING, THAT I'M STILL... ONE STEP SHORT OF FULFILLMENT...?
VIENNA, AUSTRIA ...
MEIN GOTT! WHAT IN THE WORLD IS THIS?!
YOU SAY IT IS A PORTRAIT OF MY DAUGHTER, SENT FROM FRANCE?!
MY! PERHAPS THEY WROTE OUT THE FORWARDING ADDRESS INCORRECTLY?!
THIS IS A PORTRAIT OF NONE OTHER THAN A GAUDILY DRESSED ACTRESS, NOT AN IMAGE OF THE QUEEN OF FRANCE!

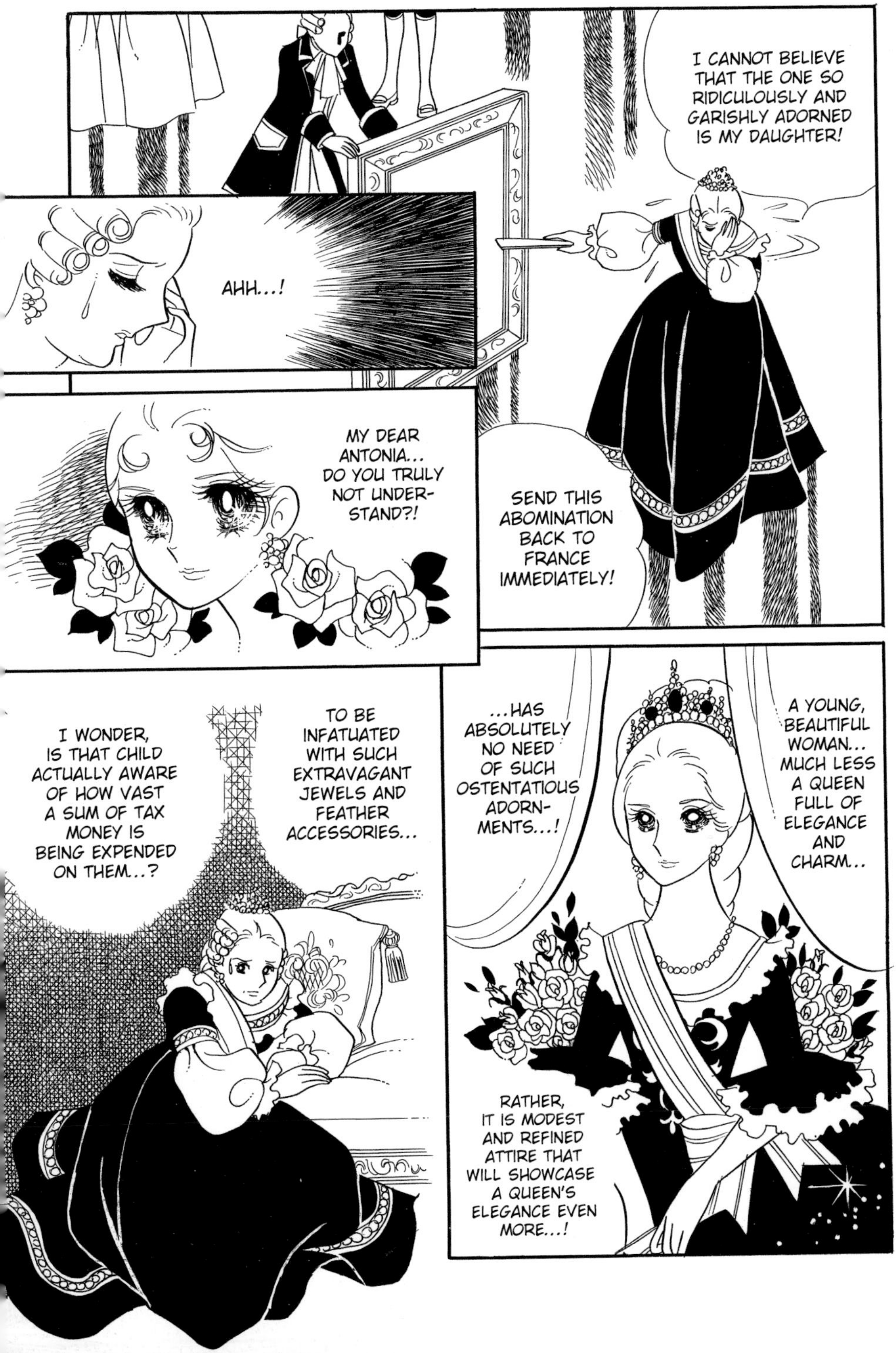
I CANNOT BELIEVE THAT THE ONE SO RIDICULOUSLY AND GARISHLY ADORNED IS MY DAUGHTER!
SEND THIS ABOMINATION BACK TO FRANCE IMMEDIATELY!
AHH...!
MY DEAR ANTONIA... DO YOU TRULY NOT UNDER-STAND?!
A YOUNG, BEAUTIFUL WOMAN... MUCH LESS A QUEEN FULL OF ELEGANCE AND CHARM...
...HAS ABSOLUTELY NO NEED OF SUCH OSTENTATIOUS ADORN-MENTS...!
RATHER, IT IS MODEST AND REFINED ATTIRE THAT WILL SHOWCASE A QUEEN'S ELEGANCE EVEN MORE...!
TO BE INFATUATED WITH SUCH EXTRAVAGANT JEWELS AND FEATHER ACCESSORIES...
I WONDER, IS THAT CHILD ACTUALLY AWARE OF HOW VAST A SUM OF TAX MONEY IS BEING EXPENDED ON THEM...?

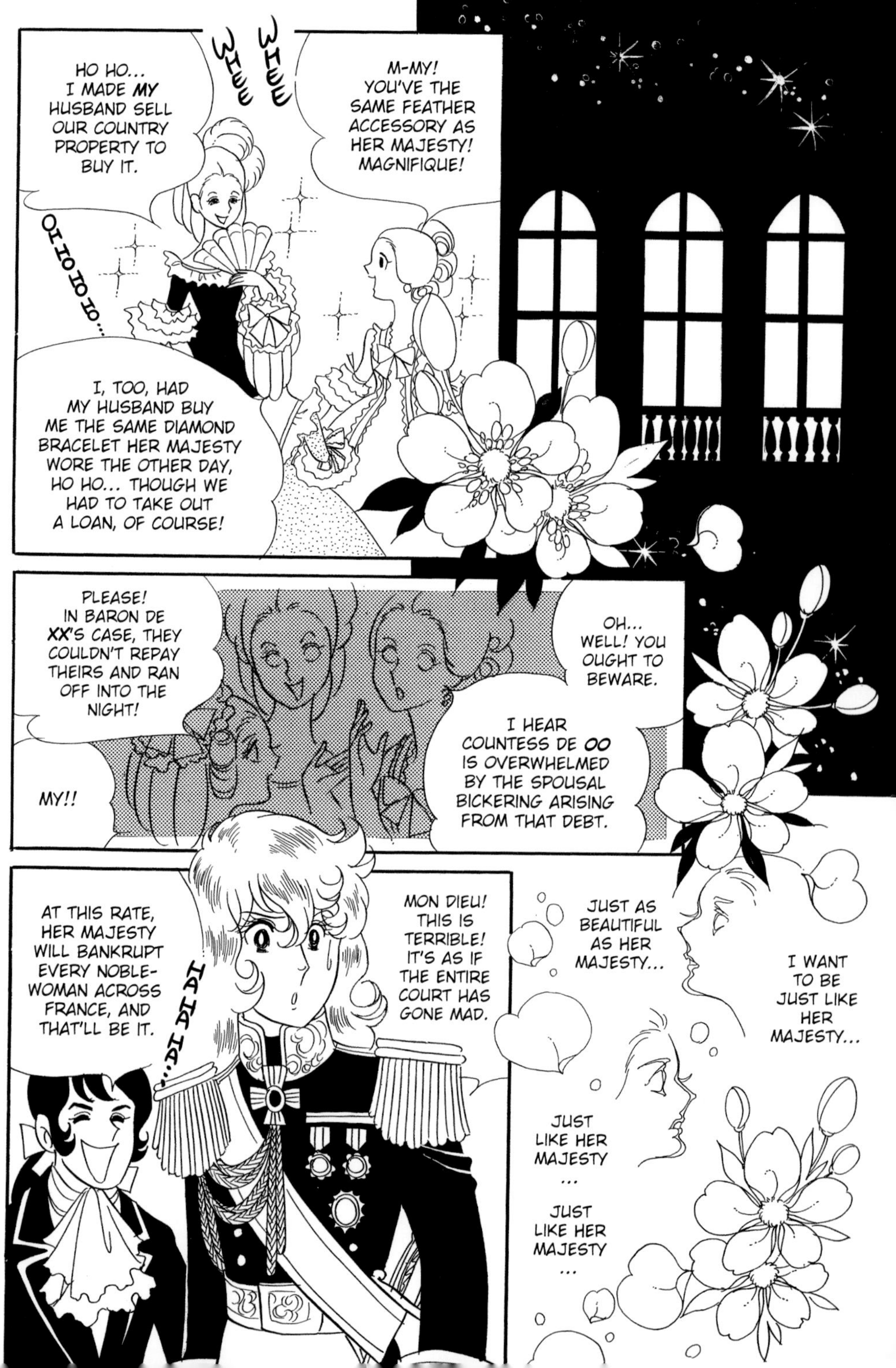
M-MY! YOU'VE THE SAME FEATHER ACCESSORY AS HER MAJESTY! MAGNIFIQUE!
WHEE WHEE
HO HO... I MADE MY HUSBAND SELL OUR COUNTRY PROPERTY TO BUY IT.
OH HO HO HO...
I, TOO, HAD MY HUSBAND BUY ME THE SAME DIAMOND BRACELET HER MAJESTY WORE THE OTHER DAY, HO HO... THOUGH WE HAD TO TAKE OUT A LOAN, OF COURSE!
OH... WELL! YOU OUGHT TO BEWARE.
I HEAR COUNTESS DE OO IS OVERWHELMED BY THE SPOUSAL BICKERING ARISING FROM THAT DEBT.
PLEASE! IN BARON DE XX'S CASE, THEY COULDN'T REPAY THEIRS AND RAN OFF INTO THE NIGHT!
MY!!
JUST AS BEAUTIFUL AS HER MAJESTY...
I WANT TO BE JUST LIKE HER MAJESTY...
JUST LIKE HER MAJESTY ...
JUST LIKE HER MAJESTY ...
MON DIEU! THIS IS TERRIBLE! IT'S AS IF THE ENTIRE COURT HAS GONE MAD.
HA HA HA...
AT THIS RATE, HER MAJESTY WILL BANKRUPT EVERY NOBLE-WOMAN ACROSS FRANCE, AND THAT'LL BE IT.

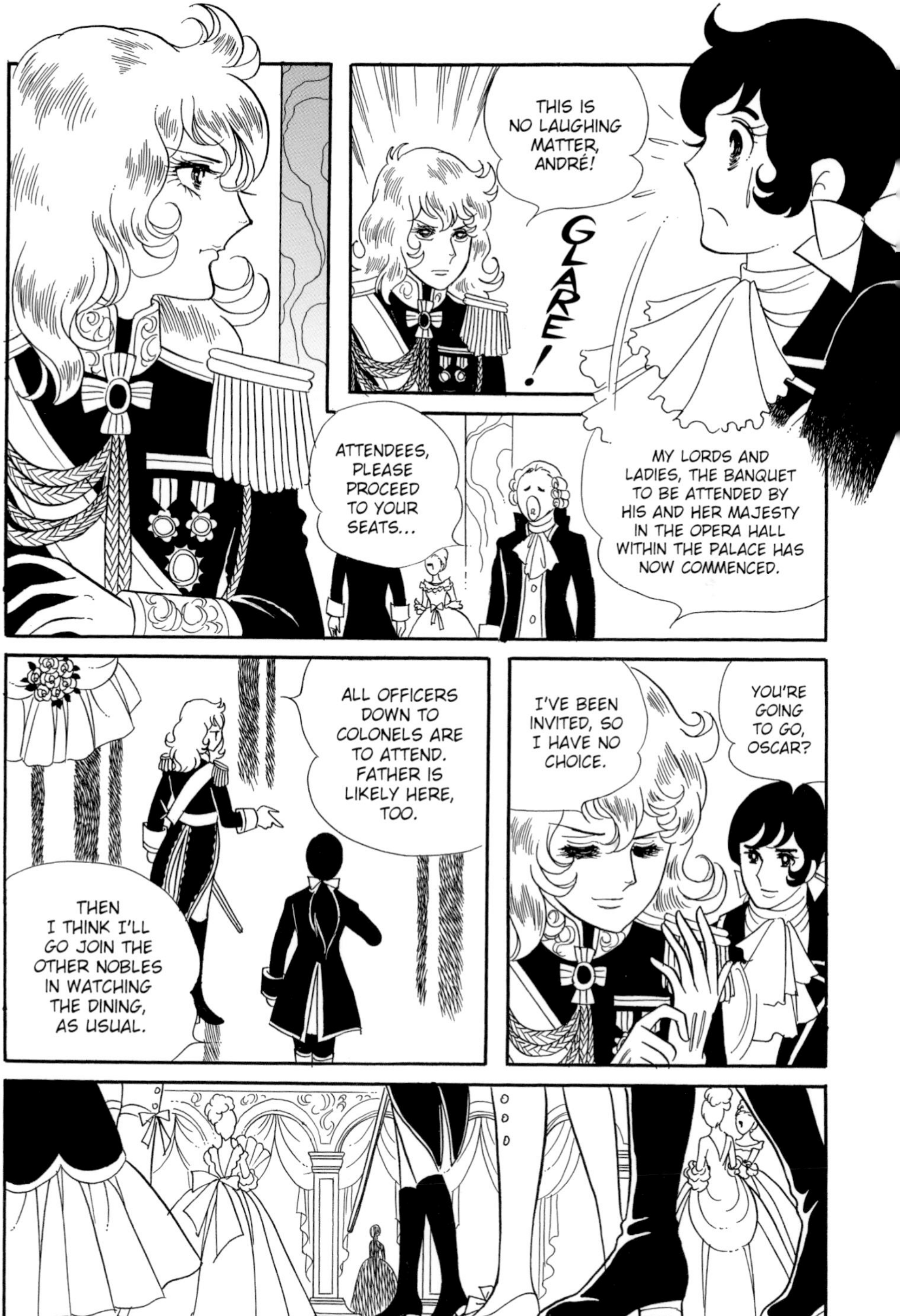
THIS IS NO LAUGHING MATTER, ANDRÉ!
GLARE!
MY LORDS AND LADIES, THE BANQUET TO BE ATTENDED BY HIS AND HER MAJESTY IN THE OPERA HALL WITHIN THE PALACE HAS NOW COMMENCED.
ATTENDEES, PLEASE PROCEED TO YOUR SEATS...
YOU'RE GOING TO GO, OSCAR?
I'VE BEEN INVITED, SO I HAVE NO CHOICE.
ALL OFFICERS DOWN TO COLONELS ARE TO ATTEND. FATHER IS LIKELY HERE, TOO.
THEN I THINK I'LL GO JOIN THE OTHER NOBLES IN WATCHING THE DINING, AS USUAL.

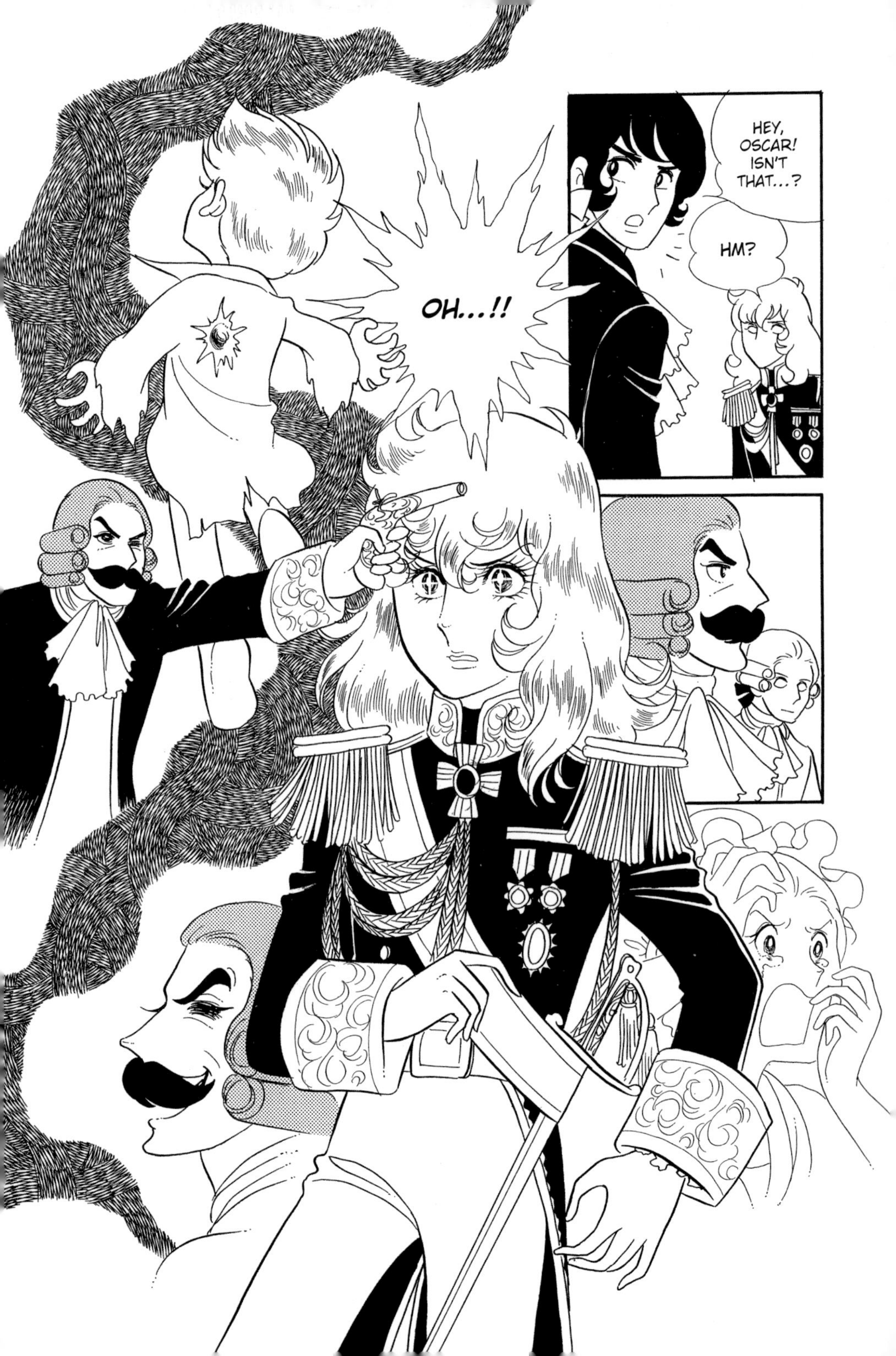
HEY, OSCAR! ISN'T THAT...?
HM?
OH...!!

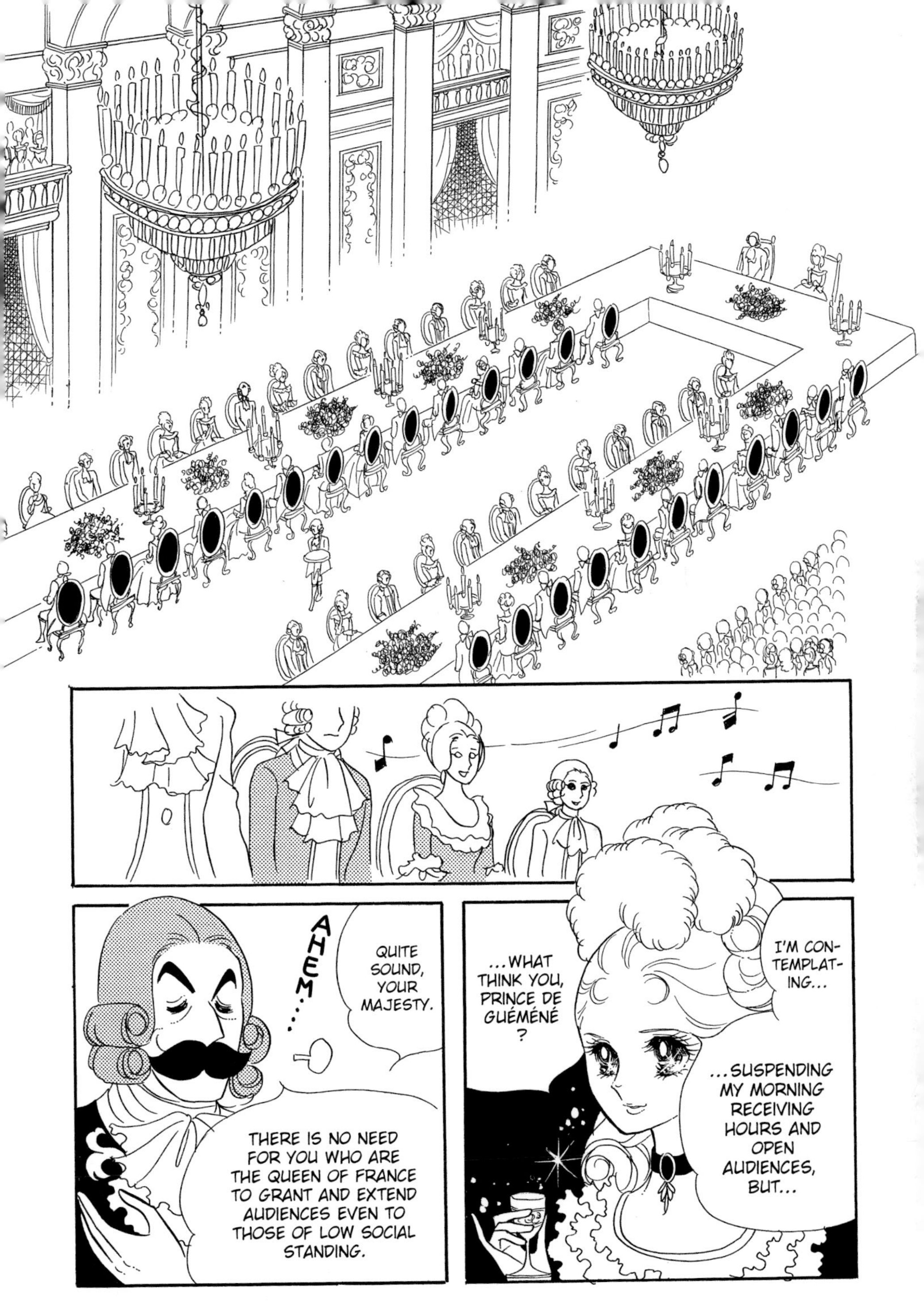
I'M CON-TEMPLAT-ING...
...SUSPENDING MY MORNING RECEIVING HOURS AND OPEN AUDIENCES, BUT...
...WHAT THINK YOU, PRINCE DE GUÉMÉNÉ?
QUITE SOUND, YOUR MAJESTY.
AHEM...
THERE IS NO NEED FOR YOU WHO ARE THE QUEEN OF FRANCE TO GRANT AND EXTEND AUDIENCES EVEN TO THOSE OF LOW SOCIAL STANDING.

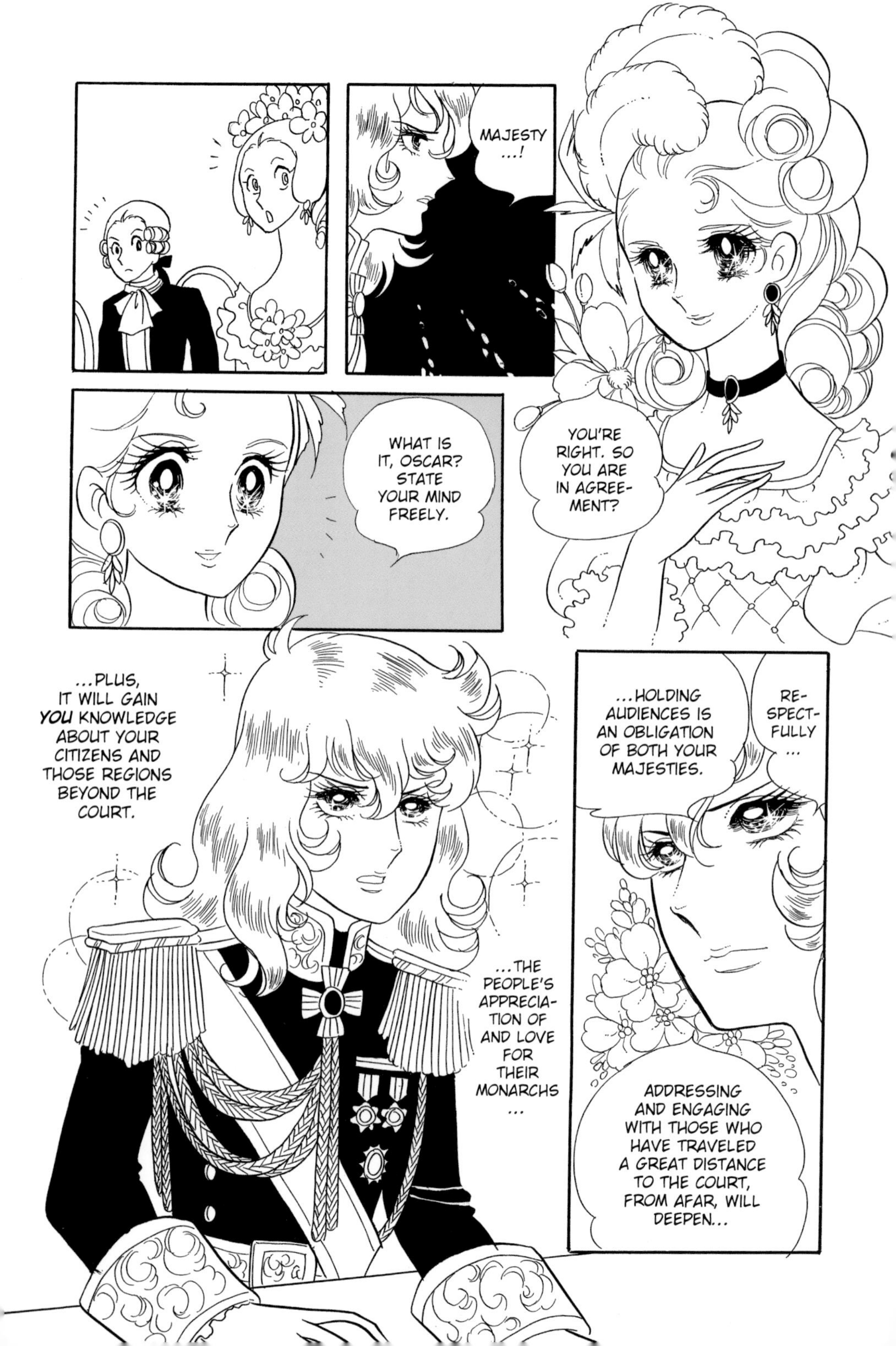
YOU'RE RIGHT. SO YOU ARE IN AGREEMENT?
MAJESTY ...!
WHAT IS IT, OSCAR? STATE YOUR MIND FREELY.
RESPECTFULLY ...
...HOLDING AUDIENCES IS AN OBLIGATION OF BOTH YOUR MAJESTIES.
ADDRESSING AND ENGAGING WITH THOSE WHO HAVE TRAVELED A GREAT DISTANCE TO THE COURT, FROM AFAR, WILL DEEPEN...
...THE PEOPLE'S APPRECIATION OF AND LOVE FOR THEIR MONARCHS ...
...PLUS, IT WILL GAIN **YOU** KNOWLEDGE ABOUT YOUR CITIZENS AND THOSE REGIONS BEYOND THE COURT.

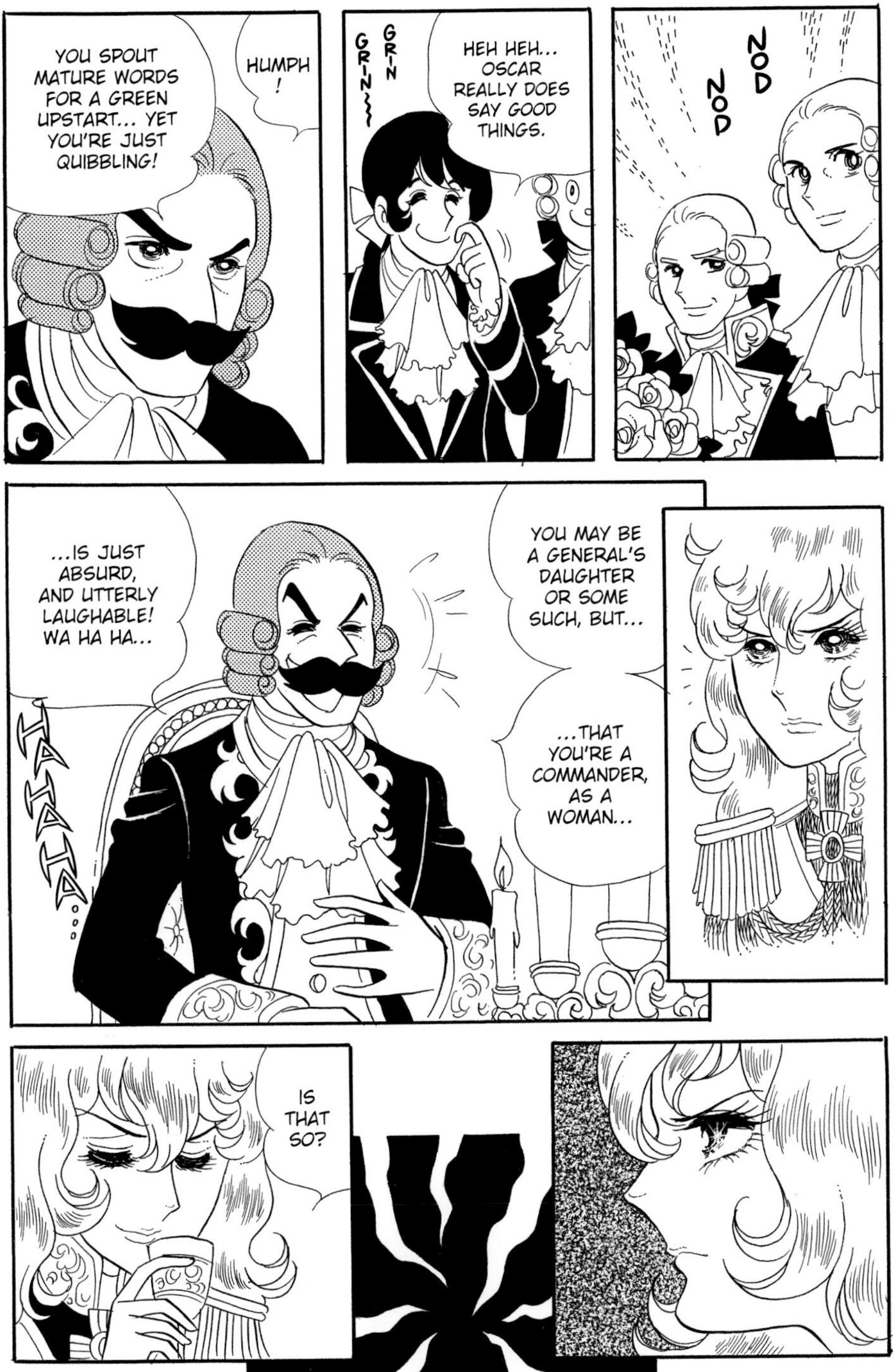
NOD
NOD
GRIN GRIN
HEH HEH... OSCAR REALLY DOES SAY GOOD THINGS.
HUMPH!
YOU SPOUT MATURE WORDS FOR A GREEN UPSTART... YET YOU'RE JUST QUIBBLING!
YOU MAY BE A GENERAL'S DAUGHTER OR SOME SUCH, BUT...
...THAT YOU'RE A COMMANDER, AS A WOMAN...
...IS JUST ABSURD, AND UTTERLY LAUGHABLE! WA HA HA...
HAHAHA...
IS THAT SO?

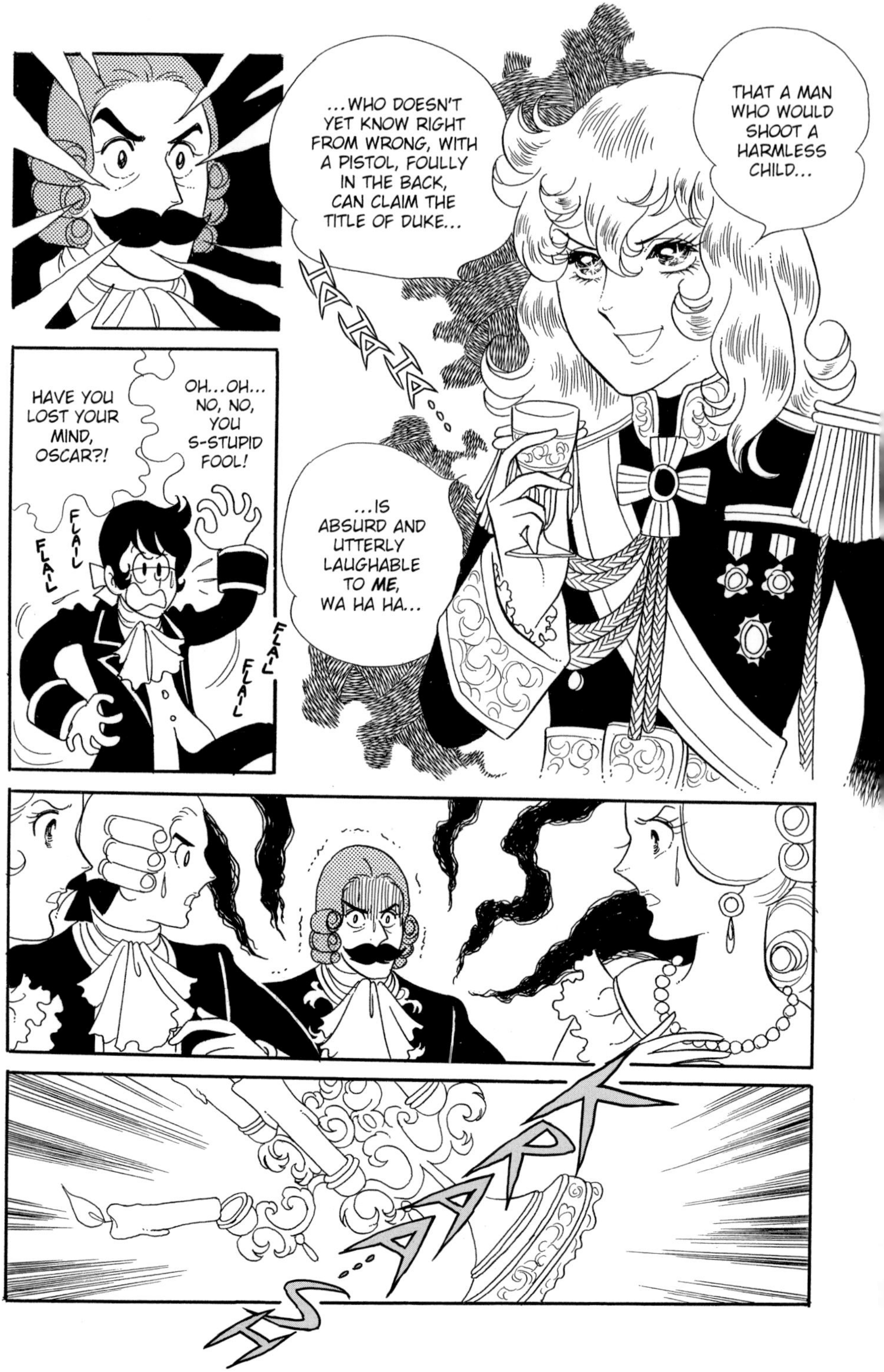
THAT A MAN WHO WOULD SHOOT A HARMLESS CHILD...
...WHO DOESN'T YET KNOW RIGHT FROM WRONG, WITH A PISTOL, FOULLY IN THE BACK, CAN CLAIM THE TITLE OF DUKE...
HA HA HA HA...
...IS ABSURD AND UTTERLY LAUGHABLE TO ME, WA HA HA...
OH...OH... NO, NO, YOU S-STUPID FOOL!
HAVE YOU LOST YOUR MIND, OSCAR?!
FLAIL FLAIL
FLAIL FLAIL
HS...AAARK

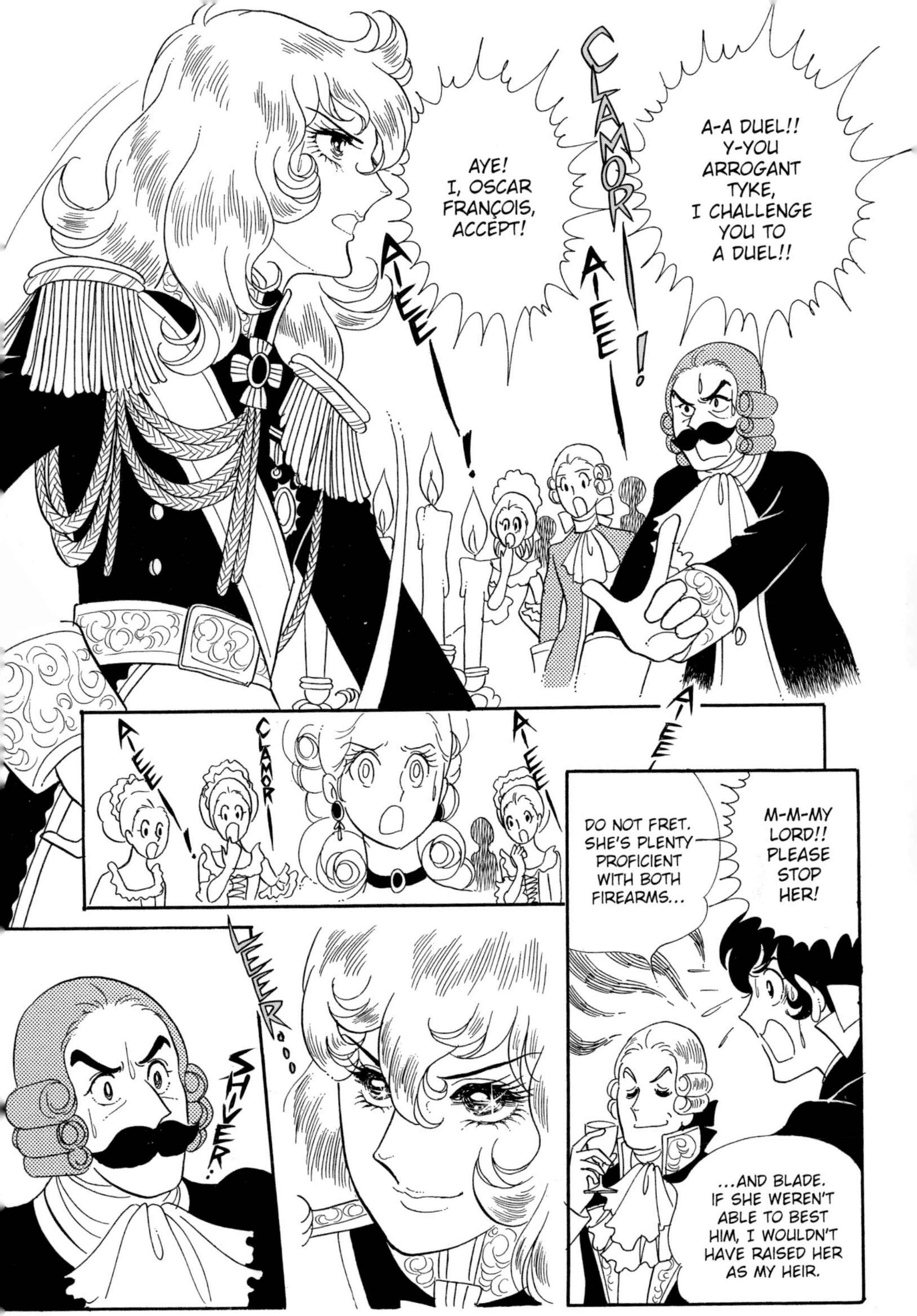
A-A DUEL!! Y-YOU ARROGANT TYKE, I CHALLENGE YOU TO A DUEL!!
CLAMOR!
AIEE--
AYE! I, OSCAR FRANÇOIS, ACCEPT!
AIEE--!
M-M-MY LORD!! PLEASE STOP HER!
DO NOT FRET. SHE'S PLENTY PROFICIENT WITH BOTH FIREARMS...
...AND BLADE. IF SHE WEREN'T ABLE TO BEST HIM, I WOULDN'T HAVE RAISED HER AS MY HEIR.
AIEE
AIEE
CLAMOR
AIEE--!
LEER...
SHIVER...

1972 WEEKLY MARGARET MAGAZINE
ISSUE 27 PREVIEW ART

♥国王夫妻のみまもる中で
オスカルが、決闘を……!!

池田理代子

バルサイユのばら

♥ OSCAR IS CHALLENGED TO A DUEL WHILE THE KING AND QUEEN LOOK ON...!!

EPISODE 15

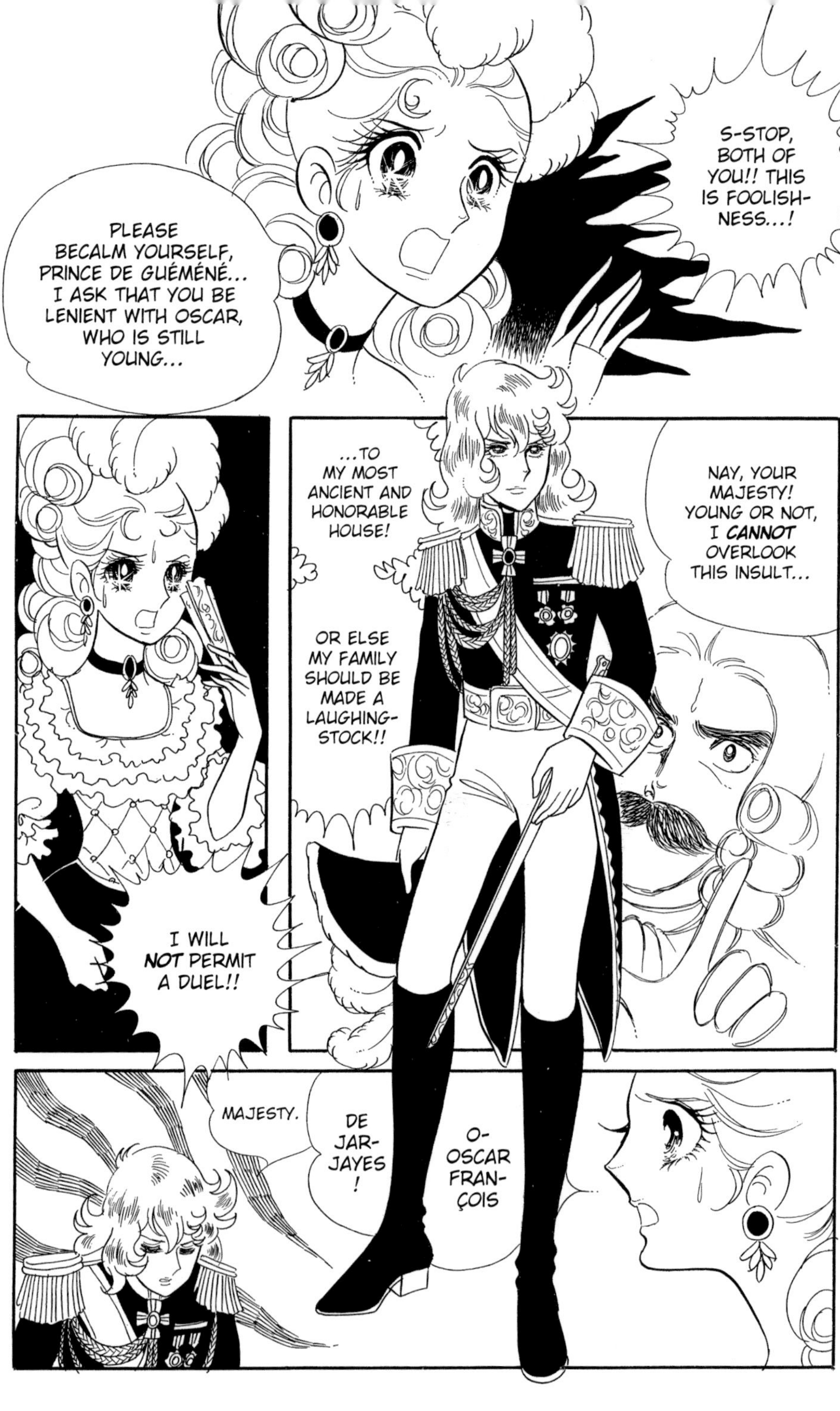
S-STOP, BOTH OF YOU!! THIS IS FOOLISHNESS...!
PLEASE BECALM YOURSELF, PRINCE DE GUÉMÉNÉ... I ASK THAT YOU BE LENIENT WITH OSCAR, WHO IS STILL YOUNG...
NAY, YOUR MAJESTY! YOUNG OR NOT, I **CANNOT** OVERLOOK THIS INSULT...
...TO MY MOST ANCIENT AND HONORABLE HOUSE!
OR ELSE MY FAMILY SHOULD BE MADE A LAUGHING-STOCK!!
I WILL **NOT** PERMIT A DUEL!!
O-OSCAR FRANÇOIS
DE JAR-JAYES!
MAJESTY.

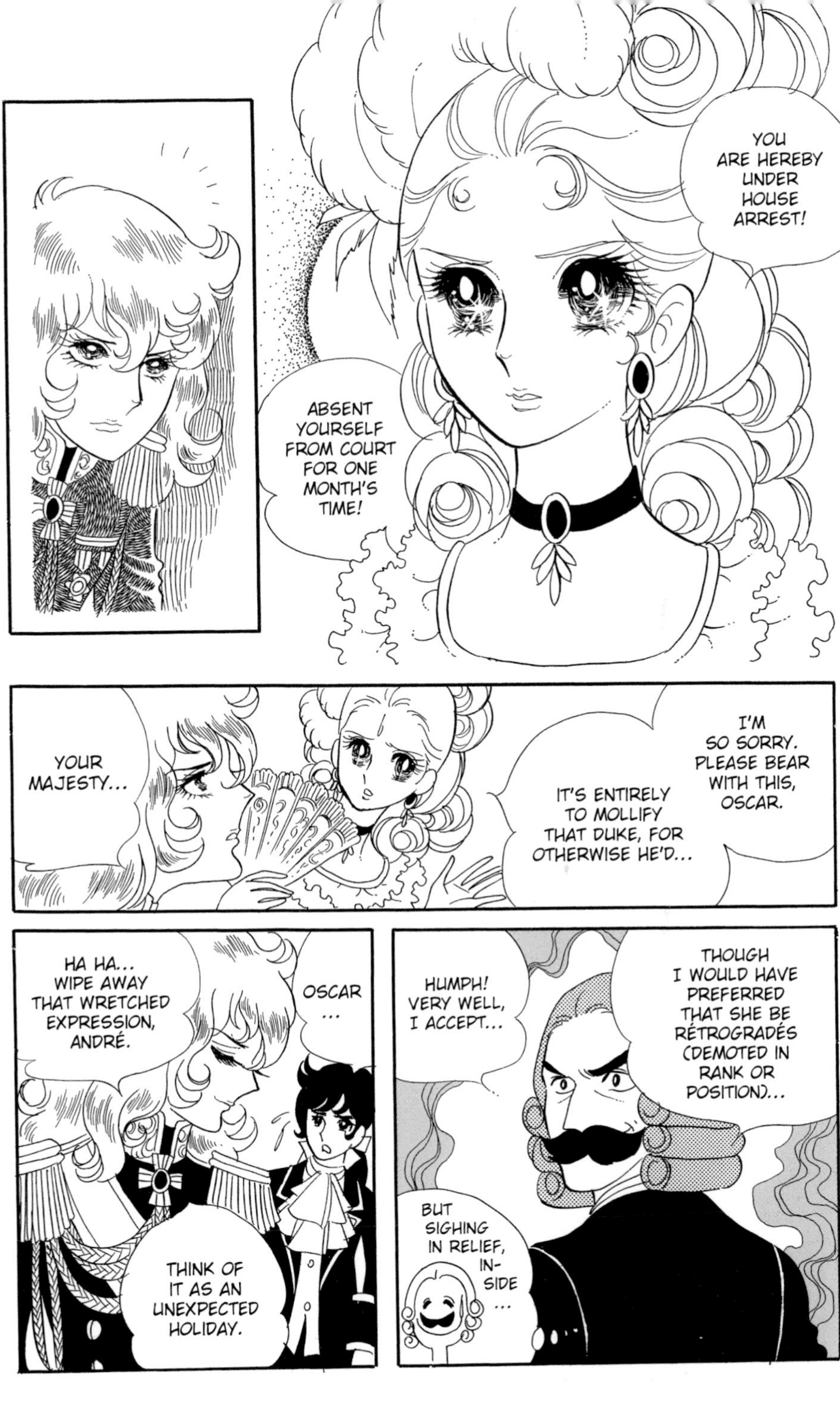
YOU ARE HEREBY UNDER HOUSE ARREST!
ABSENT YOURSELF FROM COURT FOR ONE MONTH'S TIME!
I'M SO SORRY. PLEASE BEAR WITH THIS, OSCAR.
IT'S ENTIRELY TO MOLLIFY THAT DUKE, FOR OTHERWISE HE'D...
YOUR MAJESTY...
THOUGH I WOULD HAVE PREFERRED THAT SHE BE RÉTROGRADÉS (DEMOTED IN RANK OR POSITION)...
HUMPH! VERY WELL, I ACCEPT...
BUT SIGHING IN RELIEF, IN-SIDE...
OSCAR...
HA HA... WIPE AWAY THAT WRETCHED EXPRESSION, ANDRÉ.
THINK OF IT AS AN UNEXPECTED HOLIDAY.

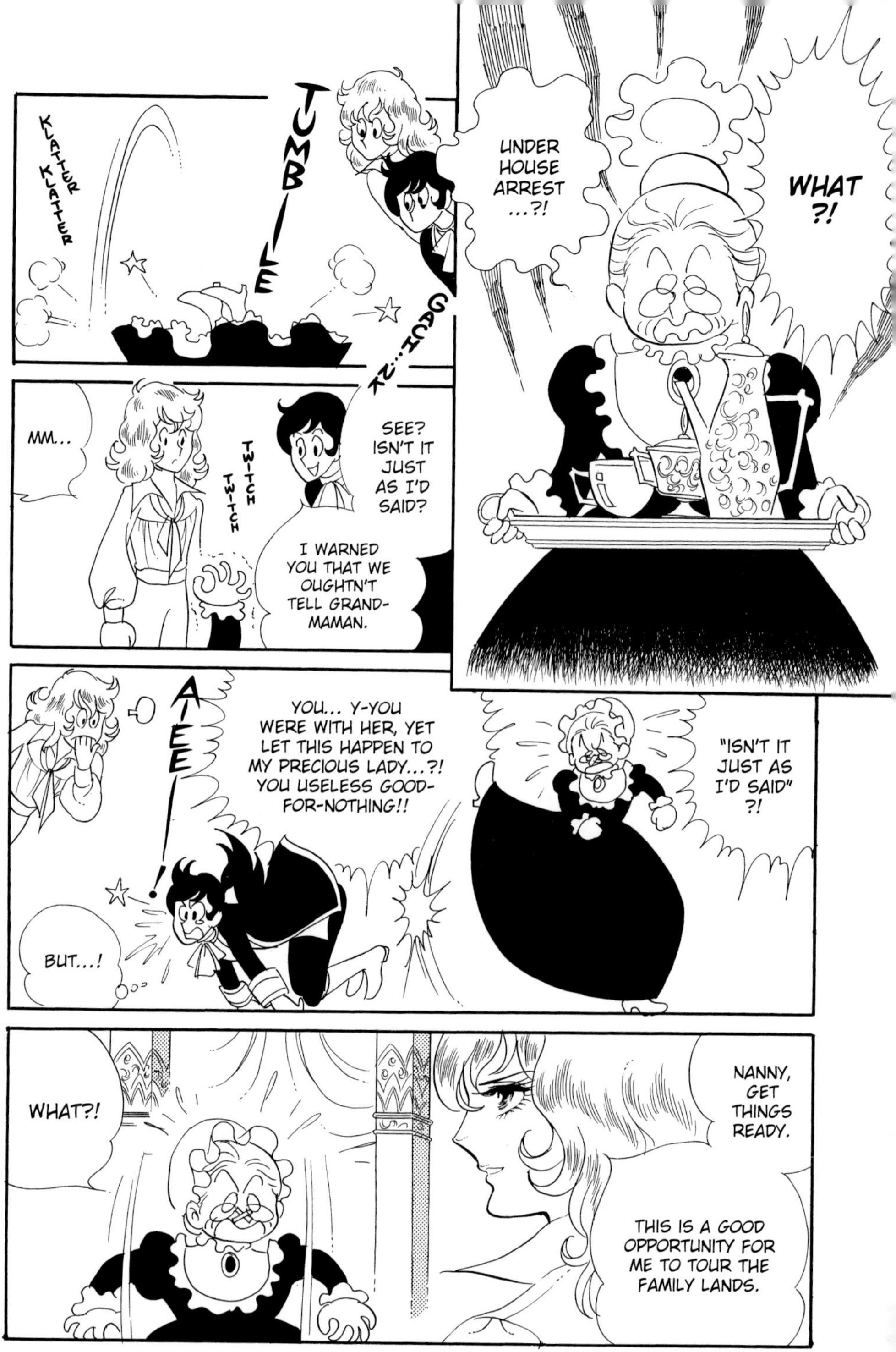
WHAT ?!
UNDER HOUSE ARREST …?!
TUMBLE
GACH…KN
KLATTER KLATTER
SEE? ISN'T IT JUST AS I'D SAID?
I WARNED YOU THAT WE OUGHTN'T TELL GRAND-MAMAN.
TWITCH TWITCH
MM…
"ISN'T IT JUST AS I'D SAID" ?!
YOU… Y-YOU WERE WITH HER, YET LET THIS HAPPEN TO MY PRECIOUS LADY…?! YOU USELESS GOOD-FOR-NOTHING!!
AIEE!!
BUT…!
NANNY, GET THINGS READY.
THIS IS A GOOD OPPORTUNITY FOR ME TO TOUR THE FAMILY LANDS.
WHAT?!

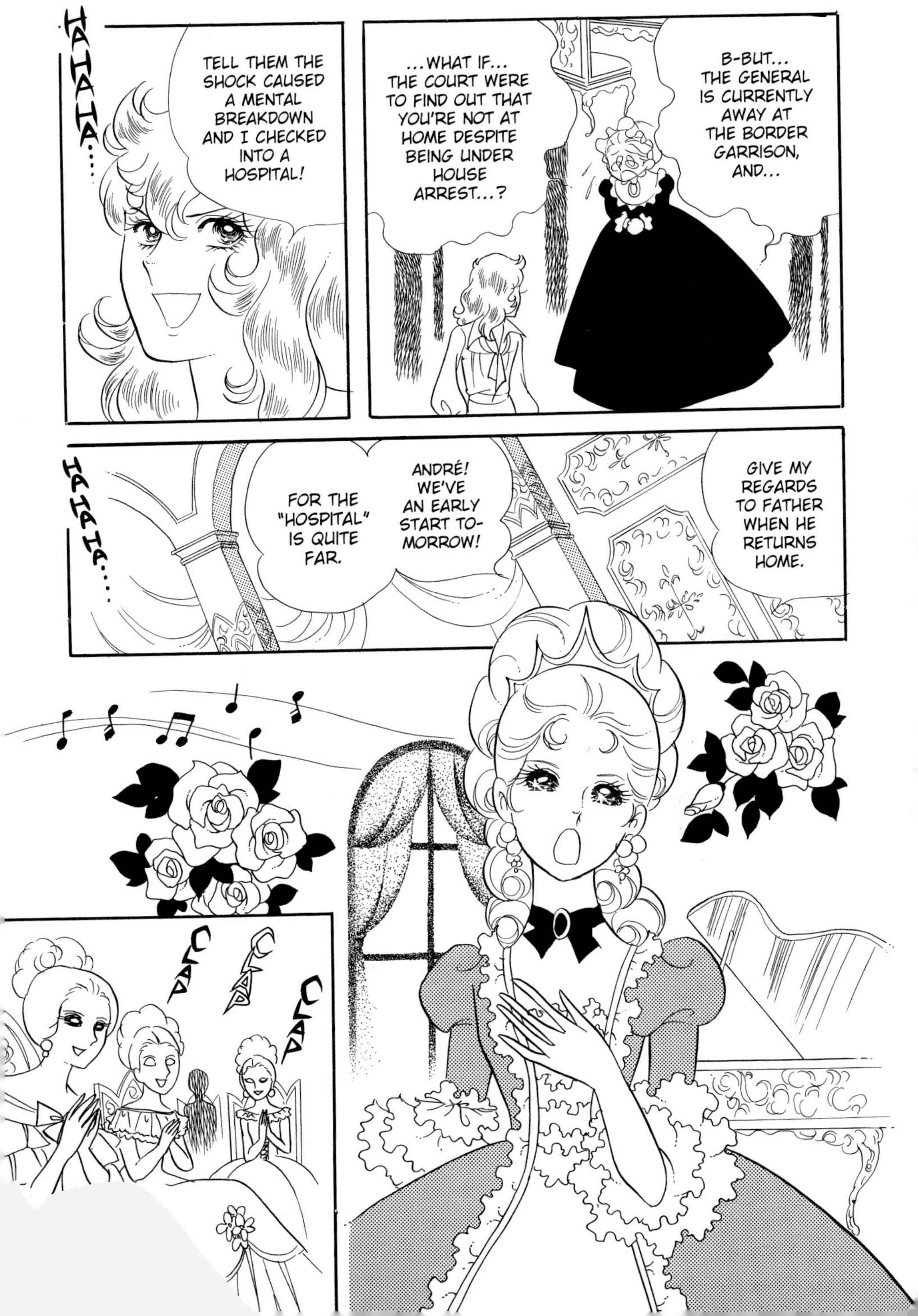
B-BUT... THE GENERAL IS CURRENTLY AWAY AT THE BORDER GARRISON, AND...
...WHAT IF... THE COURT WERE TO FIND OUT THAT YOU'RE NOT AT HOME DESPITE BEING UNDER HOUSE ARREST...?
TELL THEM THE SHOCK CAUSED A MENTAL BREAKDOWN AND I CHECKED INTO A HOSPITAL!
HAHAHA...
GIVE MY REGARDS TO FATHER WHEN HE RETURNS HOME.
ANDRÉ! WE'VE AN EARLY START TO-MORROW!
FOR THE "HOSPITAL" IS QUITE FAR.
HAHAHA...
CLAP
CLAP
CLAP

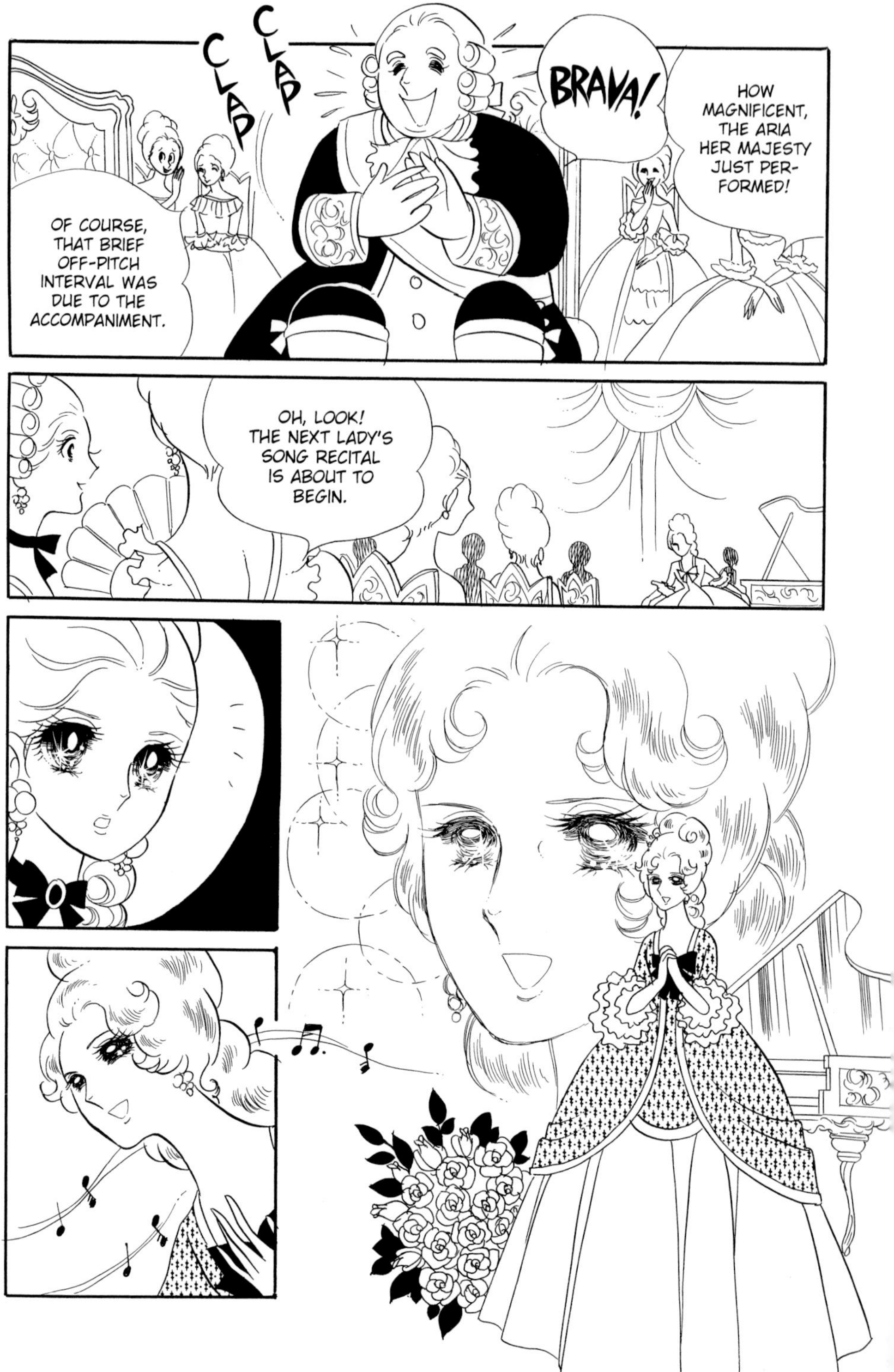
HOW MAGNIFICENT, THE ARIA HER MAJESTY JUST PERFORMED!
BRAVA!
CLAP
CLAP
OF COURSE, THAT BRIEF OFF-PITCH INTERVAL WAS DUE TO THE ACCOMPANIMENT.
OH, LOOK! THE NEXT LADY'S SONG RECITAL IS ABOUT TO BEGIN.

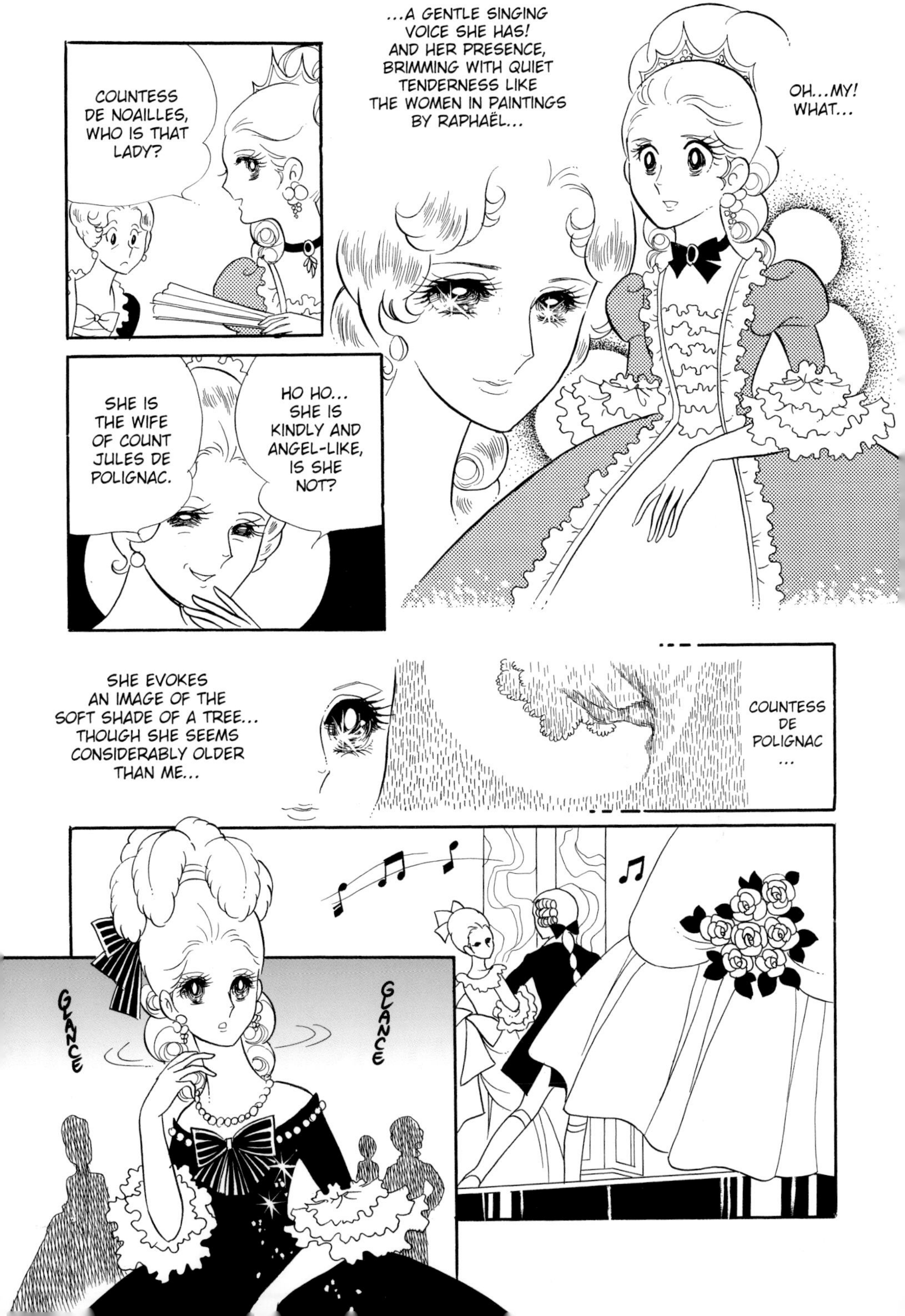
OH...MY! WHAT...
...A GENTLE SINGING VOICE SHE HAS! AND HER PRESENCE, BRIMMING WITH QUIET TENDERNESS LIKE THE WOMEN IN PAINTINGS BY RAPHAËL...
COUNTESS DE NOAILLES, WHO IS THAT LADY?
HO HO... SHE IS KINDLY AND ANGEL-LIKE, IS SHE NOT?
SHE IS THE WIFE OF COUNT JULES DE POLIGNAC.
COUNTESS DE POLIGNAC ...
SHE EVOKES AN IMAGE OF THE SOFT SHADE OF A TREE... THOUGH SHE SEEMS CONSIDERABLY OLDER THAN ME...
GLANCE
GLANCE

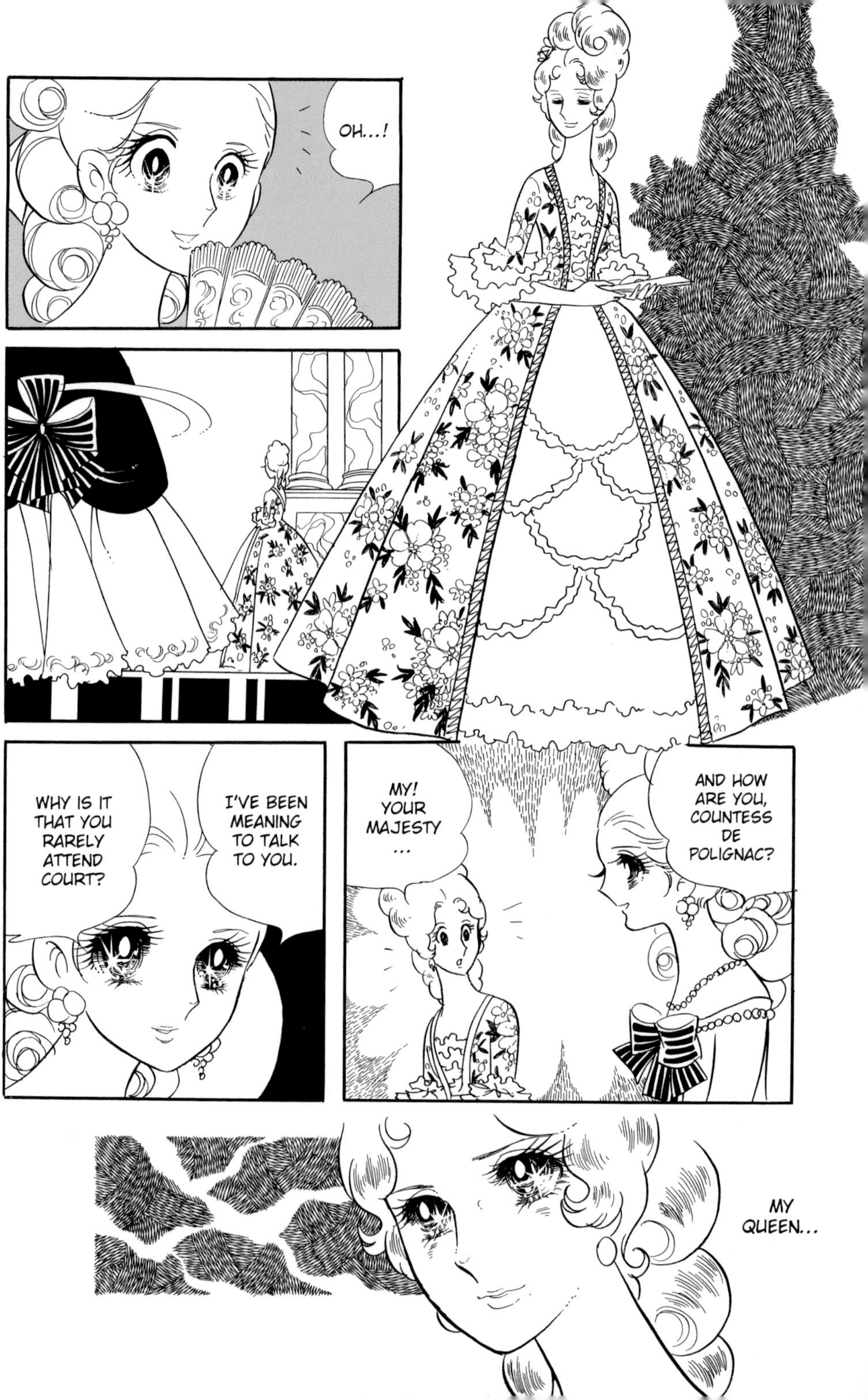
OH...!
AND HOW ARE YOU, COUNTESS DE POLIGNAC?
MY! YOUR MAJESTY ...
I'VE BEEN MEANING TO TALK TO YOU.
WHY IS IT THAT YOU RARELY ATTEND COURT?
MY QUEEN...

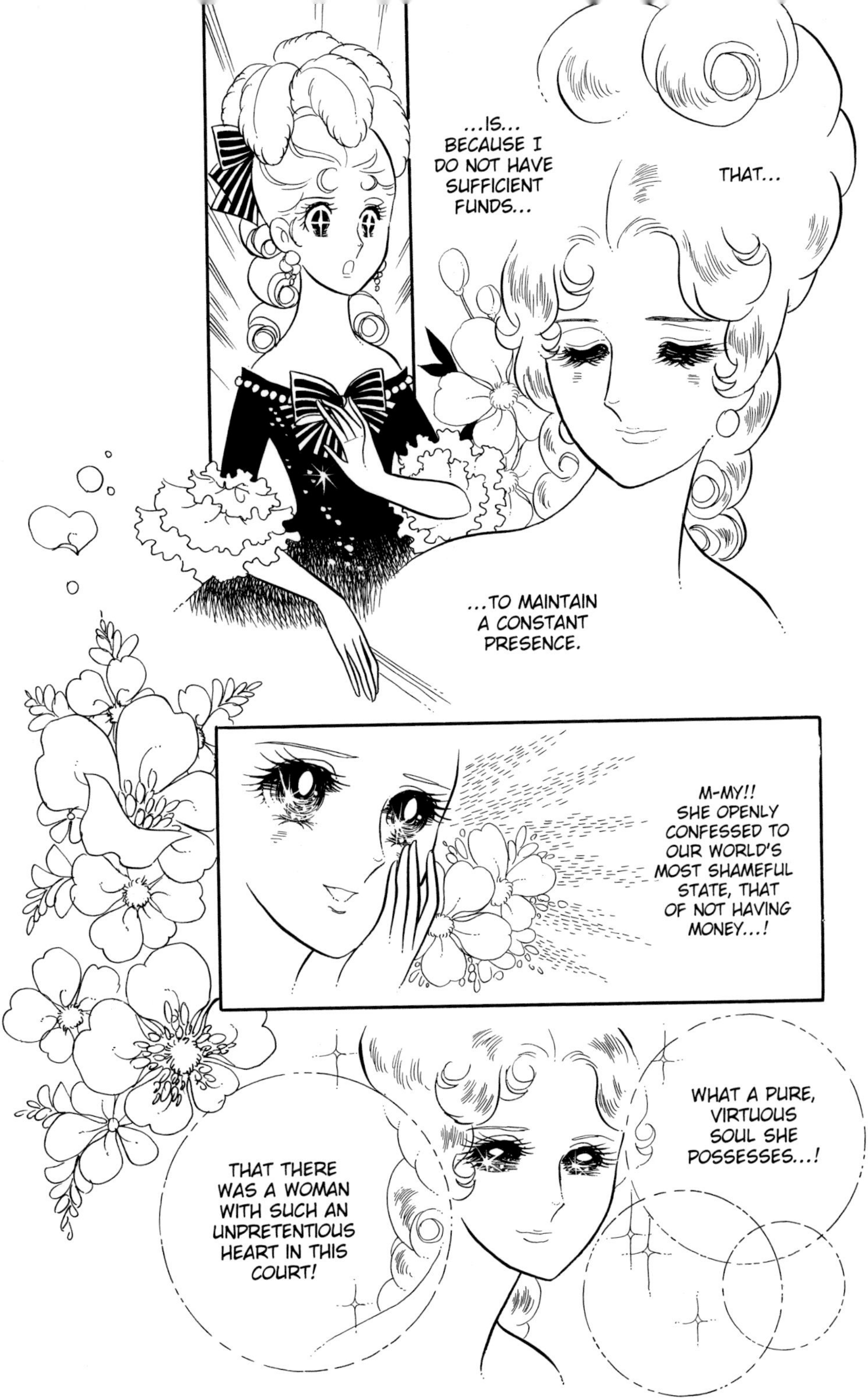
THAT...
...IS... BECAUSE I DO NOT HAVE SUFFICIENT FUNDS...
...TO MAINTAIN A CONSTANT PRESENCE.
M-MY!! SHE OPENLY CONFESSED TO OUR WORLD'S MOST SHAMEFUL STATE, THAT OF NOT HAVING MONEY...!
WHAT A PURE, VIRTUOUS SOUL SHE POSSESSES...!
THAT THERE WAS A WOMAN WITH SUCH AN UNPRETENTIOUS HEART IN THIS COURT!

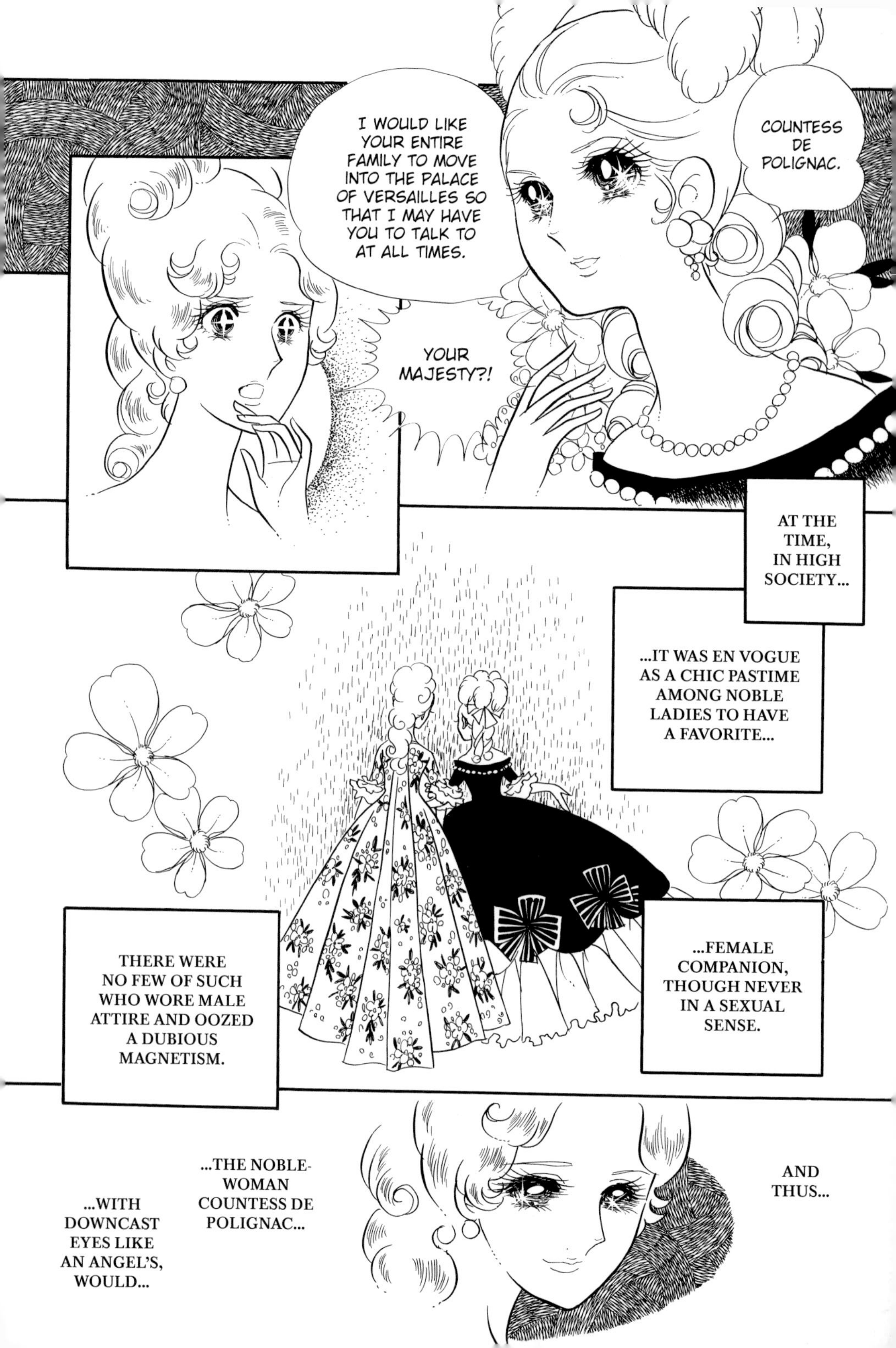
COUNTESS DE POLIGNAC.
I WOULD LIKE YOUR ENTIRE FAMILY TO MOVE INTO THE PALACE OF VERSAILLES SO THAT I MAY HAVE YOU TO TALK TO AT ALL TIMES.
YOUR MAJESTY?!
AT THE TIME, IN HIGH SOCIETY...
...IT WAS EN VOGUE AS A CHIC PASTIME AMONG NOBLE LADIES TO HAVE A FAVORITE...
...FEMALE COMPANION, THOUGH NEVER IN A SEXUAL SENSE.
THERE WERE NO FEW OF SUCH WHO WORE MALE ATTIRE AND OOZED A DUBIOUS MAGNETISM.
AND THUS...
...THE NOBLE-WOMAN COUNTESS DE POLIGNAC...
...WITH DOWNCAST EYES LIKE AN ANGEL'S, WOULD...

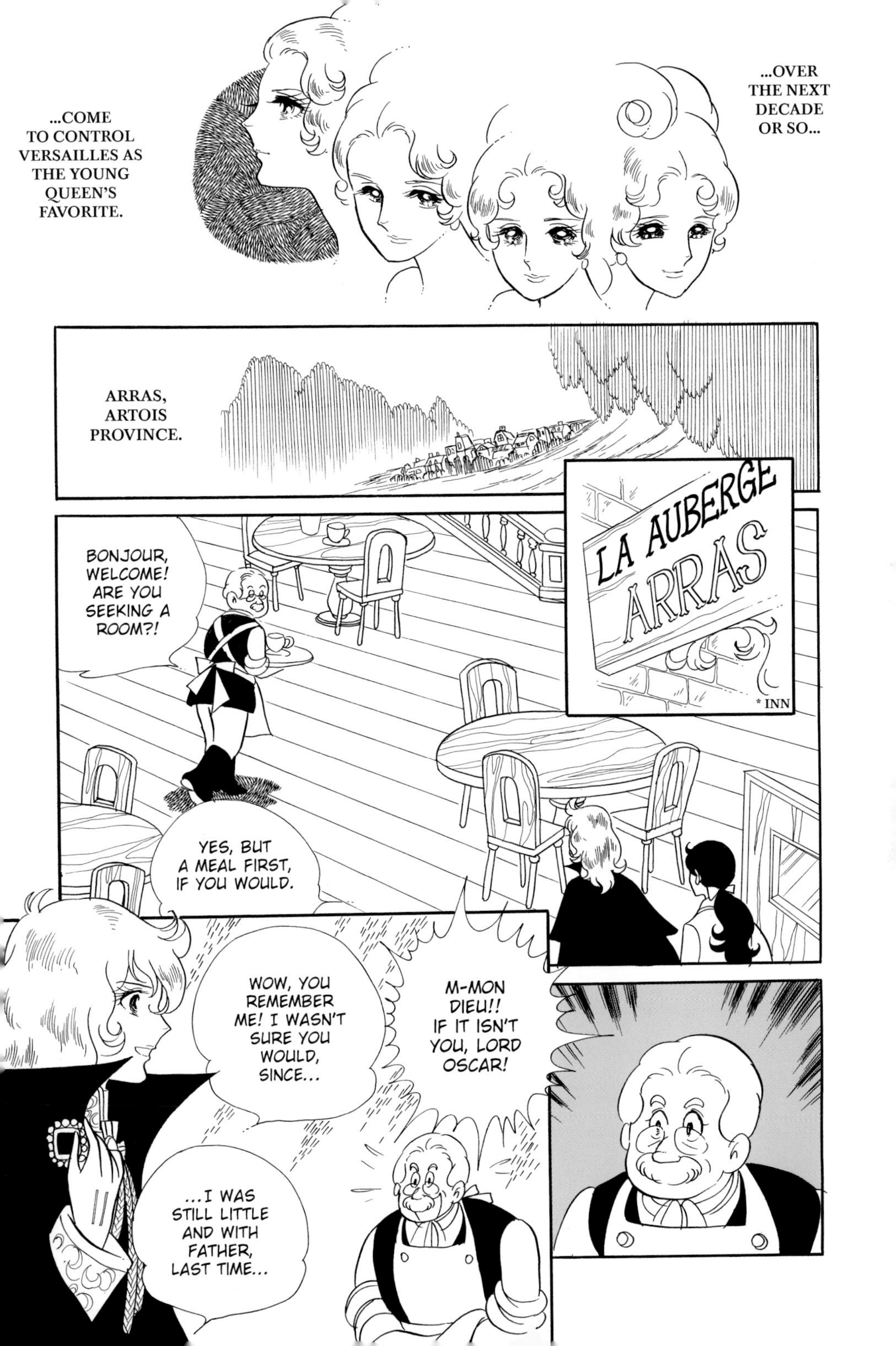
...OVER THE NEXT DECADE OR SO...
...COME TO CONTROL VERSAILLES AS THE YOUNG QUEEN'S FAVORITE.
ARRAS, ARTOIS PROVINCE.
LA AUBERGE ARRAS
* INN
BONJOUR, WELCOME! ARE YOU SEEKING A ROOM?!
YES, BUT A MEAL FIRST, IF YOU WOULD.
M-MON DIEU!! IF IT ISN'T YOU, LORD OSCAR!
WOW, YOU REMEMBER ME! I WASN'T SURE YOU WOULD, SINCE...
...I WAS STILL LITTLE AND WITH FATHER, LAST TIME...

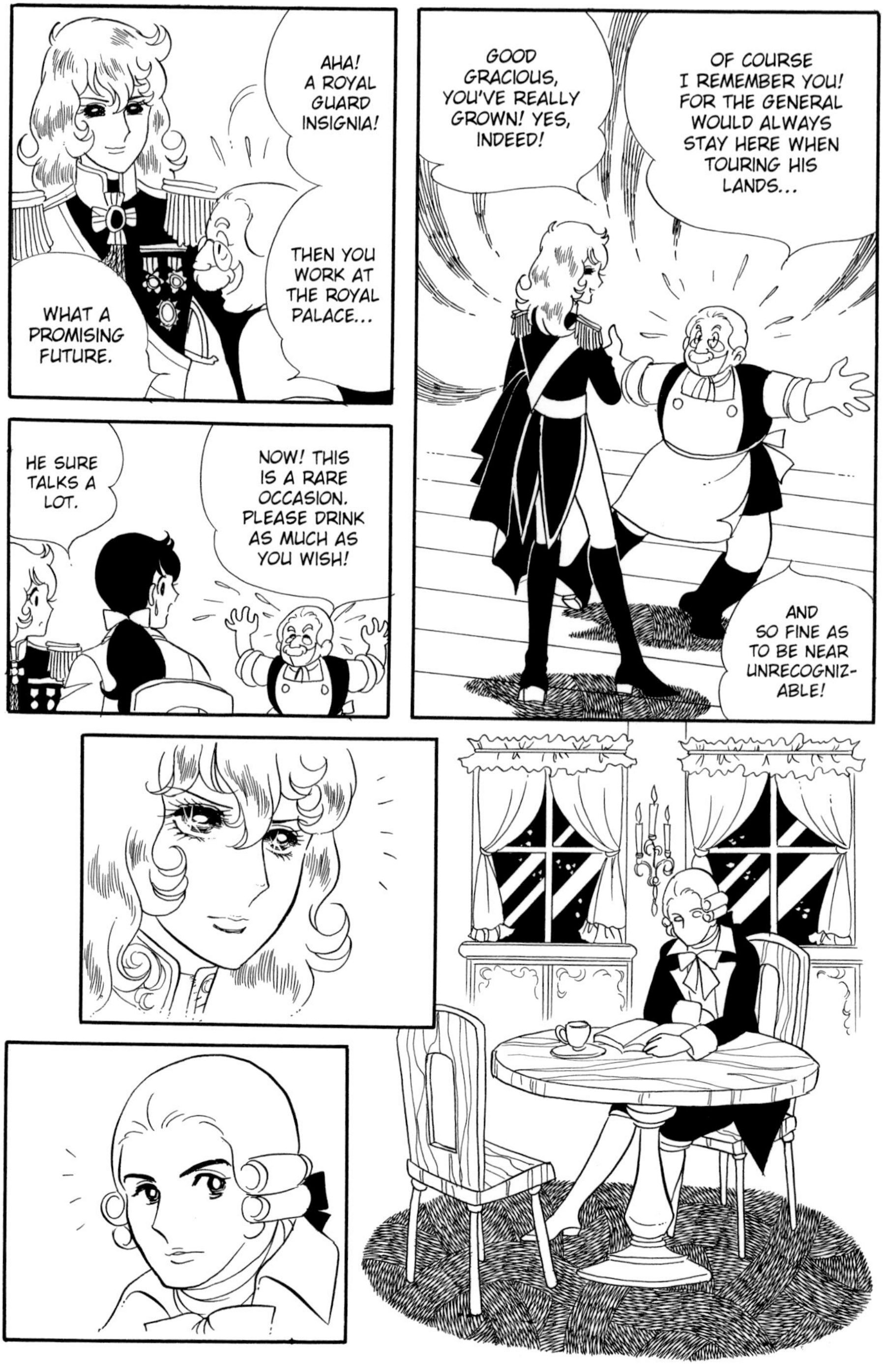
OF COURSE I REMEMBER YOU! FOR THE GENERAL WOULD ALWAYS STAY HERE WHEN TOURING HIS LANDS...
GOOD GRACIOUS, YOU'VE REALLY GROWN! YES, INDEED!
AND SO FINE AS TO BE NEAR UNRECOGNIZ-ABLE!
AHA! A ROYAL GUARD INSIGNIA!
THEN YOU WORK AT THE ROYAL PALACE...
WHAT A PROMISING FUTURE.
NOW! THIS IS A RARE OCCASION. PLEASE DRINK AS MUCH AS YOU WISH!
HE SURE TALKS A LOT.

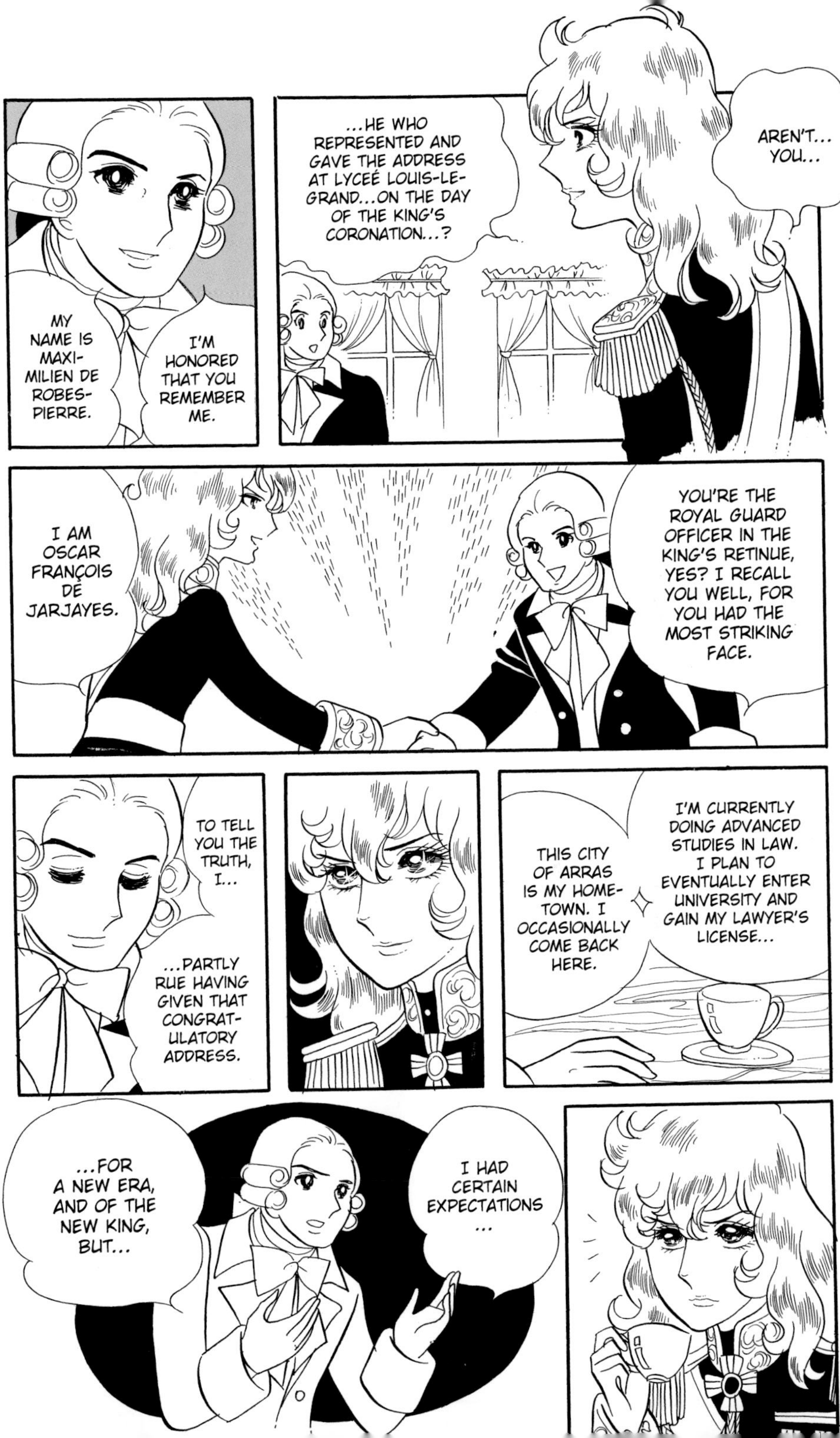
AREN'T... YOU...
...HE WHO REPRESENTED AND GAVE THE ADDRESS AT LYCEÉ LOUIS-LE-GRAND...ON THE DAY OF THE KING'S CORONATION...?
I'M HONORED THAT YOU REMEMBER ME.
MY NAME IS MAXIMILIEN DE ROBESPIERRE.
YOU'RE THE ROYAL GUARD OFFICER IN THE KING'S RETINUE, YES? I RECALL YOU WELL, FOR YOU HAD THE MOST STRIKING FACE.
I AM OSCAR FRANÇOIS DÉ JARJAYES.
I'M CURRENTLY DOING ADVANCED STUDIES IN LAW. I PLAN TO EVENTUALLY ENTER UNIVERSITY AND GAIN MY LAWYER'S LICENSE...
THIS CITY OF ARRAS IS MY HOMETOWN. I OCCASIONALLY COME BACK HERE.
TO TELL YOU THE TRUTH, I...
...PARTLY RUE HAVING GIVEN THAT CONGRATULATORY ADDRESS.
I HAD CERTAIN EXPECTATIONS...
...FOR A NEW ERA, AND OF THE NEW KING, BUT...

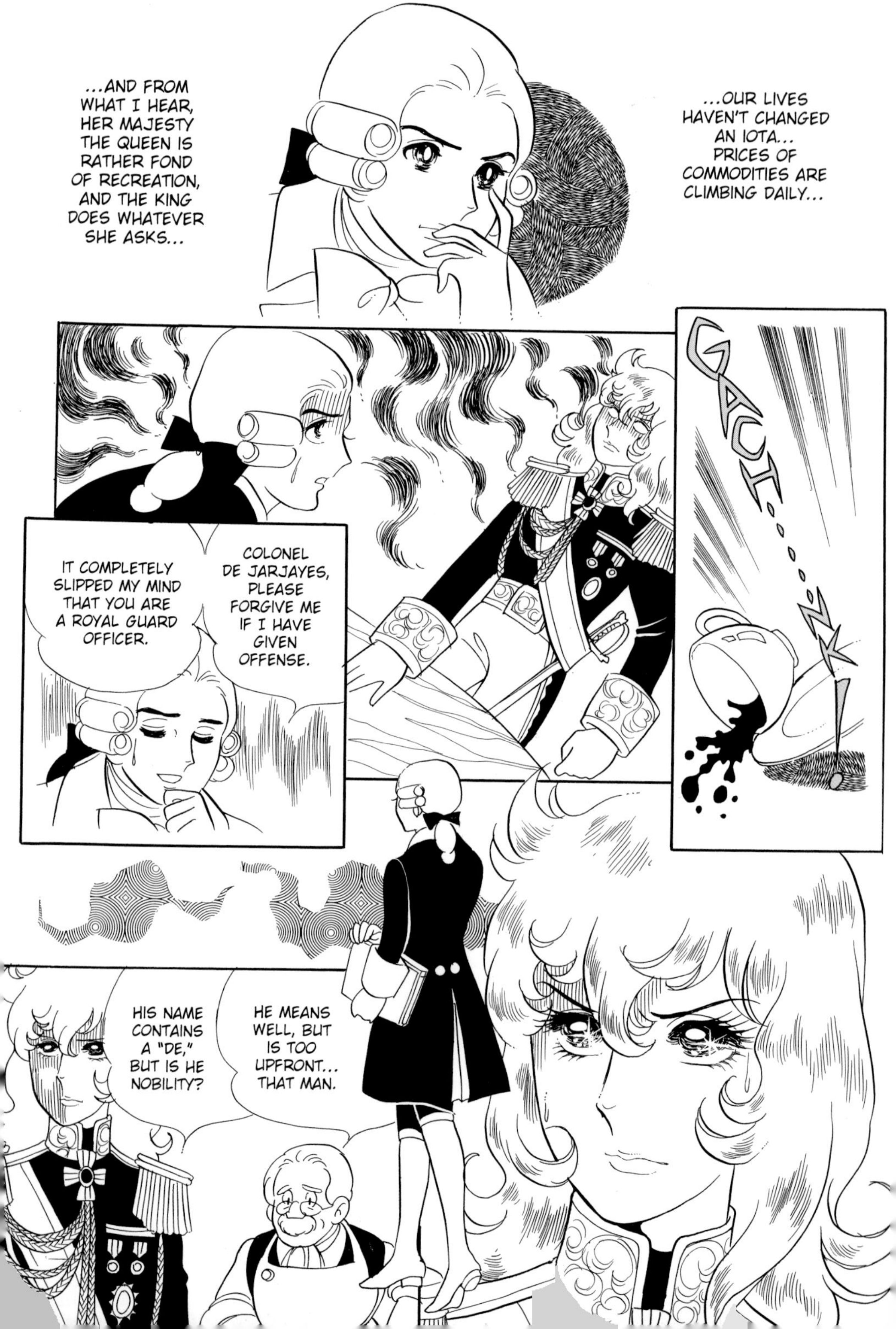
...OUR LIVES HAVEN'T CHANGED AN IOTA... PRICES OF COMMODITIES ARE CLIMBING DAILY...
...AND FROM WHAT I HEAR, HER MAJESTY THE QUEEN IS RATHER FOND OF RECREATION, AND THE KING DOES WHATEVER SHE ASKS...
GACH......NK
COLONEL DE JARJAYES, PLEASE FORGIVE ME IF I HAVE GIVEN OFFENSE.
IT COMPLETELY SLIPPED MY MIND THAT YOU ARE A ROYAL GUARD OFFICER.
HE MEANS WELL, BUT IS TOO UPFRONT... THAT MAN.
HIS NAME CONTAINS A "DE," BUT IS HE NOBILITY?

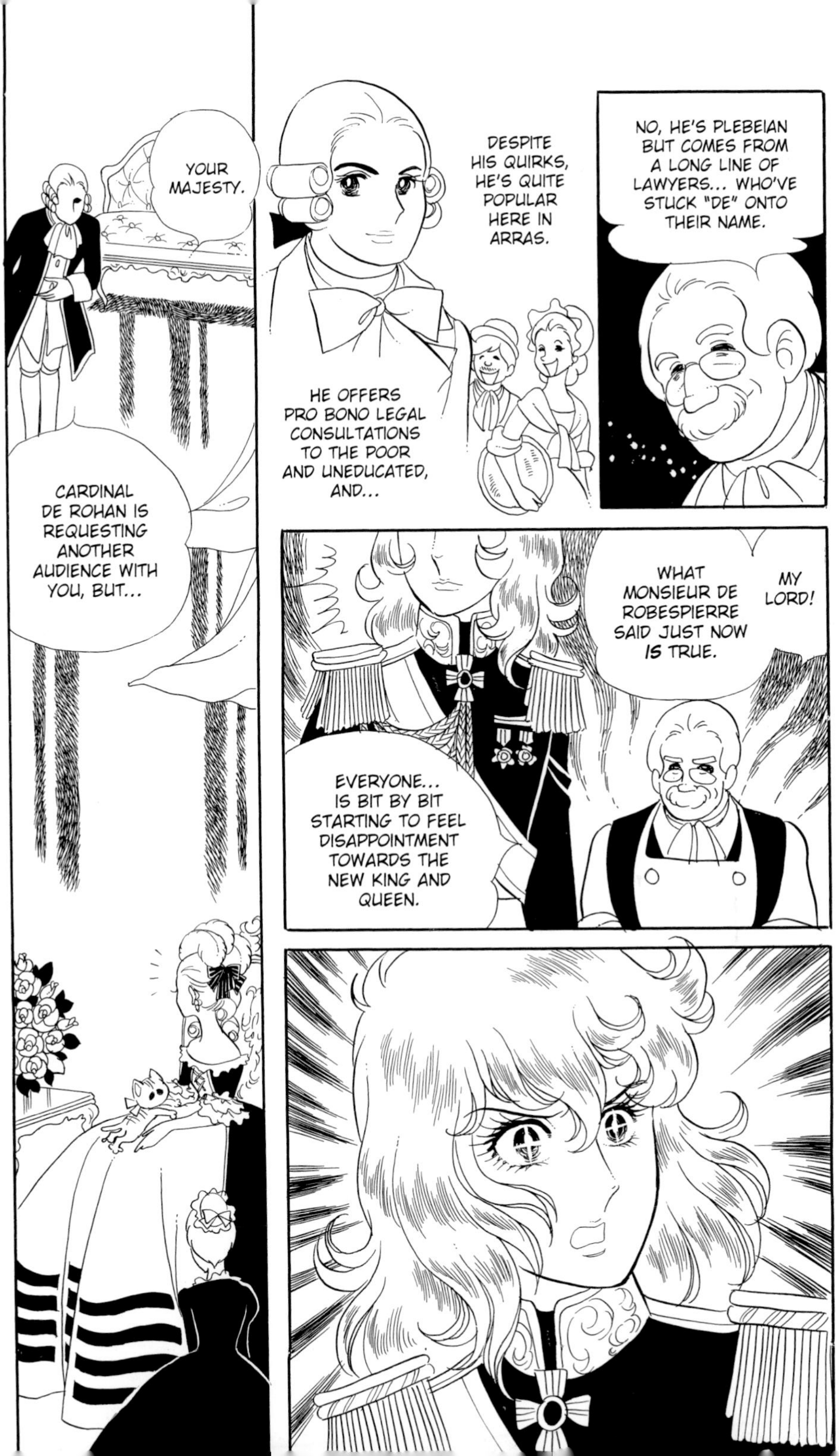
NO, HE'S PLEBEIAN BUT COMES FROM A LONG LINE OF LAWYERS... WHO'VE STUCK "DE" ONTO THEIR NAME.
DESPITE HIS QUIRKS, HE'S QUITE POPULAR HERE IN ARRAS.
HE OFFERS PRO BONO LEGAL CONSULTATIONS TO THE POOR AND UNEDUCATED, AND...
MY LORD!
WHAT MONSIEUR DE ROBESPIERRE SAID JUST NOW IS TRUE.
EVERYONE... IS BIT BY BIT STARTING TO FEEL DISAPPOINTMENT TOWARDS THE NEW KING AND QUEEN.
YOUR MAJESTY.
CARDINAL DE ROHAN IS REQUESTING ANOTHER AUDIENCE WITH YOU, BUT...

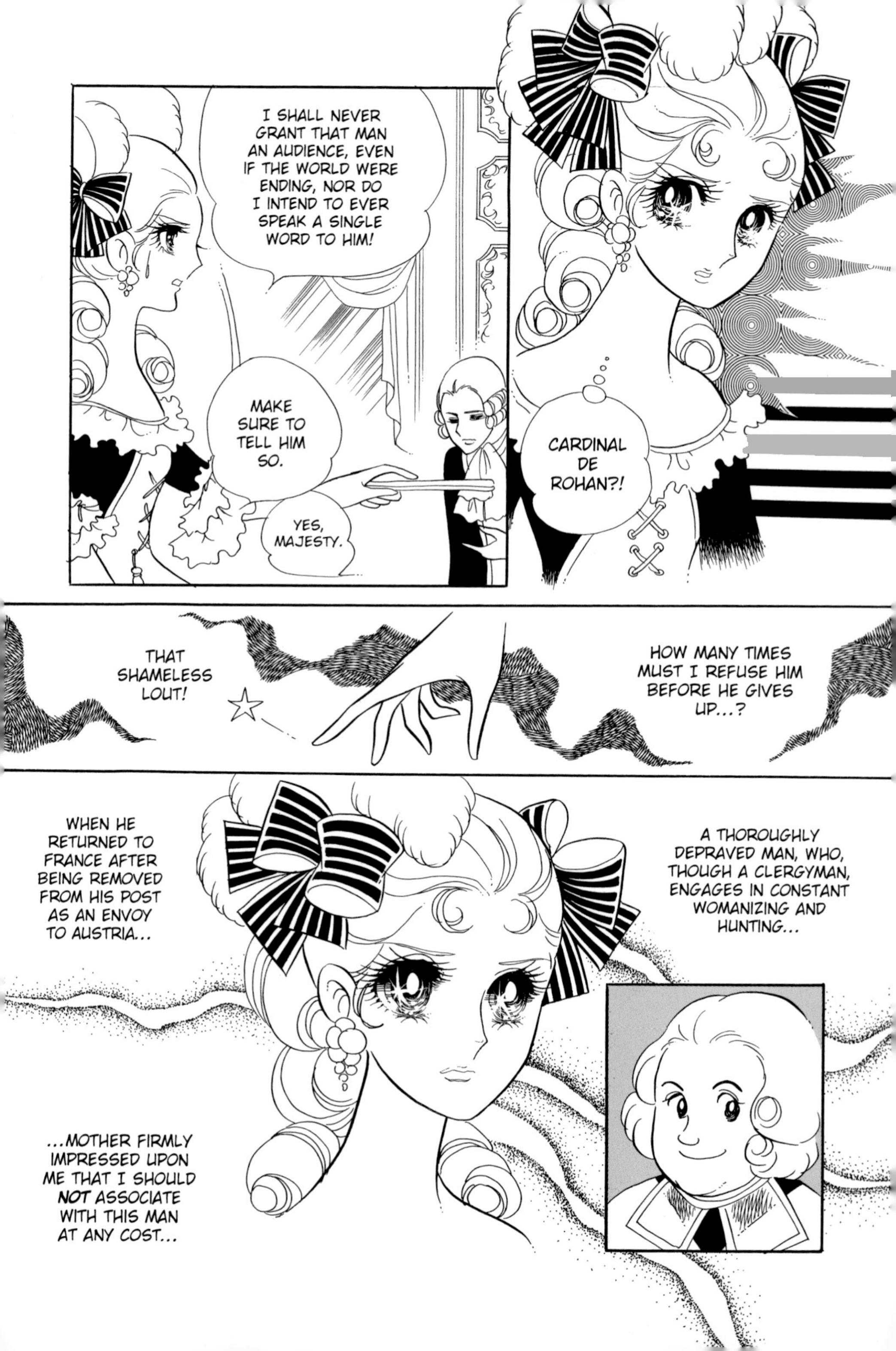
CARDINAL DE ROHAN?!
I SHALL NEVER GRANT THAT MAN AN AUDIENCE, EVEN IF THE WORLD WERE ENDING, NOR DO I INTEND TO EVER SPEAK A SINGLE WORD TO HIM!
MAKE SURE TO TELL HIM SO.
YES, MAJESTY.
HOW MANY TIMES MUST I REFUSE HIM BEFORE HE GIVES UP...?
THAT SHAMELESS LOUT!
A THOROUGHLY DEPRAVED MAN, WHO, THOUGH A CLERGYMAN, ENGAGES IN CONSTANT WOMANIZING AND HUNTING...
WHEN HE RETURNED TO FRANCE AFTER BEING REMOVED FROM HIS POST AS AN ENVOY TO AUSTRIA...
...MOTHER FIRMLY IMPRESSED UPON ME THAT I SHOULD **NOT** ASSOCIATE WITH THIS MAN AT ANY COST...

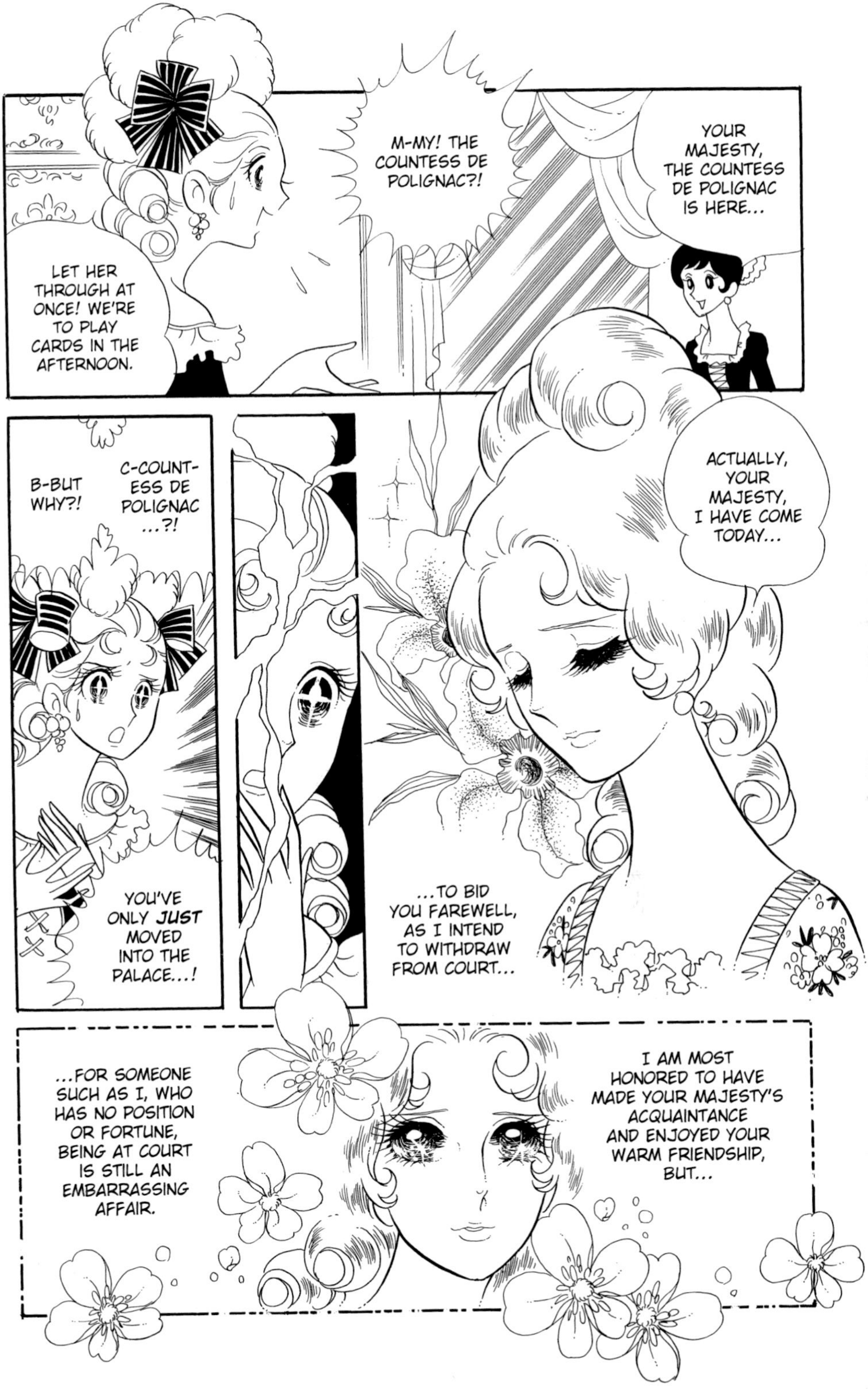
YOUR MAJESTY, THE COUNTESS DE POLIGNAC IS HERE...
M-MY! THE COUNTESS DE POLIGNAC?!
LET HER THROUGH AT ONCE! WE'RE TO PLAY CARDS IN THE AFTERNOON.
ACTUALLY, YOUR MAJESTY, I HAVE COME TODAY...
...TO BID YOU FAREWELL, AS I INTEND TO WITHDRAW FROM COURT...
C-COUNTESS DE POLIGNAC ...?!
B-BUT WHY?!
YOU'VE ONLY **JUST** MOVED INTO THE PALACE...!
I AM MOST HONORED TO HAVE MADE YOUR MAJESTY'S ACQUAINTANCE AND ENJOYED YOUR WARM FRIENDSHIP, BUT...
...FOR SOMEONE SUCH AS I, WHO HAS NO POSITION OR FORTUNE, BEING AT COURT IS STILL AN EMBARRASSING AFFAIR.

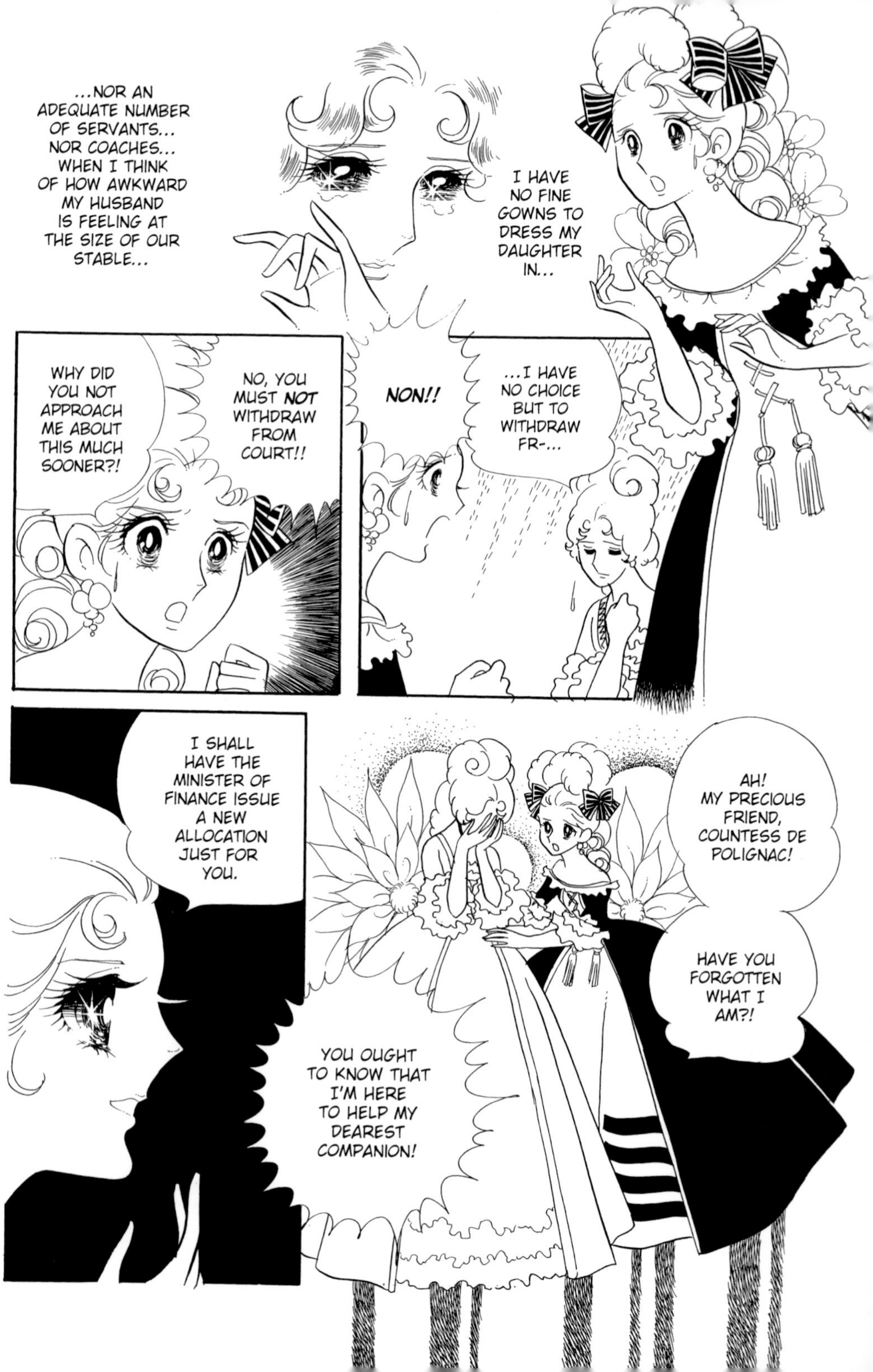
I HAVE NO FINE GOWNS TO DRESS MY DAUGHTER IN...
...NOR AN ADEQUATE NUMBER OF SERVANTS... NOR COACHES... WHEN I THINK OF HOW AWKWARD MY HUSBAND IS FEELING AT THE SIZE OF OUR STABLE...
...I HAVE NO CHOICE BUT TO WITHDRAW FR-...
NON!!
NO, YOU MUST **NOT** WITHDRAW FROM COURT!!
WHY DID YOU NOT APPROACH ME ABOUT THIS MUCH SOONER?!
AH! MY PRECIOUS FRIEND, COUNTESS DE POLIGNAC!
HAVE YOU FORGOTTEN WHAT I AM?!
YOU OUGHT TO KNOW THAT I'M HERE TO HELP MY DEAREST COMPANION!
I SHALL HAVE THE MINISTER OF FINANCE ISSUE A NEW ALLOCATION JUST FOR YOU.

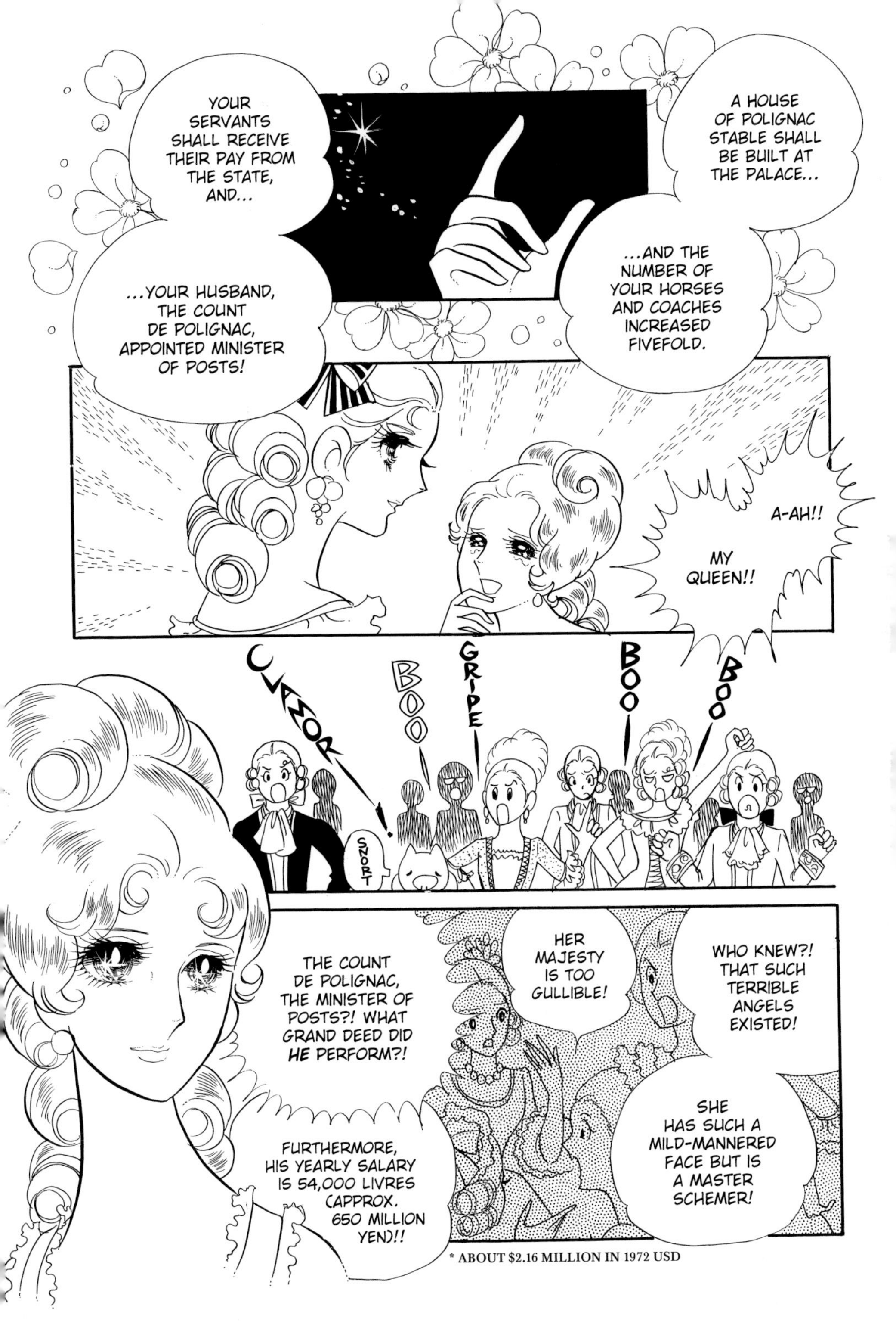
A HOUSE OF POLIGNAC STABLE SHALL BE BUILT AT THE PALACE...
...AND THE NUMBER OF YOUR HORSES AND COACHES INCREASED FIVEFOLD.
YOUR SERVANTS SHALL RECEIVE THEIR PAY FROM THE STATE, AND...
...YOUR HUSBAND, THE COUNT DE POLIGNAC, APPOINTED MINISTER OF POSTS!
A-AH!!
MY QUEEN!!
BOO
BOO
GRIPE
BOO
CLAMOR!
SNORT
WHO KNEW?! THAT SUCH TERRIBLE ANGELS EXISTED!
HER MAJESTY IS TOO GULLIBLE!
SHE HAS SUCH A MILD-MANNERED FACE BUT IS A MASTER SCHEMER!
THE COUNT DE POLIGNAC, THE MINISTER OF POSTS?! WHAT GRAND DEED DID HE PERFORM?!
FURTHERMORE, HIS YEARLY SALARY IS 54,000 LIVRES (APPROX. 650 MILLION YEN)!!

* ABOUT $2.16 MILLION IN 1972 USD

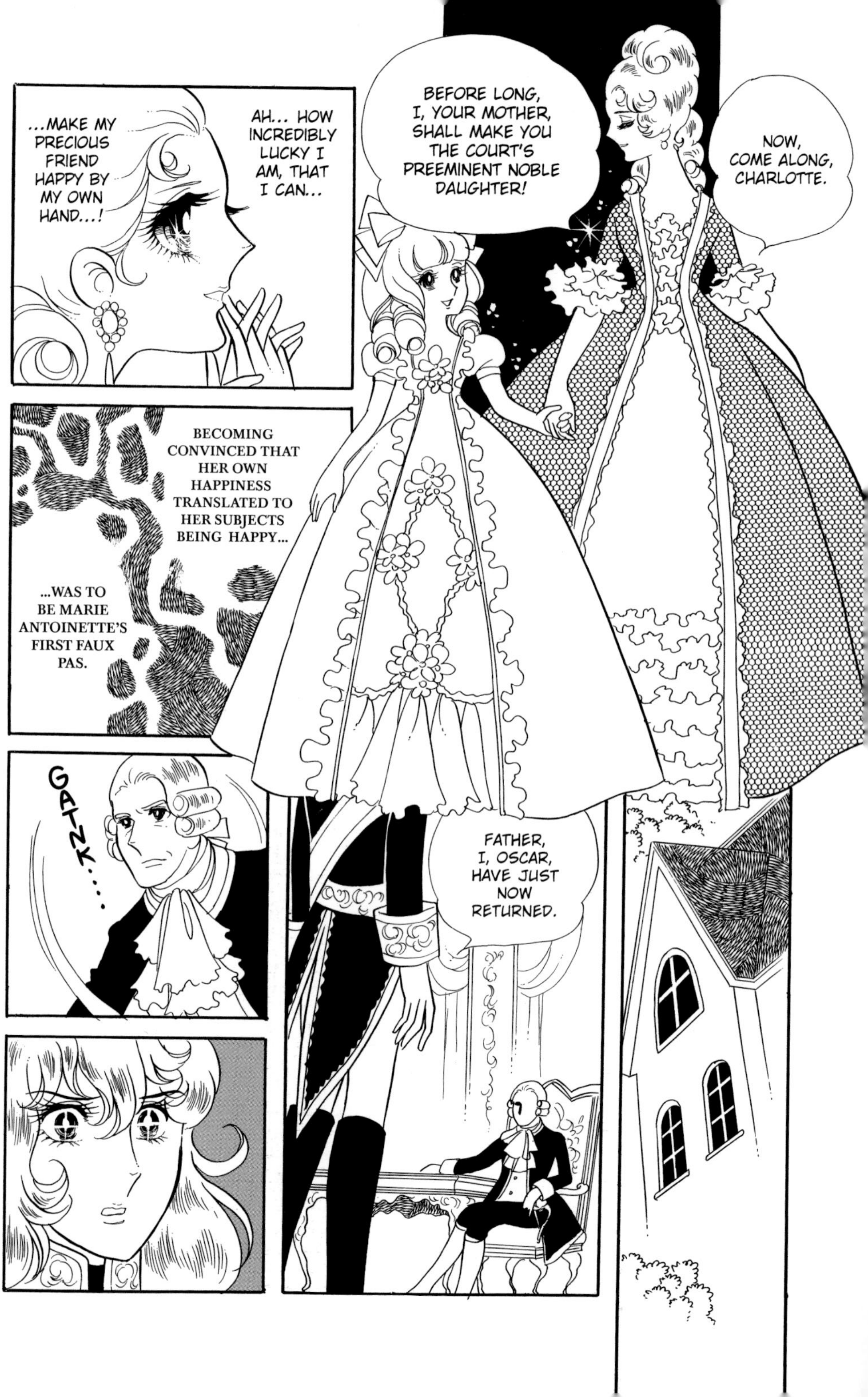
NOW, COME ALONG, CHARLOTTE.
BEFORE LONG, I, YOUR MOTHER, SHALL MAKE YOU THE COURT'S PREEMINENT NOBLE DAUGHTER!
FATHER, I, OSCAR, HAVE JUST NOW RETURNED.
AH... HOW INCREDIBLY LUCKY I AM, THAT I CAN...
...MAKE MY PRECIOUS FRIEND HAPPY BY MY OWN HAND...!
BECOMING CONVINCED THAT HER OWN HAPPINESS TRANSLATED TO HER SUBJECTS BEING HAPPY...
...WAS TO BE MARIE ANTOINETTE'S FIRST FAUX PAS.
GATNK....

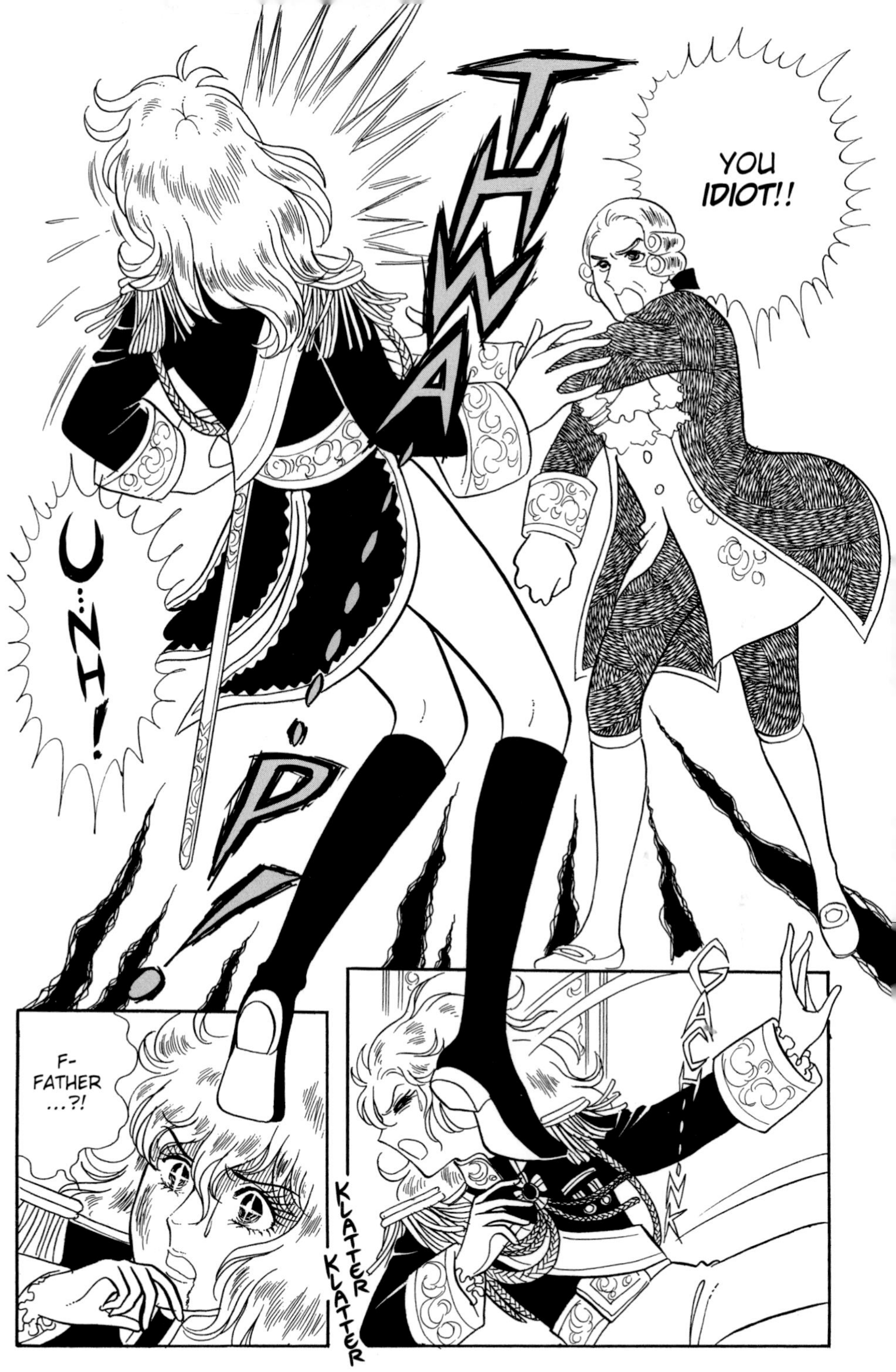
YOU IDIOT!!
THWAP!
U...NH!
GACH...NK
KLATTER KLATTER
F-FATHER ...?!

1972 WEEKLY MARGARET MAGAZINE
ISSUE 37 PREVIEW ART

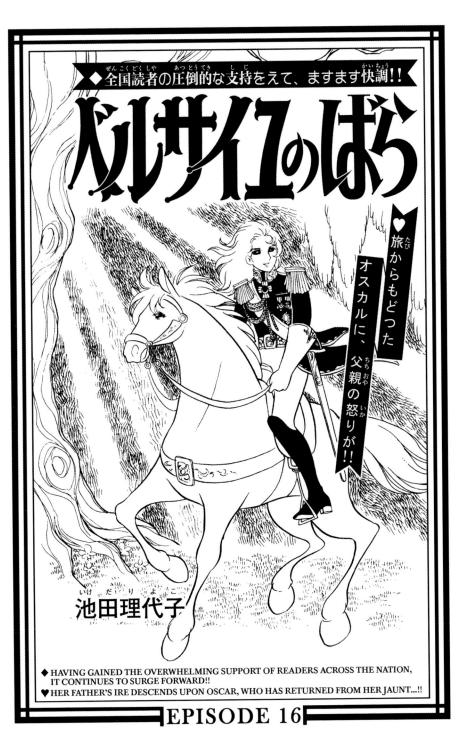

◆全国読者の圧倒的な支持をえて、ますます快調！！

ベルサイユのばら

♥旅からもどったオスカルに、父親の怒りが！！

池田理代子

◆ HAVING GAINED THE OVERWHELMING SUPPORT OF READERS ACROSS THE NATION, IT CONTINUES TO SURGE FORWARD!!
♥ HER FATHER'S IRE DESCENDS UPON OSCAR, WHO HAS RETURNED FROM HER JAUNT...!!

EPISODE 16

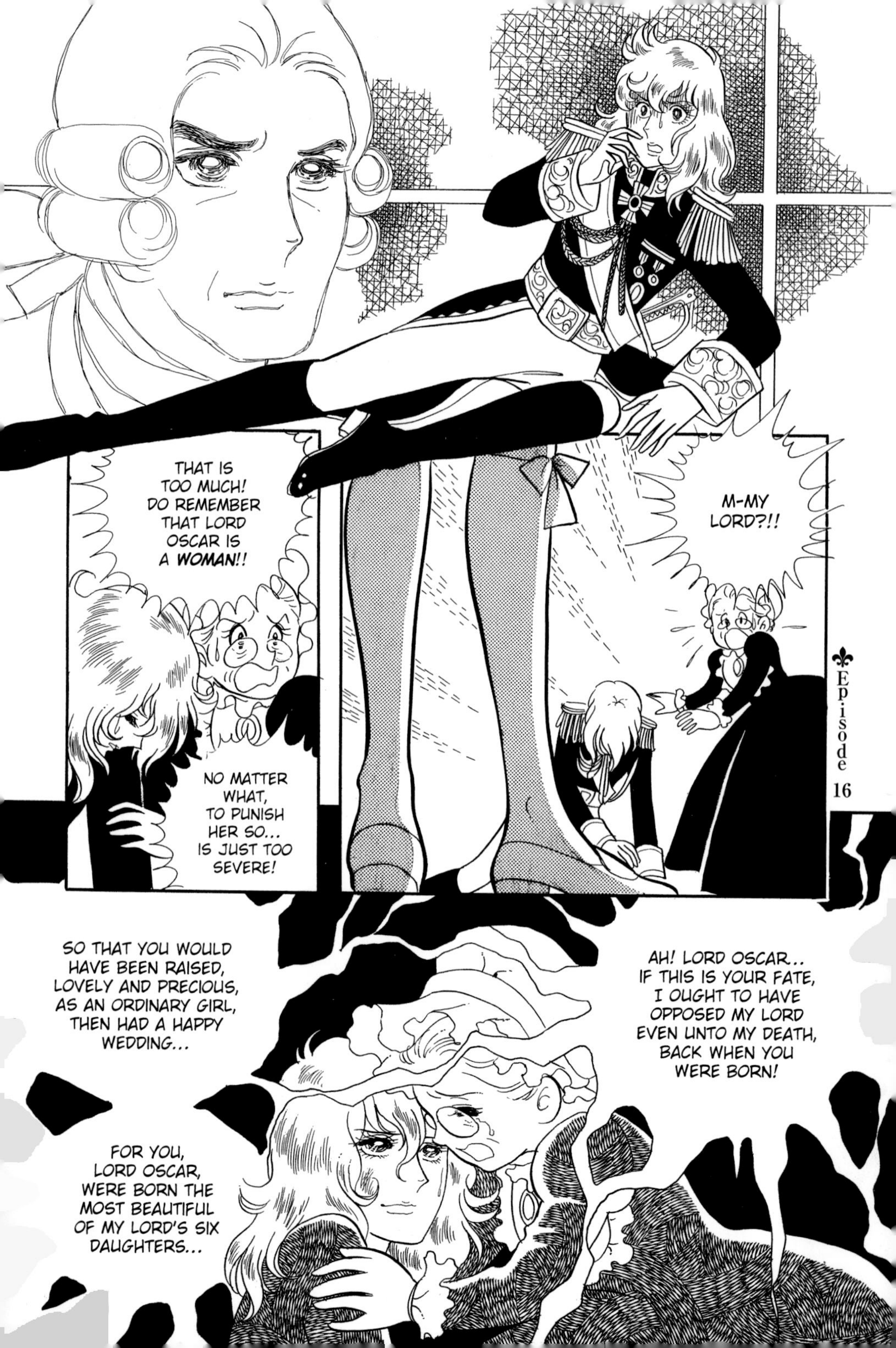
M-MY LORD?!!
THAT IS TOO MUCH! DO REMEMBER THAT LORD OSCAR IS A **WOMAN**!!
NO MATTER WHAT, TO PUNISH HER SO... IS JUST TOO SEVERE!
AH! LORD OSCAR.. IF THIS IS YOUR FATE, I OUGHT TO HAVE OPPOSED MY LORD EVEN UNTO MY DEATH, BACK WHEN YOU WERE BORN!
SO THAT YOU WOULD HAVE BEEN RAISED, LOVELY AND PRECIOUS, AS AN ORDINARY GIRL, THEN HAD A HAPPY WEDDING...
FOR YOU, LORD OSCAR, WERE BORN THE MOST BEAUTIFUL OF MY LORD'S SIX DAUGHTERS...

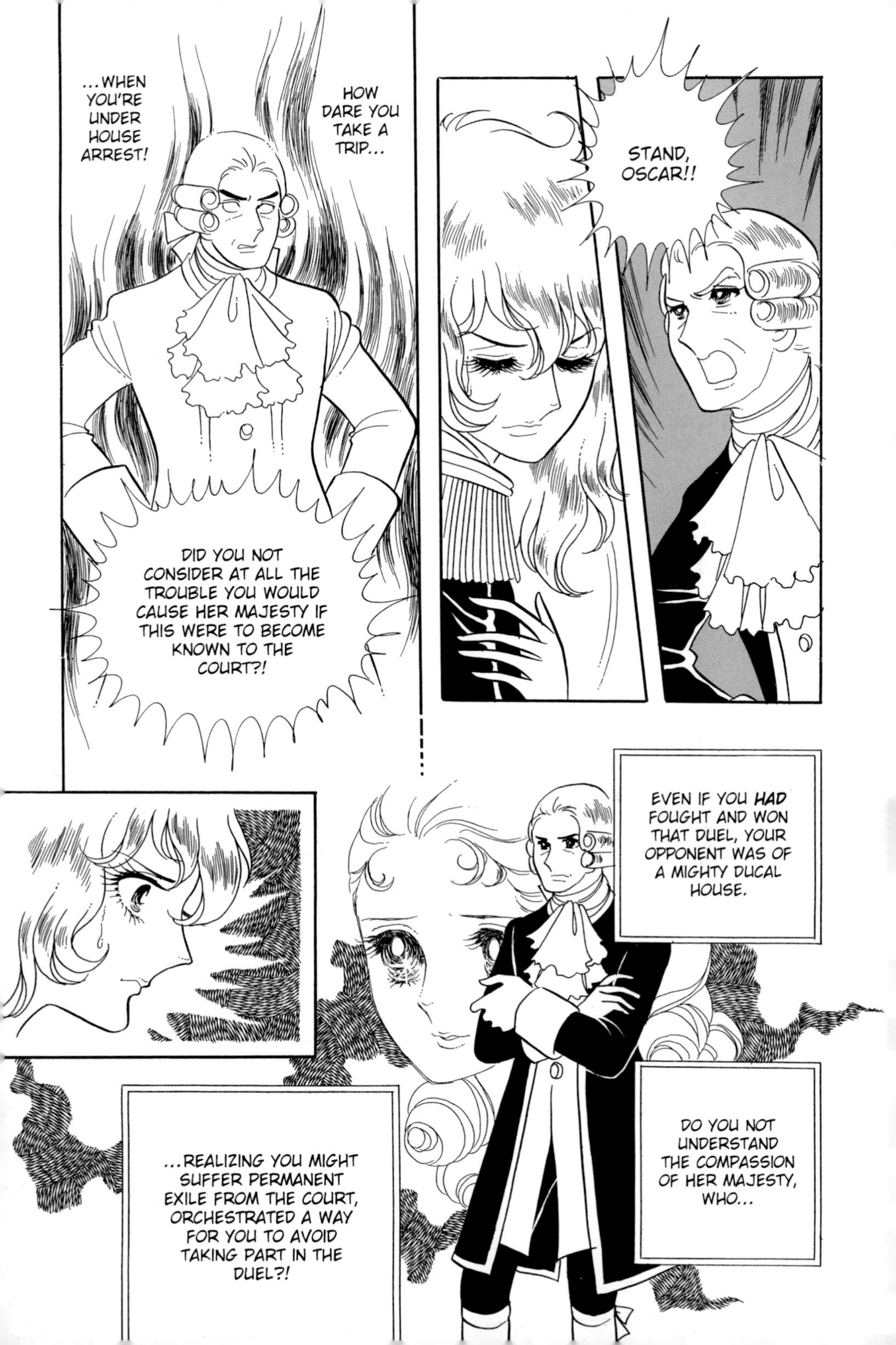
STAND, OSCAR!!
HOW DARE YOU TAKE A TRIP...
...WHEN YOU'RE UNDER HOUSE ARREST!
DID YOU NOT CONSIDER AT ALL THE TROUBLE YOU WOULD CAUSE HER MAJESTY IF THIS WERE TO BECOME KNOWN TO THE COURT?!
EVEN IF YOU **HAD** FOUGHT AND WON THAT DUEL, YOUR OPPONENT WAS OF A MIGHTY DUCAL HOUSE.
DO YOU NOT UNDERSTAND THE COMPASSION OF HER MAJESTY, WHO...
...REALIZING YOU MIGHT SUFFER PERMANENT EXILE FROM THE COURT, ORCHESTRATED A WAY FOR YOU TO AVOID TAKING PART IN THE DUEL?!

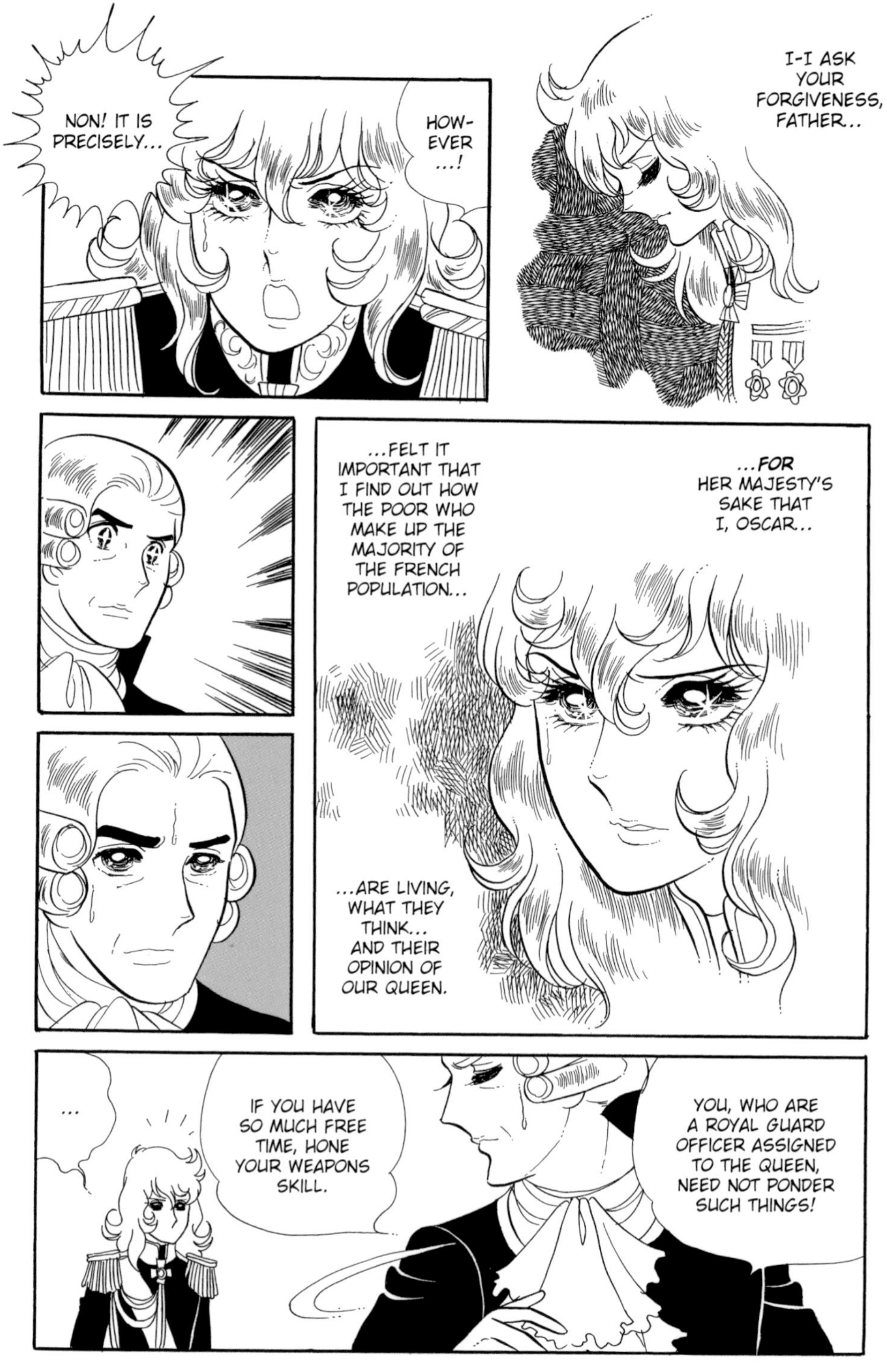
I-I ASK YOUR FORGIVENESS, FATHER...
HOW-EVER ...!
NON! IT IS PRECISELY...
...FOR HER MAJESTY'S SAKE THAT I, OSCAR...
...FELT IT IMPORTANT THAT I FIND OUT HOW THE POOR WHO MAKE UP THE MAJORITY OF THE FRENCH POPULATION...
...ARE LIVING, WHAT THEY THINK... AND THEIR OPINION OF OUR QUEEN.
YOU, WHO ARE A ROYAL GUARD OFFICER ASSIGNED TO THE QUEEN, NEED NOT PONDER SUCH THINGS!
IF YOU HAVE SO MUCH FREE TIME, HONE YOUR WEAPONS SKILL.
...

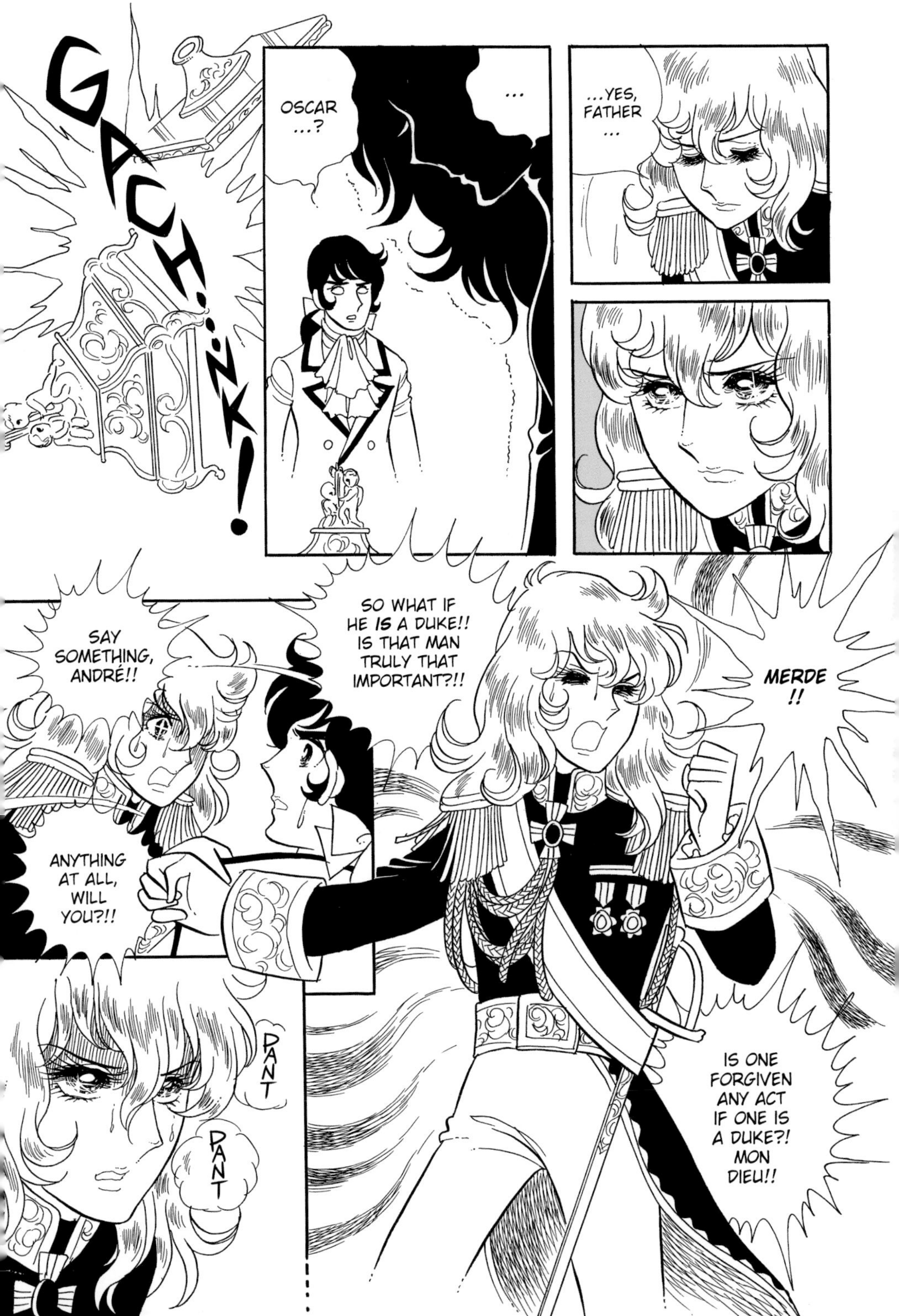
...YES, FATHER ...
...
OSCAR ...?
GACHINK!
MERDE !!
SO WHAT IF HE IS A DUKE!! IS THAT MAN TRULY THAT IMPORTANT?!!
IS ONE FORGIVEN ANY ACT IF ONE IS A DUKE?! MON DIEU!!
SAY SOMETHING, ANDRÉ!!
ANYTHING AT ALL, WILL YOU?!!
PANT
PANT

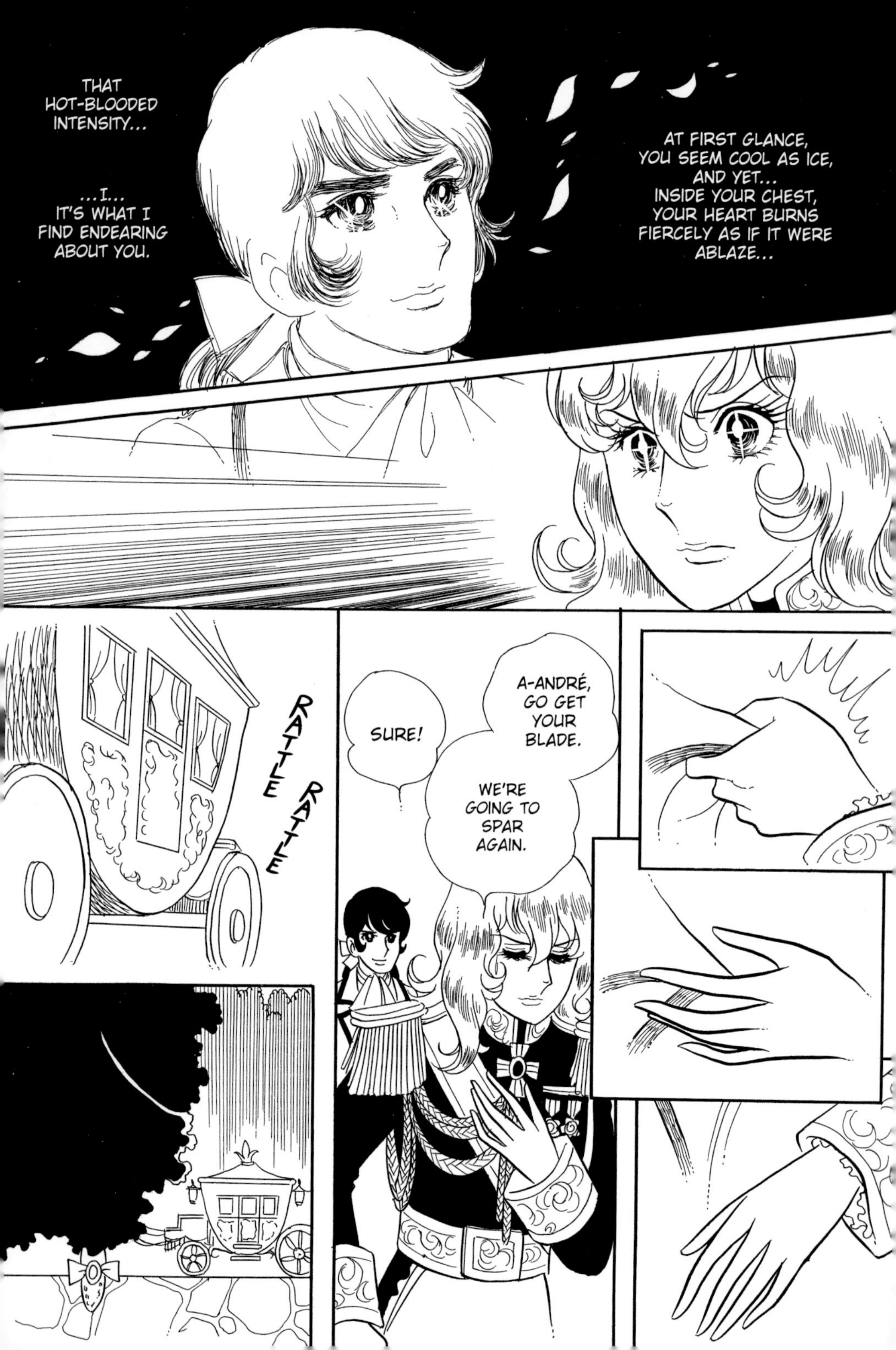
AT FIRST GLANCE, YOU SEEM COOL AS ICE, AND YET... INSIDE YOUR CHEST, YOUR HEART BURNS FIERCELY AS IF IT WERE ABLAZE...
THAT HOT-BLOODED INTENSITY...
...I... IT'S WHAT I FIND ENDEARING ABOUT YOU.
A-ANDRÉ, GO GET YOUR BLADE.
WE'RE GOING TO SPAR AGAIN.
SURE!
RATTLE RATTLE

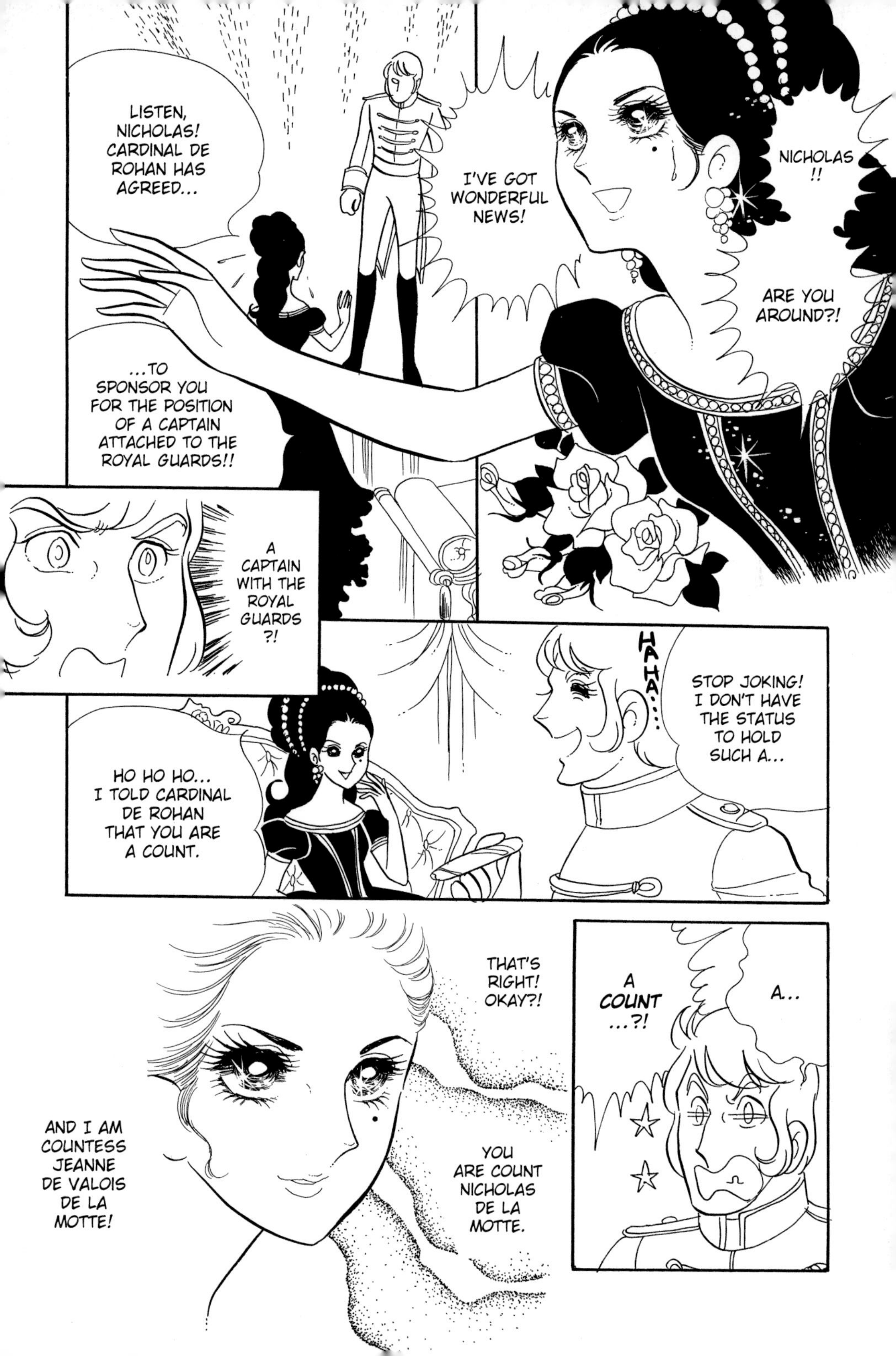
NICHOLAS !!
ARE YOU AROUND?!
I'VE GOT WONDERFUL NEWS!
LISTEN, NICHOLAS! CARDINAL DE ROHAN HAS AGREED...
...TO SPONSOR YOU FOR THE POSITION OF A CAPTAIN ATTACHED TO THE ROYAL GUARDS!!
A CAPTAIN WITH THE ROYAL GUARDS ?!
HAHA...
STOP JOKING! I DON'T HAVE THE STATUS TO HOLD SUCH A...
HO HO HO... I TOLD CARDINAL DE ROHAN THAT YOU ARE A COUNT.
A...
A COUNT ...?!
THAT'S RIGHT! OKAY?!
YOU ARE COUNT NICHOLAS DE LA MOTTE.
AND I AM COUNTESS JEANNE DE VALOIS DE LA MOTTE!

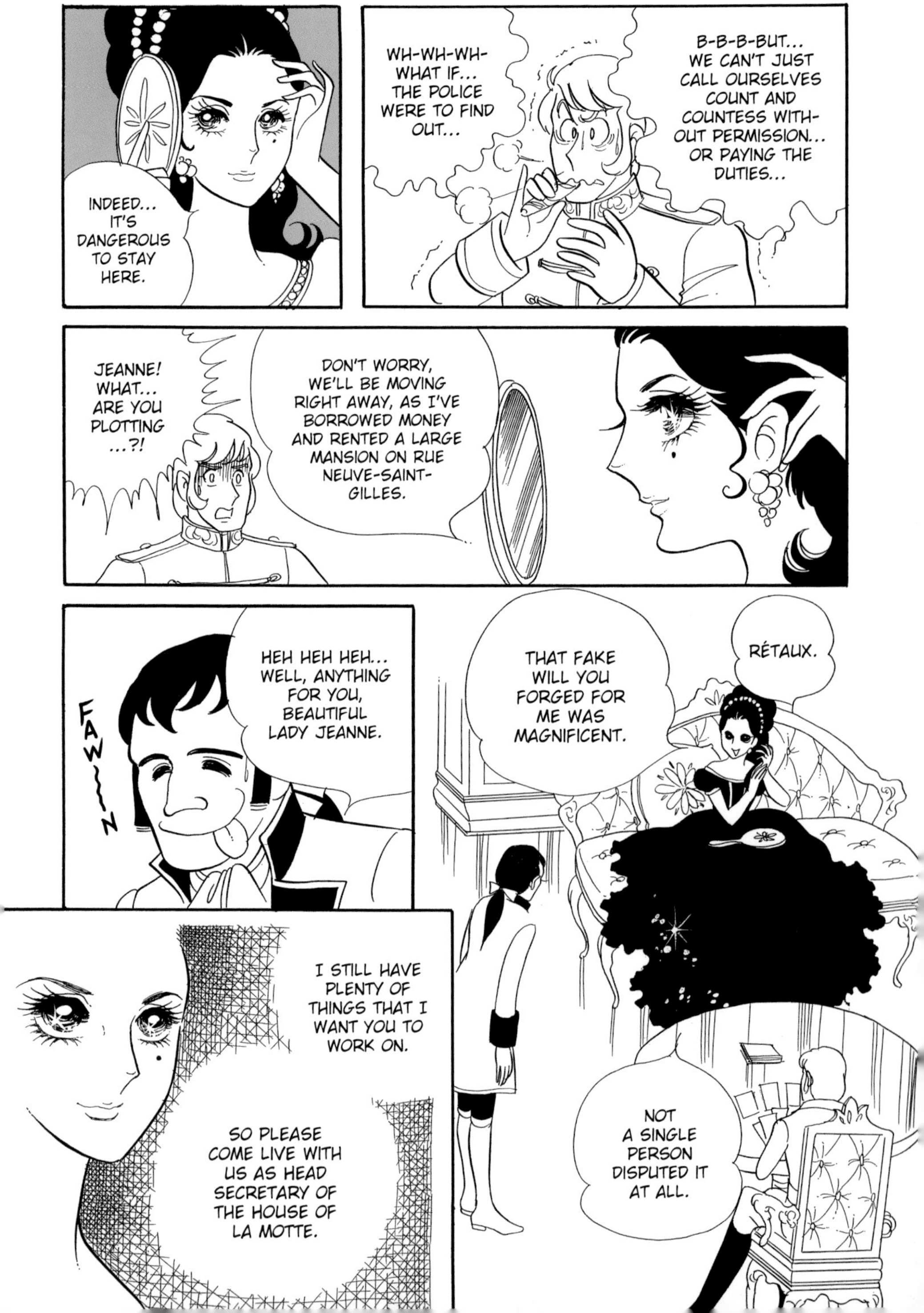
B-B-B-BUT... WE CAN'T JUST CALL OURSELVES COUNT AND COUNTESS WITHOUT PERMISSION... OR PAYING THE DUTIES...
WH-WH-WH-WHAT IF... THE POLICE WERE TO FIND OUT...
INDEED... IT'S DANGEROUS TO STAY HERE.
DON'T WORRY, WE'LL BE MOVING RIGHT AWAY, AS I'VE BORROWED MONEY AND RENTED A LARGE MANSION ON RUE NEUVE-SAINT-GILLES.
JEANNE! WHAT... ARE YOU PLOTTING ...?!
RÉTAUX.
THAT FAKE WILL YOU FORGED FOR ME WAS MAGNIFICENT.
NOT A SINGLE PERSON DISPUTED IT AT ALL.
HEH HEH HEH... WELL, ANYTHING FOR YOU, BEAUTIFUL LADY JEANNE.
FAWIIN
I STILL HAVE PLENTY OF THINGS THAT I WANT YOU TO WORK ON.
SO PLEASE COME LIVE WITH US AS HEAD SECRETARY OF THE HOUSE OF LA MOTTE.

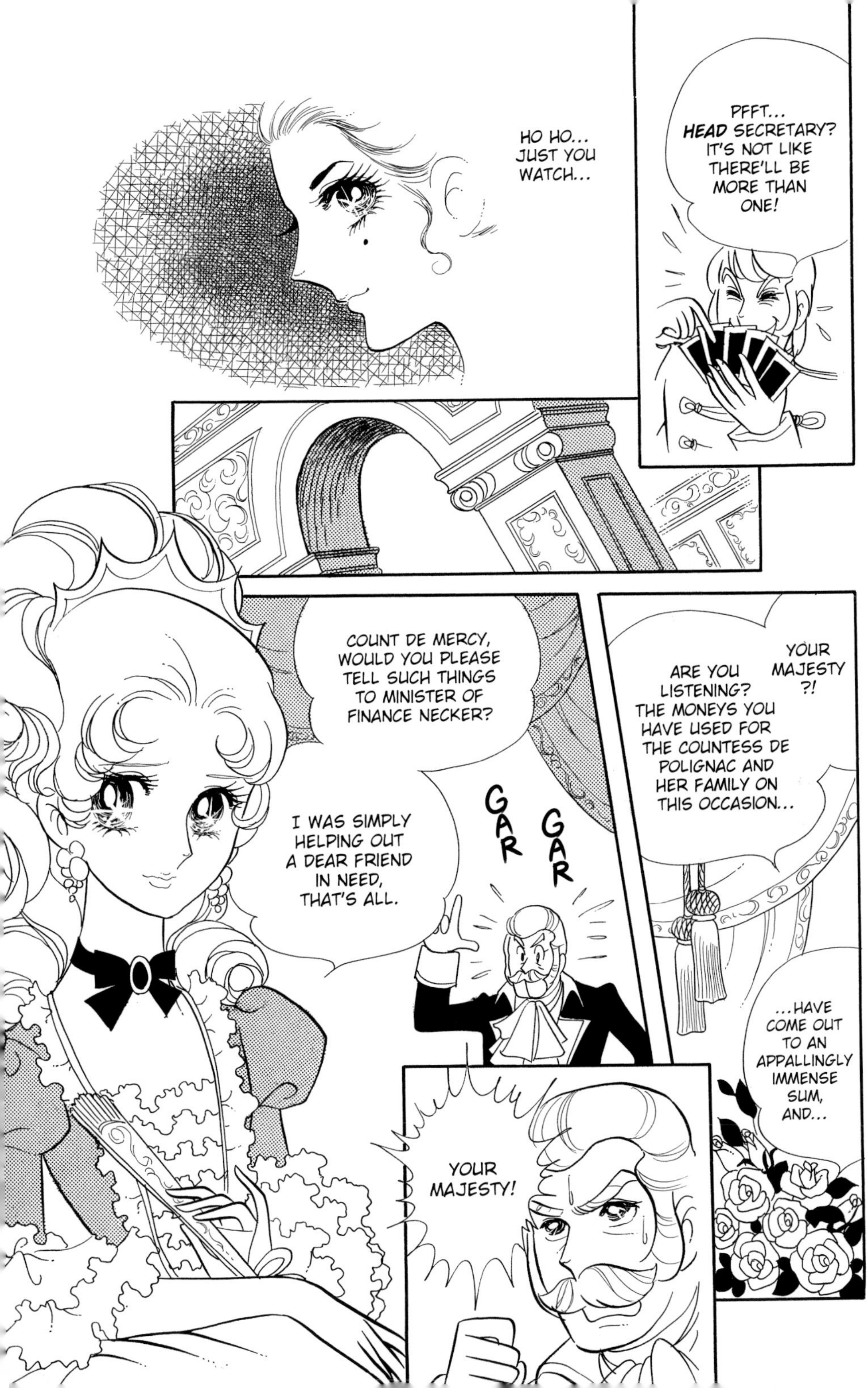
PFFT... **HEAD** SECRETARY? IT'S NOT LIKE THERE'LL BE MORE THAN ONE!
HO HO... JUST YOU WATCH...
YOUR MAJESTY ?!
ARE YOU LISTENING? THE MONEYS YOU HAVE USED FOR THE COUNTESS DE POLIGNAC AND HER FAMILY ON THIS OCCASION...
...HAVE COME OUT TO AN APPALLINGLY IMMENSE SUM, AND...
COUNT DE MERCY, WOULD YOU PLEASE TELL SUCH THINGS TO MINISTER OF FINANCE NECKER?
I WAS SIMPLY HELPING OUT A DEAR FRIEND IN NEED, THAT'S ALL.
GAR GAR
YOUR MAJESTY!

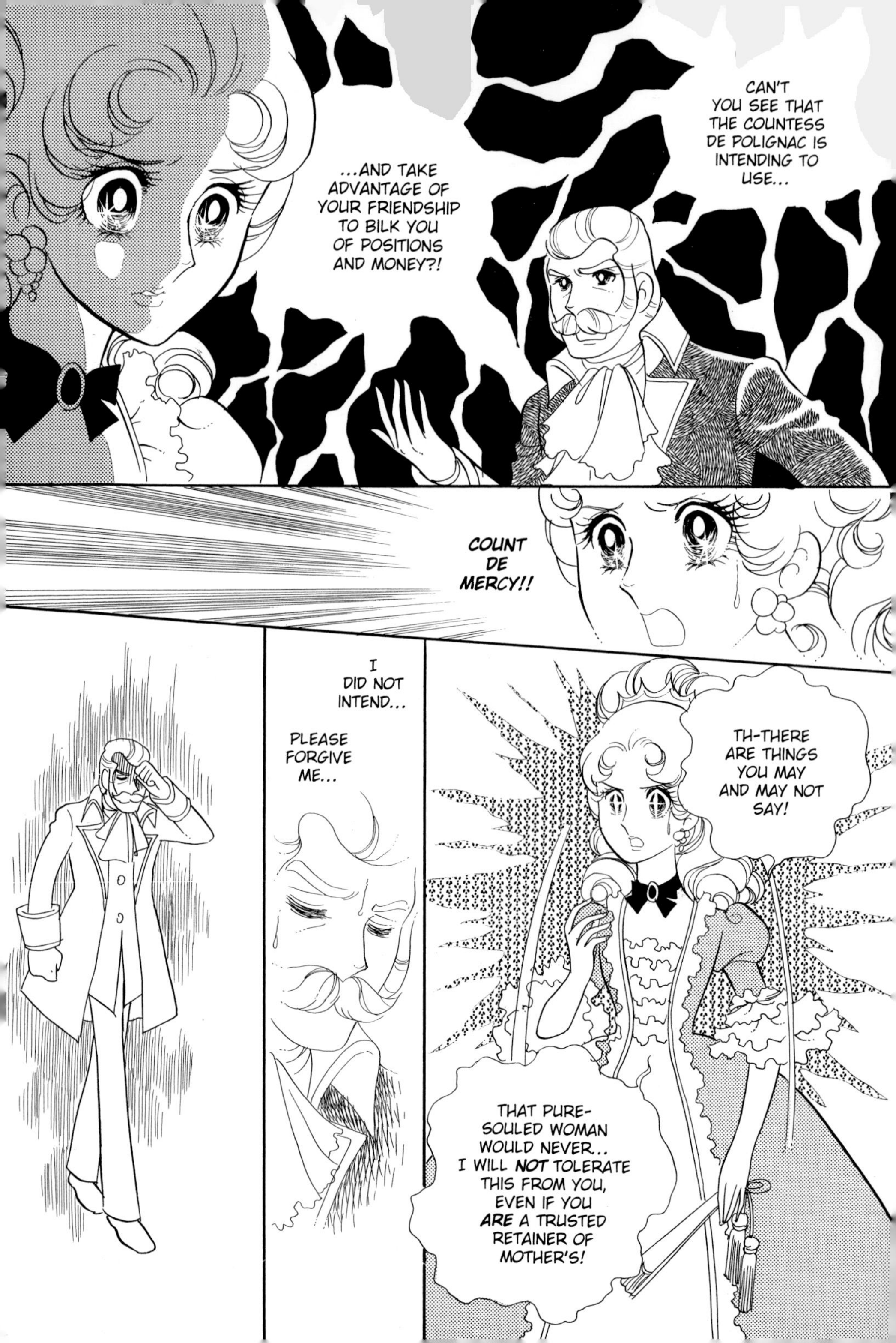
CAN'T YOU SEE THAT THE COUNTESS DE POLIGNAC IS INTENDING TO USE...
...AND TAKE ADVANTAGE OF YOUR FRIENDSHIP TO BILK YOU OF POSITIONS AND MONEY?!
COUNT DE MERCY!!
TH-THERE ARE THINGS YOU MAY AND MAY NOT SAY!
THAT PURE-SOULED WOMAN WOULD NEVER... I WILL NOT TOLERATE THIS FROM YOU, EVEN IF YOU ARE A TRUSTED RETAINER OF MOTHER'S!
I DID NOT INTEND...
PLEASE FORGIVE ME...

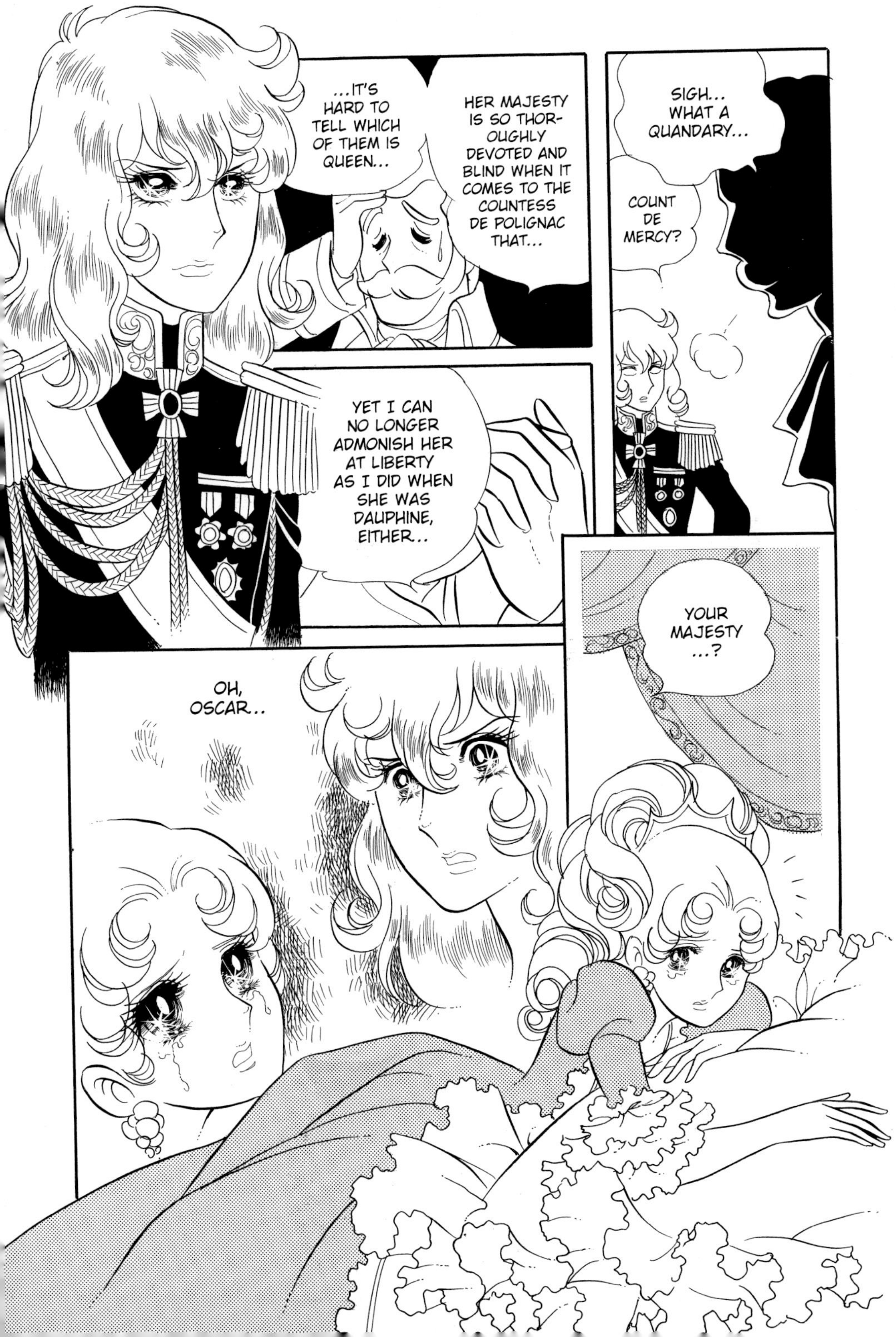
SIGH... WHAT A QUANDARY...
COUNT DE MERCY?
HER MAJESTY IS SO THOROUGHLY DEVOTED AND BLIND WHEN IT COMES TO THE COUNTESS DE POLIGNAC THAT...
...IT'S HARD TO TELL WHICH OF THEM IS QUEEN...
YET I CAN NO LONGER ADMONISH HER AT LIBERTY AS I DID WHEN SHE WAS DAUPHINE, EITHER...
YOUR MAJESTY ...?
OH, OSCAR...

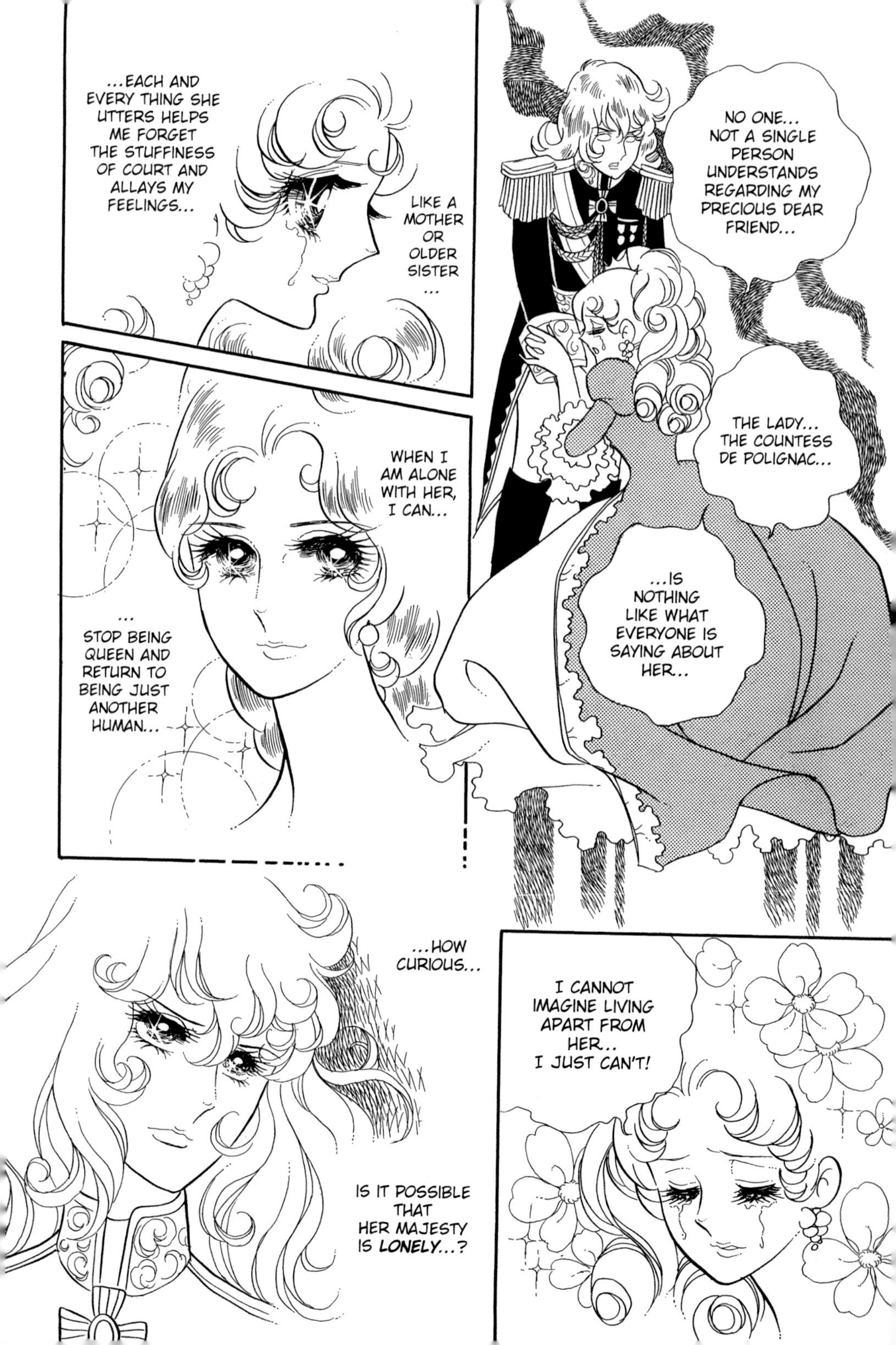

NO ONE... NOT A SINGLE PERSON UNDERSTANDS REGARDING MY PRECIOUS DEAR FRIEND...
THE LADY... THE COUNTESS DE POLIGNAC...
...IS NOTHING LIKE WHAT EVERYONE IS SAYING ABOUT HER...
...EACH AND EVERY THING SHE UTTERS HELPS ME FORGET THE STUFFINESS OF COURT AND ALLAYS MY FEELINGS...
LIKE A MOTHER OR OLDER SISTER ...
WHEN I AM ALONE WITH HER, I CAN...
... STOP BEING QUEEN AND RETURN TO BEING JUST ANOTHER HUMAN...
I CANNOT IMAGINE LIVING APART FROM HER... I JUST CAN'T!
...HOW CURIOUS...
IS IT POSSIBLE THAT HER MAJESTY IS **LONELY**...?

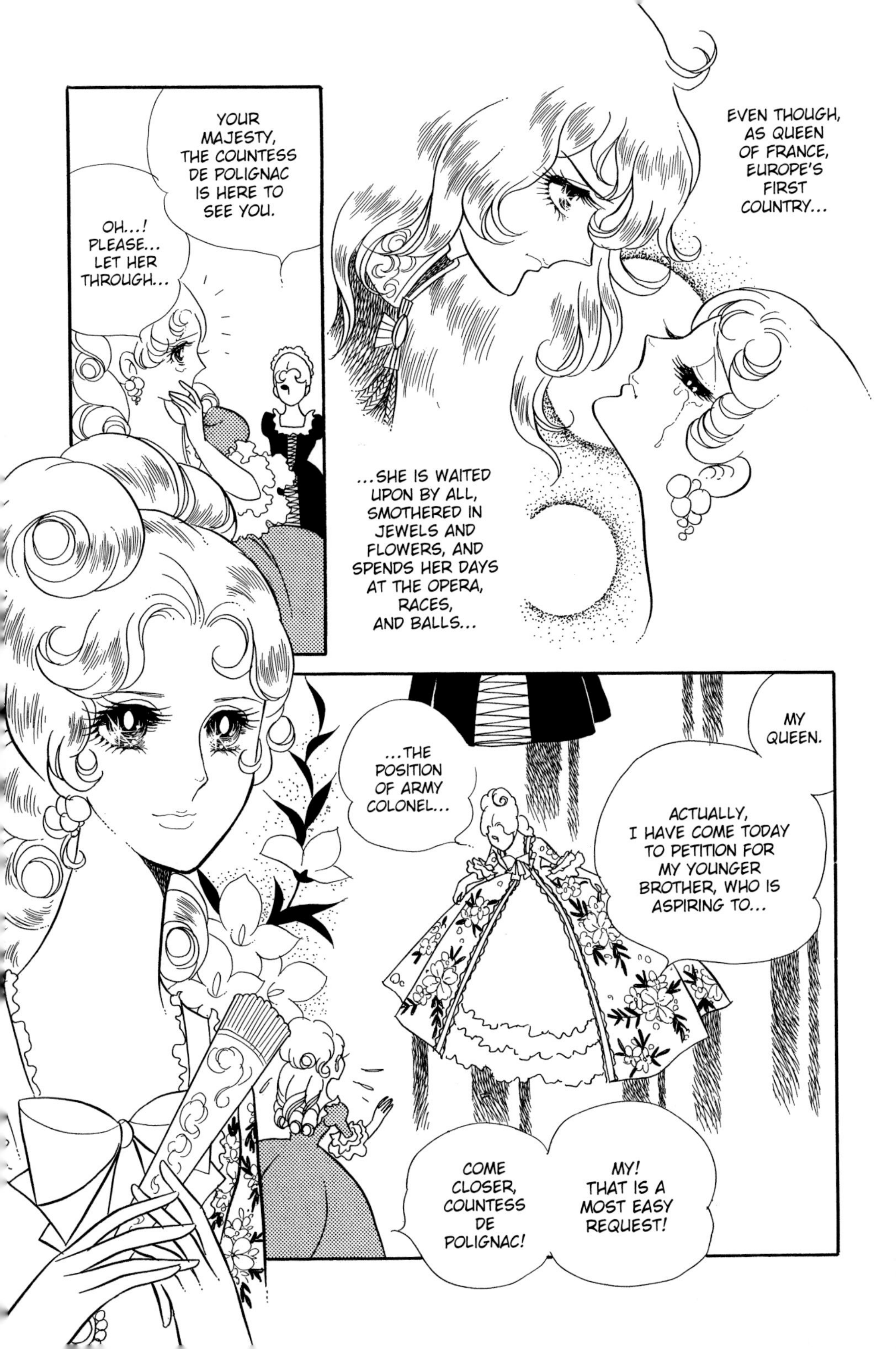
EVEN THOUGH, AS QUEEN OF FRANCE, EUROPE'S FIRST COUNTRY...
...SHE IS WAITED UPON BY ALL, SMOTHERED IN JEWELS AND FLOWERS, AND SPENDS HER DAYS AT THE OPERA, RACES, AND BALLS...
YOUR MAJESTY, THE COUNTESS DE POLIGNAC IS HERE TO SEE YOU.
OH...! PLEASE... LET HER THROUGH...
MY QUEEN.
ACTUALLY, I HAVE COME TODAY TO PETITION FOR MY YOUNGER BROTHER, WHO IS ASPIRING TO...
...THE POSITION OF ARMY COLONEL...
MY! THAT IS A MOST EASY REQUEST!
COME CLOSER, COUNTESS DE POLIGNAC!

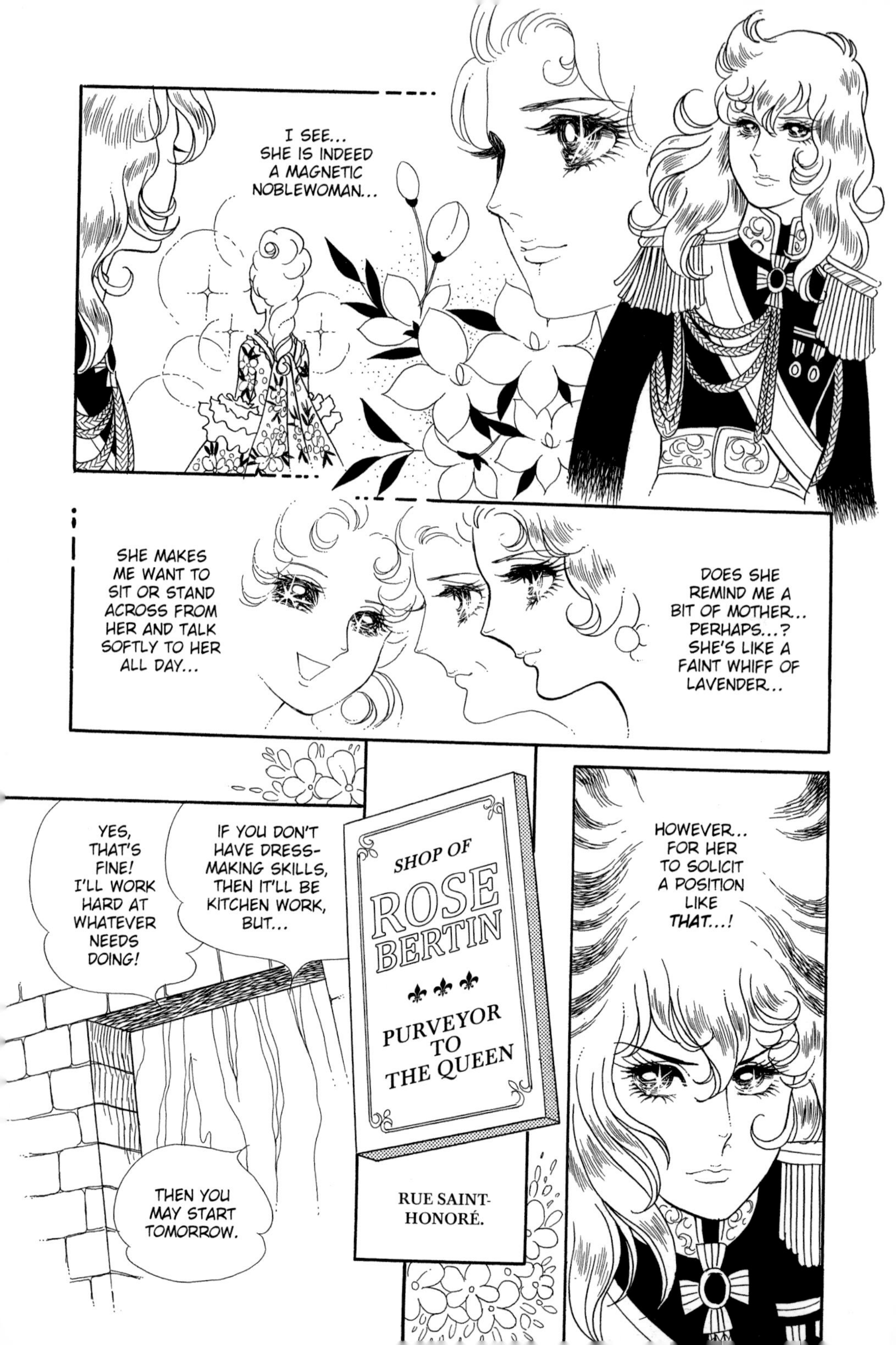
I SEE... SHE IS INDEED A MAGNETIC NOBLEWOMAN...
DOES SHE REMIND ME A BIT OF MOTHER... PERHAPS...? SHE'S LIKE A FAINT WHIFF OF LAVENDER...
SHE MAKES ME WANT TO SIT OR STAND ACROSS FROM HER AND TALK SOFTLY TO HER ALL DAY...
HOWEVER... FOR HER TO SOLICIT A POSITION LIKE *THAT*...!
SHOP OF
ROSE BERTIN
PURVEYOR TO THE QUEEN
RUE SAINT-HONORÉ.
IF YOU DON'T HAVE DRESS-MAKING SKILLS, THEN IT'LL BE KITCHEN WORK, BUT...
YES, THAT'S FINE! I'LL WORK HARD AT WHATEVER NEEDS DOING!
THEN YOU MAY START TOMORROW.

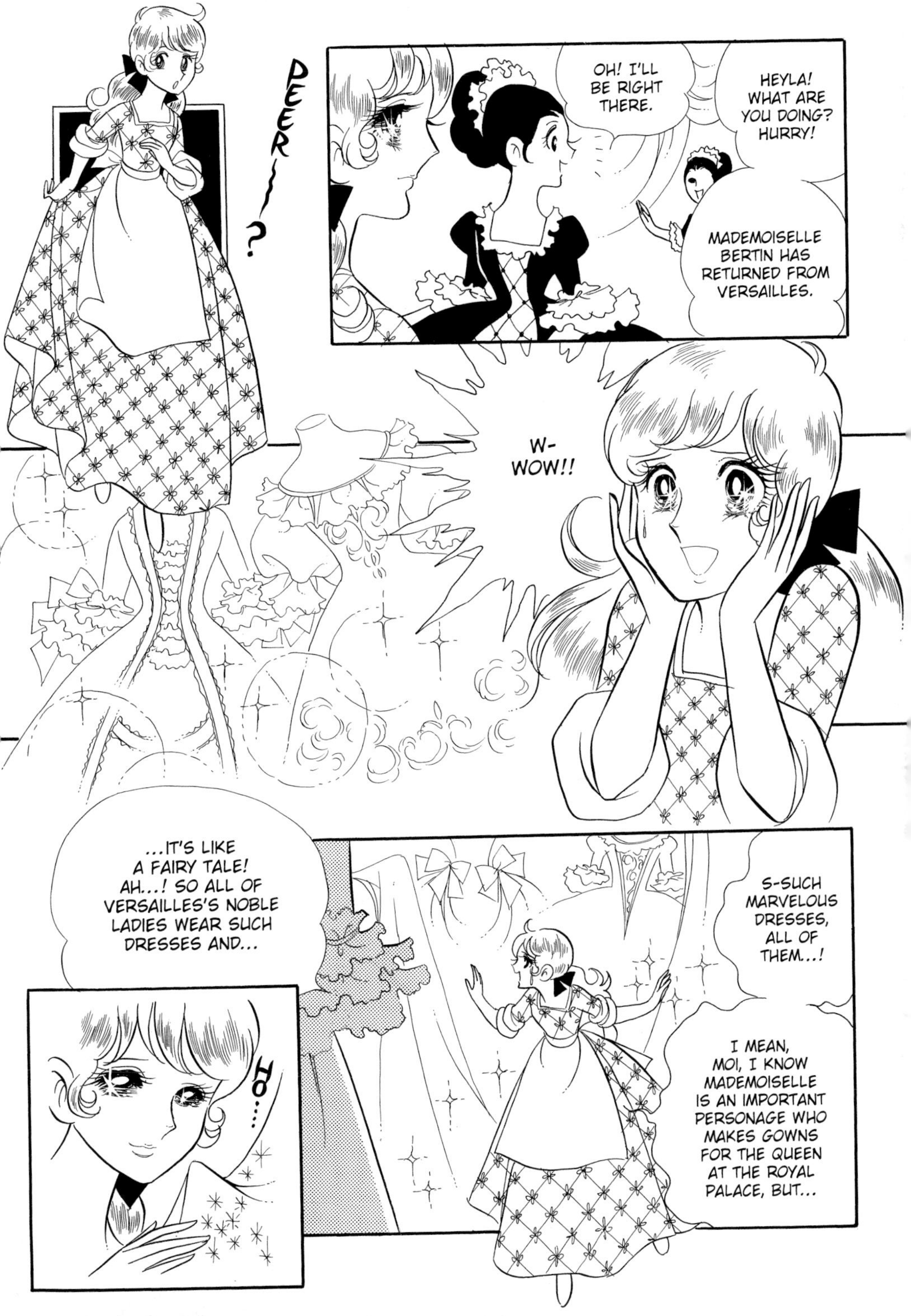
HEYLA! WHAT ARE YOU DOING? HURRY!
MADEMOISELLE BERTIN HAS RETURNED FROM VERSAILLES.
OH! I'LL BE RIGHT THERE.
PEER~~?
W-WOW!!
S-SUCH MARVELOUS DRESSES, ALL OF THEM...!
I MEAN, MOI, I KNOW MADEMOISELLE IS AN IMPORTANT PERSONAGE WHO MAKES GOWNS FOR THE QUEEN AT THE ROYAL PALACE, BUT...
...IT'S LIKE A FAIRY TALE! AH...! SO ALL OF VERSAILLES'S NOBLE LADIES WEAR SUCH DRESSES AND...
HO...

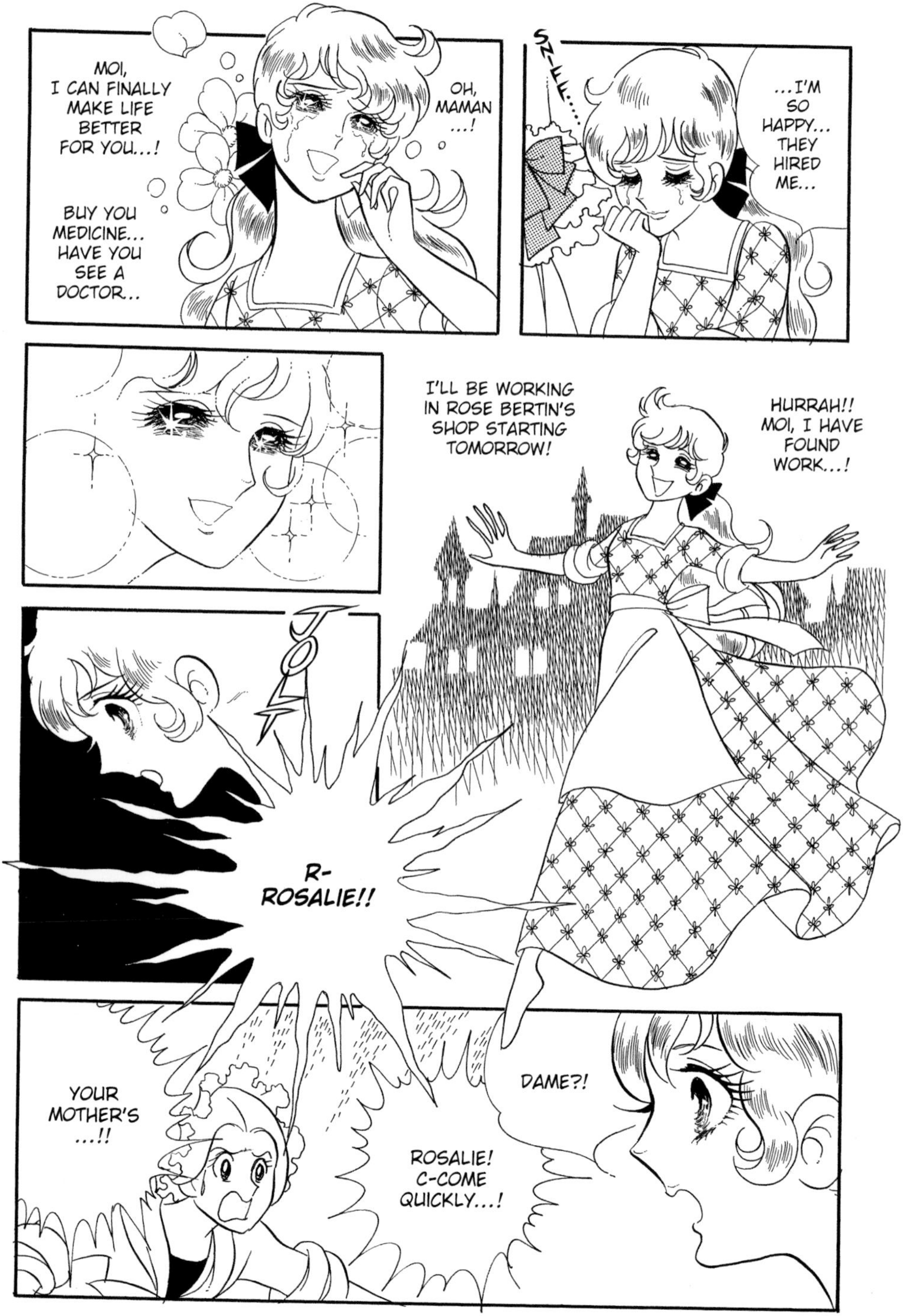
SNIFF
...I'M SO HAPPY... THEY HIRED ME...
OH, MAMAN ...!
MOI, I CAN FINALLY MAKE LIFE BETTER FOR YOU...!
BUY YOU MEDICINE... HAVE YOU SEE A DOCTOR..
HURRAH!! MOI, I HAVE FOUND WORK...!
I'LL BE WORKING IN ROSE BERTIN'S SHOP STARTING TOMORROW!
JOLT
R-ROSALIE!!
DAME?!
ROSALIE! C-COME QUICKLY...!
YOUR MOTHER'S ...!!

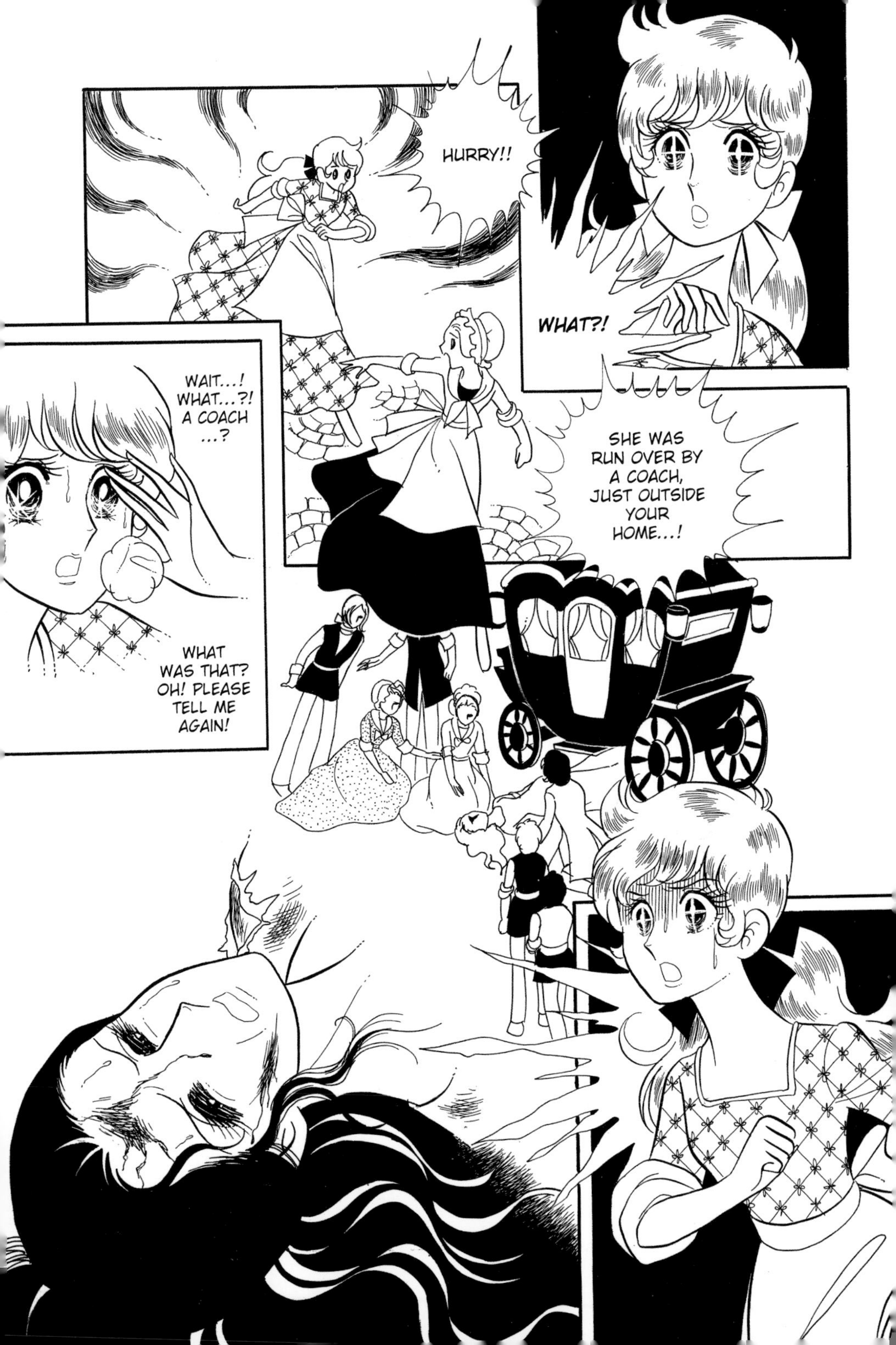
WHAT?!
HURRY!!
SHE WAS RUN OVER BY A COACH, JUST OUTSIDE YOUR HOME...!
WAIT...! WHAT...?! A COACH ...?
WHAT WAS THAT? OH! PLEASE TELL ME AGAIN!

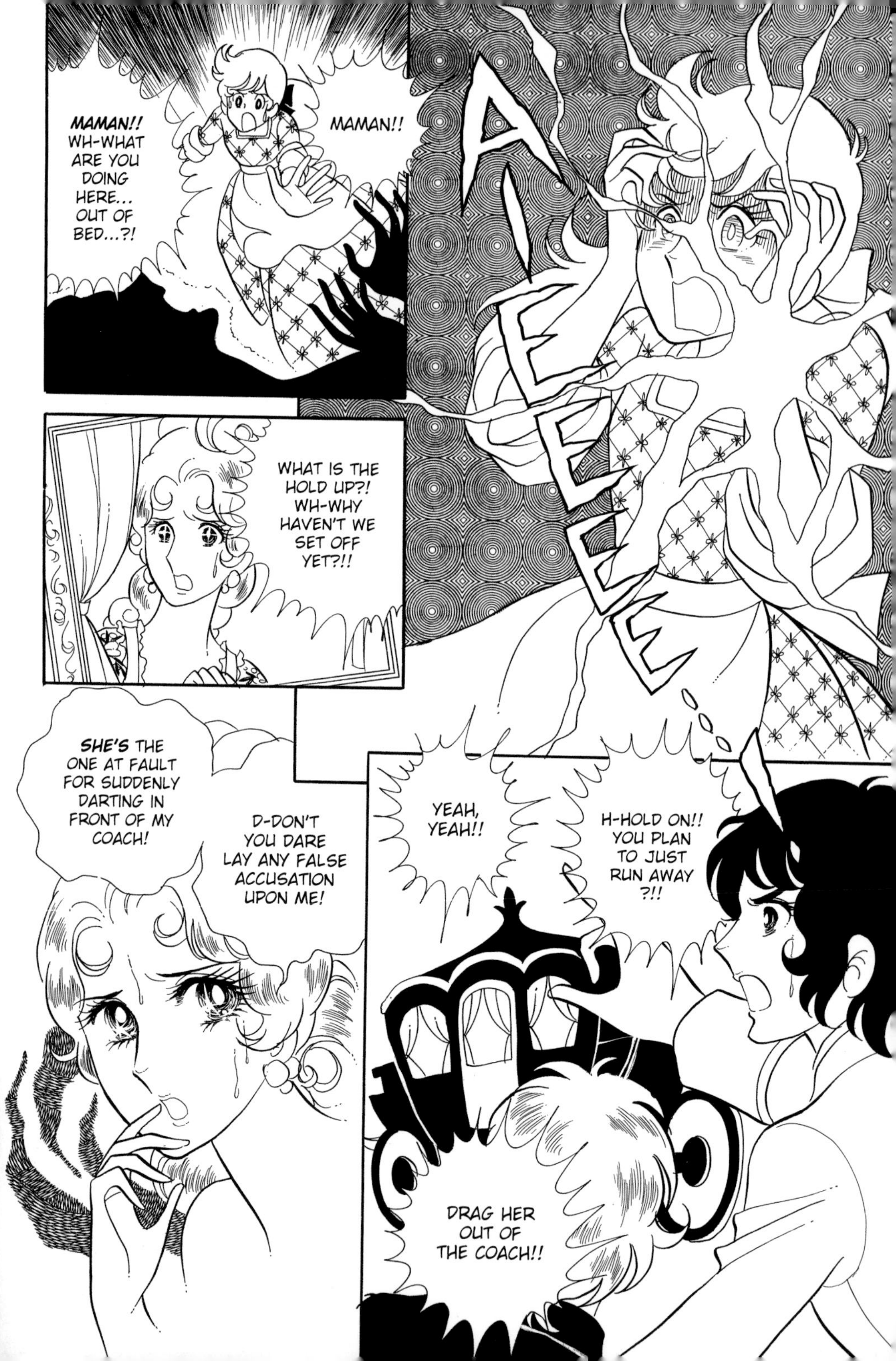
AIEEEEE...
MAMAN!!
MAMAN!! WH-WHAT ARE YOU DOING HERE... OUT OF BED...?!
WHAT IS THE HOLD UP?! WH-WHY HAVEN'T WE SET OFF YET?!!
H-HOLD ON!! YOU PLAN TO JUST RUN AWAY ?!!
YEAH, YEAH!!
DRAG HER OUT OF THE COACH!!
D-DON'T YOU DARE LAY ANY FALSE ACCUSATION UPON ME!
SHE'S THE ONE AT FAULT FOR SUDDENLY DARTING IN FRONT OF MY COACH!

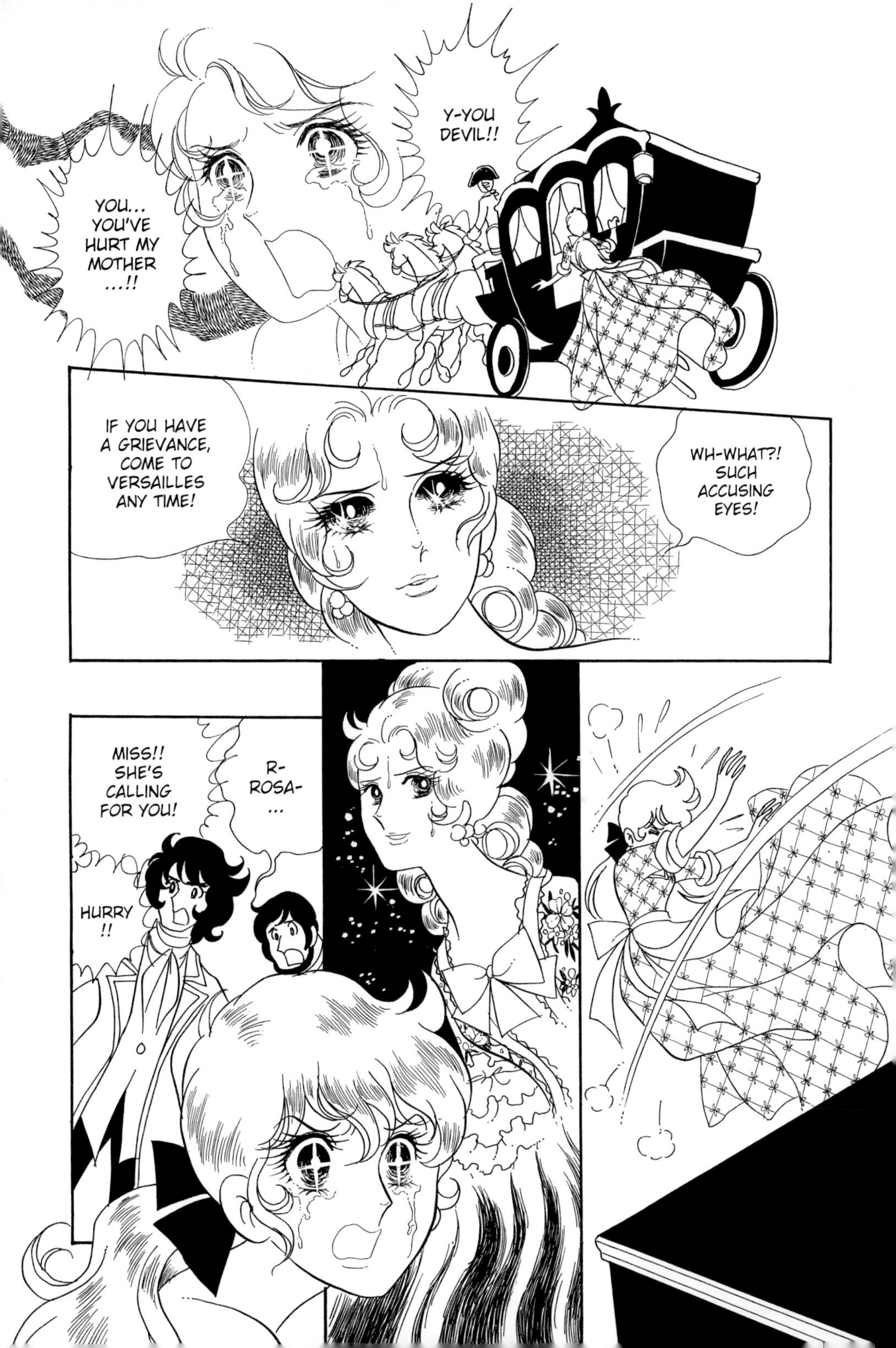
Y-YOU DEVIL!!
YOU... YOU'VE HURT MY MOTHER ...!!
WH-WHAT?! SUCH ACCUSING EYES!
IF YOU HAVE A GRIEVANCE, COME TO VERSAILLES ANY TIME!
R-ROSA-...
MISS!! SHE'S CALLING FOR YOU!
HURRY!!

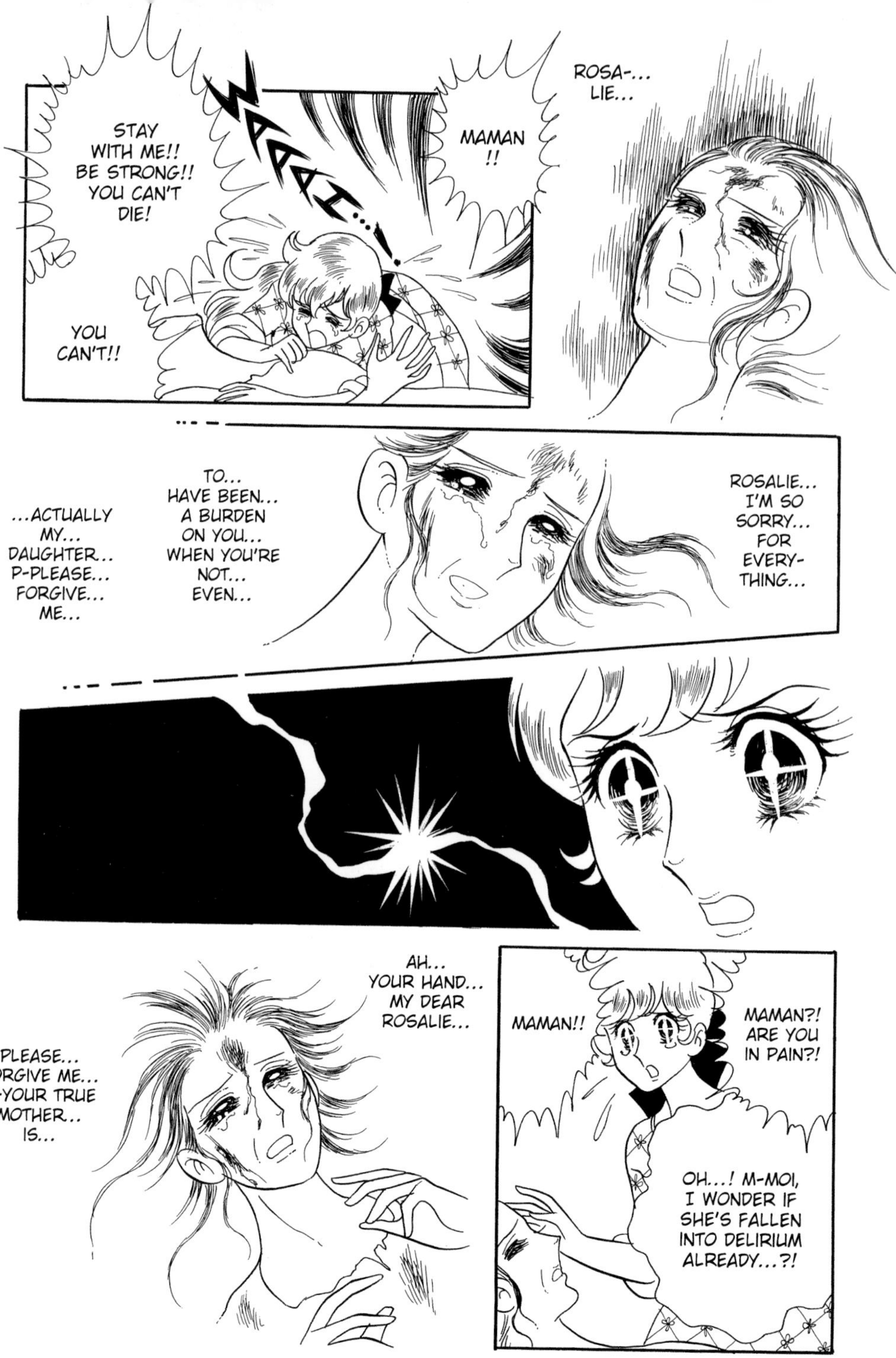
ROSA-... LIE...
MAMAN!!
WAAAI...!
STAY WITH ME!! BE STRONG!! YOU CAN'T DIE!
YOU CAN'T!!
ROSALIE... I'M SO SORRY... FOR EVERY-THING...
TO... HAVE BEEN... A BURDEN ON YOU... WHEN YOU'RE NOT... EVEN...
...ACTUALLY MY... DAUGHTER... P-PLEASE... FORGIVE... ME...
MAMAN?! ARE YOU IN PAIN?!
MAMAN!!
OH...! M-MOI, I WONDER IF SHE'S FALLEN INTO DELIRIUM ALREADY...?!
AH... YOUR HAND... MY DEAR ROSALIE...
PLEASE... FORGIVE ME... Y-YOUR TRUE MOTHER... IS...

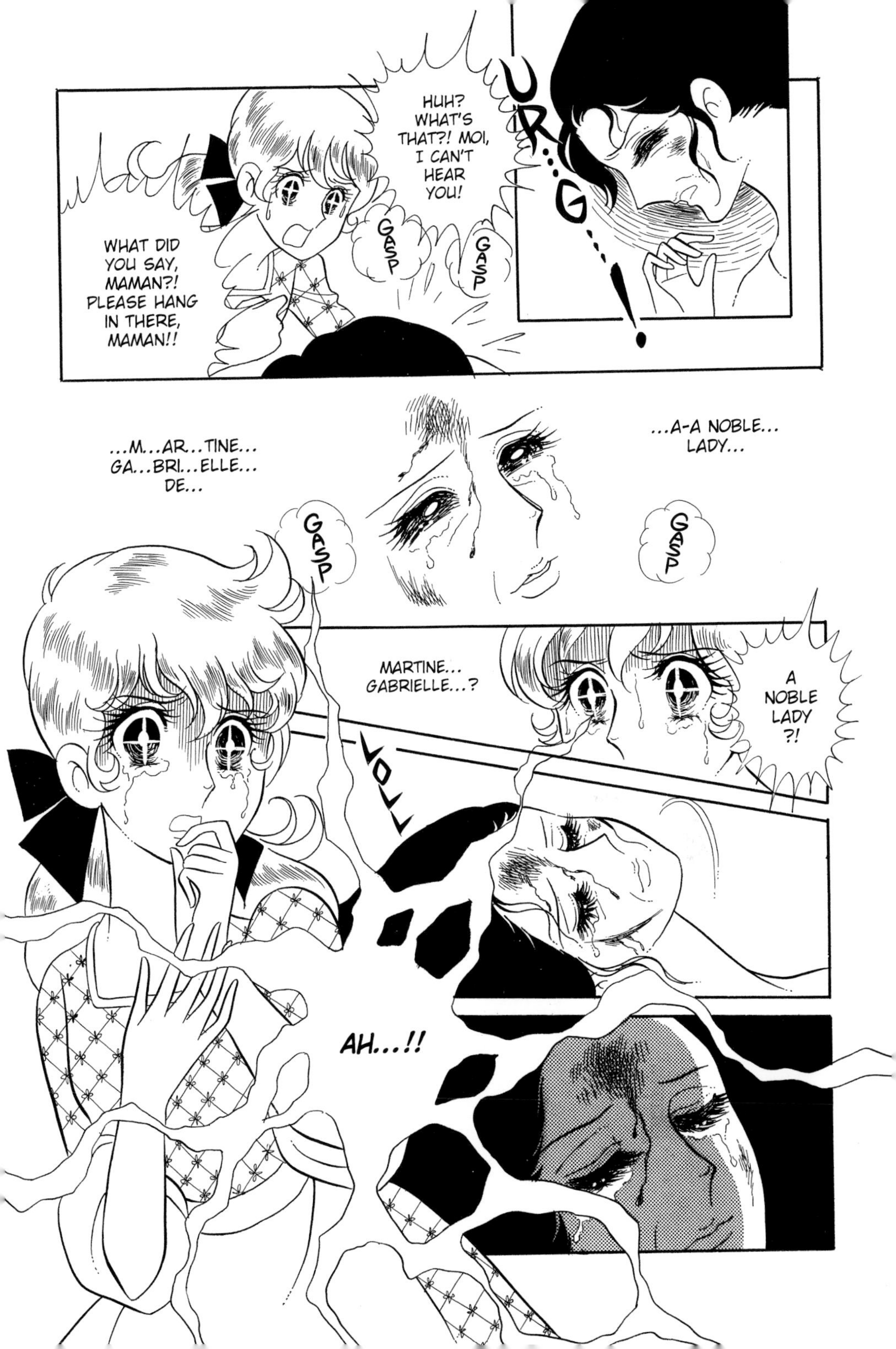
URG...!
HUH? WHAT'S THAT?! MOI, I CAN'T HEAR YOU!
GASP
GASP
WHAT DID YOU SAY, MAMAN?! PLEASE HANG IN THERE, MAMAN!!
...A-A NOBLE... LADY...
GASP
...M...AR...TINE... GA...BRI...ELLE... DE...
GASP
A NOBLE LADY?!
MARTINE... GABRIELLE...?
VOLL
AH...!!

1972 WEEKLY MARGARET MAGAZINE
ISSUE 37 BACK COVER INSERT ART

◆ THE INTRIGUES OF THE WOMAN TRYING TO USE ANTOINETTE GETS MORE INTENSE... MEANWHILE, WHAT OF ROSALIE!?

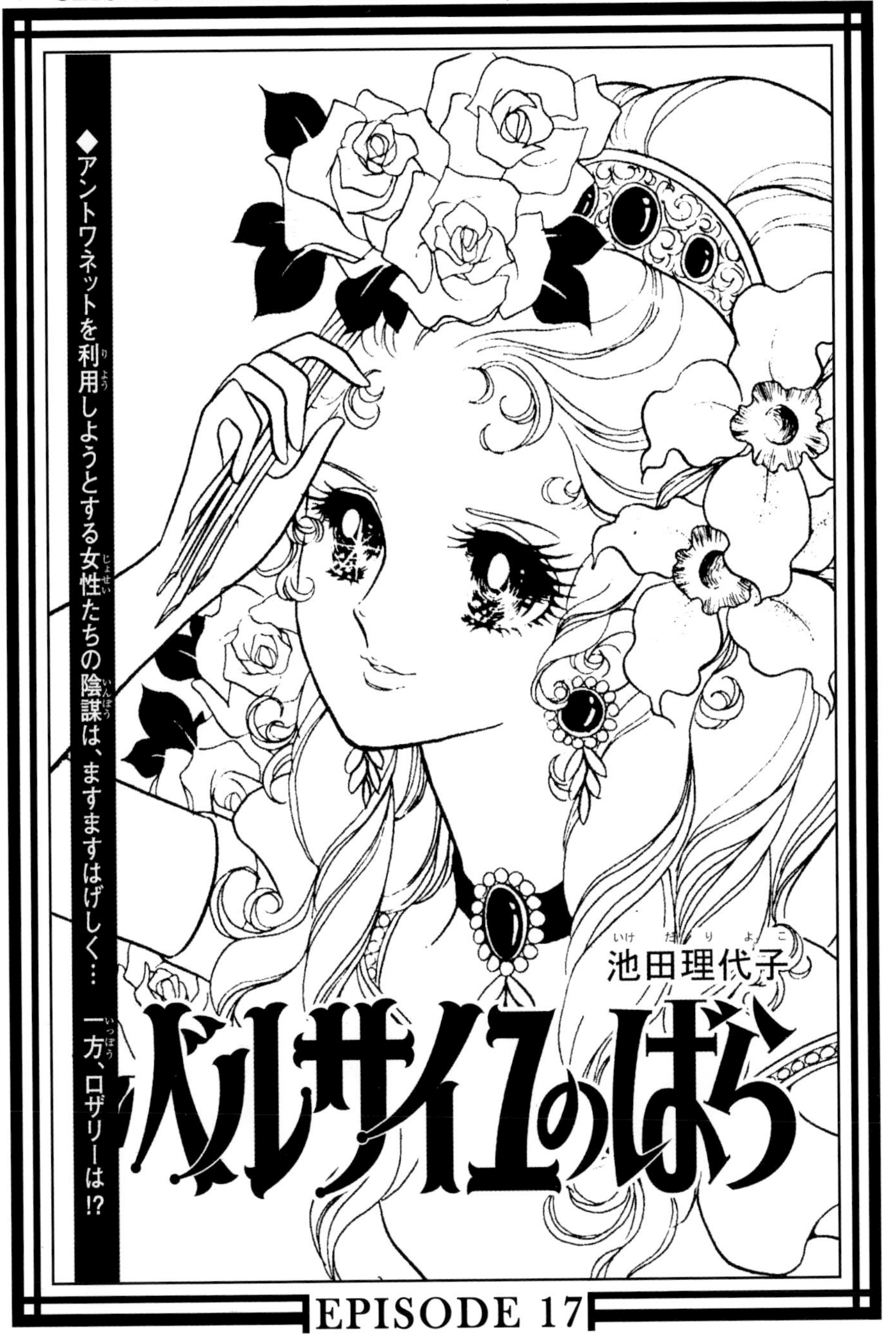
◆アントワネットを利用しようとする女性たちの陰謀は、ますますはげしく…一方、ロザリーは!?
池田理代子
ベルサイユのばら

EPISODE 17

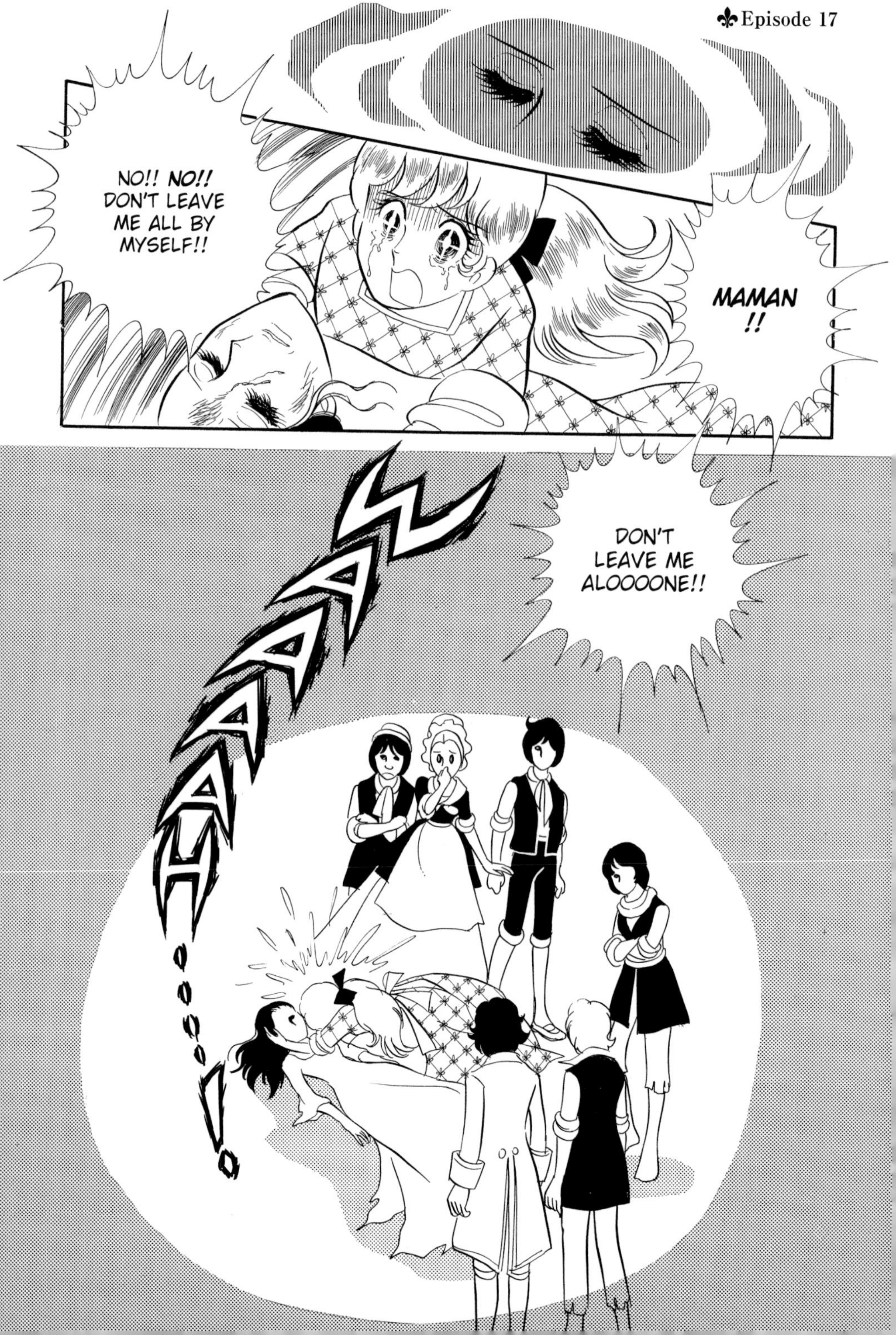
MAMAN!!
NO!! NO!! DON'T LEAVE ME ALL BY MYSELF!!
DON'T LEAVE ME ALOOOONE!!
WAAAAH......!

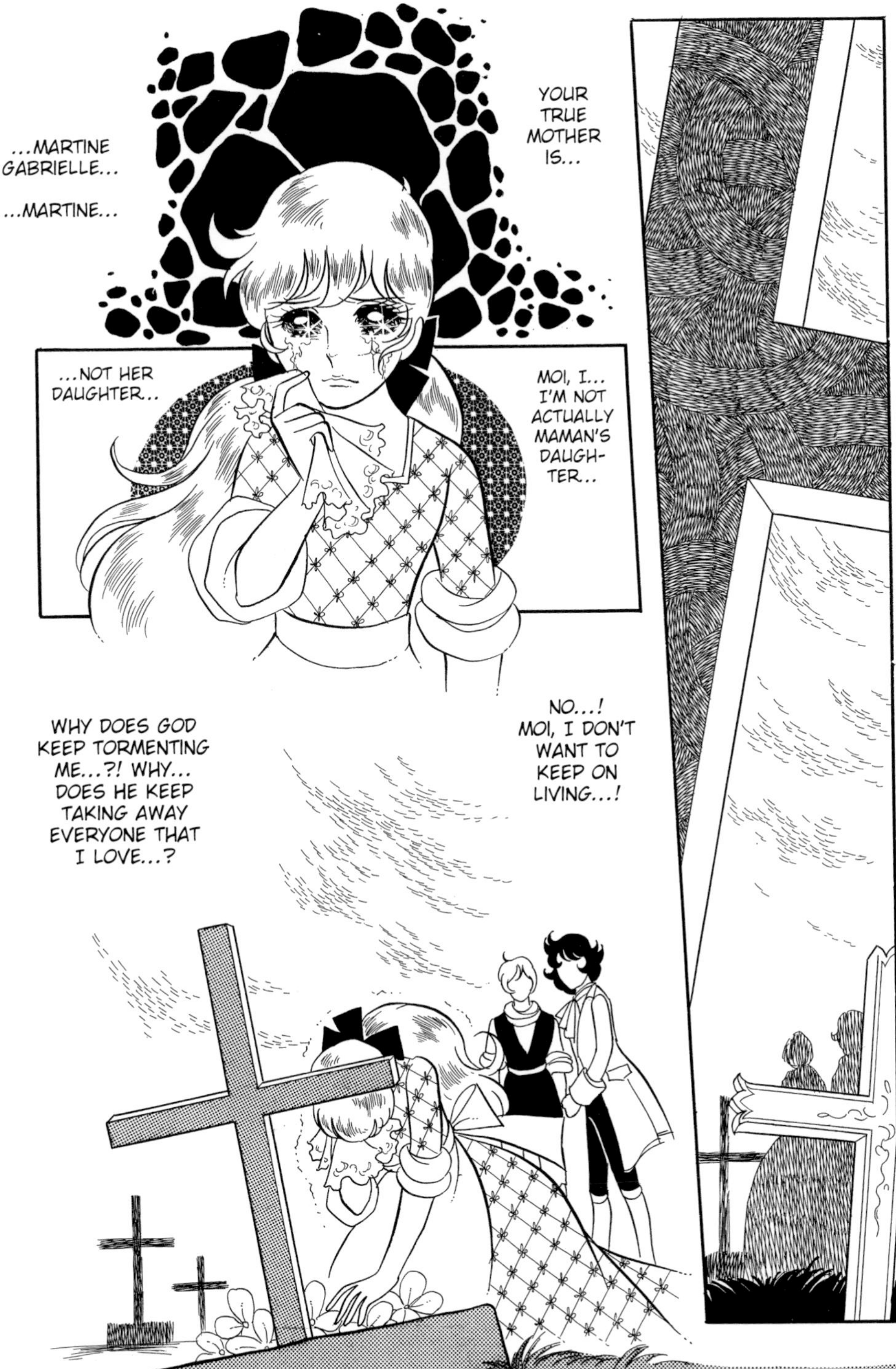
YOUR TRUE MOTHER IS...
...MARTINE GABRIELLE...
...MARTINE...
MOI, I... I'M NOT ACTUALLY MAMAN'S DAUGH-TER...
...NOT HER DAUGHTER...
NO...! MOI, I DON'T WANT TO KEEP ON LIVING...!
WHY DOES GOD KEEP TORMENTING ME...?! WHY... DOES HE KEEP TAKING AWAY EVERYONE THAT I LOVE...?

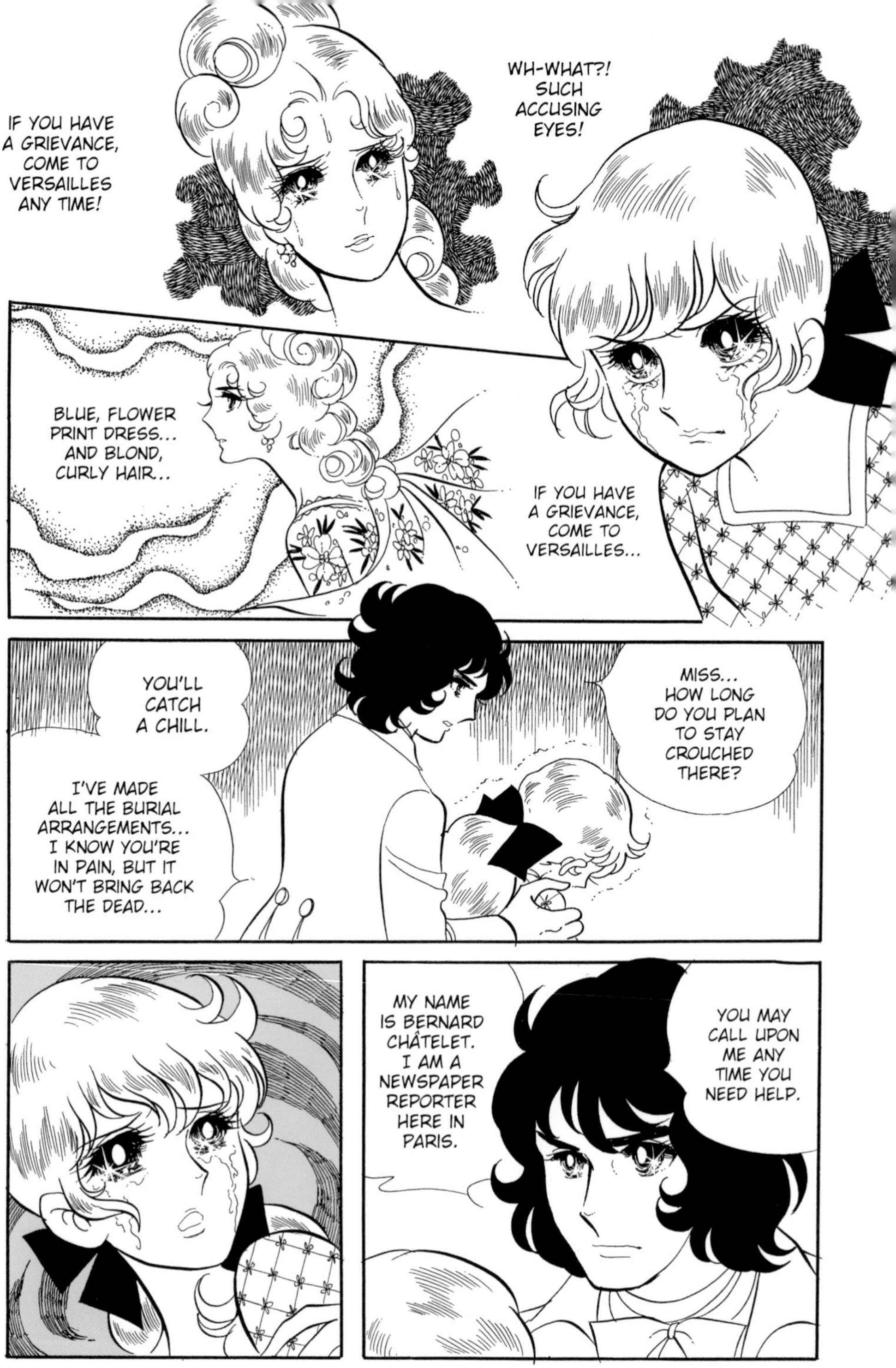
WH-WHAT?! SUCH ACCUSING EYES!
IF YOU HAVE A GRIEVANCE, COME TO VERSAILLES ANY TIME!
IF YOU HAVE A GRIEVANCE, COME TO VERSAILLES...
BLUE, FLOWER PRINT DRESS... AND BLOND, CURLY HAIR...
MISS... HOW LONG DO YOU PLAN TO STAY CROUCHED THERE?
YOU'LL CATCH A CHILL.
I'VE MADE ALL THE BURIAL ARRANGEMENTS... I KNOW YOU'RE IN PAIN, BUT IT WON'T BRING BACK THE DEAD...
MY NAME IS BERNARD CHÂTELET. I AM A NEWSPAPER REPORTER HERE IN PARIS.
YOU MAY CALL UPON ME ANY TIME YOU NEED HELP.

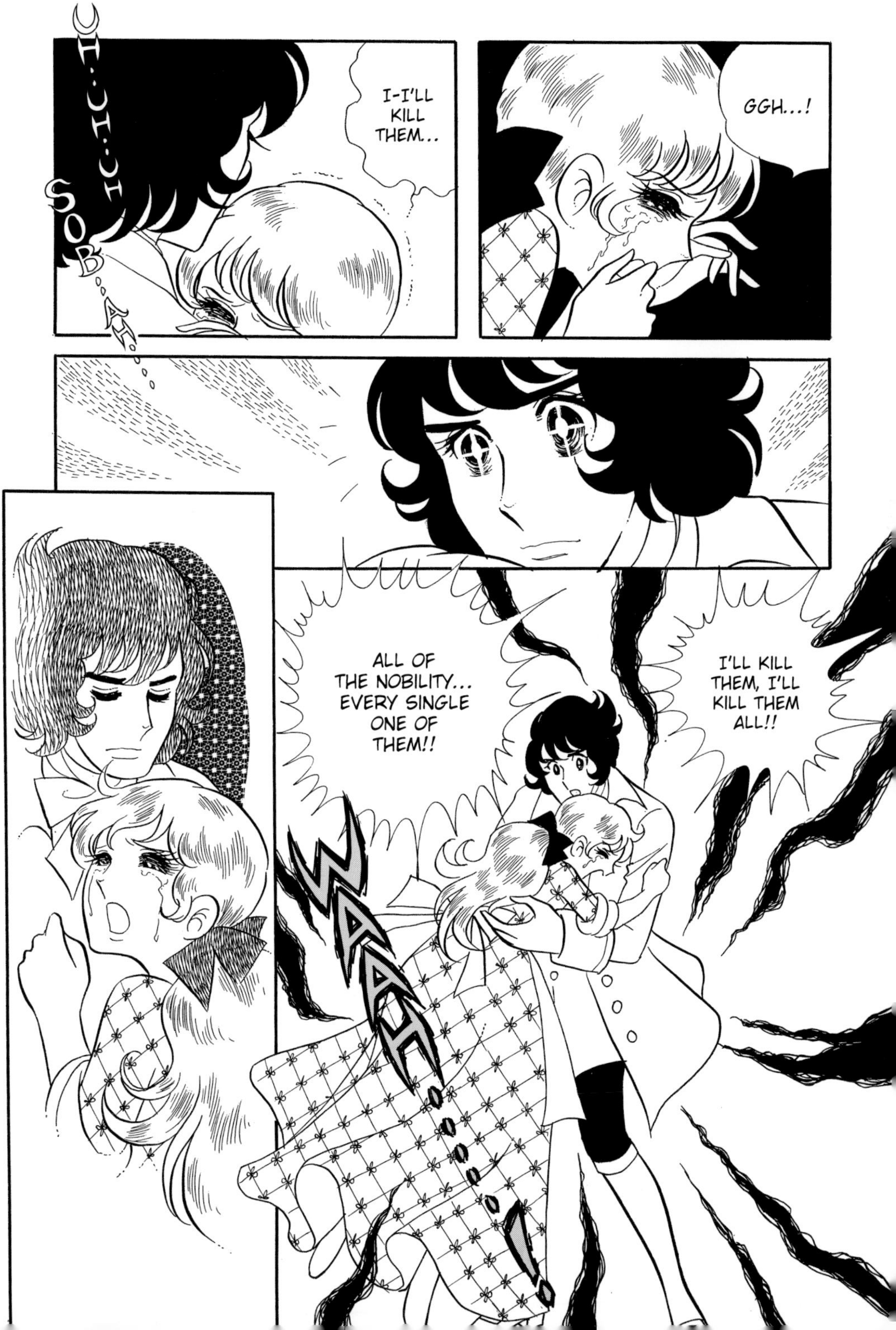
GGH...!
I-I'LL KILL THEM...
UH-UH-UH
SOB
AH...
I'LL KILL THEM, I'LL KILL THEM ALL!!
ALL OF THE NOBILITY... EVERY SINGLE ONE OF THEM!!
WAAAH!

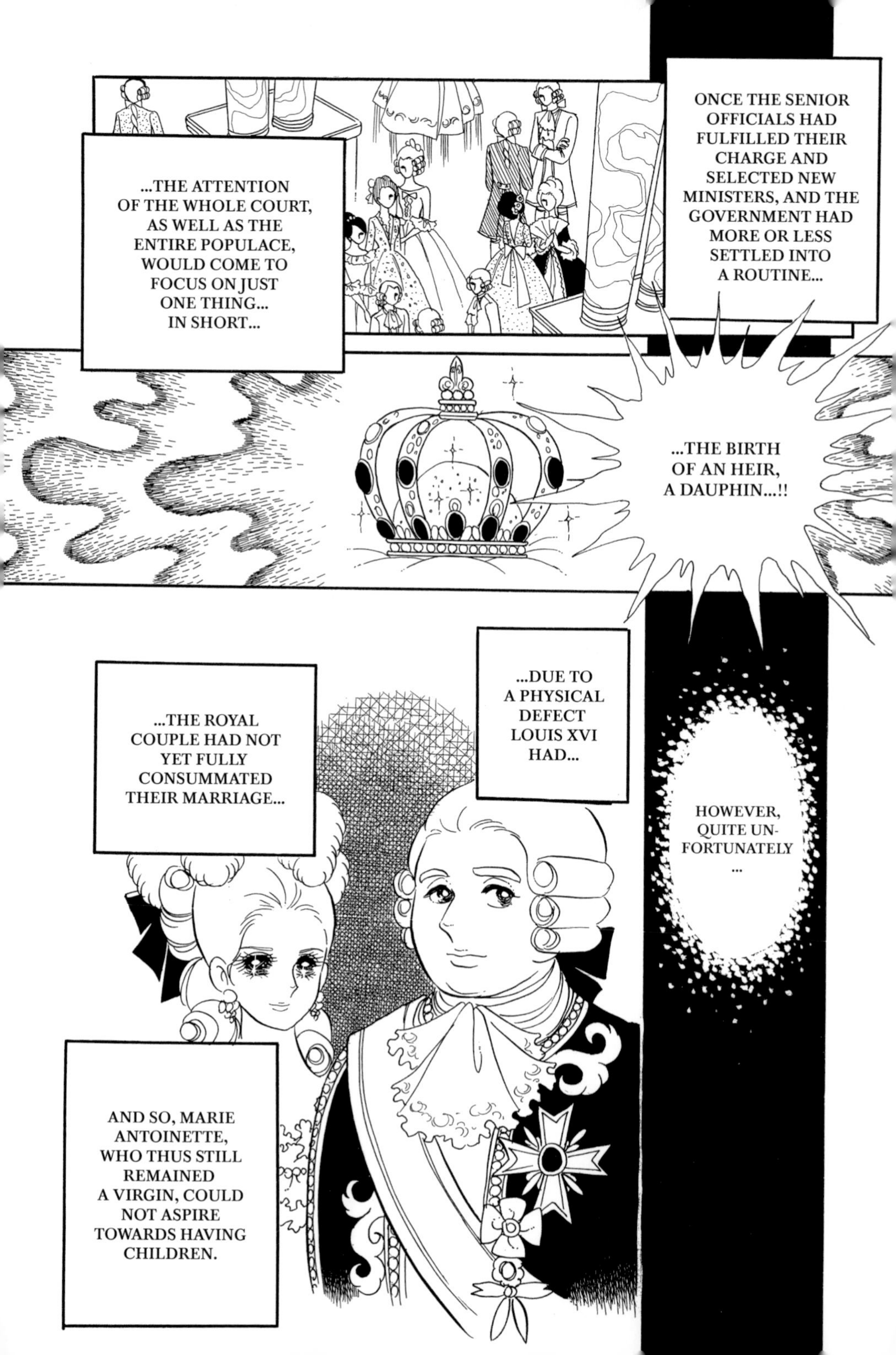
ONCE THE SENIOR OFFICIALS HAD FULFILLED THEIR CHARGE AND SELECTED NEW MINISTERS, AND THE GOVERNMENT HAD MORE OR LESS SETTLED INTO A ROUTINE...
...THE ATTENTION OF THE WHOLE COURT, AS WELL AS THE ENTIRE POPULACE, WOULD COME TO FOCUS ON JUST ONE THING... IN SHORT...
...THE BIRTH OF AN HEIR, A DAUPHIN...!!
HOWEVER, QUITE UN-FORTUNATELY ...
...DUE TO A PHYSICAL DEFECT LOUIS XVI HAD...
...THE ROYAL COUPLE HAD NOT YET FULLY CONSUMMATED THEIR MARRIAGE...
AND SO, MARIE ANTOINETTE, WHO THUS STILL REMAINED A VIRGIN, COULD NOT ASPIRE TOWARDS HAVING CHILDREN.

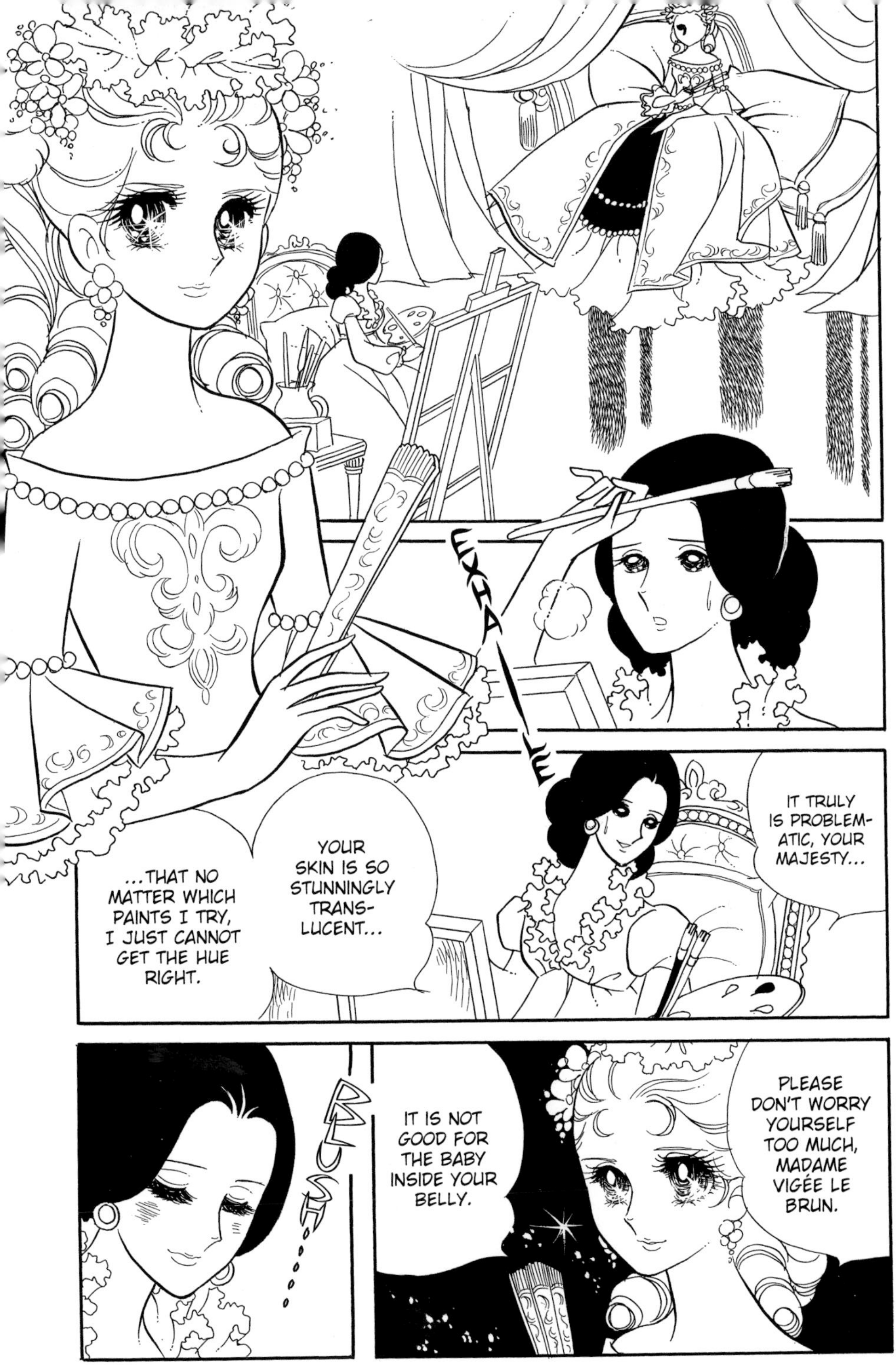
EXHALE
IT TRULY IS PROBLEM-ATIC, YOUR MAJESTY...
YOUR SKIN IS SO STUNNINGLY TRANS-LUCENT...
...THAT NO MATTER WHICH PAINTS I TRY, I JUST CANNOT GET THE HUE RIGHT.
PLEASE DON'T WORRY YOURSELF TOO MUCH, MADAME VIGÉE LE BRUN.
IT IS NOT GOOD FOR THE BABY INSIDE YOUR BELLY.
BLUSHOOOOOO

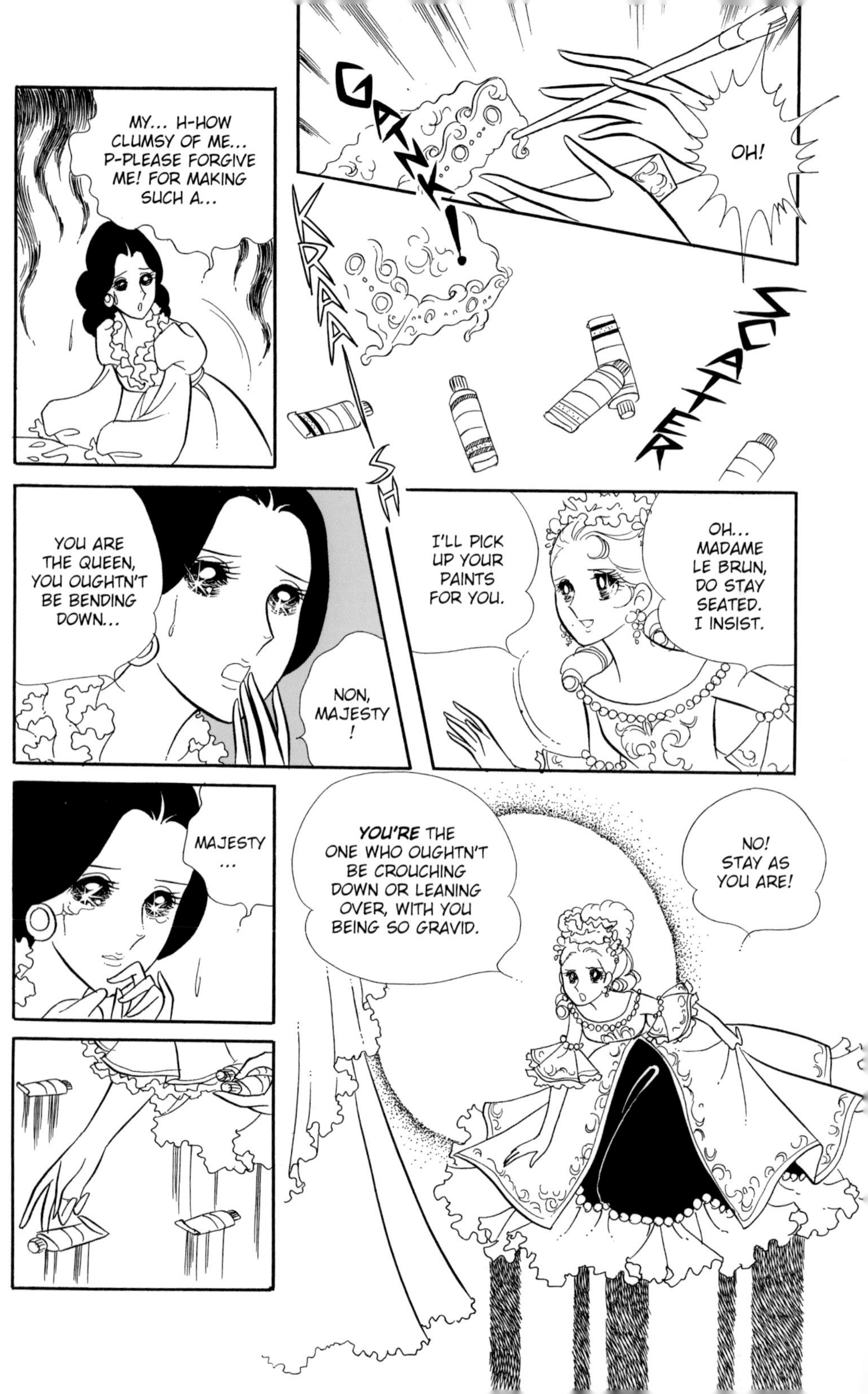
OH!
GANK!
KRAAASH
SCATTER
MY... H-HOW CLUMSY OF ME... P-PLEASE FORGIVE ME! FOR MAKING SUCH A...
OH... MADAME LE BRUN, DO STAY SEATED. I INSIST.
I'LL PICK UP YOUR PAINTS FOR YOU.
NON, MAJESTY!
YOU ARE THE QUEEN, YOU OUGHTN'T BE BENDING DOWN...
NO! STAY AS YOU ARE!
YOU'RE THE ONE WHO OUGHTN'T BE CROUCHING DOWN OR LEANING OVER, WITH YOU BEING SO GRAVID.
MAJESTY...

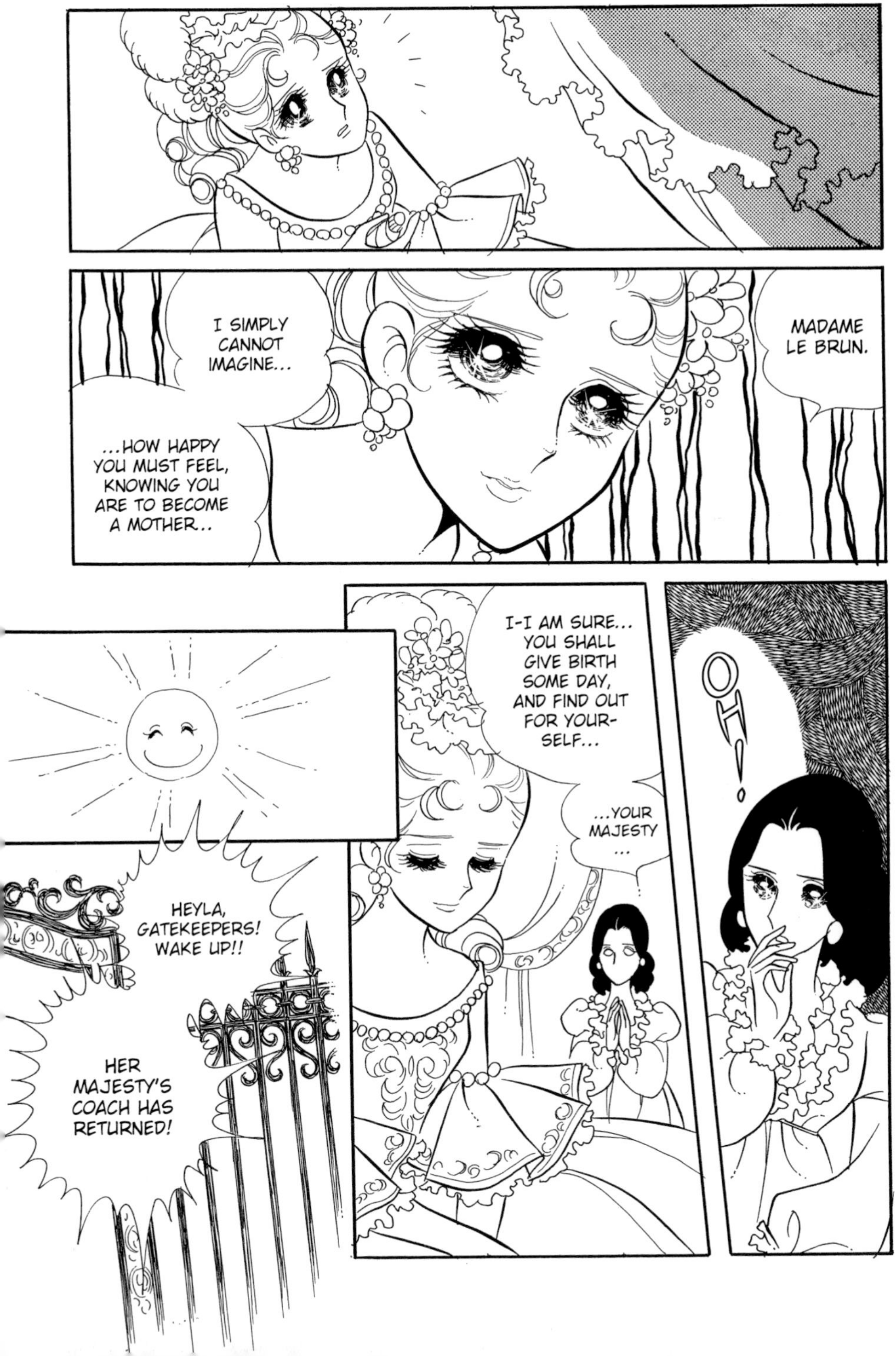
MADAME LE BRUN.
I SIMPLY CANNOT IMAGINE...
...HOW HAPPY YOU MUST FEEL, KNOWING YOU ARE TO BECOME A MOTHER...
OH!
I-I AM SURE... YOU SHALL GIVE BIRTH SOME DAY, AND FIND OUT FOR YOUR-SELF...
...YOUR MAJESTY...
HEYLA, GATEKEEPERS! WAKE UP!!
HER MAJESTY'S COACH HAS RETURNED!

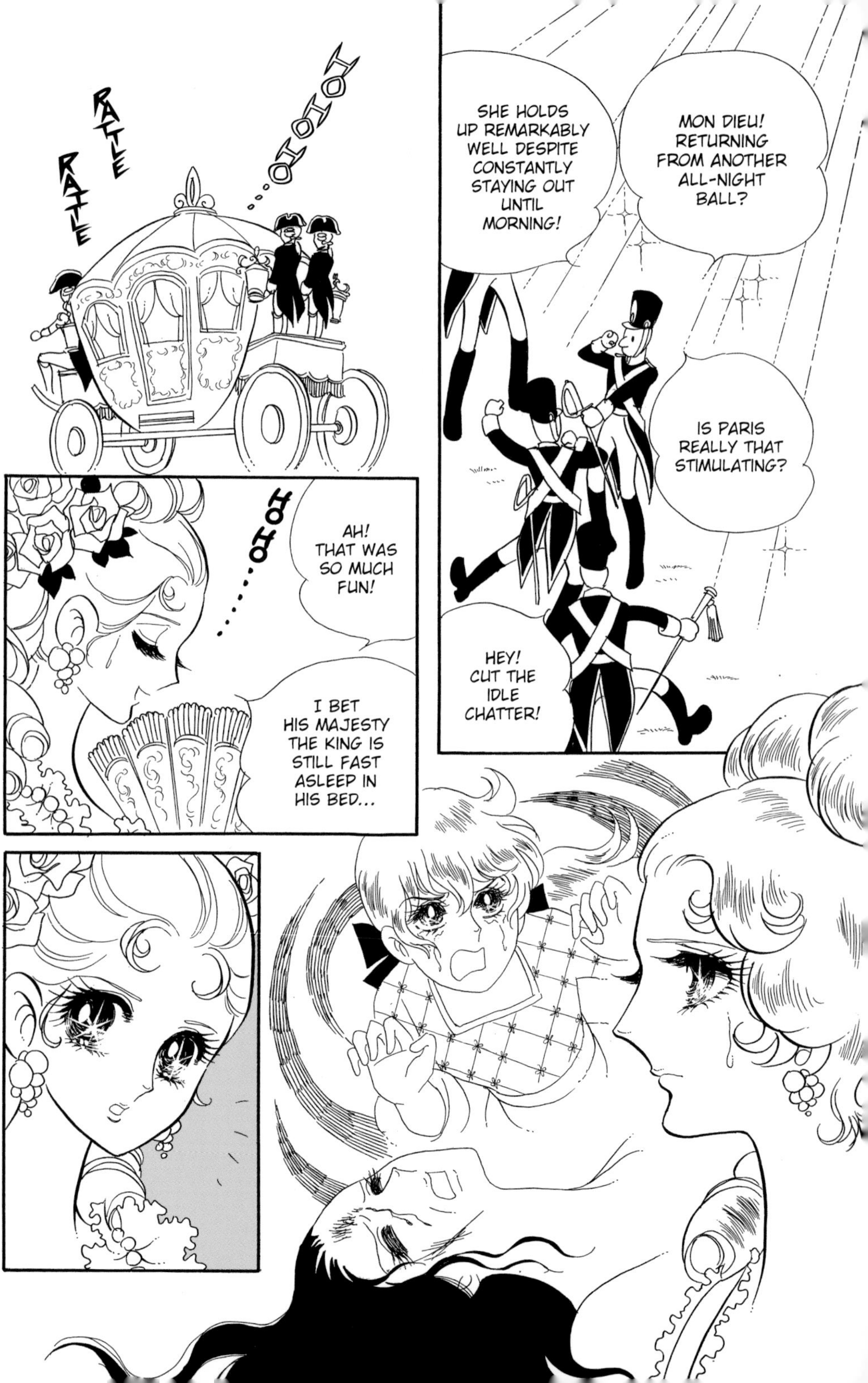
MON DIEU! RETURNING FROM ANOTHER ALL-NIGHT BALL?
SHE HOLDS UP REMARKABLY WELL DESPITE CONSTANTLY STAYING OUT UNTIL MORNING!
IS PARIS REALLY THAT STIMULATING?
HEY! CUT THE IDLE CHATTER!
RATTLE
RATTLE
HOHOHO...
HOHO...
AH! THAT WAS SO MUCH FUN!
I BET HIS MAJESTY THE KING IS STILL FAST ASLEEP IN HIS BED...

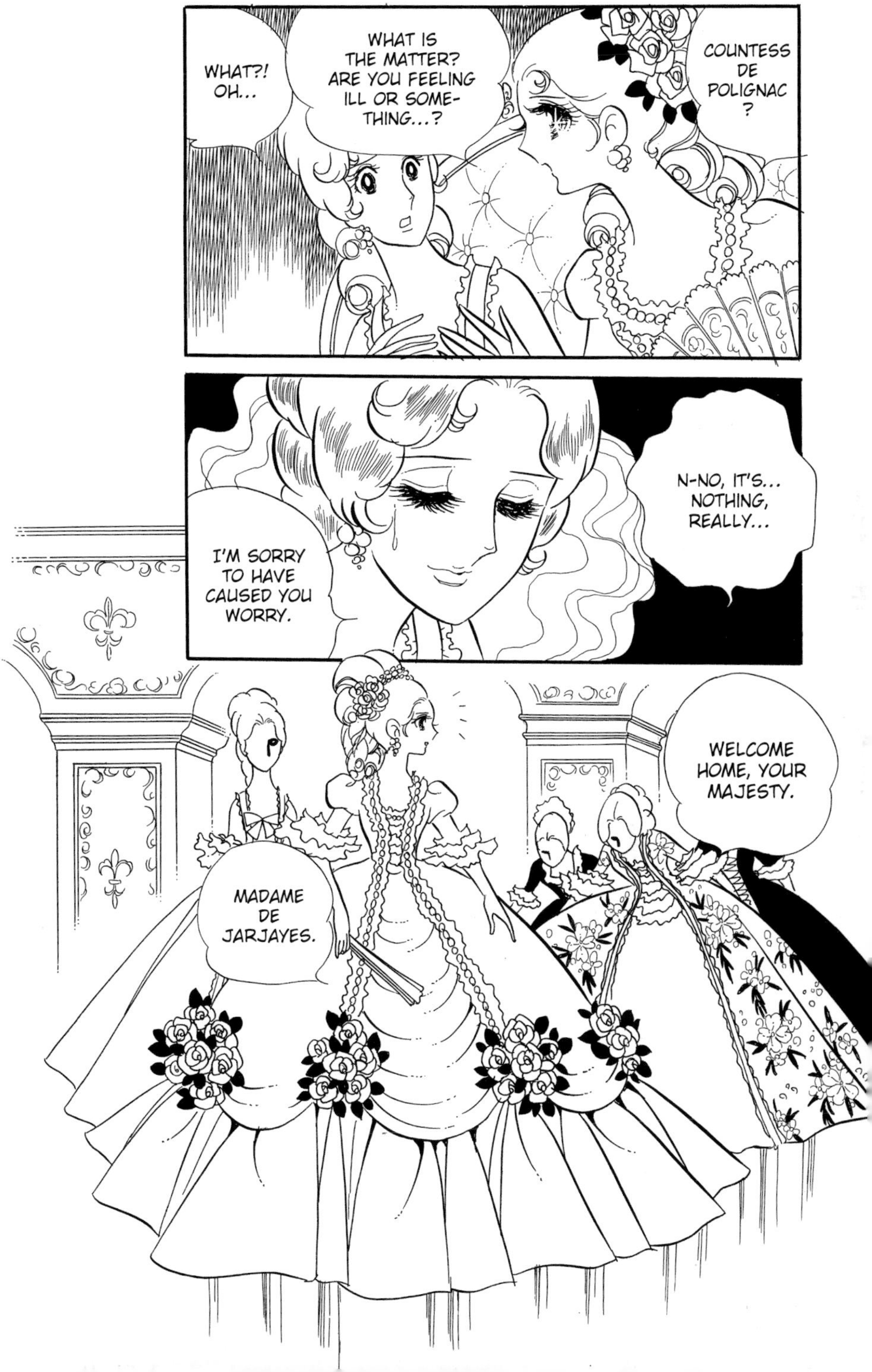
COUNTESS DE POLIGNAC?
WHAT IS THE MATTER? ARE YOU FEELING ILL OR SOMETHING...?
WHAT?! OH...
N-NO, IT'S... NOTHING, REALLY...
I'M SORRY TO HAVE CAUSED YOU WORRY.
WELCOME HOME, YOUR MAJESTY.
MADAME DE JARJAYES.

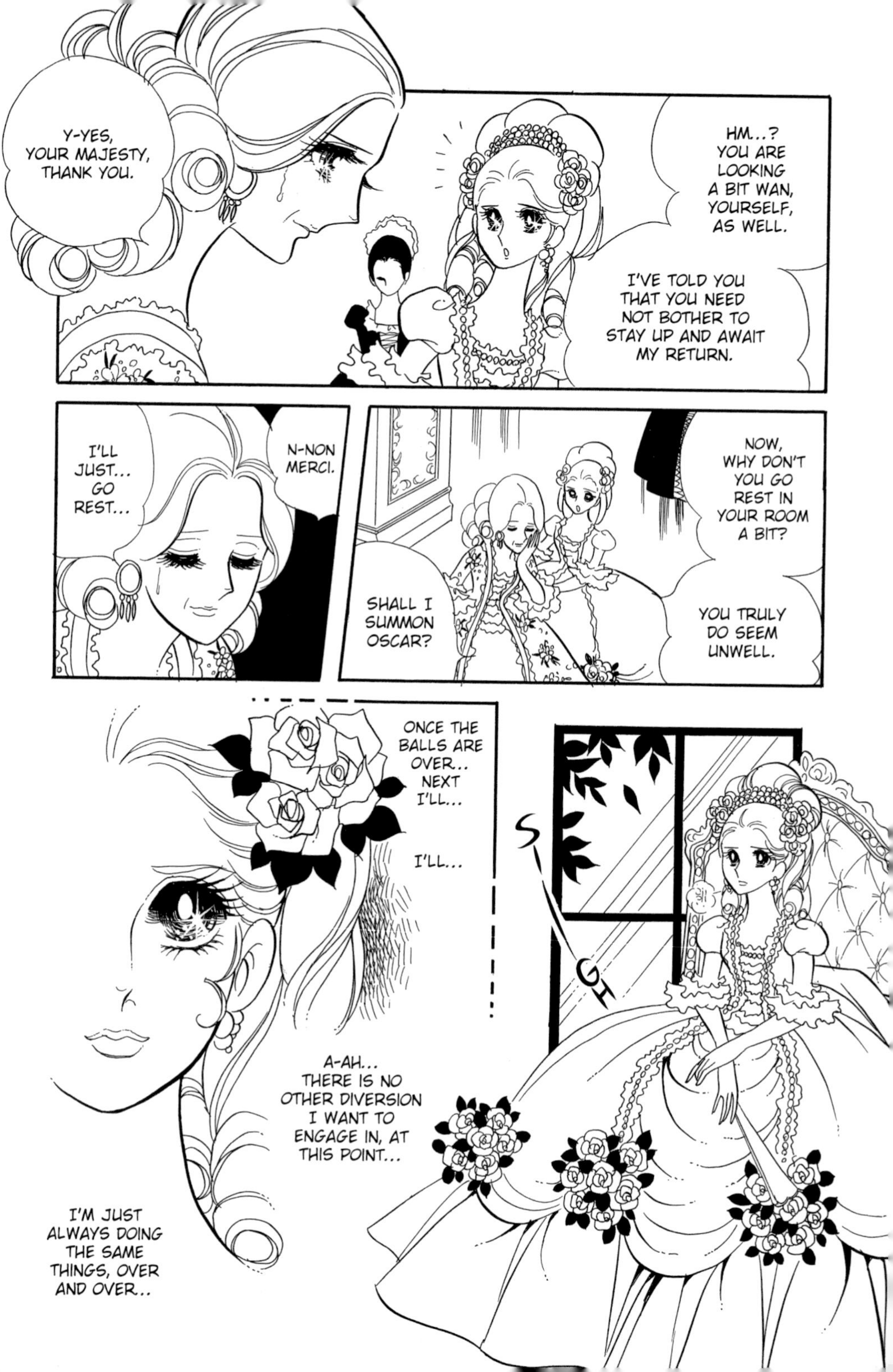
HM...? YOU ARE LOOKING A BIT WAN, YOURSELF, AS WELL.
I'VE TOLD YOU THAT YOU NEED NOT BOTHER TO STAY UP AND AWAIT MY RETURN.
Y-YES, YOUR MAJESTY, THANK YOU.
NOW, WHY DON'T YOU GO REST IN YOUR ROOM A BIT?
YOU TRULY DO SEEM UNWELL.
SHALL I SUMMON OSCAR?
N-NON MERCI.
I'LL JUST... GO REST...
SIGH
ONCE THE BALLS ARE OVER.. NEXT I'LL...
I'LL...
A-AH... THERE IS NO OTHER DIVERSION I WANT TO ENGAGE IN, AT THIS POINT...
I'M JUST ALWAYS DOING THE SAME THINGS, OVER AND OVER..

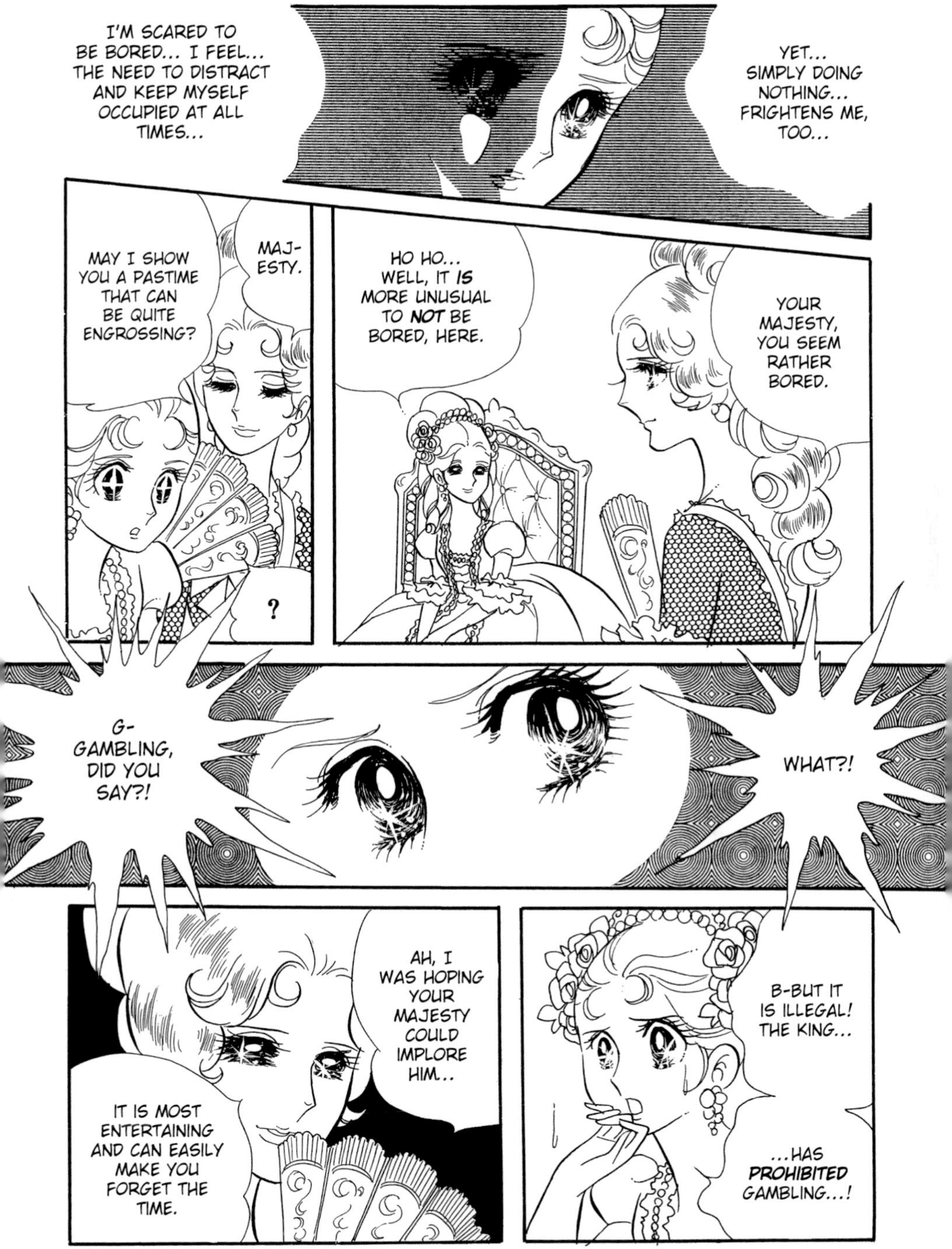

YET... SIMPLY DOING NOTHING... FRIGHTENS ME, TOO...
I'M SCARED TO BE BORED... I FEEL... THE NEED TO DISTRACT AND KEEP MYSELF OCCUPIED AT ALL TIMES...
YOUR MAJESTY, YOU SEEM RATHER BORED.
HO HO... WELL, IT **IS** MORE UNUSUAL TO **NOT** BE BORED, HERE.
MAJ-ESTY.
MAY I SHOW YOU A PASTIME THAT CAN BE QUITE ENGROSSING?
?
WHAT?!
G-GAMBLING, DID YOU SAY?!
B-BUT IT IS ILLEGAL! THE KING...
...HAS **PROHIBITED** GAMBLING...!
AH, I WAS HOPING YOUR MAJESTY COULD IMPLORE HIM...
IT IS MOST ENTERTAINING AND CAN EASILY MAKE YOU FORGET THE TIME.

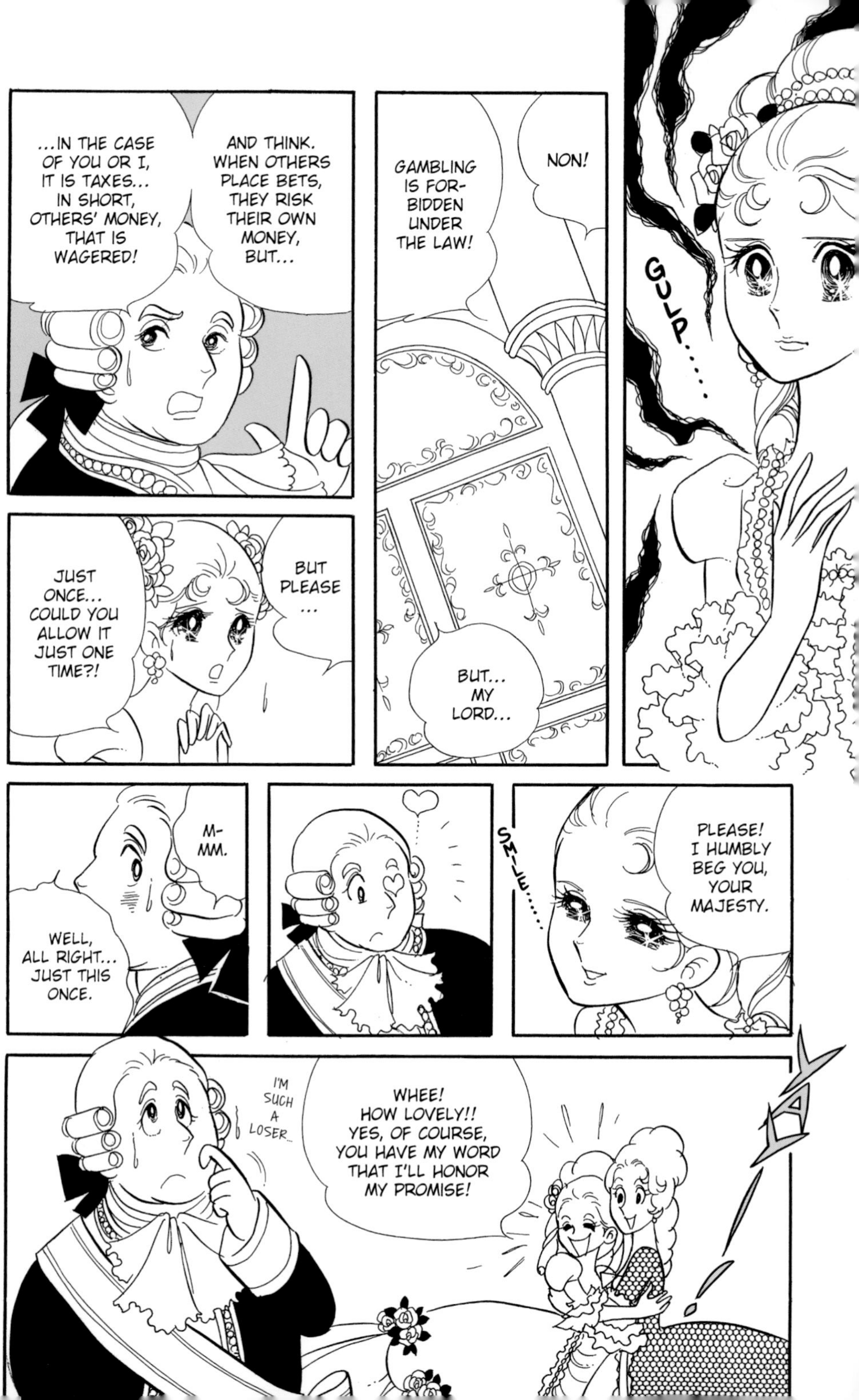
GULP....
NON!
GAMBLING IS FOR-BIDDEN UNDER THE LAW!
BUT... MY LORD...
AND THINK. WHEN OTHERS PLACE BETS, THEY RISK THEIR OWN MONEY, BUT...
...IN THE CASE OF YOU OR I, IT IS TAXES... IN SHORT, OTHERS' MONEY, THAT IS WAGERED!
BUT PLEASE ...
JUST ONCE... COULD YOU ALLOW IT JUST ONE TIME?!
PLEASE! I HUMBLY BEG YOU, YOUR MAJESTY.
SMILE....
M-MM.
WELL, ALL RIGHT... JUST THIS ONCE.
YAY!!
WHEE! HOW LOVELY!! YES, OF COURSE, YOU HAVE MY WORD THAT I'LL HONOR MY PROMISE!
I'M SUCH A LOSER...

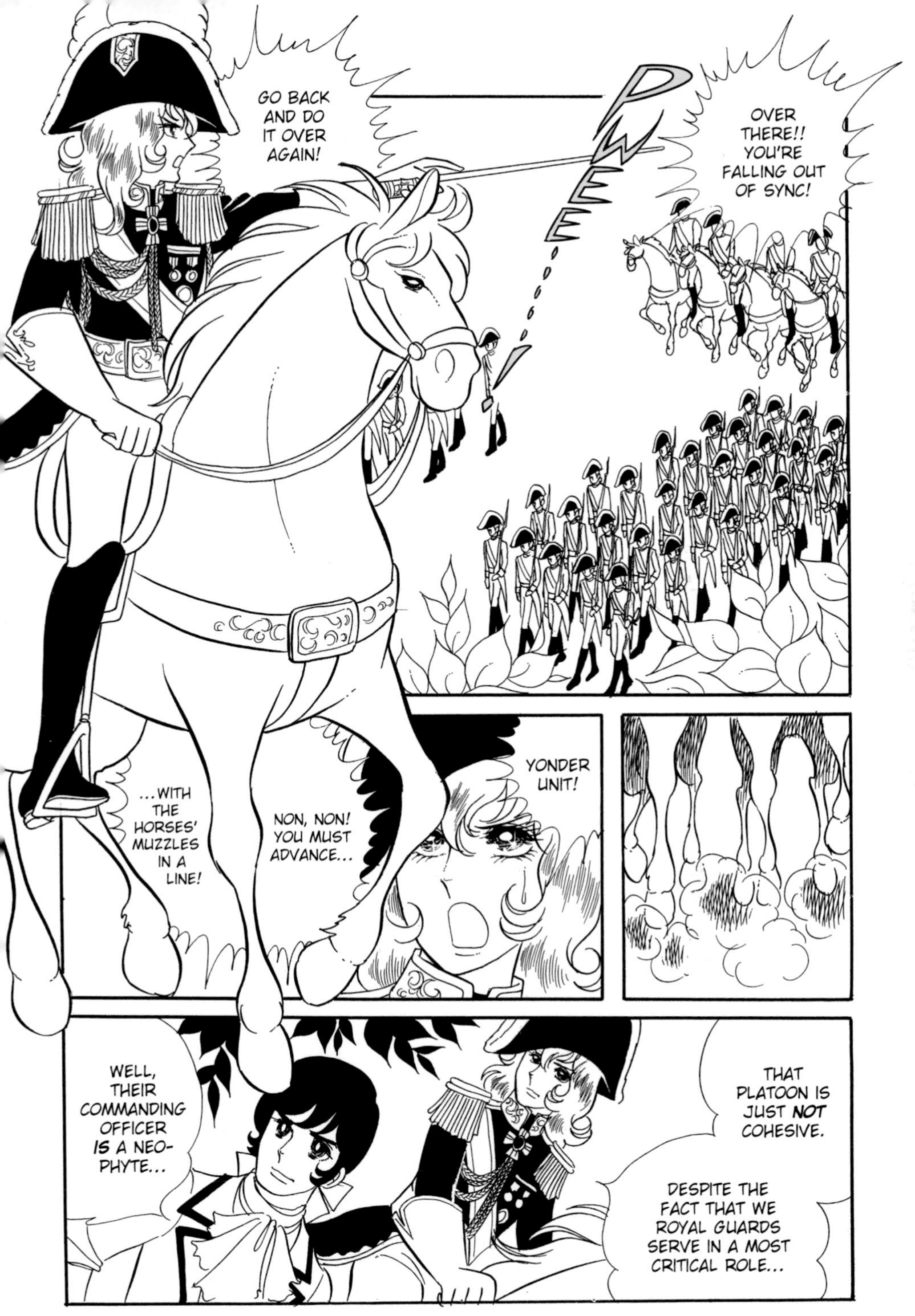

OVER THERE!! YOU'RE FALLING OUT OF SYNC!
PWEEE
GO BACK AND DO IT OVER AGAIN!
YONDER UNIT!
NON, NON! YOU MUST ADVANCE...
...WITH THE HORSES' MUZZLES IN A LINE!
THAT PLATOON IS JUST **NOT** COHESIVE.
DESPITE THE FACT THAT WE ROYAL GUARDS SERVE IN A MOST CRITICAL ROLE...
WELL, THEIR COMMANDING OFFICER **IS** A NEO-PHYTE...

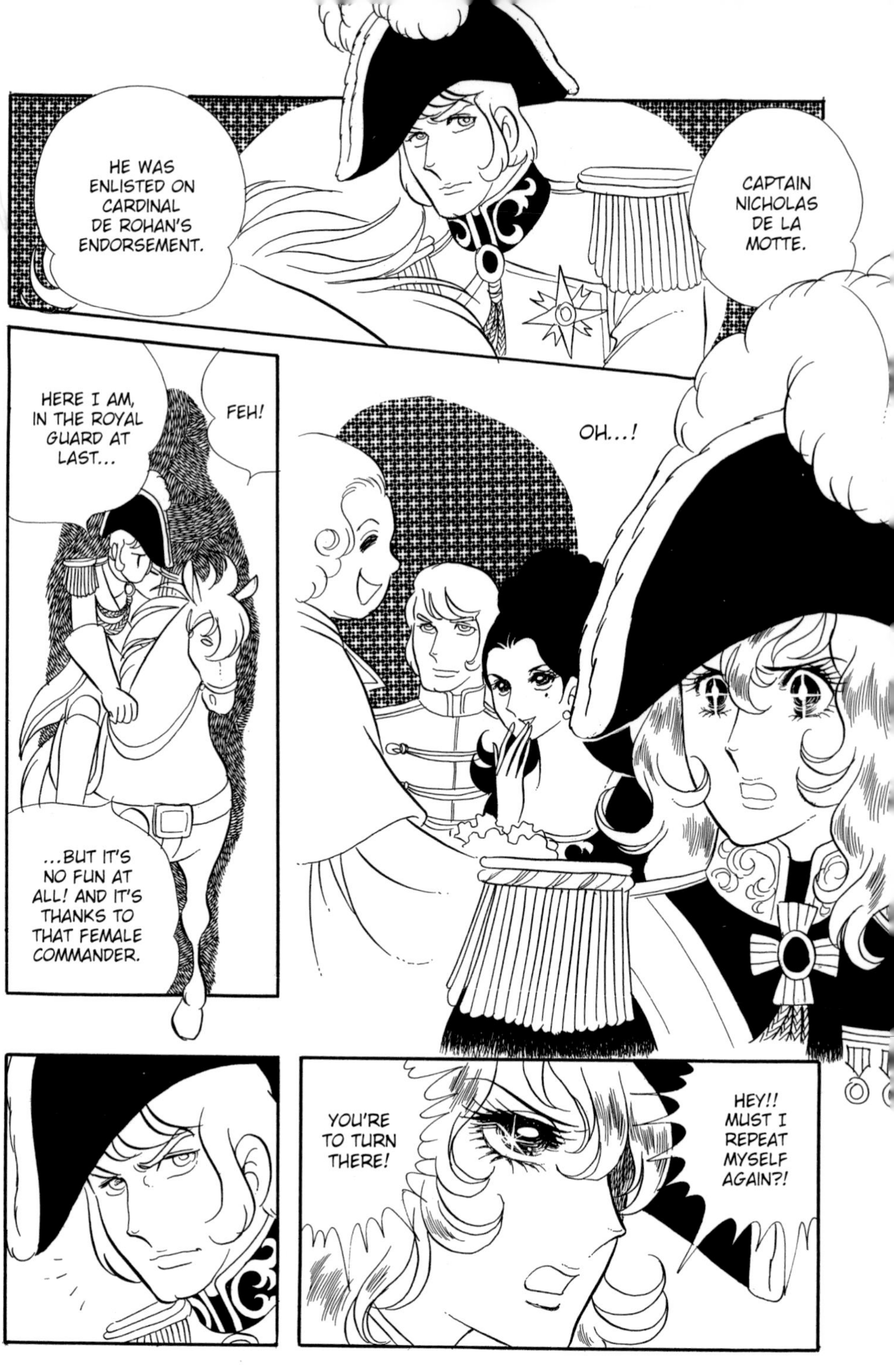
CAPTAIN NICHOLAS DE LA MOTTE.
HE WAS ENLISTED ON CARDINAL DE ROHAN'S ENDORSEMENT.
OH...!
FEH!
HERE I AM, IN THE ROYAL GUARD AT LAST...
...BUT IT'S NO FUN AT ALL! AND IT'S THANKS TO THAT FEMALE COMMANDER.
HEY!! MUST I REPEAT MYSELF AGAIN?!
YOU'RE TO TURN THERE!

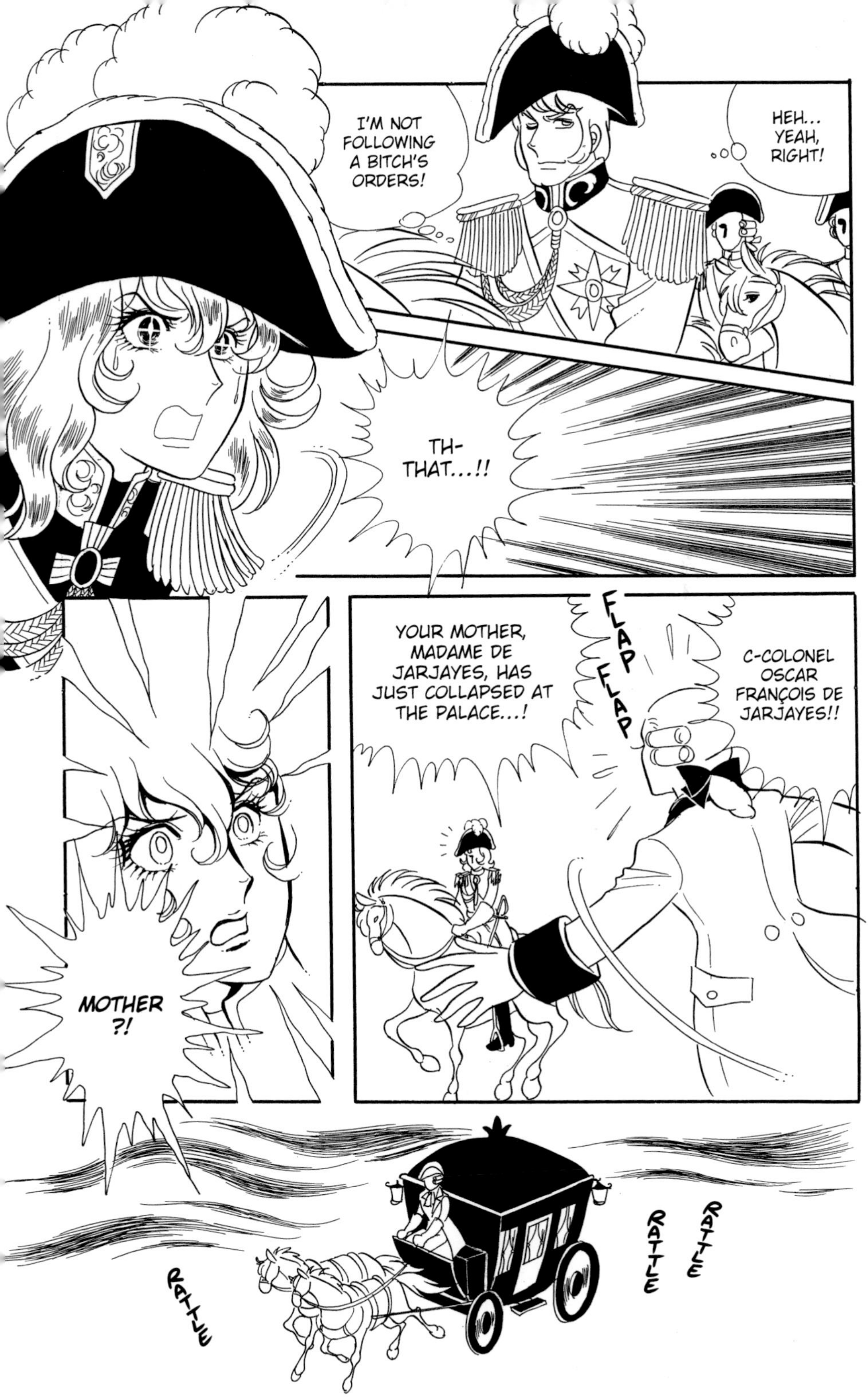
HEH... YEAH, RIGHT!
I'M NOT FOLLOWING A BITCH'S ORDERS!
TH- THAT...!!
C-COLONEL OSCAR FRANÇOIS DE JARJAYES!!
FLAP FLAP
YOUR MOTHER, MADAME DE JARJAYES, HAS JUST COLLAPSED AT THE PALACE...!
MOTHER ?!
RATTLE
RATTLE
RATTLE

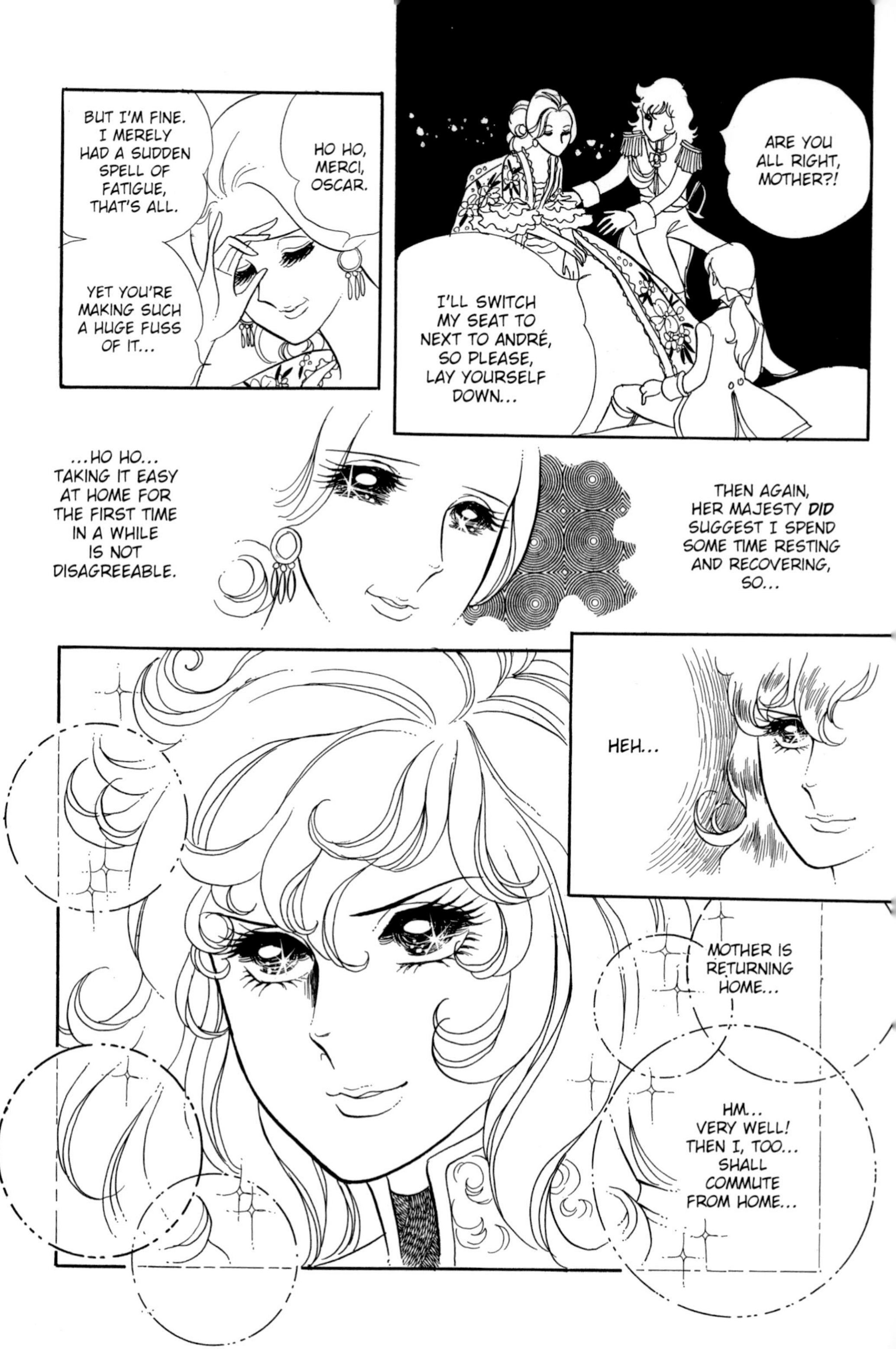
ARE YOU ALL RIGHT, MOTHER?!
I'LL SWITCH MY SEAT TO NEXT TO ANDRÉ, SO PLEASE, LAY YOURSELF DOWN...
HO HO, MERCI, OSCAR.
BUT I'M FINE. I MERELY HAD A SUDDEN SPELL OF FATIGUE, THAT'S ALL.
YET YOU'RE MAKING SUCH A HUGE FUSS OF IT...
THEN AGAIN, HER MAJESTY DID SUGGEST I SPEND SOME TIME RESTING AND RECOVERING, SO...
...HO HO... TAKING IT EASY AT HOME FOR THE FIRST TIME IN A WHILE IS NOT DISAGREEABLE.
HEH...
MOTHER IS RETURNING HOME...
HM... VERY WELL! THEN I, TOO... SHALL COMMUTE FROM HOME...

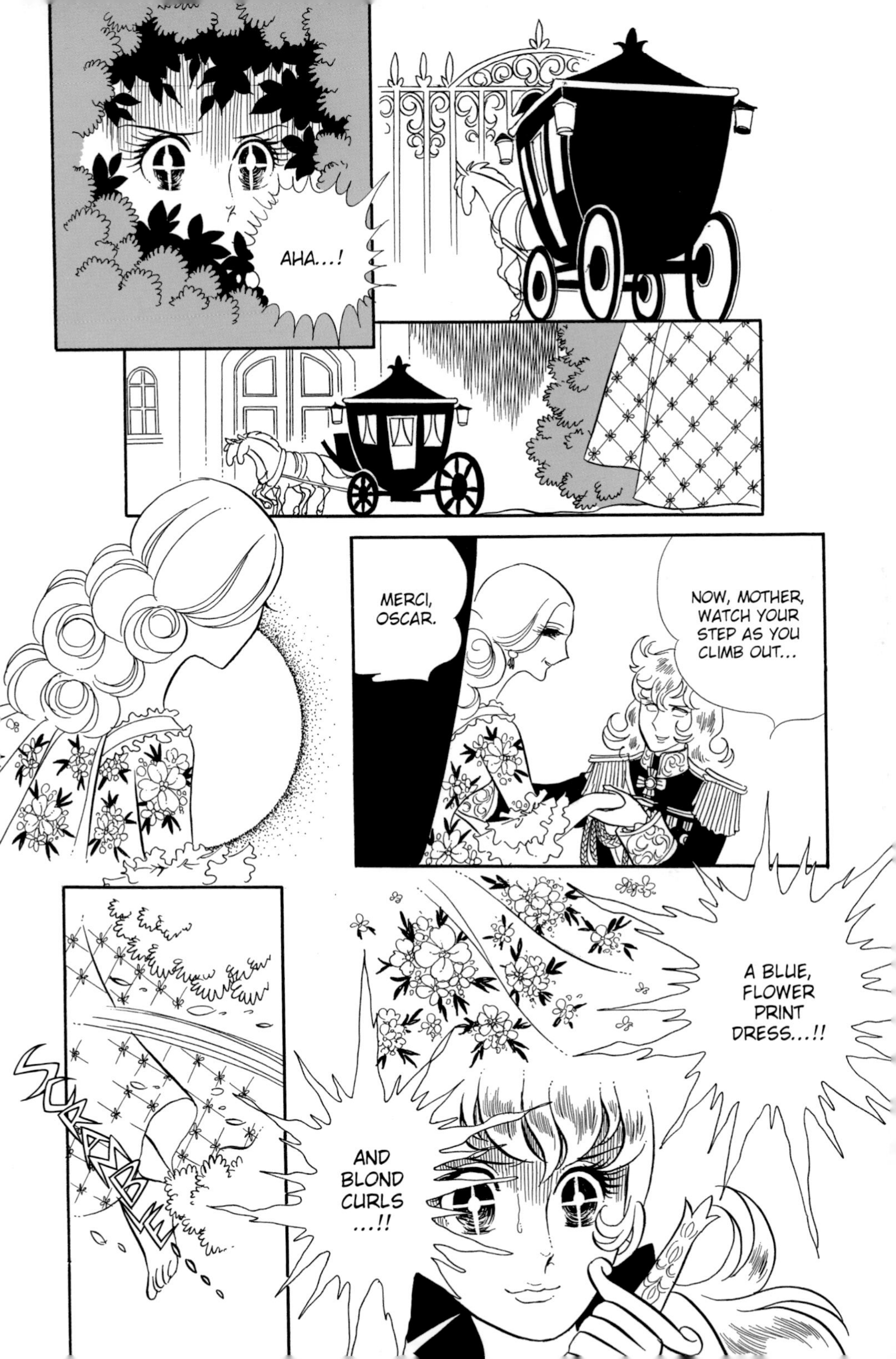
AHA...!
NOW, MOTHER, WATCH YOUR STEP AS YOU CLIMB OUT...
MERCI, OSCAR.
A BLUE, FLOWER PRINT DRESS...!!
AND BLOND CURLS ...!!
SCRAMBLE

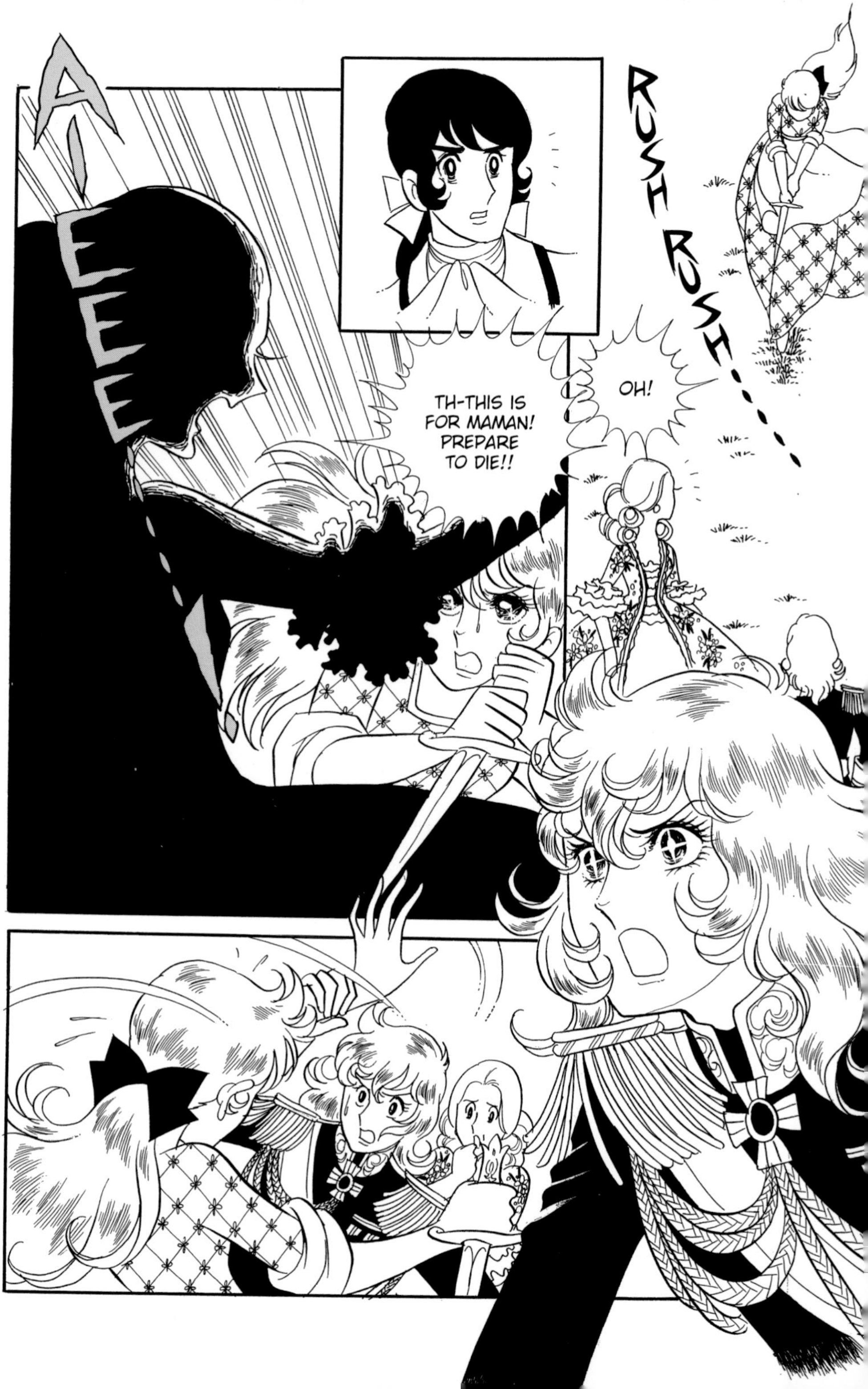

RUSH RUSH...
OH!
AIEEE...
TH-THIS IS FOR MAMAN! PREPARE TO DIE!!

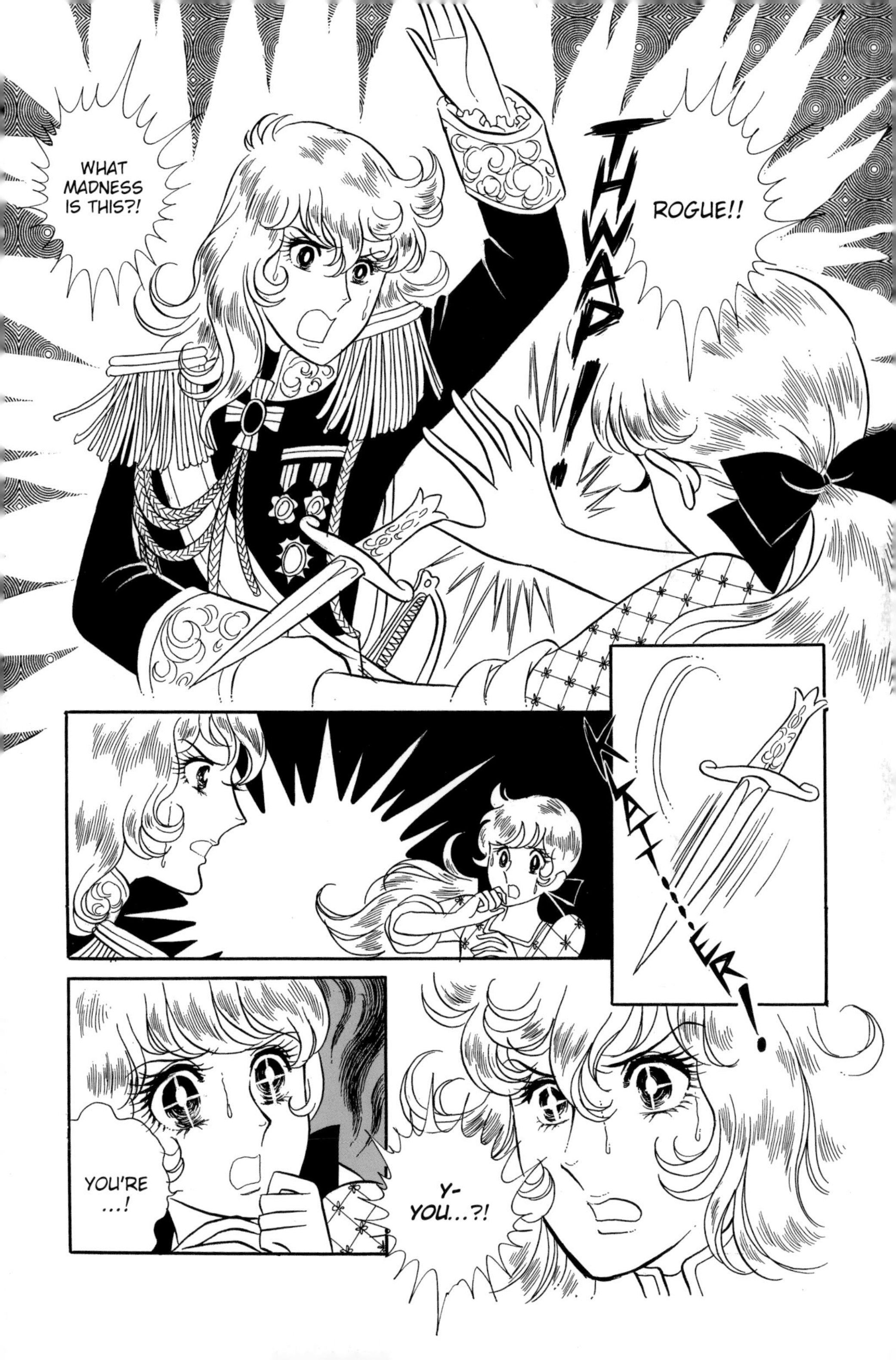
ROGUE!!
THWAP!!
WHAT MADNESS IS THIS?!
KLATT.....ER!
Y- YOU...?!
YOU'RE ...!

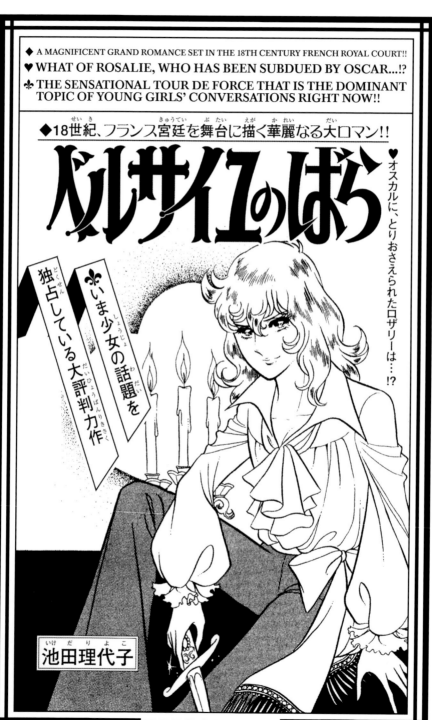

◆ A MAGNIFICENT GRAND ROMANCE SET IN THE 18TH CENTURY FRENCH ROYAL COURT!!

♥ WHAT OF ROSALIE, WHO HAS BEEN SUBDUED BY OSCAR...!?

⚜ THE SENSATIONAL TOUR DE FORCE THAT IS THE DOMINANT TOPIC OF YOUNG GIRLS' CONVERSATIONS RIGHT NOW!!

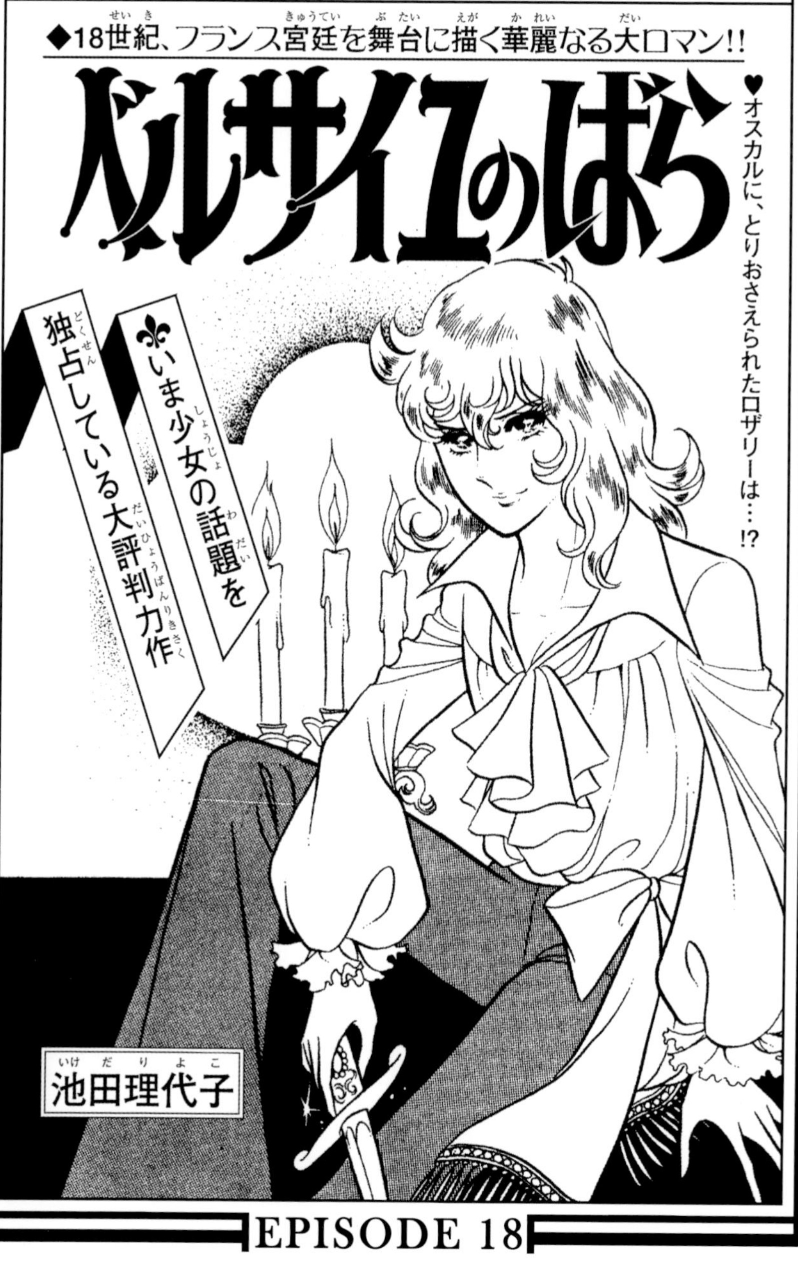
◆18世紀、フランス宮廷を舞台に描く華麗なる大ロマン!!
ベルサイユのばら
♥オスカルに、とりおさえられたロザリーは…!?
⚜いま少女の話題を
独占している大評判力作
池田理代子

EPISODE 18

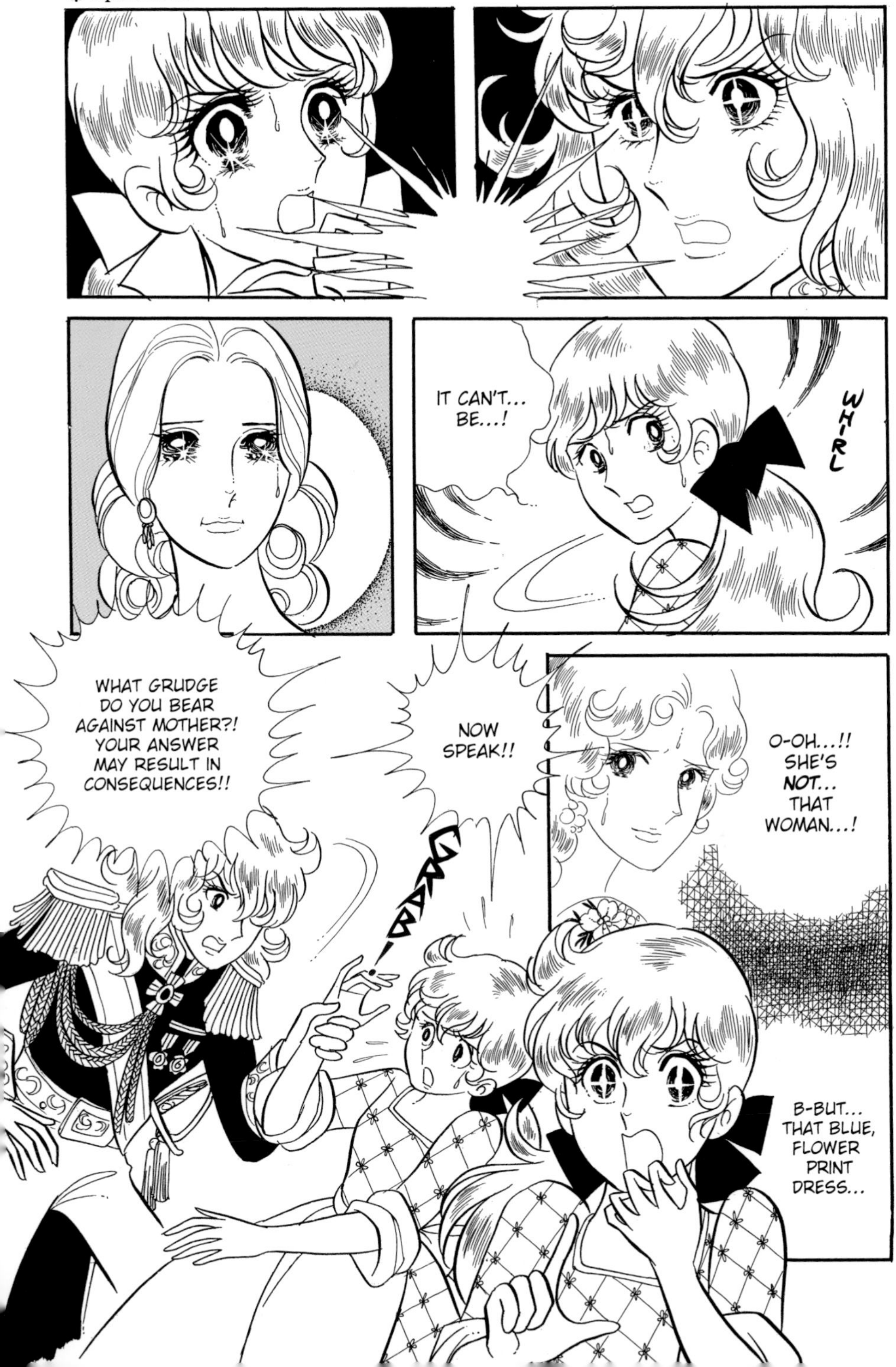
WHIRL
IT CAN'T... BE...!
O-OH...!! SHE'S **NOT**... THAT WOMAN...!
B-BUT... THAT BLUE, FLOWER PRINT DRESS...
NOW SPEAK!!
GRAB!
WHAT GRUDGE DO YOU BEAR AGAINST MOTHER?! YOUR ANSWER MAY RESULT IN CONSEQUENCES!!

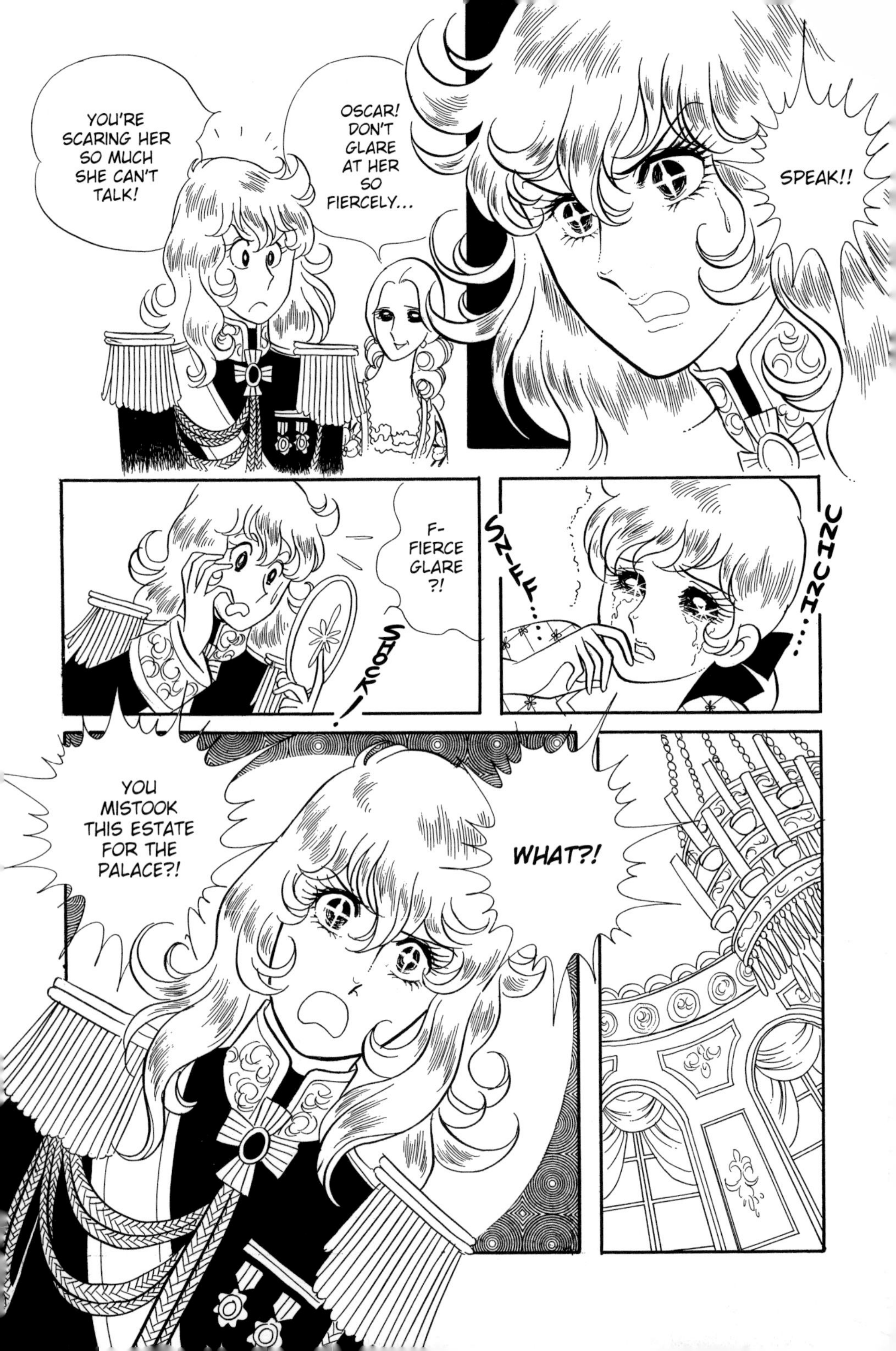
SPEAK!!
OSCAR! DON'T GLARE AT HER SO FIERCELY...
YOU'RE SCARING HER SO MUCH SHE CAN'T TALK!
SNIFF...
SNIFF...
F-FIERCE GLARE?!
SHOCK!
WHAT?!
YOU MISTOOK THIS ESTATE FOR THE PALACE?!

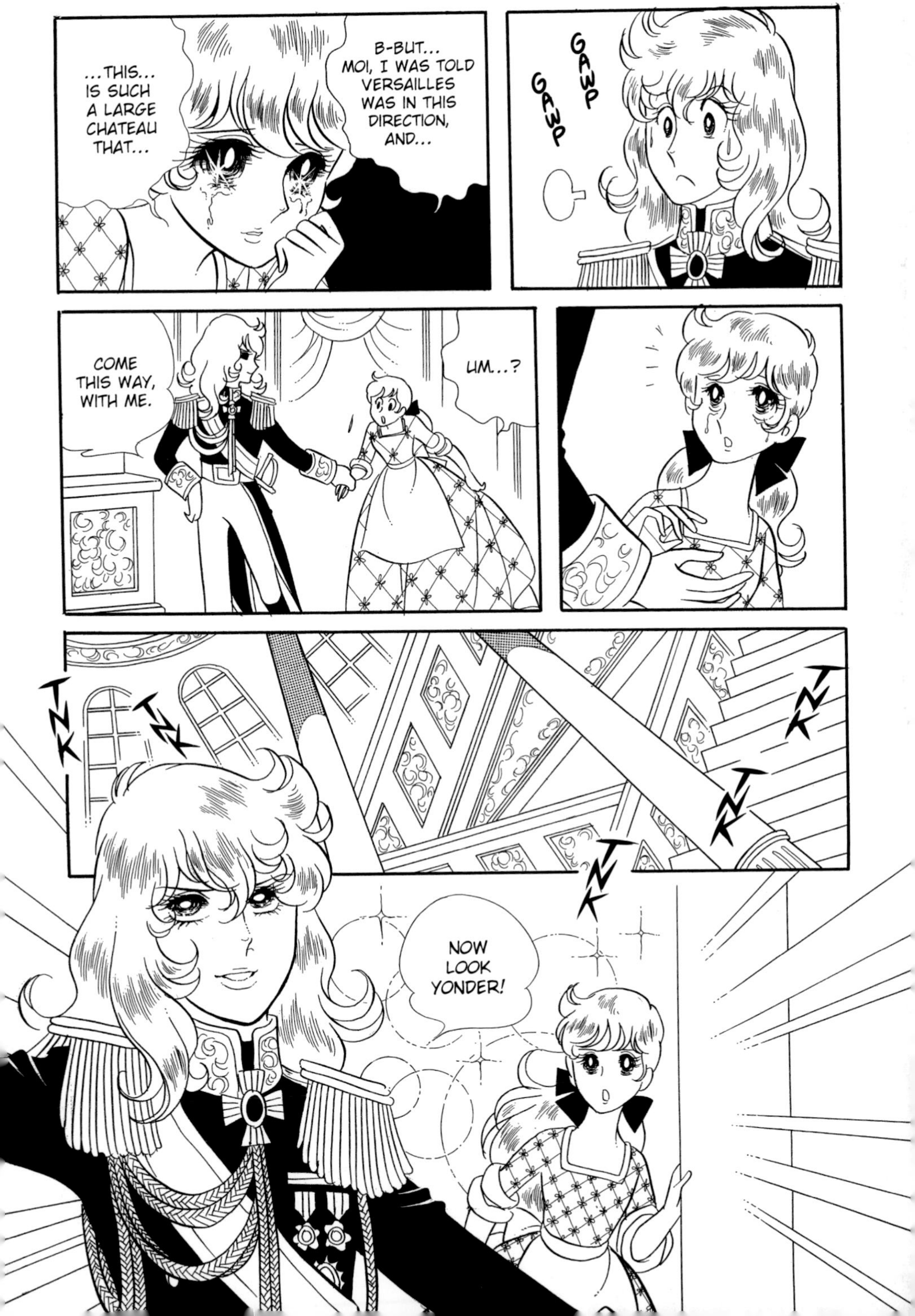
GAWP
GAWP
B-BUT... MOI, I WAS TOLD VERSAILLES WAS IN THIS DIRECTION, AND...
...THIS... IS SUCH A LARGE CHATEAU THAT...
UM...?
COME THIS WAY, WITH ME.
TNK
TNK
TNK
TNK
TNK
TNK
NOW LOOK YONDER!

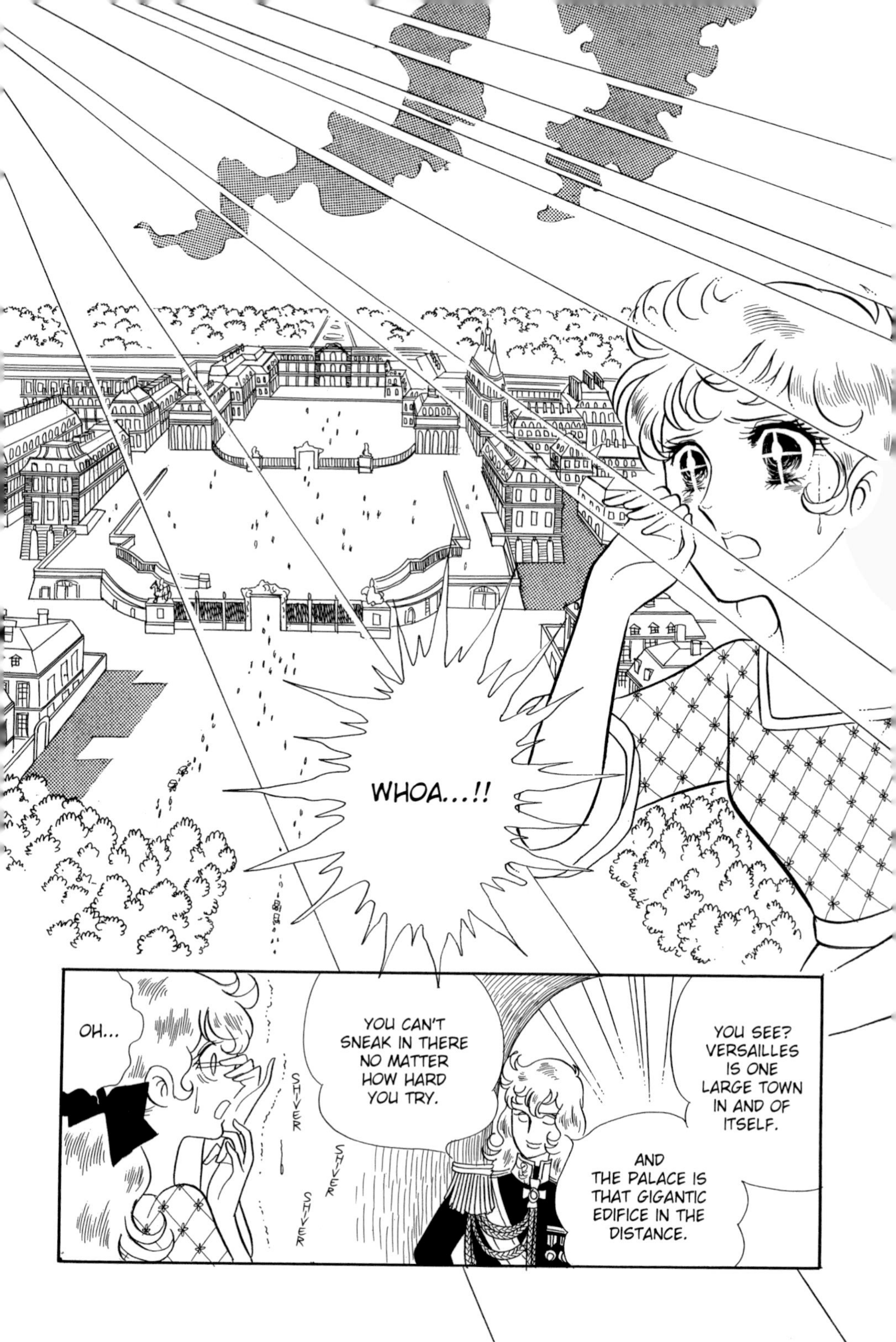
WHOA...!!
YOU SEE? VERSAILLES IS ONE LARGE TOWN IN AND OF ITSELF.
AND THE PALACE IS THAT GIGANTIC EDIFICE IN THE DISTANCE.
YOU CAN'T SNEAK IN THERE NO MATTER HOW HARD YOU TRY.
SHIVER
SHIVER
SHIVER
OH...

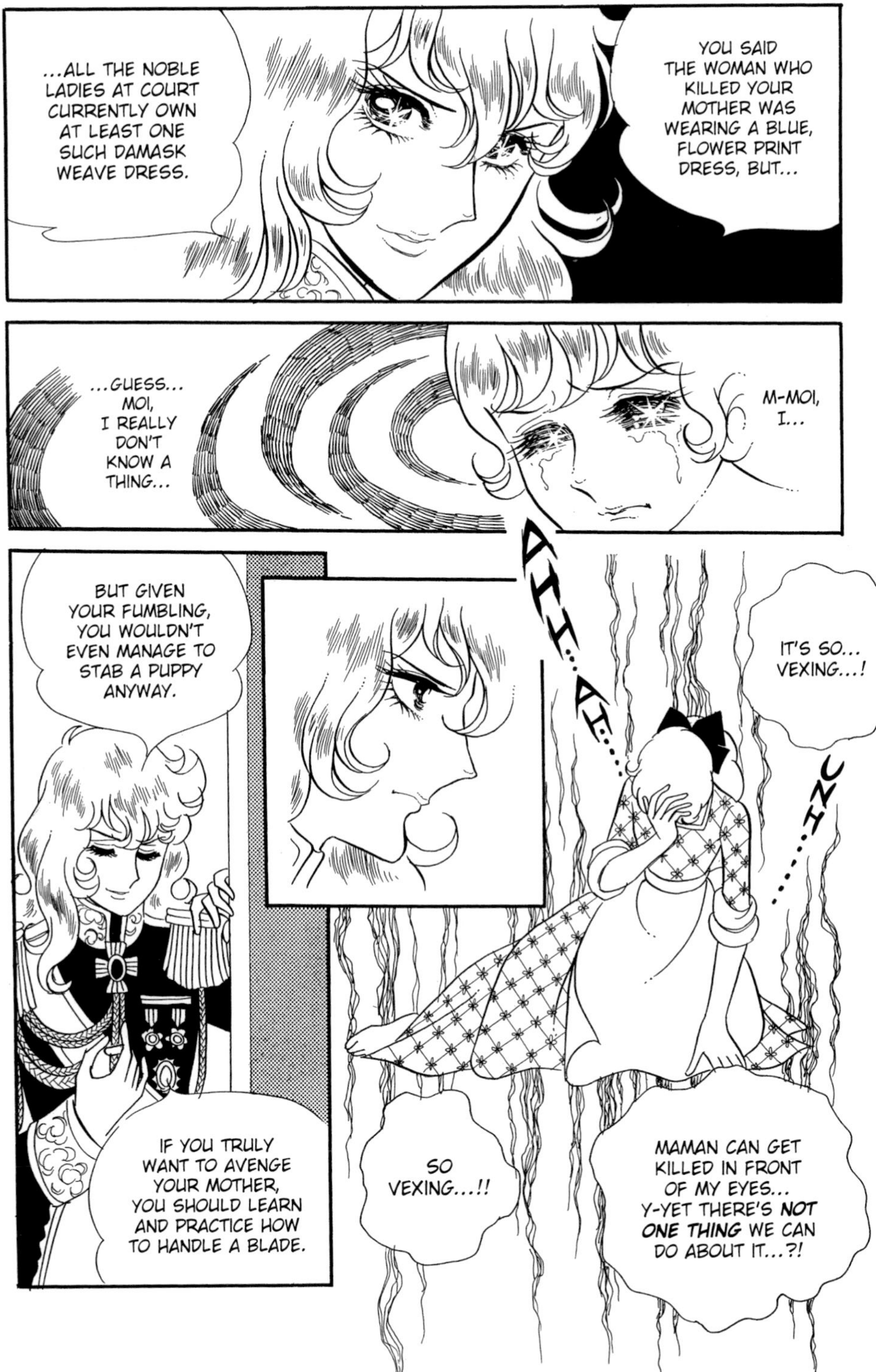
YOU SAID THE WOMAN WHO KILLED YOUR MOTHER WAS WEARING A BLUE, FLOWER PRINT DRESS, BUT...
...ALL THE NOBLE LADIES AT COURT CURRENTLY OWN AT LEAST ONE SUCH DAMASK WEAVE DRESS.
M-MOI, I...
...GUESS... MOI, I REALLY DON'T KNOW A THING...
IT'S SO... VEXING...!
AHH...AH...
UNH......
MAMAN CAN GET KILLED IN FRONT OF MY EYES... Y-YET THERE'S **NOT ONE THING** WE CAN DO ABOUT IT...?!
SO VEXING...!!
BUT GIVEN YOUR FUMBLING, YOU WOULDN'T EVEN MANAGE TO STAB A PUPPY ANYWAY.
IF YOU TRULY WANT TO AVENGE YOUR MOTHER, YOU SHOULD LEARN AND PRACTICE HOW TO HANDLE A BLADE.

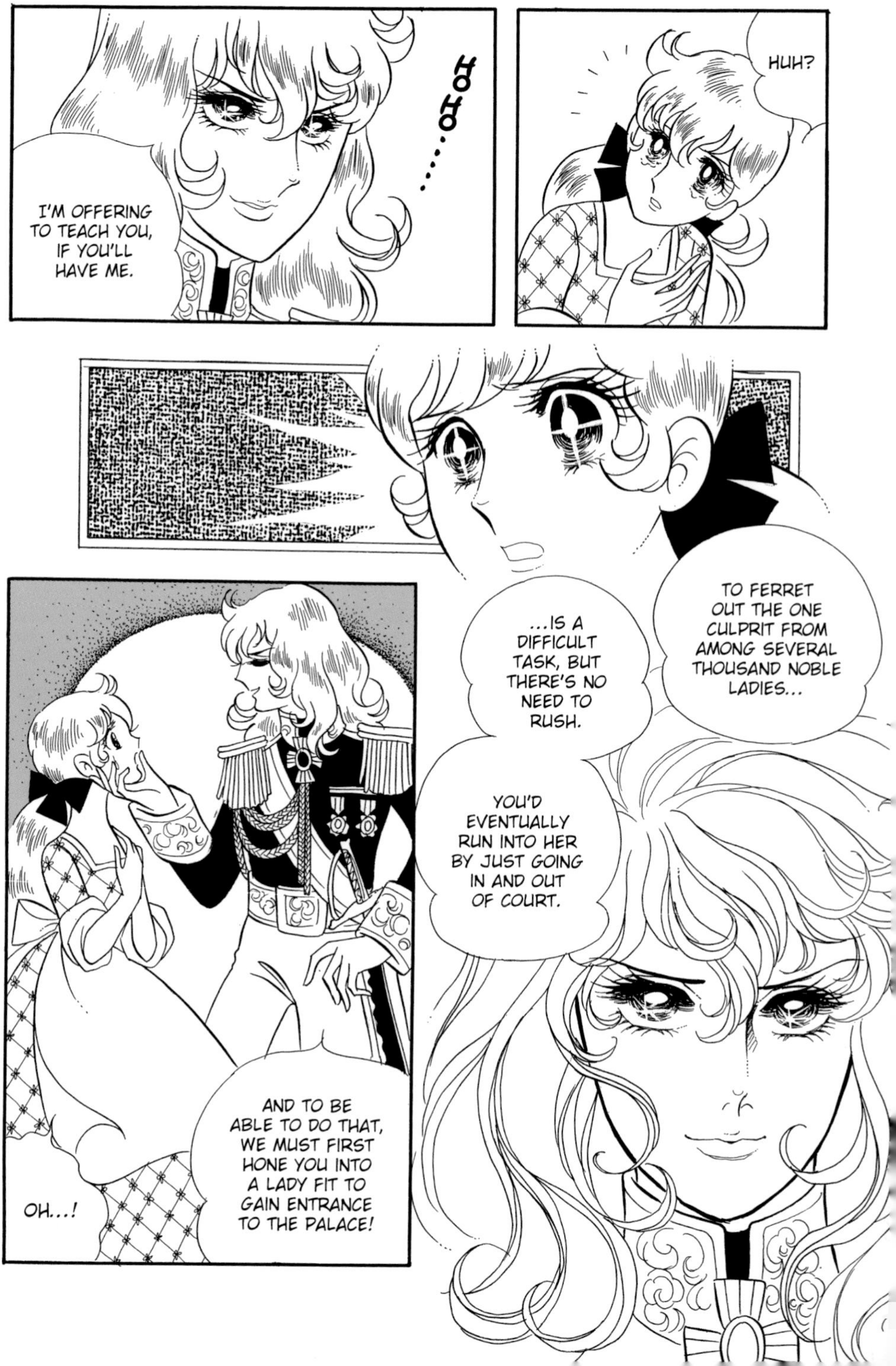
HUH?
HO HO...
I'M OFFERING TO TEACH YOU, IF YOU'LL HAVE ME.
TO FERRET OUT THE ONE CULPRIT FROM AMONG SEVERAL THOUSAND NOBLE LADIES...
...IS A DIFFICULT TASK, BUT THERE'S NO NEED TO RUSH.
YOU'D EVENTUALLY RUN INTO HER BY JUST GOING IN AND OUT OF COURT.
AND TO BE ABLE TO DO THAT, WE MUST FIRST HONE YOU INTO A LADY FIT TO GAIN ENTRANCE TO THE PALACE!
OH...!

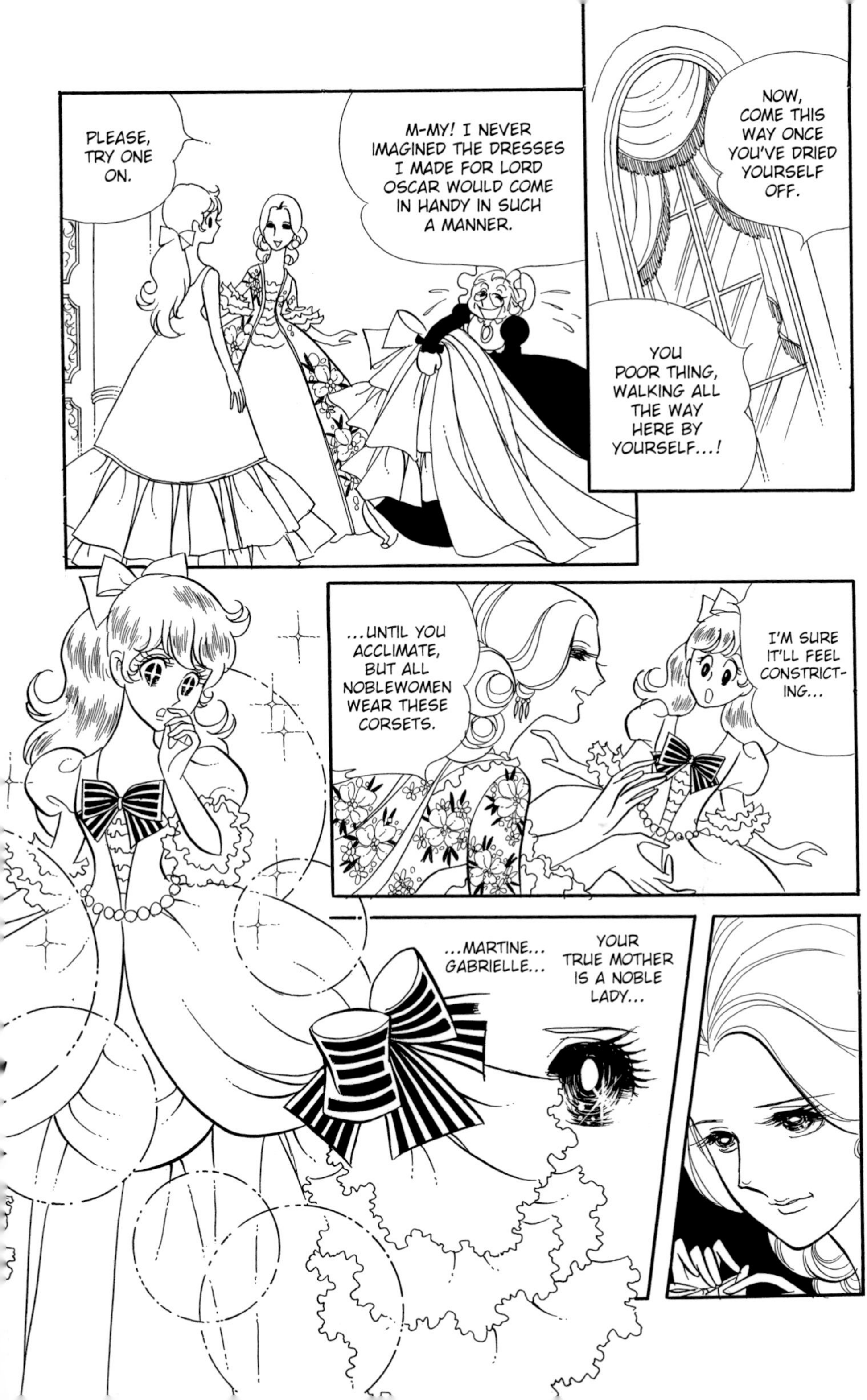

NOW, COME THIS WAY ONCE YOU'VE DRIED YOURSELF OFF.
YOU POOR THING, WALKING ALL THE WAY HERE BY YOURSELF...!
M-MY! I NEVER IMAGINED THE DRESSES I MADE FOR LORD OSCAR WOULD COME IN HANDY IN SUCH A MANNER.
PLEASE, TRY ONE ON.
I'M SURE IT'LL FEEL CONSTRICT-ING...
...UNTIL YOU ACCLIMATE, BUT ALL NOBLEWOMEN WEAR THESE CORSETS.
YOUR TRUE MOTHER IS A NOBLE LADY...
...MARTINE... GABRIELLE...

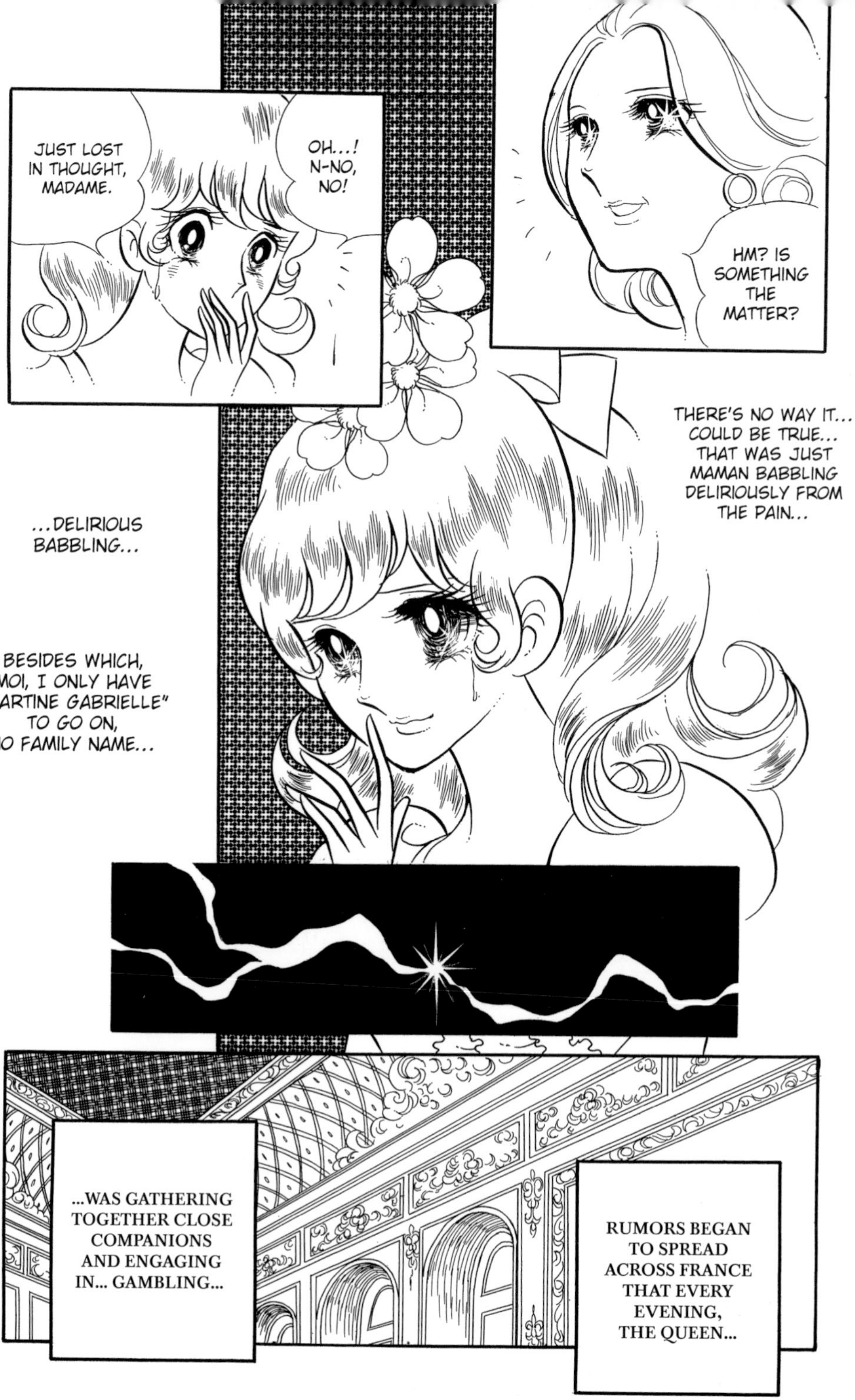
HM? IS SOMETHING THE MATTER?
OH...! N-NO, NO!
JUST LOST IN THOUGHT, MADAME.
THERE'S NO WAY IT... COULD BE TRUE... THAT WAS JUST MAMAN BABBLING DELIRIOUSLY FROM THE PAIN...
...DELIRIOUS BABBLING...
BESIDES WHICH, MOI, I ONLY HAVE "MARTINE GABRIELLE" TO GO ON, NO FAMILY NAME...
RUMORS BEGAN TO SPREAD ACROSS FRANCE THAT EVERY EVENING, THE QUEEN...
...WAS GATHERING TOGETHER CLOSE COMPANIONS AND ENGAGING IN... GAMBLING...

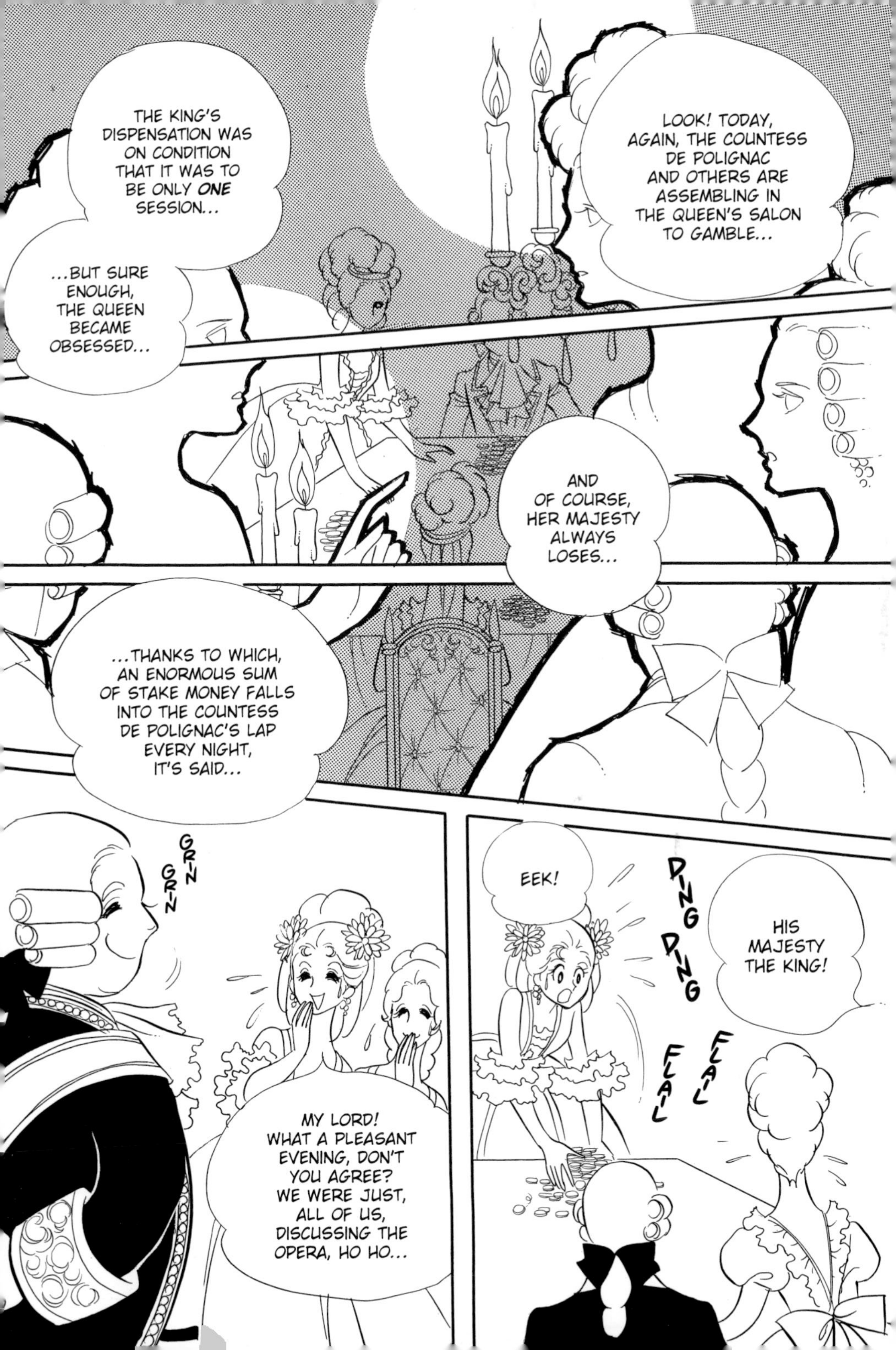

LOOK! TODAY, AGAIN, THE COUNTESS DE POLIGNAC AND OTHERS ARE ASSEMBLING IN THE QUEEN'S SALON TO GAMBLE...
THE KING'S DISPENSATION WAS ON CONDITION THAT IT WAS TO BE ONLY *ONE* SESSION...
...BUT SURE ENOUGH, THE QUEEN BECAME OBSESSED...
AND OF COURSE, HER MAJESTY ALWAYS LOSES...
...THANKS TO WHICH, AN ENORMOUS SUM OF STAKE MONEY FALLS INTO THE COUNTESS DE POLIGNAC'S LAP EVERY NIGHT, IT'S SAID...
HIS MAJESTY THE KING!
DING DING
EEK!
FLAIL FLAIL
GRIN GRIN
MY LORD! WHAT A PLEASANT EVENING, DON'T YOU AGREE? WE WERE JUST, ALL OF US, DISCUSSING THE OPERA, HO HO...

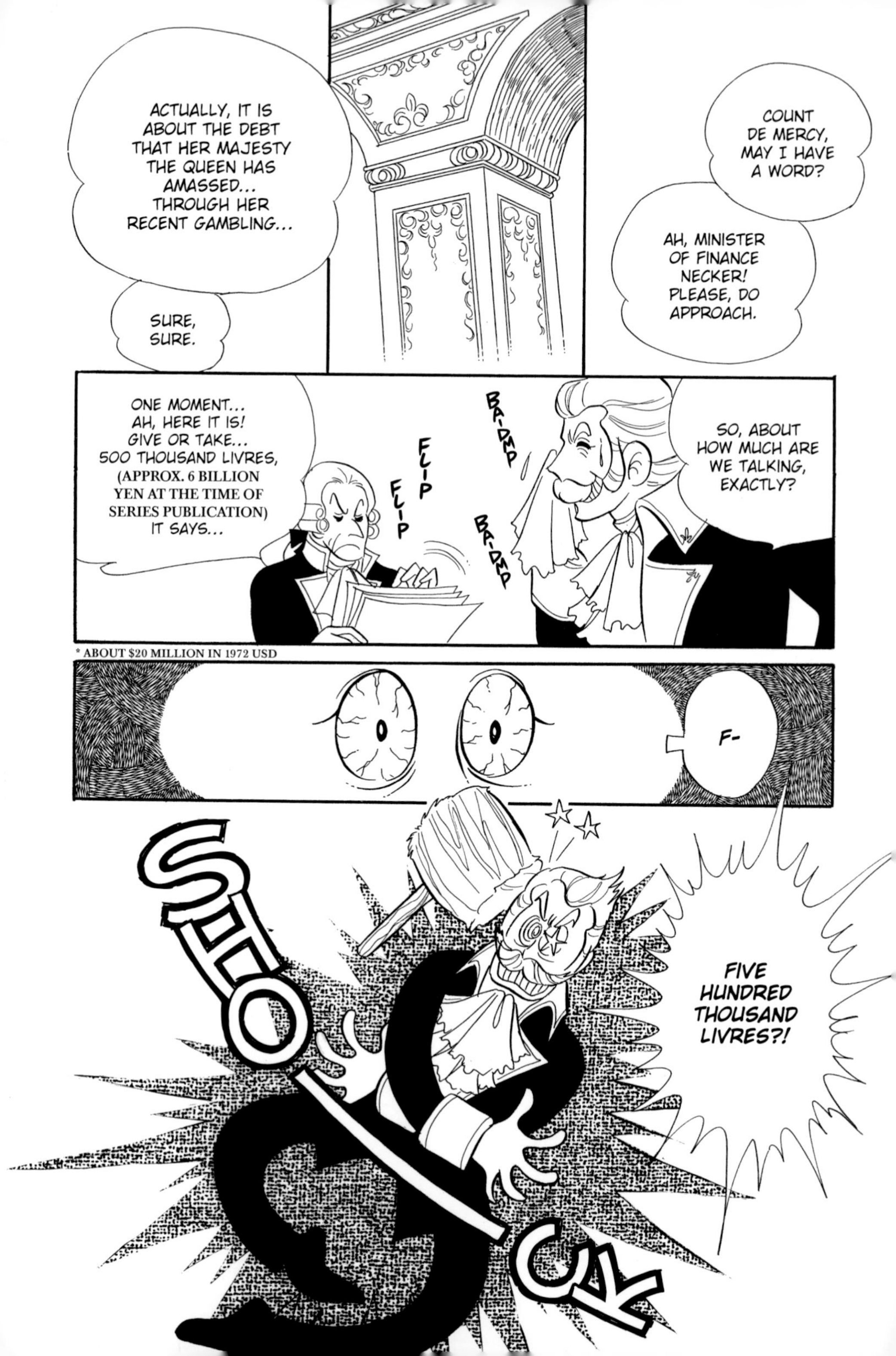
COUNT DE MERCY, MAY I HAVE A WORD?
AH, MINISTER OF FINANCE NECKER! PLEASE, DO APPROACH.
ACTUALLY, IT IS ABOUT THE DEBT THAT HER MAJESTY THE QUEEN HAS AMASSED... THROUGH HER RECENT GAMBLING...
SURE, SURE.
SO, ABOUT HOW MUCH ARE WE TALKING, EXACTLY?
BA-DMP
BA-DMP
FLIP
FLIP
ONE MOMENT... AH, HERE IT IS! GIVE OR TAKE... 500 THOUSAND LIVRES, (APPROX. 6 BILLION YEN AT THE TIME OF SERIES PUBLICATION) IT SAYS...
F-
FIVE HUNDRED THOUSAND LIVRES?!
SHOCK

* ABOUT $20 MILLION IN 1972 USD

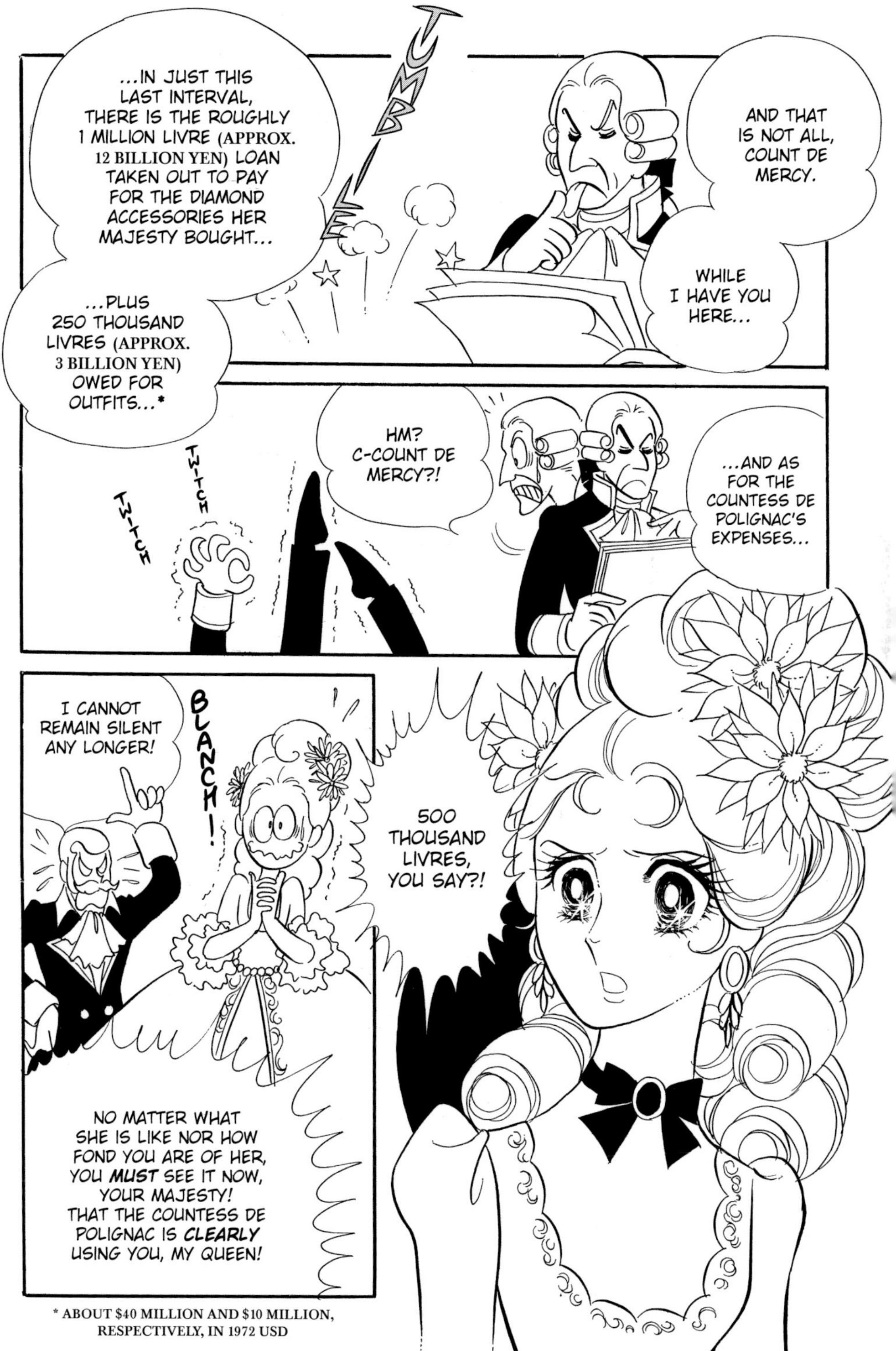
AND THAT IS NOT ALL, COUNT DE MERCY.
WHILE I HAVE YOU HERE...
...IN JUST THIS LAST INTERVAL, THERE IS THE ROUGHLY 1 MILLION LIVRE (APPROX. 12 BILLION YEN) LOAN TAKEN OUT TO PAY FOR THE DIAMOND ACCESSORIES HER MAJESTY BOUGHT...
TUMBLE
...PLUS 250 THOUSAND LIVRES (APPROX. 3 BILLION YEN) OWED FOR OUTFITS...*
...AND AS FOR THE COUNTESS DE POLIGNAC'S EXPENSES...
HM? C-COUNT DE MERCY?!
TWITCH
TWITCH
500 THOUSAND LIVRES, YOU SAY?!
BLANCH!
I CANNOT REMAIN SILENT ANY LONGER!
NO MATTER WHAT SHE IS LIKE NOR HOW FOND YOU ARE OF HER, YOU MUST SEE IT NOW, YOUR MAJESTY! THAT THE COUNTESS DE POLIGNAC IS CLEARLY USING YOU, MY QUEEN!

* ABOUT $40 MILLION AND $10 MILLION, RESPECTIVELY, IN 1972 USD

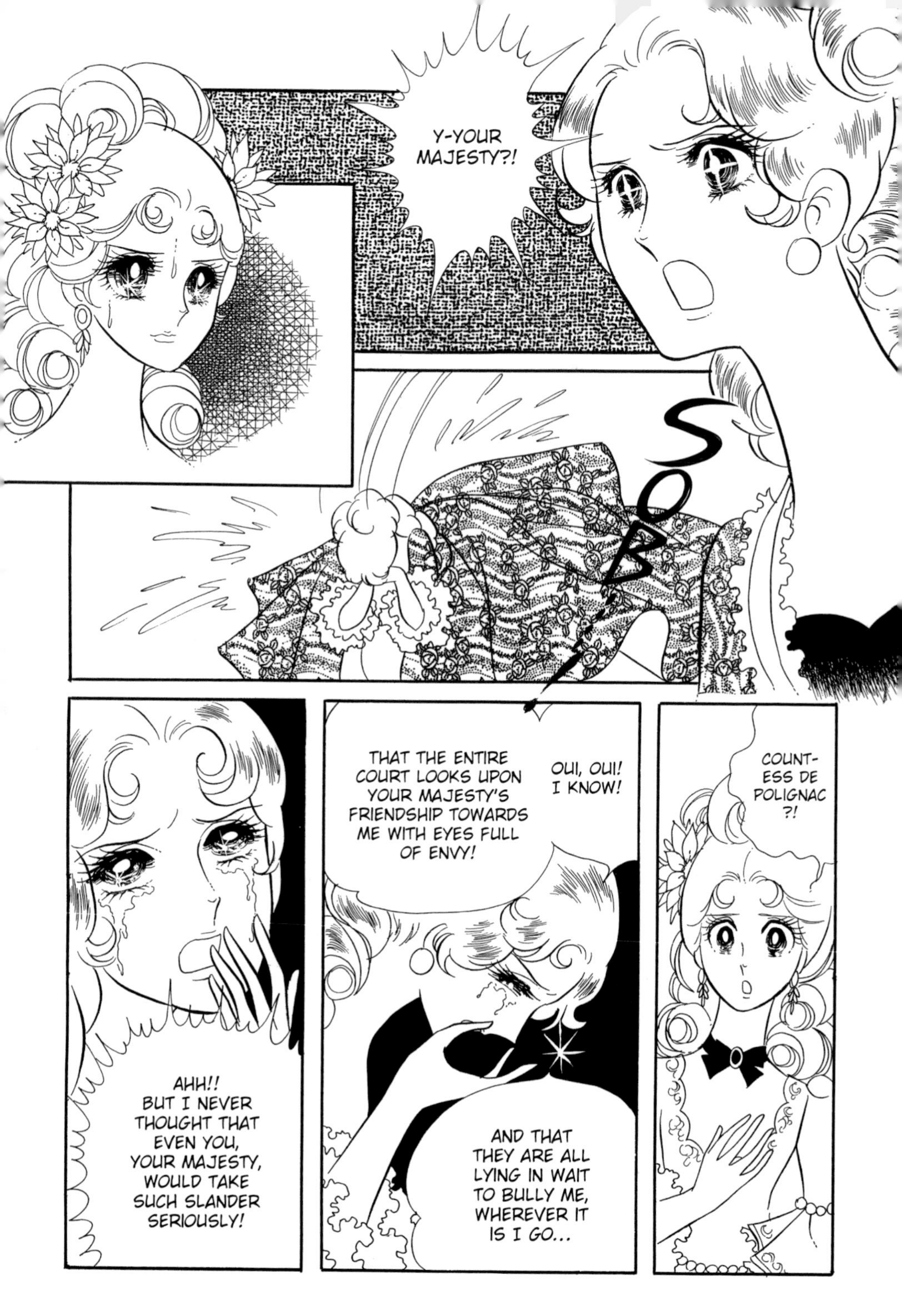
Y-YOUR MAJESTY?!
SOB...!
COUNT-ESS DE POLIGNAC ?!
OUI, OUI! I KNOW!
THAT THE ENTIRE COURT LOOKS UPON YOUR MAJESTY'S FRIENDSHIP TOWARDS ME WITH EYES FULL OF ENVY!
AND THAT THEY ARE ALL LYING IN WAIT TO BULLY ME, WHEREVER IT IS I GO...
AHH!! BUT I NEVER THOUGHT THAT EVEN YOU, YOUR MAJESTY, WOULD TAKE SUCH SLANDER SERIOUSLY!

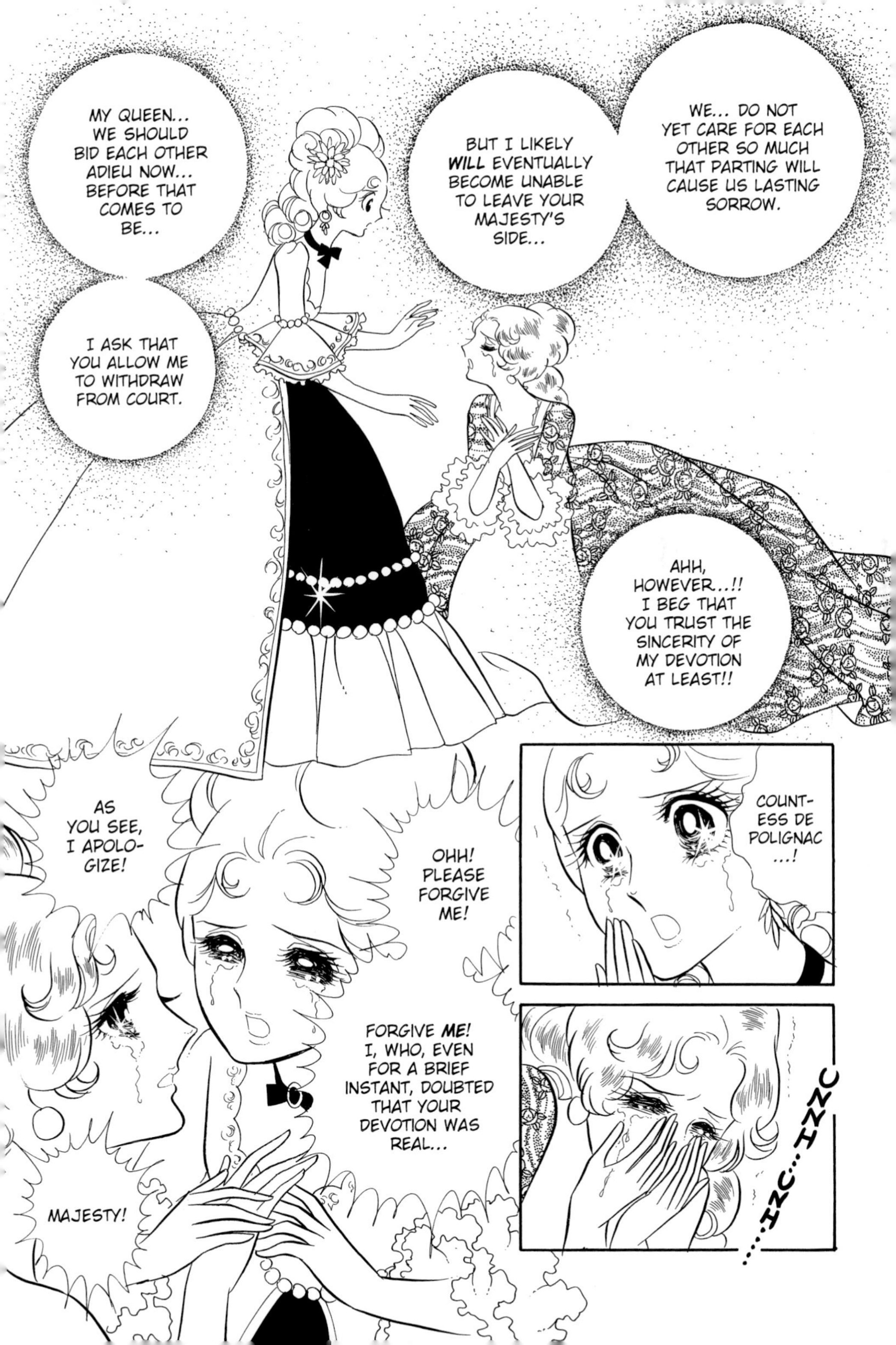
WE... DO NOT YET CARE FOR EACH OTHER SO MUCH THAT PARTING WILL CAUSE US LASTING SORROW.
BUT I LIKELY **WILL** EVENTUALLY BECOME UNABLE TO LEAVE YOUR MAJESTY'S SIDE...
MY QUEEN... WE SHOULD BID EACH OTHER ADIEU NOW... BEFORE THAT COMES TO BE...
I ASK THAT YOU ALLOW ME TO WITHDRAW FROM COURT.
AHH, HOWEVER...!! I BEG THAT YOU TRUST THE SINCERITY OF MY DEVOTION AT LEAST!!
COUNT-ESS DE POLIGNAC ...!
....HNC...HNC
OHH! PLEASE FORGIVE ME!
AS YOU SEE, I APOLO-GIZE!
FORGIVE **ME**! I, WHO, EVEN FOR A BRIEF INSTANT, DOUBTED THAT YOUR DEVOTION WAS REAL...
MAJESTY!

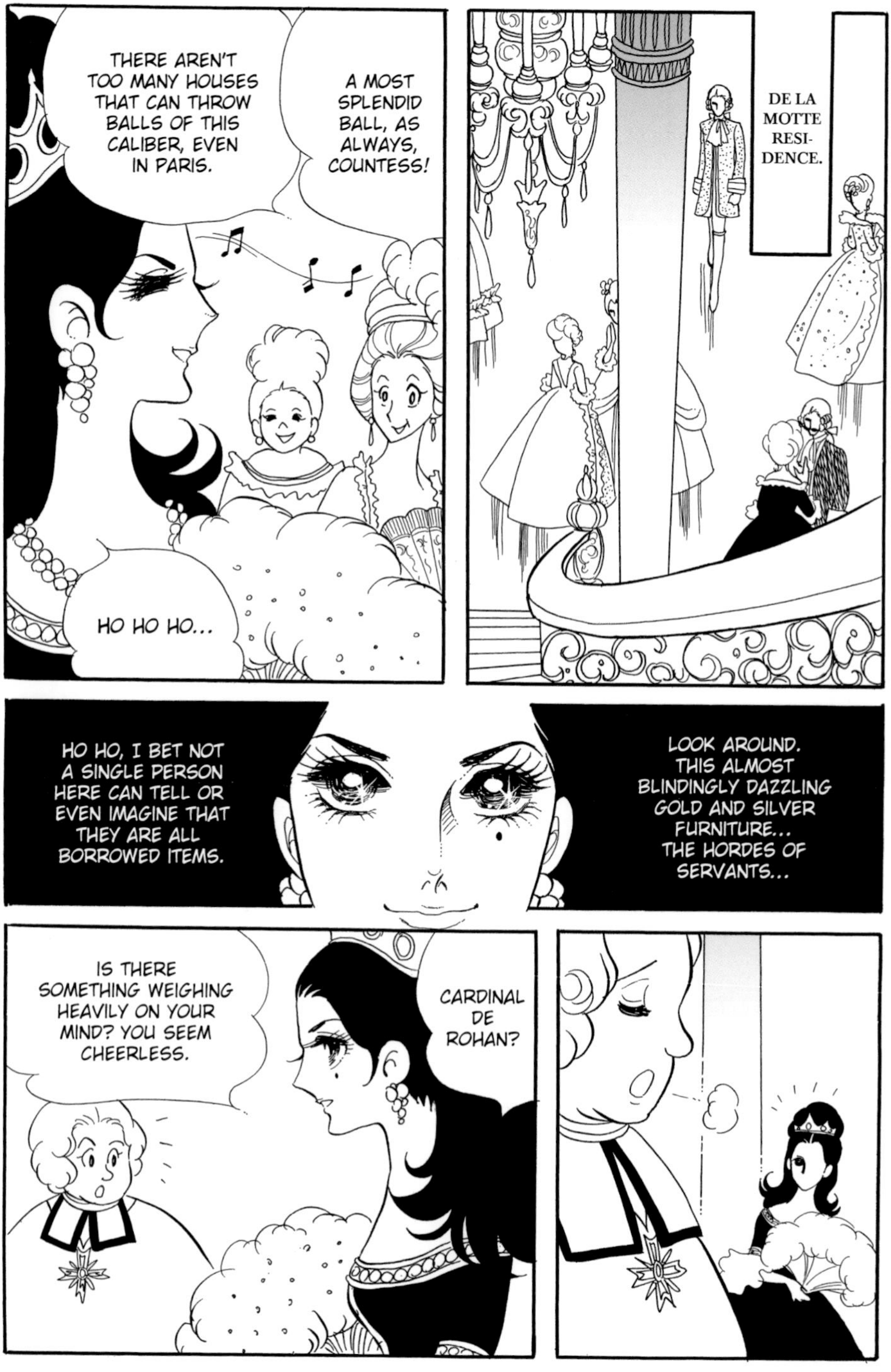
DE LA MOTTE RESIDENCE.
A MOST SPLENDID BALL, AS ALWAYS, COUNTESS!
THERE AREN'T TOO MANY HOUSES THAT CAN THROW BALLS OF THIS CALIBER, EVEN IN PARIS.
HO HO HO...
LOOK AROUND. THIS ALMOST BLINDINGLY DAZZLING GOLD AND SILVER FURNITURE... THE HORDES OF SERVANTS...
HO HO, I BET NOT A SINGLE PERSON HERE CAN TELL OR EVEN IMAGINE THAT THEY ARE ALL BORROWED ITEMS.
CARDINAL DE ROHAN?
IS THERE SOMETHING WEIGHING HEAVILY ON YOUR MIND? YOU SEEM CHEERLESS.

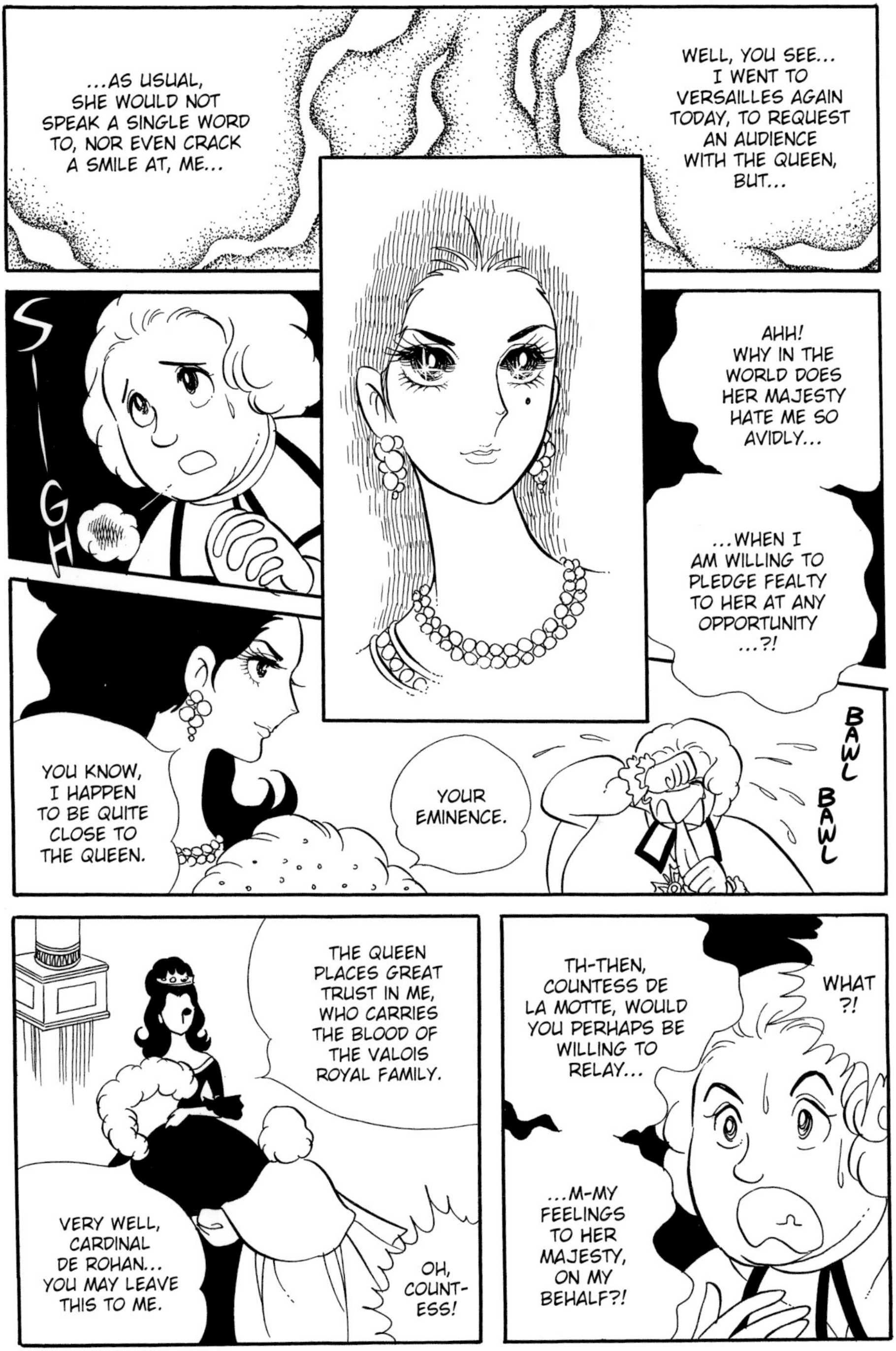
WELL, YOU SEE... I WENT TO VERSAILLES AGAIN TODAY, TO REQUEST AN AUDIENCE WITH THE QUEEN, BUT...
...AS USUAL, SHE WOULD NOT SPEAK A SINGLE WORD TO, NOR EVEN CRACK A SMILE AT, ME...
AHH! WHY IN THE WORLD DOES HER MAJESTY HATE ME SO AVIDLY...
...WHEN I AM WILLING TO PLEDGE FEALTY TO HER AT ANY OPPORTUNITY ...?!
SIGH
BAWL BAWL
YOUR EMINENCE.
YOU KNOW, I HAPPEN TO BE QUITE CLOSE TO THE QUEEN.
WHAT ?!
TH-THEN, COUNTESS DE LA MOTTE, WOULD YOU PERHAPS BE WILLING TO RELAY...
...M-MY FEELINGS TO HER MAJESTY, ON MY BEHALF?!
THE QUEEN PLACES GREAT TRUST IN ME, WHO CARRIES THE BLOOD OF THE VALOIS ROYAL FAMILY.
OH, COUNT-ESS!
VERY WELL, CARDINAL DE ROHAN... YOU MAY LEAVE THIS TO ME.

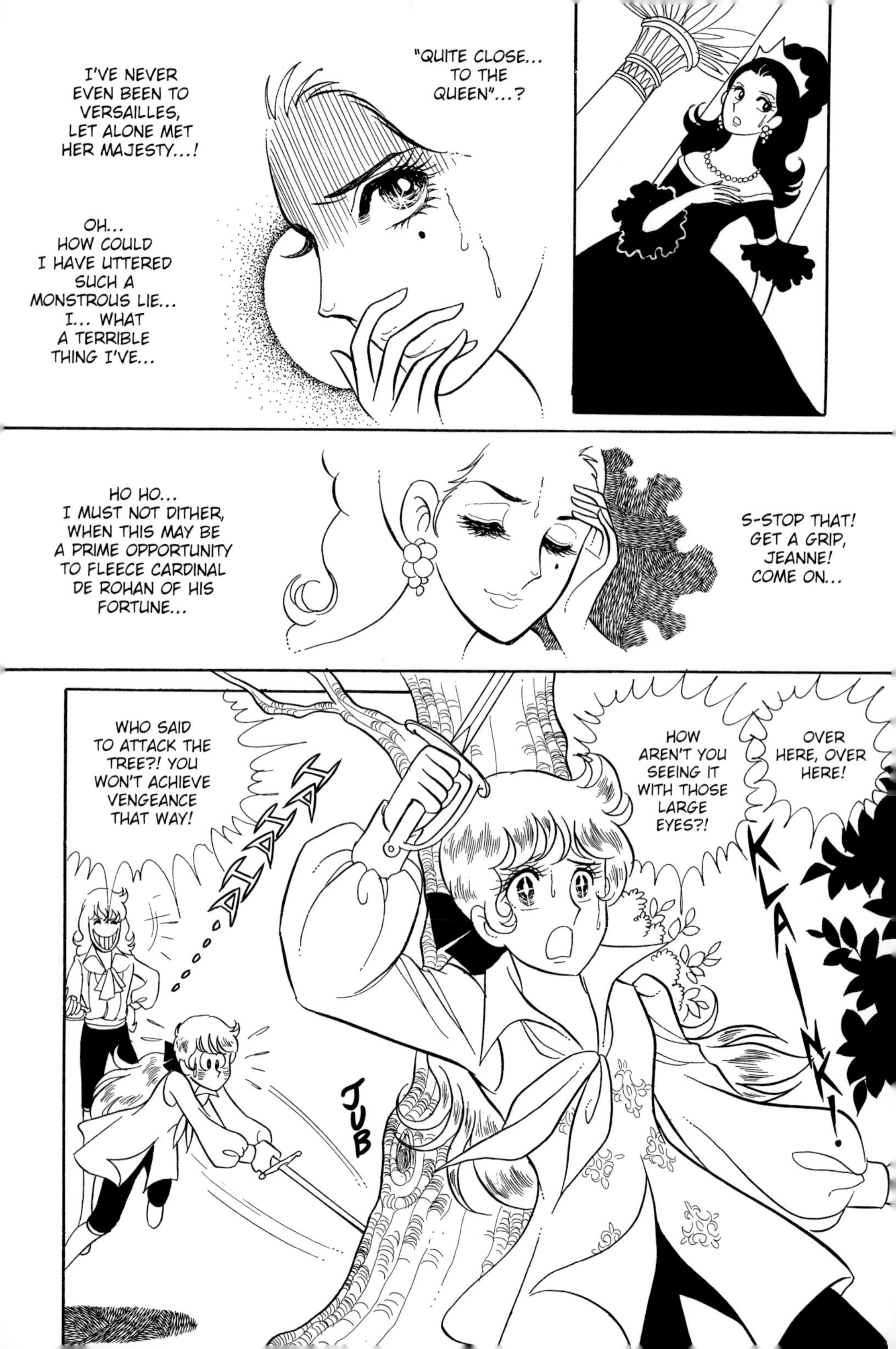
"QUITE CLOSE... TO THE QUEEN"...?
I'VE NEVER EVEN BEEN TO VERSAILLES, LET ALONE MET HER MAJESTY...!
OH... HOW COULD I HAVE UTTERED SUCH A MONSTROUS LIE... I... WHAT A TERRIBLE THING I'VE...
S-STOP THAT! GET A GRIP, JEANNE! COME ON...
HO HO... I MUST NOT DITHER, WHEN THIS MAY BE A PRIME OPPORTUNITY TO FLEECE CARDINAL DE ROHAN OF HIS FORTUNE...
OVER HERE, OVER HERE!
HOW AREN'T YOU SEEING IT WITH THOSE LARGE EYES?!
KLA-NK!
WHO SAID TO ATTACK THE TREE?! YOU WON'T ACHIEVE VENGEANCE THAT WAY!
AHAHAHA
JUB

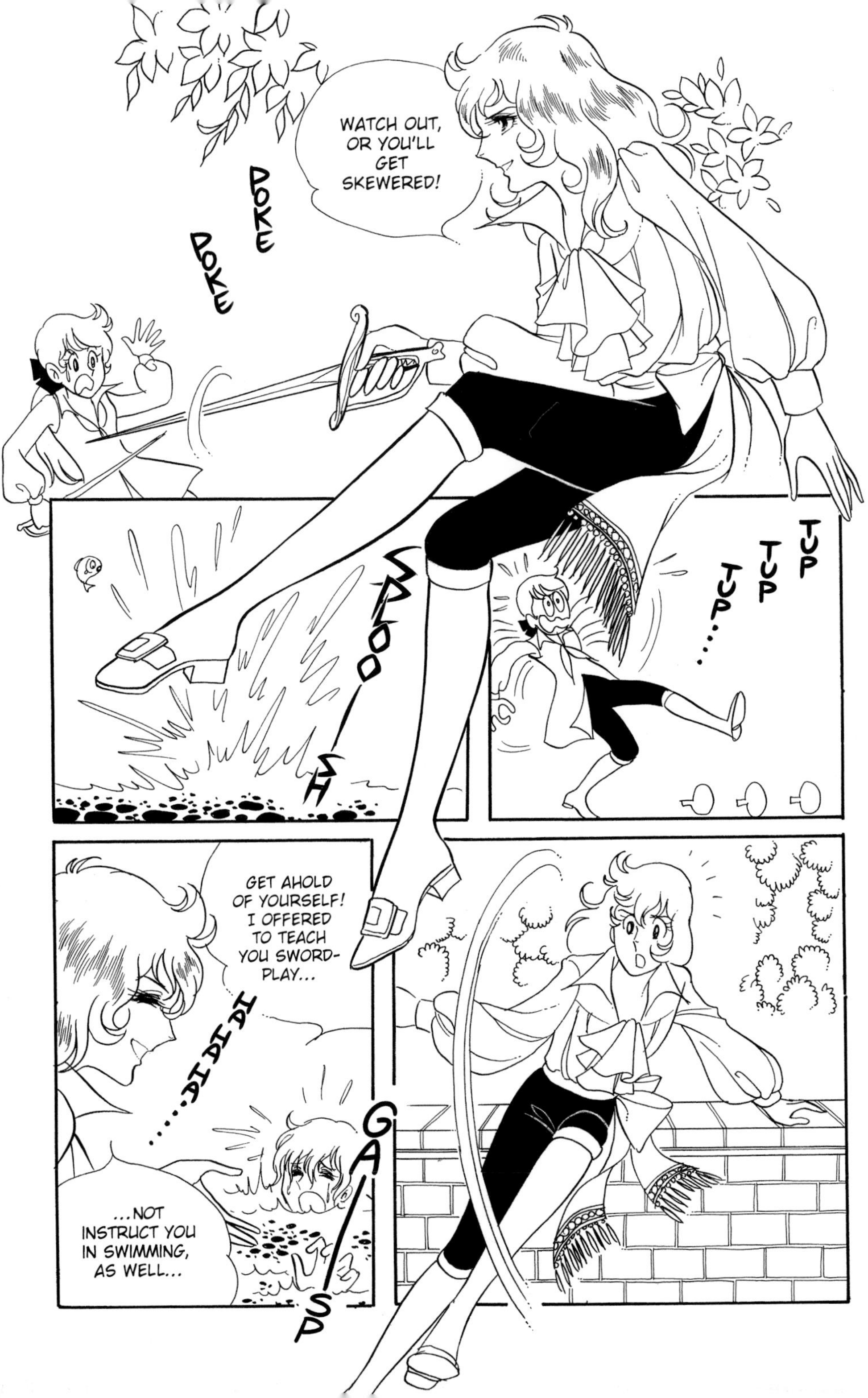
WATCH OUT, OR YOU'LL GET SKEWERED!
POKE
POKE
TUP
TUP
TUP...
SPLOO-SH
GASP
GET AHOLD OF YOURSELF! I OFFERED TO TEACH YOU SWORD-PLAY...
...NOT INSTRUCT YOU IN SWIMMING, AS WELL...
AIAIAIAI....

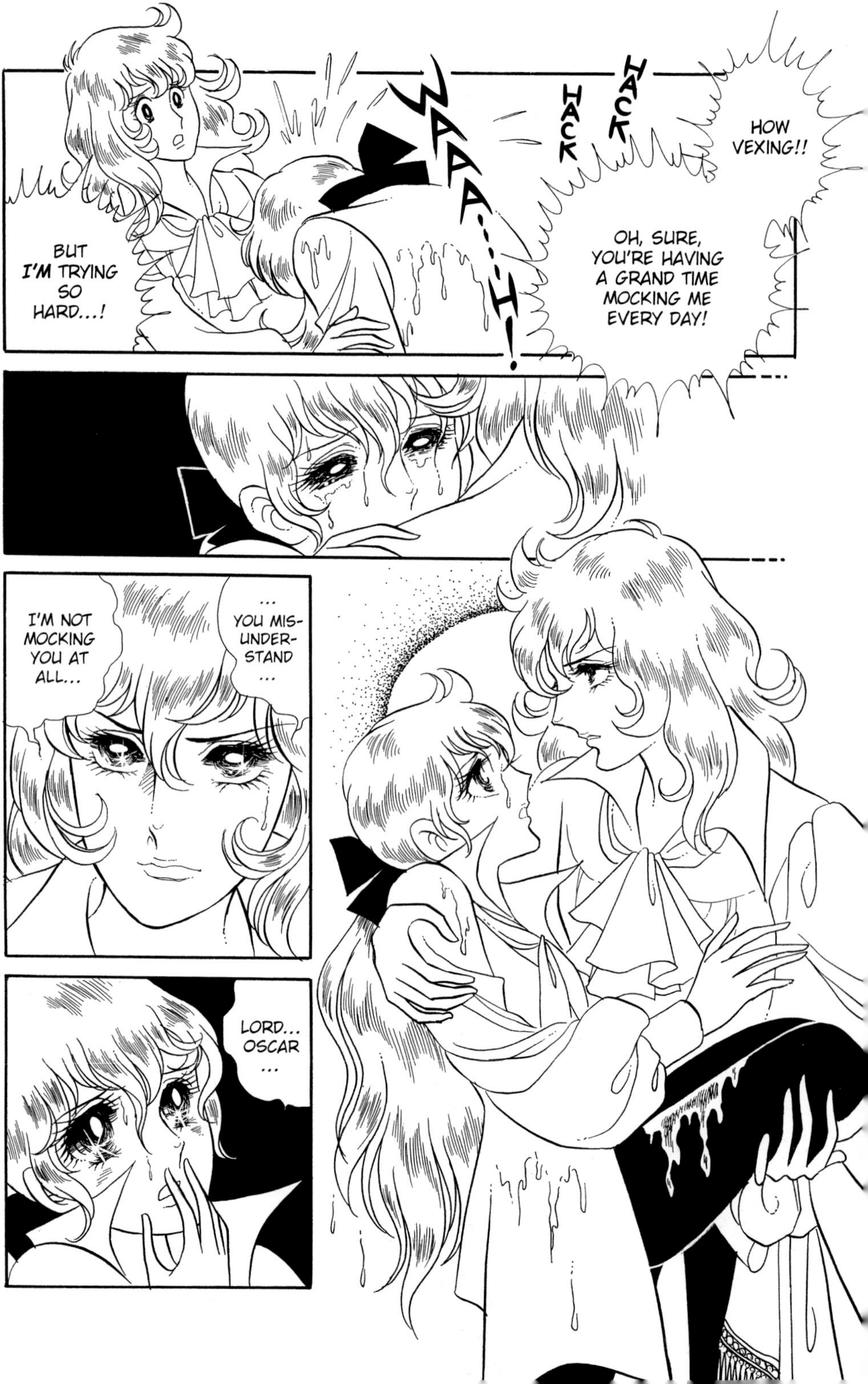
HOW VEXING!!
OH, SURE, YOU'RE HAVING A GRAND TIME MOCKING ME EVERY DAY!
HACK HACK
WAAAA...H!
BUT ***I'M*** TRYING SO HARD...!
... YOU MIS-UNDER-STAND ...
I'M NOT MOCKING YOU AT ALL...
LORD... OSCAR ...

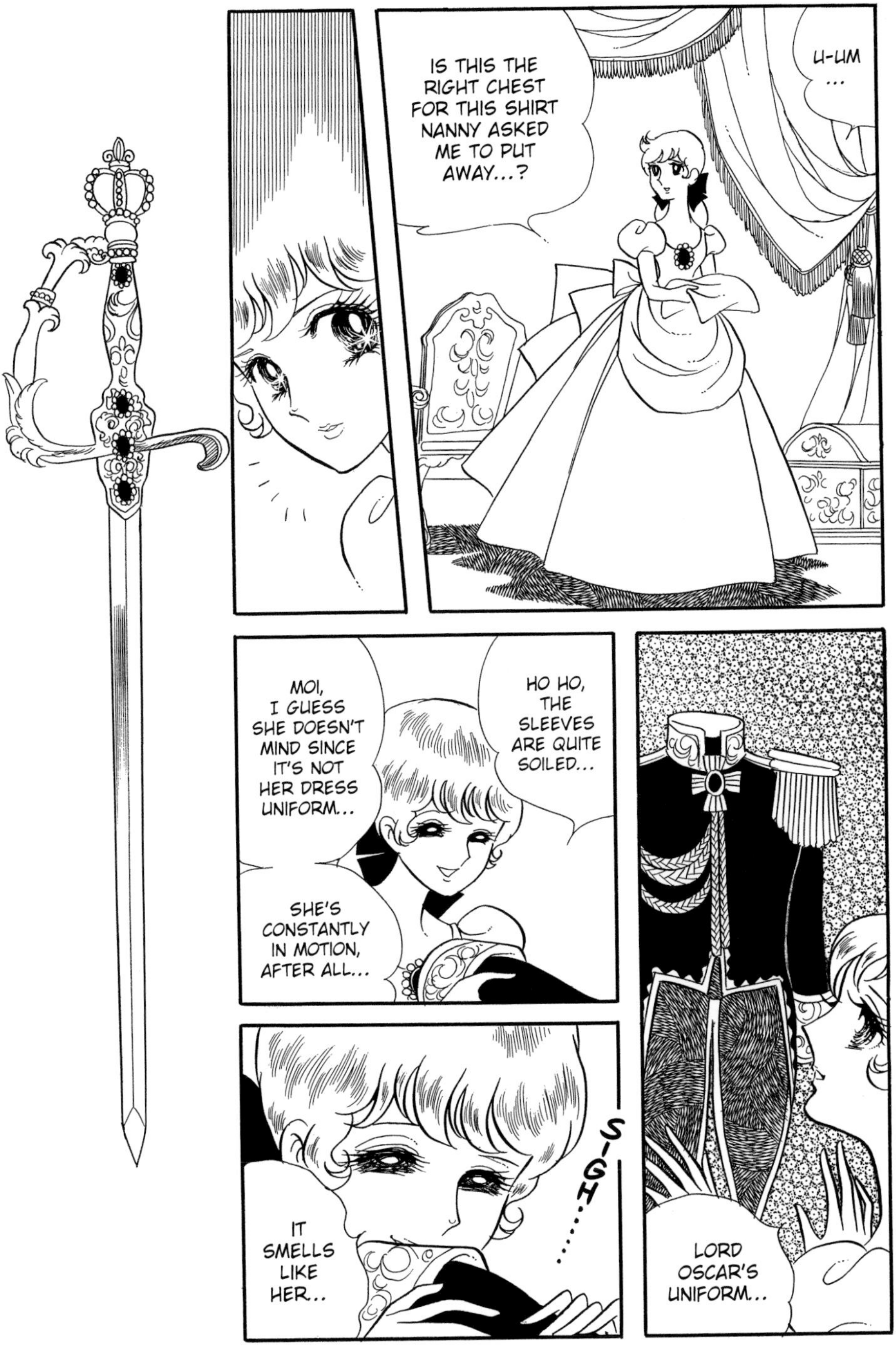
U-UM ...
IS THIS THE RIGHT CHEST FOR THIS SHIRT NANNY ASKED ME TO PUT AWAY...?
LORD OSCAR'S UNIFORM...
HO HO, THE SLEEVES ARE QUITE SOILED...
MOI, I GUESS SHE DOESN'T MIND SINCE IT'S NOT HER DRESS UNIFORM...
SHE'S CONSTANTLY IN MOTION, AFTER ALL...
SIGH....
IT SMELLS LIKE HER...

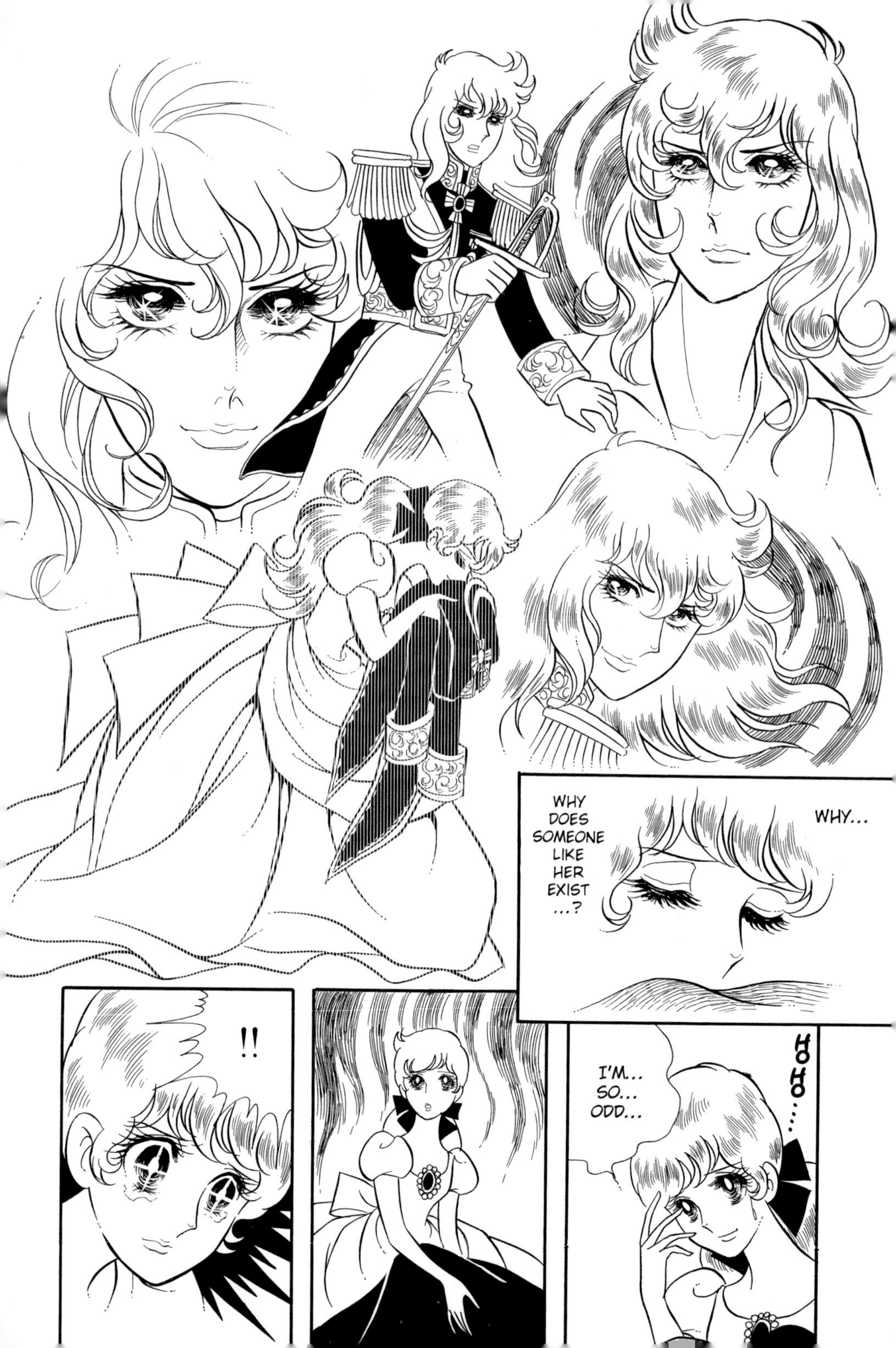
WHY...
WHY DOES SOMEONE LIKE HER EXIST ...?
HOHO....
I'M... SO... ODD...
!!

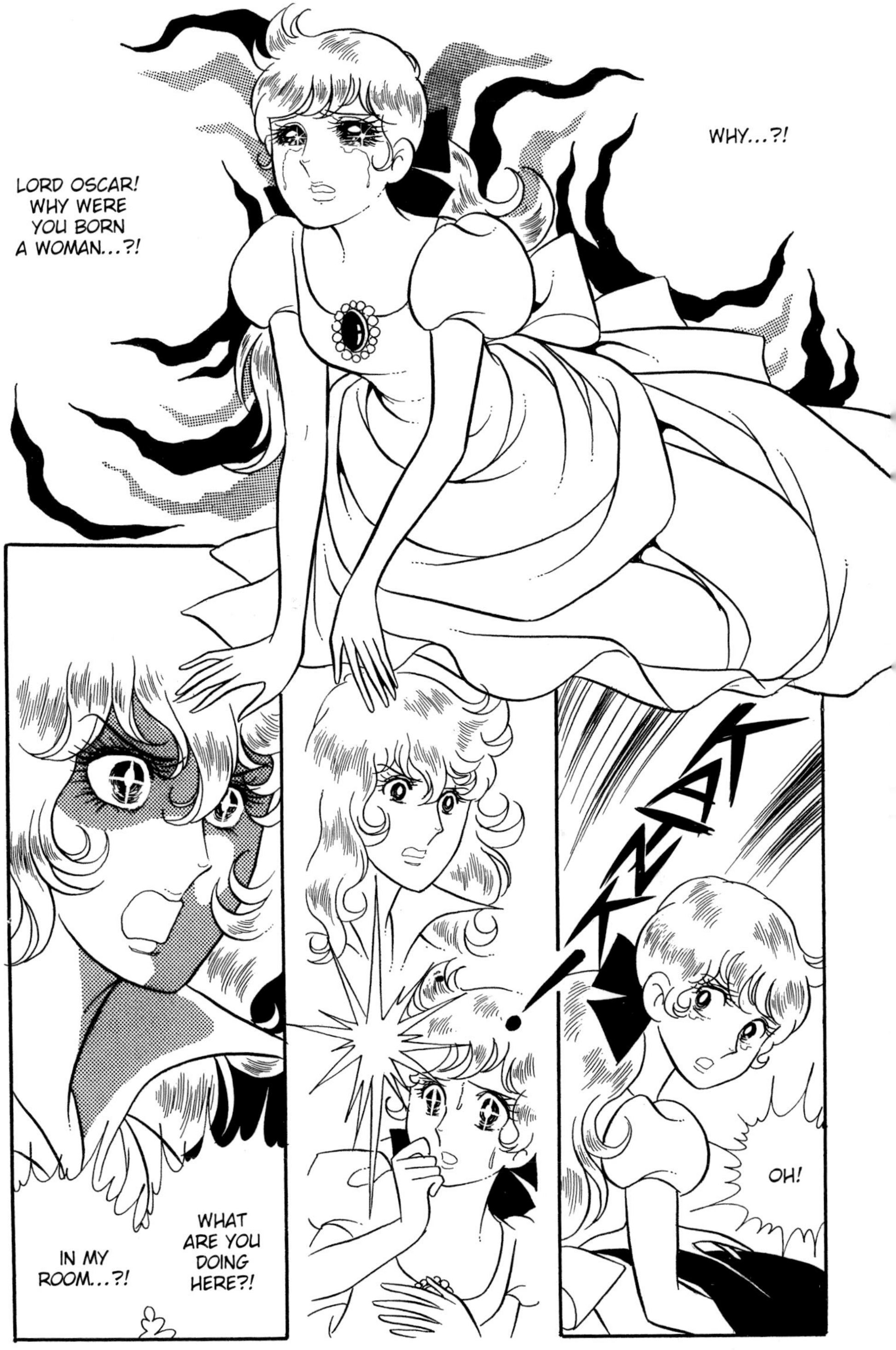
WHY...?!
LORD OSCAR! WHY WERE YOU BORN A WOMAN...?!
KANK!
OH!
WHAT ARE YOU DOING HERE?!
IN MY ROOM...?!

THE ROSE OF VERSAILLES

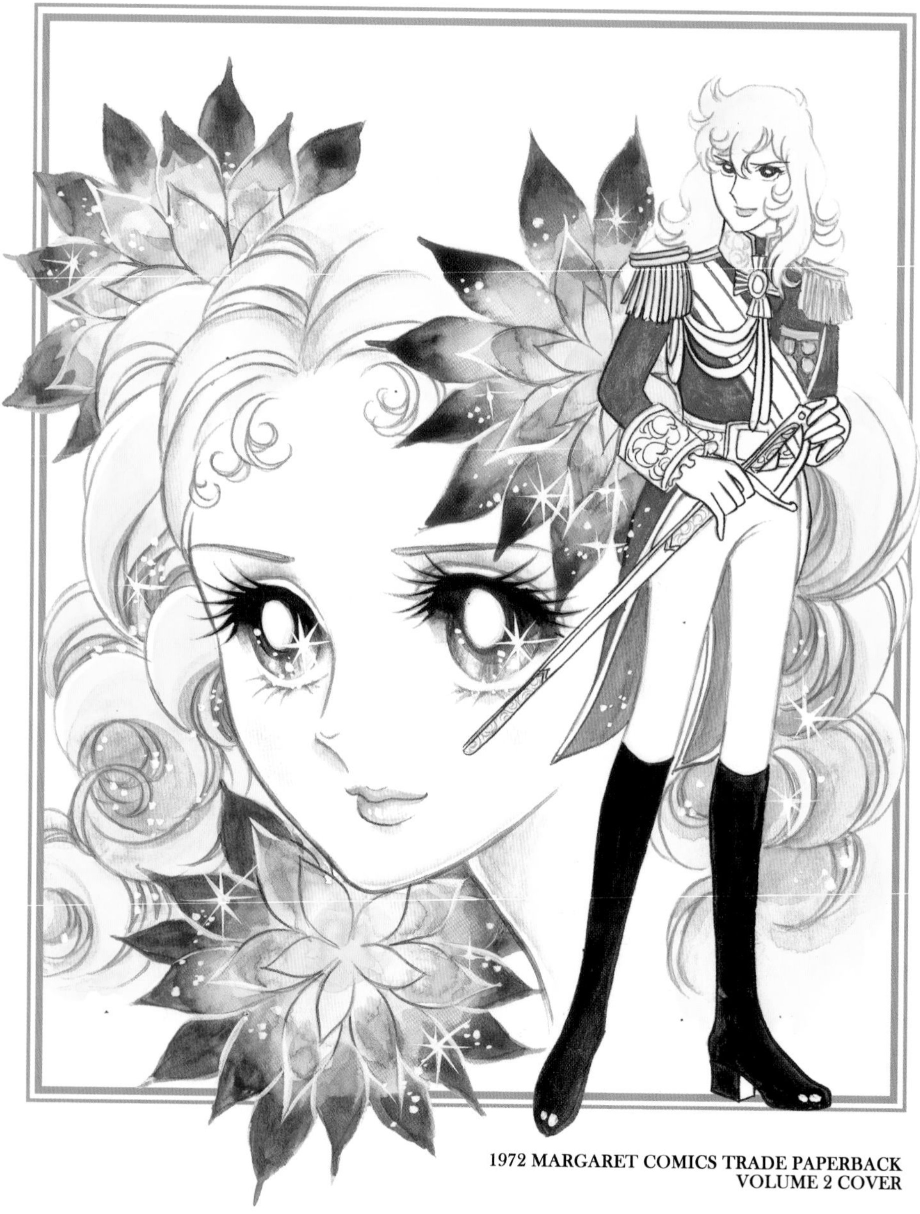

1972 MARGARET COMICS TRADE PAPERBACK
VOLUME 2 COVER

★THE HOTLY DISCUSSED TOUR DE FORCE!!
♥ROSALIE IS TROUBLED BY HER FORBIDDEN LOVE FOR OSCAR!?

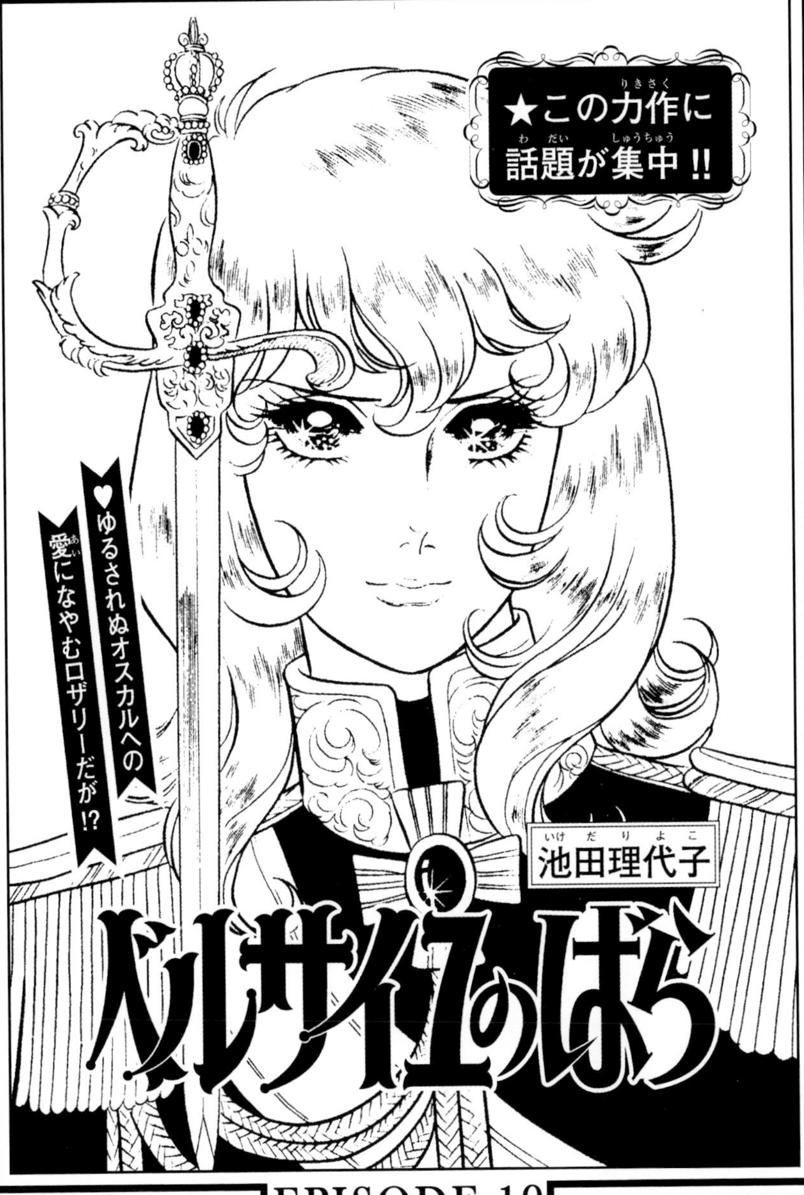
★この力作に
話題が集中!!
♥ゆるされぬオスカルへの
愛になやむロザリーだが!?
池田理代子
ベルサイユのばら

EPISODE 19

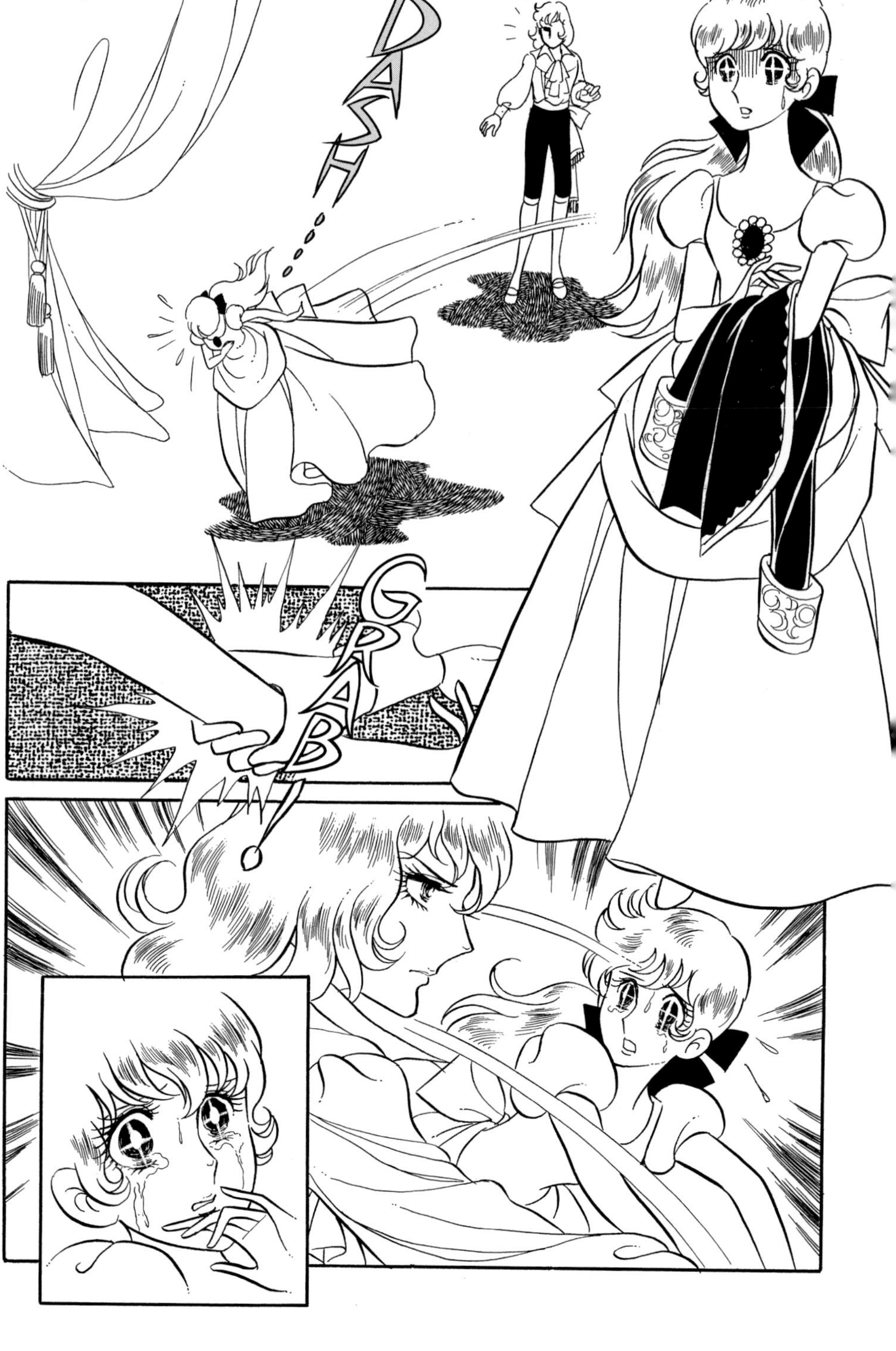
DASH
GRAB

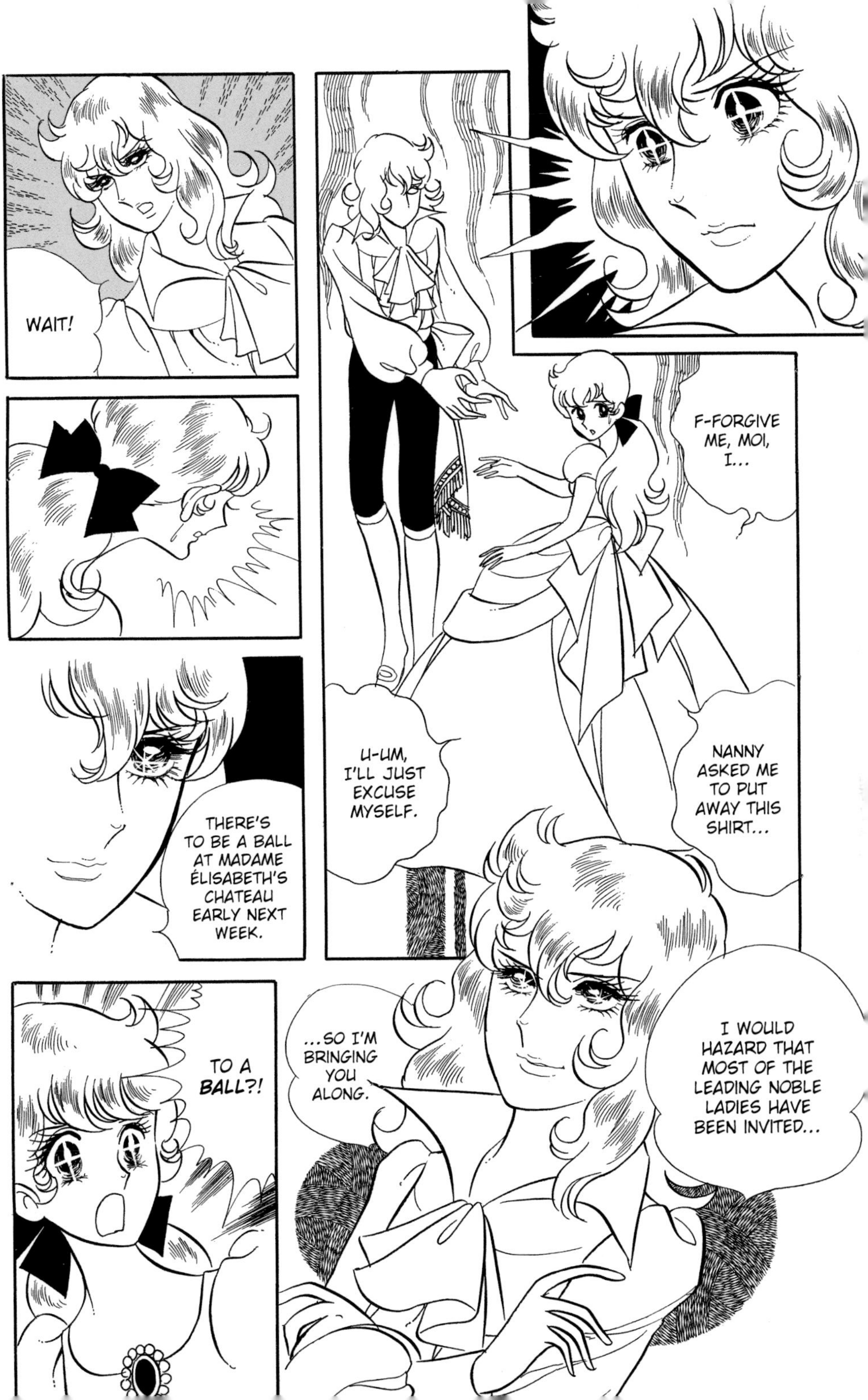
F-FORGIVE ME, MOI, I...
NANNY ASKED ME TO PUT AWAY THIS SHIRT...
U-UM, I'LL JUST EXCUSE MYSELF.
WAIT!
THERE'S TO BE A BALL AT MADAME ÉLISABETH'S CHATEAU EARLY NEXT WEEK.
I WOULD HAZARD THAT MOST OF THE LEADING NOBLE LADIES HAVE BEEN INVITED...
...SO I'M BRINGING YOU ALONG.
TO A BALL?!

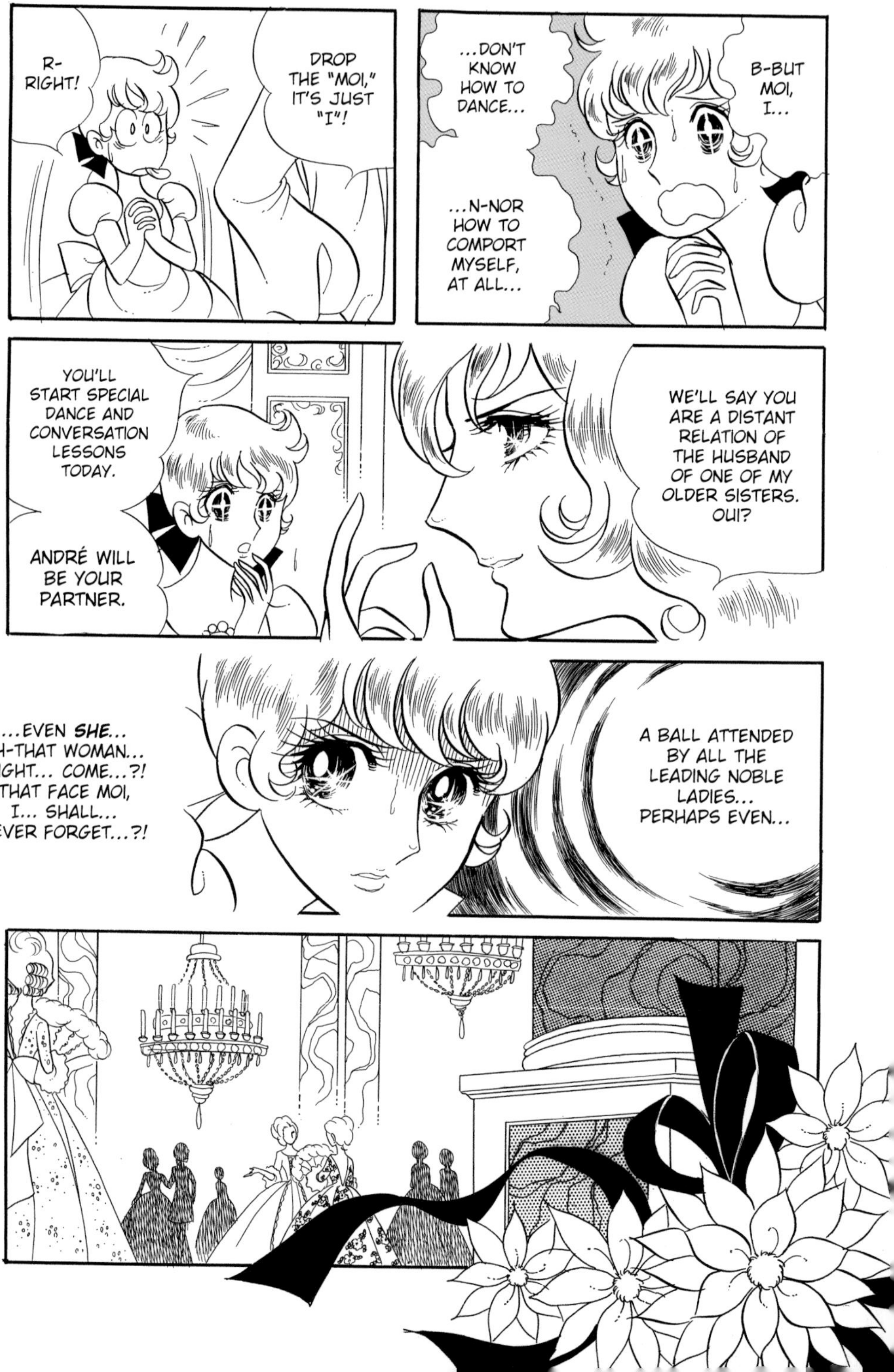
B-BUT MOI, I...
...DON'T KNOW HOW TO DANCE...
...N-NOR HOW TO COMPORT MYSELF, AT ALL...
DROP THE "MOI," IT'S JUST "I"!
R-RIGHT!
WE'LL SAY YOU ARE A DISTANT RELATION OF THE HUSBAND OF ONE OF MY OLDER SISTERS. OUI?
YOU'LL START SPECIAL DANCE AND CONVERSATION LESSONS TODAY.
ANDRÉ WILL BE YOUR PARTNER.
A BALL ATTENDED BY ALL THE LEADING NOBLE LADIES... PERHAPS EVEN...
...EVEN **SHE**... TH-THAT WOMAN... MIGHT... COME...?! THAT FACE MOI, I... SHALL... NEVER FORGET...?!

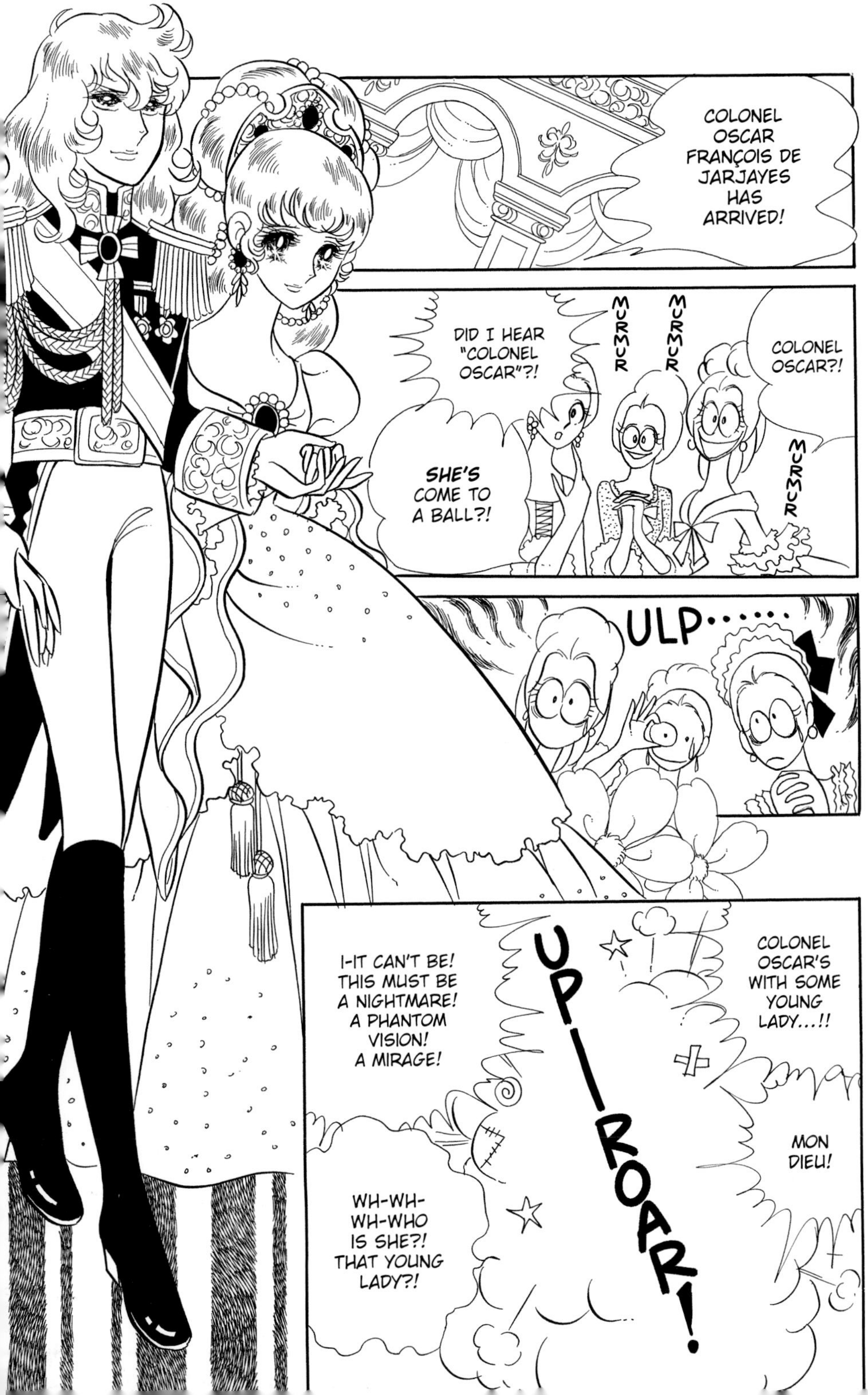
COLONEL OSCAR FRANÇOIS DE JARJAYES HAS ARRIVED!
COLONEL OSCAR?!
MURMUR
MURMUR
MURMUR
DID I HEAR "COLONEL OSCAR"?!
SHE'S COME TO A BALL?!
ULP......
COLONEL OSCAR'S WITH SOME YOUNG LADY...!!
UPROAR!
I-IT CAN'T BE! THIS MUST BE A NIGHTMARE! A PHANTOM VISION! A MIRAGE!
MON DIEU!
WH-WH-WH-WHO IS SHE?! THAT YOUNG LADY?!

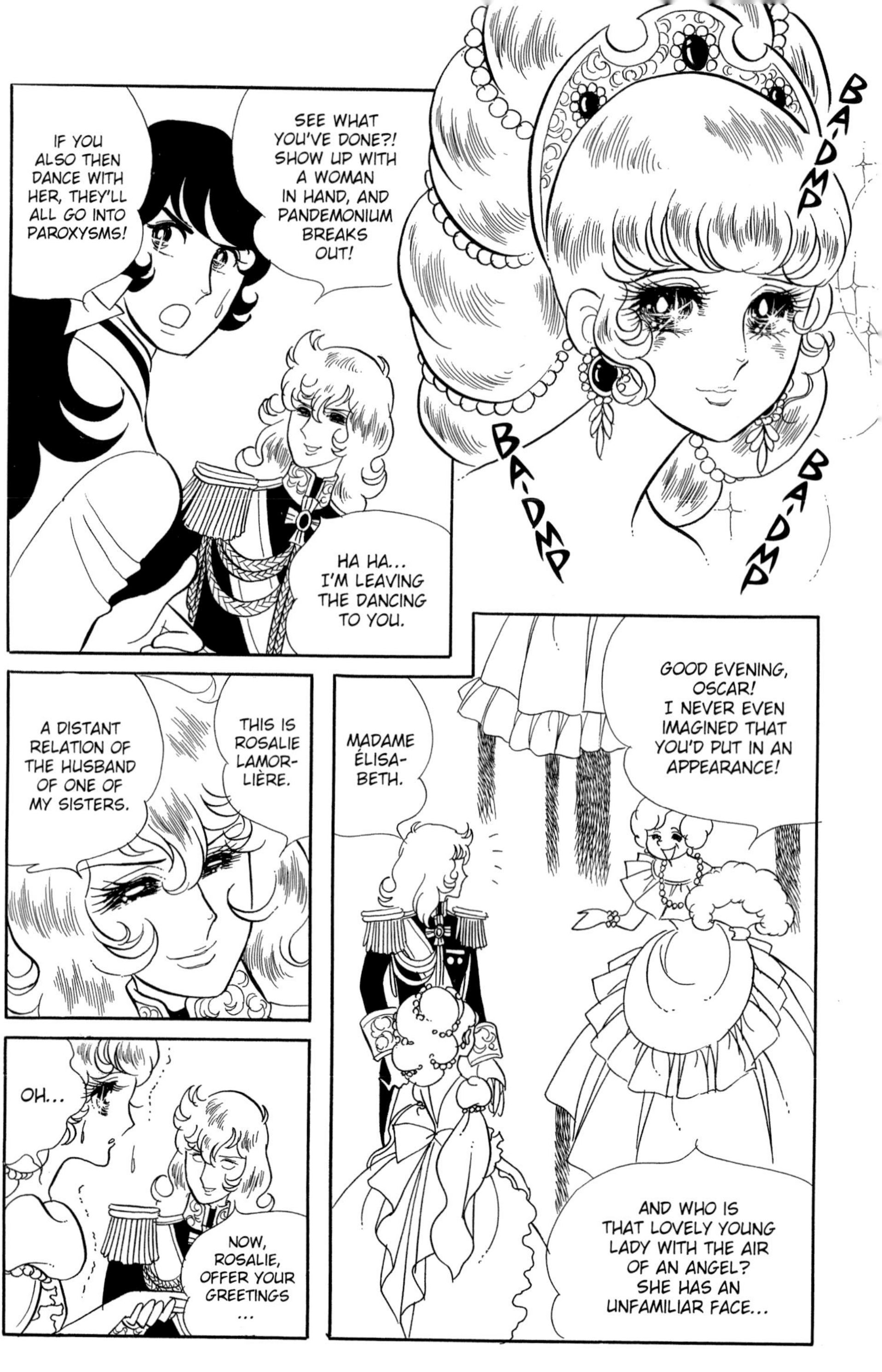
BA-DMP
BA-DMP
BA-DMP
SEE WHAT YOU'VE DONE?! SHOW UP WITH A WOMAN IN HAND, AND PANDEMONIUM BREAKS OUT!
IF YOU ALSO THEN DANCE WITH HER, THEY'LL ALL GO INTO PAROXYSMS!
HA HA... I'M LEAVING THE DANCING TO YOU.
GOOD EVENING, OSCAR! I NEVER EVEN IMAGINED THAT YOU'D PUT IN AN APPEARANCE!
MADAME ÉLISA-BETH.
AND WHO IS THAT LOVELY YOUNG LADY WITH THE AIR OF AN ANGEL? SHE HAS AN UNFAMILIAR FACE...
THIS IS ROSALIE LAMOR-LIÈRE.
A DISTANT RELATION OF THE HUSBAND OF ONE OF MY SISTERS.
OH...
NOW, ROSALIE, OFFER YOUR GREETINGS ...

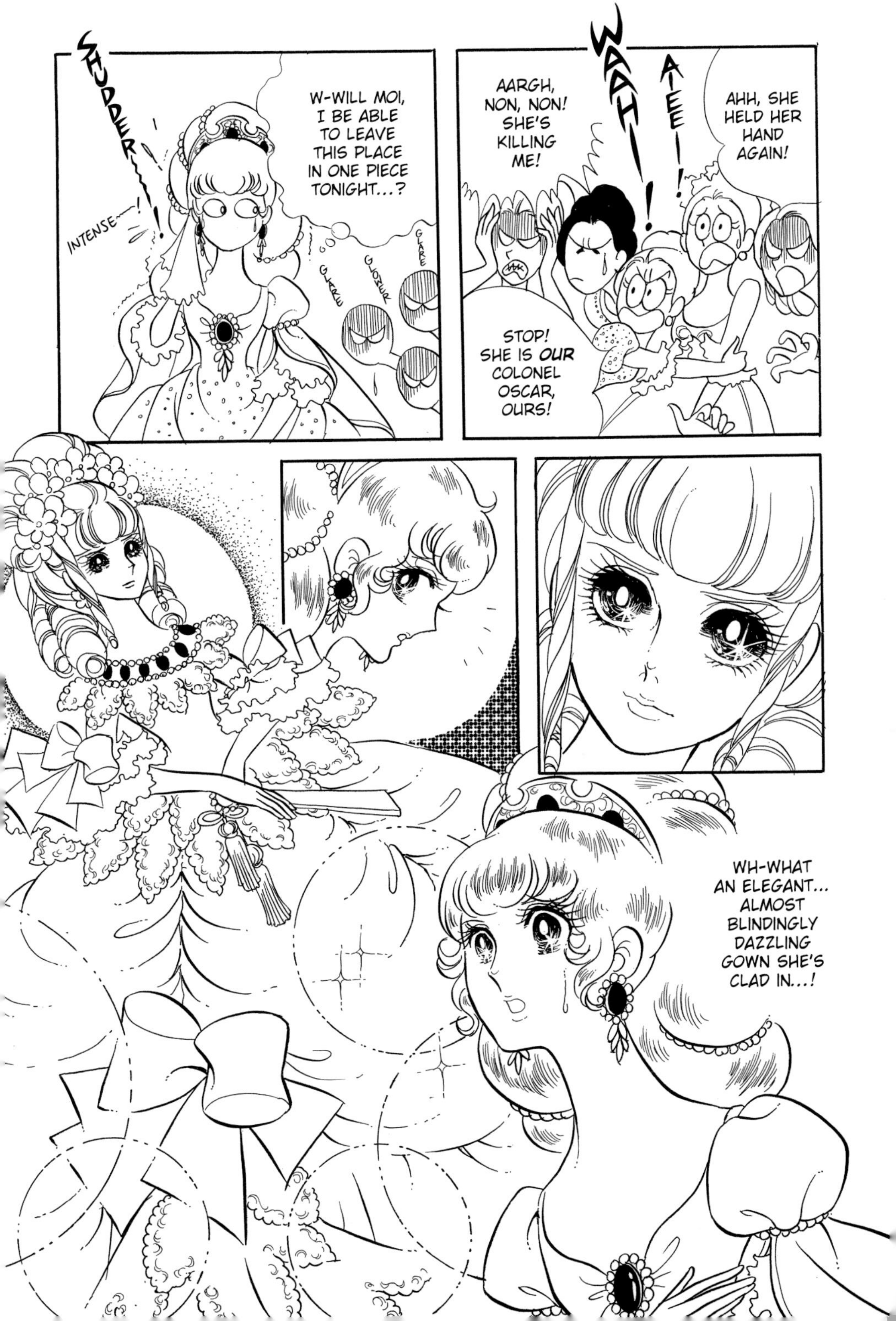
AHH, SHE HELD HER HAND AGAIN!
AIEE!
WAAH!
AARGH, NON, NON! SHE'S KILLING ME!
STOP! SHE IS **OUR** COLONEL OSCAR, OURS!
W-WILL MOI, I BE ABLE TO LEAVE THIS PLACE IN ONE PIECE TONIGHT...?
GLARE
GLOWER
GLARE
SHUDDER!
INTENSE—!
WH-WHAT AN ELEGANT... ALMOST BLINDINGLY DAZZLING GOWN SHE'S CLAD IN...!

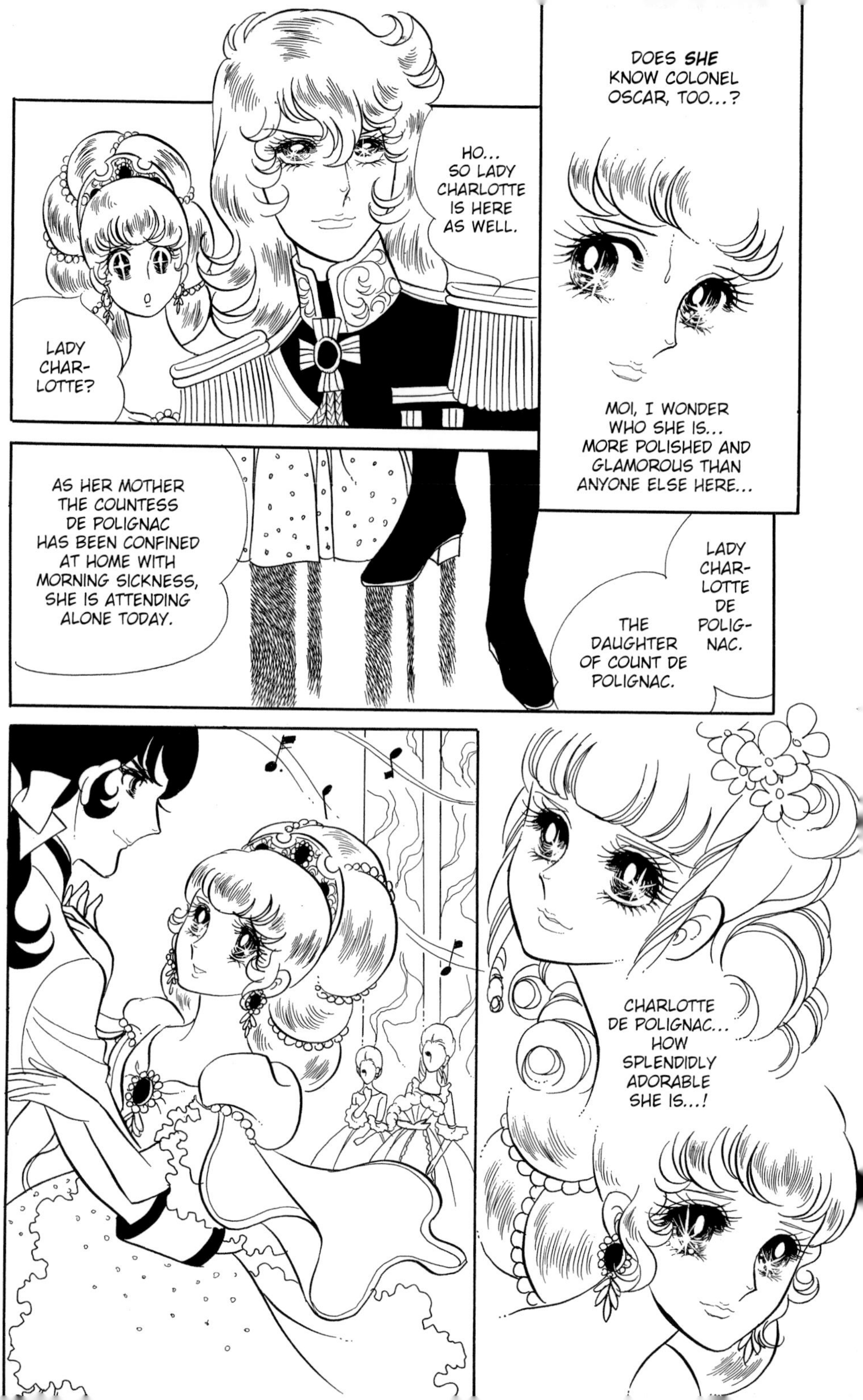

DOES **SHE** KNOW COLONEL OSCAR, TOO...?
MOI, I WONDER WHO SHE IS... MORE POLISHED AND GLAMOROUS THAN ANYONE ELSE HERE...
HO... SO LADY CHARLOTTE IS HERE AS WELL.
LADY CHAR-LOTTE?
LADY CHAR-LOTTE DE POLIG-NAC.
THE DAUGHTER OF COUNT DE POLIGNAC.
AS HER MOTHER THE COUNTESS DE POLIGNAC HAS BEEN CONFINED AT HOME WITH MORNING SICKNESS, SHE IS ATTENDING ALONE TODAY.
CHARLOTTE DE POLIGNAC... HOW SPLENDIDLY ADORABLE SHE IS...!

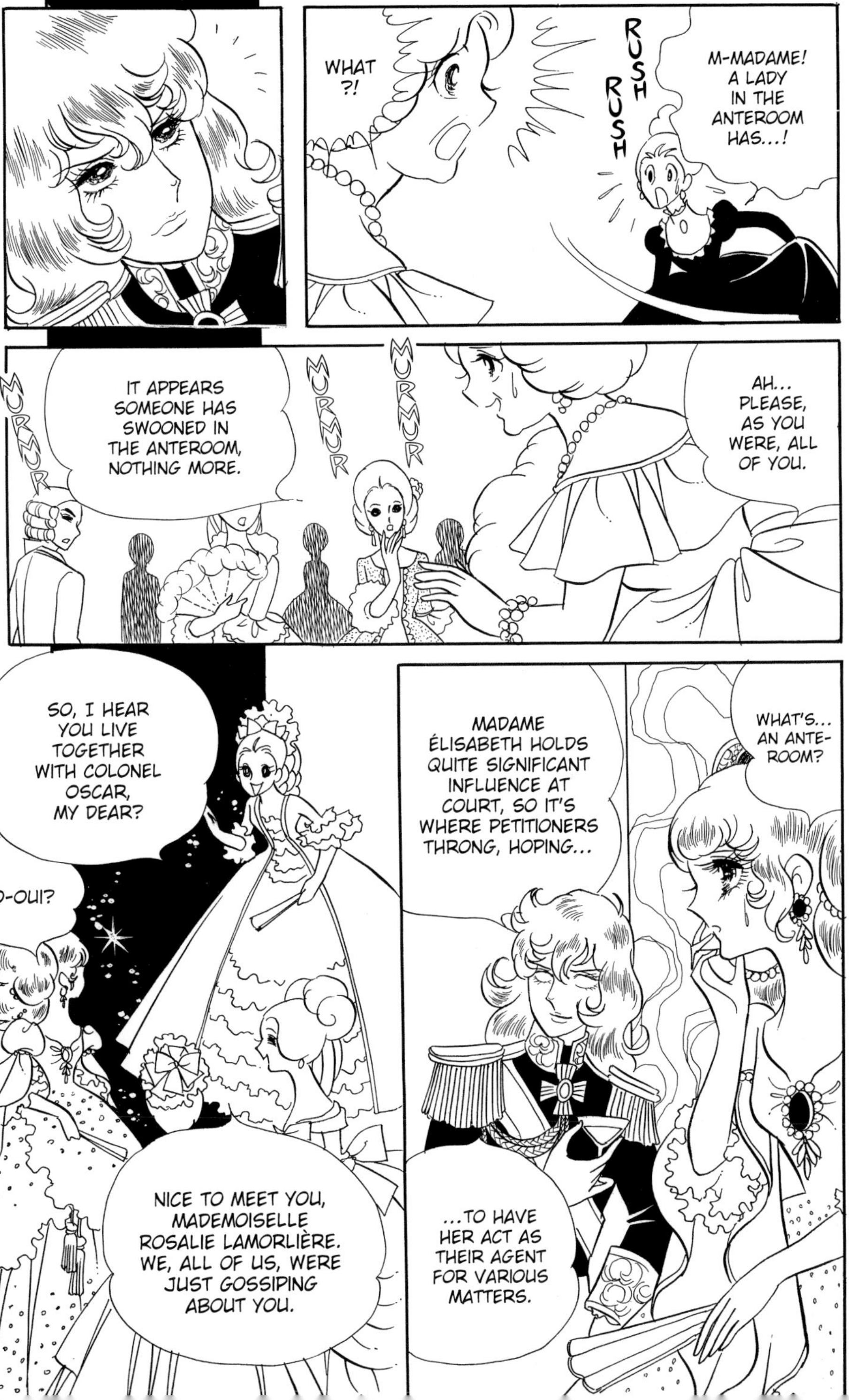
RUSH
RUSH
M-MADAME! A LADY IN THE ANTEROOM HAS...!
WHAT ?!
AH... PLEASE, AS YOU WERE, ALL OF YOU.
MURMUR
MURMUR
MURMUR
IT APPEARS SOMEONE HAS SWOONED IN THE ANTEROOM, NOTHING MORE.
WHAT'S... AN ANTE-ROOM?
MADAME ÉLISABETH HOLDS QUITE SIGNIFICANT INFLUENCE AT COURT, SO IT'S WHERE PETITIONERS THRONG, HOPING...
...TO HAVE HER ACT AS THEIR AGENT FOR VARIOUS MATTERS.
SO, I HEAR YOU LIVE TOGETHER WITH COLONEL OSCAR, MY DEAR?
O-OUI?
NICE TO MEET YOU, MADEMOISELLE ROSALIE LAMORLIÈRE. WE, ALL OF US, WERE JUST GOSSIPING ABOUT YOU.

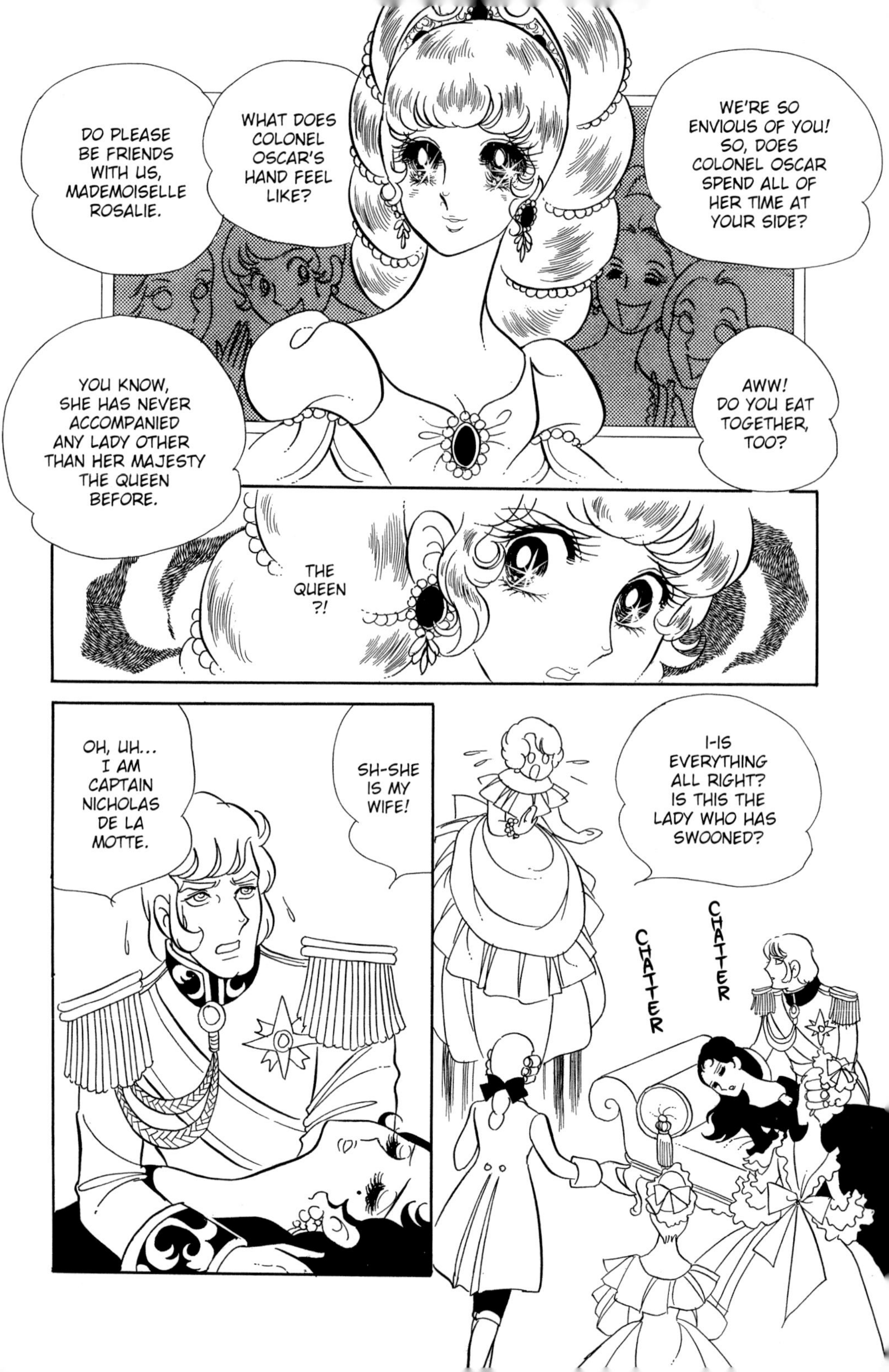
WE'RE SO ENVIOUS OF YOU! SO, DOES COLONEL OSCAR SPEND ALL OF HER TIME AT YOUR SIDE?
WHAT DOES COLONEL OSCAR'S HAND FEEL LIKE?
DO PLEASE BE FRIENDS WITH US, MADEMOISELLE ROSALIE.
AWW! DO YOU EAT TOGETHER, TOO?
YOU KNOW, SHE HAS NEVER ACCOMPANIED ANY LADY OTHER THAN HER MAJESTY THE QUEEN BEFORE.
THE QUEEN ?!
I-IS EVERYTHING ALL RIGHT? IS THIS THE LADY WHO HAS SWOONED?
CHATTER
CHATTER
SH-SHE IS MY WIFE!
OH, UH... I AM CAPTAIN NICHOLAS DE LA MOTTE.

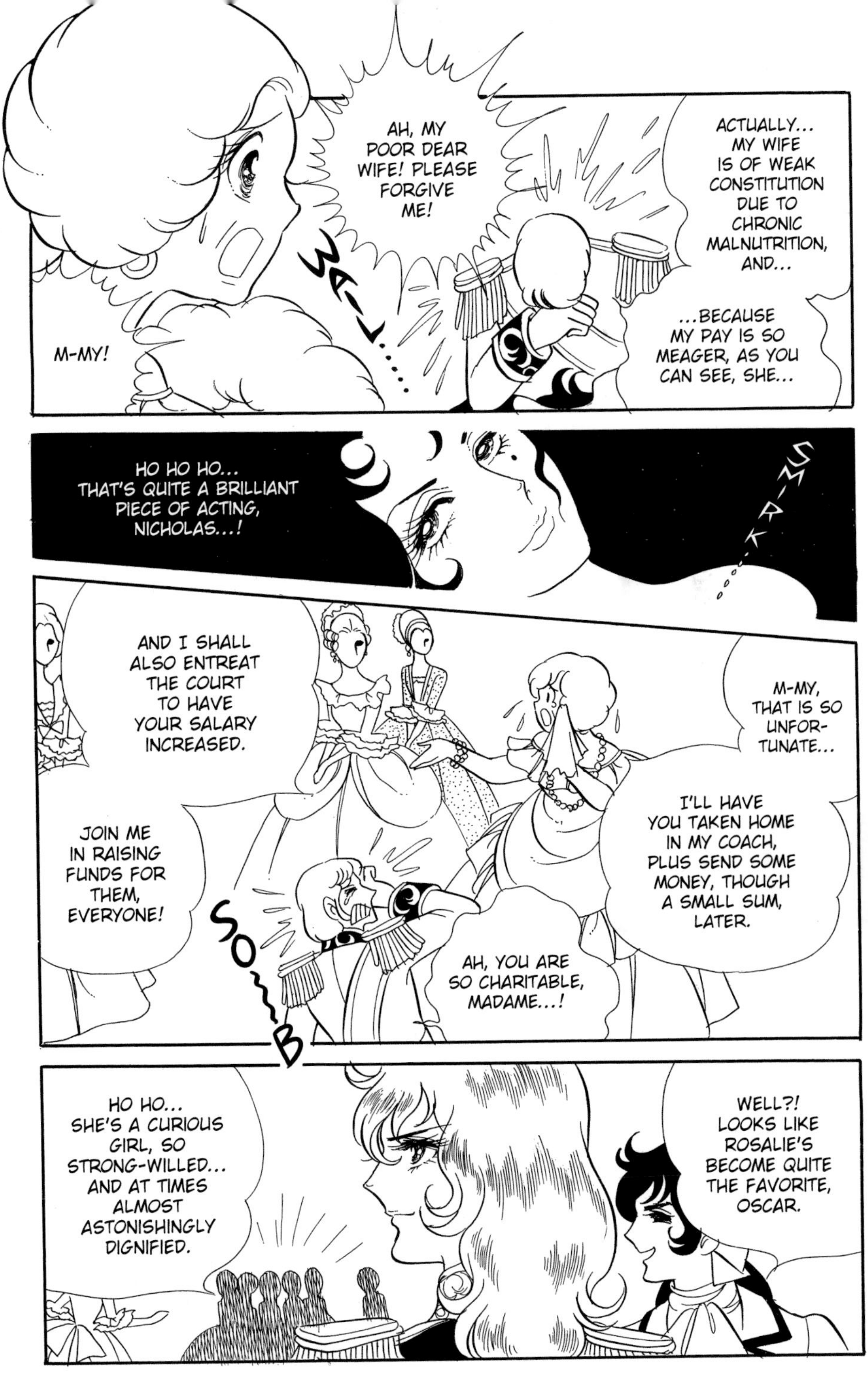
ACTUALLY... MY WIFE IS OF WEAK CONSTITUTION DUE TO CHRONIC MALNUTRITION, AND...
...BECAUSE MY PAY IS SO MEAGER, AS YOU CAN SEE, SHE...
AH, MY POOR DEAR WIFE! PLEASE FORGIVE ME!
WAIL....
M-MY!
SMIRK....
HO HO HO... THAT'S QUITE A BRILLIANT PIECE OF ACTING, NICHOLAS...!
M-MY, THAT IS SO UNFORTUNATE...
I'LL HAVE YOU TAKEN HOME IN MY COACH, PLUS SEND SOME MONEY, THOUGH A SMALL SUM, LATER.
AH, YOU ARE SO CHARITABLE, MADAME...!
SO~B
AND I SHALL ALSO ENTREAT THE COURT TO HAVE YOUR SALARY INCREASED.
JOIN ME IN RAISING FUNDS FOR THEM, EVERYONE!
WELL?! LOOKS LIKE ROSALIE'S BECOME QUITE THE FAVORITE, OSCAR.
HO HO... SHE'S A CURIOUS GIRL, SO STRONG-WILLED... AND AT TIMES ALMOST ASTONISHINGLY DIGNIFIED.

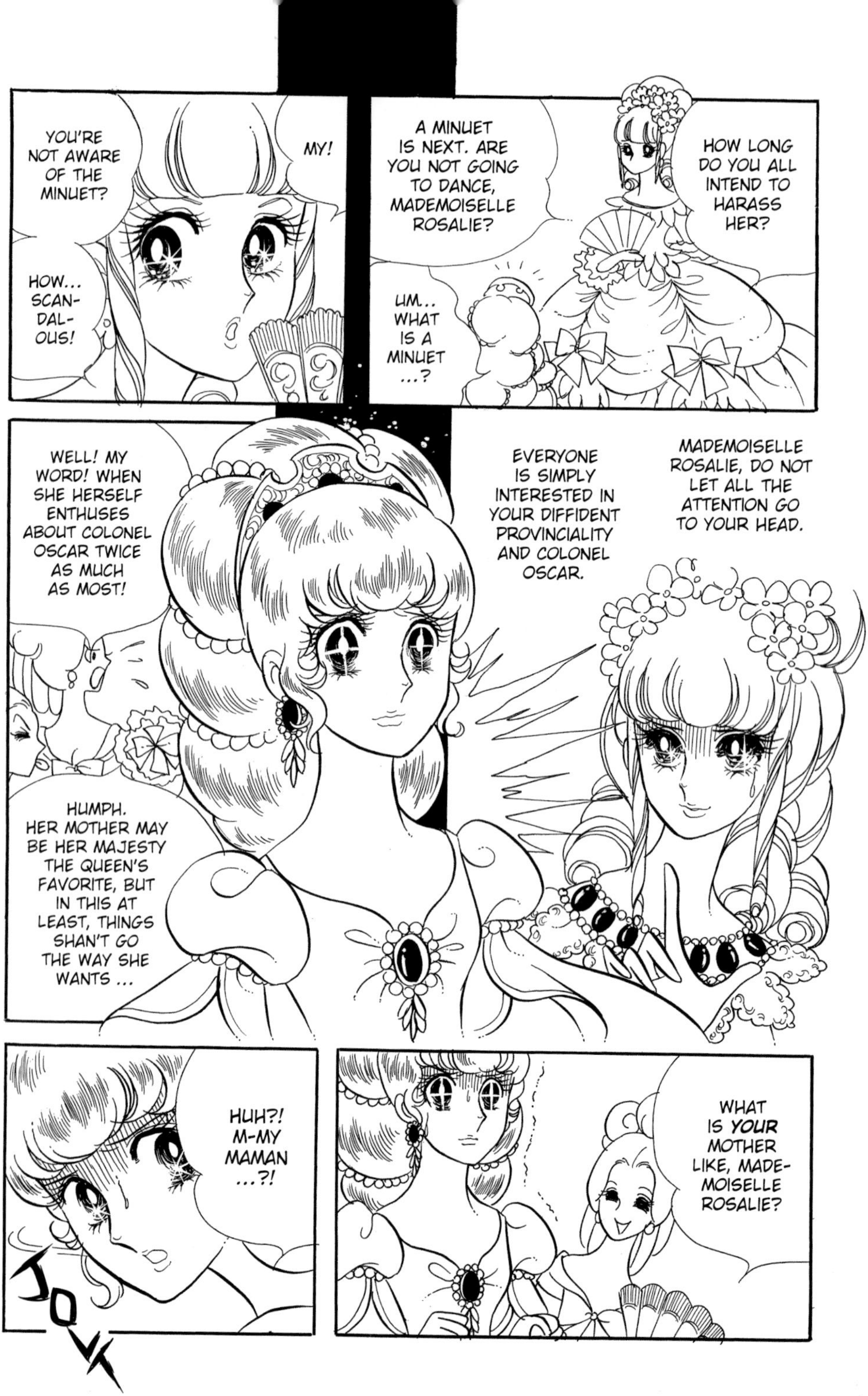
HOW LONG DO YOU ALL INTEND TO HARASS HER?
A MINUET IS NEXT. ARE YOU NOT GOING TO DANCE, MADEMOISELLE ROSALIE?
UM.. WHAT IS A MINUET ...?
MY!
YOU'RE NOT AWARE OF THE MINUET?
HOW... SCAN-DAL-OUS!
MADEMOISELLE ROSALIE, DO NOT LET ALL THE ATTENTION GO TO YOUR HEAD.
EVERYONE IS SIMPLY INTERESTED IN YOUR DIFFIDENT PROVINCIALITY AND COLONEL OSCAR.
WELL! MY WORD! WHEN SHE HERSELF ENTHUSES ABOUT COLONEL OSCAR TWICE AS MUCH AS MOST!
HUMPH. HER MOTHER MAY BE HER MAJESTY THE QUEEN'S FAVORITE, BUT IN THIS AT LEAST, THINGS SHAN'T GO THE WAY SHE WANTS ...
WHAT IS *YOUR* MOTHER LIKE, MADE-MOISELLE ROSALIE?
HUH?! M-MY MAMAN ...?!
JOLT

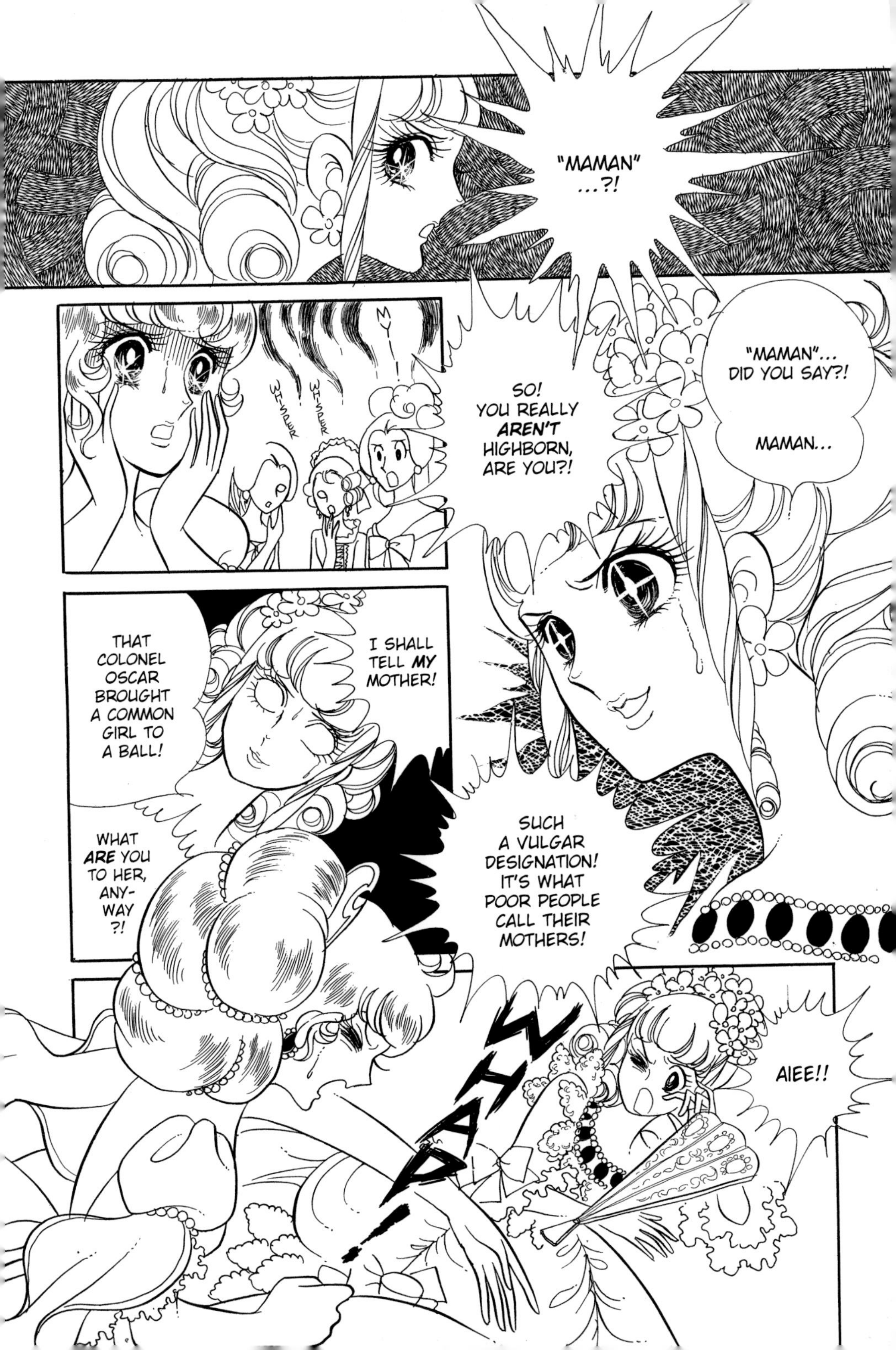
"MAMAN" ...?!
"MAMAN"... DID YOU SAY?!
MAMAN...
SO! YOU REALLY **AREN'T** HIGHBORN, ARE YOU?!
SUCH A VULGAR DESIGNATION! IT'S WHAT POOR PEOPLE CALL THEIR MOTHERS!
MY...!
WHISPER
WHISPER
I SHALL TELL **MY** MOTHER!
THAT COLONEL OSCAR BROUGHT A COMMON GIRL TO A BALL!
WHAT **ARE** YOU TO HER, ANYWAY?!
AIEE!!
WHAP!!

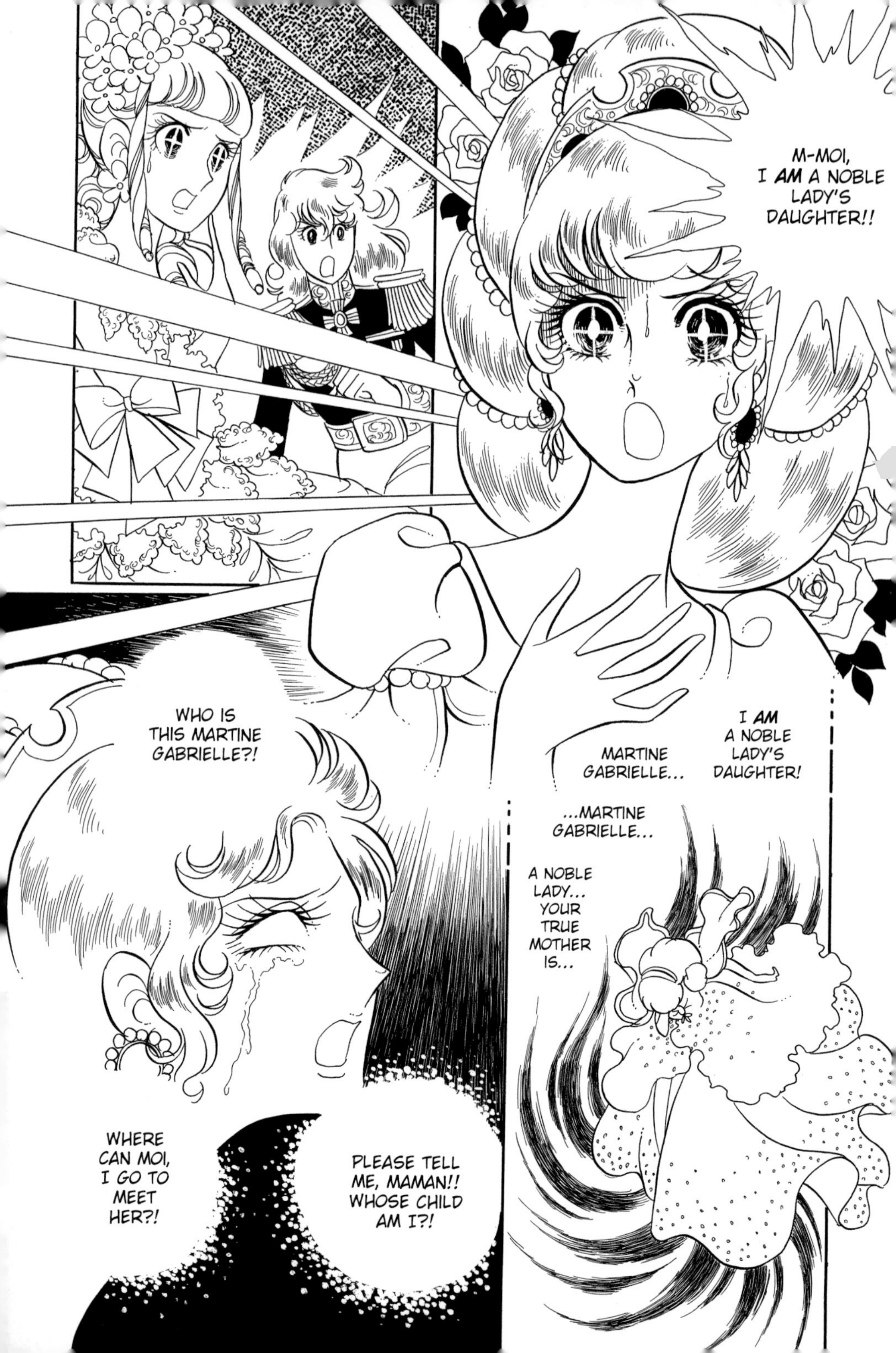
M-MOI, I **AM** A NOBLE LADY'S DAUGHTER!!
I **AM** A NOBLE LADY'S DAUGHTER!
MARTINE GABRIELLE...
...MARTINE GABRIELLE...
A NOBLE LADY... YOUR TRUE MOTHER IS...
WHO IS THIS MARTINE GABRIELLE?!
PLEASE TELL ME, MAMAN!! WHOSE CHILD AM I?!
WHERE CAN MOI, I GO TO MEET HER?!

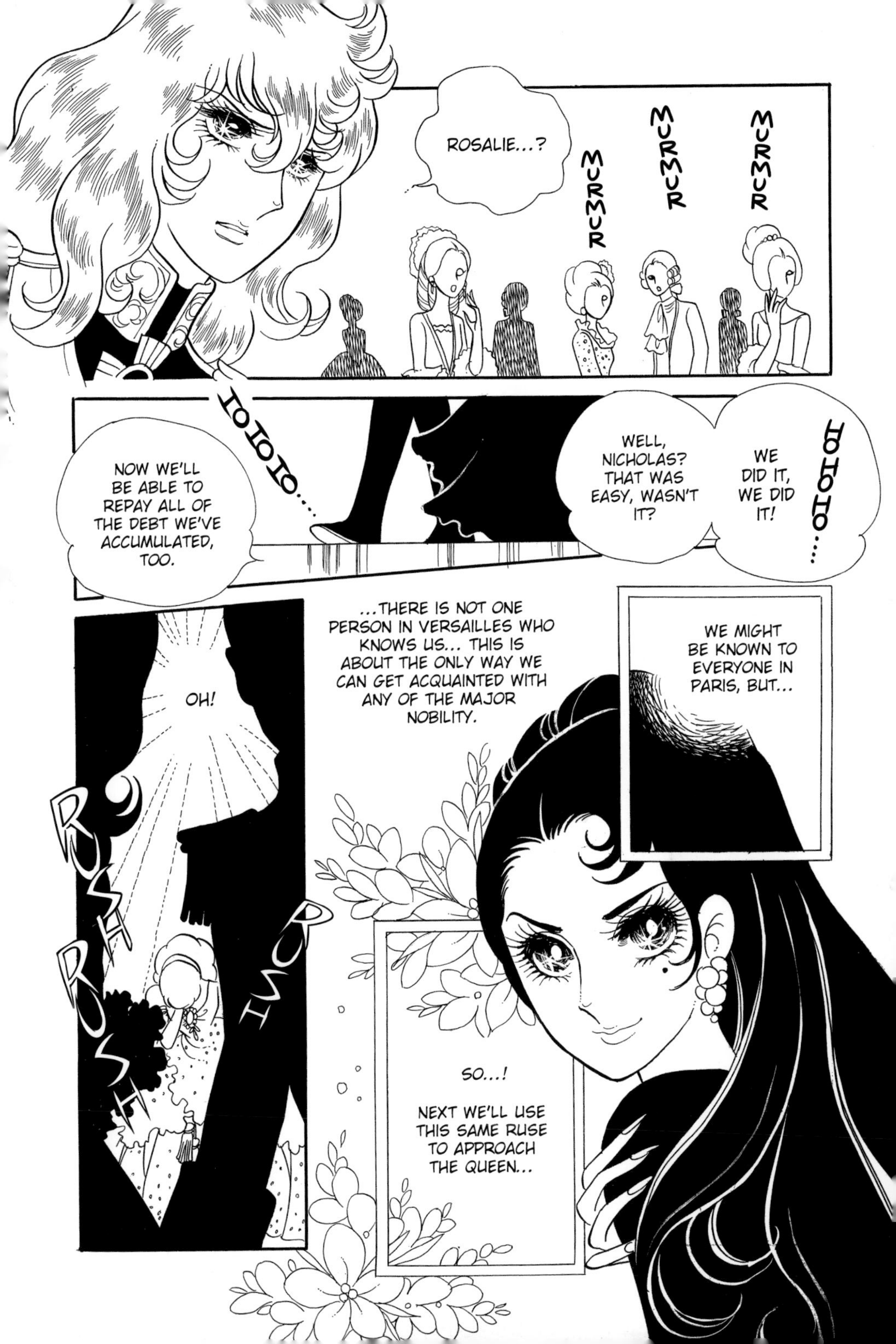
MURMUR
MURMUR
MURMUR
ROSALIE...?
HOHOHO...
WE DID IT, WE DID IT!
WELL, NICHOLAS? THAT WAS EASY, WASN'T IT?
HOHOHO...
NOW WE'LL BE ABLE TO REPAY ALL OF THE DEBT WE'VE ACCUMULATED, TOO.
WE MIGHT BE KNOWN TO EVERYONE IN PARIS, BUT...
...THERE IS NOT ONE PERSON IN VERSAILLES WHO KNOWS US... THIS IS ABOUT THE ONLY WAY WE CAN GET ACQUAINTED WITH ANY OF THE MAJOR NOBILITY.
SO...!
NEXT WE'LL USE THIS SAME RUSE TO APPROACH THE QUEEN...
OH!
RUSH
RUSH
RUSH

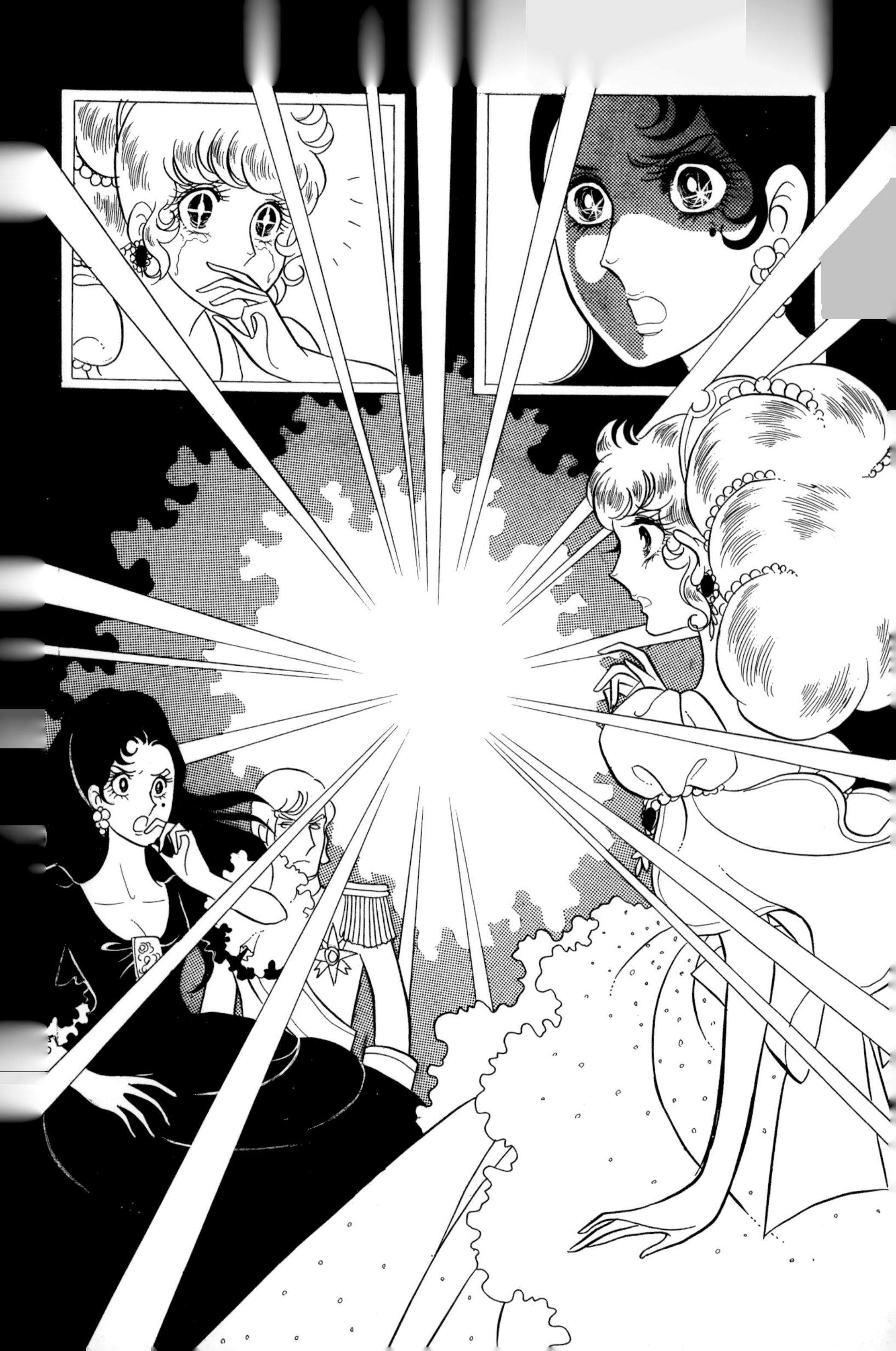

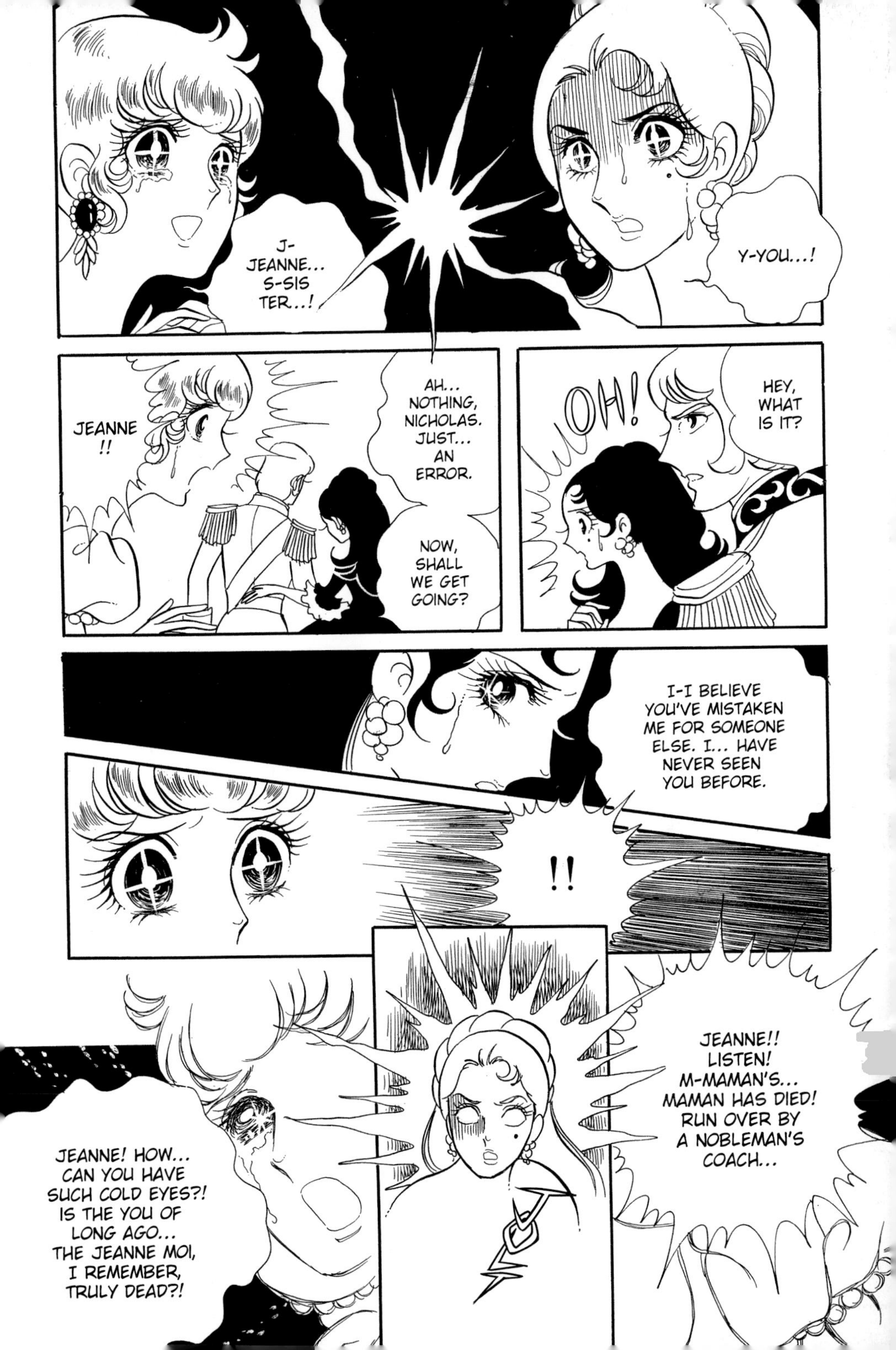
Y-YOU...!
J- JEANNE... S-SIS TER...!
HEY, WHAT IS IT?
OH!
AH... NOTHING, NICHOLAS. JUST... AN ERROR.
NOW, SHALL WE GET GOING?
JEANNE !!
I-I BELIEVE YOU'VE MISTAKEN ME FOR SOMEONE ELSE. I... HAVE NEVER SEEN YOU BEFORE.
!!
JEANNE!! LISTEN! M-MAMAN'S... MAMAN HAS DIED! RUN OVER BY A NOBLEMAN'S COACH...
JEANNE! HOW... CAN YOU HAVE SUCH COLD EYES?! IS THE YOU OF LONG AGO... THE JEANNE MOI, I REMEMBER, TRULY DEAD?!

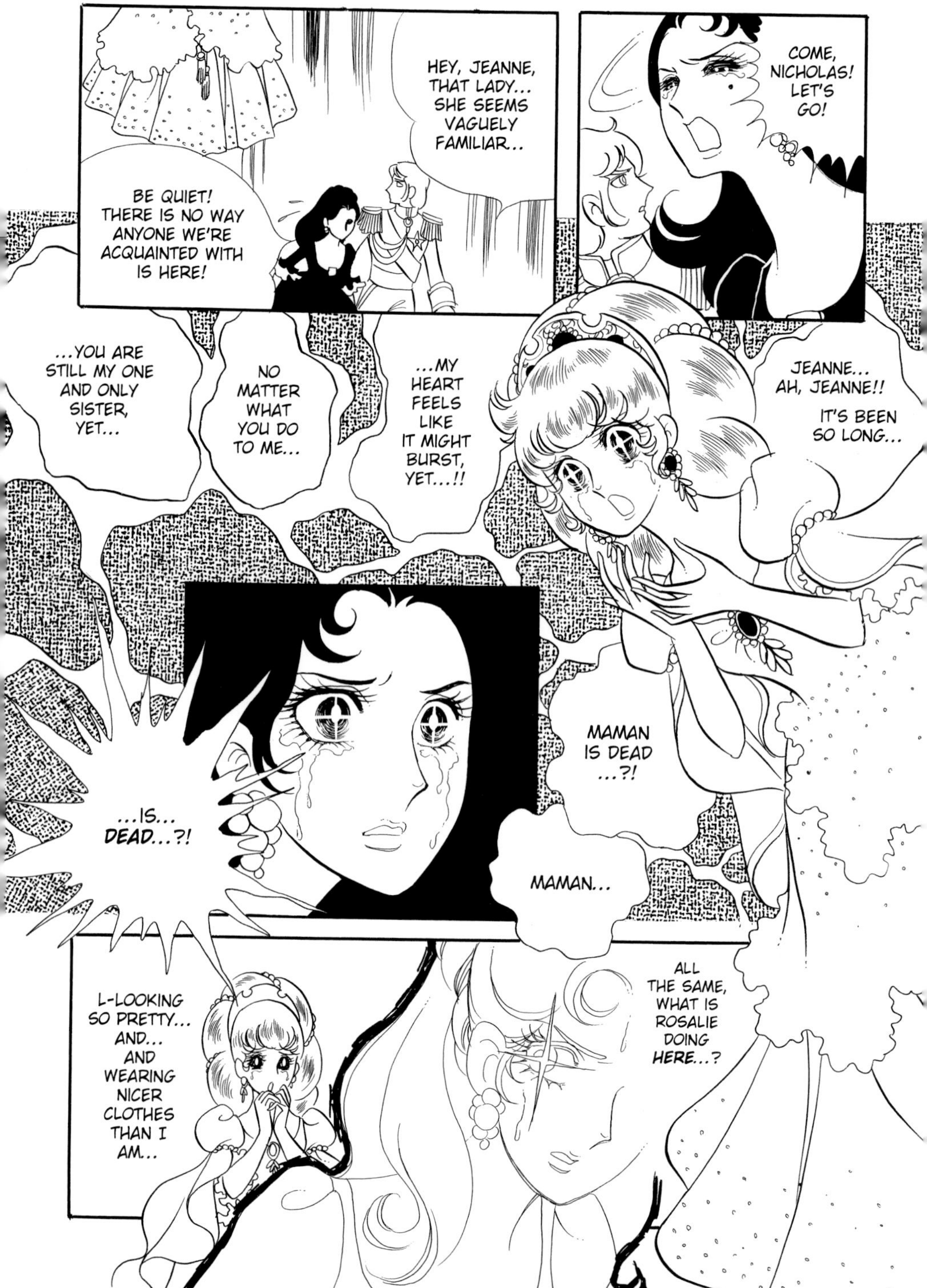
COME, NICHOLAS! LET'S GO!
HEY, JEANNE, THAT LADY... SHE SEEMS VAGUELY FAMILIAR...
BE QUIET! THERE IS NO WAY ANYONE WE'RE ACQUAINTED WITH IS HERE!
JEANNE... AH, JEANNE!!
IT'S BEEN SO LONG...
...MY HEART FEELS LIKE IT MIGHT BURST, YET...!!
NO MATTER WHAT YOU DO TO ME...
...YOU ARE STILL MY ONE AND ONLY SISTER, YET...
MAMAN IS DEAD ...?!
MAMAN...
...IS... **DEAD...?!**
ALL THE SAME, WHAT IS ROSALIE DOING **HERE...?**
L-LOOKING SO PRETTY... AND... AND WEARING NICER CLOTHES THAN I AM...

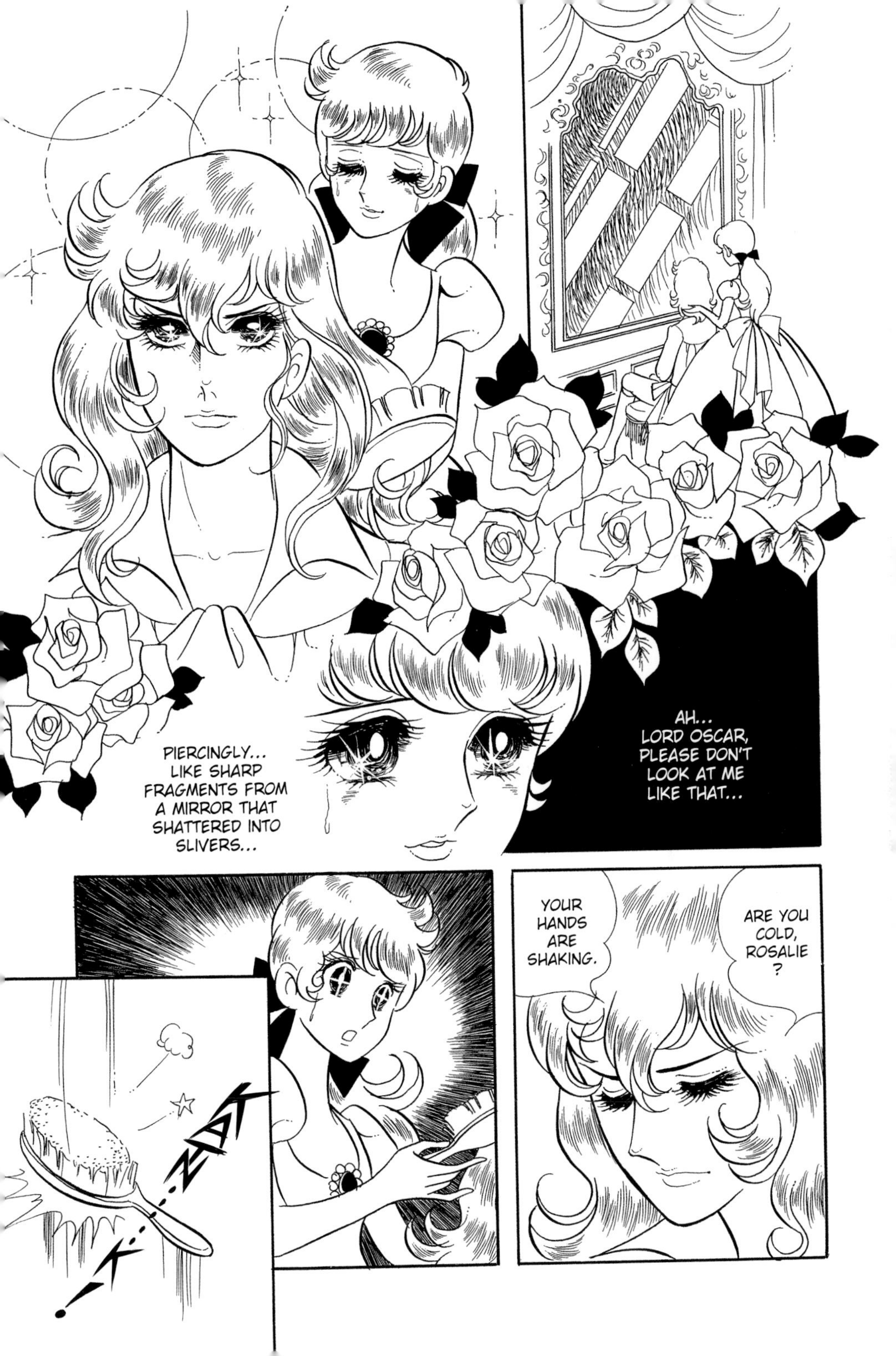
AH... LORD OSCAR, PLEASE DON'T LOOK AT ME LIKE THAT...
PIERCINGLY... LIKE SHARP FRAGMENTS FROM A MIRROR THAT SHATTERED INTO SLIVERS...
ARE YOU COLD, ROSALIE?
YOUR HANDS ARE SHAKING.

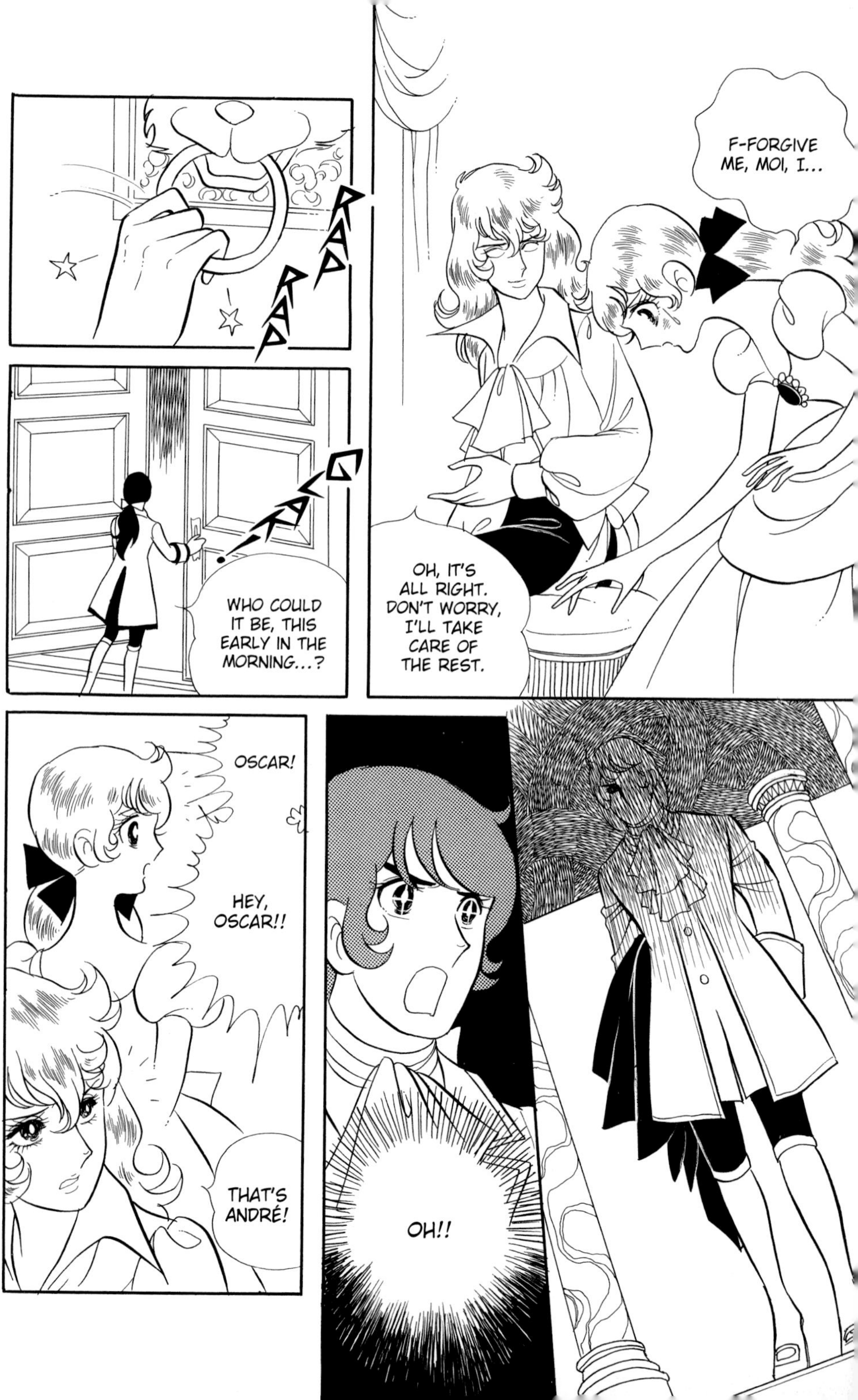
F-FORGIVE ME, MOI, I...
OH, IT'S ALL RIGHT. DON'T WORRY, I'LL TAKE CARE OF THE REST.
RAP
RAP
GLAK!
WHO COULD IT BE, THIS EARLY IN THE MORNING...?
OH!!
OSCAR!
HEY, OSCAR!!
THAT'S ANDRÉ!

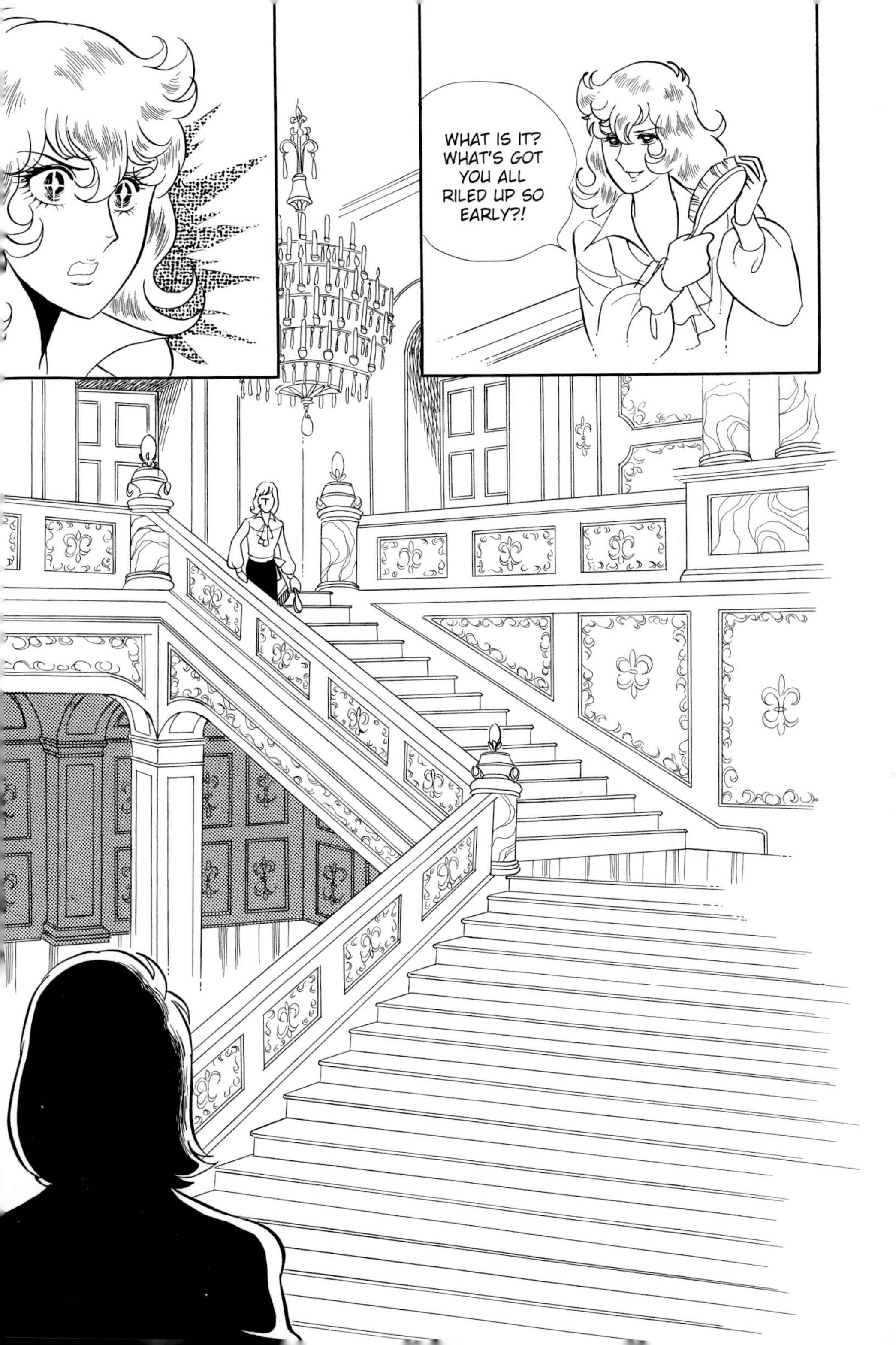
WHAT IS IT? WHAT'S GOT YOU ALL RILED UP SO EARLY?!

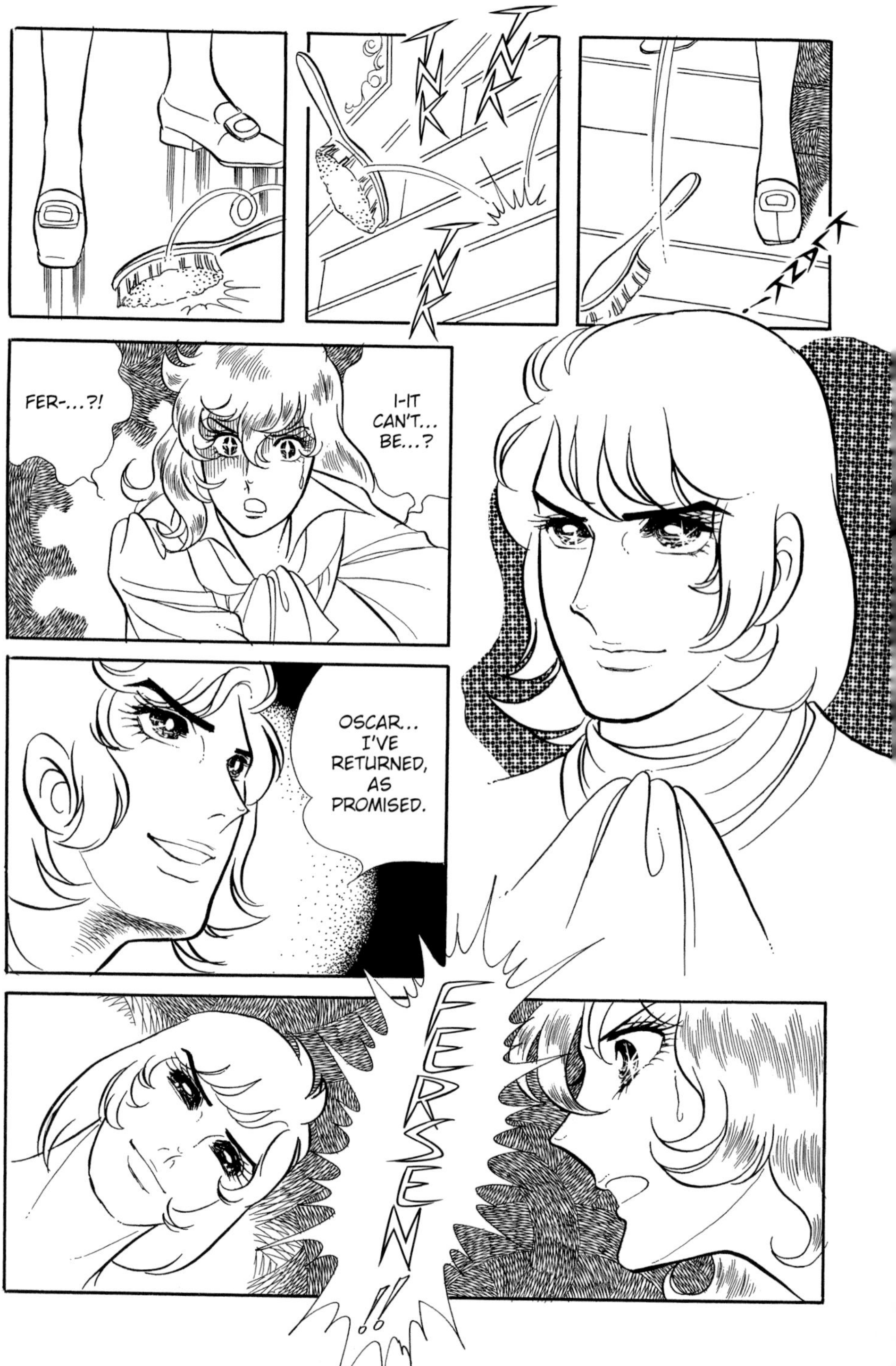

...TZAK
TINK
TINK
TINK
I-IT CAN'T... BE...?
FER-...?!
OSCAR... I'VE RETURNED, AS PROMISED.
FERSEN!!

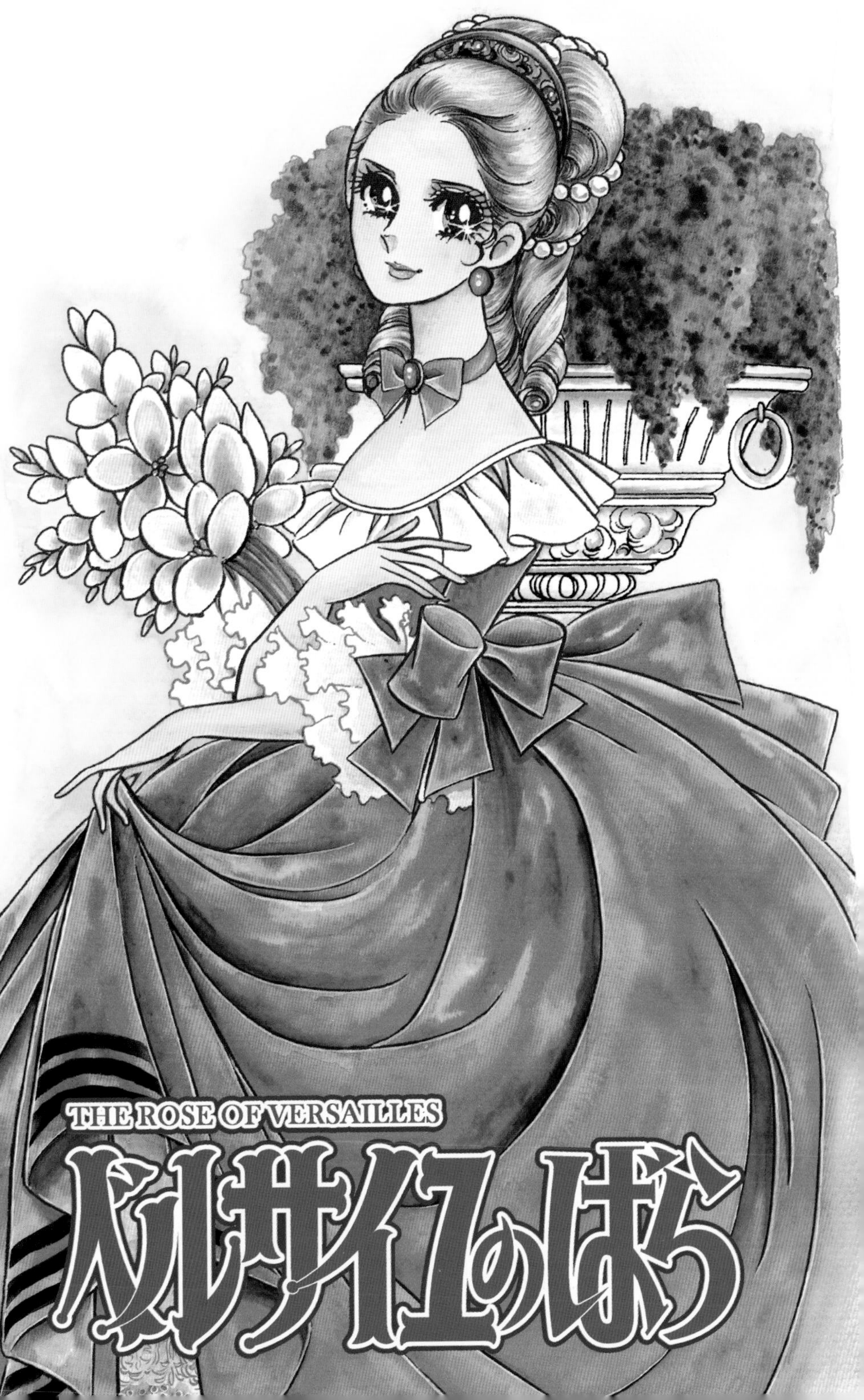
THE ROSE OF VERSAILLES
ベルサイユのばら

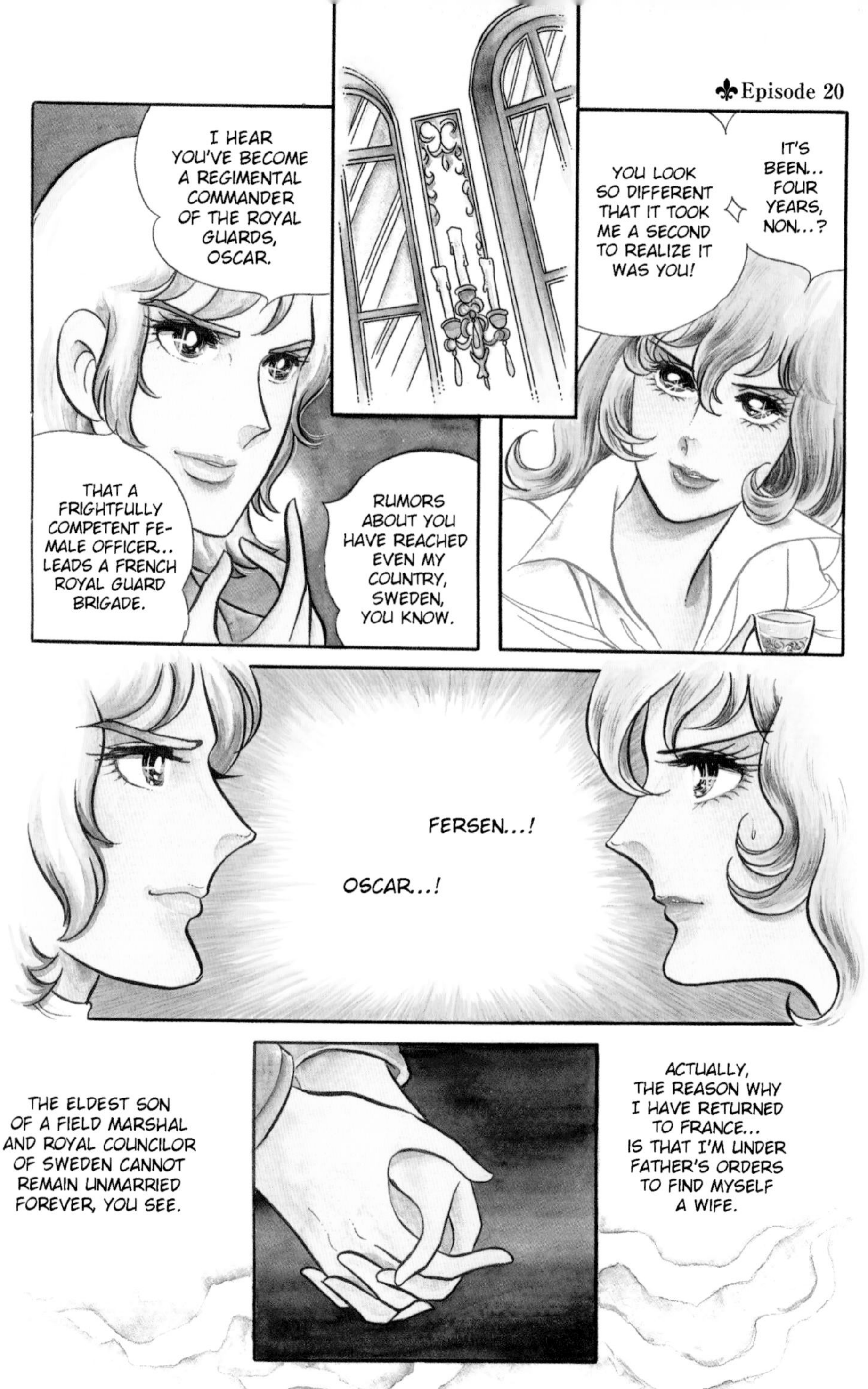
IT'S BEEN... FOUR YEARS, NON...?
YOU LOOK SO DIFFERENT THAT IT TOOK ME A SECOND TO REALIZE IT WAS YOU!
I HEAR YOU'VE BECOME A REGIMENTAL COMMANDER OF THE ROYAL GUARDS, OSCAR.
RUMORS ABOUT YOU HAVE REACHED EVEN MY COUNTRY, SWEDEN, YOU KNOW.
THAT A FRIGHTFULLY COMPETENT FE- MALE OFFICER... LEADS A FRENCH ROYAL GUARD BRIGADE.
FERSEN...!
OSCAR...!
ACTUALLY, THE REASON WHY I HAVE RETURNED TO FRANCE... IS THAT I'M UNDER FATHER'S ORDERS TO FIND MYSELF A WIFE.
THE ELDEST SON OF A FIELD MARSHAL AND ROYAL COUNCILOR OF SWEDEN CANNOT REMAIN UNMARRIED FOREVER, YOU SEE.

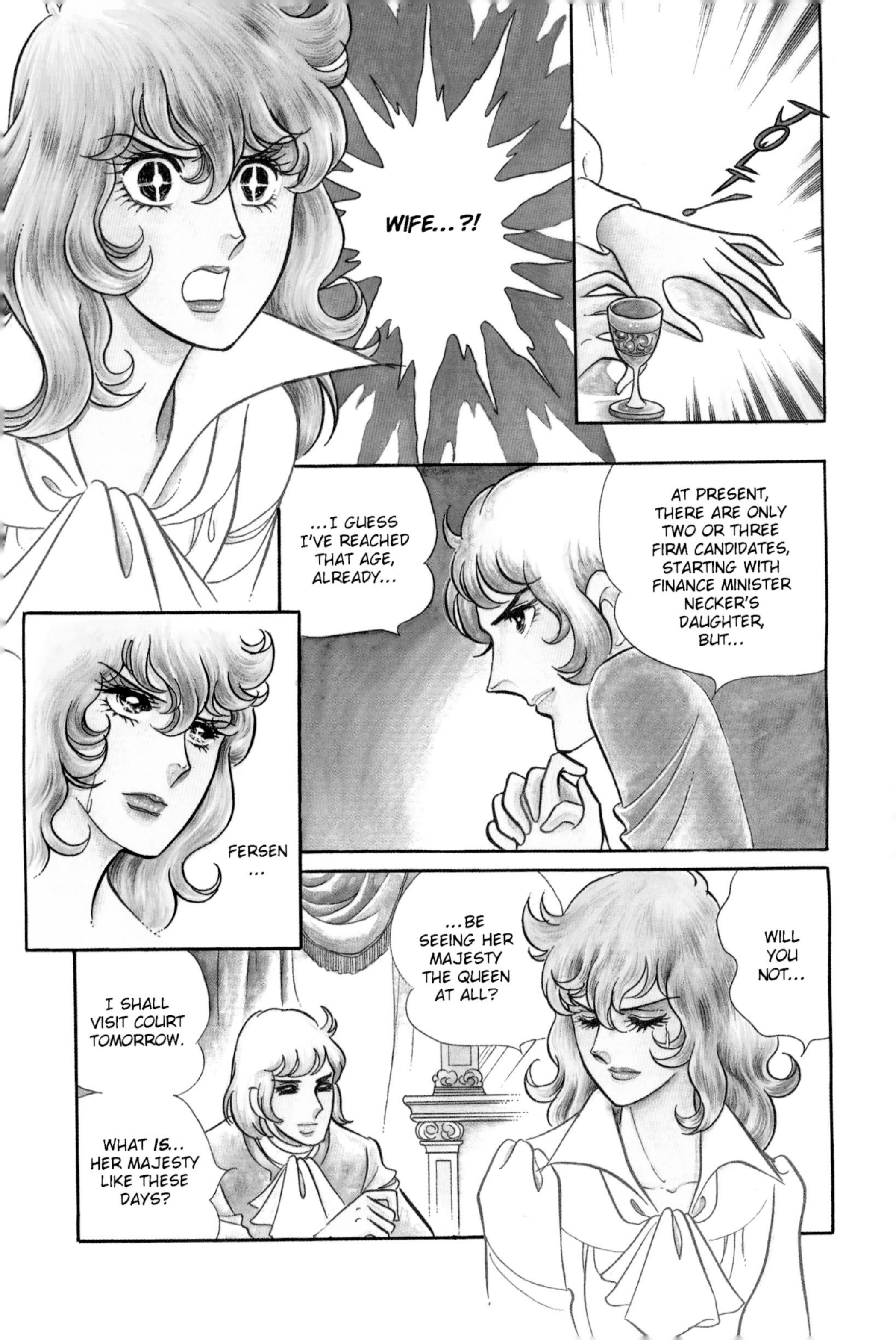
WIFE...?!
AT PRESENT, THERE ARE ONLY TWO OR THREE FIRM CANDIDATES, STARTING WITH FINANCE MINISTER NECKER'S DAUGHTER, BUT...
...I GUESS I'VE REACHED THAT AGE, ALREADY...
FERSEN ...
WILL YOU NOT...
...BE SEEING HER MAJESTY THE QUEEN AT ALL?
I SHALL VISIT COURT TOMORROW.
WHAT *IS*... HER MAJESTY LIKE THESE DAYS?

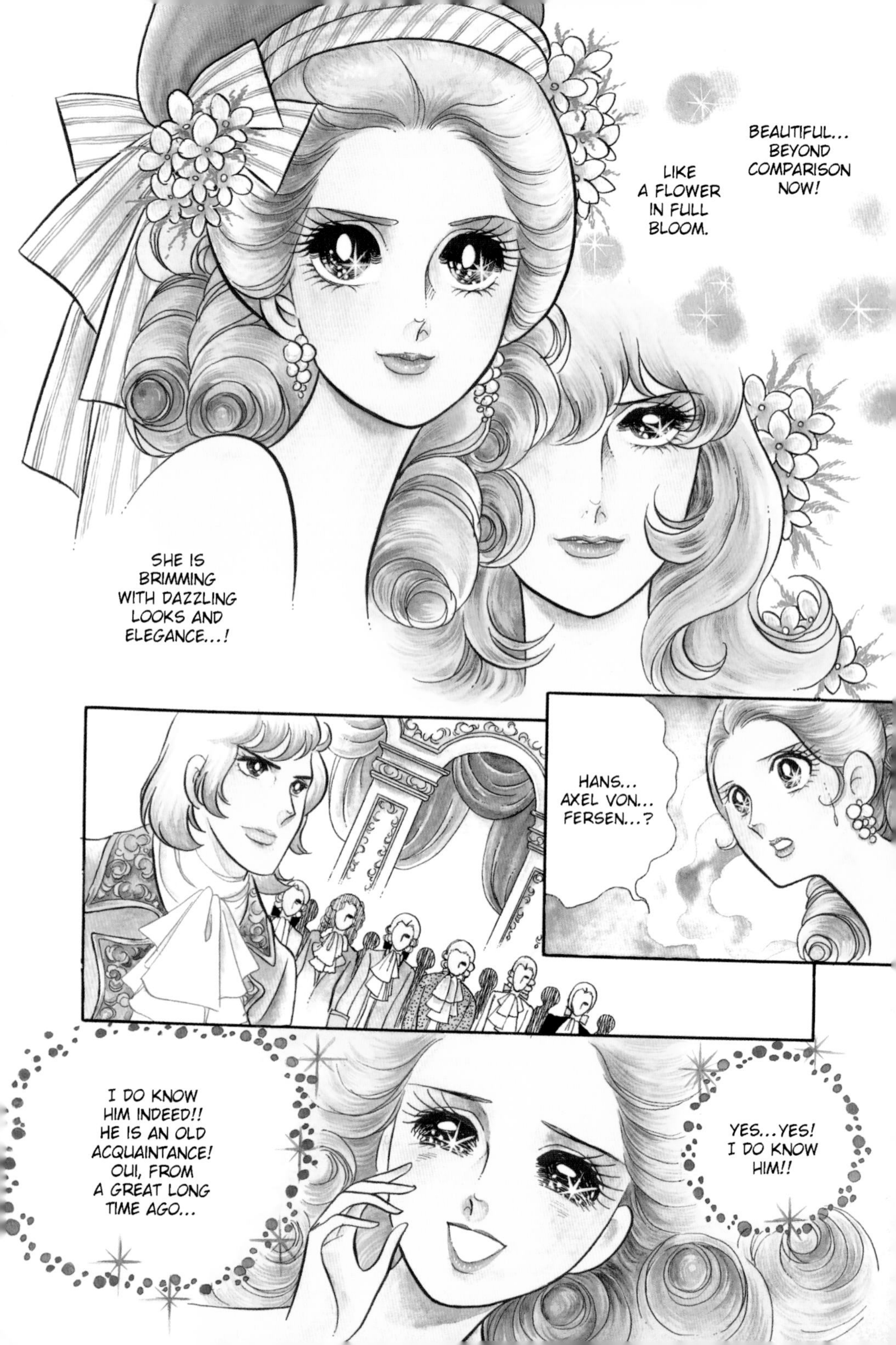
BEAUTIFUL... BEYOND COMPARISON NOW!
LIKE A FLOWER IN FULL BLOOM.
SHE IS BRIMMING WITH DAZZLING LOOKS AND ELEGANCE...!
HANS... AXEL VON... FERSEN...?
YES...YES! I DO KNOW HIM!!
I DO KNOW HIM INDEED!! HE IS AN OLD ACQUAINTANCE! OUI, FROM A GREAT LONG TIME AGO...

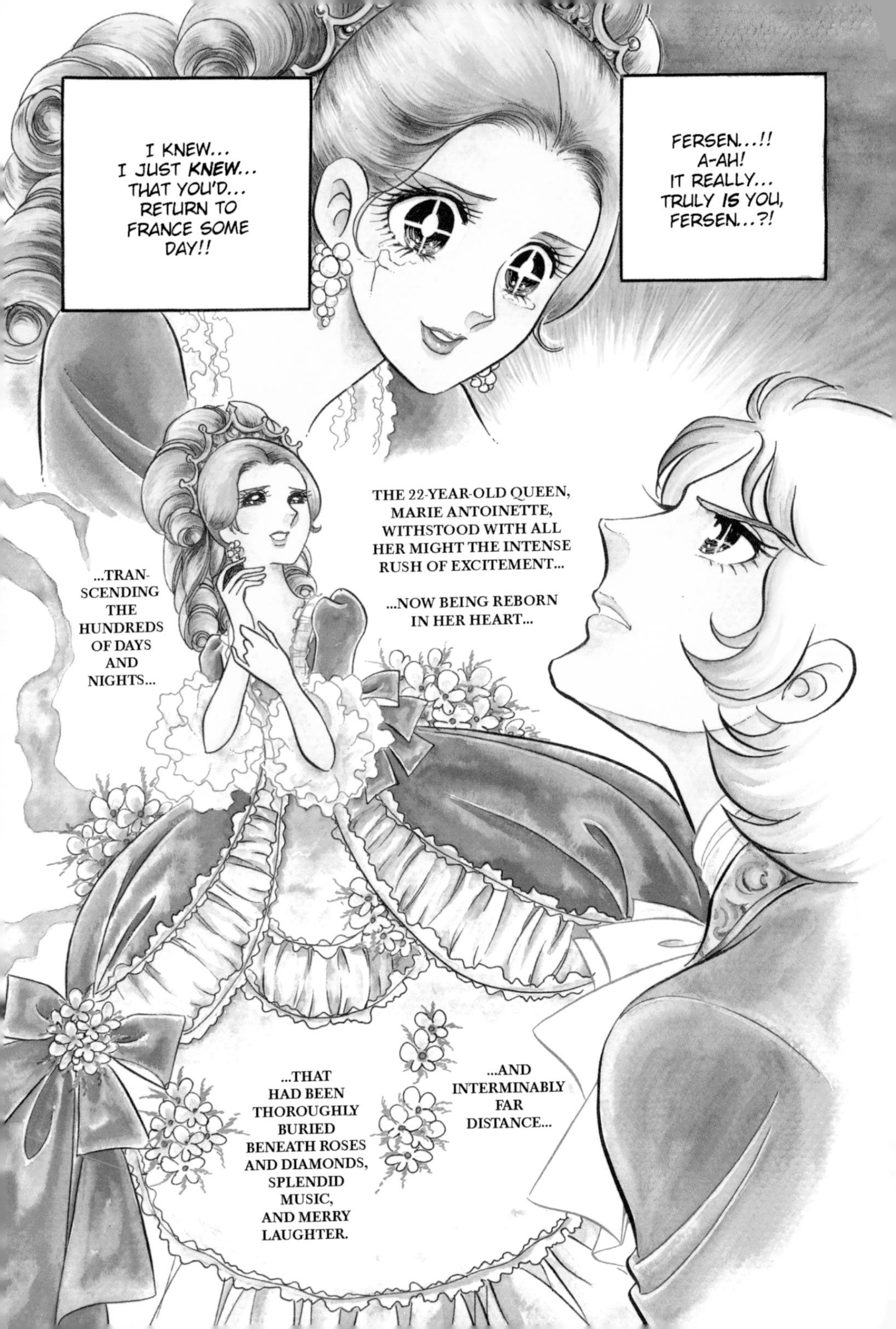
FERSEN...!! A-AH! IT REALLY... TRULY IS YOU, FERSEN...?!
I KNEW... I JUST KNEW... THAT YOU'D... RETURN TO FRANCE SOME DAY!!
THE 22-YEAR-OLD QUEEN, MARIE ANTOINETTE, WITHSTOOD WITH ALL HER MIGHT THE INTENSE RUSH OF EXCITEMENT...
...NOW BEING REBORN IN HER HEART...
...TRANSCENDING THE HUNDREDS OF DAYS AND NIGHTS...
...AND INTERMINABLY FAR DISTANCE...
...THAT HAD BEEN THOROUGHLY BURIED BENEATH ROSES AND DIAMONDS, SPLENDID MUSIC, AND MERRY LAUGHTER.

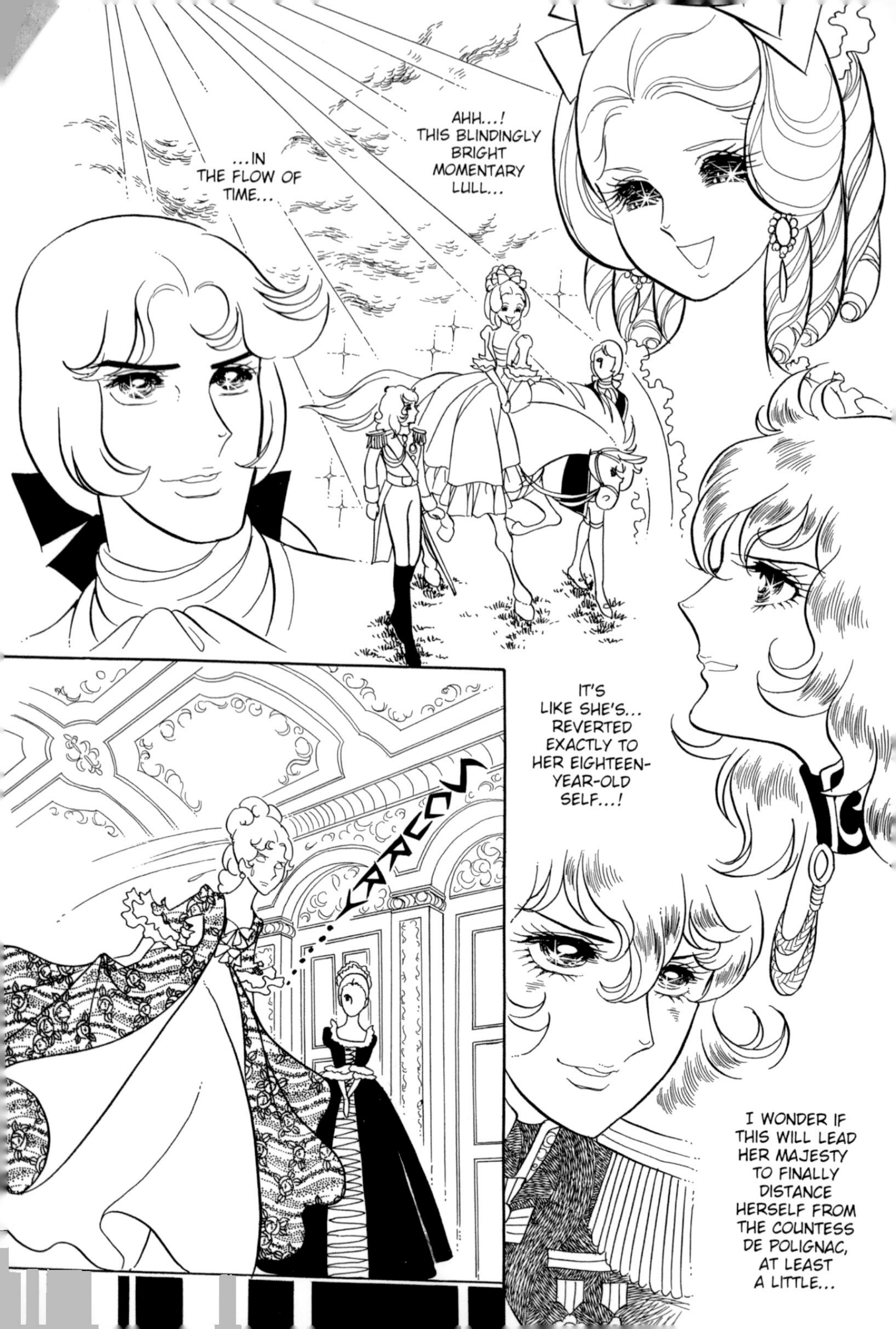
AHH...! THIS BLINDINGLY BRIGHT MOMENTARY LULL...
...IN THE FLOW OF TIME...
IT'S LIKE SHE'S... REVERTED EXACTLY TO HER EIGHTEEN-YEAR-OLD SELF...!
I WONDER IF THIS WILL LEAD HER MAJESTY TO FINALLY DISTANCE HERSELF FROM THE COUNTESS DE POLIGNAC, AT LEAST A LITTLE...

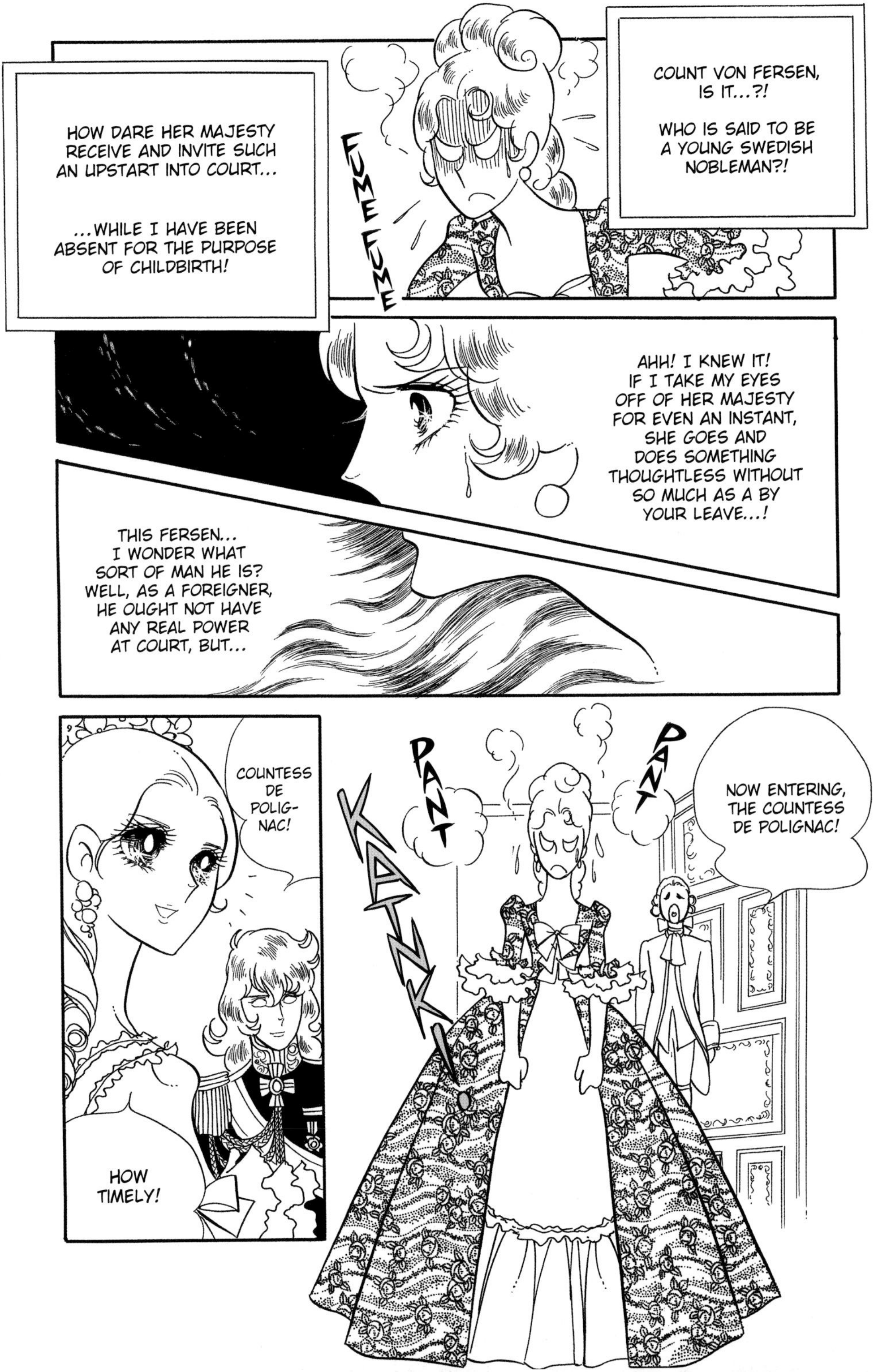
COUNT VON FERSEN, IS IT...?! WHO IS SAID TO BE A YOUNG SWEDISH NOBLEMAN?!
FUME FUME
HOW DARE HER MAJESTY RECEIVE AND INVITE SUCH AN UPSTART INTO COURT... ...WHILE I HAVE BEEN ABSENT FOR THE PURPOSE OF CHILDBIRTH!
AHH! I KNEW IT! IF I TAKE MY EYES OFF OF HER MAJESTY FOR EVEN AN INSTANT, SHE GOES AND DOES SOMETHING THOUGTLESS WITHOUT SO MUCH AS A BY YOUR LEAVE...!
THIS FERSEN... I WONDER WHAT SORT OF MAN HE IS? WELL, AS A FOREIGNER, HE OUGHT NOT HAVE ANY REAL POWER AT COURT, BUT...
NOW ENTERING, THE COUNTESS DE POLIGNAC!
PANT
PANT
KATUNK!
COUNTESS DE POLIG-NAC!
HOW TIMELY!

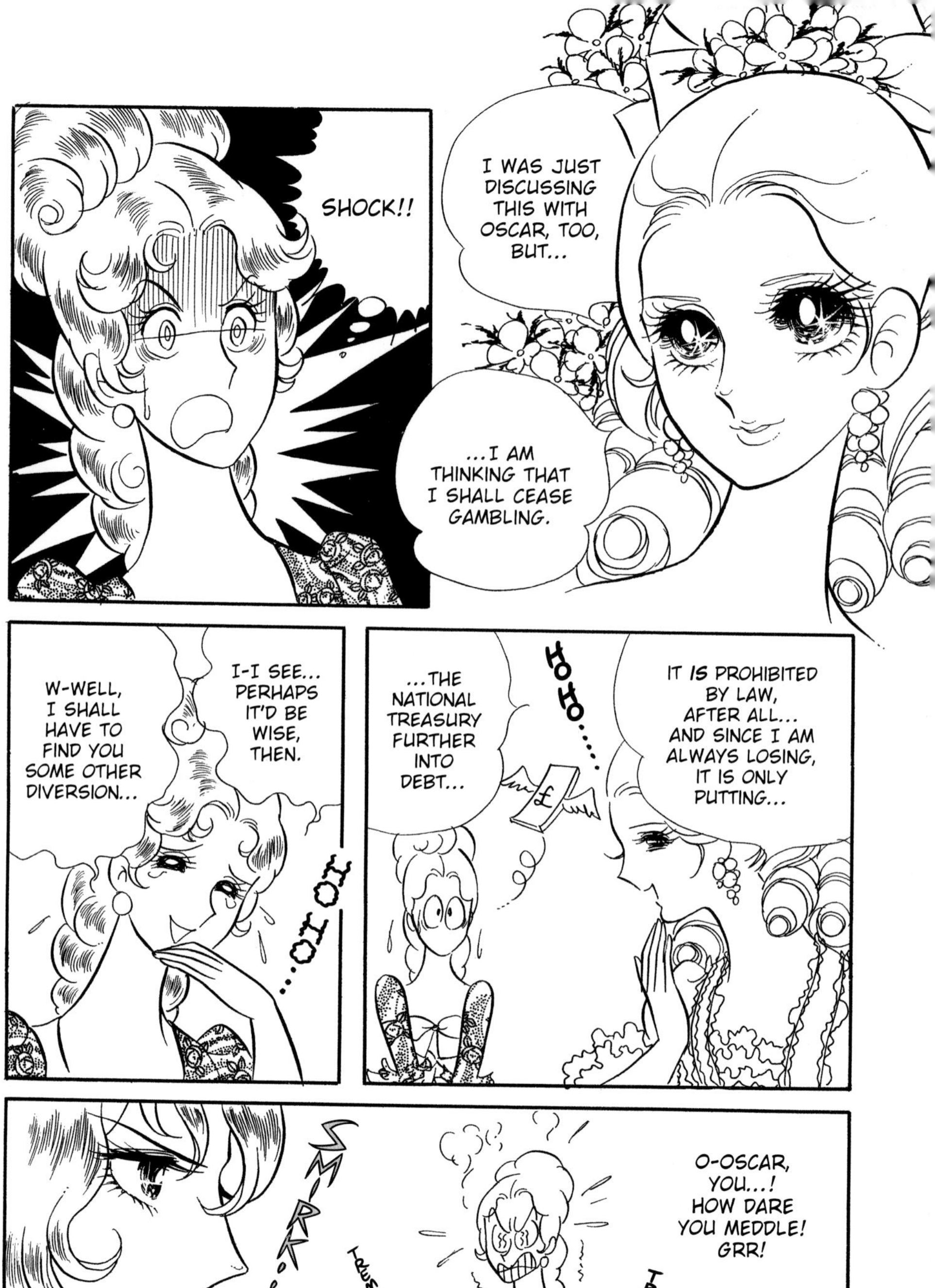
I WAS JUST DISCUSSING THIS WITH OSCAR, TOO, BUT...
...I AM THINKING THAT I SHALL CEASE GAMBLING.
SHOCK!!
IT **IS** PROHIBITED BY LAW, AFTER ALL... AND SINCE I AM ALWAYS LOSING, IT IS ONLY PUTTING...
HO HO.....
...THE NATIONAL TREASURY FURTHER INTO DEBT...
I-I SEE... PERHAPS IT'D BE WISE, THEN.
W-WELL, I SHALL HAVE TO FIND YOU SOME OTHER DIVERSION...
...OI OI
O-OSCAR, YOU...! HOW DARE YOU MEDDLE! GRR!
TREMBLE
TREMBLE
TREMBLE
SMIRK....

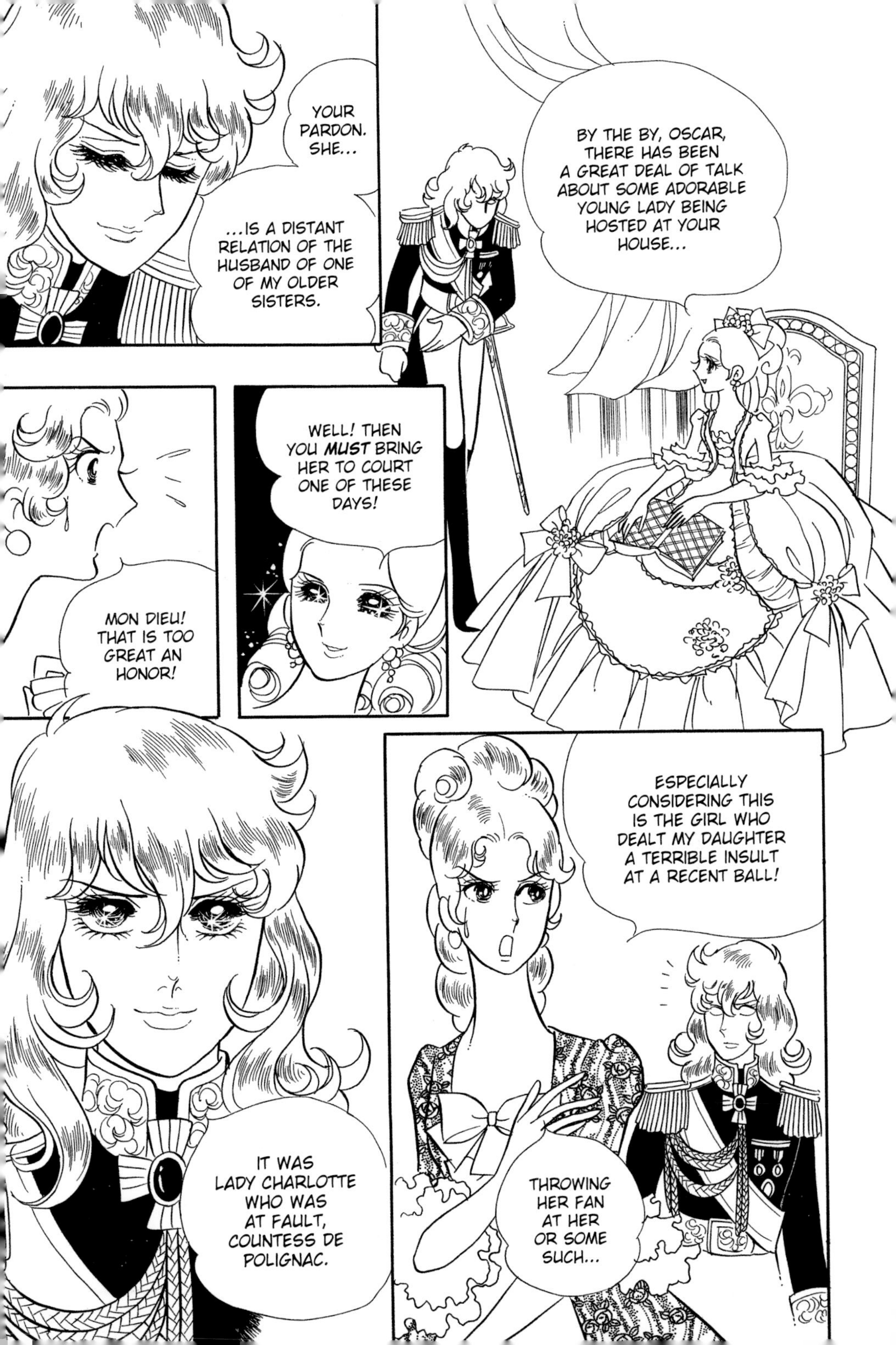
BY THE BY, OSCAR, THERE HAS BEEN A GREAT DEAL OF TALK ABOUT SOME ADORABLE YOUNG LADY BEING HOSTED AT YOUR HOUSE...
YOUR PARDON. SHE...
...IS A DISTANT RELATION OF THE HUSBAND OF ONE OF MY OLDER SISTERS.
WELL! THEN YOU **MUST** BRING HER TO COURT ONE OF THESE DAYS!
MON DIEU! THAT IS TOO GREAT AN HONOR!
ESPECIALLY CONSIDERING THIS IS THE GIRL WHO DEALT MY DAUGHTER A TERRIBLE INSULT AT A RECENT BALL!
THROWING HER FAN AT HER OR SOME SUCH...
IT WAS LADY CHARLOTTE WHO WAS AT FAULT, COUNTESS DE POLIGNAC.

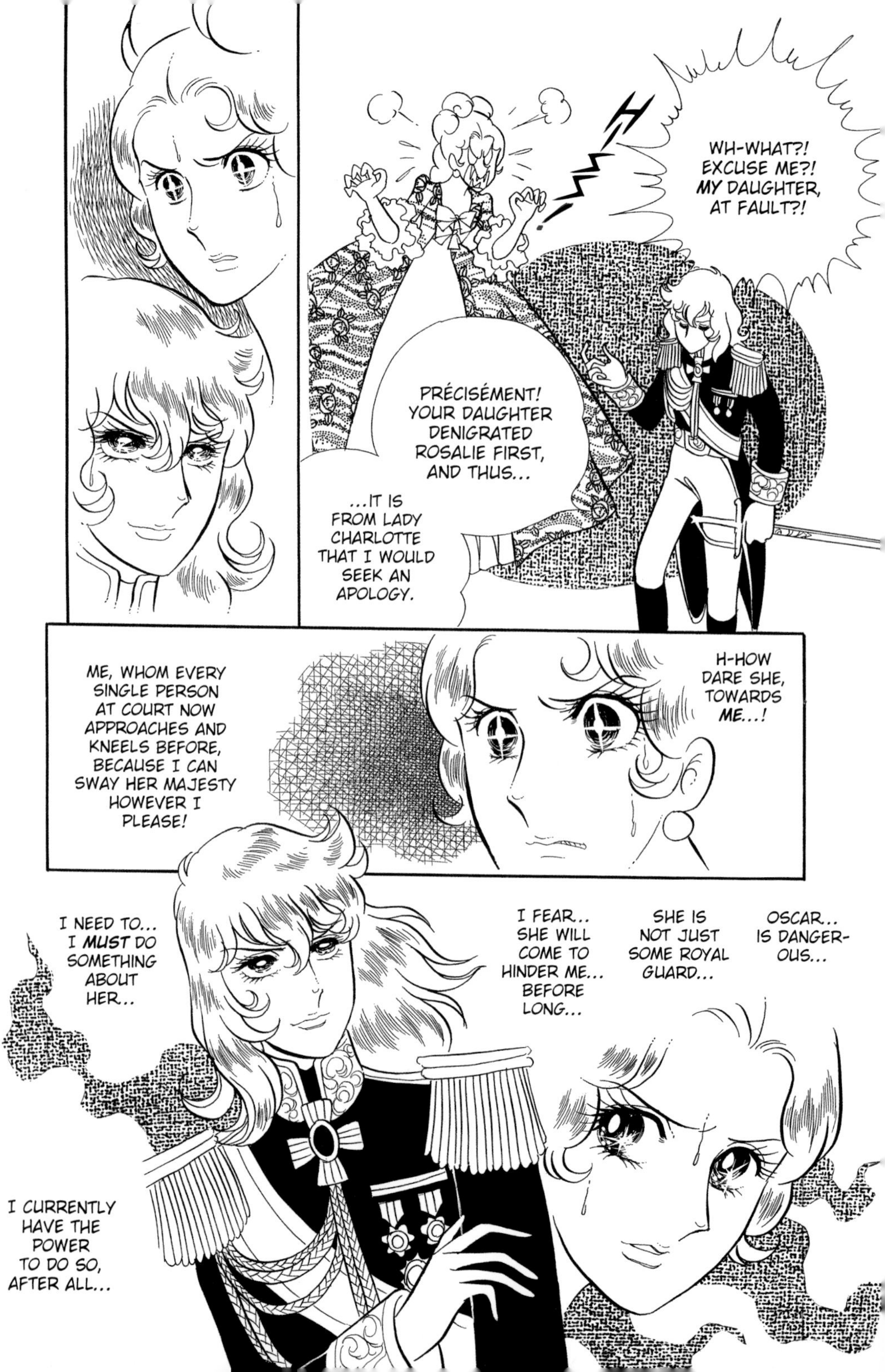
WH-WHAT?! EXCUSE ME?! MY DAUGHTER, AT FAULT?!
H-!
PRÉCISÉMENT! YOUR DAUGHTER DENIGRATED ROSALIE FIRST, AND THUS...
...IT IS FROM LADY CHARLOTTE THAT I WOULD SEEK AN APOLOGY.
H-HOW DARE SHE, TOWARDS ME...!
ME, WHOM EVERY SINGLE PERSON AT COURT NOW APPROACHES AND KNEELS BEFORE, BECAUSE I CAN SWAY HER MAJESTY HOWEVER I PLEASE!
OSCAR... IS DANGER-OUS...
SHE IS NOT JUST SOME ROYAL GUARD...
I FEAR... SHE WILL COME TO HINDER ME... BEFORE LONG...
I NEED TO... I MUST DO SOMETHING ABOUT HER...
I CURRENTLY HAVE THE POWER TO DO SO, AFTER ALL...

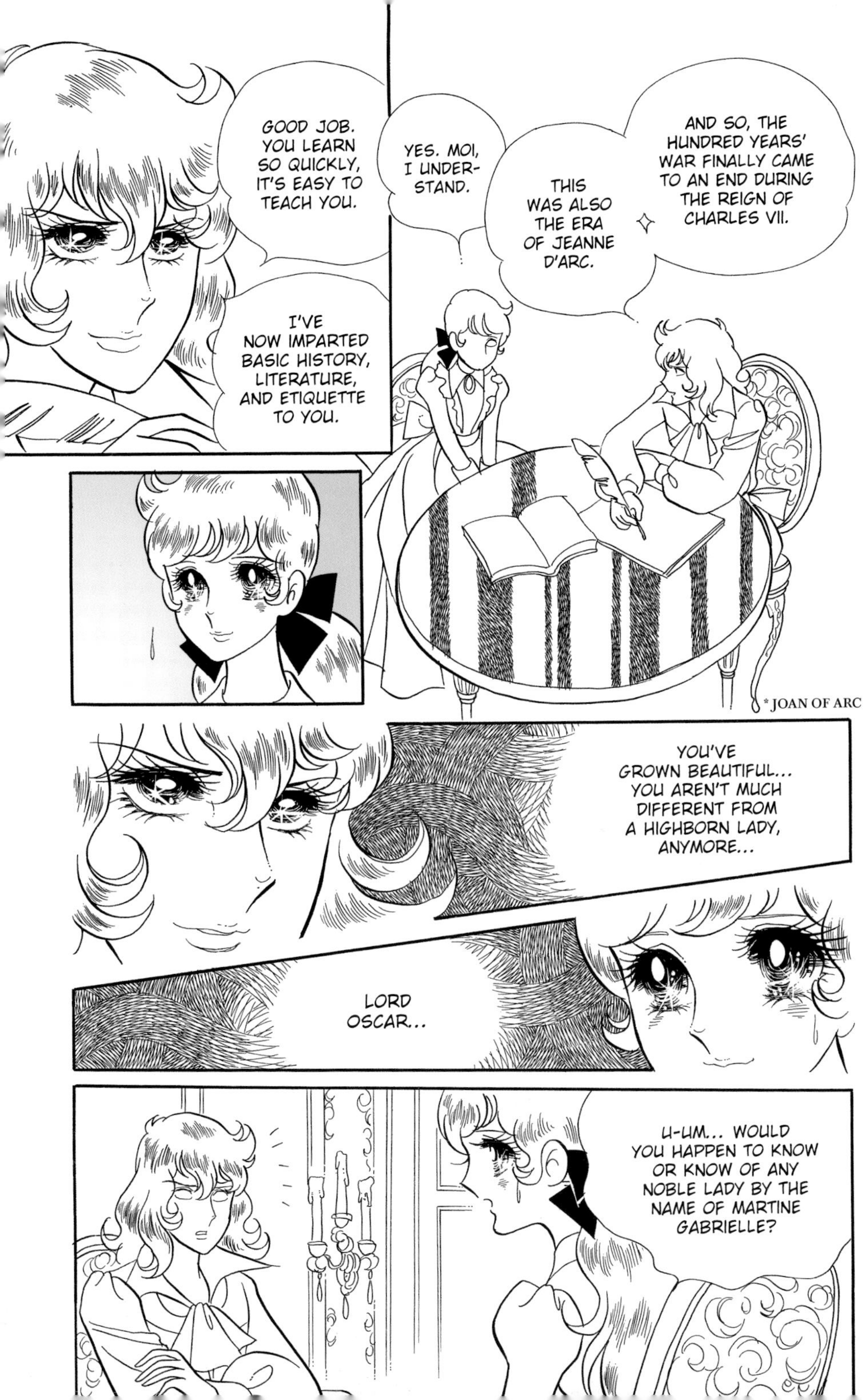
AND SO, THE HUNDRED YEARS' WAR FINALLY CAME TO AN END DURING THE REIGN OF CHARLES VII.
THIS WAS ALSO THE ERA OF JEANNE D'ARC.
YES. MOI, I UNDERSTAND.
GOOD JOB. YOU LEARN SO QUICKLY, IT'S EASY TO TEACH YOU.
I'VE NOW IMPARTED BASIC HISTORY, LITERATURE, AND ETIQUETTE TO YOU.
YOU'VE GROWN BEAUTIFUL... YOU AREN'T MUCH DIFFERENT FROM A HIGHBORN LADY, ANYMORE...
LORD OSCAR...
U-UM... WOULD YOU HAPPEN TO KNOW OR KNOW OF ANY NOBLE LADY BY THE NAME OF MARTINE GABRIELLE?

* JOAN OF ARC

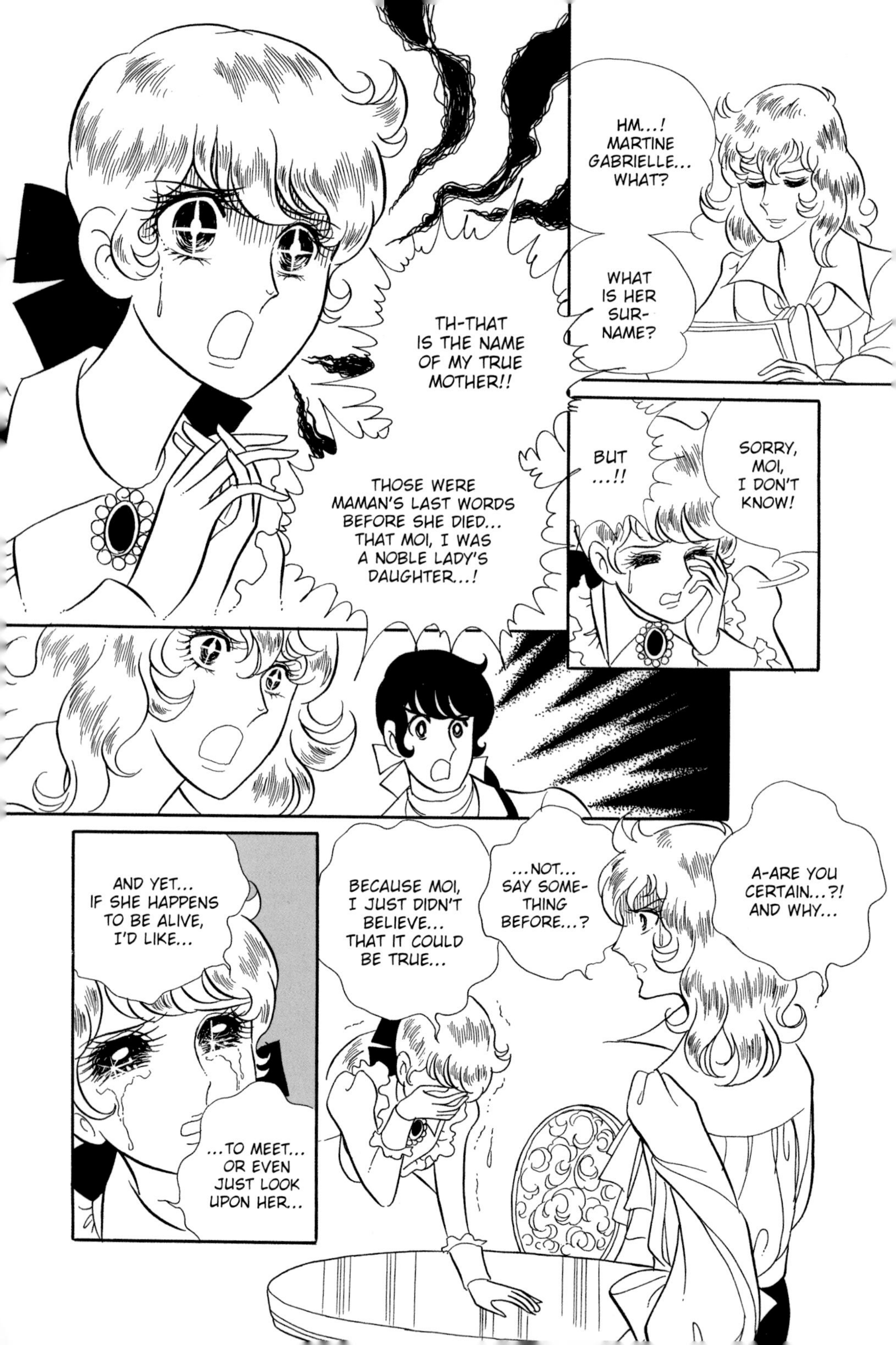
HM...! MARTINE GABRIELLE... WHAT?
WHAT IS HER SUR-NAME?
SORRY, MOI, I DON'T KNOW!
BUT ...!!
TH-THAT IS THE NAME OF MY TRUE MOTHER!!
THOSE WERE MAMAN'S LAST WORDS BEFORE SHE DIED... THAT MOI, I WAS A NOBLE LADY'S DAUGHTER...!
A-ARE YOU CERTAIN...?! AND WHY...
...NOT... SAY SOME-THING BEFORE...?
BECAUSE MOI, I JUST DIDN'T BELIEVE... THAT IT COULD BE TRUE...
AND YET... IF SHE HAPPENS TO BE ALIVE, I'D LIKE...
...TO MEET... OR EVEN JUST LOOK UPON HER...

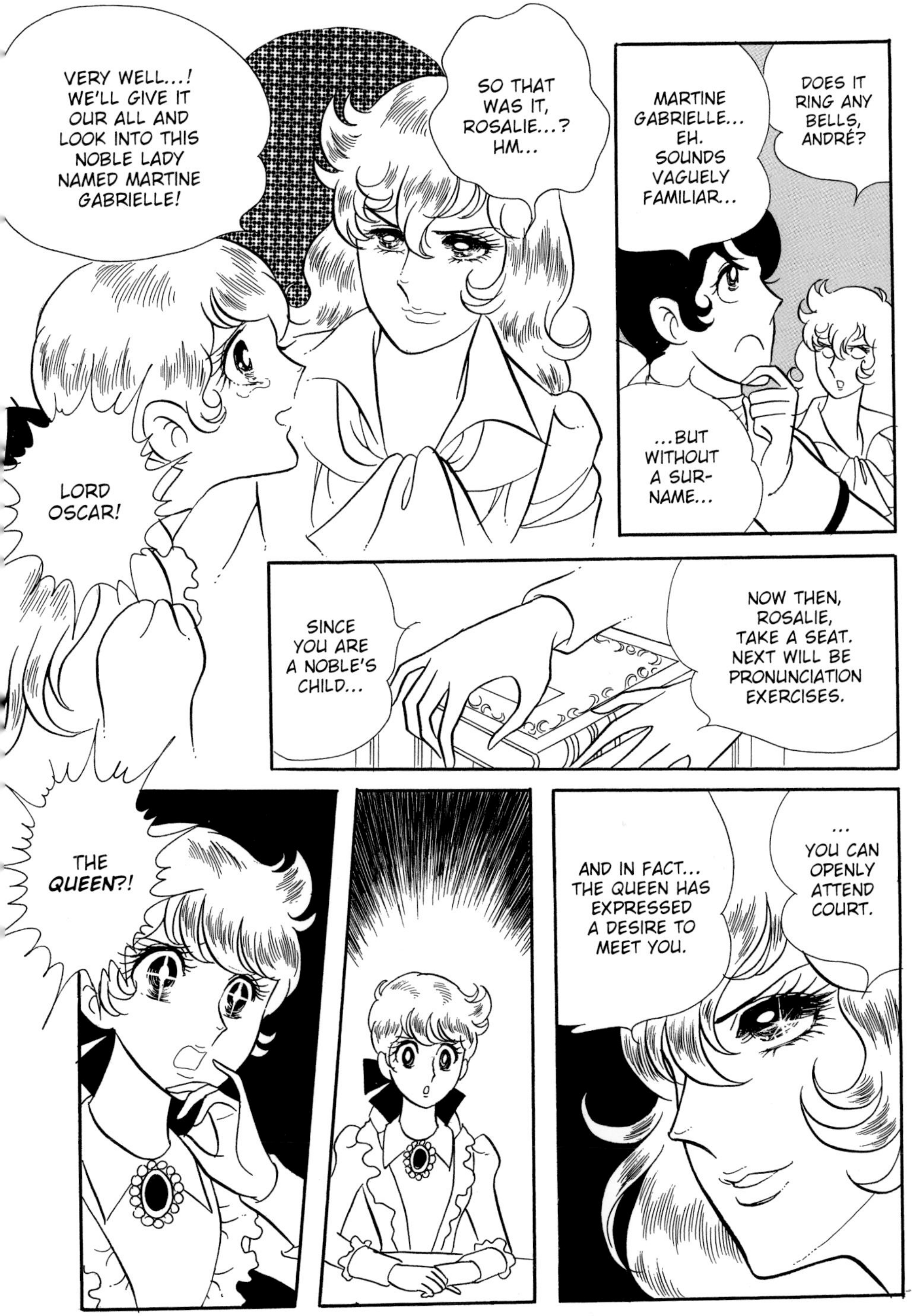
DOES IT RING ANY BELLS, ANDRÉ?
MARTINE GABRIELLE... EH. SOUNDS VAGUELY FAMILIAR...
...BUT WITHOUT A SURNAME...
SO THAT WAS IT, ROSALIE...? HM...
VERY WELL...! WE'LL GIVE IT OUR ALL AND LOOK INTO THIS NOBLE LADY NAMED MARTINE GABRIELLE!
LORD OSCAR!
NOW THEN, ROSALIE, TAKE A SEAT. NEXT WILL BE PRONUNCIATION EXERCISES.
SINCE YOU ARE A NOBLE'S CHILD...
... YOU CAN OPENLY ATTEND COURT.
AND IN FACT... THE QUEEN HAS EXPRESSED A DESIRE TO MEET YOU.
THE QUEEN?!

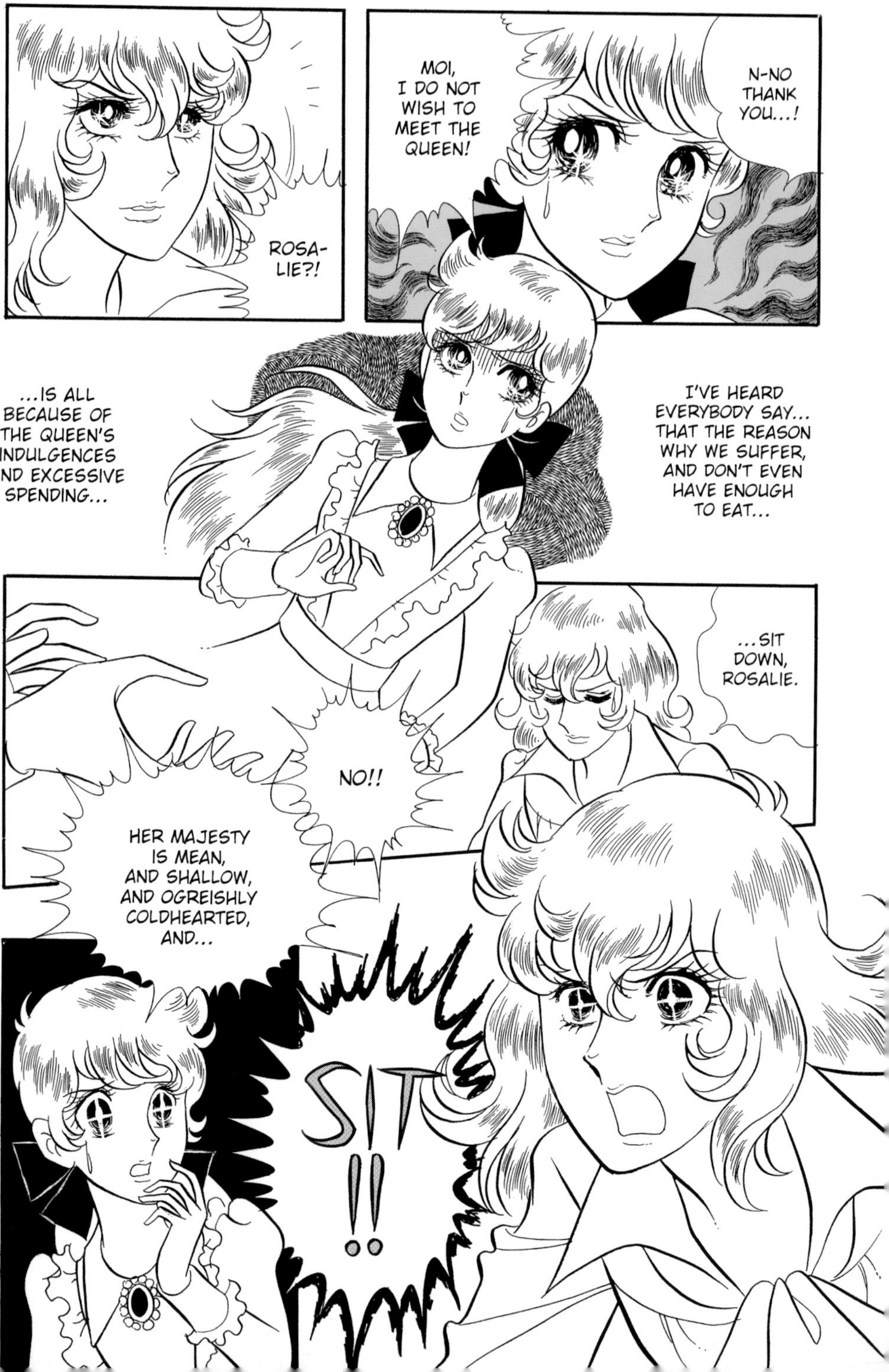
N-NO THANK YOU...!
MOI, I DO NOT WISH TO MEET THE QUEEN!
ROSA-LIE?!
I'VE HEARD EVERYBODY SAY... THAT THE REASON WHY WE SUFFER, AND DON'T EVEN HAVE ENOUGH TO EAT...
...IS ALL BECAUSE OF THE QUEEN'S INDULGENCES AND EXCESSIVE SPENDING...
...SIT DOWN, ROSALIE.
NO!!
HER MAJESTY IS MEAN, AND SHALLOW, AND OGREISHLY COLDHEARTED, AND...
SIT!!

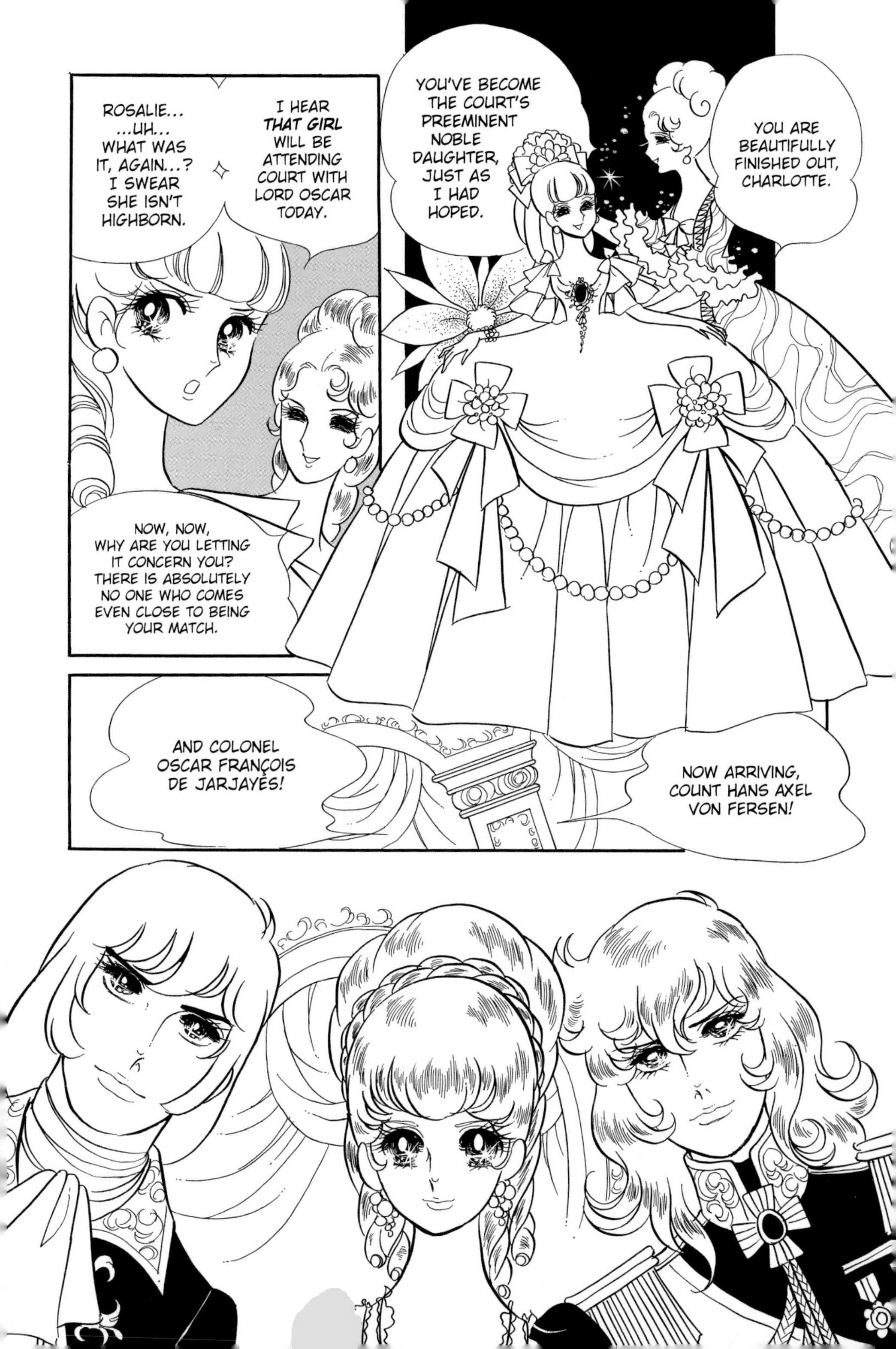
YOU ARE BEAUTIFULLY FINISHED OUT, CHARLOTTE.
YOU'VE BECOME THE COURT'S PREEMINENT NOBLE DAUGHTER, JUST AS I HAD HOPED.
I HEAR ***THAT GIRL*** WILL BE ATTENDING COURT WITH LORD OSCAR TODAY.
ROSALIE... ...UH... WHAT WAS IT, AGAIN...? I SWEAR SHE ISN'T HIGHBORN.
NOW, NOW, WHY ARE YOU LETTING IT CONCERN YOU? THERE IS ABSOLUTELY NO ONE WHO COMES EVEN CLOSE TO BEING YOUR MATCH.
NOW ARRIVING, COUNT HANS AXEL VON FERSEN!
AND COLONEL OSCAR FRANÇOIS DE JARJAYÉS!

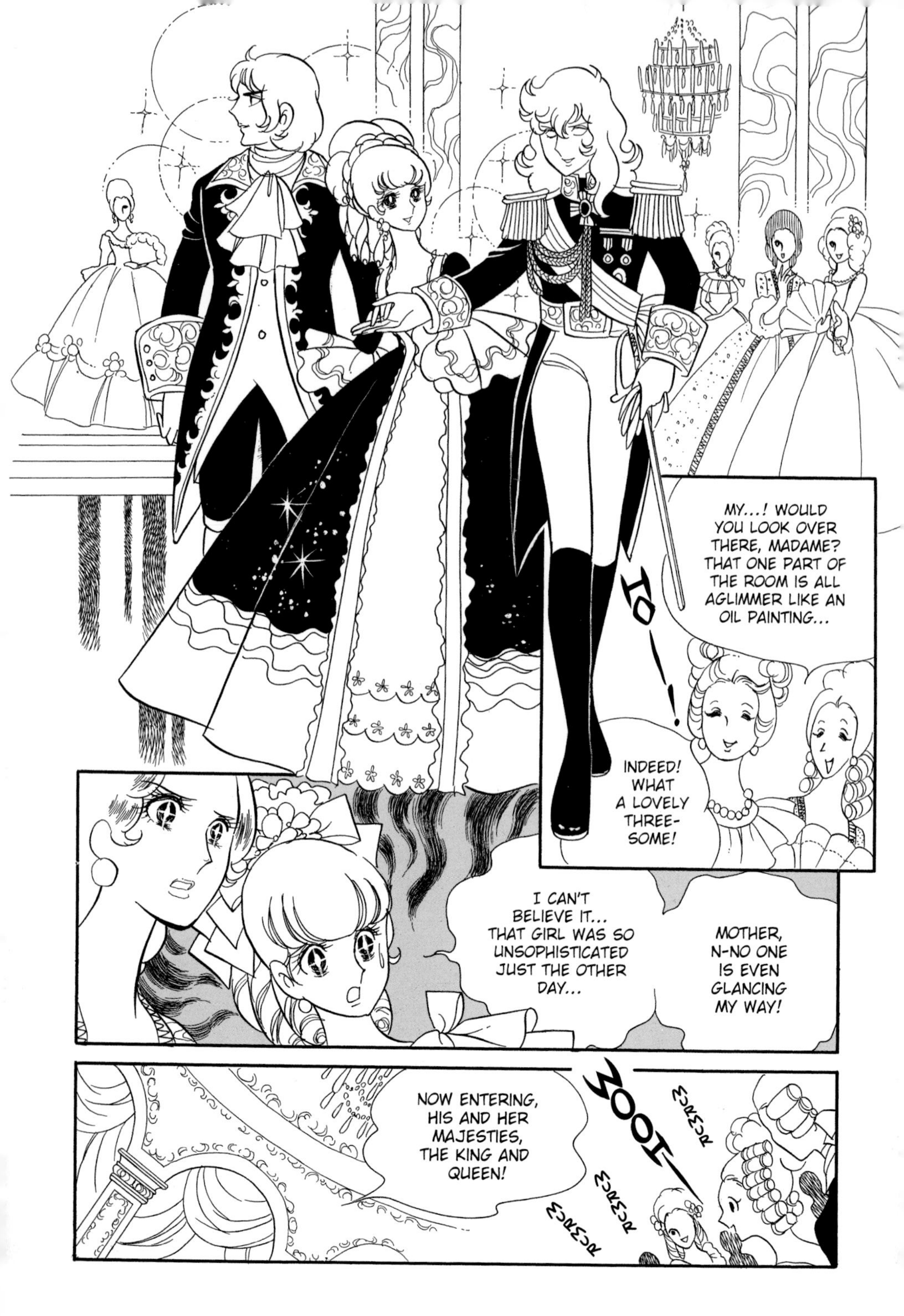
MY...! WOULD YOU LOOK OVER THERE, MADAME? THAT ONE PART OF THE ROOM IS ALL AGLIMMER LIKE AN OIL PAINTING...
TO—!
INDEED! WHAT A LOVELY THREE-SOME!
MOTHER, N-NO ONE IS EVEN GLANCING MY WAY!
I CAN'T BELIEVE IT... THAT GIRL WAS SO UNSOPHISTICATED JUST THE OTHER DAY...
MURMUR
MURMUR
MURMUR
NOW ENTERING, HIS AND HER MAJESTIES, THE KING AND QUEEN!

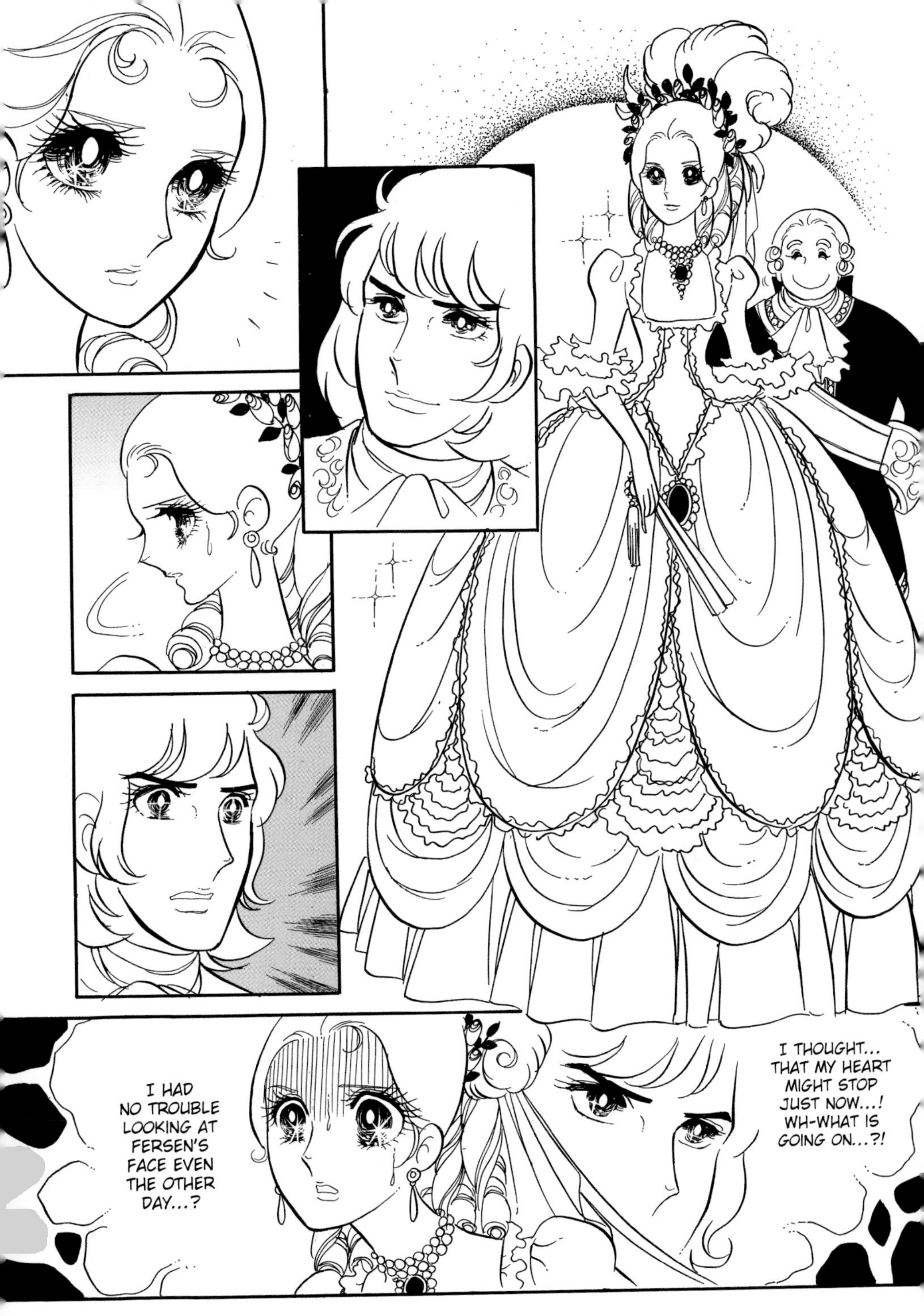
I THOUGHT... THAT MY HEART MIGHT STOP JUST NOW...! WH-WHAT IS GOING ON...?!
I HAD NO TROUBLE LOOKING AT FERSEN'S FACE EVEN THE OTHER DAY...?

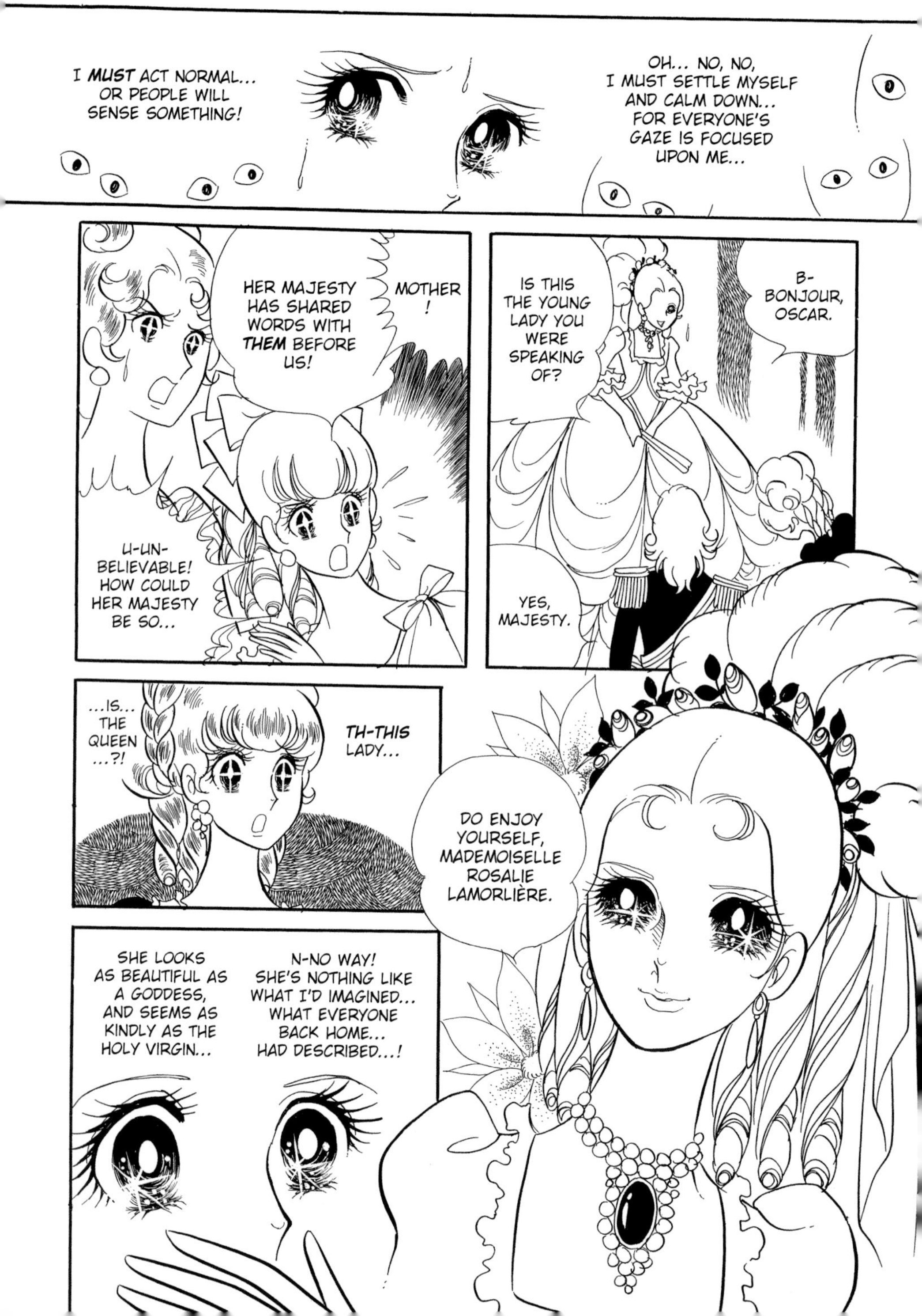
OH... NO, NO, I MUST SETTLE MYSELF AND CALM DOWN... FOR EVERYONE'S GAZE IS FOCUSED UPON ME...
I **MUST** ACT NORMAL... OR PEOPLE WILL SENSE SOMETHING!
B-BONJOUR, OSCAR.
IS THIS THE YOUNG LADY YOU WERE SPEAKING OF?
YES, MAJESTY.
MOTHER!
HER MAJESTY HAS SHARED WORDS WITH **THEM** BEFORE US!
U-UN-BELIEVABLE! HOW COULD HER MAJESTY BE SO...
DO ENJOY YOURSELF, MADEMOISELLE ROSALIE LAMORLIÈRE.
TH-THIS LADY...
...IS... THE QUEEN ...?!
N-NO WAY! SHE'S NOTHING LIKE WHAT I'D IMAGINED... WHAT EVERYONE BACK HOME... HAD DESCRIBED...!
SHE LOOKS AS BEAUTIFUL AS A GODDESS, AND SEEMS AS KINDLY AS THE HOLY VIRGIN...

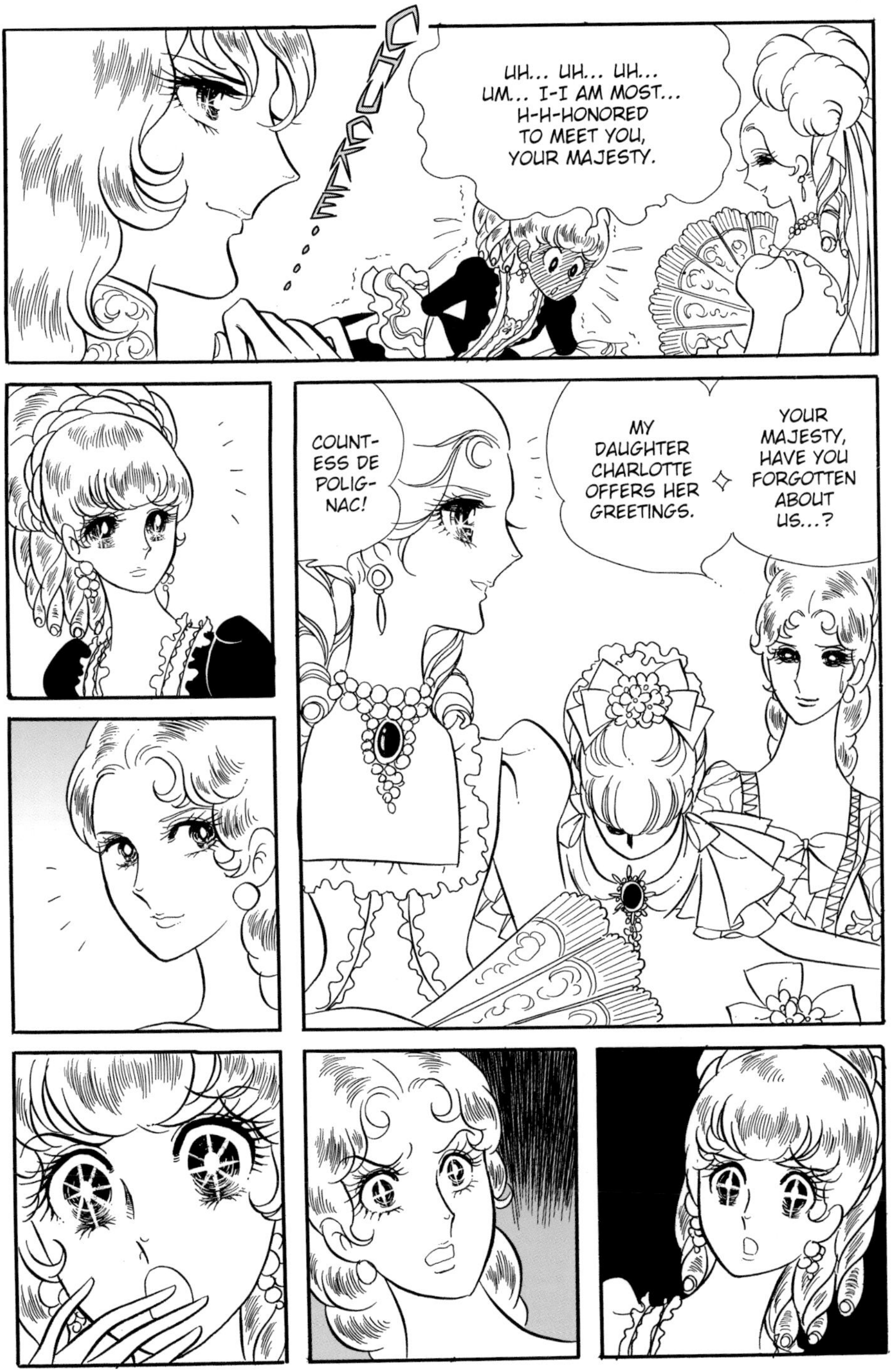
UH... UH... UH... UM... I-I AM MOST... H-H-HONORED TO MEET YOU, YOUR MAJESTY.
CHUCKLE....
YOUR MAJESTY, HAVE YOU FORGOTTEN ABOUT US...?
MY DAUGHTER CHARLOTTE OFFERS HER GREETINGS.
COUNT-ESS DE POLIG-NAC!

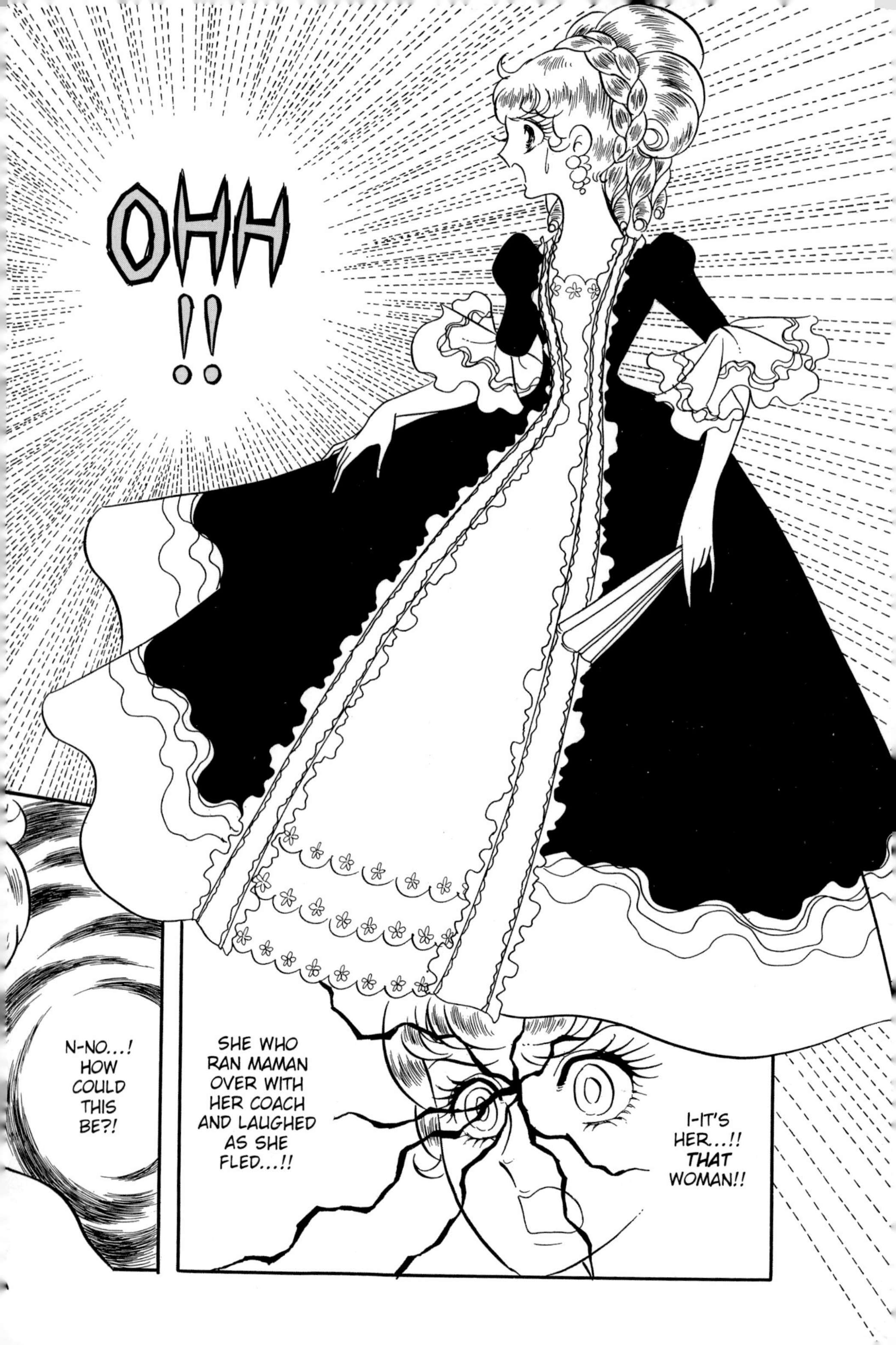
OHH!!
I-IT'S HER...!! *THAT* WOMAN!!
SHE WHO RAN MAMAN OVER WITH HER COACH AND LAUGHED AS SHE FLED...!!
N-NO...! HOW COULD THIS BE?!

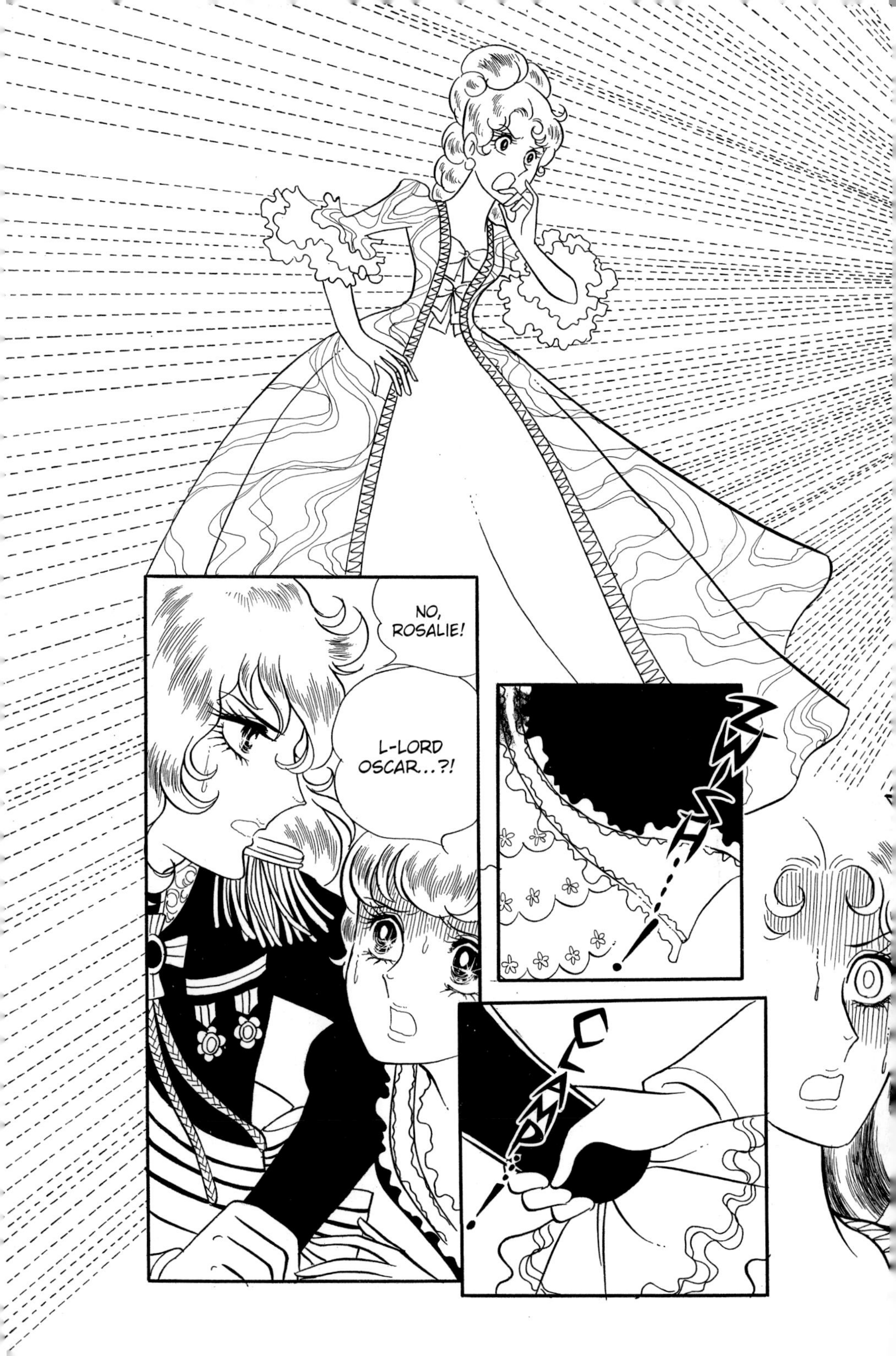
SWSH...!
CLAMP...!
NO, ROSALIE!
L-LORD OSCAR...?!

1972 WEEKLY MARGARET MAGAZINE
ISSUE 38 PREVIEW ART

♥CRITICALLY ACCLAIMED DRAMA COMING AT YOU WITH OVERWHELMING FORCE!!
♥ROSALIE FINALLY COME ACROSS HER MOTHER'S SLAYER, BUT...!?

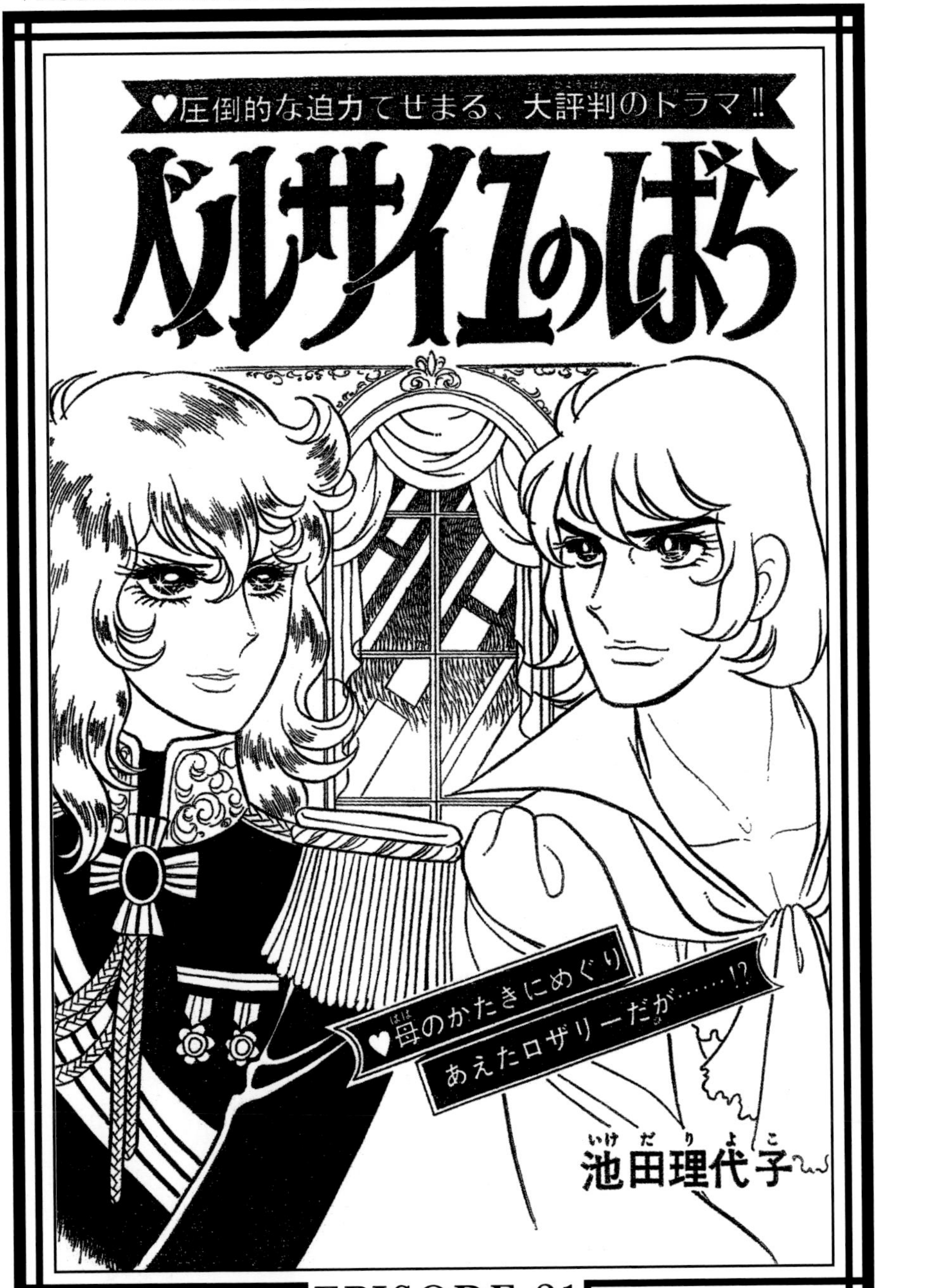

♥圧倒的な迫力でせまる、大評判のドラマ!!
ベルサイユのばら
♥母のかたきにめぐりあえたロザリーだが……!?
池田理代子
EPISODE 21

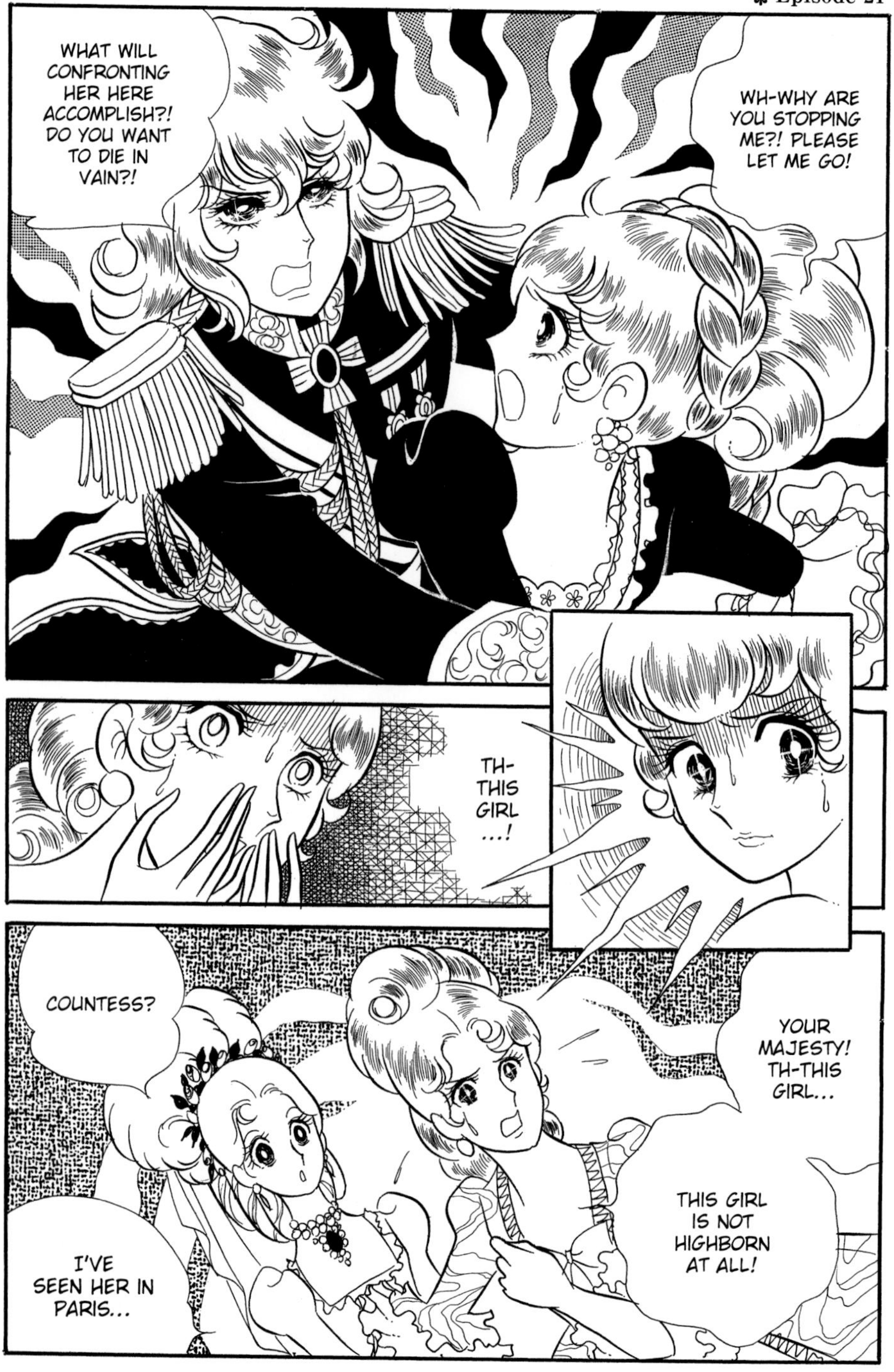
WH-WHY ARE YOU STOPPING ME?! PLEASE LET ME GO!
WHAT WILL CONFRONTING HER HERE ACCOMPLISH?! DO YOU WANT TO DIE IN VAIN?!
TH-THIS GIRL ...!
YOUR MAJESTY! TH-THIS GIRL...
COUNTESS?
THIS GIRL IS NOT HIGHBORN AT ALL!
I'VE SEEN HER IN PARIS...

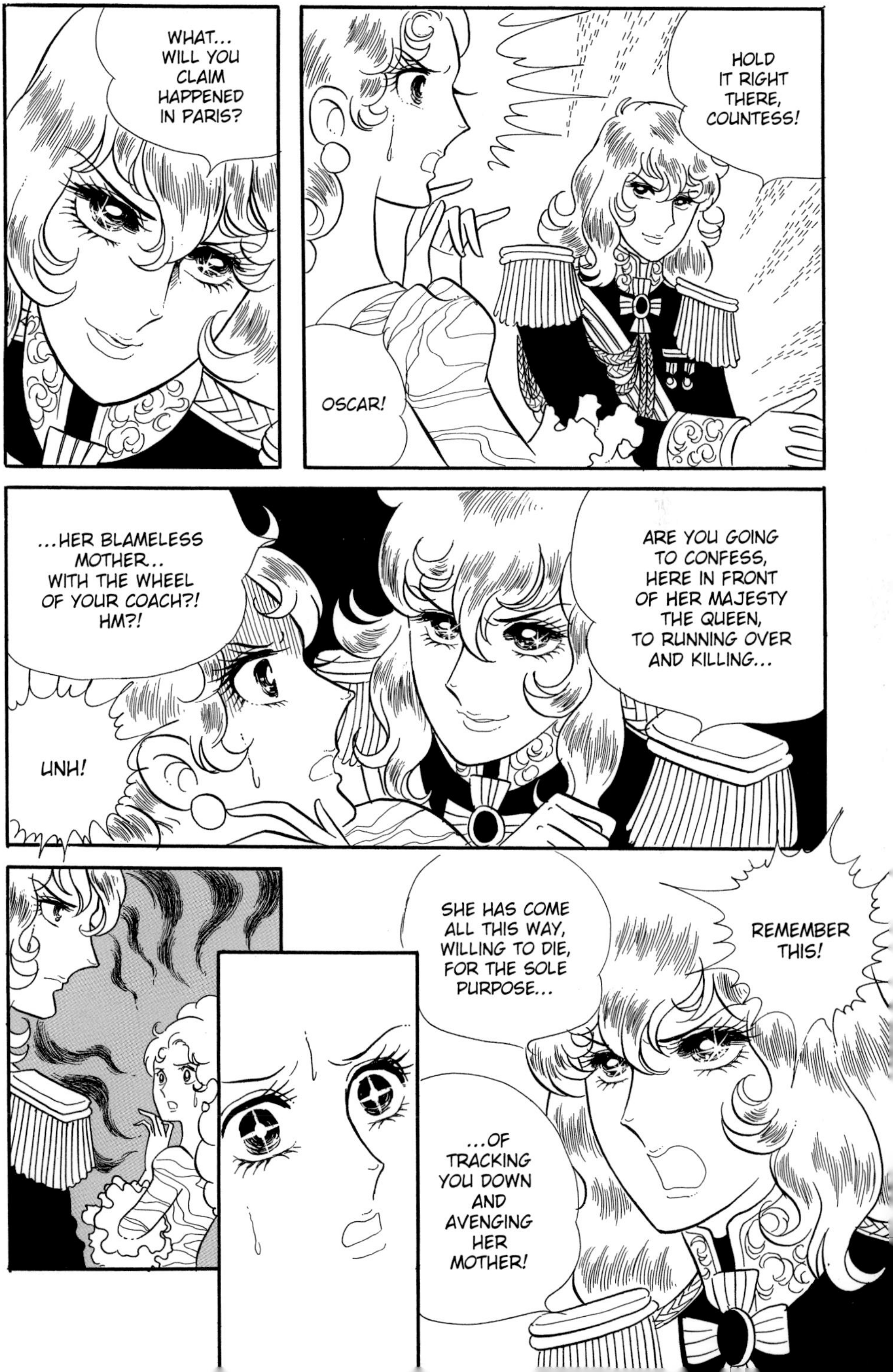
HOLD IT RIGHT THERE, COUNTESS!
OSCAR!
WHAT... WILL YOU CLAIM HAPPENED IN PARIS?
ARE YOU GOING TO CONFESS, HERE IN FRONT OF HER MAJESTY THE QUEEN, TO RUNNING OVER AND KILLING...
...HER BLAMELESS MOTHER.. WITH THE WHEEL OF YOUR COACH?! HM?!
UNH!
REMEMBER THIS!
SHE HAS COME ALL THIS WAY, WILLING TO DIE, FOR THE SOLE PURPOSE...
...OF TRACKING YOU DOWN AND AVENGING HER MOTHER!

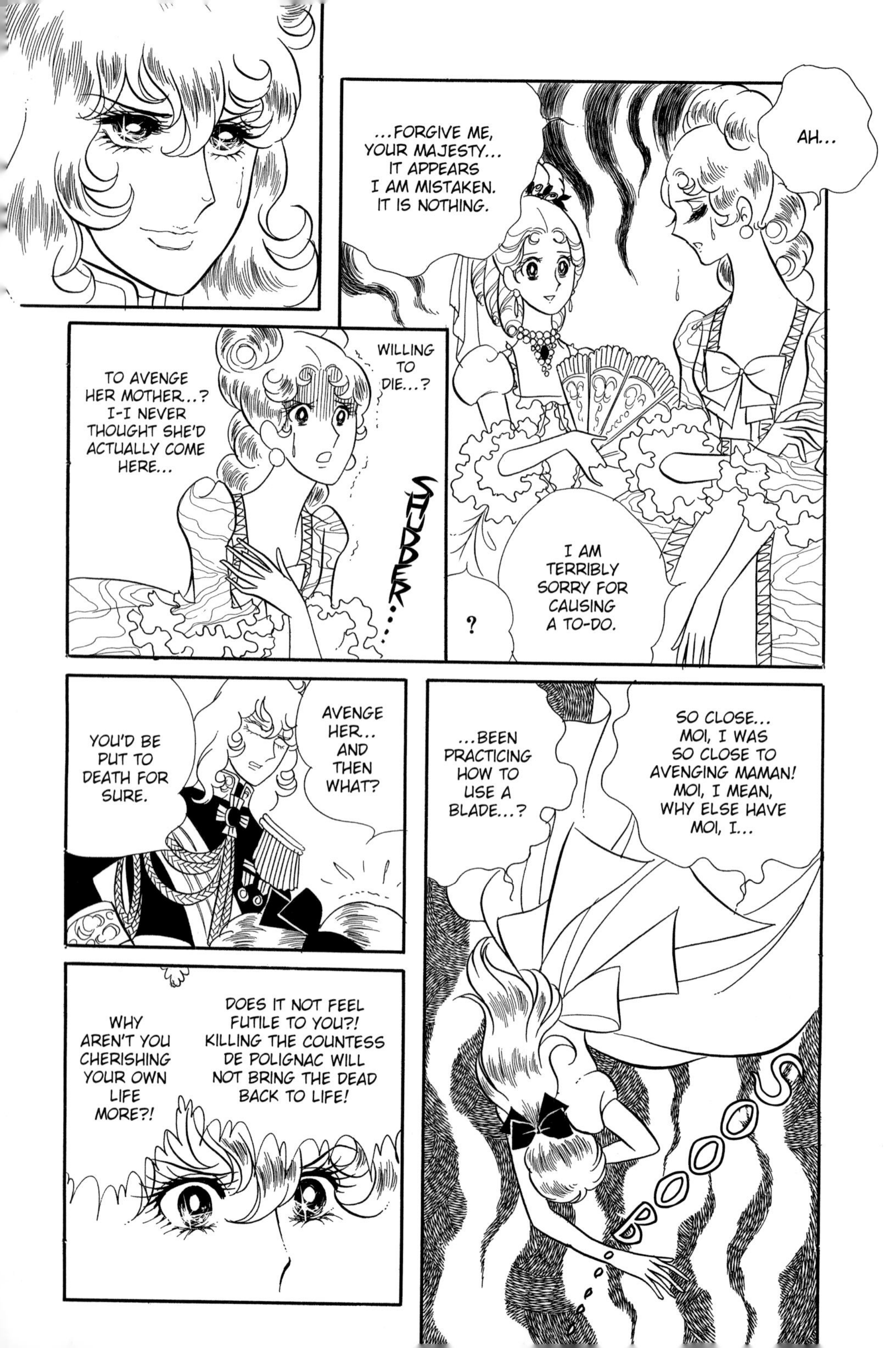
AH...
...FORGIVE ME, YOUR MAJESTY... IT APPEARS I AM MISTAKEN. IT IS NOTHING.
I AM TERRIBLY SORRY FOR CAUSING A TO-DO.
?
WILLING TO DIE...?
TO AVENGE HER MOTHER...? I-I NEVER THOUGHT SHE'D ACTUALLY COME HERE...
SHUDDER...
SO CLOSE... MOI, I WAS SO CLOSE TO AVENGING MAMAN! MOI, I MEAN, WHY ELSE HAVE MOI, I...
...BEEN PRACTICING HOW TO USE A BLADE...?
BOOOS
AVENGE HER.. AND THEN WHAT?
YOU'D BE PUT TO DEATH FOR SURE.
DOES IT NOT FEEL FUTILE TO YOU?! KILLING THE COUNTESS DE POLIGNAC WILL NOT BRING THE DEAD BACK TO LIFE!
WHY AREN'T YOU CHERISHING YOUR OWN LIFE MORE?!

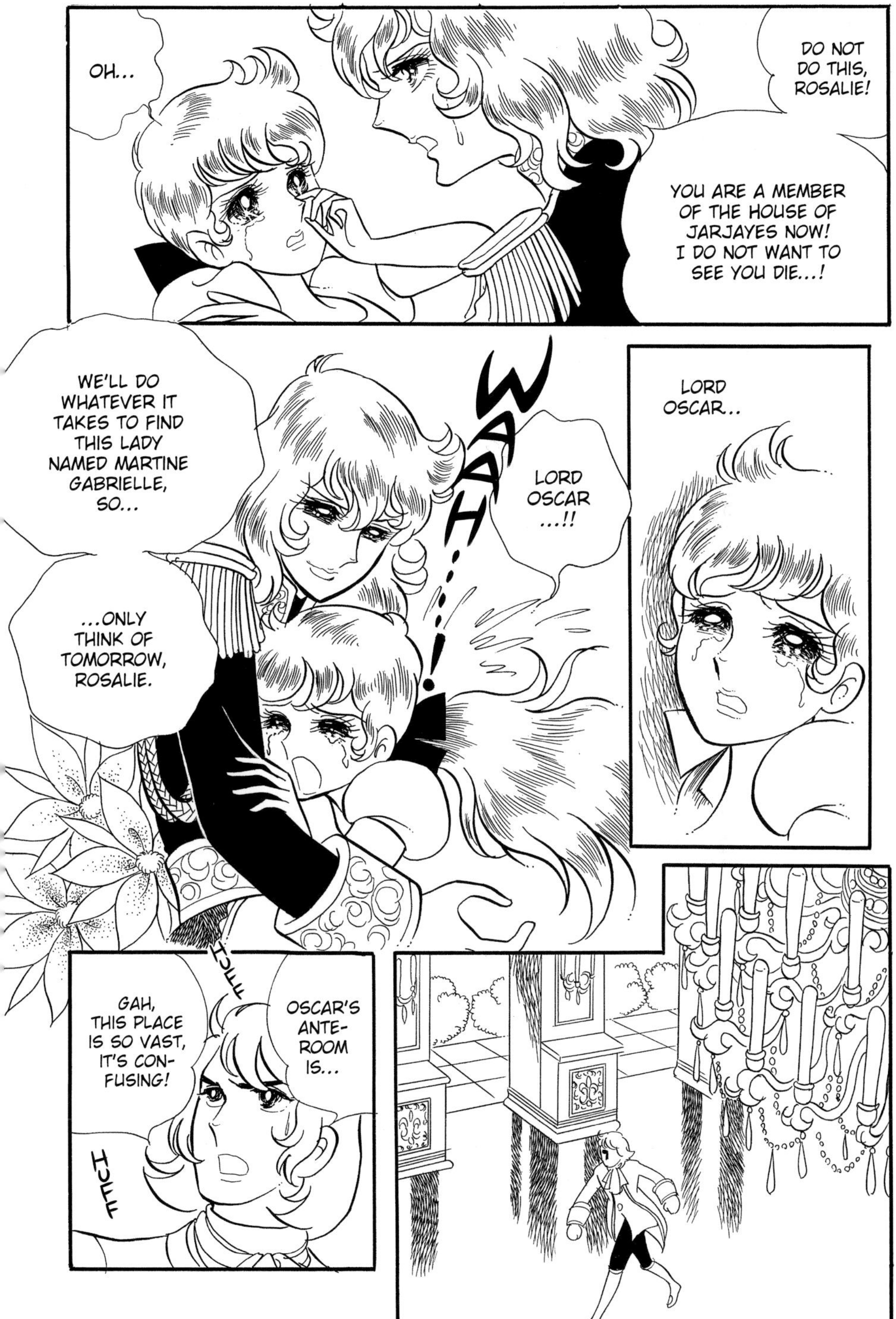
DO NOT DO THIS, ROSALIE!
YOU ARE A MEMBER OF THE HOUSE OF JARJAYES NOW! I DO NOT WANT TO SEE YOU DIE...!
OH...
LORD OSCAR...
LORD OSCAR ...!!
WAAH...!
WE'LL DO WHATEVER IT TAKES TO FIND THIS LADY NAMED MARTINE GABRIELLE, SO...
...ONLY THINK OF TOMORROW, ROSALIE.
OSCAR'S ANTE-ROOM IS...
HUFF
GAH, THIS PLACE IS SO VAST, IT'S CON-FUSING!
HUFF

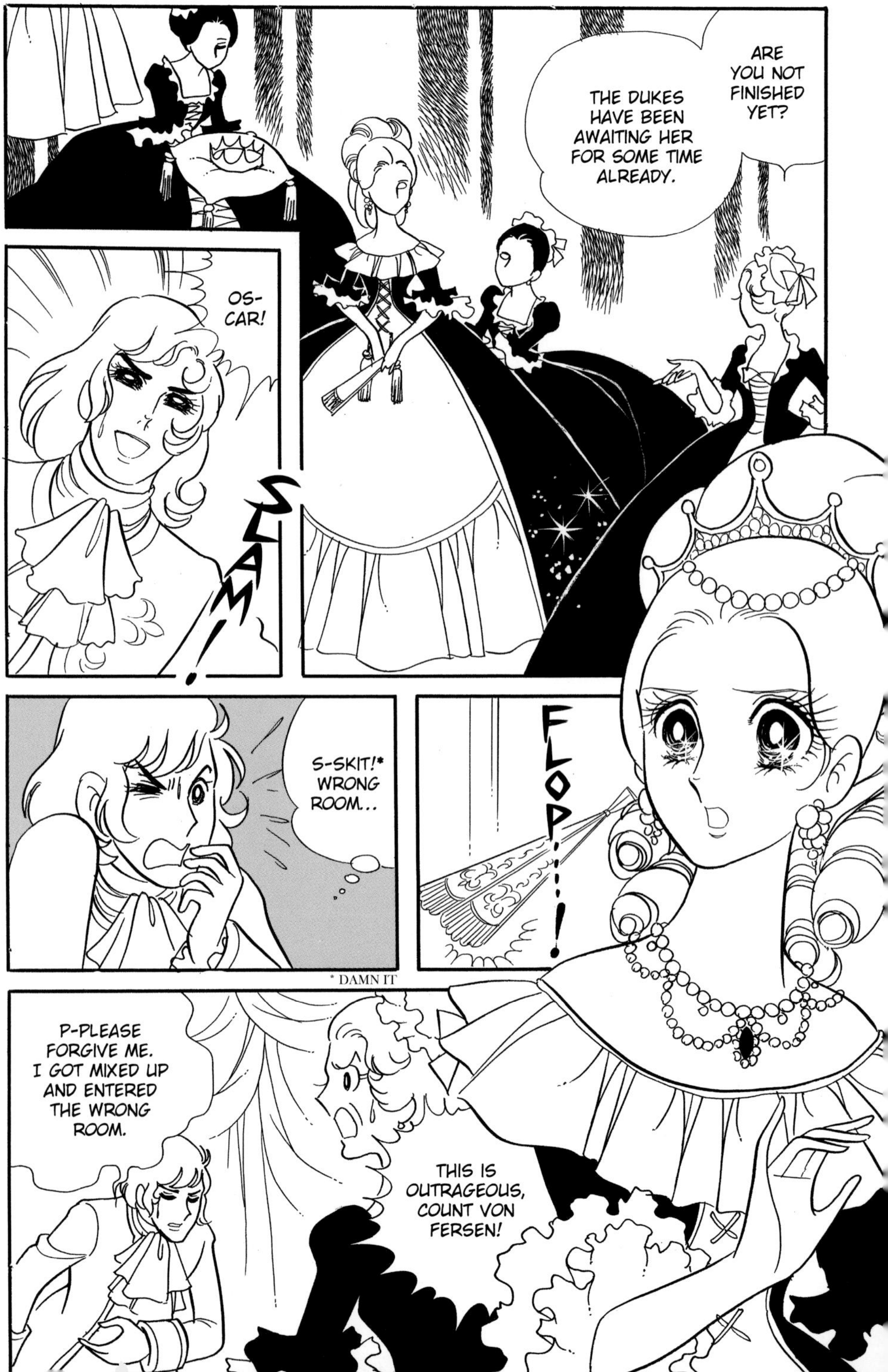
ARE YOU NOT FINISHED YET?
THE DUKES HAVE BEEN AWAITING HER FOR SOME TIME ALREADY.
OS-CAR!
SLAM!
FLOP...!
S-SKIT!* WRONG ROOM...
THIS IS OUTRAGEOUS, COUNT VON FERSEN!
P-PLEASE FORGIVE ME. I GOT MIXED UP AND ENTERED THE WRONG ROOM.

* DAMN IT

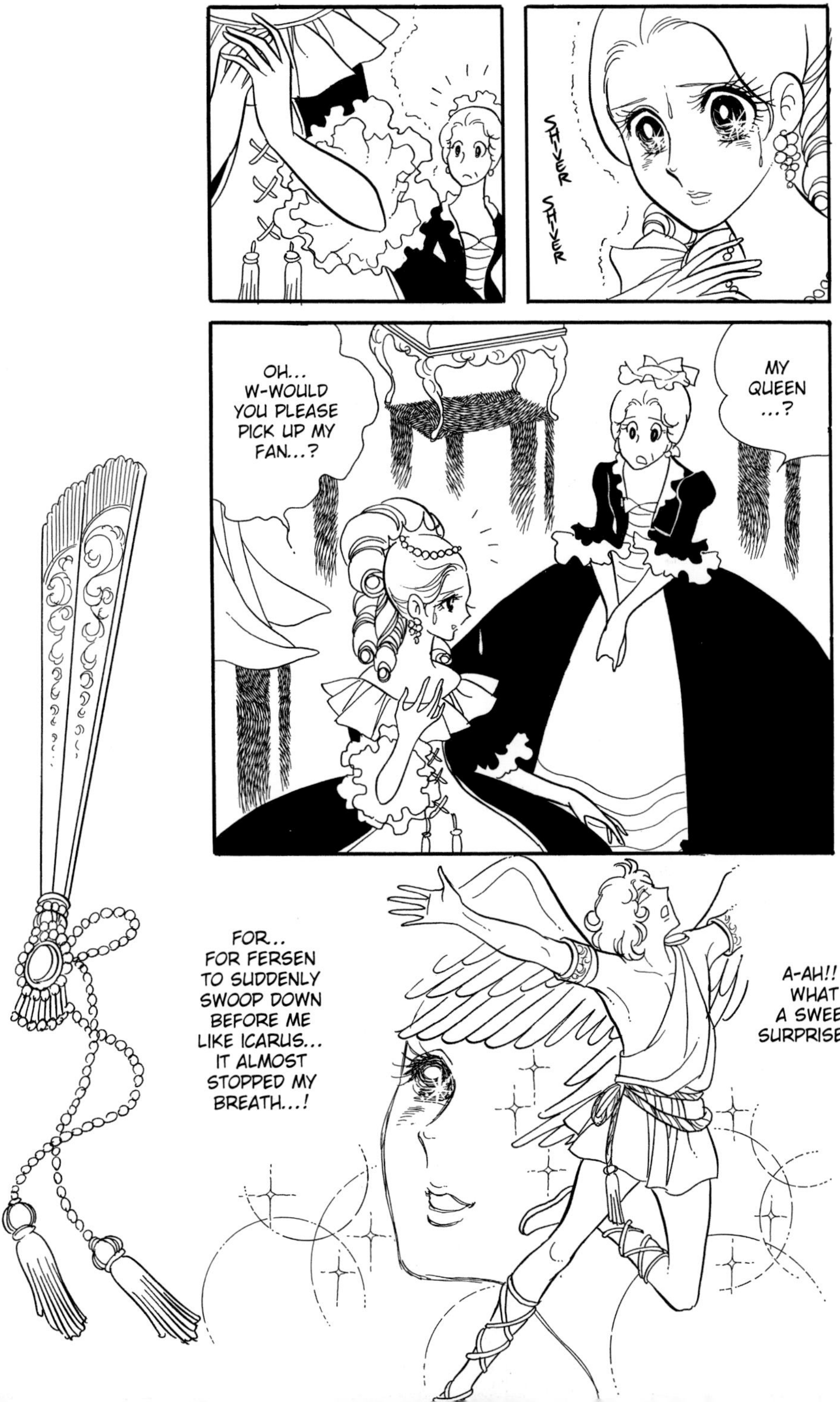
SHIVER SHIVER
MY QUEEN...?
OH... W-WOULD YOU PLEASE PICK UP MY FAN...?
A-AH!! WHAT A SWEET SURPRISE...!
FOR... FOR FERSEN TO SUDDENLY SWOOP DOWN BEFORE ME LIKE ICARUS... IT ALMOST STOPPED MY BREATH...!

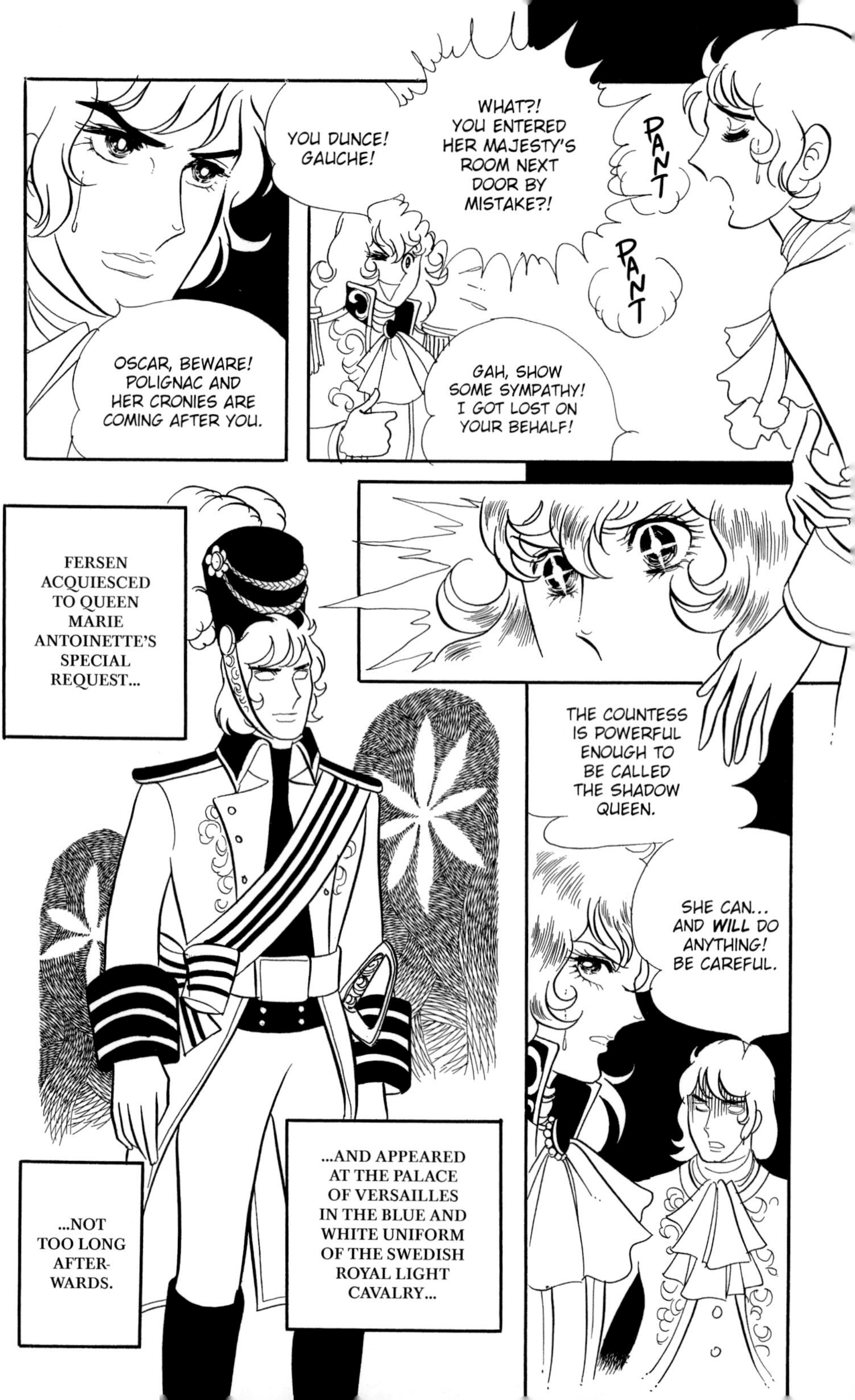
WHAT?! YOU ENTERED HER MAJESTY'S ROOM NEXT DOOR BY MISTAKE?!
PANT
PANT
YOU DUNCE! GAUCHE!
GAH, SHOW SOME SYMPATHY! I GOT LOST ON YOUR BEHALF!
OSCAR, BEWARE! POLIGNAC AND HER CRONIES ARE COMING AFTER YOU.
THE COUNTESS IS POWERFUL ENOUGH TO BE CALLED THE SHADOW QUEEN.
SHE CAN... AND **WILL** DO ANYTHING! BE CAREFUL.
FERSEN ACQUIESCED TO QUEEN MARIE ANTOINETTE'S SPECIAL REQUEST...
...AND APPEARED AT THE PALACE OF VERSAILLES IN THE BLUE AND WHITE UNIFORM OF THE SWEDISH ROYAL LIGHT CAVALRY...
...NOT TOO LONG AFTERWARDS.

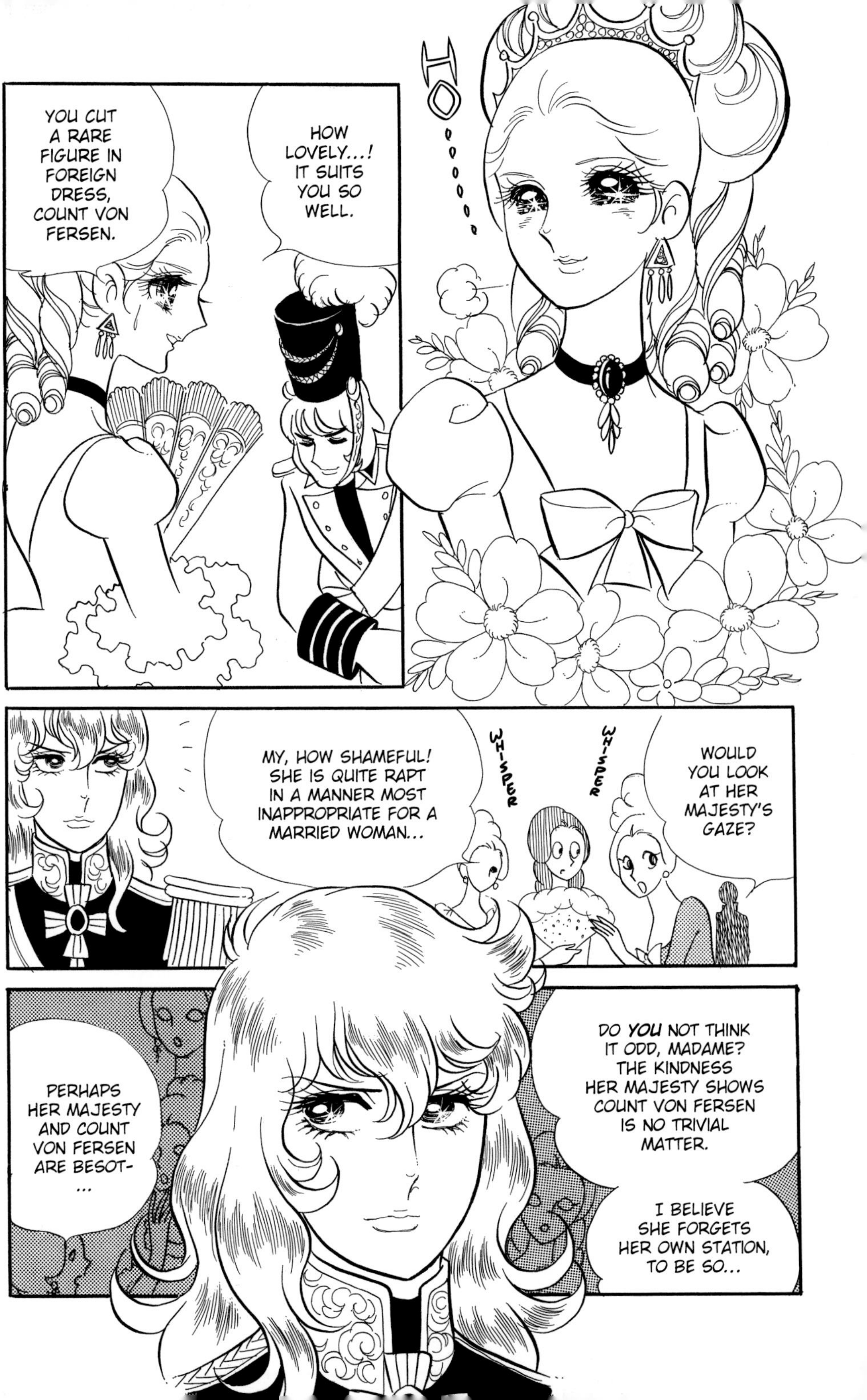
HO
HOW LOVELY...! IT SUITS YOU SO WELL.
YOU CUT A RARE FIGURE IN FOREIGN DRESS, COUNT VON FERSEN.
WOULD YOU LOOK AT HER MAJESTY'S GAZE?
WHISPER
WHISPER
MY, HOW SHAMEFUL! SHE IS QUITE RAPT IN A MANNER MOST INAPPROPRIATE FOR A MARRIED WOMAN...
DO *YOU* NOT THINK IT ODD, MADAME? THE KINDNESS HER MAJESTY SHOWS COUNT VON FERSEN IS NO TRIVIAL MATTER.
I BELIEVE SHE FORGETS HER OWN STATION, TO BE SO...
PERHAPS HER MAJESTY AND COUNT VON FERSEN ARE BESOT- ...

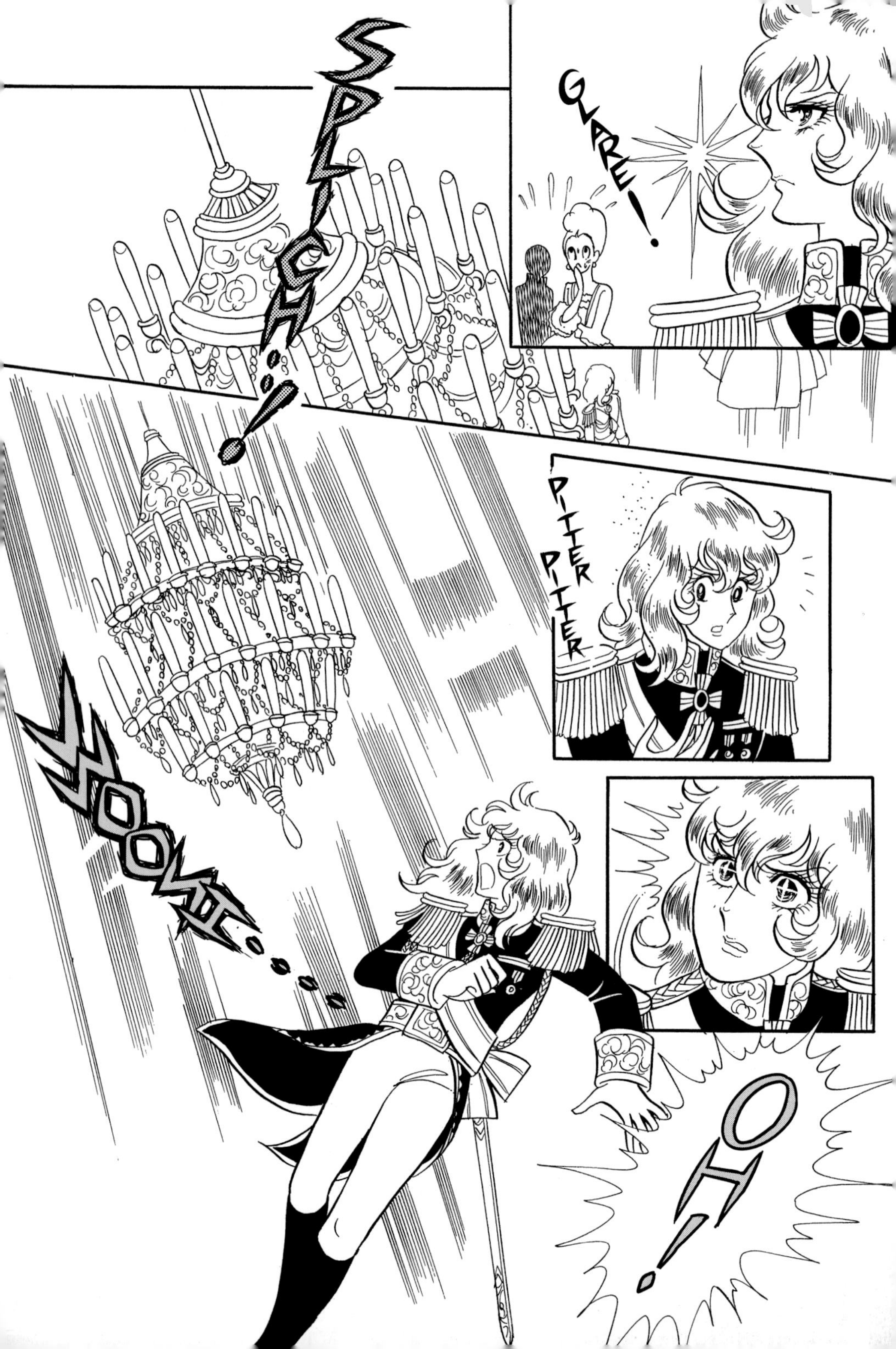
GLARE!
SPLICH..!
PITTER PITTER
WOOSH...
OH!

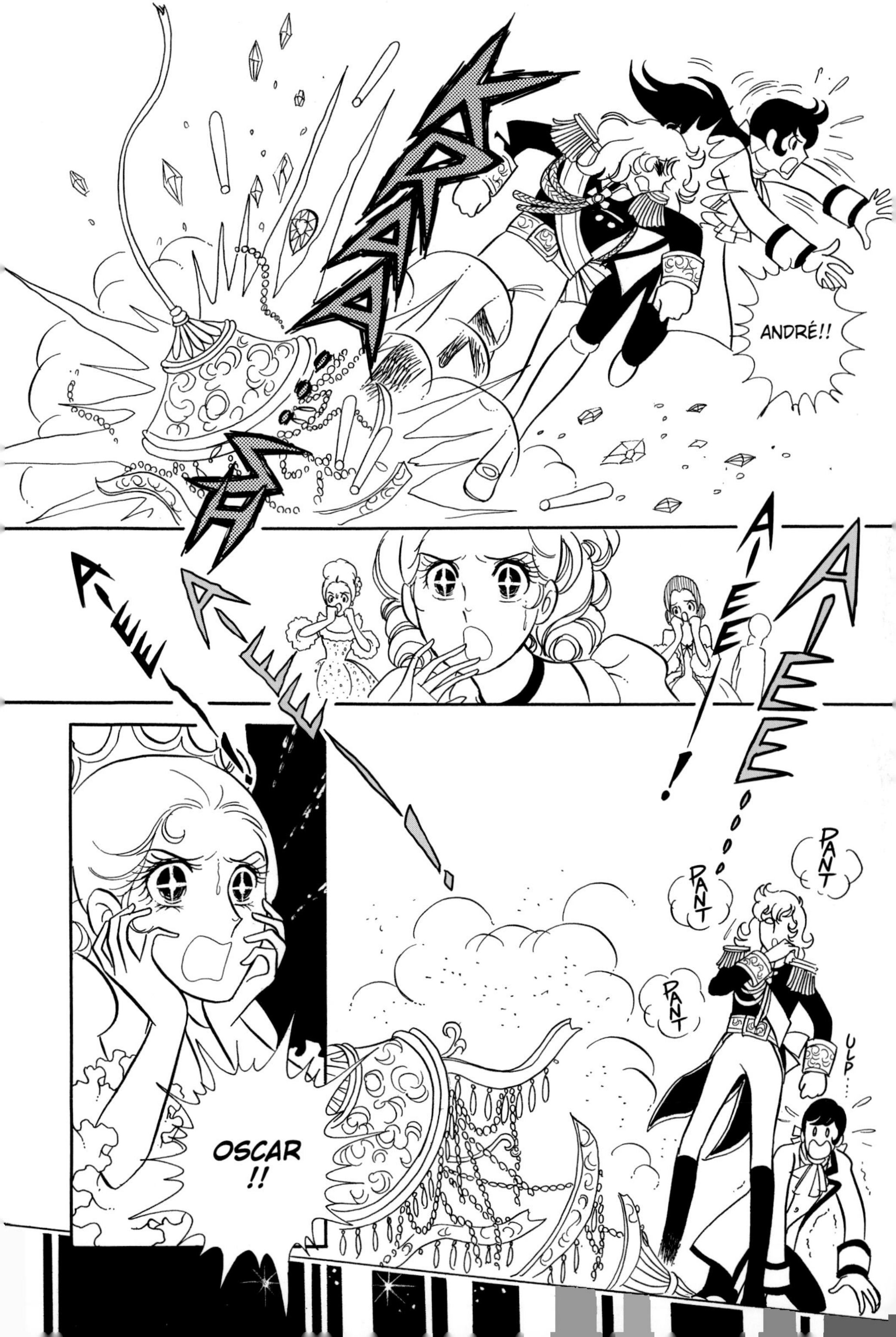
KRAAASH
ANDRÉ!!
AIEEEE!
AIEEEE.....
A-EE--!!
A-EEE--!!
PANT
PANT
PANT
ULP...
OSCAR!!

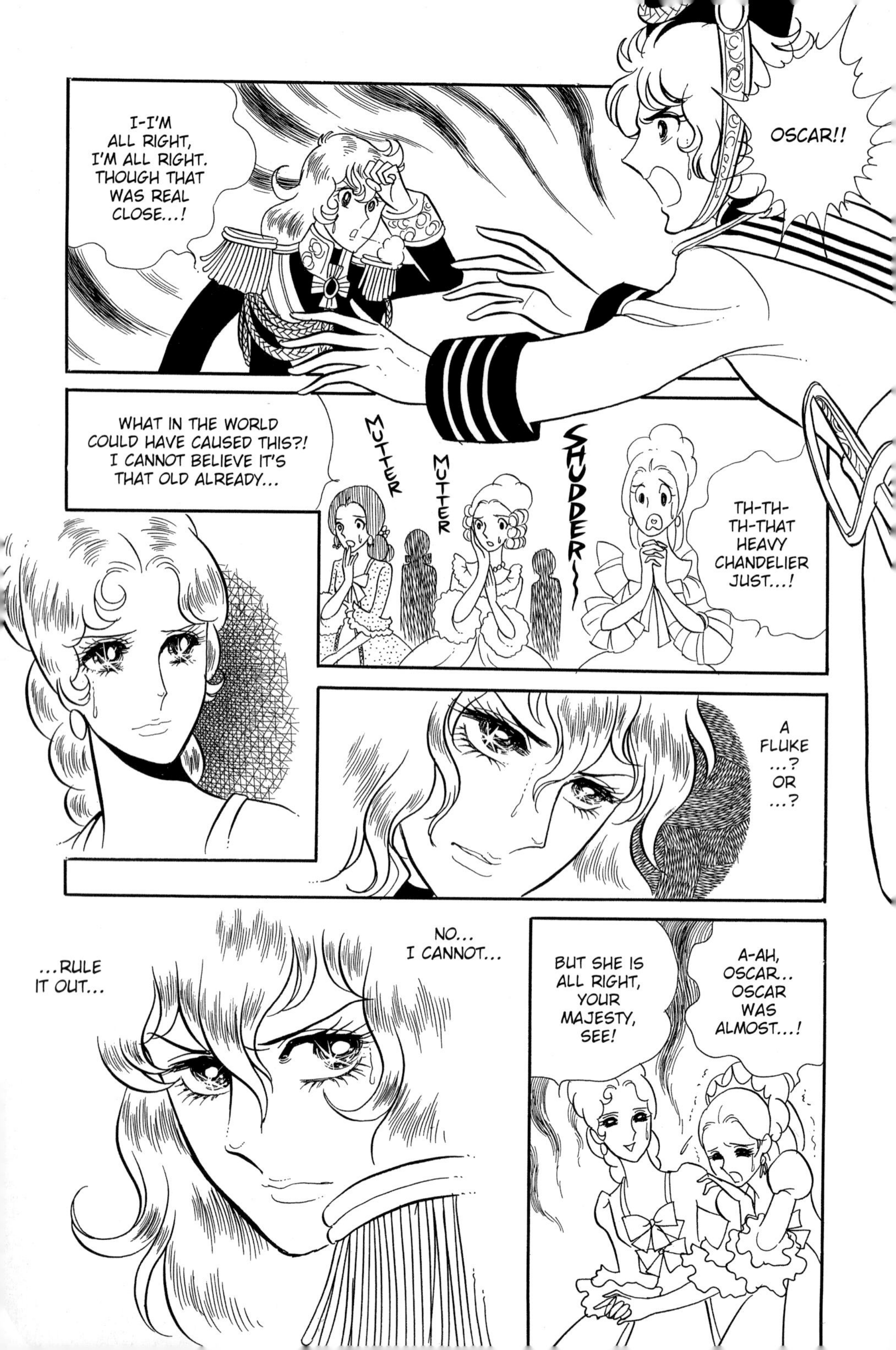
OSCAR!!
I-I'M ALL RIGHT, I'M ALL RIGHT. THOUGH THAT WAS REAL CLOSE...!
TH-TH-TH-THAT HEAVY CHANDELIER JUST...!
SHUDDER
MUTTER
MUTTER
WHAT IN THE WORLD COULD HAVE CAUSED THIS?! I CANNOT BELIEVE IT'S THAT OLD ALREADY...
A FLUKE ...? OR ...?
A-AH, OSCAR... OSCAR WAS ALMOST...!
BUT SHE IS ALL RIGHT, YOUR MAJESTY, SEE!
NO... I CANNOT...
...RULE IT OUT...

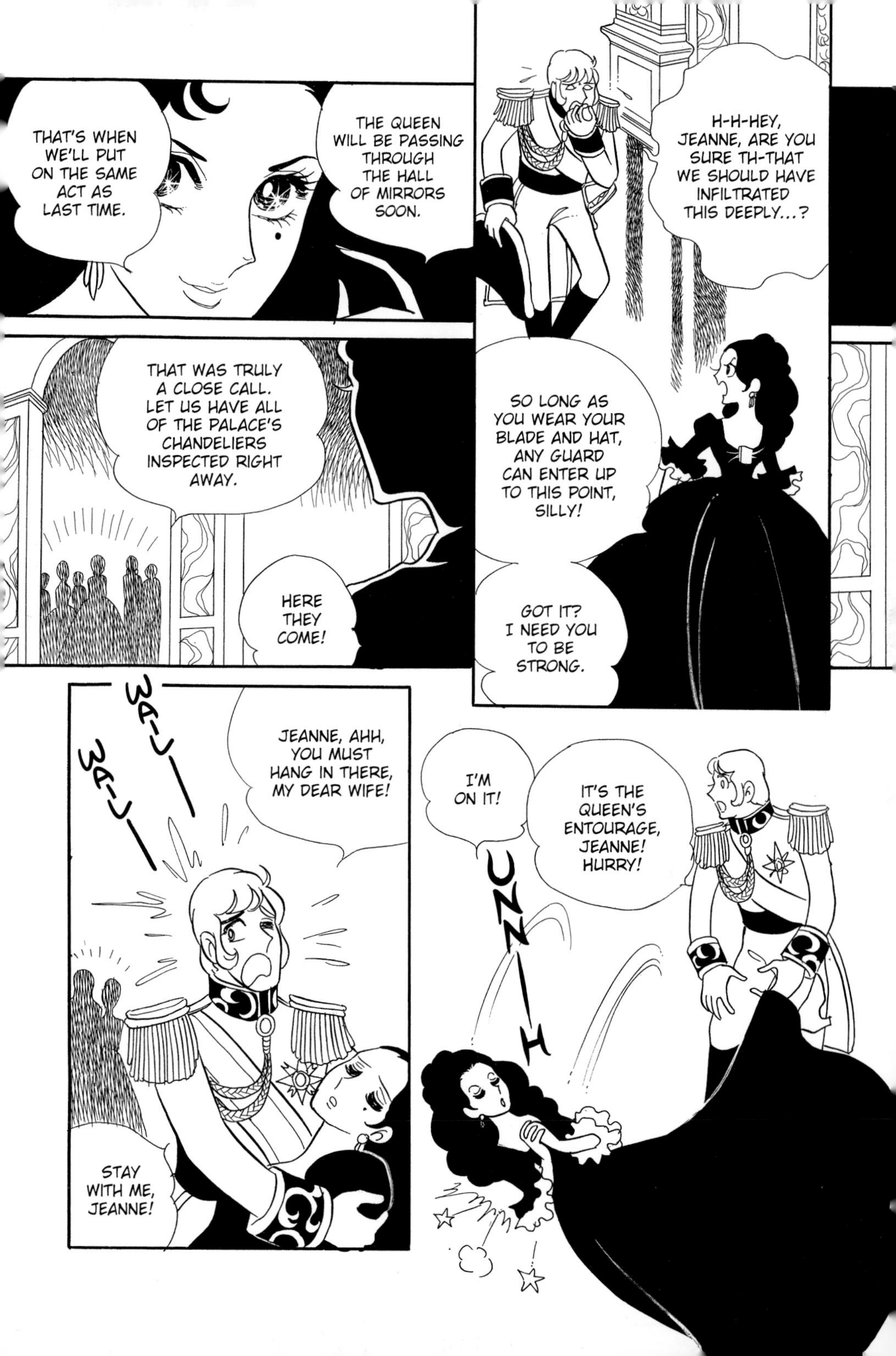

H-H-HEY, JEANNE, ARE YOU SURE TH-THAT WE SHOULD HAVE INFILTRATED THIS DEEPLY...?
SO LONG AS YOU WEAR YOUR BLADE AND HAT, ANY GUARD CAN ENTER UP TO THIS POINT, SILLY!
GOT IT? I NEED YOU TO BE STRONG.
THE QUEEN WILL BE PASSING THROUGH THE HALL OF MIRRORS SOON.
THAT'S WHEN WE'LL PUT ON THE SAME ACT AS LAST TIME.
THAT WAS TRULY A CLOSE CALL. LET US HAVE ALL OF THE PALACE'S CHANDELIERS INSPECTED RIGHT AWAY.
HERE THEY COME!
IT'S THE QUEEN'S ENTOURAGE, JEANNE! HURRY!
I'M ON IT!
UNNN—H
JEANNE, AHH, YOU MUST HANG IN THERE, MY DEAR WIFE!
WA-U—
WA-U—
STAY WITH ME, JEANNE!

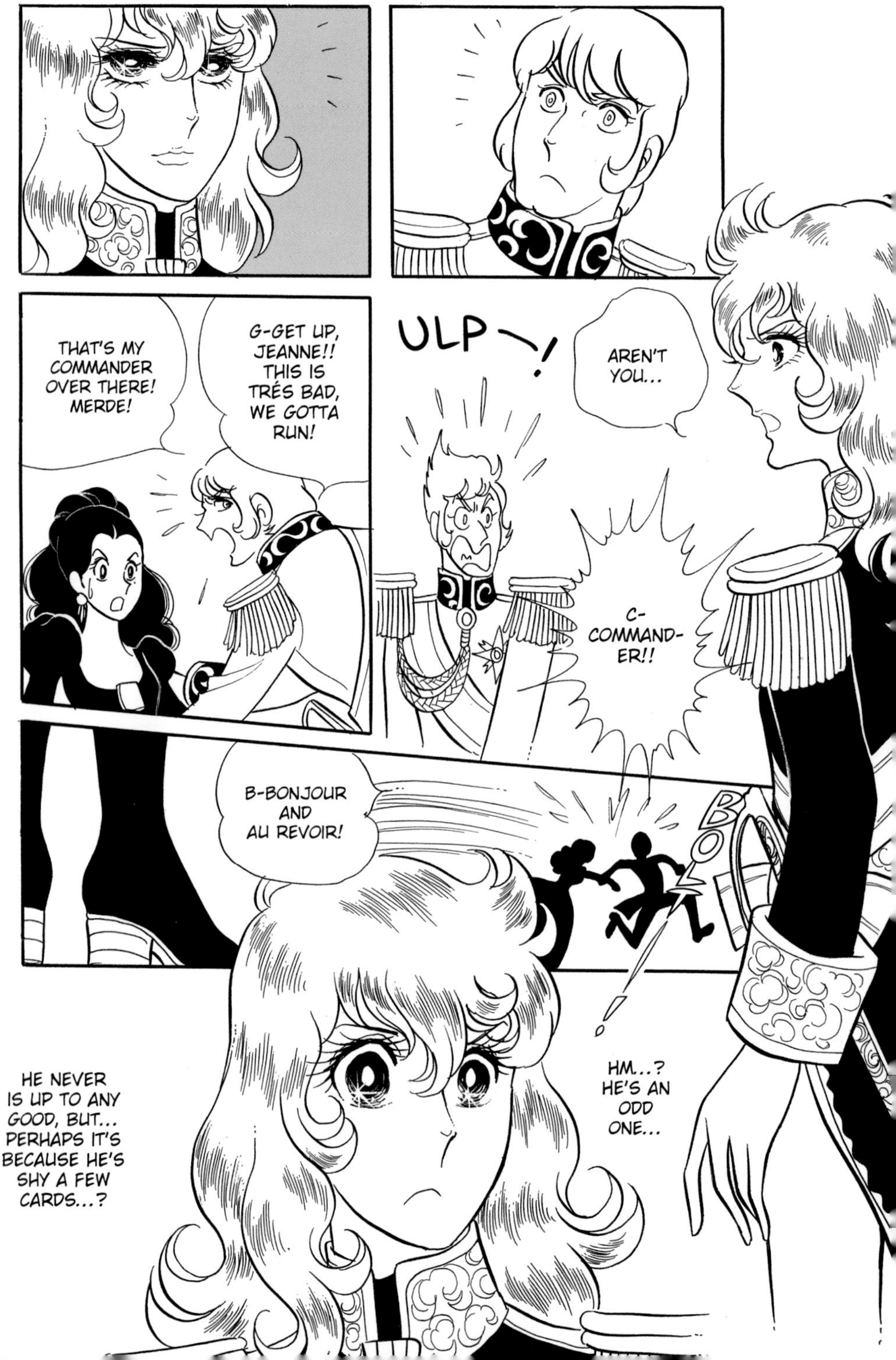
ARENT'T YOU...
ULP!
C-COMMANDER!!
G-GET UP, JEANNE!! THIS IS TRÉS BAD, WE GOTTA RUN!
THAT'S MY COMMANDER OVER THERE! MERDE!
B-BONJOUR AND AU REVOIR!
HM...? HE'S AN ODD ONE...
HE NEVER IS UP TO ANY GOOD, BUT... PERHAPS IT'S BECAUSE HE'S SHY A FEW CARDS...?

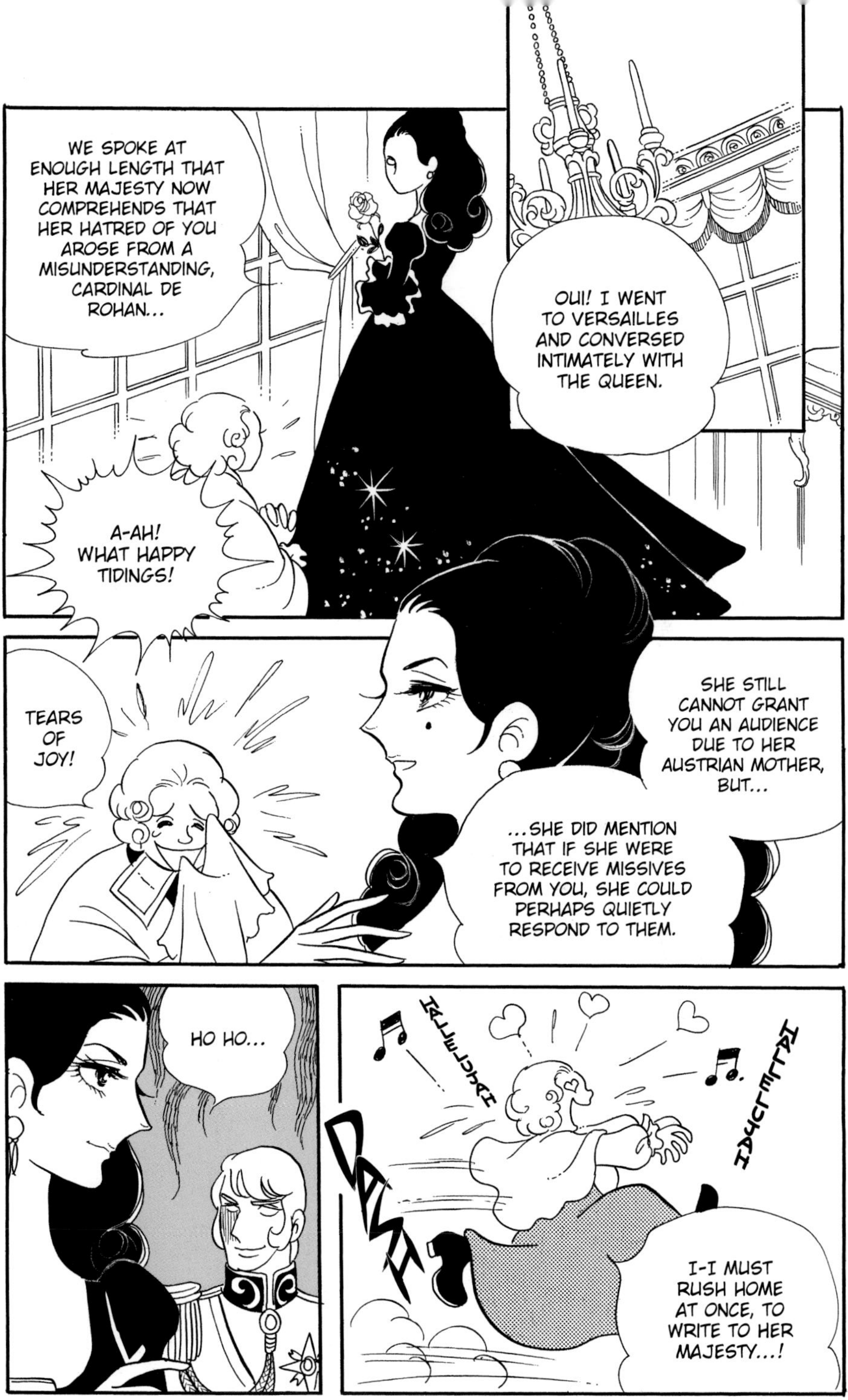
OUI! I WENT TO VERSAILLES AND CONVERSED INTIMATELY WITH THE QUEEN.
WE SPOKE AT ENOUGH LENGTH THAT HER MAJESTY NOW COMPREHENDS THAT HER HATRED OF YOU AROSE FROM A MISUNDERSTANDING, CARDINAL DE ROHAN...
A-AH! WHAT HAPPY TIDINGS!
SHE STILL CANNOT GRANT YOU AN AUDIENCE DUE TO HER AUSTRIAN MOTHER, BUT...
...SHE DID MENTION THAT IF SHE WERE TO RECEIVE MISSIVES FROM YOU, SHE COULD PERHAPS QUIETLY RESPOND TO THEM.
TEARS OF JOY!
HALLELUJAH
HALLELUJAH
DASH
I-I MUST RUSH HOME AT ONCE, TO WRITE TO HER MAJESTY...!
HO HO...

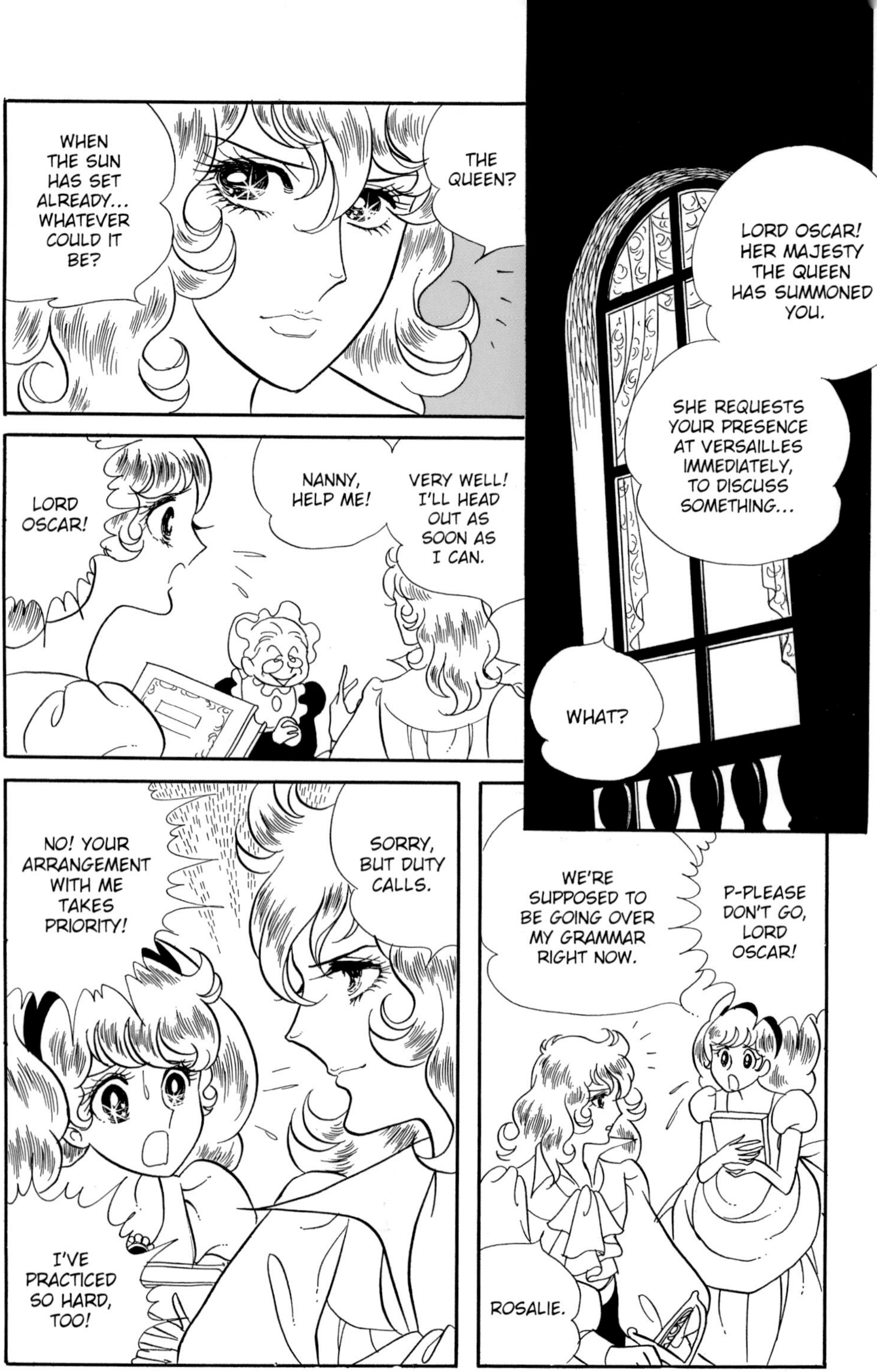
LORD OSCAR! HER MAJESTY THE QUEEN HAS SUMMONED YOU.
SHE REQUESTS YOUR PRESENCE AT VERSAILLES IMMEDIATELY, TO DISCUSS SOMETHING...
WHAT?
THE QUEEN?
WHEN THE SUN HAS SET ALREADY... WHATEVER COULD IT BE?
VERY WELL! I'LL HEAD OUT AS SOON AS I CAN.
NANNY, HELP ME!
LORD OSCAR!
P-PLEASE DON'T GO, LORD OSCAR!
WE'RE SUPPOSED TO BE GOING OVER MY GRAMMAR RIGHT NOW.
ROSALIE.
SORRY, BUT DUTY CALLS.
NO! YOUR ARRANGEMENT WITH ME TAKES PRIORITY!
I'VE PRACTICED SO HARD, TOO!

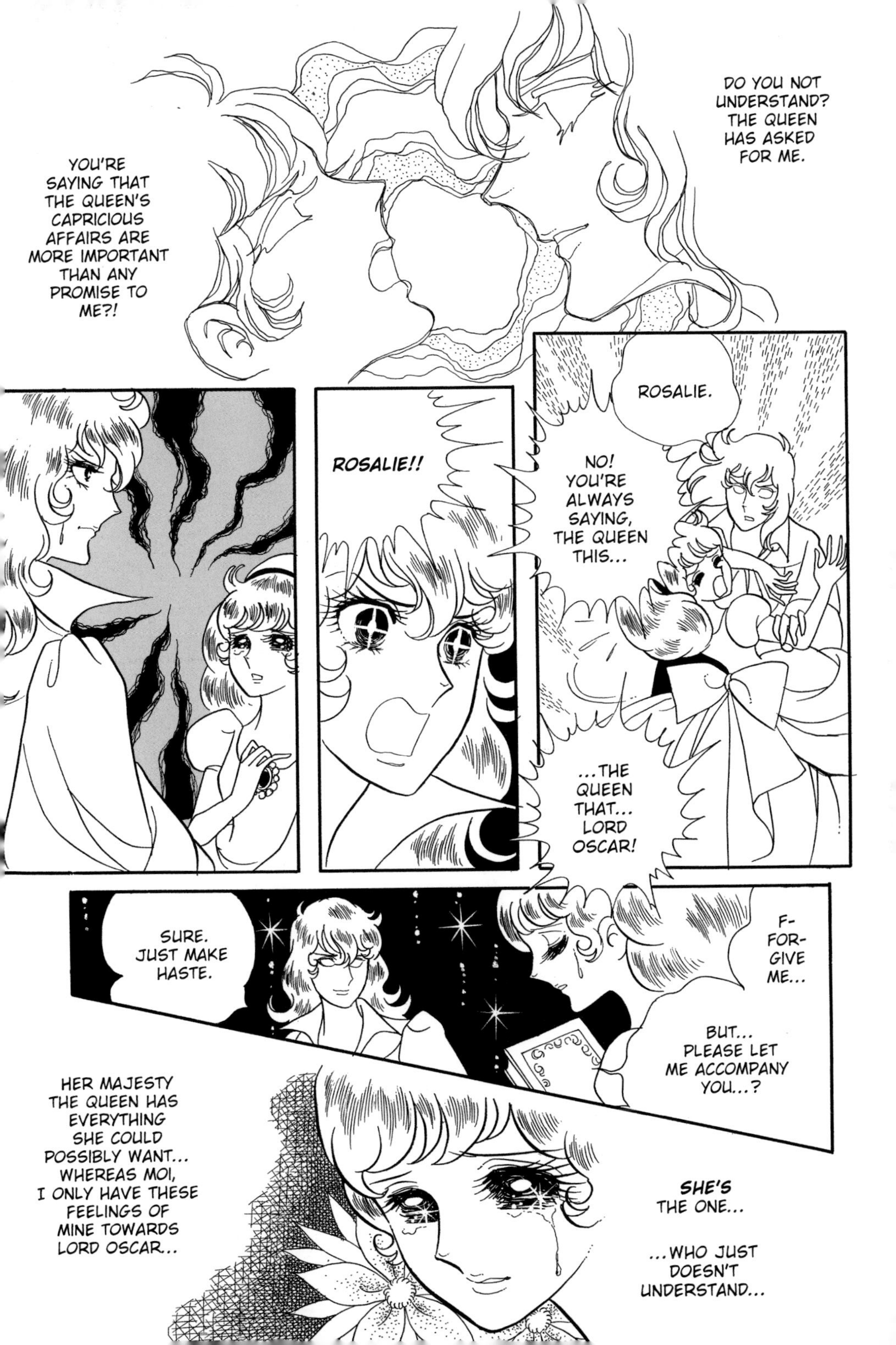
DO YOU NOT UNDERSTAND? THE QUEEN HAS ASKED FOR ME.
YOU'RE SAYING THAT THE QUEEN'S CAPRICIOUS AFFAIRS ARE MORE IMPORTANT THAN ANY PROMISE TO ME?!
ROSALIE.
NO! YOU'RE ALWAYS SAYING, THE QUEEN THIS...
...THE QUEEN THAT... LORD OSCAR!
ROSALIE!!
F-FORGIVE ME...
BUT... PLEASE LET ME ACCOMPANY YOU...?
SURE. JUST MAKE HASTE.
SHE'S THE ONE...
...WHO JUST DOESN'T UNDERSTAND...
HER MAJESTY THE QUEEN HAS EVERYTHING SHE COULD POSSIBLY WANT... WHEREAS MOI, I ONLY HAVE THESE FEELINGS OF MINE TOWARDS LORD OSCAR...

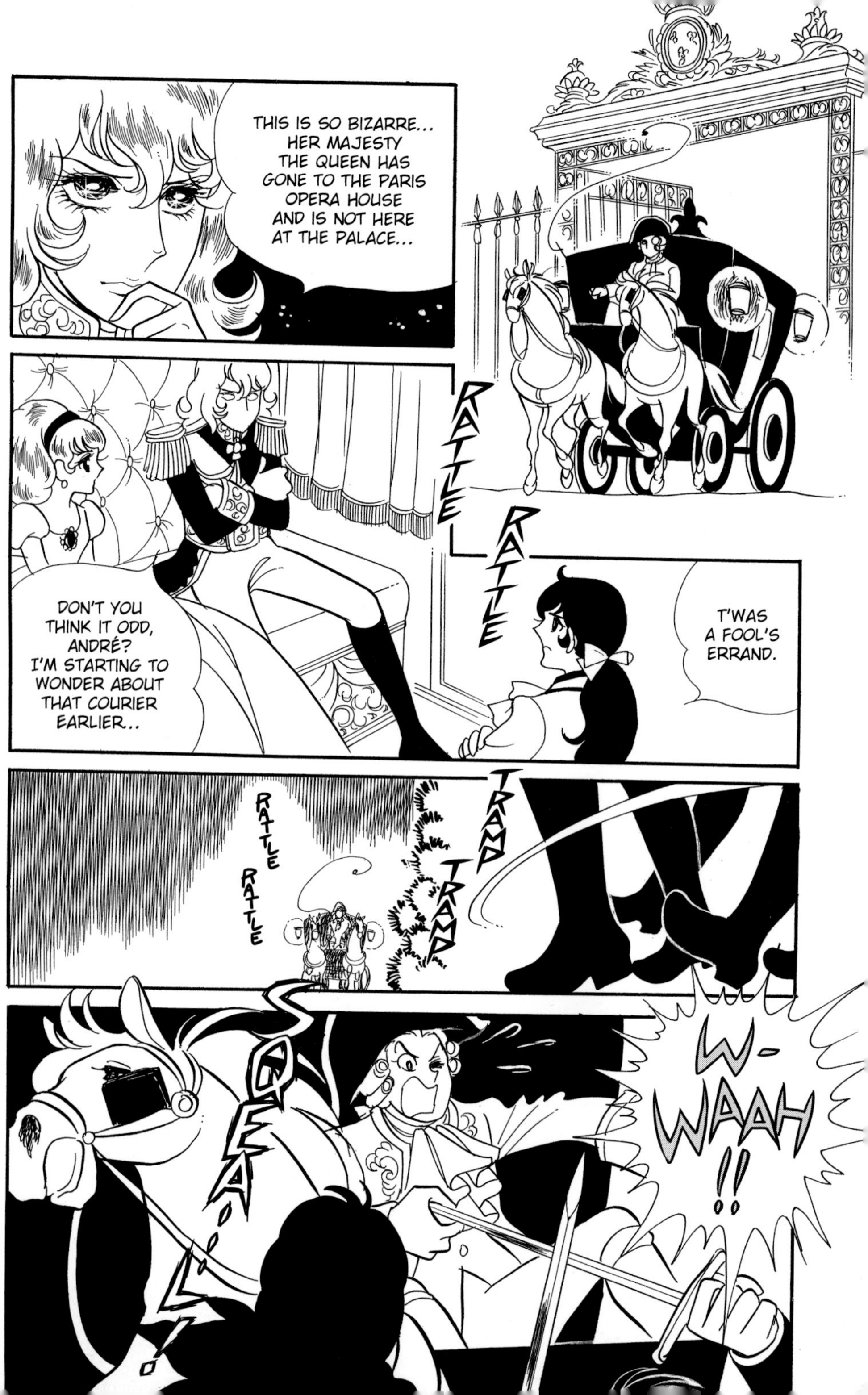
RATTLE
RATTLE
THIS IS SO BIZARRE... HER MAJESTY THE QUEEN HAS GONE TO THE PARIS OPERA HOUSE AND IS NOT HERE AT THE PALACE...
T'WAS A FOOL'S ERRAND.
DON'T YOU THINK IT ODD, ANDRÉ? I'M STARTING TO WONDER ABOUT THAT COURIER EARLIER..
TRAMP
TRAMP
RATTLE
RATTLE
W-WAAH!!
SQUEAL..!

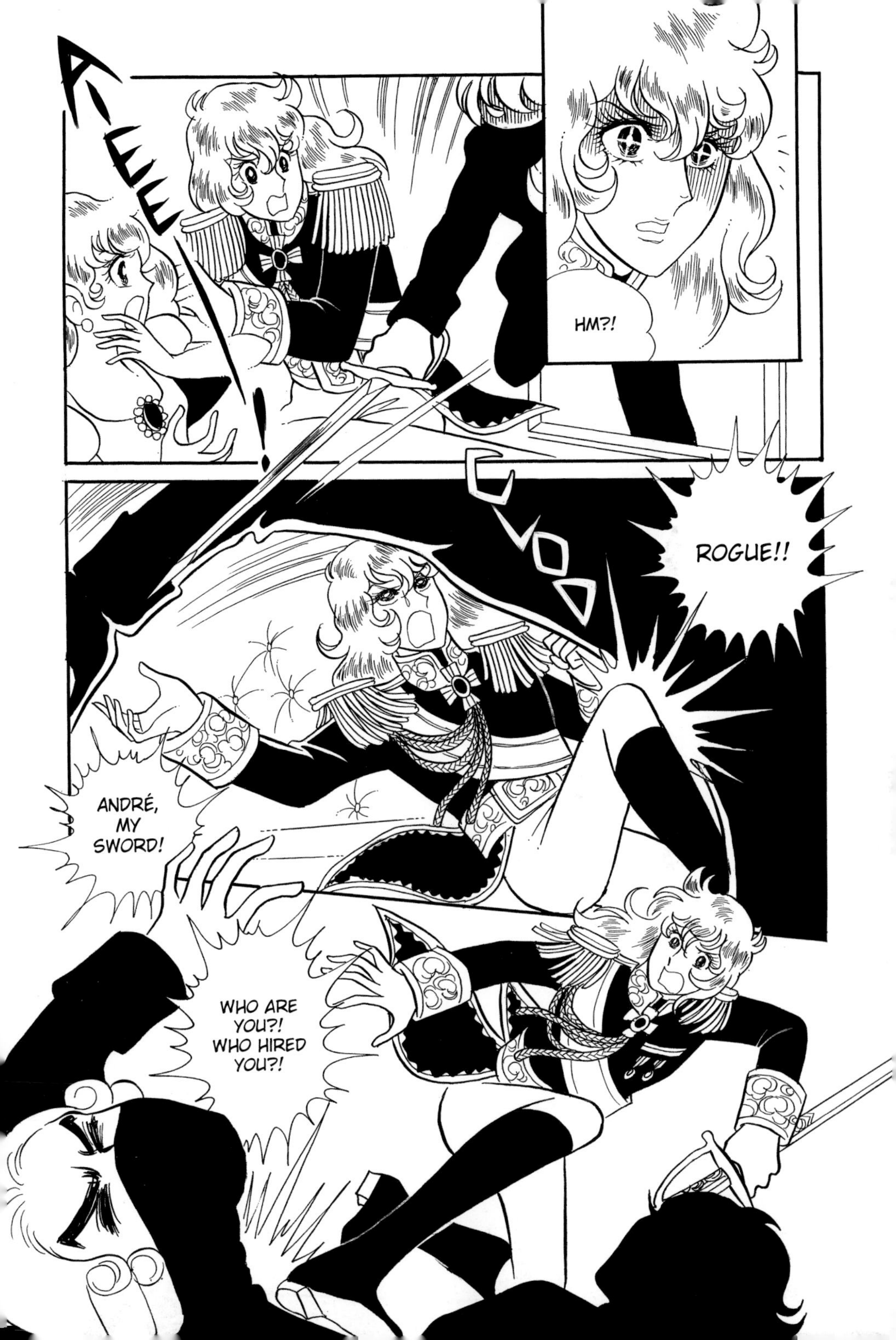
HM?!
AIEEE!
ROGUE!!
ANDRÉ, MY SWORD!
WHO ARE YOU?! WHO HIRED YOU?!

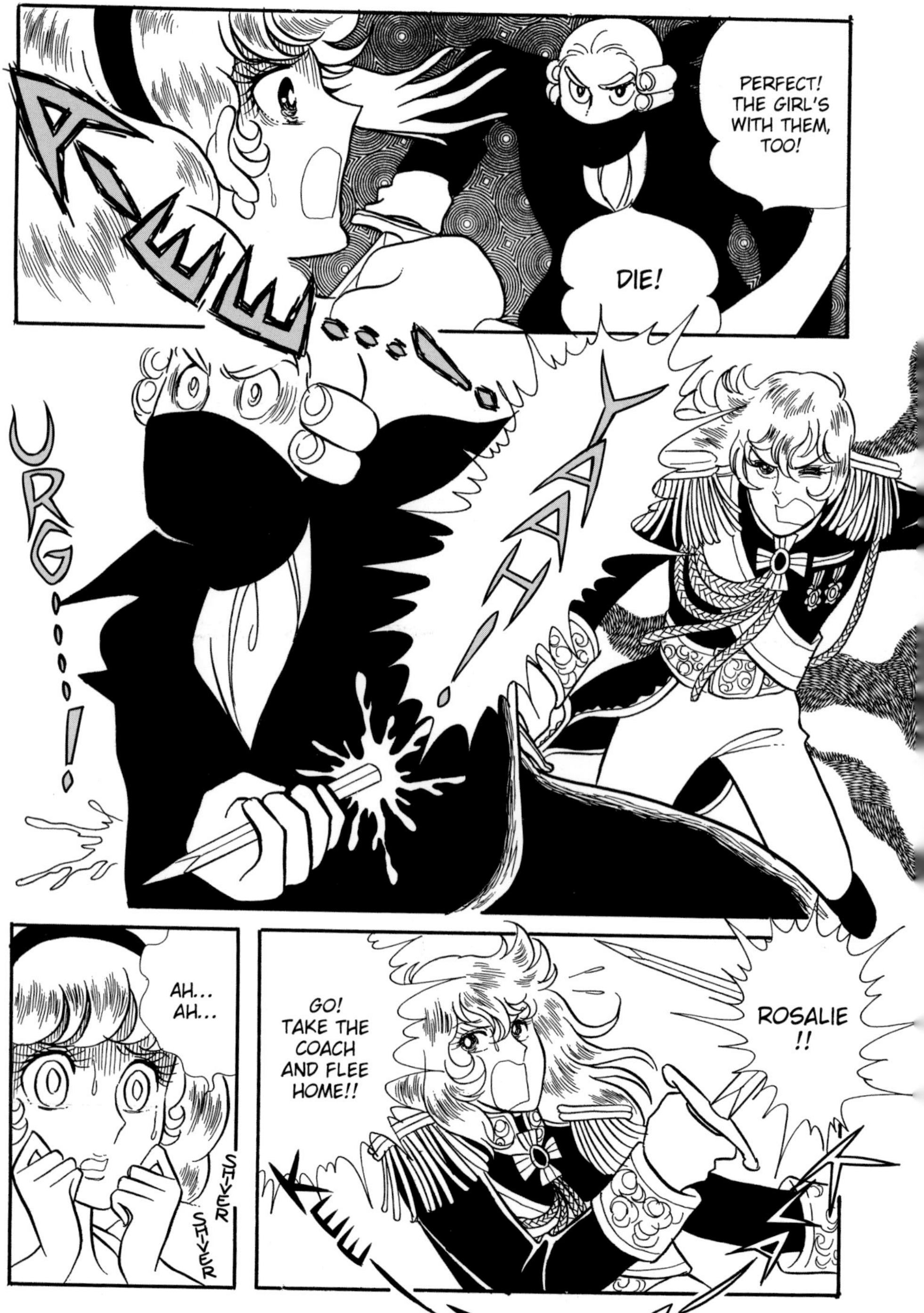
PERFECT! THE GIRL'S WITH THEM, TOO!
DIE!
HAAY!!
URG...!
ROSALIE !!
GO! TAKE THE COACH AND FLEE HOME!!
AH... AH...
SHIVER
SHIVER

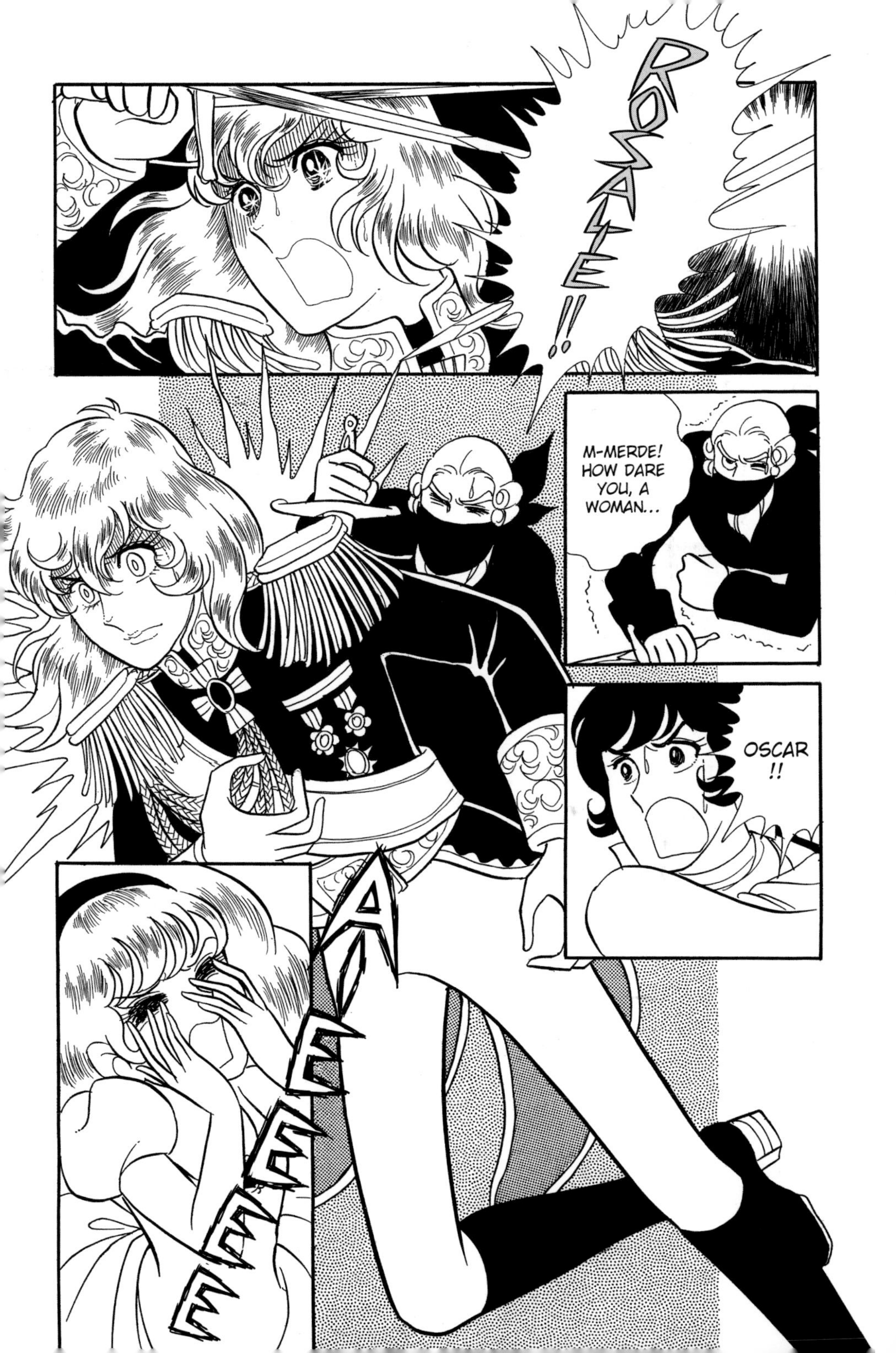
ROSALIE!!
M-MERDE! HOW DARE YOU, A WOMAN...
OSCAR!!
AEEEE

the ROSE of VERSAILLES
ベルサイユのばら

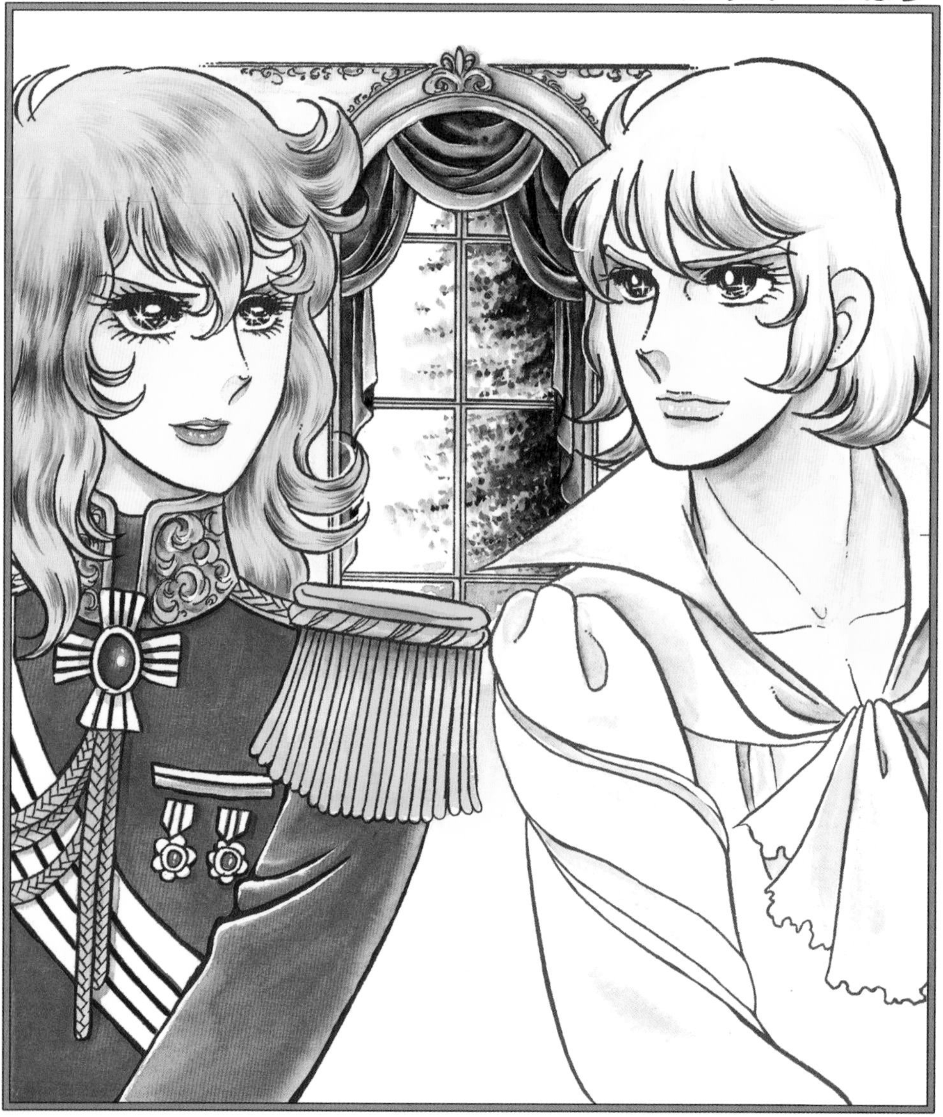

1972 WEEKLY MARGARET MAGAZINE ISSUE 41 COVER PAGE
(SPECIAL COLORIZED VERSION)

♥ HUGELY POPULAR!! A HUGE SENSATION!!

◆ WHAT OF OSCAR, WHO WAS LURED OUTSIDE AT NIGHT AND CUT DOWN FROM BEHIND!?

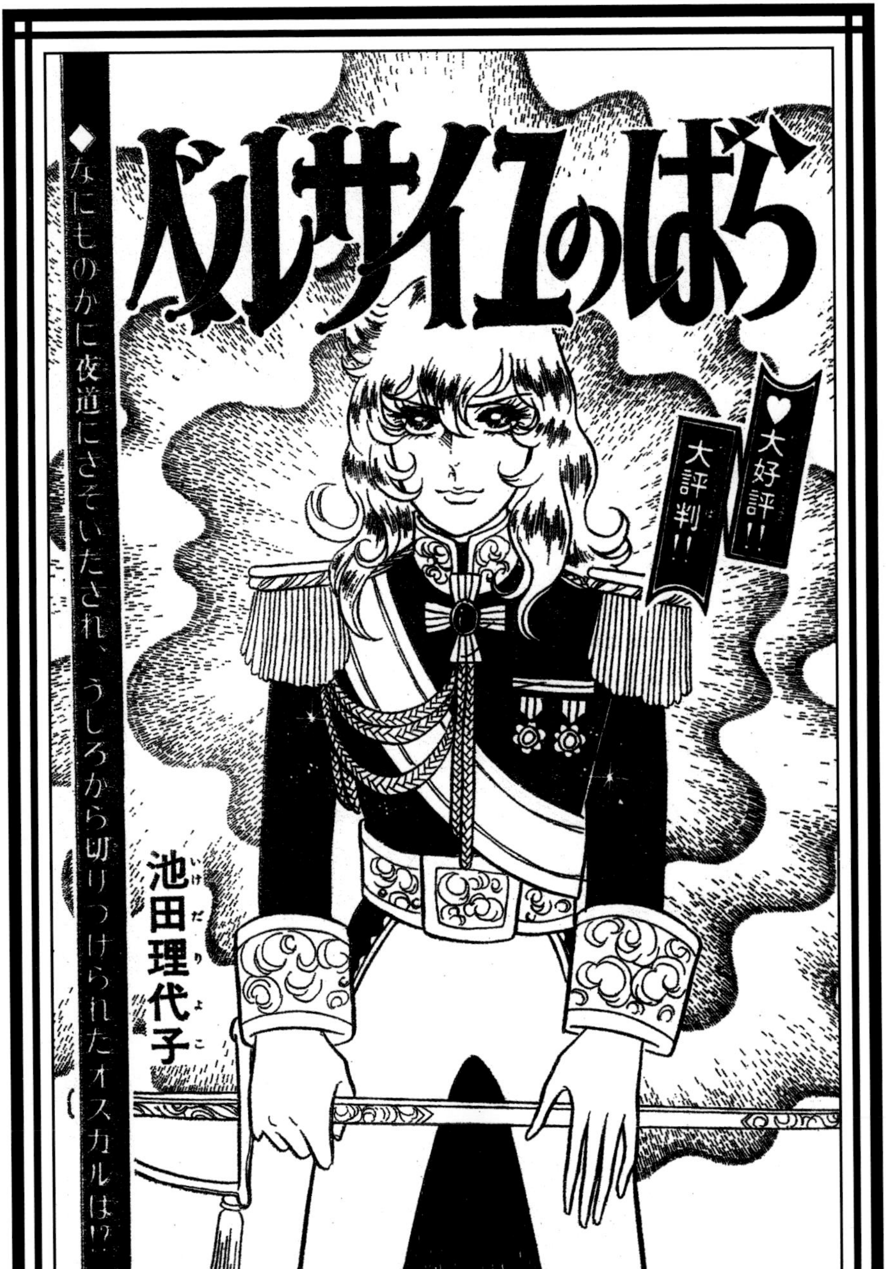
ベルサイユのばら
♥大好評!!
大評判!!
◆なにものかに夜道にさそいたされ、うしろから切りつけられたオスカルは!?
池田理代子

EPISODE 22

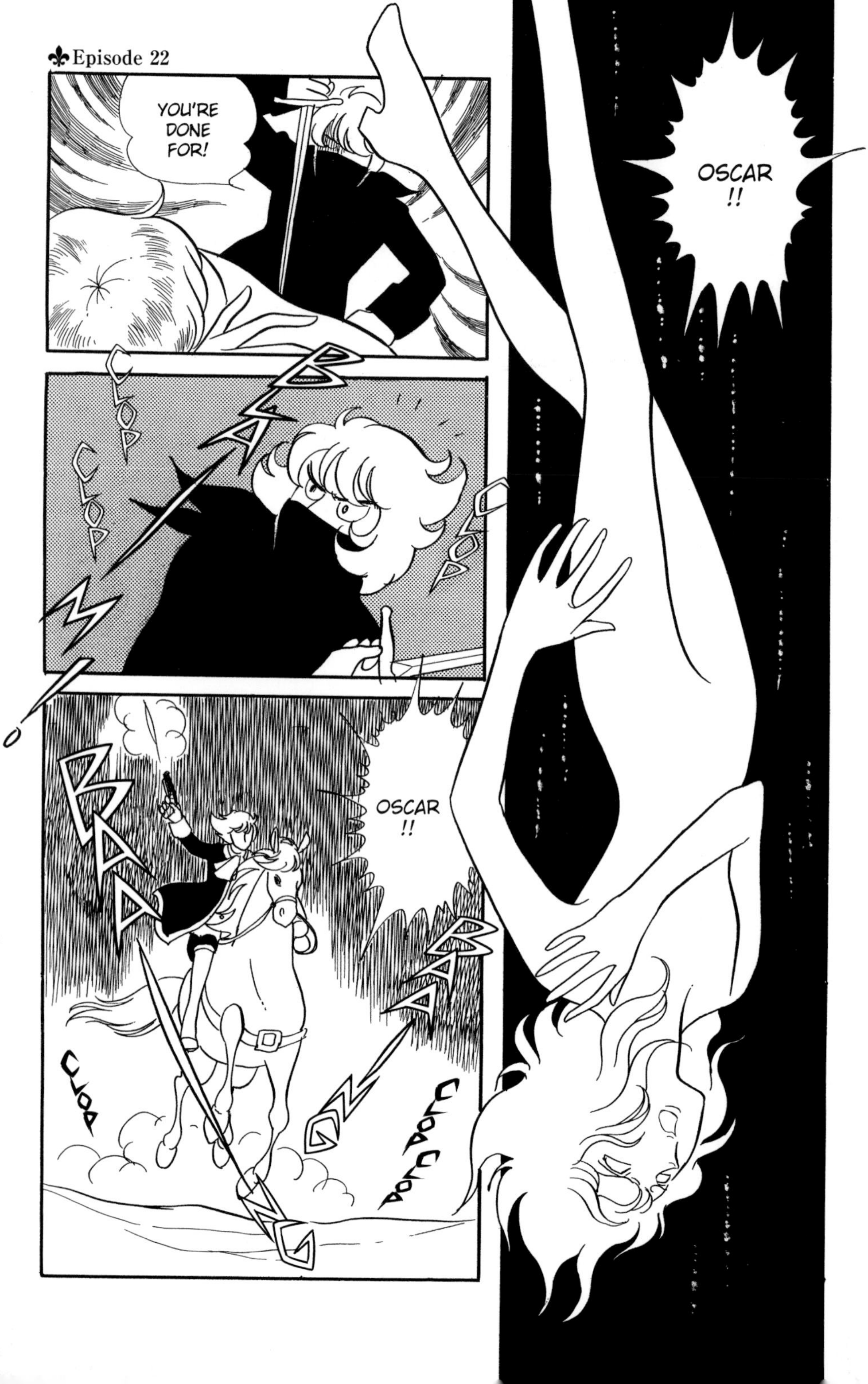
OSCAR !!
YOU'RE DONE FOR!
BLAM!!
CLOP
CLOP
CLOP
OSCAR !!
CLOP
CLOP CLOP

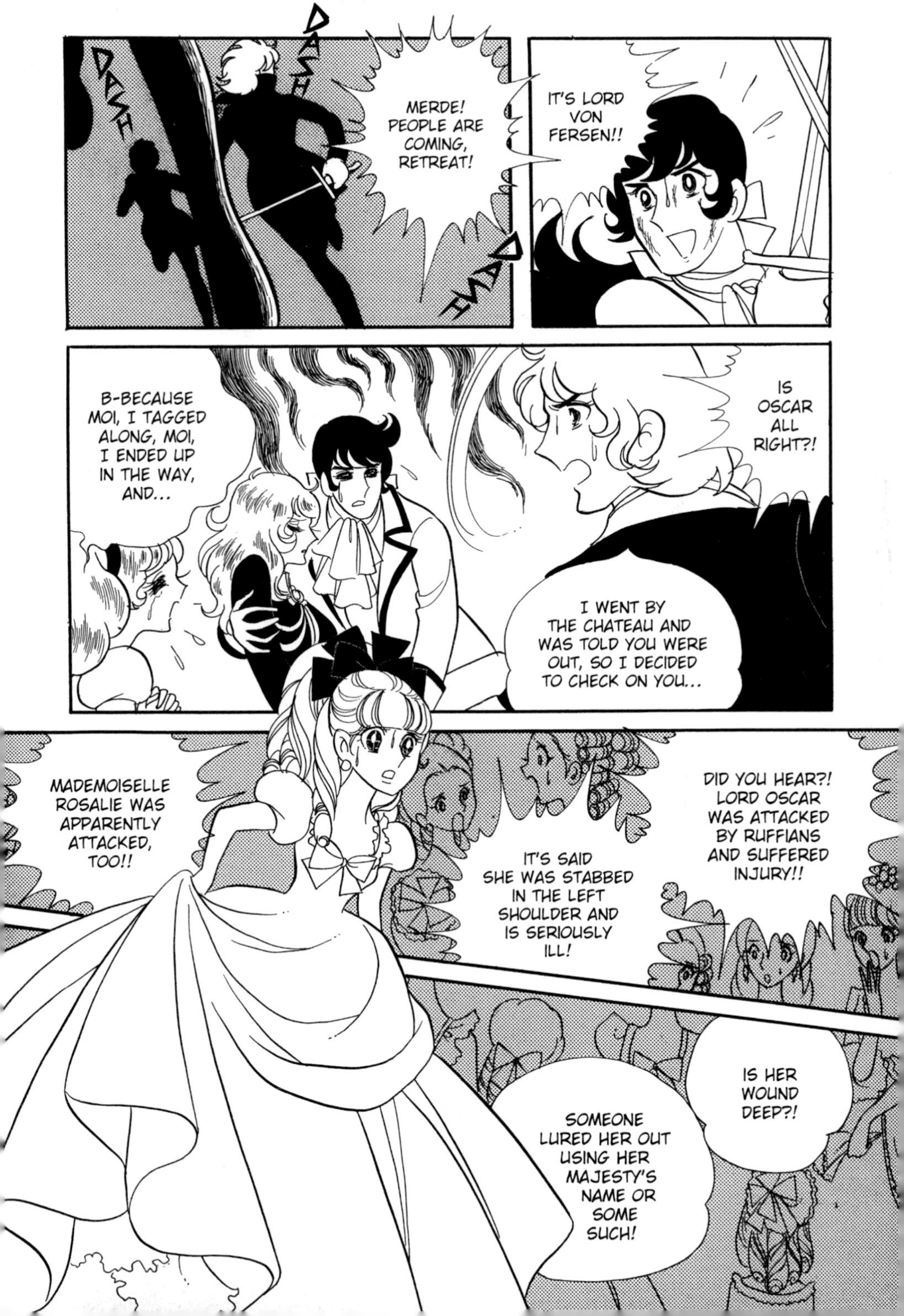
IT'S LORD VON FERSEN!!
DASH
MERDE! PEOPLE ARE COMING, RETREAT!
DASH
DASH
IS OSCAR ALL RIGHT?!
I WENT BY THE CHATEAU AND WAS TOLD YOU WERE OUT, SO I DECIDED TO CHECK ON YOU...
B-BECAUSE MOI, I TAGGED ALONG, MOI, I ENDED UP IN THE WAY, AND...
DID YOU HEAR?! LORD OSCAR WAS ATTACKED BY RUFFIANS AND SUFFERED INJURY!!
IT'S SAID SHE WAS STABBED IN THE LEFT SHOULDER AND IS SERIOUSLY ILL!
MADEMOISELLE ROSALIE WAS APPARENTLY ATTACKED, TOO!!
IS HER WOUND DEEP?!
SOMEONE LURED HER OUT USING HER MAJESTY'S NAME OR SOME SUCH!

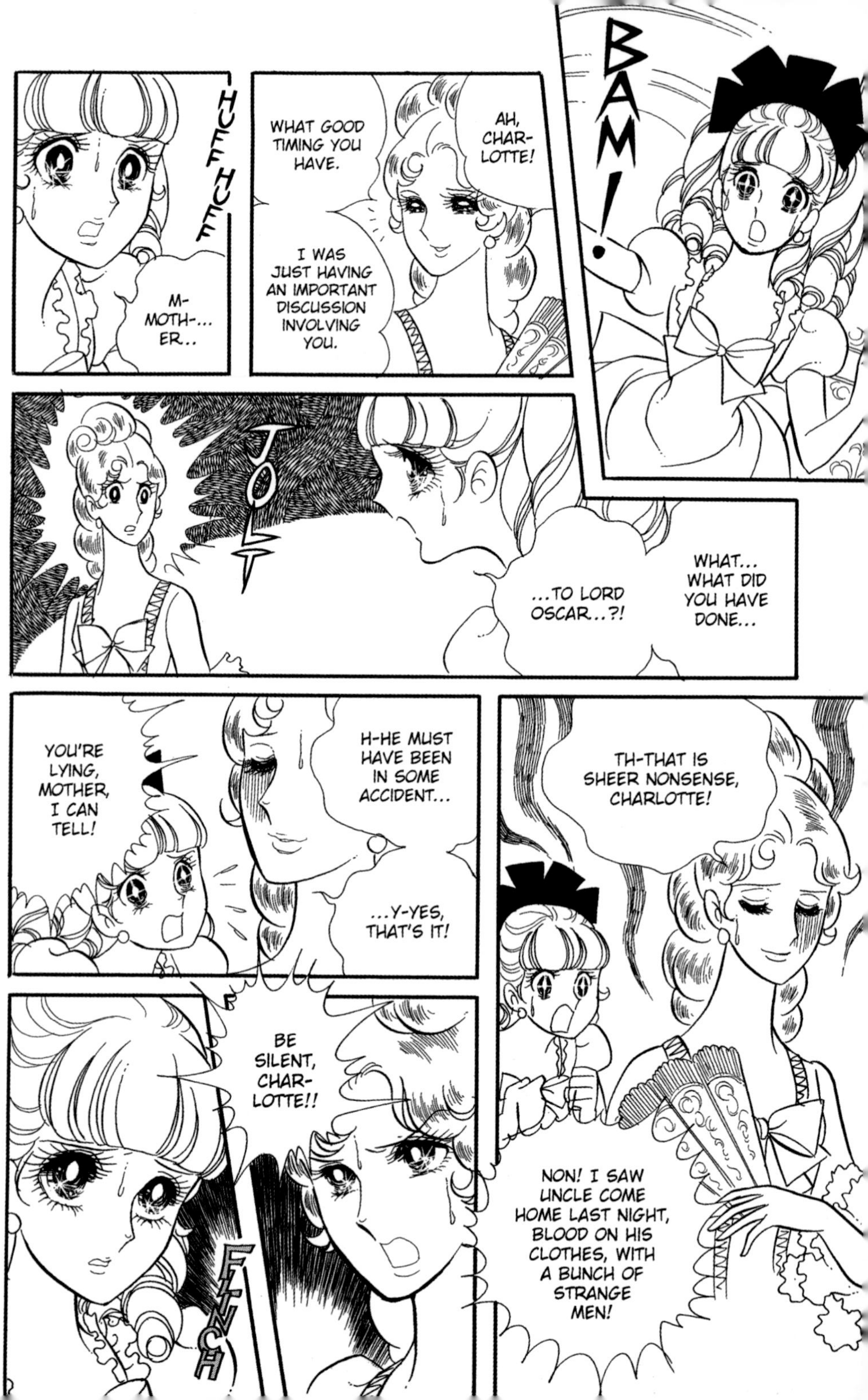
BAM!
AH, CHAR-LOTTE!
WHAT GOOD TIMING YOU HAVE.
I WAS JUST HAVING AN IMPORTANT DISCUSSION INVOLVING YOU.
HUFF HUFF
M-MOTH-... ER...
JOLT
WHAT... WHAT DID YOU HAVE DONE...
...TO LORD OSCAR...?!
TH-THAT IS SHEER NONSENSE, CHARLOTTE!
NON! I SAW UNCLE COME HOME LAST NIGHT, BLOOD ON HIS CLOTHES, WITH A BUNCH OF STRANGE MEN!
H-HE MUST HAVE BEEN IN SOME ACCIDENT...
...Y-YES, THAT'S IT!
YOU'RE LYING, MOTHER, I CAN TELL!
BE SILENT, CHAR-LOTTE!!
FLINCH

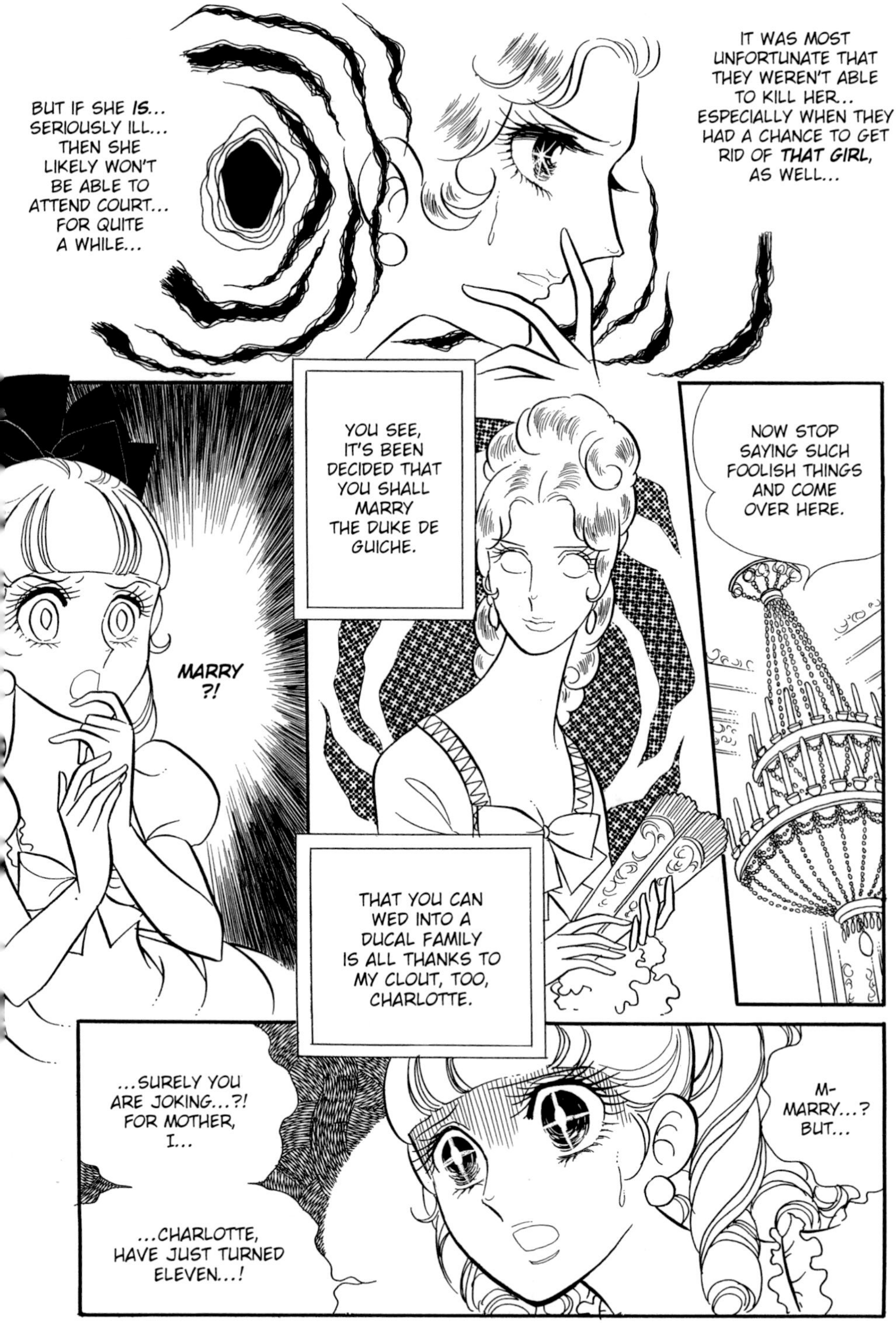
IT WAS MOST UNFORTUNATE THAT THEY WEREN'T ABLE TO KILL HER... ESPECIALLY WHEN THEY HAD A CHANCE TO GET RID OF ***THAT GIRL***, AS WELL...
BUT IF SHE ***IS***... SERIOUSLY ILL... THEN SHE LIKELY WON'T BE ABLE TO ATTEND COURT... FOR QUITE A WHILE...
NOW STOP SAYING SUCH FOOLISH THINGS AND COME OVER HERE.
YOU SEE, IT'S BEEN DECIDED THAT YOU SHALL MARRY THE DUKE DE GUICHE.
THAT YOU CAN WED INTO A DUCAL FAMILY IS ALL THANKS TO MY CLOUT, TOO, CHARLOTTE.
MARRY?!
M-MARRY...? BUT...
...SURELY YOU ARE JOKING...?! FOR MOTHER, I...
...CHARLOTTE, HAVE JUST TURNED ELEVEN...!

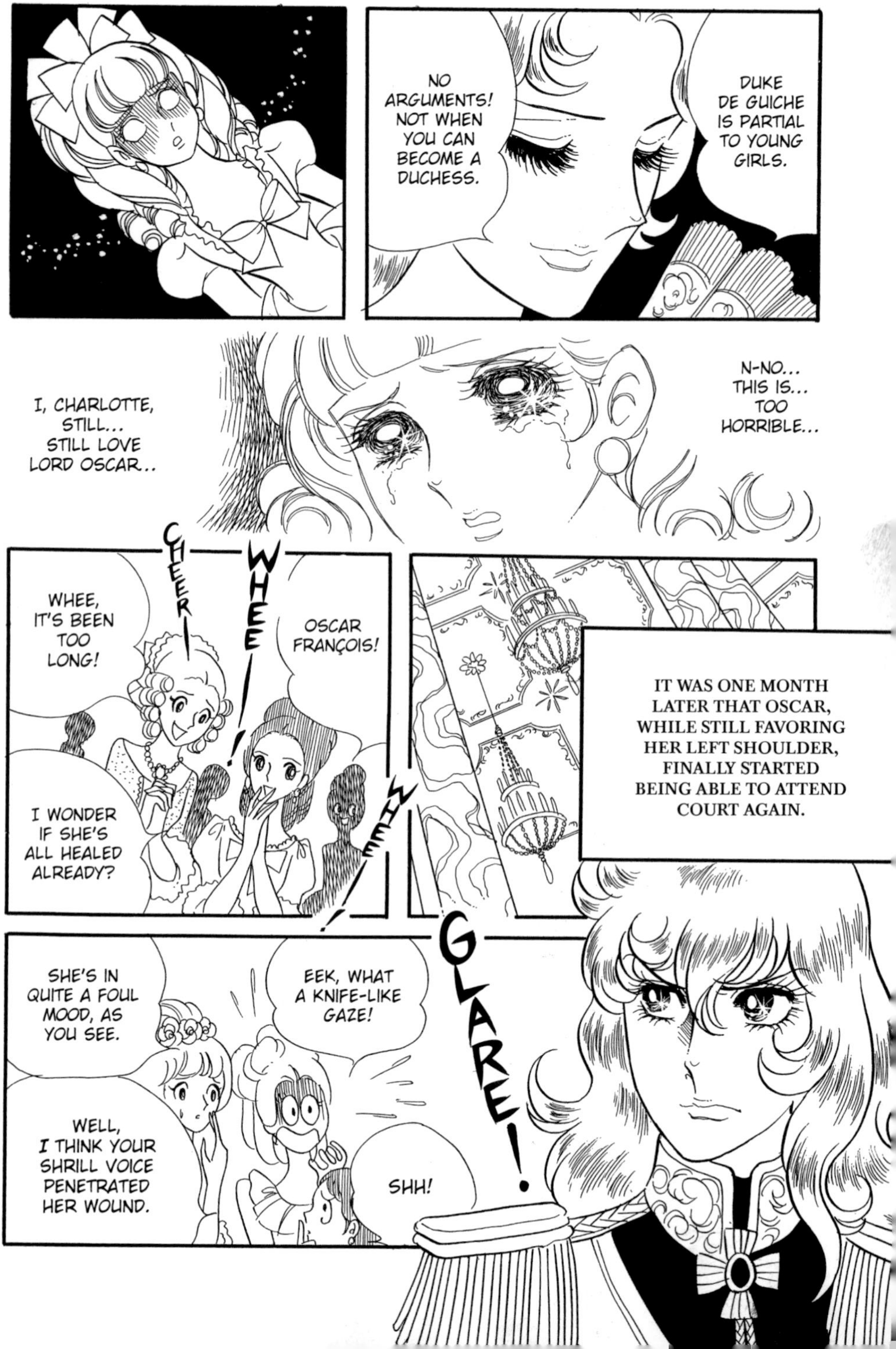
DUKE DE GUICHE IS PARTIAL TO YOUNG GIRLS.
NO ARGUMENTS! NOT WHEN YOU CAN BECOME A DUCHESS.
N-NO... THIS IS... TOO HORRIBLE...
I, CHARLOTTE, STILL... STILL LOVE LORD OSCAR...
IT WAS ONE MONTH LATER THAT OSCAR, WHILE STILL FAVORING HER LEFT SHOULDER, FINALLY STARTED BEING ABLE TO ATTEND COURT AGAIN.
OSCAR FRANÇOIS!
WHEE!
CHEER!
WHEE, IT'S BEEN TOO LONG!
I WONDER IF SHE'S ALL HEALED ALREADY?
WHEE!
GLARE!
EEK, WHAT A KNIFE-LIKE GAZE!
SHE'S IN QUITE A FOUL MOOD, AS YOU SEE.
SHH!
WELL, I THINK YOUR SHRILL VOICE PENETRATED HER WOUND.

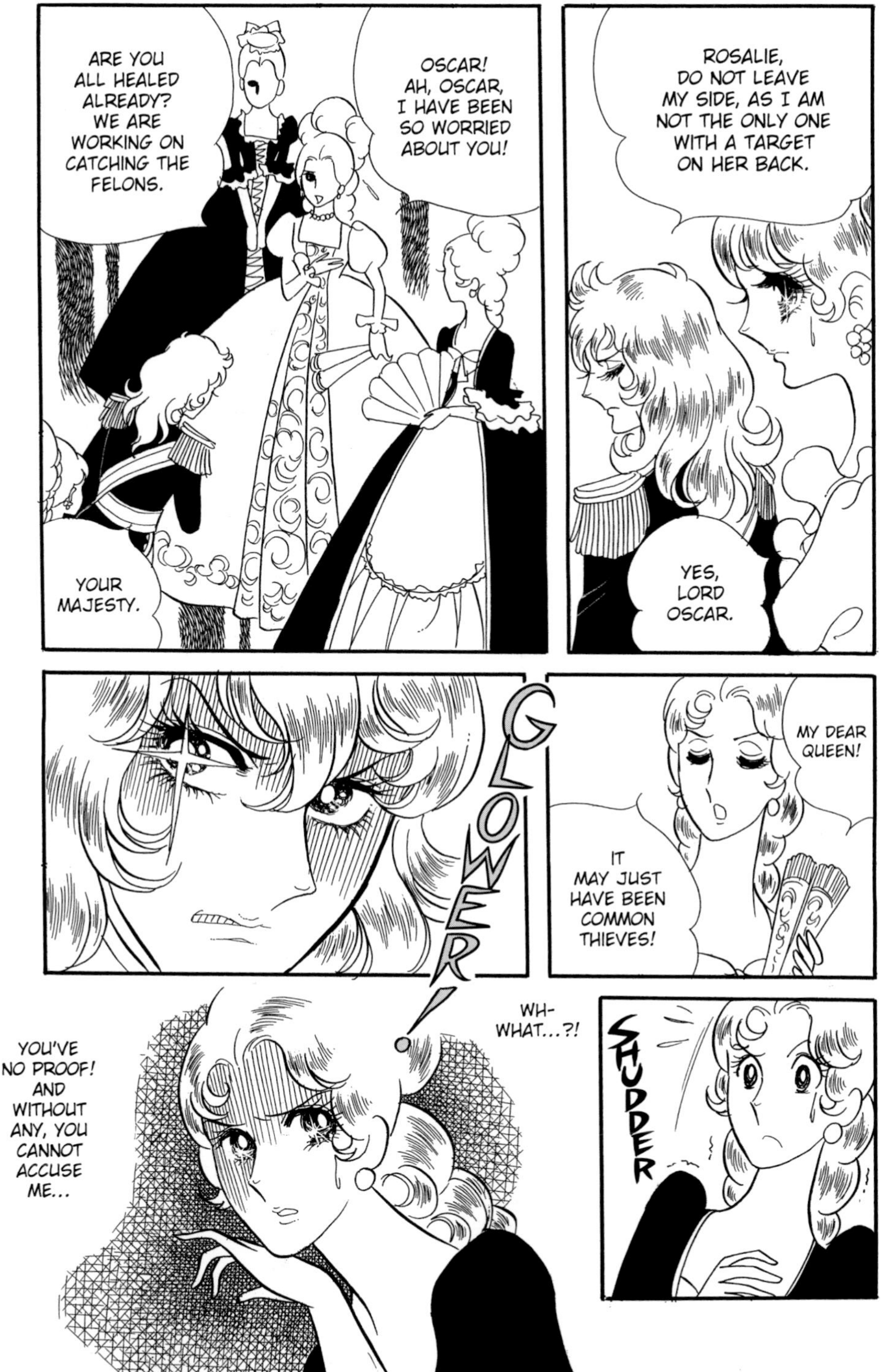
ROSALIE, DO NOT LEAVE MY SIDE, AS I AM NOT THE ONLY ONE WITH A TARGET ON HER BACK.
YES, LORD OSCAR.
OSCAR! AH, OSCAR, I HAVE BEEN SO WORRIED ABOUT YOU!
ARE YOU ALL HEALED ALREADY? WE ARE WORKING ON CATCHING THE FELONS.
YOUR MAJESTY.
MY DEAR QUEEN!
IT MAY JUST HAVE BEEN COMMON THIEVES!
GLOWER!
SHUDDER
WH- WHAT...?!
YOU'VE NO PROOF! AND WITHOUT ANY, YOU CANNOT ACCUSE ME...

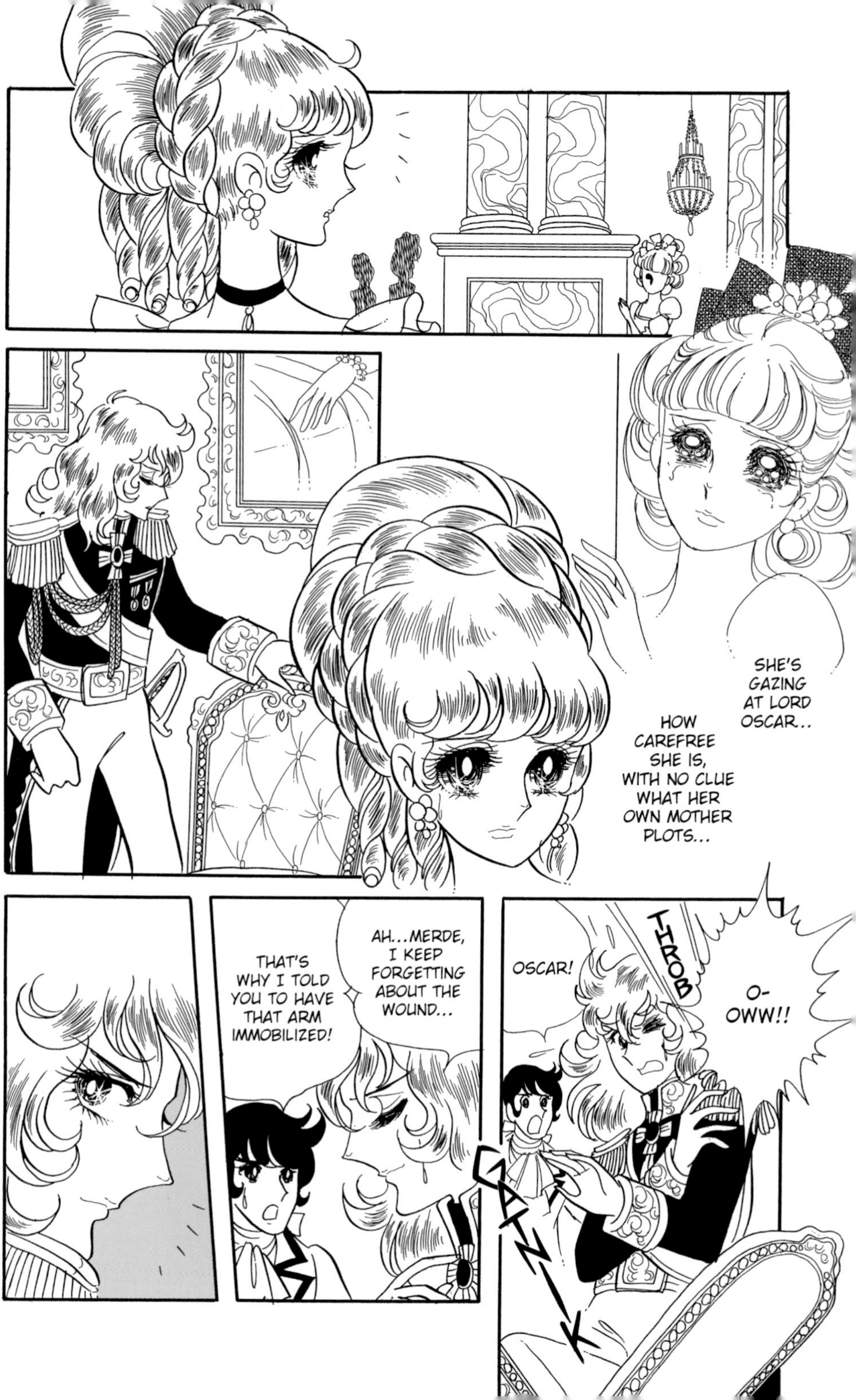
SHE'S GAZING AT LORD OSCAR...
HOW CAREFREE SHE IS, WITH NO CLUE WHAT HER OWN MOTHER PLOTS...
THROB
O-OWW!!
OSCAR!
AH...MERDE, I KEEP FORGETTING ABOUT THE WOUND...
THAT'S WHY I TOLD YOU TO HAVE THAT ARM IMMOBILIZED!

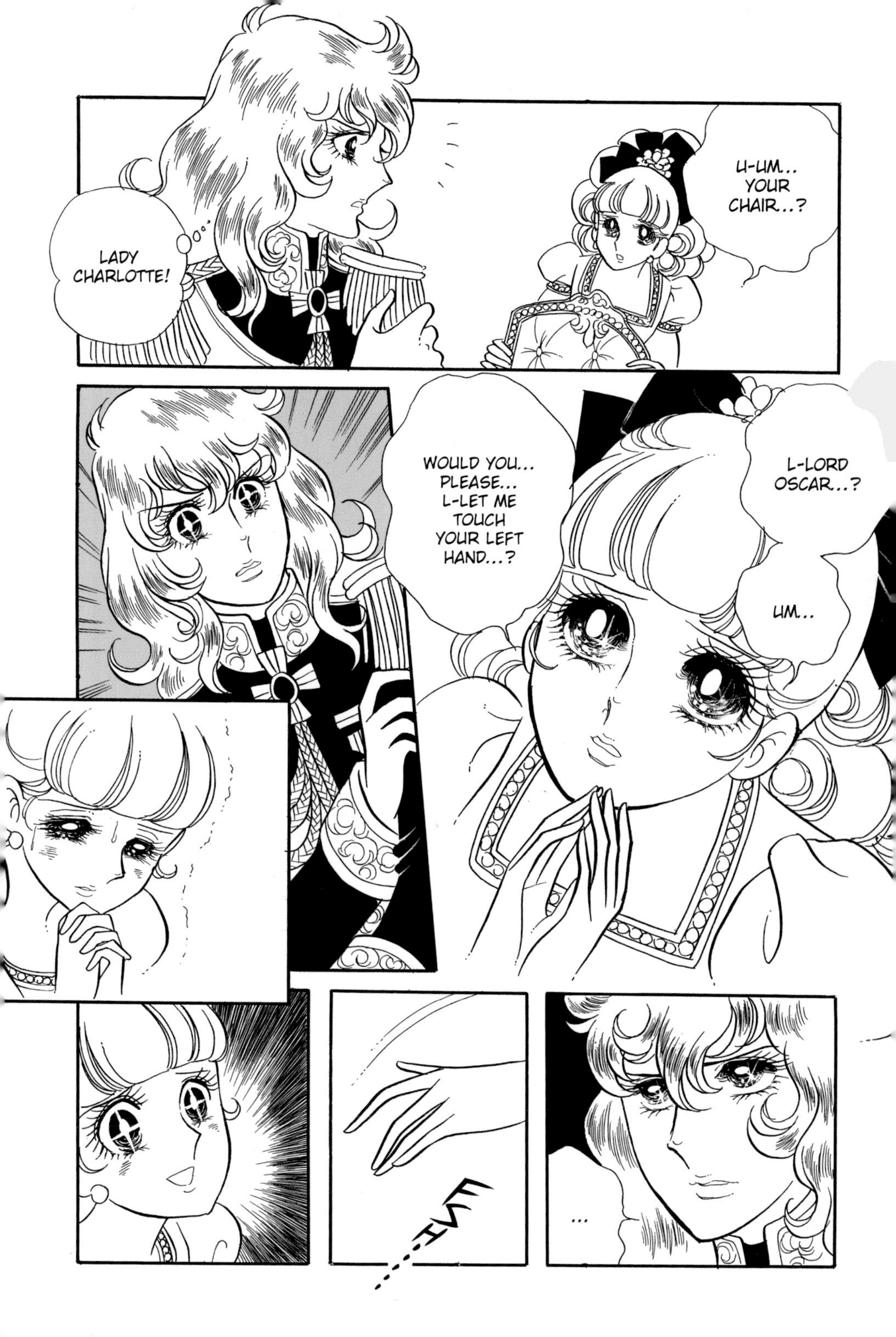
U-UM.. YOUR CHAIR..?
LADY CHARLOTTE!
L-LORD OSCAR...?
UM...
WOULD YOU... PLEASE... L-LET ME TOUCH YOUR LEFT HAND...?
...

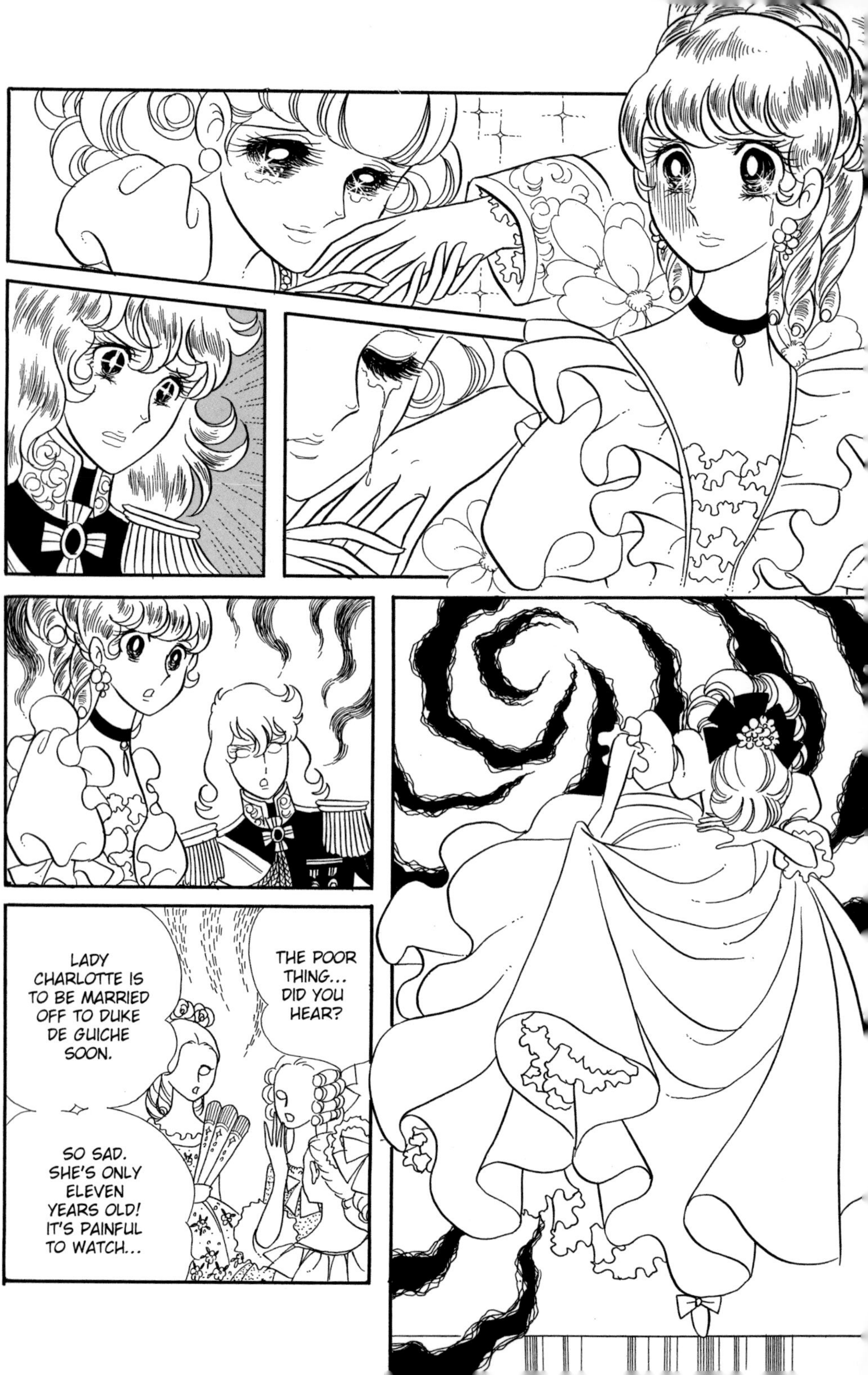
THE POOR THING... DID YOU HEAR?
LADY CHARLOTTE IS TO BE MARRIED OFF TO DUKE DE GUICHE SOON.
SO SAD. SHE'S ONLY ELEVEN YEARS OLD! IT'S PAINFUL TO WATCH...

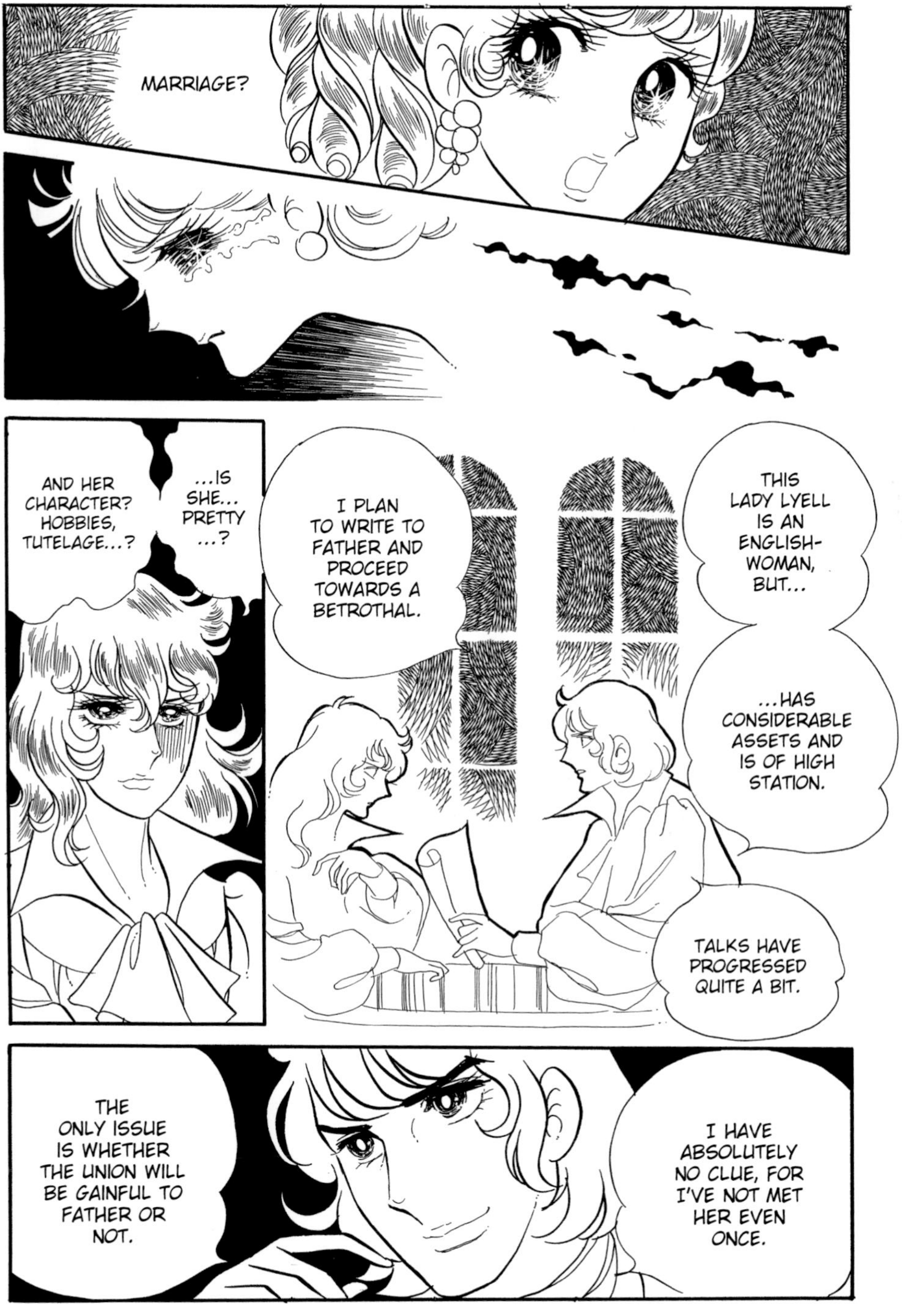
MARRIAGE?
THIS LADY LYELL IS AN ENGLISH-WOMAN, BUT...
...HAS CONSIDERABLE ASSETS AND IS OF HIGH STATION.
TALKS HAVE PROGRESSED QUITE A BIT.
I PLAN TO WRITE TO FATHER AND PROCEED TOWARDS A BETROTHAL.
...IS SHE... PRETTY ...?
AND HER CHARACTER? HOBBIES, TUTELAGE...?
I HAVE ABSOLUTELY NO CLUE, FOR I'VE NOT MET HER EVEN ONCE.
THE ONLY ISSUE IS WHETHER THE UNION WILL BE GAINFUL TO FATHER OR NOT.

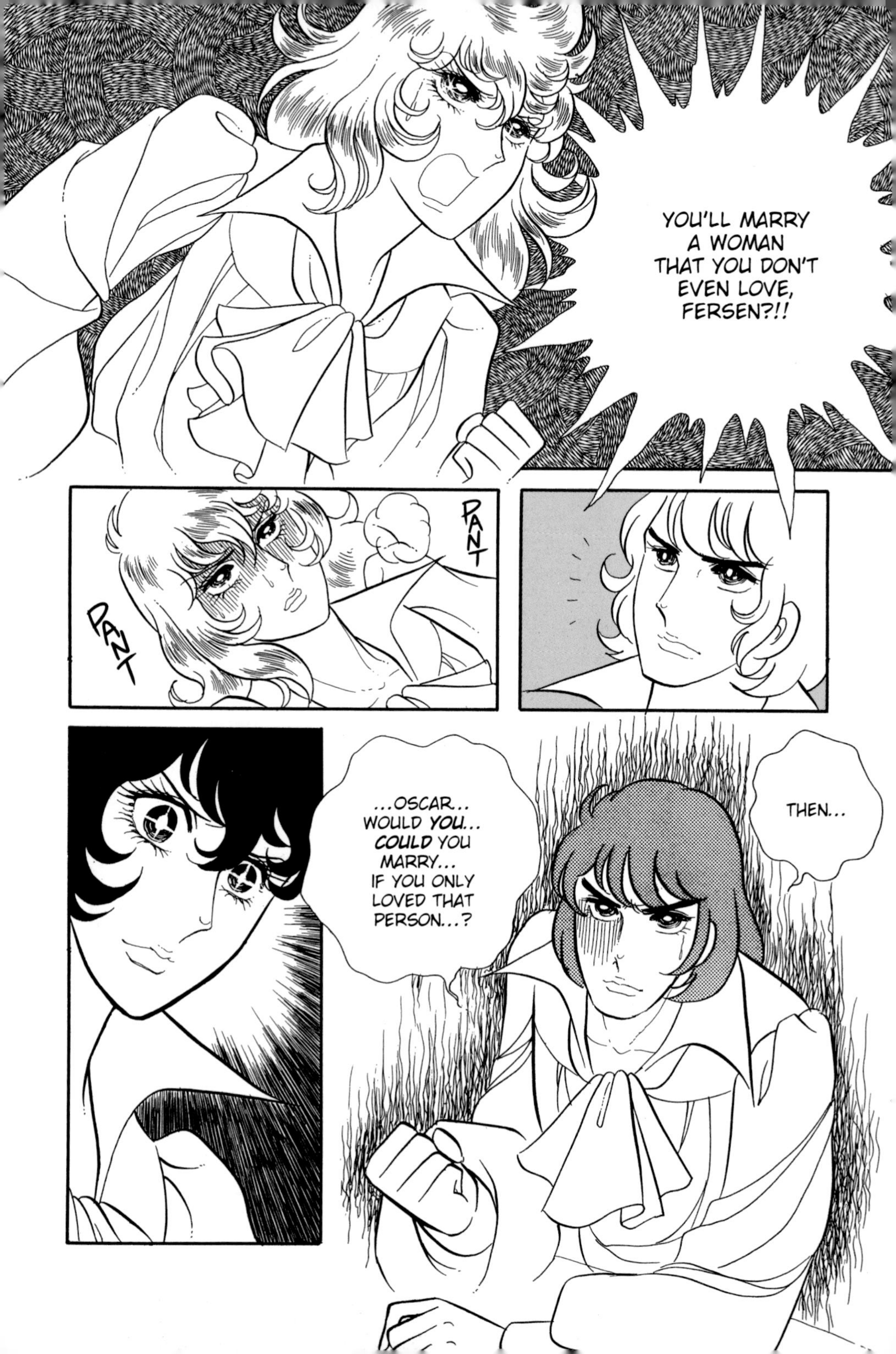
YOU'LL MARRY A WOMAN THAT YOU DON'T EVEN LOVE, FERSEN?!!
PANT
PANT
THEN...
...OSCAR... WOULD **YOU**... **COULD** YOU MARRY... IF YOU ONLY LOVED THAT PERSON...?

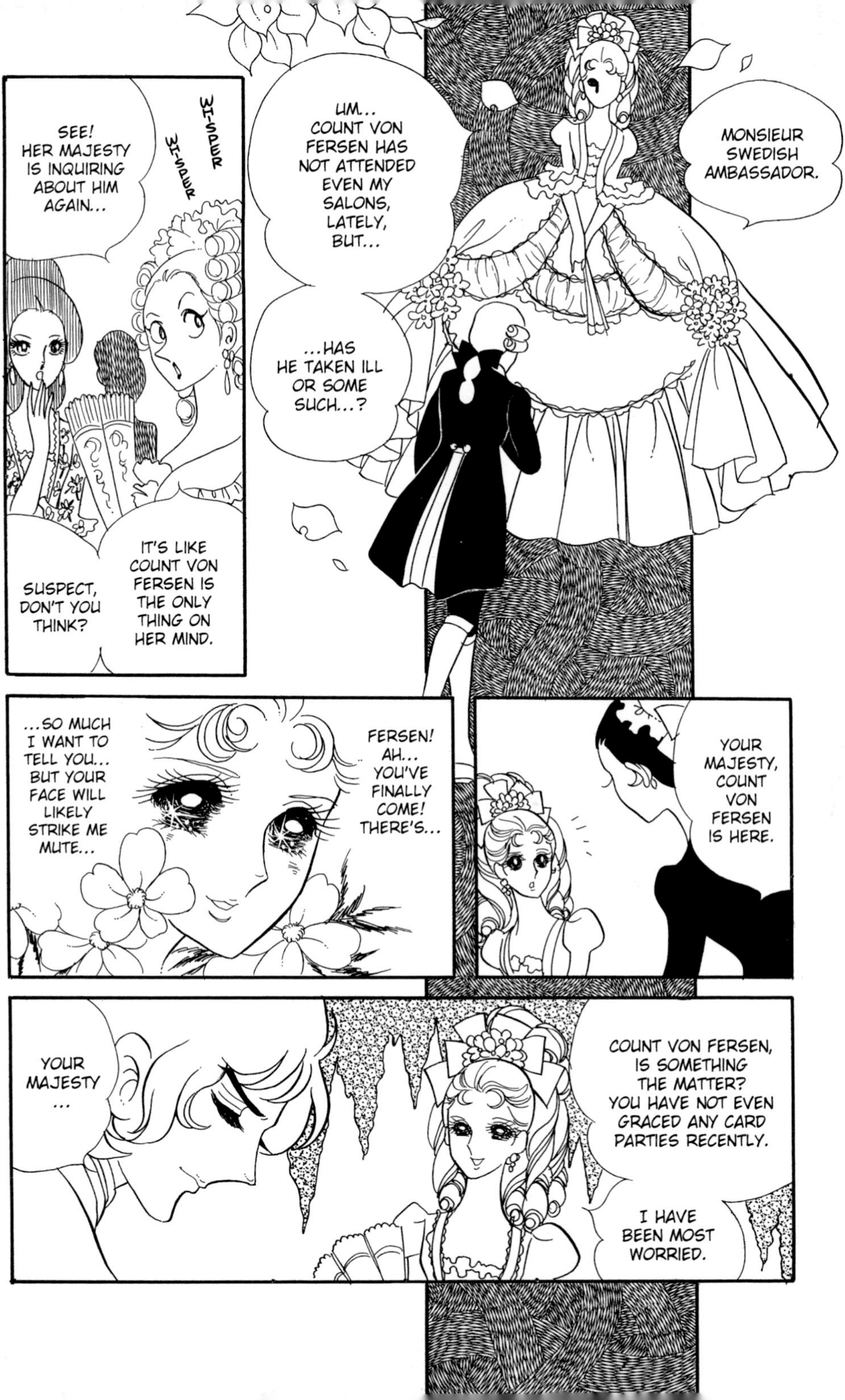
MONSIEUR SWEDISH AMBASSADOR.
UM... COUNT VON FERSEN HAS NOT ATTENDED EVEN MY SALONS, LATELY, BUT...
...HAS HE TAKEN ILL OR SOME SUCH...?
WHI-SPER
WHI-SPER
SEE! HER MAJESTY IS INQUIRING ABOUT HIM AGAIN...
IT'S LIKE COUNT VON FERSEN IS THE ONLY THING ON HER MIND.
SUSPECT, DON'T YOU THINK?
YOUR MAJESTY, COUNT VON FERSEN IS HERE.
FERSEN! AH... YOU'VE FINALLY COME! THERE'S...
...SO MUCH I WANT TO TELL YOU... BUT YOUR FACE WILL LIKELY STRIKE ME MUTE...
COUNT VON FERSEN, IS SOMETHING THE MATTER? YOU HAVE NOT EVEN GRACED ANY CARD PARTIES RECENTLY.
I HAVE BEEN MOST WORRIED.
YOUR MAJESTY ...

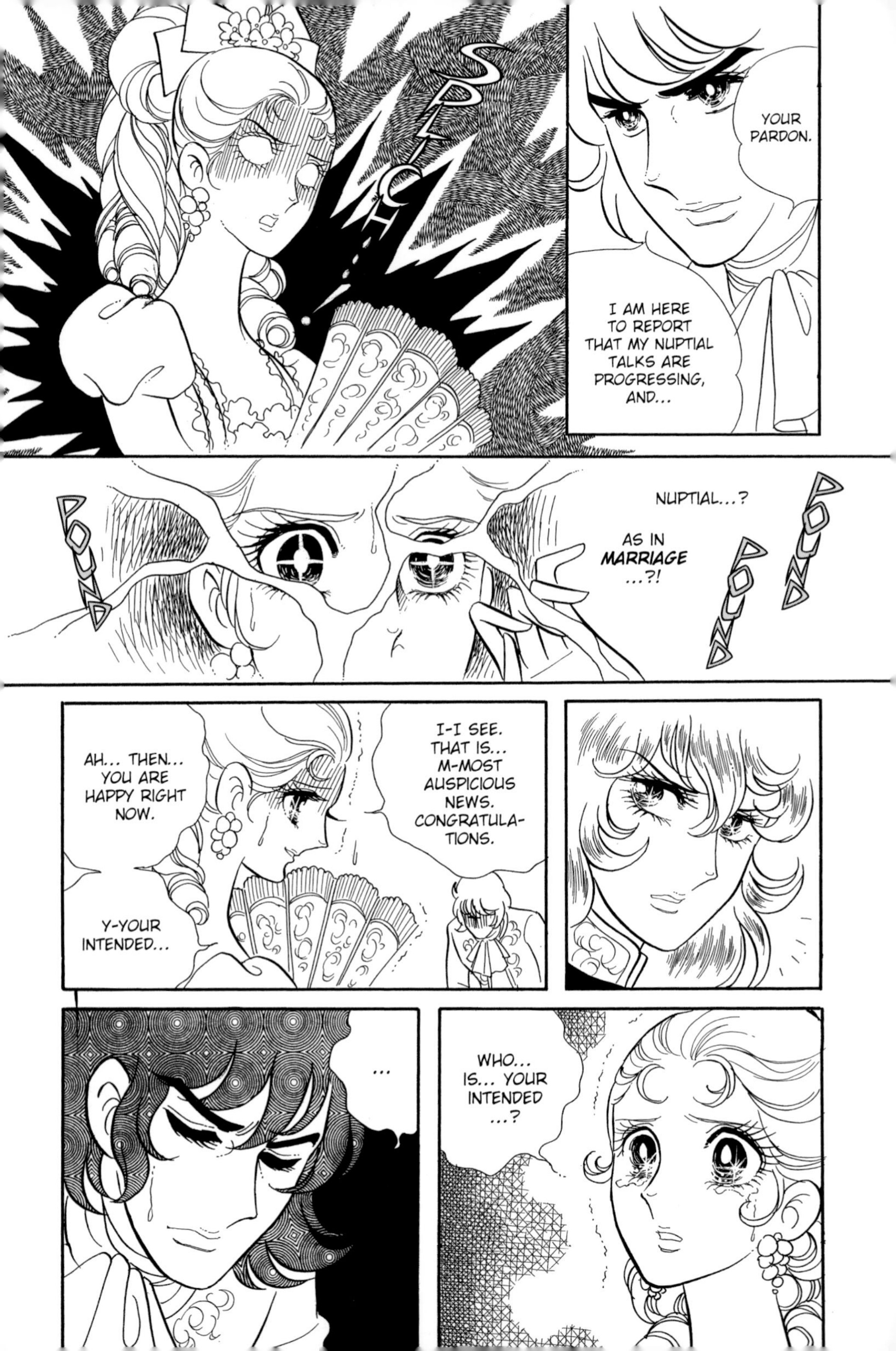
YOUR PARDON.
I AM HERE TO REPORT THAT MY NUPTIAL TALKS ARE PROGRESSING, AND...
SPLICH...
POUND
POUND
NUPTIAL...?
AS IN **MARRIAGE** ...?!
POUND
I-I SEE. THAT IS... M-MOST AUSPICIOUS NEWS. CONGRATULA-TIONS.
AH... THEN... YOU ARE HAPPY RIGHT NOW.
Y-YOUR INTENDED...
WHO... IS... YOUR INTENDED ...?
...

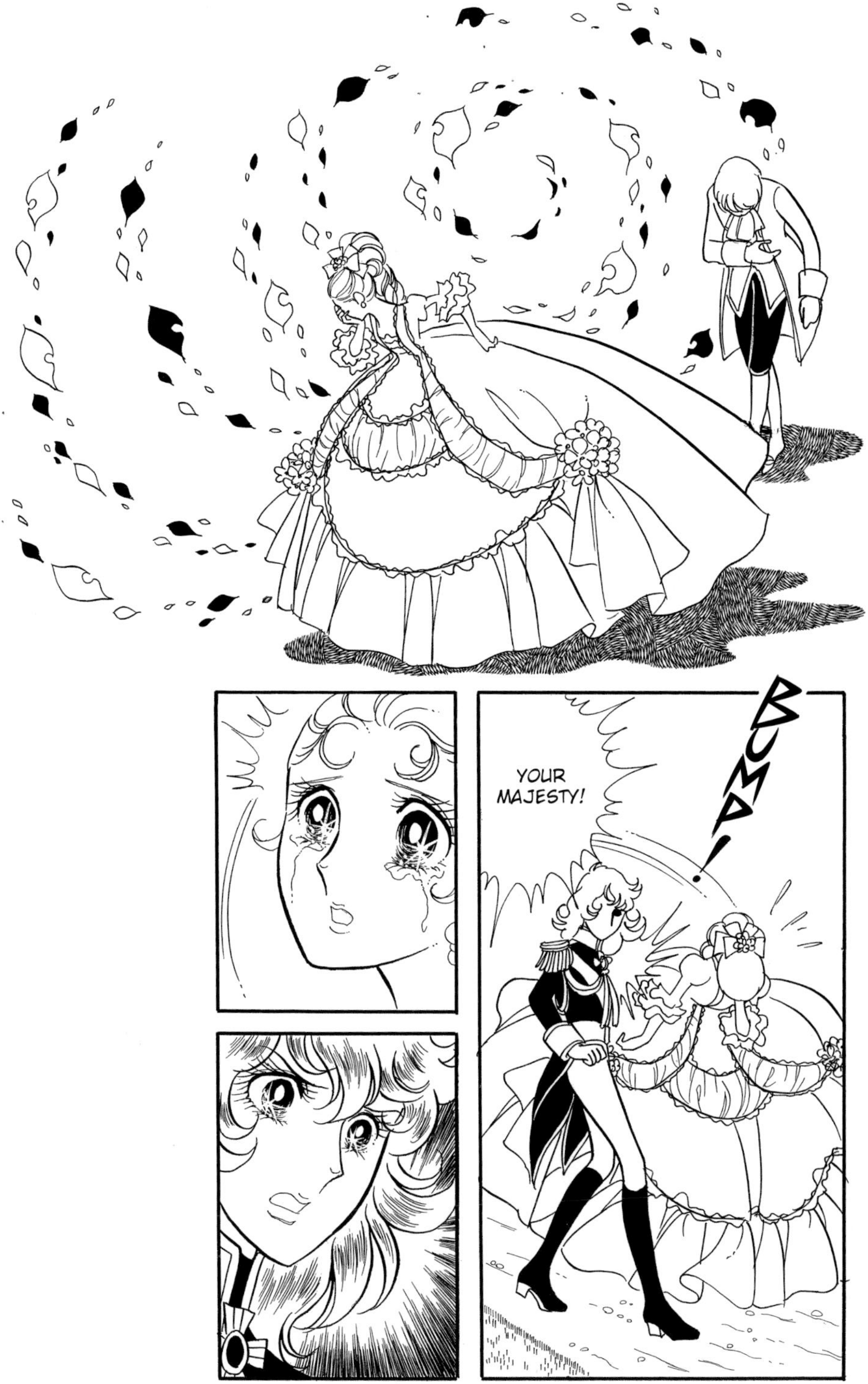
BUMP!
YOUR MAJESTY!

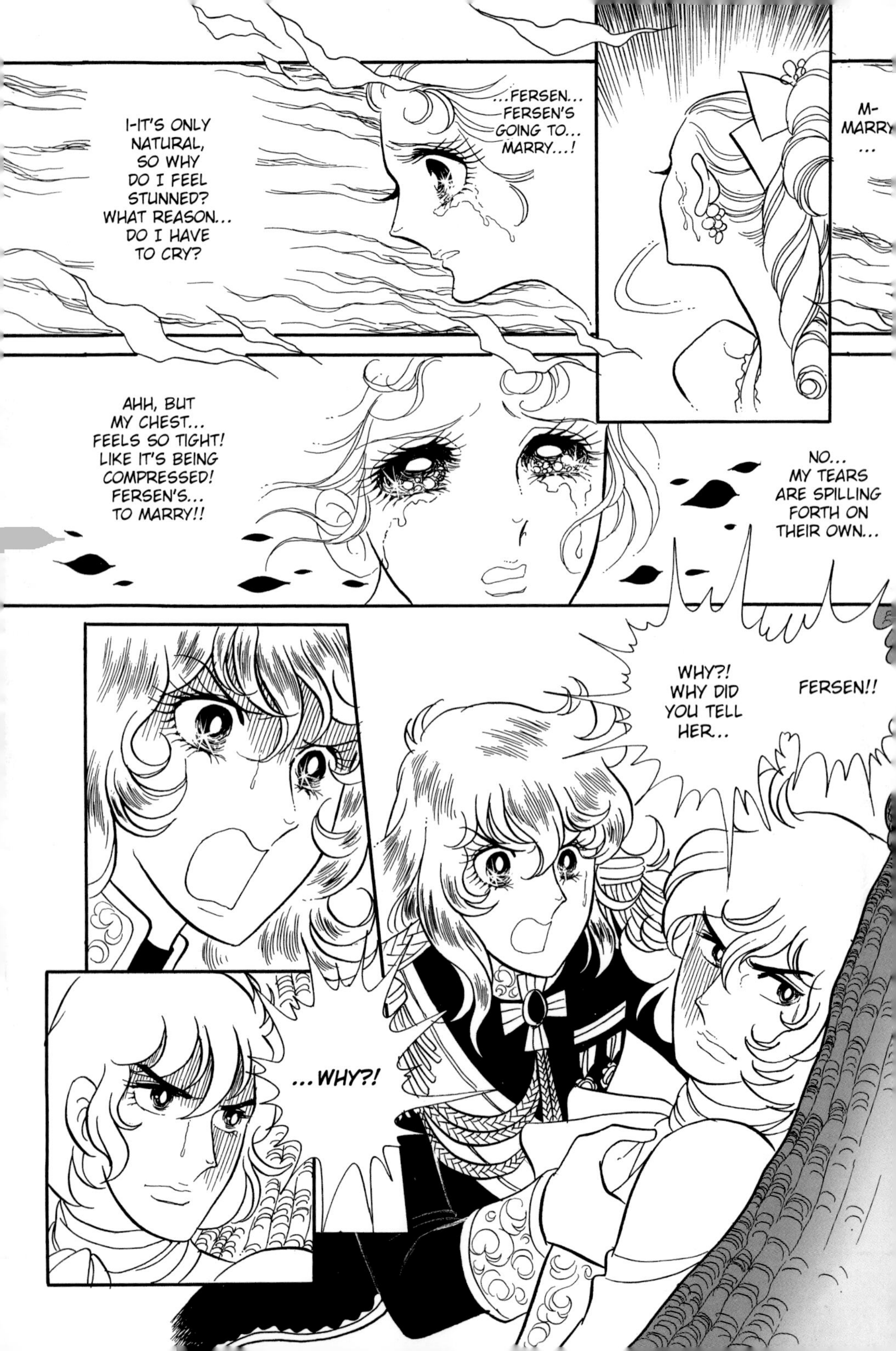
M-MARRY...
...FERSEN... FERSEN'S GOING TO... MARRY...!
I-IT'S ONLY NATURAL, SO WHY DO I FEEL STUNNED? WHAT REASON... DO I HAVE TO CRY?
NO... MY TEARS ARE SPILLING FORTH ON THEIR OWN...
AHH, BUT MY CHEST... FEELS SO TIGHT! LIKE IT'S BEING COMPRESSED! FERSEN'S... TO MARRY!!
FERSEN!!
WHY?! WHY DID YOU TELL HER...
...WHY?!

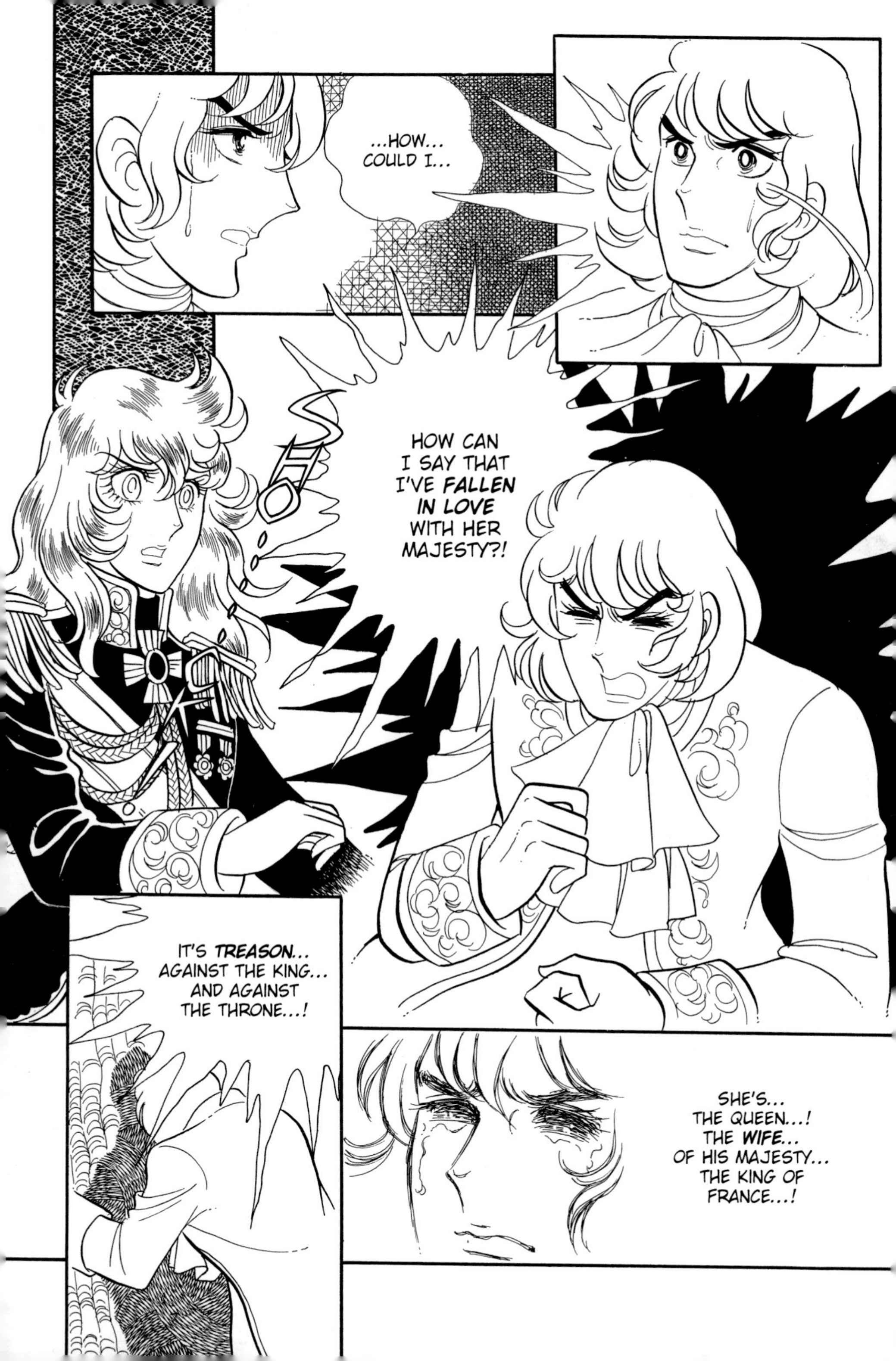
...HOW... COULD I...
HOW CAN I SAY THAT I'VE **FALLEN IN LOVE** WITH HER MAJESTY?!
SHE'S... THE QUEEN...! THE **WIFE**... OF HIS MAJESTY... THE KING OF FRANCE...!
IT'S **TREASON**... AGAINST THE KING... AND AGAINST THE THRONE...!

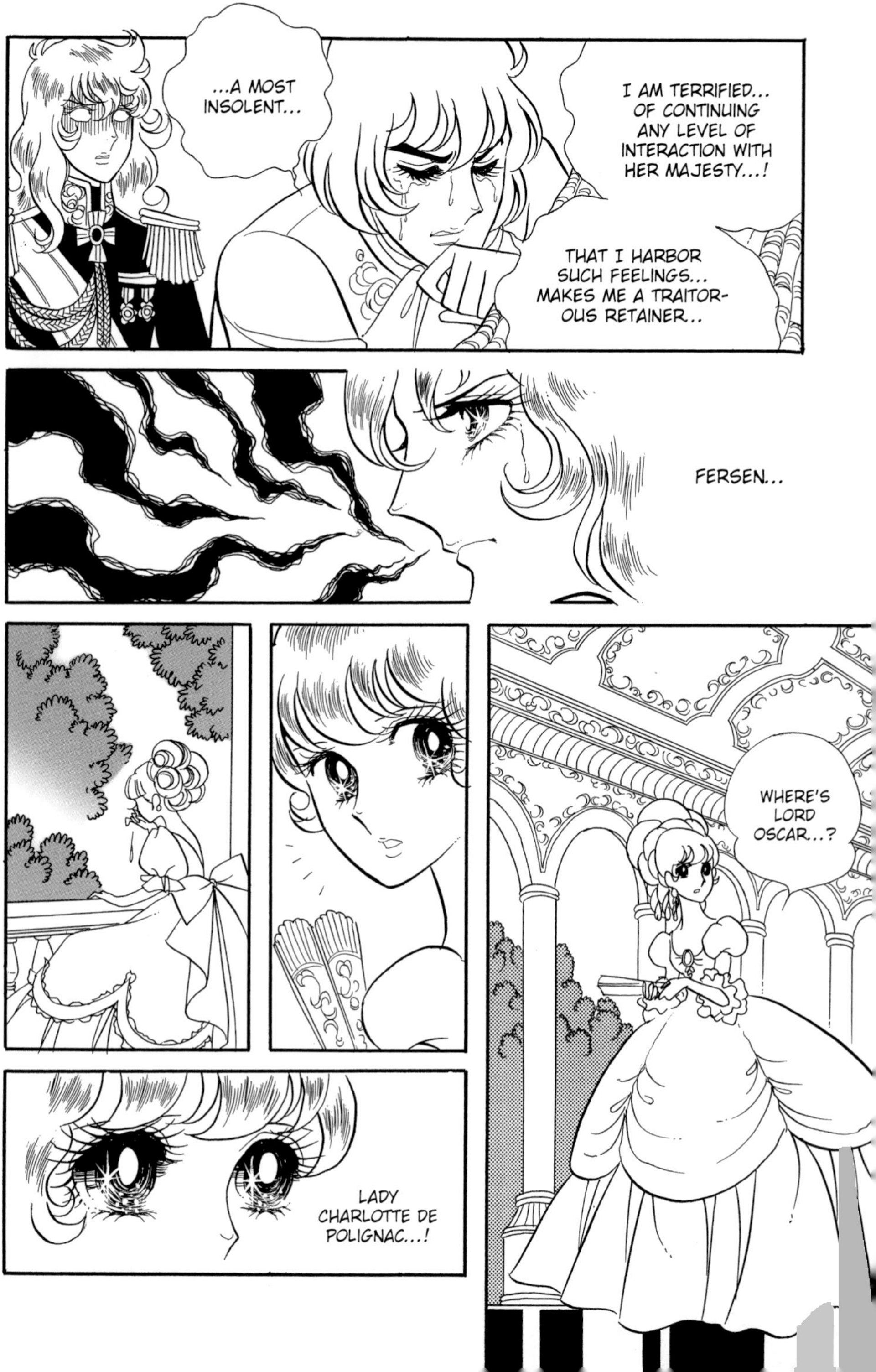
I AM TERRIFIED... OF CONTINUING ANY LEVEL OF INTERACTION WITH HER MAJESTY...!
THAT I HARBOR SUCH FEELINGS... MAKES ME A TRAITOR-OUS RETAINER...
...A MOST INSOLENT...
FERSEN...
WHERE'S LORD OSCAR...?
LADY CHARLOTTE DE POLIGNAC...!

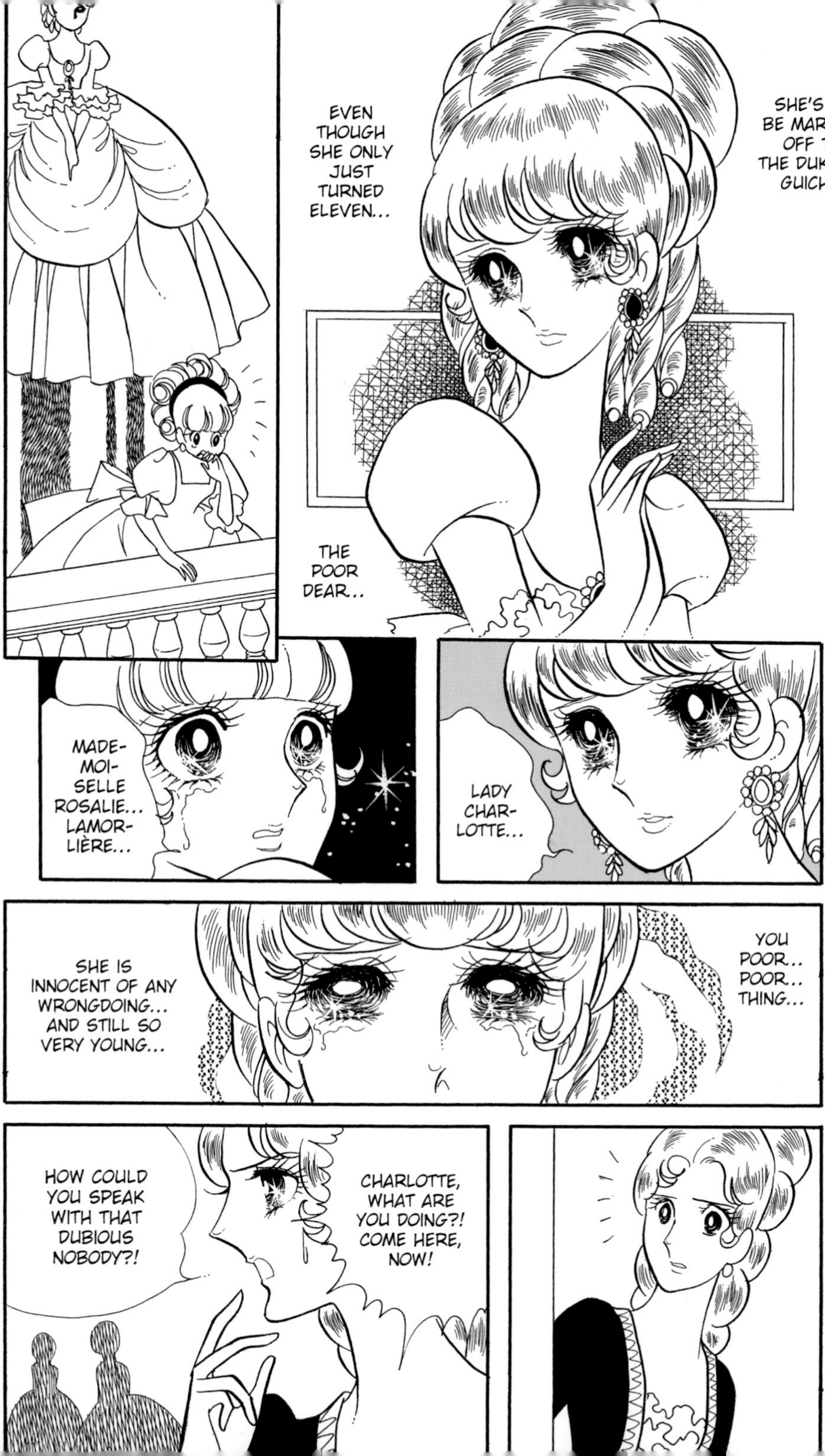
SHE'S TO BE MARRIED OFF TO THE DUKE DE GUICHE.
EVEN THOUGH SHE ONLY JUST TURNED ELEVEN...
THE POOR DEAR...
LADY CHARLOTTE...
MADEMOISELLE ROSALIE... LAMORLIÈRE...
YOU POOR.. POOR.. THING...
SHE IS INNOCENT OF ANY WRONGDOING... AND STILL SO VERY YOUNG...
CHARLOTTE, WHAT ARE YOU DOING?! COME HERE, NOW!
HOW COULD YOU SPEAK WITH THAT DUBIOUS NOBODY?!

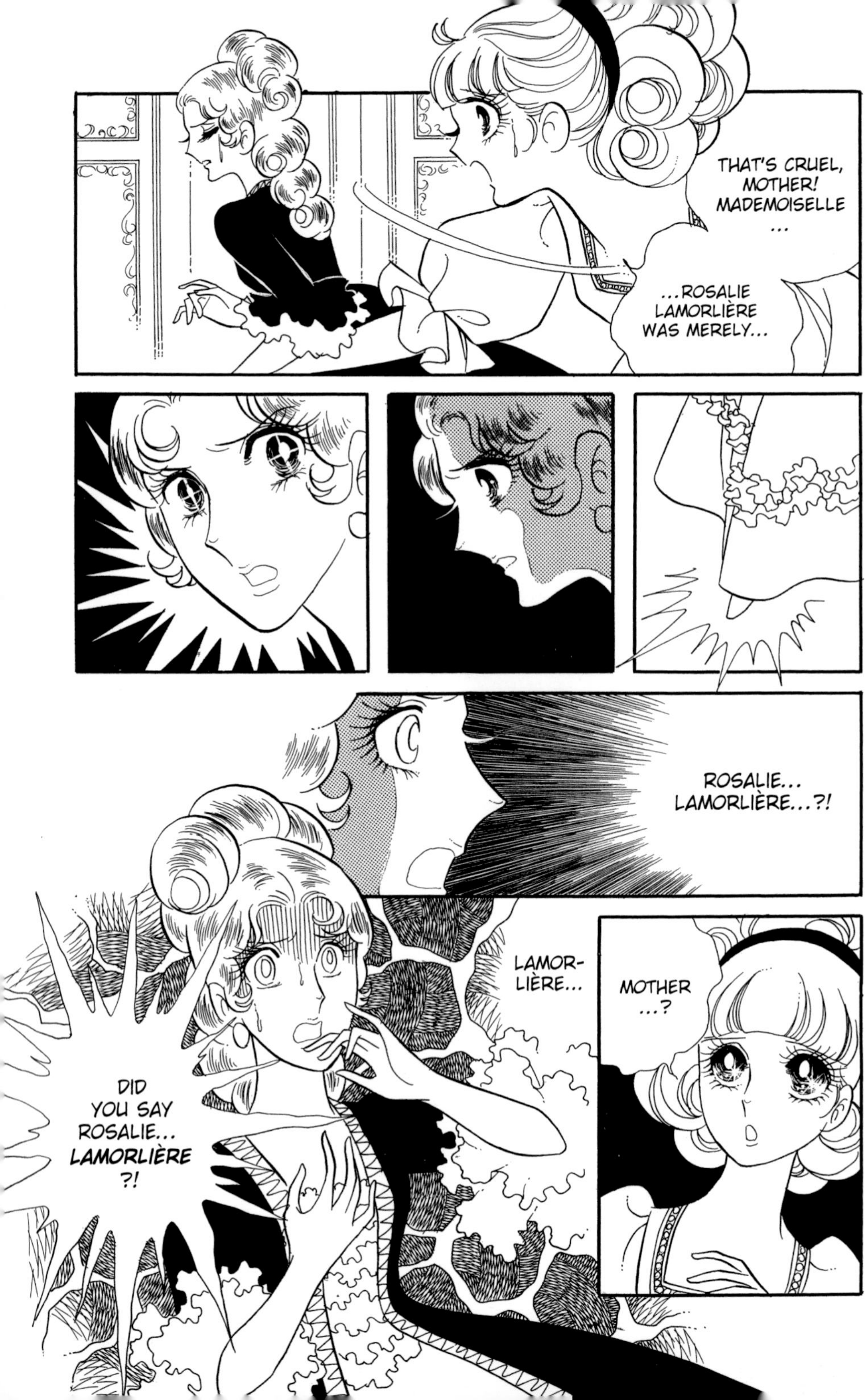
THAT'S CRUEL, MOTHER! MADEMOISELLE ...
...ROSALIE LAMORLIÈRE WAS MERELY...
ROSALIE... LAMORLIÈRE...?!
MOTHER ...?
LAMOR-LIÈRE...
DID YOU SAY ROSALIE... LAMORLIÈRE ?!

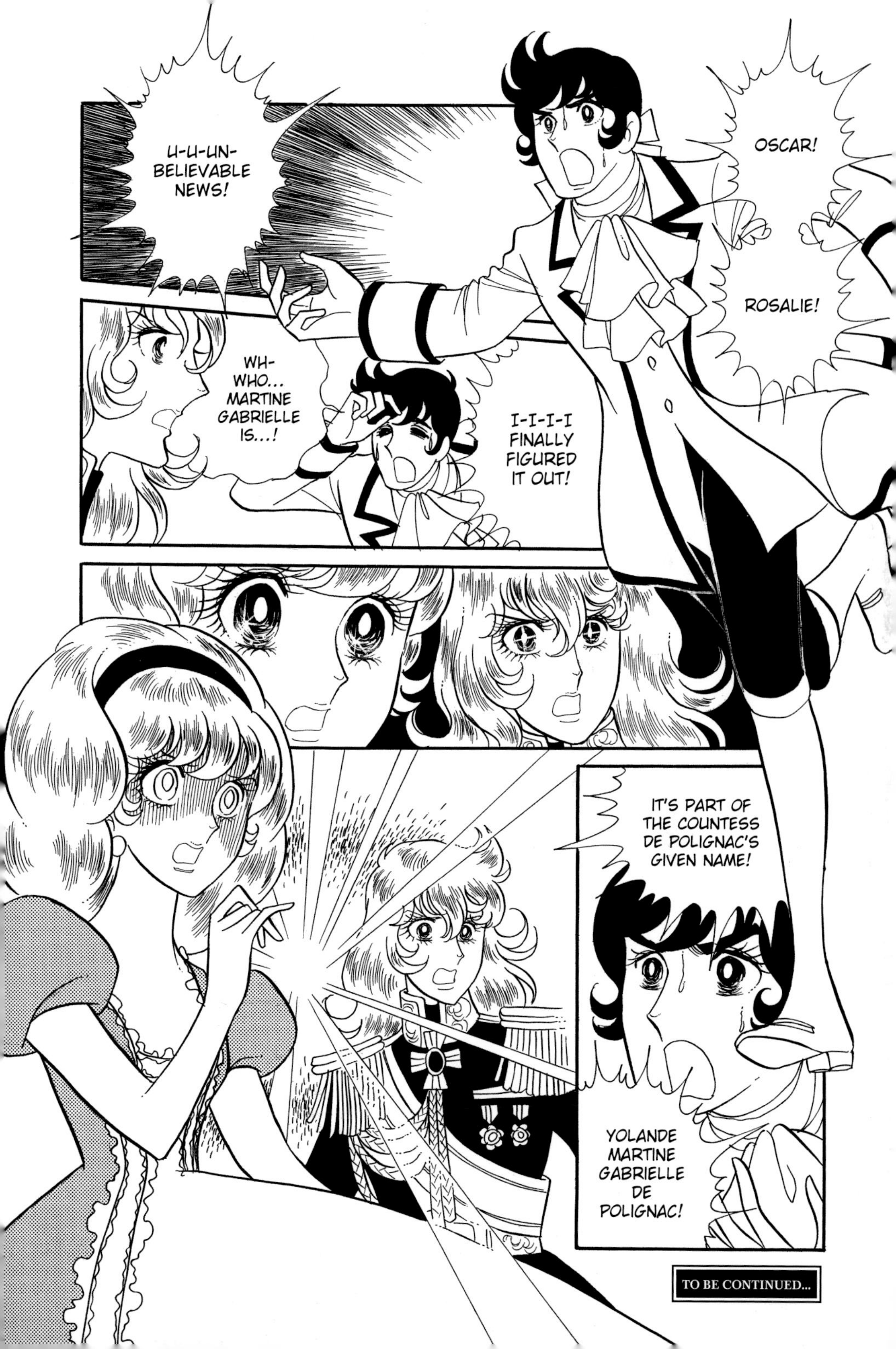
OSCAR!
ROSALIE!
U-U-UN-BELIEVABLE NEWS!
I-I-I-I FINALLY FIGURED IT OUT!
WH-WHO... MARTINE GABRIELLE IS...!
IT'S PART OF THE COUNTESS DE POLIGNAC'S GIVEN NAME!
YOLANDE MARTINE GABRIELLE DE POLIGNAC!
TO BE CONTINUED...

EXTRA COVER PAGE
ILLUSTRATIONS

The following title pages
are replaced by
special colorized art for this edition.

The original versions
are present here in this special gallery
for your enjoyment.

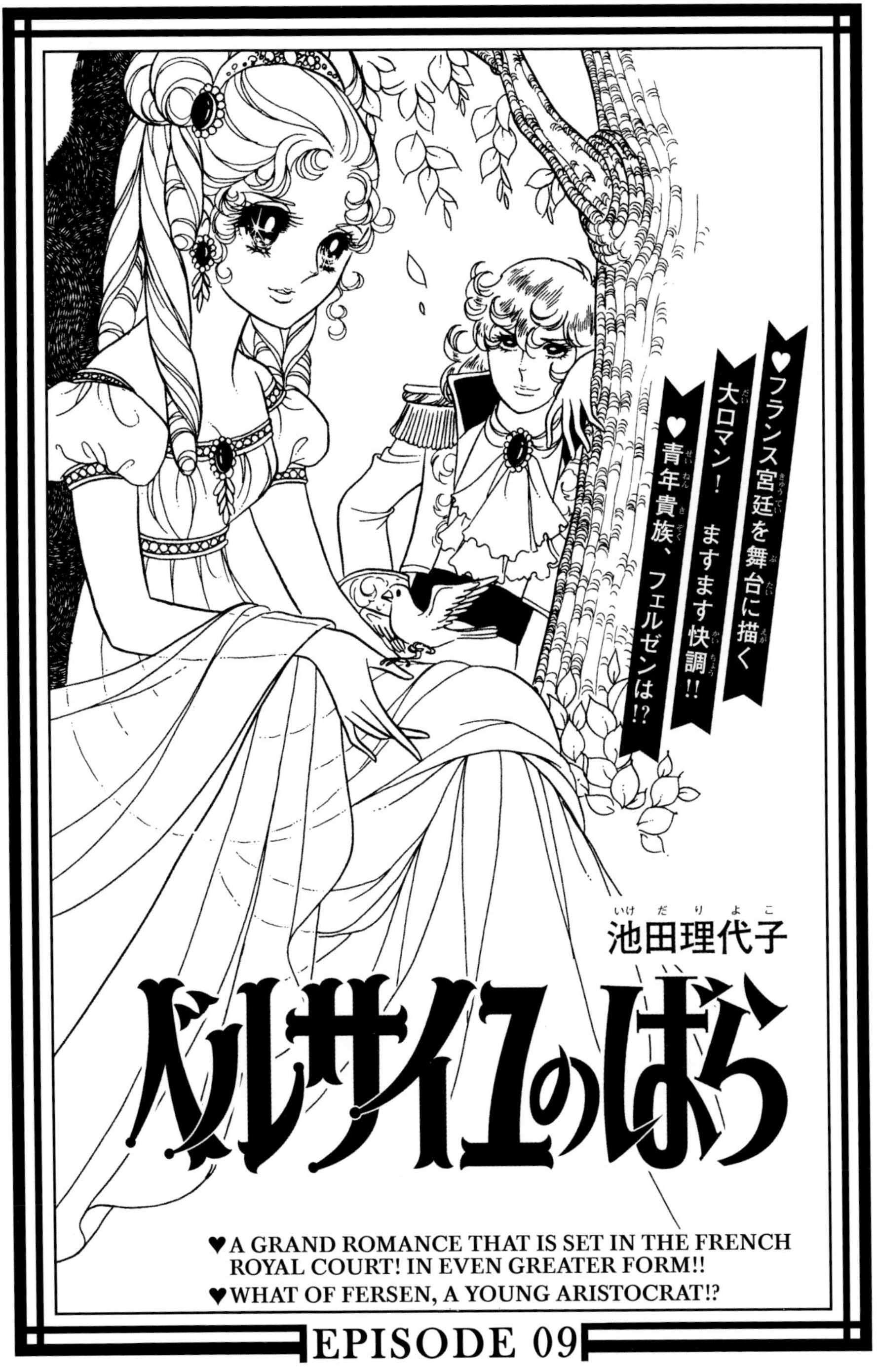
♥フランス宮廷を舞台に描く
大ロマン！ ますます快調!!
♥青年貴族、フェルゼンは!?
池田理代子
ベルサイユのばら
♥A GRAND ROMANCE THAT IS SET IN THE FRENCH ROYAL COURT! IN EVEN GREATER FORM!!
♥WHAT OF FERSEN, A YOUNG ARISTOCRAT!?
EPISODE 09

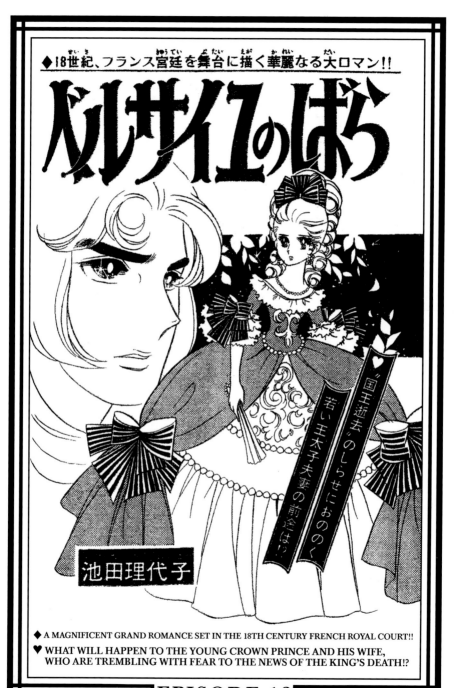

◆18世紀、フランス宮廷を舞台に描く華麗なる大ロマン!!

ベルサイユのばら

国王逝去〟のしらせにおののく
若い王太子夫妻の前途は!?

池田理代子

◆ A MAGNIFICENT GRAND ROMANCE SET IN THE 18TH CENTURY FRENCH ROYAL COURT!!

♥ WHAT WILL HAPPEN TO THE YOUNG CROWN PRINCE AND HIS WIFE, WHO ARE TREMBLING WITH FEAR TO THE NEWS OF THE KING'S DEATH!?

EPISODE 12

♥WHAT WILL OSCAR DO UPON THE SUDDEN APPEARANCE OF FERSEN!?
◆THE SENSATIONAL TOUR DE FORCE THAT IS SET IN THE FRENCH ROYAL COURT!!

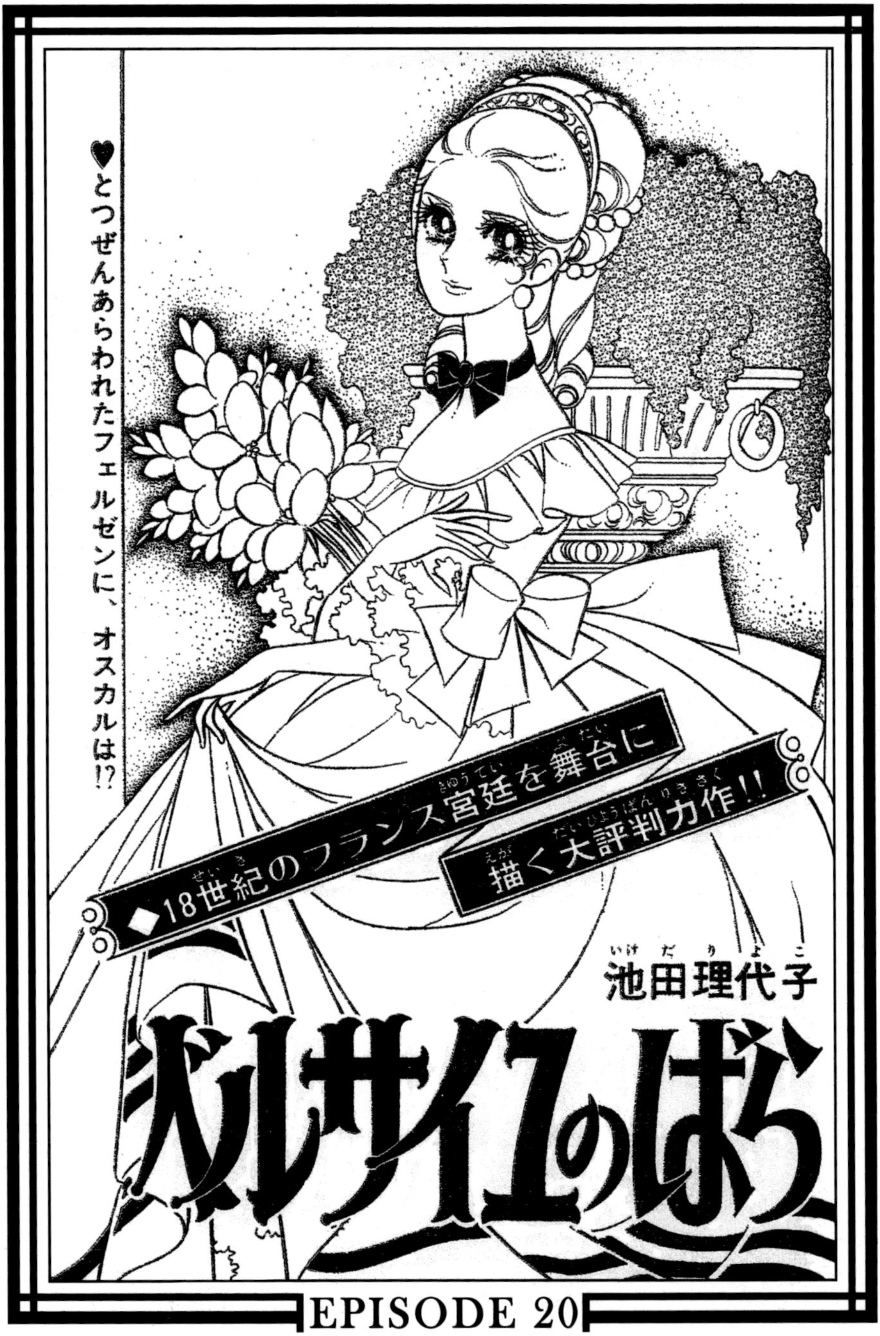
♥とつぜんあらわれたフェルゼンに、オスカルは!?
◆18世紀のフランス宮廷を舞台に
描く大評判力作!!
池田理代子
ベルサイユのばら

EPISODE 20

RIYOKO IKEDA

Manga artist, author, essayist, vocalist. Born 1947 in Osaka.

Started drawing graphic novels while enrolled at Tokyo University of Education (now University of Tsukuba), Department of Philosophy.

This work, **The Rose of Versailles**, which began serialization in **Weekly Margaret** in 1972, became the rage across near all of society, a smash hit that was adapted for the stage by the Takarazuka Revue and into anime and feature films, crossing media barriers and changing the history of shojo manga.

Since then, she has continued drawing manga works based on her deep perception of history and humankind, and written essays and critiques full of insight, to the present day.

Other representative works include **Orpheus no Mado** (**The Window of Orpheus**), which was awarded the 9th Japan Cartoonists Association Award in 1980, **Eikô no Napoleon - Eroika** (**Eroica - The Glory of Napoleon**), and **Shôtoku Taishi** (**Prince Shôtoku**).

Ms. Ikeda entered Tokyo College of Music, Voice Department, in 1995, and graduated the same institution in 1999.

In 2006, she was active as a soprano in theatrical and musical performances.

In addition, her 4-panel color comic strip **Berubara Kids** (**Rose of Versailles Kids**), serialized in the **Asahi News** Saturday edition, is drawing the interest of fans new and old.

Official webpage: http://www.ikeda-riyoko-pro.com/

VERSAILLES NO BARA Volume 1
© 1972 IKEDA RIYOKO PRODUCTION
All rights reserved.
Engish translation rights arranged with IKEDA RIYOKO PRODUCTION
through Tuttle-Mori Agency, Inc. Tokyo.

AGE: Young Adult (13+)
BISAC: CGN004050 CGN004140 CGN004130 CGN009000
LIBRARY SUBJECT: Manga, Graphic Novel, Historic Fiction, LGBTQ

www.UDONentertainment.com

First Printing: December 2019
Second Printing: September 2020
Third Printing: August 2021
Fourth Printing: March 2022
ISBN-10: 1-927925-93-2
ISBN-13: 978-1-927925-93-5

Printed in China